connect™
CORE CONCEPTS IN HEALTH

ELEVENTH EDITION

Paul M. Insel
Stanford University

Walton T. Roth
Stanford University

Boston Burr Ridge, IL Dubuque, IA Madison, WI New York
San Francisco St. Louis Bangkok Bogotá Caracas Kuala Lumpur
Lisbon London Madrid Mexico City Milan Montreal New Delhi
Santiago Seoul Singapore Sydney Taipei Toronto

Higher Education

Published by McGraw-Hill, an imprint of The McGraw-Hill Companies, Inc., 1221 Avenue of the Americas, New York, NY 10020. Copyright © 2010. All rights reserved. No part of this publication may be reproduced or distributed in any form or by any means, or stored in a database or retrieval system, without the prior written consent of The McGraw-Hill Companies, Inc., including, but not limited to, in any network or other electronic storage or transmission, or broadcast for distance learning.

4 5 6 7 8 9 0 DOW/DOW 0

ISBN: 978-0-07-338077-3
MHID: 0-07-338077-6

Editor in Chief: *Michael Ryan*
Editorial Director: *William R. Glass*
Executive Editor: *Christopher Johnson*
Marketing Manager: *William Minick*
Director of Development: *Kathleen Engelberg*
Developmental Editor: *Tim Huddleston*
Developmental Editor for Technology: *Julia D. Akpan*
Editorial Coordinator: *Lydia Kim*
Production Editor: *Carey Eisner*
Design Manager and Cover Designer: *Andrei Pasternak*
Text Designer: *Glenda King*
Manager, Photo Research: *Brian J. Pecko*
Illustrators: *John and Judy Waller*
Senior Production Supervisor: *Richard DeVitto*
Composition: *10.5/12 Berkeley Oldstyle Book by Thompson Type*
Printing: *45# New Era Thin Plus Recycle, R. R. Donnelley & Sons*

Front and Back Cover: © *Keate/Masterfile www.masterfile.com*

Credits: The credits appear at the end of the book and are considered an extension of the copyright page.

Library of Congress Cataloging-in-Publication Data

Connect core concepts in health / [compiled by] Paul M. Insel, Walton T. Roth.—11th ed.
    p. cm.
  Rev. ed. of: Core concepts in health. 10th ed. update. c2008.
  Includes bibliographical references and index.
  ISBN-13: 978-0-07-338077-3 (pbk. : alk. paper)
  ISBN-10: 0-07-338077-6 (pbk. : alk. paper)
  1. Health—Handbooks, manuals, etc. I. Insel, Paul M. II. Roth, Walton T. III. Core concepts in health.

RA776.C83 2010
613—dc22   2009007900

The Internet addresses listed in the text were accurate at the time of publication. The inclusion of a Web site does not indicate an endorsement by the authors or McGraw-Hill, and McGraw-Hill does not guarantee the accuracy of the information presented at these sites.

www.mhhe.com

BRIEF CONTENTS

PART ONE

ESTABLISHING A BASIS FOR WELLNESS

CHAPTER 1 Taking Charge of Your Health   1

CHAPTER 2 Stress: The Constant Challenge   31

CHAPTER 3 Psychological Health   63

PART TWO

UNDERSTANDING SEXUALITY

CHAPTER 4 Intimate Relationships and Communication   95

CHAPTER 5 Sex and Your Body   123

CHAPTER 6 Contraception   153

CHAPTER 7 Abortion   185

CHAPTER 8 Pregnancy and Childbirth   201

PART THREE

MAKING RESPONSIBLE DECISIONS: SUBSTANCE USE AND ABUSE

CHAPTER 9 The Use and Abuse of Psychoactive Drugs   235

CHAPTER 10 The Responsible Use of Alcohol   271

CHAPTER 11 Toward a Tobacco-Free Society   299

PART FOUR

GETTING FIT

CHAPTER 12 Nutrition Basics   329

CHAPTER 13 Exercise for Health and Fitness   379

CHAPTER 14 Weight Management   415

PART FIVE

PROTECTING YOURSELF FROM DISEASE

CHAPTER 15 Cardiovascular Health   449

CHAPTER 16 Cancer   485

CHAPTER 17 Immunity and Infection   519

CHAPTER 18 Sexually Transmitted Diseases   551

PART SIX

LIVING WELL IN THE WORLD

CHAPTER 19 Environmental Health   585

CHAPTER 20 Conventional and Complementary Medicine   615

CHAPTER 21 Personal Safety   647

PART SEVEN

ACCEPTING PHYSICAL LIMITS

CHAPTER 22 Aging: A Vital Process   679

CHAPTER 23 Dying and Death   701

APPENDIXES

APPENDIX A Nutritional Content of Popular Items from Fast-Food Restaurants   A-1

APPENDIX B A Self-Care Guide for Common Medical Problems   A-6

Credits   C-1

Index   I-1

CONTENTS

PART ONE

ESTABLISHING A BASIS FOR WELLNESS

1 TAKING CHARGE OF YOUR HEALTH 1

WELLNESS: THE NEW HEALTH GOAL 2
The Dimensions of Wellness 2
New Opportunities, New Responsibilities 3
The Healthy People Initiative 6
Health Issues for Diverse Populations 7

CHOOSING WELLNESS 12
Factors That Influence Wellness 13

REACHING WELLNESS THROUGH LIFESTYLE MANAGEMENT 15
Getting Serious About Your Health 16
Building Motivation to Change 19
Enhancing Your Readiness to Change 20
Dealing with Relapse 21
Developing Skills for Change: Creating a Personalized Plan 22
Putting Your Plan into Action 25
Staying with It 26

BEING HEALTHY FOR LIFE 26
Making Changes in Your World 26
What Does the Future Hold? 27

Tips for Today and the Future 27
Summary 27
For More Information 27
Selected Bibliography 29

2 STRESS: THE CONSTANT CHALLENGE 31

WHAT IS STRESS? 32
Physical Responses to Stressors 32
Emotional and Behavioral Responses to Stressors 34
The Stress Experience as a Whole 36

STRESS AND HEALTH 37
The General Adaptation Syndrome 37
Allostatic Load 39
Psychoneuroimmunology 39
Links Between Stress and Specific Conditions 39

COMMON SOURCES OF STRESS 41
Major Life Changes 41
Daily Hassles 41
College Stressors 41
Job-Related Stressors 42
Social Stressors 43
Environmental Stressors 44
Internal Stressors 44

MANAGING STRESS 44
Social Support 45
Communication 46
Exercise 46
Nutrition 47
Sleep 47
Time Management 48
Striving for Spiritual Wellness 50
Confiding in Yourself Through Writing 50
Cognitive Techniques 50
Relaxation Techniques 52
Counterproductive Coping Strategies 55

CREATING A PERSONAL PLAN FOR MANAGING STRESS 56
Identifying Stressors 56
Designing Your Plan 56
Getting Help 56

Tips for Today and the Future 57
Summary 57
For More Information 58
Behavior Change Strategy 59
Selected Bibliography 60

3 PSYCHOLOGICAL HEALTH 63

DEFINING PSYCHOLOGICAL HEALTH 64
Self-Actualization 64
What Psychological Health Is Not 65

MEETING LIFE'S CHALLENGES 66
Growing Up Psychologically 66
Achieving Healthy Self-Esteem 67
Being Less Defensive 70
Being Optimistic 71
Maintaining Honest Communication 71
Dealing with Loneliness 72
Dealing with Anger 72

PSYCHOLOGICAL DISORDERS 73
Anxiety Disorders 73
Mood Disorders 77
Schizophrenia 82

MODELS OF HUMAN NATURE AND THERAPEUTIC CHANGE 83
    The Biological Model 83
    The Behavioral Model 85
    The Cognitive Model 85
    The Psychodynamic Model 87
    Evaluating the Models 87

GETTING HELP 87
    Self-Help 87
    Peer Counseling and Support Groups 88
    Professional Help 89

Tips for Today and the Future 89
Summary 89
Behavior Change Strategy 90
For More Information 91
Selected Bibliography 92

PART TWO

UNDERSTANDING SEXUALITY

4 INTIMATE RELATIONSHIPS AND COMMUNICATION 95

DEVELOPING INTIMATE RELATIONSHIPS 96
    Self-Concept and Self-Esteem 96
    Friendship 97
    Love, Sex, and Intimacy 98
    Challenges in Relationships 99
    Unhealthy Relationships 101
    Ending a Relationship 102

COMMUNICATION 103
    Nonverbal Communication 103
    Communication Skills 103
    Gender and Communication 104
    Conflict and Conflict Resolution 104

PAIRING AND SINGLEHOOD 107
    Choosing a Partner 107
    Dating 107
    Living Together 109
    Same-Sex Partnerships 110
    Singlehood 111

MARRIAGE 113
    Benefits of Marriage 113
    Issues in Marriage 113
    The Role of Commitment 113
    Separation and Divorce 114

FAMILY LIFE 115
    Becoming a Parent 115
    Parenting 116
    Single Parents 117
    Stepfamilies 118
    Successful Families 118

Tips for Today and the Future 120
Summary 120
For More Information 121
Selected Bibliography 121

5 SEX AND YOUR BODY 123

SEXUAL ANATOMY 124
    Female Sex Organs 124
    Male Sex Organs 125

HORMONES AND THE REPRODUCTIVE LIFE CYCLE 127
    Differentiation of the Embryo 127
    Female Sexual Maturation 128
    Male Sexual Maturation 131
    Aging and Human Sexuality 131

SEXUAL FUNCTIONING 132
    Sexual Stimulation 133
    The Sexual Response Cycle 134
    Sexual Problems 135

SEXUAL BEHAVIOR 137
    The Development of Sexual Behavior 138
    Sexual Orientation 140
    Varieties of Human Sexual Behavior 143

Atypical and Problematic Sexual Behaviors   145
Commercial Sex   145
Responsible Sexual Behavior   146

Tips for Today and the Future   148
Summary   148
For More Information   149
Selected Bibliography   150

6   CONTRACEPTION   153

PRINCIPLES OF CONTRACEPTION   154

REVERSIBLE CONTRACEPTION   156
Oral Contraceptives: The Pill   156
Contraceptive Skin Patch   158
Vaginal Contraceptive Ring   159
Contraceptive Implants   160
Injectable Contraceptives   160
Emergency Contraception   161
The Intrauterine Device (IUD)   163
Male Condoms   164
Female Condoms   165
The Diaphragm with Spermicide   167
Lea's Shield   169
FemCap   169
The Contraceptive Sponge   169
Vaginal Spermicides   170
Abstinence, Fertility Awareness, and
    Withdrawal   171
Combining Methods   172

**PERMANENT CONTRACEPTION:
STERILIZATION**   172
Male Sterilization: Vasectomy   173
Female Sterilization   174

ISSUES IN CONTRACEPTION   175
When Is It OK to Begin Having Sexual
    Relations?   175
Contraception and Gender Differences   177
Sexuality and Contraception Education for
    Teenagers   178

**WHICH CONTRACEPTIVE METHOD IS RIGHT FOR
YOU?**   180

Tips for Today and the Future   181
Summary   181
For More Information   182
Selected Bibliography   183

7   ABORTION   185

THE ABORTION ISSUE   186
The History of Abortion in the United States   186
Current Legal Status   186
Public Opinion   188
Personal Considerations   189
Abortion Statistics   191

METHODS OF ABORTION   191
Suction Curettage   192
Manual Vacuum Aspiration   192
Multi-Fetal Pregnancy Reduction   194
Abortion After the First Trimester   194
Medical Abortion   194

COMPLICATIONS OF ABORTION   195
Possible Physical Effects   195
Unsafe Abortions   196
Possible Psychological Effects   197

Tips for Today and the Future   198
Summary   198
For More Information   198
Selected Bibliography   199

8   PREGNANCY AND CHILDBIRTH   201

PREPARATION FOR PARENTHOOD   202
Deciding to Become a Parent   202
Preconception Care   203

UNDERSTANDING FERTILITY   204
Conception   204
Infertility   206

PREGNANCY   209
Pregnancy Tests   210

Changes in the Woman's Body   210
Emotional Responses to Pregnancy   212
Fetal Development   213
The Importance of Prenatal Care   217
Complications of Pregnancy and Pregnancy Loss   222

CHILDBIRTH   224
Choices in Childbirth   224
Labor and Delivery   225
The Postpartum Period   228

Tips for Today and the Future   230
Summary   230
For More Information   231
Selected Bibliography   231

PART THREE

MAKING RESPONSIBLE DECISIONS: SUBSTANCE USE AND ABUSE

9   THE USE AND ABUSE OF PSYCHOACTIVE DRUGS   235

ADDICTIVE BEHAVIOR   236
What Is Addiction?   236
Characteristics of Addictive Behavior   237
The Development of Addiction   237
Characteristics of People with Addictions   238

Examples of Addictive Behaviors   238

DRUG USE, ABUSE, AND DEPENDENCE   240
The Drug Tradition   240
Drug Abuse and Dependence   240
Who Uses Drugs?   241
Why Do People Use Drugs?   243
Risk Factors for Dependence   244
Other Risks of Drug Use   245

HOW DRUGS AFFECT THE BODY   246
Changes in Brain Chemistry   246
Drug Factors   247
User Factors   248
Social Factors   248

REPRESENTATIVE PSYCHOACTIVE DRUGS   249
Opioids   249
Central Nervous System Depressants   249
Central Nervous System Stimulants   251
Marijuana and Other Cannabis Products   256
Hallucinogens   257
Inhalants   258

DRUG USE: THE DECADES AHEAD   259
Drugs, Society, and Families   259
Legalizing Drugs   260
Drug Testing   260
Treatment for Drug Dependence   262
Preventing Drug Abuse   264
The Role of Drugs in Your Life   265

Tips for Today and the Future   265
Summary   265
Behavior Change Strategy   266
For More Information   267
Selected Bibliography   268

10 THE RESPONSIBLE USE OF ALCOHOL 271

THE NATURE OF ALCOHOL 272
Alcoholic Beverages 272
Absorption 273
Metabolism and Excretion 273
Alcohol Intake and Blood Alcohol
    Concentration 274

ALCOHOL AND HEALTH 275
The Immediate Effects of Alcohol 275
Drinking and Driving 278
The Effects of Chronic Use 279
The Effects of Alcohol Use During Pregnancy 281
Possible Health Benefits of Alcohol 282

ALCOHOL ABUSE AND DEPENDENCE 283
Statistics on Alcohol Use 283
Abuse versus Dependence 283
Binge Drinking 283
Alcoholism 284
Gender and Ethnic Differences 287
Helping Someone with an Alcohol Problem 289

DRINKING BEHAVIOR AND RESPONSIBILITY 289
Examine Your Drinking Behavior 289
Drink Moderately and Responsibly 290
Promote Responsible Drinking in Others 291

Tips for Today and the Future 293
Summary 293
Behavior Change Strategy 294
For More Information 295
Selected Bibliography 295

11 TOWARD A TOBACCO-FREE SOCIETY 299

WHO USES TOBACCO? 300
Young People and Tobacco 301
Tobacco and Other Drugs 302

WHY PEOPLE USE TOBACCO 302
Nicotine Addiction 302
Social and Psychological Factors 303
Genetic Factors 303
Why Start in the First Place? 304

HEALTH HAZARDS 306
Tobacco Smoke: A Toxic Mix 306
The Immediate Effects of Smoking 308
The Long-Term Effects of Smoking 309
Other Forms of Tobacco Use 312

THE EFFECTS OF SMOKING ON THE NONSMOKER 315
Environmental Tobacco Smoke 315
Smoking and Pregnancy 316
The Cost of Tobacco Use to Society 316

WHAT CAN BE DONE? 318
Action at the Local Level 318
Action at the State and Federal Levels 318
International Action 318
Action in the Private Sector 319
Individual Action 320

HOW A TOBACCO USER CAN QUIT 321
The Benefits of Quitting 321
Options for Quitting 321

Behavior Change Strategy 324
Tips for Today and the Future 326
Summary 326
For More Information 326
Selected Bibliography 327

PART FOUR

GETTING FIT

12 NUTRITION BASICS 329

NUTRITIONAL REQUIREMENTS: COMPONENTS OF A HEALTHY DIET 330
Calories 330
Proteins—The Basis of Body Structure 331
Fats—Essential in Small Amounts 333
Carbohydrates—An Ideal Source of Energy 337
Fiber—A Closer Look 339
Vitamins—Organic Micronutrients 340
Minerals—Inorganic Micronutrients 342
Water—Vital but Often Ignored 342
Other Substances in Food 343

NUTRITIONAL GUIDELINES: PLANNING YOUR DIET   345

Dietary Reference Intakes   345

Dietary Guidelines for Americans   346

USDA's MyPyramid   351

The Vegetarian Alternative   356

Dietary Challenges for Special Population Groups   358

A PERSONAL PLAN: MAKING INFORMED CHOICES ABOUT FOOD   359

Reading Food Labels   360

Reading Dietary Supplement Labels   362

Protecting Yourself Against Foodborne Illness   362

Environmental Contaminants and Organic Foods   365

Additives in Food   367

Food Irradiation   367

Genetically Modified Foods   368

Food Allergies and Food Intolerances   368

Tips for Today and the Future   369

Behavior Change Strategy   370

Summary   370

For More Information   370

Selected Bibliography   372

13   EXERCISE FOR HEALTH AND FITNESS   379

WHAT IS PHYSICAL FITNESS?   380

Cardiorespiratory Endurance   380

Muscular Strength   380

Muscular Endurance   381

Flexibility   381

Body Composition   381

Skill-Related Components of Fitness   382

PHYSICAL ACTIVITY AND EXERCISE FOR HEALTH AND FITNESS   382

Physical Activity on a Continuum   383

How Much Activity Is Enough?   385

THE BENEFITS OF EXERCISE   386

Improved Cardiorespiratory Functioning   386

More Efficient Metabolism   387

Improved Body Composition   387

Disease Prevention and Management   388

Improved Psychological and Emotional Wellness   390

Improved Immune Function   390

Prevention of Injuries and Low-Back Pain   390

Improved Wellness for Life   390

DESIGNING YOUR EXERCISE PROGRAM   390

First Steps   392

Cardiorespiratory Endurance Exercises   395

Developing Muscular Strength and Endurance   396

Flexibility Exercises   399

Training in Specific Skills   400

Putting It All Together   400

GETTING STARTED AND STAYING ON TRACK   403

Selecting Instructors, Equipment, and Facilities   403

Eating and Drinking for Exercise   404

Managing Your Fitness Program   406

Tips for Today and the Future   410

Summary   410

For More Information   410

Selected Bibliography   411

Behavior Change Strategy   412

14   WEIGHT MANAGEMENT   415

BASIC CONCEPTS OF WEIGHT MANAGEMENT   416

Body Composition   416

Energy Balance   417

Evaluating Body Weight and Body Composition   417

Excess Body Fat and Wellness   419

What is the Right Weight for You?   422

FACTORS CONTRIBUTING TO EXCESS BODY FAT   423

Genetic Factors   423

Physiological Factors   424

Lifestyle Factors   424

Psychosocial Factors   425

ADOPTING A HEALTHY LIFESTYLE FOR SUCCESSFUL WEIGHT MANAGEMENT 426
    Diet and Eating Habits 429
    Physical Activity and Exercise 431
    Thinking and Emotions 431
    Coping Strategies 432

APPROACHES TO OVERCOMING A WEIGHT PROBLEM 432
    Doing It Yourself 432
    Diet Books 432
    Dietary Supplements and Diet Aids 435
    Weight-Loss Programs 435
    Prescription Drugs 437
    Surgery 437
    Psychological Help 438

BODY IMAGE 438
    Severe Body Image Problems 438
    Acceptance and Change 439

EATING DISORDERS 439
    Anorexia Nervosa 441
    Bulimia Nervosa 441
    Binge-Eating Disorder 442
    Borderline Disordered Eating 442
    Treating Eating Disorders 442

Tips for Today and the Future 443
Summary 443
Behavior Change Strategy 444
For More Information 445
Selected Bibliography 446

PART FIVE

PROTECTING YOURSELF FROM DISEASE

15 CARDIOVASCULAR HEALTH 449

THE CARDIOVASCULAR SYSTEM 450
    The Heart 450
    The Blood Vessels 451

RISK FACTORS FOR CARDIOVASCULAR DISEASE 452
    Major Risk Factors That Can Be Changed 452
    Contributing Risk Factors That Can Be Changed 458
    Major Risk Factors That Can't Be Changed 460
    Possible Risk Factors Currently Being Studied 461

MAJOR FORMS OF CARDIOVASCULAR DISEASE 465
    Atherosclerosis 465
    Heart Disease and Heart Attack 466
    Stroke 470
    Peripheral Arterial Disease 473
    Congestive Heart Failure 473

    Other Forms of Heart Disease 474

PROTECTING YOURSELF AGAINST CARDIOVASCULAR DISEASE 475
    Eat Heart-Healthy 475
    Exercise Regularly 478
    Avoid Tobacco 478
    Know and Manage Your Blood Pressure 478
    Know and Manage Your Cholesterol Levels 478
    Develop Effective Ways to Handle Stress and Anger 478

Tips for Today and the Future 478
Summary 479
For More Information 479
Behavior Change Strategy 480
Selected Bibliography 480

16 CANCER 485

WHAT IS CANCER? 486
    Metastasis 487
    The Stages of Cancer 487
    Types of Cancer 488
    The Incidence of Cancer 488

COMMON CANCERS   489

Lung Cancer   489
Colon and Rectal Cancer   490
Breast Cancer   491
Prostate Cancer   494
Cancers of the Female Reproductive Tract   495
Skin Cancer   496
Oral Cancer   498
Testicular Cancer   500
Other Cancers   500

THE CAUSES OF CANCER   501

The Role of DNA   501
Tobacco Use   504
Dietary Factors   505
Inactivity and Obesity   505
Carcinogens in the Environment   506

**DETECTING, DIAGNOSING, AND TREATING
CANCER**   507

Detecting Cancer   508
Diagnosing Cancer   508
Treating Cancer   509
Living with Cancer   512

PREVENTING CANCER   512

Tips for Today and the Future   514
Summary   514
Behavior Change Strategy   515

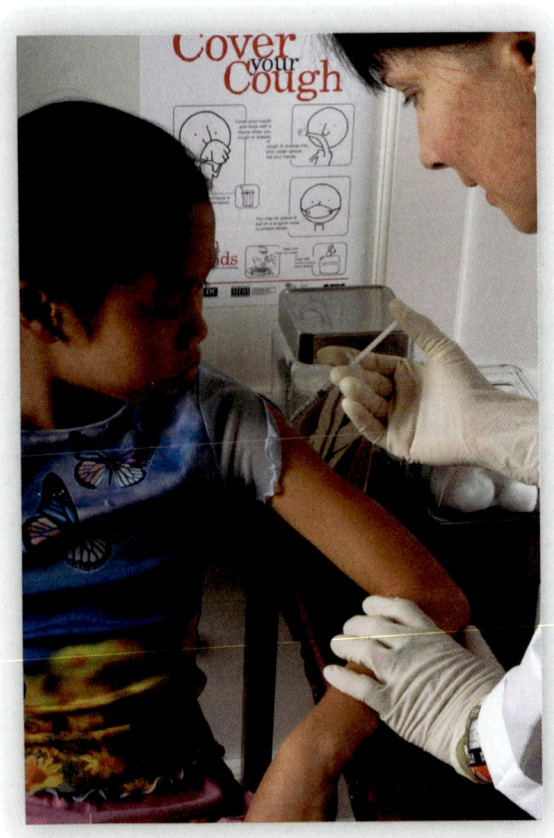

For More Information   516
Selected Bibliography   516

17 IMMUNITY AND INFECTION   519

THE CHAIN OF INFECTION   520

Links in the Chain   520
Breaking the Chain   521

THE BODY'S DEFENSE SYSTEM   521

Physical and Chemical Barriers   522
The Immune System   522
Immunization   526
Allergy: The Body's Defense System Gone
   Haywire   527

PATHOGENS AND DISEASE   530

Bacteria   530
Viruses   535
Fungi   542
Protozoa   543
Parasitic Worms   543
Prions   544
Emerging Infectious Diseases   544
Other Immune Disorders: Cancer and Autoimmune
   Diseases   546

SUPPORTING YOUR IMMUNE SYSTEM   546

Tips for Today and the Future   546
Summary   547
For More Information   548
Selected Bibliography   549

18 SEXUALLY TRANSMITTED DISEASES   551

THE MAJOR STDS   552

HIV Infection and AIDS   552
Chlamydia   566
Gonorrhea   568
Pelvic Inflammatory Disease   569
Human Papillomavirus Infection   570
Genital Herpes   572
Hepatitis B   574
Syphilis   575
Other STDs   575

WHAT YOU CAN DO   576

Education   576
Diagnosis and Treatment   576
Prevention   578

Tips for Today and the Future   580
Summary   580
For More Information   581
Selected Bibliography   581

PART SIX
LIVING WELL IN THE WORLD

19 ENVIRONMENTAL HEALTH   585

ENVIRONMENTAL HEALTH DEFINED   586

POPULATION GROWTH AND CONTROL   587
How Many People Can the World Hold?   587
Factors That Contribute to Population Growth   589

AIR QUALITY AND POLLUTION   589
Air Quality and Smog   589
The Greenhouse Effect and Global Warming   591
Thinning of the Ozone Layer   592
Energy Use and Air Pollution   594
Indoor Air Pollution   596
Preventing Air Pollution   596

WATER QUALITY AND POLLUTION   597
Water Contamination and Treatment   597
Water Shortages   598
Sewage   599
Protecting the Water Supply   599

SOLID WASTE POLLUTION   599
Solid Waste   600
Reducing Solid Waste   602

CHEMICAL POLLUTION AND HAZARDOUS WASTE   603
Asbestos   603
Lead   603
Pesticides   604
Mercury   604
Other Chemical Pollutants   605
Preventing Chemical Pollution   606

RADIATION POLLUTION   606
Nuclear Weapons and Nuclear Energy   606
Medical Use of Radiation   607
Radiation in the Home and Workplace   607
Avoiding Radiation   608

NOISE POLLUTION   608

YOU AND THE ENVIRONMENT   609

Tips for Today and the Future   610
Summary   610
For More Information   611
Selected Bibliography   612

20 CONVENTIONAL AND COMPLEMENTARY MEDICINE   615

SELF-CARE   616
Self-Assessment   616
Knowing When to See a Physician   616
Self-Treatment   617

PROFESSIONAL CARE   619

CONVENTIONAL MEDICINE   620
Premises and Assumptions of Conventional Medicine   620
The Providers of Conventional Medicine   621
Choosing a Primary Care Physician   623
Getting the Most Out of Your Medical Care   624

COMPLEMENTARY AND ALTERNATIVE MEDICINE   629
Alternative Medical Systems   629
Mind-Body Interventions   633
Biological-Based Therapies   634
Manipulative and Body-Based Methods   634
Energy Therapies   636
Evaluating Complementary and Alternative Therapies   637

PAYING FOR HEALTH CARE   638
The Current System   638
Health Insurance   639
Choosing a Policy   642

Tips for Today and the Future   642
Behavior Change Strategy   642

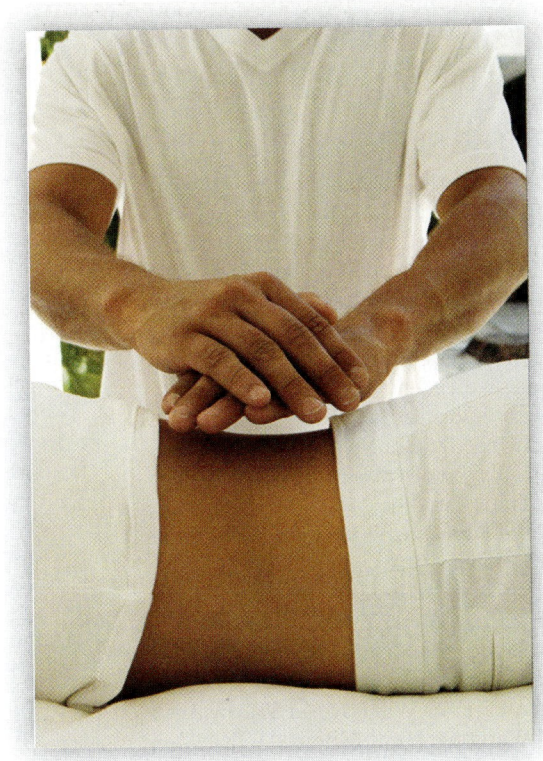

Summary   643
For More Information   643
Selected Bibliography   644

21 PERSONAL SAFETY   647

DIFFERENTIATING INJURIES   648

UNINTENTIONAL INJURIES   648
What Causes an Injury?   648
Motor Vehicle Injuries   650
Home Injuries   654
Leisure Injuries   657
Work Injuries   658

VIOLENCE AND INTENTIONAL INJURIES   659
Factors Contributing to Violence   660
Assault   662
Homicide   662
Gang-Related Violence   663
Hate Crimes   663
School Violence   663
Workplace Violence   664
Terrorism   664
Family and Intimate Violence   664
Sexual Violence   669
What You Can Do About Violence   673

PROVIDING EMERGENCY CARE   674

Tips for Today and the Future   674

Summary   675
For More Information   675
Behavior Change Strategy   676
Selected Bibliography   677

PART SEVEN
ACCEPTING PHYSICAL LIMITS

22 AGING: A VITAL PROCESS   679

GENERATING VITALITY AS YOU AGE   680
What Happens as You Age?   680
Life-Enhancing Measures: Age-Proofing   680

DEALING WITH THE CHANGES OF AGING   683
Planning for Social Changes   684
Adapting to Physical Changes   685
Handling Psychological and Mental Changes   688

AGING AND LIFE EXPECTANCY   690

LIFE IN AN AGING AMERICA   692
America's Aging Minority   692
Family and Community Resources for Older
    Adults   693
Government Aid and Policies   696
Changing the Public's Idea of Aging   696

Tips for Today and the Future   698
Summary   698
For More Information   698
Selected Bibliography   699

23 DYING AND DEATH   701

WHY IS THERE DEATH?   702

UNDERSTANDING DEATH AND DYING   702
Defining Death   702
Learning About Death   703
Denying versus Welcoming Death   704

PLANNING FOR DEATH   704
Making a Will   704
Considering Options for End-of-Life Care   705
Deciding to Prolong Life or Hasten Death   706
Completing an Advance Directive   709
Becoming an Organ Donor   710
Planning a Funeral or Memorial Service   710

COPING WITH DYING   713
Awareness of Dying   713
The Tasks of Coping   714
The Trajectory of Dying   716
Supporting a Dying Person   716

COPING WITH LOSS   717

Experiencing Grief   717

Supporting a Grieving Person   720

Helping Children Cope with Loss   720

COMING TO TERMS WITH DEATH   721

Tips for Today and the Future   721

Summary   721

For More Information   722

Selected Bibliography   723

APPENDIXES

A   NUTRITIONAL CONTENT OF POPULAR ITEMS FROM FAST-FOOD RESTAURANTS   A-1

B   A SELF-CARE GUIDE FOR COMMON MEDICAL PROBLEMS   A-6

CREDITS   C-1

INDEX   I-1

BOXES

IN THE NEWS

A "Planet in Peril": Healing the Environment   14

Coping After Violence on the Campus   45

Antidepressant Use in Young People   86

Same-Sex Marriage and Civil Unions   112

Sexsomnia: Sleep Disorders and Sex   145

Access to Emergency Contraception   162

Key Abortion Decisions and Legislation   187

Reproductive Technology   210

The Meth Epidemic   254

College Binge Drinking   285

FDA Regulation of Tobacco   318

Going Trans Fat–Free   350

Drugs and Supplements for Improved Athletic Performance   401

Are Diet Sodas Bad for You?   427

Aspirin and CVD   470

Cancer Myths and Misperceptions   507

MRSA: The Superbug?   533

Half of Americans Will Have an STD by Age 25   570

Global Warming, Local Action   593

Medical Errors, Adverse Events, and their Prevention   627

Emergency Preparedness   666

Baby Boomers: Redefining Age and Retirement   693

Profound Trauma and Loss   719

MIND/BODY/SPIRIT

Occupational Wellness   4

Stress and Your Brain   41

Paths to Spiritual Wellness   51

Are Intimate Relationships Good for Your Health?   114

Sexual Decision Making   140
Stress and Pregnancy   218
Spirituality and Drug Abuse   244
Tobacco Use and Religion: Global Views   304
Eating Habits and Total Wellness   332
Exercise and Total Wellness   383
Exercise, Body Image, and Self-Esteem   431
Anger, Hostility, and Heart Disease   460
Coping with Cancer   513
Immunity and Stress   548
Stress and Genital Herpes   573
Expressive Writing and Chronic Conditions   617
The Power of Belief: The Placebo Effect   633
Help Yourself by Helping Others   685
In Search of a Good Death   715

TAKE CHARGE

Tips for Moving Forward in the Cycle of Behavior Change   21
Motivation Boosters   26
Overcoming Insomnia   49
Meditation and the Relaxation Response   53
Breathing for Relaxation   54
Realistic Self-Talk   70
Being a Good Friend   97
Strategies for Enhancing Support in Relationships   102
Guidelines for Effective Communication   105
Strategies of Strong Families   119
Communicating About Sexuality   147
Talking with a Partner About Contraception   177
Healthy Eating During Pregnancy   220
If Someone You Know Has a Drug Problem . . .   264
Dealing with an Alcohol Emergency   277
Avoiding ETS   317
Helping a Friend or Partner Stop Using Tobacco   320
Building Motivation to Quit Smoking   322
Setting Intake Goals for Protein, Fat, and Carbohydrate   336
Choosing More Whole-Grain Foods   338
Eating for Healthy Bones   344
Judging Portion Sizes   355
Eating Strategies for College Students   360
Safe Food Handling   366
Making Time for Physical Activity   387
Determining Your Target Heart Rate Range   396
Safe Weight Training   400
Maintaining Your Exercise Program   409
Lifestyle Strategies for Successful Weight Management   433
If Someone You Know Has an Eating Disorder   443
What to Do in Case of a Heart Attack, Stroke, or Cardiac Arrest   468
Three Simple Ways to Recognize a Stroke   473
How to Perform a Breast Self-Exam   493
Testicle Self-Examination   501
Preventing HIV Infection and Other STDs   567
Don't Wait—Early Treatment of STDs Really Matters   578
Talking About Condoms and Safer Sex   579
Compact and Flourescent Bulbs   597
Making Your Letters Count   610
Recognizing the Potential for Abusiveness in a Partner   667
Preventing Date Rape   671
Staying Safe on Campus   673
Tasks for Survivors   714
Coping with Grief   720

CRITICAL CONSUMER

Evaluating Sources of Health Information   18
Alternative Remedies for Depression   83
Choosing and Evaluating Mental Health Professionals   88
Sex Enhancement Products   133
Obtaining a Contraceptive from a Health Clinic or Physician   158
Buying and Using Over-the-Counter Contraceptives   166
Making a Birth Plan   226
Choosing a Drug-Treatment Program   263
Alcohol Advertising   292
Tobacco Advertising   307
Using Food Labels   361
Using Dietary Supplement Labels   363
Choosing Exercise Footwear   405
Evaluating Fat and Sugar Substitutes   430
Is Any Diet Best for Weight Loss?   434
Choosing and Using Sunscreens and Sun-Protective Clothing   499
Avoiding Cancer Quackery   511
Preventing and Treating the Common Cold   537
Tattoos and Body Piercing   542
Getting an HIV Test   561
How to Be a Green Consumer   602
Evaluating Health News   622
Avoiding Health Fraud and Quackery   630
Choosing a Health Care Plan   641
Choosing a Bicycle Helmet   655
Choosing a Place to Live   695
A Consumer Guide to Funerals   713

DIMENSIONS OF DIVERSITY

Factors Contributing to Health Disparities Among Ethnic Minorities   10
Diverse Populations, Discrimination, and Stress   44
Ethnicity, Culture, and Psychological Disorders   75
Interfaith and Intrafaith Partnerships   108
Are There Ethnic Differences in Sexual Decision Making and Behavior?   142
Contraceptive Use Among American Women   176
Abortions Around the World   193
Ethnicity and Genetic Diseases   205
Drug Use and Ethnicity   261
Metabolizing Alcohol: Our Bodies Work Differently   274
Smoking Among U.S. Ethnic Populations   301
Ethnic Foods   348
Exercise for People with Special Health Concerns   391
Overweight and Obesity Among U.S. Ethnic Populations   426
Ethnicity and CVD   463
Ethnicity, Poverty, and Cancer   501
Poverty, Ethnicity, and Asthma   529
HIV/AIDS Around the World   554
HIV/AIDS Among African Americans and Latinos   558
Poverty and Environmental Health   604
Who Are the Uninsured?   640
Violence and Health: A Global View   665
Multicultural Wisdom About Aging   697
El Día de los Muertos: The Day of the Dead   705

GENDER MATTERS

Women's Health/Men's Health   9
Women, Men, and Stress   38
Depression, Anxiety, and Gender   80
Gender and Communication   106
Sexual Differentiation, Hormones, and the Brain   128
Men's Involvement in Contraception   178
Pregnancy Tasks for Fathers   213
Gender Differences in Drug Use and Abuse   243
Gender and Alcohol Use and Abuse   288
Gender and Tobacco Use   313
How Different Are the Nutritional Needs of Women and Men?   359
Gender Differences in Muscular Strength   398
Gender, Ethnicity, and Body Image   440
Women and CVD   462
Gender and Cancer   491
Women and Autoimmune Diseases   547
Women Are Hit Hard by STDs   568
Gender and Environmental Health   605
Health Care Visits and Gender   624
Injuries Among Young Men   649
Suicide Among Older Men   690
Why Do Women Live Longer?   691
Grief and Gender   718

ASSESS YOURSELF

Wellness: Evaluate Your Lifestyle   16
How High Is Your Stress Level?   33
Assessing Your Values   68
Are You Suffering from a Mood Disorder?   78
Are You Emotionally Intelligent?   101
Your Sexual Attitudes   142
Which Contraceptive Method Is Right for You and Your Partner?   180
Creating a Family Health Tree   207
Do You Have a Problem with Drugs?   245
Do You Have a Problem with Alcohol?   291
Nicotine Dependence: Are You Hooked?   303
Your Diet Versus MyPyramid Recommendations   357
The 1.5-Mile Run-Walk Test   407
What Triggers Your Eating?   428
Are You at Risk for CVD?   476
What's Your UV Risk?   497
Do Your Attitudes and Behaviors Put You at Risk for STDs?   577
Environmental Health Checklist   609
Personal Health Profile   626
Are You an Aggressive Driver?   651

IN FOCUS

Wellness Matters for College Students   13
Headaches: A Common Symptom of Stress   42
What Stresses Us Out?   43

Shyness 76
Myths About Suicide 82
Online Relationships 109
Sexual Activity Among College Students 141
Myths About Contraception 155
The Adoption Option 190
Abortion Myths and Misconceptions 197
Drug Use Among College Students 142
Club Drugs 252
Growing Up with Alcoholism 278
Smoking Cessation Products 323
Should You Take Supplements? 346
Classifying Activity Levels 386
Exercise Machines Versus Free Weights 399
Diabetes 421
Genetic Testing for Breast Cancer 504
The Next Influenza Pandemic—When, Not If 539
Are All Diseases Infectious? 540
College Students and STDs 571
Natural Ecosystems and Biodiversity 588
Herbal Remedies: Are They Safe 636
Cell Phones and Distracted Driving 652
Carpal Tunnel Syndrome 660
Stem Cells 681
Alzheimer's Disease 689
Hospice: Comfort and Care for the Dying 707
What Can Be Done About the Shortage of Organ Donors 712

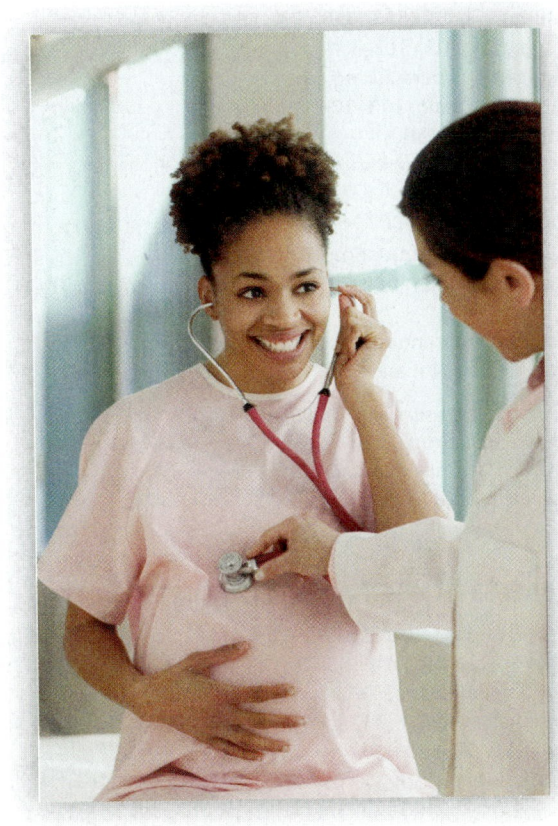

TOPICS OF SPECIAL CONCERN TO WOMEN

Aging among women, 96, 462, 691
Alcoholism, patterns among women, 288
Alcohol metabolism in women, 275
Alcohol use, special risks for women, 280, 281–282
Amenorrhea, 423
Anxiety disorders, 80
Arthritis, 391, 547, 685, 686–687
Asthma, 391, 604
Autoimmune disorders, 547
Bacterial vaginosis, 543
Body composition, 381, 387–388, 416–419
Body image, negative, 423, 438–439, 440
Breast cancer, 197, 491–494, 504
Breast self examinations, 493–494
Cancer, rates and risk factors, 488–489
Cardiovascular disease, risk among women, 462
Caregiving for older adults, 694–695, 706, 707
Carpal tunnel syndrome, 658, 660
Causes of death among women, 8, 196
Cervical cancer, 495–496
Communication styles among women, 106
Contraception, female methods, 155, 156–164, 165–171, 172–173, 174–177, 180–181
Contraceptive use and roles and responsibilities, 142, 177
Cybersex, 146
Depression, risk among women, 9, 80, 213
Dietary recommendations for women, 359
Drug use, rates of and special risks for women, 243, 252, 253, 255, 257, 260
Eating disorders, 439–443
Ectopic pregnancy, 222, 223
Environmental health risks, 589–590, 596, 603–605, 607–608
Family violence, 664–669
Female athlete triad, 422
Female genital mutilation, 138, 139
Financial planning for retirement, 684
Folic acid, 201, 204, 220, 346, 359, 477
Gender roles, 9, 36, 96, 138–139
Grief, pattern among women, 718
Health care visits, 9, 624
Health concerns and status, general, 6–10
Heart attack risk among women, 9
HIV infection rates and transmission, 552–558, 568
Hormone replacement therapy, 462
Hormones, female, 60
Infertility, female, 208
Life expectancy of women, 9
Marital status, 111, 112
Menopause, 131
Menstrual cycle, 128–131
Migraine, 42
Muscular strength, development of, 396–400
Obesity in women, 8, 129, 416, 419, 426
Osteoporosis, 342, 380, 389, 391, 688
Ovarian cancer, 496
Pap tests and pelvic exams, 107, 157, 158, 495–496, 577, 624
Parenting, single, by women, 117–118
Pelvic inflammatory disease, 136, 157, 569–570
Physical activity levels, 382, 386

Post-traumatic stress disorder, 40, 45, 76–77
Poverty rates among older women, 684, 691
Pregnancy and childbirth, 209–228, 230, 231
Premenstrual syndrome and premenstrual dysphoric disorder, 130, 131
Psychological disorders among women, 55, 62, 80
Rape, 669–672
Sexual anatomy, female, 124–125
Sexual functioning, female, 134
Sexual harassment, 672–673
Sexual health problems and dysfunctions, female, 135, 136, 137
Sexually transmitted diseases and pregnancy, 221
Sexually transmitted diseases, symptoms and special risks among women, 557, 566, 568, 576
Stalking and cyberstalking, 668
Sterilization, female, 174–175, 176
Stressors and responses to stress among women, 37, 38
Tobacco use, rates and special risks among women, 9, 301, 312, 313
Uterine cancer, 496
Violence against women, 669–672
Yeast infections, 135, 170, 171

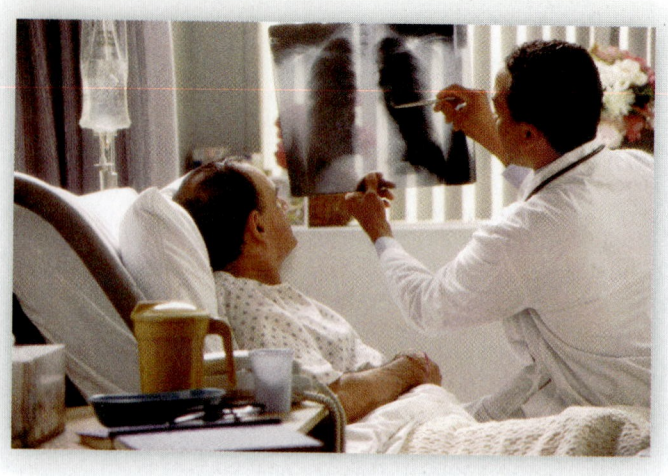

TOPICS OF SPECIAL CONCERN TO MEN

Aging among men, 132, 680, 690
Alcohol abuse and dependence, patterns among men, 287
Alcoholism in men, 273–274
Bladder cancer, 500
Body composition, 381, 387–388, 416–419
Body image, negative, 238–239, 422–423
Cancer, rates and risk factors, 386, 488, 489, 490, 491
Cardiovascular disease risk among men, 461, 462, 476
Causes of death among men, 5, 6
Cigars and pipes, 310, 314
Circumcision, 126, 556
Cluster headaches, 42
Communication styles among men, 104, 106
Contraception, male methods, 166, 172, 173–174
Contraceptive roles and responsibilities, 142, 177
Cybersex, 146
Dietary recommendations for men, 359
Drug use, rates of, 242, 243
Environmental health, 585–612
Family violence, 664–669
Firearm-related injuries, 657
Gambling, 238
Gender roles, 9, 36, 96, 138–139
Grief, pattern among men, 718
Health care visits, 8, 624
Health concerns and status, general, 6–10
Heart attack risk among men, 9
HIV infection rates and transmission, 552–558
Homicide, rates among men, 662–663
Hormones, male, 128
Infertility, male, 208
Injuries, rates of, 649
Life expectancy of men, 9
Marital status, 111, 112
Motor vehicle injuries, 650–654

Motorcycle and moped injuries, 653
Muscular strength, development of, 396–400
Obesity in men, 8, 106, 347, 416, 419, 426
Oral cancer, 313, 498, 500
Parenting, single, by men, 117–118
Poverty rates among older men, 684
Pregnancy, men's roles, 213
Prostate cancer, 494–495
Psychological disorders among men, 55, 56, 60, 62, 690
Rape, 669–672
Schizophrenia, 21, 82–83
Sexual anatomy, male, 125–127
Sexual functioning, male, 132–134
Sexual harassment, 672–673
Sexual health problems and dysfunctions, male, 136–137
Sexually transmitted diseases, symptoms and special risks among men, 9, 553, 556–559, 565
Spit tobacco, 302, 312–314
Stalking and cyberstalking, 668
Sterilization, male, 173–174
Stomach cancer, 500
Stressors and responses to stress among men, 9, 36, 37, 38
Suicide, 8, 59–60
Testicular cancer, 500
Testicular self-examination, 500
Tobacco use, rates and special risks among men, 9, 301, 312, 313
Violent behavior among men, 661–662
Violent deaths of men, 660

Note: The health issues and conditions listed here include those that disproportionately influence or affect women or men. For more information, see the Index under gender, women, men, and any of the special topics listed here.

DIVERSITY TOPICS RELATED TO ETHNICITY

Aging, attitudes toward, 697
Alcohol abuse patterns, 288–289
Alcohol metabolism, 274
Alcohol use patterns, 287–289
Asthma, 11, 590, 604
Body image, 440

Cancer, rates and risk, 500, 501, 502
Cardiovascular disease patterns and risks, 461, 463
Contraceptive use, patterns of, 176
Cystic fibrosis, 8
Death, attitudes toward, 705
Diabetes, 12, 421, 422, 494, 496
Dietary patterns and considerations, 205, 348, 352
Discrimination and health, 11, 44
Drug use, risk and protective factors, 245, 246, 261
Environmental health, 595, 604
Ethnic foods, 348
Fetal alcohol syndrome, 219, 281
Genetic disorders, 205
Glaucoma, 683
Hate crimes, 663
Health disparities, general, 6–12
Health insurance status, 640
Health status and concerns, general, 6–10, 502
Heart disease, 12
Hemochromatosis, 205
HIV/AIDS rates, 558, 566
Homicide rates, 662–663
Hypertension, 391, 453
Infant mortality, 224
Lactose intolerance, 205
Lead poisoning, 603–604

Lupus, 681
Marketing, targeted, 292, 301, 305, 307
Metabolic syndrome, 388, 427, 461–464
Osteoporosis, 342, 380, 389, 391, 688
Overweight/obesity, rates and trends, 416, 417, 426, 437
Poverty rates among older adults, 691, 692
Prostate cancer, 494–495
Psychological disorder, symptoms and rates, 74, 75
Rheumatic heart disease, 474
Sexual decision making and behavior, 143
Sexually transmitted diseases, rates of, 568, 569, 574
Sickle cell disease, 8, 205
Single-parent families, 117–118
Smoking rates, 5, 21, 300, 304, 315
Stress and discrimination, 44
Suicide rates, 7, 59
Tay-Sachs disease, 8, 205
Thallasemia, 205
Tobacco use, 1, 5, 21, 299–307
Violence, rates of, 661–665, 668
Vitamin deficiencies, 340, 342

Note: The health issues and conditions listed here include those that disproportionately influence or affect specific U.S. ethnic groups or for which patterns may appear along ethnic lines. For more information, see the Index under ethnicity, culture, names of specific population groups, and any of the topics listed here.

PREFACE

Core Concepts in Health has maintained its leadership in the field of personal health education for more than 30 years. Since we pioneered the concept of self-responsibility for personal health in 1976, millions of students have used our book to become active, informed participants in their own health care.

In keeping with twenty-first-century technology, we are adding an exciting digital dimension to the eleventh edition, reflected in the title *Connect Core Concepts in Health*. McGraw-Hill *Connect Personal Health* is an online platform that allows instructors to connect with their students and students to connect with their instructors and coursework. *Connect* adds a level of enhanced online teaching and learning potential to *Core Concepts in Health* that benefits both instructors and students. More information about *Connect* is included later in the preface.

OUR GOALS

Every edition of *Core Concepts in Health* has brought improvements and refinements, but our goals and principles have remained the same:

- To present scientifically based, accurate, up-to-date information in an accessible format
- To involve students in taking responsibility for their health and well-being
- To instill a sense of competence and personal power in students

The first of these goals means making expert knowledge about health and health care available to the individual. *Core Concepts* brings scientifically based, accurate, up-to-date information to students about topics and issues that concern them—exercise, stress, nutrition, weight management, contraception, intimate relationships, HIV infection, drugs, alcohol, and a multitude of others. Current, complete, and straightforward coverage is balanced with user-friendly features designed to make the text appealing. Written in an engaging, easy-to-read style and presented in a colorful, open format, *Core Concepts* invites the student to read, learn, and remember. Boxes, tables, artwork, photographs, and many other features highlight areas of special interest throughout the book.

Our second goal is to involve students in taking responsibility for their health. *Core Concepts* uses innovative pedagogy and unique interactive features to get students thinking about how the material they're reading relates to their lives. We invite them to examine their emotions about the issues under discussion, to consider their personal values and beliefs, to develop their critical thinking skills, and to analyze their health-related behaviors. Beyond this, for students who want to change behaviors that detract from a healthy lifestyle, we offer guidelines and tools, ranging from samples of health journals and personal contracts to detailed assessments and behavior change strategies.

Perhaps our third goal is the most important: to instill a sense of competence and personal power in the students who read the book. Everyone has the ability to monitor, understand, and affect his or her health. Although medical and health professionals possess impressive skills and have access to a huge body of knowledge that benefits everyone in our society, people can help to minimize the amount of professional care they actually require in their lifetime by taking care of themselves—taking charge of their health—from an early age. Our hope is that *Core Concepts* will continue to help young people make this exciting discovery—that they have the power to shape their futures.

ORGANIZATION AND CONTENT OF THE ELEVENTH EDITION

The book is divided into seven parts. Part One, Establishing a Basis for Wellness, includes chapters on taking charge of your health (Chapter 1), stress (Chapter 2), and psychological health (Chapter 3). Part Two, Understanding Sexuality, opens with an exploration of communication and intimate relationships, including friendship, intimate partnerships, marriage, and family (Chapter 4) and then moves on to discuss physical sexuality (Chapter 5), contraception (Chapter 6), abortion (Chapter 7), and pregnancy and childbirth (Chapter 8).

Part Three, Making Responsible Decisions: Substance Use and Abuse, opens with a discussion of addictive behavior and the different classes of psychoactive drugs (Chapter 9), followed by chapters on alcohol (Chapter 10) and tobacco (Chapter 11). Part Four, Getting Fit, includes a detailed discussion of nutrition (Chapter 12), exercise (Chapter 13), and weight management (Chapter 14).

Part Five, Protecting Yourself from Disease, deals with the most serious health threats facing Americans today—cardiovascular disease (Chapter 15), cancer (Chapter 16), infectious diseases (Chapter 17), and sexually transmitted diseases (Chapter 18). Part Six, Living Well in the World, explores environmental health (Chapter 19), conventional and complementary medicine (Chapter 20), and personal safety (Chapter 21). Part Seven, Accepting Physical Limits, explores aging (Chapter 22), and dying and death (Chapter 23).

Taken together, the chapters of the book provide students with a complete guide to promoting and protecting their health, now and through their entire lives.

CHANGES TO THE ELEVENTH EDITION

For the eleventh edition, all chapters were carefully reviewed, revised, and updated. The latest information from scientific and health-related research is incorporated in the text, and newly emerging topics and issues are discussed. The following list gives a sample of some of the topics and concerns addressed in this edition:

- Global warming and climate change; human causes and human health effects; and strategies for reducing one's environmental footprint

- The latest recommendations on physical activity and exercise from the American College of Sports Medicine, the American Cancer Society, and other organizations, as well as new information on the impact of exercise on multiple dimensions of wellness and guidelines for distinguishing light, moderate, and vigorous exercise

- Stress in America and the impact of stress on wellness, including current statistics from the American Psychological Association

- The continuing overweight and obesity epidemic, with the latest from the CDC and the National Center for Health Statistics

- The growing prevalence of diabetes, prediabetes, insulin resistance, and metabolic syndrome; their causes, warning signs, and health effects; and strategies for prevention

- Fat cells and the role of abdominal fat in chronic conditions, along with a distinction between visceral fat and subcutaneous fat and clarification of the impact of both types of fat on health

- Foodborne illness and the safety of the U.S. food supply

- Violence on school and college campuses; current statistics on personal safety, injuries, and violence from the FBI, the National Safety Council, and other organizations; and strategies for coping with violence

- Disparities in access to emergency contraception among American women

- Updated statistics on HIV/AIDS in the United States, showing that rates are higher than previously believed

- The crisis in the health care system and the effects of the faltering economy on health care for Americans

- Proposed FDA regulation of tobacco products

- The "Healthy Campus 2010" initiative

- Diet sodas and their health implications

- New hands-only CPR guidelines from the American Heart Association

- The possible role of vitamin D in heart disease and other chronic conditions and the growing use of aspirin therapy for CVD

- Exercise guidelines for older adults from the American College of Sports Medicine

- The importance of sleep in health and wellness; sleep disorders; and sleep aids and their side effects

- The importance of friendships and social connectedness in overall wellness

- Latest vaccination guidelines from the Centers for Disease Control and Prevention.

- Emerging infections and antibiotic resistance; MRSA and *Clostridium Difficile*; and strategies for prevention

(A complete, chapter-by-chapter list of changes to this edition is included on the Instructor Resource Site at www.mhhe.com/insel11e.)

For the eleventh edition, the chapter on environmental health has been moved up to highlight the importance of environmental issues in our time, and an environmental theme runs through the text, expressed in **Thinking About the Environment** boxes in each chapter. The text emphasizes that students are not just individuals but also participants in communities and citizens of a "planet in peril"—one that needs care and protection if it is to continue providing us with the means to healthy lives. The chapters on Conventional and Complementary Medicine and on Personal Safety have also been moved forward to highlight growing interest in these two important areas of personal health.

A new feature in the eleventh edition is **Quick Stats**—a marginal notation highlighting a particularly striking statistic related to the chapter topic. Quick Stats appear several times in each chapter, calling students' attention to key data. Also new to the eleventh edition are **Questions for Critical Thinking and Reflection**, which appear at the ends of major sections within chapters. These questions prompt students to think critically about chapter topics, relate them to their own lives, and probe more deeply into their own attitudes, values, and beliefs. Instructors may want to use these questions to stimulate classroom discussion.

The eleventh edition also features a new, more visually appealing design. Dozens of photos and illustrations have been added, along with new and updated graphics, more readable tables and figures, and many colorful points of interest throughout each chapter. In addition, information has been streamlined, and key data have been chunked into lists, charts, and tables to help students learn and retain important material.

FEATURES OF THE ELEVENTH EDITION

This edition of *Core Concepts in Health* builds on the features that attracted and held our readers' interest in the previous editions. One of the most popular features has always been the **boxes,** which allow us to explore a wide range of current topics in greater detail than is possible in the text itself. Each type of box is a different color and marked with a distinctive icon and label. Refer to the table of contents for a complete list of all the boxes in each category.

 Boxes with the *Connect* icon feature a student activity in *Connect*, typically a short multiple-choice quiz and a question for personal reflection. Instructors can assign the *Connect* activities to ensure that their students are getting the most from the boxes.

 **In the News** boxes focus on current health issues that have recently been highlighted in the media. Topics include environmental issues, such as global warming and climate change; violence on campus; access to emergency contraception; sleep aids and sexsomnia; same-sex marriage; health issues related to trans fats and diet sodas; and aspirin and cardiovascular disease.

 **Mind/Body/Spirit** boxes focus on spiritual wellness and the close connections between people's feelings and states of mind and their physical health. Included in Mind/Body/Spirit boxes are topics such as occupational and financial wellness, paths to spiritual wellness, benefits of being a volunteer, sexual decision making and personal values, how exercise fosters total wellness, and how stress can affect pregnancy and the immune system.

Take Charge boxes distill from each chapter the practical advice students need in order to apply information to their own lives. By referring to these boxes, students can find ways to foster friendships; to become more physically active; to stay safe when using online social networking and dating Web sites; to perform deep-breathing exercises for stress reduction; or to help a friend who has a problem with tobacco, drugs, or an eating disorder.

 **Critical Consumer** boxes help students develop and apply the critical thinking skills they need to make sound health-related choices. Critical Consumer boxes provide specific guidelines for evaluating health news and advertising, using food and dietary supplement labels to make smart choices, choosing a bicycle helmet, avoiding quackery, selecting exercise footwear, understanding health issues associated with tattooing and body piercing, getting an HIV test, and making environmentally friendly shopping choices, among others.

 Dimensions of Diversity boxes reflect and respond to the diversity of the student population. These boxes give students the opportunity to identify any specific health risks that affect them as individuals or as members of a group. Topics covered in these boxes include factors contributing to health disparities among ethnic minorities, diverse populations and stress, ethnic and cultural influences on psychological disorders, rates of smoking and alcohol use among ethnic populations, suicide among older men, exercise for people with special health concerns, links between poverty and asthma, tobacco control around the world, and the global pattern of HIV infection.

 **Gender Matters** boxes highlight key gender differences related to wellness as well as areas of particular concern to men or women. An overview of key gender-related wellness concerns is provided in Chapter 1. Topics covered in later chapters include gender differences in rates of anxiety, depression, drug use, and cancer; in responses to stress and grief; and in rates of autoimmune disorders and unintentional injuries.

 **Assess Yourself** boxes give students the opportunity to examine their behavior and identify ways that they can change their habits and improve their health. By referring to these boxes, students can examine their eating habits, evaluate their fitness level, discover if they are at increased risk for cancer or cardiovascular disease, or measure their emotional intelligence, and more.

 **In Focus** boxes highlight current wellness topics of particular interest. Topics include diabetes, headaches, carpal tunnel syndrome, herbal remedies, and growing up with alcoholism.

New to the eleventh edition are **Thinking About the Environment** boxes. Reflecting the environmental theme of this edition, these boxes highlight specific environmental issues related to the topic at hand, such as environmental factors that increase stress, the effects of the environment on mood disorders and other psychological problems, stewardship of the environment as a family value, and environmental changes and the global food supply.

In addition to the boxes, many carefully refined features and learning aids are included in the eleventh edition. Each chapter opens with **Test Your Knowledge**—a set of 4 to 6 multiple-choice and true-false questions, with answers. These self-quizzes can serve as a chapter pretest for students. The questions emphasize important points, highlight common misconceptions, and spark debate.

Vital Statistics tables and figures highlight important facts and figures in a memorable format that often reveals surprising contrasts and connections. For students who grasp a subject best when it is displayed graphically, numerically, or in a table, the Vital Statistics feature provides alternative ways of approaching and understanding the text. As noted earlier, the new feature **Quick Stats** highlights striking statistics related to chapter topics, and **Questions for Critical Thinking and Reflection** prompt students to relate chapter material to their own lives.

Like previous editions, the eleventh edition features a wealth of attractive and helpful **illustrations**. The anatomical art, which has been prepared by medical illustrators, is both visually appealing and informative. These illustrations help students understand such important information as how blood flows through the heart, how the process of conception occurs, and how to use a condom. These illustrations will particularly benefit those students who learn best from visual images.

Chapter-ending **Tips for Today and the Future** sections provide brief distillations of the major message of each chapter, followed by suggestions for a few simple things that students can try right away and in the weeks and months ahead. Tips for Today and the Future are designed to encourage students and to build their confidence by giving them easy steps they can take immediately to start changing their behaviors.

The **Behavior Change Strategies** that conclude many chapters offer specific behavior management/modification plans relating to the chapter's topic. Based on the principles of behavior management that are carefully explained in Chapter 1, these strategies will help students change unhealthy or counterproductive behaviors. Included are strategies for dealing with test anxiety, quitting smoking, developing responsible drinking habits, planning a personal exercise program, phasing in a healthier diet, and many other practical plans for change.

Two quick-reference appendixes provide students with resources they can keep and use for years to come:

- **Appendix A,** "Nutritional Content of Popular Items from Fast-Food Restaurants," provides information

on commonly ordered menu items.

- **Appendix B,** "Self-Care Guide for Common Medical Problems," provides information to help students assess and manage common symptoms, including fever, sore throat, indigestion, headache, and cuts and scrapes.

The latest emergency care guidelines for choking and cardiac arrest (the Heimlich maneuver and CPR) appear inside the back cover of the text, providing information that can save lives.

In addition, several specific learning aids have been incorporated into the text. Learning objectives labeled **Looking Ahead** appear on the opening page of each chapter, identifying major concepts and helping guide students in their reading and review of the text. Important terms appear in boldface type in the text and are defined in a **running glossary,** helping students handle a large and complex new vocabulary.

Chapter summaries offer a concise review and a way to make sure students have grasped the most important concepts in the chapter. **For More Information** sections contain annotated lists of books, newsletters, hotlines, organizations, and Web sites that students can use to extend and broaden their knowledge or pursue subjects of interest to them. Also found at the end of every chapter are **Selected Bibliographies**. A complete **Index** at the end of the book includes references to glossary terms in boldface type.

TEACHING AND LEARNING TOOLS

Available with the eleventh edition is a comprehensive package of supplementary materials designed to enhance teaching and learning.

Connect Core Concepts in Health

McGraw-Hill *Connect Personal Health* is a Web-based assignment and assessment platform that makes it easy for instructors to connect with their students and students to connect with their instructors and coursework. With *Connect,* you can choose interactive activities organized by chapter learning objectives, or you can create activities that align with your coursework. Available with *Connect Core Concepts in Health* are interactive Wellness Worksheets, video activities, Internet activities, the Fitness and Nutrition Log, the Behavior Change Workbook, and more.

Also available are activities aligned with boxes from the text. For example, in Chapter 1, there are activities associated with the Mind/Body/Spirit box on occupational wellness, the Dimensions of Diversity box on factors contributing to health disparities among ethnic minorities, and the Take Charge box on moving forward in the cycle of behavior change. You can deliver all these assignments, assessments, quizzes, and tests online and have the results automatically reported to your grade book. *Connect* is available to accompany the eleventh edition via an access code that can be packaged with each copy of the text.

With easy, 24/7 access to *Connect*, your students can practice important skills at their own pace and on their own schedule. *Connect* provides students with immediate feedback on assignments so they can see how they performed on each question. Students can conveniently complete and submit assignments for online grading, creating a paperless classroom. Every chapter-opening page in the text has the *Connect* icon and Web site address to remind students to log to study, review, and complete their assignments.

Also available is *Connect Plus*, which includes all the features of *Connect* plus an interactive, media-rich eBook—an online version of the eleventh edition text. With *Connect Plus*, students have access to a wide range of additional online resources and learning aids embedded in the eBook, including videos, key terms and definitions, chapter quizzes, student handouts, behavior change tools, links to health-related Web sites and national organizations, and appendixes on self-care and fast food. *Connect Plus* provides students with everything they need in one convenient online package to successfully complete their work wherever and whenever they choose.

Instructor's Resource Site

The **Instructor's Resource Site** (www.mhhe.com/insel11e) presents key teaching resources in an easy-to-use format. It includes the following teaching tools:

• The **Course Integrator Guide** includes learning objectives, extended chapter outlines, suggested activities, and lists of additional resources. It also describes all the print and electronic supplements available with the text and shows how to integrate them into lectures and assignments for each chapter. For the eleventh edition, the guide was prepared by Cathy Kennedy, Colorado State University.

• The **test bank** includes more than 3000 true-false, multiple-choice, and short essay questions; it also includes two 100-question multiple-choice tests that cover the content of the entire text. The answer key lists the page number in the text where each answer is found. Contributors to the test bank for the eleventh edition are Majella Smith, Los Medanos Community College; Patricia Rhea, Community College of Baltimore County, Catonsville; Leonard Williams, Tougaloo College; Cynthia Bunwell, Norfolk State University; and Karen Vail-Smith, East Carolina University.

The test bank is also available with the EZ Test **computerized testing software.** EZ Test provides a powerful, easy-to-use test maker to create printed quizzes and exams. EZ Test runs on both Windows and Macintosh

systems. For secure online testing, exams created in EZ Test can be exported to WebCT, Blackboard, PageOut, and EZ Test Online. EZ Test is packaged with a Quick Start Guide; once the program is installed, users have access to the complete User's Manual, including multiple Flash tutorials. Additional help is available at www.mhhe.com/eztest.

• The **PowerPoint slides** provide a lecture tool that you can alter or expand to meet the needs of your course. The slides include key lecture points and images from the text and other sources. For the eleventh edition, the PowerPoint presentations were created by Andrew Shim, Indiana University of Pennsylvania, and updated by Rob Hess, Community College of Baltimore County, Catonsville. As an aid for instructors who wish to create their own presentations, a complete **image bank,** including all the illustrations from the text, is also included on the Instructor's Media DVD.

• **Transparency masters and student handouts**— more than 150 in all—are provided as additional lecture resources. The transparency masters feature tables showing key statistics and data, illustrations from the text and other sources, and key points from the text. Illustrations of many body systems are also provided. The student handouts provide additional information and can be used to extend student knowledge on topics such as pre-diabetes, glycemic index, yoga for relaxation, and dealing with alcohol emergencies.

Tegrity Campus

Tegrity Campus is a service that makes class time available all the time by automatically capturing every lecture in a searchable format for students to review when they study and complete assignments. With a simple one-click start and stop process, you capture all computer screens and corresponding audio. Students replay any part of any class with easy-to-use browser-based viewing on a PC or Mac.

Educators know that the more students can see, hear, and experience class resources, the better they learn. With Tegrity Campus, students quickly recall key moments by using Tegrity Campus's unique search feature. This search helps students efficiently find what they need, when they need it, across an entire semester of class recordings. Help turn all your students' study time into learning moments immediately supported by your lecture. Contact your local sales representative for more information on Tegrity Campus.

Classroom Performance System

Classroom Performance System (CPS) brings interactivity into the classroom or lecture hall. CPS is a wireless response system that gives instructors and students immediate feedback from the entire class. Each student uses a wireless response pad similar to a television remote to respond instantly to polling or quiz questions. Contact your local sales representative for more information about CPS.

PageOut

PageOut (www.pageout.net) is a free, easy-to-use program that enables instructors to quickly develop Web sites for their courses. PageOut can be used to create a course home page, an instructor home page, a syllabus, Web links, online discussion areas, an online gradebook, and much more.

Other Resources

• **Printed versions of key supplements**—the Course Integrator Guide, test bank, transparency masters, student handouts, and Wellness Worksheets—are also available (ISBN 0-07-727324-9). The printed supplements are loose-leaf and three-hole-punched, ready to be placed in a binder.

• A set of 80 color **Transparency Acetates** is available as a lecture resource. The acetates are not duplicates of the transparency masters on the Instructor's Resource Site; many are from sources other than the text.

• Videos from **Films for Humanities** are also available.

Student Resources Available with *Connect Core Concepts in Health*

Contact your local representative to find out about packaging any of the following student resources with the text.

• More than 100 **Wellness Worksheets** (ISBN 0-07-727321-4) are available to help students become more involved in their wellness and better prepared to implement successful behavior change. The worksheets include assessment tools, Internet activities, and knowledge-based reviews of key concepts. They are available shrink-wrapped with the text in an easy-to-use pad.

• **NutritionCalc Plus** (ISBN 0-07-321925-8) is a dietary analysis program with an easy-to-use interface that allows users to track their nutrient and food group intakes, energy expenditures, and weight control goals. It generates a variety of reports and graphs for analysis, including comparisons with the latest Dietary Reference Intakes (DRIs). The ESHA database includes thousands of ethnic foods, supplements, fast foods, and convenience foods, and users can add their own foods to the food list. NutritionCalc Plus is available on CD-ROM (Windows only) or in an online version.

• **The Daily Fitness and Nutrition Journal** (ISBN 0-07-302988-2) is a handy booklet that guides students in planning and tracking a fitness program. It also helps students assess their current diet and make appropriate changes.

• The **Health and Fitness Pedometer** (ISBN 0-07-320933-3) can be packaged with copies of the text. It allows students to count their daily steps and track their level of physical activity.

• The interactive **HealthQuest CD-ROM** (ISBN 0-07-295117-6) helps students explore and change their wellness behavior. It includes tutorials, assessments, and behavior change guidelines in such key areas as stress, fitness, nutrition, cardiovascular disease, cancer, tobacco, and alcohol.

A NOTE OF THANKS

The efforts of innumerable people have gone into producing the eleventh edition of this text. The book has benefited immensely from their thoughtful commentaries, expert knowledge and opinions, and many helpful suggestions. We are deeply grateful for their participation in the project.

Academic Contributors

Thomas D. Fahey, Ed.D., California State University, Chico
Exercise for Health and Fitness

James V. Freeman, M.D., M.P.H., Stanford University
Cardiovascular Health

Michael R. Hoadley, Ph.D., Assistant Vice-President for Academic Affairs, Center for Academic Technology Support, Eastern Illinois University
Personal Safety

Paul M. Insel, Ph.D., Stanford University
Taking Charge of Your Health

Mary Iten, Ph.D., University of Nebraska at Kearney
Aging: A Vital Process

Robert Jarski, Ph.D., Professor, School of Health Sciences, Director, Complementary Medicine and Wellness Program, Oakland University
Conventional and Complementary Medicine

Nancy Kemp, M.D.
Sex and Your Body; Sexually Transmitted Diseases

John Kowalczyk, Ph.D., University of Minnesota, Duluth
Environmental Health

Inna Landres, M.D., Stanford Hospital and Clinics
Abortion

Howard Lee, M.D., M.P.H., Hematology and Oncology, San Mateo County General Hospital
Cancer

Javier Lopez-Zetina, Associate Professor, Health Science Department, California State University, Long Beach
The Use and Abuse of Psychoactive Drugs

Jacob W. Roth, M.D., Chief of Adult Psychiatry, Kaiser Permanente San Jose Medical Center Adjunct Clinical Faculty, Stanford University
Dying and Death

Walton T. Roth, M.D., Stanford University
Stress: The Constant Challenge; Psychological Health

Judith Sharlin, Ph.D., R. D., Department of Nutrition, Simmons College
Weight Management

Rachel Stern, M.S., R.D., Nutrition Consultant
The Responsible Use of Alcohol

Phillip Takakjian, Ph.D.
Intimate Relationships and Communication

Mae Tinklenberg, R.N., N.P., M.S.
Contraception

R. Elaine Turner, Ph.D., R.D., University of Florida
Nutrition Basics

Sarah Waller, M.D., Stanford University
Pregnancy and Childbirth

Patrick Zickler, Senior Health and Science Writer, Circle Solutions, Inc.
Toward a Tobacco-Free Society

Martha C. Zúñiga, Ph.D., University of California, Santa Cruz
Immunity and Infection

Academic Advisers and Reviewers of the Eleventh Edition

Rachel Abbott, University of West Georgia

Jimmy Anderson, Macon State College

Tami Ashford-Carroll, Benedict College

Debra Atkinson, Iowa State University

Faye Avard, Mississippi Valley State University

Brian Barthel, Utah Valley State College

Autumn Benner, Minnesota State University

Stephanie Bennett, University of Southern Indiana

Sheri Bollinger, Northampton Community College

Liz Brown, Rose State College

Mary Chalupsky, Eastern Connecticut State University

Michael Cleary, Slippery Rock University

Holly Clemens, Cuyahoga Community College

Nicholas DiCicco, Camden County College

Paul Finnicum, Arkansas State University

Daniel Gerber, University of Massachusetts, Amherst

Brian Goslin, Oakland University

Mary Iten, University of Nebraska at Kearney

Linda Jenuwine, Macomb Community College

Cathy Kennedy, Colorado State University

Brian Kipp, Grand Valley State University

Deneen Long, Howard University

Mary Miller, Morehead State University

Irene O'Boyle, Central Michigan University

Pam Rost, Buffalo State College

Andrea Salis, Queensborough Community College, City University of New York

Patrick Sierer, Coastal Carolina Community College

Barbara Spatz, Cuyahoga Community College

William Swanson, South Texas College

Paul Villas, University of Texas-Pan American

Debbi Ware, Gardner-Webb University

Finally, we would like to thank the members of the *Core Concepts* book team at McGraw-Hill Higher Education. We are indebted to Kirstan Price, whose dedication and extraordinary creative energies have contributed so much to the success of this book; we are also indebted to Tim Huddleston for so ably taking on the role of developmental editor for this edition. Thanks also go to Chris Johnson, executive editor; Bill Minick, marketing manager; Kate Engelberg, director of development; Julia D. Akpan, developmental editor for technology; Lydia Kim, editorial coordinator; Ron Nelms, Jr., media project manager; Carey Eisner, production editor; Randy Hurst and Rich DeVitto, production supervisors; Andrei Pasternak, design manager; Brian Pecko, photo research manager; and Marty Moga, permissions editor. To all we express our deep appreciation.

Paul M. Insel
Walton T. Roth

connect™
CORE CONCEPTS
IN HEALTH

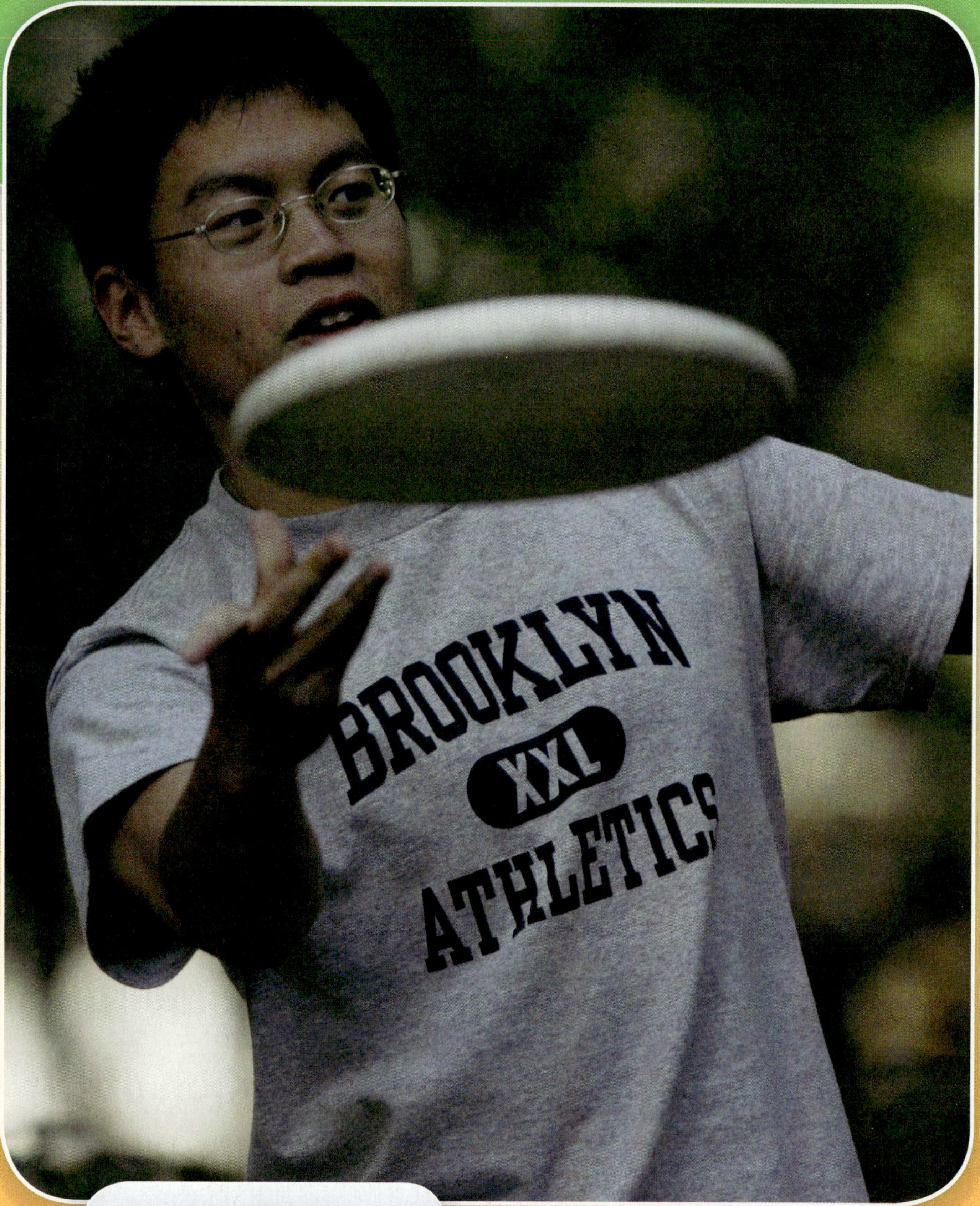
BROOKLYN
XXL
ATHLETICS

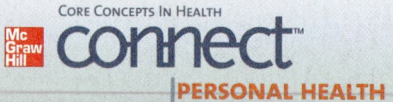

TAKING CHARGE OF YOUR HEALTH

LOOKING AHEAD >>>>>

AFTER READING THIS CHAPTER, YOU SHOULD BE ABLE TO:

- Describe the dimensions of wellness
- Identify major health problems in the United States today
- Describe the influence of gender, ethnicity, income, disability, family history, and environment on health
- Explain the importance of personal decision making and behavior change in achieving wellness
- List some available sources of health information and explain how to think critically about them
- Describe the steps in creating a behavior management plan to change a health-related behavior

TEST YOUR KNOWLEDGE

1. **Which of the following lifestyle factors is the leading preventable cause of death for Americans?**
   a. excess alcohol consumption
   b. cigarette smoking
   c. obesity

2. **The terms *health* and *wellness* mean the same thing.**
   True or false?

3. **Which of the following health-related issues affects the greatest number of college students each year?**
   a. stress
   b. colds/flu/sore throat
   c. sleep problems

4. **A person's genetic makeup determines whether he or she will develop certain diseases (such as breast cancer), regardless of that person's health habits.**
   True or false?

ANSWERS

1. **B.** Smoking causes about 500,000 deaths per year; obesity is responsible for more than 100,000; and alcohol, as many as 85,000.

2. **FALSE.** Although the words are used interchangeably, they actually have different meanings. The term *health* refers to the overall condition of the body or mind and to the presence or absence of illness or injury. The term *wellness* refers to optimal health and vitality, encompassing all the dimensions of well-being.

3. **A.** About 34% of college students suffer so much stress that it affects their academic performance. High stress levels affect overall health and wellness, making it important to manage stress.

4. **FALSE.** In many cases, behavior can tip the balance toward good health even when heredity or environment is a negative factor. For example, breast or prostate cancer may run in families, but these diseases are also associated with controllable factors, such as being overweight and inactive.

A college sophomore sets the following goals for herself:

- To join in new social circles and make new friends whenever possible
- To exercise every day
- To clean up trash and plant trees in blighted neighborhoods in her community

These goals may differ, but they have one thing in common. Each contributes, in its own way, to this student's health and well-being. Not satisfied merely to be free of illness, she wants more. She has decided to live actively and fully—not just to be healthy, but to pursue a state of overall wellness.

WELLNESS: THE NEW HEALTH GOAL

Generations of people have viewed health simply as the absence of disease. That view largely prevails today; the word **health** typically refers to the overall condition of a person's body or mind and to the presence or absence of illness or injury. **Wellness** is a relatively new concept that expands our idea of health. Beyond the simple presence or absence of disease, wellness refers to optimal health and vitality—to living life to its fullest. Although we use the words *health* and *wellness* interchangeably, there are two important differences between them:

- Health—or some aspects of it—can be determined or influenced by factors beyond your control, such as your genes, age, and family history. For example, consider a 60-year-old man with a strong family history of prostate cancer. These factors place this man at a higher-than-average risk for developing prostate cancer himself.

- Wellness is largely determined by the decisions you make about how you live. That same 60-year-old man can reduce his risk of cancer by eating sensibly, exercising, and having regular screening tests. Even if he develops the disease, he may still rise above its effects to live a rich, meaningful life. This means

choosing not only to care for himself physically but to maintain a positive outlook, keep up his relationships with others, challenge himself intellectually, and nurture other aspects of his life.

Enhanced wellness, therefore, involves making conscious decisions to control **risk factors** that contribute to disease or injury. Age and family history are risk factors you cannot control. Behaviors such as smoking, exercising, and eating a healthy diet are well within your control.

The Dimensions of Wellness

Experts have defined six dimensions of wellness:

- Physical
- Emotional
- Intellectual
- Interpersonal
- Spiritual
- Environmental

These dimensions are interrelated; each has an effect on the others. Further, the process of achieving wellness is constant and dynamic (Figure 1.1), involving change and growth. Wellness is not static; ignoring any dimension of wellness can have harmful effects on your life. The following sections briefly introduce the dimensions of wellness. Table 1.1 lists some of the specific qualities and behaviors associated with each dimension.

Physical Wellness Your physical wellness includes not just your body's overall condition and the absence of disease but your fitness level and your ability to care for yourself. The higher your fitness level, the higher your level of physical wellness will be. Similarly, as you develop the ability to take care of your own physical needs, you ensure a greater level of physical wellness. To achieve optimum physical wellness, you need to make choices that will help you avoid illnesses and injuries. The decisions you make now, and the habits you develop over your lifetime, will largely determine the length and quality of your life.

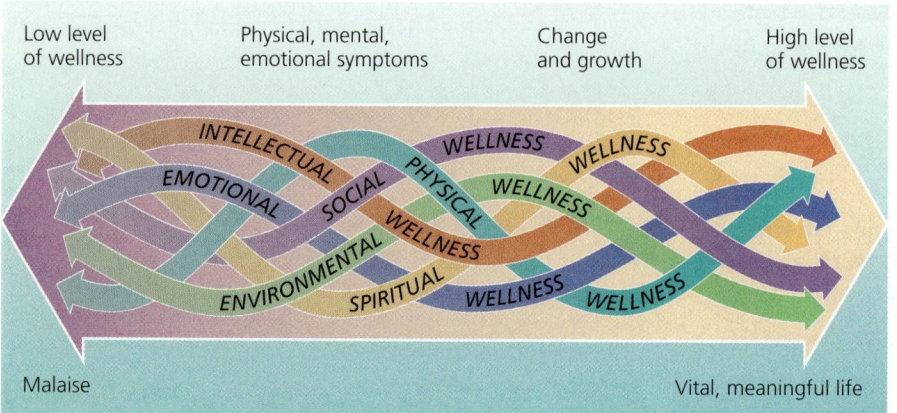

Low level of wellness | Physical, mental, emotional symptoms | Change and growth | High level of wellness

INTELLECTUAL EMOTIONAL SOCIAL PHYSICAL WELLNESS WELLNESS ENVIRONMENTAL WELLNESS SPIRITUAL WELLNESS WELLNESS

Malaise | Vital, meaningful life

FIGURE 1.1 The wellness continuum. The concept of wellness includes vitality in six interrelated dimensions, all of which contribute to overall wellness.

Table 1.1	Examples of Qualities and Behaviors Associated with the Dimensions of Wellness				
Physical	**Emotional**	**Intellectual**	**Interpersonal**	**Spiritual**	**Environmental**
• Eating well • Exercising • Avoiding harmful habits • Practicing safer sex • Recognizing symptoms of disease • Getting regular checkups • Avoiding injuries	• Optimism • Trust • Self-esteem • Self-acceptance • Self-confidence • Ability to understand and accept one's feelings • Ability to share feelings with others	• Openness to new ideas • Capacity to question • Ability to think critically • Motivation to master new skills • Sense of humor • Creativity • Curiosity • Lifelong learning	• Communication skills • Capacity for intimacy • Ability to establish and maintain satisfying relationships • Ability to cultivate support system of friends and family	• Capacity for love • Compassion • Forgiveness • Altruism • Joy • Fulfillment • Caring for others • Sense of meaning and purpose • Sense of belonging to something greater than oneself	• Having abundant, clean natural resources • Maintaining sustainable development • Recycling whenever possible • Reducing pollution and waste

Emotional Wellness Your emotional wellness reflects your ability to understand and deal with your feelings. Emotional wellness involves attending to your own thoughts and feelings, monitoring your reactions, and identifying obstacles to emotional stability. Achieving this type of wellness means finding solutions to emotional problems, with professional help if necessary.

Intellectual Wellness Those who enjoy intellectual (or mental) wellness constantly challenge their minds. An active mind is essential to wellness because it detects problems, finds solutions, and directs behavior. People who enjoy intellectual wellness never stop learning; they continue trying to learn new things throughout their lifetime. They seek out and relish new experiences and challenges.

Interpersonal Wellness Your interpersonal (or social) wellness is defined by your ability to develop and maintain satisfying and supportive relationships. Such relationships are essential to physical and emotional health. Social wellness requires participating in and contributing to your community and to society.

Spiritual Wellness To enjoy spiritual wellness is to possess a set of guiding beliefs, principles, or values that give meaning and purpose to your life, especially in difficult times. The spiritually well person focuses on the positive aspects of life and finds spirituality to be an antidote for negative feelings such as cynicism, anger, and pessimism. Organized religions help many people develop spiritual health. Religion, however, is not the only source or form of spiritual wellness. Many people find meaning and purpose in their lives on their own—through nature, art, meditation, or good works—or with their loved ones.

Environmental Wellness Your environmental wellness is defined by the livability of your surroundings. Personal health depends on the health of the planet—from the safety of the food supply to the degree of violence in society. Your physical environment either supports your wellness or diminishes it. To improve your environmental wellness, you can learn about and protect yourself against hazards in your surroundings and work to make your world a cleaner and safer place.

In addition, see the box "Occupational Wellness" (p. 4) to learn about another important aspect of wellness.

New Opportunities, New Responsibilities

Wellness is a fairly new concept. A century ago, Americans considered themselves lucky just to survive to adulthood (Figure 1.2, p. 5). A child born in 1900, for example, could expect to live only about 47 years. Many people died from common **infectious diseases** (such as pneumonia, tuberculosis, or diarrhea) and poor environmental conditions (such as water pollution and poor sanitation).

health The overall condition of body or mind and the presence or absence of illness or injury.

wellness Optimal health and vitality, encompassing all the dimensions of well-being.

risk factor A condition that increases one's chances of disease or injury.

infectious disease A disease that can spread from person to person; caused by microorganisms such as bacteria and viruses.

TERMS

Occupational Wellness

Many experts contend that occupational (or career) wellness is a seventh dimension of wellness, in addition to the six dimensions described in this chapter. Whether or not occupational wellness appears on every list of wellness dimensions, a growing body of evidence suggests that our daily work has a considerable effect on our overall wellness.

Defining Occupational Wellness

The term *occupational wellness* refers to the level of happiness and fulfillment you gain through your work. Although high salaries and prestigious titles are nice, they alone generally do not bring about occupational wellness. An occupationally well person truly likes his or her work, feels a connection to others in the workplace, and has opportunities to learn and be challenged.

Key aspects of occupational wellness include the following:

- Enjoyable work

- Job satisfaction

- Recognition and acknowledgment from managers and colleagues

- Feelings of achievement

- Opportunities to learn and grow

An ideal job draws on your passions and interests, as well as your vocational skills, and allows you to feel that you are contributing to society in your everyday work.

Financial Wellness

Another important facet of occupational wellness is financial wellness. A person's economic situation is a key factor in his or her overall well-being. People with low socioeconomic status have higher rates of death, injury, and disease; are less likely to have access to preventive health services; and are more likely to engage in unhealthy habits.

Although money and possessions in themselves won't necessarily make you happy, financial security can contribute to your peace of mind. If you are financially secure, you can worry less about daily expenses and focus on personal interests and your future. On the other hand, money problems are a source of stress for individuals and families and are a contributing factor in many divorces and suicides.

You don't need to be rich to achieve financial wellness. Instead, you need to be comfortable with your financial situation. Financially well people understand the limits of their income and live within their means by keeping expenses in check. They know how to balance a checkbook and interpret their bank statements. The financially well person may not strive to be wealthy but at least tries to save money for the future.

Achieving Occupational Wellness

How do you achieve such wellness? Career experts suggest setting career goals that reflect your personal values. For example, a career in sales may be a good way to earn a high income but may not be a good career choice for someone whose highest values involve service to others. Such a person might find more personal satisfaction in teaching or nursing.

Aside from career choices, education is a critical factor in occupational and financial wellness. For starters, learn to manage money *before* you start making it. Classes on personal money management are available through many sources and can help you on your way to financial security, whether you dream of being wealthy or not.

TERMS

chronic disease   A disease that develops and continues over a long period of time, such as heart disease or cancer.

lifestyle choice   A conscious behavior that can increase or decrease a person's risk of disease or injury; such behaviors include smoking, exercising, eating a healthy diet, and others.

Since 1900, however, life expectancy has nearly doubled, due largely to the development of vaccines and antibiotics to fight infections and to public health measures to improve living conditions. Today, a different set of diseases has emerged as our major health threat, and heart disease, cancer, and stroke are now the three leading causes of death for Americans (Table 1.2). Treating such **chronic diseases** is costly and difficult.

The good news is that people have some control over whether they develop chronic diseases. People make choices every day that increase or decrease their risks for such diseases. These **lifestyle choices** include behaviors such as smoking, diet, exercise, and alcohol use. As Table 1.3 (p. 6) makes clear, lifestyle factors contribute to many deaths in the United States, and people can influence their own health risks.

The need to make good choices is especially true for teens and young adults. For Americans age 15–24, for example, the top three causes of death are unintentional injuries (accidents), homicide, and suicide (Table 1.4, p. 6).

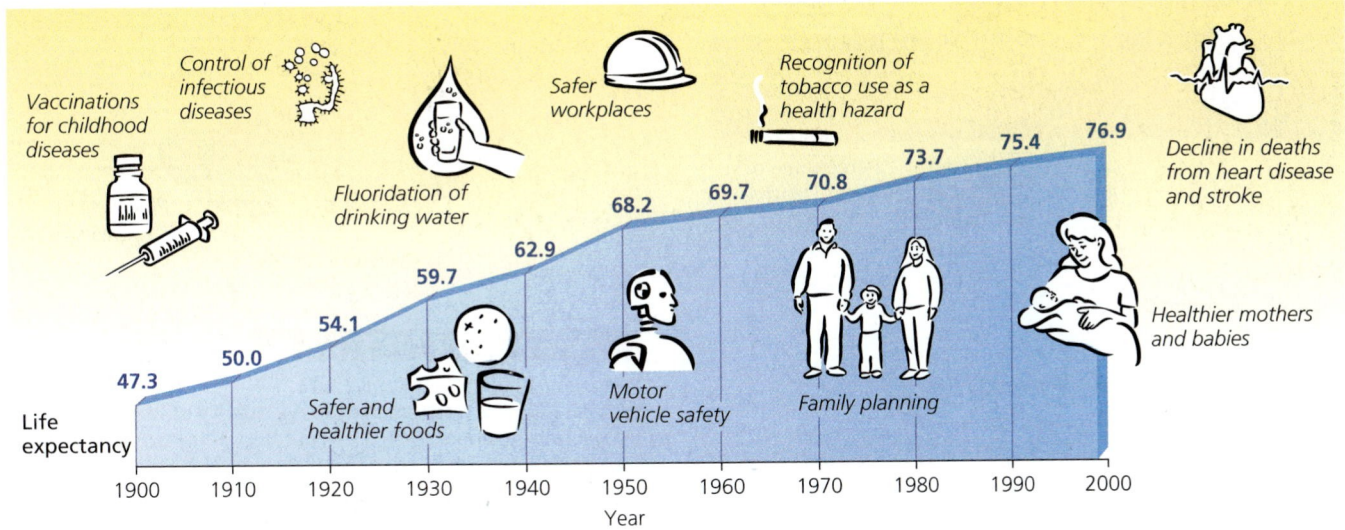

FIGURE 1.2 Public health achievements of the twentieth century. During the twentieth century, public health achievements greatly improved the quality of life for Americans. A shift in the leading causes of death also occurred, with deaths from infectious diseases declining from 33% of all deaths to just 2%. Heart disease, cancer, and stroke are now responsible for more than half of all deaths among Americans.

SOURCE: National Center for Health Statistics, Centers for Disease Control and Prevention. 1999. Ten great public health achievements—United States, 1900–1999. *Morbidity and Mortality Weekly Report* 48(50): 1141.

VITAL STATISTICS

Table 1.2   Leading Causes of Death in the United States, 2006

Rank	Cause of Death	Number of Deaths	Percent of Total Deaths*	Death Rate†	Lifestyle Factors
	All causes	2,425,901	100.0	776.4	
1	Heart disease	629,191	25.9	199.4	D I S A
2	Cancer	560,102	23.1	180.8	D I S A
3	Stroke	137,265	5.7	43.6	D I S A
4	Chronic lower respiratory diseases	124,614	5.1	40.4	S
5	Unintentional injuries (accidents)	117,748	4.9	38.5	I S A
6	Alzheimer's disease	72,914	3.0	22.7	
7	Diabetes mellitus	72,507	3.0	23.3	D I S
8	Influenza and pneumonia	56,247	2.3	17.7	S
9	Kidney disease	44,791	1.8	14.3	D I S A
10	Septicemia (systemic blood infection)	34,031	1.4	10.9	A
11	Intentional self-harm (suicide)	32,185	1.3	10.6	A
12	Chronic liver disease and cirrhosis	27,299	1.1	8.7	A
13	Hypertension (high blood pressure)	23,985	1.0	7.6	D I S A
14	Parkinson's disease	19,660	0.8	6.3	
15	Assault (homicide)	18,029	0.7	6.0	A
	All other causes	455,333	18.8		

Key
D Diet plays a part
I Inactive lifestyle plays a part
S Smoking plays a part
A Excessive alcohol use plays a part

NOTE: Although not among the overall top 15 causes of death, HIV/AIDS (approximately 12,000 deaths in 2006) is a major killer. In 2006, HIV/AIDS was the 8th leading cause of death for Americans age 15–24 years and the 6th leading cause of death for those age 25–44 years.

*Percentages may not total 100% due to rounding.

†Age-adjusted death rate per 100,000 persons.

SOURCE: National Center for Health Statistics. 2008. Deaths: Preliminary data for 2006. *National Vital Statistics Report* 56(16).

Table 1.3	Key Contributors to Death Among Americans	
	Number of Deaths per Year	Percentage of Total Deaths per Year
Tobacco	440,000	18.1
Obesity*	112,000	4.6
Alcohol consumption	85,000	3.5
Microbial agents	75,000	3.1
Toxic agents	55,000	2.3
Motor vehicles	43,000	1.8
Firearms	29,000	1.2
Sexual behavior	20,000	0.8
Illicit drug use	17,000	0.7

NOTE: The factors listed here are defined as lifestyle and environmental factors that contribute to the leading killers of Americans. Microbial agents include bacterial and viral infections like influenza and pneumonia; toxic agents include environmental pollutants and chemical agents such as asbestos.

*The number of deaths due to obesity is an area of ongoing controversy and research. Recent estimates have ranged from 112,000 to 365,000.

SOURCES: Centers for Disease Control and Prevention. 2005. *Frequently Asked Questions About Calculating Obesity-Related Risk* (http://www.cdc.gov/PDF/Frequently_Asked_Questions_About_Calculating_Obesity-Related_Risk.pdf; retrieved December 6, 2007); Mokdad, A. H., et al. 2005. Correction: Actual causes of death in the United States, 2000. *Journal of the American Medical Association* 293(3): 293–294; Mokdad, A. H., et al. 2004. Actual causes of death in the United States, 2000. *Journal of the American Medical Association* 291(10): 1238–1245.

The Healthy People Initiative

Wellness is a personal concern, but the U.S. government has financial and humanitarian interests in it, too. A healthy population is the nation's source of vitality, creativity, and wealth. Poor health drains the nation's resources and raises health care costs for all.

The national Healthy People initiative aims to prevent disease and improve Americans' quality of life. Healthy

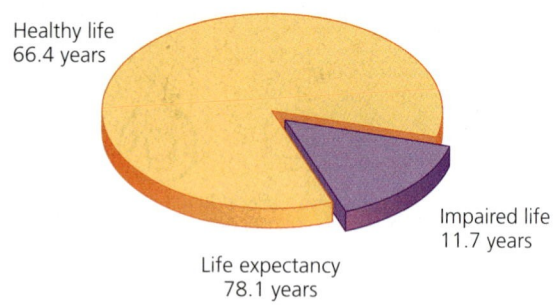

Healthy life 66.4 years

Impaired life 11.7 years

Life expectancy 78.1 years

FIGURE 1.3   Quantity of life versus quality of life. Years of healthy life as a proportion of life expectancy in the U.S. population.

SOURCES: National Center for Health Statistics. 2008. Deaths: Preliminary data for 2006. *National Vital Statistics Reports* 56(16); National Center for Health Statistics. *Healthy People 2010.* Midcourse Review. Hyattsville, Md.: Public Health Service.

People reports, published each decade since 1980, set national health goals based on 10-year agendas.

The latest report, *Healthy People 2010,* proposes two broad national goals:

• **Increase quality and years of healthy life.** One way to measure quality of life is to count the number of "sick days" people endure—days they can't function due to illness. About 18% of Americans take 14 or more sick days each year, a number that continually rises. Along those same lines, Americans increasingly describe their health as fair or poor rather than excellent or very good. Further, although the life expectancy of Americans has increased significantly in the past century, people can expect poor health to limit their activities and cause distress during the last 15% of their lives (Figure 1.3).

• **Eliminate health disparities among Americans.** Many health problems today disproportionately affect certain American populations (issues of special concern to specific groups are discussed later in this chapter). *Healthy People 2010* calls for eliminating disparities in health status, health risks, and use of preventive services among all population groups within the next decade.

Table 1.4	Leading Causes of Death Among Americans Age 15–24		
Rank	Cause of Death	Number of Deaths	Percent of Total Deaths
1	Accidents:	15,859	45.8
	Motor vehicle	10,845	31.3
	All other accidents	5,014	14.5
2	Homicide	5,596	16.2
3	Suicide	4,097	11.8
4	Cancer	1,643	4.7
5	Heart disease	1,021	2.9
	All causes	34,632	

SOURCE: National Center for Health Statistics. 2008. Deaths: Preliminary data for 2006. *National Vital Statistics Report* 56(16).

Table 1.5	Selected *Healthy People 2010* Objectives		
Objective		**Estimate of Current Status (%)**	**Goal (%)**
Increase the proportion of people age 18 and older who engage regularly in moderate physical activity.		31	50
Increase the proportion of people age 2 and older who consume at least 3 daily servings of vegetables, with at least one-third being dark-green or orange vegetables.		4	50
Increase the prevalence of healthy weight among people age 20 and older.		32	60
Reduce the proportion of adults 18 and older who use cigarettes.		21	12
Reduce the proportion of college students reporting binge drinking during the past 2 weeks.		40	20
Increase the proportion of adults who take protective measures to reduce the risk of skin cancer (sunscreens, sun-protective clothing, and so on).		71	85
Increase the use of safety belts by motor vehicle occupants.		82	92
Increase the number of residences with a functioning smoke alarm on every floor.		90	100
Increase the proportion of persons with health insurance.		83	100

SOURCE: National Center for Health Statistics. 2008. *DATA 2010: The Healthy People 2010 Database, May 2008 Edition* (http://wonder.cdc.gov/data2010/obj.htm; retrieved December 27, 2008).

Examples of individual health promotion objectives from *Healthy People 2010,* as well as estimates of how we are tracking toward the goals, appear in Table 1.5.

Healthy Campus 2010 Based on the guidelines of *Healthy People 2010* but designed specifically for college students, the *Healthy Campus 2010* program assists colleges in developing plans to improve student health. The American College Health Association's manual for the program, titled *Healthy Campus: Making It Happen,* is a companion to *Healthy People 2010.* The Healthy Campus program was developed through a broad consultation process built on scientific consensus.

Healthy Campus 2010 provides planning guidelines and more than 200 health-related objectives. Using baselines and targets for meeting these objectives, schools can customize their health programs. For example, a school might choose goals such as increasing the proportion of students who exercise at least 3 days a week, or increasing the proportion of students who follow responsible sexual practices.

Health Issues for Diverse Populations

Americans are a diverse people. Our ancestry is European, African, Asian, Pacific Islander, Latin American, and Native American. We live in cities, suburbs, and rural areas and work at every imaginable occupation. We are at heart a nation of diversity, and, though we often fall short of our goal, we strive for justice and equality among all.

When it comes to health, most differences among people are insignificant; most health issues concern us all equally. We all need to eat well, exercise, manage stress, and cultivate satisfying personal relationships. We need to know how to protect ourselves from heart disease, cancer, sexually transmitted diseases, and injuries. We need to know how to use the health care system.

But some of our differences, as individuals and as members of groups, have important implications for health. Some of us, for example, have a genetic predisposition for developing certain health problems, such as high cholesterol. Some of us have grown up eating foods that raise our risk of heart disease or obesity. Some of us live in an environment that increases the chance that we will smoke cigarettes or abuse alcohol. These health-related differences among individuals and groups can be biological—determined genetically—or cultural—acquired as patterns of behavior through daily interactions with our families, communities, and society. Many health conditions are a function of biology and culture combined. A person can have a genetic predisposition for a disease, for example, but won't actually develop the disease itself unless certain lifestyle factors are present, such as stress or a poor diet.

When we talk about health issues for diverse populations, we face two related dangers. The first is the danger of *stereotyping,* or talking about people as groups rather than as individuals. It's true that every person is an individual with a unique genetic endowment and unique life experiences. But many of these influences are shared with others of similar genetic and cultural background. Statements about these group similarities can be useful; for example, they can alert people to areas that may be of special concern for them and their families.

The second danger is that of *overgeneralizing,* or ignoring the extensive biological and cultural diversity that exists among peoples who are grouped together. Groups labeled Latino or Hispanic, for example, include Mexican Americans, Puerto Ricans, people from South and Central America, and other Spanish-speaking peoples. Similarly, the population labeled American Indian includes hundreds of recognized tribal nations, each with its own genetic and cultural heritage.

Health-related differences among groups can be identified and described in the context of several different dimensions. Those highlighted in *Healthy People 2010* are gender, ethnicity, income and education, disability, geographic location, and sexual orientation.

Sex and Gender Sex and gender profoundly influence wellness. The World Health Organization (WHO) defines **sex** as the biological and physiological characteristics that define men and women; these characteristics are related to chromosomes and their effects on reproductive organs and the functioning of the body. Menstruation in women and the presence of testicles in men are examples of sex-related characteristics. **Gender** is defined as roles, behaviors, activities, and attributes that a given society considers appropriate for men and women. A person's gender is rooted in biology and physiology, but it is shaped by experience and environment—how society responds to individuals based on their sex. Examples of gender-related characteristics that affect wellness include higher rates of smoking and drinking among men and lower earnings among women (compared with men doing similar work).

Both sex and gender have important effects on wellness, but they can be difficult to separate (see the box "Women's Health/Men's Health"). For example, more women began smoking with changes in culturally defined ideas about women's behavior (a gender issue). Because women are more vulnerable to the toxins in tobacco smoke (a sex issue), cancer rates also increased. A recent study shows that although men are more biologically likely than women to suffer from certain diseases (a sex issue), men are less likely to visit their physician for regular exams (a gender issue). As a result, 55% of American men have not seen their doctor for a checkup in the past year, and 29% of men say they wait as long as possible before seeing a doctor—even when they are sick.

Ethnicity Achieving the *Healthy People 2010* goal of eliminating all health disparities will require a national

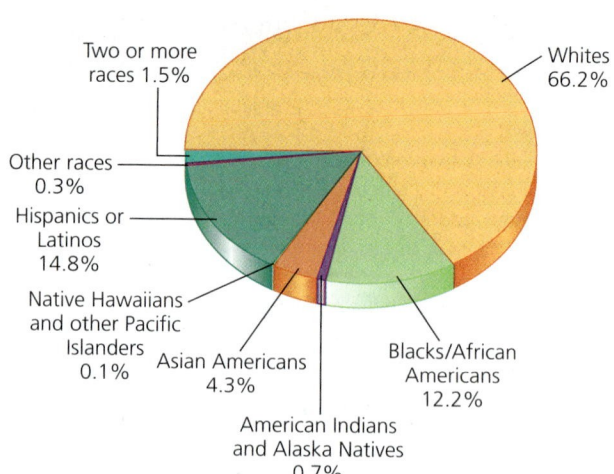

FIGURE 1.4 Distribution of the U.S. population.
SOURCE: U.S. Census Bureau. 2006. *2006 American community survey: Hispanic or Latino origin by race—Universe: Total population.* Washington, D.C.: U.S. Census Bureau.

effort to identify and address the underlying causes of ethnic health disparities. Compared with the U.S. population as a whole, American ethnic minorities have higher rates of death and disability from many causes. These disparities result from a complex mix of genetic variations, environmental factors, and health behaviors.

Some diseases are concentrated in certain gene pools, the result of each ethnic group's relatively distinct history. Sickle-cell disease is most common among people of African ancestry. Tay-Sachs disease afflicts people of Eastern European Jewish heritage and French Canadian heritage. Cystic fibrosis is more common among Northern Europeans. In addition to biological differences, many cultural differences occur along ethnic lines. Ethnic groups may vary in their traditional diets; their family and interpersonal relationships; their attitudes toward tobacco, alcohol, and other drugs; and their health beliefs and practices. All of these factors have implications for wellness. (See the box "Health Disparities Among Ethnic Minorities" on p. 10 for more information.)

The federal government collects population and health information on five broad ethnic minority groups in American society. (Figure 1.4 shows the current ethnic distribution of the United States.) Each group has some specific health concerns:

• *Latinos* are a diverse group, with roots in Mexico, Puerto Rico, Cuba, and South and Central America. Many Latinos are of mixed Spanish and American Indian descent or of mixed Spanish, Indian, and African American descent. Latinos on average have lower rates of heart disease, cancer, and suicide than the general population, but higher rates of infant mortality and a higher overall birth rate; other areas of concern include gallbladder disease and obesity. At current rates, about one in two Latinas will develop diabetes in her lifetime.

Women's Health/Men's Health

In terms of their health, women and men differ in many ways. They have different life expectancies, for one thing, and suffer from various diseases at different rates. Men and women tend to differ in some health-related behaviors, and they respond in dissimilar ways to some medications and medical treatments. The following table highlights some of the gender differences that can affect wellness.

Health Issues	Women	Men
Life expectancy	On average, live about 5 years longer but have higher rates of disabling health problems such as arthritis, osteoporosis, and Alzheimer's disease	Have a shorter life expectancy but lower rates of disabling health problems
Height and weight	Shorter on average, with a lower proportion of muscle; tend to have a "pear" shape with excess body fat stored in the hips; obesity is more common in women than men	Taller on average, with a higher proportion of muscle; tend to have an "apple" shape with excess body fat stored in the abdomen
Skills and fluencies	Score better on tests of verbal fluency, speech production, fine motor skills, and visual and working memory	Score better on tests of visual-spatial ability (such as the ability to imagine the relationships between shapes and objects when rotated in space)
Heart attacks	Experience heart attacks about 10 years later than men, on average, with a poorer 1-year survival rate; more likely to experience atypical heart attack symptoms (such as fatigue and difficulty breathing) or "silent" heart attacks that occur without chest pain	Experience heart attacks about 10 years earlier than women, on average, with a better 1-year survival rate; more likely to have "classic" heart attack symptoms (such as chest pain)
Stroke	More likely to have a stroke or die from one, but also more likely to recover language ability after a stroke that affects the left side of the brain	Less likely to die from a stroke, but also more likely to suffer permanent loss of language ability after a stroke that affects the left side of the brain
Immune response	Stronger immune systems; less susceptible to infection by certain bacteria and viruses, but more likely to develop autoimmune diseases such as lupus	Weaker immune systems; more susceptible to infection by certain bacteria and viruses, but less likely to develop autoimmune diseases
Smoking	Lower rates of smoking than men, but higher risk of lung cancer at a given level of exposure to smoke	Higher rates of smoking and spit tobacco use
Alcohol	Become more intoxicated at a given level of alcohol intake	Become less intoxicated at a given level of alcohol intake, but are more likely to use or abuse alcohol or to develop alcoholism
Stress	More likely to react to stress with a "tend-and-befriend" response that involves social support; may have a longevity advantage because of a reduced risk of stress-related disorders	More likely to react to stress with aggression or hostility; this pattern may increase the rate of stress-related disorders
Depression	More likely to suffer from depression and to attempt suicide	Lower rates of depression than women and less likely to attempt suicide, but four times more likely to succeed at suicide
Headaches	More commonly suffer migraine and chronic tension headaches	More likely to suffer from cluster headaches
Sexually transmitted diseases (STDs)	More likely to be infected with an STD during a heterosexual encounter; more likely to suffer severe, long-term effects from STDs, such as chronic infection and infertility	Less likely to be infected with an STD during a heterosexual encounter

Health Disparities Among Ethnic Minorities

In studying the underlying causes of health disparities, it is often difficult to separate the many potential contributing factors.

Income and Education

Poverty and low educational attainment are the most important factors underlying health disparities. People with low incomes and less education have higher rates of death from all causes, especially chronic disease and injury, and they are less likely to have preventive health services such as vaccinations and Pap tests. They are more likely to live in an area with a high rate of violence and many other environmental stressors. They also have higher rates of unhealthy behaviors.

Although ethnic disparities in health are significantly reduced when comparing groups with similar incomes and levels of education, they are not eliminated. For example, people living in poverty report worse health than people with higher incomes; but, within the latter group, African Americans and Latinos rate their health as worse than do whites. Infant mortality rates go down as the education level of mothers goes up; but among mothers who are college graduates, African Americans have significantly higher rates of infant mortality than whites, Latinos, and Asian Americans. These variations point to the complexity of health disparities.

Access to Appropriate Health Care

People with low incomes are less likely to have health insurance and more likely to have problems arranging for transportation to access care. They are also more likely to lack information about services and preventive care. But disparities persist even at higher income levels; for example, among nonpoor Americans, many more Latinos than whites or African Americans report having no insurance, no usual source of health care, and no health care visits within the past year. Ongoing studies continually

find that racial minorities have less access to better health care (such as complex surgery at high-volume hospitals) and receive lower quality care than whites.

Factors affecting such disparities may include the following:

• *Local differences in the availability of high-tech health care and specialists.* Minorities, regardless of income, may be more likely to live in medically underserved areas.

• *Problems with communication and trust.* People whose primary language is not English are more likely to be uninsured and to have trouble communicating with health care providers; they may also have problems interpreting health information from public health education campaigns. Language and cultural barriers may be exacerbated by an underrepresentation of minorities in the health professions.

• *Cultural preferences relating to health care.* Groups may vary in their assessment of when it is appropriate to seek medical care and what types of treatments are acceptable.

• *State and federal laws and programs.* Eligibility for Medicaid (a form of government insurance) varies by state and group. For example, Puerto Ricans are U.S. citizens and Cubans are classified as refugees, so people from these groups are immediately eligible for Medicaid; immigrants from other countries may not be able to access public insurance programs until 5 years after they enter the United States.

Culture and Lifestyle

As described in the chapter, ethnic groups may vary in health-related behaviors such as diet, tobacco and alcohol use, coping strategies, and health practices—and these behaviors can have important implications for wellness, both positive and negative. For example, African Americans are more likely to report consuming five or more servings of fruits and vegetables per day than people from

other ethnic groups. American Indians report high rates of smoking and smoking-related health problems.

Cultural background can be an important protective factor. For example, poverty is strongly associated with increased rates of depression; but some groups, including Americans born in Mexico or Puerto Rico, have lower rates of mental disorders at a given level of income and appear to have coping strategies that provide special resilience.

Discrimination

Racism and discrimination are stressful events that can cause psychological distress and increase the risk of physical and psychological problems. Discrimination can contribute to lower socioeconomic status and its associated risks. Bias in medical care can directly affect treatment and health outcomes.

Conversely, recent research shows that better health care results when doctors ask patients detailed questions about their ethnicity. (Most medical questionnaires ask patients to put themselves in a vague racial or ethnic category, such as Asian or Caucasian). Armed with more information on patients' backgrounds, medical professionals may find it easier to detect some genetic diseases or to overcome language or cultural barriers.

SOURCES: U.S. Department of Health and Human Services, Agency for Healthcare Research and Quality. 2008. *2007 National Healthcare Disparities Report.* Rockville, Md.: U.S. Department of Health and Human Services, Agency for Healthcare Research and Quality, AHRQ Pub. No. 08-0041; National Center for Health Statistics. 2008. *Early Release of Selected Estimates Based on Data from the January–June 2008 National Health Interview Survey* (http://www.cdc.gov/nchs/about/major/nhis/released200812.htm; retrieved December 27, 2008); National Center for Health Statistics. 2007. *Health, United States, 2007, with Chartbook on Trends in the Health of Americans.* Hyattsville, Md.: National Center for Health Statistics.

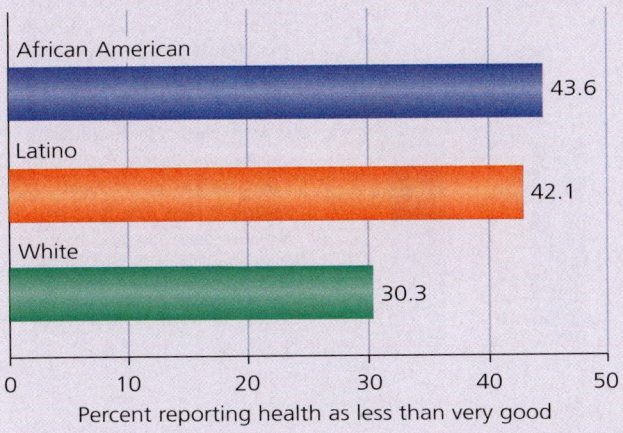

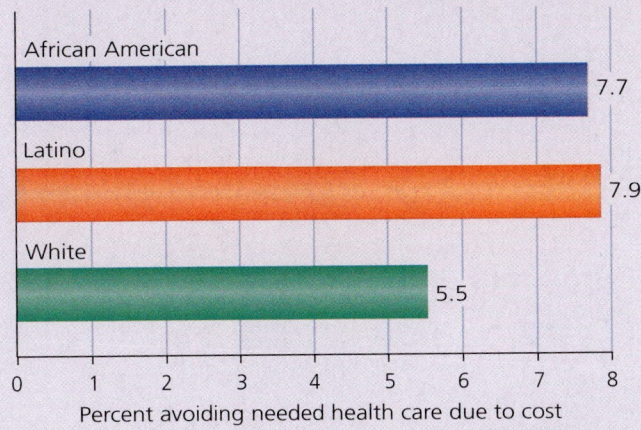

Figure 1.5   Self-rated health status and health care needs. White Americans are significantly more likely than other ethnic groups to rate their health as very good or excellent. Conversely, white Americans are less likely to avoid needed medical treatment due to the cost of health care services.

• *African Americans* have the same leading causes of death as the general population, but they have a higher infant mortality rate and lower rates of suicide and osteoporosis. Health issues of special concern for African Americans include high blood pressure, stroke, diabetes, asthma, and obesity. African American men are at significantly higher risk of prostate cancer than men in other groups, and early screening is recommended for them.

• *Asian Americans* include people who trace their ancestry to countries in the Far East, Southeast Asia, or the Indian subcontinent, including Japan, China, Vietnam, Laos, Cambodia, Korea, the Philippines, India, and Pakistan. Asian Americans have a lower death rate and a longer life expectancy than the general population. They have lower rates of coronary heart disease and obesity. However, health differences exist among these groups. For example, Southeast Asian men have higher rates of smoking and lung cancer, and Vietnamese American women have higher rates of cervical cancer.

• *American Indians and Alaska Natives* typically embrace a tribal identity, such as Sioux, Navaho, or Hopi. American Indians and Alaska Natives have lower death rates from heart disease, stroke, and cancer than the general population, but they have higher rates of early death from causes linked to smoking and alcohol use, including injuries and cirrhosis. Diabetes is a special concern for many groups; for example, the Pimas of Arizona have the highest known prevalence of diabetes of any population in the world.

• *Native Hawaiian and Other Pacific Islander Americans* trace their ancestry to the original peoples of Hawaii, Guam, Samoa, and other Pacific Islands. Pacific Islander Americans have a higher overall death rate than the general population and higher rates of diabetes and asthma. Smoking and obesity are special concerns for this group.

Disparities extend beyond health and into health care. According to the annual *National Healthcare Disparities Report* published by the U.S. Department of Health and Human Services, ethnic minorities and poor Americans consistently report their health as being less than very good, and receive lower-quality health services than do white or more affluent Americans (Figure 1.5). Although health care inequity is being addressed on the public and private fronts, and progress has been made, medical disparities still contribute to higher disease and death rates for many ethnic Americans.

Income and Education   Inequalities in income and education underlie many of the health disparities among Americans. In fact, poverty and low educational attainment are far more important predictors of poor health than any ethnic factor. Income and education are closely related, and groups with the highest poverty rates and least education have the worst health status. These Americans have higher rates of infant mortality, traumatic injury and violent death, and many diseases, including heart disease, diabetes, tuberculosis, HIV infection, and some cancers. They are more likely to eat poorly, be overweight, smoke, drink, and use drugs. They are exposed to more day-to-day stressors (such as the need to hold multiple jobs or deal with unreliable transportation) and have less access to health care services.

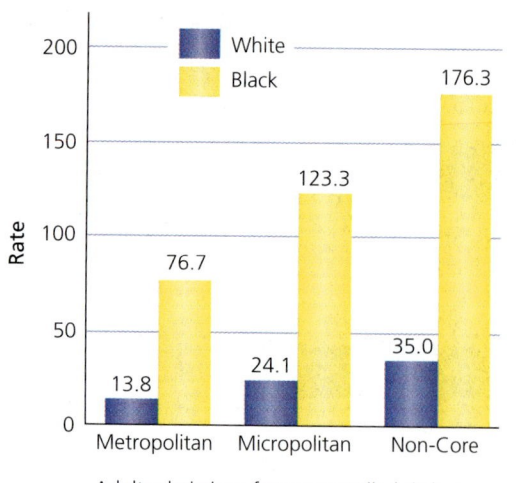

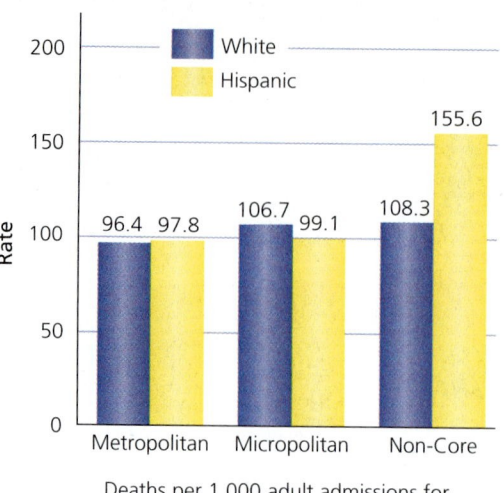

FIGURE 1.6 Health issues in rural areas. Ethnic minorities experience a higher proportion of certain diseases than whites, and this problem is compounded for people who live in rural (non-core) areas.
SOURCE: Agency for Healthcare Research and Quality 2005. *Health Care Disparities in Rural Areas: Selected Findings from the 2004 National Healthcare Disparities Report.* Rockville, Md.: Agency for Healthcare Research and Quality. AHRQ Publication No. 05-P022.

Adult admissions for uncontrolled diabetes per 100,000 population, by race and location

Deaths per 1,000 adult admissions for heart attack, by race and location

Metropolitan ≧ 50,000 inhabitants   Micropolitan = 10,000–50,000 inhabitants
Non-Core (Rural) ≦ 10,000 inhabitants

A surprising finding from a 2006 study was that poor people living in wealthy neighborhoods had higher mortality rates than poor people living in lower-income areas, perhaps because of the higher cost of living or psychosocial stressors. Many impoverished families are not only uninsured but rely on the local emergency room for their medical needs.

Disability People with disabilities have activity limitations, need assistance, or perceive themselves as having a disability. About one in five people in the United States has some level of disability, and the rate is rising, especially among younger segments of the population. People with disabilities are more likely to be inactive and overweight. They report more days of depression than people without disabilities. Many also lack access to health care services.

Geographic Location About one in four Americans currently lives in a rural area—a place with fewer than 10,000 residents. People living in rural areas are less likely to be physically active, to use safety belts, or to obtain screening tests for preventive health care. They have less access to timely emergency services and much higher rates of some diseases and injury-related death than people living in urban areas (Figure 1.6). They are also more likely to lack health insurance. Children living in dangerous neighborhoods—rural or urban—are four times more likely to be overweight than children living in safer areas.

Sexual Orientation The 1–5% of Americans who identify themselves as homosexual or bisexual make up a diverse community with varied health concerns. Their emotional wellness and personal safety are affected by factors relating to personal, family, and social acceptance of their sexual orientation. Gay, lesbian, bisexual, and transgender teens are more likely to engage in risky behaviors such as unsafe sex and drug use; they are also more likely to be depressed and to attempt suicide. HIV/AIDS is a major concern for gay men, and gay men and lesbians may have higher rates of substance abuse, depression, and suicide.

CHOOSING WELLNESS

Wellness is something everyone can have. Achieving it requires knowledge, self-awareness, motivation, and effort—but the benefits last a lifetime. Optimal health comes mostly from a healthy lifestyle, patterns of behavior that promote

QUESTIONS FOR CRITICAL THINKING AND REFLECTION
How often do you feel exuberant? Vital? Joyful? What makes you feel that way? Conversely, how often do you feel downhearted, de-energized, or depressed? What makes you feel that way? Have you ever thought about how you might increase experiences of vitality and decrease experiences of discouragement?

Wellness Matters for College Students

If you are like most college students, you probably feel pretty good about your health right now. Most college students are in their late teens or early twenties, lead active lives, have plenty of friends, and look forward to a future filled with opportunity. With all these things going for you, why shouldn't you feel good?

A Closer Look

Although most college-age people look healthy, appearances can be deceiving. Each year, thousands of students lose productive academic time to physical and emotional health problems—some of which can continue to plague them for life.

The following table shows the top 10 health issues affecting students' academic performance, according to the 2007 National College Health Assessment.

Health Issue	Students Affected (%)
Stress	32.9
Sleep difficulties	25.4
Cold/flu/sore throat	24.8
Concern for a friend or family member	18.1
Relationship problems	15.5
Depression/anxiety	15.5
Internet use/games	15.1
Death of a friend or family member	9.8
Sinus or ear infection/ bronchitis/strep throat	9.4
Attention deficit disorder	7.0

Each of these issues is related to one or more of the six dimensions of wellness, and most can be influenced by choices students make daily. Although

some troubles—such as the death of a friend—cannot be controlled, other physical and emotional concerns can be minimized by choosing healthy behaviors. For example, there are many ways to manage stress, the top health issue affecting students. By reducing unhealthy choices (such as using alcohol to relax) and by increasing healthy choices (such as using time-management techniques), even busy students can reduce the impact of stress on their lives.

The survey also estimated that, based on students' reporting of their height

and weight, more than 36% of college students are either overweight or obese. Although heredity plays a role in determining one's weight, lifestyle is also a factor in weight and weight management. In many studies over the past few decades, a large percentage of students have reported behaviors such as these:

- Overeating
- Snacking on junk food
- Frequently eating high-fat foods
- Using alcohol and binge drinking

Clearly, eating behaviors are often a matter of choice. Although students may not see (or feel) the effects of their dietary habits today, the long-term health risks are significant. Overweight and obese persons run a higher-than-normal risk of developing diabetes, heart disease, and cancer later in life. We now know with certainty that improving one's eating habits, even a little, can lead to weight loss and improved overall health.

Other Choices, Other Problems

Students commonly make other unhealthy choices. Here are some examples from the 2007 National College Health Assessment:

- Nearly 50% of students reported that they did not use a condom the last time they had vaginal intercourse.

- About 80% of students had as many as 6 drinks the last time they partied.

- Almost 19% of students had used tobacco at least once during the past month.

What choices do you make in these situations? Remember: It's never too late to change. The sooner you trade an unhealthy behavior for a healthy one, the longer you'll be around to enjoy the benefits.

SOURCE: American College Health Association. 2008. *American College Health Association— National College Health Assessment: Reference Group Executive Summary, Fall 2007.* Baltimore, Md.: American College Health Association.

and support your health now and as you get older. In the pages that follow, you'll find current information and suggestions you can use to build a better lifestyle.

Factors That Influence Wellness

Our behavior, family health history, environment, and access to health care are all important influences on wellness. These factors, which vary for both individuals and groups, can interact in ways that produce either health or disease.

Health Habits Scientific research is continuously revealing new connections between our habits and health. For ex-

ample, heart disease is associated with smoking, stress, hostile and suspicious attitudes, a poor diet, and a sedentary way of life. Unfortunately, poor health habits take hold before many Americans reach adulthood. (See the box "Wellness Matters for College Students" for more information on health habits and wellness concerns of college-age Americans.)

Other habits, however, are beneficial. Regular exercise can help prevent heart disease, high blood pressure, diabetes, osteoporosis, and depression and may reduce the risk of colon cancer, stroke, and back injury. A balanced and varied diet helps prevent many chronic diseases. As we learn more about how our actions affect our bodies and minds, we can make informed choices for a healthier life.

A "Planet in Peril": Healing the Environment

Our treatment of the environment determines—to a far greater extent than many people want to believe—how the Earth will treat us. This lesson has gradually become clear over several generations, but our troubled environment began attracting intensive worldwide attention only in the last few years. Today, the evidence is irrefutable: Our continuing abuse of the environment has led to a natural backlash that includes the extinction of entire species, shifts in global weather patterns, dying oceans, and the disappearance of polar ice fields.

Climate experts are now sounding the alarm: If we don't immediately begin reducing our impact on the environment, the damage may become irreversible. The compounded effects of humanity's environmental neglect could make our planet a much less hospitable and livable place, possibly within two or three short decades.

The Root of the Problem

Pollution, of course, is not a new problem. People have contaminated the air by burning coal, wood, and oil for millennia. Age-old industries such as forestry and mining have laid waste to vast stretches of land, and processes such as tanning and printing have dumped untold amounts of lethal toxins into the ground and water. People began to take serious notice of pollution even before the dawn of the Industrial Revolution, when a few scientists reported that the smoke from factories and trains was fouling the air, and that industrial runoff was polluting rivers.

Over time, improvements in technology made manufacturing easier and cheaper, while an increasing population and greater prosperity created an insatiable demand for manufactured goods. Industrial growth gave rise to explosive growth of urban areas—population centers that drove the need for transportation and electricity. As a result, industries

and individuals consume ever-larger amounts of fuel and other resources, creating ever more waste and pollution in the process. Combine this with the pollution generated by our use of fossil-fueled transportation, and the result is a recipe for global catastrophe.

Global Warming

Human practices affect the environment on every level. Our food chain is contaminated with pesticides, water must be cleaned of sewage and chemicals before we can drink it, and in some cities the air is so polluted with exhaust that it can actually be dangerous to breathe. But the most ravaging—and frightening—

consequence of environmental abuse is the phenomenon known as global warming: the gradual rise in the Earth's temperature that is causing polar ice caps to shrink, creating unfavorable weather patterns, and contributing to rapid devastation of land and oceans.

What causes global warming? As you will learn in Chapter 19, global warming is largely due to human activity. As we burn fossil fuels (such as coal, oil, and fuels derived from them) to power vehicles and factories, the process releases many kinds of waste gases into the skies. Some of these gases, chiefly carbon dioxide (CO_2), rise up into the air and stay there, acting as an invisible insulating blanket.

These gases create a "greenhouse" effect by trapping some of the heat that radiates from the Earth—heat that would normally dissipate through the atmosphere. By defeating the planet's natural temperature controls, CO_2 and other "greenhouse gases" are causing the Earth to get warmer.

As already mentioned, this rise in temperature can wreak havoc on the Earth, especially if temperatures increase unchecked over a long period of time. Experts are trying to determine how high Earth's temperature must climb before we reach the tipping point (when damage from climate change becomes irreversible), and how soon that point may be reached.

Reversing the Warming Trend

Until then, however, one fact is obvious. People, industries, societies, and governments must start taking action now to reduce their "imprint" on the environment. Legislation such as the Clean Water Act have helped, but it is important to understand that pollution and global warming are not problems just for governments to solve. The environment affects every person in an individual way. The more we do as individuals, the more benefits will result from our collective efforts.

This is why *Core Concepts in Health* has been revised with current environmental issues in mind. Not only does Chapter 19 examine the environment in detail, but every chapter briefly addresses the environment's impact on a specific aspect of your well-being—from the way you exercise, to the foods you eat, to your reproductive health. In each chapter, you will see a short feature called "Thinking About the Environment." This feature relates the chapter's main theme to the environment, and poses questions for you to consider or suggests actions you can take to improve the environment—and promote your personal health and wellness, as well.

Heredity/Family History Your **genome** consists of the complete set of genetic material in your cells; it contains about 25,000 genes, half from each of your parents. **Genes** control the production of proteins that serve both as the structural material for your body and as the regulators of all your body's chemical reactions

and metabolic processes. The human genome varies only slightly from person to person, and many of these differences do not affect health. However, some differences have important implications for health, and knowing your family health history can help you determine which conditions may be of special concern for you.

Chapter 8 includes more information about creating a family health tree.

Errors in our genes are responsible for about 3500 clearly hereditary conditions, including sickle-cell disease and cystic fibrosis. Altered genes also play a part in heart disease, cancer, stroke, diabetes, and many other common conditions. However, in these more common and complex disorders, genetic alterations serve only to increase an individual's risk, and the disease itself results from the interaction of many genes with other factors. An example of the power of behavior and environment can be seen in the more than 60% increase in the incidence of diabetes that has occurred among Americans since 1990. This huge increase is not due to any sudden change in our genes; it is the result of increasing rates of obesity caused by poor dietary choices and lack of physical activity.

Environment   Your environment includes not only the air you breathe and the water you drink but also substances and conditions in your home, workplace, and community. Are you frequently exposed to environmental tobacco smoke or the radiation in sunlight? Do you live in an area with poor air quality or high rates of crime and violence? Has alcohol or drug abuse been a problem in your family? These and other environmental factors all have an impact on wellness. (See the box "The Environment" for more information on current environmental issues.)

Access to Health Care   Adequate health care helps improve both quality and quantity of life through preventive care and the treatment of disease. For example, vaccinations prevent many dangerous infections, and screening tests help identify key risk factors and diseases in their early, treatable stages. As described earlier in the chapter, inadequate access to health care is tied to factors such as low income and lack of health insurance. Cost is one of many issues sur-

rounding the development of advanced health-related technologies.

Behavior *Can* Make a Difference   In many cases, behavior can tip the balance toward good health, even when heredity or environment is a negative factor. For example, breast cancer can run in families, but it also may be associated with being overweight and inactive. A woman with a family history of breast cancer is less likely to develop and die from the disease if she controls her weight, exercises regularly, and has regular mammograms to help detect the disease in its early, most treatable stage.

Similarly, a young man with a family history of obesity can maintain a normal weight by being careful to balance calorie intake against activities that burn calories. If your life is highly stressful, you can lessen the chances of heart disease and stroke by learning ways to manage and cope with stress. If you live in an area with severe air pollution, you can reduce the risk of lung disease by not smoking. You can also take an active role in improving your environment. Behaviors like these enable you to make a difference in how great an impact heredity and environment will have on your health.

REACHING WELLNESS THROUGH LIFESTYLE MANAGEMENT

As you consider the behaviors that contribute to wellness—being physically active, choosing a healthy diet, and so on—you may be doing a mental comparison with your own behaviors. If you are like most young adults, you probably have some healthy habits and some habits that place your health at risk. For example, you may be physically active and have a healthy diet but indulge in binge drinking on weekends. You may be careful to wear your safety belt in your car but smoke cigarettes or use chewing tobacco. Moving in the direction of wellness means cultivating healthy behaviors and working to overcome unhealthy ones. This approach to lifestyle management is called **behavior change.**

As you may already know from experience, changing an unhealthy habit can be harder than it looks. When you embark on a behavior change plan, it may seem like too much work at first. But as you make progress, you will gain confidence in your ability to take charge of your life.

QUESTIONS FOR CRITICAL THINKING AND REFLECTION
We frequently hear news about the ways people harm the environment, but do you ever think about the ways your environment may be harming you? How would you describe the quality of the air you breathe (indoors and outdoors) and the water you drink? Is it easy to make healthy food choices in your neighborhood? Do you find your home or school environment stressful?

genome   The complete set of genetic material in an individual's cells.

gene   The basic unit of heredity; a section of genetic material containing chemical instructions for making a particular protein.

behavior change   A lifestyle management process that involves cultivating healthy behaviors and working to overcome unhealthy ones.

TERMS

Wellness: Evaluate Your Lifestyle

All of us want optimal health. But many of us do not know how to achieve it. Taking this quiz, adapted from one created by the U.S. Public Health Service, is a good place to start. The behaviors covered in the quiz are recommended for most Americans. (Some of them may not apply to people with certain diseases or disabilities or to pregnant women, who may require special advice from their physician.) After you take the quiz, add up your score for each section.

Tobacco Use

If you never use tobacco, enter a score of 10 for this section and go to the next section.

	ALMOST ALWAYS	SOMETIMES	NEVER
1. I avoid using tobacco.	2	1	0
2. I smoke only low-tar/nicotine cigarettes *or* I smoke a pipe or cigars *or* I use smokeless tobacco.	2	1	0

Tobacco Score: _____

Alcohol and Other Drugs

	ALMOST ALWAYS	SOMETIMES	NEVER
1. I avoid alcohol *or* I drink no more than 1 (women) or 2 (men) drinks a day.	4	1	0
2. I avoid using alcohol or other drugs as a way of handling stressful situations or problems in my life.	2	1	0
3. I am careful not to drink alcohol when taking medications, such as for colds or allergies, or when pregnant.	2	1	0
4. I read and follow the label directions when using prescribed and over-the-counter drugs.	2	1	0

Alcohol and Other Drugs Score: _____

Nutrition

	ALMOST ALWAYS	SOMETIMES	NEVER
1. I eat a variety of foods each day, including seven or more servings of fruits and vegetables.	3	1	0
2. I limit the amount of total fat and saturated and trans fat in my diet.	3	1	0
3. I avoid skipping meals.	2	1	0
4. I limit the amount of salt and sugar I eat.	2	1	0

Nutrition Score: _____

Exercise/Fitness

	ALMOST ALWAYS	SOMETIMES	NEVER
1. I engage in moderate exercise for 20–60 minutes, 3–5 times a week.	4	1	0
2. I maintain a healthy weight, avoiding overweight and underweight.	2	1	0
3. I do exercises to develop muscular strength and endurance at least twice a week.	2	1	0
4. I spend some of my leisure time participating in physical activities such as gardening, bowling, golf, or baseball.	2	1	0

Exercise/Fitness Score: _____

Emotional Health

	ALMOST ALWAYS	SOMETIMES	NEVER
1. I enjoy being a student, and I have a job or do other work that I like.	2	1	0
2. I find it easy to relax and express my feelings freely.	2	1	0

You will also experience the benefits of wellness—more energy, greater vitality, deeper feelings of appreciation and curiosity, and a higher quality of life.

In the rest of this chapter, we outline a general process for changing unhealthy behaviors that is backed by research and that has worked for many people. We also offer many specific strategies and tips for change.

Getting Serious About Your Health

Before you can start changing a wellness-related behavior, you have to know that the behavior is problematic and that you *can* change it. To make good decisions, you need information about relevant topics and issues, including what resources are available to help you change.

	ALMOST ALWAYS	SOMETIMES	NEVER

3. I manage stress well   2   1   0

4. I have close friends, relatives, or others I can talk to about personal matters and call on for help.   2   1   0

5. I participate in group activities (such as church and community organizations) or hobbies that I enjoy.   2   1   0

Emotional Health Score: _____

Safety

1. I wear a safety belt while riding in a car.   2   1   0

2. I avoid driving while under the influence of alcohol or other drugs.   2   1   0

3. I obey traffic rules and the speed limit when driving.   2   1   0

4. I read and follow instructions on the labels of potentially harmful products or substances, such as household cleaners, poisons, and electrical appliances.   2   1   0

5. I avoid smoking in bed.   2   1   0

Safety Score: _____

Disease Prevention

1. I know the warning signs of cancer, diabetes, heart attack, and stroke.   2   1   0

2. I avoid overexposure to the sun and use a sunscreen.   2   1   0

3. I get recommended medical screening tests (such as blood pressure checks and Pap tests), immunizations, and booster shots.   2   1   0

4. I practice monthly breast/testicle self-exams.   2   1   0

5. I am not sexually active *or* I have sex with only one mutually faithful, uninfected partner *or* I always engage in safer sex (using condoms) *and* I do not share needles to inject drugs.   2   1   0

Disease Prevention Score: _____

What Your Scores Mean

Scores of 9 and 10 Excellent! Your answers show that you are aware of the importance of this area to your health. More important, you are putting your knowledge to work for you by practicing good health habits. As long as you continue to do so, this area should not pose a serious health risk.

Scores of 6 to 8 Your health practices in this area are good, but there is room for improvement.

Scores of 3 to 5 Your health risks are showing.

Scores of 0 to 2 You may be taking serious and unnecessary risks with your health.

Examine Your Current Health Habits Have you considered how your current lifestyle is affecting your health today and how it will affect your health in the future? Do you know which of your current habits enhance your health and which detract from it? Begin your journey toward wellness with self-assessment: Think about your own behavior, talk with friends and family members about what they've noticed about your lifestyle and your health, and take the quiz in the box "Wellness: Evaluate Your Lifestyle." Challenge any unrealistically optimistic attitudes or ideas you may hold—for example, "To protect my health, I don't need to worry about quitting smoking until I'm 40 years old," or "Being overweight won't put *me* at risk for diabetes." Health risks are very real, and health habits throughout life are important.

Evaluating Sources of Health Information

Believability of Health Information Sources

A 2007 survey conducted by the American College Health Association indicated that college students are smart about evaluating health information. They trust the health information they receive from health professionals and educators and are skeptical about popular information sources.

Rank	Source	Rank	Source
1	Health educators	8	Resident assistants/advisers
2	Health center medical staff	9	Religious centers
3	Parents	10	Internet/World Wide Web
4	Faculty/coursework	11	Friends
5	Leaflets, pamphlets, flyers	12	Magazines
6	Campus newspaper articles	13	Television
7	Campus peer educators	14	Other sources

How smart are you about evaluating health information? Here are some tips.

General Strategies

Whenever you encounter health-related information, take the following steps to make sure it is credible:

• **Go to the original source.** Media reports often simplify the results of medical research. Find out for yourself what a study really reported, and determine whether it was based on good science. What type of study was it? Was it published in a recognized medical journal? Was it an animal study or did it involve people? Did the study include a large number of people? What did the authors of the study actually report?

• **Watch for misleading language.** Reports that tout "breakthroughs" or "dramatic proof" are probably hype. A study may state that a behavior "contributes to" or is "associated with" an outcome; this does not prove a cause-and-effect relationship.

• **Distinguish between research reports and public health advice.** Do not change your behavior based on the results of a single report or study. If an agency such as the National Cancer Institute urges a behavior change, however, you should follow its advice. Large, publicly funded organizations issue such advice based on many studies, not a single report.

• **Remember that anecdotes are not facts.** A friend may tell you he lost weight on some new diet, but individual success stories do not mean the plan is truly safe or effective. Check with your doctor before making any serious lifestyle changes.

• **Be skeptical.** If a report seems too good to be true, it probably is. Be wary of information contained in advertisements. An ad's goal is to sell a product, even if there is no need for it.

• **Make choices that are right for you.** Friends and family members can be a great source of ideas and inspiration, but you need to make health-related choices that work best for you.

Internet Resources

Online sources pose special challenges; when reviewing a health-related Web site, ask these questions:

• **What is the source of the information?** Web sites maintained by government agencies, professional associations, or established academic or medical institutions are likely to present trustworthy information. Many other groups and individuals post accurate information, but it is important to look at the qualifications of the people who are behind the site. (Check the home page or click the "About Us" link.)

• **How often is the site updated?** Look for sites that are updated frequently. Check the "last modified" date of any Web page.

• **Is the site promotional?** Be wary of information from sites that sell specific products, use testimonials as evidence, appear to have a social or political agenda, or ask for money.

• **What do other sources say about a topic?** Be cautious of claims or information that appear at only one site or come from a chat room, bulletin board, or blog.

• **Does the site conform to any set of guidelines or criteria for quality and accuracy?** Look for sites that identify themselves as conforming to some code or set of principles, such as those set forth by the Health on the Net Foundation or the American Medical Association. These codes include criteria such as use of information from respected sources and disclosure of the site's sponsors.

Many people start to consider changing a behavior when friends or family members express concern, when a landmark event occurs (such as turning 30), or when new information raises their awareness of risk. If you find yourself reevaluating some of your behaviors as you read this text, take advantage of the opportunity to make a change in a structured way.

Choose a Target Behavior Changing any behavior can be demanding. This is why it's a good idea to start small, by choosing one behavior you want to change—called a **target behavior**—and working on it until you succeed.

Your chances of success will be greater if your first goal is simple, such as resisting the urge to snack between classes. As you change one behavior, make your next goal a little more significant, and build on your success.

Learn About Your Target Behavior Once you've chosen a target behavior, you need to learn its risks and benefits for you—both now and in the future. Ask these questions:

• How is your target behavior affecting your level of wellness today?

- What diseases or conditions does this behavior place you at risk for?
- What effect would changing your behavior have on your health?

As a starting point, use this text and the resources listed in the For More Information section at the end of each chapter; see the box "Evaluating Sources of Health Information" for additional guidelines.

Find Help   Have you identified a particularly challenging target behavior or mood, something like alcohol addiction, binge eating, or depression, that interferes with your ability to function or places you at a serious health risk? Help may be needed to change behaviors or conditions that are too deeply rooted or too serious for self-management. Don't be stopped by the seriousness of the problem; many resources are available to help you solve it. On campus, the student health center or campus counseling center can provide assistance. To locate community resources, consult the yellow pages, your physician, or the Internet.

Building Motivation to Change

Knowledge is necessary for behavior change, but it isn't usually enough to make people act. Millions of people have sedentary lifestyles, for example, even though they know it's bad for their health. This is particularly true of young adults, who may not be motivated to change because they feel healthy in spite of their unhealthy behaviors. To succeed at behavior change, you need strong motivation.

Examine the Pros and Cons of Change   Health behaviors have short-term and long-term benefits and costs. Consider the benefits and costs of an inactive lifestyle:

- Short-term, such a lifestyle allows you more time to watch TV and hang out with friends, but it leaves you less physically fit and less able to participate in recreational activities.
- Long-term, it increases the risk of heart disease, cancer, stroke, and premature death.

To successfully change your behavior, you must believe that the benefits of change outweigh the costs.

Carefully examine the pros and cons of continuing your current behavior and of changing to a healthier one. Focus on the effects that are most meaningful to you, including those that are tied to your personal identity and values. For example, if you see yourself as an active person who is a good role model for others, then adopting behaviors such as engaging in regular physical activity and getting adequate sleep will support your personal identity. If you value independence and control over your life, then quitting smoking will be consistent with your values and goals. To complete your analysis, ask friends and family members about the effects of your behavior on them. For example, a younger sister may tell you that your smoking habit influenced her decision to take up smoking.

The short-term benefits of behavior change can be an important motivating force. Although some people are motivated by long-term goals, such as avoiding a disease that may hit them in 30 years, most are more likely to be moved to action by shorter-term, more personal goals. Feeling better, doing better in school, improving at a sport, reducing stress, and increasing self-esteem are common short-term benefits of health behavior change. Many wellness behaviors are associated with immediate improvements in quality of life. For example, surveys of Americans have found that nonsmokers feel healthy and full of energy more days each month than do smokers, and they report fewer days of sadness and troubled sleep; the same is true when physically active people are compared with sedentary people. Over time, these types of differences add up to a substantially higher quality of life for people who engage in healthy behaviors.

Boost Self-Efficacy   When you start thinking about changing a health behavior, a big factor in your eventual success is whether you have confidence in yourself and in your ability to change. **Self-efficacy** refers to your belief in your ability to successfully take action and perform a specific task. Strategies for boosting self-efficacy include developing an internal locus of control, using visualization and self-talk, and getting encouragement from supportive people.

LOCUS OF CONTROL   Who do you believe is controlling your life? Is it your parents, friends, or school? Is it "fate"? Or is it you? **Locus of control** refers to the figurative "place" a person designates as the source of responsibility for the events in his or her life. People who believe they are in control of their own lives are said to have an *internal locus of control*. Those who believe that factors beyond their control determine the course of their lives are said to have an *external locus of control*.

For lifestyle management, an internal locus of control is an advantage because it reinforces motivation and

target behavior   An isolated behavior selected as the object for a behavior change program.

self-efficacy   The belief in one's ability to take action and perform a specific task.

locus of control   The figurative "place" a person designates as the source of responsibility for the events in his or her life.

TERMS

commitment. An external locus of control can sabotage efforts to change behavior. For example, if you believe that you are destined to die of breast cancer because your mother died from the disease, you may view monthly breast self-exams and regular checkups as a waste of time. In contrast, if you believe that you can take action to reduce your risk of breast cancer in spite of hereditary factors, you will be motivated to follow guidelines for early detection of the disease.

If you find yourself attributing too much influence to outside forces, gather more information about your wellness-related behaviors. List all the ways that making lifestyle changes will improve your health. If you believe you'll succeed, and if you recognize that you are in charge of your life, you're on your way to wellness.

VISUALIZATION AND SELF-TALK   One of the best ways to boost your confidence and self-efficacy is to visualize yourself successfully engaging in a new, healthier behavior. Imagine yourself going for an afternoon run 3 days a week or no longer smoking cigarettes. Also visualize yourself enjoying all the short-term and long-term benefits that your lifestyle change will bring. Create a new self-image: What will you and your life be like when you become a regular exerciser or a nonsmoker?

You can also use self-talk, the internal dialogue you carry on with yourself, to increase your confidence in your ability to change. Counter any self-defeating patterns of thought with more positive or realistic thoughts: "I am a strong, capable person, and I can maintain my commitment to change." See Chapter 3 for more on self-talk.

ROLE MODELS AND OTHER SUPPORTIVE INDIVIDUALS   Social support can make a big difference in your level of motivation and your chances of success. Perhaps you know people who have reached the goal you are striving for; they could be role models or mentors for you, providing information and support for your efforts. Gain strength from their experiences, and tell yourself, "If they can do it, so can I." In addition, find a buddy who wants to make the same changes you do and who can take an active role in your behavior change program. For example, an exercise buddy can provide companionship and encouragement when you might be tempted to skip your workout.

IDENTIFY AND OVERCOME BARRIERS TO CHANGE   Don't let past failures at behavior change discourage you; they can be a great source of information you can use to boost your chances of future success. Make a list of the problems and challenges you faced in any previous behavior change attempts; to this, add the short-term costs of behavior change that you identified in your analysis of the pros and cons of change. Once you've listed these key barriers to change, develop a practical plan for overcoming each one. For example, if you always smoke when you're with certain friends, decide in advance how you will turn down the next cigarette you are offered.

Enhancing Your Readiness to Change

The transtheoretical, or "stages of change," model has been shown to be an effective approach to lifestyle self-management. According to this model, you move through distinct stages as you work to change your target behavior. It is important to determine what stage you are in now so that you can choose appropriate strategies for progressing through the cycle of change. This approach can help you enhance your readiness and intention to change. Read the following sections to determine what stage you are in for your target behavior. For ideas on changing stages, see the box "Tips for Moving Forward in the Cycle of Behavior Change."

Precontemplation   People at this stage do not think they have a problem and do not intend to change their behavior. They may be unaware of the risks associated with their behavior or may deny them. They may have tried unsuccessfully to change in the past and may now think the situation is hopeless. They may also blame other people or external factors for their problems. People in the precontemplation stage believe that there are more reasons or more important reasons not to change than there are reasons to change.

Contemplation   People at this stage know they have a problem and intend to take action within 6 months. They acknowledge the benefits of behavior change but are also aware of the costs of changing—to be successful, people must believe that the benefits of change outweigh the costs. People in the contemplation stage wonder about possible courses of action but don't know how to proceed. There may also be specific barriers to change that appear too difficult to overcome.

THINKING ABOUT THE ENVIRONMENT

As you think about target behaviors you may want to change, consider your behavior toward the environment. By making simple changes to your daily routine or by using more environmentally friendly products, you can make a positive difference to the planet. For example, do you:

- Recycle paper, glass, plastic, and metal products?

- Use energy-efficient compact fluorescent light bulbs instead of standard incandescent bulbs?

- Keep your car well maintained to get the best possible gas mileage and emit the lowest possible amount of pollution?

- Avoid using aerosol products, pesticides, and other chemicals that could pollute the ground, air, or water?

For more information on the environment and environmental health, see Chapter 19.

Tips for Moving Forward in the Cycle of Behavior Change

connect™

PRECONTEMPLATION

- **Raise your awareness.** Research your target behavior and its effects.

- **Be self-aware.** Look at the mechanisms you use to resist change, such as denial or rationalization. Find ways to counteract these mechanisms.

- **Seek social support.** Friends and family members can help you identify target behaviors and understand their impact on the people around you.

- **Identify helpful resources.** These might include exercise classes or stress-management workshops offered by your school.

CONTEMPLATION

- **Keep a journal.** A record of your target behavior and the circumstances that elicit the behavior can help you plan a change program.

- **Do a cost-benefit analysis.** Identify the costs and benefits (both current and future) of maintaining your behavior and of changing it. Costs can be monetary, social, emotional, and so on.

- **Identify barriers to change.** Knowing these obstacles can help you overcome them.

- **Engage your emotions.** Watch movies or read books about people with your target behavior. Imagine what your life will be like if you don't change.

- **Create a new self-image.** Imagine what you'll be like after changing your target behavior. Try to think of yourself in new terms right now.

- **Think before you act.** Learn why you engage in the target behavior. Determine what "sets you off," and train yourself not to act reflexively.

PREPARATION

- **Create a plan.** Include a start date, goals, rewards, and specific steps you will take to change your behavior.

- **Make change a priority.** Create and sign a contract with yourself.

- **Practice visualization and self-talk.** These techniques can help prepare you mentally for challenging situations.

- **Take short steps.** Successfully practicing your new behavior for a short time—even a single day—can boost your confidence and motivation.

ACTION

- **Monitor your progress.** Keep up with your journal entries.

- **Change your environment.** Make changes that will discourage the target behavior—for example, getting rid of snack foods or not stocking the refrigerator with beer.

- **Find alternatives to your target behavior.** Make a list of things you can do to replace the behavior.

- **Reward yourself.** Rewards should be identified in your change plan. Give yourself lots of praise, and focus on your success.

- **Involve your friends.** Tell them you want to change, and ask for their help.

- **Don't get discouraged.** Real change is difficult.

MAINTENANCE

- **Keep going.** Continue using the positive strategies that worked in earlier stages.

- **Be prepared for lapses.** Don't let slip-ups set you back.

- **Be a role model.** Once you have successfully changed your behavior, you may be able to help someone else do the same thing.

Preparation People at this stage plan to take action within a month or may already have begun to make small changes in their behavior. They may be engaging in their new, healthier behavior but not yet regularly or consistently. They may have created a plan for change but may be worried about failing.

Action During the action stage, people outwardly modify their behavior and their environment. The action stage requires the greatest commitment of time and energy, and people in this stage are at risk for reverting to old, unhealthy patterns of behavior.

Maintenance People at this stage have maintained their new, healthier lifestyle for at least 6 months. Lapses may have occurred, but people in maintenance have been successful in quickly reestablishing the desired behavior. The maintenance stage can last a few months or many years.

Termination For some behaviors, a person may reach the sixth and final stage of termination. People at this stage have exited the cycle of change and are no longer tempted to lapse back into their old behavior. They have a new self-image and total self-efficacy with regard to their target behavior.

Dealing with Relapse

People seldom progress through the stages of change in a straightforward, linear way; rather, they tend to move to a certain stage and then slip back to a previous stage before resuming their forward progress. Research suggests that

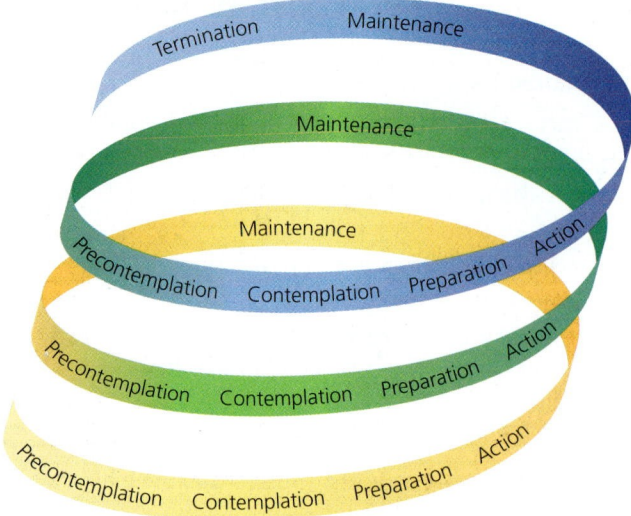

FIGURE 1.7 **The stages of change: A spiral model.**

SOURCE: Adapted from Prochaska, J. O., C. C. Diclemente, and J. C. Norcross. 1992. In Search of How People Change. *American Psychologist* 47(9): 1102–1114. Copyright © 1992 by the American Psychological Association. Reprinted by permission.

most people make several attempts before they successfully change a behavior; four out of five people experience some degree of backsliding. For this reason, the stages of change are best conceptualized as a spiral, in which people cycle back through previous stages but are further along in the process each time they renew their commitment (Figure 1.7).

If you experience a lapse—a single slip—or a relapse—a return to old habits—don't give up. Relapse can be demoralizing, but it is not the same as failure; failure means stopping before you reach your goal and never changing your target behavior. During the early stages of the change process, it's a good idea to plan for relapse so you can avoid guilt and self-blame and get back on track quickly. Follow these steps:

1. *Forgive yourself.* A single setback isn't the end of the world, but abandoning your efforts to change could have negative effects on your life.

2. *Give yourself credit for the progress you have already made.* You can use that success as motivation to continue.

3. *Move on.* You can learn from a relapse and use that knowledge to deal with potential setbacks in the future.

If relapses keep occurring or if you can't seem to control them, you may need to return to a previous stage of the behavior change process. If this is necessary, reevaluate your goals and your strategy. A different or less stressful approach may help you avoid setbacks when you try again.

Developing Skills for Change: Creating a Personalized Plan

Once you are committed to making a change, it's time to put together a plan of action. Your key to success is a well-thought-out plan that sets goals, anticipates problems, and includes rewards.

1. Monitor Your Behavior and Gather Data Keep a record of your target behavior and the circumstances surrounding it. Record this information for at least a week or two. Keep your notes in a health journal or notebook or on your computer (see the sample journal entries in Figure 1.8). Record each occurrence of your behavior, noting the following:

- What the activity was
- When and where it happened
- What you were doing
- How you felt at that time

If your goal is to start an exercise program, track your activities to determine how to make time for workouts.

2. Analyze the Data and Identify Patterns After you have collected data on the behavior, analyze the data to identify patterns. When are you most likely to overeat? What events trigger your appetite? Perhaps you are especially hungry at midmorning or when you put off eating dinner until 9:00. Perhaps you overindulge in food and drink when you go to a particular restaurant or when you're with certain friends. Note the connections between your feelings and such external cues as time of day, location, situation, and the actions of others around you.

3. Be "SMART" About Setting Goals If your goals are too challenging, you will have trouble making steady progress and will be more likely to give up altogether. If, for example, you are in poor physical condition, it will not make sense to set a goal of being ready to run a marathon within 2 months. If you set goals you can live with, it will be easier to stick with your behavior change plan and be successful.

Experts suggest that your goals meet the "SMART" criteria; that is, your behavior change goals should be:

- *Specific.* Avoid vague goals like "eat more fruits and vegetables." Instead, state your objectives in specific terms, such as "eat 2 cups of fruit and 3 cups of vegetables every day."

- *Measurable.* Recognize that your progress will be easier to track if your goals are quantifiable, so give your goal a number. You might measure your goal in terms of time (such as "walk briskly for 20 minutes a day"), distance ("run 2 miles, 3 days per week"), or some other amount ("drink 8 glasses of water every day").

Date November 5					Day M TU W TH F SA SU					
Time of day	*M/S*	*Food eaten*	*Cals.*	*H*	*Where did you eat?*	*What else were you doing?*	*How did someone else influence you?*	*What made you want to eat what you did?*	*Emotions and feelings?*	*Thoughts and concerns?*
7:30	M	1 C Crispix cereal 1/2 C skim milk coffee, black 1 C orange juice	110 40 — 120	3	home	reading newspaper	alone	I always eat cereal in the morning	a little keyed up & worried	thinking about quiz in class today
10:30	S	1 apple	90	1	hall outside classroom	studying	alone	felt tired & wanted to wake up	tired	worried about next class
12:30	M	1 C chili 1 roll 1 pat butter 1 orange 2 oatmeal cookies 1 soda	290 120 35 60 120 150	2	campus food court	talking	eating w/ friends; we decided to eat at the food court	wanted to be part of group	excited and happy	interested in hearing everyone's plans for the weekend
M/S = Meal or snack					H = Hunger rating (0–3)					

FIGURE 1.8 **Sample health journal entries.**

- *Attainable.* Set goals that are within your physical limits. For example, if you are a poor swimmer, it might not be possible for you to meet a short-term fitness goal by swimming laps. Walking or biking might be better options.
- *Realistic.* Manage your expectations when you set goals. For example, it may not be possible for a long-time smoker to quit cold turkey. A more realistic approach might be to use nicotine-replacement patches or gum for several weeks while getting help from a support group.
- *Time frame–specific.* Give yourself a reasonable amount of time to reach your goal, state the time frame in your behavior change plan, and set your agenda to meet the goal within the given time frame.

Using these criteria, a sedentary person who wanted to improve his health and build fitness might set a goal of being able to run 3 miles in 30 minutes, to be achieved within a time frame of 6 months. To work toward that goal, he might set a number of smaller, intermediate goals that are easier to achieve. For example, his list of goals might look like this:

Week	Frequency (days/week)	Activity	Duration (minutes)
1	3	Walk < 1 mile	10–15
2	3	Walk 1 mile	15–20
3	4	Walk 1–2 miles	20–25
4	4	Walk 2–3 miles	25–30
5–7	3–4	Walk/run 1 mile	15–20
⋮			
21–24	4–5	Run 2–3 miles	25–30

Of course, it may not be possible to meet these goals, but you never know until you try. As you work toward meeting your long-term goal, you may find it necessary to adjust your short-term goals. For example, you may find that you can start running sooner than you thought, or you may be able to run farther than you originally estimated. In such cases, it may be reasonable to make your goals more challenging. Otherwise, you may want to make them easier in order to stay motivated.

For some goals and situations, it may make more sense to focus on something other than your outcome goal. If you are in an early stage of change, for example, your goal may be to learn more about the risks associated with your target behavior or to complete a cost-benefit analysis. If your goal involves a long-term lifestyle change, such as reaching a healthy weight, it is better to focus on developing healthy habits than to target a specific weight loss. Your goal in this case might be exercising for 30 minutes every day, reducing portion sizes, or eliminating late-night snacks.

QUICK STATS

32% of American men and 29% of women engage in moderate physical activity 5 times each week.

—Healthy People 2010 Database, 2008

4. Devise a Plan of Action Develop a strategy that will support your efforts to change. Your plan of action should include the following steps:

Your environment contains powerful cues for both positive and negative lifestyle choices. Identifying and using the healthier options available to you throughout the day is a key part of a successful behavior change program.

- **Get what you need.** Identify resources that can help you. For example, you can join a community walking club or sign up for a smoking cessation program. You may also need to buy some new running shoes or nicotine-replacement patches. Get the items you need right away; waiting can delay your progress.
- **Modify your environment.** If there are cues in your environment that trigger your target behavior, try to control them. For example, if you normally have alcohol at home, getting rid of it can help prevent you from indulging. If you usually study with a group of friends in an environment that allows smoking, try moving to a non-smoking area. If you always buy a snack at a certain vending machine, change your route so you don't pass by it.
- **Control related habits.** You may have habits that contribute to your target behavior; modifying these habits can help change the behavior. For example, if you usually plop down on the sofa while watching TV, try putting an exercise bike in front of the set so you can burn calories while watching your favorite programs.
- **Reward yourself.** Giving yourself instant, real rewards for good behavior will reinforce your efforts. Plan your rewards; decide in advance what each one will be and how you will earn it. Tie rewards to achieving specific goals or subgoals. For example, you might treat yourself to a movie after a week of avoiding snacks. Make a list of items or events to use as rewards; they should be special to you and preferably unrelated to food or alcohol.
- **Involve the people around you.** Tell family and friends about your plan, and ask them to help. To help them respond appropriately to your needs, create a specific list of dos and don'ts. For example, ask them to support you when you set aside time to exercise or avoid second helpings at dinner.

- **Plan for challenges.** Think about situations and people that might derail your program, and develop ways to cope with them. For example, if you think it will be hard to stick to your usual exercise program during exams, schedule short bouts of physical activity (such as a brisk walk) as stress-reducing study breaks.

5. Make a Personal Contract

A serious personal contract—one that commits you to your word—can result in a higher chance of follow-through than a casual, off-hand promise. Your contract can help prevent procrastination by specifying important dates and can also serve as a reminder of your personal commitment to change.

Your contract should include a statement of your goal and your commitment to reaching it. The contract should also include details, such as the following:

- The date you will start
- The steps you will take to measure your progress
- The strategies you plan to use to promote change
- The date you expect to reach your final goal

Have someone—preferably someone who will be actively helping you with your program—sign your contract as a witness.

Figure 1.9 shows a sample behavior change contract for someone who is committing to eating more fruit

---

Behavior Change Contract

1. I, __Tammy Lau__, agree to __increase my consumption of fruit from 1 cup per week to 2 cups per day.__

2. I will begin on ___10/5___ and plan to reach my goal of __2 cups of fruit per day__ by __12/7__

3. To reach my final goal, I have devised the following schedule of mini-goals. For each step in my program, I will give myself the reward listed.
I will begin to have ½ cup of fruit with breakfast	10/5	see movie
I will begin to have ½ cup of fruit with lunch	10/26	new cd
I will begin to substitute fruit juice for soda 1 time per day	11/16	concert

   My overall reward for reaching my goal will be __trip to beach__

4. I have gathered and analyzed data on my target behavior and have identified the following strategies for changing my behavior: __Keep the fridge stocked with easy-to-carry fruit. Pack fruit in my backpack every day. Buy lunch at place that serves fruit.__

5. I will use the following tools to monitor my progress toward my final goal:
   __Chart on fridge door__
   __Health journal__

   I sign this contract as an indication of my personal commitment to reach my goal: _____Tammy Lau_____ 9/28

   I have recruited a helper who will witness my contract and __also increase his consumption of fruit; eat lunch with me twice a week.__
   _____Eric March_____ 9/28

FIGURE 1.9 A sample behavior change contract.

every day. You can apply the general behavior change planning framework presented in this chapter to any target behavior. Additional examples of behavior change plans appear in the Behavior Change Strategy sections at the end of many chapters in this text. In these sections, you wil find specific plans for quitting smoking, starting an exercise program, and making other positive lifestyle changes.

Putting Your Plan into Action

The starting date has arrived, and you are ready to put your plan into action. This stage requires commitment, the resolve to stick with the plan no matter what temptations you encounter. Remember all the reasons you have to make the change—and remember that *you* are the boss. Use all your strategies to make your plan work. Make sure your environment is change-friendly, and get as much support and encouragement from others as possible. Keep track of your progress in your health journal, and give yourself regular rewards. And don't forget to give yourself a pat on the back—congratulate yourself, notice how much better you look or feel, and feel good about how far you've come and how you've gained control of your behavior.

Staying with It

As you continue with your program, don't be surprised when you run up against obstacles; they're inevitable. In fact, it's a good idea to expect problems and give yourself time to step back, see how you're doing, and make some changes before going on. If your program is grinding to a halt, identify what is blocking your progress. It may come from one of the sources described in the following sections.

Social Influences   Take a hard look at the reactions of the people you're counting on, and see if they're really supporting you. If they come up short, connect with others who will be more supportive.

A related trap is trying to get your friends or family members to change *their* behaviors. The decision to make a major behavior change is something people come to only after intensive self-examination. You may be able to influence someone by tactfully providing facts or support, but that's all. Focus on yourself. When you succeed, you may become a role model for others.

Levels of Motivation and Commitment   You won't make real progress until an inner drive leads you to the stage of change at which you are ready to make a personal commitment to the goal. If commitment is your problem, you may need to wait until the behavior you're dealing with makes you unhappier or unhealthier; then your desire to change it will be stronger. Or you may find that changing your goal will inspire you to keep going. For more ideas, refer to the box "Motivation Boosters" (p. 26).

A beautiful day and a spectacular setting contribute to making exercise a satisfying and pleasurable experience. Choosing the right activity and doing it the right way are important elements in a successful health behavior change program.

Choice of Techniques and Level of Effort   If your plan is not working as well as you thought it would, make changes where you're having the most trouble. If you've lagged on your running schedule, for example, maybe it's because you don't like running. An aerobics class might suit you better. There are many ways to move toward your goal. Or you may not be trying hard enough. You do have to push toward your goal. If it were easy, you wouldn't need a plan.

Stress Barrier   If you hit a wall in your program, look at the sources of stress in your life. If the stress is temporary, such as catching a cold or having a term paper due, you may want to wait until it passes before strengthening your efforts. If the stress is ongoing, find healthy ways to manage it (see Chapter 2). You may even want to make stress management your highest priority for behavior change.

Procrastinating, Rationalizing, and Blaming   Be alert to games you might be playing with yourself, so you can stop them. Such games include the following:

- *Procrastinating.* If you tell yourself, "It's Friday already; I might as well wait until Monday to start," you're procrastinating. Break your plan into smaller steps that you can accomplish one day at a time.

Motivation Boosters

Changing behavior takes motivation. But how do you get motivated? The following strategies may help:

- Write down the potential benefits of the change. If you want to lose weight, your list might include increased ease of movement, energy, and self-confidence.

- Now write down the costs of not changing.

- Frequently visualize yourself achieving your goal and enjoying its benefits. If you want to manage time more effectively, picture yourself as a confident, organized person who systematically tackles important tasks and sets aside time each day for relaxation, exercise, and friends.

- Discount obstacles to change. Counter thoughts such as "I'll never have time to shop for and prepare healthy foods" with thoughts such as "Lots of other people have done it and so can I."

- Bombard yourself with propaganda. Subscribe to a self-improvement magazine. Take a class dealing with the change you want to make. Read books and watch talk shows on the subject. Post motivational phrases or pictures on your refrigerator or over your desk. Listen to motivational CDs in the car. Talk to people who have already made the change you want to make.

- Build up your confidence. Remind yourself of other goals you've achieved. At the end of each day, mentally review your good decisions and actions. See yourself as a capable person, in charge of your health.

- Create choices. You will be more likely to exercise every day if you have two or three types of exercise to choose from, and more likely to quit smoking if you've identified more than one way to distract yourself when you crave a cigarette. Get ideas from people who have been successful, and adapt some of their strategies to suit you.

- If you slip, keep trying. Research suggests that four out of five people will experience some degree of backsliding when they try to change a behavior. Only one in four succeeds the first time around. If you retain your commitment to change even when you lapse, you still are farther along the path to change than before you made the commitment. Try again. And again, if necessary.

- *Rationalizing.* If you tell yourself, "I wanted to go swimming today but wouldn't have had time to wash my hair afterward," you're making excuses. When you "win" by deceiving yourself, it isn't much of a victory.

- *Blaming.* If you tell yourself, "I couldn't exercise because Dave was hogging the elliptical trainer," you're blaming others for your own failure to follow through. Blaming is a way of taking your focus off the real problem and denying responsibility for your own actions.

BEING HEALTHY FOR LIFE

Your first few behavior change projects may never go beyond the planning stage. Those that do may not all succeed. But as you begin to see progress and changes, you'll start to experience new and surprising positive feelings about yourself. You'll probably find that you're less likely to buckle under stress. You may accomplish things you never thought possible—winning a race, climbing a mountain, quitting smoking. Being healthy takes extra effort, but the paybacks in energy and vitality are priceless.

Once you've started, don't stop. Remember that maintaining good health is an ongoing process. Tackle one area at a time, but make a careful inventory of your health strengths and weaknesses and lay out a long-range plan. Take on the easier problems first, and then use what you have learned to attack more difficult areas. Keep informed about the latest health news and trends; research is constantly providing new information that directly affects daily choices and habits.

Making Changes in Your World

You can't completely control every aspect of your health. At least three other factors—heredity, health care, and environment—play important roles in your well-being. After you quit smoking, for example, you may still be inhaling smoke from other people's cigarettes. Your resolve to eat better foods may suffer a setback when you can't find any healthy choices in vending machines.

But you can make a difference—you can help create an environment around you that supports wellness for everyone. You can help support nonsmoking areas in public places. You can speak up in favor of more nutritious foods and better physical fitness facilities. You can include non-alcoholic drinks at your parties.

QUESTIONS FOR CRITICAL THINKING AND REFLECTION

Think about the last time you made an unhealthy choice instead of a healthy one. How could you have changed the situation, the people in the situation, or your own thoughts, feelings, or intentions to avoid making that choice? What can you do in similar situations in the future to produce a different outcome?

You can also work on larger environmental challenges: air and water pollution, traffic congestion, overcrowding and overpopulation, global warming and climate change, toxic and nuclear waste, and many others. These difficult issues need the attention and energy of people who are informed and who care about good health. On every level, from personal to planetary, we can all take an active role in shaping our environment.

What Does the Future Hold?

Sweeping changes in lifestyle have resulted in healthier Americans in recent years and could have even greater effects in the years to come. In your lifetime, you can choose to take an active role in the movement toward increased awareness, greater individual responsibility and control, healthier lifestyles, and a healthier planet. Your choices and actions will have a tremendous impact on your present and future wellness. The door is open, and the time is now—you simply have to begin.

SUMMARY

- Wellness is the ability to live life fully, with vitality and meaning. Wellness is dynamic and multidimensional; it incorporates physical, emotional, intellectual, spiritual, interpersonal and social, and environmental dimensions.

- As chronic diseases have become the leading cause of death in the United States, people have recognized that they have greater control over, and greater responsibility for, their health than ever before.

- The Healthy People initiative seeks to achieve a better quality of life for all Americans. The broad goals of the *Healthy People 2010* report are to increase quality and years of healthy life and to eliminate health disparities among Americans.

- Health-related differences among people that have implications for wellness can be described in the context of gender, ethnicity, income and education, disability, geographic location, and sexual orientation.

- Although heredity, environment, and health care all play roles in wellness and disease, behavior can mitigate their effects.

- To make lifestyle changes, you need information about yourself, your health habits, and resources available to help you change.

- You can increase your motivation for behavior change by examining the benefits and costs of change, boosting self-efficacy, and identifying and overcoming key barriers to change.

- The "stages of change" model describes six stages that people move through as they try to change their behavior: precontemplation, contemplation, preparation, action, maintenance, and termination.

- A specific plan for change can be developed by (1) monitoring behavior by keeping a journal; (2) analyzing the recorded data; (3) setting specific goals; (4) devising strategies for modifying the environment, rewarding yourself, and involving others; and (5) making a personal contract.

- To start and maintain a behavior change program you need commitment, a well-developed plan, social support, and a system of rewards.

- Although we cannot control every aspect of our health, we can make a difference in helping create an environment that supports wellness for everyone.

BOOKS

American Medical Association. 2006. *American Medical Association Concise Medical Encyclopedia*. New York: Random House. *Includes more than 3000 entries on health and wellness topics, symptoms conditions, and treatments.*

Claiborn, J., and C. Pedrick. 2001. *The Habit Change Workbook: How to Break Bad Habits and Form Good Ones*. Oakland, Ca.: New Harbinger Publications. *Provides step-by-step instructions for identifying and overcoming a variety of unhealthy behaviors, such as poor eating habits, reluctance to exercise, and addictive behavior.*

Komaroff, A. L., ed. 2005. *Harvard Medical School Family Health Guide*. New York: Free Press. *Provides consumer-oriented advice for the prevention and treatment of common health concerns.*

Litin, S.C. (ed). 2004. *Mayo Clinic Family Health Book*, 3rd Ed. New York: HarperCollins Publishers. *A complete health reference for every stage of life, covering thousands of conditions, symptoms, and treatments.*

Murat, B., and G. Stewart. 2009. *Do I Need to See the Doctor? The Home-Treatment Encyclopedia—Written by Medical Doctors—That Lets You Decide*, 2nd Ed. New York: John Wiley & Sons. *Fully illustrated, easy-to-read guide to hundreds of common symptoms and ailments, designed to help consumers determine whether they can treat themselves or should seek professional medical attention.*

Prochaska, J. O., J. C. Norcross, and C. C. DiClemente. 1994. *Changing for Good: The Revolutionary Program That Explains the Six Stages of Change and Teaches You How to Free Yourself from Bad Habits*. New York: Morrow. *Outlines the authors' model of behavior change and offers suggestions and advice for each stage of change.*

U.S. Government. 2007. *2007 American Health and Medical Encyclopedia: Authoritative, Practical Guide to Health and Wellness. FDA, CDC, NIH, Surgeon General Publications (CD-ROM)*. Washington, D.C.: Progressive Management. *Contains thousands of documents from various federal agencies on myriad health issues, as well as links to dozens of health- and wellness-related Web sites.*

NEWSLETTERS

Consumer Reports on Health (800-274-7596;
    http://www.consumerreports.org/oh/index.htm)
Harvard Health Publications (877-649-9457;
    http://www.health.harvard.edu)
Harvard Men's Health Watch (877-649-9457)
Harvard Women's Health Watch (877-699-9457)
Mayo Clinic Health Letter (800-291-1128)
University of California, Berkeley, Wellness Letter (800-829-9170;
    http://www.wellnessletter.com)

ORGANIZATIONS, HOTLINES, AND WEB SITES

The Internet addresses (also called uniform resource locators, or URLs) listed here were accurate at the time of publication.
Centers for Disease Control and Prevention. Through phone, fax, and the Internet, the CDC provides a wide variety of health information.
    http://www.cdc.gov

Federal Trade Commission: Consumer Protection — Health. Includes online brochures about a variety of consumer health topics, including fitness equipment, generic drugs, and fraudulent health claims.
    http://www.ftc.gov/bcp/menus/consumer/health.shtm
FirstGov for Consumers: Health. Provides links to online brochures from a variety of government agencies.
    http://www.consumer.gov/health.htm
Healthfinder. A gateway to online publications, Web sites, support and self-help groups, and agencies and organizations that produce reliable health information.
    http://www.healthfinder.gov
Healthy Campus 2010. The American College Health Association's introduction to the Healthy Campus program.
    http://www.acha.org/info_resources/hc2010.cfm
Healthy People 2010. Provides information on Healthy People objectives and priority areas.
    http://www.healthypeople.gov
MedlinePlus. Provides links to news and reliable information about health from government agencies and professional associations; also includes a health encyclopedia and information on prescription and over-the-counter drugs.
    http://www.medlineplus.gov
National Health Information Center (NHIC). Puts consumers in touch with the organizations that are best able to provide answers to health-related questions.
    http://www.health.gov/nhic
National Institutes of Health. Provides information about all NIH activities as well as consumer publications, hotline information, and an A to Z listing of health issues with links to the appropriate NIH institute.
    http://www.nih.gov
National Wellness Institute. Serves professionals and organizations that promote optimal health and wellness.
    http://www.nationalwellness.org
National Women's Health Information Center. Provides information and answers to frequently asked questions.
    http://www.4woman.gov
Office of Minority Health Resource Center. Promotes improved health among racial and ethnic minority populations.
    http://www.omhrc.gov
Surgeon General. Includes information on activities of the Surgeon General and the text of many key reports on such topics as tobacco use, physical activity, and mental health.
    http://www.surgeongeneral.gov
World Health Organization (WHO). Provides information about health topics and issues affecting people around the world.
    http://www.who.int
The following are just a few of the many sites that provide consumer-oriented information on a variety of health issues:
    CNN Health: http://www.cnn.com/health
    FamilyDoctor.Org: http://www.familydoctor.org
    InteliHealth: http://www.intelihealth.com
    MayoClinic.com: http://www.mayoclinic.com
    MedlinePlus News: http://www.nlm.nih.gov/medlineplus/newsbydate.html
    MedPage Today Medical News: http://www.medpagetoday.com
    WebMD: http://www.webmd.com
    Yahoo Health News: http://news.yahoo.com/i/751

SELECTED BIBLIOGRAPHY

American Cancer Society. 2008. *Cancer Facts and Figures—2008*. Atlanta: American Cancer Society.

American Heart Association. 2008. *Heart Disease and Stroke Statistics—2009 Update*. Dallas: American Heart Association.

Banks, J., et al. 2006. Disease and disadvantage in the United States and in England. *Journal of the American Medical Association* 295(17): 2037–2045.

Barr, D.A. 2008. *Health Disparities in the United States: Social Class, Race, Ethnicity, and Health*. Baltimore: The Johns Hopkins University Press.

Beckman, M. 2007. Help wanted: In the pursuit of a healthy lifestyle, sheer grit only takes you so far. *Stanford Medicine Magazine* 24(3).

Bren, L. 2005. Does sex make a difference? *FDA Consumer,* July–August.

Casciano, D. A. 2005. Paving the way for safer, more effective drugs, food, and medical products. *FDA Consumer,* November–December.

Centers for Disease Control and Prevention. 2008. *Racial and Ethnic Approaches to Community Health (REACH U.S.): Finding Solutions to Health Disparities, 2008* (http://www.cdc.gov/nccdphp/publications/aag/pdf/reach.pdf; retrieved December 27, 2008).

Centers for Disease Control and Prevention. 2008. Racial/Ethnic Disparities in Self-Rated Health Status among Adults with and without Disabilities—United States, 2004–2006. *Morbidity and Mortality Weekly Report* 57(39): 1069–1073.

Finkelstein, E. A., et al. 2008. Do obese persons comprehend their personal health risks? *American Journal of Health Behavior* 32(5): 508–516.

Flegal, K.M., et al. 2005. Excess deaths associated with underweight, overweight, and obesity. Journal of the American Medical Association 293(15): 1861–1867.

Flegal, K.M., et al. 2007. Cause-specific excess deaths associated with underweight, overweight, and obesity. *Journal of the American Medical Association* 298(17): 2028–2037.

Gorman, B. K., and J. G. Read.. 2006. Gender disparities in adult health: An examination of three measures of morbidity. *Journal of Health and Social Behavior* 47(2): 95–110.

Herd, P., et al. 2007. Socioeconomic position and health: The differential effects of education versus income on the onset versus progression of health problems. *Journal of Health and Social Behavior* 48(3): 223–238.

Horneffer-Ginter, K. 2008. Stages of change and possible selves: Two tools for promoting college health. *Journal of American College Health* 56(4): 351–358.

How to keep those New Year's resolutions. 2006. *Harvard Health Letter,* January, 31.

Jemal, A., et al. 2008. Cancer statistics, 2008. *CA: A Cancer Journal for Clinicians* 58(2): 71–96.

Martin, G., and J. Pear. 2007. *Behaviour Modification: What It Is and How to Do It,* 8th ed. Upper Saddle River, N.J.: Prentice-Hall.

Mokdad, A. H., et al. 2004. Actual causes of death in the United States, 2000. *Journal of the American Medical Association* 291(10): 1238–1245.

Mokdad, A. H., et al. 2005. Correction: Actual causes of death in the United States, 2000. *Journal of the American Medical Association* 293(3): 293–294.

National Center for Health Statistics. 2006. Health behaviors of adults: United States, 2002–04. *Vital and Health Statistics* 10(230).

National Center for Health Statistics. 2007. *Health, United States, 2007, with Chartbook on Trends in the Health of Americans.* Hyattsville, Md.: National Center for Health Statistics.

National Center for Health Statistics. 2008. Deaths: Preliminary data for 2006. *National Vital Statistics Report* 56(16).

Nothwehr, F., et al. 2008. Age group differences in diet and physical activity-related behaviors among rural men and women. *Journal of Nutrition, Health and Aging* 12(3): 169–174.

Ogden, C. L., et al. 2006. Prevalence of overweight and obesity in the United States, 1999–2004. *Journal of the American Medical Association* 295(13): 1549–1555.

O'Loughlin, J., et al. 2007. Lifestyle risk factors for chronic disease across family origin among adults in multiethnic, low-income, urban neighborhoods. *Ethnicity and Disease* 17(4): 657–663.

Song, J., et al. 2006. Gender differences across race/ethnicity in use of health care among Medicare-aged Americans. *Journal of Women's Health* 15(10): 1205–1213.

U.C. Berkeley. 2007. Do men get their fair share? University of California, *Berkeley, Wellness Letter*, April, 1–2.

U.C. Berkeley. 2008. *Evaluating Web Pages: Techniques to Apply and Questions to Ask* (http://www.lib.berkeley.edu/TeachingLib/Guides/Internet/Evaluate.html; retrieved December 27, 2008).

Walker, B., and C. P. Mouton. 2008. Environmental influences on cardiovascular health. *Journal of the National Medical Association* 100(1): 98–102.

U.S. Census Bureau. 2005. *We the People: Women and Men in the United States.* Washington, D.C.: U.S. Census Bureau.

Walsh, T., et al. 2006. Spectrum of mutations in BRCA1, BRCA2, CHEK2, and TP53 in families at high risk of breast cancer. *Journal of the American Medical Association* 295: 1379–1388.

World Health Organization. 2008. Gender Inequalities and HIV/AIDS (http://www.who.int/gender/hiv_aids/en; retrieved December 27, 2008).

World Health Organization. 2008. *Why Gender and Health?* (http://www.who.int/gender/genderandhealth/en; retrieved December 27, 2008).

CORE CONCEPTS IN HEALTH

connect™

PERSONAL HEALTH

http://www.mcgrawhillconnect.com/personalhealth

STRESS: THE CONSTANT CHALLENGE

LOOKING AHEAD>>>>>

AFTER READING THIS CHAPTER, YOU SHOULD BE ABLE TO:

- Explain what stress is and how people react to it—physically, emotionally, and behaviorally
- Describe the relationship between stress and disease
- List common sources of stress
- Describe techniques for preventing and managing stress
- Put together a plan for successfully managing the stress in your life

TEST YOUR KNOWLEDGE

1. **Which of the following events can cause stress?**
   a. taking out a loan
   b. failing a test
   c. graduating from college

2. **Exercise stimulates which of the following?**
   a. analgesia (pain relief)
   b. birth of new brain cells
   c. relaxation

3. **High levels of stress can impair memory and cause physical changes in the brain.**
   True or false?

4. **Which of the following can result from chronic stress?**
   a. violence
   b. heart attack
   c. stroke

5. **Because eating induces relaxation, it is an excellent means of coping with stress.**
   True or false?

ANSWERS

1. **ALL THREE.** Stress-producing factors can be pleasant or unpleasant and can include physical challenges and goal achievement as well as events that are perceived as negative.

2. **ALL THREE.** Regular exercise is linked to improvements in many dimensions of wellness.

3. **TRUE.** Low levels of stress may improve memory, but high stress levels impair learning and memory and, over the long term, may shrink an area of the brain called the hippocampus.

4. **ALL THREE.** Chronic—or ongoing—stress can last for years. People who suffer from long-term stress may ultimately become violent toward themselves or others. They also run a greater than normal risk for certain ailments, especially cardiovascular disease.

5. **FALSE.** Eating as a means of coping with stress may lead to weight gain and to binge eating, a risky behavior associated with eating disorders.

Like the term *wellness, stress* is a word many people use without really understanding its precise meaning. Stress is popularly viewed as an uncomfortable response to a negative event, which probably describes *nervous tension* more than the cluster of physical and psychological responses that actually constitute stress. In fact, stress is not limited to negative situations; it is also a response to pleasurable physical challenges and the achievement of personal goals. Whether stress is experienced as pleasant or unpleasant depends largely on the situation and the individual. Because learning effective responses to stress can enhance psychological health and help prevent a number of serious diseases, stress management can be an important part of daily life.

As a college student, you may be in one of the most stressful times of your life (see the box "How High Is Your Stress Level?"). This chapter explains the physiological and psychological reactions that make up the stress response and describes how these reactions can be risks to good health. The chapter also presents methods of managing stress.

WHAT IS STRESS?

In common usage, the term *stress* refers to two different things: situations that trigger physical and emotional reactions, *and* the reactions themselves. This text uses the more precise term **stressor** for a situation that triggers physical and emotional reactions and the term **stress response** for those reactions. A first date and a final exam are examples of stressors; sweaty palms and a pounding heart are symptoms of the stress response. We'll use the term **stress** to describe the general physical and emotional state that accompanies the stress response. So, a person taking a final exam experiences stress.

Physical Responses to Stressors

Imagine a near miss: As you step off the curb, a car careens toward you. With just a fraction of a second to spare, you leap safely out of harm's way. In that split second of danger and in the moments following it, you experience a predictable series of physical reactions. Your body goes from a relaxed state to one prepared for physical action to cope with a threat to your life.

Two systems in your body are responsible for your physical response to stressors: the nervous system and the endocrine system. Through rapid chemical reactions affecting almost every part of your body, you are primed to act quickly and appropriately in time of danger.

Actions of the Nervous System The nervous system consists of the brain, spinal cord, and nerves. Part of the nervous system is under voluntary control, as when you tell your arm to reach for a chocolate. The part that is not under conscious supervision—for example, the part that controls the digestion of the chocolate—is the **autonomic nervous system.** In addition to digestion, it controls your heart rate, breathing, blood pressure, and hundreds of other involuntary functions.

The autonomic nervous system consists of two divisions:

- The **parasympathetic division** is in control when you are relaxed; it aids in digesting food, storing energy, and promoting growth.
- The **sympathetic division** is activated during times of arousal, including exercise, and when there is an emergency, such as severe pain, anger, or fear.

Sympathetic nerves use the neurotransmitter **norepinephrine** to exert their actions on nearly every organ, sweat gland, blood vessel, and muscle to enable your body to handle an emergency. In general, the sympathetic division commands your body to stop storing energy and to use it in response to a crisis.

Actions of the Endocrine System During stress, the sympathetic nervous system triggers the **endocrine system.** This system of glands, tissues, and cells helps control body functions by releasing **hormones** and other chemical messengers into the bloodstream to influence metabolism and other body processes. These chemicals act on a variety of targets throughout the body. Along with

TERMS

stressor Any physical or psychological event or condition that produces stress.

stress response The physical and emotional changes associated with stress.

stress The general physiological and emotional state that accompanies the stress response.

autonomic nervous system The branch of the nervous system that controls basic body processes; consists of the sympathetic and parasympathetic divisions.

parasympathetic division A division of the autonomic nervous system that moderates the excitatory effect of the sympathetic division, slowing metabolism and restoring energy supplies.

sympathetic division A division of the autonomic nervous system that reacts to danger or other challenges by almost instantly accelerating body processes.

norepinephrine A neurotransmitter released by the sympathetic nervous system onto specific tissues to increase their function in the face of increased activity; when released by the brain, causes arousal (increased attention, awareness, and alertness); also called *noradrenaline.*

endocrine system The system of glands, tissues, and cells that secrete hormones into the bloodstream to influence metabolism and other body processes.

hormone A chemical messenger produced in the body and transported in the bloodstream to target cells or organs for specific regulation of their activities.

How High Is Your Stress Level?

Many symptoms of excess stress are easy to self-diagnose. To help determine how much stress you experience on a daily basis, answer the following questions:

1. How many of the symptoms of excess stress listed in Table 2.1 (p. 36) do you experience frequently?

2. Are you easily startled or irritated?

3. Are you increasingly forgetful?

4. Do you have trouble falling or staying asleep?

5. Do you continually worry about events in your future?

6. Do you feel as if you are constantly under pressure to produce?

7. Do you often use tobacco, alcohol, or other drugs to help you relax?

8. Do you often feel as if you have less energy than you need to finish the day?

9. Do you have recurrent stomachaches or headaches?

10. Is it difficult for you to find satisfaction in simple life pleasures?

11. Are you often disappointed in yourself and others?

12. Are you overly concerned with being liked or accepted by others?

13. Have you lost interest in intimacy or sex?

14. Are you concerned that you do not have enough money?

Experiencing some of the stress-related symptoms or answering yes to a few questions is normal. However, if you experience a large number of stress symptoms or you answered yes to a majority of the questions, you are likely experiencing a high level of stress. Take time out to develop effective stress-management techniques. This chapter describes many coping strategies that can aid you in dealing with your college stressors. Additionally, your school's counseling center can provide valuable support.

---

the nervous system, the endocrine system prepares the body to respond to a stressor.

The Two Systems Together   How do both systems work together in an emergency? Let's go back to your near collision with a car. Both reflexes and higher cognitive areas in your brain quickly make the decision that you are facing a threat—and your body prepares to meet the danger. Chemical messages and actions of sympathetic nerves cause the release of key hormones, including **cortisol** and **epinephrine.** These hormones trigger the physiological changes shown in Figure 2.1 (p. 34), including these:

- Heart and respiration rates accelerate to speed oxygen through the body.

- Hearing and vision become more acute.

- The liver releases extra sugar into the bloodstream to boost energy.

- Perspiration increases to cool the skin.

- The brain releases **endorphins**—chemicals that can inhibit or block sensations of pain—in case you are injured.

Taken together, these almost-instantaneous physical changes are called the **fight-or-flight reaction.** They give you the heightened reflexes and strength you need to dodge the car or deal with other stressors. Although these physical changes may vary in intensity, the same basic set of physical reactions occurs in response to any type of stressor—positive or negative, physical or psychological.

The Return to Homeostasis   Once a stressful situation ends, the parasympathetic division of your autonomic nervous system takes command and halts the stress response. It restores **homeostasis,** a state in which blood pressure, heart rate, hormone levels, and other vital functions are maintained within a narrow range of normal. Your parasympathetic nervous system calms your body down, slowing a rapid heartbeat, drying sweaty palms, and returning breathing to normal. Gradually, your body resumes its normal "housekeeping" functions, such as digestion and temperature regulation. Damage that may have been sustained during the fight-or-flight reaction is repaired. The day after you narrowly dodge the car, you wake up feeling fine. In this way, your body can grow, repair itself, and acquire reserves of energy. When the next crisis comes, you'll be ready to respond—instantly—again.

The Fight-or-Flight Reaction in Modern Life   The fight-or-flight reaction is a part of our biological heritage, and it's a survival mechanism that has served humans well. In modern life, however, it is often absurdly inappropriate. Many of the stressors we face in everyday life do not require a physical response—for example, an exam, a mess left by a roommate, or a stop light. The

---

TERMS

cortisol   A steroid hormone secreted by the cortex (outer layer) of the adrenal gland; also called *hydrocortisone.*

epinephrine   A hormone secreted by the medulla (inner core) of the adrenal gland that affects the functioning of organs involved in responding to a stressor; also called *adrenaline.*

endorphins   Brain secretions that have pain-inhibiting effects.

fight-or-flight reaction   A defense reaction that prepares an individual for conflict or escape by triggering hormonal, cardiovascular, metabolic, and other changes.

homeostasis   A state of stability and consistency in an individual's physiological functioning.

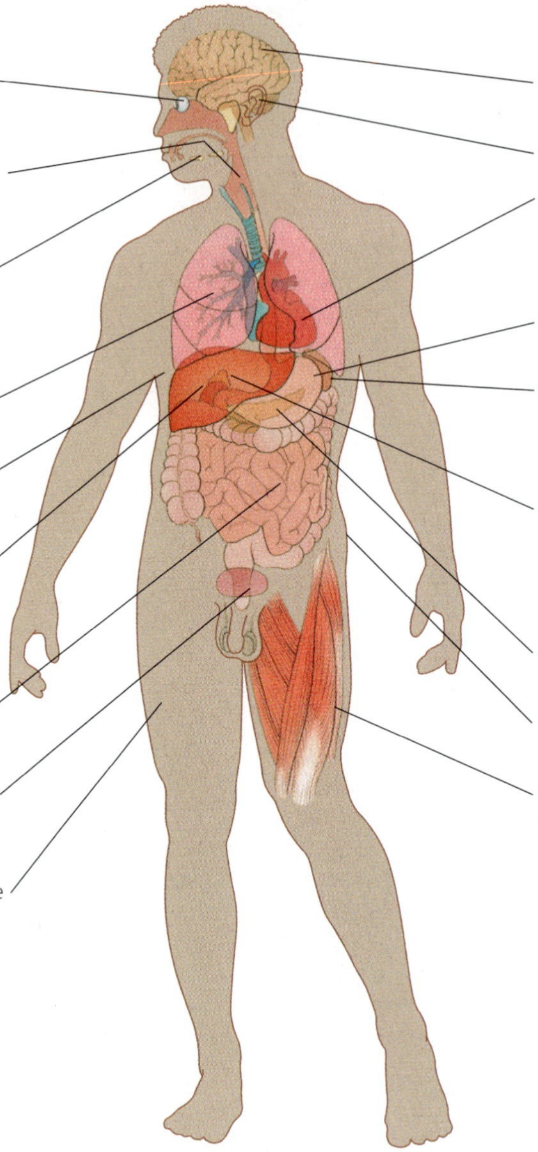

Pupils dilate to admit extra light for more sensitive vision.

Mucous membranes of nose and throat shrink, while muscles force a wider opening of passages to allow easier airflow.

Secretion of saliva and mucus decreases; digestive activities have a low priority in an emergency.

Bronchi dilate to allow more air into lungs.

Perspiration increases, especially in armpits, groin, hands, and feet, to flush out waste and cool overheating system by evaporation.

Liver releases sugar into bloodstream to provide energy for muscles and brain.

Muscles of intestines stop contracting because digestion has halted.

Bladder relaxes. Emptying of bladder contents releases excess weight, making it easier to flee.

Blood vessels in skin and viscera contract; those in skeletal muscles dilate. This increases blood pressure and delivery of blood to where it is most needed.

Endorphins are released to block any distracting pain.

Hearing becomes more acute.

Heart accelerates rate of beating, increases strength of contraction to allow more blood flow where it is needed.

Digestion, an unnecessary activity during an emergency, halts.

Spleen releases more red blood cells to meet an increased demand for oxygen and to replace any blood lost from injuries.

Adrenal glands stimulate secretion of epinephrine, increasing blood sugar, blood pressure, and heart rate; also spur increase in amount of fat in blood. These changes provide an energy boost.

Pancreas decreases secretions because digestion has halted.

Fat is removed from storage and broken down to supply extra energy.

Voluntary (skeletal) muscles contract throughout the body, readying them for action.

FIGURE 2.1 The fight-or-flight reaction. In response to a stressor, the autonomic nervous system and the endocrine system prepare the body to deal with an emergency.

fight-or-flight reaction prepares the body for physical action regardless of whether such action is a necessary or appropriate response to a particular stressor.

Emotional and Behavioral Responses to Stressors

We all experience a similar set of physical responses to stressors, which make up the fight-or-flight reaction. These responses, however, vary from person to person and from one situation to another. People's perceptions of potential stressors—and of their reactions to such stressors—also vary greatly. For example, you may feel confident about taking exams but be nervous about talking to people you don't know, while your roommate may love challenging social situations but may be very nervous about taking tests. Many factors, some external and some internal, help explain these differences.

Your cognitive (mental) appraisal of a potential stressor strongly influences how you view it. Two factors that can reduce the magnitude of the stress response are successful prediction and the perception of control. For instance, receiving course syllabi at the beginning of the term allows you to predict the timing of major deadlines and exams. Having this predictive knowledge also allows you to exert some control over your study plans and can thus help reduce the stress caused by exams.

Cognitive appraisal is highly individual and strongly related to emotions. The facts of a situation—Who? What? Where? When?—typically are evaluated fairly consistently from person to person. Evaluation with respect to

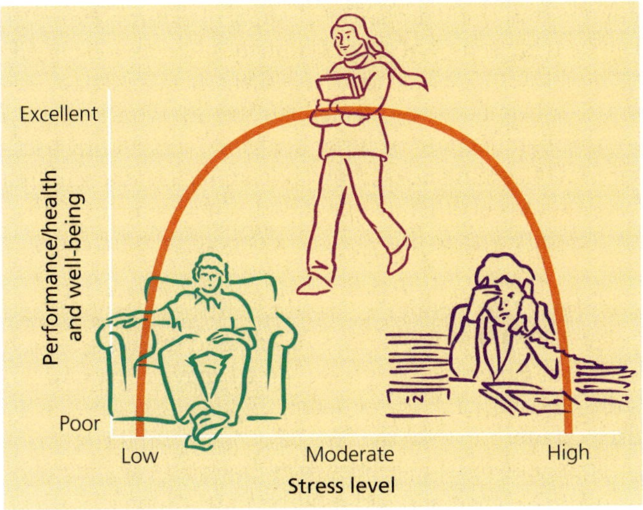

FIGURE 2.2 Stress level, performance, and well-being. A moderate level of stress challenges individuals in a way that promotes optimal performance and well-being. Too little stress, and people are not challenged enough to improve; too much stress, and the challenges become stressors that can impair physical and emotional health.

personal outcome, however, varies: What does this mean for me? Can I do anything about it? Will it improve or worsen? If an individual perceives a situation as exceeding her or his ability to cope, the result can be negative emotions and an inappropriate stress response. If, on the other hand, a person perceives a situation as a challenge that is within her or his ability to manage, more positive and appropriate responses are likely. A certain amount of stress, if coped with appropriately, can help promote optimal performance (Figure 2.2).

Effective and Ineffective Responses Common emotional responses to stressors include anxiety, depression, and fear. Although emotional responses are determined in part by inborn personality or temperament, we often can moderate or learn to control them. Coping techniques are discussed later in the chapter.

Behavioral responses to stressors—controlled by the **somatic nervous system,** which manages our conscious actions—are entirely under our control. Effective behavioral responses such as talking, laughing, exercising, meditating, learning time-management skills, and becoming more assertive can promote wellness and enable us to function at our best. Ineffective behavioral responses to stressors include overeating, expressing hostility, and using tobacco, alcohol, or other drugs.

Let's consider the individual variations demonstrated by two students, David and Amelia, responding to the same stressor—the first exam of the semester. David enters the exam with a feeling of dread and, as he reads the exam questions, responds to his initial anxiety with more anxiety. The more emotionally upset he gets, the less he can remember and the more anxious he becomes. Soon he's staring into space, imagining what will happen if he fails the course. Amelia, on the other hand, takes a deep breath to relax before she reads the questions, wills herself to focus on the answers she knows, and then goes back over the exam to deal with those questions she's not sure of. She leaves the room feeling calm, relaxed, and confident that she has done well.

As this simple example shows, avoiding destructive responses to stress and adopting effective and appropriate ones can have a direct effect on well-being.

QUICK STATS

20% of American college students suffer from test anxiety at some time during their college years.

—University of Cincinnati, Division of Student Affairs and Services

Personality and Stress Some people seem to be nervous, irritable, and easily upset by minor annoyances; others are calm and composed even in difficult situations. Scientists remain unsure just why this is or how the brain's complex emotional mechanisms work. But **personality,** the sum of cognitive, behavioral, and emotional tendencies, clearly affects how people perceive and react to stressors. To investigate the links among personality, stress, and overall wellness, researchers have looked at different constellations of characteristics, or "personality types."

- *Type A.* People with Type A personality are described as ultracompetitive, controlling, impatient, aggressive, and even hostile. Type A people have a higher perceived stress level and more problems coping with stress. They react explosively to stressors and are upset by events that others would consider only annoyances. Studies indicate that certain characteristics of the Type A pattern—anger, cynicism, and hostility—increase the risk of heart disease.
- *Type B.* The Type B personality is relaxed and contemplative. Type B people are less frustrated by daily events and more tolerant of the behavior of others.
- *Type C.* The Type C personality is characterized by anger suppression, difficulty expressing emotions, feelings of hopelessness and despair, and an exaggerated response to minor stressors. This heightened response may impair immune functions.

TERMS

somatic nervous system The branch of the peripheral nervous system that governs motor functions and sensory information, largely under conscious control.

personality The sum of behavioral, cognitive, and emotional tendencies.

Studies of Type A and C personalities suggest that expressing your emotions is beneficial but that habitually expressing exaggerated stress responses or hostility is unhealthy.

Researchers have also looked for personality traits that enable people to deal more successfully with stress. One such trait is *hardiness,* a particular form of optimism. People with a hardy personality view potential stressors as challenges and opportunities for growth and learning—not as burdens. They see fewer situations as stressful, and react less intensely to stress than nonhardy persons might. Hardy people are committed to their activities, have a sense of inner purpose and an inner locus of control, and feel at least partly in control of their lives.

The term *resilience* refers to personality traits associated with social and academic success in at-risk populations such as people from low-income families and those with mental or physical disabilities. Resilient people tend to set goals and face adversity through individual effort. There are three basic types of resilience, and each one determines how a person responds to stress:

- *Nonreactive resilience,* in which a person does not react to a stressor
- *Homeostatic resilience,* in which a person may react strongly but returns to baseline functioning quickly
- *Positive growth resilience,* in which a person learns and grows from the stress experience

Resilience is associated with emotional intelligence and violence prevention.

Can you do anything to change your personality traits and become more stress-resistant? It isn't likely. You can, however, change some of your typical behaviors and patterns of thinking, and develop positive techniques for coping with stressors. Strategies for successful stress management are described later in this chapter.

Cultural Background   Young adults from around the world come to America for a higher education; most students finish college with a greater appreciation for other cultures and worldviews. The clashing of cultures, however, can be a big source of stress for many students—especially when it leads to disrespectful treatment, harassment, or violence. It is important to remember that everyone's reaction to stress is influenced by his or her family and cultural background. Learning to accept and appreciate the cultural backgrounds of other people is both a mind-opening experience and a way to avoid stress over cultural differences.

Gender   Our **gender role**—the activities, abilities, and behaviors our culture expects of us based on our sex—can affect our experience of stress. Some behavior responses to stressors, such as crying or openly expressing anger, may be deemed more appropriate for one gender than the other.

Strict adherence to gender roles, however, can limit one's response to stress and can itself become a source of stress. Gender roles can also affect one's perception of a stressor. If a man derives most of his self-worth from his work, for example, retirement may be more stressful for him than for a woman whose self-image is based on several different roles.

See the box "Women, Men, and Stress" (p. 38) for more on gender and stress.

Experience   Past experiences can profoundly influence the evaluation of a potential stressor. Consider someone who has had a bad experience giving a speech in the past. He or she is much more likely to perceive an upcoming speech as stressful than someone who has had positive public speaking experiences.

The Stress Experience as a Whole

As Table 2.1 shows, the physical, emotional, and behavioral symptoms of excess negative stress are distinct. Even so, they are also intimately interrelated. The more intense the emotional response, for example, the stronger the physical response will be.

Effective behavioral responses can lessen stress, while ineffective ones only make it worse. Sometimes, people have such intense responses to stressors or such ineffective

Table 2.1	Symptoms of Excess Stress	
Physical Symptoms	**Emotional Symptoms**	**Behavioral Symptoms**
Dry mouth	Anxiety	Crying
Excessive perspiration	Depression	Disrupted eating habits
Frequent illnesses	Edginess	Disrupted sleeping habits
Gastrointestinal problems	Fatigue	Harsh treatment of others
Grinding of teeth	Hypervigilance	Problems communicating
Headaches	Impulsiveness	Sexual problems
High blood pressure	Inability to concentrate	Social isolation
Pounding heart	Irritability	Increased use of tobacco, alcohol, or other drugs
Stiff neck or aching lower back	Trouble remembering things	

QUESTIONS FOR CRITICAL THINKING AND REFLECTION
Think of the last time you faced a significant stressor. How did you respond? List the physical, emotional, and behavioral reactions you experienced. Did these responses help you deal with the stress, or did they interfere with your efforts to handle it?

coping techniques that they need professional help to overcome the stress in their lives.

More often, however, people can learn to handle stressors on their own. Strategies for successful stress management are described throughout this chapter. For starters, review the following list of basic stress-management strategies and consider whether any of them has ever worked for you:

- Building greater social support through meaningful relationships
- Participating in and contributing to your family and community in productive ways
- Setting higher expectations for yourself but with clear boundaries and fair, consistent expectations
- Building life skills such as decision making, effective communication, and conflict management
- Avoiding the urge to control the outcome of every situation
- Knowing your own limits and limitations
- Trusting others

THINKING ABOUT THE ENVIRONMENT
Environmental problems—whether natural or man-made—can compound other sources of stress, such as working, commuting, or taking care of a family. Consider the environment where you live, attend school, or work. Do you live with any of the following?

- Smog or other pollutants, which make the air hard to breathe
- Crowding, which makes it difficult to move around
- Poverty, which limits your choices in many aspects of life
- Crime, which can make you feel unsafe or hypervigilant

If one or more environmental factors make life more stressful for you, look for resources in your community that can help. For example, public transportation may ease your commute while helping to reduce pollution in your town. For more information on the environment and environmental health, see Chapter 19.

A person's emotional and behavioral responses to stressors depend on many different factors, including personality, gender, and cultural background. Research suggests that women are more likely than men to respond to stressors by seeking social support, a pattern referred to as tend-and-befriend.

This chapter also discusses a variety of ineffective coping behaviors and describes the destructiveness of relying on such habits to deal with stress in one's life.

STRESS AND HEALTH

According to the American Psychological Association, 77% of adult Americans reported stress-related health problems in 2007. The role of stress in health is complex, but evidence suggests that stress can increase vulnerability to many ailments. Several theories have been proposed to explain the relationship between stress and disease.

The General Adaptation Syndrome

The term **general adaptation syndrome (GAS)** describes what many believe is a universal and predictable response pattern to all stressors. As mentioned earlier, some stressors are pleasant (such as attending a party), but others are unpleasant (such as getting a bad grade). In the GAS

gender role   A culturally expected pattern of behavior and attitudes determined by a person's sex.

general adaptation syndrome (GAS)   A pattern of stress responses consisting of three stages: alarm, resistance, and exhaustion.

TERMS

Women, Men, and Stress

Men and women alike experience stress, but they experience it differently.

Women and Stress

Women are more likely than men to find themselves balancing multiple roles, such as those of student, spouse, and parent. Women who work outside the home still do most of the housework—although today's husbands are helping in greater numbers than previous generations did—and housework isn't limited to cleaning or doing laundry. For example, more than 60% of women make all decisions about their family's health care, including decisions about elderly parents. The combined pressures of home, workplace, and school can create very high stress levels.

Men and Stress

Men who fit a traditional male gender role may feel compelled to be in charge at all times. This may create tension in interpersonal situations and limit men's ability to build a support network. Such men may keenly feel the responsibility to support a family, which can compound existing pressures at home and work.

Perceptions of Stress

In late 2007, the American Psychological Association released the results of its annual "Stress in America" survey. The survey shows the different views American men and women have of their personal stress. Respondents said stress affects them in the following ways:

	Women	Men
Experience extreme stress	35%	28%
Stress has increased in past 5 years	50%	46%
Experience physical problems stemming from stress	82%	71%
Lose at least 1 hour of sleep nightly because of stress	24%	16%

The survey also shows that women are more likely than men to cope with stress through behaviors such as overeating or taking prescription medications.

Physiological Differences

Levels of testosterone (the primary male hormone, responsible for many masculine traits) increase from puberty onward, so men tend to have higher blood pressure than women of the same age. This factor contributes to greater wear on the male circulatory system, sometimes increasing a man's risk for cardiovascular disease. A part of the brain that regulates emotions, the amygdala, is sensitive to testosterone. This may be one reason that men are more likely than women to find certain situations (such as social interactions) to be stressful.

Conversely, women have higher levels of oxytocin (a hormone involved in social interaction and mood regulation) and are more likely to respond to stressors by seeking social support. This coping response may give women a longevity advantage over men by decreasing the risk of some stress-related disorders. It does not, however, free women from stress-related ailments, and women are more likely than men to suffer stress-related hypertensions, depression, and obesity.

---

theory, the stress triggered by a pleasant stressor is called **eustress**; stress brought on by an unpleasant stressor is called **distress**. The sequence of physical responses associated with GAS is the same for eustress and distress and occurs in three stages (Figure 2.3):

• *Alarm.* The alarm stage includes the complex sequence of events brought on by the fight-or-flight reaction. At this stage, the body is more susceptible to disease or injury because it is geared up to deal with a crisis. Someone in this stage may experience headaches, indigestion, anxiety, and disrupted eating or sleep patterns.

• *Resistance.* With continued stress, the body develops a new level of homeostasis in which it is more resistant to disease and injury than usual. In this stage, a person can cope with normal life and added stress.

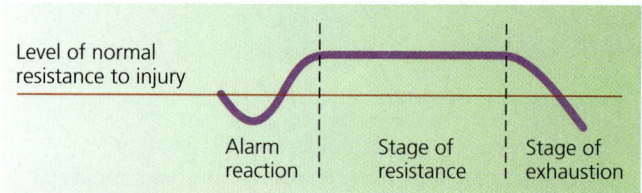

Level of normal resistance to injury

Alarm reaction | Stage of resistance | Stage of exhaustion

FIGURE 2.3 The general adaptation syndrome. During the alarm phase, a lower resistance to injury is evident. With continued stress, resistance to injury is actually enhanced. With prolonged exposure to repeated stressors, exhaustion sets in, with a return of low resistance levels seen during acute stress.

- **Exhaustion.** The first two stages of GAS require a great deal of energy. If a stressor persists, or if several stressors occur in succession, general exhaustion sets in. This is not the sort of exhaustion you feel after a long, busy day; rather, it's a life-threatening physiological state.

Allostatic Load

Although the GAS model is still viewed as a key conceptual contribution to the understanding of stress, some aspects of it are outdated. For example, increased susceptibility to disease after repeated or prolonged stress is now thought to be due to the effects of the stress response itself rather than to a depletion of resources (exhaustion state). In particular, long-term overexposure to stress hormones such as cortisol has been linked with health problems. Further, although physical stress reactions promote homeostasis (resistance stage), they also have negative effects on the body.

The long-term wear and tear of the stress response is called the **allostatic load.** An individual's allostatic load is dependent on many factors, including genetics, life experiences, and emotional and behavioral responses to stressors. A high allostatic load may be due to frequent stressors, poor adaptation to common stressors, an inability to shut down the stress response, or imbalances in the stress response of different body systems. A high allostatic load is linked with heart disease, hypertension, obesity, and reduced brain and immune system functioning. In other words, when your allostatic load exceeds your ability to cope, you are more likely to get sick.

Psychoneuroimmunology

One of the most fruitful areas of current research into the relationship between stress and disease is **psychoneuroimmunology (PNI).** PNI is the study of the interactions among the nervous system, the endocrine system, and the immune system. The underlying premise of PNI is that stress, through the actions of the nervous and endocrine systems, impairs the immune system and thereby affects health. It is important to note, however, that even large stress-induced immune changes can have small clinical (medical) consequences because they are short-term or because the immune system has redundant components and compensates for changes. In short, the immune system is remarkably flexible and capable of substantial change without compromising health. On the other hand, chronic stress in individuals predisposed to or experiencing disease may have more substantial consequences.

A complex network of nerve and chemical connections exists between the nervous and endocrine systems and the immune system. In general, increased levels of cortisol are linked to a decreased number of immune system cells, or lymphocytes (see Chapter 17 for more on the immune system). Epinephrine appears to promote the release of lymphocytes but at the same time reduces their efficiency. Scientists have identified hormone-like substances called *neuropeptides* that appear to translate stressful emotions into biochemical events, some of which impact the immune system, providing a physical link between emotions and immune function.

Different types of stress may affect immunity in different ways. For instance, during acute stress (typically lasting between 5 and 100 minutes), white blood cells move into the skin, where they enhance the immune response. During a stressful event sequence, such as a personal trauma and the events that follow, however, there are typically no overall significant immune changes. Chronic (ongoing) stressors such as unemployment have negative effects on almost all functional measures of immunity. Chronic stress may cause prolonged secretion of cortisol and may accelerate the course of diseases that involve inflammation, including multiple sclerosis, heart disease, and type 2 diabetes.

Mood, personality, behavior, and immune functioning are intertwined. For example, people who are generally pessimistic may neglect the basics of health care, become passive when ill, and fail to engage in health-promoting behaviors. People who are depressed may reduce physical activity and social interaction, which may in turn affect the immune system and the cognitive appraisal of a stressor. Optimism, successful coping, and positive problem solving, on the other hand, may positively influence immunity.

Links Between Stress and Specific Conditions

Although much remains to be learned, it is clear that people who have unresolved chronic stress in their lives or who handle stressors poorly are at risk for a wide range of health problems. In the short term, the problem might be just a cold, a stiff neck, or a stomachache. Over the long term, the problems can be more severe—cardiovascular disease (CVD), high blood pressure, impaired immune function, or accelerated aging.

QUESTIONS FOR CRITICAL THINKING AND REFLECTION

Have you ever been so stressed that you felt ill in some way? If so, what were your symptoms? How did you handle them? Did the experience affect the way you reacted to other stressful events?

TERMS

allostatic load The long-term negative impact of the stress response on the body.

psychoneuroimmunology (PNI) The study of the interactions among the nervous, endocrine, and immune systems.

Ongoing stress has been shown to make people more vulnerable to everyday ailments, such as colds and allergies.

Cardiovascular Disease During the stress response, heart rate increases and blood vessels constrict, causing blood pressure to rise. Chronic high blood pressure is a major cause of atherosclerosis, a disease in which blood vessels become damaged and caked with fatty deposits. These deposits can block arteries, causing heart attacks and strokes. The stress response can precipitate a heart attack in someone with atherosclerosis. The stress response can also cause stress cardiomyopathy ("broken heart syndrome"), a condition that mimics a heart attack but doesn't damage the heart.

Certain types of emotional responses may increase a person's risk of CVD. As described earlier, people who tend to react to situations with anger and hostility are more likely to have heart attacks than are people with a less explosive, more trusting personality.

Stress has also been linked to some of the more recently identified risk factors for CVD, including elevated cholesterol. For example, inflammation is a key component of the damage to blood vessels that leads to heart attacks. Stress increases inflammation throughout the body. Stress-induced increases in inflammatory messenger molecules are also linked to elevated levels of homocysteine and c-reactive protein (CRP), two compounds that appear to be markers for CVD risk. Stress-related depression and anger are associated with elevated homocysteine levels, and job-related exhaustion is linked to high CRP levels in some people. Elevated CRP levels have also been implicated in insulin resistance and the development of diabetes, which is in turn a risk factor for CVD. Clearly, stress reduction can improve cardiovascular health. See Chapter 15 for more on CVD.

Psychological Problems The hormones and other chemicals released during the stress response cause emotional as well as physical changes (see the box "Stress and Your Brain"). Stress also activates the enzyme PKC, which influences the brain's prefrontal cortex. Excess PKC can negatively affect focus, judgment, and the ability to think clearly. Moreover, many stressors are inherently anxiety-producing, depressing, or both. Stress has been found to contribute to psychological problems such as depression, panic attacks, anxiety, eating disorders, and post-traumatic stress disorder (PTSD). PTSD, which afflicts war veterans, rape and child abuse survivors, and others who have suffered or witnessed severe trauma, is characterized by nightmares, flashbacks, and a diminished capacity to experience or express emotion. (For more information, see Chapter 3.)

Altered Functioning of the Immune System PNI research helps explain how stress affects the immune system. Some of the health problems linked to stress-related changes in immune function include vulnerability to colds and other infections, asthma and allergy attacks, susceptibility to cancer, and flare-ups of chronic diseases such as genital herpes and HIV infection.

Other Health Problems Many other health problems may be caused or worsened by excessive stress, including the following:

- Digestive problems such as stomachaches, diarrhea, constipation, irritable bowel syndrome, and ulcers
- Tension headaches and migraines (see the box "Headaches: A Common Symptom of Stress," on p. 42)
- Insomnia and fatigue

> **QUICK STATS**
>
> **Two-thirds** of visits to family practitioners are due to stress-related issues.
>
> —American Academy of Family Physicians, 2007

Stress and Your Brain

connect™

Like a computer that registers information in response to typing on a keyboard, your brain is able to respond to and store information about changes in your environment. Unlike a computer, your brain has the attribute of *plasticity*—it physically changes its structure and function in response to experience. Plasticity allows your brain to be altered by psychological stress.

Moderate stress enhances the ability to acquire and remember information, while high levels of acute stress can impair learning. For example, people can often remember minute details following a fender bender but can't recall the events surrounding a major car crash. Thus, it is good to be a little nervous before an exam—but not too nervous.

The effects of stress on brain form and function are apparent in

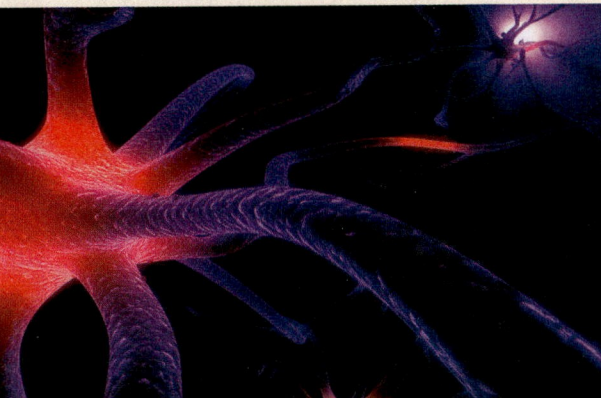

a structure called the *hippocampus*, which is involved in learning and memory. High levels of chronic stress cause brain cells (neurons) in the hippocampus to shrink in size or die, thus impairing learning and memory. New research in neuroscience has revealed that the hippocampus actually grows new neurons during adulthood. However, stress acts to reduce new cell birth in the hippocampus, reducing the replacement of lost neurons. Together, these effects of stress result in fewer neurons and fewer connections between neurons in the hippocampus, thus decreasing the capacity for information processing.

People who are depressed or who suffer from post-traumatic stress disorder have higher levels of stress hormones in their bloodstream and smaller hippocampi than others. Even in the absence of a serious disorder, it is thought that the accumulation of stress effects across the life span can contribute to brain aging. Thus, the way you cope with stress can affect the way your brain works both immediately and over the long term.

- Injuries, including on-the-job injuries caused by repetitive strain
- Menstrual irregularities, impotence, and pregnancy complications

COMMON SOURCES OF STRESS

Being able to recognize potential sources of stress is an important step in successfully managing the stress in your life.

Major Life Changes

Any major change in your life that requires adjustment and accommodation can be a source of stress. Early adulthood and the college years are associated with many significant changes, such as moving out of the family home. Even changes typically thought of as positive—graduation, job promotion, marriage—can be stressful.

Clusters of life changes, particularly those that are perceived negatively, may be linked to health problems in some people. Personality and coping skills, however, are important moderating influences. People with a strong support network and a stress-resistant personality are less likely to become ill in response to life changes than people with fewer resources.

Daily Hassles

Although major life changes are undoubtedly stressful, they seldom occur regularly. Researchers have proposed that minor problems—life's daily hassles, such as losing your keys or wallet—can be an even greater source of stress because they occur much more often.

People who perceive hassles negatively are likely to experience a moderate stress response every time they are faced with one. Over time, this can take a significant toll on health. Studies indicate that for some people, daily hassles contribute to a general decrease in overall wellness.

College Stressors

College is a time of major changes and minor hassles. For many students, college means being away from home and family for the first time. Nearly all students share stresses like the following:

- *Academic stress.* Exams, grades, and an endless workload await every college student but can be especially troublesome for young students just out of high school.
- *Interpersonal stress.* Most students are more than just students; they are also friends, children, employees, spouses, parents, and so on. Managing relationships while juggling the rigors of college life can be daunting, especially if some friends or family are less than supportive.

Headaches: A Common Symptom of Stress

More than 45 million Americans suffer from chronic, recurrent headaches. Headaches come in various types but are often grouped into three major categories: tension headaches, migraines, and cluster headaches. Other types of headaches have underlying organic causes, such as sinus congestion or infection.

Tension Headaches

Approximately 90% of all headaches are *tension headaches*, characterized by a dull, steady pain, usually on both sides of the head. It may feel as though a band of pressure is tightening around the head, and the pain may extend to the neck and shoulders. Acute tension headaches may last from hours to days, while chronic tension headaches may occur almost every day for months or even years.

Psychological stress, poor posture, and immobility are the leading causes of tension headaches. There is no cure, but the pain can sometimes be relieved with over-the-counter painkillers and with therapies such as massage, acupuncture, relaxation, hot or cold showers, and rest.

If your headaches are frequent, keep a diary with details about the events surrounding each one. If you can identify the stressors that are consistently associated with your headaches, you can begin to gain more control over the situation. If you suffer persistent tension headaches, you should consult your physician.

Migraines

Migraines typically progress through a series of stages lasting from several minutes to several days. They may produce a variety of symptoms, including throbbing pain that starts on one side of the head and may spread; heightened sensitivity to light; visual disturbances such as flashing lights; nausea; and fatigue. About 70% of migraine sufferers are women, and migraine headaches may have a genetic component.

Research suggests that people who get migraines may have abnormally excitable nerve cells in their brains. When triggered, these nerve cells send a wave of electrical activity throughout the brain, which in turn causes migraine symptoms. Potential triggers include menstruation, stress, fatigue, atmospheric changes, specific sounds or odors, and certain foods. The frequency of attacks varies from a few in a lifetime to several per week.

Keeping a headache journal can help a migraine sufferer identify headache triggers—the first step to avoiding them. In addition, many new treatments can help reduce the frequency, severity, and duration of migraines.

Cluster Headaches

Cluster headaches are extremely severe headaches that cause intense pain in and around one eye. They usually occur in clusters of one to three headaches each day over a period of weeks or months, alternating with periods of remission in which no headaches occur. About 90% of people with cluster headaches are male.

There is no known cause or cure for cluster headaches, but a number of treatments are available. During cluster periods, it is important to refrain from smoking cigarettes and drinking alcohol, because these activities can trigger attacks.

For more information on treating headaches and when a headache may signal a serious illness, see Appendix B.

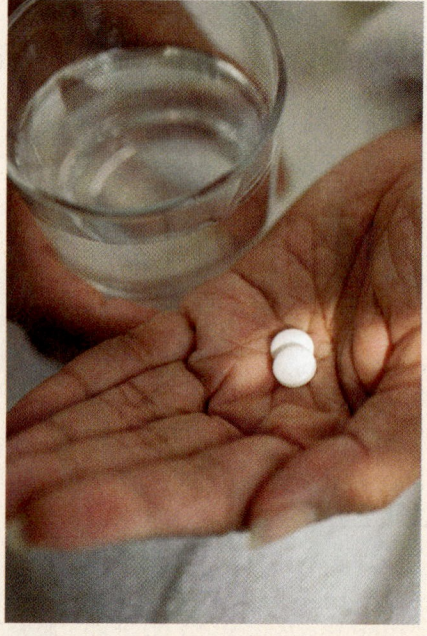

- **Time pressures.** Class schedules, assignments, and deadlines are an inescapable part of college life. But these time pressures can be drastically compounded for students who also have a job and/or family responsibilities.
- **Financial concerns.** The majority of college students need financial aid not just to cover the cost of tuition but to survive from day to day while in school. For many, college life isn't possible without a job, and the pressure to stay afloat financially competes with academic and other stressors.
- **Worries about the future.** As college life comes to an end, students face the reality of life after college. This means thinking about a career, choosing a place to live, and leaving the friends and routines of school behind.

As mentioned earlier, test anxiety is a source of stress for many students. To learn some proven techniques for overcoming test anxiety, see the Behavior Change Strategy at the end of this chapter.

Job-Related Stressors

Americans rate their jobs as a key source of stress in their lives. Tight schedules and overtime leave less time to exercise, socialize, and engage in other stress-proofing activities. More than one-third of Americans report that they always feel rushed, and nearly half say they would give up a day's pay for a day off. Worries about job performance, salary, and job security and interactions with bosses, coworkers, and customers can contribute to stress. High levels of job stress are also common for people who are

What Stresses Us Out?

In 2007, the American Psychological Association conducted a survey to determine the leading sources of stress in Americans' lives, their perceptions of stress, and the ways in which stress affects them. Americans identified the following issues as their top ten key sources of stress:

Work	74%
Money	73%
Workload	66%
Children	64%
Family responsibilities	60%
Health concerns	55%
Health problems of immediate family	55%
Health problems of other family members	53%
Housing costs	51%
Intimate relationships	47%

Work-related stress affects a large number of Americans, especially when combined with economic difficulties such as the 2008 housing/mortgage crisis. Responding to questions about work, about 52% of employed Americans stated that job stress interferes with their family lives. The same number said workplace stress was a determining factor in the decision to quit a job or look for a new one. Meanwhile, 55% reported that stress caused them to be less productive while at work.

left out of important decisions relating to their jobs. When workers are given the opportunity to shape how their jobs are performed, job satisfaction goes up and stress levels go down.

If job-related (or college-related) stress is severe or chronic, the result can be **burnout**, a state of physical, mental, and emotional exhaustion. Burnout occurs most often in highly motivated and driven individuals who come to feel that their work is not recognized or that they are not accomplishing their goals. People in the helping professions—teachers, social workers, caregivers, police officers, and so on—are also prone to burnout. For some people who suffer from burnout, a vacation or leave of absence may be appropriate. For others, a reduced work schedule, better communication with superiors, or a change in job goals may be necessary. Improving time-management skills can also help.

Nearly 40 million workdays are lost annually because of illness. Stress-related sleep disturbances, headaches, and damaged relationships are quick to arise and identify, but the effects of job stress on chronic diseases are harder to see because they take longer to develop. It's telling, however, that health care costs are nearly 50% greater for workers with high levels of stress. (For some recent statistics on job-related stress, see the box "What Stresses Us Out?".)

Social Stressors

Social networks can be real or virtual. Both types can help improve your ability to deal with stress, but any social network can also become a stressor in itself.

Real Social Networks   Although social support is a key buffer against stress, your interactions with others can themselves be a source of stress. The college years, in particular, can be a time of great change in interpersonal relationships. The larger community where you live can also act as a stressor.

Social stressors include prejudice and discrimination. You may feel stress as you try to relate to people of other ethnic or socioeconomic groups. If you are a member of a minority ethnic group, you may feel pressure to assimilate into mainstream society, or to spend as much time as possible with others who share your ethnicity or background. If English is not your first language, you may face the added burden of conducting daily activities in a language with which you are not comfortable. All these pressures can become significant sources of stress. (See the box "Diverse Populations, Discrimination, and Stress" on p. 44 for more information.)

Virtual Social Networks   New technologies can potentially be time-savers because we don't have to go home or to the office to check our e-mail or phone messages, and we can make a call on a cell phone instead of jotting down notes to pass on at a later time. Telecommuting can ease the time pressures on people who find it necessary to work from home, such as parents with young children or people with disabilities.

Increased electronic interactivity, however, can also impinge on our personal space, waste time, and cause stress. On a typical day, for example, you may check for e-mail or voice mail several times, only to find no messages waiting for you. When messages are there, you may often find that some of them are of little or no value. If you are "always on" (that is, always available by voice or text messaging), some friends or colleagues may think it's all right to contact you any time, even if you're in class or trying to work. The convenience of staying electronically connected, therefore, comes at a price.

burnout   A state of physical, mental, and emotional exhaustion.

Diverse Populations, Discrimination, and Stress

Stress is universal, but in diverse multiethnic and multicultural nations such as the United States, some groups face special stressors and have higher-than-average rates of stress-related physical and emotional problems. These groups include ethnic minorities, the poor, those with disabilities, and those with atypical sexual orientations.

Discrimination occurs when people act according to their prejudices—biased, negative attitudes toward some group. Blatant examples are painting a swastika on a Jewish studies house or defacing a sculpture depicitng a same-sex couple holding hands. More subtle examples are when an African American student notices that white shopkeepers in a mostly white college town tend to keep a close eye on him; a male-to-female transgender individual is treated with less respect by her professors and peers; a student using a wheelchair finds no accessible bathrooms; or an obese woman overhears remarks about eating and self-control.

Recent immigrants to the United States have to learn to live in a new society. This requires a balance between assimilating and changing to be like the majority, and maintaining a connection to their own culture, language, and religion. The process of acculturation is generally stressful, especially when the person's background is radically different from that of the people he or she is now living among. Parental expectations generate stress if they are too high or too low. If too high, the child may work too hard in an attempt to succeed at everything; if too low, the child may not work hard enough to succeed at anything.

Both immigrants and minorities that have lived for generations in the United States can face job- and school-related stressors because of stereotypes and discrimination. They may make less money in comparable jobs with comparable levels of education and may find it more difficult to achieve leadership positions. However, on a positive note, many who experience hardship, disability, or prejudice develop effective, goal-directed

coping skills and are successful at overcoming obstacles and managing the stress they face.

Environmental Stressors

Have you tried to eat at a restaurant where the food was great, but the atmosphere was so noisy that it put you on edge? This is an example of an environmental stress—a condition or event in the physical environment that causes stress. Examples of typical environmental stressors include the following:

- Natural disasters
- Acts of violence
- Industrial accidents
- Intrusive noises or smells

Like the noisy atmosphere of some restaurants, many environmental stressors are mere inconveniences that are easy to avoid. Others, such as pollen or construction noise, may be an unavoidable daily source of stress. For those who live in poor or violent neighborhoods or in a war-torn country, environmental stressors can be major stressors (see the box "Coping After Violence on Campus" on p. 45).

Internal Stressors

Some stressors are found not in our environment but within ourselves. We pressure ourselves to reach goals and continuously evaluate our progress and performance. Setting goals and striving to reach them can enhance self-esteem if the goals are reasonable. Unrealistic expectations, however, can be a significant source of stress and can damage self-esteem. Other internal stressors are physical and emotional states such as illness and exhaustion; these can be both a cause and an effect of unmanaged stress.

MANAGING STRESS

You can control the stress in your life by taking the following steps:

- Shore up your support system.
- Improve your communication skills.
- Develop healthy exercise, eating, and sleeping habits.
- Learn to identify and moderate individual stressors.

? QUESTIONS FOR CRITICAL THINKING AND REFLECTION

What are the top two or three stressors in your life right now? Are they new to your life—as part of your college experience—or are they stressors you've experienced in the past? Do they include both positive and negative experiences (eustress and distress)?

Coping After Violence on the Campus

Stories of violence on American campuses have become all-too familiar:

• In March 2008, an Auburn University student died from gunshot wounds sustained during a robbery. One day later, a University of North Carolina student was killed while being robbed in Chapel Hill, N.C.

• On February 14, 2008, a former Northern Illinois University student walked into one of the school's lecture halls and fatally shot five students before killing himself. Gunfire injured at least 16 other people.

• Just a few days earlier, a student at Louisiana Technical College in Baton Rouge shot two other students to death, then killed herself as classmates watched in horror.

• On April 16, 2007, a student killed 28 students and 5 teachers and injured 29 others during two attacks at Virginia Polytechnic Institute and State University (Virginia Tech). The attacker was acting out fantasies of revenge in a drama that held the nation's attention for weeks.

School shootings are not uniquely American events. They have also occurred at schools in Germany (2003) and Finland (2007)—both countries where access to guns is much more tightly controlled than in the United States.

People react to news of school violence in different ways, depending on their proximity to the event and its recency. In the case of school massacres,

people far from the site may suffer emotional reactions simply from watching endless coverage on television.

Responses to violence or reports of violence include disbelief, shock, fear, anger, resentment, anxiety, mood swings, irritability, sadness, depression, panic, guilt, apathy, feelings of isolation or powerlessness, and many of the symptoms of excess stress. Most of those affected return to normal after a few weeks or months, but a few go on to develop post-traumatic stress disorder (PTSD), a more serious condition.

In the case of the Virginia Tech shootings, the school and community mobilized quickly to respond to the expected surge in behavioral health needs generated by the attack. Hotline calls and emergency room visits increased dramatically, especially during the second and third weeks following the shootings. Information sources and support groups were established for people grieving the loss of friends, family, neighbors, or colleagues. Volunteers contacted each family that was directly affected by the shootings to offer help in making arrangements and other services.

If you are affected by a disastrous event such as a school shooting or terrorist attack, take these steps:

• Be sure that you have the best information about what happened, whether a continuing risk is present, and what you can do to avoid it. That information may be posted on Web sites or on local radio or TV stations.

• Don't expose yourself to so much media coverage that you begin to feel overwhelmed by it.

• Take care of yourself. Use the stress-relief techniques discussed in this chapter.

• Share your feelings and concerns with others. Be a supportive listener.

• If you feel able, help others in any way you can, such as by volunteering to work with victims.

• If you feel emotionally distressed days or weeks after the event, consider asking for professional help.

The effort required is well worth the time. People who manage stress effectively not only are healthier but have more time to enjoy life and accomplish goals.

Social Support

The ability to share fears, frustrations, and joys makes life richer. Having the support of friends and family members seems to contribute to the well-being of body and mind. Research supports this conclusion, as the following examples demonstrate:

• Among college students living in overcrowded apartments, a study revealed that those students with a strong social support system were less distressed by their cramped quarters than were the loners who navigated life's challenges on their own.

• Young adults who have strong relationships with their parents tend to cope with stress better than peers with poor parental relationships.

• Many studies have shown that married people live longer than single people (including those who are

> **QUICK STATS**
>
> **45%** of Hispanics have incomes below $30,000 per year; nearly 60% of those Hispanics say stress is a major concern in their lives.
>
> —American Psychological Association, 2006

divorced, widowed, or never married) and have lower mortality rates from practically all causes of death.

Social support can provide a critical counterbalance to the stress in our lives. Give yourself time to develop and maintain a network of people you can count on for emotional support, feedback, and nurturing. If you believe you don't have enough social support, consider becoming a volunteer to help build your network of friends and to enhance your spiritual wellness.

Communication

How do you communicate your wishes and needs to others? Communicating in an assertive way that respects the rights of others—while protecting your own rights—can prevent potentially stressful situations from getting out of control.

Some people have trouble either telling others what they need or saying no to the needs of others. They may suppress their feelings of anger, frustration, and resentment, and they may end up feeling taken advantage of or suffering in unhealthy relationships. At the other extreme are people who express anger openly and directly by being verbally or physically aggressive or indirectly by making critical, hurtful comments to others. Their abusive behavior pushes other people away, so they also have problems with relationships.

Better communication skills can help everyone form and maintain healthy relationships. If you typically suppress your feelings, you might want to take an assertiveness training course that can help you identify and change your patterns of communication. If you have trouble controlling your anger, you may benefit from learning anger management strategies.

Chapter 3 includes a detailed discussion of anger and its impact on health and relationships. Chapter 4 discusses strategies for building healthy relationships, including positive communication techniques.

Exercise

Exercise helps maintain a healthy body and mind and even stimulates the birth of new brain cells. Regular physical activity can also reduce many of the negative effects of stress. Consider the following examples:

- Taking a long walk can help decrease anxiety and blood pressure.

- A brisk 10-minute walk can leave you feeling more relaxed and energetic for up to 2 hours.

- People who exercise regularly react with milder physical stress responses before, during, and after exposure to stressors.

Exercise—even light activity—can be an effective antidote to stress.

- In a study, people who took three brisk 45-minute walks each week for 3 months reported that they perceived fewer daily hassles. Their sense of wellness also increased.

These findings should not be surprising, because the stress response mobilizes energy resources and readies the body for physical emergencies. If you experience stress and do not physically exert yourself, you are not completing the energy cycle. You may not be able to exercise while your daily stressors occur—during class, for example, or while sitting in a traffic jam—but you can be active at other times of the day. Physical activity allows you to expend the nervous energy you have built up and trains your body to more readily achieve homeostasis following stressful situations.

It isn't hard to incorporate light to moderate exercise into your day. For example, you may be able to walk to class or ride your bike to the store instead of driving. Plan occasional activities with a friend, such as playing tennis or going for a walk. The important thing is to find an activity that you enjoy, so it can become a habit and a regular stress reducer.

One warning: For some people, exercise can become just one more stressor in a highly stressed life. People who exercise compulsively risk overtraining, a condition characterized by fatigue, irritability, depression, and diminished athletic performance. An overly strenuous exercise program can even make you sick by compromising your immune function. (For details on creating a safe and effective exercise program, see Chapter 13.)

Nutrition

A healthy diet gives you an energy bank to draw from whenever you experience stress. Eating wisely also can enhance your feelings of self-control and self-esteem. Learning the principles of sound nutrition is easy, and sensible eating habits rapidly become second nature when practiced regularly. (For information on nutrition and healthy eating habits, see Chapter 12.)

For the purposes of managing stress, you may find it especially helpful to limit or avoid caffeine. Although one or two cups of coffee a day probably won't hurt you, caffeine is a mildly addictive stimulant that leaves some people jittery, irritable, and unable to sleep. Consuming caffeine during stressful situations can raise blood pressure and increase levels of cortisol. The following items typically contain caffeine, sometimes in high doses:

- Tea
- Cola and some other soft drinks
- Chocolate
- Cold remedies
- Aspirin products
- Weight-loss preparations

If you are concerned about your caffeine intake, read the labels of products you consume daily. You may be surprised at the amount of caffeine you are ingesting, from a variety of sources.

While your diet has an effect on the way your body handles stress, the reverse is also true. Excess stress can negatively affect the way you eat. Many people, for example, respond to stress by overeating; other people skip meals or stop eating altogether during stressful periods. Both responses are not only ineffective (they don't address the causes of stress), but potentially unhealthy.

Sleep

Most adults need 7–9 hours of sleep every night to stay healthy and perform their best. Getting enough sleep isn't just good for you physically; adequate sleep also improves mood, fosters feelings of competence and self-worth, enhances mental functioning, and supports emotional functioning.

How Sleep Works   Sleep occurs in two phases: **rapid eye movement (REM) sleep** and **non-rapid eye movement (NREM) sleep.** A sleeper goes through several cycles of non-REM and REM sleep each night.

NREM sleep actually includes four stages of successively deeper sleep. As you move through these stages of sleep, a variety of physiological changes occur, including the following:

- Blood pressure drops.
- Respiration and heart rates slow.
- Body temperature declines.
- Growth hormone is released.
- Brain wave patterns become slow and even.

During REM sleep, dreams occur. REM sleep is characterized by the rapid movement of the eyes under closed eyelids. Heart rate, blood pressure, and breathing rate rise, and brain activity increases to levels equal to or greater than those during waking hours. Muscles in the limbs relax completely, resulting in a temporary paralysis. (This total relaxation may prevent you from acting out your dreams while you're asleep.)

Sleep and Stress   Stress hormone levels in the bloodstream vary throughout the day and are related to sleep patterns. Peak concentrations occur in the early morning, followed by a slow decline during the day and evening (Figure 2.4, p. 48). Concentrations return to peak levels during the final stages of sleep and in the early morning hours. Stress hormone levels are low during non-REM sleep and increase during REM sleep. With each successive sleep cycle during the night, REM sleep lasts a little longer. This increase in REM sleep duration with each sleep cycle may underlie the progressive increase in circulating stress hormones during the final stages of sleep.

Even though stress hormones are released during sleep, it is the *lack* of sleep that has the greatest impact on stress. In someone who is suffering from **sleep deprivation** (not getting enough sleep over time), mental and physical processes steadily deteriorate. A sleep-deprived person experiences headaches, feels irritable, is unable to concentrate,

rapid eye movement (REM) sleep   The portion of the sleep cycle during which dreaming occurs.

non-rapid eye movement (non-REM) sleep   The portion of the sleep cycle that involves deep sleep; non-REM sleep includes four states of successively deeper sleep.

sleep deprivation   A lack of sleep over a period of time.

TERMS

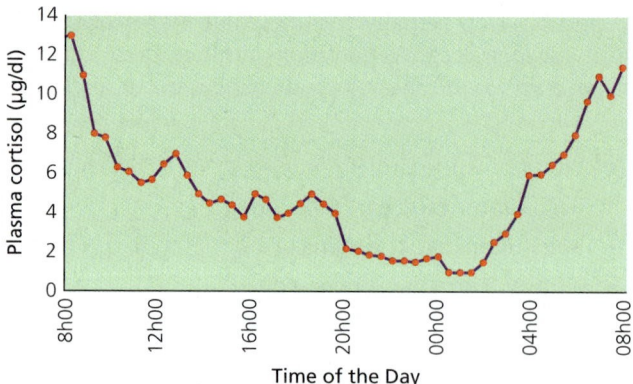

FIGURE 2.4 Changing levels of stress hormones in the bloodstream. Stress hormones, such as cortisol, fluctuate throughout the day and night and reach a high level during the last stages of sleep.

SOURCE: Palma B. D., et al. 2008. *Immune Outcomes of Sleep Disorders: The Hypothalamic-Pituitary Adrenal Axis as a Modulatory Factor, Revista Brasileiro de Psiquiatria,* vol. 29 suppl., Figure 3. 1 São Paulo May 2007.

and is more prone to forgetfulness. Poor-quality sleep has long been associated with stress and depression. A small 2008 study of female college students further associated sleep deprivation with an increased risk of suicide.

Acute sleep deprivation slows the daytime decline in stress hormones, so evening levels are higher than normal. A decrease in total sleep time also causes an increase in the level of stress hormones. Together, these changes may cause an increase in stress hormone levels throughout the day and may contribute to physical and mental exhaustion. Extreme sleep deprivation can lead to hallucinations and other psychotic symptoms, as well as to a significant increase in heart attack risk.

Sleep Problems   According to the National Sleep Foundation's 2008 Sleep in America Poll, adults sleep an average of 6 hours and 40 minutes per night. (Compare this to the recommended 7–9 hours per night.) Although many of us can attribute the lack of sleep to long work days and family responsibilities, as many as 70 million Americans suffer from chronic sleep disorders—medical conditions that prevent them from sleeping well.

TERMS

insomnia   A sleep problem involving the inability to fall or stay asleep; affects more than 50% of adults.

sleep apnea   The interruption of normal breathing during sleep.

According to the Institute of Medicine, more than 50% of adults have trouble falling asleep or staying asleep—a condition called **insomnia.** The most common causes of insomnia are lifestyle factors, such as high caffeine or alcohol intake before bedtime; medical problems, such as a breathing disorder; and stress. About 75% of people who suffer from chronic insomnia report some stressful life event at the onset of their sleeping problems. (For more information, see the box "Overcoming Insomnia," on p. 50.)

Another type of chronic sleep problem, called **sleep apnea,** occurs when a person stops breathing while asleep. Apnea can be caused by a number of factors, but it typically results when the soft tissue at the back of the mouth (such as the tongue or soft palate) "collapses" during sleep, blocking the airway. When breathing is interrupted, so is sleep, as the sleeper awakens repeatedly throughout the night to begin breathing again. In most cases, this occurs without the sleeper's even being aware of it. However, the disruption to sleep can be significant, and over time acute sleep deprivation can result from apnea. There are several treatments for apnea, including the use of medications, a special apparatus that helps keep the airway open during sleep, and surgery.

Time Management

Learning to manage your time can be crucial to coping with everyday stressors. Overcommitment, procrastination, and even boredom are significant stressors for many people. Along with gaining control of nutrition and exercise to maintain a healthy energy balance, time management is an important element in a wellness program. Try these strategies for improving your time-management skills:

• *Set priorities.* Divide your tasks into three groups: essential, important, and trivial. Focus on the first two, and ignore the third.

• *Schedule tasks for peak efficiency.* You've undoubtedly noticed you're most productive at certain times of the day (or night). Schedule as many of your tasks for those hours as you can, and stick to your schedule.

• *Set realistic goals and write them down.* Attainable goals spur you on. Impossible goals, by definition, cause frustration and failure. Fully commit yourself to achieving your goals by putting them in writing.

• *Budget enough time.* For each project you undertake, calculate how long it will take to complete. Then tack on another 10–15%, or even 25%, as a buffer.

• *Break up long-term goals into short-term ones.* Instead of waiting for or relying on large blocks of time, use short amounts of time to start a project or keep it moving.

• *Visualize the achievement of your goals.* By mentally rehearsing your performance of a task, you will be able to reach your goal more smoothly.

Overcoming Insomnia

Most people can overcome insomnia by discovering the cause of poor sleep and taking steps to remedy it. Insomnia that lasts for more than 6 months and interferes with daytime functioning requires consultation with a physician. Sleeping pills are not recommended for chronic insomnia because they can be habit-forming; they also lose their effectiveness over time.

If you're bothered by insomnia, try the following:

• Determine how much sleep you need to feel refreshed the next day, and don't sleep longer than that.

• Go to bed at the same time every night and, more important, get up at the same time every morning, 7 days a week, regardless of how much sleep you got. Don't nap for more than 30 minutes per day.

• Exercise every day, but not too close to bedtime. Your metabolism takes up to 6 hours to slow down after exercise.

• Avoid tobacco and caffeine late in the day, and alcohol before bedtime (it causes disturbed, fragmented sleep).

• If you take any medications (prescription or not), ask your doctor or pharmacist if they are known to interfere with sleep.

• Have a light snack before bedtime; you'll sleep better if you're not hungry.

• Use your bed only for sleep. Don't eat, read, study, or watch television in bed.

• Relax before bedtime with a warm bath (again, not too close to bedtime—allow about 2 hours for your metabolism to slow down afterward), a book, music, or relaxation exercises. Don't lie down in bed until you're sleepy.

• If you don't fall asleep in 15–20 minutes, or if you wake up and can't fall asleep again, get out of bed, leave the room if possible, and do something monotonous until you feel sleepy. Try distracting yourself with imagery instead of counting sheep; imagine yourself on a pleasant vacation or enjoying some beautiful scenery.

• If sleep problems persist, ask your physician for a referral to a sleep specialist in your area. You may be a candidate for a sleep study—an overnight evaluation of your sleep pattern that can uncover many sleep-related disorders.

• ***Keep track of the tasks you put off.*** Analyze the reasons you procrastinate. If the task is difficult or unpleasant, look for ways to make it easier or more fun. For example, if you find the readings for one of your classes particularly difficult, choose an especially nice setting for your reading, and then reward yourself each time you complete a section or chapter.

• ***Consider doing your least-favorite tasks first.*** Once you have the most unpleasant ones out of the way, you can work on the tasks you enjoy more.

• ***Consolidate tasks when possible.*** For example, try walking to the store so that you run your errands and exercise in the same block of time.

• ***Identify quick transitional tasks.*** Keep a list of 5- to 10-minute tasks you can do while waiting or between other tasks, such as watering your plants, doing the dishes, or checking a homework assignment.

• ***Delegate responsibility.*** Asking for help when you have too much to do is no cop-out; it's good time management. Just don't delegate the jobs you know you should do yourself.

• ***Say no when necessary.*** If the demands made on you don't seem reasonable, say no—tactfully, but without guilt or apology.

• ***Give yourself a break.*** Allow time for play—free, unstructured time when you can ignore the clock. Don't consider this a waste of time. Play renews you and enables you to work more efficiently.

• ***Avoid your personal "time sinks."*** You can probably identify your own time sinks—activities like watching television, surfing the Internet, or talking on the phone

Managing the many commitments of adult life—including work, school, and parenthood—can sometimes feel overwhelming and produce a great deal of stress. Time-management and problem-solving skills, including careful scheduling with a date book or handheld computer, can help people cope with busy days.

that consistently use up more time than you anticipate and put you behind schedule. Some days, it may be best to avoid problematic activities altogether; for example, if you have a big paper due, don't sit down for a 5-minute TV break if it is likely to turn into a 2-hour break. Try a 5-minute walk if you need to clear your head.

• **Stop thinking or talking about what you're going to do, and just do it!** Sometimes the best solution for procrastination is to stop waiting for the right moment and just get started. You will probably find that things are not as bad as you feared, and your momentum will keep you going.

Striving for Spiritual Wellness

Spiritual wellness is associated with greater coping skills and higher levels of overall wellness. It is a very personal wellness component, and there are many ways to develop it (see the box "Paths to Spiritual Wellness" on p. 51). Researchers have linked spiritual wellness to longer life expectancy, reduced risk of disease, faster recovery, and improved emotional health. Although spirituality is difficult to study, and researchers aren't sure how or why spirituality seems to improve health, several explanations have been offered.

• **Social support.** Attending religious services or participating in volunteer organizations helps people feel that they are part of a community with similar values and promotes social connectedness and caring.

• **Healthy habits.** Some of the paths to spiritual wellness may encourage healthy behaviors, such as eating a vegetarian diet or consuming less meat and alcohol, and may discourage harmful habits like smoking.

• **Positive attitude.** Spirituality can give a person a sense of meaning and purpose in life, and these qualities create a more positive attitude in the person, which in turn helps her or him cope with life's challenges.

• **Moments of relaxation.** Spiritual practices such as prayer, meditation, and immersion in artistic activities can reduce stress by eliciting the relaxation response.

Spirituality provides an ethical path to personal fulfillment that includes connectedness with self, others, and a higher power or larger reality. Spiritual wellness can make you more aware of your personal values and can help clarify them. Without an awareness of personal values, you might be driven by immediate desires and the passing demands of others. Living according to values means considering your options carefully before making a choice, choosing between options without succumbing to outside pressures

that oppose your values, and making a choice and acting on it rather than doing nothing.

Confiding in Yourself Through Writing

Keeping a diary is analogous to confiding in others, except that you are confiding in yourself. This form of coping with severe stress may be especially helpful for those who are shy or introverted and find it difficult to open up to others. Although writing about traumatic and stressful events may have a short-term negative effect on mood, over the long term, stress is reduced and positive changes in health occur. A key to promoting health and well-being through journaling is to write about your emotional responses to stressful events. Set aside a special time each day or week to write down your feelings about stressful events in your life.

Cognitive Techniques

Some stressors arise in our own minds. Ideas, beliefs, perceptions, and patterns of thinking can add to our stress level. Each of the following techniques can help you change unhealthy thought patterns to ones that will help you cope with stress. As with any skill, mastering these techniques takes practice and patience.

Think and Act Constructively Think back to the worries you had last week. How many of them were needless? Think about things you *can* control. Try to stand aside from the problem, consider the positive steps you can take to solve it, and then carry them out. Remember, if you can successfully predict that a stressor will occur, you can better control your response to it. In the evening, try to predict stressful events you might encounter the following day. Then decide how to handle them constructively. This may mean dealing positively with an unpleasant person or figuring out how to stay focused during a boring class. By taking a constructive approach, you can prevent stressors from becoming negative events and perhaps even turn them into positive experiences.

Take Control A situation often feels more stressful if you feel you're not in control of it. Time may seem to be slipping away before a big exam, for example. Unexpected obstacles may appear in your path, throwing you off course. When you feel your environment is controlling you instead of the other way around, take charge! Concentrate on what is possible to control, and set realistic goals. Be confident of your ability to succeed.

Problem-Solve Students with greater problem-solving abilities report easier adjustment to university life, higher motivation levels, lower stress levels, and higher grades. When you find yourself stewing over a problem, sit down

MIND/BODY/SPIRIT

Paths to Spiritual Wellness

Spiritual wellness means different things to different people. For many, it involves developing a set of guiding beliefs, principles, or values that give purpose and meaning to life. It helps people achieve a sense of wholeness within themselves and in their relationships with others. Spiritual wellness influences people on an individual level, as well as on a community level, where it can bond people together through compassion, love, forgiveness, and self-sacrifice.

There are many paths to spiritual wellness. One of the most common in our society is organized religion. The major religions provide paths for transforming the self in ways that can lead to greater happiness and serenity and reduce feelings of anxiety and hopelessness. For example, in Christianity, salvation means turning away from the selfish ego and to God's sovereignty and grace, where a joy is found that frees the believer from anxious self-concern and despair. *Islam* is the word for a kind of self-surrender leading to peace with God. Buddhism teaches how to detach oneself from selfish desire, leading to compassion for the suffering of others and freedom from fear-engendering illusions. Judaism emphasizes the social and ethical redemption the Jewish community can experience if it follows the laws of God.

Religions teach specific techniques for achieving these transformations of the self: prayer, both in groups and in private; meditation; the performance of rituals and ceremonies symbolizing religious truths; and good works and service to others. Religious organizations also usually offer social and material support to members who might otherwise be isolated.

Spiritual wellness does not require participation in organized religion. Many people find meaning and purpose in other ways. By spending time in nature or working on environmental issues, people can experience continuity with the natural world. Spiritual wellness can come through helping others in one's community or by promoting human rights, peace and harmony among people, and opportunities for human development on a global level. Other people develop spiritual wellness through art or through their personal relationships.

How would you define spiritual wellness and its role in your life? What beliefs and practices do you associate with your sense of spiritual wellness? To achieve overall well-being, it is important to take time out to consider what you can do to help your spiritual side flourish.

---

with a piece of paper and do some problem solving. Try this approach:

1. Define the problem in one or two sentences.
2. Identify the causes of the problem.
3. Consider alternative solutions; don't just stop with the most obvious one.
4. Weigh positive and negative consequences for each alternative.
5. Make a decision—choose a solution.
6. Make a list of what you will need to do to act on your decision.
7. Begin to carry out your list; if you're unable to do that, temporarily turn to other things.
8. Evaluate the outcome and revise your approach if necessary.

Modify Your Expectations   Expectations are exhausting and restricting. The fewer expectations you have, the more you can live spontaneously and joyfully. The more you expect from others, the more often you will feel let down. And trying to meet the expectations others have of you is often futile.

Stay Positive   If you beat up on yourself—"Late for class again! You can't even cope with college! How do you expect to ever hold down a professional job?"—change your inner dialogue. Talk to yourself as you would to a child you love: "You're a smart, capable person. You've solved other problems; you'll handle this one. Tomorrow you'll simply schedule things so you get to class with a few minutes to spare." (Chapter 3 has more information on self-talk.)

Cultivate Your Sense of Humor   When it comes to stress, laughter may be the best medicine. Even a fleeting smile produces changes in your autonomic nervous system that can lift your spirits. And a few minutes of belly laughing can be as invigorating as brisk exercise. Hearty laughter elevates your heart rate, aids digestion, eases pain, and triggers the release of endorphins and other pleasurable and stimulating chemicals in the brain. After a good laugh, your muscles go slack; your pulse and blood pressure dip below normal. You are relaxed. Cultivate the ability to laugh at yourself, and you'll have a handy and instantly effective stress reliever.

Focus on What's Important   A major source of stress is trying to store too much data. Forget unimportant details (they will usually be self-evident) and organize important information. One technique you can try is to "chunk" the important material into categories. If your next exam covers three chapters from your textbook, consider each chapter a chunk of information. Then break down each chunk into its three or four most important features. Create a mental outline that allows you to trace your way from the most general category down to the most specific details. This technique can be applied to managing daily responsibilities as well.

Relaxation Techniques

The **relaxation response** is a physiological state characterized by a feeling of warmth and quiet mental alertness. This is the opposite of the fight-or-flight reaction. When the relaxation response is triggered by a relaxation technique, heart rate, breathing, and metabolism slow down. Blood pressure and oxygen consumption decrease. At the same time, blood flow to the brain and skin increases, and brain waves shift from an alert beta rhythm to a relaxed alpha rhythm. Practiced regularly, relaxation techniques can counteract the debilitating effects of stress.

If you decide to try a relaxation technique, practice it daily until it becomes natural to you, and then use it whenever you feel the need. You may feel calmer and more refreshed after each session. You'll know you've mastered a deep relaxation technique when you start to see subtle changes in other areas of your life: You may notice you've been encountering fewer hassles, working more efficiently, or enjoying more free time. None of the techniques takes long to do.

Progressive Relaxation   Unlike most of the others, this simple method requires no imagination, willpower, or self-suggestion. You simply tense, and then relax, the muscles in your body, group by group. The technique, also known as deep muscle relaxation, helps you become aware of the muscle tension that occurs when you're under stress. When you consciously relax those muscles, other systems of the body get the message and ease up on the stress response.

Start, for example, with your right fist. Inhale as you tense it. Exhale as you relax it. Repeat. Next, contract and relax your right upper arm. Repeat. Do the same with your left arm. Then, beginning at your forehead and ending at your feet, contract and relax your other muscle groups. Repeat each contraction at least once, breathing in as you tense, breathing out as you relax. To speed up the process, tense and relax more muscles at one time—both arms simultaneously, for instance. With practice, you'll be able to relax very quickly and effectively by clenching and releasing only your fists.

Visualization   Also known as *imagery*, **visualization** lets you daydream without guilt. Athletes find that the technique enhances sports performance, and visualization is even part of the curriculum at U.S. Olympic training camps. You can use visualization to help you relax, change your habits, or perform well—whether on an exam, a stage, or a playing field.

Next time you feel stressed, close your eyes. Imagine yourself floating on a cloud, sitting on a mountaintop, or lying in a meadow. Involve all your senses; imagine the sounds, the smells, and the other sensations that would be part of the scene. Your body will respond as if your imagery were real. An alternative: Close your eyes and imagine a deep purple light filling your body. Now change the color into a soothing gold. As the color lightens, so should your distress.

Visualization can also be used to rehearse for an upcoming event and enhance performance. By experiencing an event ahead of time in your mind, you can practice coping with any difficulties that may arise. Think positively, and you can "psych yourself up" for a successful experience.

Meditation   The need to periodically stop our incessant mental chatter is so great that, from ancient times, hundreds of forms of **meditation** have developed in cultures all over the world. Meditation is a way of telling the mind to be quiet for a while. Because meditation has been at the core of many Eastern religions and philosophies, it has acquired an "Eastern" mystique that has caused some people to shy away from it. Yet meditation requires no special knowledge or background. Whatever philosophical, religious, or emotional reasons may be given for meditation, it is potentially useful for reducing stress. According to a 2008 study, college students who learned how to use meditation for stress management were able to significantly reduce their daily stress levels. Further, those students found it easier to forgive others for perceived wrongdoings and spent less time focusing on negative thoughts.

Meditation helps you tune out the world temporarily, removing you from both internal and external sources of stress. The "thinker" takes time out to become the "observer"—calmly attentive, without analyzing, judging, comparing, or rationalizing. Regular practice of this quiet awareness will subtly carry over into your daily life, encouraging physical and emotional balance no matter what confronts you. For a step-by-step description of a basic meditation technique, see the box "Meditation and the Relaxation Response."

Another form of meditation, known as *mindfulness meditation*, involves paying attention to physical sensations, perceptions, thoughts, and imagery. Instead of focusing on a word or object to quiet the mind, you observe thoughts that occur without evaluating or judging them. Development of this ability requires regular practice but

Meditation and the Relaxation Response

Here is a simple technique for eliciting the relaxation response.

The Basic Technique

1. Pick a word, phrase, or object to focus on. If you like, you can choose a word or phrase that has a deep meaning for you, but any word or phrase will work. Some meditators prefer to focus on their breathing.

2. Take a comfortable position in a quiet environment, and close your eyes if you're not focusing on an object.

3. Relax your muscles.

4. Breathe slowly and naturally. If you're using a focus word or phrase, silently repeat it each time you exhale. If you're using an object, focus on it as you breathe.

5. Keep a passive attitude. Disregard thoughts that drift in.

6. Continue for 10–20 minutes, once or twice a day.

7. After you've finished, sit quietly for a few minutes with your eyes first closed and then open. Then stand up.

Suggestions

• Allow relaxation to occur at its own pace; don't try to force it. Don't be surprised if you can't quiet your mind for more than a few seconds at a time; it's not a reason for anger or frustration. The more you ignore the intrusions, the easier doing so will become.

• If you want to time your session, peek at a watch or clock occasionally, but don't set a jarring alarm.

• The technique works best on an empty stomach, before a meal or about 2 hours after eating. Avoid times of day when you're tired—unless you want to fall asleep.

• Although you'll feel refreshed even after the first session, it may take a month or more to get noticeable results. Be patient. Eventually the relaxation response will become so natural that it will occur spontaneously, or on demand, when you sit quietly for a few moments.

---

may eventually result in a more objective view of one's perceptions. It is believed that a greater understanding of one's moment-to-moment thought processes (mindful awareness) provides a richer and more vital sense of life and improves coping. Studies also suggest that people who rate high in mindfulness are less anxious and better able to deal with stress; among people with specific health problems, mindfulness can provide substantial benefits.

Deep Breathing Your breathing pattern is closely tied to your stress level. Deep, slow breathing is associated with relaxation. Rapid, shallow, often irregular breathing occurs during the stress response. With practice, you can learn to slow and quiet your breathing pattern, thereby also quieting your mind and relaxing your body. Breathing techniques can be used for on-the-spot tension relief as well as for long-term stress reduction.

The primary goal of many breathing exercises is to change your breathing pattern from chest breathing to diaphragmatic ("belly") breathing. During the day, most adults breathe by expanding their chest and raising their shoulders rather than by expanding their abdomen. Diaphragmatic breathing, which involves free expansion of the diaphragm and lower abdomen, is the pattern of breathing characteristic of children and sleeping adults. (The diaphragm is a sheet of muscle and connective tissue that divides the chest and abdominal cavities.) Diaphragmatic breathing is slower and deeper than chest breathing. For instructions on how to perform diaphragmatic breathing, refer to the box "Breathing for Relaxation."

Yoga Hatha yoga, the most common yoga style practiced in the United States, emphasizes physical balance and breath control. It integrates components of flexibility, muscular strength and endurance, and muscle relaxation; it also sometimes serves as a preliminary to meditation. A session of yoga typically involves a series of postures, each held for a few seconds to several minutes, which involve stretching and balance and coordinated breathing. Yoga can induce the relaxation response and promote body awareness and flexibility. If you are interested in trying yoga, it's best to take a class from an experienced instructor.

> **QUICK STATS**
>
> **13.4** million Americans practice yoga, tai chi, or other mind-body exercises
>
> —Sporting Goods Manufacturers Association, 2003

Tai chi This martial art (in Chinese, *taijiquan*) is a system of self-defense that incorporates philosophical concepts from Taoism and Confucianism. In addition to self-defense, tai chi aims to bring the body into balance and harmony to promote health and spiritual growth. It teaches practitioners to remain calm and centered, to conserve and concentrate energy, and to manipulate force by becoming part of it—by "going with the flow." Tai chi is considered the gentlest of the martial arts. Instead of quick and powerful movements, tai chi consists of a series of slow, fluid, elegant movements, which reinforce the idea of moving *with* rather

Breathing for Relaxation

Controlled breathing can do more than just help you relax. It can also help control pain, anxiety, and other conditions that lead to or are related to stress. There are many methods of controlled breathing. Two of the most popular are belly breathing and tension-release breathing.

Belly Breathing

1. Lie on your back and relax.
2. Place one hand on your chest and the other on your abdomen. Your hands will help you gauge your breathing.
3. Take in a slow, deep breath through your nose and into your belly. Your abdomen should rise significantly (check with your hand); your chest should rise only slightly. Focus on filling your abdomen with air.
4. Exhale through your mouth, gently pushing out the air from your abdomen.

Tension-Release Breathing

1. Lie down or sit in a chair and get comfortable.
2. Take a slow, deep breath into your abdomen. Inhale through your nose. Try to visualize the air moving to every part of your body. As you breathe in, say to yourself, "Breathe in relaxation."
3. Exhale through your mouth. Visualize tension leaving your body. Say to yourself, "Breathe out tension."

There are many variations on these techniques. For example, sit in a chair and raise your arms, shoulders, and chin as you inhale; lower them as you exhale. Or slowly count to 4 as you inhale, then again as you exhale.

Many yoga experts suggest breathing rhythmically, in time with your own heartbeat. Relax and listen closely for the sensation of your heart beating, or monitor your pulse while you breathe. As you inhale, count to 4 or 8 in time with your heartbeat, then repeat the count as you exhale. Breathing in time with soothing music can work well, too.

Experts suggest inhaling through the nose and exhaling through the mouth. Breathe slowly, deeply, and gently. To focus on breathing gently, imagine a candle burning a few inches in front of you. Try to exhale softly enough to make the candle's flame flicker, not hard enough to blow it out.

Practice is important, too. Perform your chosen breathing exercise two or more times daily, for 5–10 minutes per session.

---

than *against* the stressors of everyday life. As with yoga, it's best to start tai chi with a class from an experienced instructor.

Listening to Music Listening to music is another method of inducing relaxation. It can influence pulse, blood pressure, and the electrical activity of muscles. Studies of newborns and hospitalized stroke patients have shown that listening to soothing, lyrical music can lessen depression, anxiety, and stress levels. Researchers have found that exposure to soothing music leads to reduced levels of the stress hormone cortisol and causes changes in the electrical activity in the brain.

To experience the stress-management benefits of music yourself, set aside a time to listen. Choose music that you enjoy and that makes you feel relaxed.

Biofeedback **Biofeedback** helps people reduce the stress response by enabling them to become more aware of their level of physiological arousal. It involves electrical monitoring of some measure of the physiological stress response, such as perspiration, heart rate, skin temperature, or muscle tension. A person receives feedback about his or her condition through the use of

Taijiquan is one of many techniques for inducing the relaxation response.

TERMS

biofeedback A technique in which monitoring devices help a person become conscious of unconscious body processes, such as body temperature or blood pressure, in order to exert some control over them.

sound (a tone or music), light, or a meter or dial. For example, as heart rate increases, the tone becomes louder; as it decreases, the tone becomes softer. In this way, people can learn to reduce their physiological stress response through conscious control even without biofeedback.

The point of biofeedback training is to learn how relaxation feels, how to induce relaxation, and how to transfer this skill to daily life (without the use of electronic equipment). In addition to monitoring equipment, biofeedback usually also requires the initial help of a therapist, stress counselor, or technician.

Other relaxation techniques include massage, hypnosis and self-hypnosis, and autogenic training. To learn more about these and other techniques for inducing the relaxation response, refer to For More Information at the end of the chapter.

Counterproductive Coping Strategies

College is a time when you'll learn to adapt to new and challenging situations and gain skills that will last a lifetime. It is also a time when many people develop habits, in response to stress, that are counterproductive and unhealthy. Such habits can last well beyond graduation.

Tobacco Use Many young adults who never smoked in high school smoke their first cigarette in college, usually at a party or bar or in a dorm with friends. Many smokers report that smoking helps them to cope with stress by providing a feeling of relaxation, giving them something to do with their hands in social situations, or breaking up monotony and routine.

Cigarettes and other tobacco products contain nicotine, a chemical that enhances the actions of neurotransmitters. Nicotine can make you feel relaxed and even increase your ability to concentrate, but it is highly addictive, and nicotine dependence itself is considered a psychological disorder. Cigarette smoke also contains substances that cause heart disease, stroke, lung cancer, and emphysema. These negative consequences far outweigh any beneficial effects, and tobacco use should be avoided. The easiest thing to do is to not start.

See Chapter 11 for more on the health effects of tobacco use and for tips on how to quit.

Use of Alcohol and Other Drugs No college experience is complete without a party or two. Letting loose, dancing, laughing, and interacting with others—all are part of college parties and all can be very effective short-term coping strategies. However, partying in college is usually associated with drinking alcohol. Keg parties and drinking games can be fun, but they contribute to binge drinking and other forms of alcohol abuse. Like nicotine,

Tobacco and alcohol use may help you relax for a little while, but long-term use is unhealthy and an ineffective way to cope with stress.

alcohol is addictive, and many alcoholics find it hard to relax without a drink. Having a few drinks might make you feel temporarily at ease, and drinking until you're intoxicated may help you forget your current stressors. However, using alcohol to deal with stress places you at risk for all the short-term and long-term problems associated with alcohol abuse. It also does nothing to address the actual causes of stress in your life. Although moderate alcohol consumption may have potential health benefits for some people, many college students have patterns of drinking that detract from wellness. For more on the responsible use of alcohol, refer to Chapter 10.

Using other psychoactive drugs to cope with stress is also usually counterproductive:

• Caffeine raises cortisol levels and blood pressure and can make you feel more stressed; caffeine also disrupts sleep. Other stimulants, such as amphetamine, can activate the stress response, and they affect the same areas of the brain that are involved in regulating the stress response.

- Marijuana use is relatively common among college students, who report that they smoke marijuana in an effort to induce relaxation and for "mind expansion." Use of marijuana causes a brief period of euphoria and decreased short-term memory and attentional abilities. Physiological effects clearly show that marijuana use doesn't cause relaxation; in fact, some neurochemicals in marijuana act to enhance the stress response, and getting high on a regular basis can elicit panic attacks. To compound this, withdrawal from marijuana may also be associated with an increase in circulating stress hormones.

- Opioids such as morphine and heroin can mimic the effects of your body's natural painkillers and act to reduce anxiety. However, tolerance to opioids develops quickly, and many users become dependent.

For more information on the use of psychoactive drugs, see Chapter 9.

Unhealthy Eating Habits   The nutrients in the food you eat provide energy and the substances needed to maintain your body. Eating is also psychologically rewarding. The feelings of satiation and sedation that follow eating produce a relaxed state. However, regular use of eating as a means of coping with stress may lead to unhealthy eating habits. In fact, a 2006 survey by the American Psychological Association revealed that about 25% of Americans use food as a means of coping with stress or anxiety. These "comfort eaters" are twice as likely to be obese as average Americans.

Certain foods and supplements are sometimes thought to fight stress. Carbohydrates may reduce the stress response by promoting activity of the parasympathetic nervous system; however, a high-carbohydrate diet can lead to excessive weight gain in sedentary people and is not recommended as a strategy for coping with stressors. In addition, some evidence suggests that greater ingestion of carbohydrates, simple sugars, and fatty foods may actually be a predisposing factor for psychological distress. Many dietary supplements are marketed for stress reduction, but supplements are not required to meet the same standards as medications in terms of safety, effectiveness, and manufacturing (see Chapters 12 and 20).

CREATING A PERSONAL PLAN FOR MANAGING STRESS

What are the most important sources of stress in your life? Are you coping successfully with these stressors? No single strategy or program for managing stress will work for everyone, but you can use the principles of behavior management described in Chapter 1 to tailor a plan specifically to your needs. The most important starting point for a successful stress-management plan is to learn to listen to your body. When you learn to recognize the stress response and the emotions and thoughts that accompany it, you'll be in a position to take charge of that crucial moment and handle it in a healthy way.

Identifying Stressors

Before you can learn to manage the stressors in your life, you have to identify them. Many experts recommend keeping a stress journal for a week or two (see Figure 2.5). Each time you feel or express a stress response, record the time and the circumstances in your journal. Note what you were doing at the time, what you were thinking or feeling, and the outcome of your response.

After keeping your journal for a few weeks, you should be able to identify your key stressors and spot patterns in how you respond to them. Take note of the people, places, events, and patterns of thought and behavior that cause you the most stress. You may notice, for example, that mornings are usually the most stressful part of your day. Or you may discover that when you're angry at your roommate, you're apt to respond with behaviors that only make matters worse. Keeping a journal allows you to be analytical about what produces the most stress in your life and fills in where your conscious memory fails you.

Designing Your Plan

Once you've identified the key stressors in your life, choose the stress reduction techniques that will work best for you and create an action plan for change. Finding a buddy to work with you can make the process more fun and increase your chances of success. Some experts recommend drawing up a formal contract with yourself.

Whether or not you complete a contract, it's important to design rewards into your plan. You might treat yourself to a special breakfast in a favorite restaurant on the weekend (as long as you eat a nutritious breakfast every weekday morning). It's also important to evaluate your plan regularly and redesign it as your needs change. Under times of increased stress, for example, you might want to focus on good eating, exercise, and relaxation habits. Over time, your new stress-management skills will become almost automatic. You'll feel better, accomplish more, and reduce your risk of disease.

Getting Help

If the techniques discussed so far don't provide you with enough relief from the stress in your life, you might want to learn more about specific areas you wish to work on. Excellent self-help guides can be found in bookstores or

Stress Journal		Date 9-1 8-09
Time	**Stressor**	**Reaction/Coping Strategy**
7:45 AM	Tara wouldn't get out of the shower	Yelled at her, started an argument
8:35 AM	Late for class	Slouched in back of room; chewed my nails
11:55 AM	Dad called to discuss credit card debt	Cried, skipped lunch and went out to smoke with Greg
5:30 PM	Power outage at dorm, couldn't study	Took a walk with Tara, made up for arguing this morning, then went to library to study
7:45 PM	Ed called, asked to borrow money	Stayed calm, put down phone and counted to 10, then explained that he already owes me $50.
8:30 PM	Ed called, angry, said he wanted to break up	Argued on phone, then went out with Tara for a drink

FIGURE 2.5   A sample stress journal.
Tracking stressful events and reactions can help you understand how you normally cope with stress.

the library. Additional resources are listed in the For More Information section at the end of the chapter.

Your student health center or student affairs office can tell you whether your campus has a peer counseling program. Such programs are usually staffed by volunteer students with special training that emphasizes maintaining confidentiality. Peer counselors can guide you to other campus or community resources or can simply provide understanding.

Support groups are typically organized around a particular issue or problem. In your area, you might find a support group for first-year students; for reentering students; for single parents; for students of your ethnicity, religion, or national origin; for people with eating disorders; or for rape survivors. The number of such groups has increased in recent years as more and more people discover how therapeutic it can be to talk with others who share the same situation.

Short-term psychotherapy can also be tremendously helpful in dealing with stress-related problems. Your student health center may offer psychotherapy on a sliding-fee scale; the county mental health center in your area may do the same. If you belong to any type of religious organization, check to see whether pastoral counseling is available. Your physician can refer you to psychotherapists in your community. Not all therapists are right for all people, so be prepared to have initial sessions with several. Choose the one you feel most comfortable with.

✳ TIPS FOR TODAY AND THE FUTURE

For the stress you can't avoid, develop a range of stress-management techniques and strategies.

RIGHT NOW YOU CAN

- Practice deep breathing for 5–10 minutes.
- Visualize a relaxing, peaceful place and imagine yourself experiencing it as vividly as possible. Stay there as long as you can.
- Do some stretching exercises.
- Get out your datebook and schedule what you'll be doing the rest of today and tomorrow. Pencil in a short walk and a conversation with a friend.

IN THE FUTURE YOU CAN

- Take a class or workshop that can help you overcome a source of stress, such as one in assertiveness training or time management.
- Find a way to build relaxing time into every day. Just 15 minutes of meditation, stretching, or massage can induce the relaxation response.

SUMMARY

- When confronted with a stressor, the body undergoes a set of physical changes known as the fight-or-flight reaction. The sympathetic nervous system and endocrine system act on many targets in the body to prepare it for action.

- Emotional and behavioral responses to stressors vary among individuals. Ineffective responses increase stress but can be moderated or changed.

- Factors that influence emotional and behavioral responses to stressors include personality, cultural background, gender, and past experiences.

- The general adaptation syndrome (GAS) has three stages: alarm, resistance, and exhaustion.

- A high allostatic load characterized by prolonged or repeated exposure to stress hormones can increase a person's risk of health problems.

- Psychoneuroimmunology (PNI) looks at how the physiological changes of the stress response affect the immune system and thereby increase the risk of illness.

- Health problems linked to stress include CVD, colds and other infections, asthma and allergies, cancer, flare-ups of chronic diseases, psychological problems, digestive problems, headaches, insomnia, and injuries.

- A cluster of major life events that require adjustment and accommodation can lead to increased stress and an increased risk of health problems. Minor daily hassles increase stress if they are perceived negatively.

- Sources of stress associated with college may be academic, interpersonal, time-related, or financial pressures.

- Job-related stress is common, particularly for employees who have little control over decisions relating to their jobs. If stress is severe or prolonged, burnout may occur.

- New and changing relationships, prejudice, and discrimination are examples of interpersonal and social stressors.

- Social support systems help buffer people against the effects of stress and make illness less likely. Good communication skills foster healthy relationships.

- Exercise, nutrition, sleep, and time management are wellness behaviors that reduce stress and increase energy.

- Cognitive techniques for managing stress involve developing new and healthy patterns of thinking, such as practicing problem solving, monitoring self-talk, and cultivating a sense of humor.

- The relaxation response is the opposite of the fight-or-flight reaction. Techniques that trigger it, including progressive relaxation, imagery, meditation, and deep breathing, counteract the effects of chronic stress. Counterproductive coping strategies include smoking, drinking, and unhealthy eating.

- A successful individualized plan for coping with stress begins with the use of a stress journal or log to identify and study stressors and inappropriate behavioral responses. Completing a contract and recruiting a buddy can help your stress-management plan succeed.

- Additional help in dealing with stress is available from self-help books, peer counseling, support groups, and psychotherapy.

FOR MORE INFORMATION

BOOKS

Blonna, R. 2007. *Coping with Stress in a Changing World.* 4th ed. New York: McGraw-Hill. *A comprehensive guide to stress management that includes separate chapters on college stressors and spirituality.*

Greenberg, J. 2009. *Comprehensive Stress Management.* 11th ed. New York: McGraw-Hill. *Provides a clear explanation of the physical, psychological, sociological, and spiritual aspects of stress and offers numerous stress-management techniques.*

Kabat-Zinn, J. 2006. *Coming to Our Senses: Healing Ourselves and the World Through Mindfulness.* New York: Hyperion. *Explores the connections among mindfulness, health, physical, and spiritual well-being.*

Pennebaker, J. W. 2004. *Writing to Heal: A Guided Journal for Recovering from Trauma and Emotional Upheaval.* Oakland, Calif.: New Harbinger Press. *Provides information about using journaling to cope with stress.*

Sapolsky, R. M. 2004. *Why Zebras Don't Get Ulcers,* 3rd ed. New York: Henry Holt. *A scientific guide to stress, stress-related diseases, and coping.*

Seaward, B. L. 2006. *Managing Stress: Principles and Strategies for Health and Well-Being,* 5th ed. Boston: Jones and Bartlett. *A comprehensive textbook for college students.*

ORGANIZATIONS AND WEB SITES

American Psychiatric Association: Healthy Minds, Healthy Lives. Provides information on mental wellness developed especially for college students.
http://www.healthyminds.org/collegementalhealth.cfm

American Psychological Association. Provides information on stress management and psychological disorders.
http://www.apa.org; http://apahelpcenter.org

Association for Applied Psychophysiology and Biofeedback. Provides information about biofeedback and referrals to certified biofeedback practitioners.
http://www.aapb.org

Benson-Henry Institute for Mind Body Medicine. Provides information about stress-management and relaxation techniques.
http://www.mbmi.org

Medical Basis for Stress. Includes information on recognizing stress and on the physiological basis of stress, self-assessments for stress levels, and techniques for managing stress.
http://www.teachhealth.com

National Institute for Occupational Safety and Health (NIOSH). Provides information and links on job stress.
http://www.cdc.gov/niosh/topics/stress

National Institute of Mental Health (NIMH). Publishes informative brochures about stress and stress management as well as other aspects of mental health.
http://www.nimh.nih.gov

National Sleep Foundation. Provides information about sleep and how to overcome sleep problems such as insomnia and jet lag.
http://www.sleepfoundation.org

Student Counseling Virtual Pamphlet Collection. Links to online pamphlets from student counseling centers; topics include stress, sleep, and time management.
http://counseling.uchicago.edu/resources/virtualpamphlets/

Dealing with Test Anxiety

Are you a person who doesn't perform as well as you should on tests? Do you find that anxiety interferes with your ability to study effectively before the test and to think clearly in the test situation? If so, you may be experiencing test anxiety. Two methods that have proven effective in helping people deal with test anxiety are systematic desensitization and success rehearsal.

Systematic Desensitization

Systematic desensitization is based on the premise that you can't feel anxiety and be relaxed at the same time.

Phase I: Constructing an Anxiety Hierarchy

Begin the first phase by thinking of ten or more situations related to your fear, such as hearing the announcement of the test date in class, studying for the test, sitting in the classroom waiting for the test to begin, reading the test questions, and so on. Write each situation on an index card, using a brief phrase to describe it on one side of the card. On the other side, list several realistic details or prompts that will help you vividly imagine yourself actually experiencing the situation. For example, if the situation is "hearing that 50% of the final grade will be based on the two exams," the prompts might include details such as "sitting in the big lecture auditorium in Baily Hall," "taking notes in my blue notebook," and "listening to Professor Smith's voice."

Next, arrange your cards in order, from least-tense to most-tense situation. Rate each situation to reflect the amount of anxiety you feel when you encounter it in real life, to confirm your anxiety hierarchy. Assign ratings on a scale of 0–100, and make sure the distances between items are fairly small and about equal. When you're sure your anxiety hierarchy is a true reflection of your feelings, number the cards.

Phase II: Learning and Practicing Muscle Relaxation

The second phase of the program involves learning to relax your muscles and to recognize when they are relaxed (see the description of progressive relaxation in this chapter). As you become proficient at this technique, you'll be able to go to a deeply relaxed state within just a few minutes. When you can do this, go on to the next phase of the program.

Phase III: Implementing the Desensitization Program

Use the quiet place where you practiced your relaxation exercises. Sit comfortably and place your stack of numbered cards within reach. Take several minutes to relax completely, and then look at the first card, reading both the brief phrase and the descriptive prompts. Close your eyes and imagine yourself in that situation for about 10 seconds. Then put the card down and relax completely for about 30 seconds. Look at the card again, imagine the situation for 10 seconds, and relax again for 30 seconds.

At this point, evaluate your current level of anxiety about the situation on the card in terms of the rating scale you devised earlier. If your anxiety level is 10 or below, relax for 2 minutes and go on to the second card. If it's higher than 10, repeat the routine with the same card until the anxiety decreases.

If you have difficulty with a particular item, go back to the previous item; then try it again. If you still can't visualize it without anxiety, try to construct three new items with smaller steps between them and insert them before the troublesome item. You should be able to move through one to four items per session.

Sessions can be conducted from twice a day to twice a week and should last no longer than 20 minutes. It's helpful to graph your progress in a way that has meaning for you.

After you have successfully completed your program, you should be desensitized to the real-life situations that previously caused anxiety. If you find that you do experience some anxiety in the real situations, take 30 seconds or a minute to relax completely, just as you did when you were practicing.

Success Rehearsal

To practice this variation on systematic desensitization, take your hierarchy of anxiety-producing situations and vividly imagine yourself successfully dealing with each one. Create a detailed scenario for each situation, and use your imagination to experience genuine feelings of confidence. Recognize your negative thoughts ("I'll be so nervous I won't be able to think straight") and replace them with positive ones ("Anxiety will keep me alert so I can do a good job").

Proceed one step at a time, thinking as you go of strategies for success that you can later implement. These might include the following:

- Before the test, find out everything you can about it—its format, the material to be covered, the grading criteria. Ask the instructor for practice materials. Study in advance; don't just cram the night before. Avoid all-nighters.

- Devise a study plan. This might include forming a study group with one or more classmates or outlining what you will study, when, where, and for how long. Generate your own questions and answer them.

- In the actual test situation, sit away from possible distractions, listen carefully to instructions, and ask for clarification if you don't understand a direction.

- During the test, answer the easiest questions first. If you don't know an answer and there is no penalty for incorrect answers, guess. If there are several questions you have difficulty answering, review the ones you have already handled. Figure out approximately how much time you have to cover each question.

- For math problems, try to estimate the answer before doing the precise calculations.

- For true-false questions, look for qualifiers such as *always* and *never*. Such questions are likely to be false.

- For essay questions, look for key words in the question that indicate what the instructor is looking for in the answer. Develop a brief outline of your answer, sketching out what you will cover. Stick to your outline, and keep track of the time you're spending on your answer. Don't get caught with unanswered questions when time is up.

- Remain calm and focused throughout the test. Don't let negative thoughts rattle you. Avoid worrying about past performance, how others are doing, or the negative consequences of a poor test grade. If you start to become nervous, take some deep breaths and relax your muscles completely for a minute or so.

The best way to counter test anxiety is with successful test-taking experiences. The more times you succeed, the more your test anxiety will recede. If you find that these methods aren't sufficient to get your anxiety under control, you may want to seek professional help.

SELECTED BIBLIOGRAPHY

American College Health Association. 2007. *American College Health Association—National College Health Assessment (ACHA—NCHA) 2007 Web Summary* (http://www.acha-ncha.org/data_highlights.html; retrieved December 27, 2008).

American Psychological Association. 2005. *The different kinds of stress* (http://www.apahelpcenter.org/articles/article.php?id=21; retrieved December 27, 2008).

American Psychological Association. 2005. *Learning to Deal with Stress* (http://helping.apa.org/articles/article.php?id=71; retrieved December 27, 2008).

American Psychological Association. 2006. *Hispanics and Stress* (http://apahelpcenter.mediaroom.com/flie.php/110/Executive+Summary+English+FINAL.pdf; retrieved December 27, 2008).

American Psychological Association. 2007. *Stress in America* (http://apahelpcenter.mediaroom.com/file.php/138/Stress+in+America+REPORT+FINAL.doc; retrieved December 27, 2008).

Ano, G. G., and E. B. Vasconcelles. 2005. Religious coping and psychological adjustment to stress: A meta-analysis. *Journal of Clinical Psychology* 61(4): 461–480.

Centers for Disease Control. 2005. *Coping with a Traumatic Event: Information for the Public* (http://www.bt.cdc.gov/masscasualties/copingpub.asp; retrieved December 27, 2008).

Cohen, S., W. J. Doyle, and A. Baum. 2006. Socioeconomic status is associated with stress hormones. *Psychosomatic Medicine* 68(3): 414–420.

Constantine, M. G., S. Okazaki, and S. O. Utsey. 2004. Self-concealment, social self-efficacy, acculturative stress, and depression in African, Asian, and Latin American international college students. *American Journal of Orthopsychiatry* 74(3): 230–241.

Frequent headaches, hidden dangers. 2006. *Consumer Reports on Health,* June.

Grossman, P., et al. 2004. Mindfulness-based stress reduction and health benefits: A meta analysis. *Journal of Psychosomatic Research* 57(1): 35–43.

Headaches. 2006. *Journal of the American Medical Association* 295(19): 2320.

How stress can make you forgetful, age faster. 2005. *Tufts University Health & Nutrition Letter,* February, 1.

Institute of Medicine Committee on Sleep Medicine and Research. 2006. *Sleep Disorders and Sleep Deprivation: An Unmet Public Health Problem,* ed. H. R. Colton and B. M. Altevogt. Washington, D.C. National Academies Press.

Lauderdale, D. S., et al. 2006. Objectively measured sleep characteristics among early-middle-aged adults: The CARDIA study. *American Journal of Epidemiology* 164(1): 17–18.

MacGeorge, Erina L., et al. 2004. Stress, social support, and health among college students after September 11, 2001. *Journal of College Student Development* 45(6): 655–670.

Mayo Foundation for Medical Education and Research. 2005. *Stress: Why you have it and how it hurts your health.* (http://www.mayoclinic.com/health/stress/SR00001; retrieved December 27, 2008).

Meier-Ewert, H. K., et al. 2004. Effect of sleep loss on C-reactive protein, an inflammatory marker of cardiovascular risk. *Journal of the American College of Cardiology* 43: 678–683.

Melamed, S., et al. 2004. Association of fear of terror with low-grade inflammation among apparently healthy employed adults. *Psychosomatic Medicine* 66(4): 484–491.

National Mental Health Association. 2006. *Coping with disaster: Tips for college students on coping with war and terrorism.* (http://www.nmha.org/reassurance/collegeWarCoping.cfm; retrieved December 27, 2008).

Nordboe, D. J., et al. 2007. Immediate Behavioral Health Response to the Virginia Tech Shootings. *Disaster Medicine and Public Health Preparedness* 1(Suppl. 1.): S31–S32.

Sax, L. J., et al. 2006. *The American Freshman: National Norms for Fall* 2005. Los Angeles: UCLA Higher Education Research Institute.

Segerstrom, S. C., and G. E. Miller. 2004. Psychological stress and the human immune system: A meta-analytic study of 30 years of inquiry. *Psychological Bulletin* 130(4): 601–630.

Stambor, Z. 2006. Stressed out nation. *Monitor on Psychology* 37(4) (http://www.apa.org/monitor/apr06/nation.html; retrieved December 27, 2008).

Steptoe, A., et al. 2004. Loneliness and neuroendocrine, cardiovascular, and inflammatory stress responses in middle-aged men and women. *Psychoneuroendocrinology* 29(5): 593–611.

Wetter, D. W., et al. 2004. Prevalence and predictors of transitions in smoking behavior among college students. *Health Psychology* 23(2): 168–177.

Wittstein, I. S., et al. 2005. Neurohumoral features of myocardial stunning due to sudden emotional stress. *New England Journal of Medicine* 352(6): 539–548.

CORE CONCEPTS IN HEALTH

connect™

|PERSONAL HEALTH

http://www.mcgrawhillconnect.com/personalhealth

PSYCHOLOGICAL HEALTH

LOOKING AHEAD>>>>>

AFTER READING THIS CHAPTER, YOU SHOULD BE ABLE TO:

- Describe what it means to be psychologically healthy
- Explain how to develop and maintain a positive self-concept and healthy self-esteem
- Discuss the importance of an optimistic outlook, good communication skills, and constructive approaches to dealing with loneliness and anger
- Describe common psychological disorders
- List the warning signs of suicide
- Describe the different types of help available for psychological problems

TEST YOUR KNOWLEDGE

1. **Normality is a key component of psychological health.**
   True or false?

2. **Trying to think rationally about what bothers you won't get you very far, because psychological problems usually are due to emotions, not thinking.**
   True or false?

3. **About how many Americans have a diagnosable psychological disorder during the course of a year?**
   a. 5%
   b. 10%
   c. 20%

4. **People with enough willpower can force themselves to snap out of their depression.**
   True or false?

5. **A person who attempts suicide but survives did not really intend to die.**
   True or false?

ANSWERS

1. **FALSE.** Normality simply means being close to average, and having unusual ideas or attitudes doesn't mean that a person is mentally ill. The fact that people's ideas are varied makes life interesting and helps people respond in creative ways to life's challenges.

2. **FALSE.** Research has shown that getting people to adopt more realistic attitudes and beliefs about themselves and others can alleviate depression.

3. **C.** Other than substance-abuse problems, the most common types of disorders are simple phobias and depression. The majority of people with psychological disorders do not receive appropriate treatment.

4. **FALSE.** Depression, a disorder strongly linked to brain chemistry, can overcome whatever willpower a person has and make it impossible for her or him to make decisions.

5. **FALSE.** A person may intend to die but miscalculate how to successfully commit suicide.

Psychological health (or *mental health*) contributes to every dimension of wellness. It can be very difficult to maintain emotional, social, or even physical wellness if you are not psychologically healthy.

Psychological health, however, is a broad concept—one that is as difficult to define as it is important to understand. That is why the first section of this chapter is devoted to explaining what psychological health is and is not. The rest of the chapter discusses a number of common psychological problems, their symptoms, and their treatments.

If life doesn't bring you the pleasure or happiness you think it should, or if you believe you should be functioning at a higher level, you should know that there are ways of getting help. This chapter will show you how.

DEFINING PSYCHOLOGICAL HEALTH

Psychological health can be defined either negatively as the absence of sickness or positively as the presence of wellness. The narrow, negative definition has two advantages: It concentrates attention on the worst problems and on the people most in need, and it avoids value judgments about the best way to lead our lives. If we think of everyone who is not severely mentally disturbed as being mentally healthy, however, we end up ignoring common problems that can be addressed. Finally, freedom from disorders is only one factor in psychological wellness.

Self-Actualization

A positive definition—psychological health as the presence of wellness—is a more ambitious outlook that encourages us to fulfill our own potential.

During the 1960s, Abraham Maslow described such an ideal of mental health in his book *Toward a Psychology of Being*. According to Maslow, there is a *hierarchy of needs*, listed here in order of decreasing importance (Figure 3.1):

- Physiological needs
- Safety
- Being loved

FIGURE 3.1 Maslow's hierarchy of needs.
SOURCE: Maslow, A. 1970. *Motivation and Personality,* 2nd ed. New York: Harper & Row.

- Maintaining self-esteem
- Self-actualization

When urgent (life-sustaining) needs—such as the need for food and water—are satisfied, less basic needs take priority. Most of us are well fed and feel reasonably safe, so we are driven by higher motives. Maslow's conclusions were based on his study of a group of visibly successful people who seemed to have lived, or be living, at their fullest. He stated that these people had achieved **self-actualization;** they had fulfilled a good measure of their human potential. Maslow suggested that self-actualized people all share certain qualities:

- *Realism.* Self-actualized people are realistic: They know the difference between what is real and what they want. As a result, they can cope with the world as it exists without demanding that it be different; they know what they can and cannot change. Just as important, realistic people accept evidence that contradicts what they want to believe. If evidence is strong enough, they adapt their belief systems accordingly.

- *Acceptance.* Psychologically healthy people accept themselves as they are. Self-acceptance requires a positive **self-concept,** or *self-image*—a positive but realistic perception of oneself. Similarly, psychological health requires an appropriately high but realistic level of **self-esteem.** People with healthy self-esteem value themselves as people; they feel good about themselves and are likely to live up to their positive self-image and enjoy successes that in turn reinforce these good feelings. Self-acceptance also

TERMS

psychological health Mental health, defined either negatively as the absence of illness or positively as the presence of wellness.

self-actualization The highest level of growth in Maslow's hierarchy.

self-concept The ideas, feelings, and perceptions one has about oneself; also called *self-image*.

self-esteem Satisfaction and confidence in oneself; the valuing of oneself as a person.

QUESTIONS FOR CRITICAL THINKING AND REFLECTION

Have you ever had a reason to feel concerned about your own psychological health? If so, what was the reason? Did your concern lead you to talk to someone about the issue, or to seek professional help? If you did, what was the outcome, and how do you feel about it now?

means being tolerant of one's own imperfections, an ability that makes it easier to accept the imperfections of others.

- **Autonomy.** Psychologically healthy people are *autonomous*, meaning they can direct themselves, acting independently of their social environment. **Autonomy** is more than physical independence; it is social, emotional, and intellectual independence, as well. Autonomous people are **inner-directed,** finding guidance from within, from their own rules and values. They have an internal locus of control and a high level of self-efficacy (see Chapter 1). By contrast, **other-directed** people often act only in response to what they feel as external pressure from others. Instead of speaking their true feelings, for example, other-directed people are more inclined to say what they believe will make other people happy.

- **Authenticity.** Autonomous people are not afraid to be themselves; sometimes, their capacity for being "real" may give them a certain childlike quality. They respond in a genuine, spontaneous way to whatever happens, without pretense or self-consciousness. Such people do not worry about being judged by others just for being themselves. This quality of genuineness is sometimes called **authenticity.**

- **Capacity for intimacy.** Healthy people can be physically and emotionally intimate. They are able to share their feelings and thoughts without fear of rejection. A psychologically healthy person is open to the pleasure of physical contact and the satisfaction of being close to others—but without being afraid of the risks involved in intimacy, such as the risk of having one's feelings hurt. (Chapters 4 and 5 discuss intimacy in more detail.)

- **Creativity.** Psychologically healthy people continually look at the world with renewed appreciation. Such appreciation can inform one's creativity, which helps explain why so many mentally healthy people are creative. They may not be great poets or painters, but they live their everyday lives in creative ways. Creative people seem to see more and to be open to new experiences; they don't fear the unknown or avoid uncertainty.

Self-actualization is an ideal to strive for. Rather than dwelling on the past, we need to concentrate on meeting current challenges in ways that lead to long-term mental wellness. We must not consider ourselves failures if we do not achieve our full potential in every way or at every moment.

What Psychological Health Is Not

Psychological health is not the same as psychological **normality.** Being mentally normal simply means being close to average. We can define normal body temperature because a few degrees above or below this temperature means physical sickness. But your ideas and attitudes can vary tremendously without your losing efficiency or feeling emotional distress. In fact, psychological diversity—with the wide range of ideas, lifestyles, and attitudes it brings about—is a valuable asset to society.

Never seeking help for personal problems does not prove you are psychologically healthy, any more than seeking help proves you are mentally ill. Unhappy people may avoid seeking help for many reasons, and severely disturbed people may not even realize they need help.

Further, we can't say people are "mentally ill" or "mentally healthy" based solely on the presence or absence of symptoms. Consider the symptom of anxiety, for example. Anxiety can help you face a problem and solve it before it becomes too big. Someone who shows no anxiety may be refusing to recognize problems or to do anything about them. A person who is anxious for good reason is likely to be judged more psychologically healthy in the long run than someone who is inappropriately calm.

Finally, we cannot judge psychological health from the way people look. All too often, a person who seems to be OK and even happy suddenly takes his or her own life. Usually, such people lack close friends who might have known their desperation. At an early age, we learn to conceal our feelings and even to lie about them. We may believe that our complaints put unfair demands on others. While suffering in silence may sometimes be a virtue, it can also prevent one from getting help.

autonomy   Independence; the sense of being self-directed.

inner-directed   Guided in behavior by an inner set of rules and values.

other-directed   Guided in behavior by the values and expectations of others.

authenticity   Genuineness.

normality   The psychological characteristics attributed to the majority of people in a population at a given time.

TERMS

MEETING LIFE'S CHALLENGES

Life is full of challenges—large and small. Everyone, regardless of heredity and family influences, must learn to cope successfully with new situations and new people. For emotional and mental wellness, each of us must continue to grow psychologically, developing new and more sophisticated coping mechanisms to suit our current lives. We must develop an adult identity that enhances our self-esteem and autonomy. We must also learn to communicate honestly, handle anger and loneliness appropriately, and avoid being defensive.

Growing Up Psychologically

Our responses to life's challenges influence the development of our personality and identity. Psychologist Erik Erikson proposed that development proceeds through a series of eight stages that extend throughout life. Each stage is characterized by a major crisis or turning point—a time of increased vulnerability as well as increased potential for psychological growth (Table 3.1).

The successful mastery of one stage is a basis for mastering the next, so early failures can have repercussions in later life. Fortunately, life provides ongoing opportunities for mastering these tasks. For example, although the development of trust begins in infancy, it is refined as we grow older. We learn to trust people outside our immediate family and to limit our trust by identifying people who are untrustworthy.

Developing an Adult Identity A primary task beginning in adolescence is the development of an adult identity: a unified sense of self, characterized by attitudes, beliefs, and ways of acting that are genuinely one's own. People with adult identities know who they are, what they are capable of, what roles they play, and their place among their peers. They have a sense of their own uniqueness but also appreciate what they have in common with others. They view themselves realistically and can assess their strengths and weaknesses without relying on the opinions of others. Achieving an identity also means that one can form intimate relationships with others while maintaining a strong sense of self.

Our identities evolve as we interact with the world and make choices about what we'd like to do and whom we'd like to model ourselves after. Developing an adult identity is particularly challenging in a heterogeneous, secular, and relatively affluent society like ours, in which many roles are possible, many choices are tolerated, and ample time is allowed for experimenting and making up one's mind.

Early identities are often modeled after parents—or the opposite of parents, in rebellion against what they represent. Over time, peers, rock stars, sports heroes, and religious figures are added to the list of possible models. In high school and college, people often join cliques that

Table 3.1	Erikson's Stages of Development		
Age	**Conflict**	**Important People**	**Task**
Birth–1 year	Trust vs. mistrust	Mother or other primary caregiver	In being fed and comforted, developing the trust that others will respond to your needs
1–3 years	Autonomy vs. shame and self-doubt	Parents	In toilet training, locomotion, and exploration, learning self-control without losing the capacity for assertiveness
3–6 years	Initiative vs. guilt	Family	In playful talking and locomotion, developing a conscience based on parental prohibitions that is not too inhibiting
6–12 years	Industry vs. inferiority	Neighborhood and school	In school and playing with peers, learning the value of accomplishment and perseverance without feeling inadequate
Adolescence	Identity vs. identity confusion	Peers	Developing a stable sense of who you are—your needs, abilities, interpersonal style, and values
Young adulthood	Intimacy vs. isolation	Close friends, sex partners	Learning to live and share intimately with others, often in sexual relationships
Middle adulthood	Generativity vs. self-absorption	Work associates, children, community	Doing things for others, including parenting and civic activities
Older adulthood	Integrity vs. despair	Humankind	Affirming the value of life and its ideals

SOURCE: Erikson, E. 1963. *Childhood and Society.* New York: Norton.

assert a certain identity, such as the "jocks," the "brains," or the "slackers." Although much of an identity is internal—a way of viewing oneself and the world—certain aspects of it can be external, such as styles of talking and dressing, ornaments like earrings, and hairstyles.

Early identities are rarely permanent. A student who works for good grades and approval one year can turn into a dropout devoted to hard rock and wild parties a year later. At some point, however, most of us adopt a more stable, individual identity that ties together the experiences of childhood and the expectations and aspirations of adulthood. Erikson's theory does not suggest that one day we suddenly assume our final identity and never change after that. Life is more interesting for people who continue evolving into more distinct individuals, rather than being rigidly controlled by their pasts. Identity reflects a lifelong process, and it changes as a person develops new relationships and roles.

Developing an adult identity is an important part of psychological wellness. Without a personal identity, we begin to feel confused about who we are; Erikson called this situation an **identity crisis.** Until we have "found ourselves," we cannot have much self-esteem, because a self is not firmly in place.

How far have you gotten in developing your adult identity? Write down a list of characteristics you think a friend who knows you well would use to describe you. Rank them from the most to the least important. Your list might include elements such as gender, socioeconomic status, ethnic and/or religious identification, choice of college or major, parents' occupations, interests and talents, attitudes toward drugs and alcohol, style of dress, the kinds of people with whom you typically associate, your expected role in society, and aspects of your personality. Which elements of your identity do you feel are permanent, and which do you think may change over time? Are there any characteristics missing from your list that you'd like to add?

Another aid to developing an adult identity is to identify possible role models. Whom do you admire and want to be like? Which characteristics of that person do you want to emulate? How did that person acquire those characteristics, and how could you follow in her or his footsteps? Some role models might be willing to be mentors to you, spending time with you and sharing their wisdom.

Developing Intimacy   Erikson's developmental stages don't end with establishing an adult identity. Learning to live intimately with others and finding a productive role for yourself in society are other tasks of adulthood—to be able to love and work.

People with established identities can form intimate relationships and sexual unions characterized by sharing, open communication, long-term commitment, and love. Those who lack a firm sense of self may have difficulty establishing relationships because they feel overwhelmed by closeness and the needs of another person. As a result, they experience only short-term, superficial relationships with others and may remain isolated.

Developing Values and Purpose in Your Life   Erikson assigned his last two stages, generativity versus self-absorption and integrity versus despair, to middle adulthood and older adulthood. But these stages are concerned with values and purpose in life, issues that need to be addressed by young people and reexamined throughout life.

Values are criteria for judging what is good and bad; they underlie our moral decisions and behavior. The first morality of the young child is to consider "good" to mean what brings immediate and tangible rewards, and "bad," whatever results in punishment. An older child will explain right and wrong in terms of authority figures and rules. But the final stage of moral development, one that not everyone attains, is being able to conceive of right and wrong in more abstract terms such as justice and virtue.

As adults we need to assess how far we have evolved morally and what values we actually have adopted. Without an awareness of our personal values, our lives may be hurriedly driven forward by immediate desires and the passing demands of others. Living according to values means doing the following:

- Considering your options carefully before making a choice
- Choosing between options without succumbing to outside pressures that oppose your values
- Making a choice and acting on it rather than doing nothing

Your actions and how you justify them proclaim to others what you stand for.

A practical exercise for clarifying your values and goals is to write a draft of your obituary for a local newspaper. How would you like to be remembered? What would you like to have achieved? What will you have done to meet those goals? This obituary should not be a glorification, but an honest, realistic appraisal. End it by summarizing in a few sentences what was most important about your life. In reading what you have written, ask yourself, "How will I have to change to be the person I want to be?"

For more on discovering your values, see the box "Assessing Your Values."

Achieving Healthy Self-Esteem

Having a healthy level of self-esteem means regarding your self, which includes all aspects of your identity, as

Assessing Your Values

Find out more about your core values by answering these questions.

- What personality traits or characteristics do you most value—for example, being friendly, patient, successful, outgoing, cooperative, loyal to family and friends? These can be characteristics you see in yourself or in others.

- What activities or accomplishments do you most value—for example, making lots of money, getting good grades, spending time with friends, making your own decisions? These can be accomplishments of your own or of others, or goals you have for the future.

- What social ideals, customs, and institutions do you value—for example, education, equality, freedom of speech, tolerance for diverse opinions?

- How well does your current lifestyle reflect your values? Can you think of some recent incidents in which you acted in accordance with your values or in ways that conflict with your values?

good, competent, and worthy of love. It is a critical component of wellness.

Developing a Positive Self-Concept   Ideally, a positive self-concept begins in childhood, based on experiences both within the family and outside it. Children need to develop a sense of being loved and being able to give love and to accomplish their goals. If they feel rejected or neglected by their parents, they may fail to develop feelings of self-worth. They may grow to have a negative concept of themselves.

Another component of self-concept is *integration*. An integrated self-concept is one that you have made for yourself—not someone else's image of you or a mask that doesn't quite fit. Important building blocks of self-concept are the personality characteristics and mannerisms of parents, which children may adopt without realizing it. Later, they may be surprised to find themselves acting like one of their parents. Eventually, such building blocks should be reshaped and integrated into a new, individual personality.

A further aspect of self-concept is *stability*. Stability depends on the integration of the self and its freedom from contradictions. People who have gotten mixed messages about themselves from parents and friends may have contradictory self-images, which defy integration and make them vulnerable to shifting levels of self-esteem. At times they regard themselves as entirely good, capable, and lovable—an ideal self—and at other times they see themselves as entirely bad, incompetent, and unworthy of love. Neither of these extreme self-concepts allow people to see themselves or others realistically, and their relationships with other people are filled with misunderstandings and ultimately with conflict.

The concepts we have about ourselves and others are an important part of our personalities. And all the components of our self-concept profoundly influence our interpersonal relationships.

Meeting Challenges to Self-Esteem   As an adult, you sometimes run into situations that challenge your self-concept. People you care about may tell you they don't love you or feel loved by you, for example, or your attempts to accomplish a goal may end in failure.

You can react to such challenges in several ways. The best approach is to acknowledge that something has gone wrong and try again, adjusting your goals to your abilities without radically revising your self-concept. Less productive responses are denying that anything went wrong and blaming someone else. These attitudes may preserve your self-concept temporarily, but in the long run they keep you from meeting the challenge.

The worst reaction is to develop a lasting negative self-concept in which you feel bad, unloved, and ineffective—in other words, to become demoralized. Instead of coping, the demoralized person gives up, reinforcing the negative self-concept and setting in motion a cycle of bad self-concept and failure. In people who are genetically predisposed to depression, demoralization can progress to additional symptoms, which are discussed later in the chapter.

NOTICE YOUR PATTERNS OF THINKING   One method for fighting demoralization is to recognize and test the negative thoughts and assumptions you may have about yourself and others. Try to note exactly when an unpleasant emotion—feeling worthless, wanting to give up, feeling depressed—occurs or gets worse, to identify the events or daydreams that trigger that emotion, and to observe whatever thoughts come into your head just before or during the emotional experience. It is helpful to keep a daily journal about such events.

AVOID FOCUSING ON THE NEGATIVE   Imagine that you are waiting for a friend to meet you for dinner, but he's 30 minutes late. What kinds of thoughts go through your head when something like this happens? You might wonder what has happened to cause the delay: Perhaps he is stuck in traffic,

A positive self-concept begins in infancy. Knowing that he's loved and valued by his parents gives this baby a solid basis for lifelong psychological health.

you think, or needs to help a roommate who has the flu. This kind of reaction is healthy for several reasons:

- *You aren't jumping to a conclusion or blaming your friend for a failure of any kind.* After all, he probably hasn't forgotten about you or decided to ditch you.

- *You are being reasonable by giving your friend the benefit of the doubt.* Things happen. Your friend probably has a good reason for not being there. He deserves a chance to explain, and may even need your help dealing with the situation that made him late.

- *You avoid personalizing the situation in such a way that you feel hurt or betrayed.* Jumping to a negative conclusion (such as "He isn't coming because he doesn't really like me") can make you feel bad unnecessarily. The same thing happens if you place blame—either on your friend or yourself—without knowing all the facts.

By contrast, people who are demoralized tend to use all-or-nothing thinking. They overgeneralize from negative events. They overlook the positive and jump to negative conclusions, minimizing their own successes and magnifying the successes of others. They take responsibility for unfortunate situations that are not their fault, then jump to more negative conclusions and more unfounded overgeneralizations. Patterns of thinking that make events seem worse than they are in reality are called **cognitive distortions.**

DEVELOP REALISTIC SELF-TALK When you react to a situation, an important piece of that reaction is your **self-talk**—the statements you make to yourself inside your own mind. To pick up on our earlier example, suppose your friend is late for a dinner date. As you wait for your friend to arrive, your self-talk has a profound effect on your reaction to his lateness.

Someone who is demoralized or wrestling with a poor self-concept might immediately react with negative self-talk: *"He isn't coming. It's my fault; he probably doesn't like me because I'm boring. I bet he's with someone else."* This type of self-talk assigns blame (not just on your friend, but on yourself), is judgmental, and jumps to an unverified conclusion about the meaning of your friend's lateness. In fact, you don't know why he is late or what he is thinking.

More rational thinking and self-talk will not only help get you through the situation without feeling upset, but will also help you avoid damaging your own self-concept. In this case, helpful self-talk is not negative, but neutral: *"He's never late for dinner. Something must be holding him up. I'll call him and make sure everything is all right."* This thinking recognizes that a problem may exist, but does not judge or assign blame.

In your own fight against demoralization, it may be hard to think of a rational response until hours or days after the event that upset you. Responding rationally can be especially hard when you are having an argument with someone else, which is why people often say things they don't mean in the heat of the moment or develop hurt feelings even when the other person had no intention of hurting them.

Once you get used to noticing the way your mind works, however, you may be able to catch yourself thinking negatively and change the process before it goes too far. This approach to controlling your reactions is not the same as positive thinking—which means substituting a positive thought for a negative one. Instead, you simply try to make your thoughts as logical and accurate as

cognitive distortion A pattern of negative thinking that makes events seem worse than they are.

self-talk The statements a person makes to himself or herself.

Realistic Self-Talk

Do your patterns of thinking make events seem worse than they truly are? Do negative beliefs about yourself become self-fulfilling prophecies? Substituting realistic self-talk for negative self-talk can help you build and maintain self-esteem and cope better with the challenges in your life. Here are some examples of common types of distorted, negative self-talk, along with suggestions for more accurate and rational responses.

Cognitive Distortion	Negative Self-Talk	Realistic Self-Talk
Focusing on negatives	School is so discouraging—nothing but one hassle after another.	School is pretty challenging and has its difficulties, but there certainly are rewards. It's really a mixture of good and bad.
Expecting the worst	Why would my boss want to meet with me this afternoon if not to fire me?	I wonder why my boss wants to meet with me. I guess I'll just have to wait and see.
Overgeneralizing	(After getting a poor grade on a paper) Just as I thought—I'm incompetent at everything.	I'll start working on the next paper earlier. That way, if I run into problems, I'll have time to consult with the TA.
Minimizing	I won the speech contest, but none of the other speakers was very good. I wouldn't have done as well against stiffer competition.	It may not have been the best speech I'll ever give, but it was good enough to win the contest. I'm really improving as a speaker.
Blaming others	I wouldn't have eaten so much last night if my friends hadn't insisted on going to that restaurant.	I overdid it last night. Next time I'll make different choices.
Expecting perfection	I should have scored 100% on this test. I can't believe I missed that one problem through a careless mistake.	Too bad I missed one problem through carelessness, but overall I did very well on this test. Next time I'll be more careful.
Believing you're the cause of everything	Sarah seems so depressed today. I wish I hadn't had that argument with her yesterday; it must have really upset her.	I wish I had handled the argument better, and in the future I'll try to. But I don't know if Sarah's behavior is related to what I said or even if she's depressed. In any case, I'm not responsible for how Sarah feels or acts; only she can take responsibility for that.
Thinking in black and white	I've got to score 10 points in the game today. Otherwise, I don't belong on the team.	I'm a good player or else I wouldn't be on the team. I'll play my best—that's all I can do.
Magnifying events	They went to a movie without me. I thought we were friends, but I guess I was wrong.	I'm disappointed they didn't ask me to the movie, but it doesn't mean our friendship is over. It's not that big a deal.

SOURCE: Adapted from Schafer, W. *Stress Management for Wellness,* 4th ed. Copyright © 2000 Wadsworth, a part of Cengage Learning, Inc. Reproduced by permission. www.cengage.com/permissions.

possible, based on the facts of the situation as you know them, and not on snap judgments or conclusions that may turn out to be false.

Demoralized people can be tenacious about their negative beliefs—so tenacious that they make their beliefs come true in a self-fulfilling prophesy. For example, if you conclude that you are so boring that no one will like you anyway, you may decide not to bother socializing. This behavior could make the negative belief become a reality.

For additional tips on changing distorted, negative ways of thinking, see the box "Realistic Self-Talk."

Being Less Defensive

Sometimes our wishes come into conflict with people around us or with our conscience, and we become frustrated and anxious. If we cannot resolve the conflict by changing the external situation, we try to resolve the conflict internally by rearranging our thoughts and feelings. Some standard **defense mechanisms** are listed in Table 3.2. The drawback of many of these coping mechanisms is that they succeed temporarily, but make finding ultimate solutions much harder.

Recognizing your own defense mechanisms can be difficult, because they've probably become habits, occurring unconsciously. But we each have some inkling about how our mind operates. By remembering the details of conflict situations you have been in, you may be able to figure out which defense mechanisms you used in successful or unsuccessful attempts to cope. Try to look at yourself as an objective, outside observer would and analyze your thoughts and behavior in a psychologically stressful situation from the past. Having insight into what strategies

Table 3.2   Defense and Coping Mechanisms

Mechanism	Description	Example
Projection	Reacting to unacceptable inner impulses as if they were from outside the self	A student who dislikes his roommate feels that the roommate dislikes him.
Repression	Expelling from awareness an unpleasant feeling, idea, or memory	The child of an alcoholic, neglectful father remembers him as a giving, loving person.
Denial	Refusing to acknowledge to yourself what you really know to be true	A person believes that smoking cigarettes won't harm her because she's young and healthy.
Passive-aggressive behavior	Expressing hostility toward someone by being covertly uncooperative or passive	A person tells a coworker, with whom she competes for project assignments, that she'll help him with a report but then never follows through.
Displacement	Shifting one's feelings about a person to another person	A student who is angry with one of his professors returns home and yells at one of his housemates.
Rationalization	Giving a false, acceptable reason when the real reason is unacceptable	A shy young man decides not to attend a dorm party, telling himself he'd be bored.
Substitution	Deliberately replacing a frustrating goal with one that is more attainable	A student having a difficult time passing courses in chemistry decides to change his major from biology to economics.
Humor	Finding something funny in unpleasant situations	A student whose bicycle has been stolen thinks how surprised the thief will be when he or she starts downhill and discovers the brakes don't work.

you typically use can lead to new, less defensive and more effective ways of coping in the future.

Being Optimistic

Many psychologists believe that pessimism is not just a symptom of everyday depression but an important root cause, as well. Pessimists not only expect repeated failure and rejection but also accept it as deserved. Pessimists do not see themselves as capable of success, and they irrationally dismiss any evidence of their own accomplishments. This negative point of view is learned, typically at a young age from parents and other authority figures. But as an optimist would tell you, that means it also has the potential to be unlearned.

Psychologist Martin Seligman points out that we are more used to refuting negative statements, such as "The problem is going to last forever and ruin everything, and it's all my fault," when they come from a jealous rival rather than from our own mind. But refuting such negative self-talk is exactly what a pessimist must learn to do in order to avoid chronic unhappiness. Pessimists must first recognize and then dispute the false, negative predictions they generate about themselves.

Maintaining Honest Communication

Another important area of psychological functioning is communicating honestly with others. It can be very frustrating for us and for people around us if we cannot express what we want and feel. Others can hardly respond to our needs if they don't know what those needs are. We must recognize what we want to communicate and then express

it clearly. For example, how do you feel about going to the party instead of a movie? Do you care if your roommate talks on the phone late into the night?

Some people know what they want others to do but don't state it clearly because they fear denial of the request, which they interpret as personal rejection. Such people might benefit from **assertiveness** training: learning to insist on their rights and to bargain for what they want. Assertiveness includes being able to say no or yes depending on the situation.

Communicating your feelings appropriately and clearly is important. For example, if you tell people you feel sad, they may have various reactions. If they feel close to you, they may express an intimate thought of their own. Or they may feel guilty because they think you're implying they have caused your sadness. They may even be angry because they feel you expect them to cheer you up.

Depending on your intention and your prediction of how a statement will be taken, you may or may not wish to make it. For example, if you say "I feel like staying home tonight," you may also be implying something different. You could really be saying "Don't bother me" or opening a negotiation about what you would be willing to do that evening, given the right event or incentive. Although this approach may help you avoid a confrontation (or even a discussion) with someone else, it is unfair because you are not really being clear about what you want.

defense mechanism   A mental mechanism for coping with conflict or anxiety.

assertiveness   Expression that is forceful but not hostile.

TERMS

Good communication means expressing yourself clearly. You don't need any special psychological jargon to communicate effectively. (For tips, see the box "Guidelines for Effective Communication" in Chapter 4.)

Dealing with Loneliness

It can be hard to strike the right balance between being alone and being with others. Some people are motivated to socialize by a fear of being alone—not the best reason to spend time with others. If you discover how to be happy by yourself, you'll be better able to cope with periods when you're forced to be alone—for example, when you've just broken off a romantic relationship or when your usual friends are away on vacation.

Unhappiness with being alone may come from interpreting it as a sign of rejection—that others are not interested in spending time with you. Before you reach such a conclusion, be sure that you give others a real chance to get to know you.

Examine your patterns of thinking: You may harbor unrealistic expectations about other people—for example, that everyone you meet must like you and, if they don't, you must be terribly flawed. You might also consider the possibility that you expect too much from new acquaintances and, sensing this, they start to draw back, triggering your feelings of rejection. Not everyone you meet is a suitable and willing person for a close or intimate relationship. Feeling pressure to have such a relationship may lead you to take up with someone whose interests and needs are remote from yours or whose need to be cared for leaves you with little time of your own. You will have traded loneliness for potentially worse problems.

Loneliness is a passive feeling state. If you decide that you're not spending enough time with people, take action to change the situation. College life provides many opportunities to meet people. If you're shy, you may have to push yourself to join a group. Look for something you've enjoyed in the past or in which you have a genuine interest.

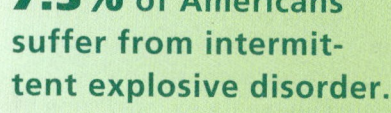

If your loneliness is the result of missing absent friends, remember that communication at a distance is cheaper and easier than ever before. For many people, e-mail and cell phones are immediate and satisfying ways to keep up with people in their lives.

Dealing with Anger

Common wisdom holds that expressing anger is beneficial for psychological and physical health. How-

College offers many antidotes to loneliness, in the forms of clubs, organized activities, sports, and just hanging out with friends.

ever, recent studies have questioned this idea by showing that overtly hostile people seem to be at higher risk for heart attacks. Angry words or actions don't contribute to psychological wellness if they damage relationships or produce feelings of guilt or loss of control. Perhaps the best way to resolve this contradiction is to distinguish between a gratuitous expression of anger and a reasonable level of self-assertiveness.

At one extreme are people who never express anger or any opinion that might offend others, even when their own rights and needs are being jeopardized. They may be trapped in unhealthy relationships or chronically deprived of satisfaction at work and at home. If you have trouble expressing your anger, consider training in assertiveness and appropriate expressions of anger to help you learn to express yourself constructively.

At the other extreme are people whose anger is explosive or misdirected—a condition called *intermittent explosive disorder (IED)*. IED is often accompanied by depression or another disorder. Explosive anger or rage, like a child's tantrum, renders individuals temporarily unable to think straight or to act in their own best interest. During an IED episode, a person may lash out uncontrollably, hurting someone else or destroying property. Anyone who expresses anger this way should seek professional help.

Managing Your Own Anger If you feel explosive anger coming on, consider the following two strategies to head it off.

First, try to *reframe* what you're thinking at that moment. You'll be less angry at another person if there is a possibility that his or her behavior was not intentionally directed against you. Imagine that another driver suddenly cuts in front of you. You would certainly be angry if you knew the other driver did it on purpose, but you probably would be less angry if you knew he simply did not see you. You might be even less upset if you consider that there may be other mitigating factors—for example, that the other driver was involved in an urgent situation of his own. If you're angry because you've just been criticized, avoid mentally replaying scenes from the past when you received similar unjust criticisms. Think about what is happening now, and try to act differently than in the past—less defensively and more analytically.

Second, until you're able to change your thinking, try to *distract* yourself. Use the old trick of counting to 10 before you respond, or start concentrating on your breathing. If needed, take a longer cooling-off period by leaving the situation until your anger has subsided. This does not mean that you should permanently avoid the issues and people who make you angry. When you've had a chance to think more clearly about the matter, return to it.

Dealing with Anger in Other People Anger can be infectious and disruptive to cooperation and communication. If someone you're with becomes very angry, respond "asymmetrically" by reacting not with anger but with calm. Try to validate the other person by acknowledging that he or she has some reason to be angry. This does not mean apologizing if you don't think you're to blame, or accepting verbal abuse, which is always inappropriate. Try to focus on solving the problem by allowing the person to explain why he or she is so angry and what can be done to alleviate the situation. Finally, if the person cannot be calmed, it may be best to disengage, at least temporarily. After a time-out, a rational problem-solving approach may become more successful.

PSYCHOLOGICAL DISORDERS

All of us have felt anxious at times, and in dealing with the anxiety we may have avoided doing something that we wanted to do or should have done. Most of us have had periods of feeling down when we became pessimistic, less energetic, and less able to enjoy life. Many of us have been bothered at times by irrational thoughts or odd feelings. Such feelings and thoughts can be normal responses to the ordinary challenges of life, but when emotions or irrational thoughts start to interfere with daily activities and rob us of our peace of mind, they can be considered symptoms of a psychological disorder.

Psychological disorders are generally the result of many factors. Genetic differences, which underlie differences in how the brain processes information and experience, are known to play an important role, especially in certain disorders. However, exactly which genes are involved, and how they alter the structure and chemistry of the brain, is still under study. Learning and life events are important, too: Identical twins often don't have the same psychological disorders in spite of having identical genes. Some people have been exposed to more traumatic events than others, leading either to greater vulnerability to future traumas or, conversely, to the development of better coping skills. Further, what your parents, peers, and others have taught you strongly influences your level of self-esteem and how you deal with frightening or depressing life events (see the box "Ethnicity, Culture, and Psychological Disorders," p. 75).

This section examines some of the more common psychological disorders, including anxiety disorders, mood disorders, and schizophrenia. (Table 3.3 on p. 74 shows the likelihood of these disorders occurring during one's lifetime and during the past year.)

Anxiety Disorders

Fear is a basic and useful emotion. Its value for our ancestors' survival cannot be overestimated; for modern humans, it provides motivation for self-protection and for learning to cope with new or potentially dangerous environmental or social situations. Only when fear is out of proportion to real danger can it be considered a problem. **Anxiety** is another word for fear, especially a feeling of fear that is not in response to any definite threat. Only

anxiety A feeling of fear that is not directed toward any definite threat.

TERMS

Table 3.3 — Prevalence of Selected Psychological Disorders Among Americans

Disorder	Men		Women	
	Lifetime Prevalence (%)	Past Year Prevalence (%)	Lifetime Prevalence (%)	Past Year Prevalence (%)
Anxiety disorders				
Simple phobia	6.7	4.4	15.7	13.2
Social phobia	11.1	6.6	15.5	9.1
Panic disorder	2.0	1.3	5.0	3.2
Generalized anxiety disorder	3.6	2.0	6.6	4.3
Obsessive-compulsive disorder	1.7	0.5	2.8	0.8
Post-traumatic stress disorder	5.0	1.5	10.4	3.5
Mood disorders				
Major depressive episode	12.0	5.5	20.4	7.7
Manic episode	1.6	1.4	1.7	1.3
Schizophrenia and related disorders	1.0	0.8	0.5	0.4
Dementia	Depends on life expectancy	6.4 (age >=65)	Depends on life expectancy	5.7 (age >=65)

NOTE: Rates of the prevalence of dementia are highly dependent on how much impairment is considered dementia and on the age range of the population.

SOURCES: Kessler, R. C., et al. 2003. The epidemiology of major depressive disorder: Results from the National Comorbidity Survey Replication (NCS-R). *Journal of the American Medical Association* 289(23): 3095–3105; U.S. Department of Health and Human Services. 1999. *Mental Health: A Report of the Surgeon General.* Rockville, Md.: DHHS; Kessler, R. C., et al. 1995. Posttraumatic stress disorder in the National Comorbidity Survey. *Archives of General Psychiatry* 52(12): 1048–1060; Kessler, R. C., et al. 1994. Lifetime and 12-month prevalence of DSM-III-R psychiatric disorders in the United States. *Archives of General Psychiatry* 51(1): 8–19; Ferri, C. P., et al. 2005. Global prevalence of dementia: A Delphi consensus. *Lancet* 366: 2112–2117; Kukull, W. A., et al. 2002. Dementia and Alzheimer disease incidence. *Archives of Neurology* 59(Nov.): 1737–1776.

when anxiety is experienced almost daily or in life situations that recur and cannot be avoided can anxiety be called a disorder. This section provides brief descriptions of the major types of anxiety disorders.

Simple Phobia The most common and most understandable anxiety disorder, **simple**, or **specific**, **phobia** is a fear of something definite like lightning or a particular animal or location. Examples of commonly feared animals are snakes, spiders, and dogs; frightening locations are often high places or enclosed spaces. Sometimes, but not always, these fears originate in bad experiences, such as being bitten by a snake. A special kind of simple phobia is fear of blood, injections, or seeing injured people. These fears usually come from a tendency to faint or become nauseated in such situations.

TERMS

simple (specific) phobia A persistent and excessive fear of a specific object, activity, or situation.

social phobia An excessive fear of being observed in public; speaking in public is the most common example.

panic disorder A syndrome of severe anxiety attacks accompanied by physical symptoms.

agoraphobia An anxiety disorder characterized by fear of being alone away from help and avoidance of many different places and situations; in extreme cases, a fear of leaving home. From the Greek for "fear of the public market."

Social Phobia The 15 million Americans with **social phobia** fear humiliation or embarrassment while being observed by others. Fear of speaking in public is perhaps the most common phobia of this kind. Extremely shy people can have social fears that extend to almost all social situations (see the box "Shyness" on p. 76). People with these kinds of fears may not continue in school as far as they could and may restrict themselves to lower-paying jobs where they do not have to come into contact with new people.

Panic Disorder People with **panic disorder** experience sudden unexpected surges in anxiety, accompanied by symptoms such as rapid and strong heartbeat, shortness of breath, loss of physical equilibrium, and a feeling of losing mental control. Such attacks usually begin in one's early twenties and can lead to a fear of being in crowds or closed places or of driving or flying. Sufferers fear that a panic attack will occur in a situation from which escape is difficult (such as while in an elevator), where the attack could be incapacitating and result in a dangerous or embarrassing loss of control (such as while driving a car or shopping), or where no medical help would be available if needed (such as when a person is alone away from home). Fears such as these lead to avoidance of situations that might cause trouble. The fears and avoidance may spread to a large variety of situations until a person is virtually housebound, a condition called **agoraphobia.** People with panic disorder can often function normally in feared situations if someone they trust accompanies them.

Ethnicity, Culture, and Psychological Disorders

connect™

Psychological disorders differ in incidence and symptoms across cultures and ethnic groups around the world. This variability is usually attributable to cultural differences—factors such as how symptoms are interpreted and communicated, whether treatment is sought, and whether a social stigma is attached to a particular symptom or disorder.

Expression of Symptoms

People from different cultures or groups may manifest or describe symptoms differently. Consider the following examples:

• In Japan, people with social phobia may be more distressed about the imagined harm their social clumsiness causes to others than about their own embarrassment.

• Older African Americans may express depression in atypical ways—for example, denying depression by taking on a multitude of extra tasks.

• Somatization, the indirect reporting of psychological distress through non-specific physical symptoms, is more prevalent among African Americans, Puerto Ricans, and Chinese Americans.

• Schizophrenia may manifest with different delusions depending on the local culture.

Differing Attitudes

It is relatively easy for Americans of northern European descent to regard an emotional problem as psychological in nature and to therefore accept a psychological treatment. For other groups, symptoms of psychological distress may be viewed as a spiritual problem, best dealt with by religious figures.

People from some groups may have little hesitation about communicating intimate, personal problems to professional care providers. However, for others, particularly men and members of certain ethnic groups, loss of emotional control may be seen as a weakness.

In addition, the use of mental health services is viewed negatively in many cultures; this stigma may partly account for the fact that African Americans and Asian American/Pacific Islanders are only about half as likely as whites to use any type of mental health service.

Assimilation

One of the largest immigrant groups in the United States is from Mexico. Surprisingly, surveys show that these immigrants are psychologically healthier than their own children born in the United States. Mexican, Cuban, and Puerto Rican Hispanics in this country come from a culture where family bonds are valued and divorce is rare. As they assimilate and begin using English exclusively, however, these family bonds tend to weaken, but less so for Cubans than for Puerto Ricans or Mexicans. With assimilation, the incidence of anxiety, depression, and substance abuse increases.

Biological Risk Factors

Biology can also play a role in the differences seen among patients of different ethnic groups. For example, psychotropic drugs are broken down in the body by a specific enzyme known as CYP2C19. Reduction of the activity of this enzyme is caused by two mutations, one of which appears to be found only in Asian populations. These "poor metabolizers" are very sensitive to medications that

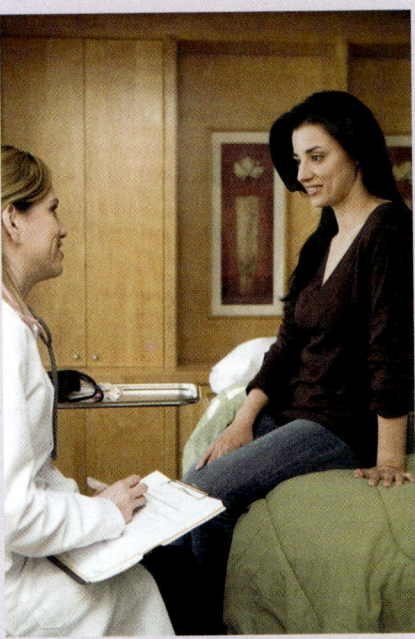

are broken down by this enzyme. The percentage of poor metabolizers among Asians is about 20%; among Latinos, about 5%; and among whites, 3%. Asian patients thus tend to have more adverse reactions to the doses of drugs standardized principally on white patients in the United States.

SOURCE: Alegria, M., et al. 2007. Understanding differences in past year psychiatric disorders for Latinos living in the US. *Social Science & Medicine* 65(2): 214–230; Kleinman, A. 2004. Culture and depression. *New England Journal of Medicine* 351(10): 951–953; Kirmayer, L. J. 2001. Cultural variations in the clinical presentation of depression and anxiety: Implications for diagnosis and treatment. *Journal of Clinical Psychiatry* 62 (Suppl. 13): 22–28; Lin, K. M. 2001. Biological differences in depression and anxiety across races and ethnic groups. *Journal of Clinical Psychiatry* 62 (Suppl. 13): 13–19.

Generalized Anxiety Disorder   A basic reaction to future threats is to worry about them. **Generalized anxiety disorder (GAD)** is a diagnosis given to people whose worries have taken on a life of their own, pushing out other thoughts and refusing banishment by any effort of will. The topics of the worrying are ordinary concerns: Will I be able to pass the exam next Friday? Where will I get money to get my car fixed?

The GAD sufferer's worrying is not completely unjustified—after all, thinking about problems can result in solving them. But this kind of thinking seems to just go around in circles, and the more you try to stop it, the more you feel at its mercy. The end result is a persistent feeling of nervousness, often accompanied by depression.

generalized anxiety disorder (GAD)   An anxiety disorder characterized by excessive, uncontrollable worry about all kinds of things and anxiety in many situations.

TERMS

Shyness

Shyness is a form of social anxiety, a fear of what others will think of one's behavior or appearance. Physical signs include a rapid heartbeat, a nervous stomach, sweating, cold and clammy hands, blushing, dry mouth, a lump in the throat, and trembling muscles. Shy people are often excessively self-critical, and their self-talk can be very negative. Their feelings of self-consciousness, embarrassment, and unworthiness can be overwhelming.

To avoid situations that make them anxious, shy people may refrain from making eye contact or speaking up in public. They may shun social gatherings and avoid college courses or job promotions that demand interpersonal interaction or public speaking.

Shyness is not the same thing as being introverted. Introverts prefer solitude to society. Shy people often long to be more outgoing, but their own negative thoughts prevent them from enjoying the social interaction they desire.

The consequences of severe shyness can include social isolation, loneliness, and lost personal and professional opportunities. Very shy people also have high rates of other anxiety and mood disorders and of substance abuse.

Shyness may be partly inherited. But for shyness, as for many health concerns, biology is not destiny. Many shy children outgrow their shyness, just as others acquire it later in life. Clearly, other factors are involved. The type of attachment between a child and his or her caregiver is important, as are parenting styles. People's experiences during critical developmental transitions, such as starting school and entering adolescence, have also been linked to shyness. For adults, the precipitating factor may be an event such as divorce or the loss of a job.

Shyness is very common, with 40–50% of Americans describing themselves as shy. However, only about 7–13% of adults are so shy that their condition interferes seriously with daily life. Recent surveys indicate that shyness rates may be rising in the United States. With the advent of technologies such as ATM machines, video games, voice mail, faxes, and e-mail, the opportunities for face-to-face interaction are diminishing. Electronic media can be a wonderful way for shy people to communicate, but they can also allow us to hide from social interaction. In fact, one study found that greater use of the Internet was associated with a decline in participants' communication with family members, a reduction in the size of their social circles, and an increase in levels of depression and loneliness.

Shyness is often undiagnosed, but help is available. Shyness classes, assertiveness training groups, and public speaking clinics are available (see the Behavior Change Strategy at the end of the chapter). For the seriously shy, effective treatments include cognitive-behavioral therapy and antidepressant drugs.

If you're shy, try to remember that shyness is widespread and that there are worse fates. Some degree of shyness has an upside. Shy people tend to be gentle,

supportive, kind, and sensitive; they are often exceptional listeners. People who think carefully before they speak or act are less likely to hurt the feelings of others. Shyness may also facilitate cooperation. For any group or society to function well, a variety of roles is required, and there is a place for quieter, more reflective individuals.

SOURCE: American Psychological Association. 2007. *Painful Shyness in Children and Adults* (http://www.apahelpcenter.org/featuredtopics/feature.php?id=5; retrieved December 29, 2008); Ebeling-Witte, S., et al. 2007. Shyness, Internet use, and personality. *Cyberpsychology and Behavior* 10(5): 713–716; Rosenthal, J., et al. 2007. Beyond shy: When to suspect social anxiety disorder. *Journal of Family Practice* 56(5): 369–374.

Obsessive-Compulsive Disorder The diagnosis of **obsessive-compulsive disorder (OCD)** is given to people with obsessions or compulsions or both.

• **Obsessions** are recurrent, unwanted thoughts or impulses. Unlike the worries of GAD, they are not ordinary concerns but improbable fears such as of suddenly committing an antisocial act or of having been contaminated by germs.

• **Compulsions** are repetitive, difficult-to-resist actions usually associated with obsessions. A common compulsion is hand washing, associated with an obsessive fear of contamination by dirt. Other compulsions are counting and repeatedly checking whether something has been done—for example, whether a door has been locked or a stove turned off.

People with OCD feel anxious, out of control, and embarrassed. Their rituals can occupy much of their time and make them inefficient at work and difficult to live with.

Post-Traumatic Stress Disorder People who suffer from **post-traumatic stress disorder (PTSD)** are reacting to severely traumatic events (events that produce a sense of terror and helplessness) such as physical violence to oneself or loved ones. Trauma occurs in personal assaults (rape, military combat), natural disasters (floods, hurricanes), and tragedies like fires and airplane or car crashes.

Symptoms include reexperiencing the trauma in dreams and in intrusive memories, trying to avoid anything associated with the trauma, and numbing of feelings. Hyperarousal, sleep disturbances, and other symptoms of anxiety and depression also commonly occur. Such symptoms can last months or even years. PTSD symptoms often decrease substantially within 3 months, but in up to one-third of PTSD cases, the individual does not fully recover. Recovery may be slower in those who have previously experienced trauma or who suffer from ongoing psychological problems.

The terrorist attacks on September 11, 2001, brought PTSD into the spotlight. Among those affected were survivors, rescue workers, passersby, residents of Manhattan in general, and to some extent, television viewers around the world who saw countless repeated images of the devastation. An estimated 150,000 New Yorkers suffered PTSD following the attacks; some were still experiencing symptoms 5 years later. Hurricane Katrina had a similarly devastating effect; in one survey, 19% of police officers and 22% of firefighters in the Gulf Coast states reported symptoms of PTSD. Soldiers wounded in combat are also at risk for PTSD; among soldiers wounded in Iraq or Afghanistan, rates of PTSD increased during the first year after the injury, suggesting that the emotional impact deepens with time. When symptoms persist, and when daily functioning is disrupted, professional help is needed.

Treating Anxiety Disorders   Therapies for anxiety disorders range from medication to psychological interventions concentrating on a person's thoughts and behavior. Both drug treatments and cognitive-behavioral therapies are effective in panic disorder, OCD, and GAD. Simple phobias are best treated without drugs.

Mood Disorders

Daily, temporary mood changes typically don't affect our overall emotional state or level of wellness. A person with a **mood disorder,** however, experiences emotional disturbances that are intense and persistent enough to affect normal functioning. The two most common mood disorders are depression and bipolar disorder.

Depression   The National Institutes of Health estimates that **depression** strikes nearly 10% of Americans annually, making it the most common mood disorder. Depression affects the young as well as adults; about 9% of adolescents age 12–17 suffer a major depressive episode each year, and nearly 50% of college students report depression severe enough to hinder their daily functioning. Depression tends to be more severe and persistent in blacks than in people of other races. Despite this, less than 50% of blacks affected by depression receive treatment for it.

Depression takes different forms but usually involves demoralization and can include the following:

- A feeling of sadness and hopelessness
- Loss of pleasure in doing usual activities
- Poor appetite and weight loss
- Insomnia or disturbed sleep
- Restlessness or, alternatively, fatigue
- Thoughts of worthlessness and guilt
- Trouble concentrating or making decisions
- Thoughts of death or suicide

A person experiencing depression may not have all of these symptoms. Sometimes instead of poor appetite and insomnia, the opposite occurs—eating too much and sleeping too long. (Depression may contribute to weight gain in young women.) People can have most of the symptoms of depression without feeling depressed, although they usually experience a loss of interest or pleasure in things. (see the Box "Are You Suffering from a Mood Disorder?").

In major depression, symptoms are often severe; a diagnosis of *dysthymic disorder* may be applied to people who experience persistent symptoms of mild or moderate depression for 2 years or longer. In some cases, depression is a clear-cut reaction to specific events, such as the loss of

TERMS

obsessive-compulsive disorder (OCD)   An anxiety disorder characterized by uncontrollable, recurring thoughts and the performing of senseless rituals.

obsession   A recurrent, irrational, unwanted thought or impulse.

compulsion   An irrational, repetitive, forced action, usually associated with an obsession.

post-traumatic stress disorder (PTSD)   An anxiety disorder characterized by reliving traumatic events through dreams, flashbacks, and hallucinations.

mood disorder   An emotional disturbance that is intense and persistent enough to affect normal function; two common types of mood disorders are depression and bipolar disorder.

depression   A mood disorder characterized by loss of interest, sadness, hopelessness, loss of appetite, disturbed sleep, and other physical symptoms.

Are You Suffering from a Mood Disorder?

You should be evaluated by a professional if you've had five or more of the following symptoms for more than 2 weeks or if any of these symptoms causes such a big change that you can't keep up your usual routine.

When You're Depressed

_____ You feel sad or cry a lot, and it doesn't go away.

_____ You feel guilty for no reason; you feel you're no good; you've lost your confidence.

_____ Life seems meaningless, or you think nothing good is ever going to happen again.

_____ You have a negative attitude a lot of the time, or it seems as if you have no feelings.

_____ You don't feel like doing a lot of the things you used to like—music, sports, being with friends, going out, and so on—and you want to be left alone most of the time.

_____ It's hard to make up your mind. You forget lots of things, and it's hard to concentrate.

_____ You get irritated often. Little things make you lose your temper; you overreact.

_____ Your sleep pattern changes: You start sleeping a lot more or you have trouble falling asleep at night; or you wake up really early most mornings and can't get back to sleep.

_____ Your eating pattern changes: You've lost your appetite or you eat a lot more.

_____ You feel restless and tired most of the time.

_____ You think about death or feel as if you're dying or have thoughts about committing suicide.

When You're Manic

_____ You feel high as a kite, like you're "on top of the world."

_____ You get unrealistic ideas about the great things you can do— things that you really can't do.

_____ Thoughts go racing through your head, you jump from one subject to another, and you talk a lot.

_____ You're a nonstop party, constantly running around.

_____ You do too many wild or risky things—with driving, with spending money, with sex, and so on.

_____ You're so "up" that you don't need much sleep.

_____ You're rebellious or irritable and can't get along at home or school or with your friends.

If you are concerned about depression in yourself or a friend, or if you are thinking about hurting or killing yourself, talk to someone about it and get help immediately.

---

a loved one or failing in school or work, whereas in other cases no trigger event is obvious.

RECOGNIZING THE WARNING SIGNS OF SUICIDE One of the principal dangers of severe depression is suicide. Although a suicide attempt can occur unpredictably and unaccompanied by depression, the chances are greater if symptoms are numerous and severe. Additional warning signs of suicide include the following:

• Expressing the wish to be dead or revealing contemplated methods

• Increasing social withdrawal and isolation

• A sudden, inexplicable lightening of mood (which can mean the person has decided to commit suicide) Certain risk factors increase the likelihood of suicide:

• A history of previous attempts

• A suicide by a family member or friend

• Readily available means, such as guns or pills

• A history of substance abuse or eating disorders

• Serious medical problems

In the United States, men have much higher suicide rates than women; white men over age 65 have the highest suicide rate (Figure 3.2). Whites and Native Americans have higher rates than most other groups, but rates among blacks have been rising. Women attempt three times as many suicides as men, yet men succeed at more than three times the rate of women (see the box "Depression, Anxiety, and Gender" on p. 80). Suicide rates among adolescents and young adults and among adults over 65 have been falling for the last two decades.

Sometimes mistaken for suicide attempts are acts of *self-injury,* including cutting, burning, hitting, and other forms of self-inflicted harm. The prevalence of self-injury is estimated at 3–4% in the general population but is higher in adolescents, especially females. In a 2007 study, 25% of college-age females surveyed said they had injured themselves intentionally. A maladaptive coping

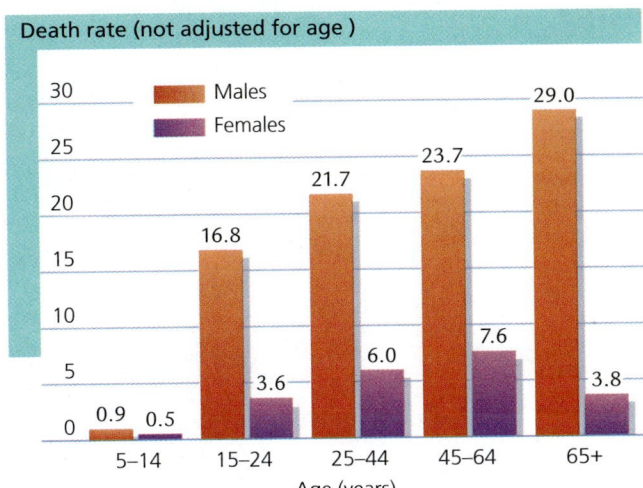

Death rate (not adjusted for age)

Males
Females

Age (years)	5–14	15–24	25–44	45–64	65+
Males	0.9	16.8	21.7	23.7	29.0
Females	0.5	3.6	6.0	7.6	3.8

(a) Suicide rate by age and gender

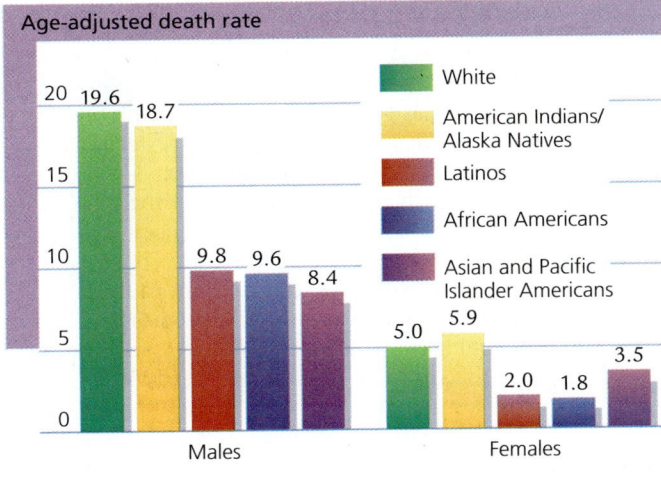

Age-adjusted death rate

White
American Indians/Alaska Natives
Latinos
African Americans
Asian and Pacific Islander Americans

Males: 19.6, 18.7, 9.8, 9.6, 8.4
Females: 5.0, 5.9, 2.0, 1.8, 3.5

(b) Suicide rate by ethnicity and gender (all ages)

VITAL STATISTICS

FIGURE 3.2   Rates of suicide per 100,000 people in the United States.   The rate of suicide varies by gender, age, and ethnicity. Rates are higher among men than women at all ages and are higher among whites compared to other groups. White men over age 65 have the highest rates of suicide. The age-adjusted national suicide rate is 10.9 per 100,000 people. These statistics are complete through 2004.

SOURCE: National Center for Health Statistics. 2007. *Health, United States, 2007.* Hyattsville, Md.: National Center for Health Statistics.

strategy, self-injury is believed to provide relief from unbearable psychological distress or pain, perhaps through the release of endorphins. A variety of psychotherapeutic interventions can help people who injure themselves. Whatever the reason behind it, however, self-harm should be taken very seriously because it may signal an increased risk for suicide. According to a 2007 British study, young persons who purposely hurt themselves were much more likely to commit suicide than the general population.

HELPING YOURSELF OR A FRIEND   If you are severely depressed or know someone who is, expert help from a mental health professional is essential. Don't be afraid to discuss the possibility of suicide with someone you fear is suicidal. You won't give them an idea they haven't already thought of (see the box "Myths About Suicide," p. 82). Asking direct questions is the best way to determine whether someone seriously intends to commit suicide. Encourage your friend to talk and to take positive steps to improve his or her situation.

Most communities have emergency help available, often in the form of a hotline telephone counseling service run by a suicide prevention agency (check the yellow pages). If you feel there is an immediate danger of suicide, do not leave the person alone. Call for help or take him or her to an emergency room.

TREATING DEPRESSION   Although treatments are highly effective, only about 35% of people who suffer from depression currently seek treatment. Treatment for depression depends on its severity and on whether the depressed

person is suicidal. The best initial treatment for moderate to severe depression is probably a combination of drug therapy and psychotherapy. Newer prescription antidepressants work well, although they may take several weeks to take effect, and patients may need to try multiple medications before finding one that works well. Therefore, when suicidal impulses are strong, hospitalization may be necessary.

Antidepressants work by affecting key neurotransmitters in the brain, including serotonin (Figure 3.3, p. 81). The herbal supplement St. John's wort may also affect serotonin levels, but it is not subject to the same testing and regulation as prescription medications (see the box "Alternative Remedies for Depression" on p. 83). Anyone who may be suffering from depression should seek a medical evaluation rather than self-treating with supplements.

Electroconvulsive therapy (ECT) is effective for severe depression when other approaches have failed, including medications and other electronic therapies such as magnetic stimulation. In ECT, an epileptic-like seizure is induced by an electrical impulse transmitted through electrodes placed on the head. Patients are given an anesthetic and a muscle relaxant to reduce anxiety and prevent injuries associated with seizures. A typical

electroconvulsive therapy (ECT)   The use of electric shock to induce brief, generalized seizures; used in the treatment of selected psychological disorders.

TERMS

Depression, Anxiety, and Gender

The common belief that females are more emotional than males has both a positive and a negative side. On the one hand, women are thought to express positive emotions more clearly than men, especially those related to sympathy and caring. On the other hand, women are more prone to negative emotions such as depression and worry.

One of the defining characteristics of a psychiatric disorder is that it interferes with daily activities and the ability to live a happy life. Thus, the higher incidence of anxiety and mood disorders in women is convincing evidence that they are more likely to suffer from emotional distress than are men.

Anxiety Disorders

Panic disorder is more than twice as common in women as in men, whereas obsessive-compulsive disorder occurs in men and women at about the same rate. In population surveys, social anxiety disorder is more common in women than in men, but men are more likely to seek treatment for it—perhaps because men are more likely to find it a barrier to success in white-collar jobs. In some surveys, PTSD is more common in women, but the incidence of PTSD depends on the incidence of traumatic events, which varies in different environments. Men are more often exposed to military combat, and women to rape. Trauma from motor vehicle crashes is a fairly common cause of PTSD in both sexes.

Depression and Suicide

Over their lifetimes, about 20% of women and 12% of men have serious depression. When women are depressed, they are more likely than men to experience guilt, anxiety, increased appetite and weight gain, and increased sleep. When women take antidepressants, they may need a lower dose than men;

at the same dosage, blood levels of medication tend to be higher in women. An issue for women who may become pregnant is whether antidepressants can harm a fetus or newborn. The best evidence indicates that the most frequently prescribed types of antidepressants do not cause birth defects, although some studies have reported withdrawal symptoms in some newborns whose mothers used certain antidepressants.

Although suicidal behavior is strongly associated with depression, and depression is more prevalent in women, many more men than women commit suicide. Overall, about three times as many women as men attempt suicide, but women's attempts are less likely to be lethal. In the United States, 60% of male suicides involve firearms.

Underlying Factors

Why women have more anxiety and depression than men is a matter of debate. Some experts think much of the difference is due to reporting bias: Women are more willing to admit to experiencing negative emotions, being stressed, or having difficulty coping. Women may also be more likely to seek treatment.

Other experts point to biologically based sex differences, particularly in the level and action of hormones. Greater anxiety and depression in women compared with men is most pronounced between puberty and menopause, when female hormones are most active. However, this period of life is also the time in which women's social roles and expectations may be the most different from those of men. Women may put more emphasis on relationships in determining self-esteem, so the deterioration of a relationship is a cause of depression that can hit women harder than men. In addition, culturally determined gender roles are more likely to place women in situations where they have less control

over key life decisions, and lack of autonomy is associated with depression.

The higher suicide rate among young men may relate to gender norms and expectations that men assert independence and physical prowess—sometimes expressed in risky, dangerous, and potentially self-destructive behavior. Such behavior, often involving drugs and alcohol and resulting in motor vehicle crashes, occurs more often in young people who later commit suicide. Even when suicidal intention is never expressed, suicidal impulses are often suspected of contributing to sudden deaths in this age group.

SOURCES: Sanz, E. J., et al. 2005. Selective serotonin reuptake inhibitors in pregnant women and neonatal withdrawal syndrome. *Lancet* 365(9458): 482–487; Kessler, R. C. 2003. Epidemiology of women and depression. *Journal of Affective Disorders* 74: 5–13; World Health Organization. 2002. *Gender and Mental Health*. Geneva: World Health Organization; Pigott, T. A. 1999. Gender differences in the epidemiology and treatment of anxiety disorders. *Journal of Clinical Psychiatry* 60(Suppl. 18): 4–15.

course of ECT includes three treatments per week for 2 to 4 weeks.

One type of depression is treated by having sufferers sit with eyes open in front of a bright light source every morning. These patients have **seasonal affective disorder (SAD)**; their depression worsens during winter months as the number of hours of daylight diminishes, then improves with the spring and summer. The American Psychiatric Association estimates that 10–20%

TERMS

seasonal affective disorder (SAD) A mood disorder characterized by seasonal depression, usually occurring in winter, when there is less daylight.

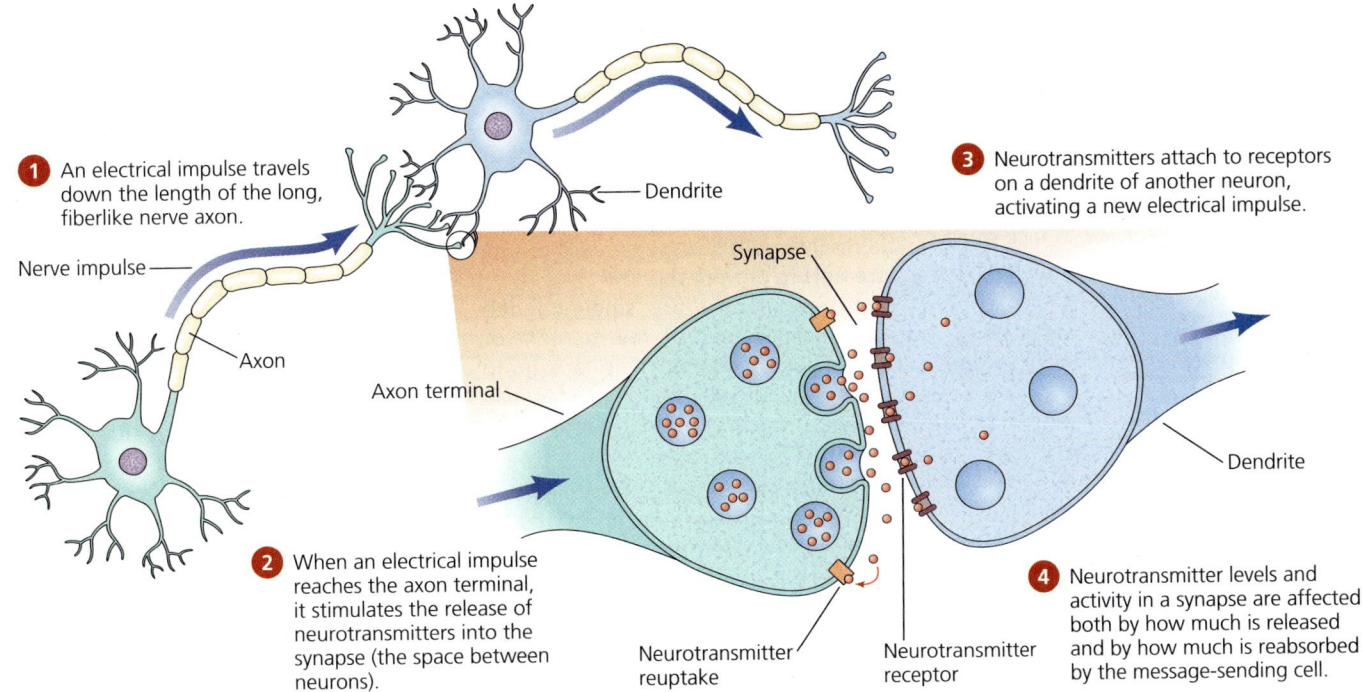

1 An electrical impulse travels down the length of the long, fiberlike nerve axon.

Nerve impulse

Axon

Dendrite

2 When an electrical impulse reaches the axon terminal, it stimulates the release of neurotransmitters into the synapse (the space between neurons).

Synapse

Axon terminal

Neurotransmitter reuptake

Neurotransmitter receptor

3 Neurotransmitters attach to receptors on a dendrite of another neuron, activating a new electrical impulse.

Dendrite

4 Neurotransmitter levels and activity in a synapse are affected both by how much is released and by how much is reabsorbed by the message-sending cell.

FIGURE 3.3 Nerve cell communication. Nerve cells (neurons) communicate through a combination of electrical impulses and chemical messages. Neurotransmitters such as serotonin and norepinephrine alter the overall responsiveness of the brain and are responsible for mood, level of attentiveness, and other psychological states. Many psychological disorders are related to problems with neurotransmitters and their receptors, and drug treatments frequently target them. For example, the antidepressant drug Prozac increases levels of serotonin by slowing the resorption (re-uptake) of serotonin.

of Americans suffer symptoms that may be linked to SAD. SAD is more common among people who live at higher latitudes, where there are fewer hours of light in winter. Light therapy may work by extending the perceived length of the day and thus convincing the brain that it is summertime even during the winter months.

Mania and Bipolar Disorder People who experience **mania**, a less common feature of mood disorders, are restless, have a lot of energy, need little sleep, and often talk nonstop. They may devote themselves to fantastic projects and spend more money than they can afford. Many manic people swing between manic and depressive states, a syndrome called **bipolar disorder** because of the two opposite poles of mood. Bipolar disorder affects men and women equally. Tranquilizers are used to treat individual manic episodes, while special drugs such as the salt lithium carbonate taken daily can prevent future mood swings. Anticonvulsants (used to prevent epileptic seizures) are also prescribed to stabilize moods; examples are Tegretol (carbamazepine) and Lamictal (lamotrigene).

THINKING ABOUT THE ENVIRONMENT

Depressive disorders such as SAD are triggered by environmental factors such as the long nights and gray skies of winter or job schedules that require one to work at night and sleep during the day. Anxiety disorders such as social phobia can be greatly compounded by living or working in a crowded area where one must deal with many other people.

If an environmental factor adds to your depression or anxiety, look for resources in your community that can help. For example, counseling can help with social anxiety, and inexpensive light treatments can relieve seasonal depression for some people. For more information on the environment and environmental health, see Chapter 19.

TERMS

mania A mood disorder characterized by excessive elation, irritability, talkativeness, inflated self-esteem, and expansiveness.

bipolar disorder A mental illness characterized by alternating periods of depression and mania.

Myths About Suicide

Myth People who really intend to kill themselves do not let anyone know about it.
Fact This belief can be an excuse for doing nothing when someone says he or she might commit suicide. In fact, most people who eventually commit suicide *have* talked about doing it.

Myth People who made a suicide attempt but survived did not really intend to die.
Fact This may be true for certain people, but people who seriously want to end their life may fail because they misjudge what it takes. Even a pharmacist may misjudge the lethal dose of a drug.

Myth People who succeed in suicide really wanted to die.

Fact We cannot be sure of that either. Some people are only trying to make a dramatic gesture or plea for help but miscalculate.

Myth People who really want to kill themselves will do it regardless of any attempts to prevent them.
Fact Few people are single-minded about suicide even at the moment of attempting it. People who are quite determined to take their life today may change their mind completely tomorrow.

Myth Suicide is proof of mental illness.
Fact Many suicides are committed by people who do not meet ordinary criteria for mental illness, although people with depression, schizophrenia, and other psychological disorders have a much higher than average suicide rate.

Myth People inherit suicidal tendencies.
Fact Certain kinds of depression that lead to suicide do have a genetic component. But many examples of suicide running in a family can be explained by factors such as psychologically identifying with a family member who committed suicide, often a parent.

Myth All suicides are irrational.
Fact By some standards all suicides may seem "irrational." But many people find it at least understandable that someone might want to commit suicide, for example, when approaching the end of a terminal illness or when facing a long prison term.

QUESTIONS FOR CRITICAL THINKING AND REFLECTION

Have you ever wondered if you were depressed? Try to recall your situation at the time. How did you feel, and what do you think brought about those feelings? What, if anything, did you do to bring about change and to feel better?

Schizophrenia

Schizophrenia can be severe and debilitating or quite mild and hardly noticeable. Although people are capable of diagnosing their own depression, they usually don't diagnose their own schizophrenia, because they often can't see that anything is wrong. This disorder is not rare; in fact, 1 in every 100 people has a schizophrenic episode sometime in his or her lifetime, most commonly starting in adolescence.

Scientists are uncertain about the exact causes of schizophrenia. Researchers have identified possible chemical and structural differences in the brains of people with the disorder as well as several genes that appear to increase risk. Schizophrenia is likely caused by a combina-

tion of genes and environmental factors that occur during pregnancy and development. For example, children born to older fathers have higher rates of schizophrenia, as do children with prenatal exposure to certain infections or medications.

Some general characteristics of schizophrenia include the following:

- *Disorganized thoughts.* Thoughts may be expressed in a vague or confusing way.

- *Inappropriate emotions.* Emotions may be either absent or strong but inappropriate.

- *Delusions.* People with delusions—firmly held false beliefs—may think that their minds are controlled by outside forces, that people can read their minds, that they are great personages like Jesus Christ or the president of the United States, or that they are being persecuted by a group such as the CIA.

- *Auditory hallucinations.* Schizophrenic people may hear voices when no one is present.

- *Deteriorating social and work functioning.* Social withdrawal and increasingly poor performance at school or work may be so gradual that they are hardly noticed at first.

None of these characteristics is invariably present. Some schizophrenic people are quite logical except on the subject of their delusions. Others show disorganized thoughts but no delusions or hallucinations.

A schizophrenic person needs help from a mental health professional. Suicide is a risk in schizophrenia, and expert treatment can reduce that risk and minimize the social consequences of the illness by shortening the period

TERMS

schizophrenia A psychological disorder that involves a disturbance in thinking and in perceiving reality.

Alternative Remedies for Depression

Mainstream therapies for depression include medications accepted as safe and effective by government regulatory agencies, certain psychotherapies, and light therapy in the case of seasonal affective disorder. Yet, in surveys, 20% of people in the United States who suffer from depression report using unconventional therapies such as acupuncture, body movement therapy, homeopathy, qigong, faith healing, or herbs or other "natural" substances. With the exception of one herb, St. John's wort (*Hypericum perforatum*), these therapies have not been shown to be effective in double-blind placebo-controlled trials. Such trials are the only scientific way to show that a treatment has healing power beyond that of a **placebo.** (See Chapter 20 for more on different types of medical research studies.)

St. John's wort, a flowering plant that grows as a weed in the United States, has been reputed to have curative properties since the time of Hippocrates in ancient Greece. Modern pharmacological studies confirm that its active ingredients produce a number of biochemical and physiological changes in animals, although it's still unclear exactly how these changes might affect depression. Data from a number of studies suggest that St. John's wort could benefit people with mild to moderate depression, but concerns have been raised about the adequacy of those trials. Recently, two carefully designed trials were conducted on St. John's wort. In one, 375 mild to moderately depressed patients were randomly assigned to receive either a placebo or an extract of St. John's wort; the extract was statistically more effective than the placebo and did not have more side effects. In the other trial, 340 depressed patients were given either St. John's wort, a placebo, or sertraline, a prescription antidepressant. In that study, St. John's wort was no more effective than the placebo—but neither was sertraline. Because many other studies have shown sertraline to have better results than a placebo, this result casts doubt as to whether the study methods were sensitive enough to detect an antidepressant effect. In any case, consumers are left without a definitive answer on the effectiveness of St. John's wort.

An advantage of St. John's wort is that it causes fewer adverse effects than conventional antidepressants. In data from three studies including about 600 depressed patients, the herb produced no more adverse effects than did the placebo. There was no evidence of sedation, gastrointestinal disturbances, or other side effects associated with other antidepressants. However, the safety of St. John's wort in pregnancy has not been established, and it may interact with, and reduce the effectiveness of, certain medications, including oral contraceptives and some medications for treating heart disease, depression, HIV infections, and seizures.

One reason for the popularity of an herb for depression is that it doesn't require a prescription or any kind of contact with a physician or a therapist; for those who are not members of a generous health care plan, an herbal remedy may also be less expensive than a prescription antidepressant. On the other hand, people suffering from depression *should* seek professional advice and not try to get along entirely with self-diagnosis and self-help. If you are depressed enough to contemplate taking St. John's wort, you need to make an appointment to talk to a professional about your depression.

Bear in mind that St. John's wort does not work for everyone, and no expert advocates it for severe depression. Also, because herbal products are classified as dietary supplements, they are not scrutinized by the regulatory agencies that oversee prescription drugs. Thus, consumers have no guarantee that the product contains the herbs and dosages listed on the label (see Chapters 12 and 20 for more on dietary supplements).

SOURCES: Trautmann-Sponsel, R. D., and A. Dienel. 2004. Safety of Hypericum extract in mildly to moderately depressed outpatients: A review based on data from three randomized, placebo-controlled trials. *Journal of Affective Disorders* 82(2): 303–307; Lecrubier, Y., et al. 2002. Efficacy of St. John's wort extract WS 5570 in major depression: A double-blind, placebo-controlled trial. *American Journal of Psychiatry* 159(8): 1361–1366; Hypericum Depression Trial Study Group. 2002. Effect of *Hypericum perforatum* (St. John's wort) in major depressive disorder: A randomized controlled trial. *Journal of the American Medical Association* 287(14): 1807–1814; Shelton, R. C., et al. 2001. Effectiveness of St. John's wort in major depression. *Journal of the American Medical Association* 285 (15): 1978–1986.

when symptoms are active. The key element in treatment is regular medication. At times medication is like insulin for diabetes—it makes the difference between being able to function or not. Sometimes hospitalization is temporarily required to relieve family and friends.

MODELS OF HUMAN NATURE AND THERAPEUTIC CHANGE

At least four different perspectives—biological, behavioral, cognitive, and psychodynamic—can be applied to human problems such as the psychological disorders discussed in this chapter. Each perspective has a distinct view of human nature, and from those views of human nature come distinct therapeutic approaches.

The Biological Model

The *biological model* emphasizes that the mind's activity depends entirely on an organic structure, the brain, whose composition is genetically determined. The activity of neurons, mediated by complex chemical reactions, gives rise to our most complex thoughts, our most ardent desires, and our most pathological behavior.

placebo A chemically inactive substance that a patient believes is an effective medical therapy for his or her condition. To help evaluate a therapy, medical researchers compare the effects of a particular therapy with the effects of a placebo. The "placebo effect" occurs when a patient responds to a placebo as if it were an active drug.

TERMS

Pharmacological Therapy   The most important kind of therapy inspired by the biological model is pharmacological therapy. A list of some of the popular medications currently used for treating psychological disorders follows. All require a prescription from a psychiatrist or other medical doctor. All have received approval from the U.S. Food and Drug Administration (FDA) as being safe and more effective than a placebo. However, as with all pharmacological therapies, these drugs may cause side effects. For example, the side effects of widely used antidepressants range from diminished appetite to loss of sexual pleasure. In addition, a patient may have to try several drugs before finding one that is effective and has acceptable side effects.

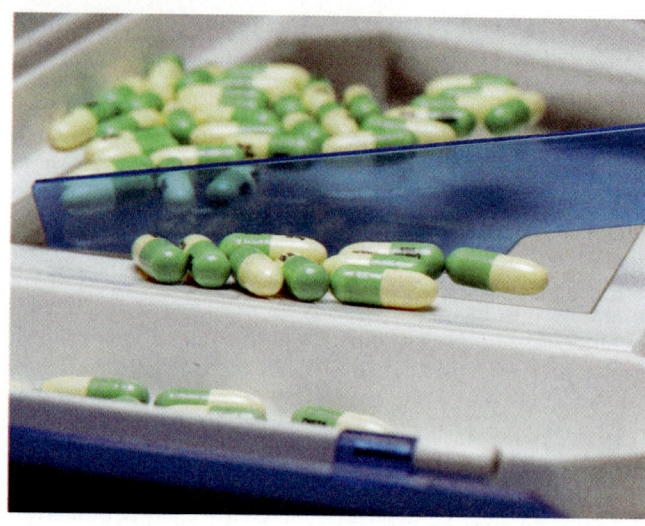

Pharmacological therapy (medication) is a common form of treatment for many psychological disorders. Medications can be very effective, but they do have risks and side effects, and they do not work for all patients.

1. *Antidepressants:* One group is called the selective serotonin re-uptake inhibitors (SSRIs) because of one of their actions, this group includes Prozac (fluoxetine), Paxil (paroxetine), Zoloft (sertraline), Luvox (fluvoxamine), Celexa (citalopram), and Lexapro (escitalopram). Another group is called the tricyclics after their chemical structure; it includes Aventyl (nortriptyline) and Elavil (amitriptyline). Nardil (phenelzine) is a monoamine oxidase inhibitor (MAOI). Antidepressants that do not fit into these groups include Effexor (venlafaxine), Welbutrin (buproprion), Serzone (nefazodone), Remeron (mirtazapine), and Cymbalta (duloxetine). Surprisingly, these antidepressants are as effective in treating panic disorder and certain kinds of chronic anxiety as they are in treating depression. They may also alleviate the symptoms of OCD.

2. *Mood stabilizers:* Lithium carbonate, Depakote (valproic acid), Lamictal (lamotrigine), and Topomax (topiramate) are prescribed as mood stabilizers. They are taken to prevent mood swings that occur in bipolar disorder and certain kinds of schizophrenia.

3. *Antipsychotics:* Older antipsychotics include Haldol (haloperidol) and Prolixin (fluphenazine); newer antipsychotics (sometimes called "atypical") are Clozaril (clozapine), Zyprexa (olanzapine), Risperdal (risperidone), Seroquel (quetiapine), Geodon (ziprasidone), Abilify (aripiprazole), and Invega (paliperidone). The drugs reduce hallucinations and disordered thinking in people with schizophrenia, bipolar disorder, and delirium, and they have a calming effect on agitated patients.

4. *Anxiolytics (antianxiety agents) and hypnotics (sleeping pills):* One of the largest and most prescribed classes of anxiolytics is the benzodiazepines, a group of drugs that includes Valium (diazepam), Librium (chlordiazepoxide), Xanax (alprazolam), and Ativan (lorazepam); Dalmane (flurazepam), Restoril (temazepam), and Halcion (triazolam) are benzodiazepines marketed as sleeping aids. Newer hypnotics are Sonata (zaleplon), Ambien (zolpidem), Lunesta (eszopiclone), and Rozerem (ramelteon).

5. *Stimulants:* Ritalin (methylphenidate) and Dexedrine (dextroamphetamine) are most commonly used for **attention-deficit/hyperactivity disorder (ADHD)** in children and less often in adults. Drugs of this type are also marketed under the names Adderall, Strattera, and Concerta. They are also used for daytime sleepiness in adults, as are purified caffeine (for example, No-Doz) and Provigil (modafinil).

6. *Anti-dementia drugs:* Dementia is an impairment in memory and thinking that occurs almost exclusively in the elderly. The most common type is Alzheimer's disease (see Chapter 22). Many people with this problem are now prescribed Aricept (donepezil) or Namenda (memantine). Other anti-dementia drugs are Exelon (rivastigmine) and Razadyne (galantamine).

Issues in the Use of Pharmacological Therapy   The discovery that many psychological disorders have a biological basis in disordered brain chemistry has led to a revolution in the treatment of many disorders, particularly depression. The new view of depression as based in brain chemistry has also lessened the stigma attached to the condition, leading more people to seek treatment, and antidepressants are now among the most widely prescribed drugs in the United States. The development of effective drugs has provided relief for many people, but

Behavioral therapy can help people overcome many kinds of fears, improving their quality of life.

To change their behavior, fearful people are taught to practice **exposure**—to deliberately and repeatedly enter the feared situation and remain in it until their fear begins to abate. A student who is afraid to speak in class might begin his behavioral therapy program by keeping a diary listing each time he makes a contribution to a classroom discussion, how long he speaks, and his anxiety levels before, during, and after speaking. He would then develop concrete but realistic goals for increasing his speaking frequency and contract with himself to reward his successes by spending more time in activities he finds enjoyable. This approach is much like the general behavior change strategy described in Chapter 1.

Although exposure to the real situation works best, exposure in one's imagination or through the virtual reality of computer simulation can also be effective. For example, in the case of someone afraid of flying, an imagined scenario would likely be vivid enough to elicit the fear necessary to practice exposure techniques.

the wide use of antidepressants has also raised many questions (see the box "Antidepressant Use in Young People" on p. 86).

Research indicates that for mild cases of depression, psychotherapy and antidepressants are about equally effective. For major depression, combined therapy is significantly more effective than either type of treatment alone. Therapy can help provide insight into factors that precipitated the depression, such as high levels of stress or a history of abuse. A therapist can also provide guidance in changing patterns of thinking and behavior that contribute to the problem.

The Behavioral Model

The *behavioral model* focuses on what people do—their overt behavior—rather than on brain structures and chemistry or on thoughts and consciousness. This model regards psychological problems as "maladaptive behavior" or bad habits. When and how a person learned maladaptive behavior is less important than what makes it continue in the present.

Behaviorists analyze behavior in terms of **stimulus, response,** and **reinforcement.** The essence of behavior therapy is to discover what reinforcements keep an undesirable behavior going and then to try to alter those reinforcements. For example, if people who fear speaking in class (the stimulus) remove themselves from that situation (the response), they experience immediate relief, which acts as reinforcement for future avoidance and escape.

The Cognitive Model

The *cognitive model* emphasizes the effect of ideas on behavior and feeling. According to this model, behavior results from complicated attitudes, expectations, and motives rather than from simple, immediate reinforcements. When behavioral therapies such as exposure work, it is because they change the way a person thinks about the feared situation and his or her ability to cope with it.

Cognitive therapy tries to expose and identify false ideas that produce feelings such as anxiety and depression. For example, a student afraid of speaking in class may harbor thoughts such as "If I begin to speak, I'll say something stupid; if I say something stupid, the teacher and my classmates will lose respect for me; then I'll get a low grade, my classmates will avoid me, and life will be hell." In cognitive therapy, these ideas will be examined

TERMS

stimulus Anything that causes a response.

response A reaction to a stimulus.

reinforcement Increasing the future probability of a response by following it with a reward.

exposure A therapeutic technique for treating fear in which the subject learns to come into direct contact with a feared situation.

Antidepressant Use in Young People

connect™

Effectiveness

Drug treatment for depression is part of a success story in which people take seriously symptoms of depression and hints of suicidal thinking in children and teens. Over the past decade, the suicide rate among adolescents has fallen. Many factors have contributed to the decline, including stricter gun laws that make it harder for young people to get guns. Drug treatment has also been considered a key factor in the decline in suicide rates.

A 2005 review of reported childhood depression cases showed that between 1995 and 2002 the number of pediatric psychotherapy sessions declined significantly while prescriptions for antidepressants rose. Most of those prescriptions were for drugs that had not been approved for use in children. To date, only one drug—fluoxetine (Prozac)—has been approved for use specifically in children and teens. Studies have found that fluoxetine causes a greater improvement than a placebo, but the combination of drug therapy and cognitive-behavioral therapy is more beneficial than either treatment alone. The placebo effect, in which people improve while taking pills containing inactive compounds, is significant in studies of depression and can exceed 30%—meaning almost a third of people receiving a placebo experience an improvement in their symptoms.

Many antidepressants other than fluoxetine, especially other SSRIs, are also prescribed to young people, but these other drugs haven't been shown to be effective for that age group. Unpublished research data indicates that some SSRIs are *not* effective in children and teens or are only slightly more effective than a placebo.

Safety

The problem associated with SSRIs is the possibility that they increase the risk of suicide in some young people, particularly in the period immediately following the start of medication use. When study results were pooled, researchers found that in the short term, about 2–3% of users have an increased risk of suicidal thoughts and actions beyond the risk inherent from depression itself.

Researchers aren't exactly sure what causes this effect. One theory is that SSRIs reverse the lethargy associated with depression more quickly than they relieve the depression itself, giving users the energy to contemplate suicide in the interim. Antidepressants may work differently on the brains of young people than on the brains of adults, so there may be as yet unidentified effects.

In October 2004, the FDA published a public health advisory about using antidepressants in children and teens. It emphasizes that young people who take antidepressants should be monitored closely, especially when starting a new medication or changing the dosage of a drug. The FDA told manufacturers to revise the labeling of their products to include a boxed warning and expanded warning statements.

Depression is a serious illness that can increase the risk of suicide, and mental health professionals and patients must balance the risks of doing nothing against the potential risks and benefits of different types of treatments. These points were emphasized by the American Academy of Child and Adolescent Psychiatry in response to the FDA advisory.

The result of the FDA advisory was a reduction of more than 20% in the number of SSRI prescriptions for this age group. Along with this reduction in prescriptions was a 15% increase in the group's suicide rate. An advisory about antidepressants in children and adolescents was issued in the Netherlands at

about the same time, with the same result: SSRI prescriptions dropped but the suicide rate increased. These statistics do not prove a cause-effect relationship but certainly are a reason for concern. For some young people, psychological treatment for depression may not have been a practical alternative to medication, because it was not available or not accepted.

SOURCES: Gibbons, R. D. 2007. Early evidence on the effects of regulators' suicidality warnings on SSRI prescriptions and suicide in children and adolescents. *American Journal of Psychiatry* 164(9): 1356–1363; Newman, T. B. 2004. Treating depression in children: A black-box warning for antidepressants in children? *New England Journal of Medicine* 351(16): 1595–1598; Brent, D. A. 2004. Treating depression in children: Antidepressants and pediatric depression—the risk of doing nothing. *New England Journal of Medicine* 351(16): 1598–1601; Treatment for Adolescents with Depression Study (TADS) Team. 2004. Fluoxetine, cognitive-behavioral therapy, and their combination for adolescents with depression. *Journal of the American Medical Association* 292(7): 807–820; Stafford, R. S., et al. 2005. Depression treatment during outpatient visits by U.S. children and adolescents. *Journal of Adolescent Health* 37(6): 434–442.

critically. If the student prepares, will he or she really sound stupid? Does every sentence said have to be exactly correct and beautifully delivered, or is that an unrealistic expectation? Will classmates' opinions be completely transformed by one presentation? Do classmates even care that much? And why does the student care so much about what *they* think? People in cognitive therapy are taught to notice their unrealistic thoughts and to substitute more realistic ones, and they are advised to repeatedly test their assumptions.

The Psychodynamic Model

The *psychodynamic model* also emphasizes thoughts. Proponents of this model, however, do not believe thoughts can be changed directly because they are fed by other unconscious ideas and impulses. Symptoms are not isolated pieces of behavior but the result of a complex set of wishes and emotions hidden by active defenses (see Table 3.2). In psychodynamic therapy, patients speak as freely as possible in front of the therapist and try to gain an understanding of the basis of their feelings toward the therapist and others. Through this process, patients gain insights that allow them to overcome their maladaptive behavior. Current therapies of this type tend to focus more on the present (the here and now) than on the past, and the therapist tries to facilitate self-exploration rather than providing explanations.

Evaluating the Models

Ignoring theoretical conflicts among psychological models, therapists have recently developed pragmatic *cognitive-behavioral therapies* that combine effective elements of both models in a single package. For example, the package for treating social anxiety emphasizes exposure as well as changing problematic patterns of thinking. Combined therapies have also been developed for panic disorder, obsessive-compulsive disorder, generalized anxiety disorder, and depression. These packages, involving ten or more individual or group sessions with a therapist and homework between sessions, have been shown to produce significant improvement.

Drug therapy and cognitive-behavioral therapies are also sometimes combined, especially in the case of depression. For anxiety disorders, both kinds of therapy are equally effective, but the effects of drug therapy last only as long as the drug is being taken, while cognitive-behavioral therapies produce longer-term improvement. For schizophrenia, drug therapy is a must, but a continuing relationship with therapists who give support and advice is also indispensable.

Psychodynamic therapies have been attacked as ineffective and endless. Of course, effectiveness is hard to demonstrate for therapies that do not focus on specific symptoms. But common sense tells us that being able to open yourself up and discuss your problems with a supportive but objective person who focuses on you and lets you speak freely can enhance your sense of self and reduce feelings of confusion and despair.

GETTING HELP

Knowing when self-help or professional help is required for mental health problems is usually not as difficult as knowing how to start or which professional to choose.

Self-Help

If you have a personal problem to solve, a smart way to begin is by finding out what you can do on your own. Some problems are specifically addressed in this book. Behavioral and some cognitive approaches are especially useful for helping yourself. They all involve becoming more aware of self-defeating actions and ideas and combating them in some way: by being more assertive; by communicating honestly; by raising your self-esteem by counteracting negative thoughts, people, and actions that undermine it; and by

Group therapy is just one of many different approaches to psychological counseling.

QUESTIONS FOR CRITICAL THINKING AND REFLECTION

Are you open to discussing the intimate details of your life, your emotions, your fears, your deepest thoughts? Have you ever truly opened up to another person in this manner? Would you be more open to this kind of sharing if it meant getting help for a psychological disorder?

Choosing and Evaluating Mental Health Professionals

College students are usually in a good position to find convenient, affordable mental health care. Larger schools typically have both health services that employ psychiatrists and psychologists and counseling centers staffed by professionals and student peer counselors. Resources in the community may include a school of medicine, a hospital, and a variety of professionals who work independently. Although independent practitioners are listed in the telephone book, it's a good idea to get recommendations from physicians, clergy, friends who have been in therapy, or community agencies rather than pick a name at random.

Financial considerations are also important. Find out how much different services will cost and what your health insurance will cover. If you're not adequately covered by a health plan, don't let that stop you from getting help; investigate low-cost alternatives. City, county, and state governments often support mental health clinics for those who can afford to pay little or nothing for treatment. Some on-campus services may be free or offered at very little cost.

The cost of treatment is linked to how many therapy sessions will be needed, which in turn depends on the type of therapy and the nature of the problem. Psychological therapies focusing on specific problems may require eight or ten sessions at weekly intervals. Therapies aiming for psychological awareness and personality change can last months or years.

Deciding whether a therapist is right for you will require meeting the therapist in person. Before or during your first meeting, find out about the therapist's background and training:

• Does she or he have a degree from an appropriate professional school and a state license to practice?

• Has she or he had experience treating people with problems similar to yours?

• How much will therapy cost?

You have a right to know the answers to these questions and should not hesitate to ask them. After your initial meeting, evaluate your impressions:

• Does the therapist seem like a warm, intelligent person who would be able to help you and interested in doing so?

• Are you comfortable with the personality, values, and beliefs of the therapist?

• Is he or she willing to talk about the techniques in use? Do these techniques make sense to you?

If you answer yes to these questions, this therapist may be satisfactory for you. If you feel uncomfortable—and you're not in need of emergency care—it's worthwhile to set up one-time consultations with one or two others before you make up your mind. Take the time to find someone who feels right for you.

Later in your treatment, evaluate your progress:

• Are you being helped by the treatment?

• If you are displeased, is it because you aren't making progress, or because therapy is raising difficult, painful issues you don't want to deal with?

• Can you express dissatisfaction to your therapist? Such feedback can improve your treatment.

If you're convinced your therapy isn't working or is harmful, thank your therapist for her or his efforts, and find another.

---

confronting, rather than avoiding, the things you fear. Get more information by seeing what books are available in the psychology or self-help sections of libraries and bookstores, but be selective. Watch out for self-help books making fantastic claims that deviate from mainstream approaches.

Some people find it helpful to express their feelings in a journal. Grappling with a painful experience in this way provides an emotional release and can help you develop more constructive ways of dealing with similar situations in the future. Research indicates that using a journal this way can improve physical as well as emotional wellness.

For some people, religious belief and practice may promote psychological health. Religious organizations provide a social network and a supportive community, and religious practices, such as prayer and meditation, offer a path for personal change and transformation.

Peer Counseling and Support Groups

Sharing your concerns with others is another helpful way of dealing with psychological health challenges. Just being able to share what's troubling you with an accepting, empathetic person can bring relief. Comparing notes with people who have problems similar to yours can give you new ideas about coping.

Many colleges offer peer counseling through a health center or through the psychology or education department. Peer counseling is usually done by volunteer students who have received special training that emphasizes confidentiality. Peer counselors may steer you toward an appropriate campus or community resource or simply offer a sympathetic ear.

Many self-help groups work on the principle of bringing together people with similar problems to share their experiences and support one another. Support groups are typically organized around a specific problem, such as eating disorders or substance abuse. Self-help groups may be listed in the phone book or the campus newspaper.

Professional Help

Sometimes self-help or talking to nonprofessionals is not enough. More objective, more expert, or more discreet help is needed. Many people have trouble accepting the need for professional help, and often those who most need help are the most unwilling to get it. You may someday find yourself having to overcome your own reluctance, or that of a friend, about seeking help.

Determining the Need for Professional Help In some cases, professional help is optional. Some people are interested in improving their psychological health in a general way by going into individual or group therapy to learn more about themselves and how to interact with others. Clearly, seeking professional help for these reasons is a matter of individual choice. In some situations, such as friction among family members or between partners, professional help can mean the difference between a painful divorce and a satisfying relationship.

Following are some strong indications that you or someone you know needs professional help:

- If depression, anxiety, or other emotional problems begin to interfere seriously with school or work performance or in getting along with others
- If suicide is attempted or is seriously considered (refer to the warning signs earlier in the chapter)
- If symptoms such as hallucinations, delusions, incoherent speech, or loss of memory occur
- If alcohol or drugs are used to the extent that they impair normal functioning during much of the week, if finding or taking drugs occupies much of the week, or if reducing their dosage leads to psychological or physiological withdrawal symptoms

Choosing a Mental Health Professional

Mental health workers belong to several different professions and have different roles. Psychiatrists are medical doctors. They are experts in deciding whether a medical disease lies behind psychological symptoms, and they are usually involved in treatment if medication or hospitalization is required. Clinical psychologists typically hold a Ph.D. degree; they are often experts in behavioral and cognitive therapies. Other mental health workers include

social workers, licensed counselors, and clergy with special training in pastoral counseling. In hospitals and clinics, various mental health professionals may join together in treatment teams.

For more on finding appropriate help, see the box "Choosing and Evaluating Mental Health Professionals."

SUMMARY

- Psychological health encompasses more than a single particular state of normality. Psychological diversity is valuable among groups of people.

- Defining psychological health as the presence of wellness means that to be healthy you must strive to fulfill your potential.

- Maslow's definition of psychological health centered on self-actualization, the highest level in his hierarchy of needs. Self-actualized people have high self-esteem and are realistic, inner-directed, authentic, capable of emotional intimacy, and creative.

- Crucial parts of psychological wellness include developing an adult identity, establishing intimate relationships, and developing values and purpose in life.

Dealing with Social Anxiety

Shyness is often the result of both high anxiety levels and lack of key social skills. To help overcome shyness, you need to learn to manage your fear of social situations and to develop social skills such as appropriate eye contact, initiating topics in conversations, and maintaining the flow of conversations by asking questions and making appropriate responses.

As described in the chapter, repeated *exposure* to the source of one's fear—in this case, social situations—is the best method for reducing anxiety. When you practice new behaviors, they gradually become easier and you experience less anxiety.

A counterproductive strategy is avoiding situations that make you anxious. Although this approach works in the short term—you eliminate your anxiety because you escape the situation—it keeps you from meeting new people and having new experiences. Another counterproductive strategy is self-medicating with alcohol or drugs. Being under their influence actually prevents you from learning new social skills and new ways to handle your anxiety.

To reduce your anxiety in social situations, try some of the following strategies:

- Remember that physical stress reactions are short-term responses to fear. Don't dwell on them—remind yourself that they will pass, and they will.

- Refocus your attention away from the stress reaction you're experiencing and toward the social task at hand. Your nervousness is much less visible than you think.

- Allow a warm-up period for new situations. Realize that you will feel more nervous at first, and take steps to relax and become more comfortable. Refer to the suggestions for deep breathing and other relaxation techniques in Chapter 2.

- If possible, take breaks during anxiety-producing situations. For example, if you're at a party, take a moment to visit the restroom or step outside. Alternate between speaking with good friends and striking up conversations with new acquaintances.

- Watch your interpretations; having a stress reaction doesn't mean that you don't belong in the group, that you're unattractive or unworthy, or that the situation is too much for you. Try thinking of yourself as excited or highly alert instead of anxious.

- Avoid cognitive distortions and practice realistic self-talk. Replace your self-critical thoughts with more supportive ones: "No one else is perfect, and I don't have to be either." "It would have been good if I had a funny story to tell, but the conversation was interesting anyway."

- Give yourself a reality check: Ask if you're really in a life-threatening situation (or just at a party), if the outcome you're imagining is really likely (or the worst thing that could possibly happen), or if you're the only one who feels nervous (or if many other people might feel the same way).

- Don't think of conversations as evaluations; remind yourself that you don't have to prove yourself with every social interaction. And remember that most people are thinking more about themselves than they are about you.

Starting and maintaining conversations can be difficult for shy people, who may feel overwhelmed by their physical stress reaction. If small talk is a problem for you, try the following strategies:

- Introduce yourself early in the conversation. If you tend to forget names, repeat your new acquaintance's name to help fix it in your mind ("Nice to meet you, Amelia").

- Ask questions, and look for shared topics of interest. Simple, open-ended questions like "How's your presentation coming along?" or "How do you know our host?" encourage others to carry the conversation for a while and help bring forth a variety of subjects.

- Take turns talking, and elaborate on your answers. Simple yes and no answers don't move the conversation along. Try to relate something in your life—a course you're taking or a hobby you have—to something in the other person's life. Match self-disclosure with self-disclosure.

- Have something to say. Expand your mind and become knowledgeable about current events and local or campus news. If you have specialized knowledge about a topic, practice discussing it in ways that both beginners and experts can understand and appreciate.

- If you get stuck for something to say, try giving a compliment ("Great presentation!" or "I love your earrings.") or performing a social grace (pass the chips or get someone a drink).

- Be an active listener. Reward the other person with your full attention and with regular responses. Make frequent eye contact and maintain a relaxed but alert posture. (See Chapter 4 for more on being an active listener.)

At first, your new behaviors will likely make you anxious. Don't give up—things *will* get easier. Create lots of opportunities to practice your new behaviors; your goal is to make them routine activities. For example, striking up a conversation with someone in a registration or movie line can help you practice your small-talk skills in a nonthreatening setting. Once you are comfortable doing that, you might try initiating brief conversations with classmates about academic topics—the upcoming midterm, for example, or an assignment. Following that, you might try something more challenging, such as discussing a more personal topic or meeting new people in a social setting.

Regular practice and stress-management skills are critical. Using these techniques, you can increase your social skills and confidence level at the same time that you decrease your anxiety. Eventually, you'll be able to sustain social interactions with comfort and enjoyment. If you find that social anxiety is a major problem for you and self-help techniques don't seem to work, consider looking into a shyness clinic or treatment program on your campus.

SOURCES: University of Texas at Dallas, Student Counseling Center. 2008 Update. *Self-Help: Overcoming Social Anxiety* (http://www.utdallas.edu/counseling/selfhelp/social-anxiety.html; retrieved December 29, 2008); Carducci, B. J. 2000. *Shyness: A Bold New Approach.* New York: Harper Paperbacks.

- A sense of self-esteem develops during childhood as a result of giving and receiving love and learning to accomplish goals. Self-concept is challenged every day; healthy people adjust their goals to their abilities.

- Using defense mechanisms to cope with problems can make finding solutions harder. Analyzing thoughts and behavior can help people develop less defensive and more effective ways of coping.

- A pessimistic outlook can be damaging; it can be overcome by developing more realistic self-talk.

- Honest communication requires recognizing what needs to be said and saying it clearly. Assertiveness enables people to insist on their rights and to participate in the give-and-take of good communication.

- People may be lonely if they haven't developed ways to be happy on their own or if they interpret being alone as a sign of rejection. Lonely people can take action to expand their social contacts.

- Dealing successfully with anger involves distinguishing between a reasonable level of assertiveness and gratuitous expressions of anger, heading off rage by reframing thoughts and distracting oneself, and responding to the anger of others with an asymmetrical, problem-solving orientation.

- People with psychological disorders have symptoms severe enough to interfere with daily living.

- Anxiety is a fear that is not directed toward any definite threat. Anxiety disorders include simple phobias, social phobias, panic disorder, generalized anxiety disorder, obsessive-compulsive disorder, and post-traumatic stress disorder.

- Depression is a common mood disorder; loss of interest or pleasure in things seems to be its most universal symptom. Severe depression carries a high risk of suicide, and suicidally depressed people need professional help.

- Symptoms of mania include exalted moods with unrealistically high self-esteem, little need for sleep, and rapid speech. Mood swings between mania and depression characterize bipolar disorder.

- Schizophrenia is characterized by disorganized thoughts, inappropriate emotions, delusions, auditory hallucinations, and deteriorating social and work performance.

- The biological model emphasizes that the mind's activity depends on the brain, whose composition is genetically determined. Therapy based on the biological model is primarily pharmacological.

- The behavioral model focuses on overt behavior and treats psychological problems as bad habits. Behavior change is the focus of therapy.

- The cognitive model considers how ideas affect behavior and feelings; behavior results from complicated attitudes, expectations, and motives, not just from simple reinforcements. Cognitive therapy focuses on changing a person's thinking.

- The psychodynamic model asserts that false ideas are fed by unconscious ideas and cannot be addressed directly. Treatment is based on psychotherapy.

- Help is available in a variety of forms, including self-help, peer counseling, support groups, and therapy with a mental health professional. For serious problems, professional help may be the most appropriate.

FOR MORE INFORMATION

BOOKS

Antony, M. M. 2008. *The Shyness & Social Anxiety Workbook: Proven, Step-by-Step Techniques for Overcoming Your Fear,* 2nd ed. Oakland, Calif.: New Harbinger. *Practical suggestions for fears of interacting with people you don't know.*

Grieco, R. 2009. *The Other Depression: Bipolar Disorder.* New York: Routledge. *Provides a complete introduction to bipolar disorder, its symptoms, and its current treatments.*

Jenkins, J., D. Keltner, and K. Oatley. 2006. *Understanding Emotions.* 2nd ed. Oxford: Blackwell. *A comprehensive guide to emotions, including current research on the neuroscience of emotions, evolutionary and cultural approaches to emotion, and the expression and communication of emotions.*

Nathan, P. E., and J. M. Gorman. 2007. *A Guide to Treatments That Work,* 3rd ed. New York: Oxford University Press. *A balanced and comprehensive report on various treatments for psychological disorders.*

Seligman, M. E. 2006. *Learned Optimism: How to Change Your Mind and Your Life* (Vintage Reprint Edition). New York: Vintage. *Introduces methods for overcoming feelings of helplessness and building a positive self-image that can contribute to emotional well-being.*

Thase, M. E., and S. S. Lang. 2006. *Beating the Blues: New Approaches to Overcoming Dysthymia and Chronic Mild Depression.* New York: Oxford University Press. *Describes strategies for changing negative thinking patterns that lead to discouragement and pessimism; also discusses newer medications and alternative therapies.*

ORGANIZATIONS, HOTLINES, AND WEB SITES

American Association of Suicidology. Provides information about suicide and resources for people in crisis.
    http://www.suicidology.org
Anxiety Disorders Association of America (ADAA). Provides information and resources related to anxiety disorders.
    http://www.adaa.org
Depression and Bipolar Support Alliance (DBSA). Provides educational materials and information about support groups.
    http://www.dbsalliance.org
Internet Mental Health. An encyclopedia of mental health information, including medical diagnostic criteria.
    http://www.mentalhealth.com
MindZone. Offers information on mental health issues specifically for teens.
    http://www.copecaredeal.org

NAMI (National Alliance on Mental Illness). Provides information and support for people affected by mental illness.

> 800-950-NAMI (Help Line)
>
> http://www.nami.org

National Hopeline Network. 24-hour hotline for people who are thinking about suicide or know someone who is; calls are routed to local crisis centers.

> 800-SUICIDE
>
> http://www.hopeline.com

National Institute of Mental Health (NIMH). Provides helpful information about anxiety, depression, eating disorders, and other challenges to psychological health.

> http://www.nimh.nih.gov

Mental Health America. Provides consumer information on a variety of issues, including how to find help.

> http://www.nmha.org

National Mental Health Information Center. A one-stop source for information and resources relating to mental health.

> http://www.mentalhealth.org

SELECTED BIBLIOGRAPHY

Adams, R. E., and J. A. Boscarino. 2006. Predictors of PTSD and delayed PTSD after disaster: The impact of exposure and psychosocial resources. *The Journal of Nervous and Mental Disease* 194(7): 485–493.

Agency for Healthcare Research and Quality. 2007. *Newer Class of Antidepressants Similar in Effectiveness, but Side Effects Differ* (http://www.ahrq.gov/news/press/pr2007/antideppr.htm; retrieved December 29, 2008).

American Psychiatric Association. 2000. *Diagnostic and Statistical Manual of Mental Disorders,* 4th ed., Text Revision *(DSM-IV-TR).* Washington, D.C.: American Psychiatric Association Press.

American Psychiatric Association. 2005. *College Mental Health Statistics* (http://www.healthyminds.org/collegestats.cfm; retrieved December 29, 2008).

Antidepressants for children and adolescents: An update. 2006. *Harvard Mental Health Letter* 22(12): 4–5.

Avagianou, P. A., and M. Zafiropoulou. 2008. Parental bonding and depression: Personality as a mediating factor. *International Journal of Adolescent Medicine & Health* 20(3): 261–269.

Brenes, G. A., 2006. Age differences in the presentation of anxiety. *Aging and Mental Health* 10(3): 298–302.

Coryell, W. H. 2006. Clinical assessment of suicide risk in depressive disorder. *CNS Spectrums* 11(6): 455–461.

Eranti, S., et al. 2007. A randomized, controlled trial with 6-month follow-up of repetitive transcranial magnetic stimulation and electroconvulsive therapy for severe depression. *American Journal of Psychiatry* 164(1): 73–81.

Favaro, A., et al. 2007. Self-injurious behavior in a community sample of young women: Relationship with childhood abuse and other types of self-damaging behaviors. *Journal of Clinical Psychiatry* 68(1): 122–131.

Fazel, S., and M. Grann. 2006. The population impact of severe mental illness on violent crime. *American Journal of Psychiatry* 163(8): 1397–1403.

Food and Drug Administration. 2005. Safeguards for children taking antidepressants strengthened. *FDA Consumer,* January/February.

Forty, L., et al. 2009. Polarity at illness onset in bipolar I disorder and clinical course of illness. *Bipolar Disorders* 11(1): 82–88.

Gunnell, D., P. K. Magnusson, and F. Rasmussen. 2005. Low intelligence test scores in 18-year-old men and risk of suicide: Cohort study. *British Medical Journal* 330(7484): 167.

Hamilton, B. E., et al. 2007. Annual Summary of Vital Statistics: 2005. *Pediatrics* 119(2): 345–360.

Hettema, J. M., et al. 2006. A population-based twin study of the relationship between neuroticism and internalizing disorders. *American Journal of Psychiatry* 163(5): 857–864.

Jones, S. H., and G. Burrell-Hodgson. 2008. Cognitive-behavioral treatment of first diagnosis bipolar disorder. *Clinical Psychology & Psychotherapy* 15(6): 367–377.

Kasper, S., et al. 2006. Superior efficacy of St. John's wort extract WS(R) 5570 compared to placebo in patients with major depression: A randomized, double-blind, placebo-controlled, multi-center trial. *BMC Medicine* 4(1): 14.

Kendler, K. S., J. Myers, and C. A. Prescott. 2005. Sex differences in the relationship between social support and risk for major depression: A longitudinal study of opposite-sex twin pairs. *American Journal of Psychiatry* 162(2): 250–256.

Licinio, J., and M. L. Wong. 2005. Opinion: Depression, antidepressants and suicidality: A critical appraisal. *Nature Reviews: Drug Discovery* 4(2): 165–171.

Lin, Y. R., et al. 2008. Evaluation of assertiveness training for psychiatric patients. *Journal of Clinical Nursing* 17(21): 2875–2883.

McGirr, A., et al. 2006. An examination of DSM-IV depressive symptoms and risk for suicide completion in major depressive disorder: A psychological autopsy study. *Journal of Affective Disorders,* 17 July.

Nemeroff, C. B. 2006. The burden of severe depression: A review of diagnostic challenges and treatment alternatives. *Journal of Psychiatric Research,* 25 July [Epub ahead of print].

Ozer, D. J., and V. Benet-Martinez. 2006. Personality and prediction of consequential outcomes. *Annual Review of Psychology* 57: 401–421.

Rothwell, J. D. 2009. *In the Company of Others: An Introduction to Communication,* 3rd ed. New York: McGraw-Hill.

Saewyc, E. M., and R. Tonkin. 2008. Surveying adolescents: Focusing on positive development. *Pediatrics & Child Health* 13(1): 43–47.

Schatzberg, A. F., J. O. Cole, and C. DeBattista. 2007. *Manual of Clinical Psychopharmacology,* 6th ed. Washington, D.C.: American Psychiatric Publishing.

Simon, G. E., and J. Savarino. 2007. Suicide attempts among patients starting depression treatment with medications or psychotherapy. *American Journal of Psychiatry* 164(7): 1029–1034.

Simon, G. 2009. Collaborative care for mood disorders. *Current Opinion in Psychiatry.* 22(1): 37–41.

Singh, N. N., et al. 2007. Individuals with mental illness can control their aggressive behavior through mindfulness training. *Behavior Modification* 31(3): 313–328.

Verhaak, P. F., et al. 2009. Receiving treatment for common mental disorders. *General Hospital Psychiatry* 31(1): 46–55.

Williams, D., et al. 2007. Prevalence and distribution of major depressive disorder in African Americans, Caribbean blacks, and non-Hispanic whites. *Archives of General Psychiatry* 64: 305–315.

Zarit, S. H., and J. M. Zarit. 2006. *Mental Disorders in Older Adults: Fundamentals of Assessment and Treatment,* 2nd ed. New York: Guilford Press.

CORE CONCEPTS IN HEALTH

connect™

PERSONAL HEALTH

http://www.mcgrawhillconnect.com/personalhealth

INTIMATE RELATIONSHIPS AND COMMUNICATION

4

LOOKING AHEAD>>>>>

AFTER READING THIS CHAPTER, YOU SHOULD BE ABLE TO:

- Explain the qualities that help people develop intimate relationships
- Describe different types of love relationships and the stages they often go through
- Identify common challenges of forming and maintaining intimate relationships
- Explain some elements of healthy and productive communication
- List some characteristics of successful families and some potential problems families face

TEST YOUR KNOWLEDGE

1. **What percentage of Americans report having no one they want to confide in?**
   a. 10%
   b. 15%
   c. 25%

2. **In a typical long-term intimate relationship, commitment tends to increase over time.**
   True or false?

3. **Jealousy is a good indicator of what?**
   a. Love
   b. Insecurity
   c. Passion

4. **What percentage of American children live in a single-parent home?**
   a. 2.8%
   b. 8%
   c. 28%

ANSWERS

1. **C.** Nearly one-quarter of Americans say they don't have a friend with whom they share intimate thoughts. The average American's circle of close friends has steadily shrunk over the last two decades.

2. **TRUE.** Although passion and physical attraction tend to decline over time, most couples become increasingly committed to their relationship as time goes by.

3. **B.** Some people think that the existence of jealousy proves the existence of love, but jealousy is actually a more accurate yardstick for measuring insecurity or possessiveness. Jealousy can destroy a relationship.

4. **C.** More than one-quarter of American children live with a single parent. In 2007, 23% of children lived with their mother, while about 5% lived with their father.

Human beings need social relationships; we cannot thrive as solitary creatures. Nor could the human species survive if adults didn't cherish and support each other, if we didn't form strong mutual attachments with our infants, and if we didn't create families in which to raise children. Simply put, people need people.

Although people are held together in relationships by a variety of factors, the foundation of many relationships is the ability to both give and receive love. Love in its many forms—romantic, passionate, platonic, parental—is the wellspring from which much of life's meaning and delight flows. In our culture, it binds us together as partners, parents, children, and friends.

Just as important, we also need to develop a healthy relationship to ourselves, which includes the ability to self-soothe, to regulate our emotions, and to be alone with ourselves at times.

DEVELOPING INTIMATE RELATIONSHIPS

People who develop successful intimate relationships believe in themselves and in the people around them. They are willing to give of themselves—to share their ideas, feelings, time, needs—and to accept what others want to give them.

Self-Concept and Self-Esteem

The principal element that we all bring to our relationships is our *selves*. To have successful relationships, we must first accept and feel good about ourselves. A positive self-concept and a healthy level of self-esteem help us love and respect others.

As discussed in Chapter 3, the roots of our identity and sense of self can be found in childhood, in the relationships we had with our parents and other family members. As adults, we probably have a sense that we're basically lovable, worthwhile people and that we can trust others if, as babies and children, we experienced the following:

- We felt loved, valued, and respected.
- Adults responded to our needs in a reasonably appropriate way.
- They gave us the freedom to explore and develop a sense of being separate individuals.

Gender Role Another thing we learn in early childhood is *gender role*—the activities, abilities, and characteristics our culture deems appropriate for us based on whether we're male or female. In our society, men have traditionally been expected to work and provide for their families; to be aggressive, competitive, and power-oriented; and to use thinking and logic to solve problems. Women have been expected to take care of home and children; to be cooperative, supportive, and nurturing; and to approach life emotionally and intuitively. Although much more egalitarian gender roles are emerging in our society, the stereotypes we absorb in childhood tend to be deeply ingrained.

Attachment Our ways of relating to others are also rooted in childhood. Some researchers have suggested that our adult styles of loving may be based on the style of **attachment** we established in infancy with our mother, father, siblings, or other primary caregiver. According to this view, people who are secure in their intimate relationships probably had a secure, trusting, mutually satisfying attachment to their mother, father, or other parenting figure. As adults, they find it relatively easy to get close to others. They don't worry about being abandoned or having someone get too close to them. They feel that other people like them and are generally well-intentioned.

People who are clinging and dependent in their relationships may have had an "anxious/ambivalent" attachment, in which a parent's inconsistent responses made them unsure that their needs would be met. As adults, they worry about whether their partners really love them and will stay with them. They tend to feel that others don't want to get as close as they do. They want to merge completely with another person, which sometimes scares others away.

People who seem to run from relationships may have had an "anxious/avoidant" attachment, in which a parent's inappropriate responses made them want to escape from his or her sphere of influence. As adults, they feel uncomfortable being close to others. They're distrustful and fearful of becoming dependent. Their partners usually want more intimacy than they do.

Even if people's earliest experiences and relationships were less than ideal, however, they can still establish satisfying relationships in adulthood. In fact, relationships in adolescence and adulthood give us a golden opportunity to work on and through unresolved issues and conflicts from the past. After all, very few people have perfect parents and perfect siblings, and no one grows up without experiencing some sort of personal pain and conflict.

People can be resilient and flexible. They have the capacity to change their ideas, beliefs, and behavior patterns. They can learn ways to raise their self-esteem; they can become more trusting, accepting, and appreciative of others; and they can acquire the communication and conflict-resolution skills required for maintaining successful relationships. Although it helps to have a good start in life, it

TERMS

attachment The emotional tie between an infant and his or her caregiver or between two people in an intimate relationship.

Being a Good Friend

How to Make Friends

• Find people with interests similar to your own. Join a club, participate in sports, do volunteer work, or join a discussion group to meet people with common interests.

• Be a good listener. Take a genuine interest in people. Solicit their opinions, and take time to listen to their problems and ideas.

• Take risks. If you meet someone interesting, ask him or her to join you for a meal or an event you would both enjoy.

How to Be a Good Friend

• Be trustworthy. Honor all confidences, and don't talk about your friend behind his or her back.

• Tell your friend about yourself. Self-disclosure—letting your friend know about your real concerns and joys—signals trust.

• Be supportive and kind. Be there when your friend is going through a rough time. Don't criticize your friend or offer unsolicited advice.

• Develop your capacity for intimacy. Intimate relationships are genuine, spontaneous, and caring.

• Don't expect perfection. Like any relationship, your friendship may go through difficult times. Talk through conflicts as they arise.

• Don't brag or boast excessively.

• Share past experiences, difficulties, and successes.

• Be altruistic; that is, be generous without expecting anything in return.

---

may be even more important to begin again, right from where you are. Most important is to be accepting and kind to ourselves as we are in the present and do our best to grow and develop emotionally.

Friendship

The first relationships we form outside the family are friendships. The friendships we form in childhood are important in our development; through them we learn about tolerance, sharing, and trust. Friendships usually include most or all of the following characteristics:

• *Companionship.* Friends are usually relaxed and happy in each other's company. They typically have common values and interests and make plans to spend time together. But real friends are also able to be tense and unhappy with each other. Unlike fair-weather friends, we need to be able to support others as we would want support from them, even on bad days.

• *Respect.* Friends have a basic respect for each other's humanity and individuality. Good friends respect each other's feelings and opinions and work to resolve their differences without demeaning or insulting each other. They also show their respect by being honest with each other (see the box "Being a Good Friend").

• *Acceptance.* Friends accept each other, "warts and all." They feel free to be themselves and express their feelings without fear of ridicule or criticism.

• *Help.* Sharing time, energy, and even material goods is important to friendship. Friends know they can rely on each other in times of need.

• *Trust.* Friends are secure in the knowledge that they will not intentionally hurt each other. They feel safe confiding in each other.

• *Loyalty.* Friends can count on each other. They stand up for each other in both word and deed.

• *Mutuality.* Friends retain their individual identities, but close friendships are characterized by a sense of mutuality—"what affects you affects me." Friends share the ups and downs in each other's lives.

• *Reciprocity.* Friendships are reciprocal. There is give-and-take between friends and the feeling that both share joys and burdens more or less equally over time.

Intimate partnerships are like friendships in many ways, but they have additional characteristics. These relationships usually include sexual desire and expression, a greater demand for exclusiveness, and deeper levels of caring. Friendships are usually considered both stabler and longer lasting than intimate partnerships. Friends are often more accepting and less critical than lovers, probably because their expectations are different. Like love relationships, friendships bind society together, providing people with emotional support and buffering them from stress.

As important as friendships are, however, the average American's social circle is shrinking—to the point that nearly 25% of Americans say they have no one they want to confide in (Table 4.1). In 2006, sociologists from Duke

Table 4.1	Average Number of Confidants: 1985 and 2004	
	Americans with This Number of Confidants	
Number	1985	2004
0	10.0%	24.6%
1	15.0	19.0
2	16.2	19.2
3	20.3	16.9
4	14.8	8.8
5	18.2	6.5
6 or more	5.4	4.9

SOURCE: McPherson, M., et al. 2006. Social isolation in America: Changes in the core discussion networks over two decades. *American Sociological Review* 71: 353–375.

University and the University of Arizona released details of a study confirming the issue. According to the study, Americans have fewer close friends than ever before. Most have only two friends they consider close enough to discuss problems with. (Compare this number to 1985, when the average American had three confidants.)

Love, Sex, and Intimacy

Love is one of the most basic and profound human emotions. It is a powerful force in all our intimate relationships. Love encompasses opposites: affection and anger, excitement and boredom, stability and change, bonds and freedom. Love does not give us perfect happiness, but it does give our lives meaning.

In many kinds of adult relationships, love is closely intertwined with sexuality. In the past, marriage was considered the only acceptable context for sexual activities, but for many people today, sex is legitimized by love. Many couples, both heterosexual and homosexual, live together in committed relationships. We now use personal standards rather than social norms to make decisions about sex. Many people, however, worry about this trend toward personal responsibility and the bypassing of

TERMS

infatuation An idealizing, obsessive attraction, characterized by a high degree of physical arousal.

traditional norms and values. They fear that the prevailing attitude about sexuality has resulted in a greater emphasis on sex over love and a permissiveness that has undermined the commitment needed to make a true loving relationship work. This casual attitude toward sex may also make it easier for people to sexualize their dependency needs.

For most people, love, sex, and commitment are closely linked ideals in intimate relationships. Love reflects the positive factors that draw people together and sustain them in a relationship. It includes trust, caring, respect, loyalty, interest in the other, and concern for the other's well-being. Sex brings excitement and passion to the relationship. It intensifies the relationship and adds fascination and pleasure.

Commitment, the determination to continue, reflects the stable factors that help maintain the relationship. Responsibility, reliability, and faithfulness are characteristics of commitment. Although love, sex, and commitment are related, they are not necessarily connected. One can exist without the others. Despite the various "faces" of love, sex, and commitment, most of us long for a special relationship that contains them all.

Other elements can be identified as features of love, such as euphoria, preoccupation with the loved one, idealization or devaluation of the loved one, and so on, but these tend to be temporary. These characteristics may include **infatuation,** which will fade or deepen into something more substantial. As relationships progress, the central aspects of love and commitment take on more importance.

Men and women tend to have different views of the relationship between love (or intimacy) and sex (or passion). Numerous studies have found that men can separate love from sex rather easily, although many men find that their most erotic sexual experiences occur in the context of a love relationship. Women generally view sex from the point of view of a relationship. Some people believe you can have satisfying sex without love—with friends, acquaintances, or strangers. Although sex with love is an important norm in our culture, it is frequently disregarded in practice, as the high incidence of extrarelational affairs attests.

The Pleasure and Pain of Love The experience of intense love has confused and tormented lovers throughout history. They live in a tumultuous state of excitement, subject to wildly fluctuating feelings of joy and despair. They lose their appetite, can't sleep, and can think of nothing but the loved one. Is this happiness? Misery? Or both?

The contradictory nature of passionate love can be understood by recognizing that human emotions have two components: physiological arousal and an emotional explanation for the arousal. Love is just one of many emotions accompanied by physiological arousal; numerous unpleasant ones can also generate arousal, such as fear,

Although passion and physical intimacy often decline with time, other aspects of a relationship—such as commitment—tend to grow as the relationship matures.

that includes external goals and projects, friends, and family. In this kind of intimate, more secure love, satisfaction comes not just from the relationship itself but also from achieving other creative goals, such as work or child rearing. The key to successful relationships is in transforming passion into an intimate love, based on closeness, caring, and the promise of a shared future.

Challenges in Relationships

Many people believe that love naturally makes an intimate relationship easy to begin and maintain, but in fact, obstacles arise and challenges occur. Even in the best of circumstances, a loving relationship will be tested. Individuals bring to a relationship diverse needs and wants, some of which emerge only at times of change or stress. Common relationship challenges relate to self-disclosure, commitment, expectations, competitiveness, and jealousy.

Is There Hidden Treasure in Our Relationships?   Obviously, we have relationships for fun, companionship, children, and support. But is that all there is to it? Is there hidden meaning to be found in our intimate relationships? Do they repeat issues and conflicts from our past *as well as* offer a way to heal and grow beyond these early-life difficulties? Some experts contend that, as adults, we unconsciously recreate relationships with others that play out the dramas of childhood. In doing so, they say, we attempt to work through and master problems from the past.

At various points in our lives, we may unconsciously play the part of our younger selves—or the part of another person (such as a parent or a sibling)—with the new emotional figure in our lives. We play these roles in the hope of getting emotionally what we didn't get as children or of giving back what we did get.

Quite often, conflicts in our later-life relationships have to do with our feelings and needs. We tend to expect too much, offer too little, or simply feel confused when it comes to our and the other's emotions. Problems in relationships are not always reflective of incompatibility and may sometimes indicate issues that are just very emotionally difficult because of past frustrations or hurt.

The good news is that our problems in relationships are the potential path to our growth as individuals as well as a couple. A man who feels he doesn't receive enough love from his partner (and didn't from his parents) may benefit from cultivating additional platonic relationships rather than hoping for complete satisfaction from one person. A woman who feels the need for more independence in a relationship (which she didn't have growing up) may grow from learning to stay with her discomfort around intimacy and see if she is gradually able to tolerate more closeness without becoming frightened or pulling back.

Ultimately, it seems that the best relationships are those in which we can be both securely connected and then

rejection, frustration, and challenge. Although experiences like attraction and sexual desire are pleasant, extreme excitement is similar to fear and is unpleasant. For this reason, passionate love may be too intense to enjoy. Over time, the physical intensity and excitement tend to diminish. When this happens, pleasure may actually increase.

The Transformation of Love   All human relationships change over time, and love relationships are no exception. At first, love is likely to be characterized by high levels of passion and rapidly increasing intimacy. After a while, passion decreases as we become habituated to it and to the person. The diminishing of romance or passionate love is often experienced as a crisis in a relationship. If a more lasting love fails to emerge, the relationship will likely break up.

Unlike passion, however, commitment does not necessarily diminish over time. When intensity diminishes, partners often discover a more enduring love. They can now move from absorption in each other to a relationship separate and be on our own at times. Developmental psychology suggests that the healthiest infants are able to feel comforted by their mother without being engulfed and can be apart from her without feeling abandoned. Most important seems to be the mother's ability to be empathically attuned to the child to know when to comfort and when to let go.

Relationships in which we can be open, expressive, and understood offer us the greatest chance to grow, develop our potential, and awaken to as much life as possible. Perhaps the larger, hidden meaning of relationships is to help us cultivate the intimacy and freedom that may have been in short supply while we were growing up. We can help ourselves and others heal and grow by offering and asking for love and compassion. We can free ourselves from the limits imposed on us from the past by challenging ourselves to see where we are afraid to go in our relationships and then going there with our partners.

Honesty and Openness   Everyone looks for honesty and openness in an intimate relationship. However, especially at the beginning of a relationship, partners tend to engage in a certain amount of pretense in an effort to present themselves in the best possible manner. It's usually best to be yourself from the start to give both you and your potential partner a chance to find out if you are comfortable with each other's beliefs, interests, and lifestyles.

Getting close to another person by sharing thoughts and feelings is emotionally risky, but it is necessary for a relationship to deepen. Take your time, and self-disclose at a slow but steady rate—one that doesn't make you feel too vulnerable or your partner too uncomfortable. Over time, you and your partner will learn more about each other and feel more comfortable sharing. In fact, intimate familiarity with your partner's life is a key characteristic of successful long-term relationships.

Unequal or Premature Commitment   Sometimes one person in an intimate partnership becomes more serious about the relationship than the other partner. In this situation, it can be very difficult to maintain a friendship without hurting the other person. Sometimes a couple makes a premature commitment, and then one of the partners has second thoughts and wants to break off the relationship. Sometimes both partners begin to realize that something is wrong, but each is afraid to tell the other. Most such problems can be dealt with only by honest and sensitive communication.

Unrealistic Expectations   Each partner brings hopes and expectations to a relationship, some of which may be unrealistic, unfair, and, ultimately, very damaging to the relationship (see the box "Are You Emotionally Intelligent?"). For example, if you believe that love will eliminate all of your problems, you may start to blame your partner for anything that goes wrong in your life. Other unrealistic expectations include the following:

- *Expecting your partner to change.* There are probably some things about your partner that you like more than others. It's OK to discuss them with your partner; however, it's unfair to demand that your partner change to meet all of your expectations. Accept the differences between your ideal and reality.

- *Assuming that your partner has all the same opinions, priorities, interests, and goals as you.* Don't assume that you think the same about everything—or that you must if the relationship is to succeed. Agreement on key issues is important, but differences can enhance a relationship as long as partners understand and respect each other's points of view.

- *Believing that a relationship will fulfill all of your personal, financial, intellectual, and social needs.* Expecting a relationship to fulfill all your needs places too much pressure on your partner and on your relationship, and it will inevitably lead to disappointment. For your own well-being, it's important to maintain some degree of autonomy and self-sufficiency.

Competitiveness   Games and competitive sports add flavor to the bonding process—as long as the focus is on fun. If one partner always feels the strong need to compete and win, it can detract from the sense of connectedness, interdependence, equality, and mutuality between partners. The same can be said for a perfectionistic need to be right in every instance—to "win" every argument.

If competitiveness is a problem for you, ask yourself if your need to win is more important than your partner's feelings or the future of your relationship. Try noncompetitive activities or an activity where you are a beginner and your partner excels. Accept that your partner's views may be just as valid and important to your partner as your own views are to you.

Balancing Time Spent Together and Apart   You may enjoy time together with your partner, but you may also want to spend time alone or with other friends. If you or your partner interpret time apart as rejection or lack of commitment, it can damage a relationship. Talk with your partner about what time apart means and share your feelings about what you expect from the relationship in terms of time together. Consider your partner's feelings carefully, and try to reach a compromise that satisfies both of you.

Differences in expectations about time spent together can mirror differences in ideas about emotional closeness.

Are You Emotionally Intelligent?

Emotional intelligence (also known as E.Q. or E.I.Q.) can be defined as the degree to which we can skillfully and adaptively deal with our emotions and those of others.

More specifically, this involves the following:

1. Recognizing feelings as they occur
2. Responding to feelings with neither impulsive, aggressive reactivity, nor suppression, denial, distraction, or avoidance
3. Being able to tolerate and contain strong emotions and soothe yourself in the presence of powerful feelings
4. Being able to use the energy of strong emotions to motivate yourself and respond skillfully to the situation at hand
5. Being able to perceive the content of feelings in order to connect the emotion to its source and understand why you are feeling a particular emotion
6. Being able to recognize and bear the feelings of others without needing to distance yourself or dissuade the other person from having their feelings

7. Being able to persist in the face of fear or frustration and cultivate resilience
8. Being able to delay gratification
9. Being able to be curious and stay open to feelings rather than close down, tighten up, or turn away from emotions
10. Being able to express a wide range of emotions in a way that is natural and to a degree that is appropriate to the particular situation

How do you cultivate emotional intelligence? The key lies in the ability to develop the overarching skill of *mindfulness*—the ability to dispassionately observe thoughts and feelings as they occur and while they're occurring. This skill is aided by cultivating a "witness" or a "watcher" in your mind and noting the arising of strong reactions with a certain detachment. By holding our reactions in a larger mental space we can make more measured, wise, and skillful responses to the situation at hand.

Mindfulness can be cultivated by simply paying more attention to the operation of our minds, slowing down our lives enough to make more detailed observations, and staying in the moment so as to maximize awareness of our-

selves and others. Although we often have a limited ability to control external events, it turns out that we have a great deal of ability to discipline, focus, and train our minds. With practice, we not only can become more emotionally intelligent but also may be able to cultivate an ongoing peace of mind that many people find so elusive.

Any romantic relationship involves giving up some degree of autonomy in order to develop an identity as a couple. But remember that every person is unique and has different needs for distance and closeness in a relationship.

Jealousy Jealousy is the angry, painful response to a partner's real, imagined, or likely involvement with a third person. Some people think that the existence of jealousy proves the existence of love, but jealousy is actually a sign of insecurity or possessiveness.

In its irrational and extreme forms, jealousy can destroy a relationship by its insistent demands and attempts at control. Jealousy is a factor in precipitating violence in dating relationships among both high school and college students, and abusive spouses often use jealousy to justify their violence. (Problems with control and violence in relationships are discussed in Chapter 21.)

People with a healthy level of self-esteem are less likely to feel jealous. When jealousy occurs in a relationship, it's important for the partners to communicate clearly with each other about their feelings.

Supportiveness Another key to successful relationships is the ability to ask for and give support. Partners need to know that they can count on each other during difficult times. If you are having trouble getting or giving the support that you or your partner needs, try some of the suggestions in the box "Strategies for Enhancing Support in Relationships" on page 102.

Unhealthy Relationships

Everyone should be able to recognize when a relationship is unhealthy. Relatively extreme examples of unhealthy relationships are those that are physically or emotionally abusive or that involve codependency; strategies for addressing these problems are presented in Chapters 21 and 9, respectively.

Even relationships that are not abusive or codependent can still be unhealthy. If your relationship lacks love and respect and places little value on the time you and your partner have spent together, it may be time to get professional help or to end the partnership. Further, if

Strategies for Enhancing Support in Relationships

• *Be aware of the importance of support.* Time and energy spent on support will help both you and your partner deal with stress and create a positive atmosphere that will help when differences or conflicts do occur.

• *Learn to ask for help from your partner.* Try different ways of asking for help and support from your partner and make note of which approaches work best for your relationship.

• *Help your partner the way she or he would like to be helped.* Some people prefer empathy and emotional support, whereas others like more practical help with problems.

• *Avoid negativity, especially when being asked for help.* Asking for help puts a person in a vulnerable position. If your partner asks for your aid, be gracious and supportive; don't use phrases like "I told you so" or "You should have just. . . ." Otherwise, your partner may learn not to ask for your help or support at all.

• *Make positive attributions.* If you're unsure about the reasons for your partner's behavior, give her or him the benefit of the doubt. For example, if your partner arrives for a date 30 minutes late and in a bad mood, assume it's because she or he had a bad day rather than attributing it to a character flaw or relationship problem. Offer appropriate support.

• *Help yourself.* Develop coping strategies for times your partner won't be available. These might include things you can do for yourself, such as going for a walk, or other people you can turn to for support.

• *Keep relationship problems separate.* Avoid bringing up relationship problems when you are offering or asking for help.

• *Avoid giving advice.* Immediately offering advice when asked for help implies that you are smarter or more capable than your partner at solving your partner's difficulty. Begin by providing emotional support and validating your partner's feelings. Then, if asked, help brainstorm solutions.

SOURCE: Plante, T., and K. Sullivan. 2000. *Getting Together and Staying Together: The Stanford Course on Intimate Relationships.* Bloomington, Ind.: 1st Books Library. Reprinted with permission of the author.

Supportiveness is a sign of commitment and compassion and is an important part of any healthy relationship.

your relationship is characterized by communication styles that include criticism, contempt, defensiveness, and withdrawal—despite real efforts to repair these destructive patterns—the relationship may not be salvageable. Consider these questions:

• Do you and your partner have more negative than positive experiences and interactions?

• Are there old hurts that you or your partner cannot forgive?

• Do you feel disrespected or unloved?

• Do you find it hard to feel positive feelings of affection for your partner?

• Does it feel as if your relationship has been a waste of time?

Spiritual leaders suggest that relationships are unhealthy when you feel that your sense of spontaneity, your potential for inner growth and joy, and your connection to your spiritual life is deadened. There are negative physical and mental consequences of being in an unhappy relationship; although breaking up is painful and difficult, it is ultimately better than living in a toxic relationship.

Ending a Relationship

Even when a couple starts out with the best of intentions, an intimate relationship may not last. Some breakups occur quickly following direct action by one or both partners, but many others occur over an extended period as the couple goes through a cycle of separating and reconciling.

Ending an intimate relationship is usually difficult and painful. Both partners may feel attacked and abandoned, but feelings of distress are likely to be more acute for the rejected partner. If you are involved in a breakup, the following suggestions may help make the ending easier:

- *Give the relationship a fair chance before breaking up.* If it's still not working, you'll know you did everything you could.

- *Be fair and honest.* If you're initiating the breakup, don't try to make your partner feel responsible.

- *Be tactful and compassionate.* You can leave the relationship without deliberately damaging your partner's self-esteem. Emphasize your mutual incompatibility, and admit your own contributions to the problem.

- *If you are the rejected person, give yourself time to resolve your anger and pain.* Mobilize your coping resources, including social support and other stress-management techniques. You may go through a process of mourning the relationship, experiencing disbelief, anger, sadness, and finally acceptance. Remember that there are actually many people with whom you can potentially have an intimate relationship.

- *Recognize the value in the experience.* You honor the feelings that you shared with your partner by validating the relationship as a worthwhile experience. Ending a close relationship can teach you valuable lessons about your needs, preferences, strengths, and weaknesses. Use your insights to increase your chance of success in your next relationship.

Use the recovery period following a breakup for self-renewal. Redirect more of your attention to yourself, and reconnect with people and areas of your life that may have been neglected as a result of the relationship. Time will help heal the pain of the loss of the relationship.

COMMUNICATION

The key to developing and maintaining any type of intimate relationship is good communication. Most of the time, we don't actually think about communicating; we simply talk and behave naturally. But when problems arise—when we feel others don't understand us or when someone accuses us of not listening—we become aware of our limitations or, more commonly, what we think are other people's limitations. Miscommunication creates frustration and distances us from our friends and partners.

Nonverbal Communication

Even when we're silent, we're communicating. We send messages when we look at someone or look away, lean forward or sit back, smile or frown. Especially important forms of nonverbal communication are touch, eye contact, and proximity. If someone we're talking to touches our hand or arm, looks into our eyes, and leans toward us when we talk, we get the message that the person is interested in us and cares about what we're saying. If a person keeps looking around the room while we're talking or takes a step backward, we get the impression the person is uninterested or wants to end the conversation.

As much as 65% of communication is non-verbal.

—Ray Birdwhistell, Anthropologist, 1970

QUICK STATS

The ability to interpret nonverbal messages correctly is important to the success of relationships. It's also important, when sending messages, to make sure our body language agrees with our words. When our verbal and nonverbal messages don't correspond, we send a mixed message.

Communication Skills

Three keys to good communication in relationships are self-disclosure, listening, and feedback.

- *Self-disclosure* involves revealing personal information that we ordinarily wouldn't reveal because of the risk involved. It usually increases feelings of closeness and moves the relationship to a deeper level of intimacy. Friends often disclose the most to each other, sharing feelings, experiences, hopes, and disappointments; married couples sometimes share less because they think they already know everything there is to know about each other.

- *Listening,* the second key of good communication, is a rare skill. Good listening skills require that we spend more time and energy trying to fully understand another person's "story" and less time judging, evaluating, blaming, advising, analyzing, or trying to control. Empathy, warmth, respect, and genuineness are qualities of skillful listeners. Attentive listening encourages friends or partners to share more and, in turn, to be attentive listeners. To connect with other people and develop real emotional intimacy, listening is essential.

? QUESTIONS FOR CRITICAL THINKING AND REFLECTION

Have you ever ended an intimate relationship? If so, how did you handle it? How did you feel after the breakup? How did the breakup affect your former partner? Did the experience help you in other relationships? If so, in what way did it help?

Conflict is an inevitable part of any intimate relationship. Couples need to develop constructive ways of resolving conflicts in order to maintain a healthy relationship.

cation. Many authorities believe that, because of the way they've been raised, men and women generally approach conversation and communication differently. According to this view, men tend to use conversation in a *competitive* way, perhaps hoping to establish dominance in relationships. When male conversations are over, men often find themselves in a one-up or a one-down position. Women tend to use conversation in a more *affiliative* way, perhaps hoping to establish friendships. They negotiate various degrees of closeness, seeking to give and receive support. Men tend to talk more—though without disclosing more—and listen less. Women tend to use good listening skills such as eye contact, frequent nodding, focused attention, and asking relevant questions.

Although these are generalized patterns, they can translate into problems in specific conversations. Even when a man and a woman are talking about the same subject, their unconscious goals may be very different. The woman may be looking for understanding and closeness, while the man may be trying to demonstrate his competence by giving advice and solving problems. Both styles are valid; the problem comes when differences in style result in poor communication and misunderstanding. See the box "Gender and Communication" on page 106 for more information.

Sometimes communication is not the problem in a relationship—the partners understand each other all too well. The problem is that they're unable or unwilling to change or compromise. Although good communication can't salvage a bad relationship, it does enable couples to see their differences and make more informed decisions.

• *Feedback*, a constructive response to another's self-disclosure, is the third key to good communication. Giving positive feedback means acknowledging that the friend's or partner's feelings are valid—no matter how upsetting or troubling—and offering self-disclosure in response. If, for example, your partner discloses unhappiness about your relationship, it is more constructive to say that you're concerned or saddened by that and want to hear more about it than to get angry, to blame, to try to inflict pain, or to withdraw. Self-disclosure and feedback can open the door to change, whereas other responses block communication and change. (For tips on improving your skills, see the box "Guidelines for Effective Communication.")

Gender and Communication

Some of the difficulties people encounter in relationships can be traced to common gender differences in communi-

Conflict and Conflict Resolution

Conflict is natural in intimate relationships. No matter how close two people become, they still remain separate individuals with their own needs, desires, past experiences, and ways of seeing the world. In fact, the closer the relationship, the more differences and the more opportunities for conflict there will be.

Conflict itself isn't dangerous to a relationship; in fact, it may indicate that the relationship is growing. But if it isn't handled in a constructive way, conflict can damage—and ultimately destroy—the relationship. Consider the following guidelines, but remember that different couples communicate in different ways around conflict.

Conflict is often accompanied by anger—a natural emotion, but one that can be difficult to handle. If we express anger aggressively, we run the risk of creating distrust, fear, and distance; if we act it out without thinking things through, we can cause the conflict to escalate; if we suppress anger, it turns into resentment and hostility. The best way to handle anger in a relationship is to recognize it as a symptom of something that requires attention and

Guidelines for Effective Communication

Getting Started

• When you want to have a serious discussion with your partner, find an appropriate time and place. Choose a block of time when you will not be interrupted or rushed and a place that is private.

• Face your partner and maintain eye contact. Use nonverbal feedback to show that you are interested and involved in the communication process.

Being an Effective Speaker

• State your concern or issue as clearly as you can.

• Use "I" statements—statements about how *you* feel—rather than statements beginning with "You," which tell another person how you think he or she feels. When you use "I" statements, you are taking responsibility for your feelings. "You" statements are often blaming or accusatory and will probably get a defensive or resentful response. The statement "I feel unloved," for example, sends a clearer, less blaming message than the statement "You don't love me."

• Focus on a specific behavior rather than on the whole person. Be specific about the behavior you like or don't like. Avoid generalizations beginning with "You always" or "You never." Such statements make people feel defensive.

• Make constructive requests. Opening your request with "I would like" keeps the focus on your needs rather than your partner's supposed deficiencies.

• Avoid blaming, accusing, and belittling. Even if you are right, you have little to gain by putting your partner down. Studies have shown that when people feel criticized or attacked, they are less able to think rationally or solve problems constructively.

• Ask for action ahead of time, not after the fact. Tell your partner what you would like to have happen in the future; don't wait for him or her to blow it and then express anger or disappointment.

Being an Effective Listener

• Provide appropriate nonverbal feedback (nodding, smiling, making eye contact, and so on).

• Don't interrupt.

• Develop the skill of reflective listening. Don't judge, evaluate, analyze, or offer solutions (unless asked to do so). Your partner may just need to have you there in order to sort out feelings. By jumping in right away to "fix" the problem, you may actually be cutting off communication.

• Don't give unsolicited advice. Giving advice implies that you know more about what a person needs to do than he or she does; therefore, it often evokes anger or resentment.

• Clarify your understanding of what your partner is saying by restating it in your own words and asking if your understanding is correct. "I think you're saying that you would feel uncomfortable having dinner with my parents and that you'd prefer to meet them in a more casual setting. Is that right?" This type of specific feedback prevents misunderstandings and helps validate the speaker's feelings and message.

• Be sure you are really listening, not off somewhere in your mind rehearsing your reply. Try to tune in to your partner's feelings as well as the words.

• Let your partner know that you value what he or she is saying and want to understand. Respect for the other person is the cornerstone of effective communication.

---

needs to be changed. When angry, partners should exercise restraint so as not to become abusive. It is important to express anger skillfully and not in a way that is out of proportion to the issue at hand.

The sources of conflict for couples change over time but primarily revolve around the basic tasks of living together: dividing the housework, handling money, spending time together, and so on. Sexual interaction is also a source of disagreement for many couples.

Although there are numerous theories on and approaches to conflict resolution, the following strategies can be helpful when negotiating with a partner:

1. *Clarify the issue.* Take responsibility for thinking through your feelings and discovering what's really bothering you. Agree that one partner will speak first and have the chance to speak fully while the other listens. Then reverse the roles. Try to understand your partner's position fully by repeating what you've heard and asking questions to clarify or elicit more information. Agree to talk only about the topic at hand and not get distracted by other issues. Sum up what your partner has said.

2. *Find out what each person wants.* Ask your partner to express his or her desires. Don't assume you know what your partner wants and don't speak for him or her.

3. *Determine how you both can get what you want.* Brainstorm to generate a variety of options.

4. *Decide how to negotiate.* Work out a plan for change; for example, one partner will do one task and the other will do another task, or one partner will do a task in exchange for something he or she wants. Be willing to compromise, and avoid trying to "win."

Gender and Communication

From an early age, parents, teachers, and society send different messages to girls and boys regarding emotion. Boys learn to suppress and bury their feelings, especially fear and other emotions that make them feel vulnerable. Girls are encouraged to express and talk about their feelings.

These differences are further reinforced by peer groups. Gender segregation is already apparent in preschool and increases throughout middle childhood for most children. Boys and girls spend most of their time with peers of the same gender, and their communication styles are very different. For example, when conflict arises, girls tend to care more about preserving their relationships, and boys care more about maintaining the game they were playing.

Research also shows that men have a more intense physiological response to certain emotions. In discussions around conflict, a man's blood pressure and heart rate rise higher and remain elevated longer. Part of the reason may be that a man's internal dialogue repeats upsetting thoughts (for example, "How could she say that? I can't take this!"). When anyone is physiologically or emotionally overwhelmed ("flooded"), productive communication is impossible.

A common pattern that arises between men and women is called "confront-withdraw." A woman approaches her male partner because she is upset and wants to talk about it. The man tries to calm her down, provides solutions he sees as rational, and/or withdraws. This response may make his partner even more upset and demanding, which causes the man to further shut down. Given what we know about gender differences, we might understand the man's response as one of self-protection, because he is entering territory that is both unknown and physically unpleasant.

In order to enjoy intimacy, men and women must work to better understand one another and develop a more compatible communication style.

Advice for Men

• When your partner raises an emotional topic, be aware of uncomfortable feelings and the desire to retreat.

• Do not run away (physically or emotionally)! Telling her to "calm down" will likely create the opposite response.

• Find a way to stay connected. This is the only way to deescalate the conflict.

• Empathize: Listen to what she is saying, and even if you disagree, communicate to her that you understand how she is feeling and where she is coming from. Often when a person feels genuinely heard, that is enough.

• Try not to think of her comments as personal attacks; instead, continue to empathize.

• You may need to calm yourself. Try taking long deep breaths, telling yourself that your partner needs to air her feelings, and remembering that she, too, wants the conflict to end.

• In some cases, a 20-minute break—during which you soothe yourself rather than think upsetting thoughts—can be helpful.

Advice for Women

• Try to be calm when approaching conflict; practice similar relaxation techniques to those described in "Advice for Men."

• Try to speak in ways that will not provoke defensiveness; complain rather than criticize, be specific, and use "I" statements.

• Try not to be critical of your partner's responses or his attempts to communicate.

• Be aware if he is withdrawing, and, if appropriate, help him to relax by using methods you have discussed previously.

SOURCE: Gottman, J. 1994. *Why Marriages Succeed or Fail . . . and How You Can Make Yours Last.* New York: Simon & Schuster.

---

5. *Solidify the agreements.* Go over the plan verbally and write it down, if necessary, to ensure that you both understand and agree to it.

6. *Review and renegotiate.* Decide on a time frame for trying out your plan, and set a time to discuss how it's working. Make adjustments as needed.

To resolve conflicts, partners have to feel safe in voicing disagreements. They have to trust that the discussion won't get out of control, that they won't be abandoned by the other, and that the partner won't take advantage of their vulnerability. Partners should follow some basic ground rules when they argue, such as avoiding ultimatums, resisting the urge to give the silent treatment, refusing to "hit below the belt," and not using sex to smooth over disagreements.

When you argue, maintain a spirit of goodwill and avoid being harshly critical or contemptuous. Remember—you care about your partner and want things to work out. See the disagreement as a difficulty that the two

QUESTIONS FOR CRITICAL THINKING AND REFLECTION

How do you handle conflict in your relationships? Do you fight intensely and then make up? Discuss, negotiate, and compromise? Avoid conflict altogether? Whatever your pattern of conflict resolution (or avoidance), where do you think you learned it? How effective is it for you? If it isn't working well, what ideas do you have for improvement?

of you have together rather than as something your partner does to you. Finish serious discussions on a positive note by expressing your respect and affection for your partner and your appreciation for having been listened to. If you and your partner find that you argue again and again over the same issue, it may be better to stop trying to resolve that problem and instead come to accept the differences between you.

PAIRING AND SINGLEHOOD

Although most people eventually marry or commit to a partner, everyone spends some time as a single person, and nearly all make some attempt, consciously or unconsciously, to find a partner. Intimate relationships are as important for singles as for couples.

Choosing a Partner

Most men and women select partners for long-term relationships through a fairly predictable process, although they may not be consciously aware of it. First attraction is based on easily observable characteristics: looks, dress, social status, and reciprocated interest. Most people pair with someone who:

- Lives in the same geographic area
- Is from a similar ethnic and socioeconomic background
- Has similar educational attainment
- Lives a similar lifestyle
- Is like them in terms of physical attraction

Once the euphoria of romantic love winds down, personality traits and behaviors become more significant factors in how the partners view each other. The emphasis shifts to basic values and future aspirations regarding career, family, and children. At some point, they decide whether the relationship feels viable and is worthy of their continued commitment.

Perhaps the most important question for potential mates to ask is, "How much do we have in common?"

Although differences add interest to a relationship, similarities increase the chances of a relationship's success. Areas in which differences can affect a relationship include values, religion, ethnicity, attitudes toward sexuality and gender roles, socioeconomic status, familiarity with each other's culture, and interactions with the extended family (see the box "Interfaith and Intrafaith Partnerships" on p. 108). Acceptance and communication skills go a long way toward making a relationship work, no matter how different the partners.

Dating

Every culture has certain rituals for pairing and finding mates. Parent-arranged marriages, still the norm in many cultures, are often very stable and permanent. Although the American cultural norm is personal choice in courtship and mate selection, the popularity of dating services and online matchmaking suggests that many people want help finding a suitable partner (see the box "Online Relationships" on p. 109).

Most Americans find romantic partners through some form of dating. They narrow the field through a process of getting to know each other. Dating often revolves around a mutually enjoyable activity, such as seeing a movie or having dinner. Traditionally, in the male-female dating pattern, the man took the lead, initiating the date, while the woman waited to be called. In this pattern, casual dating might evolve into steady or exclusive dating, then engagement, and finally marriage.

For many college students today, group activities have replaced dating as a way to meet and get to know potential partners.

Interfaith and Intrafaith Partnerships

Interfaith marriage is common among Americans; for example, about 50% of Jews and 25% of Roman Catholics marry a partner of a different faith. There are many types of interfaith partnerships, including partners from (1) two completely different religions, (2) two religions with similar roots, (3) two divisions of the same religion, or (4) two denominations from the same religious division. The latter two are often called intrafaith partnerships.

Marrying someone of a different faith can broaden the partners' worldview and enrich their lives; however, it can also be a potential stressor and a challenge to a relationship. The impact of being an interfaith couple depends on how religious the partners are. There is no specifically correct way to address religious diversity in a partnership, but the following are some potential approaches.

Withdrawal: In some couples, both partners withdraw from their respective religions. Religious differences may be minimized, but the withdrawal may not last. If a partner was observant prior to the relationship, it is likely that she or he will want to become actively involved again. This often occurs with a significant life event such as the birth of a child or death of a parent.

Conversion: In many intrafaith couples, one partner converts to the religion of the other. Religious differences are decreased, but problems can occur if the partner who converts develops resentment, has difficulties with her or his family of origin, misses the old religion, or experiences feelings of guilt or betrayal.

Compromise: Some couples convert together to a new religion, possibly to a religion or denomination at a "midpoint" between their two religions. The couple may find a happy medium that is satisfying to both. However, both may experience the problems associated with conversion.

Multifaith: Some couples join both religions—formally or informally. They may alternate places of worship weekly or make other creative arrangements. The advantage of this pattern is that both partners maintain their religions and learn more about each other. Problems may arise if the religions have conflicting values or practices.

Ecumenical: In some relationships, partners merge their religions. They may combine the "best" of each or observe only the areas where the religions intersect. They may get the best of both worlds and/or discover that their religions have more in common than they thought. In some cases, however, the original religious institutions may condemn compromise.

Diversity: In some couples, each partner chooses to follow his or her own religion. If both partners are very religious, they do not then have to give up an important part of their lives. However, some partners consider this approach undesirable because it means more time spent apart.

Do Nothing: Some couples find no need to address religious differences because neither partner is observant or committed to a religion to an extent that it is a relationship challenge. They address specific issues if and when they arise.

Couples often handle their religious differences without a problem until they marry or have children. Planning an interfaith wedding can be fraught with unique stressors, such as differing rituals and the expectations of guests from different faiths. When children arrive, decisions may need to be made about issues such as baptism, circumcision, religious upbringing, and others.

To maintain a successful partnership, couples should communicate about religious issues before getting married and having children. Discuss the importance of your religions and religious needs. Consider ways that you can honor each other's religious traditions. Learn to discuss issues relating to religion and spirituality in ways to bring you closer together.

SOURCES: Robinson, B. A. 2007. *Inter-Faith Marriages* (http://www.religioustolerance.org/ ifm_menu.htm; retrieved January 24, 2009); Robinson, B. A. 1999. *How Inter-Faith and Intra-Faith Couples Handle Religious Differences* (http://www .religioustolerance.org/ifm_diff.htm; retrieved January 24, 2009).

For many young people today, traditional dating has given way to a more casual form of getting together in groups. Greater equality between the sexes is at the root of this change. People go out in groups, rather than strictly as couples, and each person pays his or her way. A man and woman may begin to spend more time together, but often in the group context. If sexual involvement develops, it is more likely to be based on friendship, respect, and common interests than on expectations related to gender roles. In this model, mate selection may progress from getting together to living together to marriage.

Online Relationships

Worldwide, tens of millions of people use the World Wide Web to network and to find friends and partners. Social networking Web sites like Friendster, Facebook, and MySpace offer a place for profiles, photos, blogs, music, videos, and e-mail to vast numbers of people, mostly teens and young adults, seeking to connect online.

Online dating sites and forums like Match.com are also popular, especially among those out of college who are seeking an intimate partner or an expanded circle of friends.

Connecting with people online has its advantages and its drawbacks. It allows people to communicate in a relaxed way, to try out different personas, and to share things they might not share with family or friends face-to-face. Many find that it offers a sense of privacy, safety, and comfort. It is easy to put yourself out there without too much investment—you can get to know someone from the comfort of your own home, set your own pace, and start and end the relationships at any time. With millions of singles using dating forums that allow them to outline exactly what they are seeking, the Internet can increase a person's chance of finding a good match.

There are drawbacks to meeting people online, however. People often misrepresent themselves, pretending to be very different—older or younger or even of a different sex—than they really are. Investing time and emotional resources in such relationships can be painful. There have also been a few instances in which online romances have become dangerous or even deadly (see Chapter 21 for information on cyberstalking).

Because people have greater freedom to reveal only what they want to, users should also be aware of a greater tendency to idealize online partners—setting themselves up for later disappointment. If you find that your online friend seems perfect, consider that a warning sign. Looking for partners online can become like shopping—the choices available may increase your tendency to search for perfection or find fault quickly, thereby keeping you from giving people a chance. Remember what is most important to you and keep your expectations realistic.

When looking for friends and partners online, you are also reducing an important and powerful source of information: chemistry and in-person intuition. Much of our communication is transmitted through body language and tone, which are not available online and cannot be fully captured even by Web cams. Trust your feelings regarding the process of the relationship. Are you revealing more than the other person? Is there a balance in the amount of time spent talking by each of you? Is the other person respecting your boundaries? Just as in real-life dating, online relationships require you to use common sense and to trust your instincts.

If you decide to pursue an online relationship, here are some strategies that can help you have a positive experience and stay safe:

• To improve your chances of meeting people interested in you as a person, avoid sexually oriented Web sites.

• Know what you are looking for as well as what you have to offer someone else. If you are looking for a relationship, make that fact clear. Find out the other person's situation and intentions.

• Many Web sites let users upload photos. Know, however, that your photo can be downloaded by anyone, distributed to other individuals or sites, and even altered. Don't post photos unless you are completely comfortable with the potential consequences.

• Don't give out personal information, including your real full name, school, or place of employment, until you feel sure that you are giving the information to someone who is trustworthy. Do not give anyone your address or phone number over the Internet.

• Consider setting up a second e-mail account for sending and receiving dating-related e-mails.

• If someone does not respond to a message, try not to take it personally. There are many reasons why a person may not pursue the connection. Do not send multiple messages to an unresponsive person; doing so could lead to an accusation of stalking. If someone stops responding to your messages, drop the interaction completely.

• Before deciding whether to meet an online friend in person, arrange to talk over the phone a few times.

• Don't agree to meet someone face-to-face unless you feel completely comfortable about it. Always meet initially in a very public place—a museum, a coffee shop, or a restaurant, not in private, and especially not at your home. Bring along a friend to further increase your safety, let a friend know where you will be, or plan to have a friend call you during the date.

If you pursue online relationships, don't let them interfere with your other interpersonal relationships and social activities. There can be an addictive element to online dating that can become unhealthy. To maximize your emotional and interpersonal wellness, use the Internet to widen your circle of friends, not shrink it.

Living Together

According to the U.S. Census Bureau, 4.9 million opposite-sex couples and 595,000 same-sex couples were living together in 2000. The Human Rights Campaign, however, estimates that the number of same-sex couples is closer to 1.6 million. Living together, or **cohabitation,** is one of the most rapid and dramatic social changes that has ever occurred in our society. It seems to be gaining acceptance as part of the normal mate-selection process. By age 30, about half of all men and women will have cohabited. Several factors are involved in this change, including greater acceptance of premarital sex, increased availability of contraceptives, the tendency for people to wait longer before getting married, and a larger pool of single and divorced individuals.

Cohabitation is more popular among younger people than older, although a significant number of older couples live together without marrying to avoid losing a source of income, such as Social Security benefits, should they marry. Living together provides many of the benefits of marriage: companionship; a setting for an enjoyable and meaningful relationship; the opportunity to develop greater intimacy through learning, compromising, and sharing; a satisfying sex life; and a way to save on living costs.

Living together has certain advantages over marriage. For one thing, it can give the partners a greater sense of autonomy. Not bound by the social rules and expectations that are part of the institution of marriage, partners may find it easier to keep their identity and more of their independence. Cohabitation doesn't incur the same obligations as marriage. If things don't work out, the partners may find it easier to leave a relationship that hasn't been legally sanctioned.

But living together has some liabilities, too. In most cases, the legal protections of marriage are absent, such as health insurance benefits and property and inheritance rights. These considerations can be particularly serious if the couple has children, from either former relationships or the current one. Couples may feel social or family pressure to marry or otherwise change their living arrangements, especially if they have young children. The general trend, however, is toward legitimizing nonmarital partnerships; for example, some employers, communities, and states now extend benefits to unmarried domestic partners.

TERMS

cohabitation   Living together in a sexual relationship without being married.

sexual orientation   A consistent pattern of emotional and sexual attraction based on biological sex; it exists along a continuum that ranges from exclusive heterosexuality (attraction to people of the other sex) through bisexuality (attraction to people of both sexes) to exclusive homosexuality (attraction to people of one's own sex).

homosexual   Emotional and sexual attraction to people of one's own sex.

heterosexual   Emotional and sexual attraction to people of the other sex.

Although many people choose cohabitation as a kind of trial marriage, unmarried partnerships tend to be less stable than marriages. In a survey of women age 15–44 who had cohabited, fewer than half were still living—married (37%) or unmarried (10%)—with their first live-in partner, 34% had dissolved the relationship prior to marriage, and 21% had married and then divorced their partner. There is little evidence that cohabitation before marriage leads to happier or longer-lasting marriages; in fact, some studies have found slightly less marital satisfaction and slightly higher divorce rates among couples who had previously cohabited.

Same-Sex Partnerships

Regardless of **sexual orientation**, most people look for love in a close, satisfying, committed relationship. A person whose sexual orientation is lesbian, gay, or bisexual (LGB) may be involved in a **homosexual** (same-sex) relationship. Same-sex couples have many similarities with **heterosexual** couples (those who seek members of the opposite sex). According to one study, most gay men and lesbians have experienced at least one long-term relationship with a single partner. Like any intimate relationship, same-sex partnerships provide intimacy, passion, and security.

One difference between heterosexual and homosexual couples is that same-sex partnerships tend to be more egalitarian (equal) and less organized around traditional gender roles. Same-sex couples put greater emphasis on partnership than on role assignment. Domestic tasks are shared or split, and both partners usually support themselves financially.

Another difference between heterosexual and homosexual relationships is that same-sex partners often have to deal with societal hostility or ambivalence toward their relationship, in contrast to the societal approval and rights given to heterosexual couples (see the box "Same-Sex Marriage and Civil Unions" on page 112). *Homophobia*, fear or hatred of homosexuals, can be obvious, as in the case of violence or discrimination, or more subtle, such as how same-sex couples are portrayed in the media. Additional stress on a same-sex partnership may occur if an LGB individual is a member of a family or ethnic group that isn't entirely accepting of her or his sexual orientation.

Bisexual individuals involved in heterosexual relationships may feel shame or guilt around the acceptance and privileges afforded to them by their heterosexual relationship. Due to the impact of societal disapproval, community resources and support may be more important for same-sex couples as a source of identity and social support than they are for heterosexuals. Many communities offer support groups for same-sex partners and families to help them build social networks and a sense of pride and acceptance.

Greater openness has made gay men and lesbians more visible than they used to be, although they still constitute a minority of the population. Most gay men and lesbians have experienced at least one long-term relationship with a single partner.

Although many challenges for same-sex partnerships are common to all relationships, some issues are unique to LGB partnerships. Because men are not socialized to communicate about interpersonal and emotional issues, communication problems may be particularly common or acute in gay relationships. Some researchers suggest that the process of female socialization, with its emphasis on creating and maintaining intimacy, makes lesbian relationships more likely to be characterized by fusion, enmeshment, and a blurring of boundaries. Problems may also arise when one member of a same-sex relationship has come out, or publicly identified as LGB, earlier than the other; consequently, the more experienced individual may wonder and worry whether the partner's sexual orientation is transient. The less experienced member of the relationship may feel threatened by the partner's level of "outness" or involvement in the LGB community. If same-sex couples decide to seek counseling, it is important to find a therapist who is an ally to the LGB community and who has training and experience working with LGB couples.

See Chapter 5 for more information on sexual orientation, gender identity, and sexual behavior.

Singlehood

Despite the prevalence and popularity of marriage, a significant and growing number of adults in our society are unmarried—more than 110 million single individuals. The largest group of unmarried adults have never been married (Figure 4.1).

Several factors contribute to the growing number of single people. One is the changing view of singlehood, which is increasingly being viewed as a legitimate alternative to marriage. Education and career are delaying the age at which young people are marrying. The median age for marriage is now 27.1 years for men and 25.3 years for women. More young people are living with their parents as they complete their education, seek jobs, or strive for financial independence. Many other single people live together without being married. Gay people who would marry their partners if they were legally permitted to do so are counted among the single population. High divorce rates mean more singles, and people who have experienced divorce in their families may have more negative attitudes about marriage and more positive attitudes about singlehood.

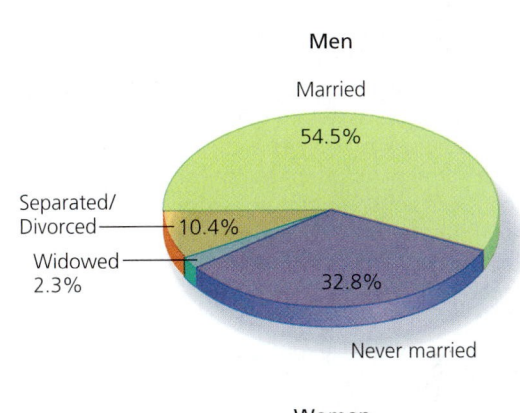

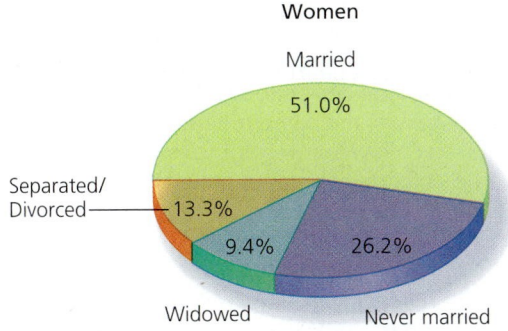

VITAL STATISTICS

FIGURE 4.1   Marital status of the U.S. population age 15 years and older.

SOURCE: U.S. Bureau of the Census. 2007. *America's Families and Living Arrangements, 2006* (http://www.census.gov/population/www/socdemo/hh-fam/cps2006.htm; retrieved January 21, 2009).

Same-Sex Marriage and Civil Unions

Marriage is often viewed primarily as a social or religious institution, but it is in fact an institution defined by state and federal statutes that confer legal and economic rights and responsibilities. According to the U.S. General Accountability Office, there are more than 1000 federal laws in which a distinction is based on marriage. Marital status affects Social Security, federal tax status, Medicaid eligibility, inheritance, medical decision making, and many other aspects of life.

The push for legal recognition of same-sex partnerships began decades ago, but it was brought to the forefront of public debate beginning in the 1990s. Supporters of same-sex marriage rights, however, have met with stiff opposition at the state and federal levels.

The majority of states and the federal government have passed laws and amendments that effectively ban same-sex marriage. A federal law called the Defense of Marriage Act (DOMA), signed by President Clinton in 1996, defines marriage as the legal union between one man and one woman and refuses federal recognition of same-sex marriages. It also allows states to refuse to recognize same-sex marriages and civil unions performed in other states or countries. (Such action might otherwise be in violation of the U.S. Constitution's provision that each state will give "full faith and credit" to the laws of other states.)

In 2004, President Bush endorsed an amendment to the U.S. Constitution, the "Federal Marriage Amendment," that would permanently ban same-sex marriage and prevent expected future legal challenges to federal and state DOMAs. Under the proposed amendment, states would still be allowed to grant civil unions. The amendment was defeated in Congress in fall 2004 and again in summer 2006.

As of late 2008, the status of same-sex marriage and civil union laws was as follows in the United States:

• Most states had enacted their own mini-DOMAs and/or passed state constitutional amendments that ban same-sex marriages and, in some cases, civil unions. Most of these states further refuse to recognize same-sex marriages from other states.

• Massachusetts began allowing same-sex marriages among its residents in 2006; same-sex non-residents cannot marry there. Connecticut legalized gay marriage in 2008.

• In 2008, Oregon granted domestic partners most of the same legal protections as marriage.

• Vermont, New Hampshire, and New Jersey all allow civil unions.

• The District of Columbia recognizes domestic partnerships. Similar types of recognition have been proposed in New York and Rhode Island, but the legislatures and courts in those states have not taken final action.

• Iowa has a DOMA, but it was overturned by a county judge in 2007. As of late 2008, the state was awaiting a decision on the issue by the Iowa Supreme Court.

• California enacted its own DOMA in 2000, but the state's Supreme Court overturned the act in 2008. After a few months of legalized same-sex marriages, California voters approved a constitutional amendment outlawing gay marriage. That amendment was immediately challenged in court.

What cases are made for and against civil union and same-sex marriage? Opponents put forth numerous arguments, including that the purpose of marriage is to procreate, that the Bible forbids same-sex unions, that homosexuals are seeking special rights, that it's bad for children and families, and that the majority of the population opposes such unions. The primary argument, however, is that same-sex marriage undermines the sanctity and validity of marriage as it is traditionally understood and thus undermines society. Rules and restrictions on who can marry preserve the value of the institution of marriage, according to this view. The underlying assumption of this position is that homosexual behavior is a choice and that people can change their orientation, though the process may be difficult.

Proponents of civil unions and same-sex marriage believe that sexual orientation is outside the control of the individual and results from genetic and environmental factors that create an unchangeable orientation. The issue of same-sex union is then seen as one of basic civil rights, in which a group is being denied rights—to publicly express their commitment to one another, to provide security for their children, and to receive the legal and economic benefits afforded to married heterosexual couples—on the basis of something as unalterable as skin color.

Both opponents and proponents of same-sex marriage point out that marriage is healthy for both men and women and is the main social institution promoting family values; both sides see this assertion as supportive of their position. What remains to be seen is how society in general is going to view same-sex marriage in the future—as a furthering of American values or as an attack on them.

QUESTIONS FOR CRITICAL THINKING AND REFLECTION

How have your life's experiences influenced your views on marriage and singlehood? If you're single now, do you plan to get married, or do you have doubts about it? If you're married, do you enjoy it, or do you have regrets? How do you explain these feelings?

Being single doesn't mean not having close relationships, however. Single people date, enjoy active and fulfilling social lives, and have a variety of sexual experiences and relationships. Other advantages of being single include more opportunities for personal and career development without concern for family obligations and more freedom and control in making life choices. Disadvantages include loneliness and a lack of companionship, as well as economic hardships (mainly for single women). Single men and women alike experience some discrimination and often are pressured to get married.

Nearly everyone has at least one episode of being single in adult life, whether prior to marriage, between marriages, following divorce or the death of a spouse, or for his or her entire life. How enjoyable and valuable this single time is depends on several factors, including how deliberately the person has chosen it; how satisfied the person is with his or her social relationships, standard of living, and job; how comfortable the person feels when alone; and how resourceful and energetic the person is about creating an interesting and fulfilling life.

MARRIAGE

The majority of Americans marry at some time in their life. Marriage continues to remain popular because it satisfies several basic needs. There are many important social, moral, economic, and political aspects of marriage, all of which have changed over the years. In the past, people married mainly for practical reasons, such as raising children or forming an economic unit. Today, people marry more for personal, emotional reasons.

Benefits of Marriage

The primary functions and benefits of marriage are those of any intimate relationship: affection, personal affirmation, companionship, sexual fulfillment, and emotional growth. Marriage also provides a setting in which to raise children, although an increasing number of couples choose to remain childless, and people can also choose to raise children without being married. Marriage is also important for providing for the future. By committing themselves to the relationship, people establish themselves with lifelong companions as well as some insurance for their later years.

Good marriages have been shown to have myriad positive effects on individuals' health (see the box "Are Intimate Relationships Good for Your Health?" on page 114).

Issues in Marriage

Although we might like to believe otherwise, love is not enough to make a successful marriage. Couples have to be strong and successful in their relationship before getting married, because relationship problems will be magnified rather than solved by marriage. The following relationship characteristics appear to be the best predictors of a happy marriage:

- The partners have realistic expectations about their relationship.
- Each feels good about the personality of the other.
- They communicate well.
- They have effective ways of resolving conflicts.
- They agree on religious/ethical values.
- They have an egalitarian role relationship.
- They have a good balance of individual versus joint interests and leisure activities.

Once married, couples must provide each other with emotional support, negotiate and establish marital roles, establish domestic and career priorities, handle their finances, make sexual adjustments, manage boundaries and relationships with their extended family, and participate in the larger community.

Marital roles and responsibilities have undergone profound changes in recent years. Many couples no longer accept traditional role assumptions, such as that the husband is solely responsible for supporting the family and the wife is solely responsible for domestic work. Today, many husbands share domestic tasks, and many wives work outside the home. In fact, over 50% of married women are in the labor force, including women with babies under 1 year of age. Although women still take most of the responsibility for home and children even when they work and although men still suffer more job-related stress and health problems than women do, the trend is toward an equalization of responsibilities.

The Role of Commitment

Coping with all these challenges requires that couples be committed to remaining in the relationship through its inevitable ups and downs. They need to be tolerant of each other's imperfections and keep their perspective and sense of humor. Commitment is based on conscious choice rather than on feelings, which, by their very nature, are transitory.

Are Intimate Relationships Good for Your Health?

Findings suggest that there are intrinsic benefits to marriage. Married people, on average, live longer than unmarried people—whether single, divorced, or widowed—and they score higher on measures of mental health. They have a lower prevalence of headaches, low-back pain, inactivity, and psychological distress. Married people consistently report being happier than unmarried people.

The benefits of intimate relationships have been demonstrated for a range of conditions: People with strong social support are less likely to catch colds. They recover better from heart attacks, live longer with heart disease, and have higher survival rates for certain cancers. Among men with prostate cancer, those who are married live significantly longer than those who are single, divorced, or widowed. Women in satisfying marriages are less likely to develop risk factors associated with cardiovascular diseases than unmarried women or women in unhappy marriages. A 2006 study found that people who never marry have a higher chance of dying prematurely than people who have been divorced, separated, or widowed.

What is it about social relationships that supports wellness? Some studies suggest that friends and partners may encourage and reinforce healthy habits, such as exercising, eating right, and seeing a physician when needed. In times of illness, a loving partner can provide both practical help (sometimes financial) and emotional support. Feeling loved, esteemed, and valued brings comfort at a time of vulnerability, reduces anxiety, and mitigates the damaging effects of stress and risks of social isolation.

Although good relationships may help the sick get better, bad relationships may have the opposite effect. The impact of relationship quality on the course of illness may be partly explained by effects of the immune system: A study of married couples whose fighting went beyond normal conflict and into criticism and name-calling found them to have weaker immune responses than couples whose arguments were more civil. Hostile couples need more time for injuries to heal; their systems tend to contain higher levels of inflammatory agents, which have been linked to long-term illness. New research shows that high marital stress is linked with risky lifestyle choices and behaviors and nonadherence to medical regimens. Similarly, unhappy marriages are associated with risk factors for heart disease, such as depression, hostility, and anger.

Marriage, of course, isn't the only support system available. Whether married, in a committed partnership, or single, if you have supportive people in your life, you are likely to enjoy better physical and emotional health than if you feel isolated and alone. So when you start planning lifestyle changes to improve your health and well-being, don't forget to nurture your relationships with family and friends. Relationships are powerful medicine.

Commitment is a promise of a shared future, a promise to be together, come what may. Committed partners put effort and energy into the relationship, no matter how they feel. They take time to attend to their partner, give compliments, and deal with conflict when necessary.

Commitment has become an important concept in recent years. To many people, commitment is a more important goal than living together or marriage.

reflects our extremely high expectations for emotional fulfillment and satisfaction in marriage (Figure 4.2). It also indicates that we no longer believe in the permanence of marriage.

The process of divorce usually begins with an emotional separation. Often one partner is unhappy and looks beyond the relationship for other forms of validation. Dissatisfaction increases until the unhappy partner decides he or she can no longer stay. Physical separation follows, although it may take some time for the relationship to be over emotionally.

Except for the death of a spouse or family member, divorce is the greatest stress-producing event in life. Research shows that divorced women are more likely to develop heart disease than married, remarried, or widowed women. Both men and women experience turmoil, depression, and lowered self-esteem during and after divorce. People experience separation distress and loneliness for about a year and then begin a recovery period of

Separation and Divorce

People marrying today have a 50–55% chance of divorcing. The high rate of divorce in the United States

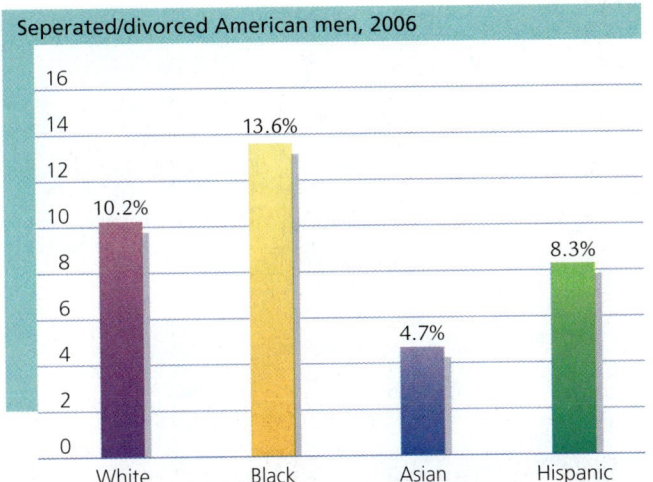

Seperated/divorced American men, 2006

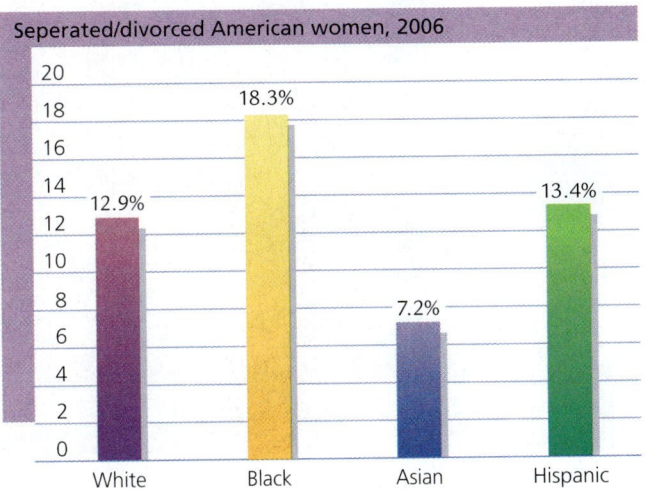

Seperated/divorced American women, 2006

FIGURE 4.2   Percentage of separated and divorced Americans, 2006.

SOURCE: U.S. Bureau of the Census. 2007. *America's Families and Living Arrangements, 2006* (http://www.census.gov/population/www/socdemo/hh-fam; retrieved January 21, 2009).

1–3 years. During this time they gradually construct a postdivorce identity, along with a new pattern of life. Most people are surprised by how long it takes to recover from divorce.

Children are especially vulnerable to the trauma of divorce, and sometimes counseling is appropriate to help them adjust to the changes in their lives. However, recent research has found that children who spend substantial time with both parents are usually better adjusted than those in sole custody arrangements and as well adjusted as their peers from intact families.

Despite the distress of separation and divorce, the negative effects are usually balanced sooner or later by the possibility of finding a more suitable partner, constructing a new life, and developing new aspects of the self. About 75% of all people who divorce remarry, often within 5 years. One result of the high divorce and remarriage rate is a growing number of stepfamilies (discussed in the next section).

FAMILY LIFE

American families are very different today than they were even a few decades ago. Currently, about half of all families are based on a first marriage; almost one-third are headed by a single parent; the remainder are remarriages or involve some other arrangement. Despite the tremendous variation apparent in American families, certain patterns can still be discerned.

Becoming a Parent

Few new parents have any preparation for the job of parenting, yet they have to assume that role literally overnight. They have to learn quickly how to hold a baby, how to change it, how to feed it, how to interpret its cries. No wonder the birth of the first child is one of the most stressful transitions for any couple.

Even couples with an egalitarian relationship before their first child is born find that their marital roles become more traditional with the arrival of the new baby. The father becomes the primary provider and protector, and the mother becomes the primary nurturer. Most research indicates that mothers have to make greater changes in their lives than fathers do. Although men today spend more time caring for their infants than ever before, women still take the ultimate responsibility for the baby. In addition, women are usually the ones who make job changes; they may quit working or reduce their hours in order to stay home with the baby for several months or more, or they may try to juggle the multiple roles of mother, homemaker, and employer/employee and feel guilty that they never have enough time to do justice to any of these roles.

Not surprisingly, marital satisfaction often declines after the birth of the first child. The wife who has stopped working may feel she is cut off from the world; the wife who is trying to fulfill duties both at home and on the job may feel overburdened and resentful. The husband may have a hard time adjusting to having to share his wife's love and attention with the baby.

But marital dissatisfaction after the baby is born is not inevitable. Couples who successfully weather the stresses

QUESTIONS FOR CRITICAL THINKING AND REFLECTION

How do you define "commitment" in a relationship? Is it simply a matter of staying faithful to a partner, or is there more? In your own relationships, what signs of commitment do you look for from your partner? What signs of commitment does your partner see in you?

of a new baby seem to have these three characteristics in common:

1. They had developed a strong relationship before the baby was born.
2. They had planned to have the child and want it very much.
3. They communicate well about their feelings and expectations.

Parenting

Sometimes being a parent is a source of unparalleled pleasure and pride—the first smile (at you), the first word, the first home run. But at other times parenting can seem like an overwhelming responsibility.

Parenting Styles   Most parents worry about their ability to raise a healthy, responsible, and well-adjusted child. Parents may wonder about the long-term impact of each decision they make on their child's well-being and personality. According to parenting experts, no one action or decision (within limits) will determine a child's personality or development; instead, what is most important is the *parenting style,* or overall approach to parenting.

Research has revealed four general styles of parenting. The four styles vary primarily according to the levels of two characteristics of the parents:

- *Demandingness* encompasses the use of discipline and supervision, the expectation that children act responsibly and maturely, and the direct response to disobedience.
- *Responsiveness* refers to a parent's warmth and his or her intent to facilitate independence and self-confidence in a child by being supportive, connected, and understanding of the child's needs.

Most parents use a blend of the four general styles but tend toward one style.

AUTHORITARIAN   *Authoritarian* parents are high in demandingness and low in responsiveness. They give orders and expect them to be obeyed, giving very little warmth or consideration to their children's special needs. They maintain a structured environment where the rules are explicit and set without input or discussion with the child. Children of authoritarian parents rate low on social competence, self-esteem, intellectual curiosity, spontaneity, and initiative. They perform fairly well in school and do not exhibit a lot of problem behavior; however, they have higher levels of depression.

AUTHORITATIVE   *Authoritative* parents are high in both demandingness and responsiveness. They set clear boundaries and expectations, but they are also loving, support-

Setting clear boundaries, holding children to high expectations, and responding with warmth to children's needs are all positive parenting strategies.

ive, and attuned to their children's needs. They are firm in their decisions but allow for a give-and-take in discussions with the intent of fostering independent thinking.

Both authoritarian and authoritative parents hold their children to high expectations. The difference is that authoritarian parents expect their children to follow their commands without question or comment and authoritative parents are more likely to explain their reasoning and allow children to express themselves. Research consistently shows that children of authoritative parents are the best adjusted and rate particularly high in social competence.

PERMISSIVE (OR INDULGENT)   *Permissive* parents are high in responsiveness and low in demandingness. They do not expect their children to act maturely but instead allow them to follow their own impulses. They are very warm, patient, and accepting, and they are focused on not stifling their child's innate creativity. They use little discipline and are often nontraditional. Children of permissive parents have difficulty with impulse-control, are immature, perform more poorly in school, have more problem behaviors, and take less responsibility for their actions. They also have higher self-esteem, better social skills, and lower levels of depression.

UNINVOLVED *Uninvolved* parents are low in both demandingness and responsiveness. They require little from their children and respond with little attention, frequency, or effort. In extreme cases, this style might reach the level of child neglect. Research has found that children of uninvolved parents perform worse in all areas measured compared with children of parents using the other styles.

Children's Temperaments
Every child has a tendency toward certain moods and a style of reacting—a temperament—that is apparent from infancy and often lasts into adulthood. Research has identified three basic temperament types; most children show aspects of different temperaments but tend toward one.

- *Easy children* are happy, content, and have regular sleeping and eating habits. They are adaptable and not easily upset.
- *Difficult children* are fussy, fearful in new situations or with strangers, and have irregular sleeping and feeding habits. They are easily upset and often hard to soothe.
- *Slow-to-warm-up children* are somewhat fussy and tend to react negatively or fearfully to new people or situations; however, they slowly warm up and adapt positively.

A match between parental style and child temperament is ideal. Difficulties tend to arise when there is a mismatch in temperaments/styles and the parent is not versed in parenting skills. For example, a parent who expects quick action in response to a command may not be a good match for a slow-to-respond child. Parents should be attuned to their child's distinct style and do their best to support the child.

According to psychologists, "optimal attunement" of the parent to the child involves allowing the child to feel close and connected without feeling engulfed or impinged upon, and also allowing for separation and aloneness without the child feeling abandoned or rejected. *Attachment parenting* advocates believe that if children are consistently held, attended to, and not allowed to be unhappy for any length of time, they will internalize the parents' consistent care and support and grow up more able to provide this for themselves and others.

Parenting and the Family Life Cycle
Parenting that is responsive and demanding is the most beneficial for children. Providing a balance of firm limits and clear structure along with high levels of warmth, nurturance, and respect for the child's own special needs and temperament as well as her or his growing independence is the

best predictor for raising a healthy child. The important thing is to keep seeking ways to promote satisfaction for all family members—including the parents! It is also important for parents to develop and maintain confidence in their parenting skills, their common sense—and, above all, their love for their children.

At each stage of the family life cycle, the relationship between parents and children changes. And with those changes come new challenges. The parents' primary responsibility to a small, helpless baby is to ensure its physical well-being around the clock. As babies grow into toddlers and begin to crawl and walk and talk, they begin to be able to take care of some of their own physical needs. For parents, the challenge at this stage is to strike a balance between giving children the freedom to explore and setting limits that will keep the children safe and secure. As children grow toward adolescence, parents need to give them increasing independence and gradually be willing to let them risk success or failure on their own.

Marital satisfaction for most couples tends to decline somewhat while the children are in school. Reasons include the financial and emotional pressures of a growing family and the increased job and community responsibilities of parents in their thirties, forties, and fifties. Once the last child has left home, marital satisfaction usually increases because the couple have time to enjoy each other once more.

Single Parents

Today the family life cycle for many women is marriage, motherhood, divorce, single parenthood, remarriage, and widowhood. According to the U.S. Census Bureau, about 28% of all children under 18 live with only one parent (Figure 4.3 on p. 118).

In some single-parent families, the traditional family life cycle is reversed and the baby comes before the marriage. In these families, the single parent is usually a teenage mother; she may very well be black or Hispanic, and she may never get married or may not marry for several years. In 2006, about 56% of all black children were living with single parents, as were 29% of Hispanic children.

Economic difficulties are the primary problem for single mothers, especially for unmarried mothers who have not finished high school and have difficulty finding work. Divorced mothers usually experience a sharp drop in income the first few years on their own, but if they have job skills or education they usually can eventually support themselves and their children adequately. Other problems for single mothers are the often-conflicting demands of playing both father and mother and the difficulty of satisfying their own needs for adult companionship and affection.

Financial pressures are also a complaint of single fathers, but they do not experience them to the extent that

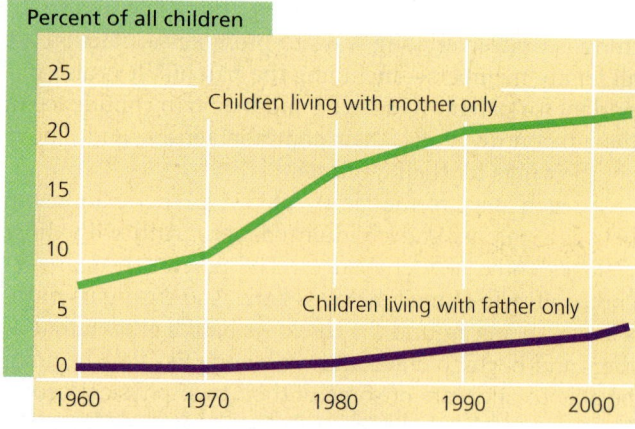

Percent of all children

Children living with mother only

Children living with father only

VITAL STATISTICS

FIGURE 4.3 **The growth of single-parent families in the United States.** Since 1960, the number of children living in single-parent families has risen from about 9% to more than 28%. Although the majority of these children live with their mother, a growing number of single-parent households are headed by fathers.

SOURCE: U.S. Bureau of the Census. 2007. *America's Families and Living Arrangements, 2006* (http://www.census.gov/population/www/socdemo/hh-fam; retrieved January 21, 2009).

single mothers do. Because they are likely to have less practice than mothers in juggling parental and professional roles, they may worry that they do not spend enough time with their children. Because single fatherhood is not as common as single motherhood, however, the men who choose it are likely to be stable, established, and strongly motivated to be with their children.

Research about the effect on children of growing up in a single-parent family is inconclusive. Evidence seems to indicate that these children tend to have less success in school and in their careers than children from two-parent families, but these effects may be associated more strongly with low educational attainment of the single parent than with the absence of the second parent. Two-parent families are not necessarily better if one of the parents spends little time relating to the children or is physically or emotionally abusive.

> **QUICK STATS**
>
> **Nearly 5%** of American children live in a home where neither parent is present.
>
> —U.S. Census Bureau, 2007

Stepfamilies

Single parenthood is usually a transitional stage: About three out of four divorced women and about four out of five divorced men will ultimately remarry. Rates are lower for widowed men and women, but overall, almost half the marriages in the United States are remarriages for the husband, the wife, or both. If either partner brings children from a previous marriage into the new family unit, a stepfamily (or "blended family") is formed.

Stepfamilies are significantly different from primary families and should not be expected to duplicate the emotions and relationships of a primary family. Research has shown that healthy stepfamilies are less cohesive and more adaptable than healthy primary families; they have a greater capacity to allow for individual differences and accept that biologically related family members will have emotionally closer relationships. Stepfamilies gradually gain more of a sense of being a family as they build a history of shared daily experiences and major life events.

Successful Families

Family life can be extremely challenging. A strong family is not a family without problems; it's a family that copes successfully with stress and crisis (see the box "Strategies of Strong Families"). Successful families are intentionally connected—members share experiences and meanings.

An excellent way to build strong family ties is to develop family rituals and routines—organized, repeated activities that have meaning for family members. Families with regular routines and rituals have healthier children, more satisfying marriages, and stronger family relationships. Some of the most common routines identified in research studies are dinnertime, a regular bedtime, and household chores; common rituals include birthdays, Christmas and other holidays, and Sunday activities. Family routines may even serve as protective factors, balancing out potential risk factors associated with single-parent families and families with divorce and remarriage. You may want to consider incorporating a regular family mealtime into your family routine, as it allows parents and children to develop closer relationships and leads to better parenting, healthier children, and better school performance.

Although there is tremendous variation in American families, researchers have proposed that six major qualities or themes appear in strong families:

1. *Commitment.* The family is very important to its members; sexual fidelity between partners is included in commitment.

2. *Appreciation.* Family members care about one another and express their appreciation. The home is a positive place for family members.

3. *Communication.* Family members spend time listening to one another and enjoying one another's company. They talk about disagreements and attempt to solve problems.

Strategies of Strong Families

Life is full of challenges; the key to life in a strong family is to work together to meet those challenges. The following are strategies used by strong families for dealing with life's difficulties:

• *Look for something positive in difficult situations.* No matter how difficult, most problems teach us something about ourselves and others that we can draw on in future situations.

• *Pull together.* Think of the problem not as one family member's difficulty but as a challenge for the family as a whole.

• *Get help outside the family.* Call on extended family members, supportive friends, neighbors, colleagues, church or synagogue members, and community professionals.

• *Create open channels of communication.* Challenges cannot be met when communication shuts down.

• *Keep things in perspective.* "These things, too, shall pass."

• *Adopt new roles in a flexible manner.* Crises often demand that individuals learn new approaches to life and take on different responsibilities.

• *Focus to minimize fragmentation.* Look at the big picture. Focusing on the details rather than the essentials can make people edgy, even hysterical.

• *Give up on worry, or put it in a box.* Worrying itself usually causes more misery than the problem at hand. Sometimes it's best to stuff the worry down or to resolve to worry 10 minutes a day and then forget about it. The mind simply has to rest.

• *Eat well, exercise, love each other, and get enough sleep.* We often forget that we are biological beings. Like kindergartners, we need a good lunch and time to play. We need to have our hair stroked, we need a good hug, and we need a good nap.

• *Create a life full of meaning and purpose.* We all face severe crises in life. These challenges are simply unavoidable. Sometimes it helps to focus on others, to offer service to the community. Giving of ourselves brings a richness and dignity to our lives, in spite of the troubles we endure.

• *Actively meet challenges head-on.* Life's disasters do not go away when we look in another direction.

• *Go with the flow to some degree.* Sometimes we are relatively powerless in the face of a crisis. Simply saying to ourselves that things will get better with time can be useful.

• *Be prepared in advance for life's challenges.* Healthy family relationships are like an ample bank balance: If our relational accounts are in order, we will be able to weather life's most difficult storms—together.

SOURCE: Olson, D. H., and J. DeFrain. 2006. *Marriages and Families: Intimacy, Diversity, and Strengths,* 5th ed. New York: McGraw-Hill.

---

4. *Time together.* Family members do things together, often simple activities that don't cost money.

5. *Spiritual wellness.* The family promotes sharing, love, and compassion for other human beings.

6. *Coping with stress and crisis.* When faced with illness, death, marital conflict, or other crises, family members pull together, seek help, and use other coping strategies to meet the challenge.

It may surprise some people that members of strong families are often seen at counseling centers. They know that the smartest thing to do in some situations is to get help. Many resources are available for individuals and families seeking counseling; people can turn to physicians, clergy, marriage and family counselors, psychologists, or other trained professionals.

THINKING ABOUT THE ENVIRONMENT

Parents can instill a lifelong sense of environmental stewardship in their children by teaching them these simple habits:

■ Recycle waste as much as possible.

■ Purchase environmentally friendly products that are manufactured from recyclable materials.

■ Turn off lights and appliances when they are not needed.

■ Shop for locally grown foods that are raised through environmentally sustainable practices.

For more information on the environment, see Chapter 19.

QUESTIONS FOR CRITICAL THINKING AND REFLECTION

Do you think of your own family as a "successful" family? Why or why not? Either way, what could you do to make your relationships in your family more successful? Are you comfortable talking to your family about these issues?

SUMMARY

- Healthy intimate relationships are an important component of the well-being of both individuals and society. Many intimate relationships are held together by love.

- Successful relationships begin with a positive sense of self and reasonably high self-esteem. Personal identity, gender roles, and styles of attachment are all rooted in childhood experiences.

- The characteristics of friendship include companionship, respect, acceptance, help, trust, loyalty, and reciprocity.

- Love, sex, and commitment are closely linked ideals in intimate relationships. Love includes trust, caring, respect, and loyalty. Sex brings excitement, fascination, and passion to the relationship.

- Common challenges in relationships relate to issues of self-disclosure, commitment, expectations, competitiveness, balancing time spent together and apart, and jealousy. Partners in successful relationships have strong communication skills and support each other in difficult times.

- The keys to good communication in relationships are self-disclosure, listening, and feedback.

- Conflict is inevitable in intimate relationships; partners need to have constructive ways to negotiate their differences.

- People usually choose partners like themselves. If partners are very different, acceptance and good communication skills are necessary to maintain the relationship.

- Most Americans find partners through dating or getting together in groups. Cohabitation is a growing social pattern that allows partners to get to know each other intimately without being married.

- Gay and lesbian partnerships are similar to heterosexual partnerships, with some differences. Partners often don't conform to traditional gender roles, and they may experience hostility or ambivalence rather than approval toward their partnership from society.

- Singlehood is a growing option in our society. Advantages include greater variety in sex partners and more freedom in making life decisions; disadvantages include loneliness and possible economic hardship, especially for single women.

- Marriage fulfills many functions for individuals and society. It can provide people with affection, affirmation, and sexual fulfillment; a context for child rearing; and the promise of lifelong companionship.

- Love isn't enough to ensure a successful marriage. Partners have to be realistic, feel good about each other, have communication and conflict-resolution skills, share values, and have a balance of individual and joint interests.

- When problems can't be worked out, people often separate and divorce. Divorce is traumatic for all involved, especially children, but the negative effects are usually balanced in time by positive ones.

- Four general parenting styles are authoritarian, authoritative, permissive, and uninvolved; the authoritative style is usually associated with the best outcomes.

- At each stage of the family life cycle, relationships change. Marital satisfaction may be lower during the child-rearing years and higher later.

- Many families today are single-parent families. Problems for single parents include economic difficulties, conflicting demands, and time pressures.

- Stepfamilies are formed when single, divorced, or widowed people remarry and create new family units. Stepfamilies gradually gain more of a sense of being a family as they build a history of shared experiences.

- Important qualities of successful families include commitment to the family, appreciation of family members, communication, time spent together, spiritual wellness, and effective methods of dealing with stress.

For resources in your area, check your campus directory for a counseling center or peer counseling program, or check the agencies listed in the Mental Health section of the phone book.

BOOKS

Brooks, J. B. 2008. *The Process of Parenting,* 7th ed. New York: McGraw-Hill. *Demonstrates how parents and caregivers can translate their love and concern for children into effective parenting behavior.*

DeGenova, M. K., and F. P. Rice. 2006. *Intimate Relationships, Marriages, and Families,* 7th ed. New York: McGraw-Hill. *A comprehensive introduction to relationships.*

McKay, M., P. Fanning, and K. Paleg. 2007. *Couple Skills: Making Your Relationship Work,* 2nd rev. ed. New York: New Harbinger. *A comprehensive guide to improving communication, resolving conflict, and developing greater intimacy and commitment in relationships.*

Miller, R., D. Perlman, and S. S. Brehm. 2008. *Intimate Relationships,* 5th ed. New York: McGraw-Hill. *A balanced presentation of both the positive and the problematic aspects of intimate relationships.*

Olson, D., and J. DeFrain. 2007. *Marriages and Families: Intimacy, Diversity, and Strengths,* 6th ed. New York: McGraw-Hill. *A comprehensive introduction to relationships and families.*

ORGANIZATIONS AND WEB SITES

American Association for Marriage and Family Therapy. Provides information on a variety of relationship issues and referrals to therapists.
http://www.aamft.org

Association for Couples in Marriage Enrichment (ACME). An organization that promotes activities to strengthen marriage; a resource for books, tapes, and other materials.
http://www.bettermarriages.org

Conflict Resolution Information Source. Provides links to a broad range of Internet resources on conflict resolution. Information covers interpersonal, marriage, family, and other types of conflicts.
http://www.crinfo.org/

Family Education Network. Provides information about education, safety, health, and other family-related issues.
http://www.familyeducation.com

Gottman Institute. Includes tips and suggestions for relationships and parenting, including an online relationships quiz.
http://www.gottman.com

Life Innovations. Provides materials for premarital counseling and marital enrichment.
http://www.prepare-enrich.com

Parents Without Partners (PWP). Provides educational programs, literature, and support groups for single parents and their children. Search the online directory for a referral to a local chapter.
http://www.parentswithoutpartners.org

United States Census Bureau. Provides current statistics on births, marriages, and living arrangements.
http://www.census.gov

Yahoo/Lesbians, Gays, and Bisexuals. A Web site and search engine that contains many links to information and support for lesbians and gays.
http://dir.yahoo.com/society_and_culture/cultures_and_groups

See also the listings for Chapters 3 and 8.

SELECTED BIBLIOGRAPHY

Bookwala, J. 2005. The role of marital quality in physical health during the mature years. *Journal of Aging and Health* 17(1): 85–104.

Centers for Disease Control and Prevention. 2004. Marital status and health: United States, 1999–2002. *Advance Data from Vital and Health Statistics,* No. 351.

Christakis, N. A., et al. 2006. Mortality after hospitalization of a spouse. *New England Journal of Medicine* 354(7): 719–730.

Egelko, B. 2006. Fight over same-sex unions hits court in San Francisco. *San Francisco Chronicle,* 10 July.

Godoy, M. 2008. *NPR: Gay Marriage Laws Interactive Map* (http://www.npr .org/news/specials/gaymarriage/map; retrieved January 24, 2009).

Holt-Lunstad, J., W. Birmingham, and B. Q. Jones. 2008. Is there something unique about marriage? *Annals of Behavioral Medicine* 35(2): 239–244.

Human Rights Campaign. 2008. Relationship Recognition in the United States (http://www.hrc.org; retrieved January 21, 2009).

Human Rights Campaign. 2008. *Statewide Marriage Laws* (http://www.hrc .org; retrieved January 21, 2009).

Madden, M., and A. Lenhart. 2006. *Online Dating.* Washington, D.C.: Pew Internet & American Life Project.

McPherson, M., L. Smith-Lovin, and M. Brashears. 2006. Social isolation in America: Changes in core discussion networks over two decades. *American Sociological Review* 71: 353–375.

Medical memo: Marital stress and the heart. 2004. *Harvard Men's Health Watch,* May.

Mookadam, F., and H. M. Arthur. 2004. Social support and its relationship to morbidity and mortality after acute myocardial infarction: Systematic overview. *Archives of Internal Medicine* 164(14): 1514–1518.

Najib, A., et al. 2004. Regional brain activity in women grieving a romantic relationship breakup. *American Journal of Psychiatry* 161(12): 2245–2256.

National Conference of State Legislatures. 2008 Update. *Same Sex Marriage, Civil Unions and Domestic Partnerships* (http://www.ncsl.org/programs/ cyf/samesex.htm; retrieved January 21, 2009).

Pleis, J. R., and M. Lethbridge-Cejku. 2007. Summary health statistics for U.S. adults: National Health Interview Survey, 2006. *Vital and Health Statistics* 10(235): 1–153.

Roisman, G. I., et al. 2008. Adult romantic relationships as contexts of human development: A multimethod comparison of same-sex couples with opposite-sex dating, engaged, and married dyads. *Developmental Psychology* 44(1): 91–101.

Schoen, R., et al. 2007. Family transitions in young adulthood. *Demography* 44(4): 807–820.

Strong, B., et al. 2005. *Human Sexuality: Diversity in Contemporary America,* 5th ed. New York: McGraw-Hill.

Wainright, J. L., S. T. Russell, and C. J. Patterson. 2004. Psychosocial adjustment, school outcomes, and romantic relationships of adolescents with same-sex parents. *Child Development* 75(6): 1886–1898.

Whisman, M. A., L. A. Uebelacker, and L. M. Weinstock. 2004. Psychopathology and marital satisfaction: The importance of evaluating both partners. *Journal of Consulting and Clinical Psychology* 72(5): 830–838.

SEX AND YOUR BODY

LOOKING AHEAD>>>>>

AFTER READING THIS CHAPTER, YOU SHOULD BE ABLE TO:

- Describe the structure and function of the female and male sex organs
- Explain the changes in sexual functioning that occur over the course of a person's life
- Describe how the sex organs function during sexual activity
- Identify common causes of sexual problems
- Outline the factors that influence sexual behavior and the various ways human sexuality can be expressed
- Describe guidelines for safe, responsible sexual behavior

TEST YOUR KNOWLEDGE

1. **Although testosterone is the primary male hormone, it is also produced in women.**
   True or false?

2. **Which of the following is a risk factor for erectile dysfunction ("impotence")?**
   a. smoking
   b. overweight
   c. physical inactivity

3. **Calcium supplements may reduce symptoms of premenstrual syndrome (PMS) in some women.**
   True or false?

4. **Alcohol consumption by young people is associated with unplanned, unprotected sexual activity and higher rates of sexually transmitted diseases (STDs).**
   True or false?

ANSWERS

1. **TRUE.** Testosterone is produced in small amounts by a woman's ovaries.

2. **ALL THREE.** 70–80% of cases of erectile dysfunction are thought to involve physical factors.

3. **TRUE.** Other self-help strategies for PMS include exercise, stress reduction, and a diet low in fat and rich in complex carbohydrates.

4. **TRUE.** Studies have shown that raising the drinking age and increasing the price of beer (through taxes) leads to a decrease in STD rates among young adults.

Humans are sexual beings. Sexual activity is the source of our most intense physical pleasures, a central ingredient in many of our intimate emotional relationships, and the key to reproduction.

Sexuality is more than just sexual behavior. It is a complex, interacting group of inborn, biological characteristics and acquired behaviors people learn in the course of growing up in a particular family, community, and society. Sexuality includes biological sex (being biologically male or female), gender (masculine and feminine behaviors), sexual anatomy and physiology, sexual functioning and practices, and social and sexual interactions with others. Our individual sense of identity is powerfully influenced by our sexuality. We think of ourselves in fundamental ways as male or female; as heterosexual or homosexual; as single, attached, married, or divorced.

Because it can arouse intense feelings, sexuality can be an emotionally charged topic. In many communities, sexual expression is regulated with restrictions and taboos, specifying which functions and behaviors are acceptable and "normal" and which are unacceptable and "abnormal." Young people in the United States are bombarded with conflicting messages about sex. The mass media suggest that the average person is a sexual athlete who continually jumps in and out of bed without using contraception, producing offspring, or contracting disease. Although parents, educators, and other responsible adults may try to present a more balanced picture, they often convey their own hidden messages as well. Ignorance, confusion, and fear are frequently the result.

Basic information about the body, sexual functioning, and sexual behavior is vital to healthy adult life. Once we understand the facts, we have a better basis for evaluating the messages we get and for making informed, responsible choices about our sexual activities. If you have questions about some aspects of your physical sexuality, this chapter will provide you with answers.

SEXUAL ANATOMY

In spite of their different appearances, the sex organs of men and women arise from the same structures and fulfill similar functions. Each person has a pair of **gonads**; ovaries are the female gonads, and testes are the male gonads. The gonads produce **germ cells** and sex hormones. The germ cells are **ova** (eggs) in females and **sperm** in males. Ova and sperm are the basic units of reproduction; their union results in the creation of a new life.

Female Sex Organs

The external sex organs, or genitals, of the female are called the **vulva** (Figure 5.1). The *mons pubis,* a rounded mass of fatty tissue over the pubic bone, becomes covered with hair during puberty (biological maturation). Below it are two paired folds of skin called the labia majora (major lips) and the labia minora (minor lips). Enclosed within these folds are the clitoris, the opening of the urethra, and the opening of the vagina.

The **clitoris** is highly sensitive to touch and plays an important role in female sexual arousal and orgasm. The clitoris consists of a shaft, glans, and spongy tissue that fills with blood during sexual excitement. The glans is the most sensitive part of the clitoris and is covered by the clitoral hood, or **prepuce,** which is formed from the upper portion of the labia minora.

The female **urethra** is a duct that leads directly from the urinary bladder to its opening between the clitoris and the opening of the vagina; it conducts urine from the bladder to the outside of the body. The female urethra is independent of the genitals.

The vaginal opening is partially covered by a membrane called the **hymen.** This membrane can be stretched or torn during athletic activity or when a woman has sexual intercourse for the first time. (The idea that an intact hymen is the sign of virginity is a myth.) The **vagina** is the

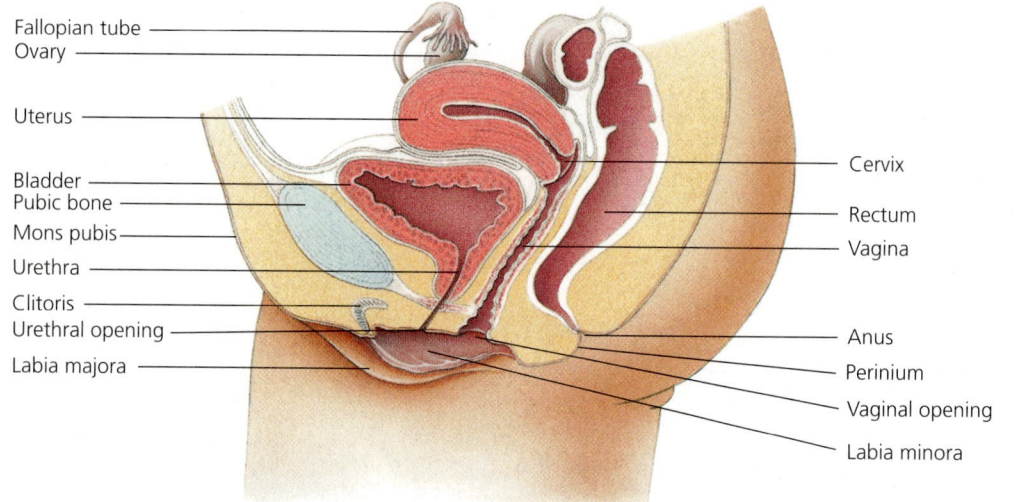

Fallopian tube
Ovary
Uterus
Bladder
Pubic bone
Mons pubis
Urethra
Clitoris
Urethral opening
Labia majora

Cervix
Rectum
Vagina
Anus
Perinium
Vaginal opening
Labia minora

FIGURE 5.1 The female sex organs.

FIGURE 5.2 The male sex organs.

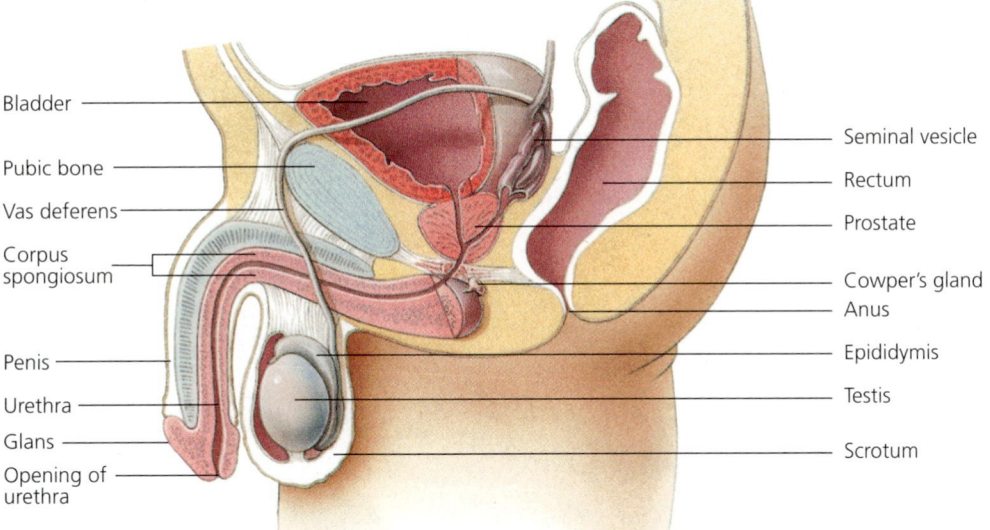

Bladder

Pubic bone

Vas deferens

Corpus spongiosum

Penis

Urethra

Glans

Opening of urethra

Seminal vesicle

Rectum

Prostate

Cowper's gland

Anus

Epididymis

Testis

Scrotum

passage that leads to the internal reproductive organs. It is the female structure for heterosexual sexual intercourse and also serves as the birth canal.

Projecting into the upper part of the vagina is the **cervix**, which is the opening of the **uterus**—or *womb*—where a fertilized egg is implanted and grows into a *fetus*.

A pair of **fallopian tubes** (or *oviducts*) extend from the top of the uterus. The end of each oviduct surrounds an **ovary** and guides the mature ovum down into the uterus after the egg exits the ovary.

Male Sex Organs

A man's external sex organs, or genitals, are the penis and the scrotum (Figure 5.2).

The **penis** consists of spongy tissue that becomes engorged with blood during sexual excitement, causing the organ to enlarge and become erect.

The **scrotum** is a pouch that contains a pair of sperm-producing male gonads, called **testes.** The scrotum maintains the testes at a temperature approximately 5°F below that of the rest of the body—that is, at about 93.6°F. The process of sperm production is extremely heat-sensitive. In hot temperatures the muscles in the scrotum relax, and the testes move away from the heat of the body. This ability to regulate the temperature of the testes is important because elevated testicular temperature can interfere with normal sperm production.

Through the entire length of the penis runs the urethra, which can carry both urine and *semen*, the sperm-carrying fluid, to the opening at the tip of the penis. Although urine and semen share a common passage, they are prevented from mixing together by muscles that control their entry into the urethra.

During its brief lifetime, a sperm takes the following route:

TERMS

sexuality   A dimension of personality shaped by biological, psychosocial, and cultural forces and concerning all aspects of sexual behavior.

gonads   The primary reproductive organs that produce germ cells and sex hormones; the ovaries and testes.

germ cells   Sperm and ova (eggs).

ovum   A germ cell produced by a female, which combines with a male germ cell (sperm) to create a fetus; plural, *ova*. Also called an *egg*.

sperm   A germ cell produced by a male, which combines with a female germ cell (ovum) to create a fetus.

vulva   The external female genitals, or sex organs.

clitoris   The highly sensitive female genital structure.

prepuce   The foreskin of the clitoris or penis.

urethra   The duct that carries urine from the bladder to the outside of the body.

hymen   A membrane that partially covers the vaginal opening.

vagina   The passage leading from the female genitals to the internal reproductive organs; the birth canal.

cervix   The end of the uterus opening toward the vagina.

uterus   The hollow, thick-walled, muscular organ in which the fertilized egg develops; the womb.

fallopian tube   A duct that guides a mature ovum from the ovary to the uterus. Also called an *oviduct*.

ovary   One of two female reproductive glands that produce ova (eggs) and sex hormones; ovaries are the female gonads.

penis   The male genital structure consisting of spongy tissue that becomes engorged with blood during sexual excitement.

scrotum   The loose sac of skin and muscle fibers that contains the testes.

testis   One of two male gonads, the site of sperm production; plural, *testes*. Also called *testicle*.

FIGURE 5.3 **Circumcised and uncircumcised penis.**

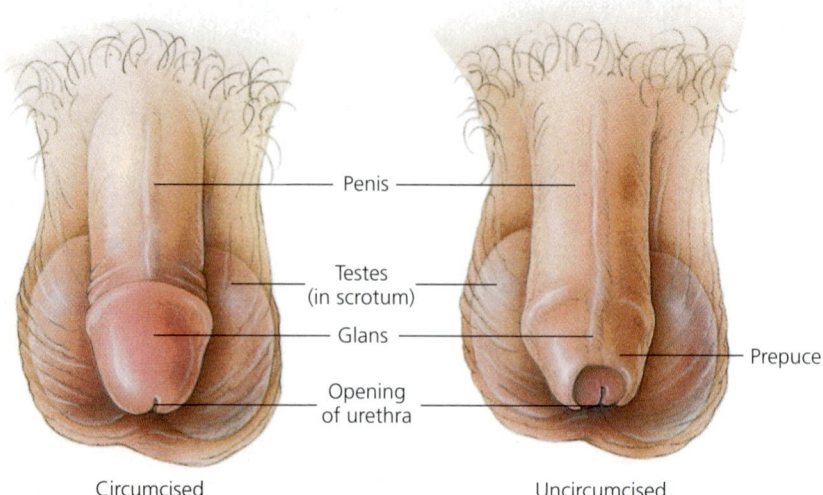

Circumcised   Uncircumcised

1. Sperm are produced inside a maze of tiny, tightly packed tubules within the testes. As they begin to mature, sperm flow into a single storage tube called the **epididymis**, which lies on the surface of each testis.

2. Sperm move from each epididymis into another tube called the **vas deferens**, which carries them upward into the abdominal cavity and through an organ called the **prostate gland**. This gland produces some of the fluid in semen, which helps transport and nourish the sperm.

3. The two *vasa deferentia* eventually merge into a pair of **seminal vesicles**, whose secretions provide nutrients for the semen.

4. On the final stage of their journey, sperm flow into the **ejaculatory ducts**, which join the urethra.

The **Cowper's glands** are two small structures flanking the urethra. During sexual arousal, these glands secrete a clear, mucuslike fluid that appears at the tip of the penis. The exact purpose of preejaculatory fluid is not known, but it is thought to help lubricate the urethra to facilitate the passage of sperm. In some men, preejaculatory fluid may contain sperm, so withdrawal of the penis before ejaculation is not a reliable form of contraception.

Circumcision The smooth, rounded tip of the penis is the highly sensitive **glans**, an important component in sexual arousal (Figure 5.3). The glans is partially covered by the foreskin, or prepuce, a retractable fold of skin that is removed by **circumcision** in about 60% of newborn males in the United States. Circumcision is performed for cultural, religious, and hygienic reasons, and rates of circumcision vary widely among different groups. Worldwide, the rate is about 30%. Most Europeans, Asians, South and Central Americans, and Africans do not perform circumcision; Jews and Muslims are the major groups who circumcise for religious reasons.

The pros and cons of this simple procedure have been widely debated. Citing research findings, proponents argue that it promotes cleanliness and reduces the risk of urinary tract infections (UTIs) in newborns and the risk of sexually transmitted diseases (STDs), including HIV, later in life. STD education and the practice of abstinence or low-risk sexual behaviors have a far greater impact on the transmission of STDs than does circumcision. However, where safer sex practices are not adhered to, circumcision can have a protective effect. Recent studies in countries with high rates of HIV infection and AIDS have shown that circumcision can reduce the risk of acquiring HIV through heterosexual contact in men by as much as 60%.

In 2007, an expert panel from the World Health Organization (WHO) recognized that male circumcision is an effective intervention for decreasing the spread of HIV, but stressed that circumcision provides only partial protection and must be combined with other preventive strategies such as condom use and limiting the number of sexual partners.

Opponents of circumcision state that it is an unnecessary surgical procedure that causes pain and puts a baby at risk for complications. They also argue that, by removing the foreskin, circumcision exposes the glans of the penis to constant irritation by clothing, thereby reducing its sensitivity; research into this issue has been inconclusive.

The American Academy of Pediatrics (AAP) takes the position (opposed by some physicians) that although circumcision has potential medical benefits, the research is

QUICK STATS

20 million or more sperm per milliliter of semen is considered a normal sperm count.

—Mayo Clinic (www.mayoclinic.com), 2008

THINKING ABOUT THE ENVIRONMENT

Research points to several possible environmental causes for sexual problems, but because studies have been scattered and produced conflicting results, scientists are now beginning exhaustive studies into these issues. Still, some researchers contend that environmental contaminants may cause a variety of sexual problems in humans. For example:

- Prenatal exposure to chemicals called phthalates may interfere with the development of sex organs in the male fetus.

- Adult exposure to pesticides may reduce sperm quality and quantity in men.

- Exposure to a number of common cleaning solvents (such as acetone) may increase a woman's chance of miscarriage.

For more information on the environment and environmental health, see Chapter 19.

not sufficient to recommend the procedure routinely. When circumcision is performed, the AAP recommends that painkilling medication be provided.

HORMONES AND THE REPRODUCTIVE LIFE CYCLE

Many cultural and personal factors help shape the expression of your sexuality, but biology also plays an important role. The sex hormones produced by the ovaries or testes have a major influence on the development and function of the reproductive system throughout life.

The sex hormones made by the testes are called **androgens,** the most important of which is *testosterone*. The female sex hormones, produced by the ovaries, belong to two groups: **estrogens** and **progestins,** the most important of which is *progesterone*. The ovaries also produce a small amount of testosterone. The cortex of the **adrenal glands** also produces androgens in both males and females.

The hormones produced by the testes, the ovaries, and the adrenal glands are regulated by the hormones of the **pituitary gland,** located at the base of the brain. This gland

QUESTIONS FOR CRITICAL THINKING AND REFLECTION

What are your personal views on circumcision? Who or what has influenced those opinions? Are the bases of your views primarily cultural, moral, or medical?

in turn is controlled by hormones produced by the **hypothalamus** in the brain.

Differentiation of the Embryo

The biological sex of an individual is determined by the fertilizing sperm at the time of conception. All human cells normally contain 23 pairs of chromosomes. In 22 of the pairs, the two partner chromosomes match. But in the twenty-third pair, the **sex chromosomes,** two configurations are possible. Individuals with two matching X chromosomes are female, and individuals with one X and one Y chromosome are male. Thus, at the time of conception, the genetic sex is established: Females are XX and males are XY (see the box "Sexual Differentiation, Hormones, and the Brain" on p. 128).

Genetic sex dictates whether the undifferentiated gonads become ovaries or testes. If a Y chromosome is present, the gonads become testes; the testes will produce

TERMS

epididymis   A storage duct for maturing sperm, located on the surface of each testis.

vas deferens   A tube that carries sperm from the epididmyis through the prostate gland to the seminal vesicles; plural, *vasa deferentia*.

prostate gland   An organ in the male reproductive system; produces some of the fluid in semen, which helps transport and nourish sperm.

seminal vesicle   A tube leading from the vas deferens to the ejaculatory duct; secretes nutrients for the semen.

ejaculatory duct   A tube that carries mature sperm to the urethra so they can exit the body upon ejaculation.

Cowper's gland   In the male reproductive system, a small organ that produces preejaculatory fluid.

glans   The rounded head of the penis or the clitoris.

circumcision   Surgical removal of the foreskin of the penis.

androgens   Male sex hormones produced by the testes in males and by the adrenal glands in both sexes.

estrogens   A class of female sex hormones, produced by the ovaries, that bring about sexual maturation at puberty and maintain reproductive functions.

progestins   A class of female sex hormones, produced by the ovaries, that sustain reproductive functions.

adrenal glands   Endocrine glands, located over the kidneys, that produce androgens (among other hormones).

pituitary gland   An endocrine gland at the base of the brain that produces follicle-stimulating hormone (FSH) and luteinizing hormone (LH), among others.

hypothalamus   A region of the brain above the pituitary gland whose hormones control the secretions of the pituitary; also involved in the nervous control of sexual functions.

sex chromosomes   The X and Y chromosomes, which determine an individual's biological sex.

Sexual Differentiation, Hormones, and the Brain

Males and females are different from each other in many ways, but we are also very similar. We develop from the same embryonic tissue. The presence or absence of androgens determines how the sex organs develop. The entire process is known as *sexual differentiation*.

As described in the chapter, each male and female reproductive structure develops from the same undifferentiated tissue, so every structure in one sex has its counterpart in the other. For example, the tissue that gives rise to the clitoris in females becomes the penis in males, and the tissue that gives rise to the labia majora in females becomes the scrotum in males. The appearance of the genitals is sometimes called *gonadal sex*.

Exposure to hormones affects more than just the reproductive organs; it also influences development of the brain. It has been demonstrated many times that males tend to perform better than females at tasks requiring spatial skills and females perform better than males on tests of verbal skills. If androgens are involved in this gender difference, we would expect genetic females exposed to androgens to do better at spatial skills

and genetic males deprived of androgens to do worse—and this is exactly what we find.

In a condition known as androgen insensitivity syndrome, genetic males do not have cell receptors for male hormones and they develop physically as females—and their spatial skills are more like those of females than males. The converse occurs when genetic females are exposed before birth to excess male hormones. In a fascinating study of twins, it was found that opposite-sex female twins had a more masculine pattern of skills and behavior compared with same-sex female twins. In opposite-sex twins, the female twin is exposed in utero to some of the androgens produced by her male twin, and these androgens influence her brain organization and thus her spatial skills.

Each person is the product of biological events that act upon the cells in the body, including the brain. However, the physical and social environment then shapes this biological foundation to produce unique individuals. Some researchers point to the human past as a way to explain sex differences in language and

visual-spatial skills. For example, the early division of labor with men as hunters and women as food gatherers, camp organizers, and child raisers may have selected for different skills based on gender, including visual-spatial skills in men and communication skills in women.

SOURCES: Cohen-Bendahan, C., et al. 2004. Prenatal exposure to testosterone and functional lateralization: A study in same-sex and opposite-sex twin girls. *Psychoneuroendocrinology* 29(7): 911–916; Sinisi, A., et al. 2003. Sexual differentiation. *Journal of Endocrinological Investigation* 26(3 Suppl.): 23–28; Joseph, R. 2000. The evolution of sex differences in language, sexuality, and visual-spatial skills. *Archives of Sexual Behavior* 29(1): 35–66.

the male hormone **testosterone.** Testosterone circulates throughout the body and causes the undifferentiated reproductive structures to develop into male sex organs (penis, scrotum, and so on). If a Y chromosome is not present, there is no testosterone and the gonads become ovaries and the reproductive structures develop into female sex organs (clitoris, labia, and so on).

Female Sexual Maturation

Although humans are fully sexually differentiated at birth, the differences between males and females are accentuated at **puberty,** the period during which the reproductive system matures, secondary sex characteristics develop, and the bodies of males and females come to appear more distinctive. The changes of puberty are induced by testosterone in the male and estrogen and **progesterone** in the female.

Physical Changes   The first sign of puberty in girls is breast development, followed by a rounding of the hips

and buttocks. As the breasts develop, hair appears in the pubic region and later in the underarms. Shortly after the onset of breast development, girls show an increase in growth rate. Breast development usually begins between ages 8 and 13, and the time of rapid body growth occurs between ages 9 and 15.

The Menstrual Cycle   A major landmark of puberty for young women is the onset of the **menstrual cycle,** the monthly ovarian cycle that leads to menstruation (loss of blood and tissue lining the uterus) in the absence of pregnancy. The timing of **menarche** (the first *menstrual period*) varies with several factors, including ethnicity, genetics, and nutritional status. The "normal" range for the onset of menstruation is wide; some girls experience menarche as young as 9 or 10, and others when they are 16 or 17 years old. The current average age of menarche in the United States is around 12 and a half years of age. Two hundred years ago, the average age of menarche was closer to 17 years. The earlier onset of menarche is probably due in large part to nutritional factors. When age at menarche is produce increasing amounts of follicle-stimulating hormone (FSH) and luteinizing hormone (LH). Under the influence of FSH, an egg-containing ovarian **follicle** begins to mature, producing increasingly higher amounts of estrogens. Stimulated by estrogen, the **endometrium**, the uterine lining, thickens with large numbers of blood vessels and uterine glands.

3. Ovulation. A surge of a potent estrogen called *estradiol* from the follicle causes the pituitary to release a large burst of LH and a smaller amount of FSH. The high concentration of LH stimulates the developing follicle to release its ovum. This event is known as **ovulation.** After ovulation, the follicle is transformed into the **corpus luteum,** which produces progesterone and estrogen. Ovulation usually occurs about 14 days prior to the onset of menstrual flow, a fact that can be used to predict the most fertile time during the menstrual cycle, useful in both fertility treatment and natural family planning methods (see Chapter 6).

4. Progestational Phase. During the progestational phase of the cycle, the amount of progesterone secreted from the corpus luteum increases and remains high until the onset of the next menses. Under the influence of estrogen and progesterone, the endometrium continues to develop, readying itself to receive and nourish a fertilized ovum. When pregnancy occurs, the fertilized egg produces the hormone human chorionic gonadotropin (HCG),

Once they reach puberty, these adolescents are biologically adults, but it will take several more years for them to become adults in social and psychological terms.

examined worldwide, menarche tends to come later to girls who live in relative poverty with diets lacking in protein and calories. Obesity is strongly correlated with earlier menarche, which may explain the current trend for earlier menarche in the United States and many other countries. Some experts worry that exposure to estrogen-like chemicals in the environment may also be contributing to earlier menarche.

The day of the onset of bleeding is considered to be day 1 of the menstrual cycle. For the purposes of our discussion, a cycle of 28 days will be used; however, normal cycles vary in length from 21 to 35 days. The menstrual cycle consists of the following four phases (Figure 5.4 on p. 130):

1. Menses. During **menses,** characterized by the menstrual flow, blood levels of hormones from the ovaries and the pituitary gland are relatively low. This phase of the cycle usually lasts from day 1 to about day 5.

2. Estrogenic Phase. The estrogenic phase begins when the menstrual flow ceases and the pituitary gland begins to

testosterone The most important androgen (male sex hormone); stimulates an embryo to develop into a male and induces the development of male secondary sex characteristics during puberty.

puberty The period of biological maturation during adolescence.

progesterone The most important progestin (female sex hormone); induces the development of female secondary sex characteristics during puberty, regulates the menstrual cycle, and sustains pregnancy.

menstrual cycle The monthly ovarian cycle, regulated by hormones; in the absence of pregnancy, menstruation occurs.

menarche The first menstrual period, experienced by most young women at some point during adolescence.

menses The portion of the menstrual cycle characterized by menstrual flow.

follicle A saclike structure within the ovary, in which eggs (ova) mature.

endometrium The lining of the uterus.

ovulation The release of a mature egg (ovum) from an ovary.

corpus luteum The part of the ovarian follicle left after ovulation, which secretes estrogen and progesterone during the second half of the menstrual cycle.

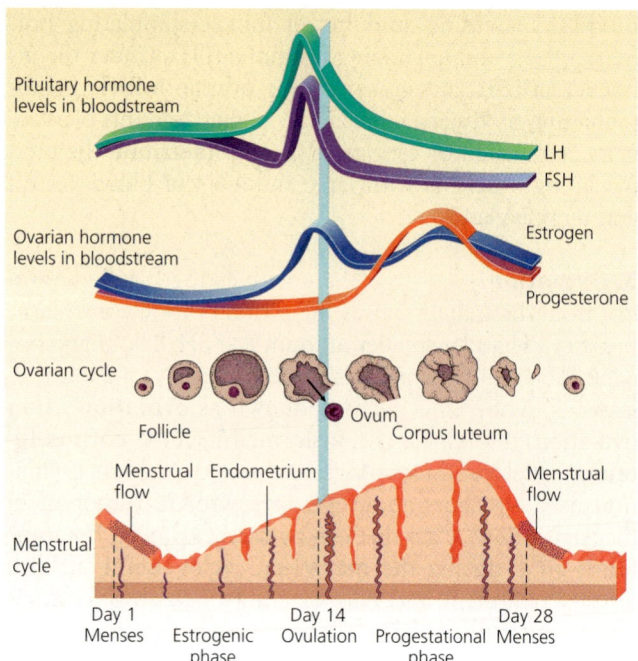

Pituitary hormone
levels in bloodstream

LH

FSH

Ovarian hormone
levels in bloodstream

Estrogen

Progesterone

Ovarian cycle

Follicle

Ovum

Corpus luteum

Menstrual
flow

Endometrium

Menstrual
flow

Menstrual
cycle

Day 1
Menses

Estrogenic
phase

Day 14
Ovulation

Progestational
phase

Day 28
Menses

FIGURE 5.4   The menstrual cycle.

which maintains the corpus luteum. Thus, levels of ovarian hormones remain high and the uterine lining is preserved, preventing menses.

If pregnancy does not occur, the corpus luteum degenerates, and estrogen and progesterone levels gradually fall. Below certain hormonal levels, the endometrium can no longer be maintained, and it begins to slough off, initiating menses. As the levels of ovarian hormones fall, a slight rise in LH and FSH occurs, and a new menstrual cycle begins.

MENSTRUAL PROBLEMS   Menstruation is a normal biological process, but it may cause physical or psychological problems. **Dysmenorrhea** is characterized by cramps in the lower abdomen, backache, vomiting, nausea, a bloated feeling, diarrhea, and loss of appetite. Some of these symptoms can be attributed to uterine muscular contractions caused by chemicals called *prostaglandins*. Any drug that blocks the effects of prostaglandins, such as aspirin or ibuprofen, will usually alleviate some of the symptoms of dysmenorrhea.

Many women experience transient physical and emotional symptoms prior to the onset of their menstrual flow. Depending on their severity, these symptoms may be categorized along a continuum: **premenstrual tension,**

premenstrual syndrome (PMS), and **premenstrual dysphoric disorder (PMDD).** Premenstrual tension symptoms are mild and may include negative mood changes and physical symptoms such as abdominal cramping and backache. More severe symptoms are classified as PMS; very severe symptoms that cause impairment in social functioning and work-related activities are classified as PMDD. All three conditions share a definite pattern: Symptoms appear prior to the onset of menses and disappear within a few days after the start of menstruation.

Symptoms associated with PMS and PMDD include physical changes such as breast tenderness, water retention (bloating), headache, and fatigue; insomnia or excessive sleep; appetite changes and food cravings; irritability, anger, and increased interpersonal conflict; mood swings; depression and sadness; anxiety and tearfulness; inability to concentrate; social withdrawal; and the sense that one is out of control or overwhelmed. The key to diagnosing PMS and PMDD is to keep a daily diary of symptoms over several menstrual cycles. PMDD is distinguished from PMS by the severity of symptoms, which in PMDD interfere significantly with work or school and with usual social activities and relationships.

Despite many research studies, the causes of PMS and PMDD are still unknown, and it is unclear why some women are more vulnerable than others. Research has focused on a variety of substances in the body that may fluctuate with the menstrual cycle. Most researchers feel that PMS is probably caused by a combination of hormonal, nutritional, and psychological factors.

Selective serotonin reuptake inhibitors (SSRIs), including Sarafem, Zoloft, Paxil, and Celexa, are the first-line treatment for PMDD. Until recently, women using SSRIs took the medication throughout the entire menstrual cycle, but it has now been shown that taking the medication during just the progestational phase of the cycle is similarly effective. Progestational phase use reduces the exposure to the drug and its associated side effects, and it lowers the cost of treatment. Antianxiety medications and progesterone have also been tested for progestational phase administration but show little positive effect in easing symptoms.

Other drug treatments include estrogen, certain oral contraceptives, diuretics to minimize water retention, and drugs such as aspirin, ibuprofen, and more potent prescription prostaglandin inhibitors that block the effects of prostaglandins. In 2006, the Yaz birth control pill was specifically approved by the FDA as a treatment for PMDD. Yaz, and a similar oral contraceptive, Yasmin, contain drospirenone, a synthetic progestin that is similar to natural progesterone and has a diuretic effect that seems to counteract some premenstrual symptoms. Yaz is also approved for the treatment of moderate acne in women who want an oral contraceptive for birth control. A number of vitamins, minerals, and other dietary supplements have also been studied for PMS relief. Only one supplement, calcium, has been shown to provide relief in rigorous clinical studies; several others show promise, but more research is needed.

The following strategies provide relief for many women, and all of them can contribute to a healthy lifestyle at any time:

- *Limit salt intake.* Salt promotes water retention and bloating.
- *Exercise.* Women who exercise experience fewer symptoms before and after menstrual periods.
- *Don't use alcohol or tobacco.* Alcohol and tobacco may aggravate certain symptoms of PMS and PMDD.
- *Eat a nutritious diet.* Choose a low-fat diet rich in complex carbohydrates from vegetables, fruits, and whole-grain breads, cereals, and pasta. Get enough calcium from calcium-rich foods and, if needed, supplements. Minimize your intake of sugar and caffeine, and avoid chocolate, which is rich in both.
- *Relax.* Stress reduction is always beneficial, and stressful events can trigger PMS symptoms. Try relaxation techniques during the premenstrual time.

If symptoms persist, keep a daily diary to track both the types of symptoms you experience and their severity. See your physician for an evaluation and to learn more about treatments that are available only with a prescription.

Male Sexual Maturation

Reproductive maturation of boys occurs about 2 years later than that of girls; it usually begins at about age 10 or 11.

Testicular growth is usually the first obvious sign of sexual maturity in boys. The penis also grows at this time, reaching adult size by about age 18. Pubic hair begins to develop after the genitals begin to increase in size, with underarm and facial hair gradually appearing. Hair on the chest, back, and abdomen increases later in development. The voice deepens as a result of the lengthening and thickening of the vocal chords. A small amount of breast development occurs in many boys during puberty. This is called *gynecomastia,* and it usually decreases after puberty. Excessive breast growth can occur in some boys, especially if they are overweight. Boys grow taller for about 6 years after the first signs of puberty, with a very rapid period of growth about 2 years after puberty starts.

Acne A not-so-welcome aspect of puberty for many boys and girls is the development of acne, technically called *acne vulgaris.* During adolescence, acne is typically worse in males; in adulthood, women tend to have more acne than men. The production of male hormones in puberty is the initial trigger for acne in most boys and girls. Acne is caused by multiple factors, including hormones, excess oil production, plugging of hair follicles (pores), infection with the bacterium *Propionibacterium acnes,* and inflammation. Fortunately, many treatments for acne exist, making control of this skin disease possible in nearly all cases.

Aging and Human Sexuality

Changes in hormone production and sexual functioning occur as we age. As a woman approaches age 50, her ovaries gradually cease to function and she enters **menopause,** the cessation of menstruation. For some women, the associated drop in hormone production causes symptoms that are troublesome. The most common physical symptom of menopause is hot flashes, sensations of warmth rising to the face from the upper chest, with or without perspiration and chills. Other symptoms include headaches, dizziness, palpitations, and joint pains. Osteoporosis—decreasing bone density—can develop, making older women more vulnerable to fractures. Some menopausal women become moody, even markedly depressed, and they may also experience fatigue, irritability, and forgetfulness.

To alleviate the symptoms of menopause and reduce the risk of heart disease and osteoporosis, millions of women have been prescribed hormone therapy (HT), a regimen of hormones that includes estrogen and progesterone. In 2002, an ongoing study of HT involving more than 16,000 women was halted because the women taking HT for long periods suffered more strokes, heart attacks, and blood clots and had a higher incidence of breast cancer than women in the study taking a placebo. The risks for such health problems were small but significant enough to halt the study. The positive findings from this study were a reduction in hip fractures and a reduced risk

TERMS

dysmenorrhea Painful or problematic menstruation.

premenstrual tension Mild physical and emotional changes associated with the time before the onset of menses; symptoms can include abdominal cramping and backache.

premenstrual syndrome (PMS) A disorder characterized by physical discomfort, psychological distress, and behavioral changes that begin after ovulation and cease when menstruation begins.

premenstrual dysphoric disorder (PMDD) Severe form of PMS, characterized by symptoms serious enough to interfere with work or school or with social activities and relationships.

menopause The cessation of menstruation, occurring gradually around age 50.

of colon cancer among the women taking HT. Many women who were taking HT stopped and many more never started as a result of the publicity surrounding the 2002 study. In 2007, analysis of data on breast cancer in the United States showed a decline in 2003 and 2004, possibly because fewer women took HT (although other factors may also be responsible for the decline in breast cancer). At around the same time, scientists reanalyzed the original 2002 data on HT and found that women who started HT close to the time of menopause tended to have a reduced risk of cardiovascular disease, while women who took HT several years after going through menopause had a higher risk of heart disease.

All this information is quite confusing, but the bottom line seems to be that the benefits of HT may outweigh the risks in women close to the time of menopause who have distressing symptoms not relieved by any other treatment. As a result of these findings, women taking HT were advised to consult their health care providers about their personal risks and benefits. (See Chapters 12, 15, and 22 for more information on osteoporosis, heart disease, and HT.)

As a result of decreased estrogen production during menopause, the vaginal walls become thin, and lubrication in response to sexual arousal diminishes; sexual intercourse may become painful. Hormonal treatment or the use of lubricants during intercourse can minimize these problems.

Between the ages of 35 and 65, men experience a gradual decline in testosterone production resulting in the aging male syndrome, sometimes referred to as *male menopause* or *andropause*. Experts generally prefer the term *aging male syndrome* because the process is much more gradual than female menopause. Symptoms vary widely among men, but most men experience at least some of the following symptoms as they age: loss of muscle mass, increased fat mass, decreased sex drive, erectile problems, depressed mood, irritability, difficulties with concentration, increased urination, loss of bone mineral density, and sleep difficulties. In some cases, treatment with testosterone can help. While taking testosterone can be very harmful in young healthy men, older men with low testosterone levels may benefit from carefully prescribed testosterone treatment.

As men get older, they depend more on direct physical stimulation for sexual arousal. They take longer to achieve an erection and find it more difficult to maintain; orgasmic contractions are less intense. Older men with erectile dysfunction are often prescribed medications such as Viagra or even more successful therapies that combine medication with a testosterone gel applied to the skin; see the section on sexual dysfunction later in the chapter for more information.

Unlike women, who are born with all the eggs they will ever have and stop being fertile at menopause, men continue to produce sperm throughout their lives and can sometimes father children when they are well into their eighties and even nineties. Starting at about age 30, however, men become gradually less fertile. Regardless of the age of their female partners, couples in which the male is over age 35 have a 50% lower pregnancy rate than cou-

Although sexual physiology changes as people get older, many men and women readily adjust to these alterations.

ples in which the man is 30 years old or younger. Men who are over age 40 are more likely to produce children with health problems such as autism, schizophrenia, and Down syndrome.

As women and men age, sexual activity can continue to be a source of pleasure and satisfaction for them. A recent study of sexuality in older Americans found that three-fourths of 57–64-year-olds were sexually active (defined as having at least one sexual partner in the last year). Half of those age 65–74, and about one-fourth of people age 75–85, remained sexually active.

SEXUAL FUNCTIONING

In this section, we discuss sexual physiology—how the sex organs function during sexual activity—and problems that can occur with sexual functioning. Sexual activity is based on stimulus and response. Erotic stimulation leads to sexual arousal (excitement), which may culminate in the intensely pleasurable experience of orgasm. But sexual activity should not be thought of only in terms of the sex

Sex Enhancement Products

The search for substances that can enhance sexual function and pleasure probably began long before recorded history. Among the huge variety of herbal and animal concoctions that have been reputed to improve sexual function are ginseng, raw oysters, bear gallbladder, rhinoceros horn, and tiger penis. Although research has shown that none of these products works, people continue to sell these materials, sometimes at extremely high prices, to gullible buyers. The demand for exotic animal parts has contributed to the endangerment of some of these species.

Check your junk e-mail folder and it's likely to be full of advertisements for products that supposedly increase sexual prowess. Recently, a number of these products have been shown to contain potentially dangerous ingredients. For example, the Food and Drug Administration (FDA) has cautioned against many dietary supplements sold online as "all natural" sexual enhancement products under names such as Zimaxx, Libidus, Neophase, Nasutra, Vigor25, Actra-Rx, 4Evron, True Man, and Energy Max. These products have been shown to contain the same or very similar compounds as those found in prescription drugs for erectile dysfunction such as Viagra, despite their claims of being herbal or "all natural." No mention of these Viagra-like compounds is found on their labels, though many of them contain full- or even double-strength doses of these drugs.

The FDA is concerned that these falsely labeled products could have potentially dangerous or even lethal side effects, especially if they are taken by people who are being treated with heart drugs that contain nitrates. Nitrates are common compounds found in many drugs used to treat heart disease and high blood pressure. Nitrates cause blood vessels to dilate, as does Viagra. When the two types of drugs are used together, blood pressure can plummet, potentially resulting in fainting, falls, heart attacks, or strokes.

People with heart disease who take nitrates are usually instructed not to take Viagra-like medications, so they may be especially tempted to try sexual enhancement products that are marketed as "natural" or "herbal." Other types of nitrate compounds, such as amyl nitrate, are used as recreational drugs (sometimes called "poppers") and can be very dangerous when combined with Viagra-like drugs.

Another potentially dangerous group of products that are marketed for sexual enhancement online includes male sex hormones such as testosterone and DHEA (dehydroepiandrosterone). These hormones are potentially dangerous and should never be used without medical supervision. Side effects of male hormones include acne, testicular atrophy, infertility, enlarged breasts, baldness, and accelerated growth of preexisting prostate cancer. Nonprescription hormone products sold on the Internet are of particular concern because there is no guarantee of the actual strength or purity of the ingredients, or even whether the product contains any of the advertised hormone at all.

Another example of a potentially unsafe product sold on the Internet for sexual improvement is Yohimbine, an extract of tree bark. It is marketed as a dietary supplement for low libido, erectile dysfunction, and female sexual problems. These nonprescription forms of yohimbine are problematic because the FDA does not monitor dietary supplements for strength, purity, quality, effectiveness, or safety. A prescription form of Yohimbine (Yohimbine hydrochloride) is, like all prescription drugs, regulated by the FDA. Yohimbine can cause blood pressure changes and rapid and/or irregular heart beat.

Aggressive marketing of these sexual enhancement products on the Internet and television makes it likely that they will harm more and more people. Any product that purports to enhance sexual function, especially if it is sold online without medical supervision, should be viewed with healthy skepticism.

SOURCES: Many herbal sex pills carry hidden heart risk. 2007: *Sacramento Bee*, 13 November, A5; Mayo Clinic. 2006. *DHEA* (http://www.mayoclinic.com/health/dhea/NS_patient-dhea; retrieved January 29, 2009); Mayo Clinic. 2007. *Yohimbe* (http://www.mayoclinic.com/health/drug-information/DR601453; retrieved January 29, 2009); U.S. National Library of Medicine. 2006. *Yohimbe Bark Extract* (http://www.nlm.nih.gov/medlineplus/druginfo/natural/patient-yohimbe.html; retrieved January 29, 2009).

organs. Responses to sexual stimulation involve not just the genitals but the entire body—and the mind as well.

Sexual Stimulation

Sexual excitement can come from many sources, both physical and psychological. Although physical stimuli have an obvious and direct effect, some people believe

psychological stimuli—thoughts, fantasies, desires, perceptions—are even more powerfully erotic. Regardless of the source of erotic stimuli, all stimulation has a physical basis, which is given meaning by the brain.

Physical Stimulation Physical stimulation comes through the senses: We are aroused by things we see, hear, taste, smell, and feel. Most often, sexual stimuli come from other people, but they may also come from books, photographs, paintings, songs, films, or other sources.

The most obvious and effective physical stimulation is touching. Even though culturally defined practices vary and individual people have different preferences, most sexual encounters eventually involve some form of touching with hands, lips, and body surfaces. Kissing, caressing, fondling, and hugging are as much a part of sexual encounters as they are of expressing affection.

QUESTIONS FOR CRITICAL THINKING AND REFLECTION

Think about your own experience as you matured sexually during puberty and adolescence. In what ways did these changes affect your life? How did they contribute to the person you are today?

The most intense form of stimulation by touching involves the genitals. The clitoris and the glans of the penis are particularly sensitive to such stimulation. Other highly responsive areas include the vaginal opening, the nipples, the breasts, the insides of the thighs, the buttocks, the anal region, the scrotum, the lips, and the earlobes. Such sexually sensitive areas, or **erogenous zones,** are especially susceptible to sexual arousal for most people, most of the time. Often, though, what determines the response is not *what* is touched but how, for how long, and by whom. Under the right circumstances, touching any part of the body can cause sexual arousal.

Psychological Stimulation Sexual arousal also has an important psychological component, regardless of the nature of the physical stimulation. Fantasies, ideas, memories of past experiences, and mood can all generate sexual excitement. Erotic thoughts may be linked to an imagined person or situation or to a sexual experience from the past. Fantasies may involve activities a person doesn't actually wish to experience in reality, usually because they're dangerous, frightening, or forbidden.

Arousal is also powerfully influenced by emotions. How you feel about a person and how the person feels about you matter tremendously in how sexually responsive you are likely to be. Even the most direct forms of physical stimulation carry emotional overtones. Kissing, caressing, and fondling express affection and caring. The emotional charge they give to a sexual interaction is at least as significant to sexual arousal as the purely physical stimulation achieved by touching.

The Sexual Response Cycle

Men and women respond physiologically with a predictable set of reactions, regardless of the nature of the stimulation (Figure 5.5).

Two physiological mechanisms explain most genital and bodily reactions during sexual arousal and orgasm. These mechanisms are vasocongestion and muscular tension. **Vasocongestion** is the engorgement of tissues that

results when more blood flows into an organ than is flowing out. Thus, the penis becomes erect on the same principle that makes a garden hose become stiff when the water is turned on. Increased muscular tension culminates in rhythmical muscular contractions during orgasm.

Four phases characterize the sexual response cycle:

1. In the *excitement phase,* the penis becomes erect as its tissues become engorged with blood. The testes expand and are pulled upward within the scrotum. In women, the clitoris, labia, and vaginal walls are similarly engorged with blood. Tension increases in the vaginal muscles, and the vaginal walls become moist with lubricating fluid.

2. The *plateau phase* is an extension of the excitement phase. Reactions become more marked. In men, the penis becomes harder, and the testes become larger. In women, the lower part of the vagina swells, as its upper end expands and vaginal lubrication increases.

3. In the *orgasmic phase,* or **orgasm,** rhythmic contractions occur along the man's penis, urethra, prostate gland, seminal vesicles, and muscles in the pelvic and anal regions. These involuntary muscular contractions lead to the ejaculation of **semen,** which consists of sperm cells from the testes and secretions from the prostate gland and seminal vesicles. In women, contractions occur in the lower part of the vagina and in the uterus, as well as in the pelvic region and the anus.

4. In the *resolution phase,* all the changes initiated during the excitement phase are reversed. Excess blood drains from tissues, the muscles in the region relax, and the genital structures return to their unstimulated state.

More general physical reactions accompany the genital changes in both men and women. Beginning with the excitement phase, nipples become erect, the woman's breasts begin to swell, and in both sexes the skin of the chest becomes flushed; these changes are more marked in women. The heart rate doubles by the plateau phase, and respiration becomes faster. During orgasm, breathing becomes irregular and the person may moan or cry out. A feeling of warmth leads to increased sweating during the resolution phase. Deep relaxation and a sense of well-being pervade the body and the mind.

Male and female reactions during the sexual response cycle differ somewhat. Generally, the male pattern is more uniform, whereas the female pattern is more varied. For instance, the female excitement phase may lead directly to orgasm, or orgasmic and plateau phases may be fused.

Male orgasm is marked by the ejaculation of semen. After ejaculation, men enter a *refractory period,* during which they cannot be restimulated to orgasm. Women do not have a refractory period, and immediate restimulation to orgasm is possible for some women.

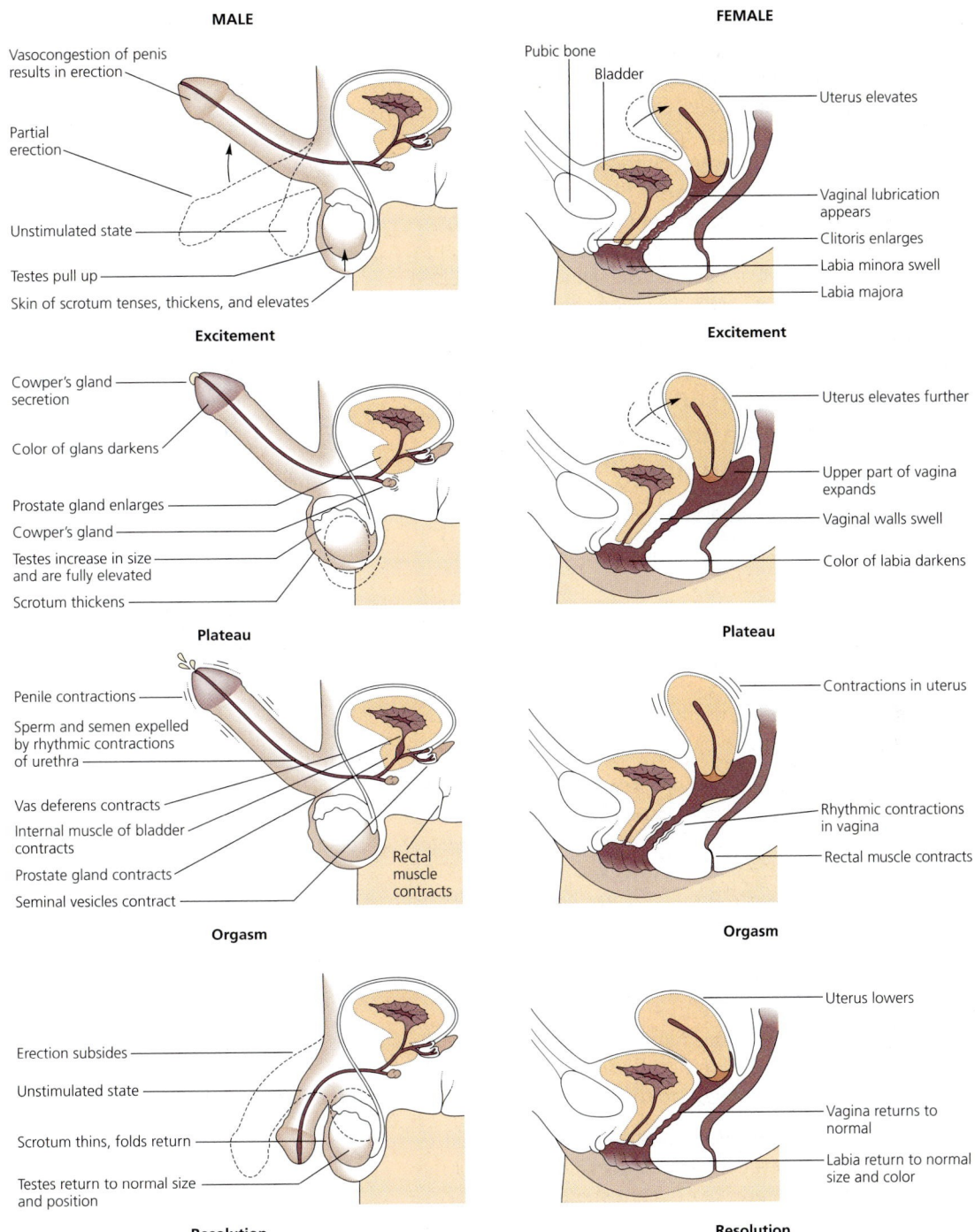

FIGURE 5.5 Stages of the sexual response cycle.

MALE

Vasocongestion of penis results in erection

Partial erection

Unstimulated state

Testes pull up

Skin of scrotum tenses, thickens, and elevates

Excitement

Cowper's gland secretion

Color of glans darkens

Prostate gland enlarges

Cowper's gland

Testes increase in size and are fully elevated

Scrotum thickens

Plateau

Penile contractions

Sperm and semen expelled by rhythmic contractions of urethra

Vas deferens contracts

Internal muscle of bladder contracts

Prostate gland contracts

Seminal vesicles contract

Rectal muscle contracts

Orgasm

Erection subsides

Unstimulated state

Scrotum thins, folds return

Testes return to normal size and position

Resolution

FEMALE

Pubic bone

Bladder

Uterus elevates

Vaginal lubrication appears

Clitoris enlarges

Labia minora swell

Labia majora

Excitement

Uterus elevates further

Upper part of vagina expands

Vaginal walls swell

Color of labia darkens

Plateau

Contractions in uterus

Rhythmic contractions in vagina

Rectal muscle contracts

Orgasm

Uterus lowers

Vagina returns to normal

Labia return to normal size and color

Resolution

Sexual Problems

Both physical and psychological factors can interfere with sexual functioning. Disturbances in sexual desire, performance, or satisfaction are referred to as **sexual dysfunctions.**

Common Sexual Health Problems Some problems with sexual functioning are due to treatable or preventable infections or other sexual health problems. Conditions that affect women include the following:

- *Vaginitis,* inflammation of the vagina, is caused by a variety of organisms: *Candida* (yeast infection), *Trichomonas* (trichomoniasis), and the overgrowth of a variety of bacteria (bacterial vaginosis). Symptoms include vaginal discharge, vaginal irritation, and pain during intercourse. (See Chapters 17 and 18 for more information.)
- *Endometriosis* is the growth of endometrial tissue (tissue normally found lining the uterus) outside the uterus. It occurs most often in women of childbearing age, and pain in the lower abdomen and pelvis is the most common

symptom. Painful premenstrual intercourse may occur. Endometriosis can cause serious problems if left untreated because the endometrial tissue can scar and partially or completely block the oviducts, causing infertility (difficulty conceiving) or sterility (the inability to conceive). Endometriosis is treated with hormone therapy and/or surgery.

• *Pelvic inflammatory disease (PID)* is an infection of the uterus, oviducts, or ovaries caused when microorganisms spread to these areas from the vagina. Approximately 50–75% of PID cases are caused by sexually transmitted organisms associated with diseases such as gonorrhea and chlamydia. PID can cause scarring of the oviducts, resulting in infertility or sterility. Symptoms include pain in the abdomen and pelvis, fever, and possibly pain during intercourse. (Sexually transmitted diseases are discussed in detail in Chapter 18.)

Sexual health problems that affect men include the following:

• *Prostatitis* is inflammation or infection of the prostate gland. Prostatitis can be acute (sudden) or chronic (gradual and long-lasting). The symptoms of *acute bacterial prostatitis* usually appear suddenly and may include fever, chills, flu-like symptoms, pain in the lower back or groin, problems with urination, and painful ejaculation. Acute prostatitis is treated with antibiotics. It is potentially serious, so any man with these symptoms needs to seek immediate medical attention.

Chronic prostatitis is more common in men over age 40. It can be caused by infection or inflammation of the prostate and is sometimes difficult to diagnose and treat.

• *Testicular cancer* occurs most commonly in men in their twenties and thirties. A rare cancer, it has a very high cure rate if detected early. Every man should perform testicular self-exams regularly (see Chapter 16).

TERMS

erectile dysfunction The inability to have or maintain an erection.

premature ejaculation Involuntary orgasm before or shortly after the penis enters the vagina or anus; ejaculation that takes place sooner than desired.

retarded ejaculation The inability to ejaculate when one wishes to during intercourse.

orgasmic dysfunction The inability to experience orgasm.

masturbation Self-stimulation for the purpose of sexual arousal and orgasm.

Sexual Dysfunctions The term *sexual dysfunction* encompasses disturbances in sexual desire, performance, or satisfaction. A wide variety of physical conditions and drugs may interfere with sexual functioning; psychological causes and problems in intimate relationships can be important factors in many cases.

COMMON SEXUAL DYSFUNCTIONS Common sexual dysfunctions in men include **erectile dysfunction** (previously called *impotence*), the inability to have or maintain an erection sufficient for sexual intercourse; **premature ejaculation**, ejaculation before or just on penetration of the vagina or anus; and **retarded ejaculation**, the inability to ejaculate once an erection is achieved. Many men experience occasional difficulty achieving an erection or ejaculating because of excessive alcohol consumption, fatigue, or stress.

Female sexual problems generally involve either a lack of desire to have sex, the failure to become physically aroused even when sex is desired, the failure to have an orgasm (**orgasmic dysfunction**), or pain during sexual contact. All of these problems can have physical and psychological components. Many medical problems can influence a woman's desire and ability to respond sexually. Hormonal factors, especially menopause, also have a major influence. Psychological and social issues such as relationship difficulties, family stresses, depression, and past sexual trauma are all frequent causes of sexual dysfunction.

Orgasmic dysfunction has been the subject of a great deal of discussion over the years, as people debated the nature of the female orgasm and what constitutes dysfunction in women. Many women experience orgasm but not during intercourse, or they experience orgasm during intercourse only if the clitoris is directly stimulated at the same time. In general, the inability to experience orgasm under certain circumstances is a problem only if the woman considers it so.

TREATING SEXUAL DYSFUNCTION Most forms of sexual dysfunction are treatable. The first step is to have a physical examination to find a possible medical cause. Heart disease and diabetes, for example, may cause erectile dysfunction; in fact, erectile dysfunction is often the first sign of a serious medical condition. This is one reason why men who buy drugs online to treat their erectile disfunction without first getting a good medical evaluation may be missing out on the opportunity to diagnose and treat a potentially life-threatening disease (see the box "Sex Enhancement Products" on p. 133). Up to 80% of all erectile problems are thought to be due to physical factors, particularly vascular problems involving restriction of blood flow. Smoking affects blood flow in the penis and is an independent risk factor for erectile dysfunction.

Alcohol, and many prescription and nonprescription drugs can inhibit sexual response. In particular, antidepressant drugs (especially the widely used selective serotonin re-uptake inhibitors such as Prozac) are believed to cause sexual dysfunction in up to one-half of people who take them. Switching to a different antidepressant often helps, and sometimes drugs such as Viagra are used to counteract the side effects of antidepressants.

Other common medications that can inhibit sexual response include certain drugs that treat high blood pressure. Patients are sometimes reluctant to tell their physician that they are having sexual problems, and may even stop taking their blood pressure medication for this reason. Letting the doctor know about sexual and other side effects is crucial because most of the time the problem can be solved by switching to a different medication. Newer antihypertensive drugs are highly effective and do not usually have sexual side effects.

Many treatments are available, particularly for erectile dysfunction. In 1998, Viagra (sildenafil citrate), the first-ever prescription pill for erectile dysfunction, was introduced. Since then, two other oral medications with actions similar to Viagra, Cialis (tadalafil) and Levitra (vardenafil), have been approved by the FDA. All three work by enhancing the effects of nitric oxide, a chemical that relaxes smooth muscles in the penis. This increases the amount of blood flow and allows a natural erection to occur in response to sexual stimulation. The medications are generally safe for healthy men, but they should not be used by men who have a high risk of heart attack or stroke. They are effective in about 70% of users, but there are potential side effects, including headaches, indigestion, facial flushing, back pain, visual and hearing disturbances, and changes in blood pressure. Viagra, Cialis, and Levitra should never be taken by anyone who takes nitrate medication (usually prescribed for heart problems). Also, the recreational drugs amyl nitrate or nitrite (sometimes called "poppers") should never be combined with drugs for erectile dysfunction. The combination of nitrates and Viagra-like drugs can cause a sudden potentially lethal drop in blood pressure.

Viagra use by men between the ages of 18 and 45 has risen dramatically—possibly due to use of the drug for recreational purposes. The drug may cut the refractory period in men who do not have erectile dysfunction; younger men may also be using it to cope with performance anxiety or the effects of other drugs, such as antidepressants.

Although Viagra is not approved by the FDA for use by women, a growing number of women are trying the drug. Research findings are mixed as to whether Viagra can increase sex drive and satisfaction levels in women. Recent studies have shown, however, that the drug can help women with sexual dysfunction caused by their use of antidepressant drugs.

Other treatments for erectile dysfunction in men are available. Prostaglandin E can be administered with a fine needle into the penis or placed into the tip of the penis as a tiny suppository about the size of a grain of rice; it works by relaxing the smooth muscles lining the blood vessels in the penis. A prostaglandin topical cream called Alprostadil can be applied to the penis to improve erectile func-

tion. For a small number of men with testosterone deficiency, hormone replacement therapy is an option. There are also vacuum devices that pull blood into the

penis, and in cases where other treatments are unsuccessful, penile implants can be used. Exercise may also help improve erectile function, especially exercises that target the muscles of the pelvic floor.

Even when there is a physical reason for sexual dysfunction, emotional and social factors frequently compound the problem. Many people with no obvious physical disorder have sexual problems because of psychological and social issues. Too often, sexual difficulties are treated with drugs when nondrug strategies may be more appropriate. Psychosocial causes of dysfunction include troubled relationships, a lack of sexual skills, irrational attitudes and beliefs, anxiety, and psychosexual trauma, such as sexual abuse or rape. Many of these problems can be addressed by sex therapy. A therapist may recommend books or films to help counter sexual myths and teach sexual skills. A therapist can also promote open discussion between partners and suggest specific techniques.

Women who seek treatment for orgasmic dysfunction often have not learned what types of stimulation will excite them and bring them to orgasm. Most sex therapists treat this problem with **masturbation** (genital self-stimulation). Women are taught about their own anatomy and sexual responses and then are encouraged to experiment with masturbation until they experience orgasm. Once they can masturbate to orgasm, they can transfer this learning to sexual intercourse with a partner.

Substances being tested for the treatment of female sexual dysfunction include prostaglandin creams and testosterone patches. A prostaglandin cream that improves blood flow to the clitoris is currently being developed under the name Femprox, and may be available to treat female sexual arousal disorder in the future. Another option is a device that creates suction over the clitoris to increase blood flow and sensitivity.

SEXUAL BEHAVIOR

Many behaviors stem from sexual impulses, and sexual expression takes a variety of forms. Probably the most basic aspect of sexuality is reproduction. But sexual excitement and satisfaction are aspects of sexual behavior separate from reproduction. The intensely pleasurable sensations of arousal and orgasm are probably the strongest motivators for human sexual behavior. People are infinitely varied in the ways they seek to experience erotic pleasure.

QUESTIONS FOR CRITICAL THINKING AND REFLECTION

If you are sexually active, would you consider using a product such as Viagra even if you didn't need it? Are you fully aware of the potential side effects of such products? In your opinion, would the potential benefits outweigh the risks?

The Development of Sexual Behavior

Sexual behavior is a product of many factors, including genetics, physiology, psychology, and social and cultural influences. Our behavior is shaped by the interplay of our biological predispositions and our life experiences.

Gender Roles and Gender Identity As mentioned in Chapters 2 and 4, your *gender role* is everything you do in your daily life that expresses your maleness or femaleness to others, including dress, speech patterns, and mannerisms. Your **gender identity** is your personal, inner sense of being male or female.

Biological sex, gender role, and gender identity are usually in agreement, but some people experience conflict among them. For example, a male who feels trapped in the body of a male and who wants to be a female appears to others as a male, but his gender identity is that of a female. The umbrella term *transgender* is often used to describe any individual whose appearance, personal characteristics, or behavior differs from the social and cultural norms for males and females. Transgender individuals include the following:

- *Transsexual* men and women, who feel their biological sex does not match their gender identity. Transsexuals may seek sex reassignment, which involves surgery to change the appearance of the genitals and hormonal treatments to induce secondary sex characteristics such as breasts or facial hair.

- *Transvestites,* who enjoy wearing clothing identified with the other gender. Cross-dressing covers a broad range of behaviors, from wearing one article of clothing of the other sex in a private location to wearing an entire outfit in public.

- *Intersexed individuals,* who were born with ambiguous genitals—neither fully female nor fully male—due to genetic or hormonal abnormalities. Inter-

sexed individuals may or may not have undergone surgery as infants to assign them to a particular sex.

- Men or women, regardless of sexual orientation, whose appearance, characteristics, or behavior is perceived as gender-atypical in their society or culture.

BIOLOGICAL AND CULTURAL INFLUENCES Some gender characteristics are determined biologically, such as the genitals a person is born with and the secondary sex characteristics that develop at puberty. Others are defined by society and learned in the course of growing up. From birth, children are encouraged to behave in ways their culture deems appropriate for one sex or the other. In our society, parents usually give children gender-specific names, clothes, and toys, and children may model their own behavior after their same-sex parent. Family and friends create an environment that teaches the child how to act appropriately as a girl or a boy. Teachers, television, books, and even strangers model these gender roles.

Gender roles vary from one society to another and from one time to another. In the United States today, for example, many women shave their legs and wear makeup; in some Muslim countries, women wear robes and veils that conceal their face and body. Each set of behaviors expresses some learned aspect of the female gender role in that society, and each set would be inappropriate in the other society. Standards of sexual attractiveness also vary from one culture to another.

An extreme example of how cultural traditions can affect gender roles and sexual activity is female genital mutilation, or "female circumcision." Each year in 28 African countries, parts of Asia and the Middle East, and immigrant communities elsewhere, 3 million female children undergo this procedure. In some cases, only the hood of the clitoris is removed. In others, the entire clitoris, the labia minora, and parts of the labia majora are removed. The sides of the labia majora may be sewn together, leaving only a small opening for the passage of urine and menstrual blood. The effects of these painful procedures can include bleeding, infection, the inability to enjoy sex, and infertility. Women who have endured genital mutilation commonly have difficulty during labor and childbirth. Children of such women are at far greater risk of dying during or after childbirth.

The practice probably developed as a way of controlling women's sexuality and ensuring that a woman would be a virgin when she married. Upon marriage, the husband reopens the labia to allow intercourse and childbirth.

Many countries now have laws against female genital mutilation. The WHO and other groups are trying to educate people about the negative medical consequences of this practice.

GENDER-ROLE FLEXIBILITY Historically, gender roles have tended to emphasize the differences between males and females, but new gender roles are emerging in our society that reflect more of a mix of male and female characteristics and behaviors. This tendency toward **androgyny** greatly

---

TERMS

gender identity A person's personal, internal sense of maleness or femaleness.

androgyny The state of being neither overtly male nor female.

nocturnal emissions Orgasm and ejaculation (wet dream) during sleep.

Our sense of gender identity and many of our gender-role behaviors are overwhelmingly influenced by cultural factors. This young boy is learning gender-specific behaviors by imitating his father.

broadens the range of experiences available to both males and females. Androgynous adults are less stereotyped in their thinking; in how they look, dress, and act; in how they divide work in the home; in how they think about jobs and careers; and in how they express themselves sexually. Women in our society today are able, and even expected, to be much more assertive, competitive, ambitious, and powerful than they were allowed to be in the past; likewise, men can be more sensitive, articulate, nurturing, and emotionally expressive.

Gender, Sexuality, and the Mass Media   Many of our ideas about sexuality and gender roles are shaped by the mass media. Media images of sexuality are often more influential than the family in shaping the sexual attitudes and behaviors of adolescents and college students. Yet these images are usually unrealistic and help perpetuate stereotypes of women and men in our society. The mass media rarely portray people negotiating safer sex or communicating seriously about other sexual issues.

Childhood Sexual Behavior   The capacity to respond sexually is present at birth. Ultrasound studies suggest that boys experience erections in the uterus. After birth,

both sexes have the capacity for orgasm, though many babies may not experience it. As people grow, many discover this capacity through self-exploration. Sexual behaviors

gradually emerge in childhood; self-exploration and touching the genitals are common forms of play, observed among infants as young as 6 months. They gradually lead to more deliberate forms of masturbation, with or without orgasm.

Children often engage in sexual play with playmates by exploring each other's genitals. These activities are often part of games like "playing house" or "playing doctor." By age 12, 40% of boys have engaged in sex play; the peak exploration age for girls is 9, by which time 14% have had such experiences.

Adolescent Sexuality   A person who has experienced puberty is biologically an adult. But in psychological and social terms, people take 5–10 more years to attain full adult status. This discrepancy between biological and social maturity creates considerable confusion over what constitutes appropriate sexual behavior during adolescence.

Sexual fantasies and dreams become more common and explicit in adolescence than at earlier ages, often as an accompaniment to masturbation. Research has shown that about 80% of teenage boys and 55% of teenage girls masturbate more or less regularly. Once puberty is reached, orgasm in boys is accompanied by ejaculation. Teenage boys also experience **nocturnal emissions** ("wet dreams"). Some girls also have orgasmic dreams.

Sexual interaction during adolescence usually takes place between peers in the context of dating. Sexual intimacy is usually expressed in such relationships through petting and necking, which may involve kissing, caressing, and stimulating the breasts and genitals. These activities lead to arousal but may not culminate in orgasm.

Many American teenagers also engage in premarital sexual relations. Recent surveys indicate that the average age of first sexual intercourse is about 17 years old. Almost half (46%) of 15–19-year-olds in the United States have had sex at least once. Rates for premarital sex vary considerably from one group to another, however, based on ethnic, educational, socioeconomic, religious, geographic, and other factors. First-time intercourse is affected by these same factors, plus psychological readiness, fear of consequences, being in love, going steady, peer pressure, and the need to act like an adult, gain popularity, or rebel. A mother's relationship with her daughter influences the timing of first intercourse. Girls who perceive that their mother disapproves of their having sex are more likely to delay first intercourse.

Sexual Decision Making

Choosing to have sex can change a relationship as well as an individual's life. In making decisions about sexual activity, you owe it to yourself and your partner to think and talk honestly about your choices. Consider the following issues:

• *Your background, beliefs, and goals.* What are your religious, moral, and/or personal values regarding relationships and sex? What are your priorities at this time, and how will a sexual relationship fit into your goals and plans for the future? Are you physically, emotionally, and financially ready to accept the potential consequences of the choices you make?

• *Your relationship with your partner.* How do you feel about your partner and your relationship? Do you respect and trust each other? Do you feel comfortable talking about sexual issues, and have you discussed contraception, pregnancy, and safer sex? How do you think having sex will affect your relationship and how you feel about yourself and your partner? What does having sex mean to each of you?

• *Your reasons for having sex.* What reasons do you have for moving into a sexual relationship? Are you being honest with yourself and your partner about this?

Personal decisions about sex should always be respected. You have the right to make your own choices and to do only what you feel comfortable with. When you make choices about sex based on self-respect, along with physical, emotional, and spiritual considerations, you'll be more likely to feel good about your decisions—now and in the future.

Adolescent sexual behaviors are not confined to heterosexual relationships. Beginning in childhood, sex play involves members of one's own sex as well as of the other sex. Homosexual attractions, with or without sexual encounters, are common in adolescence. For many these are youthful experiments and don't mean that participants will ultimately be homosexual. For some, they may be a factor in adult sexual orientation. Most adult gay men and women trace their preferences to childhood.

Adult Sexuality   Early adulthood is a time when people make important life choices—a time of increasing responsibility in terms of interpersonal relationships and family life (see the box "Sexual Decision Making"). In recent years, there has been a trend toward marriage at a later age than in past decades. And before marriage, more young adults are driven by a need to become sexually knowledgeable (see the box "Sexual Activity Among College Students"). Today, more people in their twenties believe that becoming sexually experienced rather than preserving virginity is an important prelude to selecting a mate. Take the quiz in the box "Your Sexual Attitudes" on page 142 to explore your own beliefs and opinions about sex.

Individual motivations for engaging in sexual activities change with age. Younger men state that they engage in sex for physical reasons, whereas women of the same age state that they engage in sex for emotional reasons. As men and women get older, their motives change; men more often engage in sex for emotional reasons, and women more often for physical reasons. In the oldest age groups, women's and men's motives for sex are actually the reverse of those of the earliest age groups. In addition to age, factors such as ethnicity, educational attainment, and living arrangements also influence adult choices about sexuality; see the box "Are There Ethnic Differences in Sexual Decision Making and Behavior?" on page 143.

Sexuality in Illness and Disability   Any disease or disability that affects mobility, well-being, self-esteem, or body image has the potential to affect sexual expression. People with chronic diseases or disabilities often have special needs regarding their sexual behavior. They may also confront the perception that they are asexual. Sexuality is integral to all of us, regardless of our physical status.

The diagnosis of a chronic illness or the onset of a disability usually requires major adjustments in many areas of life, including sexuality. At first, sexual activity may take a low priority because of fear and the loss of self-esteem. Individuals and couples can learn to become creative about sexual expression and develop new approaches based on the limitations of the disability. Developing a positive body image is often a particularly important, and difficult, adjustment for people with physical illness or limitations.

Sexual Orientation

Sexual orientation is a consistent pattern of emotional and sexual attraction based on biological sex. It exists along a continuum that ranges from exclusive heterosexuality (attraction to people of the other sex) through bi-

Sexual Activity Among College Students

The popular perception of college students is that they are young, attractive, and highly sexually active. But how close are these stereotypes to reality? In a 2006 survey of nearly 95,000 college students, about one-third of the respondents said they had never had a sexual partner or were currently not sexually active. Of those students who reported having sex with a partner, the vast majority said they had only one partner. Only a small group—about 1 in 10 students—reported having had three or more sexual partners in the last year.

Students tend to grossly overestimate the sexual activity level of their peers, mirroring the popular perception of college students. In the survey, students guessed that their peers had more than twice as many sex partners as they actually did.

Slightly more than half of all students said they had not had sexual intercourse in the last 30 days. When asked what types of intercourse they engaged in, most sexually active students reported participating in either vaginal or oral intercourse. Anal intercourse was relatively rare, with only about 1 in 20 students reporting having had anal sex one or more times in the last month. Once again, students wildly overestimated the frequency of all types of intercourse among their fellow students; more than half of the students who were polled guessed that the typical student at their college was participating in anal sex, while in reality only a small minority of college students report having had anal sex.

Judging from the results of this large survey, condom use among college students is far from consistent. Only about 18% of students reported using a condom every time they had vaginal intercourse in the last month. Birth control pills were the most popular contraceptive, with condoms a close second. The vast majority of students do not use condoms when they engage in oral sex. When asked about condom use during anal sex—which is among the riskiest of all sexual behaviors in terms of acquiring a sexually transmitted disease—the majority of students who reported this activity did not use a condom the last time they had anal sex.

Among the college men polled in this study, 93% described themselves as heterosexual, as did 95% of women. About

4% of men identified themselves as gay and 1% of women identified themselves as lesbian. Another 2% of college men and 3% of women classified themselves as bisexual. Less than 1% of college students described themselves as transgendered.

---

sexuality (attraction to people of both sexes) to exclusive homosexuality (attraction to people of one's own sex). The terms *straight* and *gay* are often used to refer to heterosexuals and homosexuals, respectively, and female homosexuals are also referred to as *lesbians*.

Sexual orientation involves feelings and self-concept, and individuals may or may not express their sexual orientation in their behavior. In national surveys, about 2–6% of men identify themselves as homosexuals and about 1.5% of women identify themselves as lesbians. It is difficult to gauge the accuracy of these estimates because people may not tell the truth in surveys that probe very sensitive and private aspects of their lives.

Heterosexuality The great majority of people are heterosexual. The heterosexual lifestyle usually includes all the behavior and relationship patterns described in Chapter 4: dating, engagement and/or living together, and marriage.

Homosexuality Homosexuality exists in almost all cultures. The major difference between heterosexuals and homosexuals is in their choice of sex partners. Homosexual individuals are as varied and different from one another as are heterosexuals. Just like heterosexuals, lesbians and gay men may be in long-term, committed relationships or they may date different people.

Bisexuality Some bisexual individuals are involved with partners of both sexes at the same time, whereas others may alternate between same-sex partners and partners of the other sex ("serial bisexuality"). The largest group of bisexuals consists of married men who have secret sexual involvements with men but who rarely have female sexual contacts outside marriage.

The Origins of Sexual Orientation Many theories try to account for the development of sexual orientation. At this time, most experts agree that sexual orientation results from multiple genetic, biological, cultural, social, and psychological factors.

Scientists are now looking for genetic markers associated with sexual orientation in males. This study, funded by the National Institutes of Health, will examine the DNA of 1000 pairs of gay brothers and their families. Twin studies are another way of looking at the genetic contribution to sexual identity. Identical twins share the same DNA, so if sexual orientation were entirely genetically determined, we would expect that if one identical

Your Sexual Attitudes

For each statement, circle the response that most closely reflects your position.

		AGREE	NOT SURE	DISAGREE
1.	Sex education encourages young people to have sex.	1	2	3
2.	Homosexuality is a healthy, normal expression of sexuality.	3	2	1
3.	Members of the other sex will think more highly of you if you remain mysterious.	1	2	3
4.	It's better to wait until marriage to have sex.	1	2	3
5.	Abortion should be a personal, private choice for a woman.	3	2	1
6.	It's natural for men to have more sexual freedom than women do.	1	2	3
7.	Condoms should not be made available to teenagers.	1	2	3
8.	Access to pornography should not be restricted for adults.	3	2	1
9.	A woman who is raped usually does something to provoke it.	1	2	3
10.	Contraception is the woman's responsibility.	1	2	3
11.	Feminism has had a positive influence on society.	3	2	1
12.	Masturbation is a healthy expression of sexuality.	3	2	1
13.	I have many friends of the other sex.	3	2	1
14.	Prostitution should be legalized.	3	2	1
15.	Women use sex for love; men use love for sex.	1	2	3
16.	Our society is too sexually permissive.	1	2	3
17.	The man should be the undisputed head of the household.	1	2	3
18.	Having sex just for pleasure is OK.	3	2	1

Scoring

1–18	Traditional attitude about sexuality
19–36	Ambivalent or mixed attitude about sexuality
37–54	Open, progressive attitude about sexuality

twin was homosexual, the other would be as well. But studies of many identical twins (both gay and lesbian) show that the odds are between 30% and 50% that both twins will have the same sexual orientation. These studies provide evidence that our genes make an important but limited contribution to our sexual orientation.

Exposure to hormones before birth also has a major impact on sexual orientation. Experiments with mice show that exposure to sex hormones early in development determines whether they will ultimately be sexually attracted to male or female mice. The situation is much more complicated in humans, but most researchers believe that the hormonal environment in the womb probably has an important influence on sexual orientation.

Researchers have also compared the brain structure of homosexual and heterosexual men. Although some differences have been found, they are not consistent across all studies. Also, even if brain structure differences exist, it is unclear whether they are the cause or an effect of differences in sexual orientation.

Several studies have shown that the more older brothers a boy has, the more likely he will grow up to be gay. The odds of being gay go up 33% with each older brother. There are numerous theories to explain this phenomenon. One intriguing, but unproven, theory suggests that mothers with multiple biological sons may develop antibodies against proteins produced by male fetuses. The immune response by the mother may affect the fetal development of later sons, resulting in an increased chance of homosexuality.

Many psychological theories have also been proposed. Researchers have looked at how much contact children have with members of the two sexes, at the types of relationships children have with their parents, and at family dynamics. Early negative experiences with heterosexuality or positive experiences with homosexuality have also been proposed as possible influences. The significant growth of single-parent families over the past 40 years has not been accompanied by large shifts in sexual orientation among Americans, so it is unlikely that family dynamics or early learning experiences are strong factors in determining sexual orientation. In addition, parents' sexual orientation seems to have little impact on children's sexual orientation. Studies of children raised by gay or lesbian parents show that these children's ultimate sexual orientation is similar to that of children raised by heterosexual parents.

Are There Ethnic Differences in Sexual Decision Making and Behavior?

In general, researchers have found that ethnicity contributes to differences in sexual behaviors—but that other variables are equally important. Those variables include age, income, educational attainment, and living arrangements.

In a study comparing low-income women from different groups, there was one area in which ethnicity appeared to have an influence independent of other factors. When the women were asked who makes the decision about the timing and type of sexual activity, 80% of Latinas stated it was a mutual decision with their partner. White women were also likely to report mutual decision making (64%). African American women were less likely to report a mutual decision (47%) but more likely to report that they made the decision themselves (31%). Only 6% of Latinas and 13% of white women reported that they made the decision as to the timing and type of sexual activity with their partners.

Vaginal intercourse was the most common behavior among all the participants in the study, followed by oral sex and then anal sex. African American women were less likely to engage in oral sex (26%) compared with white women (58%) and Latinas (56%). Among women with high educational attainment, rates of oral sex went up for white women and down for African American women. Rates of oral sex were also lower for older African American women and Latinas.

African American women in the survey reported more sexual partners in the past 6 months compared with white women and Latinas. However, women of all ethnicities who were not living with a partner were more likely to report multiple sexual partners, and fewer African American women in this study were living with a partner. Thus, living arrangement was a more important factor than ethnicity in influencing the number of sexual partners.

Ethnic differences also exist in sexual issues among college students. A recent study found that African American and Latino students reported higher levels of unwanted noncondom use compared with white students. Unwanted noncon-

dom use refers to a situation in which an individual intends to use condoms with her or his partner but then does not because of the influence of the partner.

SOURCES: Smith, L. 2003. Partner influence on noncondom use: Gender and ethnic differences. *Journal of Sex Research* 40(4): 346–350; Quadagno, D., et al. 1998. Ethnic differences in sexual decisions and sexual behaviors. *Archive of Sexual Behavior* 27(1): 57–75.

So far, most studies on the origin of sexual orientation have focused on males. The factors that determine sexual orientation in women may be even more complex. Perhaps the most important message is that sexual orientation is most likely the result of the complex interaction of biological, psychological, and social factors, possibly different in the case of each individual.

Varieties of Human Sexual Behavior

Some sexual behaviors are aimed at self-stimulation only, whereas other practices involve interaction with a partner. Some people choose not to express their sexuality at all.

Celibacy Continuous abstention from sexual activities, termed **celibacy,** can be a conscious and deliberate choice, or it can be necessitated by circumstances. Health considerations and religious and moral beliefs may lead some people to celibacy, particularly until marriage or until an acceptable partner appears.

Many people use the related term *abstinence* to refer to avoidance of just one sexual activity—intercourse. The use of abstinence to prevent pregnancy and sexually transmitted diseases is discussed in Chapters 6 and 18.

Autoeroticism and Masturbation The most common form of **autoeroticism** is **erotic fantasy,** creating imaginary experiences that range from fleeting thoughts to elaborate scenarios.

Masturbation involves manually stimulating the genitals, rubbing them against objects, or using stimulating devices such as vibrators. Although commonly associated with adolescence, masturbation is practiced by many throughout adult life. It may be used as a substitute for sexual intercourse or as part of sexual activity with a partner. Masturbation gives a person control over the pace, time, and method of sexual release and pleasure.

Touching and Foreplay Touching is integral to sexual experiences, whether in the form of massage, kissing, fondling, or holding. Our entire body surface is a sensory organ, and touching almost anywhere can enhance intimacy

celibacy	Continuous abstention from sexual activity.
autoeroticism	Behavior aimed at sexual self-stimulation.
erotic fantasy	Sexually arousing thoughts and daydreams.

TERMS

This couple's physical experiences together will be powerfully affected by their emotions, ideas, and values and by the quality of their relationship.

and sexual arousal. Touching can convey a variety of messages, including affection, comfort, and a desire for further sexual contact.

During arousal, many men and women manually and orally stimulate each other by touching, stroking, and caressing their partner's genitals. Men and women vary greatly in their preferences for the type, pacing, and vigor

---

---

of such **foreplay.** Working out the details to accommodate each other's pleasure is a key to enjoying these activities. Direct communication about preferences can enhance sexual pleasure and protect both partners from physical and psychological discomfort.

Oral-Genital Stimulation   **Cunnilingus** (the stimulation of the female genitals with the lips and tongue) and **fellatio** (the stimulation of the penis with the mouth) are common practices. Oral sex may be practiced either as part of foreplay or as a sex act culminating in orgasm. Although prevalence varies in different populations, 90% of men, 88% of women, and more than 50% of teens report that they have engaged in oral sex. A recent study showed that more teens age 15–19 had engaged in oral sex than vaginal intercourse. The most common reasons given for postponing vaginal sex were avoidance of pregnancy, and the desire to remain technically a virgin.

Like all acts of sexual expression between two people, oral sex requires the cooperation and consent of both partners. If they disagree about its acceptability, they need to discuss their feelings and try to reach a mutually pleasing solution.

Anal Intercourse   About 10% of heterosexuals and 50% of homosexual males regularly practice anal stimulation and penetration by the penis or a finger. The receiver does not usually reach orgasm from anal intercourse, though men usually experience orgasm while penetrating.

Because the anus is composed of delicate tissues that tear easily under such pressure, anal intercourse is one of the riskiest of sexual behaviors associated with the transmission of HIV and all other sexually transmitted infections. Anal intercourse is also associated with increased risk of anal cancer, hemorrhoids, anal fissures, prolapsed rectum, and fecal incontinence. The use of condoms is highly recommended for anyone engaging in anal sex. Special care and precaution should be exercised if anal sex is practiced—cleanliness, lubrication, and gentle entry at the very least. Anything that is inserted into the anus should not subsequently be put into the vagina unless it has been thoroughly washed. Bacteria normally present in the anus can cause vaginal infections.

Sexual Intercourse   For most adults, most of the time, **sexual intercourse** (*coitus*) is the ultimate sexual experience. Men and women engage in vaginal intercourse to fulfill both sexual and psychological needs. In a 2006 study by the National Center for Health Statistics, 87% of men age 15–44 and 98% of women in the same age group reported having had vaginal intercourse. The most common heterosexual practice is the man inserting his erect penis into the woman's dilated and lubricated vagina after sufficient arousal.

Much has been written on how to enhance pleasure through various coital techniques, positions, and practices.

Sexsomnia: Sleep Disorders and Sex

A man accused of sexual assault claims he is not guilty of rape because he was sound asleep and completely unaware of his actions. Could he be telling the truth? Sleep experts say that such behavior while asleep is possible, although it is relatively uncommon.

Sexual arousal during sleep is normal and usually perfectly safe since it generally occurs during the rapid eye movement, or dreaming, phase of sleep when we are semiparalyzed. But some people have episodes of abnormal sleep in which they are able to perform complex physical activities without any awareness of what they are doing. They have no memory of these episodes once they are fully awake. This category of sleep disorder, called *parasomnia,* includes sleepwalking, sleep talking, sleep eating, sleep driving, and sleep sex.

Sexsomnia is a recently coined term for sleep sex disorder. Sleep researchers have observed this phenomenon in the laboratory and have correlated it with abnormal brain wave activity similar to that seen in other parasomnias. Sexsomnia has been in the news recently because several defendants in sexual assault cases have been acquitted when they were found to not be responsible for their actions due to sexsomnia. These cases have received considerable publicity, but it is important to remember that only a few cases of sexsomnia have been documented in medical literature and that the disorder is probably rather rare.

Another recent development that has brought attention to the disorder is the finding that popular sleep medications (called *sedative-hypnotic* drugs) seem to cause a phenomenon similar to the parasomnias in some people. There are reports of these people driving, making phone calls, and preparing and eating food while asleep. A few people report having sex while apparently asleep after taking these drugs.

As a result of these reports, the FDA has requested that the manufacturers of 13 sleep medications (including Ambien and Lunesta) include warnings about complex sleep behaviors on their labels. In addition, the FDA requested further clinical research into the potential side effects of these drugs.

SOURCES: Schenk, C. H., et al. 2007. Sleep and sex: What can go wrong? *Sleep* 30(6): 683–702; U.S. Food and Drug Administration. 2007. *FDA Requests Label Change for All Sleep Disorder Drug Products* (http://www.fda.gov/bbs/topics/news/2007/new01587.html; retrieved January 29, 2009).

For a woman, the key factor in physical readiness for coitus is adequate vaginal lubrication, and in psychological readiness, being aroused and receptive. For a man, the setting and the partner must arouse him to attain and maintain an erection. Psychological factors and the quality of the relationship are more important to overall sexual satisfaction than sophisticated or exotic sexual techniques.

Atypical and Problematic Sexual Behaviors

In American culture, many kinds of sexual behavior are accepted. However, some types of sexual expression are considered harmful; they may be illegal, classified as mental disorders, or both. Because sexual behavior occurs on a continuum, it is sometimes difficult to differentiate a behavior that is simply atypical from one that is harmful (see the box "Sexsomnia: Sleep Disorders and Sex"). When attempting to evaluate an unusual sexual behavior, experts consider the issues of consent between partners and whether physical or psychological harm is done to the individual or to others.

The term *paraphilia* is used to describe certain sexual behaviors that are atypical and cause harm to self or others. Clinically, the term may be used for a sexual behavior that causes significant distress to the individual involved or to other people. Paraphilias of clinical concern are characterized by recurring, intense sexual fantasies and urges that involve nonhuman objects, the suffering or humiliation of oneself or one's partner, or children or other non-consenting individuals. Examples are peeping into strangers' homes, making obscene phone calls, and having sexual contact with children. The effects of paraphilic behavior on others range from minor upset to serious physical and long-term psychological harm. Paraphilias are considered mental disorders by the American Psychiatric Association.

The use of force and coercion in sexual relationships is one of the most serious problems in human interactions. The most extreme manifestation of **sexual coercion**—forcing a person to submit to another's sexual desires—is rape, but sexual coercion occurs in many subtler forms, such as sexual harassment. Sexual coercion—including rape, the sexual abuse of children, and sexual harassment—is discussed in detail in Chapter 21.

Commercial Sex

Conflicting feelings about sexuality are apparent in the attitudes of Americans toward commercial sex: prostitution and sexually oriented materials in a variety of formats. Our

> **49.5%** of college students reported having vaginal intercourse at least once in the last 30 days.
>
> —American College Health Association—
> National College Health Assessment, 2007
>
> QUICK STATS

society condemns sexually explicit material and prostitution, but it also provides their customers.

Pornography Derived from the Greek word meaning "the writing of prostitutes," **pornography** (*porn*) is now often defined as obscene literature, art, or movies. A major problem in identifying pornographic material is that different people and communities have different opinions about what is obscene. Differing definitions of obscenity have led to many legal battles over potentially pornographic materials. Currently, the sale and rental of pornographic materials is restricted so that only adults can legally obtain them; materials depicting children in sexual contexts are illegal in any format or setting.

Many people distinguish between "soft porn" and "hard porn" materials. Soft porn, often marketed for couples, typically includes an apparently loving couple having sex in a relaxed setting. There is mutual kissing and touching, and both partners are shown as having a positive experience. In hard porn, there is usually little mutual touching, and only the male appears to enjoy the experience. Hard porn sometimes explicitly depicts sexual violence and exploitation. Hard porn materials tend to be the focus of more criticism than soft porn materials.

Much of the debate about pornography focuses on whether it is harmful. Some people argue that adults who want to view pornographic materials in the privacy of their own homes should be allowed to do so. Others feel that the exposure to explicit sexual material can lead to delinquent or criminal behavior, such as rape or the sexual abuse of children. Currently, there is no reliable evidence that pornography by itself leads to violence or paraphilic behavior, and debate is likely to continue.

Online Porn and Cybersex The appearance of thousands of sexually oriented Web sites has expanded the number of people with access to pornography, and has made it more difficult for authorities to enforce laws regarding porn. People who might have hesitated to buy magazines or rent videos in person can now access sexually explicit materials online. Of special concern is the increased availability of child pornography, which previously could be acquired only with great difficulty and at great legal risk. Online porn is now a multibillion-dollar industry.

In addition to (or instead of) viewing porn online, hundreds of thousands of people also use the Internet to engage in **cybersex,** or *virtual sex.* Cybersex is erotic interaction between people who are communicating over a network such as the Internet; the participants are not in physical contact with each other. People can engage in cybersex in many different ways, such as visiting sexually oriented Web sites, joining cybersex chat rooms, participating in videoconferences via Web cams, or even by exchanging e-mail messages. Participants may have sexually explicit discussions, share private photographs, or engage in fantasy role playing online. Many cybersex participants report feeling some degree of sexual excitement; some masturbate while viewing erotic images online or engaging in sexual chat.

Although many people view cybersex as a safe form of sexual expression, it is not without problems. It can be addictive, and some cybersex addicts report spending more than 50 hours a week online for sexual purposes. People who become addicted to cybersex or viewing online porn may become isolated and perform poorly at work or school. Their addiction may also have a negative impact on their interpersonal relationships.

Prostitution The exchange of sexual services for money is **prostitution.** Prostitutes may be men, women, or children, and the buyer of a prostitute's services is nearly always a man. Except in parts of Nevada, prostitution is illegal in the United States.

Sex with a prostitute provides the customer with sexual release without commitment, the expectation of intimacy, or fear of rejection. Some men patronize prostitutes to have sex with a different type of partner than usual or to engage in a type of sex their usual partner will not permit. Most customers are white, middle-class, middle-aged, and married. Although they come from a wide variety of backgrounds, prostitutes are usually motivated to join the profession because of money.

AIDS is a major concern for prostitutes and their customers. Many prostitutes are injection drug users or are involved with men who are. The rate of HIV infection among prostitutes varies widely, but in some parts of the country it is as high as 25–50%.

Responsible Sexual Behavior

Healthy sexuality is an important part of adult life. It can be a source of pleasurable experiences and emotions and an important part of intimate partnerships. But sexual behavior also carries many responsibilities, as well as potential consequences such as pregnancy, STDs, and emotional changes in the relationship. Every sexually active person should be aware of these consequences and accept responsibility for them.

Open, Honest Communication Each partner needs to clearly indicate what sexual involvement means to him or

Communicating About Sexuality

To talk with your partner about sexuality, follow the general suggestions for effective communication given in Chapter 4. Getting started may be the most difficult part. Some people feel more comfortable if they begin by talking about talking—that is, initiating a discussion about why people are so uncomfortable talking about sexuality. Talking about sexual histories—how partners first learned about sex or how family and cultural background influenced sexual values and attitudes—is another way to get started. Reading about sex can also be a good beginning: Partners can read an article or book and then discuss their reactions.

Be honest about what you feel and what you want from your partner. Cultural and personal obstacles to discussing sexual subjects can be difficult to overcome, but self-disclosure is important for successful relationships. Research indicates that when one partner openly discusses attitudes and feelings, the other partner is more likely to do the same. If your partner seems hesitant to open up, try asking open-ended or either/or questions: "Where do you like to be touched?" or "Would you like to talk about this now or wait until later?"

If something is bothering you about your sexual relationship, choose a good time to initiate a discussion with your partner. Be specific and direct but also tactful. Focus on what you actually observe, rather than on what you think

the behavior means. "You didn't touch or hug me when your friends were around" is an observation. "You're ashamed of me around your friends" is an inference about your partner's feelings. Try focusing on a specific behavior that concerns you rather than on the person as a whole—your partner can change behaviors but not his or her entire personality. For example, you could say "I'd like you to take a few minutes away from studying to kiss me" instead of "You're so caught up in your work, you never have time for me."

If you are going to make a statement that your partner may interpret as criticism, try mixing it with something positive: "I love spending time with you, but I feel annoyed when you. . . ." Similarly, if your partner says something that upsets you, don't lash back. An aggressive response may make you feel better in the short run, but it will not help the communication process or the quality of the relationship.

If you want to say no to some sexual activity, say no unequivocally. Don't send mixed messages. If you are afraid of hurting your partner's feelings, offer an alternative if it's appropriate: "I am uncomfortable with that. How about . . .?"

If you're in love, you may think that the sexual aspects of a relationship will work out magically without discussion. However, partners who never talk about sex deny themselves the opportunity to increase their closeness and improve their relationship.

---

her. Does it mean love, fun, a permanent commitment, or something else? The intentions of both partners should be clear. For strategies on talking about sexual issues with your partner, see the box "Communicating About Sexuality."

Agreed-On Sexual Activities No one should pressure or coerce a partner. Sexual behaviors should be consistent with the sexual values, preferences, and comfort level of both partners. Everyone has the right to refuse sexual activity at any time.

Sexual Privacy Intimate relationships involving sexual activity are based on trust, and that trust can be violated if partners reveal private information about the relationship to others. Sexual privacy also involves respecting other people—not engaging in activities in the presence of others that would make them uncomfortable. The question of how to handle bringing a partner back to a shared dorm room is something that many college students must address. Roommates should be respectful of one another and discuss the situation in advance to avoid embarrassing encounters.

Using Contraception If pregnancy is not desired, contraception should be used during sexual intercourse. Both partners need to take responsibility for protecting against

unwanted pregnancy. Partners should discuss contraception before sexual involvement begins. (See Chapter 6 for more information on contraception.)

Safer Sex Both partners should be aware of and practice safer sex to guard against sexually transmitted diseases (STDs). The U.S. Surgeon General stated in his 2001 *Call to Action to Promote Sexual Health and Responsible Sexual Behavior* that the United States faces a significant challenge to the sexual health of its people due to the high levels of STDs. Many sexual behaviors carry the risk of STDs, including HIV infection. Partners should be honest about their health and any medical conditions and work out a plan for protection. (For more information on STDs and safer sex practices, see Chapter 18.)

Sober Sex The use of alcohol or drugs in sexual situations increases the risk of unplanned, unprotected sexual activity. This is particularly true of young adults, many of whom engage in episodes of binge drinking during social events. The link between intoxication and unsafe sex is illustrated by a recent study that found that states with higher drinking ages and higher beer taxes have lower rates of STDs. Alcohol and drugs impair judgment and should not be used in association with sexual activity.

Aside from the dangers of mixing alcohol and sex, alcohol has a negative impact on sexual performance in both men and women. Although alcohol may lower sexual inhibition and make people more likely to attempt a sexual encounter, too much alcohol makes it difficult for a man to achieve or keep an erection, decreases vaginal lubrication in women, and makes orgasm more difficult to achieve in both sexes. Chronic overuse of alcohol reduces testosterone in men, ultimately causing erectile dysfunction, infertility, and body changes such as enlarged breasts. Women who overuse alcohol often experience menstrual abnormalities and decreased sexual function. Similarly, cigarette smoking has a powerful negative effect on sexual function, primarily because it decreases blood flow to the genitals.

TIPS FOR TODAY AND THE FUTURE

A healthy sexual life is built on acceptance of yourself and good communication with your partner.

RIGHT NOW YOU CAN

- Deal with any sexual question or problem you've been avoiding. Unless you're sure it isn't a physical problem, see your doctor.
- Articulate to yourself exactly what your beliefs are about sexual relationships. Consider whether you are acting in accordance with your beliefs.
- If you're in a sexual relationship, consider the information you and your partner have shared about sex. Are you comfortable that you and your partner know enough about each other to have a safe, healthy sexual relationship?

IN THE FUTURE YOU CAN

- If you're in a sexual relationship, or if you plan to begin one, open (or reopen) a dialog with your partner about sex. Make time to talk at length about the responsibilities and consequences of a sexual relationship.

QUESTIONS FOR CRITICAL THINKING AND REFLECTION

If you are sexually active or plan to become active soon, how open have you been about communicating with your partner? Are you aware of your partner's feelings about sex and his or her comfort level with certain activities? Do you and your partner share the same views on contraception, STD prevention, and ethical issues about sex?

Responsible sexual behavior includes discussing potential consequences openly and honestly.

SUMMARY

- The female external sex organs are called the vulva; the clitoris plays an important role in sexual arousal and orgasm.

- The vagina leads to the internal sex organs, including the uterus, oviducts, and ovaries.

- The male external sex organs are the penis and the scrotum; the glans of the penis is an important site of sexual arousal.

- Internal sexual structures include the testes, vasa deferentia, seminal vesicles, and prostate gland.

- The fertilizing sperm determines the sex of the individual. Specialized genes on the Y chromosome initiate the process of male sexual differentiation in the embryo.

- Hormones initiate the changes that occur during puberty: The reproductive system matures, secondary sex characteristics develop, and the bodies of males and females become more distinctive.

- The menstrual cycle consists of four phases: menses, the estrogenic phase, ovulation, and the progestational phase.

- The ovaries gradually cease to function as women approach age 50 and enter menopause. The pattern of male sexual responses changes with age, and testosterone production gradually decreases.

- Sexual activity is based on stimulus and response. Stimulation may be physical or psychological.

- Vasocongestion and muscle tension are the primary physiological mechanisms of sexual arousal.

- The sexual response cycle has four stages: excitement, plateau, orgasm, and resolution.

- Physical and psychological problems can both interfere with sexual functioning.

- A treatment for sexual dysfunction first addresses any underlying medical conditions and then looks at psychosocial problems.

- Some gender characteristics are determined biologically, and others are defined by society. Children learn traits and behaviors traditionally deemed appropriate for one sex or the other.

- The ability to respond sexually is present at birth. Sexual behaviors emerging in childhood include self-exploration, perhaps leading to masturbation.

- Although puberty defines biological adulthood, people take 5–10 more years to reach social maturity.

- Sexual fantasies and dreams and nocturnal emissions characterize adolescent sexuality.

- A person's sexual orientation can be heterosexual, homosexual, or bisexual. Possible influences include genetics, hormonal factors, and early childhood experiences.

- Human sexual behaviors include celibacy, erotic fantasy, masturbation, touching, cunnilingus, fellatio, anal intercourse, and coitus.

- To evaluate whether an atypical sexual behavior is problematic, experts consider the issues of consent between partners and whether the behavior results in physical or psychological harm.

- Pornography and prostitution are examples of the commercialization of sex; sexual stimulation is exchanged for money.

- Responsible sexuality includes open, honest communication; agreed-on sexual activities; sexual privacy; using contraception; safer sex practices; sober sex; and taking responsibility for consequences.

BOOKS

Carlson, K. J., S. A. Eisenstat, and T. Ziporyn. 2004. *The New Harvard Guide to Women's Health.* Cambridge, Mass.: Belknap Press; Simon, H. B. 2004. *The Harvard Medical School Guide to Men's Health: Lessons from the Harvard Men's Health Studies.* New York: Free Press. *These books provide research-based information about a wide variety of health issues, including sexuality, contraception, and sexually transmitted diseases.*

Halbreich, U. 2003. New advances in premenstrual syndromes (PMS/PMDD). *Psychoneuroendocrinology* [Special Issue] 28(Suppl. 3). *An entire issue devoted to all aspects of PMS and PMDD, including symptoms, treatments, and possible causes.*

Kelly, G. F. 2007. *Sexuality Today,* 9th ed. New York: McGraw-Hill. *An accessible approach that highlights cross-cultural examples, popular topics and issues, and case studies featuring college-age individuals.*

Marcus, E. 2005. *Is It a Choice? Answers to 300 of the Most Frequently Asked Questions About Gays and Lesbian People,* 3rd ed. San Francisco: Harper. *Candid and informative information on coming out, family roles, and politics.*

Omoto, A. M., and H. S. Kurtzman, eds. 2006. *Sexual Orientation and Mental Health: Examining Identity and Development in Lesbian, Gay, and Bisexual People.* Washington, D.C.: American Psychological Association. *Covers topics in mental health as well as sexual behavior, work satisfaction, and the well-being of children of same-sex couples.*

Strong, B., et al. 2008. *Human Sexuality: Diversity in Contemporary America,* 6th ed. New York: McGraw-Hill. *A comprehensive introduction to human sexuality.*

Taverner, W. J. 2006. *Taking Sides: Clashing Views on Controversial Issues in Human Sexuality,* 9th ed. New York: McGraw-Hill. *Includes pro and con position statements on sexuality issues relating to biology, behavior, and legal and social issues.*

ORGANIZATIONS AND WEB SITES

American Association of Sex Educators, Counselors, and Therapists (AASECT). Certifies sex educators, counselors, and therapists and provides listings of local therapists dealing with sexual problems.
    http://www.aasect.org

Center for Young Women's Health. Includes information about topics such as menstruation, gynecological exams, eating disorders, body piercing, and sexual health.
    http://www.youngwomenshealth.org

The Kinsey Institute for Research in Sex, Gender, and Reproduction. One of the oldest and most respected institutions doing research on sexuality.
    http://www.kinseyinstitute.org

Sexuality Information and Education Council of the United States (SIECUS). Provides information on many aspects of sexuality and has an extensive library and numerous publications.
    http://www.siecus.org

Talking with Kids. Provides advice for parents about talking with children about difficult issues, including sex, relationships, and STDs.

    http://www.talkingwithkids.org

U.S. Food and Drug Administration/Consumer Drug Information. Provides information and cautions about the use of drugs to treat sexual dysfunction in men.

    http://www.fda.gov/cder/drug/DrugSafety/DrugIndex.htm

See also the listings for Chapters 4, 6–8, and 18.

SELECTED BIBLIOGRAPHY

Agot, K. E., et al. 2004. Risk of HIV-1 in rural Kenya: A comparison of circumcised and uncircumcised men. *Epidemiology* 15(2): 157–163.

American College Health Association. August 2007 Update. *American College Health Association—National College Health Assessment (ACHA-NCHA) Web Summary* (http://www.acha-ncha.org/data_highlights.html; retrieved January 27, 2009).

American Psychological Association. 2008. *Answers to Your Questions About Sexual Orientation and Homosexuality* (http://www.apa.org/topics/orientation.html; retrieved January 27, 2009).

Bogaert, A. F. 2006. Biological versus nonbiological older brothers and men's sexual orientation. *Proceedings of the National Academy of Sciences* 103(28): 10771–10774.

Centers for Disease Control and Prevention. 2004. Teenagers in the United States: Sexual activity, contraceptive use, and childbearing, 2002. *Vital and Health Statistics* 23(24).

Centers for Disease Control and Prevention. 2005. Percentage of never-married teens aged 15–19 years who reported ever having sexual intercourse, by sex and age group—United States, 1995 and 2002. *Morbidity and Mortality Weekly Report* 54(30): 751.

Cleveland Clinic. 2005. *Sexual Dysfunction in Females* (http://www.clevelandclinic.org/health/health-info/docs/2400/2420.asp?index=9123; retrieved January 27, 2009).

Consumer Reports On Health. 2006. *Healthy Sex: His and Hers* (http://www.consumerreports.org/mg/treatment-centers/sexual-health/free-highlights/manage-your-health/healthy_sex.htm; retrieved January 27, 2009).

Dailar, Cynthia. 2006. *Guttmacher Policy Review* (http://www.guttmacher.org/pubs/gpr/09/3/gpr090312.html; retrieved January 27, 2009).

Delate, T., V. Simmons, and B. Motheral. 2004. Patterns of use of sildenafil among commercially insured adults in the United States, 1998–2002. *International Journal of Impotence Research* 16: 313–318.

Gades, N. M., et al. 2005. Association between smoking and erectile dysfunction: A population-based study. *American Journal of Epidemiology* 161(4): 346–351.

Hershberger, S. L., and N. L. Segal. 2004. The cognitive, behavioral, and personality profiles of male monozygotic triplet set discordant for sexual orientation. *Archives of Sexual Behavior* 33(5): 497–514.

Hijazi, R. A., and G. R. Cunningham. 2004. Andropause: Is androgen replacement therapy indicated for the aging male? *Annual Review of Medicine* 56: 117–137.

Hutcheson, J. C. 2004. Male neonatal circumcision: Indications, controversies and complications. *Urologic Clinics of North America* 31(3): 461–471.

Laumann, E. O., et al. 2005. Sexual problems among women and men aged 40–80 y: Prevalence and correlates identified in the Global Study of Sexual Attitudes and Behaviors. *International Journal of Impotence Research* 17(1): 39–57.

Lee, J. M., et al. 2007. Weight status in young girls and the onset of puberty. *Pediatrics* 119(3): 624–630.

Lewis, B. H., et al. 2006. Medical implications of the male biological clock. *Journal of the American Medical Association* 296(19): 2369–2371.

Lindau, S. T., et al. 2007. A study of sexuality and health among older adults in the United States. *New England Journal of Medicine* 357(8): 762–774.

National Center for Health Statistics. 2006. Fertility, contraception, and fatherhood: Data on men and women from Cycle 6 (2002) of the National Survey of Family Growth. *Vital Health Statistics* 23(26).

National Institutes of Health. 2007. *Decrease in Breast Cancer Rates Related to Reduction in Use of Hormone Replacement Therapy* (http://www.nih.gov/news/pr/apr2007/nci-18a.htm; retrieved January 27, 2009).

Nelson, C. P., et al. 2005. The increasing incidence of newborn circumcision: Data from the nationwide inpatient sample. *Journal of Urology* 173(3): 978–981.

Pills for erectile dysfunction: Now there are three. 2004. *Harvard Men's Health Watch,* April.

Rossouw, J. E., et al. 2007. Postmenopausal hormone therapy and risk of cardiovascular disease by age and years since menopause. *Journal of the American Medical Association* 297(13): 1465–1477.

Sulak, P. J., S. J. Herbelin, D. D. Fix, and T. J. Kuehl. 2006. Impact of an adolescent sex education program that was implemented by an academic medical center. *American Journal of Obstetrics and Gynecology* 195(1): 78–84.

U.S. Department of Health and Human Services. 2007. *Aging Male Syndrome* (http://womenshealth.gov/mens/sexual/ams.cfm; retrieved January 27, 2009).

Wang, L., et al. 2004. Stress and dysmenorrhoea: A population based prospective study. *Occupational and Environmental Medicine* 61(12): 1021–1026.

WebMD. 2007. *Acne vulgaris* (http://www.emedicine.com/derm/topic2.htm; retrieved January 27, 2009).

World Health Organization. 2007. *WHO and UNAIDS Announce Recommendations from Expert Consultation on Male Circumcision for HIV Prevention* (http://www.who.int/hiv/mediacentre/news68/en/print.html; retrieved January 27, 2009).

World Health Organization. 2008. *Female Genital Mutilation.* (http://www.who.int/gb/ebwha/pdf_files/EB122/B122_R13-en.pdf; retrieved January 27, 2009).

Yawman, D., et al. 2006. Pain relief for neonatal circumcision: A follow-up of residency training practices. *Ambulatory Pediatrics* 6(4): 210–214.

http://www.mcgrawhillconnect.com/personalhealth

CONTRACEPTION

LOOKING AHEAD >>>>>

AFTER READING THIS CHAPTER, YOU SHOULD BE ABLE TO:

- Explain how contraceptives work
- Interpret information about a contraceptive method's effectiveness, risks, and benefits
- List the most popular contraceptives and discuss their advantages, disadvantages, and effectiveness
- Discuss issues related to contraception, including nonmarital sexual relationships, gender differences, sex education for teenagers, and communication between partners
- Choose a method of contraception based on the needs of the user and the safety and effectiveness of the method

TEST YOUR KNOWLEDGE

1. **Which of the following contraceptive methods offers the best protection against pregnancy? Which offers the best protection against sexually transmitted diseases?**
   a. oral contraceptives
   b. injectable contraceptives
   c. male condoms
   d. diaphragm with spermicidal foam

2. **Sperm can survive only about 24 hours inside a woman's body.**
   True or false?

3. **Hand lotion, petroleum jelly, and baby oil are good choices for condom lubricants.**
   True or false?

4. **Worldwide, which of the following is the most commonly used contraceptive method?**
   a. oral contraceptives
   b. sterilization
   c. male condoms
   d. diaphragms

5. **Emergency contraception is now available without a prescription to women 18 and older.**
   True or false?

ANSWERS

1. **B AND C.** Injectable contraceptives are the most effective at preventing pregnancy; male condoms are the most effective against sexually transmitted diseases.

2. **FALSE.** Sperm usually live about 72 hours within the woman's body, but can live up to 6 or 7 days.

3. **FALSE.** Only water-based lubricants such as K-Y Jelly should be used as condom lubricants. Any product that contains mineral oil can cause latex condoms to disintegrate, beginning within 60 seconds of being applied.

4. **B.** Sterilization is the most popular method of contraception used around the world. Although male sterilization is less expensive and less prone to complications, female sterilization is far more commonly practiced.

5. **TRUE.** In August 2006, the Food and Drug Administration approved the over-the-counter sale of Plan B, an emergency contraception product, for women 18 and older. In most states, women younger than 18 need a prescription to purchase Plan B. It is stocked behind the counter in pharmacies because proof of age is required to purchase it.

People have always had a compelling interest in managing fertility and preventing unwanted pregnancies, a practice commonly known as **birth control.** Records dating to the fourth century B.C. describe the use of foods, herbs, drugs, douches, and sponges to prevent **conception,** which is the fusion of an ovum and sperm that creates a fertilized egg. Early attempts at **contraception** (blocking conception through the use of a device, substance, or method) were based on the same principle as many modern birth control methods.

Today, women and men can choose from many different types of **contraceptives** to avoid unwanted pregnancies. Modern contraceptives take a wide variety of forms and work in different ways. Modern contraceptive methods are much more predictable and effective than in the past, and people in developed countries now have many options when it comes to making decisions about their sexual and contraceptive behavior.

Worldwide, however, the situation is quite different. People in many countries have little access to contraceptive information and supplies. The World Health Organization estimates that 80 million women worldwide have unintended or unwanted pregnancies every year and 500,000 women die from complications of pregnancy and chilbirth.

VITAL STATISTICS

Table 6.1 — Intended versus Unintended Pregnancies in the United States: 2001

Total pregnancies	6,404,000
Intended	51%
Unintended	49%
Unintended pregnancies ending in abortion	42%
Pregnancy rate*	104
Abortion rate*	21
Unintended birth rate*	22

*Per 1000 women

SOURCE: Finer, L. B., and S. K. Henshaw. 2006. Disparities in rates of unintended pregnancy in the United States, 1994 and 2001. *Perspectives on Sexual and Reproductive Health* 38(2): 90–96.

Table 6.1 shows the numbers of intended and unintended pregnancies in the United States in 2001 (the most recent year for which complete data are available). About 44% of unintended pregnancies were carried to term that year; another 42% ended in abortion. The remainder ended in loss of the fetus for some other reason.

In addition to preventing pregnancy, many types of contraception play an important role in protecting against **sexually transmitted diseases (STDs).** Being informed about the realities and risks and making responsible decisions about sexual and contraceptive behavior are crucial components of lifelong wellness. But because such decisions are emotional, complex, and difficult, people tend to avoid them or to deal with them ineffectively.

Biological, social, and media pressures often encourage sexual activity at ever-younger ages, but few forces in the United States support a factual, realistic discussion of the importance of either postponing sexual intercourse or using contraception when intercourse is chosen. Americans' superficial approaches to sexual education are clearly ineffective: The United States has one of the highest teen pregnancy rates of all developed nations. Because many women's lives are severely affected by unplanned child rearing and because the option of abortion is becoming more restricted, the problem of unplanned, unwanted pregnancies is more serious than the numbers show.

This chapter provides basic information on the various contraceptive methods, including their advantages and disadvantages; STDs are discussed in Chapter 18.

PRINCIPLES OF CONTRACEPTION

There are a variety of effective approaches to contraception, including the following:

- **Barrier methods** work by physically blocking the sperm from reaching the egg. Diaphragms, con-

TERMS

birth control   The practice of managing fertility and preventing unwanted pregnancies.

conception   The fusion of ovum and sperm, resulting in a fertilized egg, or *zygote*.

contraception   The prevention of conception through the use of a device, substance, or method.

contraceptive   Any agent or method that can prevent conception.

sexually transmitted disease (STD)   Any of several contagious diseases contracted through intimate sexual contact.

barrier method   A contraceptive that acts as a physical barrier, blocking the sperm from uniting with the egg.

hormonal method   A contraceptive that alters the biochemistry of a woman's body, preventing ovulation and making it more difficult for sperm to reach an egg if ovulation does occur.

natural method   An approach to contraception that does not use drugs or devices; requires avoiding intercourse during the period of the woman's menstrual cycle when an egg is likely to be present at the site of conception and the risk of pregnancy is greatest.

surgical method   Sterilization of a male or female, to permanently prevent the transport of sperm or eggs to the site of conception.

contraceptive failure rate   The percentage of women using a particular contraceptive method who experience an unintended pregnancy in the first year of use.

continuation rate   The percentage of people who continue to use a particular contraceptive after a specified period of time.

Myths About Contraception

Myth Taking birth control pills for a few days before having sex gives reliable protection against pregnancy.

Fact Instructions for taking birth control pills must be followed carefully to provide effective contraception. With most pills, this means starting them with a menstrual period and then taking one every day.

Myth Pregnancy never occurs when unprotected intercourse takes place just before or just after a menstrual period.

Fact Menstrual cycles may be irregular, and ovulation may be unpredictable.

Myth During sexual relations, sperm enter the vagina only during ejaculation and never before.

Fact The small amount of fluid secreted before ejaculation may contain sperm. This is why withdrawing the penis from the vagina just prior to ejaculation is not an effective method of contraception.

Myth If semen is deposited just outside the vaginal entrance, pregnancy cannot occur.

Fact Although sperm usually live about 72 hours within the woman's body, they can live up to 6 or 7 days and are capable of traveling through the vagina and up into the uterus and oviducts.

Myth Douching immediately after sexual relations can prevent sperm from reaching and fertilizing an egg.

Fact During ejaculation (within the vagina), some sperm begin to enter the cervix and uterus. Because these sperm are no longer in the vagina, it is impossible to remove them by douching after sexual relations. Douching may actually push the sperm up farther.

Myth A woman who is breastfeeding does not have to use any contraceptive method to prevent pregnancy.

Fact Frequent and regular breastfeeding may at times prevent ovulation, but not consistently and reliably. Ovulation and pregnancy may occur before the first period after delivering a baby.

Myth Women can't become pregnant the first time they have intercourse.

Fact *Any time* intercourse without protection takes place, pregnancy may result. There is nothing unique about first intercourse that prevents this.

Myth Taking a "rest" from the pill periodically is necessary for safety.

Fact There are no known medical benefits from taking a prolonged break from oral contraceptive use; the risks and benefits of ongoing pill use should be evaluated for each individual. Pregnancy commonly occurs when one method of contraception is stopped and not immediately replaced by another method.

Myth Pregnancy is impossible if partners have sex while standing up.

Fact Sperm can travel and reach the egg regardless of body position.

---

doms, and several other methods are based on this principle.

- **Hormonal methods,** such as oral contraceptives (birth control pills), alter the biochemistry of the woman's body, preventing ovulation (the release of the egg) and producing changes that make it more difficult for the sperm to reach the egg if ovulation does occur.

- **Natural methods** of contraception are based on the fact that egg and sperm have to be present at the same time if fertilization is to occur.

- **Surgical methods**—female and male sterilization—more or less permanently prevent transport of the sperm or eggs to the site of conception.

All contraceptive methods have advantages and disadvantages that make them appropriate for some people but not for others or the best choice at one period of life but not at another. Factors that affect the choice of method include effectiveness, convenience, cost, reversibility, side effects and risks, and protection against STDs. Later in this chapter, we help you sort through these factors to decide on the method that's best for you. (See the box "Myths About Contraception" to make sure you're not basing your current choices on common misinformation.)

Contraceptive effectiveness is partly determined by the reliability of the method itself—the failure rate if it were always used exactly as directed ("perfect use"). Effectiveness is also determined by characteristics of the user, including fertility of the individual, frequency of intercourse, and how consistently and correctly the method is used. This "typical use" **contraceptive failure rate** is based on studies that directly measure the percentage of women experiencing an unintended pregnancy in the first year of contraceptive use. For example, the 8% failure rate of oral contraceptives means 8 out of 100 typical users will become pregnant in the first year. This failure rate is likely to be lower for women who are consistently careful in following instructions and higher for those who are frequently careless; the "perfect use" failure rate is 0.3%.

About 400 eggs are released through ovulation during a woman's fertile life.

—**American College of Obstetricians and Gynecologists, 2008**

QUICK STATS

Another measure of effectiveness is the **continuation rate**—the percentage of people who continue to use the method after a specified period of time. This measure is

A careful explanation by a health care professional will help this couple choose a contraceptive method that is right for them.

important because many unintended pregnancies occur when a method is stopped and not immediately replaced with another. Thus, a contraceptive with a high continuation rate would be more effective at preventing pregnancy than one with a low continuation rate.

REVERSIBLE CONTRACEPTION

Reversibility is an extremely important consideration for young adults when they choose a contraceptive method, because most people either plan to have children or at least want to keep their options open until they're older.

Oral Contraceptives: The Pill

About a century ago, a researcher noted that ovulation does not occur during pregnancy. Further research re-

QUESTIONS FOR CRITICAL THINKING AND REFLECTION

Prior to reading this section, how familiar were you with the principles of contraception? Did you know as much as you thought? Does this kind of information make you feel as though you should be more or less directly responsible for the contraceptive choices in your life?

vealed the hormonal mechanism: During pregnancy, the corpus luteum secretes progesterone and estrogen in amounts high enough to suppress ovulation. (See Chapter 5 for a complete discussion of the menstrual cycle.) **Oral contraceptives (OCs),** or *birth control pills,* prevent ovulation by mimicking the hormonal activity of the corpus luteum. The active ingredients in OCs are estrogen and progestins, laboratory-made compounds that are closely related to progesterone. Today, OCs are the most widely used form of contraception among unmarried women and are second only to sterilization among married women.

In addition to preventing ovulation, the birth control pill has other backup contraceptive effects. It inhibits the movement of sperm by thickening the cervical mucus, alters the rate of ovum transport by means of its hormonal effects on the oviducts, and may prevent implantation by changing the lining of the uterus, in the unlikely event that a fertilized ovum reaches that area.

The most common type of OC is the *combination pill.* Each 1-month packet contains a 3-week supply of pills that combine varying types and amounts of estrogen and progestin. Most packets also include a 1-week supply of inactive pills to be taken following the hormone pills; others simply instruct the woman to take no pills at all for 1 week before starting the next cycle. During the week in which no hormones are taken, a light menstrual period occurs. Many different types of combination pills are available.

Newer use schedules include a variety of extended-cycle regimens. With the pills Seasonale and Seasonique, for example, a woman takes active pills for 84 consecutive days, then inactive pills for a week; this pattern reduces the number of menstrual periods from 13 per year to just 4 per year. With the pill Lybrel, active pills are taken indefinitely. This and other new OCs are specifically packaged for extended use. Other OCs with hormones similar to the prepackaged brands may be used in the same way. When taken without a break, Lybrel can stop a woman's monthly periods. Changing the menstrual cycle has not been linked with any major health risks. More long-range research is needed.

Another, much less common, type of OC is the *minipill,* a small dose of a synthetic progesterone taken every day of the month. Because the minipill contains no estrogen, it has fewer side effects and health risks, but it is associated with more irregular bleeding patterns.

A woman is usually advised to start the first cycle of pills with a menstrual period to increase effectiveness and eliminate the possibility of unsuspected pregnancy. If pregnancy has been ruled out, the pill can be started immediately. She must take each month's pills completely and according to instructions. Taking a few pills just prior to having sexual intercourse will not provide effective contraception.

Hormonal adjustments that occur during the first cycle or two may cause slight bleeding between periods. This spotting is considered normal. If the pill is not started with a menstrual period, full effectiveness cannot be guaranteed during the first week. A backup method is recommended during the first week and any subsequent cycle in which the woman forgets to take any pills.

OC use was once linked to possible increased risks of heart attack and stroke. However, these risks have been substantially reduced by the use of lower-dosage pills (those with 50 micrograms or less of estrogen) and the identification of women at higher risk for complications.

Advantages Oral contraceptives are very effective in preventing pregnancy. Nearly all unplanned pregnancies result because the pills were not taken as directed. The pill is relatively simple to use and does not hinder sexual spontaneity. Most women also enjoy the predictable regularity of periods, as well as the decrease in cramps and blood loss. For young women, the reversibility of the pill is especially important; **fertility**—the ability to reproduce—returns after the pill is discontinued (although not always immediately).

Medical advantages include a decreased incidence of benign breast disease, iron-deficiency anemia, pelvic inflammatory disease (PID), ectopic pregnancy, colon and rectal cancer, endometrial cancer (in the lining of the uterus), and ovarian cancer. Women who have never used the pill are twice as likely to develop endometrial or ovarian cancer as those who have taken it for at least 5 years.

Disadvantages Although oral contraceptives lower the risk of PID, they do not protect against HIV infection or other STDs in the lower reproductive tract. OCs have been associated with increased cervical chlamydia. Regular condom use is recommended for an OC user, unless she is in a long-term, mutually monogamous relationship with an uninfected partner.

The hormones in birth control pills influence all tissues of the body and can lead to a variety of disturbances. Symptoms of early pregnancy—morning nausea and swollen breasts, for example—may appear during the first few months of OC use. They usually disappear by the fourth cycle. Other side effects include depression, nervousness, changes in sex drive, dizziness, generalized headaches, migraine, bleeding between periods, and changes in the lining of the walls of the vagina, with an increase in clear or white vaginal discharge. Chloasma, or "mask of pregnancy," sometimes occurs, causing brown "giant freckles" to appear on the face. Acne may develop or worsen but, in most women, using the pill causes acne to clear up, and it is sometimes prescribed for that purpose.

Serious side effects have been reported in a small number of women. These include blood clots, stroke, and heart attack, concentrated mostly in older women who smoke or have a history of circulatory disease. Recent studies have shown no increased risk of stroke or heart attack for healthy, young, nonsmoking women on lower-dosage pills. OC users may be slightly more prone to high blood pressure, blood clots in the legs and arms, and benign liver tumors that may rupture and bleed.

OC use is associated with little, if any, increase in breast cancer and a slight increase in cervical cancer; however, earlier detection and other variables such as number of sexual partners may account for much of this increase. The link between OC use and cervical cancer appears to pertain primarily to women infected with human papillomavirus, an STD.

Birth control pills are not recommended for women with a history of blood clots (or a close family member with unexplained blood clots at an early age), heart disease or stroke, migraines with changes in vision, any form of cancer or liver tumor, or impaired liver function. Women with certain other health conditions or behaviors, including migraines without changes in vision, high blood pressure, cigarette smoking, and sickle-cell disease, require close monitoring.

When deciding whether to use OCs, each woman needs to weigh the benefits against the risks. To make an informed decision, she should seek the help of a health care professional (see the box "Obtaining a Contraceptive from a Health Clinic or Physician" on p. 158). A woman can take several steps to decrease her risk from OC use:

1. Request a low-dosage pill. (OCs recommended for most new users contain 30–35 micrograms of estrogen.)

2. Stop smoking.

3. Follow the dosage carefully and consistently.

4. Be alert to preliminary danger signals, which can be remembered with the word ACHES:

   Abdominal pain (severe)

   Chest pain (severe), cough, shortness of breath or sharp pain on breathing in

   Headaches (severe), dizziness, weakness, or numbness, especially if one-sided

   Eye problems (vision loss or blurring) and/or speech problems

   Severe leg pain (calf or thigh)

5. Have regular checkups to monitor blood pressure, weight, and urine, and have an annual examination of the thyroid, breasts, abdomen, and pelvis.

6. Have regular **Pap tests** to check for early cervical changes.

---

oral contraceptive (OC) Any of various hormone compounds (estrogen and progestins) in pill form that prevent conception by preventing ovulation.

fertility The ability to reproduce.

Pap test A scraping of cells from the cervix for examination under a microscope to detect cancer.

TERMS

Obtaining a Contraceptive from a Health Clinic or Physician

If you are a woman who is considering a method of contraception that requires a prescription or professional fitting or insertion, you'll need to go to a health clinic or a physician to get it. Many of the female methods—including the hormonal methods, IUDs, and the diaphragm and cervical cap—require at least an initial professional visit.

The thought of visiting a physician's office or health clinic to discuss and obtain contraception makes many people nervous. Remember that the people in the office are health care professionals who will not pass moral judgment on you. They are dedicated to meeting your health care needs. Knowing what to expect can help you get more from your visit.

Before Your Visit

You can prepare for a more successful visit by doing the following:

1. Pull together your personal and family medical history. Make sure it's accurate and up-to-date.

2. Review the section in this chapter titled "Which Contraceptive Method Is Right for You?" Carefully consider each topic, and discuss it with your partner if that would be helpful.

3. Write down any questions you have. Decide what you need to learn about your contraceptive options.

4. If you have questions about sexually transmitted diseases or other aspects of sexuality, write those down, too.

5. If you like, plan to have your partner, a friend, or a family member accompany you to your appointment.

During Your Visit

When you arrive, you'll probably be asked to fill out forms covering your background and medical history. A physician or staff member will then review the various contraceptive methods with you and answer your questions. She or he can help you evaluate the key factors affecting your choice of method, including health risks, lifestyle factors, cost, and protection against STDs. Blood and urine samples may be taken for lab tests.

The Physical Exam

Your physical exam will probably include a check of your breasts, external genitals, and abdomen, plus a Pap test and possible screening for certain STDs. The exam will help ensure that you can safely use the method you have chosen, as well as protect your overall health. If this is your first pelvic exam and/or you feel nervous or uncomfortable, tell the clinician, and ask her or him to explain each step of the examination.

For the pelvic exam, you will be asked to lie on your back on an examination table, with your feet in metal stirrups and your knees bent. The exam doesn't usually hurt. An instrument called a *speculum* will be inserted into the vagina to hold it open so the clinician can look at the cervix and vaginal walls. For the Pap test, the clinician will scrape some cells from the cervix and place them on a glass slide. These cells will be analyzed for any signs of cancer. You may feel a slight pressure while the cells are collected. The clinician will also check your internal organs by placing two gloved fingers into the vagina and the other hand on the lower abdomen. He or she will palpate (examine by touching) the uterus and ovaries to check for any abnormalities.

If you're getting a diaphragm or a cervical cap, you will be fitted for it at this time. The clinician will probably try different sizes to find the best fit and then will show you how to insert and remove it.

Following Your Exam

After your exam, a health care worker will either provide you with your contraceptive, arrange for a further appointment (if necessary), or give you a prescription. Make sure you know exactly how to use the method you've chosen. Written instructions and information may be available. Be sure you have a phone number you can call if you have questions later.

For most women, the known, directly associated risk of death from taking birth control pills is much lower than the risk of death from pregnancy (Table 6.2).

Effectiveness   Oral contraceptive effectiveness varies substantially because it depends so much on individual factors. If taken exactly as directed, the failure rate is extremely low (0.3%). However, among average users, lapses such as forgetting to take a pill do occur, and a typical first-year failure rate is 8.7%. The continuation rate for OCs also varies; the average rate is 68% after 1 year.

Contraceptive Skin Patch

The contraceptive skin patch, Ortho Evra, is a thin, 1¾-inch square patch that slowly releases an estrogen and a progestin into the bloodstream. The contraceptive patch prevents pregnancy in the same way as combination OCs, following a similar schedule. Each patch is worn continuously for 1 week and is replaced on the same day of the week for 3 consecutive weeks. The fourth week is patch-free, allowing a woman to have her menstrual period.

The patch can be worn on the upper outer arm, abdomen, buttocks, or upper torso (excluding the breasts); it is designed to stick to skin even during bathing or swimming. If a patch should fall off for more than a day, the FDA advises starting a new 4-week cycle of patches and using a backup method of contraception for the first week. Patches should be discarded according to the manufacturer's directions to avoid leakage of hormones into the environment.

Advantages   With both perfect and typical use, the patch is as effective as OCs in preventing pregnancy. Compliance seems to be higher with the patch than with OCs,

Table 6.2 Contraceptive Risks

Contraceptive Method	Risk of Death in Any Given Year
Oral contraceptives	
Nonsmoker	1 in 66,700
Age less than 35	1 in 200,000
Age 35–44	1 in 28,600
Heavy smoker (25 or more cigarettes/day)	1 in 1,700
Age less than 35	1 in 5,300
Age 35–44	1 in 700
IUDs	1 in 10,000,000
Barrier methods, spermicides	none
Fertility awareness methods, withdrawal	none
Sterilization	
Laparoscopic tubal ligation	1 in 38,500
Hysterectomy	1 in 1,600
Vasectomy	1 in 1,000,000
Pregnancy and childbirth	1 in 10,000

SOURCE: Hatcher, R. A., et al. 2004. *Contraceptive Technology*, 18th rev. ed. New York: Ardent Media. Reprinted by permission of Ardent Media, Inc.

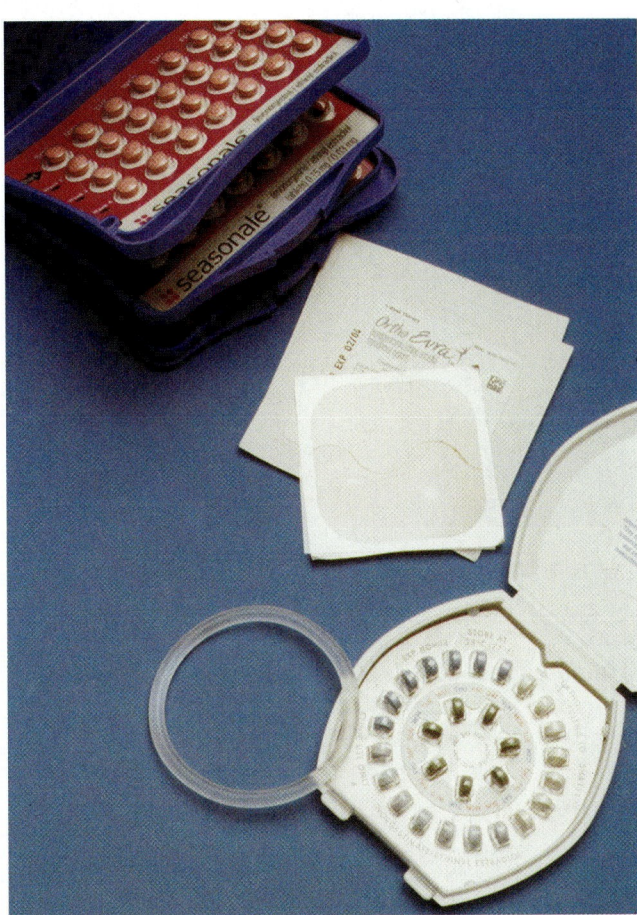

Reversible hormonal contraceptives are available in several forms. Shown here are the patch, the ring, and birth control pills.

probably because the patch requires weekly instead of daily action. Medical benefits are likely to be comparable to those of OCs.

Disadvantages With patch use, additional measures must be taken to protect against STDs. Minor side effects are similar to those of OCs, although breast discomfort may be more common in patch users. Some women also experience skin irritation around the patch. More serious complications are thought to be similar to those of OCs, including an increased risk of side effects among women who smoke. However, because Ortho Evra exposes users to higher doses of estrogen than most OCs, patch use may further increase the risk of blood clots and other adverse effects.

Effectiveness With perfect use, the patch's failure rate is very low (0.3%) in the first year of use. The typical failure rate is assumed to be lower than the pill's 8.7%, because consistent use is better among patch users. The product appears to be less effective when used by women weighing more than 198 pounds.

Vaginal Contraceptive Ring

The NuvaRing is a vaginal ring that is molded with a mixture of progestin and estrogen. The 2-inch ring slowly releases hormones and maintains blood hormone levels comparable to those found with OC use; it prevents pregnancy in the same way as OCs. A woman inserts the ring anytime during the first 5 days of her menstrual period and leaves it in place for 3 weeks. During the fourth week, which is ring-free, her next menstrual period occurs. A new ring is then inserted. Rings should be discarded according to the manufacturer's directions to avoid leakage of hormones into the environment.

Backup contraception must be used for the first 7 days of the first ring use or if the ring has been removed for more than 3 hours during use. A diaphragm is not recommended as a backup contraceptive with the NuvaRing because the ring may interfere with the placement of a diaphragm. Diaphragm use is discussed on p. 167.

Advantages The NuvaRing offers 1 month of protection with no daily or weekly action required. It does not require a fitting by a clinician, and exact placement in the vagina is not critical as it is with a diaphragm. Medical benefits are probably similar to those of OCs.

Disadvantages The NuvaRing gives no protection against STDs. Side effects are roughly comparable to those seen with OC use, except for a lower incidence of nausea and vomiting. Other side effects may include vaginal discharge, vaginitis, and vaginal irritation. Medical risks also are similar to those found with OC use.

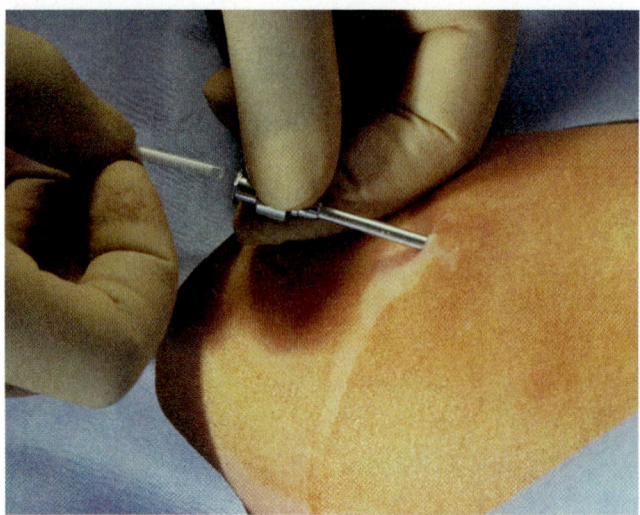

Only trained health professionals can insert a contraceptive implant.

Effectiveness   As with the pill and patch, the perfect use failure rate is around 0.3% and the typical use failure rate is likely to be lower than the pill's 8.7%.

Contraceptive Implants

Contraceptive implants are placed under the skin of the upper arm and deliver a small but steady dose of progestin (a synthetic progesterone) over a period of years. One such implant, called Implanon, is a single implant that was approved for use in the United States in 2006. This device is effective for 3 years.

The progestins in implants have several contraceptive effects. They cause hormonal shifts that may inhibit ovulation and affect development of the uterine lining. The hormones also thicken the cervical mucus, inhibiting the movement of sperm. Finally, they may slow the transport of the egg through the fallopian tubes. Contraceptive implants are best suited for women who wish to have continuous and long-term protection against pregnancy.

Advantages   Contraceptive implants are highly effective. After insertion of the implants, no further action is required; contraceptive effects are quickly reversed upon removal. Because implants, unlike the combination pill, contain no estrogen, they carry a lower risk of certain side effects, such as blood clots and other cardiovascular complications. In addition, the progestin is released at a steady rate, in smaller quantities than are found in oral contraceptives. The thickened cervical mucus resulting from implant use has a protective effect against PID.

Disadvantages   Like the pill, an implant provides no protection against HIV infection and STDs in the lower reproductive tract. Although the implants are barely visible, their appearance may bother some women. Only spe-

cially trained practitioners can insert or remove the implants, and removal is sometimes difficult.

The most common side effects of contraceptive implants are menstrual irregularities, including longer menstrual periods, spotting between periods, or having no bleeding at all. The menstrual cycle usually becomes more regular after 1 year of use. Less common side effects include headaches, weight gain, breast tenderness, nausea, acne, and mood swings. Cautions and more serious health concerns are similar to those associated with oral contraceptives but are less common.

Effectiveness   The overall failure rate for Implanon is estimated at about 0.1%.

Injectable Contraceptives

Hormonal contraceptive injections were developed in the 1960s and are currently being used in at least 80 countries throughout the world. The first injectable contraceptive approved for use in the United States was Depo-Provera, which uses long-acting progestins. Injected into the arm or buttocks, Depo-Provera is usually given every 12 weeks, although it actually provides effective contraception for a few weeks beyond that. As another progestin-only contraceptive, it prevents pregnancy in the same ways as implants.

Advantages   Injectable contraceptives are highly effective and require little action on the part of the user. Because the injections leave no trace and involve no ongoing supplies, injectables allow women almost total privacy in their decision to use contraception. Depo-Provera has no estrogen-related side effects; it requires only periodic injections rather than the minor surgical procedures of implant insertion and removal.

Disadvantages   Injectable contraceptives provide no protection against HIV infection and STDs in the lower reproductive tract. A woman must visit a health care facility every 3 months to receive the injections. The side effects of Depo-Provera are similar to those of implants; menstrual irregularities are the most common, and after 1 year of using Depo-Provera many women have no menstrual bleeding at all. Weight gain is a common side effect. After discontinuing the use of Depo-Provera, women may experience temporary infertility for up to 12 months.

Reasons for not using Depo-Provera are similar to those for not using implants. Although early animal studies indicated that Depo-Provera increases the risk of breast and other cancers, the FDA has concluded that worldwide studies and years of human use have shown the risk of cancer in humans to be minimal or nonexistent. Extended use of Depo-Provera is associated with decreased bone density, a risk factor for osteoporosis (see Chapter 12); women who use Depo-Provera are advised to do weight-bearing exercise and take 1000 mg of calcium daily. Women are advised to use Depo-Provera as a long-term contraceptive (longer than 2 years, for example) only if other methods are inadequate. Studies have found that bone density rebounds when use of Depo-Provera stops.

Effectiveness   The perfect use failure rate is 0.3% for Depo-Provera. With typical use, the failure rate increases to 6.7% in the first year of use. The 1-year continuation rate for Depo-Provera is about 56%.

Emergency Contraception

Emergency contraception (EC) refers to postcoital methods—those used after unprotected sexual intercourse. An emergency contraceptive may be appropriate if a regularly used method has failed (for example, if a condom breaks) or if unprotected sex has occurred. Sometimes called the "morning-after pill," emergency contraceptives are designed only for emergency use and should not be relied on as a regular birth control method.

Until recently the most frequently used emergency contraceptive was a two-dose regimen of certain oral contraceptives. Researchers are still uncertain precisely how OCs work as emergency contraceptives. Opponents of their use argue that if they act by preventing implantation of a fertilized egg, they may actually be **abortifacients;** however, recent evidence indicates that prevention of implantation is not their primary mode of action. Postcoital pills appear to work primarily by inhibiting or delaying ovulation and by altering the transport of sperm and/or eggs; they do not affect a fertilized egg already implanted in the uterus.

Plan B is a newer product specifically designed for emergency contraception. It contains two progestin-only pills. The first pill should be taken as soon as possible (no more than 120 hours) after inadequately protected sex. The second pill should be taken 12 hours after the first. Both pills may be taken together in a single dose with little change in effectiveness or side effects. If taken within 24 hours after intercourse,

Plan B may prevent as many as 95% of expected pregnancies. Overall, Plan B reduces pregnancy risk by about 89%. It is most effective if initiated in the first 12 hours. Possible side effects are similar to those associated with the OC regimen and can include nausea, stomach pain, headache, dizziness, and breast tenderness.

In August 2006, the FDA approved the use of Plan B as an over-the-counter (OTC) drug for women age 18 and older. Prior to that time, it was available to all women by prescription and in some states directly from pharmacists. It remains a prescription drug for those under age 18. Plan B is stocked behind the counter because proof of age or a prescription is required to purchase it.

Because of concerns about the drug's use by young teens, the manufacturer of Plan B, Duramed, agreed to a rigorous program of labeling, packaging, education, distribution, and monitoring called Convenient Access, Responsible Education (CARE). Among other things, Duramed has committed not to distribute Plan B through convenience stores or other retail outlets where younger women might have access to it without a prescription.

Easy access to emergency contraception is important because the sooner the drug is taken, the more effective it is. Some clinicians advise women to keep a package of emergency contraception on hand in case their regular contraception method fails. Research has found that ready access to emergency contraception does *not* lead to an increase in unprotected intercourse, unintended pregnancies, or STDs.

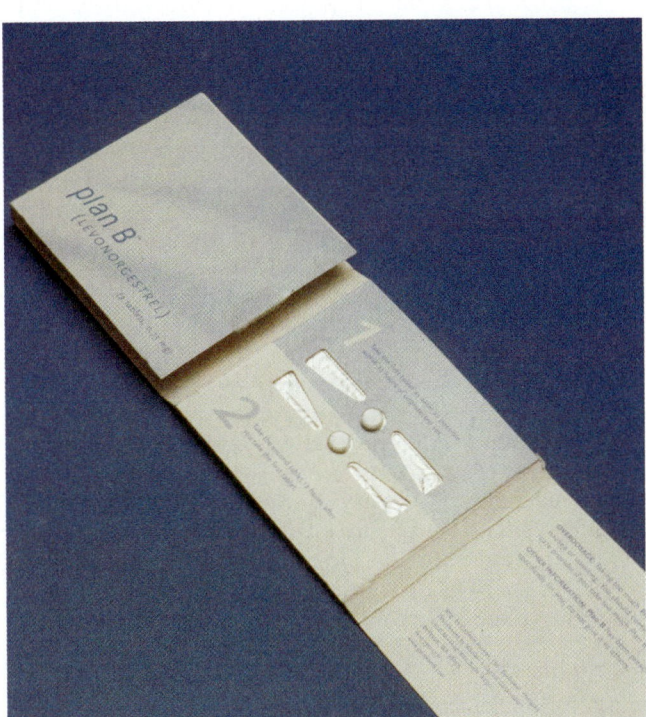

Emergency hormonal contraceptives can significantly reduce the risk of pregnancy if taken within 72 hours of unprotected intercourse. The most commonly used regimens for emergency contraception involve taking two doses of hormones about 12 hours apart.

emergency contraception   A birth control method used after unprotected sexual intercourse has occurred.

abortifacient   An agent or substance that induces abortion.

TERMS

Even though the FDA approved the emergency contraceptive drug Plan B for over-the-counter sale to adults in 2006, many women still have trouble getting emergency contraception (EC) when they need it most.

Soon after the start of Plan B sales, media outlets reported that some pharmacists were refusing to dispense the drug, even to women who had a doctor's prescription for it. (Under FDA rules, women younger than 18 must have a prescription in order to buy Plan B.) Most of these pharmacists—and in some cases, pharmacy management, physicians, and hospitals—claimed a moral or religious basis for declining to distribute Plan B. The drug, they contended, is more an abortifaciant than a contraceptive, because it might interfere with the implantation of a fertilized egg in a woman's uterus.

As a result, an untold number of women, some of whom claim to have been sexually assaulted, found their requests for emergency contraception being turned down by doctors, pharmacists, and even some emergency room staff. In most cases, the women have been able to obtain the drug from another medical

professional, but many of them say the experience left them humiliated as well as inconvenienced.

The controversy over Plan B has raised an important but difficult question about the role of religion among health care providers, especially pharmacists. That is, should a doctor or pharmacist be allowed to refuse treatment if he or she feels the treatment is immoral or contrary to his or her religious beliefs? As an example, many doctors refuse to perform abortions because they view it as an act of murder; our society and the government do not force these doctors to do abortions. By the same token, then, can we force pharmacists to distribute Plan B if they are morally opposed to the drug?

Many Plan B proponents contend that health care professionals who refuse to provide the drug—regardless of the reason—are jeopardizing the physical and emotional health of patients. Proponents also argue the issue of fairness: If a pharmacy sells some types of contraceptives, such as condoms and standard birth control pills, then it should sell *all* forms of contraception, including EC. At the very least, say Plan B supporters, if pharmacists or doctors refuse to dispense the drug, they should be willing to direct patients to other professionals who will provide it. (There are numerous stories of health care providers simply turning women away without offering any kind of helpful information.)

State legislatures and courts have jumped into the fray, as well. According to the Guttmacher Institute, 16 states now require emergency room staff to provide emergency contraception to women who have been sexually assaulted; in 11 other states, EC must be made available on request to assault victims.

A few states have adopted legislation encouraging pharmacists to provide EC services; in nine states, for example, pharmacists can provide Plan B without a prescription under certain circumstances. Another two states require pharmacists to fill all valid prescriptions that are presented to them.

However, a few other states have placed restrictions on access to EC, and five states have regulations that specifically allow pharmacists or pharmacies to refuse to sell any kind of contraceptives, including EC.

A number of pharmacists have filed suits in several states to overturn regulations that require them to dispense Plan B; a few of these suits have been successful. Many experts believe that the rights of individual health care providers to deny certain services on religious grounds may ultimately prevail over a woman's right to receive emergency contraceptive services.

It's important to remember, however, that only a small percentage of doctors, pharmacies, and hospitals have refused to provide EC to women who need it. Many more support a woman's right to receive such services, especially in cases involving sexual assault.

In 2007, the American College of Obstetricians and Gynecologists (ACOG) released a position statement on the issue of "conscientious refusal" to provide reproductive medical services. The group urged doctors who object to EC to give patients prior notice of their objections while continuing to give accurate medical information about health services such as contraception and abortion. When doctors refuse to perform the actual services, the ACOG urges them to refer patients to other doctors who are willing to provide them.

Meantime, women who are at risk of unwanted pregnancy should consider talking to their doctor about emergency contraception. Many doctors write prescriptions for Plan B proactively (before it is actually needed), so women can have the drug on hand in case of an emergency. This precautionary step can allow a woman to take the drug as soon as it's needed, without spending time trying to get it.

Women who have trouble getting EC may find help from organizations such as Planned Parenthood (http://www.plannedparenthood.org). Web sites such as Princeton University's Emergency Contraception site (http://ec.princeton.edu) enable visitors to search for EC providers by ZIP code.

Despite FDA approval, not all physicians, hospitals, or pharmacists make emergency contraception available, even in cases of sexual assault. (See the box "Access to Emergency Contraception" for more information.) So-called refusal or conscience clauses, originally designed to allow physicians to refuse to perform abortions because of personal moral or religions objections, are being applied to a wider range of health care activities and participants. Increasingly, however, states are requiring pharmacies to carry Plan B. Call the Emergency Contraception Hotline (888-NOT-2-LATE) for more information about access.

Intrauterine devices, discussed in the next section, can also be used for emergency contraception: If inserted within 5 days of unprotected intercourse, they are even more effective than OCs. However, because their use is more complicated, they are not used nearly as frequently.

The Intrauterine Device (IUD)

The **intrauterine device (IUD)** is a small plastic device placed in the uterus as a contraceptive. Two IUDs are now available in the United States: the Copper T-380A (also known as the ParaGard), which gives protection for up to 10 years, and the Levonorgestral IUD (Mirena), which releases small amounts of progestin and is effective for up to 5 years.

Researchers do not know exactly how IUDs prevent pregnancy. Current evidence suggests that they work primarily by preventing fertilization. IUDs may cause biochemical changes in the uterus and affect the movement of sperm and eggs; although less likely, they may also interfere with implantation of fertilized eggs. Mirena slowly releases very small amounts of hormones, which impedes fertilization or implantation.

An IUD must be inserted and removed by a trained professional. It can be inserted at any time during the menstrual cycle, as long as the woman is not pregnant. The device is threaded into a sterile inserter, which is introduced through the cervix; a plunger pushes the IUD into the uterus. The threads protruding from the cervix are trimmed so that only 1–1½ inches remain in the upper vagina (Figure 6.1).

Advantages Intrauterine devices are highly reliable and are simple and convenient to use, requiring no attention except for a periodic check of the string position. They do not require the woman to anticipate or interrupt sexual activity. According to the American College of Obstetricians and Gynecologists, IUD use reduces the risk of developing endometrial cancer by as much as 40%. Usually IUDs have only localized side effects, and in the absence of complications they are considered a fully reversible contraceptive. In most cases, fertility is restored as soon as the IUD is removed. The risks of ectopic pregnancy and uterine cancer are both decreased with IUD use. The long-term expense of using an IUD is low.

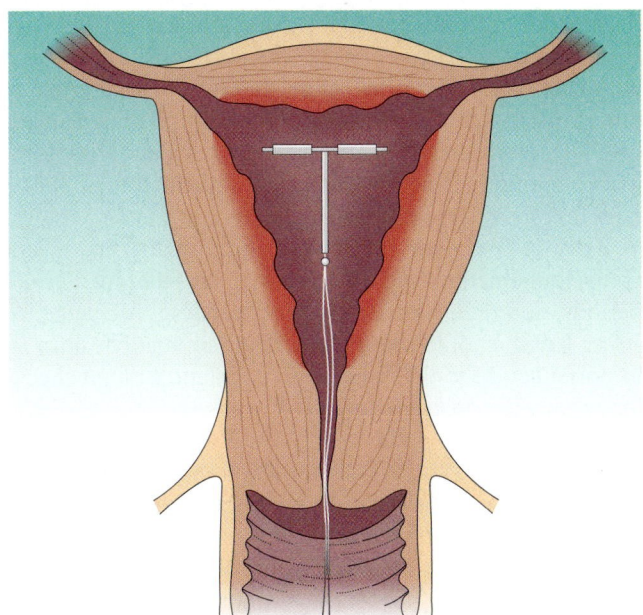

FIGURE 6.1 An IUD (Copper T-380A) properly positioned in the uterus. The attached threads that protrude from the cervix into the upper vagina allow the woman to check to make sure that the IUD is in place.

Disadvantages Most side effects of IUD use are limited to the genital tract. Heavy menstrual flow and bleeding and spotting between periods may occur, although with Mirena menstrual periods tend to become shorter and lighter over time. Another side effect is pain, particularly uterine cramps and backache, which seem to occur most often in women who have never been pregnant. Spontaneous expulsion of the IUD happens to 5–6% of women within the first year, most commonly during the first months after insertion. The older the woman is and the more children she has had, the less likely she is to expel the device. In about 1 of 1000 insertions, the IUD punctures the wall of the uterus and may migrate into the abdominal cavity.

A serious but rare complication of IUD use is pelvic inflammatory disease (PID). Most pelvic infections among IUD users occur shortly after insertion, are relatively mild, and can be treated successfully with antibiotics. However, early and adequate treatment is critical—a lingering infection can lead to tubal scarring and subsequent infertility.

Some physicians advise against the use of IUDs by young women who have never been pregnant because of the increased incidence of side effects in this group and the risk of infection with the possibility of subsequent infertility.

intrauterine device (IUD) A plastic device inserted into the uterus as a contraceptive.

TERMS

IUDs are not recommended for women of any age who are at high risk for STDs. They are also unsuitable for women with suspected pregnancy, large tumors of the uterus or other anatomical abnormalities, irregular or unexplained bleeding, or rheumatic heart disease. No evidence has been found linking IUD use to an increased risk of cancer. IUDs offer no protection against STDs.

Early IUD danger signals are abdominal pain, fever, chills, foul-smelling vaginal discharge, irregular menstrual periods, and other unusual vaginal bleeding. A change in string length should also be noted. An annual checkup is important and should include a Pap test and a blood check for anemia if menstrual flow has increased.

Effectiveness   The typical failure rate of IUDs during the first year of use is 0.6% for the ParaGard and 0.1% for Mirena. Effectiveness can be increased by periodically checking to see that the device is in place and by using a backup method for the first few months after IUD insertion. If pregnancy occurs, the IUD should be removed to safeguard the health of the woman and to maintain the pregnancy. The continuation rate of IUDs is about 80% after 1 year of use.

Male Condoms

The **male condom** is a thin sheath designed to cover the penis during sexual intercourse. Most brands available in the United States are made of latex, although condoms made of polyurethane are also now available. Condoms prevent sperm from entering the vagina and provide protection against disease. Condoms are the most widely used barrier method and the third most popular of all contraceptive methods used in the United States, after the pill and female sterilization.

Condom sales have increased dramatically in recent years, primarily because they are the only method that provides substantial protection against HIV infection as well as some protection against other STDs. At least one-third of all male condoms are bought by women. This figure will

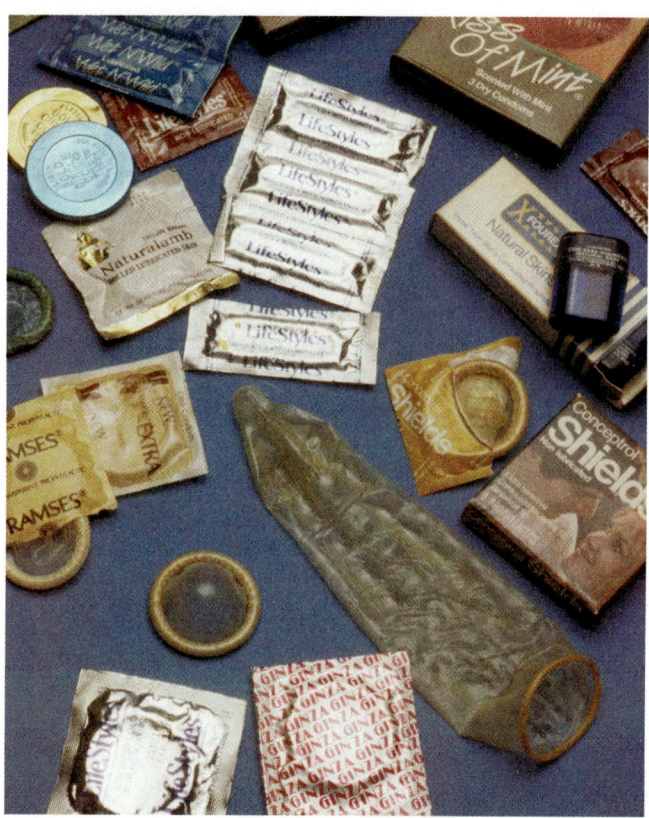

Condoms come in a variety of sizes, textures, and colors; some brands have a reservoir tip designed to collect semen. Used consistently and correctly, condoms provide the most reliable protection available against HIV infection for sexually active people.

probably increase as more women become aware of the serious risks associated with STDs and assume the right to insist on condom use.

The man or his partner must put the condom on the penis before it is inserted into the vagina, because the small amounts of fluid that may be secreted unnoticed prior to **ejaculation** often contain sperm capable of causing pregnancy. The rolled-up condom is placed over the head of the erect penis and unrolled down to the base of the penis, leaving a half-inch space (without air) at the tip to collect semen (Figure 6.2). Some brands of condoms have a reservoir tip designed for this purpose. Uncircumcised men must first pull back the foreskin of the penis. Partners must be careful not to damage the condom with fingernails, rings, or other rough objects.

Prelubricated condoms are available containing the **spermicide** nonoxynol-9, the same agent found in many of the contraceptive creams that women use. However, spermicidal condoms are no more effective than condoms without spermicide, even though they cost more. Furthermore, these condoms have been associated with urinary tract infections in women and, if they cause tissue irritation, an increased risk of HIV transmission.

If desired, users can lubricate their own condoms with contraceptive foam, creams, or jelly. If vaginal irritation

TERMS

male condom   A sheath, usually made of thin latex (synthetic rubber), that covers the penis during sexual intercourse; used for contraception and to prevent STDs.

ejaculation   An abrupt discharge of semen from the penis after sexual stimulation.

spermicide   A chemical agent that kills sperm.

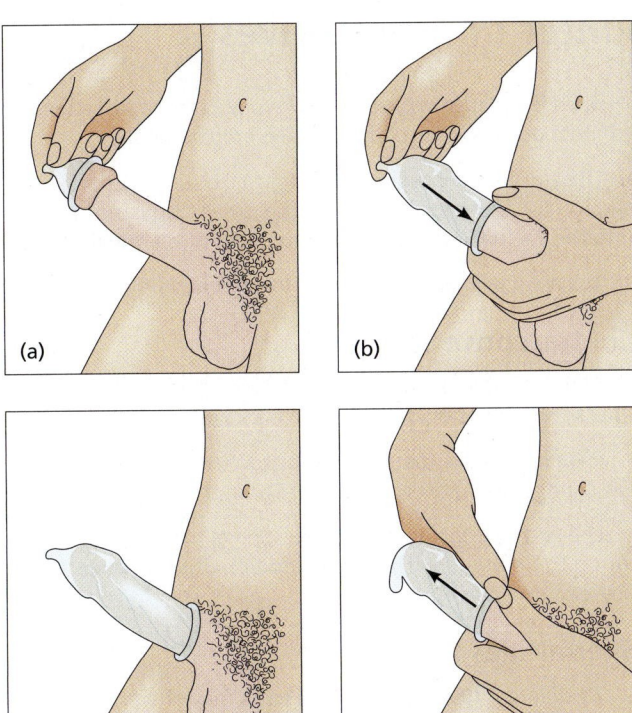

FIGURE 6.2 Use of the male condom. (a) Place the rolled-up condom over the head of the erect penis. Hold the top half-inch of the condom (with air squeezed out) to leave room for semen. (b) While holding the tip, unroll the condom onto the penis. Gently smooth out any air bubbles. (c) Unroll the condom down to the base of the penis. (d) To avoid spilling semen after ejaculation, hold the condom around the base of the penis as the penis is withdrawn. Remove the condom away from your partner, taking care not to spill any semen.

occurs with these products, water-based preparations such as K-Y Jelly can be used. Any products that contain mineral or vegetable oil—including baby oil, many lotions, regular petroleum jelly, cooking oils (corn oil, shortening, butter, and so on), and some vaginal lubricants and anti-fungal or anti-itch creams—should never be used with latex condoms. Such products can cause latex to begin to disintegrate within 60 seconds, thus greatly increasing the chance of condom breakage. (Polyurethane is not affected by oil-based products.)

When the man loses his erection after ejaculating, the condom loses its tight fit. To avoid spilling semen, the condom must be held around the base of the penis as the penis is withdrawn. If any semen is spilled on the vulva, sperm may find their way to the uterus.

Advantages Condoms are easy to purchase and are available without prescription or medical supervision (see the box "Buying and Using Over-the-Counter Contraceptives" on p. 166). In addition to being free of medical side effects (other than occasional allergic reactions), latex condoms help protect against STDs. A recent study determined that condoms may also protect women from human papilloma virus (HPV), which causes cervical cancer.

Condoms made of polyurethane are appropriate for people who are allergic to latex. However, they are more likely to slip or break than latex condoms, and therefore may give less protection against STDs and pregnancy. (Lambskin condoms permit the passage of HIV and other disease-causing organisms, so they can be used only for pregnancy prevention, not the prevention of STDs.) Except for abstinence, correct and consistent use of latex male condoms offers the most reliable available protection against the transmission of HIV.

Disadvantages The two most common complaints about condoms are that they diminish sensation and interfere with spontaneity. Although some people find these drawbacks serious, others consider them only minor disadvantages. Many couples learn to creatively integrate condom use into their sexual practices. Indeed, it can be a way to improve communication and share responsibility in a relationship.

Effectiveness In actual use, the failure rate of condoms varies considerably. First-year rates among typical users average about 17.4%. With perfect use, the first-year failure rate is about 2%. At least some pregnancies happen because the condom is carelessly removed after ejaculation. Some may also occur because of breakage or slippage, which may happen 1–2 times in every 100 instances of use for latex condoms and up to 10 times in every 100 instances for polyurethane condoms. Breakage is more common among inexperienced users. Other contributing factors include poorly fitting condoms, insufficient lubrication, excessively vigorous sex, and improper storage (because heat destroys rubber, latex condoms should not be stored for long periods in a wallet or a car's glove compartment). To help ensure quality, condoms should not be used past their expiration date or more than 5 years past their date of manufacture (2 years for those with spermicide).

If a condom breaks or is carelessly removed, the risk of pregnancy can be reduced somewhat by the immediate use of a vaginal spermicide. Some clinicians recommend keeping emergency contraceptive pills on hand. If the emergency contraceptive Plan B is taken within 1 hour of inadequately protected sex, the failure rate is only about 0.14%. The most common cause of pregnancy with condom users is "taking a chance"—that is, occasionally not using a condom at all—or waiting to use it until after preejaculate fluid (which may contain some sperm) has already entered the vagina.

Female Condoms

A female condom is a latex or polyurethane pouch that can be inserted into a woman's vagina. Although the female condom is preferred in certain situations because it requires less participation on the part of the male partner, its overall popularity remains far below that of the male condom.

Buying and Using Over-the-Counter Contraceptives

You can buy several types of contraceptives without a prescription. These have several advantages—they are readily accessible and relatively inexpensive, they are moderately effective at preventing pregnancy, and some offer some protection against HIV infection and other STDs. But like all methods, over-the-counter contraceptives work only if they are used correctly. The following guidelines can help you maximize the effectiveness of your method of choice.

Male Condoms

• *Buy latex condoms.* If you're allergic to latex, use a polyurethane condom or wear a lambskin condom under a latex one. Lambskin condoms provide no STD protection; polyurethane condoms are more likely to slip or break than latex. Spermicidal condoms provide no additional protection against pregnancy or STDs.

• *Buy and use condoms while they are fresh.* Packages have an expiration date or a manufacturing date. Don't use a condom after the expiration date or more than 5 years after the manufacturing date (2 years if it contains spermicide).

• *Try different styles and sizes.* Male condoms come in a variety of textures, colors, shapes, lubricants, and sizes. Shop around until you find a brand that's right for you. Condom widths and lengths vary by about 10–20%. A condom that is too tight may be uncomfortable and more likely to break; one that is too loose may slip off.

• *Use "thinner" condoms with caution.* Condoms advertised as "thinner" are often no thinner than others, and the thinnest ones tend to break more easily.

• *Don't remove the condom from an individual sealed wrapper until you're ready to use it.* Open the packet carefully. Don't use a condom if it's gummy, dried out, or discolored. Keep extra condoms on hand.

• *Store condoms correctly.* Don't leave condoms in extreme heat or cold, and don't carry them in a pocket wallet.

• *Use only water-based lubricants.* Never use oil-based lubricants like Vaseline or hand lotion, as they may cause a latex condom to break. Avoid oil-based vaginal products.

• *Use male condoms correctly* (see Figure 6.2). Use a new condom every time you have intercourse. Misuse is by far the leading reason that condoms fail.

• *Use emergency contraceptive pills if a condom slips or breaks.*

Female Condoms

• *Make sure your condom comes with the necessary supplies and information.* The FC female condom comes individually wrapped. With your condom, you should receive a leaflet containing instructions and a small bottle of additional lubricant.

• *Buy and use female condoms while they are fresh.* Check the expiration dates on the condom packet and the lubricant bottle.

• *Buy several condoms.* Buy one or more for practice before using one during sex. Have a backup in case you have a problem with insertion or use.

• *Read the leaflet instructions carefully.* Practice inserting the condom and checking that it's in the proper position.

• *Use the female condom correctly.* Make sure the penis is inserted into the pouch and that the outer ring is not pushed into the vagina. Add lubricant around the outer ring if needed.

• *Use emergency contraception pills if a condom slips or breaks.*

Contraceptive Sponges

• *Buy and use contraceptive sponges when they are fresh.* Check the expiration date on each package.

• *Read and follow the package instructions carefully.* Moisten the sponge with water and place high in the vagina.

• *Use each sponge only once.* The sponge may be left in place for up to 24 hours without the addition of spermicide for repeated intercourse.

Spermicides

• *Try different types of spermicides.* You may find one type easier or more convenient to use. Foams come in aerosol cans and are similar to shaving cream in consistency. Foams are thicker than creams, which are thicker than jellies. Foams, creams, and jellies usually require applicators; spermicidal suppositories and films do not.

• *Read and follow the package directions carefully.* Cans of foam must be shaken before use. Jellies and creams are often inserted with an applicator just outside the entrance to the cervix. Suppositories and film must be placed with a finger.

• *Pay close attention to the timing of use.* Follow the package instructions for inserting the spermicide at the appropriate time before intercourse actually occurs. Spermicides have a fairly narrow window of effectiveness. Be sure to also allow the recommended amount of time for suppositories and films to dissolve.

• *Use an additional full dose for each additional act of intercourse.*

• *Leave the spermicide in place for 8 hours after the last act of intercourse.*

• *Consider using spermicides with another form of birth control.* These include a condom, diaphragm, or cervical cap. Combined use provides greater protection against pregnancy.

Emergency Contraceptive Pills

Plan B pills are highly effective when taken soon after unprotected intercourse. If you are 18 or older, you can purchase Plan B over the counter. It is stocked behind the counter, so you will have to request it from the pharmacist and show proof of age. It is not available at convenience stores or other retail outlets where younger women might have access to it without a prescription. To maximize effectiveness, follow the instructions on the package carefully.

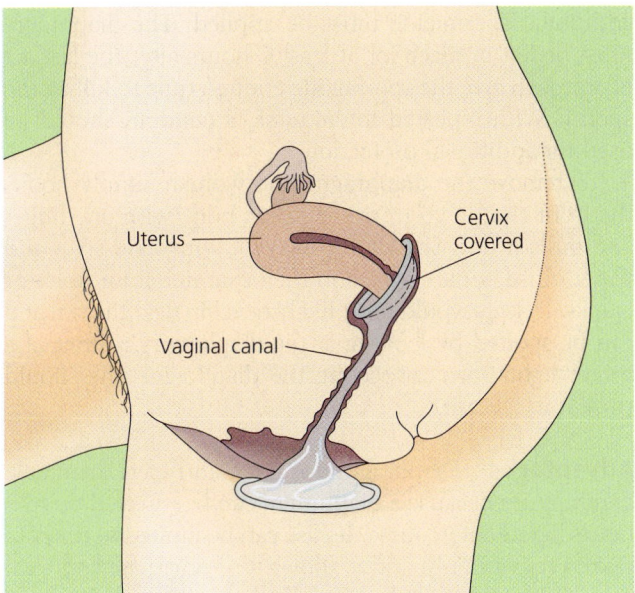

FIGURE 6.3 **The female condom properly positioned.**

The female condom currently available is a disposable device that comes in one size and consists of a soft, loose-fitting polyurethane sheath with two flexible rings (Figure 6.3). The ring at the closed end is inserted into the vagina and placed at the cervix much like a diaphragm. The ring at the open end remains outside the vagina. The walls of the condom protect the inside of the vagina.

The directions that accompany the condom should be followed closely. It can be inserted up to 8 hours before intercourse and should be used with the supplied lubricant or a spermicide to prevent penile irritation. As with male condoms, users need to take care not to tear the condom during insertion or removal. Following intercourse, the woman should remove the condom immediately, before standing up. By twisting and squeezing the outer ring, she can prevent the spilling of semen. A new condom should be used for each act of sexual intercourse. A female condom should not be used with a male condom because when the two are used together slippage is more likely to occur.

Advantages For many women, the greatest advantage of the female condom is the control it gives them over contraception and STD prevention. (Partner cooperation is still important, however.) Female condoms can be inserted before sexual activity and are thus less disruptive than male condoms. Because the outer part of the condom covers the area around the vaginal opening as well as the base of the penis during intercourse, it offers potentially better protection against genital warts or herpes. The polyurethane pouch can be used by people who are allergic to latex. And because polyurethane is thin and pliable, there is little loss of sensation.

When used correctly, the female condom should theoretically provide protection against HIV transmission and STDs comparable to that of the latex male condom. However, in research involving typical users, the female condom was less effective in preventing both pregnancy and STDs. With careful instruction and practice, effectiveness can be improved.

Disadvantages As with the traditional condom, interference with spontaneity is likely to be a common complaint. The outer ring, which hangs visibly outside the vagina, may be bothersome during foreplay; if so, couples may choose to put the device in just before intercourse. During coitus, both partners must take care that the penis is inserted into the pouch, not outside it, and that the device does not slip inside the vagina. Female condoms, like male condoms, are made for one-time use. A single female condom costs about four times as much as a single male condom.

Effectiveness The typical first-year failure rate of the female condom is 27%. For women who follow instructions carefully and consistently, the failure rate is considerably lower—about 5%. Although the female condom rarely breaks during use, slippage occurs in nearly one in ten users. The risk of being exposed to semen is higher if the relationship is new or short-term, if intercourse is very active, and if there is a large disparity between vagina and penis sizes. Having Plan B available as a backup contraceptive is recommended.

The Diaphragm with Spermicide

Before oral contraceptives were introduced, about 25% of all American couples who used any form of contraception relied on the **diaphragm.** Many diaphragm users switched to the pill or IUDs, but the diaphragm offers advantages that are important to some couples.

The diaphragm is a dome-shaped cup of thin rubber stretched over a collapsible metal ring. When correctly used with spermicidal cream or jelly, the diaphragm covers the cervix, blocking sperm from entering the uterus.

Diaphragms are available only by prescription. Because of individual anatomical differences among women, a diaphragm must be carefully fitted by a trained clinician to ensure both comfort and effectiveness. The fitting should be checked with each routine annual medical examination, as well as after childbirth, abortion, or a weight change of more than 10 pounds.

The woman spreads spermicidal jelly or cream on the diaphragm before inserting it and checking its placement (Figure 6.4 on p. 168). If more than 6 hours elapse between the time of insertion and the time of intercourse,

diaphragm A contraceptive device consisting of a flexible, dome-shaped cup that covers the cervix and prevents sperm from entering the uterus.

TERMS

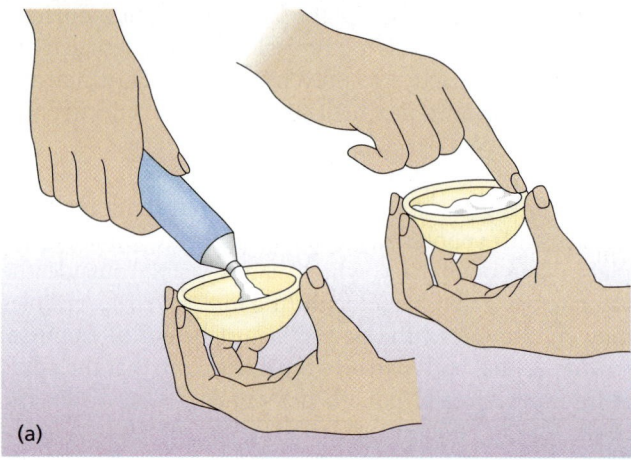

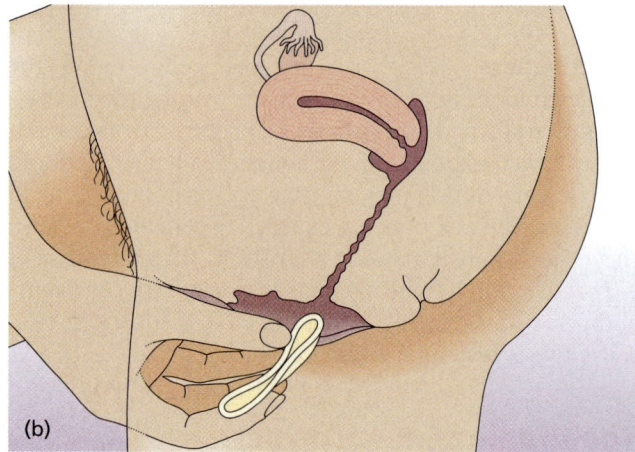

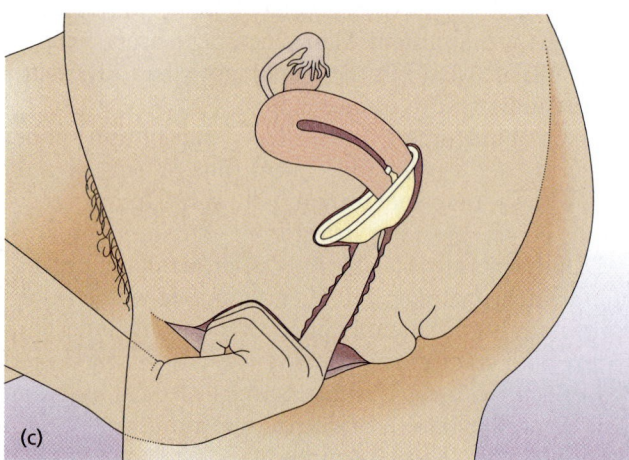

FIGURE 6.4 Use of the diaphragm. Wash your hands with soap and water before inserting the diaphragm. It can be inserted while squatting, lying down, or standing with one foot raised. (a) Place about a tablespoon of spermicidal jelly or cream in the concave side of the diaphragm, and spread it around the inside of the diaphragm and around the rim. (b) Squeeze the diaphragm into a long, narrow shape between the thumb and forefinger. Insert it into the vagina, and push it up along the back wall of the vagina as far as it will go. (c) Check its position to make sure the cervix is completely covered and that the front rim of the diaphragm is tucked behind the pubic bone.

additional spermicide must be applied. The diaphragm must be left in place for at least 6 hours after the last act of coitus to give the spermicide enough time to kill all the sperm. With repeated intercourse, a condom should be used for additional protection.

To remove the diaphragm, the woman simply hooks the front rim down from the pubic bone with one finger and pulls it out. She should wash it with mild soap and water, rinse it, pat it dry, and then examine it for holes or cracks. Defects would most likely develop near the rim and can be spotted by looking at the diaphragm in front of a bright light. After inspecting the diaphragm, she should store it in its case.

Advantages Diaphragm use is less intrusive than male condom use because a diaphragm can be inserted up to 6 hours before intercourse. Its use can be limited to times of sexual activity only, and it allows for immediate and total reversibility. The diaphragm is free of medical side effects (other than rare allergic reactions).

When used along with spermicidal jelly or cream, it offers significant protection against gonorrhea and possibly chlamydia, STDs that are transmitted only by semen and for which the cervix is the sole site of entry. Diaphragm use can also protect the cervix from semen infected with the human papillomavirus, which causes cervical cancer. However, the diaphragm is unlikely to protect against STDs that can be transmitted through vaginal or vulvar surfaces (in addition to the cervix), including HIV infection, genital herpes, and syphilis.

Disadvantages Diaphragms must always be used with a spermicide, so a woman must keep both of these somewhat bulky supplies with her whenever she anticipates sexual activity. Diaphragms require extra attention, since they must be cleaned and stored with care to preserve their effectiveness. Some women cannot wear a diaphragm because of their vaginal or uterine anatomy. In other women, diaphragm use can cause an increase in bladder infections and may need to be discontinued if repeated infections occur.

Diaphragms have also been associated with a slightly increased risk of **toxic shock syndrome (TSS),** an occasionally fatal bacterial infection. To reduce the risk of TSS, a woman should wash her hands carefully with soap and water before inserting or removing the diaphragm, should not use the diaphragm during menstruation or when abnormal vaginal discharge is present, and should never leave the device in place for more than 24 hours.

Effectiveness The diaphragm's effectiveness depends mainly on whether it is used properly. In actual practice, women rarely use it correctly every time they have intercourse. With perfect use, the failure rate is about 6%. Typical failure rates are 16% during the first year of use. The main causes of failure are incorrect insertion, inconsistent use, and inaccurate fitting. Sometimes, too, the

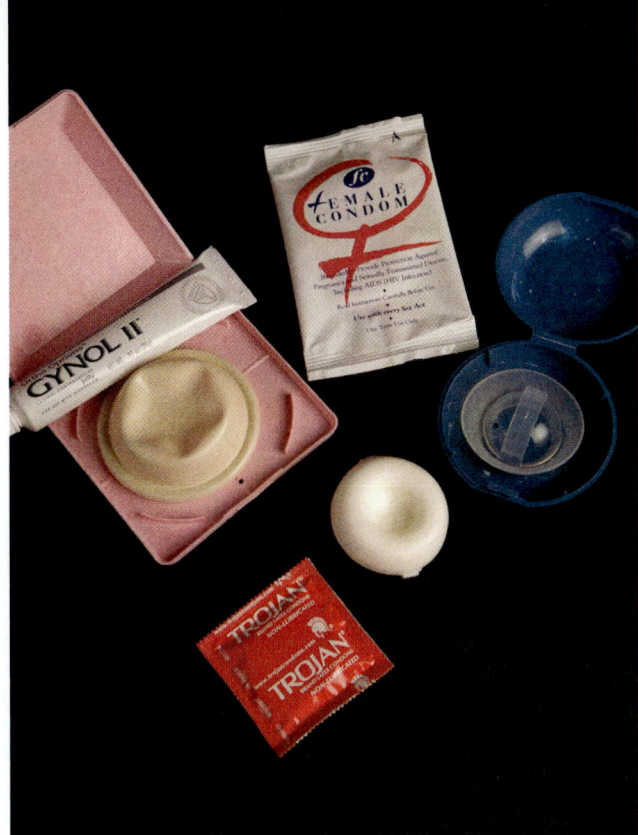

Many contraceptive methods work by blocking sperm from entering the cervix. Barrier methods pictured here are the diaphragm, the female condom, the male condom, the sponge, and the FemCap cervical cap.

vaginal walls expand during sexual stimulation, causing the diaphragm to be dislodged. If a diaphragm slips during intercourse, a woman may choose to use emergency contraception.

Lea's Shield

Lea's Shield is a one-size-fits-all diaphragm-like device, available by prescription. Made of silicone rubber, it can be used by women who are allergic to latex, and it is not damaged by petroleum-based products. The shield has a valve that allows the flow of air and fluids from the cervix as well as a loop that aids in insertion and removal. The device may be inserted at any time prior to intercourse, but should be left in place for 8 hours after last intercourse; it can be worn for up to 48 hours. Like the diaphragm, it must be used with spermicide. Studies completed thus far have reported advantages, disadvantages, and failure rates similar to those of the diaphragm.

FemCap

FemCap, another barrier device, is a small flexible cup that fits snugly over the cervix and is held in place by suction. This cervical cap is a clear silicone cup with a brim around the dome to hold spermicide and trap sperm and a removal strap over the dome. It comes in three sizes and must be fitted by a trained clinician. It is used like a diaphragm, with a small amount of spermicide placed in the cup and on the brim before insertion.

Advantages Advantages of the cervical cap are similar to those associated with diaphragm use and include partial STD protection. It is an alternative for women who cannot use a diaphragm because of anatomical reasons or recurrent urinary tract infections. Because the cap fits tightly, it does not require backup condom use with repeated intercourse. It may be left in place for up to 48 hours.

Disadvantages Along with most of the disadvantages associated with the diaphragm, difficulty with insertion and removal is more common for cervical cap users. Because there may be a slightly increased risk of TSS with prolonged use, the cap should not be left in place for more than 48 hours.

Effectiveness Studies indicate that the average failure rate for the cervical cap is 16% for women who have never had a child and 32% for women who have had a child. Failure rates drop significantly with perfect use.

The Contraceptive Sponge

The **sponge** is a round, absorbent device about 2 inches in diameter with a polyester loop on one side (for removal) and a concave dimple on the other side, which helps it fit snugly over the cervix. The sponge is made of polyurethane and is presaturated with the same spermicide that is used in contraceptive creams and foams. The spermicide is activated when moistened with a small amount of water just before insertion. The sponge, which can be used only

toxic shock syndrome (TSS) A bacterial disease usually associated with tampon use; can also occur in men; symptoms include weakness, cold and clammy hands, fever, nausea, and headache. TSS can progress to life-threatening complications, including very low blood pressure (shock) and kidney and liver failure.

FemCap A small flexible cup that fits over the cervix, to be used with spermicide.

sponge A contraceptive device about 2 inches in diameter that fits over the cervix and acts as a barrier, spermicide, and seminal fluid absorbent.

once, acts as a barrier, as a spermicide, and as a seminal fluid absorbent.

Advantages   The sponge offers advantages similar to those of the diaphragm and cervical cap, including partial protection against some STDs. In addition, sponges can be obtained without a prescription or professional fitting, and they may be safely left in place for 24 hours without the addition of spermicide for repeated intercourse.

Disadvantages   Reported disadvantages include difficulty with removal and an unpleasant odor if the sponge is left in place for more than 18 hours. Allergic reactions, such as irritation of the vagina, are more common with the sponge than with other spermicide products, probably because the overall dose contained in each sponge is significantly higher than that used with other methods. (A sponge contains 1 gram of spermicide compared with the 60–100 mg present in one application of other spermicidal products.) If irritation of the vaginal lining occurs, the risk of yeast infections and STDs (including HIV) may increase.

Because the sponge has also been associated with toxic shock syndrome, the same precautions must be taken as described for diaphragm use. A sponge user should be especially alert for symptoms of TSS when the sponge has been difficult to remove or was not removed intact.

Effectiveness   The typical effectiveness of the sponge is the same as the diaphragm (16% failure rate during the first year of use) for women who have never experienced childbirth. For women who have had a child, however, sponges are significantly less effective than diaphragms. One possible explanation is that the sponge's size may be insufficient to adequately cover the cervix after childbirth. To ensure effectiveness, the user should carefully check the expiration date on each sponge, as shelf life is limited.

Vaginal Spermicides

Spermicidal compounds developed for use with a diaphragm have been adapted for use without a diaphragm by combining them with a bulky base. Foams, creams, jellies, suppositories, and films are all available. Foam is sold in an aerosol bottle or a metal container with an ap-

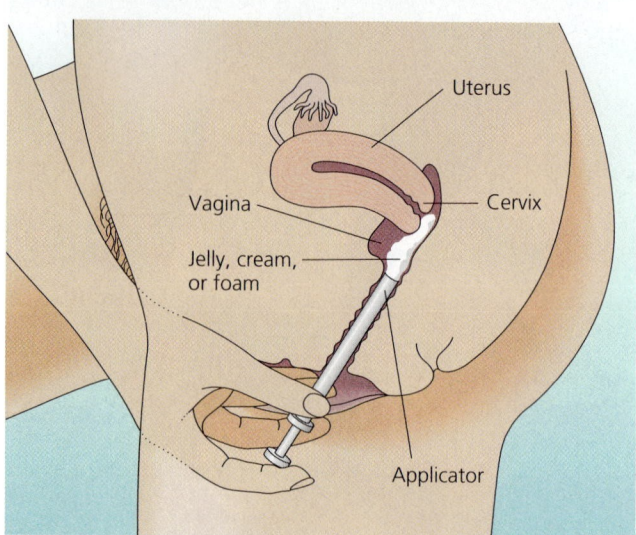

FIGURE 6.5   The application of vaginal spermicide.

plicator that fits on the nozzle. Creams and jellies are sold in tubes with an applicator that can be screwed onto the opening of the tube (Figure 6.5).

Foams, creams, and jellies must be placed deep in the vagina near the cervical entrance and must be inserted no more than 60 minutes before intercourse. After an hour, their effectiveness is drastically reduced, and a new dose must be inserted. Another application is also required before each repeated act of coitus. If the woman wants to **douche,** she should wait for at least 6 hours after the last intercourse to make sure that there has been time for the spermicide to kill all the sperm; douching is not recommended, however, because it can irritate vaginal tissue and increase the risk of various infections.

The spermicidal suppository is small and easily inserted like a tampon. Because body heat is needed to dissolve and activate the suppository, it is important to wait at least 15 minutes after insertion before having intercourse. The suppository's spermicidal effects are limited in time, and coitus should take place within 1 hour of insertion. A new suppository is required for every act of intercourse.

The Vaginal Contraceptive Film (VCF) is a paper-thin 2-inch square of film that contains spermicide. It is folded over one or two fingers and placed high in the vagina, as close to the cervix as possible. In about 15 minutes the film dissolves into a spermicidal gel that is effective for up to 1 hour. A new film must be inserted for each act of intercourse.

Advantages   The use of vaginal spermicides is relatively simple and can be limited to times of sexual activity. They are readily available in most drugstores and do not require a prescription or a pelvic examination. Spermicides allow for complete and immediate reversibility, and the only medical side effects are occasional allergic reactions. Vaginal spermicides may provide limited protection against some STDs but should never be used instead of condoms for reliable protection.

Disadvantages   When used alone, vaginal spermicides must be inserted shortly before intercourse, so their use may be seen as an annoying disruption. Some women find the slight increase in vaginal fluids after spermicide use unpleasant. Spermicides can alter the balance of bacteria in the vagina. Because this may increase the occurrence of yeast infections and urinary tract infections, women who are especially prone to these infections may want to avoid spermicides. Also, this method does not protect against gonorrhea, chlamydia, or HIV. Overuse of spermicides can irritate vaginal tissues; if this occurs, the risk of HIV transmission may increase.

Effectiveness   The effectiveness rates of vaginal spermicides vary widely, depending partly on how consistently and carefully instructions are followed. The typical failure rate is about 29% during the first year of use. Foam is probably the most effective form of spermicide, because its effervescent mass forms a denser and more evenly distributed barrier to the cervical opening. Creams and jellies provide only minimal protection unless used with a diaphragm or cervical cap.

Spermicide is generally recommended only in combination with other barrier methods or as a backup to other contraceptives. Plan B provides a better backup than spermicides, however.

Abstinence, Fertility Awareness, and Withdrawal

Millions of people throughout the world do not use any of the contraceptive methods described earlier, either because of religious conviction, cultural prohibitions, poverty, or lack of information and supplies. If they use any method at all, they are likely to use one of the following relatively "natural" methods of attempting to prevent conception.

Abstinence   The decision not to engage in sexual intercourse for a chosen period of time, or **abstinence,** has been practiced throughout history for a variety of reasons. Until relatively recently, many people abstained because they had no other contraceptive measures. Today, few American women rely on periodic abstinence as a contraceptive method. For those who do, other methods may simply seem unsuitable. Concern about possible side effects, STDs, and unwanted pregnancy may be factors. For others, the most important reason for choosing abstinence is a moral one, based on cultural or religious beliefs or strongly held personal values (see the box "Sexual Decision Making" in Chapter 5). Many people feel that sexual intercourse is appropriate only for married couples or for people in serious, committed relationships. Abstinence may also be considered the wisest choice in terms of one's emotional needs. A period of abstinence, for example, may be useful as a time to focus energies on other aspects of one's life.

Couples may choose abstinence to allow time for their relationship to grow. A period of abstinence allows partners to get to know each other better and to develop trust and respect for each other. Many couples who choose to abstain from sexual intercourse in the traditional sense turn to other mutually satisfying alternatives. These may include dancing, massage, hugging, kissing, petting, mutual masturbation, and oral-genital sex.

The Fertility Awareness Method   The basis for the **fertility awareness method (FAM)** is abstinence from coitus during the fertile phase of a woman's menstrual cycle. Ordinarily, only one egg is released by the ovaries each month, and it lives about 24 hours unless it is fertilized. Sperm deposited in the vagina may be capable of fertilizing an egg for up to 6–7 days, so conception can theoretically occur only during 8 days of any cycle. Predicting which 8 days is difficult. It is done by using either the calendar method or the temperature method. Information on cyclical changes of the cervical mucus can also help determine the time of ovulation.

The *calendar method* is based on the knowledge that the average woman releases an egg 14–16 days before her next period begins. Few women menstruate with complete regularity, so a record of the menstrual cycle must be kept for 12 months, during which time some other method of contraception must be used. The first day of each period is counted as day 1. To determine the first fertile, or "unsafe," day of the cycle, subtract 18 from the number of days in the shortest cycle (Figure 6.6 on p. 172). To determine the last unsafe day of the cycle, subtract 11 from the number of days in the longest cycle.

A variation of the calendar method known as the Standard Days Method (SDM) can be used by women with regular menstrual cycles between 26 and 32 days long. Couples must avoid unprotected intercourse on days 8 through 19 of the woman's cycle. Some women who use SDM use a string of color-coded beads to track their fertile days.

The *temperature method* is based on the knowledge that a woman's body temperature drops slightly just before ovulation and rises slightly after ovulation. A woman using the temperature method records her basal (resting) body temperature (BBT) every morning before getting out of bed and before eating or drinking anything. Once the temperature pattern is apparent (usually after about 3 months), the

> **4%** of women who practice some sort of contraception rely on withdrawal as their birth control method.
>
> —Guttmacher Institute, 2008
>
> QUICK STATS

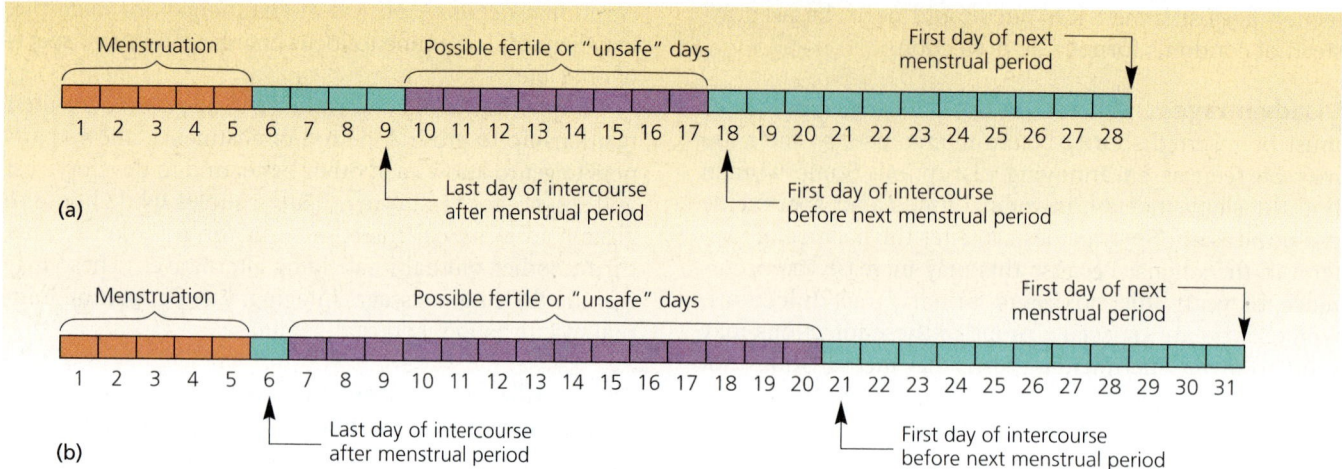

FIGURE 6.6 **The fertility awareness method of contraception.** This chart shows the safe and unsafe days for (a) a woman with a regular 28-day cycle and (b) a woman with an irregular cycle ranging from 25 to 31 days.

unsafe period for intercourse can be calculated as the interval from day 5 (day 1 is the first day of the period) until 3 days after the rise in BBT. To arrive at a shorter unsafe period, some women combine the calendar and temperature methods, calculating the first unsafe day from the shortest cycle of the calendar chart and the last unsafe day as the third day after a rise in BBT.

The *mucus method* (or Billings method) is based on changes in the cervical secretions throughout the menstrual cycle. During the estrogenic phase, cervical mucus increases and is clear and slippery. At the time of ovulation, some women can detect a slight change in the texture of the mucus and find that it is more likely to form an elastic thread when stretched between thumb and finger. After ovulation, these secretions become cloudy and sticky and decrease in quantity. Infertile, safe days are likely to occur during the relatively dry days just before and after menstruation. These additional clues have been found to be helpful by some couples who rely on the fertility awareness method. One problem that may interfere with this method is that vaginal infections or vaginal products or medication can also alter the cervical mucus.

FAM is not recommended for women who have very irregular cycles—about 15% of all menstruating women. Any woman for whom pregnancy would be a serious problem should not rely on FAM alone, because the fail-ure rate is high—approximately 25% during the first year of use. FAM offers no protection against STDs.

Withdrawal   In **withdrawal,** or *coitus interruptus,* the male removes his penis from the vagina just before he ejaculates. Withdrawal has a relatively high failure rate because the male has to overcome a powerful biological urge. In addition, because preejaculatory fluid may contain viable sperm, pregnancy can occur even if the man withdraws prior to ejaculation. Sexual pleasure is often affected because the man must remain in control and the sexual experience of both partners is interrupted.

The failure rate for typical use is about 18% in the first year. Men who are less experienced with sexual intercourse and withdrawal or who have difficulty in foretelling when ejaculation will occur have higher failure rates. Withdrawal does not protect against STDs.

Combining Methods

Couples can choose to combine the preceding methods in a variety of ways, both to add STD protection and/or to increase contraceptive effectiveness. For example, condoms are strongly recommended along with OCs whenever there is a risk of STDs (Table 6.3). Foam may be added to condom use to increase protection against both STDs and pregnancy. For many couples, and especially for women, the added benefits far outweigh the extra effort and expense.

Table 6.4 summarizes the effectiveness of available contraceptive methods.

PERMANENT CONTRACEPTION: STERILIZATION

Sterilization is permanent, and it is highly effective at preventing pregnancy. For these reasons, it is becoming

Table 6.3 — Contraceptive Methods and STD Protection

Method	Level of Protection
Hormonal methods	Do not protect against HIV or STDs in lower reproductive tract; increase risk of cervical chlamydia; provide some protection against PID.
IUD	Does not protect against STDs; associated with PID in first month after insertion.
Latex or polyurethane male condom	Best method for protection against STDs (if used correctly); does not protect against infections from lesions that are not covered by the condom. (Lambskin condoms do not protect against STDs.)
Female condom	Theoretically should reduce the risk of STDs, but research results are not yet available.
Diaphragm, sponge, or cervical cap	Protects against cervical infections and PID. Diaphragms, sponges, and cervical caps should not be relied on for protection against HIV.
Spermicide	Modestly reduces the risk of some vaginal and cervical STDs; does not reduce the risk of HIV, chlamydia, or gonorrhea. If vaginal irritation occurs, infection risk may increase.
FAM	Does not protect against STDs.
Sterilization	Does not protect against STDs.
Abstinence	Complete protection against STDs (as long as all activities that involve the exchange of body fluids are avoided).

QUESTIONS FOR CRITICAL THINKING AND REFLECTION

If you are sexually active, do you use any of the reversible methods described in the preceding sections? Based on the information given here, do you believe you are using your contraceptive perfectly, or in a way that increases your risk of an unintended pregnancy?

Table 6.4 — Contraceptive Effectiveness

Method	First-Year Failure Rates Typical Use	Perfect Use
Pill	8.7%	0.3%
Patch	8.0%	0.3%
Ring	8.0%	0.3%
Implant	1.0%	0.05%
Injectable (3-month)	6.7%	0.3%
ParaGard IUD	1.0%	0.6%
Mirena IUD	0.1%	0.1%
Male condom	17.4%	2.0%
Female condom	27.0%	5.0%
Diaphragm	16.0%	6.0%
Cervical cap		
Never had a child	16.0%	9.0%
Have had a child	32.0%	26.0%
Sponge		
Never had a child	16.0%	9.0%
Have had a child	32.0%	20.0%
Spermicides	29.0%	18.0%
Periodic abstinence	25.3%	
Withdrawal	18.4%	4.0%
Vasectomy	0.2%	0.1%
Tubal sterilization	0.7%	0.5%

SOURCE: Guttmacher Institute. 2008. *In Brief: Facts on Contraceptive Use.* New York: Guttmacher Institute.

an increasingly popular method of contraception. At present it is the most commonly used method both in the United States and in the world. It is especially popular among couples who have been married 10 or more years, and who have had all the children they intend to have. Sterilization does not protect against STDs.

An important consideration in choosing sterilization is that, in most cases, it cannot be reversed. Although the chances of restoring fertility are being increased by modern surgical techniques, such operations are costly, and pregnancy can never be guaranteed. Some couples choosing male sterilization store sperm to extend the option of childbearing.

Some studies indicate that male sterilization is preferable to female sterilization for a variety of reasons. The overall cost of a female procedure is about four times that of a male procedure, and women are much more likely than men to experience both minor and major complications following the operation. Furthermore, feelings of regret seem to be somewhat more prevalent in women than in men after sterilization. Men seeking sterilization are typically white, married, relatively affluent and well educated, and privately insured.

Although some physicians will perform surgery for sterilization on request, most require a thorough discussion with both partners before the operation. Most physicians also recommend that people who have religious conflicts, psychological problems related to sex, or unstable marriages not be sterilized. Young couples who might later change their minds are also frequently advised not to undergo sterilization.

Male Sterilization: Vasectomy

The procedure for male sterilization, **vasectomy,** involves severing the vasa deferentia, two tiny ducts that transport sperm from the testes to the seminal vesicles. The testes continue to produce sperm, but the sperm are absorbed into the body. Because the testes contribute only about 10% of the total seminal fluid, the actual quantity of ejaculate is only slightly reduced. Hormone production from the testes continues with very little change, and secondary sex characteristics are not altered.

Vasectomy is ordinarily performed in a physician's office and takes about 30 minutes. A local anesthetic is injected into the skin of the scrotum near the vasa. Small incisions are made at the upper end of the scrotum where it joins the body, and the vas deferens on each side is exposed, severed, and tied off or sealed by electrocautery. Some doctors seal each of the vasa with a plastic clamp, which is the size of a grain of rice. The incisions are then closed with sutures, and a small dressing is applied (Figure 6.7). Pain and swelling are usually slight and can be relieved with ice compresses, aspirin, and the use of a scrotal support. Bleeding and infection occasionally develop but are usually easily treated. Fewer complications occur with an alternative procedure involving a midline puncture rather than incisions; many physicians in the United States now perform this "no-scalpel" vasectomy. After either procedure, most men are ready to return to work in 2 days.

Men can have sex again as soon as they feel no further discomfort, usually after about a week. Another method of contraception must be used for at least 3 months after vasectomy, however, because sperm produced before the operation may still be present in the semen. Microscopic examination of a semen sample can confirm that sperm are no longer present in the ejaculate.

Vasectomy is highly effective. In a small number of cases, a severed vas rejoins itself, so some physicians advise yearly examination of a semen sample. The overall failure rate for vasectomy is 0.2%. No strong links have been found between vasectomy and chronic diseases, and the bulk of the evidence now indicates that men with vasectomies are not at increased risk for heart disease, prostate cancer, or testicular cancer.

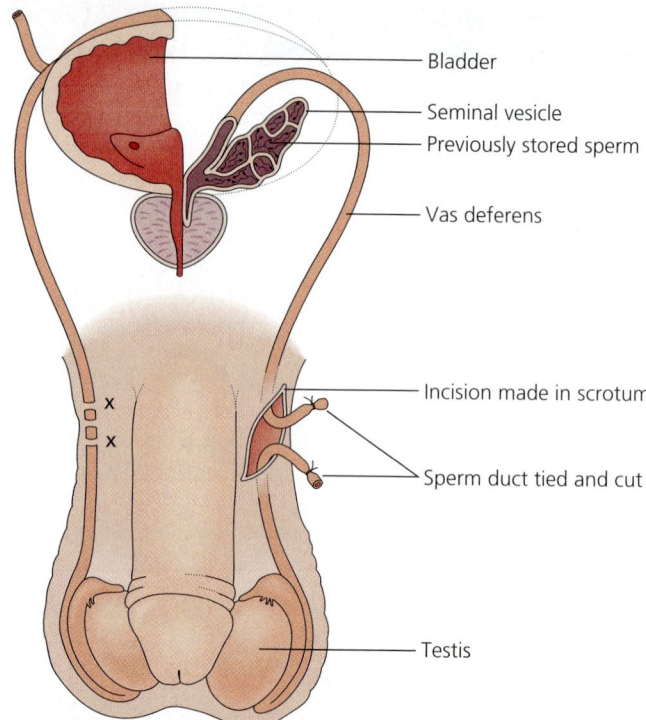

FIGURE 6.7 Vasectomy. This surgical procedure involves severing the vasa deferentia, thereby preventing sperm from being transported and ejaculated.

Labels: Bladder · Seminal vesicle · Previously stored sperm · Vas deferens · Incision made in scrotum · Sperm duct tied and cut · Testis

About one-half of vasectomy reversals are successful. In at least half of all men who have had vasectomies, the process of absorbing sperm (instead of ejaculating it) results in antisperm antibodies that may interfere with later fertility. The length of time between the vasectomy and the reversal surgery may also be an important predictor of reversal success.

Female Sterilization

The most common method of female sterilization involves severing or blocking the oviducts, thereby preventing eggs from reaching the uterus and sperm from entering the fallopian tubes. Ovulation and menstruation continue, but the unfertilized eggs are released into the abdominal cavity and absorbed. Although progesterone levels in the blood may decline slightly, hormone production by the ovaries and secondary sex characteristics are generally not affected.

Tubal sterilization (also called *tubal ligation*) is most commonly performed by a method called **laparoscopy**. A laparoscope, a tube containing a small light, is inserted through a small abdominal incision, and the surgeon looks through it to locate the fallopian tubes. Instruments are passed either through the laparoscope or through a second small incision, and the two fallopian tubes are sealed off with ties or staples or by electrocautery (Figure 6.8). General anesthesia is usually used. The operation

TERMS

tubal sterilization   Severing or blocking the oviducts to prevent eggs from reaching the uterus; also called *tubal ligation*.

laparoscopy   Examining the internal organs by inserting a tube containing a small light through an abdominal incision.

hysterectomy   Total or partial surgical removal of the uterus.

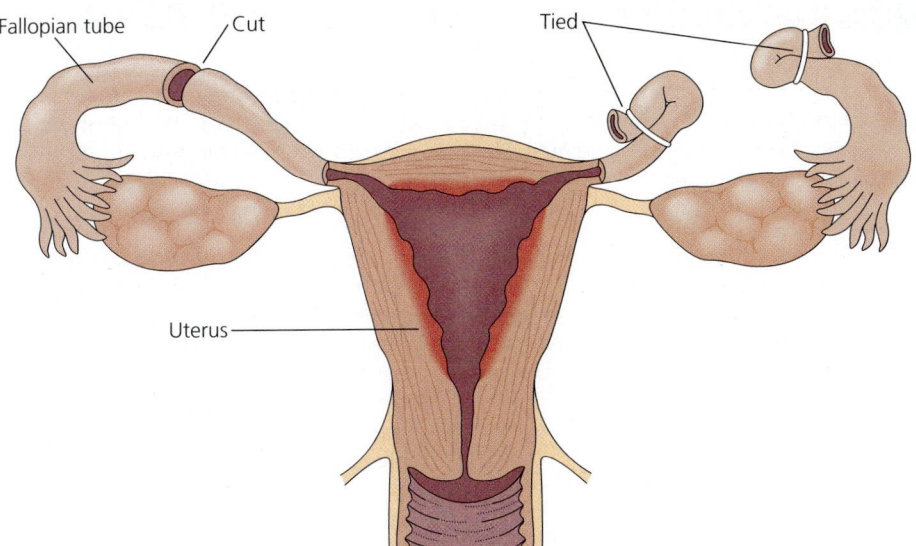

Fallopian tube — Cut — Tied

Uterus —

FIGURE 6.8 Tubal sterilization. This procedure involves severing or blocking the fallopian tubes, thereby preventing eggs from traveling from the ovaries to the uterus. It is a more complex procedure than vasectomy.

takes about 15 minutes, and women can usually leave the hospital 2–4 hours after surgery. Tubal sterilization can also be performed shortly after a vaginal delivery, or in the case of cesarean section immediately after the uterine incision is repaired.

Although tubal sterilization is somewhat riskier than vasectomy, with a rate of minor complications of about 6–11%, it is the more common procedure (see the box "Contraceptive Use Among American Women" on p. 176). Potential problems include bowel injury, wound infection, and bleeding. Serious complications are rare, and the death rate is low.

The failure rate for tubal sterilization is about 0.7%. When pregnancies occur, an increased percentage of them are ectopic. Because reversibility rates are low and the procedure is costly, female sterilization should be considered permanent.

A new female sterilization device called the Essure System consists of tiny springlike metallic implants that are inserted through the vagina and into the fallopian tubes, using a special catheter. Within several months, scar tissue forms over the implants, blocking the tubes. A backup method may be used until a test shows that the tubes are occluded. Placement of the device doesn't require an incision or general anesthesia, and recovery time is quicker

than that following tubal sterilization. Only clinicians with specialized training and equipment can perform this procedure.

In late 2007, the Food and Drug Administration's Obstetrics and Gynecology Devices Panel recommended FDA approval of a new method for blocking a woman's fallopian tubes. The procedure—potentially to be marketed under the commercial name Adiana—involves using a catheter to create small lesions just inside the entrance to each fallopian tube. A small device, the size of a grain of rice, is then placed in each tube. As the lesions heal, healthy new tissue grows on and around the device, eventually blocking the fallopian tube. Based on the manufacturer's studies, the FDA advisory panel estimated that Adiana's 1-year failure rate was about 1.1%.

Hysterectomy, removal of the uterus, is the preferred method of sterilization for only a small number of women, usually those with preexisting menstrual problems. Because of the risks involved, hysterectomy is not recommended unless the woman has disease or damage of the uterus and future surgery appears inevitable.

ISSUES IN CONTRACEPTION

The subject of contraception is closely tied to several issues that receive a lot of attention in the United States, such as premarital sexual relations, gender differences, and sexuality education for teens.

When Is It OK to Begin Having Sexual Relations?

Answers to this question strongly affect a society's approach to contraception. Opinions on the appropriate age or time to begin having sex often determine one's views on sexuality education and contraception accessibility.

QUESTIONS FOR CRITICAL THINKING AND REFLECTION

What are your personal views on sterilization? Do you think it could be an option for you one day? Do you believe people should forego considering sterilization until they have reached a certain point in their life? If so, what is that point? When does sterilization become the best option, if ever?

About 62 million women in the United States are in their childbearing years (15–44) and thus face decisions about contraception. About 62% of these women use some form of contraception. Most of the remaining 38% are either sterile, pregnant or trying to become pregnant, or not sexually active.

Only 7% of American women are fertile, sexually active, not seeking pregnancy, *and* not using contraceptives; this small group accounts for almost half of the 3 million unintended pregnancies that occur each year. The unintended pregnancies that occur among contraceptive users are usually the result of inconsistent or incorrect use of methods. For example, one-third of barrier method users report not using their method every time they have intercourse.

Oral contraceptives and female sterilization are the two most popular methods among American women (see figure). However, choice of contraceptive method and consistency of use vary with age, marital status, and other factors:

• *Age:* Sterilization is much more common among older women, particularly those who are over 35 years of age and/or who have had children. Young women in their teens and twenties are more likely to use the pill or condoms. Older women, however, are more likely to use reversible methods consistently—they are less likely to miss pills and more likely to use barrier methods during every act of intercourse.

• *Marital status:* Women who are or were married have much higher rates of sterilization than women who have never been married. Those who have never been married have high rates of OC and condom usage.

• *Ethnicity:* Overall rates of contraceptive use and use of OCs are highest among white women. Female sterilization, implants, and injectables are more often used by African American women and Latinas, and IUD use is highest among Latinas. Condom use is highest among Asian American women and similar across other ethnic groups. Male sterilization is much more common among white men than among men of other ethnic groups.

• *Socioeconomic status and educational attainment:* Low socioeconomic status and low educational attainment are associated with high rates of female sterilization and low rates of pill and condom use. However, women who are poor or have low educational attainment and who use OCs have higher rates of consistent use than women who are wealthier or have more education. About 20% of women age 15–44 lack adequate health insurance, increasing the cost and difficulty of obtaining contraceptives.

Some trends in contraceptive use may also reflect the differing priorities and experiences of women and men. For example, female sterilization is more expensive and carries greater health risks than male sterilization—yet it is more than twice as common. (Worldwide, female sterilization is more than four times as common as male sterilization.) This pattern may reflect culturally defined gender roles and the fact that women are more directly affected by unintended pregnancy. In surveys, women rate pregnancy prevention as the single most important factor when choosing a contraceptive method; in contrast, men rate STD prevention as equally important.

SOURCES: Frost, L. J., et al. 2007. Factors associated with contraceptive use and nonuse, United States, 2004. *Perspectives on Sexual and Reproductive Health* 39(2): 90–99; Guttmacher Institute. 2008. *In Brief: Facts on Contraceptive Use.* New York: Guttmacher Institute; Ryan, S., et al. 2007. Knowledge, perceptions, and motivations for contraception: Influence on teens' contraceptive consistency. *Youth & Society* 39(2) 182–208.

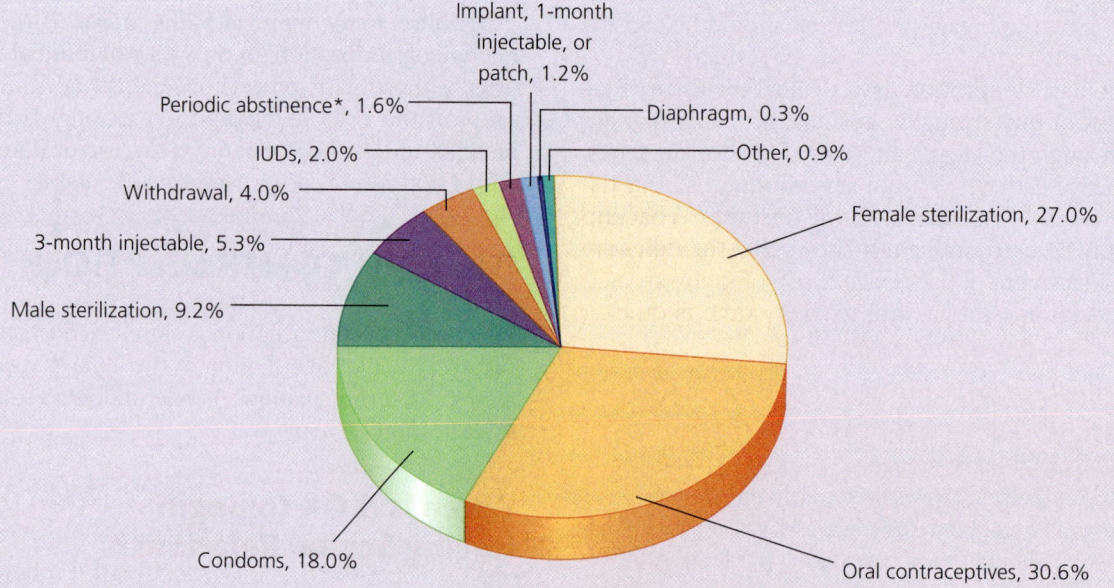

- Implant, 1-month injectable, or patch, 1.2%
- Periodic abstinence*, 1.6%
- IUDs, 2.0%
- Withdrawal, 4.0%
- 3-month injectable, 5.3%
- Male sterilization, 9.2%
- Condoms, 18.0%
- Diaphragm, 0.3%
- Other, 0.9%
- Female sterilization, 27.0%
- Oral contraceptives, 30.6%

Contraceptive use among American women age 15–44 years.

*Includes women using either the calendar method or natural family planning.

Talking with a Partner About Contraception

Many people have a difficult time talking about contraception with a potential sex partner. How should you bring it up? And whose responsibility is it, anyway? Talking about the subject may be embarrassing at first, but imagine the possible consequences of *not* talking about it. An unintended pregnancy or a sexually transmitted disease could profoundly affect you for the rest of your life. Talking about contraception is one way of showing that you care about yourself, your partner, and your future.

Before you talk with your partner, explore your own thoughts and feelings. Find out the facts about different methods of contraception, and decide which one you think would be most appropriate for you. If you're nervous about having this discussion with your partner, it may help to practice with a friend.

Pick a good time to bring up the subject. Don't wait until you've started to have sex. A time when you're both feeling comfortable and relaxed will improve your chances of having a good discussion. Tell your partner what you know about contraception and how you feel about using it, and talk about what steps you both need to take to get and use a method you can live with. Listen to what your partner has to say, and try to understand his or her point of view. You may need to have more than one discussion, and it may take some time for both of you to feel comfortable with the subject. *But don't have sex until this issue is resolved.*

If you want your partner to be involved but he or she isn't interested in talking about contraception, or if he or she leaves all the responsibility for it up to you, consider whether this is really a person you want to be sexually involved with. If you decide to go ahead with the involvement, you may want to enlist the support of a friend, family member, or health care worker to help you make and implement decisions about contraception.

Americans have a wide range of opinions on this issue: only after marriage; when 18 years or older; when in a loving, stable relationship; when the partners have completed their education and/or could support a child; whenever both partners feel ready and are using protection against pregnancy and STDs.

Opinions about appropriate sexual behavior shift from one decade to another. Although attitudes became more liberal during the 1960s and 1970s, people started having more restrictive views in the 1980s and 1990s. Today, the most common reasons for disapproving of sex are the risk of exposure to STDs, the risk of pregnancy, and moral or religious beliefs. According to recent data, most of today's young Americans are somewhat permissive regarding premarital sex. Although many approve of sexual relations for couples who are seriously dating or engaged to be married, they are less accepting of sexual intercourse on a first date or at the casual dating stage.

As more women consider careers for themselves and therefore often delay childbearing and even marriage, the likelihood of sexual activity and the critical need for pregnancy and STD prevention only increase. As a result, making decisions about sexual activity and contraception becomes even more important to those starting college or a career. Unfortunately, however, many individuals in this age group—even those who protect their health in all other areas of their life—end up taking high risks in their sexual behavior. Ambivalence and a lack of communication about who will "take charge" are common. (For guidelines on improving your own communication, see the box "Talking with a Partner About Contraception.") Alcohol and drug use are also strongly linked to risky sexual behavior.

THINKING ABOUT THE ENVIRONMENT

Overpopulation is a key contributor to the global environmental crisis, and is due in some part to the lack of contraception and family planning services in many parts of the world. In many central African nations, for example, less than 20% of the population use any type of contraception. The shortage of contraceptive services is a particular problem in undeveloped countries, where more than 30% of pregnancies are unplanned. In these regions, resources such as food, clean water, and fuel are already in short supply and serious environmental degradation has already occurred.

As populations grow—driven in large part by unplanned pregnancies—competition increases for scarce resources. In response to the problem of overpopulation, international organizations such as the World Health Organization and the United Nations are making efforts to increase global awareness of contraception and to make contraceptive methods more readily available.

For more information on the environment and environmental health, see Chapter 19.

Contraception and Gender Differences

The consequences of not using contraception are markedly different for men and women. In past years, women have accepted the primary responsibility of contraception, along with related side effects and health risks, partly because of the wider spectrum of methods available to them and partly because women have greater personal investment in preventing pregnancy and childbearing. Men still have very few contraceptive options, with condoms being the only reversible method currently available. Recently,

Men's Involvement in Contraception

What can be done to increase men's involvement in contraception? Health care professionals are taking the following approaches:

• Develop programs and campaigns that stress the importance of information, counseling, and medical care relating to sexual and reproductive matters from adolescence on. Men are less likely than women to seek regular checkups, but regular care for men would benefit men in their own right and both men and women as individuals, couples, and families.

• Recruit and train male health workers, who can be important advocates and role models for healthful behaviors. Expand educational material and clinical programs that focus on male contraception and reproductive health.

• Focus on men as obstacles to women's contraceptive use and as an untapped group of potential users. Educate men about the ways in which stereotypical views of male or female sexuality can inhibit good reproductive health for both men and women. Stress the importance of shared responsibility.

• Develop educational and clinical programs specifically targeted at young men. Men in their early twenties are most likely to engage in risky sexual behaviors and to have adverse reproductive health outcomes. Surveys indicate that most men use a condom the first time they have intercourse, but condom use subsequently declines—and there is much greater reliance on female contraceptive methods.

What can individuals do? Men can increase their participation in contraception in the following ways:

• Initiate and support communication regarding contraception and STD protection.

• Buy and use condoms whenever appropriate.

• Help pay contraceptive costs.

• Be available for shared responsibility in the resolution of an unintended pregnancy, should one occur.

however, men's participation has become critical, since condom use is central to safer sex even when OCs or other methods are being used by women.

Although dependent primarily on the cooperation of the man, condom use and the prevention of STDs have potentially greater consequences for the woman. Whereas men may suffer only local and short-term effects from the most common diseases (not including HIV infection), women face an increased risk of serious long-term effects, such as cervical cancer and/or pelvic infection with associated infertility, from these same prevalent STDs. In addition, women are more likely than men to contract HIV from an infected partner. In other words, although dependent on the male, condom use is clearly a more important issue for women. The female condom may offer a helpful alternative, but the cooperation of the male partner is still needed to ensure correct use.

Worldwide, condom use is increasing, but it remains low in developing countries, where it is often difficult for women to negotiate safer sex and condom use. The World Health Organization reports that the main factor in poor sexual health around the world is gender inequality.

The experience of an unintended pregnancy is also very different for men and women. Although men do suffer emotional stress from such an unexpected occurrence (and sometimes share financial and/or custodial responsibilities), women are much more intimately affected, obviously by the biological process of pregnancy itself as well as the outcome: abortion, adoption, or parenting. In addition, our societal attitudes are more severely punitive toward the woman and place much greater responsibility and blame on her when an unintended pregnancy occurs. Fortunately, there is growing interest in the roles and responsibilities of men in family planning (see the box "Men's Involvement in Contraception").

Sexuality and Contraception Education for Teenagers

Sexuality education and pregnancy prevention programs for teenagers are an important, though controversial, issue. Opinion in the United States is sharply divided on this subject. Certain groups are concerned that more sexuality education and especially the availability of contraceptives will lead to more sexual activity and promiscuity. They maintain that greater access to improved contraception was a key factor contributing to the sexual revolution in the 1960s and that the ensuing liberal sexual attitudes have been generally more destructive than helpful. They point to an increase in divorce, a rise in STDs, and a general relaxing of standards of morality as related negative effects.

Many in this group urge that sexuality education be handled in the home, where parents can instill moral values, including premarital abstinence. According to some in this group, young people should primarily be taught to "just say no." They see most public education about contraception, especially facilities that make supplies available, as only increasing the problem.

Other groups argue that encouraging the public availability of contraceptive information and supplies does not necessarily result in an increase in promiscuous sexual behavior, pointing to the fact that many young teenagers are already pregnant when they first visit a health care facility. These groups assert that parents are not effectively dealing with the issues and that a broader, coordinated approach involving public institutions, including schools, is needed, along with parental input. Many current programs focus on postponing sexual involvement but also emphasize contraceptive use for individuals who are sexually active. Increased availability of contraceptive information and methods is considered a necessary and realistic part of this approach.

The urgency of this debate has only increased with recent statistics. After falling steadily for more than a decade, the birth rate for American teenagers jumped in 2006, and remains significantly higher than rates in other developed countries. The teen pregnancy rate in the United States is nearly twice that in Canada and Great Britain, for example, and approximately 4 times that in France, 5 times that in Germany, and 9 times that in the Netherlands. The teen abortion rate in the United States is nearly 8 times higher than in Germany, 7 times higher than in the Netherlands, and 3 times higher than in France. The rate of gonorrhea among U.S. teens is more than 50 times higher than the rate in the Netherlands or France; rates of HIV infection, syphilis, and chlamydia among teens are also much higher in the United States. Levels of sexual activity and age at first intercourse do not differ significantly in these countries, but sexually active U.S. teens are less likely to use any contraceptive method and particularly less likely to use one of the more effective hormonal methods.

Reports by the Guttmacher Institute and Advocates for Youth have noted some attitudes and programs in other developed countries that may help explain their lower teen pregnancy rates:

• Childbearing is strongly regarded as adult behavior, to be considered when young people have completed their education, are in stable relationships, and are financially independent from their parents. This attitude is weaker and varies across regions and groups in the United States.

How old should people be when they become sexually active? The answer depends on the personal values, beliefs, and experiences of the individuals involved.

• Young people who are sexually active are expected to protect themselves and their partners from pregnancy and STDs, and state or public schools typically provide comprehensive information about prevention. More than one-third of U.S. school districts currently provide abstinence-only sexuality education.

• In many European countries, governments support large, long-term public education campaigns promoting responsible sexual behavior. These campaigns are direct and humorous, focus on safety and pleasure, and utilize many outlets, including the Internet, television, films, radio, and billboards.

• Young people in other developed countries typically have easier access to contraceptives and reproductive health services than do young people in the United States. Contraceptives are typically free or are inexpensive through national health insurance. U.S. teens may encounter logistical, financial, or legal barriers to contraceptive access. Some states have or are considering parental notification laws that would apply to minors seeking prescription contraceptives at family planning clinics. Surveys indicate that such laws are likely to increase the number of teens using no contraception or less effective over-the-counter contraceptives.

Sexuality and contraceptive education remains a volatile issue. Studies show that sexually active students who

QUESTIONS FOR CRITICAL THINKING AND REFLECTION
Do you feel your sexual education up to this point in your life has been complete? Do you feel it has prepared you to have a healthy, safe, and responsible sexual life?

Which Contraceptive Method Is Right for You and Your Partner?

If you are sexually active, you need to use the contraceptive method that will work best for you. A number of factors may be involved in your decision. The following questions will help you sort out these factors and choose an appropriate method. Answer yes (Y) or no (N) for each statement as it applies to you and, if appropriate, your partner.

_____ 1. I like sexual spontaneity and don't want to be bothered with contraception at the time of sexual intercourse.

_____ 2. I need a contraceptive immediately.

_____ 3. It is very important that I do not become pregnant now.

_____ 4. I want a contraceptive method that will protect me and my partner against sexually transmitted diseases.

_____ 5. I prefer a contraceptive method that requires the cooperation and involvement of both partners.

_____ 6. I have sexual intercourse frequently.

_____ 7. I have sexual intercourse infrequently.

_____ 8. I am forgetful or have a variable daily routine.

_____ 9. I have more than one sex partner.

_____ 10. I have heavy periods with cramps.

_____ 11. I prefer a method that requires little or no action or bother on my part.

_____ 12. I am a nursing mother.*

_____ 13. I want the option of conceiving immediately after discontinuing contraception.

_____ 14. I want a contraceptive method with few or no side effects.

If you answered yes to the statements whose numbers are listed in the left-hand column below, the method in the right-hand column might be a good choice for you.

1, 3, 6, 10, 11, 12	Oral contraceptives
1, 3, 6, 8, 10, 11	Contraceptive patch, vaginal ring
1, 3, 6, 8, 10, 11, 12	Contraceptive injectables
1, 3, 6, 8, 11, 12, 13	IUD
2, 4, 5, 7, 8, 9, 12, 13, 14	Condoms (male and female)
2, 5, 7, 8, 12, 13, 14	Vaginal spermicides and sponge
5, 7, 12, 13, 14	Diaphragm and spermicide, cervical cap
5, 7, 13, 14	FAM and withdrawal

*Progestin-only hormonal contraceptives (the minipill and Depo-Provera injections) are safe for use by nursing mothers; contraceptives that include estrogen are not usually recommended.

---

receive comprehensive sexuality education are more likely to use contraceptives and that those who are not sexually active are not encouraged to initiate having sex. Abstinence-only school programs, on the other hand, do not appear to reduce the number of teens who are having sex. Although a great deal of focus has been placed on HIV and STDs prevention, the nearly 1 million U.S. teenage pregnancies that occur each year are a serious public health problem and warrant much greater national attention.

WHICH CONTRACEPTIVE METHOD IS RIGHT FOR YOU?

The process of choosing and using a contraceptive method can be complex and varies from one couple to another. Each person must consider many variables in deciding

which method is most acceptable and appropriate for her or him. Key considerations include those listed here:

1. *Health risks.* When considering any contraceptive method, determine whether it may pose a risk to your health. For example, IUDs are not recommended for young women without children because of an increased risk of pelvic infection and subsequent infertility. Hormonal methods should be used only after a clinical evaluation of your medical history. Other methods have only minor and local side effects. Talk with your physician about the potential health effects of different methods for you.

2. *The implications of an unplanned pregnancy.* Many teens and young adults fail to consider how their life would be affected by an unexpected pregnancy. When considering contraception (or deciding

whether to have sex in the first place), think about the potential consequences of your choices.

3. *STD risk.* STDs are another potential consequence of sex. In fact, several activities besides vaginal intercourse (such as oral sex) can put you at risk for an STD. Condom use is of critical importance whenever any risk of STDs is present. This is especially true when you are not in an exclusive, long-term relationship or if you are a woman taking the pill, because cervical changes that occur during hormone use may increase vulnerability to certain diseases. Abstinence or activities that don't involve intercourse or any other exchange of body fluids can be a satisfactory alternative for some people.

4. *Convenience and comfort level.* The hormonal methods are generally ranked high in this category, unless there are negative side effects and health risks or for-

getting to take pills is a problem for you. If this is the case for you, a vaginal ring may be a good alternative to the pill. Some people think condom use disrupts spontaneity and lowers penile sensitivity. (Creative approaches to condom use and improved quality can decrease these concerns.) The diaphragm, cervical cap, contraceptive sponge, female condom, and spermicides can be inserted before intercourse begins but are still considered a significant inconvenience by some.

5. *Type of relationship.* Barrier methods require more motivation and sense of responsibility from *each* partner than hormonal methods do. When the method depends on the cooperation of one's partner, assertiveness is necessary, no matter how difficult. This is especially true in new relationships, when condom use is most important. When sexual activity is infrequent, a barrier method may make more sense than an IUD or one of the hormonal methods.

6. *Ease and cost of obtaining and maintaining each method.* Investigate the costs of different methods. If you have insurance, find out if it covers any of the costs.

7. *Religious or philosophical beliefs.* For some, abstinence and/or FAM may be the only permissible contraceptive methods.

Whatever your needs, circumstances, or beliefs, *do* make a choice about contraception. Not choosing anything is the one method known *not* to work. (To help make a choice that's right for you, take the quiz in the box "Which Contraceptive Method Is Right for You and Your Partner?") This is an area in which taking charge of your health has immediate and profound implications for your future. The method you choose today won't necessarily be the one you'll want to use your whole life or even next year. But it should be one that works for you right now.

QUESTIONS FOR CRITICAL THINKING AND REFLECTION

What are the most important factors influencing your personal decisions about contraception? List these factors in order of their priority to you, and determine whether you have given each factor full consideration in choosing a contraceptive method.

TIPS FOR TODAY AND THE FUTURE

Your decisions about contraception are among the most important you will make in your life.

RIGHT NOW YOU CAN

- Visualize the kind of life you want to have in the future. Does your vision include a family? If so, how far in the future do you see this happening? If you're sexually active now, are you confident that you're doing everything possible to prevent an unwanted pregnancy?
- If you're sexually active, discuss your contraceptive method with your partner. Make sure you are using the method that works best for you.
- Work with your partner to choose a backup contraceptive method to use in case your primary method isn't effective enough.

IN THE FUTURE YOU CAN

- Talk to your physician about contraception and get his or her advice on choosing the best method.
- Occasionally discuss your contraceptive method with your partner to make sure it continues to meet your needs. A change in health status or lifestyle may make a different form of contraception preferable in the future.

- Barrier methods of contraception physically prevent sperm from reaching the egg; hormonal methods are designed to prevent ovulation, fertilization, and/or implantation; and surgical methods permanently block the movement of sperm or eggs to the site of conception.

- The choice of contraceptive method depends on effectiveness, convenience, cost, reversibility, side effects and risk factors, and protection against STDs. Measures of effectiveness include failure rate and continuation rate.

- Hormonal methods may include a combination of estrogen and progestins or progesterone alone. Hormones may be delivered via pills, patch, vaginal ring, implants, or injections.

- Hormonal methods prevent ovulation, inhibit the movement of sperm, and affect the uterine lining so that implantation is prevented.

- The most commonly used emergency contraceptives are two-dose regimens of OCs and Plan B, which is now available without a prescription to women 18 and older.

- How IUDs work is not clearly understood; they may cause biochemical changes in the uterus, affect movement of sperm and eggs, or interfere with the implantation of the egg in the uterus.

- Male condoms are simple to use, immediately reversible, and provide STD protection; female condoms are available but are more difficult to use.

- The diaphragm, Lea's Shield, cervical cap, and contraceptive sponge cover the cervix and block sperm from entering; all are used with or contain spermicide.

- Vaginal spermicides come in the form of foams, creams, jellies, suppositories, and film.

- So-called natural methods include abstinence, withdrawal, and fertility awareness method (FAM); the latter is based on avoiding intercourse during the fertile phase of a woman's menstrual cycle.

- Combining methods can increase contraceptive effectiveness and help protect against STDs.

- Vasectomy—male sterilization—involves severing the vasa deferentia. Female sterilization involves severing or blocking the oviducts so that the egg cannot reach the uterus.

- Key issues in contraception include decisions about when it is OK to have sex, gender differences in the significance of contraception, and sexuality education and contraception accessibility for teens.

- Issues to be considered in choosing a contraceptive include the individual health risks of each method, the implications of an unplanned pregnancy, STD risk, convenience and comfort level, type of relationship, the cost and ease of obtaining and maintaining each method, and religious or philosophical beliefs.

FOR MORE INFORMATION

Boston Women's Health Book Collective. 2005. *Our Bodies, Ourselves—A New Edition for a New Era.* New York: Simon & Schuster. *Broad coverage of many women's health concerns, with extensive coverage of contraception.*

Glasier, A., and B. Winikoff. 2005. *Fast Facts: Contraception,* 2nd ed. Oxford: Health Press. *Basic facts and figures related to contraceptive methods. Succinct and easy to read.*

Guillebaud, J. 2007. *Contraception Today,* 6th ed. London: Informa Healthcare. *A pocket guide popular with clinicians, but also useful to the layperson.*

Hatcher, R. A., et al. 2008. *Contraceptive Technology,* 19th ed. New York: Ardent Media. *A reliable source of up-to-date information on contraception.*

Zieman, M., et al. 2007. *A Pocket Guide to Managing Contraception, 2007–2009 ed.* Tiger, Ga.: Bridging the Gap Foundation. *An easy-to-use, reliable source of contraceptive information.*

ORGANIZATIONS, HOTLINES, AND WEB SITES

The Guttmacher Institute. A nonprofit institute for reproductive health research, policy analysis, and public education.
  http://www.agi-usa.org

Ann Rose's Ultimate Birth Control Links Page. A Web site with information on methods of birth control and decision-making strategies.
  http://www.ultimatebirthcontrol.com

Association of Reproductive Health Professionals. Offers educational materials about family planning, contraception, and other reproductive health issues; the Web site includes an interactive questionnaire to help people choose contraceptive methods.
  http://www.arhp.org

Emergency Contraception Hotline. Provides information and referrals.
  888-NOT-2-LATE

Emergency Contraception Web Site. Provides extensive information about emergency contraception; sponsored by the Office of Population Research at Princeton University.
  http://www.not-2-late.com

It's Your Sex Life. Provides information about sexuality, relationships, contraceptives, and STDs; geared toward teenagers and young adults.
  http://www.itsyoursexlife.com

Kaiser Family Foundation: Women's Health Policy: Contraception. Provides information and reports focused on how policies impact reproductive health care and access to contraceptives.
  http://www.kff.org/womenshealth/contraception.cfm

Managing Contraception. Provides brief descriptions and tips for using many forms of contraception.
  http://www.managingcontraception.com

Planned Parenthood Federation of America. Provides information on family planning, contraception, and abortion and provides counseling services.
  http://www.plannedparenthood.org

Reproductive Health Online (Reproline). Presents information on contraceptive methods currently available and those under study for future use.
  http://www.reproline.jhu.edu

The following are some of the many organizations focusing on family planning and reproductive health issues worldwide:

Family Health International
  http://www.fhi.org

Global Reproductive Health Forum at Harvard
  http://www.hsph.harvard.edu/Organizations/healthnet

International Planned Parenthood Federation
  http://www.ippf.org

Safe Motherhood
  http://www.safemotherhood.org

United Nations Population Fund
  http://www.unfpa.org

See also the listings for Chapters 5, 7, 8, and 18.

SELECTED BIBLIOGRAPHY

Advance provision of emergency contraception for pregnancy prevention (full review). 2007. *Cochrane Database of Systematic Reviews* (2): CD005497.

Afable-Munsuz, A., and C. D. Brindis. 2006. Acculturation and the sexual and reproductive health of Latino youth in the United States: A literature review. *Perspectives on Sexual and Reproductive Health* 38(4): 208–219.

Anawalt, B. D. 2007. Update on the development of male hormonal contraceptives. *Current Opinion in Investigational Drugs* 8(4): 318–323.

Beckman, L. J., et al. 2006. Women's acceptance of the diaphragm: The role of relationship factors. *Journal of Sex Research* 43(4): 297–306.

Beksinska, M. E., et al. 2007. Bone mineral density in adolescents using norethisterone enanthate, depot-medroxyprogesterone acetate or combined oral contraceptives for contraception. *Contraception* 75(6): 438–443.

Bethea, A. 2007. Birth control costs climb at colleges. *Charlotte* (N.C.) *Observer*, 15 October.

Boonstra, H. D. 2007. Under increased pressure, abstinence-only advocates intensify campaign to protect their funding. *Guttmacher Policy Review* 10(3): 20.

Brohet, R. M., et al. 2007. Oral contraceptives and breast cancer risk in the international BRCA 1/2 carrier cohort study: A report from EMBRACE, GENEPSO, GEO-HEBON, and the IBCCS Collaborating Group. *Journal of Clinical Oncology* 25(25): 3831–3836.

Burkman, R. T. 2007. Transdermal hormonal contraception: Benefits and risks. *American Journal of Obstetrics and Gynecology* 197(2): 134.e1–134.e6.

Chamley, L. W., and G. N. Clarke. 2007. Antisperm antibodies and conception. *Seminars in Immunopathology* 29(2): 169–184.

Coffee, A. L., et al. 2007. Long-term assessment of symptomatology and satisfaction of an extended oral contraceptive regimen. *Contraception* 75(6): 444–449.

Cook, L. A., et al. 2007. Scalpel versus no-scalpel incision for vasectomy. *Cochrane Database of Systematic Reviews,* 18 April (2): CD004112.

Cook, L. A., et al. 2007. Vasectomy occlusion techniques for male sterilization. *Cochrane Database of Systematic Reviews,* 18 April (2): CD003991.

Curtis, K. M., et al. 2007. Neoplasia with use of intrauterine devices. *Contraception* 75(6 Suppl. 1): S60–S69.

Frost, J. J., et al. 2007. Factors associated with contraceptive use and nonuse, United States, 2004. *Perspectives on Sexual and Reproductive Health* 39(2): 90–99.

Frye, C. A. 2006. An overview of oral contraceptives: Mechanism of action and clinical use. *Neurology* 66(6 Suppl. 3): S29–S36.

Gilliam, M., et al. 2007. Factors associated with willingness to use the contraceptive vaginal ring. *Contraception* 76(1): 30–34.

Gordon, L., et al. 2007. Clinical inquiries. What hormonal contraception is most effective for obese women? *Journal of Family Practice* 56(6): 471–473.

Grimes, D. A., et al. 2007. Steroid hormones for contraception in men. *Cochrane Database of Systematic Reviews,* 18 April (2): CD004316.

Hampton, T. 2007. Study examines effects of advance access to emergency contraception. *Journal of the American Medical Association* 297(19): 2067–2068.

Isley, M. M., and A. Edelman. 2007. Contraceptive implants: An overview and update. *Obstetrics and Gynecology Clinics of North America* 34(1): 73–90.

Jick, S., et al. 2007. Further results on the risk of nonfatal venous thromboembolism in users of the contraceptive transdermal patch compared to users of oral contraceptives containing norgestimate and 35 micrograms of ethinyl estradiol. *Contraception* 76(1): 4–7.

Kalmuss, D., and C. Tatum. 2007. Patterns of men's use of sexual and reproductive health services. *Perspectives on Sexual and Reproductive Health* 39(2): 74–81.

Lurie, G., et al. 2007. Association of estrogen and progestin potency of oral contraceptives with ovarian carcinoma risk. *Obstetrics and Gynecology* 109(3): 597–607.

Macaluso, M., et al. 2007. Efficacy of the male latex condom and of the female polyurethane condom as barriers to semen during intercourse: A randomized clinical trial. *American Journal of Epidemiology* 166(1): 88–96.

MacIsaac, L., and E. Espey. 2007. Intrauterine contraception: The pendulum swings back. *Obstetrics and Gynecology Clinics of North America* 34(1): 91–111.

Mann, J. R., and C. Stine. 2007. The roles of abstinence and contraception in declining pregnancy rates. *American Journal of Public Health* 97(6): 969–970.

Margolis, K. L., et al. 2007. A prospective study of oral contraceptive use and risk of myocardial infarction among Swedish women. *Fertility and Sterility* 88(2): 310–316.

Meirik, O., and T. M. Farley. 2007. Risk of cancer and the oral contraceptive pill. *British Medical Journal* 335(7621): 621–622.

Moreau, C., et al. 2007. Oral contraceptive tolerance: Does the type of pill matter? *Obstetrics and Gynecology* 109(6): 1277–1285.

Nettleman, M. D., et al. 2007. Reasons for unprotected intercourse: Analysis of the PRAMS survey. *Contraception* 75(5): 361–366.

Padian, N. S., et al. 2007. Diaphragm and lubricant gel for prevention of HIV acquisition in southern African women: A randomized controlled trial. *Lancet* 370(9583): 251–261.

Pei, K., et al. 2007. Weekly contraception with mifepristone. *Contraception* 75(1): 40–44.

Petersen, R., et al. 2007. Pregnancy and STD prevention counseling using an adaptation of motivational interviewing: A randomized controlled trial. *Perspectives on Sexual and Reproductive Health* 39(1): 21–28.

Prine, L. 2007. Emergency contraception, myths and facts. *Obstetrics and Gynecology Clinics of North American* 34(1): 127–136.

Rocca, C. H., et al. 2007. Beyond access: Acceptability, use and nonuse of emergency contraception among young women. *American Journal of Obstetrics and Gynecology* 196(1): 29.e1–29.e6.

Roumen, F. J. 2007. The contraceptive vaginal ring compared with the combined oral contraceptive pill: A comprehensive review of randomized controlled trials. *Contraception* 75(6): 420–429.

Sanderson, C. A., and D. J. Yopyk. 2007. Improving condom use intentions and behavior by changing perceived partner norms: An evaluation of condom promotion videos for college students. *Health Psychology* 26(4): 481–487.

Santelli, J. S., et al. 2007. Exploring recent declines in adolescent pregnancy in the United States: The contribution of abstinence and increased contraceptive use. *American Journal of Public Health* 97: 150–158.

Shtarkshall, R. A., et al. 2007. Sex education and sexual socialization: Roles for educators and parents. *Perspectives on Sexual and Reproductive Health* 39(2): 116–119.

Sonfield, A. 2007. Popularity disparity: Attitudes about the IUD in Europe and the United States. *Guttmacher Policy Review* 10(4): 19–24.

Swica, Y. 2007. The transdermal patch and the vaginal ring: Two novel methods of combined hormonal contraception. *Obstetrics and Gynecology Clinics of North America* 34(1): 31–42.

Westhoff, C., et al. 2007. Initiation of oral contraceptives using a quick start compared with a conventional start: A randomized controlled trial. *Obstetrics and Gynecology* 109(6): 1270–1276.

Westhoff, C. L., et al. 2007. Oral contraceptive discontinuation: Do side effects matter? *American Journal of Obstetrics and Gynecology* 196(4): 412.e1–412.e6; discussion 412.e6–412.e7.

Whittaker, P. G., et al. 2007. Characteristics associated with emergency contraception use by family planning patients: A prospective cohort study. *Perspectives on Sexual and Reproductive Health* 39(3): 158–166.

Witte, S. S., et al. 2006. Promoting female condom use to heterosexual couples: Findings from a randomized clinical trial. *Perspectives on Sexual and Reproductive Health* 38(3): 148–154.

Zurawin, R. K., and L. Ayensu-Coker. 2007. Innovations in contraception: A review. *Clinical Obstetrics and Gynecology* 50(2): 425–439.

ABORTION

LOOKING AHEAD>>>>>

AFTER READING THIS CHAPTER, YOU SHOULD BE ABLE TO:

- Describe the history and current legal status of abortion in the United States
- Explain the current debate over abortion, including the main points of the pro-choice and pro-life points of view
- Describe the methods of abortion available in the United States
- List possible physical and psychological effects of abortion

TEST YOUR KNOWLEDGE

1. **About what percentage of abortions in the United States take place in the first 12 weeks of pregnancy?**
   a. 60%
   b. 70%
   c. 80%
   d. 90%

2. **A majority of Americans are in favor of the right to a legal abortion in some circumstances.**
   True or false?

3. **The procedure known as "partial birth abortion" is one of the most commonly used methods of abortion.**
   True or false?

4. **At what point during pregnancy is a fetus generally considered to become viable, meaning it can survive outside the womb?**
   a. 12 weeks
   b. 24 weeks
   c. 48 weeks

5. **Since the U.S. Supreme Court made abortion legal in all 50 states in its 1973 *Roe v. Wade* decision, more than half the states have enacted their own laws regulating abortion.**
   True or false?

ANSWERS

1. **D.** Nearly 90% of all abortions take place in the first 12 weeks of pregnancy; more than 60% take place in the first 9 weeks.

2. **TRUE.** Current polls indicate that about 28% of Americans favor the right to legal abortion in all circumstances, and an additional 53% favor the right in some circumstances. About 17% of Americans think that abortion should be illegal in all circumstances.

3. **FALSE.** This method of abortion (correctly called *intact dilation and extraction*) is performed only rarely, representing 0.17% of all abortions in the United States.

4. **B.** Today, most clinicians define this point as 24 weeks of gestation. When the fetus is considered viable, a state may regulate and even bar all abortions except those considered necessary to preserve the mother's life or health.

5. **TRUE.** Currently, 36 states prohibit abortion after a certain point in pregnancy. However, these laws typically allow exceptions, such as when the mother's life or health is endangered, and they may not create an "undue burden" for women seeking an abortion.

Few issues are as complex and emotionally charged as abortion. In the United States, public attention has focused on the legal definition of abortion and the issue of restricting its practice. These far-reaching questions are important, but the most difficult aspects of abortion are personal—especially for women who must decide whether to have an abortion.

Because most women who undergo abortions are young, many college students have personal experience with unintended pregnancy and abortion. Therefore, college students are in a good position not just to debate the larger issues surrounding abortion, but also to address the complex human factors involved in preventing pregnancy and dealing with unintended pregnancy.

This chapter offers basic information on abortion and discusses some current areas of controversy.

THE ABORTION ISSUE

The word **abortion,** by strict definition, means the expulsion of an embryo or fetus from the uterus before it is sufficiently developed to survive outside the uterus. As commonly used, however, the term *abortion* refers only to those expulsions that are artificially induced by mechanical means or drugs. The term **miscarriage** is generally used when referring to a *spontaneous abortion*—one that occurs naturally with no causal intervention. In this chapter, *abortion* refers to a deliberately induced expulsion.

The History of Abortion in the United States

For more than two centuries, abortion policy in the United States followed English common law, which made the practice a crime only when performed after "quickening" (fetal movement that begins at about 20 weeks). There was little public objection to this policy until the early 1800s, when an anti-abortion movement began, led primarily by physicians who questioned the doctrine of quickening and who objected to the growing practice of abortion by untrained persons.

This anti-abortion drive attracted little attention until the mid-1800s, when newspaper advertisements for abortion preparations became common and concern grew that women were using abortion as a means of birth control or to cover up extramarital activity. By the 1900s abortion

was illegal in every state. These anti-abortion laws stayed in effect until the 1960s, when courts began to invalidate them on the grounds of constitutional vagueness and violation of the right to privacy (see the box "Key Abortion Decisions and Legislation").

Current Legal Status

In 1973, the U.S. Supreme Court made abortion legal in the landmark case of *Roe v. Wade*. To replace the restrictions most states still imposed at that time, the justices devised new standards to govern abortion decisions. They divided pregnancy into three parts, or trimesters, giving a woman less choice about abortion as her pregnancy advances toward full term.

In the first trimester, the abortion decision must be left to the judgment of the pregnant woman and her physician. During the second trimester, similar rights remain up to the point when the fetus becomes **viable**—that is, capable of surviving outside of the uterus. Today, most clinicians define this point as 24 weeks of gestation. When the fetus is considered viable, a state may regulate and even bar all abortions except those considered necessary to preserve the mother's life or health.

Since 1973, repeated campaigns have been waged to overturn the *Roe v. Wade* decision and to ban abortion altogether. Although abortion remains legal throughout the United States, subsequent rulings by the Supreme Court allow states to regulate abortion throughout pregnancy as long as an "undue burden" is not imposed on women seeking the procedure. As a result, states have passed a variety of laws that have had the effect of reducing women's access to abortion. Between 1995 and 2006, the number of state laws restricting abortion more than quadrupled. For example:

- In 24 states where pre-abortion counseling is required, counseling must be followed by a waiting period before an abortion can be performed.

- In 34 states, parents must give consent or at least be notified before a minor can undergo an abortion.

- 36 states prohibit abortions after a specified point in pregnancy except in cases where the mother's life or health is endangered, where the pregnancy is the result of rape or incest, or where severe fetal abnormalities have been detected. These restrictions and their exceptions vary by state.

- In 32 states and the District of Columbia, the use of state funds for abortions is restricted except when the mother's life is in danger or the pregnancy is the result of rape or incest.

Research into the effects of state restrictions has yielded mixed results. Some studies indicate that parental consent and notification laws may result in minors' traveling out of state to get abortions. Mandatory delay laws have

TERMS

abortion   The artificially induced expulsion of an embryo or fetus from the uterus.

miscarriage   A naturally occurring spontaneous abortion.

viable   Capable of surviving outside of the uterus.

Key Abortion Decisions and Legislation

1700s to mid-1800s Abortion is generally legal throughout the United States.

Mid-1800s to mid-1900s Abortion becomes illegal in all 50 states, with certain exceptions that vary by state (for example, to save the life of the mother). The federal Comstock Act of 1873 makes it illegal to distribute or possess information about, or devices or medications for, contraception or abortion.

1965 *Griswold v. Connecticut:* The Supreme Court overturns a law prohibiting use of contraceptives by married couples, stating that it violates the right of marital privacy guaranteed in the Bill of Rights.

1967–1973 Some states rewrite their abortion laws, including four states that repeal abortion bans.

1972 *Eisenstadt v. Baird:* The Supreme Court overturns a law banning distribution of contraceptives to unmarried adults, stating that the ban violates the equal protection clause of the constitution.

1973 *Roe v. Wade:* The Supreme Court strikes down a Texas law banning abortion and rules that abortion is encompassed within the constitutional right to privacy.

1976 *Planned Parenthood of Central Missouri v. Danforth:* The Supreme Court rules against a statute that requires married women to obtain their spouse's approval before having an abortion and requires minors to obtain written parental consent.

1980 *Harris v. McRae:* The Supreme Court upholds restrictions on Medicaid funding for abortions except as needed to protect the life of the mother or in other special circumstances.

1986 *Thornburgh v. American College of Obstetricians and Gynecologists:* The Supreme Court strikes down a law requiring any woman seeking an abortion to receive a state-scripted lecture from her physician about potential risks and possible alternatives.

1989 *Webster v. Reproductive Health Services:* The Supreme Court upholds a state law prohibiting the use of public facilities for abortions that are not medically necessary and requiring physicians to do viability testing on fetuses of more than 20 weeks' gestation.

1991 *Rust v. Sullivan:* The Supreme Court rules that clinics receiving federal Title X (family planning) funding can be prohibited from counseling, referring, or providing information about abortions.

1992 *Planned Parenthood of Southeastern Pennsylvania v. Casey:* The Supreme Court upholds the *Roe* decision but allows states to restrict abortion access as long as the restrictions do not impose an undue burden on women seeking abortions. It upholds a provision requiring minors to obtain consent from one parent or a judge (judicial bypass) to obtain an abortion.

1994 Congress passes the Freedom of Access to Clinics Act, making it a crime to injure, intimidate, or interfere through threats, force, or physical obstruction with a woman's right to obtain reproductive health services, including abortion.

2000 The FDA approves mifepristone (RU-486), the abortion pill.

2000 *Stenberg v. Carhart:* The Supreme Court finds a Nebraska law banning partial-birth abortion unconstitutional because it lacks an exception for the health of the mother and imposes an undue burden on women seeking abortions.

2003 Congress passes and President Bush signs the Partial Birth Abortion Ban Act with no exception to the ban in cases of risk to a woman's health.

2004 The Partial Birth Abortion Ban Act is declared unconstitutional by federal judges in San Francisco, New York, and Lincoln, Nebraska. Also, the Freedom of

Choice Act (FOCA) is introduced in the Senate. At the federal level, FOCA would prohibit state and federal government entities from denying or interfering with a woman's right to choose to bear a child, to terminate a pregnancy before viability, or to terminate a pregnancy after viability when termination is necessary to protect the mother's life or health.

2007 *Gonzales v. Carhart:* The Supreme Court upholds the Partial Birth Abortion Ban Act and imposes a nationwide ban on a rare but controversial abortion procedure, called intact dilation and extraction (intact D & E).

SOURCES: Cornell University Legal Information Institute. 2009. *U.S. Supreme Court Decisions* (http://supct.law.cornell.edu/supct/; retrieved February 3, 2009); CBS News. 2007. *Abortion Timeline* (http://www.cbsnews.com/htdocs/abortion/timeline.html; retrieved February 3, 2009); National Public Radio. 2003. *History of the Abortion Debate: Timeline of Significant Supreme Court Decisions* (http://www.npr.org/news/specials/roevwade/timeline.html; retrieved February 3, 2009). Planned Parenthood. 2008. *Abortion Issues.* (http://www.plannedparenthood.org/issues-action/abortion-issues-5946.html; retrieved February 3, 2009).

been found to influence the number and timing of abortions. Future research may help to determine whether such restrictions place an undue burden on women seeking abortions.

Further, Congress has barred the use of federal Medicaid funds to pay for abortions, except when a woman's life is in danger or in cases of rape or incest. Currently, 17 states provide nonfederal public money to assist some poor women seeking medically necessary abortions. Concerns have been raised that a two-tiered system has been created—one for women with means and another for those without. The overall abortion rate declined 25% between 1990 and 2005, but the rate among women of low socioeconomic status rose during this period. Women below the federal poverty threshold have an abortion rate more than four times that of higher-income women.

Legal and legislative efforts have also targeted procedures and medications that can be used to induce abortion. One such drug, Mifepristone, is discussed in detail later in the chapter.

Public Opinion

Along with the legal debates are ongoing arguments between pro-life and pro-choice groups regarding the ethics of abortion.

Pro-choice groups believe that the decision to end or continue a pregnancy is a personal matter. Pro-life groups oppose abortion on the basis of their belief that life begins at conception.

Central to the pro-life position is the belief that the fertilized egg must be valued as a human being from the moment of conception and that abortion at any time is equivalent to murder. This group holds that any woman who has sexual intercourse knows that pregnancy is a possibility, and should she willingly have intercourse and get pregnant, she is morally obligated to carry the pregnancy through. Pro-life followers encourage adoption for women who feel they are unable to raise the child and point out the number of couples seeking babies for adoption. Pro-life supporters do not consider the availability of legal abortion as essential to women's well-being but view it instead as having an overall destructive effect on our traditional morals and values.

In contrast, the pro-choice viewpoint holds that distinctions must be made between the stages of fetal development and that preserving the fetus early in pregnancy (or *gestation*) is not always the ultimate moral concern. Members of this group maintain that women must have the freedom to decide whether and when to have children; they argue that pregnancy can result from contraceptive failure or other factors out of a woman's control. (All contraceptive methods except abstinence have the potential for failure.) When pregnancy occurs, pro-choice supporters believe that the most moral decision possible must be determined according to each situation and that, in some cases, greater injustice could result if abortion were not an option. If legal abortions were not available, pro-choice supporters say, "back-alley shops" and do-it-yourself techniques, with their many health risks, as well as the births of unplanned children, would again grow in number. Others argue that discrimination in health care would result, since wealthy women could more easily make the travel arrangements necessary for a legal abortion elsewhere.

Both pro-choice and pro-life groups are likely to remain active, seeking to advance their positions both by promoting legislation and by supporting political candidates who share their views.

Some people strongly identify exclusively with either the pro-life or the pro-choice stance, but many have moral beliefs that are a mixture of the two. Many people instinctively feel that the fetus gains increasing human value as a pregnancy advances. In this view, first-trimester abortion is acceptable but later-term abortion should be performed only when the mother's health is in jeopardy. Although the most vocal groups in the abortion debate tend to paint a black-and-white picture, the majority of Americans view abortion as a complex issue without any easy answers.

In general, U.S. public opinion on abortion seems to change depending on the specific situation. Many individuals approve of legal abortion as an option when destructive health or welfare consequences could result from continuing pregnancy, but they do not advocate abortion as a simple way out of an inconvenient situation. Overall, most adults in the United States ap-

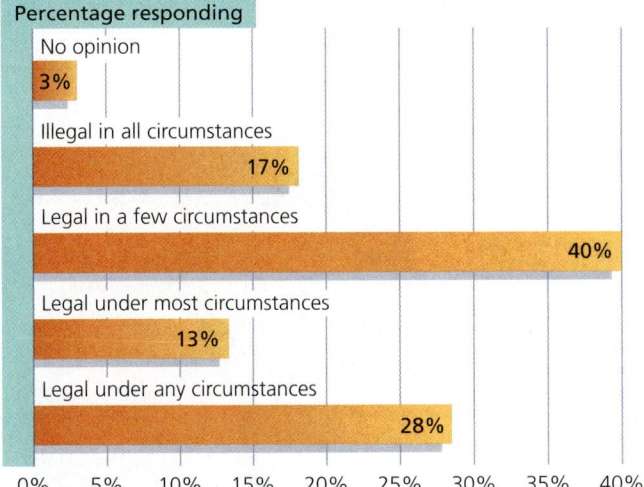

No opinion 3%

Illegal in all circumstances 17%

Legal in a few circumstances 40%

Legal under most circumstances 13%

Legal under any circumstances 28%

0% 5% 10% 15% 20% 25% 30% 35% 40%

VITAL STATISTICS

FIGURE 7.1 Public opinion about abortion.

SOURCE: "Public Opinion About Abortion," from http://www.gallup.com/poll/27628/Public-Divided-ProChoice-vs-ProLife-Abortion-Labels.aspx. Reprinted with permission from Gallup, Inc.

VITAL STATISTICS

Table 7.1 Views on Abortion

1. Should abortion be legal in the following circumstances?

	Yes
The woman's life is endangered.	85%
The woman's physical health is endangered.	77%
The pregnancy was caused by rape or incest.	76%
The woman's mental health is endangered.	63%
There is evidence that the baby is physically impaired.	56%
The woman or family cannot afford to raise the child.	35%

2. Should abortion be legal during the following stages of pregnancy?

	Yes
In the first 3 months	66%
In the second 3 months	25%
In the last 3 months	10%

SOURCE: Gallup, Inc. 2008. *Gallup's Pulse of Democracy: Abortion* (http://www.gallup.com/poll/1576/Abortion.aspx; retrieved February 3, 2009).

prove of legal abortion and are opposed to overturning the basic right to abortion established in *Roe v. Wade* (Figure 7.1). However, the amount of public support varies considerably depending on the circumstances surrounding the abortion request (Table 7.1).

42% of Americans identify themselves as pro-life; 53% identify themselves as pro-choice.

—Gallup, Inc., 2008

QUICK STATS

THINKING ABOUT THE ENVIRONMENT

A miscarriage, a pregnancy that ends on its own before the 20th week of gestation, is a common outcome of pregnancy. The American College of Gynecologists and Obstetricians estimates that 15–25% of pregnancies end in miscarriage—often before the mother even realizes she is pregnant.

Miscarriages occur for a variety of reasons, such as chromosomal abnormalities, maternal health problems, and infections. But experts also believe that many spontaneous abortions may be associated with exposure to environmental toxins. Some environmental substances are encountered by choice or as a result of lifestyle; these include tobacco smoke, alcohol, recreational drugs, prescription and over-the-counter medications, and some herbal remedies.

Other environmental toxins may be found in or around a woman's home or workplace. For example, some reports indicate that miscarriage rates are higher in agricultural areas where pesticides are routinely applied to crops. In workplaces where exposure to radiation or heavy metals is possible, a woman's chance of miscarriage may be greatly increased.

For more information on the environment and environmental health, see Chapter 19.

Personal Considerations

For the pregnant woman who is considering abortion, the usual legal and moral arguments may sound meaningless as she attempts to weigh the many short- and long-term ramifications for all lives directly concerned. If she chooses abortion, can she accept that decision in terms of her own religious and moral beliefs? What are her long-range feelings likely to be regarding this decision? What are her partner's feelings regarding abortion, and how will she deal with his response? Does she have a supportive relative or friend who will help her through this time of emotional adjustment? Which medical facility offering abortions would be most suitable for her? What about transportation and costs?

For the woman who decides against abortion and chooses instead to continue the pregnancy, there are other questions. If she decides to raise the child herself, will she have the resources to do it well? Is a supportive, lasting relationship with her partner likely? If not, how does she

The Adoption Option

Between 1952 and 1972, nearly 9% of unmarried pregnant women gave their children up for adoption; currently, however, less than 1% of women choose to place a child for adoption. This decline is probably due to a variety of factors, including increased rates of contraceptive use and an easing of the social stigma of single parenthood. The drop in adoption rates in the 1970s probably reflected an increase in the abortion rate following the 1973 legalization of abortion; however, since 1990 adoption rates have remained steady, while the abortion rate has declined, indicating that women are not choosing abortion over adoption.

Women who place their children for adoption tend to come from higher socioeconomic backgrounds and to have higher levels of educational attainment than those who choose to keep their babies or have an abortion. They are also likely to have greater educational and vocational goals for themselves than those who keep their children. Often, women who choose adoption come from supportive families who assist them throughout the experience.

If you are pregnant and considering adoption, make sure you explore all possibilities before you make a final choice. The decision to go through an unwanted pregnancy and then give the baby to another family is difficult and takes tremendous love, maturity, and courage. Adoption is permanent: The adoptive parents will raise your child and have legal authority for his or her welfare. Think about your life now and in the future as you weigh alternatives.

There are many people who can help you consider your options, including your partner, friends, family members, or a professional counselor at a crisis pregnancy center, a family planning clinic, or a family services, social services, or adoption agency. A counselor should always treat you with respect and be willing to discuss all your options with you—keeping the baby, having an abortion, or arranging an adoption.

There are two types of adoptions, confidential and open. In confidential adoption, the birth parents and the adoptive parents never know each other. Adoptive parents will be given any information, such as medical information, that they would need to help take care of the child. A later meeting between the child and birth parents is possible in confidential adoption, however, if the birth parents leave information with the agency or lawyer who handled the adoption and/or in a national adoption registry.

In an open adoption, the birth parents and adoptive parents know something about each other. There are different levels of openness, ranging from reading a brief description of prospective adoptive parents to meeting them and sharing full information. Birth parents may also be able to stay in touch with the family by visiting, calling, or writing.

In all states, you can work with a licensed child-placing (adoption) agency. In most, you can also work directly with an adopting couple or their attorney; this is called a private or independent adoption. Prospective adoptive parents can be located through personal ads, a physician, adoptive parent support groups, national matching services, and family members and friends. To find an agency or lawyer who will arrange the type of adoption you want, ask about their rules and procedures. For example, will you receive financial help and counseling? Will you be able to have the amount of information about the adoptive parents and the amount of contact with the baby that you want? If your baby is a child of color and it is important to you that the adoptive parents are of the same ethnic or racial background, ask if the agency or attorney has such families approved and waiting for placement. Some agencies specialize in finding families for children of color.

You will also need to consider the reaction and rights of the birth father. A

woman can choose to have an abortion without the consent or knowledge of the father, but once the baby is born, the father has certain rights. These rights vary from state to state but, at a minimum, most states require that the birth father be notified of the adoption. In some states, the birth father may be able to take the child even if the mother prefers that the child go to an adoptive family.

As with abortion, there are emotional and physical risks associated with pregnancy, childbirth, and adoption. Throughout the adoption process, make sure that you have the help you need and that you carefully consider all your options. Deciding how to handle an unplanned pregnancy is important, and you have the power to make your own decisions.

SOURCES: Child Welfare Information Gateway. 2007. *Are You Pregnant and Thinking About Adoption?* (http://www.childwelfare.gov/pubs/f _pregna/index.cfm; retrieved February 3, 2009); Child Welfare Information Gateway. 2006. *Voluntary Relinquishment for Adoption: Numbers and Trends* (http://www.childwelfare.gov/pubs/s _place.cfm; retrieved February 3, 2009).

feel about being a single parent? Are family members available to help with the many demands of child rearing? If she is young, what will be the effects on her own growth? Will she be able to continue with her educational and personal goals? What about the ongoing financial responsibilities?

If the pregnant woman considers adoption, she will have to try to predict what her emotional responses will be throughout the full-term pregnancy and the adoption process. What are her long-range feelings likely to be? What is the best setting for her during her pregnancy? How can she best continue with the rest of her life and her long-term goals? What type of adoption would be most appropriate? (The box "The Adoption Option" addresses some of these questions.)

Abortion Statistics

Abortions are fairly common in the United States. Among American women, about 50% of all pregnancies are unintended; about 40% of such pregnancies end in abortion. About 22% of all pregnancies—wanted and unwanted—end in abortion, not including those that end in miscarriage. More than 45 million legal abortions were performed in the United States between 1973 and 2005.

After the Supreme Court's ruling in *Roe v. Wade,* the number of abortions rapidly increased in the United States (Figure 7.2). According to the Guttmacher Institute (a private organization that tracks statistics on contraception and abortion), nearly 750,000 abortions occurred in 1973; the number rose each year after that, until hitting a peak of 1.6 million in 1990. The number has steadily declined since then, with just over 1.2 million legal abortions reported in 2005, the most recent year for which data is available.

The number of late-term abortions has dropped over time, as well. In 2005, 89% of abortions occurred during the first 12 weeks (the first trimester) of pregnancy; about 1% were performed after the 20th week.

The Guttmacher Institute estimates that about 50% of American women will experience an unintended pregnancy by age 45, and more than one-third will have an abortion. Based on national research, the majority of American women who get abortions share the following characteristics:

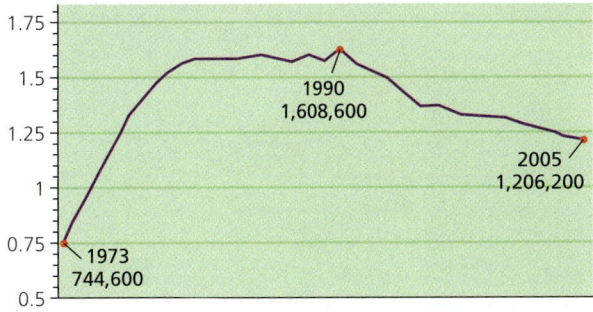

Number of reported abortions (in millions)

FIGURE 7.2   Number of reported abortions in the United States, 1973–2005.

SOURCE: Jones, R. K., et al. 2008. Abortion in the United States: Incidence and Access to Services, 2005. *Perspectives on Sexual and Reproductive Health* 40(1): 6–16.

- Are under age 25
- Have previously given birth
- Have never been married
- Are poor
- Live in a metropolitan area

238 abortions were performed for every **1000** live births in the United States in **2004.**
—CDC, 2008

QUICK STATS

Black and Hispanic women are more likely to have an abortion than white women. This disparity is likely due to limited access to and funds for contraception. Figures 7.3 and 7.4 provide some more statistical information about American women who choose to have abortions. (For a broader perspective, see the box "Abortion around the World" on p. 193.)

METHODS OF ABORTION

Abortion methods can be divided into two categories: surgical and medical. Surgical abortion is by far the most common, accounting for about 87% of all abortions performed in the United States in 2005. Medical abortion, in which one or more drugs are used to induce abortion, accounted for 13% of all U.S. abortions in 2005. Medical abortions are discussed in detail later in this chapter.

Emergency contraception—pills taken or IUDs inserted immediately after unprotected sexual intercourse—are generally not considered abortifacients (agents that produce abortion) from a medical viewpoint, because they act before implantation of the fertilized egg, if one

By woman's age

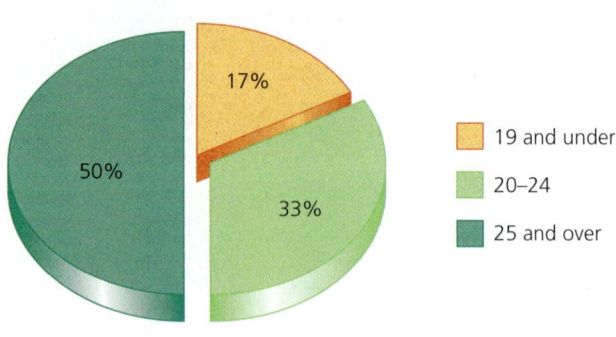

- 17%
- 50%
- 33%

Legend:
- 19 and under
- 20–24
- 25 and over

By gestation period

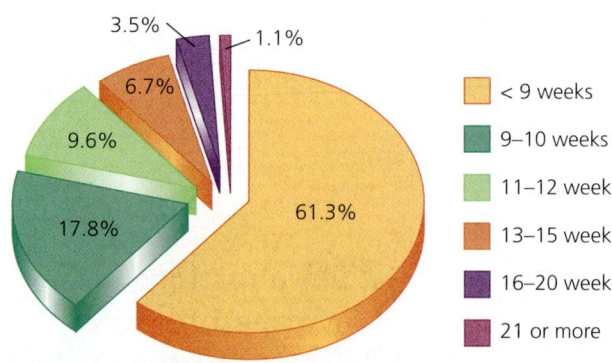

- 3.5%
- 1.1%
- 6.7%
- 9.6%
- 17.8%
- 61.3%

Legend:
- < 9 weeks
- 9–10 weeks
- 11–12 weeks
- 13–15 weeks
- 16–20 weeks
- 21 or more

VITAL STATISTICS

FIGURE 7.3   Distribution of abortions by the woman's age and by the weeks of gestation: 2005.

SOURCE: Guttmacher Institute. 2008. *In Brief: Facts on Induced Abortion in the United States* (http://www.guttmacher.org/pubs/fb_induced_abortion.html; retrieved February 3, 2009).

is present (see Chapter 6). Therefore, these topics are not discussed here.

Suction Curettage

First developed in China in 1958, **suction curettage** (commonly known as *dilation and curettage,* or *D & C*) is the most common method for abortions performed from the 6th to the 12th week of pregnancy. It is used in about 90% of all abortions performed in the United States. The procedure can be done quickly, usually on an outpatient basis, and the risk of complications is small.

TERMS

suction curettage   Removal of the embryo or fetus by means of suction; also called *dilation and curettage (D & C).*

manual vacuum aspiration (MVA)   The vacuum aspiration of uterine contents shortly after a missed period using a handheld syringe.

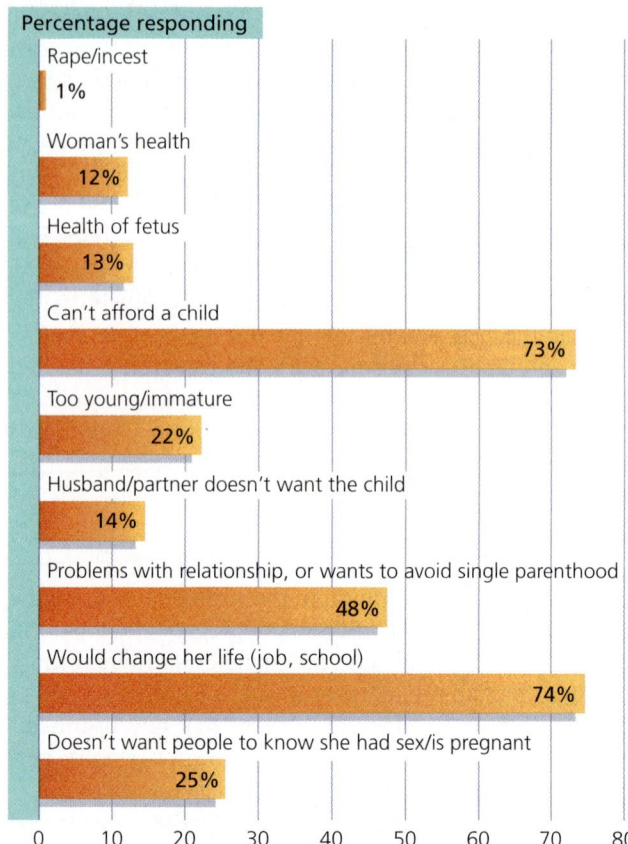

Percentage responding

Reason	%
Rape/incest	1%
Woman's health	12%
Health of fetus	13%
Can't afford a child	73%
Too young/immature	22%
Husband/partner doesn't want the child	14%
Problems with relationship, or wants to avoid single parenthood	48%
Would change her life (job, school)	74%
Doesn't want people to know she had sex/is pregnant	25%

FIGURE 7.4   The reasons women choose abortions.   The respondents in this study were allowed to give more than one answer.

SOURCE: Finer, L. B., et al. 2005. Reasons U.S. women have abortions: Quantitative and qualitative perspectives. *Perspectives on Sexual and Reproductive Health* 37(3): 110–118.

A sedative may be given, along with a local anesthetic. A speculum is inserted into the vagina, and the cervix is cleansed with a surgical solution. The cervix is dilated and a suction curette, a specially designed tube, is then inserted into the uterus (Figure 7.5 on p. 194). The curette is attached to the rubber tubing of an electric pump, and suction is applied. In 20–30 seconds, the uterus is emptied. Moderate cramping is common during evacuation. To ensure that no fragments of tissue are left in the uterus, the doctor usually scrapes the uterine lining with a metal curette, an instrument with a spoonlike tip. The entire suction curettage procedure takes 5–10 minutes.

After a few hours in a recovery area, the woman can return home. She is usually instructed not to have intercourse or use tampons for several weeks after the abortion and to return for a postabortion examination. This follow-up exam is important to verify that the abortion was complete and that no signs of infection are present.

Manual Vacuum Aspiration

For more than 30 years, gynecologists have used **manual vacuum aspiration (MVA)** to manage incomplete

DIMENSIONS OF DIVERSITY

Abortion Around the World

The legal status, availability, and safety of abortion vary widely around the world. According to the World Health Organization (WHO), there were about 80 million unplanned pregnancies worldwide in 2003, the most recent year for which data is available. That year, nearly 42 million abortions occurred. The WHO estimates that 20 million of those abortions were illegal and unsafe. The vast majority of unsafe abortions occur in developing countries with restrictive abortion laws and where access to family planning and abortion services is limited.

About 60% of the world's population lives in countries where abortion is permitted either without restriction or, more commonly, for a wide range of reasons but with certain restrictions. This is not the case in many developing countries, which tend to have the most restrictive laws regarding abortion; in fact, more than 100 countries do not permit abortion even in cases of rape or incest. The following table shows the grounds on which abortion is legally permitted in 193 countries, as of 2001.

Ground	Permitted	Not Permitted
To save the woman's life	189	4
To preserve physical health	122	71
To preserve mental health	120	73
Rape or incest	83	110
Fetal impairment	76	117
Economic/social reasons	63	130
On request	52	141

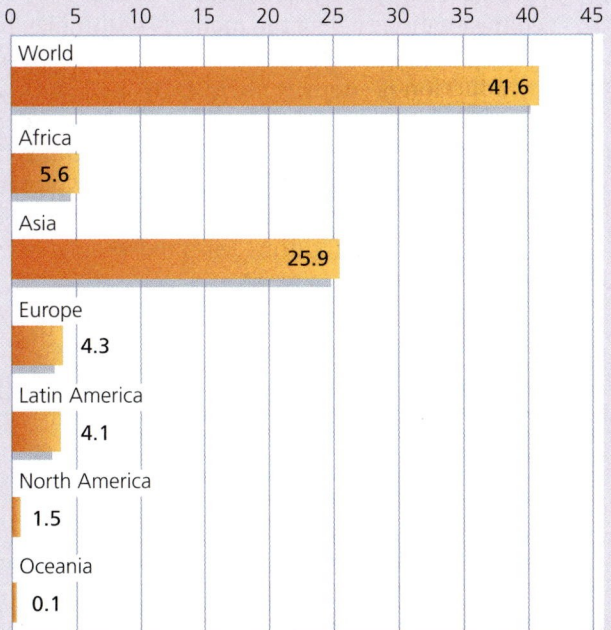

Abortions performed each year (millions)

Many countries with strict anti-abortion laws have high rates of abortion. Because the procedure is commonly performed secretly and in unsafe conditions, those countries also have high rates of serious complications. The WHO estimates that 5 million women suffer complications from unsafe abortions each year, and about 70,000 of these women die from their complications.

Legal status is not the only factor that determines whether a woman has access to safe abortion services. The way laws are interpreted can be just as critical. For example, in some countries that allow abortion for mental health reasons, the law is interpreted to allow the majority of women seeking abortions to obtain them; in other countries with similar laws, few abortions are allowed. Enforcement of abortion laws is also a factor, and varies from country to country.

Strict enforcement of anti-abortion laws tends to disproportionately affect poor women because wealthier women can pay to obtain discreet, safe abortions from private physicians, avoiding the more tightly regulated public hospitals. Younger women have a much higher rate of unsafe abortions. The WHO estimates, for example, that women under 30 account for more than 60% of unsafe abortions in the world's developing regions.

The attitudes and beliefs of the medical community also influence the availability of abortion services. In Nigeria, for example, many physicians will perform abortions in spite of legal bans because the medical community believes in the need for safe abortion services. On the flip side, major medical associations in Poland and the Republic of Ireland have adopted guidelines that are stricter than their country's laws.

The number and location of abortion providers and the cost of abortion services also influence the true availability of abortion in a particular country, regardless of its actual legal status. Community and physician opposition to abortion has left parts of the United States, Austria, and Germany without abortion providers, despite the fact that abortion is legal in all three countries. In contrast, policies in Denmark go beyond just permitting safe abortion to ensuring that services are widely available. There, each county must have at least one hospital with the capability of providing abortion services, and the services are free.

SOURCES: Guttmacher Institute. 2007. *In Brief: Facts on Induced Abortion Worldwide* (http://www.guttmacher.org/pubs/fb_IAW.html; retrieved February 3, 2009); World Health Organization. 2007. *Unsafe Abortion: Global and Regional Estimates of Incidence of Unsafe Abortion and Associated Mortality in 2003*, 5th ed. Geneva: World Health Organization; Rao, K. A., and A. Faundes. 2006. Access to safe abortion within the limits of the law. *Best Practice and Research Clinical Obstetrics and Gynaecology* 20(3): 421–432; Ahman, E. L., and I. H. Shah. 2006. Contraceptive use, fertility, and unsafe abortion in developing countries. *European Journal of Contraception and Reproductive Health Care* 11(2): 126–131.

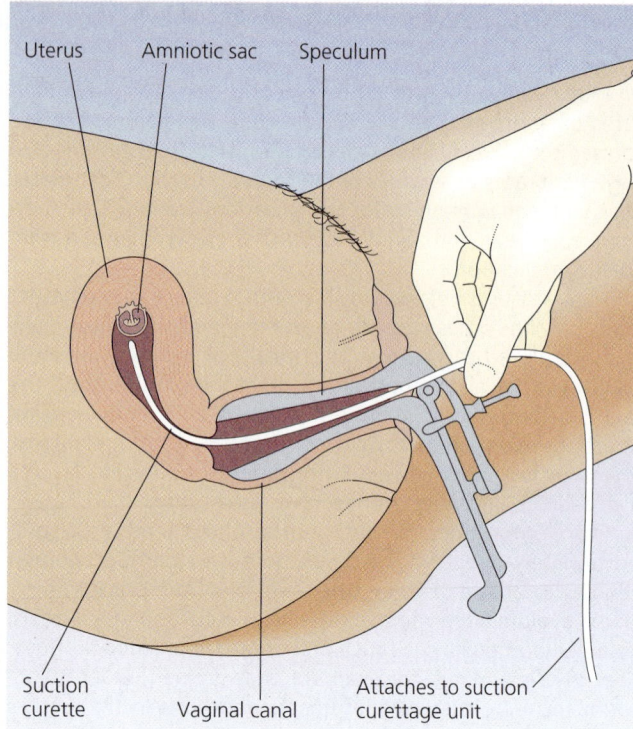

Uterus   Amniotic sac   Speculum

Suction curette   Vaginal canal   Attaches to suction curettage unit

FIGURE 7.5 Suction curettage. This procedure takes 5–10 minutes and can be performed up to the 12th week of pregnancy.

abortions, for endometrial sampling in nonpregnant women, and for elective abortion. During this procedure, as in suction curettage, the woman receives a local anesthetic and her cervix is dilated. A plastic tube attached to a handheld syringe is inserted through the cervix and into the uterus. The syringe provides gentle suction, which empties the uterus.

MVA has several advantages over the traditional D & C. Manual vacuum aspiration may be used earlier in pregnancy, can be performed in the office, and does not require an electric pump or additional equipment. It is also significantly cheaper than suction curettage, does not require electricity, and can be performed by mid-level providers such as midwives and nurses. For these reasons, MVA is ideal for low-resource settings. A number of recent studies have shown that the two techniques have equivalent safety profiles and low rates of complications when done up to 10 weeks of gestation.

Multi-Fetal Pregnancy Reduction (MFPR)

Multi-fetal (twin and higher multiple) pregnancies are associated with high fetal morbidity and mortality rates. **Multi-fetal pregnancy reduction (MFPR)** is a procedure that reduces the number of fetuses in a multiple pregnancy. It is usually performed during the first trimester. In the most common method of MFPR, the fetal heart is injected with potassium chloride. The dead fetus is then absorbed by the mother's body. Multi-fetal reduction re-

duces the risk of preterm delivery for the remaining fetus and improves maternal pregnancy outcomes.

Abortion After the First Trimester

Only about one in ten abortions is performed after the 12th week of pregnancy. The method most commonly used for abortion from 13 to 24 weeks of pregnancy is **dilation and evacuation (D & E)**. The cervix is opened using dilators, which gradually expand the cervix overnight while the woman is at home. The next day, the uterus is emptied using surgical instruments and an aspirating machine. The more advanced the pregnancy, the higher the incidence of complications such as bleeding, infection, or incomplete abortion. When performed by a trained provider, however, complication rates are very low.

Intact dilation and extraction (known controversially as *partial birth abortion*) is a surgical abortion wherein an intact fetus is removed from the uterus. Occasionally, the skull is collapsed after fetal limbs and body are delivered to allow it to pass more easily through the cervix. This procedure is performed only rarely, representing 0.17% of all abortions in the United States. Experts say that intact dilation and extraction can be useful when certain fetal anomalies are present, such as severe hydrocephalus (swelling of the fetus's head), and that the procedure may be the safest option for the mother in some circumstances. Intact dilation and extraction became illegal after the 2007 Supreme Court ruling in the case of *Gonzales v. Carhart,* even in situations where the mother's health may be in jeopardy.

Labor induction is another infrequently used method of late abortion. Prostaglandins, chemicals that cause uterine contractions, are used to induce labor, sometimes in conjunction with injections of salt or urea into the uterus. The delivery of the fetus usually occurs in 6–24 hours. The woman is hospitalized during this process.

Medical Abortion

Medical abortion is generally used in very early pregnancy, within 49 days of the last menstrual period. The

multi-fetal pregnancy reduction (MFPR) A method of abortion used to reduce the number of fetuses in a multiple-fetus pregnancy.

dilation and evacuation (D & E) The method of abortion most commonly used between 13 and 24 weeks of pregnancy. Following dilation of the cervix, both vacuum aspiration and curettage instruments are used as needed.

intact dilation and extraction A rarely used method of late-term abortion, wherein an intact fetus is removed from the uterus.

labor induction An infrequently used method of late-term abortion, in which chemicals are used to induce abortion and labor.

TERMS

combination of drugs that is given causes the embryo and products of conception to be passed out through the vagina, as in a natural miscarriage. An ultrasound may be performed before giving the medication to make sure that the pregnancy dates are accurate, because complication rates for medical abortion are higher if the pregnancy is more advanced.

Advantages and Disadvantages of Medical Abortion

Medical abortion is generally safer than surgical abortion because it involves no anesthesia or surgical risks. Some women feel that medical abortion allows them to take more control of the procedure and gives them more privacy than a surgical abortion would. Medical abortion can also be done very early in pregnancy.

The major disadvantages of medical abortion are that the process takes days or even weeks to complete (early surgical abortion generally takes less than an hour and can be done under sedation) and that bleeding after the procedure is often heavier and lasts longer than with surgical abortion. Medical abortion also generally requires more clinic visits than surgical abortion. The cost to the patient is generally about the same.

Drugs Used for Medical Abortion

Mifepristone, misoprostol, and methotrexate are three widely used drugs for medical abortion. Mifepristone blocks the effect of progesterone that is produced by the ovaries after implantation of the fertilized egg. The loss of progesterone support causes the uterine lining and any fertilized egg to shed. Mifepristone is currently approved for use up to 49 days following the last menstrual period. A woman takes a dose of mifepristone and follows it up two days later with a second drug, the prostaglandin analog misoprostol, which induces contractions. The two-drug regimen has a rate of completed abortion of about 92–95%; the success rate is highest early in pregnancy.

Side effects include nausea, vomiting, diarrhea, and abdominal pain. Vaginal bleeding is often more prolonged than with surgical abortion (9–16 days), but total blood loss is similar. In a few cases, bleeding is heavy, and a follow-up suction curettage is necessary to complete the abortion in a small percentage of women. This is generally done in the emergency room at the hospital, or at a clinic. With mifepristone and misoprostol, abortion can take anywhere from a few hours to several weeks; about 50% of abortions occur within 4 hours, and 75% within 24 hours. Two weeks after taking mifepristone, a woman must return to her health care provider for a follow-up visit to ensure that the abortion is complete.

Since the FDA's approval of mifepristone in 2000, several deaths have been reported with the drug's use. In 2006, the FDA investigated the deaths of five American women after intravaginal administration of the second medication, misoprostol, which is currently FDA-approved only for oral use. The five deaths were all linked to sepsis (blood or tissue poisoning) caused by a *Clostridium* species bacterial infection. *Clostridium* species bacteria are normally present in the vagina in up to 10% of women. At the end of the investigation, the FDA concluded that there was no established causal link between the deaths and mifepristone. The FDA also updated the black box warning for Mifeprex, to inform patients of the sepsis cases, and to alert them to signs and symptoms of possible sepsis.

Most recently, cases of *Clostridium* sepsis have been identified after spontaneous miscarriage, childbirth, and other gynecologic procedures (where neither mifepristone nor misoprostol were used). There are ongoing studies looking at the risk factors for the rare development of sepsis from *Clostridium* bacteria after a medical termination and other procedures.

Methotrexate can also be used with prostaglandin for early medical abortion. Methotrexate stops the embryonic or fetal cells from dividing; it is followed by a dose of prostaglandin in a regimen similar to that for mifepristone. With this combination of drugs, 80–85% of women will abort within 2 weeks; up to 95% will abort within 30 days. Mifepristone acts quicker than methotrexate, has fewer side effects, and is slightly more effective. For these reasons, mifepristone has become the preferred drug for medical abortion. However, methotrexate may be used if there is suspicion of ectopic pregnancy (pregnancy implanting outside of the uterus) or in settings where mifepristone is not available.

COMPLICATIONS OF ABORTION

Along with questions regarding the actual procedure of abortion, many people have concerns about possible aftereffects. More information is gradually being gathered on this important subject.

Possible Physical Effects

The incidence of immediate problems following an abortion (infection, bleeding, trauma to the cervix or uterus, and incomplete abortion requiring repeat curettage) varies widely. The potential for problems is significantly reduced by a woman's good health, early timing of the abortion, use of the suction method, performance by a well-trained clinician, and the availability and use of prompt follow-up care. (For more information, see the box "Abortion Myths and Misconceptions" on p. 197.)

QUESTIONS FOR CRITICAL THINKING AND REFLECTION

What is your stand on the issue of late-term abortion? Do you feel it is never acceptable, or is it acceptable under certain circumstances? If so, what are those circumstances?

Problems related to infection can be minimized through preabortion testing and treatment for gonorrhea, chlamydia, and other infections. Some clinicians routinely give antibiotics after an abortion, while others treat only those women who have a history or current symptoms of pelvic infection. Postabortion danger signs are as follows:

- Fever above 100°F
- Abdominal pain or swelling, cramping, or backache
- Abdominal tenderness (to pressure)
- Prolonged or heavy bleeding
- Foul-smelling vaginal discharge
- Vomiting or fainting
- Delay in resuming menstrual periods (6 weeks or more)

Some cramping and bleeding are an expected part of ending a pregnancy. In rare cases, life-threatening bleeding, infections, or other problems can occur following a miscarriage, surgical abortion, or medical abortion. Prompt medical attention should be sought if heavy bleeding, severe abdominal pain, or fever occurs. Excessive bleeding during or after an abortion is rare with early suction curettage. In later-stage pregnancies, the use of uterus-contracting medication significantly reduces the risk of bleeding. Some pain medications may increase bleeding, so patients should check with their physician about appropriate medications for postoperative pain.

Incomplete abortion means that some pregnancy tissue has remained in the uterus. With this condition, or when blood clots form in the uterus shortly after an abortion, severe cramping and signs of infection can occur, and a repeat suction curettage is usually needed. On rare occasions, a pregnancy may continue after an incomplete abortion. The recommended follow-up exam is important to establish that the abortion was complete.

Missed ectopic pregnancy is another potentially serious problem that can surface after an abortion. Surgical abortion techniques remove tissue from the uterus but will miss an ectopic pregnancy developing outside of the uterus. If an ectopic pregnancy goes untreated, the embryo can eventually become large enough to rupture the fallopian tube, causing potentially catastrophic bleeding. Tissue removed during an abortion is normally examined for evidence that the gestational sac or embryo has been removed. If there is any doubt, ultrasound and follow-up pregnancy testing can reveal whether an ectopic pregnancy is present.

Table 7.2	Abortion Risks
	Risk of Death in Any Given Year
Legal abortion	
Before 9 weeks	1 in 262,800
9–12 weeks	1 in 100,100
13–15 weeks	1 in 34,400
After 15 weeks	1 in 10,200
Illegal abortion	1 in 3,000
Pregnancy and childbirth	1 in 10,000

SOURCES: Hatcher, R. A., et al. 2004. *Contraceptive Technology*, 18th ed. New York: Ardent Media; Carlson, K. J., S. A. Eisenstat, and T. Ziporyn. 2004. *The New Harvard Guide to Women's Health*. Cambridge, Mass.: Harvard University Press.

For Rh-negative women, dangerous sensitization (the buildup of antibodies) can be minimized by an injection of Rh-immune globulin given within 72 hours of the procedure.

The overall risk of death is low. Mortality rates have decreased substantially since abortion was legalized in 1973 (Table 7.2).

Unsafe Abortions

Unsafe abortion is defined as abortion done either by people lacking the necessary skills or in an environment lacking minimal medical standards. These include abortions in countries where the law is restrictive, or abortions that do not meet legal requirements in countries where the law is not restrictive.

In 2003, 48% of all abortions were unsafe; the majority of them took place in developing countries. Poor women in rural areas, where trained providers may not be available or affordable, are at highest risk of undergoing unsafe abortions. In undeveloped regions, many methods of abortion are based on cultural or traditional practices and include repeated blows to the abdomen; insertion of stones, twigs, or sharp wire objects into the vagina and cervix; and drinking or flushing the vagina with caustic substances.

Immediate complications from unsafe abortions include severe bleeding, uterine perforation, tearing of the cervix, damage to genitals and abdomen, infection, and sepsis. Long-term complications include pelvic inflammatory disease and infertility. Globally, an estimated 5 million women are hospitalized and 70,000 women die every year from complications related to unsafe abortions. The actual numbers may be much greater because women may not present themselves to the hospital or may not be identified as victims of unsafe abortion.

The root causes of unsafe abortions are unmet needs for contraception, restrictive abortion laws, and prohibitive costs of a safe abortion. Unsafe and safe abortions correspond in large part with illegal and legal abortions. Higher restrictive abortion laws do not lower abortion incidence; rather, they increase the rates of un-

Abortion Myths and Misconceptions

Because abortion is still taboo for many Americans, a great deal of misinformation has circulated about it. Many mistruths and misconceptions have taken hold, some of which have been around for generations.

Still, much new information is only now coming to light about abortion and its effects. Here are three common misperceptions about abortion, and recent scientific findings relating to them.

Abortion and Future Pregnancies

Many people believe that an abortion can cause problems with future pregnancies, or even render a woman infertile. Some earlier studies identified a history of prior induced abortion as a risk factor for preterm delivery in a subsequent pregnancy. All these studies, however, were flawed because they did not adjust for other risk factors for poor pregnancy outcomes such as smoking and sexually transmitted diseases.

More recent reviews of both first- and second-trimester abortions found that

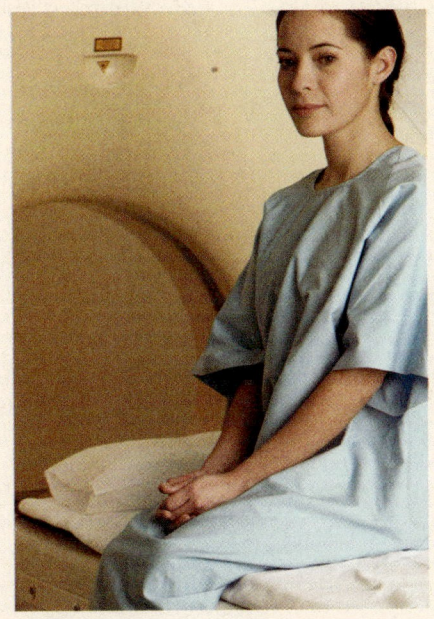

women whose first pregnancy ended in abortion had no greater risk of spontaneous mid-trimester loss or preterm delivery. Studies of medical abortion have also shown no adverse effects on the outcome of a subsequent pregnancy.

Abortion and Endometriosis

Endometriosis is a chronic, painful condition affecting many women of reproductive age. A single highly advertised study reported an increased risk of endometriosis with abortion. Other studies have shown no link between endometriosis and induced abortion, and the majority of medical experts do not believe that abortion is a risk factor for endometriosis.

Abortion and Breast Cancer

A few small studies have reported that women who have abortions have an increased risk of breast cancer. However, several subsequent larger studies, including a study of 1.5 million Danish women, found no connection between abortion and breast cancer. The Early Reproductive Events and Breast Cancer Workshop convened by the National Cancer Institute in 2003 concluded that abortion is not associated with an increase in breast cancer risk.

---

safe abortions. For example, in South Africa, the rates of infection from abortion decreased by 50% after a more liberal abortion law went into effect in 1996. Improving access to contraceptive services dramatically decreases rates for both safe and unsafe abortions.

Possible Psychological Effects

After an exhaustive review completed in 1988, the then surgeon general, C. Everett Koop, concluded that the available evidence failed to demonstrate either a negative or a positive long-term impact of abortion on mental health. More recent research has resulted in the same general conclusion. The frequency of any psychiatric diagnoses in women who have undergone an abortion procedure is no higher than in women with no such history.

The psychological side effects of abortion, however, are less clearly defined than the physical ones. Responses vary and depend on the individual woman's psychological makeup, family background, current personal and social relationships, cultural attitudes, and many other factors. A woman who has specific goals with a somewhat structured life may be able to incorporate her decision to have an abortion as the unequivocally best and most acceptable course more easily than a woman who feels uncertain about her future.

Although many women experience great relief after an abortion and virtually no negative feelings, some go through a period of ambivalence. Along with relief, they often feel a mixture of other responses, such as guilt, regret, loss, sadness, and/or anger. When a woman feels she was pressured into sexual intercourse or into the abortion, she may feel bitter. If she had strongly believed abortion to be immoral, she may wonder if she is still a good person. Many of these feelings are strongest immediately after the abortion, when hormonal shifts are occurring; such feelings often pass quite rapidly. Others take time to resolve and fade only slowly. It is important for a woman to realize that a mixture of feelings is natural.

For a woman who experiences psychological or emotional effects after an abortion, talking with a close friend or family member can be very helpful. Supportive people can help her feel positive about herself and her decision. Although a legal and common procedure in the United States, abortion is still treated very secretively in most of our society, so it is easy for a woman to feel isolated and alone. Many clinical centers that offer abortions make peer counseling available. Other women find they can identify with case histories in books written on abortion, which can help them deal with their own reactions. Unresolved emotions may persist, and a woman should seek professional counseling.

QUESTIONS FOR CRITICAL THINKING AND REFLECTION

Suppose you are in the position of lending support to a friend who has gone through an abortion. What sort of physical or emotional signals would you look for? What kind of support would you be willing to offer?

TIPS FOR TODAY AND THE FUTURE

You may never have to face an unintended pregnancy, but you should know what choices you would have, as well as where you stand on the issue of abortion.

RIGHT NOW YOU CAN

- Examine your feelings about the possibility of becoming a parent, especially if it were to happen unintentionally.
- Consider your views on the morality of abortion, and whether it is acceptable under certain circumstances.

IN THE FUTURE YOU CAN

- If you are sexually active or plan to become sexually active, talk to your partner about abortion. Do you share similar views and feelings, or are they different? How would you resolve conflicts about this issue?
- If you are sexually active, reexamine your contraceptive method and make sure you have made the right choice. Remember that no method of contraception is 100% effective.

SUMMARY

- The common use of the word *abortion* refers only to artificially induced expulsion of the fetus. The term *miscarriage* is used to describe a naturally occurring spontaneous abortion.

- Until the mid-1800s, abortion in the United States was legal if it took place before the 20th week of pregnancy; more restrictive laws passed by the various states remained in effect until they began to be invalidated by courts in the 1960s.

- The 1973 *Roe v. Wade* Supreme Court case devised new standards to govern abortion decisions; based on the trimesters of pregnancy, it limited a woman's choices as her pregnancy advanced.

- Although the Supreme Court continued to uphold its 1973 decision, later rulings gave states further power to regulate abortion.

- The controversy between pro-life and pro-choice viewpoints focuses on the issue of when life begins. Pro-life groups believe that a fertilized egg is a human life from

the moment of conception and that any abortion is a murder. Pro-choice groups distinguish between stages of fetal development and argue that a woman should make the final decision regarding her pregnancy.

- Overall public opinion in the United States supports legal abortion in at least some circumstances and opposes overturning *Roe v. Wade*. Opinion changes according to individual situations.

- Most people agree that abortions performed late in pregnancy present personal, medical, philosophical, and social problems.

- The woman considering abortion must think about her own religious and moral beliefs, her long-range reactions, support from others, and the cost and availability of the procedure.

- In suction curettage, the preferred method of abortion from the 6th to the 12th week of pregnancy, an electric pump is used to remove the uterine contents; also, the physician scrapes the uterine lining with a metal curette.

- Manual vacuum aspiration is the aspiration of the uterine contents using suction provided by a handheld syringe.

- The most common abortion method after the first trimester is dilation and evacuation (D & E), in which the uterus is emptied using aspiration and surgical instruments.

- Intact dilation and extraction and labor induction are rarely used methods of late-term abortion. The intact dilation and extraction method became illegal in 2007, following a Supreme Court ruling.

- Multi-fetal pregnancy reduction (MFPR) is a method of abortion used to reduce the number of fetuses in a multiple-fetus pregnancy.

- Medical abortion is performed with a combination of drugs very early in pregnancy; drugs used include mifepristone, misoprostol, and methotrexate.

- Physical complications following abortion can be minimized by overall good patient health, early timing, use of the suction method, a well-trained physician, and follow-up care.

- Psychological aftereffects of abortion vary with the individual. Many women go through a period of ambivalence; the strongest feelings usually occur immediately after the abortion. Having a supportive partner, friend, and/or family member can be helpful.

FOR MORE INFORMATION

BOOKS

Adamec, C. A., and L. C. Miller. 2006. *The Encyclopedia of Adoption* (Facts on File Library of Health and Living), 3rd ed. New York: Facts on File, Inc. *Covers a wide range of adoption-related issues, such* as gay/lesbian adoptions, the rights of birth fathers, transracial adoptions, and international adoptions.

Alters, S. M., ed. 2008. *Abortion: An Eternal Social and Moral Issue.* Farmington Hills, Mich.: Gale Cengage. *A brief reference outlining legal, political, and ethical issues.*

Davenport, D. 2006. *The Complete Book of International Adoption.* New York: Broadway Books. *A detailed look at the process of adopting children from different countries.*

National Abortion and Reproductive Rights Action League Foundation. 2008. *Who Decides? A State-by-State Review of Abortion and Reproductive Rights.* Washington, D.C.: NARAL Foundation. *An in-depth annual review of the legal status of reproductive rights in the United States.*

ORGANIZATIONS AND WEB SITES

Child Welfare Information Gateway. A clearinghouse of information on many aspects of child-raising, including adoption.
    http://www.childwelfare.gov
Guttmacher Institute. Publishes books and fact sheets on reproductive health issues; its journal, *The Guttmacher Policy Review,* provides timely analysis of national reproductive health policy debates.
    http://www.guttmacher.org
Guttmacher Institute State Center. National and state-by-state analysis of public policies on reproductive rights and abortion.
    http://www.guttmacher.org/statecenter
MedlinePlus: Abortion. Managed by the National Library of Medicine and the National Institutes of Health, this site provides a list of informational resources on various aspects of abortion.
    http://www.nlm.nih.gov/medlineplus/abortion.html
National Abortion and Reproductive Rights Action League. Provides information on the politics of the pro-choice movement. Also provides information on the abortion laws and politics in each state.
    http://www.naral.org
National Abortion Federation. Provides information and resources on the medical and political issues relating to abortion; managed by health care providers.
    http://www.prochoice.org
National Adoption Center. A national agency focused on finding adoptive homes for children with special needs or who are currently in foster care.
    http://www.adopt.org
National Right to Life Committee. Provides information on alternatives to abortion and the politics of the pro-life movement.
    http://www.nrlc.org
Planned Parenthood Federation of America. Provides information on family planning, contraception, and abortion and provides counseling services.
    http://www.plannedparenthood.org.

See also the listings for Chapters 5, 6, and 8.

SELECTED BIBLIOGRAPHY

Ashok, P. W., et al. 2005. Patient preference in a randomized study comparing medical and surgical abortion at 10–13 weeks gestation. *Contraception* 71(2): 143–148.

Beral, V., et al. 2004. Breast cancer and abortion: Collaborative reanalysis of data from 53 epidemiological studies, including 83,000 women with breast cancer from 16 countries. *Lancet* 363(9414): 1007–1016.

Boonstra, H., et al. 2006. *Abortion in Women's Lives.* New York: Guttmacher Institute.

Broen, A. N., et al. 2006. Predictors of anxiety and depression following pregnancy termination: A longitudinal five-year follow-up study. *Acta Obstetricia et Gynecologica Scandinavica* 85(3): 317–323.

Centers for Disease Control and Prevention. 2005. *Clostridium sordellii* toxic shock syndrome after medical abortion with mifepristone and intravaginal misoprostol—United States and Canada, 2001–2005. *Morbidity and Mortality Weekly Report* 54 (29): 724.

Chen A., et al. 2004. Mifepristone-induced early abortion and outcome of subsequent wanted pregnancy. *American Juornal of Epidemiology* 160(2): 110–117.

Cohen, A. L., et al. 2007. Toxic shock associated with *Clostridium sordellii* and *Clostridium perfringens* after medical and spontaneous abortion. *Obstetrics and Gynecology* 110(5): 1027–1033.

Cohen, S. A. 2007. New Data on Abortion Incidence, Safety Illuminate Key Aspects of Worldwide Abortion Debate. *Guttmacher Policy Review* 10(4): 2–5.

Derbyshire, S. W. G. 2006. Can fetuses feel pain? *British Medical Journal* 332(7546): 909–912.

Espey, E., et al. 2005. Abortion education in medical schools: A national survey. *American Journal of Obstetrics and Gynecology* 192(2): 640–643.

Fiala, C., and K. Gemzel-Danielsson. 2006. Review of medical abortion using mifepristone in combination with a prostaglandin analogue. *Contraception* 74(1): 66–86.

Finer, L. B., and S. K. Henshaw. 2006. Disparities in rates of unintended pregnancy in the United States, 1994 and 2001. *Perspectives on Sexual and Reproductive Health* 38(2): 90–96.

Fischer, M., et al. 2005. Fatal toxic shock syndrome associated with *Clostridium sordellii* after medical abortion. *New England Journal of Medicine* 353(22): 2352–2360.

Goldberg, A. B., et al. 2004. Manual versus electric vacuum aspiration for early first-trimester abortion: A controlled study of complication rates. *Obstetrics and Gynecology* 103(1): 101–107.

Grimes, D. A. 2006. Estimation of pregnancy-related mortality risk by pregnancy outcome, United States, 1991 to 1999. *American Journal of Obstetrics and Gynecology* 194(1): 92–94.

Grimes, D. A., et al. 2006. Unsafe Abortion: The preventable pandemic. *Lancet* 368: 908–919.

Guttmacher Institute. 2008. *Facts on Induced Abortion in the United States.* (http://www.guttmacher.org/pubs/fb_induced_abortion.html; retrieved February 3, 2009).

Guttmacher Institute. 2009. *An Overview of Abortion Laws: State Policies in Brief* (http://www.guttmacher.org/statecenter/spibs/spib_OAL.pdf; retrieved February 3, 2009).

Henshaw, S. K., and L. B. Finer. 2003. 13th Survey of all known U.S. abortion providers by AGI. *Perspectives on Sexual and Reproductive Health* 35(1): 6–15.

Ho, P. C. 2006. Women's perceptions on medical abortion. *Contraception* 74(1): 11–15.

International Planned Parenthood. 2007. *The Health Dangers of Unsafe Abortion* (http://www.ippf.org/en/Resources/Articles/The+health+dangers+of+unsafe+abortion.htm; retrieved February 3, 2009).

Niinimaki, M., et al. 2006. A randomized study comparing efficacy and patient satisfaction in medical or surgical treatment of miscarriage. *Fertility and Sterility* 86(2): 367–372.

Planned Parenthood. 2007. *Abortion After the First Trimester in the United States* (http://www.plannedparenthood.org/news-articles-press/politics-policy-issues/abortion-access/trimester-abortion-6140.htm; retrieved February 3, 2009).

Rorbye, D., M. Norgaard, and L. Nilas. 2005. Medical versus surgical abortion: Comparing satisfaction and potential confounders in a partly randomized study. *Human Reproduction* 20(3): 834–838.

Sedgh, G., et al. 2007. Induced abortion: Estimated rates and trends worldwide. *Lancet* 379: 1338–1345.

Sit, D., et al. 2007. Psychiatric outcomes following medical and surgical abortion. *Human Reproduction* 22(3):878–884.

Strauss, L. T., et al. 2006. Abortion surveillance—United States, 2003. *Morbidity and Mortality Weekly Report* 55(SS-11): 1–32.

Van de Velde, M., et al. 2006. Fetal pain perception and pain management. *Seminars in Fetal and Neonatal Medicine* 11(4): 232–236.

PREGNANCY AND CHILDBIRTH

8

LOOKING AHEAD >>>>>

AFTER READING THIS CHAPTER, YOU SHOULD BE ABLE TO:

- List key issues to consider when deciding about parenthood
- Explain the process of conception, and describe the most common causes and treatments for infertility
- Describe the physical and emotional changes a pregnant woman typically experiences
- Discuss the stages of fetal development
- List the important components of good prenatal care
- Describe the process of labor and delivery

TEST YOUR KNOWLEDGE

1. **What is the approximate annual cost of raising one child?**
   a. $5,500–$11,000
   b. $8,250–$16,500
   c. $11,000–$22,000

2. **What is the leading cause of female infertility?**
   a. growths in the uterus
   b. exposure to radiation
   c. tubal factors such as blockages and previous infection

3. **Before conception and in the early weeks of pregnancy, adequate intake of which of the following nutrients can reduce the risk of spina bifida and other neural tube defects?**
   a. iron
   b. folic acid
   c. calcium

4. **Cigarette smoking before or during pregnancy is linked to which of the following?**
   a. congenital anomalies
   b. low birth weight
   c. miscarriage
   d. central nervous system defects

ANSWERS

1. **C.** According to the U.S. Department of Agriculture, a two-parent family will spend from $11,000 to $22,000 per year, depending on the family's income level, to raise a single child to age 18.

2. **C.** If left untreated, the STDs gonorrhea and chlamydia can lead to tubal scarring and blockage.

3. **B.** It is recommended that all reproductive-age women consume 400 µg of folic acid from fortified foods and/or supplements each day to reduce the risk of spina bifida and other neural tube defects.

4. **ALL FOUR.** Maternal smoking during pregnancy is associated with many types of birth defects and low birth weight. Lower measured intelligence levels and increased frequencies of behavioral and psychological abnormalities have been reported in children and adults whose mothers smoked cigarettes during pregnancy. Also, the risk of having a miscarriage is 20–80% higher among women who smoke cigarettes during pregnancy.

Deciding whether to become a parent is one of the most important choices a person can ever make. Yet many people approach this decision with only a vague notion of what is involved in pregnancy and childbirth. This may help explain why about half of the more than 4.2 million babies born every year in the United States are from unintentional pregnancies.

Previous generations of Americans assumed that virtually every married couple would have children. Today, however, with changing cultural expectations and more sophisticated contraceptive technology, you can choose whether and when to have a child. As a result of these changes, the average age of first-time mothers in the United States has increased steadily, from 21.4 years in 1970 to 25.0 years in 2006.

The more you know about conception and pregnancy, fetal development and prenatal care, childbirth and parenting, the more capable you will be of making intelligent, informed decisions about them. This chapter presents information you can use both now and later in your life to make the choices about pregnancy and childbirth that are right for you.

PREPARATION FOR PARENTHOOD

Before you decide whether or when to become a parent, you should consider your suitability and readiness. If you elect to have a child, there are actions you can take before the pregnancy begins to help ensure a healthy outcome for all.

Deciding to Become a Parent

Many factors must be taken into account when you are considering parenthood. Some issues are relevant to both men and women; others apply only to women.

Health and Age   Generally speaking, healthier women tend to have more trouble-free pregnancies and healthier babies. Women who are considering motherhood should see their doctor for a complete medical checkup to catch problems that might interfere with pregnancy or childbirth. For example, high blood pressure and diabetes may require ongoing attention; if uncontrolled, these health problems can pose life-threatening dangers to mother or child.

A mother's age can also be a factor in pregnancy and childbirth. Teenagers and women over age 35 have a higher incidence of certain problems that can affect the health of both mother and baby. In fact, most experts automatically classify a pregnancy as "high-risk" if the mother is over age 30, especially if it is her first pregnancy.

Emotional Preparedness   Just as they need to be physically prepared, parents also need to be emotionally ready to have a child. A new baby is totally helpless and relies on adults for everything. For parents, this means being strong and stable enough to handle the responsibility and being mature enough to give up certain freedoms in order to care for a child.

Financial Circumstances   Parenthood is financially draining, even for families with steady incomes and health insurance. According to a 2008 report from the U.S. Department of Agriculture, a two-parent family will spend from $11,000 to $22,000 per year, depending on the family's income level, to raise an only child to age 18. The expense increases about 77% with each additional child.

Table 8.1 shows the average annual cost of raising the younger child in a family with two children, based on the family's average annual income range. These figures do not include the costs of a private education or college.

If you are planning to have a child, try to make sure you are prepared financially—especially during the first few years, when the costs of diapers, furniture, pediatrician visits, and other necessities quickly add up. It makes good sense for all expecting parents to consult with a financial planner, regardless of income level. A qualified financial planner can help new parents see their larger financial picture and focus on issues such as taxes, insurance needs, and saving for long-term goals as well as emergencies.

Relationships   The stress and expense of child rearing can strain any relationship, even a healthy one. This is why it is important for couples to plan for parenting. Through open, honest discussion, partners should make sure they are both ready to take the step of having a child. Both should be equally committed to parenthood and agree on matters of child care, housework, and other day-to-day responsibilities. Couples with relationship problems should work together to resolve their issues—with professional help, if necessary—before adding a child to the mix.

New parents also need a strong support network of friends and family members who can lend a hand when things get tough. Many first-time parents count on their own parents and siblings for aid with child care or household chores. It can be easy, however, to alienate family and friends with too many requests for assistance. To avoid this problem, parents-to-be should include members of their support network in the planning process, to figure out who will be able to help, in what ways, and at what times.

Future Plans   Having a child can put other life plans on hold, especially if the pregnancy is unintended. Anyone considering parenthood should make sure that it will fit

Table 8.1	Average Per-Year Cost of Raising a Second Child: 2007		
	Before-Tax Income		
Child's Age	Less Than $45,800	45,800– $77,100	More Than $77,100
0–2	$7,830	$10,960	$16,290
3–5	$8,020	$11,280	$16,670
6–8	$8,000	$11,130	$16,310
9–11	$7,950	$10,930	$15,980
12–14	$8,830	$11,690	$16,810
15–17	$8,810	$12,030	$17,500
Total	$148,320	$204,060	$298,680

SOURCE: Lino, Mark. 2008. *Expenditures on Children by Families, 2007.* U.S. Department of Agriculture, Center for Nutrition Policy and Promotion. Miscellaneous Publication No. 1528-2007.

with other goals. Otherwise, it may be necessary to postpone or cancel educational or career plans.

An important aspect of this planning is child care. New parents should figure out whether they will need child care services (such as a day-care center or a private caregiver) in order to work or attend school. The cost and availability of such services can be a deciding factor in determining whether parents can pursue their future plans. According to a 2008 report from the National Association of Child Care Resource and Referral Agencies (NACCRRA), day-care costs for an infant in the United States range from $4,542 to $14,591 a year ($379 to $1,216 monthly).

Attitude and Aptitude   Before having a child, it's important for parents to recognize whether they have the right attitude about child rearing. If one parent is devoted to a child but the other views parenting as a burden, the partnership and the child will suffer. Before deciding to become a parent, it's a good idea to spend time with young children and see how you respond to them. It is also wise to talk to people who have raised children, and see if their experiences strike a positive chord in you.

Parents-to-be should also ask themselves how much they know about caring for a child and seek help according to their needs. Certain skills—such as diaper changing, bathing, and feeding—are essential but easy to learn and quickly become routine with a little practice. Other important parenting attributes, such as patience and the ability to stay calm in a crisis, aren't easily acquired if you don't already have them.

Luckily, there are many good sources of information for first-time parents. The best place to start is a family physician or pediatrician. Many hospitals offer free or low-cost classes on labor, delivery, breastfeeding, and basic child care for expecting parents. In many communities, organizations pair new parents with experienced ones who can act as mentors and provide advice and guidance on many child-rearing issues.

Beliefs   Some people question the value of bringing more people into an already overcrowded world. They feel that humans have already fulfilled the biblical directive to be fruitful and multiply. People with such concerns may feel more comfortable with the decision not to have children.

Preconception Care

The birth of a healthy baby depends in part on the mother's overall wellness *before* conception. The U.S. Public Health Service recommends that all women receive health care to help them prepare for pregnancy. **Preconception care** should include an assessment of health risks, the promotion of healthy lifestyle behaviors, and any treatments necessary to reduce risk. Following are some of the issues, tests, and treatments you and your partner may encounter during preconception care:

- *Preexisting conditions.* Medical conditions such as diabetes, epilepsy, asthma, high blood pressure, and anemia can cause problems during pregnancy. These conditions should be treated and monitored throughout pregnancy.

- *Medications.* Some medications and dietary supplements harm the **fetus** (the unborn baby from the 9th week after conception to the moment of birth), so a pregnant woman may need to change or stop taking certain drugs.

- *Prior pregnancies.* Problems with previous pregnancies or deliveries—such as miscarriage, premature birth, or delivery complications—may be due to a treatable physical condition.

- *Age.* As mentioned earlier, a woman's age may place her at risk for certain problems during pregnancy. A pregnant teenager, for example, may require special nutrition to meet her own growing body's needs and those of her baby. A woman over age 35 may need genetic

preconception care   Health care in preparation for pregnancy.

fetus   The developmental stage of a human from the 9th week after conception to the moment of birth.

TERMS

testing due to the increased risk of her baby's developing Down syndrome.

- **Tobacco, alcohol, and caffeine use.** These substances can harm a developing fetus. Women who smoke, drink, or consume caffeine should stop before becoming pregnant. (See Chapters 9–11 for more information on these and other substances.)

- **Infections.** A woman who has any type of infection should be treated for the infection before getting pregnant, if possible. This is good advice for men, too, to avoid transmitting an infection to their partner. A woman may need to be vaccinated against hepatitis B, rubella (German measles), varicella (chicken pox), and other communicable diseases if she is at risk for them. Testing for tuberculosis and some STDs can ensure treatment prior to pregnancy. (See Chapter 17 for more on infectious diseases.)

- **HIV.** Any woman who is at risk of HIV infection should be tested before getting pregnant; her partner should be tested, as well. (See Chapter 18 for more on HIV and AIDS.)

- **Diet.** Good nutrition is essential to a healthy pregnancy. Nutritional counseling can help a woman create a plan for healthy eating before and during pregnancy. Diet is especially important for any woman with special nutritional needs or an eating disorder, or who is overweight or obese. Physicians commonly prescribe prenatal vitamin supplements to pregnant women. The U.S. Public Health Service recommends that all women of childbearing age take extra folic acid to reduce the risk of neural tube defects that can arise in the fetus. (See Chapter 12 for more information on nutrition.)

- **DES.** From the 1940s to the early 1970s, many pregnant women were given a drug called diethylstilbestrol (DES) to prevent miscarriage. Daughters

of those women are at risk for a variety of problems with conception and pregnancy. These woman may need special monitoring and care.

- **Multiple births.** If twins or multiple births run in a woman's family, she is more likely to have multiple births, too. Multiple births are also more prevalent in mothers who are obese, over 40, or using certain reproductive technologies to get pregnant.

- **Genetic diseases.** If either partner has a family history of any genetic disease, then genetic counseling may be in order before pregnancy. Genetic testing can determine whether the mother or father is a carrier for a specific disease. With counseling, a couple can decide how best to deal with the possibility of transferring a disease to a child. Members of some ethnic groups are at higher risk for genetic disorders; for more information on these disorders, see the box "Ethnicity and Genetic Diseases."

Additional tests or changes in behavior may be recommended for prospective parents who have recently traveled outside the United States; work with chemicals, radiation, or toxic substances; participate in physically demanding or hazardous activities or occupations; or face significant psychosocial risks, including homelessness, an unsafe home environment, or mental illness.

UNDERSTANDING FERTILITY

Conceiving a child is a highly complex process. Although many couples conceive readily, others can testify to the difficulties that can be encountered.

Conception

The process of conception involves the **fertilization** of an ovum (egg) from a woman by a sperm from a man (Figure 8.1 on p. 206). Every month during a woman's fertile years, her body prepares itself for conception and pregnancy. In one of her ovaries an egg matures and is released from its follicle. The egg, about the size of a pinpoint, travels through an oviduct, or fallopian tube, to the uterus in 3–4 days. The endometrium, or lining of the uterus, has already thickened for the implantation of a **fertilized egg,** or *zygote*. If the egg is not fertilized, it lasts about 24 hours and then disintegrates. It is expelled along with the uterine lining during menstruation.

Sperm cells are produced in the man's testes and ejaculated from his penis into the woman's vagina during sexual intercourse (except in cases of artificial insemination or assisted reproduction; see p. 208). Sperm cells are much smaller than eggs. The typical ejaculate contains millions of sperm, but only a few complete the journey through the uterus and up the fallopian tube to the egg. Many sperm cells do not survive the acidic environment of the vagina.

QUESTIONS FOR CRITICAL THINKING AND REFLECTION

If you don't have children now, do you plan to have them someday? Have you given any thought to the skills and qualities that make a good parent? Given what you know about yourself today, do you think you will make a good parent? What skills or qualities do you think you need to develop?

TERMS

fertilization   The initiation of biological reproduction: the union of the nucleus of an egg cell with the nucleus of a sperm cell.

fertilized egg   The egg after penetration by a sperm; a *zygote*.

Ethnicity and Genetic Diseases

Genes carry the chemical instructions that determine the development of hundreds of individual traits, including disease risks, in every human being. Many traits and conditions involve multiple genes and environmental influences. Some diseases, however, can be traced to a mutation in a single gene.

Children inherit one set of genes from each parent. If only one copy of an abnormal gene is necessary to produce a disease, then it is called a *dominant* gene. Diseases caused by dominant genes seldom skip a generation; anyone who carries the gene will probably get the disease.

If two copies of an abnormal gene (one from each parent) are necessary for a disease to occur, then the gene is called *recessive.* Many diseases caused by recessive genes occur disproportionately in certain ethnic groups. Prospective parents who come from the same ethnic group can be tested for any recessive diseases that are known to occur in that group. If both parents are carriers, each of their children will have about a 25% chance of developing the disease.

The following list describes a few common conditions with proven genetic links in certain ethnic populations. If there is a history of any of these conditions in your family and you plan to have children, genetic tests and counseling can help assess the risk to your prospective offspring.

• *Sickle-cell disease* occurs in about 1 out of every 500 African American births and in 1 out of every 36,000 Hispanic American births, according to the CDC. In this disease, red blood cells, which carry oxygen to the body's tissues, change shape; the normally disc-shaped cells become sickle-shaped. The altered cells carry less oxygen and can block small blood vessels.

People who inherit one gene for sickle-cell disease (about 1 in 12 African Americans) experience only mild symptoms; those with two genes become severely, often fatally, ill.

If you are at risk for sickle-cell disease, you should take care to reduce stress and respond to minor infections, because red blood cells become sickle-shaped when the body is under stress. You should also have regular checkups and appropriate treatment, if required.

• *Hemochromatosis* ("iron overload") affects about 1 in 200 people. At highest risk are people of Northern European (especially Irish), Mediterranean, and Hispanic descent. In hemochromatosis, the body absorbs and stores up to ten times the normal amount of iron. Iron deposits form in the joints, liver, heart, and pancreas. If untreated, the disease can cause organ failure and death.

Early symptoms are often vague and include weakness, lethargy, darkening of the skin, and joint pain. Early detection and treatment are necessary to prevent damage. Treatment involves reducing iron stores by removing blood from the body (a process known as phlebotomy or "bloodletting").

• *Tay-Sachs disease*, another recessive disorder, occurs in about 1 in 3000 Jews of Eastern European ancestry. People with Tay-Sachs disease cannot properly metabolize fat. As a result, the brain and other nerve tissues deteriorate. Affected children show weakness in their movements and eventually develop blindness (by age 12–18 months) and seizures. This disease is fatal, and death usually occurs by age 6. No effective treatment is currently available.

• *Cystic fibrosis* occurs in 1 in 2500–3000 Caucasians; about 1 in 29 carries one copy of the cystic fibrosis gene. Because essential enzymes of the pancreas are deficient, the body cannot properly absorb nutrients. Thick mucus impairs functioning in the lungs and intestinal tracts of people with this disease. Cystic fibrosis is often fatal in early childhood, but treatments are increasingly effective in reducing symptoms and prolonging life. In some cases, symptoms do not appear until early adulthood.

• *Thalassemia* is a blood disease found most often among Italians, Greeks, and to a lesser extent African Americans and Asians. When inherited from one parent, this form of anemia is mild; when two genes are present, the disease is severe and can cause fetal death.

Children with this condition require repeated blood transfusions, eventually resulting in a damaging iron buildup. New interventions, such as genetic engineering, bone marrow transplants, and chemicals that bind with excess iron and remove it from the body, offer promise. Transplantation of stem cells from the umbilical cord blood of an unaffected sibling or donor is already being used in some cases.

If you are at risk of carrying thalassemia, you should get regular checkups and monitor your health for symptoms, and learn ways to manage symptoms if they start to occur.

• *Lactose intolerance*, or intolerance to lactose-containing foods (primarily dairy products), is a common problem that often has a genetic component. In Europe and the United States, the prevalence is as high as 20% in Caucasians, 80–95% in Native Americans, 65–75% among Africans and African Americans, and 50% in Hispanics. The prevalence exceeds 90% in some populations in eastern Asia.

Clinical symptoms of lactose intolerance include diarrhea, abdominal pain, and flatulence after ingestion of milk or milk-containing products. These symptoms result from low intestinal lactase levels, which are commonly due to the reduced genetic expression of the enzyme lactase-phlorizin hydrolase. Genetically regulated reduction of lactase activity determined by racial or ethnic factors is the underlying mechanism of lactose malabsorption in healthy individuals.

If you suspect lactose intolerance, see your doctor for a lactose absorption test. In the absence of a correctable underlying disease, lactose malabsorption is treated by reducing lactose intake, finding alternatives to foods containing lactose, taking an enzyme substitute, and maintaining calcium and vitamin D intake.

Other health problems that have a hereditary component and that disproportionately affect certain ethnic groups include diabetes, osteoporosis, high blood pressure, alcoholism, and certain cancers. Later chapters discuss many of these links.

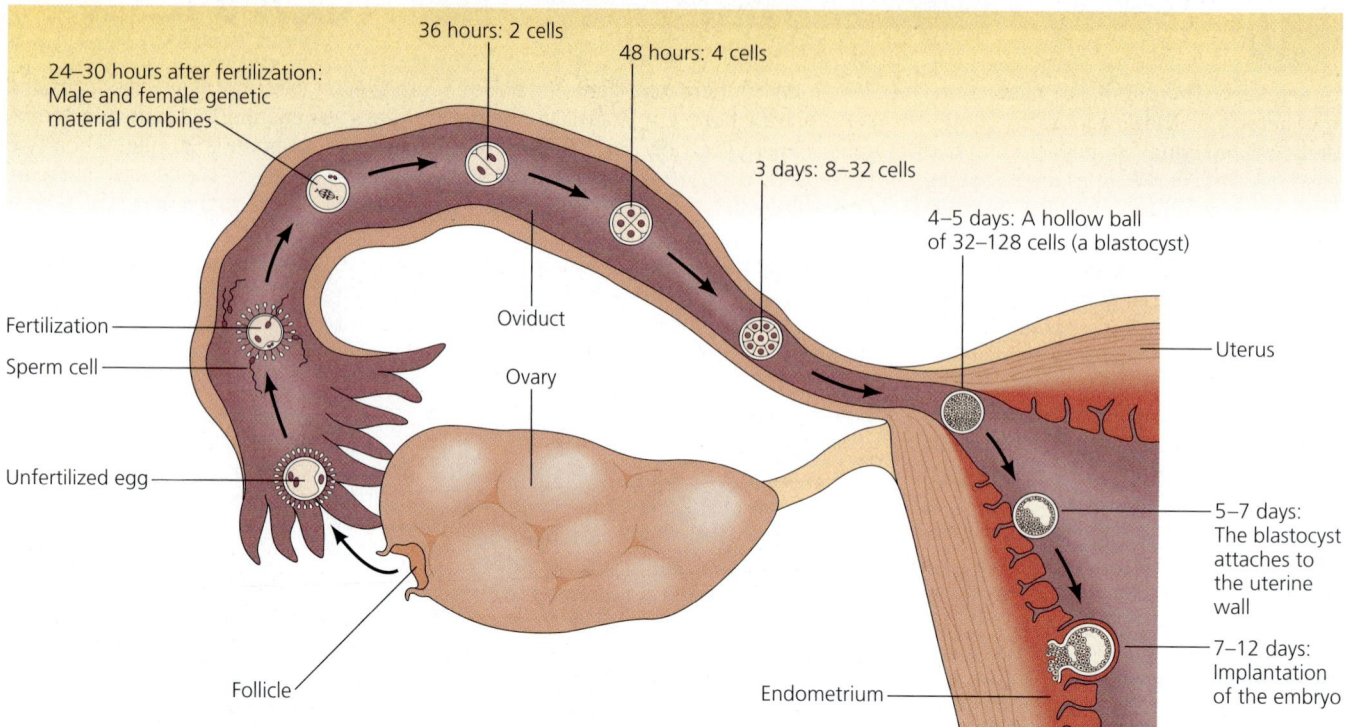

24–30 hours after fertilization: Male and female genetic material combines

36 hours: 2 cells

48 hours: 4 cells

3 days: 8–32 cells

4–5 days: A hollow ball of 32–128 cells (a blastocyst)

Fertilization

Sperm cell

Unfertilized egg

Follicle

Oviduct

Ovary

Uterus

Endometrium

5–7 days: The blastocyst attaches to the uterine wall

7–12 days: Implantation of the embryo

FIGURE 8.1 **Fertilization and early development of the embryo.**

Once through the cervix and into the uterus, many sperm cells are diverted to the wrong oviduct or get stuck along the way. Of those that reach the egg, only one will penetrate its hard outer layer. As sperm approach the egg, they release enzymes that soften this outer layer. Enzymes from hundreds of sperm must be released in order for the egg's outer layer to soften enough to allow one sperm cell to penetrate. The first sperm cell that bumps into a spot that is soft enough can swim into the egg cell. It then merges with the nucleus of the egg, and fertilization occurs. The sperm's tail, its means of locomotion, gets stuck in the outer membrane and drops off, leaving the sperm head inside the egg. The egg then releases a chemical that makes it impenetrable by other sperm.

The ovum carries the hereditary characteristics of the mother and her ancestors; sperm cells carry the hereditary characteristics of the father and his ancestors. Each parent cell—egg or sperm—contains 23 chromosomes, each of which contains **genes**, packages of chemical in-

structions for the developing baby. Genes provide the blueprint for a unique individual (see the box "Creating a Family Health Tree").

As soon as fertilization occurs, the zygote starts to undergo the cell division that begins the growth process. It continues to divide as it travels through the oviduct to the uterus. Upon reaching the uterus, the cluster of cells, now called a *blastocyst*, becomes implanted in the endometrium.

The usual course of events is that one egg and one sperm unite to produce one fertilized egg and one baby. But if the ovaries release two (or more) eggs during ovulation and if both eggs are fertilized, twins will develop. These twins will be no more alike than siblings from different pregnancies, because each will have come from a different fertilized egg. Twins who develop this way are referred to as **fraternal twins**; they may be the same sex or different sexes. About 70% of twins are fraternal. Twins can also develop from the division of a single fertilized egg into two cells that develop separately. Because these babies share all genetic material, they will be **identical twins.** The most serious complication of multiple births is preterm delivery (delivery before the fetus is adequately mature). Studies show that the more fetuses a woman carries simultaneously, the shorter the gestational period will be.

Infertility

Millions of couples have difficulty conceiving. **Infertility** is defined as the inability to conceive after trying for a year or more. It affects about 15% of the reproductive-age

TERMS

gene The basic unit of heredity; a section of a chromosone containing chemical instructions for making a particular protein.

fraternal twins Twins who develop from separate fertilized eggs; not genetically identical.

identical twins Twins who develop from the division of a single zygote; genetically identical.

infertility The inability to conceive after trying for a year or more.

Creating a Family Health Tree

The genetic inheritance that each of us receives from our parents—and that our children receive from us—contains more than just physical characteristics, such as eye and hair color. Heredity also contributes to our risk of developing certain diseases and disorders. For certain uncommon illnesses such as hemophilia and sickle-cell disease, heredity is the primary cause; if your parents pass on the necessary genes, you'll get the disease. But heredity plays a subtler role in many other diseases, which are caused at least in part by environmental influences such as infection, cancer-causing chemicals, and physical inactivity. Although your genes alone will not produce those diseases, they can determine how susceptible you are. Researchers have found a genetic influence in many common disorders, including heart disease, diabetes, depression, asthma, alcoholism, and certain forms of cancer.

Knowing that a specific disease runs in your family can save your life. It allows you to watch for early warning signs and get screening tests more often than you otherwise would. Changing health habits, too, can be valuable for people with a family history of certain diseases. An individual with a family history of high cholesterol and early heart disease can increase physical activity and pay special attention to diet.

In general, the more relatives with a genetically transmitted disease and the closer they are to you, the greater your risk. However, nongenetic factors—such as health habits—can also play a role. Signs of strong hereditary influence include early onset of the disease, appearance of the disease largely or exclusively on one side of the family, onset of the same disease at the same age in more than one relative, and developing the disease despite good health habits.

You can put together a simple family health tree by compiling a few key facts on your primary relatives: siblings, parents, aunts and uncles, and grandparents. Those facts include the date of birth, major diseases, health-related conditions and habits, and, for deceased relatives, the age at death as well as the cause. Because certain diseases are more common in particular ethnic groups, also record the ethnic background of each grandparent. Next, create a tree, using the example here as a guide. Then show your tree to a physician or genetic counselor, who can help you target the health behaviors and screening tests that are most important for you and help you determine whether genetic testing might be appropriate.

A Sample Family Health Tree and What It Means

The 55-year-old woman who prepared this family tree has a strong family history of osteoporosis on her mother's side. Based on this, her physician may suggest a bone density test to help gauge her risk and recommend bone-healthy lifestyle changes. She also has several close relatives on her father's side of the family who had high cholesterol levels and had heart attacks at an early age. These risk factors significantly increase her chance of having a heart attack.

The woman has two aunts who died of breast cancer, but there are several reasons not to be overly concerned. Aunts are second-degree relatives, more distantly related to her than her mother or sister (first-degree relatives). In addition, they came from different sides of the family, and they developed the disease quite late in life. Given these factors, it is likely that these cases of breast cancer did not have a significant genetic origin.

Looking at her family history can help this woman make important decisions about behaviors such as moderate alcohol consumption, which may lower the risk of heart attack but which may also slightly increase the risk of breast cancer. Based on her family history, her physician may recommend bone density testing to determine her risk of dangerous fractures and recommend medication and a heart-healthy diet to reduce her unhealthy cholesterol level and overall heart attack risk.

SOURCES: From "Prepare for the Future: Know Your Ancestors" and "Creating a Family Health Tree" © 1999 by Consumers Union of U.S., Inc. Yonkers, NY 10703-1057, a nonprofit organization. Reprinted with permission from the September 1999 issue of *Consumer Reports on Health*® for educational purposes only. No commercial use or reproduction permitted. www.ConsumerReports.org.

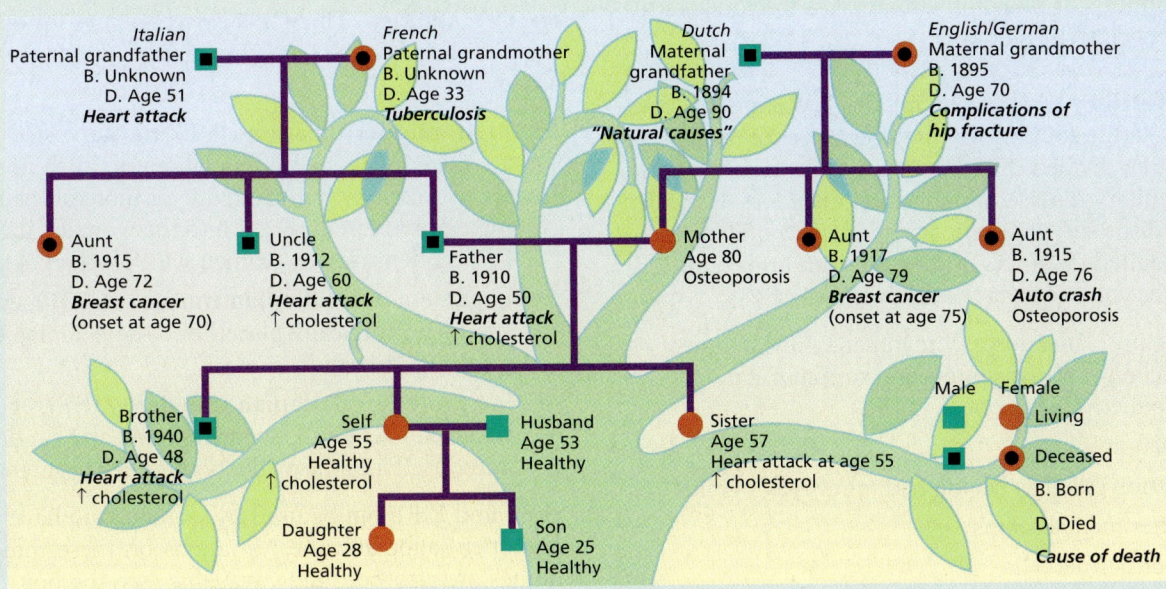

137,085 twins were born in the United States in 2006.

—CDC, 2009

population of the United States. Over a million couples seek treatment for infertility each year. Although the focus is often on women (where the cause of infertility is found in 40% of cases), 20% of the factors contributing to infertility are male, and in 30% of infertile couples, both partners have problems. Therefore, it is important that each individual be evaluated.

Female Infertility   Female infertility usually results from one of two key causes—tubal blockage (40%) or failure to ovulate (40%). An additional 10% of cases of infertility are due to anatomical abnormalities, benign growths in the uterus, thyroid disease, and other uncommon conditions; the remaining 10% of cases are unexplained.

Blocked fallopian tubes are most commonly the result of *pelvic inflammatory disease (PID),* a serious complication of several sexually transmitted diseases. Each year, PID renders more than 100,000 American women infertile. Most cases of PID are associated with untreated cases of chlamydia or gonorrhea. More than 1 million cases of PID are treated each year, but physicians estimate that just as many may go untreated because of an absence of symptoms. Tubal blockages can also be caused by prior surgery or by *endometriosis,* a condition in which endometrial (uterine) tissue grows outside of the uterus. This tissue responds to hormones and can cause pelvic pain, bleeding, scarring, and adhesions. Endometriosis is typically treated with hormonal therapy and surgery.

Age impacts fertility; beginning at around age 30, a woman's fertility naturally begins to decline. Age is probably the main factor in ovulation failure. Exposure to toxic chemicals or radiation also appears to reduce fertility, as does cigarette smoking.

Male Infertility   Male factor infertility accounts for about 20% of infertile couples. The leading causes of male infertility can be divided into four main categories: hypothalamic pituitary disease or congenital disorders, testicular disease, disorders of sperm transport, and unexplained. Some acquired disorders of the testes can lead to infertility, such as damage from the following causes:

- Drug use (large doses of marijuana, for example, cause lower sperm counts and suppress certain reproductive hormones)
- Radiation
- Infection (such as having had mumps as a child)
- Environmental toxins
- Hyperthermia
- Smoking

The sons of mothers who took DES may have increased sperm abnormalities and fertility problems. Studies have identified a link between infertility and overweight and obesity in men, although the mechanism responsible for the relationship was not clear.

Treating Infertility   The cause of infertility can be determined for about 85% of infertile couples. Most cases of infertility are treated with conventional medical therapies. Surgery can repair oviducts, clear up endometriosis, and correct anatomical problems in both men and women. Fertility drugs can help women ovulate, although they may cause multiple births. If these conventional treatments don't work, couples can turn to **assisted reproductive technology (ART)** techniques, as described in the following sections.

Most infertility treatments are expensive and emotionally draining, however, and their success is hard to predict. Some infertile couples choose not to try to have children, whereas others turn to adoption. One measure you can take now to avoid infertility is to protect yourself against STDs and to treat promptly and completely any disease you do contract. Also, couples who are ready should consider trying to conceive prior to the woman's late 30s to decrease the probability of age-related infertility.

INTRAUTERINE INSEMINATION   Male infertility can sometimes be overcome by collecting and concentrating the man's sperm and introducing it by syringe into a woman's vagina or uterus, a procedure known as **artificial (intrauterine) insemination.** To increase the probability of success, the woman is often given fertility drugs to induce ovulation prior to the insemination procedure. The sperm can be provided by the woman's partner or, if there are severe problems with his sperm or he carries a serious genetic disorder, by a donor. Donor sperm are also used by single women and lesbian couples who wish to conceive using artificial insemination. The success rate is about 60–70%.

IVF, GIFT, AND ZIFT   Three related techniques for overcoming infertility involve removing mature eggs from a woman's ovary.

- In **in vitro fertilization (IVF),** the harvested eggs are mixed with sperm in a laboratory dish. If eggs are successfully fertilized, one or more of the resulting embryos are inserted into the woman's uterus. IVF is often used by women with blocked oviducts.
- In **gamete intrafallopian transfer (GIFT),** eggs and sperm are surgically placed into the fallopian tubes prior to fertilization.
- In **zygote intrafallopian transfer (ZIFT),** eggs are fertilized outside the woman's body and surgically introduced into the oviducts after they begin to divide.

GIFT and ZIFT can be used by women who have at least one open fallopian tube. Variations on these three techniques are also becoming available (see the box "Reproductive Technology" on p. 210).

138,198 ART procedures were performed in the United States in 2006, resulting in more than 54,600 babies.

—CDC, 2009

major area of their lives. They may lose perspective on the rest of their lives as they focus more and more on the reasons for their infertility and on treatment. Infertile couples may need to set their own limits on how much treatment they are willing to undergo.

Support groups for infertile couples can provide help in this difficult situation, but there are few easy answers to infertility. If treatment is unsuccessful, couples must mourn the loss of the children they will never bear. They will need to make some kind of decision about their future—whether to pursue plans for adoption or another treatment or to adjust to childlessness and go on with their lives.

IVF, GIFT, and ZIFT have drawbacks. Success rates vary from about 27% to 51%. They cost between $8000 and $12,000 per procedure and may require five or more cycles to produce one live birth. They also increase the chance of multiple births, which in turn increases the risk of premature birth and maternal complications, including pregnancy-related hypertension and diabetes.

SURROGATE MOTHERHOOD   Surrogate motherhood involves a contract between an infertile couple and a fertile woman who agrees to carry a fetus. The surrogate mother agrees to be artificially inseminated by the father's sperm or to undergo IVF with the couple's embryo, to carry the baby to term, and to give it to the couple at birth. In return, the couple pays her for her services (typically around $50,000). There are thought to be several hundred births to surrogate mothers each year in the United States.

Emotional Responses to Infertility   Couples who seek treatment for infertility have often already confronted the possibility of not being able to become biological parents. Many infertile couples feel they have lost control over a

PREGNANCY

Pregnancy is usually discussed in terms of **trimesters**—three periods of about 3 months (or 13 weeks) each. During the first trimester, the mother experiences a few physical changes and some fairly common symptoms. During the second trimester, often the most peaceful time of pregnancy, the mother gains weight, looks noticeably pregnant, and may experience a general sense of well-being if she is happy about having a child. The third trimester is the hardest for the mother because she must breathe, digest, excrete, and circulate blood for herself and the growing fetus. The weight of the fetus, the pressure of its body on her organs, and its increased demands on her system cause discomfort and fatigue and may make the mother increasingly impatient to give birth.

assisted reproductive technology (ART)   Advanced medical techniques used to treat infertility.

artificial (intrauterine) insemination   The introduction of semen into the vagina by artificial means, usually by syringe.

in vitro fertilization (IVF)   Combining egg and sperm outside of the body and inserting the fertilized egg into the uterus.

gamete intrafallopian transfer (GIFT)   Surgically introducing eggs and sperm into the fallopian tube prior to fertilization.

zygote intrafallopian transfer (ZIFT)   Surgically introducing a fertilized egg into the fallopian tube.

trimester   One of the three 3-month periods of pregnancy.

TERMS

Reproductive Technology

Research into the areas of genetics and cloning promise more breakthroughs for ART treatments. Below are a few of the most advanced techniques currently in use and under study.

Use of donor eggs, donor sperm, and/or donor embryos is fairly common in ART treatments. The use of donor eggs and embryos has allowed women in their fifties to complete pregnancy and deliver a baby. The resulting offspring is no more genetically related to the woman than an adopted child would be. Use of ART in women of this age is controversial.

Intracytoplasmic sperm injection (ICSI), in which a single sperm is injected into a mature egg, was originally developed to overcome cases of severe male infertility; it is now used for a broader range of conditions. Some studies have linked ICSI to an increase in genetic and birth defects in offspring. In addition, ICSI allows men who are infertile due to Y chromosome defects to have children, even though any sons they have will inherit the defect and also be infertile.

Cryopreservation of ovarian tissue and/or unfertilized eggs has been studied as a possible means of preserving fertility in women undergoing cancer therapy. In 2004, the first woman gave birth after having ovarian tissue removed and frozen prior to cancer chemotherapy and then reimplanted. This technique could potentially be used in women who choose to delay childbearing.

Freezing embryos is common in ART because multiple eggs are usually harvested and fertilized during IVF. If the initial IVF cycle is unsuccessful, the backup embryos can be used for additional attempts. Once ART treatment is completed, couples may choose to donate leftover embryos for use by another infertile couple or to have them destroyed. A more controversial potential use of extra embryos is for the creation of stem cell lines (see Chapter 22).

Preimplantation genetic diagnosis, in which embryos created through IVF undergo genetic analysis before implantation in the womb, was originally developed to help couples at risk for genetic diseases. Some physicians now offer it for sex selection in couples who have no fertility problems. This is considered controversial because a particular gender isn't a disease that needs to be prevented, and there remains the difficult question of what becomes of the "wrong sex" embryos—freezing, donation, destruction, or use in research.

Injection of cytoplasm (the material in a cell that surrounds the nucleus) from a younger woman's egg into an older woman's egg can be used as a possible means of reducing genetic errors in the older woman's egg. These errors occur in so-called mitochondrial DNA, genetic material in the cytoplasm of the cell that is passed along unchanged to offspring.

Nuclear transfer, a technique related to cytoplasm injection, uses cloning technology—the transfer of the nucleus from an older woman's egg into an egg from a younger woman from which the nucleus has been removed. In cytoplasm injection and nuclear transfer, the offspring carry

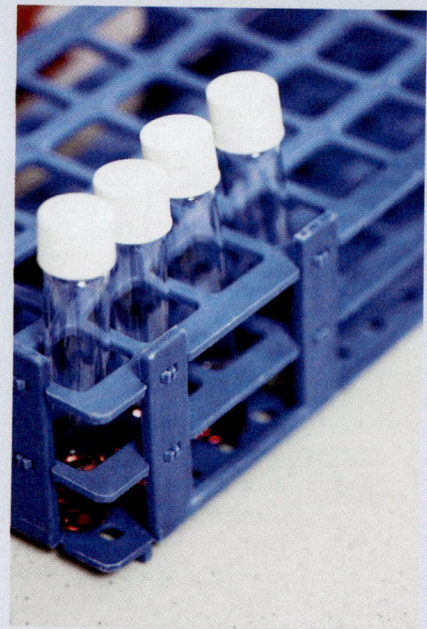

DNA from two women—nuclear DNA from one woman and mitochondrial DNA from a second woman—and so have three genetic "parents."

What about cloning? **Cloning** is different from any of the techniques discussed here because it is a form of asexual reproduction. A clone carries the genes of only one person, not two. However, as described above, the cloning technique of nuclear transfer could potentially be used in the treatment of infertility. Nuclear transfer could theoretically also be used to create a child that is the genetic offspring of two people of the same sex.

Pregnancy Tests

The earliest tests for pregnancy are chemical tests designed to detect the presence of **human chorionic gonadotropin (HCG)**, a hormone produced by the implanted fertilized egg. These tests may be performed as early as 2 weeks after fertilization.

Home pregnancy test kits, which are sold without a prescription in drugstores, include a small sample of red blood cells coated with HCG antibodies, to which the woman adds a small amount of her urine. If the concentration of HCG is great enough, it will clump together with the HCG antibodies, indicating that the woman is pregnant. Home pregnancy tests can be very reliable, but the instructions must be followed carefully. If a home test done at the time of a missed menstrual period is negative, retesting after another week is recommended. In the first day or two following a missed period, the concentration of HCG may be too low to be detected by the test.

Changes in the Woman's Body

Hormonal changes begin as soon as the egg is fertilized, and for the next 9 months the woman's body nourishes the fetus and adjusts to its growth. Let's take a closer look at the changes of early, middle, and late pregnancy (Figure 8.2).

Early Signs and Symptoms

Early recognition of pregnancy is important, especially for women with physical problems and nutritional deficiencies. The following symptoms are not absolute indications of pregnancy, but they are reasons to visit a gynecologist:

- *A missed menstrual period.* If an egg has been fertilized and implanted in the uterine wall, the endometrium is retained to nourish the embryo. A woman who misses a period after having intercourse may be pregnant.

- *Slight bleeding.* Slight bleeding follows implantation of the fertilized egg in about 14% of pregnant women. Because this happens about the time a period is expected, the bleeding is sometimes mistaken for menstrual flow. It usually lasts only a few days.

- *Nausea.* About two-thirds of pregnant women feel nauseated, probably as a reaction to increased levels of progesterone and other hormones. Although this nausea is often called *morning sickness,* some women have it all day long. It frequently begins during the 6th week and disappears by the 12th week. In some cases, it lasts throughout the pregnancy.

- *Breast tenderness.* Some women experience breast tenderness, swelling, and tingling, usually described as different from the tenderness experienced before menstruation.

- *Increased urination.* Increased frequency of urination can occur soon after the missed period.

- *Sleepiness, fatigue, and emotional upset.* These symptoms result from hormonal changes. Fatigue can be surprisingly overwhelming in the first trimester but usually improves significantly around the third month of pregnancy.

The first reliable physical signs of pregnancy can be distinguished about 4 weeks after a woman misses her menstrual period. A softening of the uterus just above the cervix, called *Hegar's sign,* and other changes in the cervix and pelvis are apparent during a pelvic examination. The labia minora and the cervix may take on a purple color rather than their usual pink hue.

Four weeks after a woman misses her menstrual period, she would be considered to be about 8 weeks pregnant because pregnancy is calculated from the time of a woman's last menstrual period rather than from the time of actual fertilization. (The timing of ovulation and fertilization is often difficult to determine.) Although a woman should see her physician to determine her due date, due dates can be approximated by subtracting 3 months from the date of the last menstrual period and then adding 7 days. For example, a woman whose last menstrual period began on September 20th would have a due date of about June 27th.

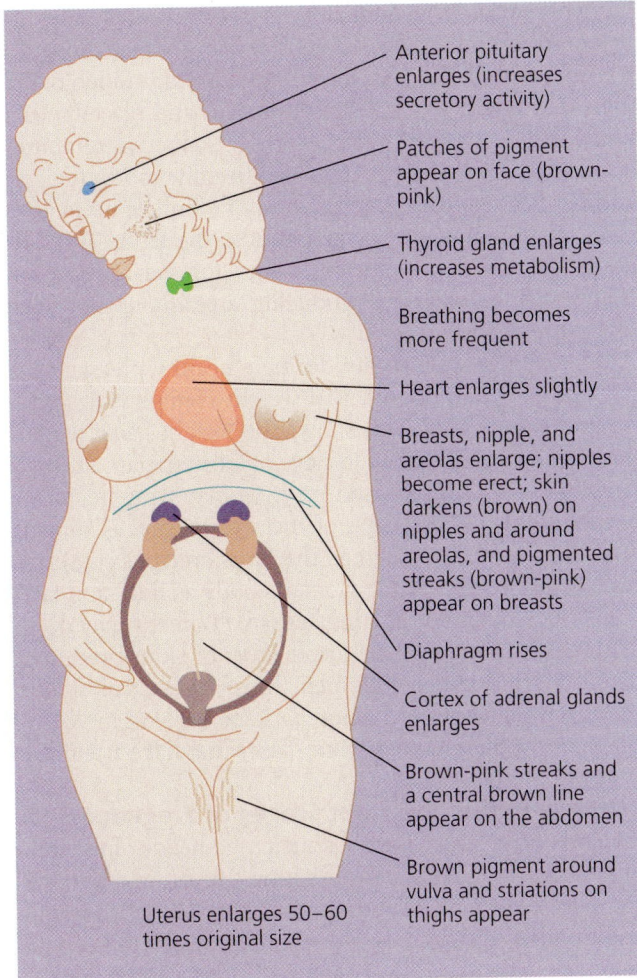

Anterior pituitary enlarges (increases secretory activity)

Patches of pigment appear on face (brown-pink)

Thyroid gland enlarges (increases metabolism)

Breathing becomes more frequent

Heart enlarges slightly

Breasts, nipple, and areolas enlarge; nipples become erect; skin darkens (brown) on nipples and around areolas, and pigmented streaks (brown-pink) appear on breasts

Diaphragm rises

Cortex of adrenal glands enlarges

Brown-pink streaks and a central brown line appear on the abdomen

Brown pigment around vulva and striations on thighs appear

Uterus enlarges 50–60 times original size

FIGURE 8.2   Physiological changes during pregnancy.

Continuing Changes in the Woman's Body

The most obvious changes during pregnancy occur in the reproductive organs. During the first 3 months, the uterus enlarges to about three times its nonpregnant size, but it still cannot be felt in the abdomen. By the 4th month, it is large enough to make the abdomen protrude. By the 7th or 8th month, the uterus pushes up into the rib cage, which makes breathing slightly more difficult. The breasts enlarge and are sensitive; by week 8, they may tingle or throb. The pigmented area around the nipple, the areola, darkens and broadens.

Other changes are going on as well. Early in pregnancy, the muscles and ligaments attached to bones begin to soften and stretch. The joints between the pelvic bones loosen and spread, making it easier to have a baby but

human chorionic gonadotropin (HCG)   A hormone produced by the fertilized egg that can be detected in the urine or blood of the mother within a few weeks of conception.

cloning   Asexual reproduction in which offspring are genetically identical to one parent.

TERMS

harder to walk. The circulatory system becomes more efficient to accommodate the blood volume, which increases by 50%, and the heart pumps it more rapidly. Much of the increased blood flow goes to the uterus and placenta (the organ that exchanges nutrients and waste between mother and fetus). The mother's lungs also become more efficient, and her rib cage widens to permit her to inhale up to 40% more air. Much of the oxygen goes to the fetus. The kidneys become highly efficient, removing waste products from fetal circulation and producing large amounts of urine by midpregnancy.

The average weight gain during a healthy pregnancy is 27.5 pounds, although actual weight change varies with the individual. Table 8.2 shows the weight gains recommended by the American College of Obstetricians and Gynecologists (ACOG), based on a woman's prepregnancy weight status. About 60% of the weight gain is directly related to the baby (such as the fetus and placenta); the rest accumulates over the woman's body as fluid and fat.

As the woman's skin stretches, small breaks may occur in the elastic fibers of the lower layer of skin, producing *stretch marks* on her abdomen, hips, breasts, or thighs. Increased pigment production darkens the skin in 90% of pregnant women, especially in places that have stretched.

Changes During the Later Stages of Pregnancy
By the end of the 6th month, the increased needs of the fetus place a burden on the mother's lungs, heart, and kidneys. Her back may ache from the pressure of the baby's weight and from having to throw her shoulders back to keep her balance while standing (Figure 8.3). Her body retains more water, perhaps up to 3 extra quarts of fluid. Her legs, hands, ankles, or feet may swell, and she may be bothered by leg cramps, heartburn, or constipation. Despite discomfort, both her digestion and her metabolism are working at top efficiency.

The uterus prepares for childbirth with preliminary contractions, called *Braxton Hicks contractions*. Unlike true labor contractions, these are usually short, irregular, and painless. The mother may only be aware that at times her abdomen is hard to the touch. These contractions become more frequent and intense as the delivery date approaches.

In the 9th month, the baby settles into the pelvic bones, usually head down, fitting snugly. This process, called **lightening,** allows the uterus to sink down about 2 inches, producing a visible change in the mother's profile. Pelvic

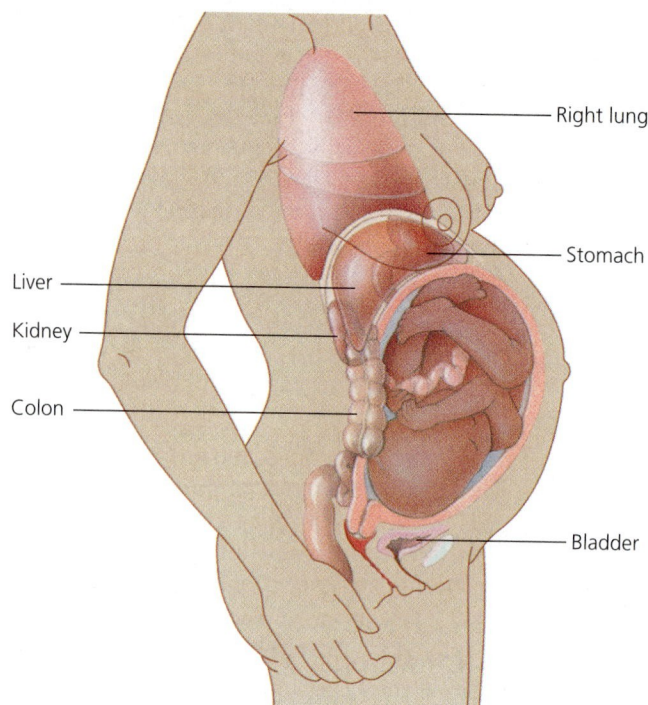

FIGURE 8.3 **The fetus during the third trimester of pregnancy.**

pressure increases, and pressure on the diaphragm lightens. Breathing becomes easier; urination becomes more frequent. Sometimes, after a first pregnancy, the baby doesn't settle down into the pelvis until labor begins.

Emotional Responses to Pregnancy

Rapid changes in hormone levels can cause a pregnant woman to experience unpredictable emotions. A large part of pregnancy is beyond the woman's control—her changing appearance, her energy level, her variable moods—and some women need extra support and reassurance to keep on an even keel. Hormonal changes can also make women feel exhilarated and euphoric, although for some women such moods are temporary.

Like the physical changes that accompany pregnancy, emotional responses also change as the pregnancy develops. During the first trimester, the pregnant woman may fear that she may miscarry or that the child will not be normal. Education about pregnancy and childbirth and support from her partner, friends, relatives, and health care professionals are important antidotes to these fears (see the box "Pregnancy Tasks for Fathers").

During the second trimester, the pregnant woman can feel the fetus move within her, and worries about miscarriages usually begin to diminish. She may look and feel happy and be delighted as her pregnancy begins to show. However, she may also worry that her increasing size makes her unattractive. Reassurance from her partner can ease these fears.

Table 8.2	Recommended Weight Gain During Pregnancy	
Status	**Weight Gain (pounds)**	
Underweight	28–40	
Normal	25–35	
Overweight	15–25	
Obese	15 or more	

Pregnancy Tasks for Fathers

Before the Pregnancy

• *Consider your lifestyle and health habits.* A healthy lifestyle can help boost fertility and improve pregnancy outcome. Being too thin or too heavy may lower a man's sperm count, as may marijuana use. Men who smoke and drink have a lower concentration of sperm and a lower percentage of active sperm. Exposure to chemicals on the job may also affect pregnancy.

• *Check your budget, financial situation, and insurance status.* Make sure your finances are in order, and that you have as much life, health, and disability insurance as you can afford. See a financial planner for advice. Try putting away extra money every month now—both to practice living on a tighter budget and to actually save up for the baby.

• *Get any necessary health checks and genetic counseling.* See the discussion of potential health concerns in the section on "Preconception Care."

During the Pregnancy

• *Help your partner stay healthy during the pregnancy.* If you smoke, quit; secondhand smoke is dangerous for the developing fetus. Support your partner by making other lifestyle changes and/or joining her in any changes she's making; for example, drink nonalcoholic beverages, take walks with her, and get extra sleep.

• *Help around the home and with planning for the baby.* Help shop for necessities, and help get your home ready for a baby. Pregnancy is hard work, so providing extra help with household chores and errands can be an important element of support. (Due to the risk of infection by toxoplasmosis, pregnant women should avoid handling cat litter; if you and your partner have a cat, emptying the litter box should be your job.)

• *Be involved.* Go to all the prenatal visits, birth preparation or education classes, hospital and nursery tours, and so on. Learn more about pregnancy, childbirth, and parenting by reading books, visiting Internet sites, and talking with other parents.

After the Baby Arrives

• *Help meet your baby's needs.* If your job allows, take parental leave to help with the new baby. Support the new mother by helping with baby care (feeding, diaper changes), laundry, shopping, and other chores. Take turns or join the mother when the baby needs care or feeding during the night; one survey found that more than half of fathers continue to sleep or pretend to be asleep when their babies cry during the night.

• *Support your partner, and reach out to others for help.* It is normal for a new mother to be tired and to experience mood changes, and some men also experience anxiety about their new role. Good communication between partners and help from supportive relatives and friends can help new parents adjust.

• *Give mom some time off.* A new mother needs time to recover from childbirth, even after she leaves the hospital or birthing center. This is especially true if the delivery was difficult, if a cesarean section was performed, or if an episiotomy was required. Aside from pitching in with daily chores, the father can aid the mother's recuperation by taking the baby for a few hours at a time. If the baby is being bottlefed, the dad may be able to take charge for a morning, an afternoon, or even the entire day.

The third trimester is the time of greatest physical stress during the pregnancy. A woman may find that her physical abilities are limited by her size. Because some women feel physically awkward and sexually unattractive, they may experience periods of depression. But many also feel a great deal of happy excitement and anticipation. The fetus may already be looked on as a member of the family, and both parents may begin talking to the fetus and interacting with it by patting the mother's belly. The upcoming birth will probably be a focus for both the woman and her partner.

Fetal Development

Now that we've seen what happens to the mother's body during pregnancy, let's consider the development of the fetus (Figure 8.4, p. 214).

The First Trimester About 30 hours after the egg is fertilized, the cell divides, and this process of cell division repeats many times. As the cluster of cells drifts down

Up to 20% of pregnant woman have symptoms of major depression.

—March of Dimes Foundation, 2007

lightening   A process in which the uterus sinks down because the baby's head settles into the mother's pelvic area.

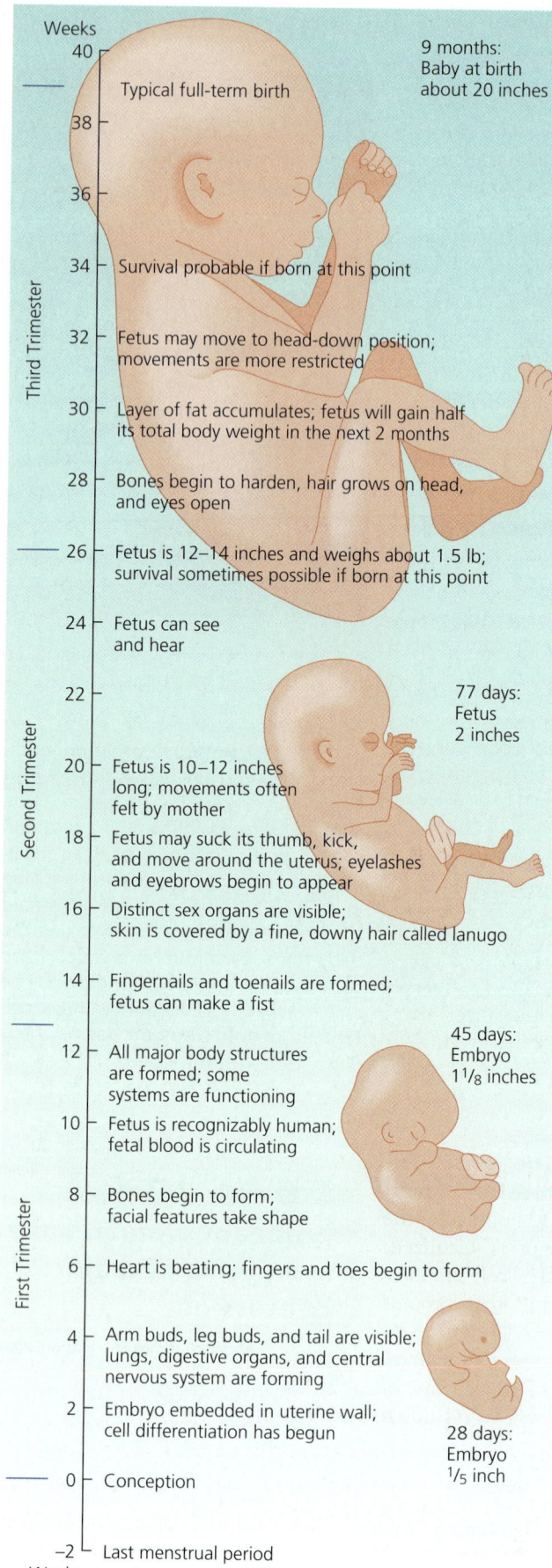

Weeks

40 — Typical full-term birth

9 months:
Baby at birth
about 20 inches

38

36

Third Trimester

34 — Survival probable if born at this point

32 — Fetus may move to head-down position; movements are more restricted

30 — Layer of fat accumulates; fetus will gain half its total body weight in the next 2 months

28 — Bones begin to harden, hair grows on head, and eyes open

26 — Fetus is 12–14 inches and weighs about 1.5 lb; survival sometimes possible if born at this point

24 — Fetus can see and hear

22 —

77 days:
Fetus
2 inches

Second Trimester

20 — Fetus is 10–12 inches long; movements often felt by mother

18 — Fetus may suck its thumb, kick, and move around the uterus; eyelashes and eyebrows begin to appear

16 — Distinct sex organs are visible; skin is covered by a fine, downy hair called lanugo

14 — Fingernails and toenails are formed; fetus can make a fist

12 — All major body structures are formed; some systems are functioning

45 days:
Embryo
1 1/8 inches

10 — Fetus is recognizably human; fetal blood is circulating

8 — Bones begin to form; facial features take shape

First Trimester

6 — Heart is beating; fingers and toes begin to form

4 — Arm buds, leg buds, and tail are visible; lungs, digestive organs, and central nervous system are forming

2 — Embryo embedded in uterine wall; cell differentiation has begun

28 days:
Embryo
1/5 inch

0 — Conception

−2 — Last menstrual period

Weeks

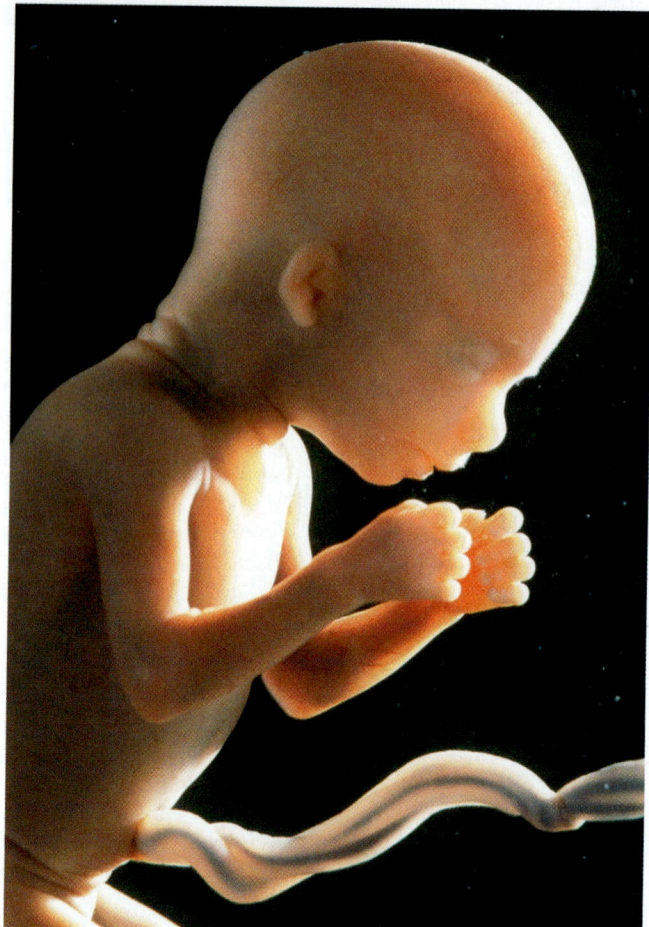

By the 4th month, the fetus is growing rapidly and is about 10 inches long. Weighing about 6 ounces, it moves vigorously in the uterus and can suck its thumb, frown, and turn its head.

the oviduct, several different kinds of cells emerge. The entire set of genetic instructions is passed to every cell, but each cell follows only certain instructions; if this were not the case, there would be no different organs or body parts. For example, all cells carry genes for hair color and eye color, but only the cells of the hair follicles and irises (of the eye) respond to that information.

On about the fourth day after fertilization, the cluster, now about 32–128 cells and hollow, arrives in the uterus; this is a **blastocyst**. On about the sixth or seventh day, the blastocyst attaches to the uterine wall, usually along the upper curve; over the next few days, it becomes firmly implanted and begins to draw nourishment from the endometrium, the uterine lining.

The blastocyst becomes an **embryo** by about the end of the 2nd week after fertilization. The inner cells of the blastocyst separate into three layers. One layer becomes inner body parts, the digestive and respiratory systems;

FIGURE 8.4   A chronology of milestones in prenatal development.

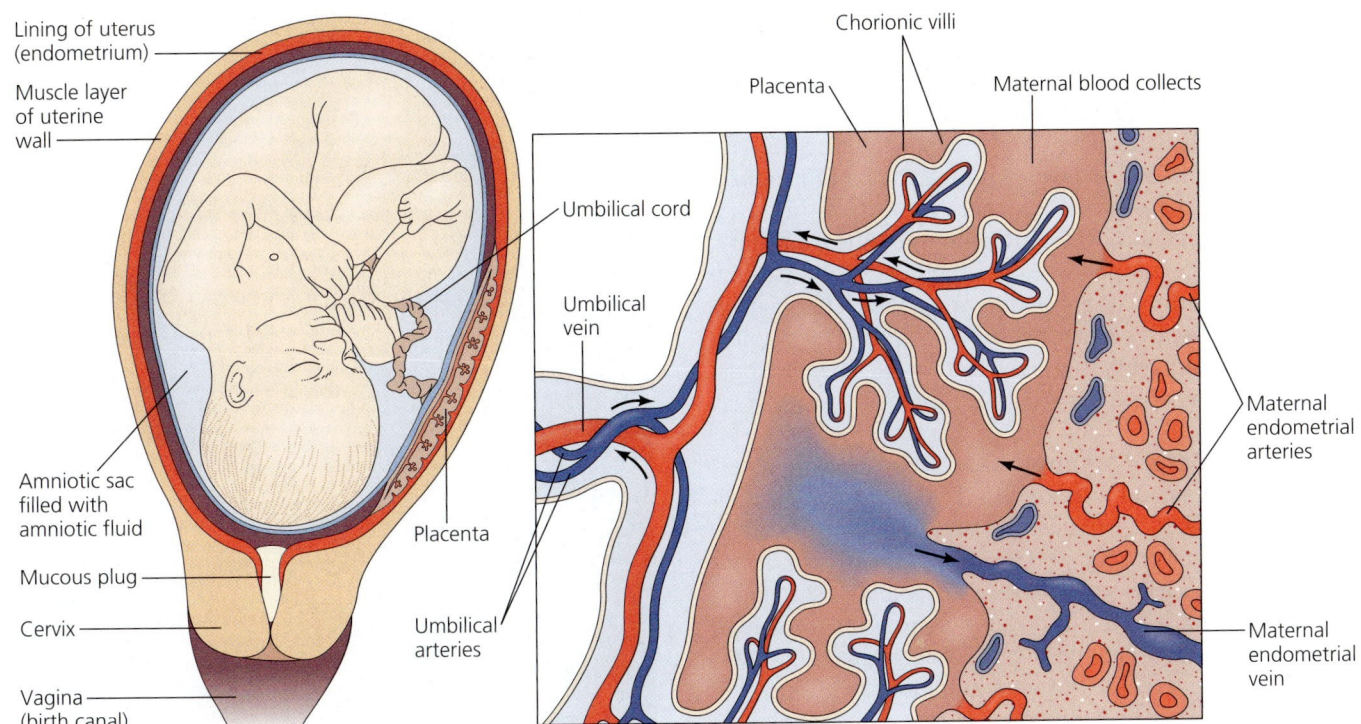

Lining of uterus (endometrium)

Muscle layer of uterine wall

Amniotic sac filled with amniotic fluid

Mucous plug

Cervix

Vagina (birth canal)

Umbilical cord

Umbilical vein

Placenta

Umbilical arteries

Chorionic villi

Placenta

Maternal blood collects

Maternal endometrial arteries

Maternal endometrial vein

FIGURE 8.5   A cross-sectional view of the fetus in the uterus and an enlargement of the placenta.

the middle layer becomes muscle, bone, blood, kidneys, and sex glands; and the third layer becomes the skin, hair, and nervous tissue.

The outermost shell of cells becomes the **placenta, umbilical cord,** and **amniotic sac** (Figure 8.5). A network of blood vessels called *chorionic villi* eventually forms the placenta. The human placenta allows a two-way exchange of nutrients and waste materials between the mother and the fetus. The placenta brings oxygen and nutrients to the fetus and transports waste products out. The placenta does not provide a perfect barrier between the fetal circulation and the maternal circulation, however. Some blood cells are exchanged and certain substances, such as alcohol, pass freely from the maternal circulation through the placenta to the fetus.

The period between weeks 2 and 9 is a time of rapid differentiation and change. All the major body structures are formed during this time, including the heart, brain, liver, lungs, and sex organs; the eyes, nose, ears, arms, and legs also appear. Some organs begin to function—the heart begins to beat, and the liver starts producing blood cells. Because body structures are forming, the developing organism is vulnerable to damage from environmental influences such as drugs and infections (discussed in detail in sections that follow).

By the end of the 2nd month, the brain sends out impulses that coordinate the functioning of other organs. The embryo is now a fetus, and most further changes will be in the size and refinement of working body parts. In the 3rd month, the fetus begins to be quite active. By the

end of the first trimester, the fetus is about an inch long and weighs less than 1 ounce.

The Second Trimester   To grow during the second trimester, to about 14 inches and 1.5 pounds, the fetus must have large amounts of food, oxygen, and water, which come from the mother through the placenta. All body systems are operating, and the fetal heartbeat can be heard with a stethoscope. The mother can detect fetal movements beginning in the 4th or 5th month. Against great odds, a fetus born prematurely at the end of the second trimester might survive.

The Third Trimester   The fetus gains most of its birth weight during the last 3 months. Some of the weight is fatty

blastocyst   A stage of development, days 6–14, before the cell cluster becomes the embryo and placenta.

embryo   The stage of development between blastocyst and fetus; about weeks 2–8.

placenta   The organ through which the fetus receives nourishment and empties waste via the mother's circulatory system; after birth, the placenta is expelled from the uterus.

umbilical cord   The cord connecting the placenta and fetus, through which nutrients pass.

amniotic sac   A membranous pouch enclosing and protecting the fetus; also holds amniotic fluid.

tissue under the skin that insulates the fetus and supplies food. The fetus needs a great deal of calcium, iron, and nitrogen from the food the mother eats. Some 85% of the calcium and iron she consumes goes into the fetal bloodstream.

Although the fetus may live if it is born during the 7th month, it needs the fat layer acquired in the 8th month and time for the organs, especially the respiratory and digestive organs, to develop. It also needs the immunity supplied by the antibodies in the mother's blood during the final 3 months. The antibodies protect the fetus against many of the diseases to which she has acquired immunity. Breast milk can help the baby further resist infections because it also contains maternal antibodies.

Diagnosing Fetal Abnormalities About 3% of babies are born with a major birth defect. Information about the health and sex of a fetus can be obtained prior to birth through prenatal testing.

Ultrasonography (also called *ultrasound*) uses high-frequency sound waves to create a **sonogram,** or visual image, of the fetus in the uterus. Sonograms show the position of the fetus, its size and gestational age, and the presence of certain anatomical problems. Sonograms can sometimes be used to determine the sex of the fetus. Sonograms are considered safe for a pregnant woman and the fetus, but the FDA advises against "keepsake" sonograms performed for no medical purpose.

Amniocentesis involves the removal of fluid from the uterus with a long, thin needle inserted through the abdominal wall. It is usually performed between 15 and 18 weeks into the pregnancy, although earlier amniocentesis is available. A genetic analysis of the fetal cells in the fluid can reveal the presence of chromosomal disorders, such as Down syndrome, and some genetic diseases, including Tay-Sachs disease. The sex of the fetus can also be determined. Most amniocentesis tests are performed on pregnant women over age 35, who have a greater risk of chromosomal abnormalities, or in cases where the fetus is known to be at risk for a particular chromosomal or genetic defect. Amniocentesis carries a slight risk (a 0.3–0.7% chance of miscarriage).

Another prenatal test is **chorionic villus sampling (CVS),** which can be performed earlier in pregnancy than amniocentesis, between weeks 10 and 12. This procedure involves removal through the cervix (by catheter) or abdomen (by needle) of a tiny section of chorionic villi, which contain fetal cells that then can be analyzed. When CVS first became available, it was associated with a higher risk of miscarriage than amniocentesis, but by 2003 the two procedures were found to be equally safe.

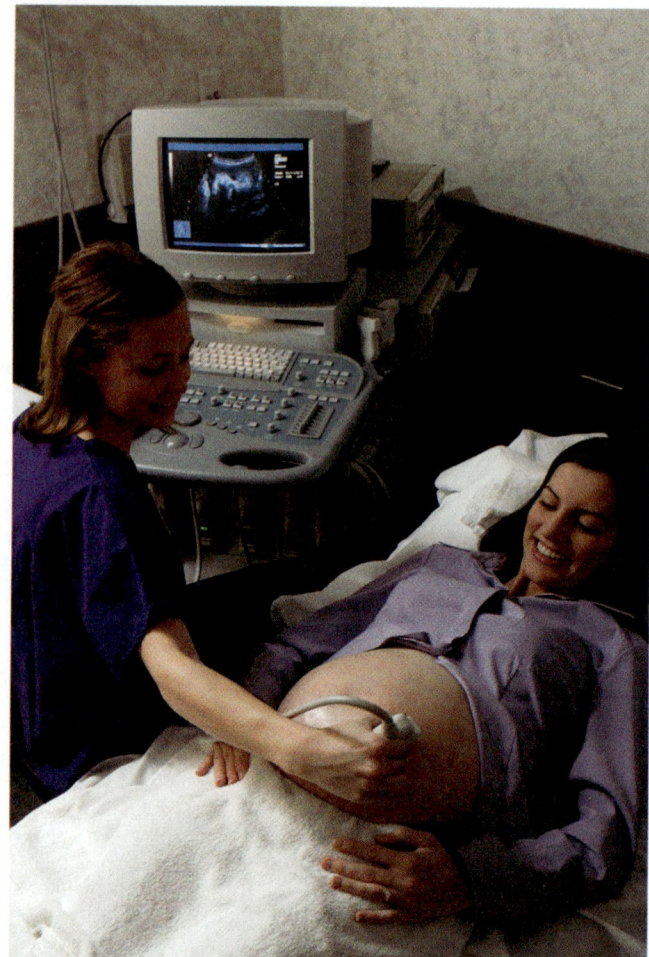

Ultrasonography provides information about the position, size, and physical condition of a fetus in the uterus.

The **quadruple marker screen (QMS)** is a maternal blood test that can be used to help identify fetuses with neural tube defects, Down syndrome, and other anomalies. Blood is taken from the mother at 16–19 weeks of pregnancy and analyzed for four hormone levels—human chorionic gonadotropin (HCG), unconjugated estriol, alpha-fetoprotein (AFP), and inhibin-A. The hormone levels are compared to appropriate standards, and the results are used to estimate the probability that the fetus has particular anomalies. QMS is a screening test rather than a diagnostic test; in the case of abnormal QMS results, parents may choose further testing such as ultrasonography or amniocentesis.

A new first trimester screening test for Down syndrome combines ultrasound evaluation of nuchal translucency (the thickness of the back of the fetus's neck) with maternal blood testing. This test can be done between the 10th and 14th week of pregnancy. If results indicate an increased risk of abnormality, further diagnostic studies such as amniocentesis can be done for confirmation.

Genetic counselors explain the results of the different tests so that parents can understand their implications. If a fetus is found to have a defect, it may be carried to term, aborted, or, in rare instances, treated while still in the uterus. Results of most current screening tests are not available until after week 12 of pregnancy; consequently, if abortion is chosen, it is likely to involve one of the more medically complex and physically difficult methods (see Chapter 7). Researchers are searching for new fetal screening techniques that are less invasive and that can be done earlier in pregnancy.

Fetal Programming Amniocentesis, CVS, and QMS look for chromosomal, genetic, and other anomalies that typically cause immediate problems. A new area of study known as *fetal programming theory* focuses on how conditions in the womb may influence the risk of adult diseases. For example, researchers have linked low birth weight to an increased risk of heart disease, high blood pressure, obesity, diabetes, and schizophrenia; high birth weight in female infants, however, has been linked to an increased risk of breast cancer in later life.

How might conditions during gestation affect the risk of adult diseases? A number of studies have looked at groups of people born in areas of poverty or at times of famine, when pregnant women were unable to eat properly. The poor prenatal conditions that stunt the growth of a developing fetus and lead to low birth weight may also affect specific organs. For example, if energy is limited, resources may be directed toward the developing fetal brain and away from other organs, including the liver and kidneys. Later in life, a small liver may be unable to clear cholesterol from the bloodstream, thereby increasing cholesterol levels and raising the risk of heart disease; undersized kidneys may be less able to regulate blood pressure. The fetus may also respond to limited resources by developing a permanently thrifty metabolism that triggers increased appetite and fat storage—leading to a greater risk of adult obesity and diabetes. Stress, both physical and emotional, increases maternal levels of the hormone cortisol, which in turn may permanently affect an infant's system of blood pressure regulation (see the box "Stress and Pregnancy" on p. 218).

Hormones may also be involved in the link between high birth weight and increased risk of breast cancer. Growth factors that contribute to high birth weight include leptin, insulin, and estrogen. Exposure to high levels of these in the womb may alter developing breast tissue in such a way that, when exposed to estrogen later in life, breast cells may be more likely to become malignant.

Although fetal programming theory is not yet embraced by all scientists, these studies emphasize that everything that occurs during pregnancy can have an impact on the developing fetus. In the future, people may be able to use information about their birth weight and other indicators of gestational conditions just as they can now use family history and genetic information—to alert them to special health risks and to help them improve their health.

Prenatal care is essential to the health of both mother and baby.

The Importance of Prenatal Care

Adequate prenatal care—as described in the following sections—is essential to the health of both mother and baby. All physicians recommend that women start getting regular prenatal checkups as soon as they become pregnant. Typically, this means one checkup per month during the first 8 months, then one checkup per week during the final month. About 84% of pregnant women begin

TERMS

ultrasonography The use of high-frequency sound waves to view the fetus in the uterus; also known as *ultrasound*.

sonogram The visual image of the fetus produced by ultrasonography.

amniocentesis A process in which amniotic fluid is removed and analyzed to detect possible birth defects.

chorionic villus sampling (CVS) Surgical removal of a tiny section of chorionic villi to be analyzed for genetic defects.

quadruple marker screen (QMS) A measurement of four hormones, used to assess the risk of fetal abnormalities.

Stress and Pregnancy

High levels of stress can have the same adverse effects on a pregnant woman as they do on anyone else (see Chapter 2). However, recent research suggests that stress can also affect the course of pregnancy and the health of the fetus.

Researchers have linked high levels of stress to miscarriage, preterm labor, and low birth weight. In one study, women who reported high levels of job stress were found to have a risk of miscarriage two to three times higher than that of less-stressed women. Other studies have found that pregnant women who experience major life changes, traumatic experiences, or high levels of pregnancy-related anxiety are at greater risk for preterm labor and for having a low-birth-weight infant.

Stress hormones may constrict blood flow to the placenta, depriving the fetus of the oxygen and nutrients needed for growth and development. Stress hormones also play a role in triggering labor, so high hormone levels may also increase the risk of preterm labor.

Stress may also affect the behavior of a pregnant woman; negative coping techniques such as use of tobacco, alcohol, and other drugs can adversely affect a developing fetus. On the flip side, social support during pregnancy has been linked to improved fetal growth and healthy birth weight.

The time in pregnancy in which stress is experienced may be important in determining its effects. A study of earthquake survivors found that women who were in their first trimester when the earthquake occurred were at increased risk for preterm labor; women further along in their pregnancies experienced no such increase in risk. Researchers hypothesize that hormones produced in the later stages of pregnancy may protect both mother and fetus from the effects of stress.

High levels of stress have also been linked to birth defects. Although the overall risk of birth defects is very low, women who experience severe emotional trauma around the time of conception or during the first trimester are more likely to have an infant with defects of the skull, spine, palate, or limbs. The relationship between stress and birth defects has been found to be significantly greater in women with lower levels of education, suggesting that chronic stressors and behaviors that go along with low educational attainment and low income may increase the impact of stressful life events on fetal development.

Researchers have studied the long-term effects of stress by looking at children of pregnant Dutch women who experienced high levels of physical and emotional stress during the "Hunger Winter" of 1944–1945, when the Nazis block-

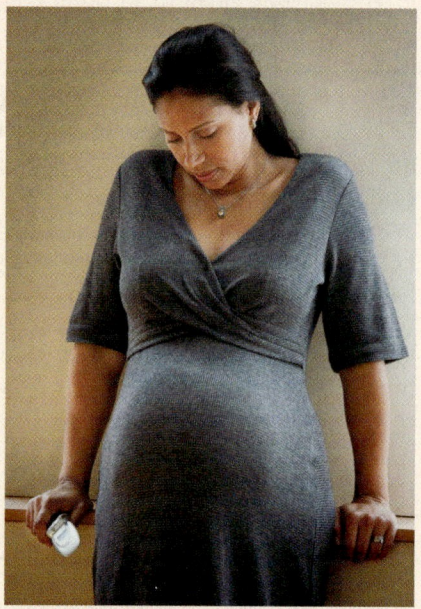

aded the western Netherlands. Fetuses exposed to the famine early in development were found to be at increased risk of central nervous system defects and, as adults, obesity and schizophrenia.

Although most American women do not experience such extreme stressors during pregnancy, these studies reinforce the importance of adequate prenatal care, including stress management and social support.

---

receiving adequate prenatal care during the first trimester; about 3.5% wait until the last trimester or receive no prenatal care at all.

Regular Checkups

In the woman's first visit to her obstetrician, she will be asked for a detailed medical history of herself and her family. The physician or midwife will note any hereditary conditions that may assume increased significance during pregnancy. The tendency to develop gestational diabetes (diabetes during pregnancy only), for example, can be inherited; appropriate treatment during pregnancy reduces the risk of serious harm.

The woman is given a complete physical exam and is informed about appropriate diet. She returns for regular checkups throughout the pregnancy, during which her blood pressure and weight gain are measured, her urine is analyzed, and the size and position of the fetus are monitored. Regular prenatal visits also give the mother a chance to discuss her concerns and assure herself that everything is proceeding normally. Physicians, midwives, health educators, and teachers of childbirth classes can provide the mother with invaluable information.

Blood Tests

A blood sample is taken during the initial prenatal visit to determine blood type and detect possible anemia or Rh incompatibilities. The **Rh factor** is a blood protein. If an Rh-positive father and an Rh-negative mother conceive an Rh-positive baby, the baby's blood will be incompatible with the mother's. If some of the baby's blood enters the mother's bloodstream during delivery, she will develop antibodies to it just as she would toward a virus. If she has subsequent Rh-positive babies, the antibodies in the mother's blood, passing through the placenta, will destroy the fetus's red blood cells, possibly leading to jaundice, anemia, mental retardation, or death. This condition is completely treatable with a serum called

Rh-immune globulin, which destroys Rh-positive cells as they enter the mother's body and prevents her from forming antibodies to them. Rh-immune globulin is given to Rh-negative mothers in the third trimester and again after the birth if the baby is found to be Rh-positive.

Blood may also be tested for evidence of hepatitis B, syphilis, rubella immunity, thyroid problems, and, with the mother's permission, HIV infection.

Prenatal Nutrition   A nutritious diet throughout pregnancy is essential for both the fetus and the mother. Not only does the baby get all its nutrients from the mother, but it also competes with her for nutrients not sufficiently available to meet both their needs. When a woman's diet is low in iron or calcium, the fetus receives most of it, and the mother may become deficient in the mineral. To meet the increased nutritional demands of her body, a pregnant woman shouldn't just eat more; she should make sure that her diet is nutritionally adequate (see the box "Healthy Eating During Pregnancy" on p. 220).

Avoiding Drugs and Other Environmental Hazards

In addition to the food the mother eats, the drugs she takes and the chemicals she is exposed to affect the fetus. Everything the mother ingests may eventually reach the fetus in some proportion. Some drugs harm the fetus but not the mother because the fetus is in the process of developing and because the proper dose for the mother is a massive dose for the fetus.

During the first trimester, when the major body structures are rapidly forming, the fetus is extremely vulnerable to environmental factors such as viral infections, radiation, drugs, and other **teratogens**, any of which can cause **congenital malformations**, or birth defects (see Table 8.3). The most susceptible body parts are those growing most rapidly at the time of exposure. The rubella

(German measles) virus, for example, can cause a congenital malformation of a delicate system such as the eyes or ears, leading to blindness or deafness, if exposure occurs during the first trimester, but it does no damage later in the pregnancy. Similarly, the drug thalidomide taken early in pregnancy prevents the formation of arms and legs in fetuses, but taken later, when limbs are already formed, it causes no damage. Other drugs can cause damage throughout prenatal development.

ALCOHOL   Alcohol is a potent teratogen. Getting drunk just one time during pregnancy may be enough to cause brain damage in a fetus. A high level of alcohol consumption during pregnancy is associated with miscarriages, stillbirths, and, in live babies, **fetal alcohol syndrome (FAS)**. A baby born with FAS is likely to suffer from a small head and body size, unusual facial characteristics, congenital heart defects, defective joints, impaired vision, mental impairment, and abnormal behavior patterns. Researchers now doubt that any level of alcohol consumption is safe, and they recommend total abstinence during pregnancy (see Chapter 10).

> **QUICK STATS**
>
> ## Up to 1.5 in 1000 babies born in the United States have FAS.
>
> —CDC, 2006

TOBACCO   About 10% of all mothers smoke during their pregnancy. Pregnant women who smoke should quit, and nonsmoking pregnant women should avoid places where people smoke. Smoking during pregnancy increases the risk of miscarriage, low birth weight, immune system impairment, and infant death; it may also cause genetic damage or physical deformations. If nicotine levels in a mother's bloodstream are high, fetal breathing rate and movement become more rapid; the fetus may also metabolize cancer-causing by-products of tobacco.

Infants of women who smoke during pregnancy have poorer lung function at birth, and exposure to secondhand smoke after birth increases a baby's susceptibility

Table 8.3	Most Common Birth Defects
Category	**Annual Cases***
Chromosomal	6916
Oro-facial	6776
Cardiovascular	6527
Musculoskeletal	5799
Neural tube	5210
Gastrointestinal	2883
Eye	834

*Case numbers for neural tube defects are actual (1999–2000); case numbers for other types of birth defects are estimates (1999–2001).

SOURCES: Centers for Disease Control and Prevention. 2006. Improved national prevalence estimates for 18 selected major birth defects—United States, 1999–2001. *Morbidity and Mortality Weekly Report* 54(51 & 52): 1301–1305; Centers for Disease Control and Prevention. 2004. Spina bifida and anencephaly before and after folic acid mandate—United States, 1995–1996 and 1999–2000. *Morbidity and Mortality Weekly Report* 53(17): 362–365.

> **TERMS**
>
> **Rh factor**   A protein found in blood; Rh incompatibility between a mother and fetus can jeopardize the fetus's health.
>
> **teratogen**   An agent or influence that causes physical defects in a developing fetus.
>
> **congenital malformation**   A physical defect existing at the time of birth, either inherited or caused during gestation.
>
> **fetal alcohol syndrome (FAS)**   A combination of birth defects caused by excessive alcohol consumption by the mother during pregnancy.

Healthy Eating During Pregnancy

To maintain her own health and help the fetus grow, a woman needs to consume about 250–500 extra calories per day during pregnancy. Breast-feeding an infant requires even more energy—about 500 or more extra calories per day.

Healthy Choices

To ensure a balanced intake of key nutrients, pregnant women should follow the U.S. Department of Agriculture's Food Guide, which is based on five basic food groups. For a moderately active pregnant woman consuming about 2400 calories per day, the daily recommended intake from each group is as follows:

• Fruits: 2 cups

• Vegetables: 3 cups total, including a mixture of legumes (dry beans and peas) and dark green, orange, or deep yellow, and starchy vegetables

• Grains: 8 ounce-equivalents, with 1 slice of bread or $1/2$ cup of cooked grains being the equivalent of 1 ounce; half of daily grain servings should be whole grains

• Lean meat, poultry, fish, dry beans, eggs, and nuts: 6.5 ounces of lean meat or the equivalent

• Milk, yogurt, and cheese: 3 cups

Fats, oils, and sweets should be used sparingly according to total energy needs. A pregnant woman must also drink enough—about 11 cups of liquid from beverages and foods. See Chapter 12 for a more detailed discussion of the Food Guide.

Supplements

Some physicians may prescribe vitamin and mineral supplements for women who are pregnant or lactating or who are trying to get pregnant. Adequate vitamin and mineral intake is important for many reasons. For example, women with low levels of vitamin D are more likely to have low-birth-weight babies.

Adequate intake of the B vitamin folate before conception and during pregnancy has been shown to decrease the risk of neural tube defects, including spina bifida. Any woman capable of becoming pregnant should consume at least 400 µg (0.4 mg) of folic acid (the synthetic form of folate) daily from fortified foods and/or supplements, in addition to folate from a varied diet. Pregnant women should have 600 µg every day. For women who have already had a pregnancy involving a fetus with a neural tube defect, the CDC recommends consulting with a physician about taking a much larger amount of folic acid (4 mg), starting 1 month before conception and continuing through the first trimester. Folate is found naturally in leafy green vegetables, legumes, citrus fruits, and most berries. Since 1998, when the FDA mandated fortification of enriched grain products with folic acid, the incidence of neural tube defects has declined by as much as 32%. However, a 2006 study found that folate intake is still well below FDA targets.

It is important that a pregnant woman not supplement beyond her physician's advice because some vitamins and minerals are harmful if taken in excess. It is also important not to take herbal dietary supplements without consulting a physician; few dietary supplements have been tested for safety during pregnancy, and some have been shown to be dangerous.

Food Safety

Pregnant women should pay special attention to food safety because foodborne pathogens can be particularly dangerous during pregnancy. Two such pathogens are *Listeria monocytogenes* and *Toxoplasma gondii*. *Listeria* is a bacterium most often found in undercooked or ready-to-eat meat, poultry, or seafood; soft cheeses; products made with unpasteurized milk; and unpasteurized juice. Listeriosis causes flulike symptoms in pregnant women; if the fetus is infected, the result can be miscarriage, premature birth, or birth defects.

T. gondii, a parasite carried by cats, can also contaminate food or soil. Toxoplasmosis is typically caused by eating undercooked meat or poultry or unwashed fruits and vegetables, cleaning a litter box, or handling contaminated soil. Toxoplasmosis causes few symptoms in pregnant women, but if passed to the fetus it may cause miscarriage or mental impairment.

One further food safety recommendation for pregnant women relates to fish. Most types of fish are good choices for a healthy diet, but a few types can be contaminated with mercury or industrial pollutants. The FDA advises pregnant women not to eat swordfish, shark, king mackerel, or tilefish and to limit overall fish consumption to 12 ounces per week. Pregnant women are also advised to check with their local health departments before consuming any game fish.

For detailed information on food safety, see Chapter 12.

---

to pneumonia and bronchitis. If a mother who smokes breast-feeds, her infant will be exposed to tobacco chemicals through breast milk. See Chapter 11 for more on the effects of smoking.

CAFFEINE Caffeine, a powerful stimulant, puts both mother and fetus under stress by raising the level of the hormone epinephrine. Caffeine also reduces the blood supply to the uterus. One study found that consuming the amount of caffeine in five or more cups of coffee a day doubled the risk of miscarriage. Coffee, colas, strong black tea, and chocolate are high in caffeine, as are some over-the-counter medications. A pregnant woman should limit her caffeine intake to no more than the equivalent of two cups of coffee per day.

DRUGS Some prescription drugs, such as some blood pressure medications, can harm the fetus, so they should be used only under medical supervision. Many babies born to women who use antidepressants during pregnancy suffer withdrawal symptoms after birth. In 2005, the FDA placed a "black box" warning on the antidepres-

Table 8.4 Selected Environmental Factors Associated with Problems in a Fetus or Infant

Agent or Condition	Potential Effects
Accutane (acne medication)	Small head, mental impairment, deformed or absent ears, heart defects, cleft lip and palate
Alcohol	Unusual facial characteristics, small head, heart defects, mental impairment, defective joints
Chlamydia	Eye infections, pneumonia
Cigarette smoking	Miscarriage, stillbirth, low birth weight, respiratory problems, sudden infant death
Cocaine	Miscarriage, stillbirth, low birth weight, small head, defects of genital and urinary tracts
Cytomegalovirus (CMV)	Small head, mental impairment, blindness
Diabetes (insulin-dependent)	Malformations of the brain, spine, and heart
Gonorrhea	Eye infection leading to blindness if untreated
Herpes	Brain damage, death
HIV infection	Impaired immunity, death
Lead	Reduced IQ, learning disorders
Marijuana	Impaired fetal growth, increase in alcohol-related fetal damage
Mercury	Brain damage
Propecia (hair loss medication)	Abnormalities of the male sex organs
Radiation (high dose)	Small head, growth and mental impairment, multiple birth defects
Rubella (German measles)	Malformation of eyes or ears causing deafness or blindness; small head; mental impairment
Syphilis	Fetal death and miscarriage, prematurity, physical deformities
Tetracycline	Pigmentation of teeth, underdevelopment of enamel
Vitamin A (excess)	Miscarriage; defects of the head, brain, spine, and urinary tract

sant paroxetine, which had been shown to cause fetal cardiac defects. Accutane, an anti-acne drug, may have caused over 1000 cases of severe birth defects in the 1980s. Over-the-counter drugs should be used only under a physician's direction. Large doses of vitamin A, for example, can cause birth defects.

Recreational drugs, such as cocaine, are thought to increase the risk of major birth defects. Marijuana use may also interfere with fertility treatments, and methamphetamine use is associated with underweight babies.

STDS AND OTHER INFECTIONS Infections, including those that are sexually transmitted, are another serious problem for the fetus. The most common cause of life-threatening infections in newborns is Group B streptococcus (GBS), a type of bacterium that can cause pneumonia, meningitis, and blood infections. About 25% of all pregnant women carry GBS but do not become ill, so routine screening close to the time of delivery is recommended. A woman who carries GBS or who develops a fever during labor will be given intravenous antibiotics at the time of labor to reduce the risk of passing GBS to her baby.

Syphilis can infect and kill a fetus; if the baby is born alive, it will have syphilis. Penicillin taken by the mother during pregnancy cures syphilis in both mother and fetus. Gonorrhea can infect the baby during delivery and cause blindness. Because gonorrhea is often asymptomatic, in many states the eyes of newborns are routinely treated with erythromycin ointment to destroy gonorrheal bacteria. All pregnant women should be tested for hepatitis B, a virus that can pass from the mother to the infant at birth. Infants of infected mothers can be immunized shortly after birth.

Herpes simplex can damage the baby's eyes and brain and cause death, and no cure has yet been discovered for it. Genital herpes can be transmitted to the baby during delivery if the mother's infection is in the active phase. If this is the case, the baby may be delivered by cesarean section. An initial outbreak of herpes can be dangerous if it occurs during pregnancy because the virus may pass through the placenta to the fetus. For this reason, it is important to know if the pregnant woman or her partner has a history of herpes.

The human immunodeficiency virus (HIV), which causes AIDS, can be passed to the fetus by an HIV-infected mother during pregnancy, labor and delivery, or breast-feeding. Nationwide, more than 9000 children under age 13 have been diagnosed with AIDS, and many more are infected with HIV. The babies most at risk are those whose mothers inject drugs or are the sex partners of men who inject drugs. HIV testing is critical for any woman at risk for HIV, and some physicians recommend routine testing for all pregnant women. Antiviral drugs, given to an HIV-infected mother during pregnancy and delivery and to her newborn immediately following birth, reduce the rate of HIV transmission from mother to infant from 25% to 5% or less. Of course, women should also take all the necessary precautions against HIV infection during pregnancy. (See Chapter 18 for more on HIV and other STDs.)

Environmental factors affecting fetal or infant development are summarized in Table 8.4.

Prenatal Activity and Exercise Physical activity during pregnancy contributes to mental and physical wellness. Women can continue working at their jobs until late in their pregnancy, provided the work isn't so physically demanding that it jeopardizes their health. At the same time, pregnant women need more rest and sleep to maintain their own well-being and that of the fetus.

A moderate exercise program during pregnancy does not adversely affect pregnancy or birth; in fact, regular exercise appears to improve a woman's chance of an on-time delivery and may reduce the risk of pregnancy-related diabetes. The amniotic sac protects the fetus, and normal activities will not harm it. A woman who exercised before becoming pregnant can often continue her program, with appropriate modifications to maintain her comfort and safety. A pregnant woman who hasn't been exercising and wants to start should first consult a physician.

The U.S. Department of Health and Human Services recommends 30 minutes of moderate exercise most days, unless physical complications prevent exercise. Regular cardio-respiratory endurance exercise is recommended. Walking, swimming, and stationary cycling are all good choices; more strenuous activities that could result in a fall are best delayed until after the birth.

Kegel exercises, to strengthen the pelvic floor muscles, are recommended for pregnant women. These exercises are performed by alternately contracting and releasing the muscles used to stop the flow of urine. Each contraction should be held for about 5 seconds. Kegel exercises should be done several times a day, for a total of about 50 repetitions daily.

Prenatal exercise classes are valuable because they teach exercises that tone the body muscles involved in birth, especially those of the abdomen, back, and legs. Toned-up muscles aid delivery and help the body regain its nonpregnant shape afterward.

Preparing for Birth   Childbirth classes are almost a routine part of the prenatal experience for both mothers and fathers these days. These classes typically teach the details of the birth process as well as relaxation techniques to help deal with the discomfort of labor and delivery. The mother learns and practices a variety of techniques so she will be able to choose what works best for her during labor when the time comes. The father typically acts as a coach, supporting his partner emotionally and helping her with her breathing and relaxing. He remains with her throughout labor and delivery, even when a cesarean section is performed.

Complications of Pregnancy and Pregnancy Loss

About 31% of mothers-to-be suffer complications during pregnancy. Some complications may prevent full-term development of the fetus or affect the health of the infant at birth. As discussed earlier in the chapter, exposure to harmful substances, such as alcohol or drugs, can harm the fetus. Other complications are caused by physiological problems or genetic abnormalities.

Ectopic Pregnancy   In an **ectopic pregnancy**, the fertilized egg implants and begins to develop outside of the uterus, usually in an oviduct (Figure 8.6). More than 100,000 ectopic pregnancies are reported each year in the United States. Ectopic pregnancies account for 9% of all maternal deaths.

Ectopic pregnancies usually occur because the fallopian tube is blocked, most often as a result of pelvic inflammatory disease; smoking also increases a woman's risk for ectopic pregnancy. The embryo may spontaneously abort, or the embryo and placenta may continue to expand until they rupture the oviduct. Sharp pain on one side of the abdomen or in the lower back, usually in about the 7th or 8th week, may signal an ectopic pregnancy, and there may be irregular bleeding. If bleeding from a rupture is severe, the woman may go into shock, characterized by low blood pressure, a fast pulse, weakness, and fainting.

Surgical removal of the embryo and the oviduct may be necessary to save the mother's life, although microsurgery can sometimes be used to repair the damaged oviduct. If diagnosed early, before the oviduct ruptures, ectopic pregnancy can often be successfully treated without surgery. The incidence of ectopic pregnancy has more than quadrupled in the past 25 years.

Spontaneous Abortion   A spontaneous abortion, or miscarriage, is the termination of pregnancy before the 20th week. About 15–20% of all clinically diagnosed pregnancies end in miscarriage, and many women have miscarriages without knowing they were pregnant. About 30% of miscarriages occur before the 12th week of pregnancy. Most—about 60%—are due to chromosomal abnormalities in the fetus. Certain occupations that involve exposure to chemicals may increase the likelihood of a spontaneous abortion.

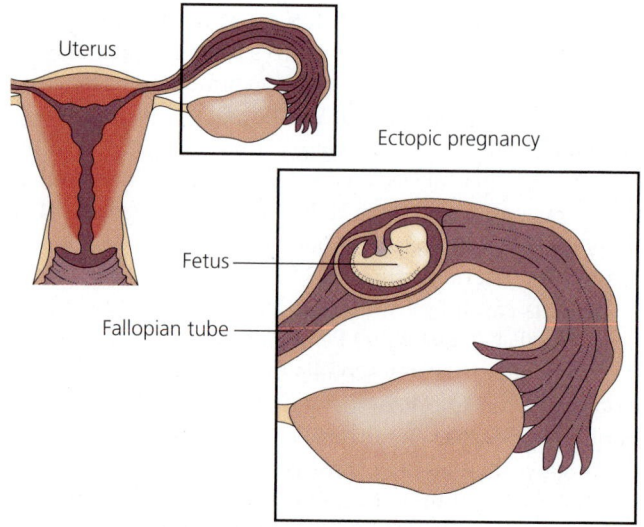

Uterus

Ectopic pregnancy

Fetus

Fallopian tube

FIGURE 8.6.   Ectopic pregnancy in a fallopian tube.

Vaginal bleeding (spotting) is usually the first sign that a pregnant woman may miscarry. She may also develop pelvic cramps, and her symptoms of pregnancy may disappear. (Note: Mild cramping is common in pregnancy and is usually not associated with miscarriage.)

One miscarriage doesn't mean that later pregnancies will be unsuccessful, and about 70–90% of women who miscarry eventually become pregnant again. About 1% of women suffer three or more miscarriages, possibly because of anatomical, hormonal, genetic, or immunological factors.

Stillbirth The terms *fetal death, fetal demise, stillbirth,* and *stillborn* all refer to the delivery of a fetus that shows no signs of life. Each year, over 3 million stillbirths occur worldwide. In the United States, the stillbirth rate is a little more than 6 in 1000. Risk factors for stillbirth include smoking, advanced maternal age, obesity, multiple gestations, and chronic disease. Race is also a factor; black women have twice as many stillbirths as white women.

Preeclampsia A disease unique to human pregnancy, **preeclampsia** is characterized by elevated blood pressure and the appearance of protein in the urine. Symptoms include headache, right upper-quadrant abdominal pain, vision changes (referred to as *scotomata*), and notable increased swelling and weight gain. If preeclampsia is untreated, patients can develop seizures, a condition called **eclampsia**. Other potential complications of preeclampsia are liver and kidney damage, bleeding, fetal growth restriction, and even fetal death.

The incidence of preeclampsia is commonly cited to be about 5%, but wide variations are reported. The incidence is related to race and ethnicity as well as to environmental factors and family history. It affects women at all reproductive ages. The incidence of eclampsia in the United States in 1998 was about 1 in 3250.

Women with mild preeclampsia may be monitored closely as outpatients and placed on home bed rest. More severe cases may require hospitalization for close medical management and early delivery.

Placenta Previa In **placenta previa**, the placenta either completely or partially covers the cervical opening, preventing the mother from delivering the baby vaginally. As a result, the baby must be delivered by cesarean section. This condition occurs in 1 in 250 live births. Risk factors include prior cesarean delivery, multiple pregnancies, intrauterine surgery, smoking, multiple gestations, and advanced maternal age. Previas often present as painless bright red vaginal bleeding and may be associated with contractions. They represent 20% of bleeding in the third trimester.

Placental Abruption In **placental abruption**, a normally implanted placenta prematurely separates from the uterine wall. Patients experience abdominal pain, vaginal

bleeding, and uterine tenderness. It represents 30% of all bleeding in the third trimester. The condition also increases the risk of fetal death. The risk factors for developing a placental abruption are maternal age, tobacco smoking, cocaine use, multiple gestation, trauma, preeclampsia, hypertension, and preterm premature rupture of membranes.

Gestational Diabetes During gestation, about 4% of all pregnant women develop **gestational diabetes (GDM),** in which the body loses its ability to use insulin properly. In these women, diabetes occurs only during pregnancy. The condition stems from placental secretion of certain hormones, including growth hormone, cortisol, placental lactogen, and progesterone. GDM arises when pancreatic function is not sufficient to overcome the insulin resistance created by these pregnancy-related hormones. Women diagnosed with GDM have an increased risk of developing type 2 diabetes later in life. It is important to accurately diagnose and treat GDM as it can lead to preeclampsia, polyhydramnios (increased levels of amniotic fluid), large fetuses, birth trauma, operative deliveries, perinatal mortality, and neonatal metabolic complications.

Preterm Labor When a pregnant woman goes into labor before the 37th week of gestation, she is said to undergo *preterm labor.* Preterm labor is one of the most common reasons for hospitalizing pregnant women, but verifying true preterm labor can be difficult. About 30–50% of preterm labors resolve themselves, with the pregnancy continuing to full term. In other cases, interventions may be required to delay labor and allow gestation to continue.

Labor Induction If pregnancy continues well beyond the baby's due date, it may be necessary to induce labor artificially. This is one of the most common obstetrical procedures and is typically offered to pregnant women who have not delivered and are 7–14 days past their due date. Labor can be artificially induced in several ways.

---

ectopic pregnancy A pregnancy in which the embryo develops outside of the uterus, usually in the fallopian tube.

preeclampsia A condition of pregnancy characterized by high blood pressure, and protein in the urine.

eclampsia A severe, potentially life-threatening form of preeclampsia, characterized by seizures.

placenta previa A complication of pregnancy in which the placenta covers the cervical opening, preventing the mother from delivering the baby vaginally.

placental abruption A complication of pregnancy in which a normally implanted placenta prematurely separates from the uterine wall.

gestational diabetes (GDM) A form of diabetes that occurs during pregnancy.

Low Birth Weight and Premature Birth A **low-birth-weight (LBW)** baby is one that weighs less than 5.5 pounds at birth. LBW babies may be **premature** (born before the 37th week of pregnancy) or full-term. Babies who are born small even though they're full-term are referred to as *small-for-date* or *small-for-gestational-age* babies. Low birth weight affected about 8% of babies born in 2006 in the United States. About half of all cases are related to teenage pregnancy, cigarette smoking, poor nutrition, and poor maternal health. Other maternal factors include drug use, stress, depression, and anxiety. Adequate prenatal care is the best way to prevent LBW.

Full-term LBW babies tend to have fewer problems than premature infants. In the United States in 2006, about 13% of babies were born prematurely. Many of the premature infant's organs are not sufficiently developed. Even mild prematurity increases an infant's risk of dying in the first month or year of life. Premature infants are subject to respiratory problems and infections. They may have difficulty eating because they may be too small to suck a breast or bottle and their swallowing mechanism may be underdeveloped. As they get older, premature infants may have problems such as learning difficulties, behavior problems, poor hearing and vision, and physical awkwardness.

Infant Mortality The U.S. rate of **infant mortality**, the death of a child of less than 1 year of age, is near its lowest point ever; however, it remains far higher than that of most of the developed world. The United States ranks low among the world's developed countries for low infant mortality, with 6.3 deaths for every 1000 live births. Poverty and inadequate health care are key causes; in some inner-city areas, the infant mortality rate approaches that of developing countries, with more than 20 deaths per 1000 births. The infant mortality rate among African Americans is 2.4 times higher than that of white infants.

Other causes of infant death are congenital problems, infectious diseases, and injuries. In **sudden infant death syndrome (SIDS)**, an apparently healthy infant dies suddenly while sleeping. About 2250 infant deaths are attributed to SIDS each year.

The number of SIDS deaths has decreased since 1992, when the "Back to Sleep" campaign was instituted to make people aware that putting babies to bed on their backs rather than on their stomachs significantly reduces the risk of SIDS. Research suggests that abnormalities in the brainstem, the part of the brain that regulates breathing, heart rate, and other basic functions, underline the risk for SIDS. Risk is greatly increased for infants with these innate differences if they are exposed to environmental risks, such as sleeping face down; being exposed to tobacco smoke, alcohol, or other drugs; or sleeping on a soft mattress or with fluffy bedding, pillows, or stuffed toys. Overbundling a baby or keeping a baby's room too warm also increases the risk of SIDS; because of this, SIDS deaths are more common in the colder months. Exposure to nitrous dioxide air pollution is also under investigation as a possible contributing factor. Several studies have found that the use of a pacifier significantly reduces the risk of SIDS.

Coping with Loss Parents form a deep attachment to their children even before birth, and those who lose an infant before or during birth usually experience deep grief. Initial feelings of shocked disbelief and numbness may give way to sadness, anger, crying spells, and preoccupation with the loss. Physical sensations such as tightness in the chest or stomach, loss of appetite, and sleeplessness may also occur. For the mother, physical exhaustion and hormone imbalances can compound the emotional and physical stress.

Experiencing the pain of loss is part of the healing process. A support group or professional counseling is also often helpful. Planning the next pregnancy, with a physician's input, can be an important step toward recovery, as long as the mind and body are given time to heal.

CHILDBIRTH

By the end of the 9th month of pregnancy, most women are tired of being pregnant; both parents are eager to start a new phase of their lives. Most couples find the actual process of birth to be an exciting and positive experience.

Choices in Childbirth

Many couples today can choose the type of practitioner and the environment they want for the birth of their child. A high-risk pregnancy is probably best handled by a specialist physician in a hospital with a nursery, but for low-risk births, many options are available.

In 2006, 99% of babies in the United States were delivered in hospitals. Many hospitals have introduced alternative birth centers in response to criticisms of traditional

QUICK STATS

4500 infants die suddenly of unexplained causes (including SIDS) each year in the United States.

—CDC, 2008

> **? QUESTIONS FOR CRITICAL THINKING AND REFLECTION**
>
> Do you know anyone who has lost a child to miscarriage, stillbirth, or a birth defect? If so, how did they cope with their loss? What would you do to help someone in this situation?

hospital routines. Alternative birth centers provide a comfortable, emotionally supportive environment in close proximity to up-to-date medical equipment.

Parents can choose to have their baby delivered by a physician (an obstetrician or family practitioner) or by a certified nurse-midwife. Certified nurse-midwives are registered nurses with special training in obstetrical techniques. They are usually less expensive than physicians, and they are often part of a complete medical team that includes a backup physician in case of emergency. Nurse-midwives can usually participate in births in any setting, although this may vary according to hospital policy, state law, and the midwife's preferences. About 1 in 20 babies each year is delivered by a nurse-midwife.

Many mothers-to-be are accompanied in the delivery room by a labor companion, called a *doula*. A doula is a woman who has either been through childbirth or has extensive experience with birth. She stays with the laboring woman continuously and provides emotional and tangible support, information, and advocacy. Supportive labor companions may improve labor progress by reducing maternal anxiety. Studies show that the presence of a knowledgeable doula can shorten the duration of labor, increase the rate of spontaneous vaginal birth, and reduce the use of narcotic painkillers, forceps delivery, and cesarean birth.

A small number of American women elect to give birth at home or in birth facilities that offer low-technology care. In 2006, nearly 25,000 home births were reported. The ACOG recommends against home births, especially for women with certain conditions such as diabetes or high blood pressure. Other groups, such as the American College of Nurse Midwives, support out-of-hospital births for healthy women with a low risk of complications.

It's important for prospective parents to discuss all aspects of labor and delivery with their physician or midwife beforehand so they can learn what to expect and can state their preferences. For more information, see the box "Making a Birth Plan" on p. 226.

Labor and Delivery

The birth process occurs in three stages (Figure 8.7, p. 227). **Labor** begins when hormonal changes in both the mother and the baby cause strong, rhythmic uterine **contractions** to begin. These contractions exert pressure on the cervix and cause the lengthwise muscles of the uterus to pull on the circular muscles around the cervix, causing effacement (thinning) and dilation (opening) of the cervix. The contractions also pressure the baby to descend into the mother's pelvis, if it hasn't already. The entire process of labor and delivery usually takes between 2 and 36 hours, depending on the size of the baby, the baby's position in the uterus, the size of the mother's pelvis, the strength of the uterine contractions, the number of prior deliveries, and other factors. The length of labor is generally shorter for second and subsequent births.

The First Stage of Labor   The first stage of labor averages 13 hours for a first birth, although there is a wide variation among women. It begins with cervical effacement and dilation and continues until the cervix is completely dilated (10 centimeters). Contractions usually last about 30 seconds and occur every 15–20 minutes at first, more often later. The prepared mother relaxes as much as possible during these contractions to allow labor to proceed without being blocked by tension. Early in the first stage, a small amount of bleeding may occur as a plug of slightly bloody mucus that blocked the opening of the cervix during pregnancy is expelled. In some women, the amniotic sac ruptures and the fluid rushes out; this is sometimes referred to as the "water breaking."

The last part of the first stage of labor, called **transition,** is characterized by strong and frequent contractions, much more intense than in the early stages of labor. Contractions may last 60–90 seconds and occur every 1–3 minutes. During transition the cervix opens completely, to a diameter of about 10 centimeters. The head of the fetus usually measures 9–10 centimeters; thus once the cervix has dilated completely, the head can pass through. Many women report that transition, which normally lasts about 30–60 minutes, is the most difficult part of labor.

The Second Stage of Labor   The second stage of labor begins with complete cervical dilation and ends with the delivery of the baby. The baby is slowly pushed down, through the bones of the pelvic ring, past the cervix, and into the vagina, which it stretches open. The mother bears down with the contractions to help push the baby down and out. Some women find this the most difficult part of labor; others find that the contractions and bearing down bring a sense of relief. The baby's back bends, the head turns to fit through the narrowest parts of the passageway, and the soft bones of the baby's skull move together and overlap as it is squeezed through the pelvis. When the top

Making a Birth Plan

A variety of birth situations can have positive physical and psychological outcomes. Parents should choose what is appropriate for their medical circumstances and what feels most comfortable to them. Prospective parents should discuss their preferences in the following areas with their physician or midwife:

1. Who will be present at the birth? The father? Friends? Children and other relatives? Will young siblings be allowed to visit the mother and new baby?

2. What type of room will the mother be in during labor, delivery, and recovery? How many times will she be moved?

3. What types of tables, beds, or birthing chairs are available? What type of environment can be created for the birth? Can specific music be played?

4. Will the mother receive any routine preparation, such as an enema, intravenous feeding, or shaving of the pubic area?

5. What is the policy regarding food and drink during labor? Will the mother have the option of walking around or taking a shower or bath during labor?

6. Under what circumstances does the physician or midwife administer drugs to induce or augment labor? The use of these drugs tends to change the course of labor and carries a small risk.

7. Is **electronic fetal monitoring (EFM)** typically used during labor? About 75% of all births are electronically monitored, but there is disagreement among medical authorities about the risks or benefits of EFM. The American College of Obstetricians and Gynecologists offers periodic monitoring using a stethoscope rather than EFM for low-risk pregnancies.

8. Under what circumstances will an **episiotomy,** an incision at the base of the vaginal opening, be performed? Are any steps taken to avoid it?

9. Under what circumstances will forceps or vacuum extraction be used? In some cases of fetal distress, the use of forceps or vacuum extraction may be necessary to save the infant's life, but some authorities believe these techniques are overused.

10. What types of medications are typically used during labor and delivery? Some form of anesthetic is usually administered during most hospital deliveries, as are hormones that intensify the contractions and shrink the uterus after delivery. Different types of anesthetics, including short-acting narcotics, regional nerve blocks, and local anesthetics, may be available; each has different effects on the mother and the fetus.

11. Under what conditions or circumstances does the physician perform a cesarean section? If prospective parents are concerned, they should research the cesarean frequency rates of different physicians before they make their final choice.

12. Who will "catch" the baby as she or he is born? Who will cut the umbilical cord?

13. What will be done to the baby immediately after birth? What kinds of tests and procedures will be done on the baby, and when?

14. How often will the baby be brought to the mother while they remain in the hospital or birthing center? Can the baby stay in the mother's room rather than in the nursery? This practice is known as **rooming-in.**

15. How will the baby be fed—by breast or bottle? Will feeding be on a schedule or on demand? Is there someone with breastfeeding expertise available to answer questions if necessary?

---

of the head appears at the vaginal opening, the baby is said to be crowning.

As the head of the baby emerges, the physician or midwife will remove any mucus from the mouth and nose, wipe the baby's face, and check to ensure that the umbilical cord is not around the neck. With a few more contractions, the baby's shoulders and body emerge. As the baby is squeezed through the pelvis, cervix, and vagina, the fluid in the lungs is forced out by the pressure on the baby's chest. Once this pressure is released as the baby emerges from the vagina, the chest expands and the lungs fill with air for the first time. The baby will still be connected to the mother via the umbilical cord, which is not cut until it stops pulsating. The baby will appear wet and often is covered with a cheesy substance. The baby's head may be oddly shaped at first, due to the molding of the soft plates of bone during birth, but it usually takes on a more rounded appearance within 24 hours.

The Third Stage of Labor　　In the third stage of labor, the uterus continues to contract until the placenta is expelled. This stage usually takes 5–30 minutes. It is important that the entire placenta be expelled; if part remains in the uterus, it may cause infection or bleeding. Breastfeeding soon after delivery helps control uterine bleeding because it stimulates the secretion of a hormone that makes the uterus contract.

The baby's physical condition is assessed with the **Apgar score,** a formalized system for assessing the baby's need for medical assistance. Heart rate, respiration, color, reflexes, and muscle tone are individually rated with a score of 0–2, and a total score between 0 and 10 is given at 1 and 5 minutes after birth. A score of 7–10 at 5 minutes is considered normal. Most newborns are also tested for 29 specific disorders, some of which are life-threatening. The American Academy of Pediatrics endorses these tests, but they are not routinely performed in every state.

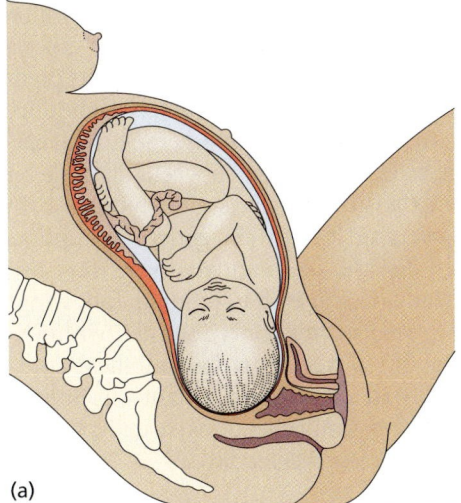

(a)

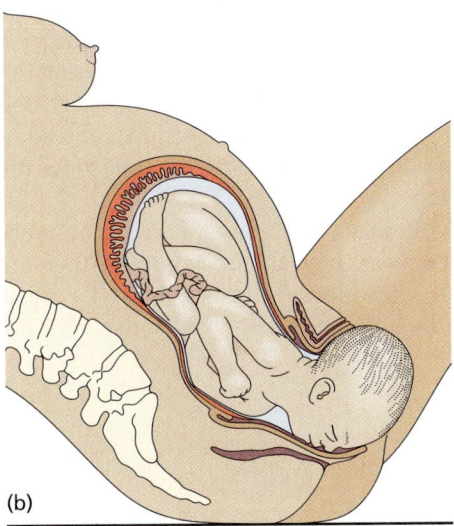

(b)

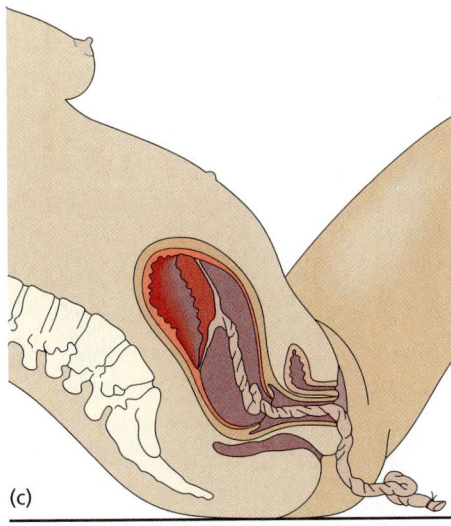

(c)

FIGURE 8.7 Birth: labor and delivery.   (a) The first stage of labor; (b) the second stage of labor: delivery of the baby; (c) the third stage of labor: expulsion of the placenta.

Pain Relief During Labor and Delivery   Women vary in how much pain they experience in childbirth. First babies are typically the most challenging to deliver, as the birth canal has never stretched to this extent before. It is recommended that women and their partners learn about labor and what kinds of choices are available for pain relief. Childbirth preparation courses are a good place to start, and communicating with one's obstetrician or midwife is essential to assess the approaches that will be available. Breathing and relaxation techniques such as Lamaze or Bradley have been used effectively, and they are often modified by the laboring women to be even more effective. Forms of hypnosis can also be used.

The most commonly employed medical intervention for pain relief is the epidural. This procedure involves placing a thin plastic catheter between the vertebrae in the lower back. Medication that reduces the transmission of pain signals to the brain is given through this catheter. Local anesthetic drugs are given in low concentration in order to minimize weakening of the leg muscles so that the mother can effectively push during the birth. The amount of medication given is quite low and does not accumulate in the baby or interfere with the baby's transition after birth. The mother is awake and is an active participant in the birth.

Women can also elect to have narcotics, such as fentanyl or demerol, given for pain relief during labor, but these medications usually provide less pain relief than the epidural and, if given shortly before the birth, can cause the baby to be less vigorous at birth. Local anesthesia is available for repair of any tear or episiotomy if the mother has not used an epidural for the labor.

Cesarean Deliveries   In a **cesarean section**, the baby is removed through a surgical incision in the abdominal wall and uterus. Cesarean sections are necessary when a baby cannot be delivered vaginally—for example, if the baby's head is bigger than the mother's pelvic girdle or if the baby is in an unusual position. If the mother has a serious health condition such as high blood pressure, a cesarean may be safer for her than labor and a vaginal delivery. Cesareans are more common among women

TERMS

electronic fetal monitoring (EFM)   The use of an external or internal electronic monitor during labor to measure uterine contractions and fetal heart rate.

episiotomy   An incision made to widen the vaginal opening to facilitate birth and prevent uncontrolled tearing during delivery.

rooming-in   The practice of allowing the mother and baby to remain together in the hospital or birth center after delivery.

Apgar score   A formalized system for assessing a newborn's need for medical assistance.

cesarean section   A surgical incision through the abdominal wall and uterus, performed to deliver a fetus.

who are overweight or have diabetes. Other reasons for cesarean delivery include abnormal or difficult labor, fetal distress, and the presence of a dangerous infection like herpes that can be passed to the baby during delivery. A growing number of cesareans are performed on low-risk mothers; researchers hope further analysis will help determine if the trend is due to patient choice, physician choice, or a combination of the two.

Repeat cesarean deliveries are also very common. About 90% of American women who have had one child by cesarean have subsequent children delivered the same way. Although the risk of complications from a vaginal delivery after a previous cesarean delivery is low, there is a small (1%) risk of serious complication to the mother and baby if the previous uterine scar opens during labor (uterine rupture). For this reason, women and their doctors may choose to deliver by elective repeat caesarean.

Cesarean section is the most common hospital procedure performed in the United States, and the current cesarean delivery rate is the highest it has ever been, despite the efforts of U.S. health officials to reduce it. Like any major surgery, cesarean section carries some risk and should be performed only for valid medical reasons (not convenience). Women who have cesarean sections can remain conscious during the operation if they are given a regional anesthetic, and the father may be present.

The Postpartum Period

The **postpartum period,** a stage of about 3 months following childbirth, is a time of critical family adjustments. Parenthood begins literally overnight, and the transition can cause considerable stress.

Following a vaginal delivery, mothers usually leave the hospital within 1–3 days (after a cesarean section, they usually stay 3–5 days). Uterine contractions will occur from time to time for several days after delivery, especially during nursing, as the uterus begins to return to its prebirth size. It usually takes 6–8 weeks for a woman's reproductive organs to return to their prebirth condition. She will have a bloody discharge called *lochia* for 3–6 weeks after the birth.

Within the first few days after birth, a baby will undergo screening for certain genetic conditions such as sickle-cell disease; the mandated tests vary by state. The baby's head—if somewhat pointed following a vaginal delivery—will become more rounded within a few days. It takes about a week for the umbilical cord stump to shrivel and fall off. Regular infant checkups for health screenings and immunizations usually begin when the infant is only a few weeks old.

Breastfeeding   Currently, about 74% of mothers breastfeed their infants for a short time after delivery, up from about 10% in 1970. **Lactation,** the production of milk, begins about 3 days after childbirth. Prior to that time (sometimes as early as the second trimester), **colostrum** is secreted by the nipples. Colostrum contains antibodies that help protect the newborn from infectious diseases and is also high in protein.

The American Academy of Pediatrics recommends breastfeeding exclusively for 6 months, then in combination with solid food until the baby is 1 year of age, and then for as long after that as a mother and baby desire.

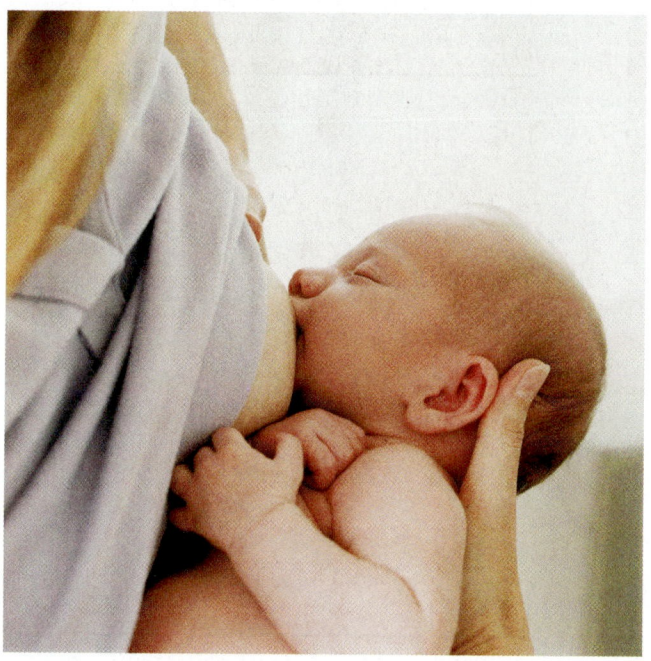

Breastfeeding can enhance the bond between mother and child. The American Academy of Pediatrics recommends breastfeeding exclusively for 6 months and then in combination with solid food until the baby is at least 1 year of age.

TERMS

postpartum period   The period of about 3 months after delivering a baby.

lactation   The production of milk.

colostrum   A yellowish fluid secreted by the mammary glands around the time of childbirth until milk comes in, about the third day.

postpartum depression   An emotional low that may be experienced by the mother following childbirth.

Currently, only 11% of U.S. mothers breast-feed exclusively for 6 months. Human milk is perfectly suited to the baby's nutritional needs and digestive capabilities, and it supplies the baby with antibodies. Breastfeeding decreases the incidence of infant ear infections, allergies, anemia, diarrhea, and bacterial meningitis. Preschoolers who were breastfed as babies are less likely to be overweight, and school-age children who were breastfed are less anxious and better able to cope with stress. Breastfeeding even has a beneficial effect on blood pressure and cholesterol levels later in life.

Breastfeeding is beneficial to the mother, as well. It stimulates contractions that help the uterus return to normal more rapidly, contributes to postpregnancy weight loss, and may reduce the risk of ovarian cancer, breast cancer, and postmenopausal hip fracture. Nursing also provides a sense of closeness and emotional well-being for mother and child. For women who want to breast-feed but who have problems, help is available from support groups, books, or a lactation consultant.

For some women, physical problems such as tenderness or infection of the nipples can make breastfeeding difficult. If a woman has an illness or requires drug treatment, she may have to bottle-feed her baby because drugs and infectious agents may show up in breast milk. Breastfeeding can be restrictive, making it especially difficult for working mothers. Employers rarely provide nursing breaks, so bottlefeeding or the use of a breast pump (to express milk for use while the mother is away from her infant) may be the only practical alternatives. Bottlefeeding makes it easier to tell how much milk an infant is taking in, and bottlefed infants tend to sleep longer. Bottlefeeding also allows the father or other caregiver to share in the nurturing process. Both breastfeeding and bottlefeeding can be part of loving, secure parent-child relationships.

When a mother doesn't nurse, menstruation usually begins within about 10 weeks. Breastfeeding can prevent the return of menstruation for 6 months or longer because the hormone prolactin, which aids milk production, suppresses hormones vital to the development of mature eggs. However, ovulation—and pregnancy—can occur before menstruation returns, so breastfeeding is not a reliable contraceptive method; if a woman wishes to avoid pregnancy, she should use a more reliable method. If the mother becomes pregnant while still nursing, she needs to make sure that she is receiving adequate nutrition, because the energy requirement for both breastfeeding and gestating is immense. With proper counseling, breastfeeding can continue until near delivery.

Postpartum Depression   Many women experience fluctuating emotions during the postpartum period as hormone levels change. The physical stress of labor, as well as dehydration, blood loss, and other physical factors, contributes to lowering the woman's stamina. About 50–80% of new mothers experience "baby blues," characterized by episodes of sadness, weeping, anxiety, headache, sleep disturbances, and irritability. A mother may feel lonely and anxious about caring for her infant. About 5–9% of new mothers experience **postpartum depression,** a more disabling syndrome characterized by despondency, mood swings, guilt, and occasional hostility. Rest, sharing feelings and concerns with others, and relying on supportive relatives and friends for assistance are usually helpful in dealing with mild cases of the baby blues or postpartum depression, which generally lasts only a few weeks. If the depression is serious, professional treatment may be needed. Some men also seem to get a form of postpartum depression, characterized by anxiety about their changing role and feelings of inadequacy. Both mothers and fathers need time to adjust to their new roles as parents.

Attachment   Another feature of the postpartum period is the development of attachment—the strong emotional tie that grows between the baby and the adult who cares for the baby. Parents can foster secure attachment relationships in the early weeks and months by responding sensitively to the baby's true needs. Parents who respond appropriately to the baby's signals of gazing, looking away, smiling, and crying establish feelings of trust in their child. They feed the baby when she's hungry, for example; respond when she cries; interact with her when she gazes, smiles, or babbles; and stop stimulating her when she frowns or looks away. A secure attachment relationship helps the child develop and function well socially, emotionally, and mentally.

For most people, the arrival of a child provides a deep sense of joy and accomplishment. However, adjusting to parenthood requires effort and energy. Talking with friends and relatives about their experiences during the first few weeks or months with a baby can help prepare new parents for the period when the baby's needs may require all the energy that both parents have to expend. But the pleasures of nurturing a new baby are substantial, and many parents look back on this time as one of the most significant and joyful of their lives.

QUESTIONS FOR CRITICAL THINKING AND REFLECTION

If you are a woman, what are your views on labor and delivery options? If you have a child in the future, which facility, delivery, and pain management options do you think you would prefer? If you are a man, what are your views on participating in delivery? What role would you want to play?

SUMMARY

- Factors to consider when deciding if and when to have a child include physical health and age; financial circumstances; relationship with your partner; educational, career, and child care plans; emotional readiness for parenthood; social support system; personal qualities, attitudes toward children, and aptitude for parenting; and philosophical or religious beliefs.

- Preconception care examines factors such as preexisting medical conditions, current medications, age of the mother, lifestyle behaviors, infections, nutritional status, and family history of genetic disease.

- Fertilization is a complex process culminating when a sperm penetrates the membrane of the egg released from the woman's ovary.

- Infertility affects about 10% of the reproductive-age population of the United States. The leading causes of infertility in women are blocked oviducts and ovulation disorders. Exposure to toxins, injury to the testicles, and infection can cause infertility in men.

- Early signs and symptoms of pregnancy include a missed menstrual period; slight bleeding; nausea; breast tenderness; increased urination; fatigue and emotional upset; and a softening of the uterus just above the cervix.

- During pregnancy, the uterus enlarges until it pushes up into the rib cage; the breasts enlarge and may secrete colostrum; the muscles and ligaments soften and stretch; and the circulatory system, lungs, and kidneys become more efficient.

- The fetal anatomy is almost completely formed in the first trimester and is refined in the second; during the third trimester, the fetus grows and gains most of its weight, storing nutrients in fatty tissues.

- Prenatal tests include ultrasound, amniocentesis, chorionic villus sampling, and quadruple marker screening.

- Health care during pregnancy includes a complete history and physical at the beginning, followed by regular checkups and monitoring of blood pressure, weight gain, and size and position of the fetus.

- Important elements of prenatal care include good nutrition; avoiding drugs, alcohol, tobacco, infections, and other harmful environmental agents or conditions; regular physical activity; and childbirth classes.

- Pregnancy usually proceeds without major complications. Problems that can occur include ectopic pregnancy, spontaneous abortion, preeclampsia, and low birth weight. The loss of a fetus or infant is deeply felt by most parents, who need time to grieve and heal.

- Couples preparing for childbirth may have many options to choose from, including type of practitioner and facility.

- The first stage of labor begins with contractions that exert pressure on the cervix, causing effacement and dilation. The second stage begins with complete cervical dilation and ends when the baby emerges. The third stage of labor is expulsion of the placenta.

- During the postpartum period, the mother's body begins to return to its prepregnancy state, and she may begin to breast-feed. Both mother and father must adjust to their new roles as parents, as they develop a strong emotional tie to their baby.

FOR MORE INFORMATION

BOOKS

American College of Obstetricians and Gynecologists. 2005. *Your Pregnancy and Birth,* 4th ed. Washington, D.C.: ACOG. *Advice on conception, pregnancy, prenatal care, and delivery options.*

Beer, A. E., et al. 2006. *Is Your Body Baby-Friendly? Unexplained Infertility, Miscarriage, and IVF Failure Explained and Treated.* Chicago: AJR Publishing. *Covers many issues facing women and couples who are trying to overcome infertility.*

Lees, C., et al. 2007. *Pregnancy and Birth: Your Questions Answered.* London: Dorling Kindersley. *Answers hundreds of common questions about conception, pregnancy, and delivery.*

Lichtman, R., et al. 2005. *Dr. Guttmacher's Pregnancy, Birth & Family Planning,* updated ed. New York: New American Library. *A complete guide to contraception, conception, pregnancy, and childbirth.*

Riley, L. 2006. *Healthy Eating During Pregnancy.* New York: Meredith Books. *Provides up-to-date dietary information and meal-planning guides for pregnant women.*

Wynbrandt, J. 2007. *Encyclopedia of Genetic Disorders and Birth Defects.* New York: Facts on File, Inc. *A detailed overview of many types of birth defects, both inherited and noninherited.*

ORGANIZATIONS AND WEB SITES

American College of Obstetricians and Gynecologists (ACOG). Provides written materials relating to many aspects of preconception care, pregnancy, and childbirth.

> http://www.acog.org

The American Society for Reproductive Medicine. Provides up-to-date information on all aspects of infertility.

> http://www.asrm.org

Centers for Disease Control and Prevention, National Center on Birth Defects and Developmental Disabilities. Provides information about a variety of topics related to birth defects, including fetal alcohol syndrome and the importance of folic acid.

> http://www.cdc.gov/ncbddd

Childbirth.Org. Contains medical information and personal stories about all phases of pregnancy and birth.

> http://www.childbirth.org

Generational Health. Helps you create a family health tree online and provides information about detection and screening for any conditions that are common in your family history.

> http://www.generationalhealth.com

Health Resources and Services Administration (HRSA): Maternal and Child Health. Provides publications, videos, and other resources relating to maternal, infant, and family health.

> http://www.ask.hrsa.gov/MCH.cfm

International Council on Infertility Information Dissemination. A Web site that includes information on current research and treatments for infertility.

> http://www.inciid.org

La Leche League International. Provides advice and support for breastfeeding mothers.

> http://www.lalecheleague.org

The March of Dimes. Provides public education materials on many pregnancy-related topics, including preconception care, genetic screening, diet and exercise, and the effects of smoking and drinking during pregnancy.

> http://www.marchofdimes.com

National Institute of Child Health and Human Development. Provides information about reproductive and genetic problems; sponsors the "Back to Sleep" campaign to fight SIDS.

> http://www.nichd.nih.gov

Resolve. Provides information, support, and referrals for people facing infertility.

> http://www.resolve.org

SELECTED BIBLIOGRAPHY

American Academy of Pediatrics Section on Breastfeeding. 2005. Breast-feeding and the use of human milk. *Pediatrics* 115(2): 496 – 506.

American Academy of Pediatrics Task Force on Sudden Infant Death Syndrome. 2005. The Changing Concept of Sudden Infant Death Syndrome. *Pediatrics* 116(5): 1245–1255.

Centers for Disease Control and Prevention. 2009. *2006 Assisted Reproductive Technology (ART) Success Rates: National Summary and Fertility Clinic Reports.* Atlanta: Centers for Disease Control and Prevention.

Centers for Disease Control and Prevention. 2006. *Preconception Health and Care, 2006* (http://www.cdc.gov/ncbddd/preconception/documents/At-a-glance-4-11-06.pdf; retrieved January 29, 2009).

Centers for Disease Control and Prevention. 2007. Breastfeeding trends and updated national health objectives for exclusive breastfeeding—United States, birth years 2000–2004. *Morbidity and Mortality Weekly Report* 56(30): 760–763.

Central Intelligence Agency. 2009. *The World Factbook: Rank Order—Infant Mortality Rate* (https://www.cia.gov/cia/publications/factbook/rankorder/2091rank.html; retrieved January 29, 2009).

Child Health Alert. 2006. *Does caffeine in pregnancy cause birth defects?* 24: 2.

de la Chica, R. A., et al. 2005. Chromosomal instability in amniocytes from fetuses of mothers who smoke. *Journal of the American Medical Association* 293(10): 1212–1222.

De Sutter, P. 2006. Rational diagnosis and treatment of infertility. *Best Practice & Research: Clinical Obstetrics & Gynaecology,* 9 June [epub].

Declercq, E., F. Menacker, and M. MacDorman. 2005. Rise in "no indicated risk" primary caesareans in the United States, 1991–2001: Cross sectional analysis. *British Medical Journal* 330(7482): 71–72.

Duncombe, D., et al. 2006. Vigorous exercise and birth outcomes in a sample of recreational exercisers: A prospective study across pregnancy. *The Australian & New Zealand Journal of Obstetrics & Gynaecology* 46(4): 288–292.

Gorman, C. 2006. What alcohol does to a child. *Time,* 5 June.

Harrison, E. C., and J. S. Taylor. 2006. IVF therapy for unexplained infertility. *American Family Physician* 73(1): 63 – 65.

Jimenez-Chillaron, J. C., et al. 2005. Beta-cell secretory dysfunction in the pathogenesis of low birth weight–associated diabetes. *Diabetes* 54(3): 702 – 711.

Keim, S. A., and M. A. Klebanoff. 2006. Aspirin use and miscarriage risk. *Epidemiology* 17(4): 435 – 439.

Lavender, T., et al. 2006. Caesarean section for non-medical reasons at term. *Cochrane Database of Systematic Reviews* 19(3).

Leguizamon, G. F., and N. P. Zeff. 2006. Hypertension and the pregnancy complicated by diabetes. *Current Diabetes Reports* 6(4): 297 – 304.

Levine, R. J., et al. 2005. Urinary placental growth factor and risk of pre-eclampsia. *Journal of the American Medical Association* 293(1): 77 – 85.

Lino, Mark. 2008. *Expenditures on Children by Families, 2007.* U.S. Department of Agriculture, Center for Nutrition Policy and Promotion. Miscellaneous Publication No. 1528-2007.

Macfarlane, A., and Tuffnell, D. 2006. Diabetes and pregnancy. *British Medical Journal* 333(7560): 157 – 158.

Mannion, C. A., et al. 2006. Association of low intake of milk and vitamin D during pregnancy with decreased birth weight. *Canadian Medical Association Journal* 174(9): 1273 – 1277.

McCormack, V. A., et al. 2005. Birth characteristics and adult cancer incidence: Swedish cohort of over 11,000 men and women. *International Journal of Cancer,* 7 February [epub].

National Association of Child Care Resources and Referral Agencies. 2008. *Parents and the High Price of Child Care* (http://www.naccrra.org/docs/reports/price_report/Price_Report_2008.pdf; retrieved January 29, 2009).

National Center for Health Statistics. 2009. Births: Final data for 2006. *National Vital Statistics Reports* 57(7): 1–102.

Pattenden, S., et al. 2006. Parental smoking and children's respiratory health: Independent effects of prenatal and postnatal exposure. *Tobacco Control* 15(4): 294–301.

Scollan-Koliopoulos, M., et al. 2006. Gestational diabetes management: Guidelines to a healthy pregnancy. *Nurse Practitioner* 31(6): 14–23.

U.S. Census Bureau. 2006. *International Database: IDB Data-Access—User Configurable, Table 010: Infant Mortality Rates and Life Expectancy at Birth, by Sex: All Countries, 2006* (http://www.census.gov/cgi-bin/ipc/idbsprd; retrieved August 5, 2006).

U.S. Department of Health and Human Services and U.S. Department of Agriculture. 2005. *Dietary Guidelines for Americans, 2005,* 6th ed. Washington, D.C.: U.S. Government Printing Office.

Voelker, R. 2005. The business of baby pictures: Controversy brews over "keepsake" fetal ultrasounds. *Journal of the American Medication Association* 293(1): 25–27.

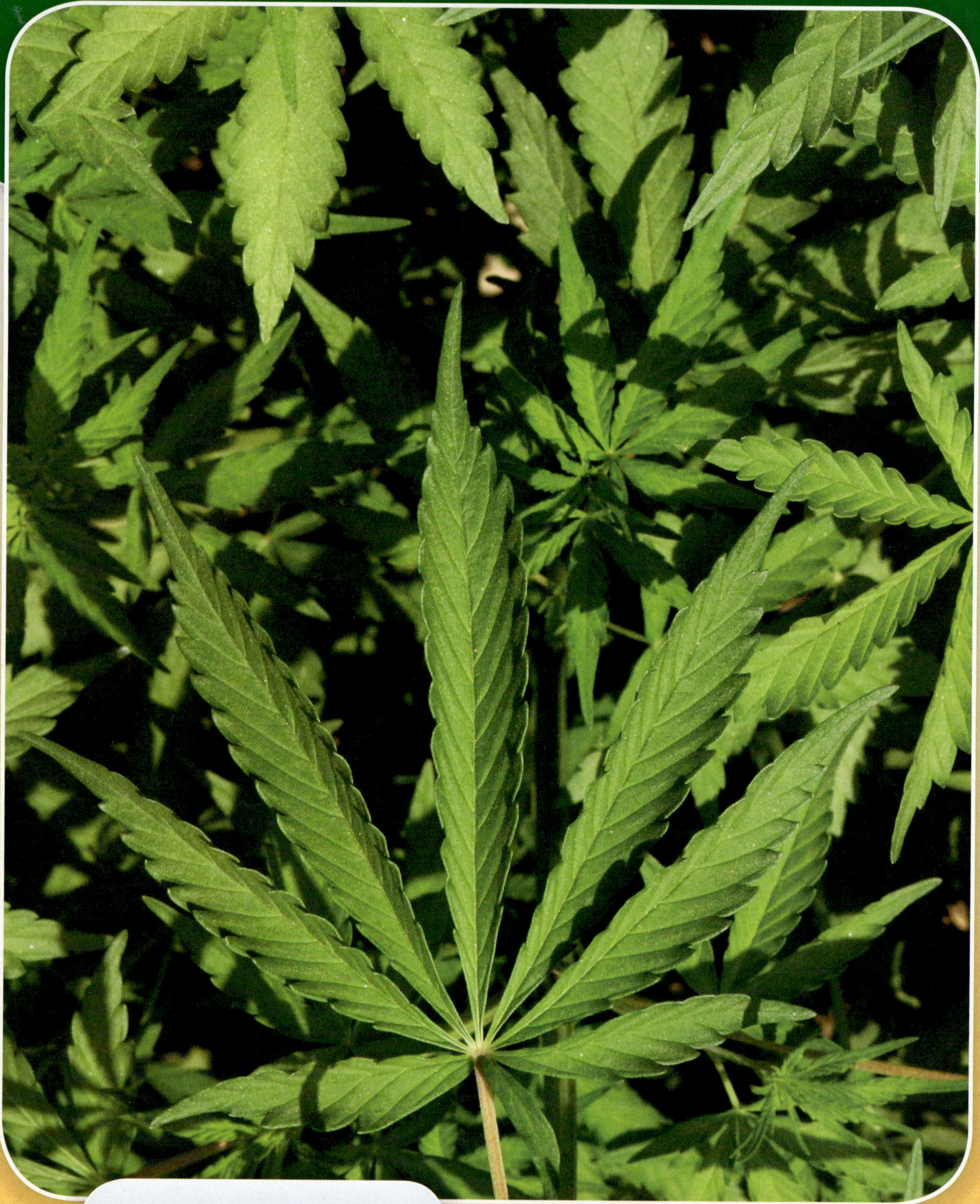

CORE CONCEPTS IN HEALTH

PERSONAL HEALTH

http://www.mcgrawhillconnect.com/personalhealth

THE USE AND ABUSE OF PSYCHOACTIVE DRUGS

9

LOOKING AHEAD>>>>>

AFTER READING THIS CHAPTER, YOU SHOULD BE ABLE TO:

- Define and discuss the concepts of addictive behavior, substance abuse, and substance dependence
- Explain factors contributing to drug use and dependence
- List the major categories of psychoactive drugs and describe their effects, methods of use, and potential for abuse and dependence
- Discuss social issues related to psychoactive drug use and its prevention and treatment
- Evaluate the role of drugs and other addictive behaviors in your life and identify your risk factors for abuse or dependence

TEST YOUR KNOWLEDGE

1. **Addictions always involve drugs that cause physical withdrawal symptoms when the person stops taking them.**
   True or false?

2. **Which of the following is the most widely used illegal drug among college students?**
   a. cocaine
   b. hallucinogens
   c. marijuana
   d. heroin

3. **Caffeine use can produce physical dependence.**
   True or false?

4. **Which of the following drugs is most addictive?**
   a. marijuana
   b. nicotine
   c. LSD

5. **About what percentage of street drugs contain the promised primary ingredient?**
   a. 50%
   b. 66%
   c. 75%

ANSWERS

1. **FALSE.** Both assertions in this statement are wrong. Addiction does not always involve a drug, but even when it does, withdrawing from that drug may not result in physical symptoms.

2. **C.** Marijuana ranks first, followed (in order) by hallucinogens and cocaine. Alcohol remains by far the most popular drug among college students.

3. **TRUE.** Regular users of caffeine develop physical tolerance, needing more caffeine to produce the same level of alertness. Many also experience withdrawal symptoms, such as headaches and irritability, when they decrease their intake.

4. **B.** Nicotine is believed to be the most highly addictive psychoactive drug.

5. **A.** This figure is even lower for drugs that are difficult to obtain or manufacture. Street drugs may be sold in unsafe dosages and are typically mixed ("cut") with cheaper and often more hazardous substances.

The use of **drugs** for both medical and social purposes is widespread in America (Table 9.1). Many people believe that every problem has or should have a chemical solution. For fatigue, many turn to caffeine; for insomnia, sleeping pills; for anxiety or boredom, alcohol or other recreational drugs. Advertisements, social pressures, and the human desire for quick solutions to life's difficult problems all contribute to the prevailing attitude that drugs can ease all pain. Unfortunately, using drugs can—and often does—have serious consequences.

The most serious consequences are abuse and addiction. The drugs most often associated with abuse are **psychoactive drugs**—those that alter a person's experiences or consciousness. In the short term, psychoactive drugs can cause **intoxication**, a state in which sometimes unpredictable physical and emotional changes occur. A person who is intoxicated may experience potentially serious changes in physical functioning. His or her emotions and judgment may be affected in ways that lead to uncharacteristic and unsafe behavior. In the long term, recurrent drug use can have profound physical, emotional, and social effects.

This chapter introduces the concept of addictive behavior, then focuses on the major classes of psychoactive drugs, their effects, their potential for abuse and addiction, and other issues related to their use. Alcohol and nicotine—two of the most widely used and most harmful psychoactive drugs—are discussed in Chapters 10 and 11.

ADDICTIVE BEHAVIOR

Although addiction is most often associated with drug use, many experts now extend the concept of addiction to other behaviors. **Addictive behaviors** are habits that have gotten out of control, with resulting negative effects on a

Table 9.1 — Nonmedical Drug Use Among Americans, 2007

	Percentage Using Substance in the Past 30 Days	
	College Students (age 18–25)	All Americans (age 12 and older)
Illicit Drugs	19.7	8.0
Tobacco (all forms)	41.8	28.6
Cigarettes	36.2	24.2
Smokeless tobacco	5.3	3.2
Cigars	11.8	5.4
Pipe tobacco	1.2	0.8
Alcohol	61.2	51.1
Binge alcohol use	41.8	23.3
Marijuana and hashish	16.4	5.8
Cocaine	1.7	0.8
Crack	0.2	0.2
Heroin	0.1	0.1
Methamphetamine	0.4	0.2
Hallucinogens	1.5	0.4
LSD	0.2	0.1
PCP	0.0	0.0
Ecstasy	0.7	0.2
Inhalants	0.4	0.2
Nonmedical use of psychotherapeutics	6.0	2.8
Pain relievers	4.6	2.1
OxyContin	0.5	0.1
Tranquilizers	1.7	0.7
Stimulants	1.1	0.4
Sedatives	0.2	0.1

SOURCE: Office of Applied Studies, Substance Abuse and Mental Health Services Administration. 2008. *Results from the 2007 National Survey on Drug Use and Health: National Findings* (http://oas.samhsa.gov/nsduh.htm; retrieved February 3, 2009).

person's health. Looking at the nature of addiction and a range of addictive behaviors can help us understand similar behaviors when they involve drugs.

What Is Addiction?

The word *addiction* tends to be a highly charged one for most people. Most of us think of true addiction as a habitual and uncontrollable behavior, usually involving the use of a drug. Some people think of addiction as a moral flaw or a personal weakness. Others think addictions arise from certain personality traits, genetic factors, or socioeconomic influences. Views on the causes of addictions have an impact on our attitudes toward people with addictive disorders, as well as on the approaches to treatment.

Historically, the term *addiction* was applied only when the habitual use of a drug produced chemical changes in

TERMS

drug Any chemical other than food intended to affect the structure or function of the body.

psychoactive drug A drug that can alter a person's consciousness or experience.

intoxication The state of being mentally affected by a chemical (literally, a state of being poisoned).

addictive behavior Any habit that has gotten out of control, resulting in a negative effect on one's health.

addiction Psychological or physical dependence on a substance or behavior, characterized by a compulsive desire and increasing need for the substance or behavior, and by harm to the individual and/or society.

habituation Similar to addiction, involving the routine use of a substance, but without the level of compulsion or increasing need that characterizes addiction.

the user's body. One such change is physical tolerance, in which the body adapts to a drug so that the initial dose no longer produces the original emotional or psychological effects. This process, caused by chemical changes, means the user has to take larger and larger doses of the drug to achieve the same high. (Tolerance is discussed in greater detail later in the chapter.) The concept of addiction as a disease process, one based in brain chemistry rather than a moral failing, has led to many advances in the understanding and treatment of drug addiction.

As scientists have learned about addictive behaviors, they have been able to distinguish between different levels of addiction. In particular, the concepts of drug **addiction** and drug **habituation** have been defined over the past few decades to help explain how drug use impacts people's lives in different ways. These two terms are often differentiated as follows:

- *Drug addiction* is defined by four important characteristics: the compulsive desire for a drug, the need to increase the dosage associated with psychological and physical dependence, harmful effects to the individual, and harm to society.

- *Drug habituation* (or habit) is often considered to mean a lesser version of addiction. While sharing the same behavioral patterns with drug addiction, drug habituation is defined by the routine use of a drug but without reaching a level of compulsion or increased need for greater dosage associated with drug addiction. Further, drug habituation is accompanied by psychological but not physical dependence.

Distinguishing among different levels of drug addiction is important for developing and implementing successful prevention and treatment strategies for drug use. The definitions of drug addiction and drug habituation, however, are under continuous debate.

Some scientists think that other behaviors may share some of the chemistry of drug addiction. They suggest that activities like gambling, eating, exercising, and sex trigger the release of brain chemicals that cause a pleasurable rush in much the same way that psychoactive drugs do. The brain's own chemicals thus become the "drug" that can cause addiction. These theorists suggest that all addictions—whether to drugs or to pleasurable activities—have a common mechanism in the brain. In this view, addiction is partly the result of our own natural wiring.

The view that addiction is based in our brain chemistry does *not* imply that people are not responsible for their addictive behavior. Many experts believe that it is inaccurate and counterproductive to think of all bad habits and excessive behaviors as diseases. They point to other factors, especially lifestyle and personality traits, that play key roles in the development of addictive behaviors.

Characteristics of Addictive Behavior

It is often difficult to distinguish between a healthy habit and one that has become an addiction. Experts have identified some general characteristics typically associated with addictive behaviors:

- *Reinforcement.* Addictive behaviors are reinforcing. Some aspect of the behavior produces pleasurable physical and/or emotional states or relieves negative ones.

- *Compulsion or craving.* The individual feels a strong compulsion—a compelling need—to engage in the behavior, often accompanied by obsessive planning for the next opportunity to perform it.

- *Loss of control.* The individual loses control over the behavior and cannot block the impulse to do it.

- *Escalation.* Addiction often involves a pattern of escalation, in which more and more of a particular substance or activity is required to produce its desired effects.

- *Negative consequences.* The behavior continues despite serious negative consequences, such as problems with academic or job performance, personal relationships, and health; legal or financial troubles are also typical.

The Development of Addiction

We all engage in activities that are potentially addictive. Some of these activities can be good for you if they are done appropriately and in moderation. But if a behavior starts to be excessive, it may become an addiction.

An addiction often starts when a person does something to bring pleasure or avoid pain. The activity may be drinking a beer, using the Internet, playing the lottery, or going shopping. If it works, the person is likely to repeat it. He or she becomes increasingly dependent on the behavior, and tolerance may develop—that is, the person needs more of the behavior to feel the same effect. Eventually, the behavior becomes a central focus of the person's life, and there is a deterioration in other areas, such as school performance or relationships. The behavior no longer brings pleasure, but it is necessary to avoid the pain of going without it. What started as a seemingly innocent way of feeling good can become a prison.

Although many common behaviors are potentially addictive, most people who engage in them do not develop problems. The reason lies in the combination of factors that are involved in the development of addiction, including personality, lifestyle, heredity, the social and physical environment, and the nature of the substance or behavior in question. For a behavior to become an addiction, these diverse factors must come together in a certain way. For example, nicotine (the psychoactive drug in tobacco) has a very high potential for physical addiction; but a person must submit to the temptation to start using tobacco—whether prompted by peer pressure, stress, or personality traits—in order to develop an addiction to it.

Characteristics of People with Addictions

The causes and course of an addiction are extremely varied, but people with addictions seem to share some characteristics. Many use a substance or activity as a substitute for healthier coping strategies. People vary in their ability to manage their lives, and those who have the most trouble dealing with stress and painful emotions may be more susceptible to addiction.

Some people may have a genetic predisposition to addiction to a particular substance; such predispositions may involve variations in brain chemistry. People with addictive disorders usually have a distinct preference for a particular addictive behavior. They also often have problems with impulse control and self-regulation, and tend to be risk takers.

Examples of Addictive Behaviors

Some behaviors that are not related to drugs can become addictive for some people.

Compulsive or Pathological Gambling Compulsive gamblers cannot control the urge to gamble, even in the face of financial and personal ruin. Most compulsive gamblers seek excitement even more than money. Increasingly larger bets are necessary to produce the desired level of excitement. When financial resources become strained, the person may lie or steal to pay off debts. The consequences of compulsive gambling are not just financial; the suicide rate of compulsive gamblers is 20 times higher than that of the general population.

The American Psychiatric Association (APA) recognizes pathological gambling as a mental disorder and lists ten characteristic behaviors, including preoccupation with gambling, unsuccessful efforts to cut back or quit, using gambling to escape problems, and lying to family members to conceal the extent of involvement with gambling. Gambling is often linked to other risky behaviors, and many compulsive gamblers also have drug and alcohol abuse problems.

In the United States, it is estimated that 1% of adults are compulsive (pathological) gamblers, and another 2% are

Many college students have gotten caught up in the poker craze. By some estimates, the number of college-age poker players has doubled in recent years.

"problem gamblers." In a recent survey of more than 10,000 students from more than 100 colleges, 42% of students reported having gambled at least once in the past year, and about 3% reported gambling at least once a week.

Compulsive Exercising When taken to a compulsive level, even healthy activities may develop into harmful addictions. For example, compulsive exercising has been widely studied and is now recognized as a serious departure from normal behavior. Compulsive exercising is often accompanied by more severe psychiatric disorders such as anorexia nervosa and bulimia (Chapter 14). Traits frequently associated with compulsive exercising include an excessive preoccupation and dissatisfaction with body image, the use of laxatives or vomiting to lose weight, and the development of other obsessive-compulsive symptoms.

Experts don't completely agree on what frequency and intensity of physical activity constitute compulsive exercising. Many compulsive exercisers, however, get involved in physical activities that cause bodily harm. For example, research has shown that professional bodybuilders, when compared to recreational exercisers engaged in weight lifting, are often dissatisfied with muscle size. Because of their preoccupation with muscle size, and because of the frequency and intensity of their workouts, some bodybuilders face an increased risk of injuries due to harmful weight-lifting practices.

Work Addiction   The term *workaholic* is often used to describe individuals with an excessive preoccupation with work and work-related activities. Work addiction, however, is actually based on a set of symptoms, including the following:

- An intense work schedule
- The inability to limit one's own work schedule
- The inability to relax, even when away from work
- Failed attempts at curtailing the intensity of work (in some cases)

Many of these traits are also seen in other types of addiction such as alcoholism—hence the popularity of the word *workaholism*.

Work addiction is a serious concern for various reasons. Someone suffering from this addiction is likely to neglect other areas of his or her life. For example, work addicts may tend to exercise less, spend less time with family and friends, and stay away from social activities.

Further, work addiction typically coincides with a well-known risk factor for cardiovascular disease—the Type A personality (Chapter 15). Traits associated with Type A personality include competitiveness, ambition, drive, time urgency, restlessness, and hyperalertness.

Many researchers see work addiction as a culture-bound disorder arising from a workplace that encourages these harmful behavioral patterns. The changing landscape of the modern workplace is likely to make work addiction a source of disability for a growing number of people.

Sex and Love Addiction   More controversial is the notion of addiction to sex or love. Some researchers believe that the initial rush of arousal and erotic or romantic chemistry produces an effect in the brain comparable to that of taking amphetamines or morphine. After a time, the brain becomes desensitized, and the addict must then seek his or her next rush by pursuing a new partner. According to this view, cheating on a partner, having many partners, and sexually victimizing others are behaviors parallel to drug-seeking behavior. Behaviors associated with sex addiction include an extreme preoccupation with sex, a compulsion to have sex repeatedly within a short period of time, spending a great deal of time and energy looking for partners or engaging in sex, using sex as a means of relieving painful feelings, and suffering negative emotional, personal, and professional consequences as a result of sexual activities.

Some experts are reluctant to call compulsive sexual activity a true addiction. However, even therapists who challenge the concept of sex addiction recognize that some people become overly preoccupied with sex, cannot seem to control their sex drive, and act in potentially harmful ways in order to obtain satisfaction. This pattern

Because the Internet provides easy access to so many different kinds of content, many Americans experience Internet addiction.

of sexual behavior seems to meet the criteria for addictive behaviors discussed earlier.

Compulsive Buying or Shopping   A compulsive buyer repeatedly gives in to the impulse to buy more than he or she needs or can afford. Compulsive spenders usually buy luxury items rather than daily necessities. Compulsive buyers are usually distressed by their behavior and its social, personal, and financial consequences. Some experts link compulsive shopping with neglect or abuse during childhood; it also seems to be associated with eating disorders, depression, and bipolar disorder.

Internet Addiction   In the decade since the Internet became widely available, millions of Americans have become compulsive Internet users. To spend more time online, Internet addicts skip important school, social, or recreational activities; compulsive Internet users often spend their work time online, a fact that has led many employers to adopt strict Internet usage policies. Despite negative financial, social, or academic consequences, compulsive Internet users don't feel able to stop. As with other addictive behaviors, online addicts may be using their behavior to alleviate stress or avoid painful emotions.

According to a 2006 study, 5–10% of the U.S. population may experience Internet addiction. Another study showed that Internet addicts spent an average of 38 hours online every week. There is concern that the number of Internet addicts will continue growing as the Internet becomes evermore accessible.

Other behaviors that can become addictive include eating, watching TV, and playing video games. Any substance or activity that becomes the focus of a person's life at the expense of other needs and interests can be damaging to health.

DRUG USE, ABUSE, AND DEPENDENCE

The substances most commonly associated with addiction are psychoactive drugs. Drugs are chemicals other than food that are intended to affect the structure or function of the body. They include prescription medicines such as antibiotics and antidepressants; nonprescription or over-the-counter (OTC) substances such as alcohol, tobacco, and caffeine products; and illegal substances such as LSD and heroin. The use of drugs is not new in society; drug use has a long history.

The Drug Tradition

Using drugs to alter consciousness is an ancient and universal pursuit. People have used alcohol for celebration and intoxication for thousands of years. People in all parts of the world have exploited the psychoactive properties of various local plants, such as the coca plant in South America and the opium poppy in the Far East.

In the nineteenth century, chemists began extracting the active chemicals from medicinal plants, such as morphine from the opium poppy and cocaine from the coca leaf. This was the beginning of modern **pharmacy,** the art of compounding drugs, and of **pharmacology,** the science and study of drugs. From this point on, a variety of drugs began to be produced, including codeine, LSD, methamphetamine, and heroin.

For generations, the manufacture and sale of these new drugs were not regulated. Pure morphine or cocaine could be purchased by mail order, and the makers of patent medicines and tonics included potentially addictive drugs in their products without informing consumers of either the ingredients or the dangers. The earliest version of the soft drink Coca-Cola contained cocaine, for example, which accounted for the lift it provided.

Drug addiction among middle-class Europeans and North Americans was more common by 1900 than at any time before or since. Concerns about drug addiction and the need to regulate drug sales and manufacture led in the early 1900s to the passage of federal drug laws in the United States. Middle-class use of regulated drugs dropped, and drug use became restricted to, and increasingly identified with, criminal subcultures.

Nonmedical (recreational) drug use expanded in America during the 1960s and 1970s, reaching a peak in 1979. Drug use rates then declined until the early to mid-1990s, when drug use rates began to rise in certain age groups. Between 2002 and 2007, however, use of illicit drugs, including marijuana and methamphetamine, declined among youths age 12–17, as did use of alcohol and tobacco. In young adults age 18–25, overall drug use remained stable during the same period, although there was a significant increase in nonmedical use of narcotic pain relievers.

Drug Abuse and Dependence

The APA's *Diagnostic and Statistical Manual of Mental Disorders* is the authoritative reference for defining all sorts of behavioral disorders, including those related to drugs. The APA has chosen not to use the term *addiction,* in part because it is so broad and has so many connotations. Instead, the APA refers to two forms of substance (drug) disorders: substance abuse and substance dependence. Both are maladaptive patterns of substance use that lead to significant impairment or distress. Although the APA's definitions are more precise and more directly related to drug use, they clearly encompass the general characteristics of addictive behavior described in the preceding section.

Abuse   As defined by the APA, **substance abuse** involves one or more of the following:

- Recurrent drug use, resulting in a failure to fulfill major responsibilities at work, school, or home
- Recurrent drug use in situations in which it is physically hazardous, such as before or while driving a car
- Recurrent drug-related legal problems
- Continued drug use despite persistent social or interpersonal problems caused or exacerbated by the effects of the drug

The pattern of use may be constant or intermittent, and **physical dependence** may or may not be present. For example, a person who smokes marijuana once a week and cuts classes because he or she is high is abusing marijuana, even though he or she is not physically dependent.

Dependence   **Substance dependence** is a more complex disorder and is what many people associate with the idea of addiction. The seven specific criteria the APA uses to diagnose substance dependence are listed below. The first two are associated with physical dependence; the final five are associated with compulsive use. To be considered dependent, one must experience a cluster of three or more of these symptoms during a 12-month period.

1. *Developing tolerance to the substance.* When a person requires increased amounts of a substance to achieve

the desired effect or notices a markedly diminished effect with continued use of the same amount, he or she has developed **tolerance.**

2. *Experiencing withdrawal.* In an individual who has maintained prolonged, heavy use of a substance, a drop in its concentration within the body can result in unpleasant physical and cognitive **withdrawal** symptoms. Withdrawal symptoms are different for different drugs. For example, nausea, vomiting, and tremors are common for alcohol, opioids, and sedatives. Some drugs have no significant withdrawal symptoms.

3. *Taking the substance in larger amounts or over a longer period than was originally intended.*

4. *Expressing a persistent desire to cut down or regulate substance use.*

5. *Spending a great deal of time obtaining the substance, using the substance, or recovering from its effects.*

6. *Giving up or reducing important social, school, work, or recreational activities because of substance use.*

7. *Continuing to use the substance in spite of recognizing that it is contributing to a psychological or physical problem.*

If a drug-dependent person experiences either tolerance or withdrawal, he or she is considered physically dependent. However, not everyone who experiences tolerance or withdrawal is drug dependent. For example, a hospital patient who is prescribed therapeutic doses of morphine to relieve pain may develop a tolerance to the drug and experience withdrawal symptoms when the prescription is discontinued. But without showing any signs of compulsive use, this individual would not be considered dependent.

Conversely, dependence can occur without a physical component, based solely on compulsive use. For example, people with at least three symptoms of compulsive use of marijuana who show no signs of tolerance or withdrawal are suffering from substance dependence. In general, dependence problems that involve physical dependence carry a greater risk of immediate general medical problems and higher relapse rates.

Who Uses Drugs?

The use and abuse of drugs occur at all income and education levels, among all ethnic groups, and at all ages (see the box "Drug Use Among College Students" on p. 242). Society is concerned with the casual or recreational use of illegal drugs because it is not really possible to know when drug use will lead to abuse or dependence. Some casual users develop substance-related problems; others do not. Some psychoactive drugs are more likely than others to lead to dependence (Table 9.2), but some users

TERMS

pharmacy The art of compounding drugs from various substances.

pharmacology The science and study of drugs.

substance abuse A maladaptive pattern of using any substance that persists despite adverse social, psychological, or medical consequences. The pattern may be intermittent, with or without tolerance and physical dependence.

physical dependence The result of physiological adaptation that occurs in response to the frequent presence of a drug; typically associated with tolerance and withdrawal.

substance dependence A cluster of cognitive, behavioral, and physiological symptoms that occur in someone who continues to use a substance despite suffering significant substance-related problems, leading to significant impairment or distress; also known as *addiction.*

tolerance Lower sensitivity to a drug so that a given dose no longer exerts the usual effect and larger doses are needed.

withdrawal Physical and psychological symptoms that follow the interrupted use of a drug on which a user is physically dependent; symptoms may be mild or life-threatening.

Table 9.2	Psychoactive Drugs and Their Potential for Producing Dependence	
	Potential for Dependence	
Drug	**Physical**	**Psychological**
Alcohol	Possible	Possible
Amphetamine	Possible	High
Barbiturates	High	Moderate
Chloral hydrate	Moderate	Moderate
Cocaine	Possible	High
Codeine	Moderate	Moderate
Crack cocaine	High	High
Hashish	Unknown	Moderate
Heroin	High	High
Ice (smoked methamphetamine)	High	High
LSD	None	Unknown
Marijuana	Unknown	Moderate
Methaqualone	High	High
Opium	High	High
PCP	Unknown	High
Psilocybin	None	Unknown

SOURCES: U.S. Department of Health and Human Services, Substance Abuse and Mental Health Services Administration. 2007. *Drugs of Abuse* (http://ncadi.samhsa.gov/govpubs/rop926; retrieved February 3, 2009); Beers, M. H., et al. 2006. *The Merck Manual of Diagnosis and Therapy,* 18th ed. New York: Wiley.

Drug Use Among College Students

Drug use in college has long been recognized as a significant health problem that affects many students. By some measures of substance abuse, double-digit prevalence is still the defining characteristic of drug use on college campuses for certain drugs.

According to the most recent survey data from the Substance Abuse and Mental Health Services Administration (SAMHSA), 19.7% of young adults age 18–25 reported using an illicit drug in the past 30 days (see Table 9.1). This number represents a slight decline from 2005 and 2006. The same survey shows that past-month tobacco use decreased and binge drinking remained steady among college-age Americans, while marijuana and cocaine use decreased slightly.

Other surveys show that recreational drug use is fairly common among college students. According to the 2007 American College Health Association—National College Health Assessment, more than 12% of college students reported using marijuana at least once in the past 30 days. Another 1.2% said they had used cocaine at least once in the past 30 days, and nearly 2% reported using amphetamines.

Drug use on college campuses has been examined extensively, and many experts believe that no single factor can explain the widespread impact of this phenomenon. Family history, peer pressure, depression, anxiety, low self-esteem,

and the dynamics of college life (for example, the drive to compete and distorted perception of drug use among peers) have been suggested as potential explanations for drug use among college students.

Excessive alcohol use often accompanies illicit drug use. In fact, the term *AOD* (Alcohol and Other Drug) has been developed to refer to this type of substance use among college students. Further, AOD use and depression and/or anxiety are generally recognized as coexisting conditions that require a comprehensive approach to prevention and treatment.

Despite the growing awareness among college counselors and other health professionals who work with college students, it is not entirely clear whether anxiety and depression precede the onset of alcohol and drug use, or early pre-college exposure to alcohol and drug use may exacerbate more serious psychiatric disorders by the time a student enters college. A third line of research suggests that AOD use, depression, and anxiety share common causes such as genetic predisposition and/or family history.

However, one aspect of drug use among college students remains clear: AOD use has dramatic consequences for the educational, family, and community life of students. Poor academic performance has been linked with AOD use. Further, driving while intoxicated remains one of the most dangerous outcomes associated with AOD use affecting families and communities.

Several AOD prevention programs are now under way at college campuses. Since the late 1980s, several federal laws have been enacted to provide resources and a legislative framework for addressing AOD use at schools. The 1989 Drug-free School and Communities Act and the 1998 Higher Education Amendment are examples of concerted federal legislative efforts to encourage the development of educational policies for preventing alcohol and other drug use and providing assistance to college students at risk for these harmful behaviors.

---

of even heroin or cocaine do not meet the APA's criteria for substance dependence.

It isn't possible to accurately predict which drug users will become abusers, but young people at a high risk of *trying* drugs share certain characteristics:

- *Being young.* People who start using drugs when they're very young have a greater risk of dependence and health consequences.

- *Being male.* Males are twice as likely as females to abuse illicit drugs (see the box "Gender Differences in Drug Use and Abuse").

- *Being a troubled adolescent.* Teens are more likely to try drugs if they have poor self-image or self-control, use tobacco, or suffer from certain mental or emotional problems.

- *Being a thrill-seeker.* A sense of invincibility is a factor in drug experimentation.

- *Being in a dysfunctional family.* A chaotic home life or parental abuse increases the risk of drug use. The same is true for children from a single-parent home or whose parents didn't complete high school.

- *Being in a peer group that accepts drug use.* Young people who are uninterested in school and earn poor grades are more likely to try drugs.

- *Being poor.* Young people who live in disadvantaged areas are more likely to be around drugs at a young age.

- *Dating young.* Adolescent girls who date boys two or more years older than themselves are more likely to use drugs.

GENDER MATTERS

Gender Differences in Drug Use and Abuse

Men are more likely than women to use, abuse, and be dependent on illicit drugs. Rates of use are similar in males and females age 12–17, but among those 18 and older, more men than women use drugs and have problems associated with drug use (see table). Men account for about 80% of arrests for drug abuse violations, 70% of admissions for treatment, and 65% of drug-related deaths.

There are also gender differences in why and how young people use drugs. Young males tend to use alcohol or drugs for sensation seeking or to enhance their social status, factors tied to culturally based gender roles. Young women tend to use drugs to improve mood, increase confidence, and reduce inhibitions. Boys are likelier to receive offers to use drugs in public settings, whereas girls are likelier to receive offers in a private place such as a friend's residence.

Despite overall lower rates of drug use, females may have unique biological vulnerabilities to certain drugs, and they may move more quickly from use to abuse. Major life transitions, including the physical and emotional changes associated with puberty, increase the risk

of drug use and abuse for girls more so than for boys. Certain other drug abuse risk factors are also more common in female adolescents, including depression, low self-esteem, eating disorders, and a history of physical or sexual abuse.

Adolescent boys and girls share some protective factors relating to drug abuse, including positive family relationships and extracurricular activities; religious involvement is protective for both boys and girls but may be more protective for girls.

Among older men and women, marriage, children, and employment are associated with lower rates of drug abuse and dependence. Rates of drug abuse and dependence among married adults are less than half of those among unmarried adults. Similar patterns are seen when comparing adults who live with children versus those who do not live with children and adults who are employed versus those who are unemployed.

National Survey Results: Percent Reporting in Past Year

	Males	Females
Illicit drug use*	17.4	11.6
Age 12–17	19.4	18.0
Age 18–25	37.2	29.1
Age 26 and older	13.5	7.9
Drove under the influence of an illicit drug	5.7	2.4
Illicit drug or alcohol abuse or dependence	12.5	5.7
Treatment for drug dependence	1.3	0.5

*Illicit drugs include marijuana/hashish, cocaine, heroin, hallucinogens, inhalants, and prescription-type psychotherapeutics used nonmedically.

SOURCE: Office of Applied Studies, Substance Abuse and Mental Health Services Administration. 2008. *Results from the 2007 National Survey on Drug Use and Health: National Findings* (http://oas.samhsa.gov/nsduh.htm; retrieved February 3, 2009).

What about people who *don't* use drugs? As a group, nonusers also share some characteristics. Not surprisingly, people who perceive drug use as risky and who disapprove of it are less likely to use drugs than those who believe otherwise. Drug use is also less common among people who have positive self-esteem and self-concept and who are assertive, independent thinkers who are not controlled by peer pressure. Self-control, social competence, optimism, academic achievement, and regular church attendance are also linked to lower rates of drug use (see the box "Spirituality and Drug Abuse" on p. 244).

Home environments are also influential: Coming from a strong family, one that has a clear policy on drug use, is another characteristic of people who don't use drugs. Young people who communicate openly with their parents and feel supported by them are also less likely to use drugs.

Why Do People Use Drugs?

Young people, especially those from middle-class backgrounds, are frequently drawn to drugs by the allure of

the exciting and illegal. They may be curious, rebellious, or vulnerable to peer pressure. Young people may want to imitate adult models in their lives or in the movies. Most people who take illicit drugs do so experimentally, typically trying the drug one or more times but not continuing. The main factors in the initial choice of a drug are whether it is available and whether peers are using it.

Although some people use drugs because they have a desire to alter their mood or are seeking a spiritual experience, others are motivated primarily by a desire to escape boredom, anxiety, depression, feelings of worthlessness, or other distressing symptoms of psychological problems. They use drugs as a way to cope with the difficulties they are experiencing in life. The common practice in our society of seeking a drug solution to every problem is a factor in the widespread reliance on both illicit and prescription drugs.

For people living in poverty in the inner cities, many of these reasons for using drugs are magnified. The problems are more devastating, the need for escape more compelling. Furthermore, the buying and selling of drugs provide access to an unofficial, alternative economy that may seem like an opportunity for success.

Spirituality and Drug Abuse

Although there are diverse religious viewpoints on drug use, many religions infer some link between psychoactive drugs and spirituality. Some religions use drugs in the quest for spiritual transcendence: American Indian, Polynesian, African, and other indigenous religions have used psychoactive drugs such as peyote, khat, alcohol, and hashish for expanding consciousness and developing personal spirituality. Other religions view psychoactive drugs as a threat to spirituality. In Islam, for example, the consumption of alcohol and certain other drugs is strictly forbidden.

In studies of American teens and adults, spiritual or religious involvement is generally associated with a lower risk of trying psychoactive drugs and, for those who do use drugs, a lower risk of heavy use and dependence. The mechanism for this protective effect is unclear; possibilities include the adoption of a strict code of behavior or set of principles that forbids drug use, the presence of a social support system for abstinence or moderation, and the promotion of values that include avoidance of drug use.

The relationship between religious faith and avoidance of drug use appears to be even stronger in teens than in adults. One study found that teens who felt they had a personal relationship with the divine and/or who belonged to a more fundamentalist religious denomination were less likely to engage in substance use and abuse than other teens.

Teens who attend 25 or more religious services per year are about half as likely to use illicit drugs as teens who attend services less frequently. Overall, people who spend time regularly engaging in spiritual practices such as prayer and transcendental meditation have lower rates of drug abuse.

People with current substance-abuse problems tend to have lower rates of religious affiliation and involvement and lower levels of spiritual wellness, characterized by a lack of a sense of meaning in life. One of the hallmarks of drug dependence is spending increasing amounts of time and energy obtaining and using drugs; such a pattern of behavior inevitably reduces the resources an individual puts toward developing physical, emotional, and spiritual wellness.

Among people in treatment for substance abuse, higher levels of religious faith and spirituality may contribute to the recovery process. A study of people recovering from alcohol or other drug abuse found that spirituality and religiousness were associated with increased coping skills, greater optimism about life, greater resilience to stress, and greater perceived social support.

More research is needed to clarify the relationships among spirituality, religion, drug use, and recovery. One of the difficulties in conducting research in this area is the difficulty in defining and measuring spirituality and religious involvement. Spirituality is a complex part of human nature, involving behavior, be-

lief, and experience. And although behaviors such as the spiritual practices of prayer or meditation can be measured, it is more difficult to determine what such practices mean to an individual and her or his overall sense of self.

SOURCES: Brown, A. E., et al. 2006. Alcohol recovery and spirituality: Strangers, friends, or partners? *Southern Medical Journal* 99(6): 654–657; Substance Abuse and Mental Health Network. 2004. Religious beliefs and substance use among youths. *NSDUH Report*, January; Dunn, M. S. 2005. The relationship between religiosity, employment, and political beliefs on substance use among high school seniors. *Journal of Alcohol and Drug Education* 49(1): 73.

Risk Factors for Dependence

Why do some people use psychoactive drugs without becoming dependent, whereas others aren't as lucky? The answer seems to be a combination of physical, psychological, and social factors. Research indicates that some people may be born with certain characteristics of brain chemistry or metabolism that make them more vulnerable to drug dependence. Other research suggests that people who were exposed to drugs while still in the womb may have an increased risk of abusing drugs themselves later in life.

Psychological risk factors for drug dependence include difficulty in controlling impulses and a strong need for excitement, stimulation, and immediate gratification. Feelings of rejection, hostility, aggression, anxiety, or depres-

sion are also associated with drug dependence. People may turn to drugs to blot out their emotional pain.

People with mental illnesses have a very high risk of substance dependence. Research shows that about one-third of people with psychological disorders also have a substance-dependence problem and about one-third of those have another mental disorder. People with two or more coexisting mental disorders are referred to as having **dual (co-occurring) disorders.** Diagnosis of psychologi-

> **dual (co-occurring) disorder**   The presence of two or more mental disorders simultaneously in the same person; for example, drug dependence and depression.

TERMS

Do You Have a Problem with Drugs?

Answer yes (Y) or no (N) to the following questions:

_____ 1. Do you take the drug regularly?

_____ 2. Have you been taking the drug for a long time?

_____ 3. Do you always take the drug in certain situations or when you're with certain people?

_____ 4. Do you find it difficult to stop using the drug? Do you feel powerless to quit?

_____ 5. Have you tried repeatedly to cut down or control your use of the drug?

_____ 6. Do you need to take a larger dose of the drug in order to get the same high you're used to?

_____ 7. Do you feel specific symptoms if you cut back or stop using the drug?

_____ 8. Do you frequently take another psychoactive substance to relieve withdrawal symptoms?

_____ 9. Do you take the drug to feel "normal"?

_____ 10. Do you go to extreme lengths or put yourself in dangerous situations to get the drug?

_____ 11. Do you hide your drug use from others? Have you ever lied about what you're using or how much you use?

_____ 12. Do people close to you ask you about your drug use?

_____ 13. Are you spending more and more time with people who use the same drug as you?

_____ 14. Do you think about the drug when you're not high, figuring out ways to get it?

_____ 15. If you stop taking the drug, do you feel bad until you can take it again?

_____ 16. Does the drug interfere with your ability to study, work, or socialize?

_____ 17. Do you skip important school, work, social, or recreational activities in order to obtain or use the drug?

_____ 18. Do you continue to use the drug despite a physical or mental disorder or despite a significant problem that you know is made worse by drug use?

_____ 19. Have you developed a mental or physical condition or disorder because of prolonged drug use?

_____ 20. Have you done something dangerous or that you regret while under the influence of the drug?

The more times you answer yes, the more likely it is that you are developing a dependence on the drug. If your answers suggest dependence, talk to someone at your school health clinic or to your physician about taking care of the problem before it gets worse.

---

cal problems among people with substance dependence can be very difficult because drug intoxication and withdrawal can mimic the symptoms of a mental illness.

Social factors that may influence drug dependence include growing up in a family in which a parent or sibling abused drugs, belonging to a peer group that emphasizes and encourages drug abuse, and living in poverty. Because they have easy access to drugs, health care professionals are also at a higher risk. To determine whether you are at risk, take the quiz in the box "Do You Have a Problem with Drugs?"

Other Risks of Drug Use

Dependence is not the only serious potential consequence of drug use. In 2005, 1.4 million emergency room visits were related to drug misuse or abuse (Table 9.3).

Intoxication People who are under the influence of drugs—intoxicated—may act in uncharacteristic and unsafe ways because both their physical and mental functioning are impaired. They are more likely to be injured from a variety of causes, including falls, drowning,

Table 9.3	Emergency Room (ER) Visits Involving Drug Use/Abuse: 2005*	
Reason for ER Visit	**Estimated Visits**	**Percentage of Visits**
Illicit drugs only	450,296	30%
Pharmaceuticals only	395,617	27
Alcohol only in patients younger than 21	98,364	7
Illicit drugs and alcohol	199,008	14
Alcohol and pharmaceuticals	138,477	10
Illicit drugs and pharmaceuticals	110,652	8
Illicit drugs with pharmaceuticals and alcohol	56,740	4
Total	**1,449,154**	**100%**

*U.S. hospitals received 108 million emergency room visits in 2005. About 1% of those visits involved drug use or abuse by the patient. (Note: percentages shown here may not equal 100 due to rounding.)

SOURCE: Substance Abuse and Mental Health Services Administration, Office of Applied Studies. 2007. *Drug Abuse Warning Network, 2005: National Estimates of Drug-Related Emergency Department Visits.* Rockville, Md.: Substance Abuse and Mental Health Services Administration, DAWN Series D-29, DHHS Publication No. (SMA) 07-4256.

More than 4 million Americans have injected heroin, cocaine, or a stimulant at least once in their life.

—SAMHSA, 2008

and automobile crashes; to engage in unsafe sex, increasing their risk for sexually transmitted diseases and unintended pregnancy; and to be involved in incidents of aggression and violence, including sexual assault.

Unexpected Side Effects Psychoactive drugs have many physical and psychological effects beyond the alteration of consciousness. These effects range from nausea and constipation to paranoia, depression, and heart failure. Some drugs also carry the risk of fatal overdose.

Unknown Drug Constituents There is no quality control in the illegal drug market, so the composition, dosage, and toxicity of street drugs is highly variable. Studies indicate that half of all street drugs don't contain their promised primary ingredient; in some cases, a drug may be present in unsafe dosages or mixed with other drugs to boost the effects. Careless manufacturing practices can result in the presence of toxic contaminants.

Risks Associated with Injection Drug Use Heroin and related substances are the most commonly injected drugs, but users can also inject cocaine, amphetamines, and other drugs. Many injection drug users (IDUs) share or reuse needles, syringes, and other injection equipment, which can easily become contaminated with the user's blood. Small amounts of blood can carry enough human immunodeficiency virus (HIV) and hepatitis C virus (HCV) to be infectious. In 2006, injection drug use accounted for about 13% of all new HIV/AIDS cases; many more were attributed to sexual contact with IDUs. Injection drug use also accounts for the majority of HCV infections.

Unsterile injection practices can cause skin and soft tissue infections, which can progress to gangrene and be fatal if untreated. Other risks include endocarditis (infection of the heart valves), tuberculosis, and tetanus.

The surest way to prevent diseases related to injection drug use is never to inject drugs. Those who inject drugs should use a new needle and syringe with each injection and should use sterile water and other equipment to prepare drugs. Bleach or boiling water may kill some viruses and bacteria, but they are not foolproof sterilization methods. Many viruses can survive in a syringe for a month or more.

Syringe exchange programs (SEPs)—where IDUs can trade a used syringe for a new one—have been advocated to help slow the spread of HIV and reduce the rates and cost of other health problems associated with injection drug use. Opponents of SEPs argue that supplying addicts with syringes gives them the message that illegal drug use is acceptable and could thus exacerbate the nation's drug problem. However, studies have shown that well-implemented SEPs do not increase the use of drugs, and most offer AIDS counseling and provide referrals to drug treatment programs. Getting people off drugs is clearly the best solution, but there are far more IDUs than treatment facilities can currently handle.

Legal Consequences Many psychoactive drugs are illegal, so using them can result in large fines and/or imprisonment. According to the Federal Bureau of Investigation (FBI), law enforcement officials made 1.8 million arrests for drug abuse violations (13% of all arrests) in 2007—more arrests than for any other offense that year.

HOW DRUGS AFFECT THE BODY

The drugs discussed in this chapter have complex and variable effects, many of which can be traced to changes in brain chemistry. However, the same drug may affect different people differently or the same person in different ways under different circumstances. Beyond a fairly predictable general change in brain chemistry, the effects of a drug may vary depending on drug factors, user factors, and social factors.

Changes in Brain Chemistry

Psychoactive drugs produce most of their key effects by acting on brain chemistry in a characteristic fashion. Before any changes in brain chemistry can occur, however, molecules of the drug have to be carried to the brain through the bloodstream via a particular route of administration. A drug that is taken by mouth has to dissolve in the stomach, be absorbed into the bloodstream through the lining of the small intestine, and then pass through the liver, heart, and lungs before returning to the heart to be carried via arteries to the brain. A drug that is already

QUESTIONS FOR CRITICAL THINKING AND REFLECTION

Have you ever tried a psychoactive drug for fun? What were your reasons for trying it? Who were you with, and what were the circumstances? What was your experience like? What would you tell someone else who was thinking about trying a drug?

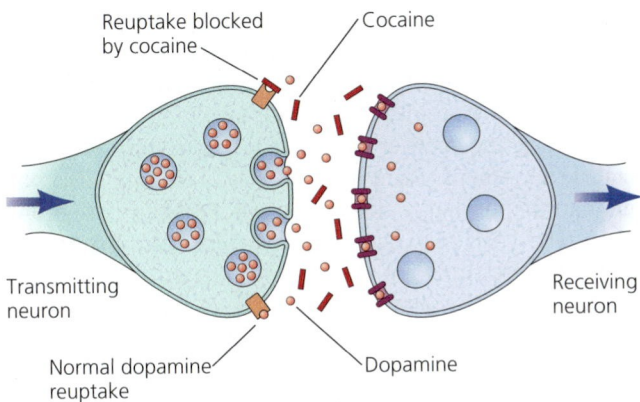

FIGURE 9.1 **Effect of cocaine on brain chemistry.** Under normal circumstances, the amount of dopamine at a synapse is controlled in part by the reuptake of dopamine by the transmitting neuron. Cocaine blocks the removal of dopamine from a synapse; the resulting buildup of dopamine causes continuous stimulation of the receiving neurons.

Method of use (or route of administration) is one variable in the overall effect of a drug on the body.

dissolved and is injected directly into the bloodstream will reach the brain in much less time, and drugs that are inhaled and absorbed by the lungs travel to the brain even more rapidly. The more quickly a drug reaches the brain, the more likely the user is to become dependent.

Once a psychoactive drug reaches the brain, it acts on one or more **neurotransmitters,** either increasing or decreasing their concentration and actions. Cocaine, for example, affects dopamine, a neurotransmitter thought to play a key role in the process of reinforcement—the brain's way of telling itself "That's good; do the same thing again." When a neurotransmitter is released by one neuron to signal another neuron, its level or concentration is controlled in part by the reuptake or resorption of the neurotransmitter by the releasing neuron. Cocaine inhibits the resorption of dopamine, thereby increasing the concentration of dopamine in the synapse and lengthening the time of its action (Figure 9.1). The euphoria produced by cocaine is thought to be a result of its effect on dopamine. Heroin, nicotine, alcohol, and amphetamines also affect dopamine levels through their effects on the brain.

The duration of a drug's effect depends on many factors and may range from 5 minutes (crack cocaine) to 12 or more hours (LSD). As drugs circulate through the body, they are metabolized by the liver and eventually excreted by the kidneys in urine. Small amounts may also be eliminated in other ways, including in sweat, in breast milk, and via the lungs.

Drug Factors

When different drugs or dosages produce different effects, the differences are usually caused by one or more of five different drug factors:

1. The **pharmacological properties** of a drug are its overall effects on a person's body chemistry, behavior, and psychology. The pharmacological properties also include the amount of a drug required to exert various effects, the time course of these effects, and other characteristics, such as a drug's chemical composition.

2. The **dose-response function** is the relationship between the amount of drug taken and the type and intensity of the resulting effect. Many psychological

neurotransmitter A brain chemical that transmits nerve impulses.

pharmacological properties The overall effects of a drug on a person's behavior, psychology, and chemistry.

dose-response function The relationship between the amount of a drug taken and the intensity and type of the resulting effect.

effects of drugs reach a plateau in the dose-response function, so that increasing the dose does not increase the effect any further. With LSD, for example, the maximum changes in perception occur at a certain dose, and no further changes in perception take place if higher doses are taken. However, all drugs have more than one effect, and the dose-response functions usually are different for different effects. This means that increasing the dose of any drug may begin to result in additional effects, which are likely to be increasingly unpleasant or dangerous at high doses.

3. The **time-action function** is the relationship between the time elapsed since a drug was taken and the intensity of its effect. The effects of a drug are greatest when concentrations of the drug in body tissues are changing fastest, especially if they are increasing.

4. The person's *drug use history* may influence the effects of a drug. A given amount of alcohol, for example, will generally affect a habitual drinker less than an occasional drinker. Tolerance to some drugs, such as LSD, builds rapidly. To experience the same effect, a user has to abstain from the drug for a period of time before that dosage will again exert its original effects.

5. The *method of use* (or *route of administration*) has a direct effect on how strong a response a drug produces. Methods of use include ingestion, inhalation, injection, and absorption through the skin or tissue linings. Drugs are usually injected in one of three ways: intravenously (IV, or mainlining), intramuscularly (IM), or subcutaneously (SC, or skin popping).

User Factors

Certain physical and psychological characteristics also help determine how a person will respond to a drug. Body mass is one variable. The effects of a certain dose of a drug on a 100-pound person will be twice as great as on a 200-pound person. Other variables include general health and genetic factors. For example, some people have an inherited ability to rapidly metabolize a cough suppressant called dextromethorphan, which also has psychoactive properties. These people must take a higher-than-normal dose to get a given cough-suppressant effect.

If a person's biochemical state is already altered by another drug, this too can make a difference. Some drugs intensify the effects of other drugs, as is the case with alcohol and sedatives. Some drugs block the effects of other drugs, such as when a tranquilizer is used to relieve anxiety caused by cocaine. Interactions between drugs, including many prescription and OTC medications, can be unpredictable and dangerous.

One physical condition that requires special precautions is pregnancy. It can be risky for a woman to use any drugs at all during pregnancy, including alcohol and common OTC preparations like cough medicine. The risks are greatest during the first trimester, when the fetus's body is rapidly forming and even small biochemical alterations in the mother can have a devastating effect on fetal development. Even later, the fetus is more susceptible than the mother to the adverse effects of any drugs she takes. The fetus may even become physically dependent on a drug being taken by the mother and suffer withdrawal symptoms after birth.

Sometimes a person's response to a drug is strongly influenced by the user's expectations about how he or she will react (the psychological *set*). With large doses, the drug's chemical properties seem to have the strongest effect on the user's response. But with small doses, psychological (and social) factors are often more important. When people strongly believe that a given drug will affect them a certain way, they are likely to experience those effects regardless of the drug's pharmacological properties. In one study, regular users of marijuana reported a moderate level of intoxication (**high**) after using a cigarette that smelled and tasted like marijuana but contained no THC, the active ingredient in marijuana. This is an example of the **placebo effect**—when a person receives an inert substance yet responds as if it were an active drug. (The placebo effect is discussed in more detail in Chapter 20.) In other studies, subjects who smoked low doses of real marijuana that they believed to be a placebo experienced no effects from the drug. Clearly, the user's expectations had a greater effect on the smokers than the drug itself.

Social Factors

The *setting* is the physical and social environment surrounding the drug use. If a person uses marijuana at home with trusted friends and pleasant music, the effects are likely to be different from the effects if the same dose is taken in an austere experimental laboratory with an impassive research technician. Similarly, the dose of alcohol

---

time-action function   The relationship between the time elapsed since a drug was taken and the intensity of its effect.

high   The subjectively pleasing effects of a drug, usually felt quite soon after the drug is taken.

placebo effect   A response to an inert or innocuous medication given in place of an active drug.

opioid   Any of several natural or synthetic drugs that relieve pain and cause drowsiness and/or euphoria; examples are opium, morphine, and heroin; also called a *narcotic*.

euphoria   An exaggerated feeling of well-being.

depressant, or sedative-hypnotic   A drug that decreases nervous or muscular activity, causing drowsiness or sleep.

central nervous system (CNS)   The brain and spinal cord.

TERMS

QUESTIONS FOR CRITICAL THINKING AND REFLECTION

Has an over-the-counter medication (such as a decongestant) ever made you feel strange, drowsy, or even high? Did you expect to react to the medication that way? Do such reactions influence the way you use over-the-counter drugs?

that produces mild euphoria and stimulation at a noisy, active cocktail party might induce sleepiness and slight depression when taken at home while alone.

REPRESENTATIVE PSYCHOACTIVE DRUGS

The following sections introduce six representative groups of psychoactive drugs (Figure 9.2 on p. 250): opioids, central nervous system (CNS) depressants, central nervous system stimulants, marijuana and other cannabis products, hallucinogens, and inhalants. Some of these drugs are classified according to how they affect the body; others—the opioids and the cannabis products—are classified according to their chemical makeup.

Opioids

Also called *narcotics,* **opioids** are natural or synthetic (laboratory-made) drugs, such as opium, morphine, heroin, methadone, codeine, hydrocodone, oxycodone, meperidine, and fentanyl. Opioids relieve pain, cause drowsiness, and induce **euphoria.** Especially in small doses, opioids have beneficial medical uses, including pain relief and cough suppression. Opioids tend to reduce anxiety and produce lethargy, apathy, and an inability to concentrate. Opioid users become less active and less responsive to frustration, hunger, and sexual stimulation. These effects are more pronounced in novice users; with repeated use, many effects diminish.

Opioids are typically injected or absorbed into the body from the stomach, intestines, nasal membranes (from snorting or sniffing), or lungs (from smoking). Effects depend on the method of administration. If brain levels of the drug change rapidly, more immediate effects will result. Although the euphoria associated with opioids is an important factor in their abuse, many people experience a feeling of uneasiness when they first use these drugs. Users also often feel nauseated and vomit, and they may have other unpleasant sensations. Even so, the abuse of opioids often results in dependence. Tolerance can develop rapidly and be pronounced. Withdrawal symptoms include cramps, chills, sweating, nausea, tremors, irritability, and feelings of panic.

Rates of heroin use have always been low, but there are periodic episodes of increased use among some groups. Use among college students remains below 1%, but between 1991 and 2000 heroin use among high school seniors more than doubled, mostly due to increased rates of sniffing or smoking the drug. Although these users avoid the special disease risks of injection drug use, including HIV infection, dependence can readily result from sniffing and smoking heroin. In addition, the potentially high but variable purity of street heroin poses a risk of unintentional overdose. Symptoms of overdose include respiratory depression, coma, and constriction of the pupils; death can result.

Nonmedical use of prescription pain relievers that contain oxycodone and hydrocodone, including Oxycontin and Vicodin, has increased in recent years. When taken as prescribed in tablet form, these drugs treat moderate to severe chronic pain and do not typically lead to abuse. However, like other opioids, use of prescription painkillers can lead to abuse and dependence. Oxycodone and hydrocodone can be abused orally; the long-acting form of oxycodone is also sometimes crushed and snorted or dissolved and injected, providing a powerful heroin-like high. When taken in large doses or combined with other drugs, oxycodone and hydrocodone can cause fatal respiratory depression.

Central Nervous System Depressants

Central nervous system **depressants,** also known as **sedative-hypnotics,** slow down the overall activity of the **central nervous system (CNS).** The result can range

THINKING ABOUT THE ENVIRONMENT

Most substance-abuse research has focused on interpersonal and intrapersonal characteristics associated with an individual's drug use. Recently, however, there has been increasing interest in environmental factors that may influence substance abuse. For example, the proximity of commercial outlets selling alcohol has been suggested as an important determinant of heavy alcohol use.

Spatial and spatially related features of the environment—such as land use, urban sprawl, quality of housing, neighborhood characteristics, and density of particular commercial outlets—are emerging topics in substance-abuse research. The term *built environment* has been proposed to refer to attributes of an area or neighborhood that cannot be linked directly to the residents of that area, but which may be associated with substance abuse and adverse consequences of drug use.

For more information on the environment and health, see Chapter 19.

Category	Representative drugs	Street names	Appearance	Methods of use	Short-term effects
Opioids 	Heroin	Dope, H, junk, brown sugar, smack	White/dark brown powder; dark tar or coal-like substance	Injected, smoked, snorted	Relief of anxiety and pain; euphoria; lethargy, apathy, drowsiness, confusion, inability to concentrate; nausea, constipation, respiratory depression
	Opium	Big O, black stuff, hop	Dark brown or black chunks	Swallowed, smoked	
	Morphine	M, Miss Emma, monkey, white stuff	White crystals, liquid solution	Injected, swallowed, smoked	
	Oxycodone, codeine, hydrocodone	Oxy, O.C., killer, Captain Cody, schoolboy, vike	Tablets, powder made from crushing tablets	Swallowed, injected, snorted	
Central nervous system depressants 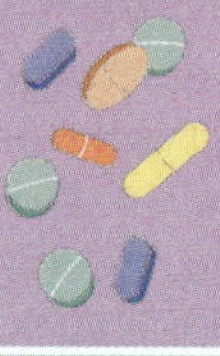	Barbiturates	Barbs, reds, red birds, yellows, yellow jackets	Colored capsules	Swallowed, injected	Reduced anxiety, mood changes, lowered inhibitions, impaired muscle coordination, reduced pulse rate, drowsiness, loss of consciousness, respiratory depression
	Benzodiazepines (e.g., Valium, Xanax, Rohypnol)	Candy, downers, tranks, roofies, forget-me pill	Tablets	Swallowed, injected	
	Methaqualone	Ludes, quad, quay	Tablets	Injected, swallowed	
	Gamma hydroxy butyrate (GHB)	G, Georgia home boy, grievous bodily harm	Clear liquid, white powder	Swallowed	
Central nervous system stimulants 	Amphetamine, methamphetamine	Bennies, speed, black beauties, uppers, chalk, crank, crystal, ice, meth	Tablets, capsules, white powder, white crystals	Injected, swallowed, smoked, snorted	Increased heart rate, blood pressure, metabolism; increased mental alertness and energy; nervousness, insomnia, impulsive behavior; reduced appetite
	Cocaine, crack cocaine	Blow, C, candy, coke, flake, rock, toot	White powder, beige pellets or rocks	Injected, smoked, snorted	
	Ritalin	JIF, MPH, R-ball, Skippy	Tablets	Injected, swallowed, snorted	
Marijuana and other cannabis products 	Marijuana	Dope, grass, joints, Mary Jane, reefer, skunk, weed	Dried leaves and stems	Smoked, swallowed	Euphoria, slowed thinking and reaction time, confusion, anxiety, impaired balance and coordination, increased heart rate
	Hashish	Hash, hemp, boom, gangster	Dark, resin-like compound formed into rocks or blocks	Smoked, swallowed	
Hallucinogens 	LSD	Acid, boomers, blotter, yellow sunshines	Blotter paper, liquid, gelatin tabs, pills	Swallowed, absorbed through mouth tissues	Altered states of perception and feeling; nausea; increased heart rate, blood pressure; delirium; impaired motor function; numbness, weakness
	Mescaline (peyote)	Buttons, cactus, mesc	Brown buttons, liquid	Swallowed, smoked	
	Psilocybin	Shrooms, magic mushrooms	Dried mushrooms	Swallowed	
	Ketamine	K, special K, cat valium, vitamin K	Clear liquid, white or beige powder	Injected, snorted, smoked	
	PCP	Angel dust, hog, love boat, peace pill	White to brown powder, tablets	Injected, swallowed, smoked, snorted	
	MDMA (ecstasy)	X, peace, clarity, Adam	Tablets	Swallowed	
Inhalants 	Solvents, aerosols, nitrites, anesthetics	Laughing gas, poppers, snappers, whippets	Household products, sprays, glues, paint thinner, petroleum products	Inhaled through nose or mouth	Stimulation, loss of inhibition, slurred speech, loss of motor coordination, loss of consciousness

FIGURE 9.2 Commonly abused drugs and their effects.

SOURCES: The Partnership for a Drug-Free America. 2006. *Drug Guide by Name* (http://www.drugfree.org/portal/drug_guide; retrieved August 7, 2006); U.S. Drug Enforcement Agency. 2006. *Photo Library* (http://www.usdoj.gov/dea/photo_library.html; retrieved August 7, 2006); U.S. Drug Enforcement Agency. 2005. *Drug Information* (http://www.usdoj.gov/dea/concern.concern.htm; retrieved August 7, 2006); National Institute on Drug Abuse. 2004. *Commonly Abused Drugs* (http://www.drugabuse.gov/DrugPages/DrugsofAbuse.html; retrieved August 7, 2006).

from mild **sedation** to death, depending on the various factors involved—which drug is used, how it's taken, how tolerant the user is, and so on. CNS depressants include alcohol (Chapter 10), barbiturates, and other sedatives.

Types The various types of barbiturates are similar in chemical composition and action, but they differ in how quickly and how long they act. Drug users call barbiturates "downers" or "downs" and refer to specific brands by names that describe the color and design of the capsules. People usually take barbiturates in capsules, but they may also inject them.

Antianxiety agents, also called sedatives or **tranquilizers,** include the benzodiazepines such as Xanax, Valium, Librium, clonazepam (Klonopin), and flunitrazepam (Rohypnol, also called roofies). Other CNS depressants include methaqualone (Quaalude), ethchlorvynol (Placidyl), chloral hydrate ("mickey"), and gamma hydroxy butyrate (GHB, or "liquid ecstasy").

Effects CNS depressants reduce anxiety and cause mood changes, impaired muscular coordination, slurring of speech, and drowsiness or sleep. Mental functioning is also affected, but the degree varies from person to person and also depends on the kind of task the person is trying to do. Most people become drowsy with small doses, although a few become more active.

Medical Uses Barbiturates, antianxiety agents, and other sedative-hypnotics are widely used to treat insomnia and anxiety disorders and to control seizures. Some CNS depressants are used for their calming properties in combination with **anesthetics** before operations and other medical or dental procedures.

From Use to Abuse People are usually introduced to CNS depressants either through a medical prescription or through drug-using peers. The use of Rohypnol and GHB is often associated with dance clubs and raves (see the box "Club Drugs" on p. 252). The abuse of CNS depressants by a medical patient may begin with repeated use for insomnia and progress to dependence through increasingly larger doses at night, coupled with a few capsules at stressful times during the day.

Most CNS depressants, including alcohol, can lead to classical physical dependence. Tolerance, sometimes for up to 15 times the usual dose, can develop with repeated use. Tranquilizers have been shown to produce physical dependence even at ordinary prescribed doses. Withdrawal symptoms can be more severe than those accompanying opioid dependence and are similar to the DTs of alcoholism (see Chapter 10). They may begin as anxiety, shaking, and weakness but may turn into convulsions and possibly cardiovascular collapse and death.

35 million prescriptions for sleeping pills were filled in the United States in 2004.

—National Institutes of Health, 2006

QUICK STATS

While intoxicated, people on depressants cannot function well. They are confused and are frequently obstinate, irritable, and abusive. Even prescription use of benzodiazepines has been associated with an increased risk of automobile crashes. After long-term use, depressants like alcohol can lead to poor health and brain damage, with impaired ability to reason and make judgments.

Overdosing with CNS Depressants Too much depression of the central nervous system slows respiration and may stop it entirely. CNS depressants are particularly dangerous in combination with another depressant, such as alcohol. People who combine depressants with alcohol account for thousands of emergency room visits and hundreds of overdose deaths each year. Rohypnol is ten times more potent than Valium and can be fatal if combined with alcohol. GHB is often produced clandestinely, resulting in widely varying degrees of purity; it has been responsible for many poisonings and a number of deaths.

Central Nervous System Stimulants

CNS **stimulants** speed up the activity of the nervous or muscular system. Under their influence, the heart rate accelerates, blood pressure rises, blood vessels constrict, the pupils of the eyes and the bronchial tubes dilate, and gastric and adrenal secretions increase. There is greater muscular tension and sometimes an increase in motor activity. Small doses usually make people feel more awake and alert, less fatigued and bored. The most common CNS stimulants are cocaine, amphetamines, nicotine (Chapter 11), ephedrine, and caffeine.

Cocaine Usually derived from the leaves of coca shrubs that grow high in the Andes in South America, cocaine is a potent CNS stimulant. For centuries, natives of the Andes have chewed coca leaves both for pleasure and to increase their endurance. For a short time during the nineteenth century, some physicians were enthusiastic about the use of cocaine to cure alcoholism and addiction to the painkiller morphine. Enthusiasm waned after the drug's adverse side effects became apparent.

TERMS

sedation The induction of a calm, relaxed, often sleepy state.

tranquilizer A CNS depressant that reduces tension and anxiety.

anesthetic A drug that produces a loss of sensation with or without a loss of consciousness.

stimulant A drug that increases nervous or muscular activity.

Club Drugs

Club drugs are part of the popular dance culture of clubs and raves—all-night dance parties held in fields or abandoned buildings. Some people refer to club drugs as soft drugs because they see them as recreational—for the casual, weekend user—rather than as addictive. But club drugs have many potential negative effects and are particularly potent and unpredictable when mixed with alcohol. Substitute drugs are often sold in place of club drugs, putting users at risk for taking dangerous combinations of unknown drugs.

MDMA *(ecstasy, E, X, XTC, Adam, hug drug, lover's speed):* Taken in pill form, MDMA (methylenedioxymethamphetamine) is a stimulant with mildly hallucinogenic and amphetamine-like effects. Users may experience euphoria, increased energy, and a heightened sense of belonging. In club settings, using MDMA can produce dangerously high body temperature and potentially fatal dehydration; some users experience confusion, depression, anxiety, paranoia, muscle tension, involuntary teeth clenching,

blurred vision, nausea, and seizures. Even low doses can affect concentration, judgment, and driving ability. Tolerance can develop, leading users to take the drug more frequently, to use higher doses, or to combine MDMA with other drugs to enhance the drug's effects.

In addition to MDMA, many ecstasy tablets include other drugs such as methamphetamine, ephedrine, or cocaine. At high doses or mixed with other drugs, MDMA is extremely dangerous; most deaths linked to MDMA have occurred as a result of multidrug toxicity or traumatic injuries.

MDMA increases the activity of three neurotransmitters: serotonin, dopamine, and norepinephrine. Increases in serotonin are likely the cause of the drug's mood-elevating effects, but use of MDMA can deplete the brain of serotonin and may cause an emotional let-down (sadness, irritability, etc.) in the days following use.

MDMA users perform worse than nonusers on complex cognitive tasks of memory, attention, and general intelligence. Long-term effects may include physical symptoms and psychological problems such as confusion or paranoia. Research suggests that pregnant women who use MDMA are at increased risk for having a baby with congenital malformations and long-term impairment in memory and other cognitive functions.

LSD *(acid, boomers, yellow sunshines, red dragon):* A potent hallucinogen, LSD (lysergic acid diethylamide) is sold in tablets or capsules, in liquid form, or on small squares of paper called blotters. LSD increases heart rate and body temperature and may cause nausea, tremors, sweating, numbness, and weakness.

Ketamine *(special K, vitamin K, K, cat valium, jet):* A veterinary anesthetic that can be taken in powdered or liquid form, ketamine may cause hallucinations and impaired attention and memory. At higher doses, ketamine can cause delirium, amnesia, high blood pressure, and

potentially fatal respiratory problems. Tolerance to ketamine develops rapidly.

GHB *(Georgia home boy, G, grievous bodily harm, liquid ecstasy):* GHB (gamma hydroxybutyrate) can be produced in clear liquid, white powder, tablet, and capsule form. GHB is a CNS depressant that in large doses or when taken in combination with alcohol or other depressants can cause sedation, loss of consciousness, respiratory arrest, and death. GHB may cause prolonged and potentially life-threatening withdrawal symptoms.

Some products sold as dietary supplements for bodybuilding, weight loss, or insomnia contain the chemically similar compounds GBL (gamma butyrolactone) or BD (butanediol). It is illegal to sell products containing GHB, GBL, or BD for human consumption. The FDA has issued several warnings to prevent such items from being sold to the public.

Rohypnol *(roofies, roche, forget-me pill):* Taken in tablet form, Rohypnol (flunitrazepam) is a sedative that is ten times more potent than Valium. Its effects, which are magnified by alcohol, include reduced blood pressure, dizziness, confusion, gastrointestinal disturbances, and loss of consciousness. Users of Rohypnol may develop physical and psychological dependence on the drug.

Several club drugs are used as "date rape drugs." Because they can be added to beverages surreptitiously, these drugs may be unknowingly consumed by intended rape victims. In addition to depressant effects, some drugs also cause *anterograde amnesia*, the loss of memory of things occurring while under the influence of the drug. Because of concern about such drugs, Congress passed the "Drug-Induced Rape Prevention and Punishment Act," which increased federal penalties for use of any controlled substance to aid in sexual assault (see Chapter 21)

Cocaine—also known as coke or snow—quickly produces a feeling of euphoria, which makes it a popular recreational drug. Cocaine use surged in popularity during the early 1980s, when the drug's high price made it a status drug. The introduction of crack cocaine during the 1980s made the drug available in smaller quantities and at lower prices to more people. The typical recreational user shifted rapidly from wealthy professionals snorting powdered cocaine to poor inner-city smokers of crack cocaine. In the general population, cocaine use peaked in 1985 with an estimated 3% of adult Americans reporting use.

METHODS OF USE Cocaine is usually snorted and absorbed through the nasal mucosa or injected intravenously, providing rapid increases of the drug's concentration in the blood and therefore fast, intense effects. Another method of use involves processing cocaine with baking soda and water, yielding the ready-to-smoke form of cocaine known as crack. Crack is typically available as small beads or pellets smokable in glass pipes. The tiny but potent beads can be handled more easily than cocaine powder and marketed in smaller, less expensive doses.

EFFECTS The effects of cocaine are usually intense but short-lived. The euphoria lasts from 5 to 20 minutes and ends abruptly, to be replaced by irritability, anxiety, or slight depression. When cocaine is absorbed via the lungs, by either smoking or inhalation, it reaches the brain in about 10 seconds, and the effects are particularly intense. This is part of the appeal of smoking crack. The effects from IV injections occur almost as quickly—in about 20 seconds. Since the mucous membranes in the nose briefly slow absorption, the onset of effects from snorting takes 2–3 minutes. Heavy users may inject cocaine intravenously every 10–20 minutes to maintain the effects.

The larger the cocaine dose and the more rapidly it is absorbed into the bloodstream, the greater the immediate—and sometimes lethal—effects. Sudden death from cocaine is most commonly the result of excessive CNS stimulation that causes convulsions and respiratory collapse, irregular heartbeat, extremely high blood pressure, blood clots, and possibly heart attack or stroke. Although rare, fatalities can occur in healthy young people; among people age 18–59, cocaine users are seven times more likely than nonusers to have a heart attack. Chronic cocaine use produces inflammation of the nasal mucosa, which can lead to persistent bleeding and ulceration of the septum between the nostrils. The use of cocaine may also cause paranoia and/or aggressiveness.

Although the use of cocaine decreased in the general U.S. population after 1985, cocaine is responsible for more deaths and emergency room visits than any other illicit drug (Table 9.4). This presumably reflects the fact that smoking crack is more toxic than snorting powdered cocaine. Most deaths result from people using cocaine in combination with another substance, such as alcohol or heroin.

ABUSE AND DEPENDENCE When steady cocaine users stop taking the drug, they experience a sudden "crash" characterized by depression, agitation, and fatigue, followed by a period of withdrawal. Their depression can be temporarily relieved by taking more cocaine, so its continued use is reinforced. A binge cocaine user may go for weeks or months without using any cocaine and then take large

Table 9.4	Illicit Drugs in Emergency Room (ER) Visits: 2005
Drug	**Estimated Visits**
Cocaine	448,481
Heroin	164,572
Marijuana	242,200
Stimulants	138,950
Amphetamines	35,827
Methamphetamine	108,905
Ecstasy	10,752
GHB	1,861
Rohypnol	596
Ketamine	275
LSD	1,864
PCP	7,535
Misc. hallucinogens	3,792
Inhalants	4,312
Others	1,755

SOURCE: Substance Abuse and Mental Health Services Administration, Office of Applied Studies. 2007. *Drug Abuse Warning Network, 2005: National Estimates of Drug-Related Emergency Department Visits.* Rockville, Md.: Substance Abuse and Mental Health Services Administration, DAWN Series D-29, DHHS Publication No. (SMA) 07-4256.

amounts repeatedly. Although not physically dependent, a binge cocaine user who misses work or school and risks serious health consequences is clearly abusing the drug.

COCAINE USE DURING PREGNANCY Cocaine rapidly passes from the mother's bloodstream into the placenta and can have serious effects on the fetus. A woman who uses cocaine during pregnancy is at higher risk for miscarriage, premature labor, and stillbirth. She is more likely to deliver a low-birth-weight baby who has a small head circumference. Her infant may be at increased risk for defects of the genitourinary tract, cardiovascular system, central nervous system, and extremities. It is difficult to pinpoint the effects of cocaine because many women who use cocaine also use tobacco and/or alcohol.

Infants whose mothers use cocaine may also be born intoxicated. They are typically irritable and jittery and do not eat or sleep normally. These characteristics may affect their early social and emotional development because it may be more difficult for adults to interact with them. Cocaine also passes into breast milk and can intoxicate a breastfeeding infant.

Amphetamines Amphetamines (uppers) are a group of synthetic chemicals that are potent CNS stimulants. Some common drugs in this family are amphetamine (Benzedrine), dextroamphetamine (Dexedrine), and methamphetamine (Methedrine). Crystal methamphetamine (ice), a smokable, high-potency form of methamphetamine, is popular in some cities. Easy to manufacture, ice is cheaper than crack and produces a similar but longer-lasting euphoria. The use of ice can quickly lead to dependence.

The Meth Epidemic

As its name suggests, methamphetamine is similar to the stimulant amphetamine. Meth, however, is more addictive and dangerous than most forms of amphetamine because it is more toxic and its effects last longer. Once taken, the drug causes the brain to release high amounts of dopamine, a key neurotransmitter. Methamphetamine is highly addictive; many casual users rapidly become regular users.

What Are Meth's Effects?

By stimulating dopamine activity in the brain, meth increases the user's ability to stay awake and perform physical activity. Meth's other short-term effects can include euphoria, rapid breathing, increased body temperature (hyperthermia), insomnia, tremors, anxiety, and convulsions.

In the long term, methamphetamine's effects can be devastating. Severe weight loss, heart attack, stroke, hallucinations, violence, paranoia, and psychotic behavior have all been linked to meth addiction. Brain damage similar to that found in Parkinson's disease and Alzheimer's disease has been reported in long-term meth users. Meth use causes extensive tooth decay and tooth loss, a condition referred to as "meth mouth." The drug takes a severe toll on the user's heart, increasing heart rate and blood pressure, damaging blood vessels, and causing irregular heartbeat. Such damage can be fatal.

Who Uses Meth?

According to estimates from the Substance Abuse and Mental Health Services Administration, about 1.3 million Americans have used meth at least once in the past year. The highest rates of use are among young adults age 18–25.

Although methamphetamine is often called "poor man's cocaine," its users are not all poor or poorly educated; rather, they span the socioeconomic spectrum. The drug spread east from the West Coast and is now found in all 50 states, in rural, suburban, and urban areas. Meth producers are finding ways to attract younger users, such as by designing candy-flavored meth, which makes the drug easier to take and more appealing to children. Many drug enforcement and government officials say methampethamine is the number-one drug problem in the United States today.

Related Issues

Along with the physical problems suffered by meth users, the drug has led to a growing array of social and emotional problems. For example, because meth diminishes the user's judgment, many meth addicts engage in unsafe sex—often with injection drug users—when they're high. As a result, meth users face an increased risk of infection from a variety of transmittable diseases, especially HIV and hepatitis C. Meth use is also associated with domestic violence and family breakdown.

Another problem unique to meth is its do-it-yourself appeal to users and dealers. The drug is relatively easy to make, using commonly available chemicals, and clandestine meth labs in residential living rooms and basements have sprung up across the country. One of the chemicals used in making meth is pseudoephedrine, a drug found in products used to relieve nasal or sinus con-

gestion, such as Sudafed and other cold and allergy medications. To limit access to this drug, Congress passed the Combat Methamphetamine Epidemic Act of 2005 as part of the Patriot Act, requiring behind-the-counter sale of products containing pseudoepinehprine and two other drugs used to make meth.

Methamphetamine production is also very dangerous. The use of caustic and highly explosive chemicals puts meth "cooks" at risk for injury and death from explosion and fire.

Treatment Options

At this time, there are few treatment options for meth addiction. Cognitive behavioral therapy is widely viewed as the best approach; therapy helps users identify the root causes of their addiction and teaches them skills needed to effectively quit using the drug. In some cases, antidepressants or antianxiety medications are prescribed, but there currently is no single effective pharmacological treatment for methamphetamine addiction. In studies, the drug Prometa has been effective in helping meth addicts break their addiction. Further studies are under way.

According to the CDC's 2007 Youth Risk Behavior Surveillance, 4.5% of American high school students reported using methamphetamine at least once during their lifetime (see the box "The Meth Epidemic" above).

EFFECTS Small doses of amphetamines usually make people feel more alert. Amphetamines generally increase motor activity but do not measurably alter a normal, rested person's ability to perform tasks calling for challenging motor skills or complex thinking. When amphetamines do improve performance, it is primarily by counteracting fatigue

and boredom. Amphetamines in small doses also increase heart rate and blood pressure and change sleep patterns.

Amphetamines are sometimes used to curb appetite, but after a few weeks the user develops tolerance and higher doses are necessary. When people stop taking the drug, their appetite usually returns, and they gain back the weight they lost unless they have made permanent changes in eating behavior.

FROM USE TO ABUSE Much amphetamine abuse begins as an attempt to cope with a temporary situation. A student cramming for an exam or an exhausted long-haul truck driver can go a little longer by taking amphetamines, but the results can be disastrous. The likelihood of making bad judgments significantly increases. The stimulating effects may also wear off suddenly, and the user may precipitously feel exhausted or fall asleep ("crash").

Another problem is **state dependence,** the phenomenon whereby information learned in a certain drug-induced state is difficult to recall when the person is not in that same physiological state. Test performance may deteriorate when students use drugs to study and then take tests in their normal, nondrug state. (Users of antihistamines may also experience state dependence.)

Methamphetamine intoxication leads to unsafe and uncharacteristic behavior. It has been linked to high-risk sexual activity and increased rates of STDs, including HIV infection (Chapter 18).

DEPENDENCE Repeated use of amphetamines, even in moderate doses, often leads to tolerance and the need for increasingly larger doses. The result can be severe disturbances in behavior, including a temporary state of paranoid **psychosis,** with delusions of persecution and episodes of unprovoked violence. If injected in large doses, amphetamines produce a feeling of intense pleasure, followed by sensations of vigor and euphoria that last for several hours. As these feelings wear off, they are replaced by feelings of irritability and vague uneasiness. Long-term use of amphetamines at high doses can cause paranoia, hallucinations, delusions, and incoherence.

Methamphetamine users have signs of brain damage similar to those seen in Parkinson's disease patients that appear to persist even after drug use ceases, causing impaired memory and motor coordination. Withdrawal symptoms may include muscle aches and tremors, profound fatigue, deep depression, despair, and apathy. Chronic high-dose use is often associated with pronounced psychological cravings and obsessive drug-seeking behavior.

Women who use amphetamines during pregnancy risk premature birth, stillbirth, low birth weight, and early infant death. Babies born to amphetamine-using mothers have a higher incidence of cleft palate, cleft lip, and deformed limbs. They may also experience symptoms of withdrawal from amphetamines.

Ritalin A stimulant with amphetamine-like effects, Ritalin (methylphenidate) is used to treat attention-deficit/

hyperactivity disorder (ADHD). When taken orally at prescribed levels, it has little potential for abuse. When injected or snorted, however, dependence and tolerance can rapidly result.

Ephedrine Although somewhat less potent than amphetamine, ephedrine does produce stimulant effects. Ephedrine has been linked to heart arrhythmia, stroke, psychotic reactions, seizures, and some deaths, and it may be particularly dangerous at high doses or when combined with another stimulant such as caffeine. The FDA has banned the sale of ephedrine (see Chapter 14).

Caffeine Caffeine is probably the most popular psychoactive drug and also one of the most ancient. It is found in coffee, tea, cocoa, soft drinks, headache remedies, and OTC preparations like NōDōz. (Table 9.5 lists typical levels of caffeine in several popular beverages.) In ordinary doses, caffeine produces greater alertness and a sense of well-being. It also decreases feelings of fatigue or boredom; using caffeine may enable a person to keep at physically tiring or repetitive tasks longer. Such use is usually followed, however, by a sudden letdown. Caffeine does not noticeably influence a person's ability to perform complex mental tasks unless fatigue, boredom, or other factors have already affected normal performance.

Caffeine mildly stimulates the heart and respiratory system, increases muscular tremor, and enhances gastric secretion. Higher doses may cause nervousness, anxiety, irritability, headache, disturbed sleep, and gastric irritation or peptic ulcers. In people with high blood pressure, caffeine can cause blood pressure to rise even further above normal; in people with type 2 diabetes, caffeine may cause glucose and insulin levels to rise after meals.

Some people, especially children, are quite vulnerable to the adverse effects of caffeine. They become wired: hyperactive and overly sensitive to any stimulation in their environment. In rare instances, the disturbance is so severe that there is misperception of their surroundings—a toxic psychosis.

Drinks containing caffeine are rarely harmful for most people, but some tolerance develops, and withdrawal symptoms of irritability, headaches, and even mild depression do occur. Thus, although we don't usually think of caffeine as a dependence-producing drug, for some people it is. People can usually avoid problems by simply decreasing their daily intake of caffeine; if intake is decreased gradually, withdrawal symptoms can be reduced or avoided. About 80–90% of American adults consume caffeine regularly; the average daily intake is about 280 mg.

TERMS

state dependence A situation in which information learned in a drug-induced state is difficult to recall when the effect of the drug wears off.

psychosis A severe mental disorder characterized by a distortion of reality; symptoms might include delusions or hallucinations.

Table 9.5	Caffeine Content of Popular Beverages	

	Serving Size	Typical Caffeine Level (mg)*
Coffee		
Regular coffee, brewed	8 oz.	95
Regular coffee, instant	8 oz.	93
Espresso	1 oz.	64
Decaffeinated coffee, brewed	8 oz.	5
Decaffeinated coffee, instant	8 oz.	2
Tea		
Regular tea, brewed	8 oz.	47
Snapple Iced Tea	16 oz.	18
Nestea	12 oz.	17
SoBe Green Tea	8 oz.	14
Lipton Brisk Iced Tea, Lemon	12 oz.	10
Decaffeinated tea, brewed	8 oz.	2
Green tea, brewed	8 oz.	Varies
Soda		
Code Red Mountain Dew	12 oz.	54
Mello Yello	12 oz.	53
Diet Coke	12 oz.	47
Dr. Pepper, Diet Dr. Pepper	12 oz.	41
Sunkist Orange Soda	12 oz.	41
Pepsi	12 oz.	38
Coca-Cola Classic, Cherry Coca-Cola, Diet Cherry Coca-Cola, Diet Pepsi	12 oz.	35
A&W Crème Soda	12 oz.	29
Barq's Root Beer	12 oz.	23
Energy Drinks		
No Name	8.4 oz.	280
SoBe No Fear	16 oz.	174
Monster Energy, Rockstar	16 oz.	160
SoBe Adrenaline Rush	16 oz.	152
Full Throttle, Full Throttle Fury	16 oz.	144
AMP Energy Drink	16 oz.	143
Red Bull	8.3 oz.	76
Vault	8 oz.	47

*Caffeine levels vary greatly by brand of product, manner of preparation, and amount consumed. The amounts shown here are averages based on tests conducted by a variety of organizations. The U.S. Food and Drug Administration limits the amount of caffeine in cola and pepper soft drinks to 71 milligrams per 12-ounce serving. To find the exact amount of caffeine in any product, check that product's label.

SOURCES: Center for Science in the Public Interest. 2007. *Caffeine Content of Food & Drugs* (http://www.cspinet.org/new/cafchart.html; retrieved February 3, 2009); Mayo Clinic. 2007. *How Much Caffeine Is in Your Daily Habit?* (http://www.mayoclinic.com/health/caffeine/AN01211; retrieved February 3, 2009); U.S. Department of Agriculture, Agricultural Research Service. 2007. *USDA National Nutrient Database for Standard Reference, Release 20* (http://www.ars.usda.gov/ba/bhnrc/ndl; retrieved February 3, 2009).

Marijuana and Other Cannabis Products

Marijuana is the most widely used illegal drug in the United States (cocaine is second). More than 40% of Americans have tried marijuana at least once; among 21–25-year-olds, more than 54% have tried marijuana. In 2007, 12.6% of college students reported using marijuana at least once within the past month.

Marijuana is a crude preparation of various parts of the Indian hemp plant *Cannabis sativa,* which grows in most parts of the world. THC (tetrahydrocannabinol) is the main active ingredient in marijuana. Based on THC content, the potency of marijuana preparations varies widely. Marijuana plants that grow wild often have less than 1% THC in their leaves. When selected strains are cultivated by separation of male and female plants (*sinsemilla*), the bud leaves from the flowering tops may contain 7–8% THC. Hashish, a potent preparation made from the thick resin that exudes from the marijuana leaves, may contain up to 14% THC.

These various preparations have all been known and used for centuries, so the frequently heard claim that today's marijuana is more potent than the marijuana of the 1970s is not strictly true. However, a greater proportion of the marijuana sold today is the higher-potency (and more expensive) sinsemilla; hence, the average potency of street marijuana has increased.

Marijuana is usually smoked, but it can also be ingested. The classification of marijuana is a matter of some debate. For this reason, it is treated separately here.

Short-Term Effects and Uses As is true with most psychoactive drugs, the effects of a low dose of marijuana are strongly influenced both by the user's expectations and by past experiences. At low doses, marijuana users typically experience euphoria, a heightening of subjective sensory experiences, a slowing down of the perception of passing time, and a relaxed, laid-back attitude. These pleasant effects are the reason this drug is so widely used. With moderate doses, these effects become stronger, and the user can also expect to have impaired memory function, disturbed thought patterns, lapses of attention, and feelings of **depersonalization,** in which the mind seems to be separated from the body.

The effects of marijuana in higher doses are determined mostly by the drug itself rather than by the user's expectations and setting. Very high doses produce feelings of depersonalization, as well as marked sensory distortion and changes in body image (such as a feeling that the body is very light). Inexperienced users sometimes think these sensations mean they are going crazy and become anxious or even panicky. Unexpected reactions are the leading reason for emergency room visits by users of marijuana or hashish.

depersonalization A state in which a person loses the sense of his or her reality or perceives his or her body as unreal.

hallucinogen Any of several drugs that alter perception, feelings, or thoughts; examples are LSD, mescaline, and PCP.

TERMS

Marijuana is the most widely used illegal drug in the United States.

Long-Term Effects The most probable long-term effect of smoking marijuana is respiratory damage, including impaired lung function and chronic bronchial irritation. Although there is no evidence linking marijuana use to lung cancer, it may cause changes in lung tissue that promote cancer growth. Marijuana users may be at increased risk for emphysema and cancer of the head and neck; among people with chronic conditions like cancer and AIDS, marijuana use is associated with increased risk of fatal lung infections. (These are key reasons the Institute of Medicine recommended the development of alternative methods of delivering the potentially beneficial compounds in marijuana.) Heavy users may experience learning problems, as well as subtle impairments of attention and memory that may or may not be reversible following long-term abstinence. Long-term use may also decrease testosterone levels and sperm counts and increase sperm abnormalities.

Heavy marijuana use during pregnancy may cause impaired fetal growth and development, low birth weight, and increased risk of ectopic pregnancy. Marijuana may act synergistically with alcohol to increase the damaging effects of alcohol on the fetus. THC rapidly enters breast milk and may impair an infant's early motor development.

Dependence Regular users of marijuana can develop tolerance; some develop dependence, and researchers estimate that 1.5% of Americans meet the APA criteria for marijuana dependence. Withdrawal symptoms may occur in the majority of dependent or heavy users; common symptoms include anger or aggression, irritability, nervousness or restlessness, sleep difficulties, and decreased appetite or weight loss.

Physiologically, marijuana increases heart rate and dilates certain blood vessels in the eyes, which creates the characteristic bloodshot eyes. The user may also feel less inclined toward physical exertion and may feel particularly hungry or thirsty. THC affects parts of the brain controlling balance, coordination, and reaction time; thus marijuana use impairs driving performance. The combination of alcohol and marijuana is even more dangerous: Even a low dose of marijuana, when combined with alcohol, significantly impairs driving performance and increases crash risk.

In 1999, the Institute of Medicine determined that some compounds in marijuana may have legitimate medical use. For example, marijuana has been shown to ease pain, reduce nausea, and increase appetite. These benefits led several states to approve the use of "medical marijuana" by extremely ill patients, with physician monitoring. However, because growing, selling, or possessing marijuana is a federal crime, the Supreme Court has held that state laws permitting medical marijuana use cannot supersede federal law. This means anyone who uses marijuana for medical reasons—even in a state that approves

Hallucinogens

Hallucinogens are a group of drugs whose predominant pharmacological effect is to alter the user's perceptions, feelings, and thoughts. Hallucinogens include the following:

- LSD (lysergic acid diethylamide)
- Mescaline
- Psilocybin
- STP (4-methyl-2,5-dimethoxyamphetamine)
- DMT (dimethyltryptamine)

- MDMA (3,4-methylene-dioxymethamphetamine)
- Ketamine
- PCP (phencyclidine)

These drugs are most commonly ingested or smoked.

LSD LSD is one of the most powerful psychoactive drugs. Tiny doses will produce noticeable effects in most people, such as an altered sense of time, visual disturbances, an improved sense of hearing, mood changes, and distortions in how people perceive their bodies. Dilation of the pupils and slight dizziness, weakness, and nausea may also occur. With larger doses, users may experience a phenomenon known as **synesthesia**, feelings of depersonalization, and other alterations in the perceived relationship between the self and external reality.

Many hallucinogens induce tolerance so quickly that after only one or two doses their effects decrease substantially. The user must then stop taking the drug for several days before his or her system can be receptive to it again. These drugs cause little drug-seeking behavior and no physical dependence or withdrawal symptoms.

The immediate effects of low doses of hallucinogens are largely determined by expectations and setting. Many effects are hard to describe because they involve subjective and unusual dimensions of awareness—the **altered states of consciousness** for which these drugs are famous. For this reason, hallucinogens have acquired a certain aura not associated with other drugs. People have taken LSD in search of a religious or mystical experience or in the hope of exploring new worlds. During the 1960s, some psychiatrists gave LSD to their patients to help them talk about their repressed feelings.

A severe panic reaction, which can be terrifying in the extreme, can result from taking any dose of LSD. It is impossible to predict when a panic reaction will occur. Some LSD users report having had hundreds of pleasurable and ecstatic experiences before having a bad trip, or bummer. If the user is already in a serene mood and feels no anger or hostility and if he or she is in secure surroundings with trusted companions, a bad trip may be less likely, but a tranquil experience is not guaranteed.

Even after the drug's chemical effects have worn off, spontaneous flashbacks and other psychological disturbances can occur. **Flashbacks** are perceptual distortions and bizarre thoughts that occur after the drug has been entirely eliminated from the body. Although they are relatively rare phenomena, flashbacks can be extremely distressing. They are often triggered by specific psychological cues

associated with the drug-taking experience, such as certain mood states or even types of music.

Other Hallucinogens Most other hallucinogens have the same general effects as LSD, but there are some variations. For example, a DMT or ketamine high does not last as long as an LSD high; an STP high lasts longer. MDMA has both hallucinogenic and amphetamine-like properties. Tolerance to MDMA develops quickly, and high doses can cause anxiety, delusions, and paranoia. (See the box "Club Drugs" on p. 252 for more on MDMA.)

PCP reduces and distorts sensory input, especially proprioception, the sensation of body position and movement; it creates a state of sensory deprivation. PCP was initially used as an anesthetic but was unsatisfactory because it caused agitation, confusion, and delirium (loss of contact with reality). Because it can be easily made, PCP is often available illegally and is sometimes used as an inexpensive replacement for other psychoactive drugs.

The effects of ketamine are similar to those of PCP—confusion, agitation, aggression, and lack of coordination—but they tend to be less predictable. Tolerance to either drug can develop rapidly.

Mescaline, derived from the peyote cactus, is the ceremonial drug of the Native American Church. It causes effects similar to LSD, including altered perception and feeling; increased body temperature, heart rate, and blood pressure; weakness and trembling; and sleeplessness. Mescaline is expensive, so most street mescaline is diluted LSD or a mixture of other drugs. Hallucinogenic effects can be obtained from certain mushrooms (*Psilocybe mexicana,* or "magic mushrooms"), certain morning glory seeds, nutmeg, jimsonweed, and other botanical products, but unpleasant side effects, such as dizziness, have limited the popularity of these products.

Inhalants

Inhaling certain chemicals can produce effects ranging from heightened pleasure to delirium and death. Inhalants fall into several major groups:

- Volatile solvents, which are found in products such as paint thinner, glue, and gasoline
- Aerosols, which are sprays that contain propellants and solvents

synesthesia A condition in which a stimulus evokes not only the sensation appropriate to it but also another sensation of a different character, such as when a color evokes a specific smell.

altered states of consciousness Profound changes in mood, thinking, and perception.

flashback A perceptual distortion or bizarre thought that recurs after the chemical effects of a drug have worn off.

TERMS

Inhalant use is difficult to monitor and control because inhalants are found in many inexpensive and legal products.

- Nitrites, such as butyl nitrite and amyl nitrite
- Anesthetics, which include nitrous oxide, or laughing gas

Inhalant use tends to be highest among younger adolescents and declines with age; in 2007, 3.9% of teens age 12–17 had used inhalants during the past year, as had 1.6% of young adults age 18–25.

Inhalant use is difficult to control because inhalants are easy to obtain. They are present in a variety of seemingly harmless products, from dessert-topping sprays to underarm deodorants, that are both inexpensive and legal. Us-

? QUESTIONS FOR CRITICAL THINKING AND REFLECTION

Do you know any young teens who may be at risk for using inhalants? If so, would you try to intervene in some way? What would you tell a youngster to convince him or her to stop inhaling chemicals?

ing the drugs also requires no illegal or suspicious paraphernalia. Inhalant users get high by sniffing, snorting, "bagging" (inhaling fumes from a plastic bag), or "huffing" (placing an inhalant-soaked rag in the mouth).

Although different in makeup, nearly all inhalants produce effects similar to those of anesthetics, which slow down body functions. Low doses may cause users to feel slightly stimulated; at higher doses, users may feel less inhibited and less in control. Sniffing high concentrations of the chemicals in solvents or aerosol sprays can cause a loss of consciousness, heart failure, and death. High concentrations of any inhalant can also cause death from suffocation by displacing the oxygen in the lungs and central nervous system. Deliberately inhaling from a bag or in a closed area greatly increases the chances of suffocation. Other possible effects of the excessive or long-term use of inhalants include damage to the nervous system (impaired perception, reasoning, memory, and muscular coordination); hearing loss; increased risk of cancer; and damage to the liver, kidneys, and bone marrow.

DRUG USE: THE DECADES AHEAD

Drug research will undoubtedly provide new information, new treatments, and new chemical combinations in the decades ahead. New psychoactive drugs may present unexpected possibilities for therapy, social use, and abuse. Making honest and unbiased information about drugs available to everyone, however, may cut down on their abuse.

Although the use of some drugs, both legal and illegal, has declined dramatically since the 1970s, the use of others has held steady or increased. Mounting public concern has led to great debate and a wide range of opinions about what should be done. Efforts to combat the problem include workplace drug testing, tougher law enforcement and prosecution, and treatment and education. With drugs entering the country on a massive scale from South America, Southeast Asia, and elsewhere and being distributed through tightly controlled drug-smuggling organizations and street gangs, it remains to be seen how effective any program will be.

Drugs, Society, and Families

The economic cost of drug abuse is staggering. According to the National Institute on Drug Abuse, the cost to society of illicit drug abuse alone is $181 billion annually. That figure exceeds $500 billion when combined with the costs of alcohol and tobacco use, including health care, criminal justice, and lost productivity. But the costs are more than just financial; they are also paid in human pain and suffering.

The relationship between drugs and crime is complex. The criminal justice system is inundated with people accused of crimes related to drug possession, sale, or use. The FBI reports that more than 1.8 million arrests are made annually for drug violations; at any given time, more than 100,000 people are in jail for violating drug laws. Many assaults and murders are committed when people try to acquire or protect drug territories, settle disputes about drugs, or steal from dealers. Violence and the use of guns are more common in neighborhoods where drug trafficking is prevalent. Addicts commit more robberies and burglaries than criminals not on drugs. People under the influence of drugs, especially alcohol, are more likely to commit violent crimes like rape and murder than people who do not use drugs. Although often associated with poor inner-city areas and ethnic minorities, drug-related problems affect all groups and every area of the country (see the box "Drug Use and Ethnicity: Risk Factors and Protective Factors").

Drug use is also a health care issue for society. In the United States, illegal drug use leads to more than 800,000 emergency room admissions and nearly 20,000 deaths annually. Although it is in the best interest of society to treat addicts who want help, there is not nearly enough space in treatment facilities to help the millions of Americans who need immediate treatment. Drug addicts who want to quit, especially those among the urban poor, often have to wait a year or more for acceptance into a residential care or other treatment program.

Drug abuse also takes a toll on individuals and families. Children born to women who use drugs such as alcohol, tobacco, or cocaine may have long-term health problems. Drug use in families can become a vicious cycle. Observing adults around them using drugs, children assume it is an acceptable way to deal with problems. Problems such as abuse, neglect, lack of opportunity, and unemployment become contributing factors to drug use and serve to perpetuate the cycle.

QUICK STATS

Only **17.8%** of Americans in need of treatment for illicit drug use problems actually received treatment at a specialized facility.

—SAMHSA, 2008

Legalizing Drugs

Pointing out that many of the social problems associated with drugs are related to prohibition rather than to the effects of the drugs themselves, some people have argued for various forms of drug legalization or decriminalization. Proposals range from making drugs such as marijuana and heroin available by prescription to allowing licensed dealers to sell some of these drugs to adults. Proponents argue that legalizing some currently illicit drugs—but putting controls on them similar to those used for alcohol, tobacco, and prescription drugs—could eliminate many of the problems related to drug use.

Opponents of drug legalization argue that allowing easier access to drugs would expose many more people to possible abuse and dependence. Drugs would be cheaper and easier to obtain, and drug use would be more socially acceptable. Legalizing drugs could cause an increase in drug use among children and teenagers. Opponents point out that alcohol and tobacco are major causes of disease and death in our society and that they should not be used as models for other practices.

Drug Testing

The workplace is another segment of our society where drug use is common. According to data from recent surveys, the majority of substance users hold full-time jobs and constitute a significant public health problem in the workplace. Drug use in the workplace not only creates health problems for individual users, but it has a negative effect on productivity and on safety of coworkers. People who use drugs at work face higher rates of absenteeism, poor health, and a greater likelihood of harming themselves or others in the workplace.

Statistics from the federal government show that 8.2% of full-time workers used illicit drugs between 2002 and 2004. In absolute numbers, approximately 16.4 million current illicit drug users and nearly 15 million heavy alcohol users were full-time workers during that period. Illicit drug use is highest among workers in the food industry and construction sectors, while heavy alcohol use is greatest among construction, mining, and repair workers. Premature death, illness, and disability—factors associated with the economic and health burden of lost productivity—are estimated to run as high as $114 billion for drug use and $179 billion for heavy alcohol use.

The extent of the problem has given rise to the development of workplace policies to help workers regain their health and well-being. According to survey data collected during the period 2002–2004, nearly half of full-time workers were aware of written policies on drug and alcohol use in the workplace. Workplace policies developed to address the problem often include drug testing and referral services. Despite controversial aspects of drug testing in the workplace, a growing number of U.S. workers recognize the need for such screening.

Most drug testing involves a urine test; a test for alcohol involves a blood test or a breath test. The accuracy of these tests has improved in recent years, so there are fewer opportunities for people to cheat or for the tests to yield inaccurate results. If a person tests positive for drugs, the employer may provide drug counseling or treatment, suspend the employee until he or she tests negative, or fire the individual.

Drug Use and Ethnicity: Risk Factors and Protective Factors

Surveys of the U.S. population find a variety of trends in drug use and abuse among ethnic groups (see table). In addition to these general trends, there are also trends relating to specific drugs; for example, hallucinogen use is relatively prevalent among whites and Latinos, inhalant use among Native Hawaiians and Pacific Islander Americans.

However, as is true for many areas of health, ethnic trends are influenced by a complex interplay of other factors:

- *Educational status:* Adults with four or more years of college are more likely to have *tried* illicit drugs than are people of the same age who never finished high school, but *current* drug use is lower among college graduates than among people with less education. Among teens, poor school performance is associated with increased risk for illicit drug use.

- *Employment status:* Most adult drug users are employed, but rates of current drug use are much higher among people who are unemployed or who work part-time compared with those who are employed full-time.

- *Parental education and socioeconomic status:* Students from poor families have higher rates of *early* drug use compared with students from wealthier families, but by the twelfth grade, the differences disappear. Socioeconomic status and parental education are closely linked.

- *Geographic area:* Current drug use in the United States is highest in the West and South; drug use is also higher in met-

ropolitan and urban areas compared with more rural areas. People living in communities with high rates of poverty, crime, and unemployment have higher than average rates of drug use and abuse. Specific drugs may also be more available—and their abuse more prevalent—in certain regions or communities.

Strong cultural identity is associated with reduced risk of drug use and abuse among all groups. Some factors believed to contribute to lower rates of drug use among these groups include the following:

- *Parental and community disapproval of drug and alcohol use:* Parents of Asian American children tend to have more restrictive drug and alcohol use norms than African American and white parents. Black parents tend to monitor their children's activities and friendships more closely than white parents. Parental disapproval of drug use is often tied to greater perceived risk of drug use—and lower rates of drug use—among teens.

- *Close family ties:* Asian American teens are the likeliest to come from intact homes. Respect for authority and family loyalty are strongly valued among many Asian American populations. Black teens, although least likely to come from intact homes, often come from single-parent households with close extended family ties. Teens from cohesive and stable families are less likely to use drugs.

- *Focus on schooling and education:* Teens from families who value educa-

tion and where parents help with homework and limit weeknight time with friends have lower rates of drug use. Asian Americans have twice the rate of college graduation compared with other groups.

SOURCES: Johnston, L. D., et al. 2008. *Monitoring the Future: National Results on Adolescent Drug Use: Overview of Key Findings, 2007.* Bethesda, Md.: National Institute on Drug Abuse; Office of Applied Studies, Substance Abuse and Mental Health Services Administration. 2008. *Results from the 2007 National Survey on Drug Use and Health: National Findings* (http://oas.samhsa.gov/nhsda.htm; retrieved May 1, 2008).

National Survey Results, 2007

	Lifetime Drug Use	Past Year Drug Use	Past Month Drug Use Age 12–17	Age 18–25	Age 26 and Older	All Ages	Past Year Illicit Drug Dependence
White	50.3	14.9	10.2	21.9	5.9	8.2	2.7
Black or African American	43.1	16.0	9.4	18.7	7.5	9.5	3.7
Hispanic or Latino	34.2	12.2	8.1	14.6	4.3	6.6	2.5
Asian American	22.8	7.2	6.0	11.7	2.6	4.2	1.1
American Indian and Alaska Native	54.6	18.4	N/A	N/A	8.5	12.6	4.0
Native Hawaiian and Pacific Islander American	N/A	13.3	N/A	9.0	N/A	N/A	3.6
Two or more races	51.5	22.1	9.2	25.9	9.1	11.8	5.1

Note: Results shown in percentages of each population group.

N/A = Data not available for 2007.

The FDA has approved several over-the-counter home drug testing kits designed to allow parents to check their children for drug use. Urine samples are collected at home; preliminary results may be available immediately, but final results require that the sample be sent to a laboratory for analysis. Many experts, including the American Academy of Pediatrics, advise against the use of home tests in cases of suspected drug use; instead, they recommend a comprehensive evaluation by a qualified health professional.

Treatment for Drug Dependence

Treatment for drug dependence is sometimes characterized by discrete episodes of short-term abstinence and relapse. Regardless of the therapeutic approach used for drug dependence, many individuals undergoing treatment will often slide back into their drug habits. Often, this backsliding results in worsening of the original substance-abuse problem. For some substances, the period from abstinence to relapse occurs within one year after treatment.

Preventing relapse and maintaining long-term cessation of drug use is an exceedingly complex medical goal. Medical interventions based on pharmaceutical aids to enhance the individual's long-term commitment to change and stay drug-free remains a distant and elusive goal. Relapse prevention research is instead increasingly focusing on the need to expand the behavioral repertoire of skills needed to decrease the risk of recidivism among individuals receiving drug-treatment services.

Medication-Assisted Treatment   Medications are increasingly being used in addiction treatment—to reduce the craving for the abused drug or to block or oppose its effects. Perhaps the best-known medication for drug abuse is methadone, a synthetic drug used as a substitute for heroin. Use of methadone prevents withdrawal reactions and reduces the craving for heroin; it enables dependent people to function normally in social and vocational activities, although they remain dependent on methadone. The narcotic buprenorphine, approved in 2002 for treatment of opioid addiction, also reduces cravings. Many other medications are under study; drugs used specifically in the treatment of nicotine and alcohol dependence are discussed in Chapters 10 and 11.

Medication therapy is relatively simple and inexpensive and is therefore popular among patients, health care providers, and insurance companies. However, the relapse rate is high. Combining drug therapy with psy-

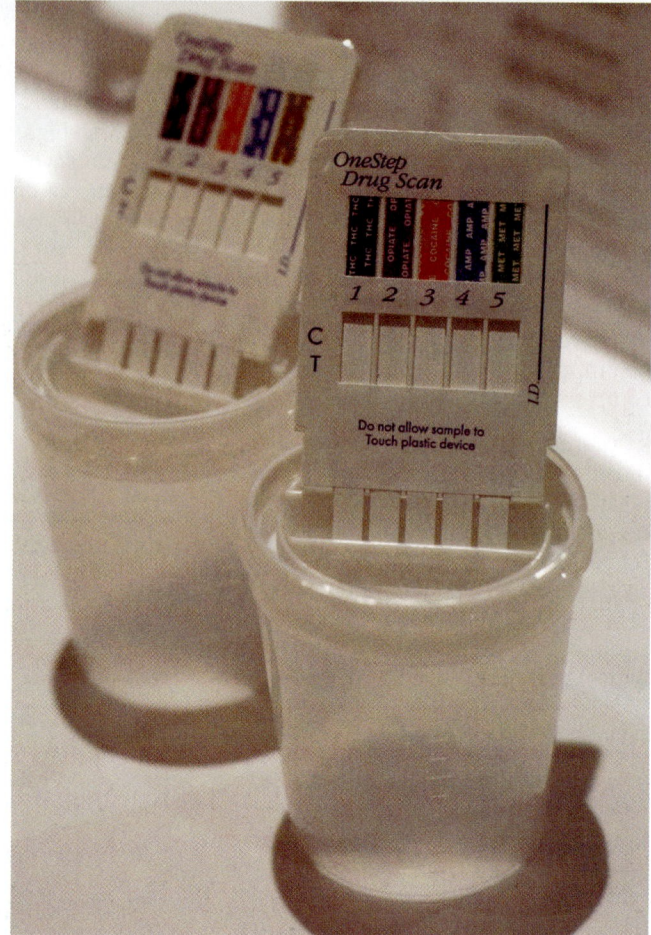

Many companies test current and prospective employees for drug use.

chological and social services improves success rates, underscoring the importance of psychological factors in drug dependence.

Treatment Centers   Treatment centers offer a variety of short-term and long-term services, including hospitalization, detoxification, counseling, and other mental health services. The therapeutic community is a specific type of center, a residential program run in a completely drug-free atmosphere. Administered by ex-addicts, these programs use confrontation, strict discipline, and unrelenting peer pressure to attempt to resocialize the addict with a different set of values. Halfway houses, transitional settings between a 24-hour-a-day program and independent living, are an important phase of treatment for some people. Strategies for evaluating programs are given in the box "Choosing a Drug-Treatment Program."

Self-Help Groups and Peer Counseling   Groups such as Alcoholics Anonymous (AA) and Narcotics Anonymous (NA) have helped many people. People treated in

Choosing a Drug-Treatment Program

When evaluating different facilities or programs for drug treatment, consider the following issues:

• *What type of treatment or facility is most appropriate?* Intensive outpatient treatment is available through many community mental health centers, as well as through specialized drug-treatment facilities. Such programs typically require several sessions per week, combining individual therapy, group counseling, and attendance at 12-step meetings. Residential, or inpatient, facilities may be associated with a medical facility such as a hospital, or they may be freestanding programs that focus solely on substance-abuse treatment. Some residential treatment programs last longer or cost more per week than many health insurance plans will cover.

• *How will treatment be paid for?* Many health insurance plans limit residential treatment to a maximum of 3 weeks or less. They may also require that you first attempt a less expensive form of treatment before they will approve coverage for a residential facility.

• *Is there likely to be a need for medical support?* Chronic alcoholics or abusers of other CNS depressants may experience life-threatening seizures or other withdrawal symptoms during the first few days of detoxification. Malnutrition is common among substance abusers, and injection drug users may suffer from local infections and bloodborne diseases such as hepatitis or HIV infection. Medical problems such as these are best handled in an inpatient program with good medical support.

• *What is the level of professional training of the staff?* Is there a medical doctor on-site or making frequent visits? Are there trained nurses? Licensed psychologists or social workers? Many successful programs are staffed primarily by recovering alcoholics or drug users. Do those staff members have training and certification as addiction specialists or some other license or certificate?

• *Does the program provide related services, such as family and job counseling and post-treatment follow-up?* These types of services are extremely important for the long-term success of drug-abuse treatment.

• *Can you visit the facility and speak with the staff and clients?* A prospective client and his or her family should be allowed to visit any treatment center or program.

---

drug substitution programs or substance-abuse treatment centers are often urged or required to join a self-help group as part of their recovery. These groups follow a 12-step program. Group members' first step is to acknowledge that they have a problem over which they have no control. Peer support is a critical ingredient of these programs, and members usually meet at least once a week. Each member is paired with a sponsor to call on for advice and support if the temptation to relapse becomes overwhelming. With such support, thousands of substance-dependent people have been able to recover, remain abstinent, and reclaim their lives. Chapters of AA and NA meet on some college campuses; community-based chapters are listed in the phone book and in local newspapers.

Many colleges also have peer counseling programs, in which students are trained to help other students who have drug problems. A peer counselor's role may be as limited as referring a student to a professional with expertise in substance dependence for an evaluation or as involved as helping arrange a leave of absence from school for participation in a drug-treatment program. Most peer counseling programs are founded on principles of strict confidentiality. Peer counselors may also be able to help students who are concerned about a classmate or loved one with an apparent drug problem (see the box "If Someone You Know Has a Drug Problem . . ." on p. 264). Information about peer counseling programs is usually available from the student health center.

Harm Reduction Strategies Recognizing that many attempts at treatment are at first unsuccessful and that a drug-free society may be an unobtainable goal, some experts advocate the use of harm reduction strategies. The goal of harm reduction is to minimize the negative effects of drug use and abuse; a common example is the use of designated drivers to reduce alcohol-related motor vehicle crashes. In terms of illicit drugs, drug substitution programs such as methadone maintenance are one form of harm reduction; although participants remain drug dependent, the negative individual and social consequences of their drug use is reduced. Syringe exchange programs, designed to reduce transmission of HIV and hepatitis C, are another harm reduction approach. Some experts have also suggested free testing of street drugs for purity and potency to help users avoid unintentional toxicity or overdose.

Codependency Many treatment programs also offer counseling for those who are close to drug abusers. Drug abuse takes a toll on friends and family members, and counseling can help people work through painful feelings of guilt and powerlessness. **Codependency,** in which a

codependency A relationship in which a non–substance-abusing partner or family member is controlled by the abuser's behavior; codependent people frequently engage in enabling behaviors.

TERMS

If Someone You Know Has a Drug Problem . . .

Changes in behavior and mood in someone you know may signal a growing dependence on drugs. Signs that a person's life is beginning to focus on drugs include the following:

- Sudden withdrawal or emotional distance

- Rebellious or unusually irritable behavior

- A loss of interest in usual activities or hobbies

- A decline in school performance

- A sudden change in the chosen group of friends

- Changes in sleeping or eating habits

- Frequent borrowing of money or stealing

- Secretive behavior about personal possessions, such as a backpack or the contents of a drawer

- Deterioration of physical appearance

If you believe a family member or friend has a drug problem, obtain information about resources for drug treatment available on your campus or in your community. Communicate your concern, provide him or her with information about treatment options, and offer your support during treatment. If the person continues to deny having a problem, you may want to talk with an experienced counselor about setting up an intervention—a formal, structured confrontation designed to end denial by having family, friends, and other caring individuals present their concerns to the drug user. Participants in an intervention would indicate the ways in which the individual is hurting others as well as himself or herself. If your friend or family member agrees to treatment, encourage him or her to attend a support group such as Narcotics Anonymous or Alcoholics Anonymous. And finally, examine your relationship with the abuser for signs of codependency. If necessary, get help for yourself; friends and family of drug users can often benefit from counseling.

person close to the drug abuser is controlled by the abuser's behavior, sometimes develops. Codependent people may come to believe that love, approval, and security are contingent on their taking care of the abuser. People can become codependent naturally because they want to help when someone they love becomes dependent on a drug. They may assume that their good intentions will persuade the drug user to stop.

Codependent people often engage in behaviors that remove or soften the effects of drug use on the user—so-called *enabling* behaviors. However, the habit of enabling can inhibit a drug-dependent person's recovery because the person never has to experience the consequences of his or her behavior. Often, the enabler is dependent, too—on the patterns of interaction in the relationship. People who need to take care of people often marry people who need to be taken care of. Children in these families often develop the same behavior pattern as one of their parents, by either becoming helpless or becoming a caregiver. For this reason, many treatment programs involve the whole family.

Have you ever been an enabler in a relationship? You may have, if you've ever done any of the following:

- Given someone one more chance to stop abusing drugs, then another, and another . . .

- Made excuses or lied for someone to his or her friends, teachers, or employer

- Joined someone in drug use and blamed others for your behavior

- Loaned money to someone to continue drug use

- Stayed up late waiting for or gone out searching for someone who uses drugs

- Felt embarrassed or angry about the actions of someone who uses drugs

- Ignored the drug use because the person got defensive when you brought it up

- Not confronted a friend or relative who was obviously intoxicated or high on a drug

If you come from a codependent family or see yourself developing codependency relationships or engaging in enabling behaviors, consider acting now to make changes in your patterns of interaction. Remember, you cannot cause or cure drug dependence in another person.

Preventing Drug Abuse

Obviously, the best solution to drug abuse is prevention. Government attempts at controlling the drug problem tend to focus on stopping the production, importation, and distribution of illegal drugs. Creative effort also has to be put into stopping the demand for drugs. Developing persuasive antidrug educational programs offers the best hope for solving the drug problem in the future. Indirect approaches to prevention involve building young people's self-esteem, improving their academic skills, and increasing their recreational opportunities. Direct approaches involve giving information about the adverse effects of drugs and teaching tactics that help students resist peer pressure to use drugs in various situations. Developing strategies for resisting peer pressure is one of the more effective techniques.

Prevention efforts need to focus on the different motivations individuals have for using and abusing specific drugs at different ages. For example, grade-school children seem receptive to programs that involve their parents or well-known adults such as professional athletes. Adolescents in junior or senior high school are often more responsive to peer counselors. Many young adults tend to be influenced by efforts that focus on health education. For all ages, it is important to provide nondrug alternatives—such as recreational facilities, counseling, greater opportunities for leisure activities, and places to socialize—that speak to the individual's or group's specific reasons for using drugs. Reminding young people that most people, no matter what age, are *not* users of illegal drugs, do *not* smoke cigarettes, and do *not* get drunk frequently is a critical part of preventing substance abuse.

QUESTIONS FOR CRITICAL THINKING AND REFLECTION

Do you know someone who may have a drug problem? What steps, if any, have you taken to help that person? If you were using drugs and felt that things had gone out of control, what would you want your friends to do for you?

TIPS FOR TODAY AND THE FUTURE

RIGHT NOW YOU CAN

- If you are a regular caffeine user, look for ways to cut back.
- Consider whether you or someone you know might benefit from drug counseling. Find out what types of services are available on campus or in your area.

IN THE FUTURE YOU CAN

- Study the drug-related attitudes of people you know. For example, talk to two older adults and two fellow students about their attitudes toward legalizing marijuana. What are the differences in their opinions, and how do they account for them?
- Analyze media portrayals of drug use. As you watch TV shows and movies, take note of the way they depict drug use among people of different ages and backgrounds. How realistic are the portrayals, in your view? Think about the influence they have on you and your peers.

The Role of Drugs in Your Life

Where do you fit into this complex picture of drug use and abuse? Chances are that you've had experience with OTC and prescription drugs, and you may or may not have had experience with one or more of the drugs described in this chapter. You probably know someone who has used or abused a psychoactive drug. Whatever your experience has been up to now, it's likely that you will encounter drugs at some point in your life. To make sure you'll have the inner resources to resist peer pressure and make your own decision, cultivate a variety of activities you enjoy doing, realize that you are entitled to have your own opinion, and don't neglect your self-esteem.

Before you try a psychoactive drug, consider the following questions:

- *What are the risks involved?* Many drugs carry an immediate risk of injury or death. Most involve the longer-term risk of abuse and dependence.

- *Is using the drug compatible with your goals?* Consider how drug use will affect your education and career objectives, your relationships, your future happiness, and the happiness of those who love you.

- *What are your ethical beliefs about drug use?* Consider whether using a drug would cause you to go against your personal ethics, religious beliefs, social values, or family responsibilities.

- *What are the financial costs?* Many drugs are expensive, especially if you become dependent on them.

- *Are you trying to solve a deeper problem?* Drugs will not make emotional pain go away; in the long run, they will only make it worse. If you are feeling depressed or anxious, seek help from a mental health professional instead of self-medicating with drugs.

Like all aspects of health-related behavior, making responsible decisions about drug use depends on information, knowledge, and insight into yourself. Many choices are possible; making the ones that are right for you is what counts.

SUMMARY

- Addictive behaviors are reinforcing. Addicts experience a strong compulsion for the behavior and a loss of control over it; an escalating pattern of abuse with serious negative consequences may result.

- The sources or causes of addiction include heredity, personality, lifestyle, and environmental factors. People may use an addictive behavior as a means of alleviating stress or painful emotions.

Changing Your Drug Habits

This behavior change strategy focuses on one of the most commonly used drugs—caffeine. If you are concerned about your use of a different drug or another type of addictive behavior, you can devise your own plan based on this one and on the steps outlined in Chapter 1.

Because caffeine supports certain behaviors that are characteristic of our culture, such as sedentary, stressful work, you may find yourself relying on coffee (or tea, chocolate, or cola) to get through a busy schedule. Such habits often begin in college. Fortunately, it's easier to break a habit before it becomes entrenched as a lifelong dependency.

When you are studying for exams, the forced physical inactivity and the need to concentrate even when fatigued may lead you to overuse caffeine. But caffeine doesn't help unless you are already sleepy. And it does not relieve any underlying condition (you are just more tired when it wears off). How can you change this pattern?

Self-Monitoring

Keep a log of how much caffeine you eat or drink. Use a measuring cup to measure coffee or tea. Using Table 9.5, convert the amounts you drink into an estimate expressed in milligrams of caffeine. Be sure to include all forms, such as chocolate bars and OTC medications, as well as caffeine candy, colas, cocoa or hot chocolate, chocolate cake, tea, and coffee.

Self-Assessment

At the end of the week, add up your daily totals and divide by 7 to get your daily average in milligrams. How much is too much? At more than 250 mg per day, you may well be experiencing some adverse symptoms. If you are experiencing at least five of the following symptoms, you may want to cut down.

- Restlessness
- Nervousness
- Excitement
- Insomnia
- Flushed face
- Excessive sweating
- Gastrointestinal problems
- Muscle twitching
- Rambling thoughts and speech
- Irregular heartbeat
- Periods of inexhaustibility
- Excessive pacing or movement

Set Limits

Can you restrict your caffeine intake to a daily total, and stick to this contract? If so, set a cutoff point, such as one cup of coffee. Pegging it to a specific time of day can be helpful, because then you won't confront a decision at any other point (and possibly fail). If you find you cannot stick to your limit, you may want to cut out caffeine altogether; abstinence can be easier than moderation for some people. If you experience caffeine withdrawal symptoms (headache, fatigue), you may want to cut your intake more gradually.

Find Other Ways to Keep Up Your Energy

If you are fatigued, it makes sense to get enough sleep or exercise more, rather than drowning the problem in coffee or tea. Different people need different amounts of sleep; you may also need more sleep at different times, such as during a personal crisis or an illness. Also, exercise raises your metabolic rate for hours afterward—a handy fact to exploit when you want to feel more awake and want to avoid an irritable caffeine jag. And if you've been compounding your fatigue by not eating properly, try filling up on complex carbohydrates such as whole-grain bread or crackers instead of candy bars.

Tips on Cutting Out Caffeine Here are some more ways to decrease your consumption of caffeine:

- Keep some noncaffeinated drinks on hand, such as decaffeinated coffee, herbal teas, mineral water, bouillon, or hot water.
- Alternate between hot and very cold liquids.
- Fill your coffee cup only halfway.
- Avoid the office or school lunchroom or cafeteria and the chocolate sections of the grocery store. (Often people drink coffee or tea and eat chocolate simply because they're available.)
- Read labels of over-the-counter medications to check for hidden sources of caffeine.

- Many common behaviors are potentially addictive, including gambling, shopping, sexual activity, Internet use, eating, and working.

- Drug abuse is a maladaptive pattern of drug use that persists despite adverse social, psychological, or medical consequences.

- Drug dependence involves taking a drug compulsively, which includes neglecting constructive activities because of it and continuing to use it despite experiencing adverse effects resulting from its use. Tolerance and withdrawal symptoms are often present.

- Reasons for using drugs include the lure of the illicit; curiosity; rebellion; peer pressure; and the desire to alter one's mood or escape boredom, anxiety, depression, or other psychological problems.

- Psychoactive drugs affect the mind and body by altering brain chemistry. The effect of a drug depends on the properties of the drug and how it's used (drug factors), the physical and psychological characteristics of the user (user factors), and the physical and social environment surrounding the drug use (social factors).

- Opioids relieve pain, cause drowsiness, and induce euphoria; they reduce anxiety and produce lethargy, apathy, and an inability to concentrate.

- CNS depressants slow down the overall activity of the nerves; they reduce anxiety and cause mood changes, impaired muscular coordination, slurring of speech, and drowsiness or sleep.

- CNS stimulants speed up the activity of the nerves, causing acceleration of the heart rate, a rise in blood pressure, dilation of the pupils and bronchial tubes, and an increase in gastric and adrenal secretions.

- Marijuana usually causes euphoria and a relaxed attitude at low doses; very high doses produce feelings of depersonalization and sensory distortion. The long-term effects may include chronic bronchitis and cancer; use during pregnancy may impair fetal growth.

- Hallucinogens alter perception, feelings, and thought and may cause an altered sense of time, visual disturbances, and mood changes.

- Inhalants are present in a variety of harmless products; they can cause delirium. Their use can lead to loss of consciousness, heart failure, suffocation, and death.

- Economic and social costs of drug abuse include the financial costs of law enforcement, treatment, and health care and the social costs of crime, violence, and family problems. Drug testing and drug legalization have been proposed to address some of the problems related to drug abuse.

- Approaches to treatment include medication, treatment centers, self-help groups, and peer counseling; many programs also offer counseling to family members.

FOR MORE INFORMATION

BOOKS

Aue, P. W. 2006. *Teen Drug Abuse: Opposing Viewpoints.* San Diego: Greenhaven Press. *Explores key issues relating to drug use and abuse by teenagers.*

Hanson, G. R., et al. 2008. *Drugs and Society,* 10th ed. Boston: Jones & Bartlett. *Discusses the impact of drug abuse on individuals' lives and on the broader society.*

Karch, S. B. 2006. *Drug Abuse Handbook,* 2nd ed. London: CRC Press. *Explores drug abuse from a variety of perspectives, including clinical and criminological.*

Ksir, C., C. L. Hart, and O. S. Ray. 2008. *Drugs, Society, and Human Behavior,* 12th ed. New York: McGraw-Hill. *Examines drugs and be-* havior from the behavioral, pharmacological, historical, social, legal, and clinical perspectives.

Lessa, N. R., et al. 2006. *Wiley Concise Guides to Mental Health: Substance Use Disorders.* New York: Wiley. *A clearly written introduction to the diagnosis and treatment of various kinds of substance abuse.*

Murphy, P. J. M., and M. Shlafer. 2006. *Over-the-Counter Drugs of Abuse.* New York: Chelsea House Publications. *An up-to-date discussion of nonprescription medicines and their abuse.*

Rosen Publishing. 2006. *Drug Abuse and Society Series.* New York: Rosen Publishing. *A series of short books, each exploring a different type of drugs—from prescription medicine to club drugs—and their use and abuse.*

ORGANIZATIONS, HOTLINES, AND WEB SITES

Center for On-Line Addiction. Contains information about Internet and cybersex addiction.
   http://netaddiction.com
ClubDrugs.Org. Provides information on drugs commonly classified as "club drugs."
   http://www.clubdrugs.org
Do It Now Foundation. Provides youth-oriented information about drugs.
   http://www.doitnow.org
Drug Enforcement Administration: Drugs of Abuse. Provides basic facts about major drugs of abuse, including penalties for drug trafficking.
   http://www.dea.gov/concern/concern.htm
Gamblers Anonymous. Includes questions to help diagnose gambling problems and resources for getting help.
   http://www.gamblersanonymous.org
Higher Education Center for Alcohol and Other Drug Abuse and Violence Prevention. Gives information about alcohol and drug abuse on campus and links to related sites.
   http://www.edc.org/hec
Indiana Prevention Resource Center. A clearinghouse of information and links on substance-abuse topics, including specific psychoactive drugs and issues such as drug testing and drug legalization.
   http://www.drugs.indiana.edu
Narcotics Anonymous (NA). Similar to Alcoholics Anonymous, NA sponsors 12-step meetings and provides other support services for drug abusers.
   http://www.na.org
There are also 12-step programs that focus on specific drugs:
   Cocaine Anonymous
      http://www.ca.org
   Marijuana Anonymous
      http://www.marijuana-anonymous.org
National Center on Addiction and Substance Abuse (CASA) at Columbia University. Provides information about the costs of substance abuse to individuals and society.
   http://www.casacolumbia.org
National Clearinghouse for Alcohol and Drug Information. Provides statistics, information, and publications on substance abuse, including resources for people who want to help friends and family members overcome substance-abuse problems.
   http://ncadi.samhsa.gov

National Council on Problem Gambling. Provides information and help for people with gambling problems and their families, including a searchable directory of counselors.

http://www.ncpgambling.org

National Drug Information, Treatment, and Referral Hotlines. Sponsored by the SAMHSA Center for Substance Abuse Treatment, these hotlines provide information on drug abuse and on HIV infection as it relates to substance abuse; referrals to support groups and treatment programs are available.

800-662-HELP

800-729-6686 (Spanish)

800-487-4889 (TDD for hearing impaired)

National Institute on Drug Abuse. Develops and supports research on drug-abuse prevention programs; fact sheets on drugs of abuse are available on the Web site or via recorded phone messages, fax, or mail.

http://www.drugabuse.gov

Substance Abuse and Mental Health Services Administration (SAMHSA). Provides statistics, information, and other resources related to substance-abuse prevention and treatment.

http://www.samhsa.gov

See also the listings for Chapters 10 and 11.

SELECTED BIBLIOGRAPHY

American Psychiatric Association. 2000. *Diagnostic and Statistical Manual of Mental Disorders,* Fourth Edition, Text Revision. *(DSM-IV-TR).* Washington, D.C.: American Psychiatric Association.

Beers, M. H., et. al. 2006. *The Merck Manual of Diagnosis and Therapy,* 18th ed. New York: Wiley.

Braine, N. 2004. Long-term effects of syringe exchange on risk behavior and HIV prevention. *AIDS Education and Prevention* 16(3): 264–275.

Budney, A. J., et al. 2004. Review of the validity and significance of cannabis withdrawal syndrome. *American Journal of Psychiatry* 161(11): 1967–1977.

Centers for Disease Control and Prevention. 2006. Methamphetamine Use and HIV Risk Behaviors Among Heterosexual Men. *Morbidity and Mortality Weekly Report* (55)10: 273–277.

Colfax, G., et al. 2005. Longitudinal patterns of methamphetamine, popper (amyl nitrite), and cocaine use and high-risk sexual behavior among a cohort of San Francisco men who have sex with men. *Journal of Urban Health,* 28 February [epub].

Compton, W. M., et al. 2004. Prevalence of marijuana use disorder in the United States. *Journal of the American Medical Association* 291(17): 2114–2121.

Delaney-Black, V., et al. 2004. Prenatal cocaine: Quantity of exposure and gender moderation. *Journal of Developmental and Behavioral Pediatrics* 25(4): 254–263.

Grant, J. E., et al. 2006. Multicenter investigation of the opioid antagonist nalmefene in the treatment of pathological gambling. *American Journal of Psychiatry* 163(2): 303–312.

Hurd, Y. L., et al. 2005. Marijuana impairs growth in mid-gestation fetuses. *Neurotoxicology and Teratology* 27(2): 221–229.

Iannone, M., et al. 2006. Electrocortical effects of MDMA are potentiated by acoustic stimulation in rats. *BMC Neuroscience* 7: 13.

Jefferson, D. J. 2005. America's most dangerous drug. *Newsweek,* 8 August, 41–48.

Johnston, L. D., et al. 2008. *Monitoring the Future: National Results on Adolescent Drug Use: Overview of Key Findings, 2007.* Bethesda, Md.: National Institute on Drug Abuse.

Juliano, L. M., and R. R. Griffiths. 2004. A critical review of caffeine withdrawal: Empirical validation of symptoms and signs, incidence, severity, and associated features. *Psychopharmacology* 176(1): 1–29.

Kim, S. W., et al. 2006. Pathological gambling and mood disorders: Clinical associations and treatment implications. *Journal of Affective Disorders* 92(1): 109–116.

Lane, J. D., et al. 2004. Caffeine impairs glucose metabolism in type 2 diabetes. *Diabetes Care* 27(8): 2047–2048.

Lynch, W. J., P. K. Maciejewski, and M. N. Potenza. 2004. Psychiatric correlates of gambling in adolescents and young adults grouped by age at gambling onset. *Archives of General Psychiatry* 61(11): 1116–1122.

Mahowald, M. L., J. A. Singh, and P. Majeski. 2005. Opioid use by patients in an orthopedics spine clinic. *Arthritis and Rheumatology* 52(1): 312–321.

McBride, B. F., et al. 2004. Electrocardiographic and hemodynamic effects of a multicomponent dietary supplement containing ephedra and caffeine. *Journal of the American Medical Association* 291(4): 216–221.

McCusker, R. R., et al. 2006. Caffeine content of energy drinks, carbonated sodas, and other beverages. *Journal of Analytical Toxicology* 30(2): 112–114.

Messinis, L., et al. 2006. Neuropsychological deficits in long-term frequent cannabis users. *Neurology* 66(5): 737–739.

National Institute on Drug Abuse. 2008. *NIDA InfoFacts: Treatment Approaches for Drug Addiction* (http://www.drugabuse.gov/infofacts/treatmeth.html; retrieved February 3, 2009).

Office of Applied Studies, Substance Abuse and Mental Health Services Administration. 2008. *Results from the 2007 National Survey on Drug Use and Health: National Findings* (http://oas.samhsa.gov/nhsda.htm; retrieved February 3, 2009).

Opioid abuse. 2004. *Journal of the American Medical Association* 291(11): 1394.

Parrott, A. C. 2005. Chronic tolerance to recreational MDMA (3,4-methylenedioxymethamphetamine) or ecstasy. *Journal of Psychopharmacology* 19(1): 71–83.

Ramaekers, J. G., et al. 2004. Dose-related risk of motor vehicle crashes after cannabis use. *Drug and Alcohol Dependence* 73(2): 109–119.

Ren, S., et al. 2006. Effect of long-term cocaine use on regional left ventricular function as determined by magnetic resonance imaging. *American Journal of Cardiology* 97(7): 1085–1088.

Savoca, M. R., et al. 2005. Association of ambulatory blood pressure and dietary caffeine in adolescents. *American Journal of Hypertension* 18(1): 116–120.

Singer, L. T., et al. 2004. Cognitive outcomes of preschool children with prenatal cocaine exposure. *Journal of the American Medical Association* 291(20): 2448–2456.

Substance Abuse and Mental Health Services Administration. 2005 Nonmedical oxycodone users: A comparison with heroin users. *The NSDUH Report,* January.

Substance Abuse and Mental Health Services Administration, Office of Applied Studies. 2007. *Drug Abuse Warning Network, 2005: National Esti-*

mates of Drug-Related Emergency Department Visits. Rockville, Md.: Substance Abuse and Mental Health Services Administration, DAWN Series D-29, DHHS Publication No. (SMA) 07-4256.

Wareing, M., et al. 2005. Visuo-spatial working memory deficits in current and former users of MDMA ("ecstasy"). *Human Psychopharmacology* 20(2): 115–23.

Waska, R. 2006. Addictions and the quest to control the object. *American Journal of Psychoanalysis* 66(1): 43–62.

Zakzanis, K. K., and Z. Campbell. 2006. Memory impairment in now abstinent MDMA users and continued users: A longitudinal follow-up. *Neurology* 66(5): 740–741.

THE RESPONSIBLE USE OF ALCOHOL

10

LOOKING AHEAD>>>>>

AFTER READING THIS CHAPTER, YOU SHOULD BE ABLE TO:

- Explain how alcohol is absorbed and metabolized by the body
- Describe the immediate and long-term effects of drinking alcohol
- Define moderate alcohol consumption and discuss its possible benefits
- Describe the different forms of alcohol abuse and their consequences
- Evaluate the role of alcohol in your life, and list strategies for using it responsibly

TEST YOUR KNOWLEDGE

1. **"Moderate drinking" is having three or fewer drinks per day.**
   True or false?

2. **Approximately how many adults in the United States do not drink any alcohol?**
   a. 1 in 10
   b. 1 in 5
   c. 1 in 3

3. **If a man and a woman of the same weight drink the same amount of alcohol, the woman will become intoxicated more quickly than the man.**
   True or false?

4. **Drinking too much alcohol in too short a time can cause death from alcohol poisoning.**
   True or false?

5. **Drinking coffee will help you sober up.**
   True or false?

ANSWERS

1. **FALSE.** Moderate drinking is no more than one drink per day for women and no more than two drinks per day for men.

2. **C.** Most adults drink lightly and occasionally; a small number of heavy drinkers, about 7% of adults, consume more than half of all the alcohol in the United States. Overall, college students drink less alcohol but are more likely to binge-drink than young adults who are not in college. Nonstudents are more likely to be or become dependent on alcohol.

3. **TRUE.** Women are usually smaller than men, have a higher percentage of body fat, and have a less active form of a stomach enzyme that breaks down alcohol. These factors cause them to become intoxicated more quickly and to a greater degree.

4. **TRUE.** Consuming a number of drinks over a period of several hours is likely to cause intoxication, followed by a hangover; chugging the same amount in an hour or less can be lethal.

5. **FALSE.** Once alcohol has been absorbed by the body, nothing speeds its metabolism.

Throughout history, alcohol has been more popular than any other psychoactive drug in the Western world, despite numerous prohibitions against it. Alcohol has a somewhat contradictory role in human life. Used in moderation, alcohol can enhance social occasions by loosening inhibitions and creating a pleasant feeling of relaxation. But alcohol use can also be unhealthy. Like other drugs, alcohol has physiological effects on the body that can impair functioning in the short term and cause devastating damage in the long term. For some people, alcohol becomes an addiction, leading to a lifetime of recovery or, for a few, to debilitation and death. Many of our slang expressions for intoxication reflect its less positive aspects; we describe someone who is drunk as being "smashed," "bombed," or "wasted."

The use of alcohol is a complex issue, one that demands conscious thought and informed decisions. In our society, some people choose to drink in moderation while some choose not to drink at all. Still others realize too late that they've made an unwise choice—when they become dependent on alcohol, are involved in an alcohol-related car crash, or simply wake up to discover they've done something they regret.

This chapter discusses the complexities of alcohol use and provides information that will help you make choices that are right for you.

THE NATURE OF ALCOHOL

If you have ever been around people who are drinking, you probably noticed that alcohol seems to affect different people in different ways. One person may seem to get drunk after just a drink or two, while another appears to tolerate a great deal of alcohol without becoming intoxicated. These differences make alcohol's effects on the body seem mysterious and help explain why there are many misconceptions about alcohol use. The following sections describe how alcohol works in the body.

Alcoholic Beverages

Technically speaking, there are many kinds of **alcohol**, and each is an organic compound. In this book, however, the term *alcohol* refers only to ethyl alcohol (or ethanol, often abbreviated as ETOH). Several kinds of alcohol are similar to ethyl alcohol, such as methanol (wood alcohol) and isopropyl alcohol (rubbing alcohol), but they are highly toxic; if consumed, these forms of alcohol can cause serious illness, blindness, and even death.

Common Alcoholic Beverages   There are several basic types of alcoholic beverages; ethanol is the psychoactive ingredient in each of them:

- Beer is a mild intoxicant brewed from a mixture of grains. By volume, beer usually contains 3–6% alcohol.
- Ales and malt liquors, which are similar to beer, typically contain 6–8% alcohol by volume.
- Wines are made by fermenting the juices of grapes or other fruits. During *fermentation,* sugars from the fruit react with yeast to create ethanol and other by-products. In table wines, the concentration of alcohol is about 9–14%. A more potent type of wine, called *fortified wine,* is so called because extra alcohol is added during its production. Fortified wines—such as sherry, port, and Madeira—contain about 20% alcohol.
- Hard liquor—such as gin, whiskey, rum, tequila, vodka, and liqueur—is made by *distilling* brewed or fermented grains or other plant products. Hard liquors usually contain 35–50% alcohol but can be much stronger.

The concentration of alcohol in a beverage is indicated by its **proof value,** which is two times the percentage concentration. For example, if a beverage is 100 proof, it contains 50% alcohol. Two ounces of 100-proof whiskey contain 1 ounce of pure alcohol. The proof value of hard liquor can usually be found on the bottle's label.

"Standard Drinks" Versus Actual Servings   When discussing alcohol consumption, the term **one drink** (or *a standard drink*) means the amount of a beverage that typically contains about 0.6 ounce of alcohol. Figure 10.1 shows the amounts of popular beverages that are considered to be one standard drink, based on their alcohol content.

People don't always limit themselves to one drink. In fact, a typical serving of most alcoholic beverages is larger (sometimes significantly larger) than a single standard drink. This is particularly true of mixed drinks, which often include more than one type of hard liquor. Alcoholic beverages are usually purchased in packages that contain multiple servings, as shown in Table 10.1.

Caloric Content   Alcohol provides 7 calories per gram, and the alcohol in one drink (14–17 grams) supplies about 100–120 calories. Most alcoholic beverages also

alcohol   The intoxicating ingredient in fermented or distilled beverages; a colorless, pungent liquid.

proof value   Two times the percentage of alcohol by volume; a beverage that is 50% alcohol by volume is 100 proof.

one drink   The amount of a beverage that typically contains about 0.6 ounce of alcohol; also called *a standard drink.*

metabolism   The chemical transformation of food and other substances in the body into energy and wastes.

TERMS

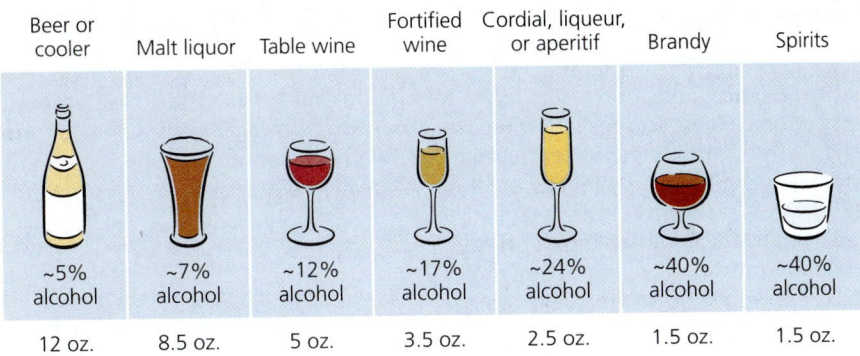

FIGURE 10.1 **One drink of various alcoholic beverages.**

SOURCE: Department of Health and Human Services. 2007. *The Surgeon General's Call to Action to Prevent and Reduce Underage Drinking.* Washington, D.C.: Department of Health and Human Services, Office of the Surgeon General.

Beer or cooler — ~5% alcohol — 12 oz.
Malt liquor — ~7% alcohol — 8.5 oz.
Table wine — ~12% alcohol — 5 oz.
Fortified wine — ~17% alcohol — 3.5 oz.
Cordial, liqueur, or aperitif — ~24% alcohol — 2.5 oz.
Brandy — ~40% alcohol — 1.5 oz.
Spirits — ~40% alcohol — 1.5 oz.

contain some carbohydrate, so, for example, one beer provides about 150 total calories. The "light" in light beer refers to calories; a light beer typically has close to the same alcohol content as a regular beer and about 100 calories. A 5-ounce glass of red wine has 100 calories; white wine has 96. A 3-ounce margarita supplies 157 calories, a 6-ounce cosmopolitan has 143 calories, and a 6-ounce rum and Coke contains about 180 calories.

Absorption

When a person ingests alcohol, about 20% is rapidly absorbed from the stomach into the bloodstream. About 75% is absorbed through the upper part of the small intestine. Any remaining alcohol enters the bloodstream further along the gastrointestinal tract. Once in the bloodstream, alcohol produces feelings of intoxication. The rate of absorption is affected by a variety of factors. For example, the carbonation in a beverage like champagne increases the rate of alcohol absorption. Artificial sweeteners (commonly used in drink mixers) have been shown to have the same effect. Food in the stomach slows the rate of absorption, as does the drinking of highly concentrated alcoholic beverages such as hard liquor. But remember: *All* alcohol a person consumes is eventually absorbed.

Metabolism and Excretion

Alcohol is quickly transported throughout the body by the blood. Because alcohol easily moves through most biological membranes, it is rapidly distributed throughout most body tissues. The main site of alcohol **metabolism** is the liver, though a small amount of alcohol is metabolized in the stomach. Alcohol can be metabolized by several processes. Most is converted first to acetaldehyde, then to acetate, which is ultimately burned for energy or converted to fat. The enzymes needed for this process vary slightly among individuals, creating differences in how people react to alcohol. (See the box "Metabolizing Alcohol: Our Bodies Work Differently" on p. 274.)

About 2–10% of ingested alcohol is not metabolized in the liver or other tissues but is excreted unchanged by the lungs, kidneys, and sweat glands. Excreted alcohol causes the telltale smell on a drinker's breath and is the basis of breath and urine analyses for alcohol levels. Although such analyses do not give precise measurements of alcohol concentrations in the blood, they provide a reasonable approximation if done correctly.

Alcohol readily enters the human brain, crossing the restrictive layer of cells that ordinarily shields that organ. There, alcohol affects neurotransmitters, the chemicals that carry messages between brain cells. The ability of brain cells to receive these messages is changed, and networks

Table 10.1	Serving Sizes Versus Standard Drinks of Common Alcoholic Beverages	
Beverage	**Serving/Container Size**	**No. of Standard Drinks**
Beer	12 oz.	1
	16 oz.	1.3
	22 oz.	2
	40 oz.	3.3
Malt liquor	12 oz.	1.5
	16 oz.	2
	22 oz.	2.5
	40 oz.	4.5
Table wine	750 mL (25 oz.) bottle	5
Hard liquor (80 proof)	1 mixed drink	1 or more
	1 pint (16 oz.) bottle	11
	1 fifth (25 oz.) bottle	17
	1.75 L (59 oz.) bottle	39

SOURCE: Department of Health and Human Services. 2007. *The Surgeon General's Call to Action to Prevent and Reduce Underage Drinking.* Washington, D.C.: Department of Health and Human Services, Office of the Surgeon General.

Do you notice that you react differently to alcohol than some of your friends? If so, you may be witnessing genetic differences in alcohol metabolism that are associated with ethnicity. Alcohol is metabolized mainly in the liver, where it is converted by an enzyme (alcohol dehydrogenase) to a toxic substance called acetaldehyde. Acetaldehyde is responsible for many of alcohol's noxious effects. Ideally, it is quickly broken down by another enzyme (acetaldehyde dehydrogenase).

But some people, primarily those of Asian descent, have inherited ineffective or inactive variations of the latter enzyme. Other people, including some of African descent and some Jewish population groups, have forms of alcohol dehydrogenase that metabolize alcohol to acetaldehyde unusually quickly. In either case, the result is a buildup of acetaldehyde when these people drink alcohol.

They experience a reaction called *flushing syndrome*. Their skin feels hot, their heart and respiration rates increase, and they may get a headache, vomit, or break out in hives. The severity of their reaction is affected by the inherited form of their alcohol-metabolizing enzymes. Drinking makes some people so uncomfortable that it's unlikely they could ever become addicted to alcohol.

The body's response to acetaldehyde is the basis for treating alcohol abuse with the drug disulfiram (Antabuse), which inhibits the action of acetaldehyde dehydrogenase. When a person taking disulfiram ingests alcohol, acetaldehyde levels increase rapidly, and he or she develops an intense flushing reaction along with weakness, nausea, vomiting, and other disagreeable symptoms.

How people behave in relation to alcohol is influenced in complex ways by many factors, including social and cultural ones. But in this case at least, individual choices and behavior are strongly influenced by a specific genetic characteristic.

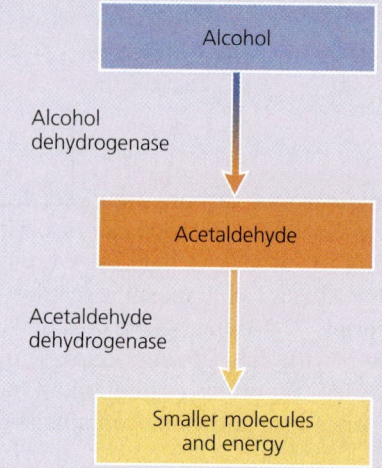

within the brain that connect different brain regions are disrupted. These changes are temporary, creating many of the immediate effects of drinking alcohol.

With chronic heavy usage, however, alcohol's effects become permanent, resulting in permanent disruption of brain function and changes in brain structure. Alcohol interferes with the production of new brain cells in unborn children, young children, adolescents, and young adults in whom the brain continues to develop until about age 21. Even in mature adults, new brain cells are produced to replace damaged ones, and alcohol is likely to affect that process as well.

Alcohol Intake and Blood Alcohol Concentration

Blood alcohol concentration (BAC), a measure of intoxication, is determined by the amount of alcohol consumed in a given amount of time and by individual factors:

- *Body weight:* In most cases, a smaller person develops a higher BAC than a larger person after drinking the same amount of alcohol (Figure 10.2). A smaller person has less overall body tissue into which alcohol can be distributed.

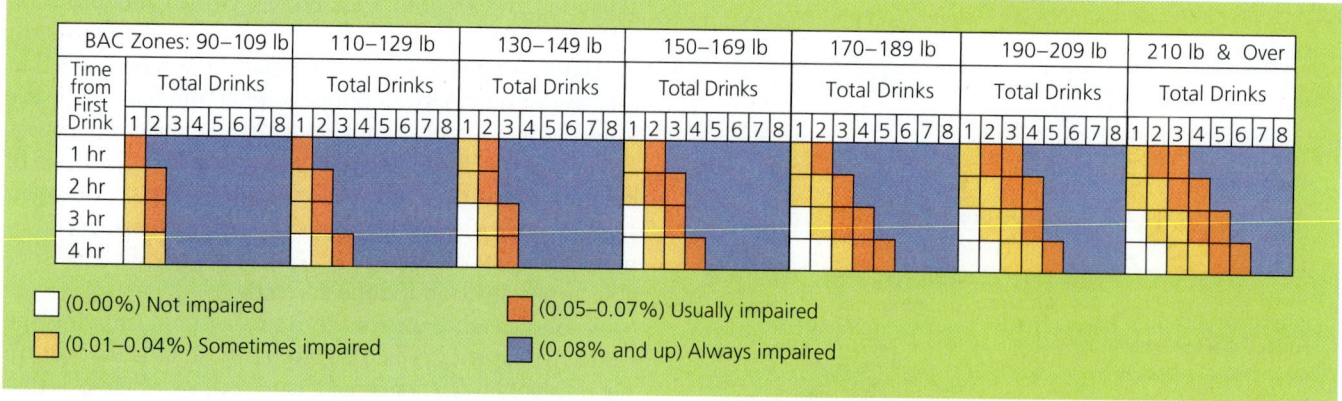

FIGURE 10.2 Approximate blood alcohol concentration and body weight. This chart illustrates the BAC an average person of a given weight would reach after drinking the specified number of drinks in the time shown. The legal limit for BAC is 0.08%; for drivers under 21 years of age, many states have zero-tolerance laws that set BAC limits of 0.01% or 0.02%.

Table 10.2 — The Effects of Alcohol

BAC (%)	Common Behavioral Effects	Hours Required to Metabolize Alcohol
0.00–0.05	Slight change in feelings, usually relaxation and euphoria. Decreased alertness.	2–3
0.05–0.10	Emotional instability, with exaggerated feelings and behavior. Reduced social inhibitions. Impairment of reaction time and fine motor coordination. Increasingly impaired during driving. Legally drunk at 0.08%.	3–6
0.10–0.15	Unsteadiness in standing and walking. Loss of peripheral vision. Driving is extremely dangerous.	6–10
0.15–0.30	Staggering gait. Slurred speech. Pain and other sensory perceptions greatly impaired.	10–24
More than 0.30	Stupor or unconsciousness. Anesthesia. Death possible at 0.35% and above. Can result from rapid or binge drinking with few earlier effects.	More than 24

- *Percent body fat:* A person with a higher percentage of body fat will usually develop a higher BAC than a more muscular person of the same weight. Alcohol does not concentrate as much in fatty tissue as in muscle and most other tissues, in part because fat has fewer blood vessels.

- *Sex:* Women metabolize less alcohol in the stomach than men do because the stomach enzyme that breaks down alcohol before it enters the bloodstream is four times more active in men than in women. This means that more unmetabolized alcohol is released into the bloodstream in women. Because women are also generally smaller than men and have a higher percentage of body fat, women will have a higher BAC than men after consuming the same amount of alcohol. Hormonal fluctuations may also affect the rate of alcohol metabolism, making a woman more susceptible to high BACs at certain times during her menstrual cycle (usually just prior to the onset of menstruation).

BAC also depends on the balance between the rate of alcohol absorption and the rate of alcohol metabolism. A man who weighs 150 pounds and has normal liver function metabolizes about 0.3 ounce of alcohol per hour, the equivalent of about half a 12-ounce bottle of beer or a 5-ounce glass of wine.

The rate of alcohol metabolism varies among individuals and is largely determined by genetic factors and drinking behavior. Chronic drinking activates enzymes that metabolize alcohol in the liver, so people who drink frequently metabolize alcohol at a more rapid rate than nondrinkers. Although the rate of alcohol absorption can be slowed by factors like food, the metabolic rate *cannot* be influenced by exercise, breathing deeply, eating, drinking coffee, or taking other drugs. The rate of alcohol metabolism is the same whether a person is asleep or awake.

If a person absorbs slightly less alcohol each hour than he or she can metabolize in an hour, the BAC remains low. People can drink large amounts of alcohol this way over a long period of time without becoming noticeably intoxicated; however, they do run the risk of significant long-term health hazards (described later in the chapter). If a person drinks alcohol more quickly than it can be metabolized, the BAC will steadily increase, and he or she will become more and more drunk (Table 10.2). Think of a quantity of alcohol drunk over a period of 2 or 3 hours—enough to cause intoxication and a hangover the next day. Now, imagine chugging that same quantity in an hour or less. Drinking that much alcohol so quickly could be lethal.

ALCOHOL AND HEALTH

The effects of alcohol consumption on health depend on the individual, the circumstances, and the amount of alcohol consumed.

The Immediate Effects of Alcohol

BAC is a primary factor determining the effects of alcohol (see Table 10.2). At low concentrations, alcohol tends to make people feel relaxed and jovial, but at higher

blood alcohol concentration (BAC) The amount of alcohol in the blood in terms of weight per unit volume; used as a measure of intoxication.

TERMS

concentrations people are more likely to feel angry, sedated, or sleepy. Alcohol is a CNS depressant, and its effects vary because body systems are affected to different degrees at different BACs. At any given BAC, the effects of alcohol are more pronounced when the BAC is rapidly increasing than when it is slowly increasing, steady, or decreasing. The effects of alcohol are more pronounced if a person drinks on an empty stomach, because alcohol is absorbed more quickly and the BAC rises more quickly.

Low Concentrations of Alcohol   The effects of alcohol can first be felt at a BAC of about 0.03–0.05%. These effects may include light-headedness, relaxation, and a release of inhibitions. Most drinkers experience mild euphoria and become more sociable. When people drink in social settings, alcohol often seems to act as a stimulant, enhancing conviviality or assertiveness. This apparent stimulation occurs because alcohol depresses inhibitory centers in the brain.

Higher Concentrations of Alcohol   At higher concentrations, the pleasant effects tend to be replaced by more negative ones: interference with motor coordination, verbal performance, and intellectual functions. The drinker often becomes irritable and may be easily angered or given to crying. When the BAC reaches 0.1%, most sensory and motor functioning is reduced, and many people become sleepy. Vision, smell, taste, and hearing become less acute. At 0.2%, most drinkers are completely unable to function, either physically or psychologically, because of the pronounced depression of the central nervous system, muscles, and other body systems. Coma usually occurs at a BAC of 0.35%, and any higher level can be fatal.

Small doses of alcohol may improve sexual functioning for individuals who are especially anxious or self-conscious, but higher doses often have negative effects, such as reduced erectile response. (Chronic effects of heavy drinking include reduction of testosterone levels and impairment of sperm production.)

Alcohol causes blood vessels near the skin to dilate, so drinkers often feel warm; their skin flushes, and they may sweat more. Flushing and sweating contribute to heat loss, however, so the internal body temperature falls. High doses of alcohol may impair the body's ability to regulate temperature, causing it to drop sharply, especially if the surrounding temperature is low. Drinking alcoholic beverages to keep warm in cold weather does not work and can even be dangerous.

Since alcohol is a sedative, it induces sleepiness. But for those using alcohol as a sleep aid, its utility is short-lived, because people quickly build up a tolerance to it. Moreover, large amounts of alcohol disturb normal sleep patterns. The sleep that follows drinking becomes poor quality after some hours, fitful and unrefreshing as the person dreams, awakens, and often stays wakeful. Alcohol can also cause or worsen sleep apnea, a breathing disorder in which the air passage at the back of the mouth narrows or closes during sleep. The condition, evidenced by loud snoring and gasping for breath, greatly reduces the restfulness of sleep. All of these sleep disturbances adversely affect next-day performance and alertness. Performance is further impaired if total sleep time is inadequate. Fatigue and sleepiness compromise memory, response time, and ability to perform difficult tasks. These effects become cumulative if, over time, alcohol use and insufficient sleep become routine.

Alcohol Hangover   Alcohol's effects wear off slowly, and anyone who has experienced a severe hangover knows they are no laughing matter. The symptoms include headache, shakiness, nausea, diarrhea, fatigue, and impaired mental functioning. Table 10.2 shows how much time is needed to metabolize alcohol. But even after sobering up, at high BACs the resulting hangover can continue to leave a person impaired.

A hangover is probably caused by a combination of the toxic products of alcohol breakdown, dehydration, and hormonal effects. During a hangover, heart rate and blood pressure increase, making some individuals more vulnerable to heart attacks. Electroencephalography (brain wave measurement) shows diffuse slowing of brain waves for up to 16 hours after BAC drops to zero. Studies of pilots, drivers, and skiers all indicate that coordination and cognition are impaired in a person with a hangover, increasing the risk of injury.

The best treatment for hangover is prevention. Nearly all men can expect a hangover if they drink more than five or six drinks; for women, the number is three or four drinks. Drinking less, drinking at a slower pace, and consuming food and plenty of nonalcoholic liquids decrease the risk of hangover. If you get a hangover, remember that your ability to drive is definitely impaired, even after your BAC has returned to zero.

Alcohol Poisoning   Acute alcohol poisoning occurs much more frequently than most people realize, and all too often it causes death. Drinking large amounts of alcohol over a short period of time can rapidly raise the BAC into the lethal range. Alcohol, either alone or in combination with other drugs, is responsible for more toxic overdose deaths than any other drug.

Death from alcohol poisoning may be caused either by central nervous system and respiratory depression or by inhaling fluid or vomit into the lungs. The amount of alcohol it takes to make a person unconscious is dangerously close to a fatal dose. Although passing out may prevent someone from drinking more, BAC can keep rising during unconsciousness, because the body continues absorbing ingested alcohol into the bloodstream. Special care should be taken to ensure the safety of anyone who has been drinking heavily, especially if the person becomes unconscious (see the box "Dealing with an Alcohol Emergency").

Dealing with an Alcohol Emergency

Remember: Being very drunk is potentially life-threatening. Helping a drunken friend could save a life.

• Be firm but calm. Don't engage the person in an argument or discuss her drinking behavior while she is intoxicated.

• Get the person out of harm's way—don't let her drive or wander outside. Don't let her drink any more alcohol.

• If the person is unconscious, don't assume she is just "sleeping it off." Place her on her side with her knees up. This position will help prevent choking if the person should vomit.

• Stay with the person—you need to be ready to help if she vomits or stops breathing.

• Don't try to give the person anything to eat or drink, including coffee or other drugs. Don't give cold showers or try to make her walk around. None of these things help anyone to sober up, and they can be dangerous.

Call 911 immediately in any of the following instances:

• You can't wake the person even with shouting or shaking.

• The person is taking fewer than 8 breaths per minute or her breathing seems shallow or irregular.

• You think the person took other drugs in addition to alcohol.

• The person has had an injury, especially a blow to the head.

• The person drank a large amount of alcohol within a short period of time and then became unconscious. Death caused by alcohol poisoning most often occurs when the blood alcohol level rises very quickly due to rapid ingestion of alcohol.

If you aren't sure what to do, call 911. You may save a life.

Using Alcohol with Other Drugs Alcohol-drug combinations are a leading cause of drug-related deaths. Using alcohol while taking a medication that can cause CNS depression increases the effects of both drugs, potentially leading to coma, respiratory depression, and death. Such drugs include barbiturates, Valium-like drugs, narcotics such as codeine, and OTC antihistamines such as Benadryl. For people who consume three or more drinks per day, use of OTC pain relievers like aspirin, ibuprofen, or acetaminophen increases the risk of stomach bleeding or liver damage. Some antibiotics and diabetes medications can also interact dangerously with alcohol.

Many illegal drugs are especially dangerous when combined with alcohol. Life-threatening overdoses occur at much lower doses when heroin and other narcotics are combined with alcohol. When cocaine and alcohol are used together, a toxic substance called cocaethylene is formed; this substance is responsible for more than half of all cocaine-related deaths.

The safest strategy is to avoid combining alcohol with any other drug—prescription, over-the-counter, or illegal. If in doubt, ask your pharmacist or physician before using any drug in combination with alcohol, or just don't do it.

Alcohol-Related Injuries and Violence The combination of impaired judgment, weakened sensory perception, reduced inhibitions, impaired motor coordination, and increased aggressiveness and hostility that characterizes alcohol intoxication can be dangerous. Through homicide, suicide, automobile crashes, and other traumatic incidents, alcohol use is linked to more than 75,000 American deaths each year. The majority of people who attempt suicide have been drinking. Among successful suicides, alcohol use is common, as well; a recent analysis of 5550 suicide deaths found that one-third involved alcohol. Alcohol use more than triples the chances of fatal injuries during leisure activities such as swimming and boating, and more than half of all fatal falls and serious burns happen to people who have been drinking.

Alcohol and Aggression Alcohol use contributes to over 50% of all murders, assaults, and rapes. Not surprisingly, alcohol is frequently found in the bloodstream of victims as well as perpetrators. In 2007, more than 2,600,000 arrests were made for alcohol-related offenses. However, only some people become violent under alcohol's influence. These people are often predisposed to aggressive behavior, are highly impulsive, and may have an underlying psychiatric condition called *antisocial personality disorder*. Their bad behavior—repeated criminal acts, deceitfulness, impulsiveness, repeated fights or assaults, and disregard for the safety of others—worsens under alcohol's influence. They are also more likely to become alcohol dependent. Alcohol is an important component of gang life, affirming masculinity and male togetherness, and contributing to gang violence.

Alcohol abuse can wreak havoc on home life. Marital discord and domestic violence often exist in the presence of excess alcohol. Heavy drinking by parents is associated with abuse of their children, typically emotional or

Growing Up with Alcoholism

For a child growing up in a household where alcoholism exists, family life can take a painful toll. Whether the alcoholic is a parent, a sibling, or another relative living with the family, the dysfunctional environment's effects start in childhood and can last throughout adulthood. Children from households where there is alcoholism—particularly the children of alcoholics (COAs)—deal with constant stress, anxiety, and embarrassment. Many, feeling that the alcohol abuse was somehow their fault, carry a burden of guilt from early childhood on. Nevertheless, most COAs somehow escape the major damage to which dysfunctional family life contributes: mental illness, alcohol dependence, and alcohol abuse.

In such households there is often neglect, with household activities revolving around the needs of the alcoholic. The child may witness or be the victim of verbal or physical abuse. The child may simply learn that drinking is an accepted approach to problem solving.

The presence of an alcoholic parent or close relative affects the health and well-being of all members of the household. Other family members are frequently the target of the alcoholic's verbal or physical abuse and all too often have their own problems with alcohol. Nondrinking female spouses of heavy drinkers experience high levels of psychological distress. A recent California study found that both adults and children in the households of alcohol abusers had more medical problems than people from non-abusive households and, not surprisingly, also incurred greater health care costs.

But children are most vulnerable, and an environment of alcoholism results in poor health early on. A very young child is almost completely dependent on the attention and reasonable actions of his caregivers, who may be unable to respond appropriately when the child gets sick. As the child gets older, the caregivers' inability to provide adequate supervision leaves the child vulnerable in other ways.

Yet, the outlook for COAs is not as grim as one might expect, given the hurdles these individuals must overcome. Even though their risk of illness, alcohol dependence, and alcohol abuse is greater than for those without a history of family alcoholism, an impressive majority of COAs are not alcohol abusers or alcoholics. In 2001–2002, the National Institute on Alcohol Abuse and Addiction (NIAAA) undertook a comprehensive, in-depth survey on alcohol use, interviewing more than 43,000 Americans age 18 and older. The following table shows some of the survey's results.

Although adults with a family background of alcoholism were more likely to drink currently, and to drink more heavily, a sizeable proportion had chosen to never drink, and even more had used alcohol in the past but had abstained for at least a year.

The likelihood of problematic alcohol use is also greater among adults with a family background of alcoholism. In the NIAAA survey, approximately 6% of these adults abused alcohol, and 7.4% were alcohol dependent. By comparison, 3.4% of respondents without such a family history abused alcohol, and 2.3% were alcohol dependent. Thus, about three times as many people with a family history of alcoholism became alcoholics.

Alcohol Status	No Family Alcoholism	Family History of Alcoholism
Current Drinker (1 or more drinks in past 12 months)	61%	71%
Current Heavier Drinker (Men: more than 2 drinks/day; Women: more than 1 drink/day)	8%	14%
Former Drinker (no drinks in past 12 months)	16%	20%
Lifetime Abstainer	23%	9%

psychological abuse. Links between parental drinking and physical or sexual abuse are not found consistently, but when such mistreatment does take place, the damaging effect is often long-lasting and associated with alcohol misuse in the grown child. (See the box "Growing Up with Alcoholism" above.)

Alcohol and Sexual Decision Making Alcohol seriously affects a person's ability to make wise decisions about sex. A recent survey of college students revealed that frequent binge drinkers were five times more likely to engage in unplanned sexual activity and five-and-a-half times more likely to have unprotected sex than non–binge drinkers. Heavy drinkers are also more likely to have multiple sex partners and to engage in other forms of high-risk sexual behavior. For all these reasons, rates of sexually transmitted infections (including HIV) and unwanted pregnancy are higher among people who drink heavily than among people who drink moderately or not at all.

Women who binge-drink are at increased risk for rape and other forms of nonconsensual sex. The laws regarding sexual consent are clear: A person who is very drunk or passed out cannot consent to sex. Having sex with a person who is drunk or unconscious is sexual assault.

Drinking and Driving

Drunk driving remains a serious problem in the United States. In 2007, about 32% of more than 41,000 crash fatalities involved drivers with a BAC of 0.08% or higher. These statistics have changed little in the past decade. Each year, more than 275,000 people are injured in alcohol-related (BAC of 0.01% or higher) car crashes—an average of

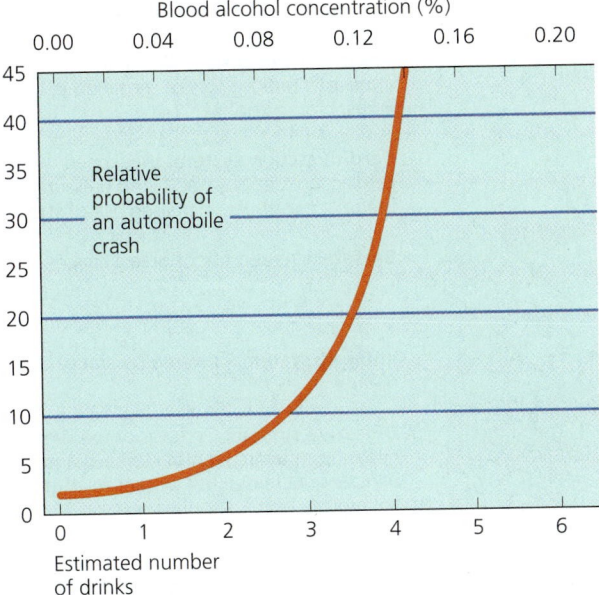

Blood alcohol concentration (%)

Relative probability of an automobile crash

Estimated number of drinks

FIGURE 10.3 The dose-response relationship between BAC and automobile crashes.

one person injured every 2 minutes. In the 2007 National Survey on Drug Use and Health, 13.7% of Americans age 18 and older admitted to using alcohol before driving. Meantime, 94% of Americans say they consider drunk driving a major safety issue.

People who drink and drive are unable to drive safely because their judgment is impaired, their reaction time is slower, and their coordination is reduced. Some driving skills are affected at BACs of 0.02% and lower; at 0.05%, visual perception, reaction time, and certain steering tasks are all impaired. Any amount of alcohol impairs your ability to drive safely, and fatigue augments alcohol's effects.

The *dose-response function* (see Chapter 9) is the relationship between the amount of alcohol or drug consumed and the type and intensity of the resulting effect. Higher doses of alcohol are associated with a much greater probability of automobile crashes (Figure 10.3). A person driving with a BAC of 0.14% is more than 40 times more likely to be involved in a crash than someone with no alcohol in his or her blood. For those with a BAC above 0.14%, the risk of a fatal crash is estimated to be 380 times higher. The risks for young drivers are even greater than indicated in Figure 10.3, even at very low BACs. Younger drivers have less experience with both driving and alcohol, which results in significant impairment with BACs as low as 0.02%.

In addition to an increased risk of injury and death, driving while intoxicated can have serious legal consequences. Drunk driving is against the law. Since 2003, the legal limit for BAC has been 0.08% in all states and the District of Columbia. There are stiff penalties for drunk driving, including fines, loss of license, confiscation of

vehicle, and jail time. Under current zero-tolerance laws in many states, drivers under age 21 who have consumed *any* alcohol may have their license suspended. Increasingly, states are passing laws against having open containers of alcohol in a vehicle and are allowing stricter punishment for repeat offenders.

If you are out of your home and drinking, find alternative transportation or have a *designated driver* who doesn't drink and can provide safe transportation home. The responsibility can be rotated for different occasions. Remember, you risk more than your own life when you drink and drive. Causing serious injury or death results in lifelong feelings of sadness and guilt for the driver and grief for friends and families of victims.

It's more difficult to protect yourself against someone else who drinks and drives. Learn to be alert to the erratic driving that signals an impaired driver. Warning signs include wide, abrupt, and illegal turns; straddling the center line or lane marker; driving against traffic; driving on the shoulder; weaving, swerving, or nearly striking an object or another vehicle; following too closely; erratic speed; driving with headlights off at night; and driving with the window down in very cold weather. If you see any of these signs, try the following strategies:

- If the driver is ahead of you, maintain a safe following distance. Don't try to pass.
- If the driver is behind you, turn right at the nearest intersection, and let the driver pass.
- If the driver is approaching your car, move to the shoulder and stop. Avoid a head-on collision by sounding your horn or flashing your lights.
- When approaching an intersection, slow down and stay alert for vehicles that don't appear to be slowing.
- Make sure your safety belt is fastened and children are in approved safety seats.
- Report suspected impaired drivers to the nearest police station by phone.

The Effects of Chronic Abuse

Because alcohol is distributed throughout most of the body, it can affect many different organs and tissues (Figure 10.4 on p. 280). Problems associated with chronic or habitual excessive use of alcohol include diseases of the digestive and cardiovascular systems and some cancers. Drinking during pregnancy risks the health of both the woman and the developing fetus.

The Digestive System Even in the short term, alcohol can alter the functioning of the liver. Within just a few days of heavy alcohol consumption, fat begins to accumulate in liver cells, resulting in the development of "fatty liver." If drinking continues, inflammation of the liver can

IMMEDIATE EFFECTS

Central nervous system: Impaired reaction time and motor coordination; impaired judgment and sedation; coma and death at high BACs

Senses: Less acute vision, smell, taste, and hearing

Stomach: Nausea, inflammation, and bleeding

Skin: Flushing; sweating; heat loss and hypothermia; formation of broken capillaries

Sexual functioning: In men, reduced erection response

EFFECTS OF CHRONIC USE

Brain: Damaged/destroyed brain cells; impaired memory; loss of sensation in limbs; brain atrophy

Cardiovascular system: Weakened cardiac muscle; elevated blood pressure; irregular heartbeat; increased risk of stroke

Breast: Increased risk of breast cancer

Immune system: Lowered resistance to disease

Digestive system: Cirrhosis of the liver; hepatitis; inflammation of stomach and pancreas; increased risk of cancers of the lip, mouth, larynx, esophagus, liver, rectum, stomach, and pancreas

Kidney: Kidney failure associated with end-stage liver disease

Nutrition: Nutrient deficiencies; obesity

Reproductive system: In women, menstrual irregularities and increased risk of having children with fetal alcohol syndrome (FAS); in men, impotence and impaired sperm production

Bone: Increased risk of osteoporosis; increased risk of fractures from frequent falls

FIGURE 10.4   The immediate and long-term effects of alcohol abuse.

occur, resulting in alcoholic hepatitis, a frequent cause of hospitalization and death in alcoholics. Both fatty liver and alcoholic hepatitis are potentially reversible if the person stops drinking. With continued alcohol use, however, liver cells are progressively damaged and then permanently destroyed. The destroyed cells are replaced by fibrous scar tissue, a condition known as **cirrhosis.** As cirrhosis develops, a drinker may gradually lose his or her capacity to tolerate alcohol, because there are fewer and fewer healthy cells remaining in the liver to metabolize it.

As with most health hazards, the risk of cirrhosis depends on an individual's susceptibility, largely genetically determined, and the amount of alcohol consumed over time. Some people show signs of cirrhosis after a few years of consuming three or four drinks per day. Women gen-

erally develop cirrhosis at lower levels of alcohol consumption than men. Heavy drinkers who also inject drugs place themselves at risk of acquiring infection with hepatitis C virus (HCV); the combination of alcohol abuse and HCV infection greatly increases the risk for cirrhosis and liver cancer.

Signs of cirrhosis can include jaundice (a yellowing of the skin and white part of the eyes) and the accumulation of fluid in the abdomen and lower extremities. Some people with cirrhosis have no obvious outward signs of the disease. Treatment for cirrhosis includes correcting nutrient deficiencies and complete abstinence from alcohol. People with cirrhosis who continue to drink have only a 50% chance of surviving 5 or more years.

Alcohol can inflame the pancreas, causing nausea, vomiting, abnormal digestion, and severe pain. Acute alcoholic pancreatitis generally occurs in binge drinkers. Unlike cirrhosis, which usually occurs after years of fairly heavy alcohol use, pancreatitis can occur after just one or two severe binge-drinking episodes. Acute pancreatitis is often fatal; in survivors it can develop into a chronic condition.

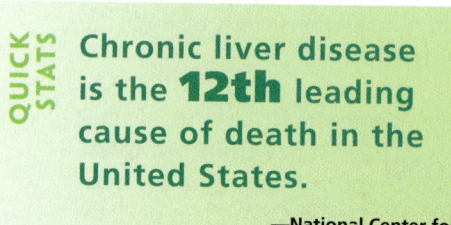

QUICK STATS

Chronic liver disease is the 12th leading cause of death in the United States.

—National Center for Health Statistics, 2008

Overuse of alcohol is a common cause of bleeding in the gastrointestinal tract. Cirrhosis frequently results in development of enlarged, fragile esophageal and rectal veins, which can easily burst or tear with potentially fatal results. Enlarged esophageal veins are especially vulnerable when the drinker vomits after an alcoholic binge. Even a relatively small amount of alcohol can cause painful irritation of the lining of the stomach.

The Cardiovascular System

The effects of alcohol on the cardiovascular system depend on the amount of alcohol consumed. Moderate doses of alcohol—one drink or less a day for women and one to two drinks a day for men—may reduce the risk of heart disease and heart attack in some people. (The possible health benefits of alcohol are discussed later in this chapter.)

However, higher doses of alcohol have harmful effects on the cardiovascular system. In some people, more than two drinks a day will elevate blood pressure, making stroke and heart attack more likely. Some alcoholics show a weakening of the heart muscle, a condition known as **cardiac myopathy.** Binge drinking can cause "holiday heart," a syndrome characterized by serious abnormal heart rhythms, which usually appear within 24 hours of a binge episode.

Cancer

In 2000, the U.S. Department of Health and Human Services added alcoholic beverages to its list of known human carcinogens. Chronic alcohol consumption is a clear risk factor for cancers of the mouth, throat, larynx, and esophagus. (These cancers are also associated with use of tobacco, with which alcohol frequently acts as a cocarcinogen.) Five or six daily drinks, especially combined with smoking, increase risk of these cancers by a factor of 50 or more. Alcohol also is largely responsible for the most common form of liver cancer, and continued heavy drinking in people with hepatitis accelerates progression to this cancer. In all alcohol-related cancers, however, genetics and other biological factors play important roles, and help explain why some chronic alcohol abusers do not get cancer.

Alcohol increases the risk of breast cancer, but the risks of light to moderate drinking are unclear and somewhat controversial. Recent studies show that breast cancer risk, although still small, begins to increase at two to three drinks per day, and continues to rise with increasing numbers of daily drinks. The kind of alcohol does not seem to matter. Women at otherwise increased risk of breast cancer (for example, those with a family history of breast or ovarian cancer) should carefully weigh the risks of even moderate drinking.

Brain Damage

Brain damage due to chronic alcohol abuse is also tempered by an individual's physiology and genetics. Imaging studies document that many alcoholics experience brain shrinkage with loss of both grey and white matter, reduced blood flow, and slowed metabolic rates in some brain regions. To some extent, brain shrinkage can be reversed over time with abstinence. About half of the alcoholics in the United States have cognitive impairments, ranging from mild to severe. These include memory loss, dementia, and compromised problem-solving and reasoning abilities. Malnutrition, particularly thiamine deficiency, contributes to severe brain damage and the disabling condition known as Wernicke-Korsakoff syndrome.

Mortality

Excessive alcohol consumption is a factor in several of the leading causes of death for Americans. Average life expectancy among alcoholics is about 15 years less than among nonalcoholics. About half the deaths caused by alcohol are due to chronic conditions such as cirrhosis and cancer; the other half are due to acute conditions or events such as car crashes, falls, and suicide. Because many deaths from acute conditions occur in youths and young adults, alcohol is responsible for 2.3 million years of potential life lost each year.

The Effects of Alcohol Use During Pregnancy

During pregnancy, alcohol and its metabolic product acetaldehyde readily cross the placenta, potentially harming the developing fetus. Damage to the fetus depends on the amount of alcohol consumed and the stage of the pregnancy. Early in pregnancy, heavy drinking can cause spontaneous abortion or miscarriage. Alcohol in early pregnancy can also cause a collection of birth defects known as **fetal alcohol syndrome (FAS).** Children with FAS have a characteristic mixture of deformities that can include a small head, abnormal facial structure, heart defects, and other physical abnormalities. Their physical and mental growth is slower than normal, and most are mentally impaired.

Because rapid brain development continues throughout pregnancy, the fetal brain stays vulnerable to alcohol use until delivery. Although effects of drinking later in pregnancy do not typically cause the characteristic physical deformities of FAS, getting drunk just once during the final 3 months of pregnancy could damage fetal brain cells.

TERMS

cirrhosis A disease in which the liver is severely damaged by alcohol, other toxins, or infection.

cardiac myopathy Weakening of the heart muscle through disease.

fetal alcohol syndrome (FAS) A characteristic group of birth defects caused by excessive alcohol consumption by the mother, including facial deformities, heart defects, and physical and mental impairments.

FAS is a permanent, incurable condition that causes lifelong disability; it is among the most common preventable causes of mental retardation in the Western world. Full-blown FAS occurs in up to 15 out of every 10,000 live births in the United States. About three times as many babies are born with **alcohol-related neurodevelopmental disorder (ARND)**. Children with ARND appear physically normal but often have significant learning and behavioral disorders. As adults, they are more likely to develop substance abuse problems and to have criminal records. The whole range of FAS and ARND is commonly called *fetal alcohol spectrum disorder (FASD)*.

No one is sure exactly how much alcohol causes FASD or ARND. Like other untoward effects of alcohol, genetics and individual differences in metabolism, along with environmental factors such as diet, are thought to affect vulnerability. A 2002 study found that children born to mothers who drank as little as one and a half alcoholic drinks per week during their pregnancy weighed less and were shorter at age 14 than children of mothers who drank nothing during pregnancy. This is one of the first studies to show a significant difference between the children of nondrinkers and those of light drinkers. The children's smaller size may be a marker for subtle, persistent alcohol damage. Therefore, no amount of alcohol during pregnancy is considered safe.

Women who are trying to conceive, or who are sexually active without using effective contraception, should abstain from alcohol to avoid inadvertently harming their baby in the first few days or weeks of pregnancy, before they know they're expecting. Binge drinking among women of childbearing age is a particular concern. In 1989, labels on alcoholic beverages were required to carry a warning on the dangers of drinking during pregnancy.

Any alcohol consumed by a nursing mother quickly enters the breast milk. What impact this has on the child or on the mother's milk production is a matter of controversy. Dosage may again be the key issue. However, many physicians advise nursing mothers to abstain from drinking alcohol because of the belief that any amount may have negative effects on the baby's brain development.

Experts warn that there is no safe level of alcohol consumption during pregnancy.

Possible Health Benefits of Alcohol

Numerous studies have shown that, on average, light to moderate drinkers (no more than one drink per day for women, and one to two drinks per day for men) live longer than either abstainers or heavy drinkers.

The risks and benefits of drinking alcohol vary considerably with the age of the drinker. If you are 35 or younger, your odds of dying *increase* in direct proportion to the amount of alcohol you drink. Among people under age 35, even light drinkers have slightly higher mortality rates than nondrinkers. In other words, young adults who drink *any* amount of alcohol are more likely to die than nondrinkers of the same age. By contrast, alcohol consumption appears to confer health benefits primarily to older individuals.

The clearest evidence of benefit relates to coronary heart disease (CHD). The lowest rates of CHD deaths occur with moderate alcohol use, which in studies had a positive effect on both healthy people and individuals at risk for CHD. (CHD is discussed in detail in Chapter 15.) In a 2006 study of men age 50 and over, those who drank moderately each day reduced their risk of CHD by about 40%, compared to men who never drank. The difference was not as great in women. Moderate drinking may improve heart health by raising blood levels of HDL (the beneficial form of cholesterol), by thinning the blood, and

QUESTIONS FOR CRITICAL THINKING AND REFLECTION

Have you ever witnessed or been involved in an alcohol emergency? Did you consider the situation to be an emergency at the time? What were the circumstances surrounding the event? How did the people involved deal with it?

by reducing inflammation and the risk of dangerous blood clots, all of which can contribute to the risk of a heart attack. Individuals with heart disease or with strong risk factors should talk with their doctors about the possible health benefits of moderate drinking.

Some evidence also suggests that moderate drinkers may be less likely to develop or better able to manage a variety of other conditions, including diabetes, high blood pressure, strokes, arterial blockages in the legs, cognitive decline (including Alzheimer's disease), and benign prostate enlargement. It is still unclear if these effects are due to the alcohol itself or to the nonalcoholic components of alcoholic drinks (the substances that give each different kind of beverage its distinctive character).

Research is under way to determine whether the apparent health benefits of wine are due to the alcohol or to some other substance found in wine. Some experts believe that the apparent benefit of wine may merely reflect the fact that wine drinkers tend to be more affluent and to have healthier lifestyles than non–wine drinkers.

ALCOHOL ABUSE AND DEPENDENCE

Abuse of and dependence on alcohol affect more than just the drinker. Friends, family members, coworkers, strangers that drinkers encounter on the road, and society as a whole pay the physical, emotional, and financial costs of the misuse of alcohol.

Statistics on Alcohol Use

The CDC estimates that about 60% of Americans age 18 and older drink alcohol routinely or infrequently. Approximately 15% of Americans are former drinkers, and 25% are lifetime abstainers.

According to the National Survey on Drug Abuse and Health for 2007, almost 7% of Americans were classified as heavy alcohol users. Heavy drinkers account for over half of all the alcohol consumed, as well as a disproportionate amount of the social, economic, and medical costs of alcohol abuse (estimated at over $180 billion per year). Excessive alcohol use is responsible for 75,000 deaths per year among Americans and is the third leading lifestyle-related cause of death.

Abuse Versus Dependence

As explained in Chapter 9, the American Psychiatric Association's *Diagnostic and Statistical Manual of Mental Disorders* makes a distinction between substance abuse and substance dependence.

Alcohol abuse is recurrent alcohol use that has negative consequences, such as drinking in dangerous situations (before driving, for instance), or drinking patterns that result in academic, professional, interpersonal, or legal difficulties. One does not have to be an alcoholic to have problems with alcohol. The person who drinks only once a month, perhaps after an exam, but then drives while intoxicated is an alcohol abuser.

Alcohol dependence, or **alcoholism**, involves more extensive problems with alcohol use, usually involving physical tolerance and withdrawal. Alcoholism is discussed in greater detail later in the chapter.

How can you tell if you or someone you know is becoming alcohol-dependent? Look for the following warning signs:

- Drinking alone or secretively
- Using alcohol deliberately and repeatedly to perform or get through difficult situations
- Feeling uncomfortable on certain occasions when alcohol is not available
- Escalating alcohol consumption beyond an already established drinking pattern
- Consuming alcohol heavily in risky situations, such as before driving
- Getting drunk regularly or more frequently than in the past
- Drinking in the morning or at other unusual times

Binge Drinking

The National Institute on Alcohol Abuse and Alcoholism defines **binge drinking** as a pattern of alcohol use that

TERMS

alcohol-related neurodevelopmental disorder (ARND)   Cognitive and behavioral problems seen in people whose mothers drank alcohol during pregnancy.

alcohol abuse   The use of alcohol to a degree that causes physical damage, impairs functioning, or results in behavior harmful to others.

alcohol dependence   A pathological use of alcohol or impairment in functioning due to alcohol; characterized by tolerance and withdrawal symptoms; alcoholism.

alcoholism   A chronic psychological disorder characterized by excessive and compulsive drinking.

binge drinking   Periodically drinking alcohol to the point of severe intoxication.

brings a person's BAC up to 0.08% or above (typically four drinks for men or three drinks for women), consumed within about 2 hours. The National Survey on Drug Use and Health defines binge drinking as having five or more drinks within about 2 hours, at least once within 30 days; the 2007 survey estimated that 23% of people over the age of 12 were binge drinkers. Almost 7% were heavy drinkers, defined as having five or more drinks on the same occasion on each of 5 or more days in the past 30 days.

Among Americans under 21 years old, most drinking is in the form of a binge. However, a sizeable number of those 25 years or older are binge drinkers, and about 75% of the alcohol consumed by adults in the United States meets the definition of binge drinking.

Binge drinking has a profound effect on students' lives (see the box "College Binge Drinking"). Frequent binge drinkers were found to be three to seven times more likely than non–binge drinkers to engage in unplanned or unprotected sex, to drive after drinking, and to get hurt or injured (Table 10.3). Binge drinkers were also more likely to miss classes, get behind in schoolwork, and argue with friends. The more frequent the binges, the more problems the students encountered. Despite their experiences, fewer than 1% of the binge drinkers identified themselves as problem drinkers.

Alcoholism

As mentioned earlier, alcoholism, or alcohol dependence, is usually characterized by tolerance to alcohol and withdrawal symptoms. Everyone who drinks—even nonalcoholics—develops tolerance after repeated alcohol use.

Patterns and Prevalence Alcoholism occurs among people of all ethnic groups and at all socioeconomic levels. The stereotype of the homeless, impoverished alcoholic actually accounts for fewer than 5% of all alcohol-dependent people and usually represents the final stage of a drinking career that began years earlier. There are different patterns of alcohol dependence, including these four common ones:

1. Regular daily intake of large amounts.
2. Regular heavy drinking limited to weekends.
3. Long periods of sobriety interspersed with binges of daily heavy drinking lasting for weeks or months.
4. Heavy drinking limited to periods of stress.

Once established, alcoholism often exhibits a pattern of exacerbations and remissions. The person may stop drinking and abstain from

VITAL STATISTICS

Table 10.3	The Effects of Binge Drinking on College Students	
	Percentage of Students Experiencing Problems	
Alcohol-Related Problem	**Non–Binge Drinkers**	**Frequent Binge Drinkers**
Drove after drinking alcohol	18	58
Did something they regretted	17	62
Argued with friends	10	43
Engaged in unplanned sex	9	41
Missed a class	9	60
Got behind in schoolwork	9	42
Had unprotected sex	4	21
Got hurt or injured	4	28
Got into trouble with police	2	14
Had five or more of these problems since school year began	4	48

SOURCE: Wechsler, H., and B. Wuethrich. 2003. *Dying to Drink: Confronting Binge Drinking on College Campuses,* reprint ed. Emmaus, Pa.: Rodale.

alcohol for days or months after a frightening problem develops. After a period of abstinence, an alcoholic often attempts controlled drinking, which almost inevitably leads to an escalation in drinking and more problems. Alcoholism is not hopeless, however; many alcoholics do achieve permanent abstinence.

Health Effects Tolerance and withdrawal can have a serious impact on health. As described in Chapter 9, *tolerance* means that a drinker needs more alcohol to achieve intoxication or the desired effect, that the effects of continued use of the same amount of alcohol are diminished, or that the drinker can function adequately at doses or a BAC that would produce significant impairment in a casual user. Heavy users of alcohol may need to consume about 50% more than they originally needed in order to experience the same degree of intoxication.

When alcoholics stop drinking or sharply decrease their intake, they experience withdrawal. Symptoms include trembling hands (shakes, or jitters), a rapid pulse and accelerated breathing rate, insomnia, nightmares, anxiety, and gastrointestinal upset. These symptoms usu-

College Binge Drinking

College binge drinking, a serious problem for decades, has recently come under a harsh spotlight due largely to highly publicized alcohol-related tragedies on campus. Deaths from alcohol overdose, alcohol-related injuries (including motor vehicle crashes), violent crimes, student riots, and serious vandalism have all drawn attention to the epidemic of heavy drinking on college campuses.

To many people, heavy drinking is considered a normal and integral part of college life. But research has shown that heavy drinking has had a devastating impact on far too many students—drinkers and nondrinkers alike—as well as on their families and communities.

Drinking on campus is pervasive. Approximately 80% of college students drink alcohol; that's more than use cigarettes, marijuana, or cocaine combined. Much of the current data on college drinking comes from the ongoing Harvard School of Public Health Alcohol Study, the first large-scale study of the subject. Their research on college students across the United States shows that nearly half (44%) of students binge-drink. Other sources estimate that about 40% binge-drink, and about 20% binge three or more times over a two-week period.

The consequences of college drinking are alarming. Every year, an estimated 1700 college students age 18–24 die from overdoses and alcohol-related injuries. Another 600,000 sustain unintentional alcohol-related injuries, 700,000 are assaulted by other students who have been drinking, and 100,000 are victims of alcohol-related date rape or sexual assault.

These statistics have shocked many students, administrators, and parents into demanding changes in college attitudes and policies regarding alcohol. In response, the Task Force of the National Advisory Council on Alcohol Abuse and Alcoholism was formed. Its report documents the extent of the alcohol problem and is a call to action for colleges and their surrounding communities to re-examine their alcohol policies and overhaul the campus drinking culture. These efforts, according to the Task Force, must focus on three levels:

1. Ultimately, *individual students* must take responsibility for their own behavior, but programs that encourage and support development of healthy attitudes toward alcohol are often needed. These programs should target students at increased risk of developing alcohol problems: first-year students, Greek organization members, and athletes. Treatment should be readily available for problem drinkers.

2. The *student body as a whole* must work to discourage alcohol abuse. This effort might include promoting alcohol-free activities, reducing the availability of alcohol, and avoiding social and commercial promotion of alcohol on campus. There should be an environment of acceptance of students who choose to abstain, and disapproval of students who drink to excess. Fraternities, sororities, eating clubs, and other campus organizations should be held accountable if underage or otherwise inappropriate alcohol use takes place on their premises.

3. *Colleges and surrounding communities* must cooperate to discourage excessive drinking. College administrators, law enforcement, bar and liquor store owners, residents who live near campus, and the court system must all do their part to reduce the availability of cheap alcohol and to enforce existing laws. Those who enable students to drink irresponsibly must be held accountable.

The United States Surgeon General, in his 2007 Call to Action to Prevent and Reduce Underage Drinking, suggests eliminating alcohol sponsorship of athletic events and other social activities. He also recommends implementing responsible alcohol policies, and possibly restricting sale of alcohol, at campus facilities such as sports stadiums, campus pubs, and concert halls.

Working together, students, faculty, administrators, parents, and the community have begun to put an end to the destructive culture of heavy drinking on college campuses. At some schools, there is an effort to shift classes to Fridays and even Saturdays, after it was found that binge drinking increases when students don't have Friday classes. Increasingly, incoming students are required to take a 3-hour online class about alcohol. And there is stricter punishment for underage drinking and public drunkenness on some campuses, with the likelihood of suspension for repeat offenders.

Many colleges have instituted bans on ads for alcoholic drinks in college newspapers and during broadcasts of college athletic events. Flyers, posters, and other promotions for cheap drinks such as two-for-one specials, happy hours, all you can drink, and ladies' night, are banned on many campuses, as well. Bars and restaurants that cater to students are discouraged from offering these cheap alcohol incentives.

---

ally begin 5–10 hours after alcohol intake is decreased and improve after 4–5 days. After a week, most people feel much better, but occasionally anxiety, insomnia, and other symptoms persist for 6 months or more.

More severe withdrawal symptoms occur in about 5% of alcoholics. These include seizures (sometimes called rum fits), confusion, and **hallucinations.** Still less common is **delirium tremens (the DTs),** a medical emergency characterized by severe disorientation, confusion, epileptic-like seizures, and vivid hallucinations, often of vermin and small animals. The mortality rate from DTs can be as high as 15%, especially in very debilitated people with preexisting medical illnesses.

Alcoholics face all the physical health risks associated with intoxication and chronic drinking described earlier in the chapter. Some of the damage is compounded by nutritional deficiencies that often accompany alcoholism. A mental problem associated with alcohol use is profound memory gaps (commonly known as blackouts), which are sometimes filled by conscious or unconscious lying.

The specific health effects of alcoholism tend to vary from person to person. For example, one individual may suffer from problems with memory and CNS defects and have no liver or gastrointestinal problems. Another person with a similar drinking and nutritional history may have advanced liver disease but no memory gaps.

Social and Psychological Effects

Alcohol use causes more serious social and psychological problems than all other forms of drug abuse combined. For every person who is an alcoholic, another three or four people are directly affected. In a 2004 Gallup poll, about a third of Americans reported that alcohol had been a source of trouble in their family.

Alcoholics frequently suffer from mental disorders in addition to their substance dependence. Alcoholics are much more likely than nonalcoholics to suffer from clinical depression, panic disorder, schizophrenia, and antisocial personality disorders. People with anxiety or panic attacks may try to use alcohol to lessen their anxiety, even though alcohol often makes these disorders worse. Alcoholics also often have other substance-abuse problems.

Causes of Alcoholism

The precise causes of alcoholism are unknown, but many factors are probably involved. Studies of twins and adopted children clearly demonstrate the importance of genetics. If one of a pair of fraternal twins is alcoholic, then the other has about twice the chance of becoming alcoholic. For the identical twin of an alcoholic, the risk of alcoholism is about four times that of the general population. These risks persist even when the twins have little contact with each other or their biological parents. Similarly, adoption studies show an increased risk among children of alcoholics, even if they were adopted at birth into nondrinking families. Alcoholism in adoptive parents, contrarily, doesn't make individuals more or less likely to become alcoholic. Some studies suggest that as much as 50–60% of a person's risk for alcoholism is determined by genetic factors.

Not all children of alcoholics become alcoholic, however, and it is clear that other factors are involved. A person's risk of developing alcoholism may be increased by certain personality disorders, having grown up in a violent or otherwise troubled household, and imitating the alcohol abuse of peers and other role models. People who begin drinking excessively in their teens are especially prone to binge drinking and alcoholism later in life. Common psychological features of individuals who abuse alcohol are denial ("I don't have a problem") and rationalization ("I drink because I need to socialize with my customers"). Certain social factors have also been linked with alcoholism, including urbanization, disappearance of the extended family, a general loosening of kinship ties, increased mobility, and changing values.

Treatment

Some alcoholics recover without professional help. How often this occurs is unknown, but possibly as many as one-third stop drinking on their own or reduce their drinking enough to eliminate problems. Often these spontaneous recoveries are linked to an alcohol-related crisis, such as a blackout or alcohol-related automobile crash, a health problem, or the threat of being fired. Not all alcoholics must hit bottom before they are motivated to stop. People vary markedly in what induces them to change their behavior.

Most alcoholics, however, require a treatment program of some kind in order to stop drinking. Many different kinds of programs exist. No single treatment works for everyone, so a person may have to try different programs before finding the right one.

Although treatment is not successful for all alcoholics, considerable optimism has replaced the older view that nothing could be done. Many alcoholics have patterns of drinking that fluctuate widely over time. These fluctuations indicate that their alcohol abuse is a response to environmental factors, such as life stressors or social pressures, and therefore may be influenced by treatment.

One of the oldest and best-known recovery programs is Alcoholics Anonymous (AA). AA consists of self-help groups that meet several times each week in many communities and follow a 12-step program. Important steps for people in these programs include recognizing that they are "powerless over alcohol" and must seek help from a "higher power" in order to regain control of their lives. By verbalizing these steps, the alcoholic directly addresses the denial that is often prominent in alcoholism and other addictions. Many AA members have a sponsor of their choosing who is available by phone 24 hours a day for individual support and crisis intervention. AA convincingly shows the alcoholic that abstinence can be achieved and also provides a sober peer group of people who share the same identity—that of recovering alcoholics. Many AA members find that it works best in combination with counseling and medical care.

Other recovery approaches are available. Some, like Rational Recovery and Women for Sobriety, deliberately avoid any emphasis on higher spiritual powers. A more controversial approach to problem drinking is offered by the group Moderation Management, which encourages people to manage their drinking behavior by limiting intake or abstaining.

Al-Anon is a companion program to AA for families and friends of alcoholics. In Al-Anon, spouses and others explore how they enabled the alcoholic to drink by deny-

QUICK STATS

2.7 million
Americans were treated for alcohol use, or problems relating to its use, in 2007.

—SAMSHA, 2008

ing, rationalizing, or covering up his or her drinking and how they can change this codependent behavior.

Employee assistance programs and school-based programs represent another approach to alcoholism treatment. These programs can deal directly with work and campus issues, often important sources of stress for the alcohol abuser. They encourage effective coping responses for internal and external stressors.

Inpatient hospital rehabilitation is useful for some alcoholics, especially if they have serious medical or mental problems or if life stressors threaten to overwhelm them. When the person returns to the community, however, it is critical that there be some form of active, continuing, long-term treatment. Patients who return to a spouse or family often need to address issues involving those significant others, and to establish new routines and shared recreational activities that do not involve drinking.

There are also several medical treatments for alcoholism. All of these work best in combination with counseling or other nonpharmacological programs:

- *Disulfiram* (Antabuse) inhibits the metabolic breakdown of acetaldehyde and causes patients to flush and feel ill when they drink, thus theoretically inhibiting impulse drinking. However, disulfiram is potentially dangerous if the user continues to drink.

- *Naltrexone* (ReVia, Depade) binds to a brain pleasure center that reduces the craving for alcohol and decreases its pleasant, reinforcing effects. When taken correctly, naltrexone usually does not make the user feel ill.

- *Injectable naltrexone* (Vivtrol) acts the same as oral naltrexone, but it is a single monthly shot administered by a health professional. Compliance with a monthly regimen may be better for some alcoholics.

- *Acamprosate* (Campral) helps people maintain abstinence after they have stopped drinking. It is unclear how acamprosate works, but it appears to act on brain pathways related to alcohol abuse.

As of 2007, at least 15 drugs to treat alcoholism were undergoing clinical trials, either alone, in combination, or in combination with counseling therapies.

In people who abuse alcohol and have significant depression or anxiety, the use of antidepressant or antianxiety medication can improve both mental health and drinking behavior. In addition, drugs such as diazepam (Valium) are sometimes prescribed to replace alcohol during initial stages of withdrawal. Such chemical substitutes are usually useful for only a week or so, because alcoholics are at particularly high risk for developing dependence on other drugs.

Alcohol-treatment programs are successful in achieving an extended period of sobriety for about half of those who participate. Success rates of conventional treatment programs are about the same for men and women and for people from different ethnic groups. Women, minorities,

Table 10.4 Users and Abusers of Alcohol in the U.S., by Demographic Characteristics: 2007

	Past Year Prevalence (Percentage)	
	Alcohol Use	Alcohol Abuse or Dependence
Gender		
Men	69.5	10.6
Women	62.2	4.6
Ethnicity		
White	70.4	8.0
Black or African American	54.5	6.3
American Indian and Alaska Native	59.3	10.9
Native Hawaiian and other Pacific Islander	72.3	7.3
Asian American	49.6	4.3
Hispanic or Latino	57.2	7.0
Two or more races	64.3	8.6
Total Population	**65.7**	**7.5**

SOURCE: Office of Applied Studies, Substance Abuse and Mental Health Services Administration. 2008. *Results from the 2007 National Survey on Drug Use and Health: National Findings* (http://oas.samhsa.gov/nsduh; retrieved February 4, 2009).

and the poor often face major economic and social barriers to receiving treatment. Most inpatient treatment programs are financially out of reach for people of low income or those without insurance coverage. AA remains the mainstay of treatment for most people and is often a component of even the most expensive treatment programs. Special AA groups exist in many communities for young people, women, gay men and lesbians, non–English speakers, and a variety of interest groups.

Gender and Ethnic Differences

Alcohol abusers come from all socioeconomic levels and cultural groups, but there are notable differences in patterns of drinking between men and women and among different ethnic groups (Table 10.4).

Men Among white American men, excessive drinking often begins in the teens or twenties and progresses gradually through the thirties until the individual is clearly identifiable as an alcoholic by the time he is in his late thirties or early forties. Other men remain controlled drinkers until later in life, sometimes becoming alcoholic in association with retirement, the loss of friends and loved ones, boredom, illness, or psychological disorders. (See the box "Gender and Alcohol Use and Abuse.")

Gender and Alcohol Use and Abuse

Men are more likely than women to drink alcohol, to abuse alcohol, and to have alcohol dependency. Men account for the majority of alcohol-related deaths and injuries in the United States, the greater proportion occurring in men age 35 and younger. Most alcohol-related deaths and injuries among men result from incidents involving intoxication, such as motor vehicle crashes, falls, drowning, suicide, and homicide.

A variety of factors contribute to the higher rates of alcohol use and abuse among men. Traditional or stereotypic gender roles and ideas regarding masculinity and drinking behavior may promote excessive alcohol consumption among men. Young men in particular are also more likely to engage in all types of risky health behaviors. Men drive more miles, drive more dangerously, and are more likely to drive while intoxicated. They tend to have greater access to firearms, contributing to their increased rates of suicide and homicide. Men may also be more likely than women to use alcohol to cope with stress and other life challenges.

Women are not immune to alcohol problems, however, and rates of alcohol abuse and dependence among women have increased in the past decade. Whether a woman is a "social drinker," a binge drinker, or a heavy daily user, the impact of alcohol on her will be different from and generally greater than the impact of comparable use on a man. And because of the social stigma attached to problem drinking, particularly among women, women are less likely to seek early treatment.

Women become intoxicated at lower doses of alcohol than men, and they tend to experience the adverse physical effects of chronic drinking sooner and at lower levels of alcohol consumption than men. Female alcoholics have higher death rates than male alcoholics, including death rates from cirrhosis. They develop alcohol liver disease and alcohol-related brain damage after a comparatively shorter period of heavy drinking and a lower level of drinking than men. Some alcohol-related health problems are unique to women, including an increased risk of breast cancer, menstrual disorders, infertility, and,

in pregnant women, giving birth to a child with FAS.

Women from all walks of life and all ethnic groups can develop alcohol problems, but those who have never married or are divorced are more likely to drink heavily than married or widowed women. Women who have multiple life roles, such as parent, worker, and spouse, are less vulnerable to alcohol problems than women who have fewer roles.

Women The progression of alcoholism in women is usually different. Women tend to become alcoholic at a later age and with fewer years of heavy drinking. It is not unusual for women in their forties or fifties to become alcoholic after years of controlled drinking. Women alcoholics develop cirrhosis and other medical complications somewhat more often than men. Women alcoholics may have more medical problems because they are less likely to seek early treatment. In addition, there may be an inherently greater biological risk for women who drink.

African Americans Although as a group African Americans use less alcohol than most other groups (including whites), they face disproportionately high levels of alcohol-related birth defects, cirrhosis, cancer, hypertension, and other medical problems. In addition, blacks are more

likely than members of other ethnic groups to be victims of alcohol-related homicides, criminal assaults, and injuries. African American women are more likely to abstain from alcohol use than white women, but among black women who drink there is a higher percentage of heavy drinkers. Urban black males commonly start drinking excessively and develop serious neurological illnesses at an earlier age than urban white males. They also have a higher rate of alcoholism-related suicide.

AA groups of predominantly African Americans are effective, perhaps because essential elements of AA—sharing common experiences, mutual acceptance of one another as human beings, and trusting a higher power—are already a part of African American culture. Treatments that use the extended family and occupational training are also effective.

Latinos Drinking patterns among Latinos vary significantly, depending on their specific cultural background and how long they and their families have lived in the United States. Drunk driving and cirrhosis are the most common causes of alcohol-related death and injury among Hispanic men. Hispanic women are more likely to abstain from alcohol than white or black women, but those who do drink are at special risk for problems. Treating the entire family as a unit is an important part of treatment because family pride, solidarity, and support are important aspects of Latino culture. Some Hispanics may do better if treatment efforts are integrated with the techniques of folk healers and spiritists.

Asian Americans   As a group, Asian Americans have lower-than-average rates of alcohol abuse. However, acculturation may somewhat weaken the generally strong Asian taboos and community sanctions against alcohol misuse. For many Asian Americans, though, the genetically based physiological aversion to alcohol remains a deterrent to abuse. Ethnic agencies, health care professionals, and ministers seem to be the most effective sources of treatment, when needed.

American Indians and Alaska Natives   Alcohol abuse is one of the most widespread and severe health problems among American Indians and Alaska Natives, especially for adolescents and young adults. Excessive drinking varies from tribe to tribe but is generally high in both men and women. The rate of alcoholism among American Indians is twice that of the general population, and the death rate from alcohol-related causes is about eight times higher. Treatment may be more effective if it reflects tribal values.

Helping Someone with an Alcohol Problem

Helping a friend or relative with an alcohol problem requires skill and tact. Start by making sure you are not enabling someone to continue excessively using alcohol. Enabling takes many forms, such as making excuses for the alcohol abuser—for example, saying "he has the flu" when it is really a hangover.

Another important step is open, honest labeling—"I think you have a problem with alcohol." Such explicit statements usually elicit emotional rebuttals and may endanger a relationship. However, you are not helping your friends by allowing them to deny their problems with alcohol or other drugs. Taking action shows that you care.

Even when problems are acknowledged, there is usually reluctance to get help. You can't cure a friend's drinking problem, but you can guide him or her to appropriate help. Your best role might be to obtain information about the available resources and persistently encourage their use. Consider making an appointment for your friend at the student health center and then go with him or her to the appointment. Most student health centers will be able to recommend local options for self-help groups and formal treatment; the counseling center is another excellent source for help. You can also check the phone book and the Internet for local chapters of AA and other groups (see For More Information at the end of the chapter). And don't underestimate the power of families to help. An honest phone call to your friend's parents could save a life if your friend is in serious trouble with alcohol.

DRINKING BEHAVIOR AND RESPONSIBILITY

The responsible use of alcohol means keeping your BAC low, so that your behavior is always under your control. In addition to controlling your own drinking, you can promote responsible alcohol use in others.

Examine Your Drinking Behavior

When you want to drink responsibly, it's helpful to know, first of all, why you drink. The following are common reasons given by college students:

19% of college students age 18–24 meet the criteria for alcohol abuse or dependence.

—NIAAA, 2007

QUICK STATS

- "It lets me go along with my friends."
- "It makes me less self-conscious and more social."
- "It makes me less inhibited."
- "It relieves depression, anxiety, tension, or worries."
- "It enables me to experience a different state of consciousness."

If you drink alcohol, what are your reasons for doing so?

After examining your reasons for drinking, take a closer look at your drinking behavior. Is it moderate and responsible? Or do you frequently overindulge and suffer negative consequences? The Behavior Change Strategy at the end of the chapter explains how to keep and analyze a record of your drinking. The CAGE screening test can help you determine whether you, or someone close to you, may have a drinking problem. Answer yes or no to the following questions:

QUESTIONS FOR CRITICAL THINKING AND REFLECTION
Do you know anyone with a serious alcohol problem? From what you have read in this chapter, would you say that person abuses alcohol or is dependent on it? What effects, if any, has this person's problem had on your life? Have you thought about getting support or help?

Our attitudes about alcohol use are usually based on our experiences and observations of the world around us. For example, you may not think of alcohol as being an important part of life if you grew up in a household where alcohol was served only at special events or as an occasional accompaniment to dinner.

On the other hand, if your parents or other family members drank heavily or made a big deal of having alcohol on hand for most occasions, then you may have a similar view of alcohol and be more inclined to use it frequently.

The college environment can play an important role in shaping students' attitudes about drinking. Does it seem as if everyone at your college drinks? Do you feel pressure to drink, even when you don't want to? Many students feel pressured to use alcohol or illegal drugs. But even though it may seem like everyone drinks, about one-fifth of college students are nondrinkers. Remember: The majority of American adults drink moderately or not at all. Perceptions about the drinking habits of others can be misleading.

Have you ever felt you should
Cut down on your drinking?

Have people
Annoyed you by criticizing your drinking?

Have you ever felt bad or
Guilty about your drinking?

Have you ever had an
Eye-opener (a drink first thing in the morning to steady your nerves or get rid of a hangover)?

One "yes" response suggests a possible alcohol problem; if you answered yes to more than one question, it is highly likely that a problem exists. For a more detailed evaluation of your drinking habits, complete the AUDIT questionnaire in the box "Do You Have a Problem with Alcohol?" If the results of either assessment test indicate a potential problem, get help right away.

Drink Moderately and Responsibly

Sometimes people lose control when they misjudge how much they can drink. At other times, they set out deliberately to get drunk. Following are some strategies for keeping your drinking and your behavior under control:

By choosing a designated driver, these men are ensuring a safe trip home.

- *Drink Slowly.* Sip your drinks rather than gulp them. Do not drink alcoholic beverages to quench your thirst. Avoid drinks made with carbonated mixers, especially if you're thirsty; you'll be more likely to gulp them down.
- *Space Your Drinks.* Drink nonalcoholic drinks at parties, or alternate them with alcoholic drinks. Learn to refuse a round: "I've had enough for right now." Parties are easier for some people if they hold a glass of something nonalcoholic that has ice and a twist of lime floating in it so it looks like an alcoholic drink.
- *Eat Before and While Drinking.* Avoid drinking on an empty stomach. Food in your stomach will not prevent the alcohol from eventually being absorbed, but it will slow down the rate somewhat and lower the peak BAC. In restaurants, order your food before you order a drink. Try to have something to eat before you go out to a party where alcohol will be served.
- *Know Your Limits and Your Drinks.* Learn how different BACs affect you. In a safe setting such as your home, with your roommate or a friend, see how a set amount—say, two drinks in an hour—affects you. A good

Do You Have a Problem with Alcohol?

The Alcohol Use Disorders Test (AUDIT) is a screening tool for problem drinking. It can also be used for self-assessment. For each question, choose the answer that best describes your behavior. Then total your scores.

Questions	Points					Your Score
	0	1	2	3	4	
1. How often do you have a drink containing alcohol?	Never	Monthly or less	2–4 times a month	2–3 times a week	4 or more times a week	_____
2. How many drinks containing alcohol do you have on a typical day when you are drinking?	1 or 2	3 or 4	5 or 6	7–9	10 or more	_____
3. How often do you have 6 or more drinks on one occasion?	Never	Less than monthly	Monthly	Weekly	Daily or almost daily	_____
4. How often during the past year have you found that you were not able to stop drinking once you had started?	Never	Less than monthly	Monthly	Weekly	Daily or almost daily	_____
5. How often during the past year have you failed to do what was normally expected because of drinking?	Never	Less than monthly	Monthly	Weekly	Daily or almost daily	_____
6. How often during the past year have you needed a first drink in the morning to get yourself going after a heavy drinking session?	Never	Less than monthly	Monthly	Weekly	Daily or almost daily	_____
7. How often during the past year have you had a feeling of guilt or remorse after drinking?	Never	Less than monthly	Monthly	Weekly	Daily or almost daily	_____
8. How often during the past year have you been unable to remember what happened the night before because you had been drinking?	Never	Less than monthly	Monthly	Weekly	Daily or almost daily	_____
9. Have you or someone else been injured as a result of your drinking?	No	Yes, but not in the past year (2 points)		Yes, during the past year (4 points)		_____
10. Has a relative, friend, doctor, or other health worker been concerned about your drinking or suggested you cut down?	No	Yes, but not in the past year (2 points)		Yes, during the past year (4 points)		_____
					Total	_____

A total score of 8 or more indicates a strong likelihood of hazardous or harmful alcohol consumption. Even if you score below 8, if you are encountering drinking-related problems with your academic performance, job, relationships, health, or the law, you should consider seeking help.

SOURCE: Sanders, J. B. et al. 1993, *Development of the Alcohol Use Disorders Identification Test (AUDIT):* WHO collaborative project on early detection of persons with harmful alcohol consumption-II. Addiction, 88(6), Appendix, p. 803. Reprinted by permission of Blackwell Publishers..

test is walking heel to toe in a straight line with your eyes closed or standing with your feet crossed and trying to touch your finger to your nose with your eyes closed.

Be aware that in different settings your performance, and especially your ability to judge your behavior, may change. At a given BAC, you will perform less well when surrounded by activity and boisterous companions than you will in a quiet test setting with just one or two other people. This impairment results partially because alcohol reduces your ability to perform when your brain is bombarded by multiple stimuli.

Promote Responsible Drinking in Others

Although you cannot completely control the drinking behavior of others, there are things you can do to help promote responsible drinking.

Encourage Responsible Attitudes Our society teaches us attitudes toward drinking that contribute to alcohol-related problems. Many of us have difficulty expressing disapproval about someone who has drunk too much,

Alcohol Advertising

To be a careful and informed health consumer, you need to consider the effects that advertisements have on you.

Alcohol manufacturers spend $6 billion every year on advertising and promotions. They claim that the purpose of their advertising is to persuade adults who already drink to choose a certain brand. But in reality, ads cleverly engage young people and children—never overtly suggesting that young people should drink, but clearly linking alcohol and good times.

Alcohol ads are common during televised sporting events and other shows popular with teenagers. Studies show that the more TV adolescents watch, the more likely they are to take up drinking in their teens. New alcoholic drinks geared to the tastes of young people are heavily promoted. "Hard lemonade" and other fruity or sweetened drinks ("alcopops" or "low-alcohol refreshers") have been described by teens as a way to get drunk without suffering the bitter taste of most alcoholic beverages. Though only recently introduced, these drinks have been tried by almost half of 14–18-year-olds.

Alcohol manufacturers also reach out to young people at youth-oriented activities like concerts and sporting events. Product logos are heavily marketed through sales of T-shirts, hats, and other items. Many colleges allow alcohol manufacturers to advertise at campus events in exchange for sponsorship.

What is the message of all these advertisements? Think about the alcohol ads you've seen. Many give the impression that drinking alcohol is a normal part of everyday life and good times. This message seems to work well on the young, many of whom believe that heavy-duty drinking at parties is normal and fun. The use of famous musicians, athletes, or actors in commercials increases the appeal of alcohol by associating it with fame, wealth, sex, and popularity. Many beer advertisements, for example, portray beer drinking as a critical part of one's success in finding an attractive mate.

What ads don't show is the darker side of drinking. You never see hangovers, car crashes, slipping grades, or violence. Although some ads include a brief message such as "know when to say when," the impact of such cautions is small compared to that of the image of happy, attractive young people having fun while drinking.

The next time you see an advertisement for alcohol, take a critical look. What is the message of the ad? What audience is being targeted, and what is the ad implying about alcohol use? Be aware of its effect on you.

---

and we are amused by the antics of a funny drunk. We accept the alcohol industry's linkage of drinking with virility or sexuality (see the box "Alcohol Advertising"). And many people treat nondrinkers as nonconformists in social settings. Recognize that the choice to abstain is neither odd nor unusual. More than one-third of adults do not drink at all or drink very infrequently. Most adults are capable of enjoying their leisure time without alcohol or drugs. In hazardous situations, such as driving or operating machinery, abstinence is the only appropriate choice.

Be a Responsible Host   When you are the host, serve nonalcoholic beverages as well as alcohol. Have only enough alcohol on hand for each guest to have a moderate amount. Don't put out large kegs of beer, as these invite people to overindulge. For parties hosted by a dorm, fraternity, or other campus group, don't allow guests to have unlimited drinks for a single admission fee, as this also encourages binge drinking.

Always serve food along with alcohol, and stop serving alcohol an hour or more before people will leave. If possible, arrange carpools with designated nondrinking drivers in advance. Remind your guests who are under 21 about the new zero-tolerance laws in many states—even a single drink can result in an illegal BAC. Insist that guests who drink too much take a taxi, ride with someone else, or stay overnight rather than drive.

Plan social functions with no alcohol at all. Outdoor parties, hikes, and practically every other type of social occasion can be enjoyable without alcohol. If that doesn't seem possible to you, then examine your drinking patterns and attitudes toward alcohol. If you can't have fun without drinking, you may have a problem with alcohol.

Hold the Drinker Responsible   The individual who consumes alcohol must take full responsibility for his or her behavior. Pardoning unacceptable behavior fosters the attitude that the behavior is caused by the drug. The drinker is thereby excused from responsibility and learns to expect minimal adverse consequences for bad behavior. The opposite approach—holding the individual fully accountable—is a more effective policy. For example, alcohol-impaired drivers who receive strict penalties have fewer subsequent rearrests than those who receive only mandatory treatment. Other people's drunkenness can impinge on your living or study environment. Speak up against this behavior—and insist on your rights.

Take Community Action   Consider joining an action group such as Students Against Destructive Decisions (SADD). Through lesson plans, peer counseling, and the promotion of better communication between students and parents, SADD helps students avoid the dangers of drinking, drug use, impaired driving, and other destructive choices.

QUESTIONS FOR CRITICAL THINKING AND REFLECTION

Are you aware of the campus and community resources that can help someone overcome an alcohol problem? For example, does your school offer alternatives to keg parties or other events where alcohol is traditionally provided? Are there dorms, Greek organizations, or clubs whose members agree to abstain from alcohol? Are counseling services readily available to students?

TIPS FOR TODAY AND THE FUTURE

The responsible use of alcohol means drinking in moderation or not at all.

RIGHT NOW YOU CAN

- Consider whether there is a history of alcohol abuse or dependence in your family.
- Think about your current drinking habits. For example, count the number of parties you attended in the past month and how many drinks you had at each one.
- Take stock of the number of alcoholic beverages in your home. Does there always seem to be a lot on hand? Do you find yourself purchasing alcohol frequently? What do your purchasing habits say about your drinking?

IN THE FUTURE YOU CAN

- Think about the next party you plan to attend. Decide how much you will drink at the party, and how you will get home afterward.
- Watch your friends' behavior at events where drinking is involved. Do any of them show signs of a drinking problem? If so, consider what you can do to help.

SUMMARY

- Although alcohol has long been a part of human celebrations, it is a psychoactive drug capable of causing addiction.

- After being absorbed into the bloodstream in the stomach and small intestine, alcohol is transported throughout the body. The liver metabolizes alcohol as blood circulates through it.

- If people drink more alcohol each hour than the body can metabolize, blood alcohol concentration (BAC) increases. The rate of alcohol metabolism depends on a variety of individual factors.

- Alcohol is a CNS depressant. At low doses, it tends to make people feel relaxed.

- At higher doses, alcohol interferes with motor and mental functioning; at very high doses, alcohol poisoning, coma, and death can occur. Effects may be increased if alcohol is combined with other drugs.

- Alcohol use increases the risk of injury and violence; drinking before driving is particularly dangerous, even at low doses.

- Continued alcohol use has negative effects on the digestive and cardiovascular systems and increases cancer risk and overall mortality.

- Pregnant women who drink risk giving birth to children with a cluster of birth defects known as fetal alcohol syndrome (FAS). Even occasional drinking during pregnancy can cause brain injury in the fetus.

- Moderate drinking may decrease the risk of coronary heart disease in some people.

- Alcohol abuse involves drinking in dangerous situations or drinking to a degree that causes academic, professional, interpersonal, or legal difficulties.

- Alcohol dependence, or alcoholism, is characterized by more extensive problems with alcohol, usually involving tolerance and withdrawal.

- Binge drinking is a common form of alcohol abuse on college campuses that has negative effects on both drinking and nondrinking students.

- Physical consequences of alcoholism include the direct effects of tolerance and withdrawal, as well as all the problems associated with chronic drinking. Psychological problems include memory loss and additional mental disorders such as depression.

- Treatment approaches include mutual support groups like AA, job- and school-based programs, inpatient hospital programs, and pharmacological treatments.

- Helping someone who abuses alcohol means avoiding being an enabler, and obtaining information about available resources and persistently encouraging their use.

- Strategies for keeping drinking under control include examining attitudes about drinking and drinking behavior, drinking slowly, spacing drinks, eating before and while drinking, and knowing one's limits.

- Strategies for promoting responsible drinking in others include encouraging responsible attitudes, being a responsible host, holding the drinker responsible for his or her actions, learning about prevention programs, and taking community action.

Developing Responsible Drinking Habits

How much do you drink? Is it the right amount for you? You may know the answer to this question already, or you may not have given it much thought. Many people learn through a single unpleasant experience how alcohol affects them. Others suffer ill effects but choose to ignore or deny them.

To make responsible and informed choices about using alcohol, consider, first, whether there is any history of alcohol abuse in your family. If someone in your family is dependent on alcohol, you have a higher-than-average likelihood of becoming dependent too. Second, consider whether you are dependent on other substances or behaviors. Do you smoke, drink strong coffee every day, or use other drugs regularly? Does some habit control your life? Some people have more of a tendency to become addicted than others, and a person with one addiction is often likely to have other addictions as well. If this is the case for you, again you may need to be more cautious with alcohol.

Keep a Record

Once you have answered these questions, find out more about your alcohol-related behavior by keeping track of your drinking for 2 weeks in your health journal. Keep a daily alcohol behavior record like the one illustrated in Chapter 1 for eating behavior. Include information on the following:

- *The drinking situation,* including type of drink, time of day, how fast you drank it, where you were, and what else you were doing.

- *Your internal state,* including what made you want to drink and your feelings, thoughts, and concerns at the time. Note how others influenced you.

- *The consequences of drinking,* including any changes in your feelings or behavior while or after you were drinking, such as silliness, assertiveness, aggressiveness, or depression.

Analyze Your Record

Next, analyze your record to detect patterns of feelings and environmental cues. Do you always drink when you're at a certain place or with certain people? Do you sometimes drink just to be sociable, when you don't really want a drink and would be satisfied with a nonalcoholic beverage? Refer to the list of warning signs of alcohol abuse given in the text. Are any of them true for you? For example, do you feel uncomfortable in a social situation if alcohol is *not* available?

Set Goals

Now that you've analyzed your record, think about whether you want to change any of your behaviors. Would you do better academically if you drank less? Has drinking had a negative impact on any of your relationships? Have you risked infection and unplanned pregnancy by having unprotected sex while drunk? Do you depend on alcohol in order to have a good time? Have you been injured while drinking? If you drink and drive or if you feel you are becoming dependent on alcohol, it is time to change your drinking behavior. Decide on goals that will give you the best health and safety returns, such as a beer or a glass of wine with dinner, one drink per hour at a party, or no alcohol at all.

Devise a Plan

Refer to your health journal to see what kinds of patterns your drinking falls into and where you can intervene to break the behavior chain. If you have determined that your life would be improved if you changed your drinking habits, now is the time to make changes. For some people, simple changes in the environment such as stocking the refrigerator with alternative beverages like juices or sparkling water can be helpful. If you feel self-conscious about ordering a nonalcoholic drink when you're out with a group, try recruiting a friend to do the same. If it's too difficult to avoid drinking in some situations, such as at a bar or a beer party, you may decide to avoid those situations for a period of time.

Examine your friendships. If drinking is becoming a problem for you and some of your friends drink heavily, you may need to think about letting those relationships go. If you find support groups helpful, check with your college counseling center or health clinic; most schools sponsor peer group activities for those who are working to change their drinking habits. Local chapters of AA and other organizations may have groups geared toward college-age people.

Instead of drinking, try other activities that produce the same effect. For example, if you drink to relieve anxiety or tension, try adding 20–30 minutes of exercise to your schedule to help manage stress. Or try doing a relaxation exercise or going for a brisk walk to help reduce anxiety before a party or date. If you drink to relieve depression or to stop worrying, consider finding a trustworthy person (perhaps a professional counselor) to talk to. If you drink to feel more comfortable sexually, consider ways to improve communication with your partner so you can deal with sexual issues more openly. When these activities are successful, they will reinforce your responsible drinking decisions and make it more likely that you'll make the same decisions again in the future.

For other ways to monitor and control your drinking behavior, see the suggestions in the section "Drinking Behavior and Responsibility."

Reward Yourself and Monitor Your Progress

If changing your drinking behavior turns out to be difficult, it may be a clue that drinking is becoming a problem for you—all the more reason to get it under control now. Be sure to reward yourself as you learn to drink responsibly (or not at all). You may lose weight, look better, feel better, and have higher self-esteem as a result. Keep track of your progress in your health journal, and use the strategies described in Chapter 1 for maintaining your program. Remember, when you establish sensible drinking habits, you're planning not just for this week or month—but for your whole life.

FOR MORE INFORMATION

BOOKS

Auth, J. 2007. *Emmy's Questions.* St. Augustine, Fla.: Morningtide Press. *A young girl's experience growing up in an alcoholic household; for children age 9–12.*

Herrick, C. 2007. *100 Questions & Answers About Alcoholism & Drug Addiction.* Boston: Jones and Bartlett. *Answers a range of specific questions about alcohol abuse, dependence, and treatment options.*

Kinney, J. 2007. *Loosening the Grip: A Handbook of Alcohol Information,* 9th ed. New York: McGraw-Hill. *A fascinating book about alcohol, including information on physical effects, abuse, alcoholism, and cultural aspects of alcohol use.*

Lu, K. 2006. *Media and College Binge-Drinking: Direct and Indirect Media Influences on Drinking Norm.* Ann Arbor: ProQuest/UMI. *A quantitative review of the effect of the media on students' perceptions about drinking.*

Seaman, B. 2006. *Binge: Campus Life in an Age of Disconnection and Excess.* New York: Wiley. *An exploration of campus life at 12 residential colleges and universities, with discussions on the effects of student isolation, peer pressure, and drinking on today's students.*

Wholey, D. 2007. *Why Do I Keep Doing That?* Deerfield Beach, Fla.: Health Communications. *An optimistic approach to breaking self-destructive habits.*

Zailckas, K. 2006. *Smashed: Story of a Drunken Girlhood* (reprint ed.). New York: Penguin. *A young woman writes about her experiences of drinking through high school and college; also includes information from surveys and research into the effects of alcohol use.*

ORGANIZATIONS, HOTLINES, AND WEB SITES

Al-Anon Family Group Headquarters. Provides information and referrals to local Al-Anon and Alateen groups. The Web site includes a self-quiz to determine if you are affected by someone's drinking.

888-4AL-ANON

http://www.al-anon.alateen.org

Alcoholics Anonymous (AA) World Services. Provides general information on AA, literature on alcoholism, and information about AA meetings and related 12-step organizations.

212-870-3400

http://www.aa.org

AlcoholScreening.Org. Provides information about alcohol and health, referrals for treatment and support groups, and a drinking self-assessment.

http://www.alcoholscreening.org

Alcohol Treatment Referral Hotline. Provides referrals to local intervention and treatment providers.

800-ALCOHOL

Bacchus and Gamma Peer Education Network. An association of college- and university-based peer education programs that focus on prevention of alcohol abuse.

http://www.bacchusgamma.org

Betty Ford Center. In addition to its residential treatment program, the center offers symposia, newsletters, and programs for children of alcoholics.

800-434-7365

http://www.bettyfordcenter.org

The College Alcohol Study. Harvard School of Public Health. Provides information about and results from the recent studies of binge drinking on college campuses.

http://www.hsph.harvard.edu/cas

College Drinking Prevention. Includes information about alcohol, including myths about alcohol use and an interactive look at how alcohol affects the body.

http://www.collegedrinkingprevention.gov

Facts on Tap. Provides information about alcohol and college life, sex and alcohol, and children of alcoholics, as well as suggestions for students who have been negatively affected by other students' alcohol use.

http://www.factsontap.org

HadEnough.Org. Provides information and a self-quiz on binge drinking among college students.

http://www.hadenough.org

Higher Education Center for Alcohol and Other Drug Prevention. Provides support for campus alcohol and illegal drug prevention efforts; a Web site gives information about alcohol and drug abuse on campus and links to related sites.

http://www.edc.org/hec

Moderation Management Network. Controversial self-help program designed to help early problem drinkers limit their drinking; not intended for serious alcohol abusers or alcoholics.

http://www.moderation.org

Mothers Against Drunk Driving (MADD). Supports efforts to develop solutions to the problems of drunk driving and underage drinking; provides news, information, and brochures about many topics, including a guide for giving a safe party.

http://www.madd.org

National Association for Children of Alcoholics (NACoA). Provides information and support for children of alcoholics.

888-554-COAS

http://www.nacoa.net

National Clearinghouse for Alcohol and Drug Information/Prevention Online. Provides statistics and information on alcohol abuse, including resources for people who want to help friends and family members overcome alcohol-abuse problems.

http://ncadi.samhsa.gov

National Council on Alcoholism and Drug Dependence (NCADD). Provides information and counseling referrals.

212-269-7797; 800-NCA-CALL (24-hour Hope Line)

http://www.ncadd.org

National Institute on Alcohol Abuse and Alcoholism (NIAAA). Provides booklets and other publications on a variety of alcohol-related topics, including fetal alcohol syndrome, alcoholism treatment, and alcohol use and minorities.

http://www.niaaa.nih.gov

Rational Recovery. A free self-help program that offers an alternative to 12-step programs; the emphasis is on learning the skill of abstinence.

http://www.rational.org

See also the listings for Chapter 9.

SELECTED BIBLIOGRAPHY

Addolorato, G., et al. 2006. Baclofen: A new drug for the treatment of alcohol dependence. *International Journal of Clinical Practice* 60(8): 1003–1008.

Anton, R. F., et al. 2006. Combined pharmacotherapies and behavioral interventions for alcohol dependence: The COMBINE study: A randomized controlled trial. *Journal of the American Medical Association* 295(17): 2003–2017.

Callahan, M. 2006. Cocktail confidential. *Health,* June, 169–171.

Centers for Disease Control and Prevention. 2004. Alcohol-attributable deaths and years of potential life lost, United States, 2001. *Morbidity and Mortality Weekly Report* 53(37): 866–870.

Clifasefi, S. L., et al. 2006. Blind drunk: The effects of alcohol on inattentional blindness. *Applied Cognitive Psychology* 20(5): 697–704.

College Drinking Prevention. 2007. *A Snapshot of Annual High-Risk College DrinkingConsequences*(http://www.collegedrinkingprevention.gov/StatsSummaries/snapshot.aspx; retrieved February 4, 2009).

Collins, G. B., et al. 2006. Drug adjuncts for treating alcohol dependence. *Cleveland Clinic Journal of Medicine* 73(7): 641–644.

Costello, R. M. 2006. Long-term mortality from alcoholism: A descriptive analysis. *Journal of Studies on Alcohol* 67(5): 694–699.

Dawson, D. A., et al. 2005. Recovery from DSM-IV alcohol dependence: United States, 2001–2002. *Addiction* 100(3): 281–292.

Department of Health and Human Services. 2007. *The Surgeon General's Call to Action to Prevent and Reduce Underage Drinking.* Washington, D.C.: Department of Health and Human Services, Office of the Surgeon General.

Gruenewald, P. J., and L. Remer. 2006. Changes in outlet densities affect violence rates. *Alcoholism: Clinical and Experimental Research* 30(7): 1184–1193.

Heilig, M., and M. Egli. 2006. Pharmacological treatment of alcohol dependence: Target symptoms and target mechanisms. *Pharmacology and Therapeutics* 111(3): 855–876.

Hingson, R., et al. 2005. Magnitude of alcohol-related mortality and morbidity among U.S. college students ages 18–24. *Annual Review of Public Health* 26: 259–279.

Hingson, R. W., et al. 2006. Age at drinking onset and alcohol dependence: Age at onset, duration, and severity. *Archives of Pediatrics and Adolescent Medicine* 160(7): 739–746.

Krampe, H., et al. 2006. Follow-up of 180 alcoholic patients for up to 7 years after outpatient treatment: Impact of alcohol deterrents on outcome. *Alcohol: Clinical and Experimental Research* 30(1): 86–95.

Mayo Clinic. 2006. Pain relievers and alcohol: A potentially risky combination. *Mayo Clinic Health Letter,* May.

McCaig, L. F., and E. N. Nawar. 2006. National Hospital Ambulatory Medical Care Survey: 2004 emergency department summary. *Advance Data from Vital and Health Statistics* No. 372. Hyattsville, Md.: National Center for Health Statistics.

Miller, T. R., et al. 2006. Societal costs of underage drinking. *Journal of Studies on Alcohol* 67(4): 519–528.

Monti, P. M., et al. 2005. Adolescence: Booze, brains, and behavior. *Alcoholism: Clinical and Experimental Research* 29(2): 207–220.

National Center for Health Statistics. 2008. Deaths: Preliminary data for 2006. *National Vital Statistics Reports* 56(16).

National Institute on Alcohol Abuse and Alcoholism. 2006. *Young Adult Drinking.* Alcohol Alert No. 68. Bethesda, Md.: National Institute on Alcohol Abuse and Alcoholism.

Nelson, T. F., et al. 2005. The state sets the rate: The relationship of college binge drinking rates and selected state alcohol control policies. *American Journal of Public Health* 95(3): 441–446.

Office of Applied Studies, Substance Abuse and Mental Health Services Administration. 2008. *Results from the 2007 National Survey on Drug Use and Health: National Findings* (http://www.drugabusestatistics.samhsa.gov; retrieved February 4, 2009).

Perreira, K. M., and K. E. Cortes. 2006. Explaining Race/Ethnicity and Nativity Differences in Alcohol and Tobacco Use During Pregnancy. *American Journal of Public Health,* 27 July [epub].

Slutska, W. S. 2005. Alcohol use disorders among US college students and their non-college-attending peers. *Archives of General Psychiatry* 62(3): 321–327.

Willford, J., et al. 2006. Moderate prenatal alcohol exposure and cognitive status of children at age 10. *Alcoholism: Clinical and Experimental Research* 30(6): 1051–1059.

TOWARD A TOBACCO-FREE SOCIETY

11

LOOKING AHEAD>>>>>

AFTER READING THIS CHAPTER, YOU SHOULD BE ABLE TO:

- List the reasons people start using tobacco and why they continue to use it
- Explain the short- and long-term health risks associated with tobacco use
- Discuss the effects of environmental tobacco smoke on nonsmokers
- Describe the social costs of tobacco, and list actions that have been taken to combat smoking in the public and private sectors
- Prepare plans to stop using tobacco and to avoid environmental tobacco smoke

TEST YOUR KNOWLEDGE

1. **"Light" or low-tar cigarettes are safer than regular cigarettes.**
   True or false?

2. **Which of the following substances is found in tobacco smoke?**
   a. acetone (nail polish remover)
   b. ammonia (cleaner)
   c. hexamine (lighter fluid)
   d. toluene (industrial solvent)

3. **Every day in the United States, about 1000 teens start smoking.**
   True or false?

4. **Cigarette smoking increases the risk for which of the following conditions?**
   a. facial wrinkling
   b. miscarriage
   c. impotence

5. **A person who quits smoking now will reduce his or her risk of lung cancer within 10 years.**
   True or false?

ANSWERS

1. **FALSE.** Smokers who choose "light" or low-tar cigarettes do not reduce tar intake or smoking-related disease risks, nor is there any evidence that switching to "light" cigarettes helps smokers quit.

2. **ALL FOUR.** Tobacco contains thousands of chemical substances, including many that are poisonous or linked to the development of cancer.

3. **TRUE.** Roughly 1300 teenagers start smoking every day in the United States.

4. **ALL THREE.** Cigarette smoking reduces the quality of life and is the leading preventable cause of death in the United States.

5. **TRUE.** The lung cancer rate of a former smoker is 50% of that of a continuing smoker within 10 years of quitting.

S moking is the leading cause of preventable death in the United States. Each year, in fact, nearly 440,000 Americans die prematurely from tobacco-related causes (Figure 11.1). Tobacco use accounts for nearly one of every five adult deaths.

Smoking affects the health of people at all stages of life and from all walks of life. On average, a male smoker loses about 13 years from his life; a female smoker loses nearly 15 years. Nonsmokers also suffer, especially the children of parents who smoke. Exposure to environmental tobacco smoke (ETS) kills thousands of nonsmokers every year.

In spite of these facts—and despite increasing public and private efforts to restrict smoking—nearly 71 million Americans are smokers, with thousands more joining their ranks every day. This chapter discusses the reasons people use tobacco, the negative impact of smoking, and the measures being taken to stop this public health threat.

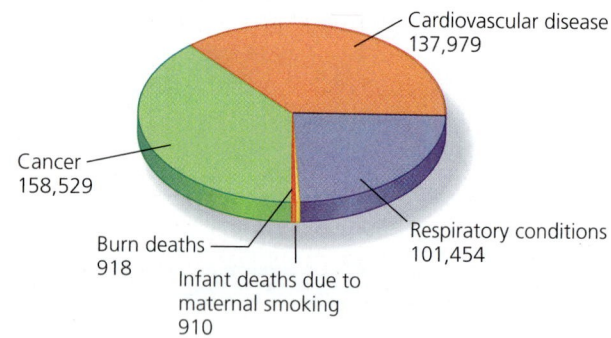

(a) Mortality: Deaths per year due to smoking

Cardiovascular disease 137,979

Cancer 158,529

Burn deaths 918

Infant deaths due to maternal smoking 910

Respiratory conditions 101,454

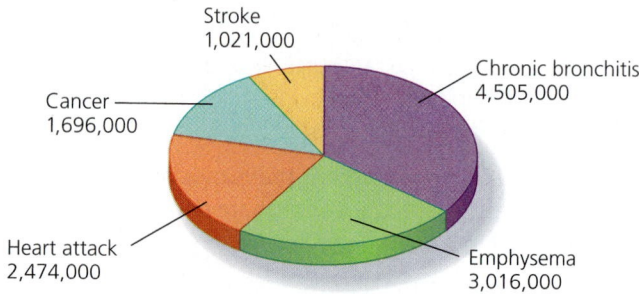

(b) Morbidity: Number of people with chronic illnesses due to smoking

Stroke 1,021,000

Chronic bronchitis 4,505,000

Cancer 1,696,000

Heart attack 2,474,000

Emphysema 3,016,000

VITAL STATISTICS

FIGURE 11.1 Annual mortality and morbidity among smokers attributable to smoking.

SOURCES: Centers for Disease Control and Prevention. 2003. Cigarette smoking attributable morbidity—United States, 2000. *Morbidity and Mortality Weekly Report* 52(35): 842–844; Centers for Disease Control and Prevention. 2005. Annual smoking-attributable mortality, years of potential life lost, and productivity losses—United States, 1997–2001. *Morbidity and Mortality Weekly Report* 54(25): 625–628.

WHO USES TOBACCO?

According to the 2007 National Survey on Drug Use and Health, nearly 71 million Americans, including nearly 13.7 million college-age Americans, reported using a tobacco product at least once in the preceding month. Based on early results from the 2008 National Health Interview Survey, nearly 21% of Americans age 18 and older described themselves as current smokers, meaning they smoke cigarettes every day or most days.

Smoking rates reported in such surveys are essentially unchanged from those reported in 2004, suggesting that a decades-long decline in smoking prevalence has stalled. Until 2004, smoking rates had dropped steadily from a high of roughly 42% in 1964, when a report from the U.S. Surgeon General linked smoking and lung cancer.

In 2006, nearly 24% of men and 18% of women smoked cigarettes (Table 11.1). Rates of smoking varied, based on gender, age, ethnicity, and education level (see the box "Smoking Among U.S. Ethnic Populations"). Adults with less than a twelfth-grade education were much more likely to smoke cigarettes than those with a college degree. The reverse is true for cigars; cigar smoking is most common among the affluent and those with high educational attainment.

For more than a decade, there has been a gradual increase in the number of "occasional smokers" (people who smoke on some days but not daily). Most such smokers are young adults age 18–25 who say they smoke only

Table 11.1	Who Smokes?		
	Percentage of Smokers		
	Men	**Women**	**Total**
Ethnic Group (age ≥ 18)			
White	24.3	19.7	21.9
Black	27.6	19.2	23.0
Asian	16.8	4.6	10.4
American Indian/ Alaskan Native	35.6	29.0	32.4
Latino	20.1	10.1	15.2
Education (age ≥ 25)			
≤ 8 years	22.3	12.3	17.4
9–11 years	40.1	36.4	35.4
12 years (no diploma)	27.9	23.3	25.6
GED	51.3	40.2	46.0
12 years (diploma)	27.6	20.4	23.8
Associate degree	25.4	17.8	21.2
Undergraduate degree	10.8	8.4	9.6
Graduate degree	7.3	5.8	6.6
Total	**23.9**	**18.0**	**20.8**

SOURCE: Centers for Disease Control and Prevention. 2007. Cigarette smoking among adults—United States, 2006. *Morbidity and Mortality Weekly Report* 56(44): 1157–1161.

Smoking Among U.S. Ethnic Populations   connect™

The overall rate of tobacco use among Americans age 12 and older was 28.6% in 2007. That means on average that any group of a dozen people is likely to include three or four who use tobacco. But averages include wide variations among populations, and ethnic differences appear in the earliest stages of tobacco use.

About 20% of all U.S. high school students described themselves as "current cigarette users" in 2007. African American students (11.6%) were less likely than either whites (23.2%) or Latinos (16.2%) to smoke in high school. Similarly, far more white students (10.4%) described themselves as "frequent" smokers than did Latinos (4.2%) or blacks (3.9%).

Use of smokeless tobacco shows an even greater disparity. White high school students are nearly ten times more likely to use spit tobacco than are African American students, and about two times more likely than Latino students. White students (14.8%) smoke cigars only slightly more often than Latino students (12.7%) or black students (10%).

Wide ethnic variations also exist among smokers over 18 years old. Almost 33% of American Indian and Alaska Native adults are smokers. Only 10% of Asian American adults smoke, about half the rate for the general population.

Within broad ethnic categories, even greater variation occurs. Among people grouped under the broad category Latinos, 30% of Puerto Ricans but only 19% of Central or South Americans are smokers. There are higher smoking rates among population groups who trace their origins to Southeast Asia (for example, Vietnam, Cambodia, or Laos) than among other population groups within the general Asian American grouping (for example, people from the

Philippines, China, or Japan). Time in the United States, English proficiency, and level of educational attainment also influence smoking rates.

In populations of Asian and Pacific Islander Americans, rates of smoking are much higher among men than among women, regardless of country of origin. Although smoking among women decreases with age in the general population, smoking rates among Asian and Pacific Islander women increase with age. Asian and Pacific Islander Americans, male and female, who smoke tend to smoke fewer cigarettes per day (a half a pack daily or less) than whites who smoke.

The variations between and within ethnic populations reflect a complex interplay of social, environmental, and cultural factors. For example, in some Latino populations, strong parental disapproval of smoking, particularly for girls, holds

down the rate of smoking initiation. For other groups, smoking may have a mature and masculine aura, thereby promoting smoking. In some populations, socioeconomic factors may limit access to stop-smoking programs; prevention programs may also not be available to non–English speaking groups.

Tobacco companies understand the value of marketing strategies based on ethnic, cultural, age, and other differences. In 2004, a New York Supreme Court justice ruled that Brown & Williamson Tobacco Company was illegally appealing to young people with its "Kool MIXX" marketing campaign, which focused on hip-hop music and culture. R. J. Reynolds Tobacco Company (RJRT) extensively marketed its "Exotic Blends"—fruit- and spice-flavored, premium-priced, and imaginatively packaged versions of Camel cigarettes—to minority communities and to women. To increase Camel cigarette sales in the gay and lesbian community, RJRT developed a marketing plan designated Project Sub Culture Urban Marketing, or "Project SCUM." The campaign identified gays, "rebellious generation X," and street people as markets where "opportunity exists for a cigarette manufacturer to dominate."

SOURCES: Office of Applied Studies, Substance Abuse and Mental Health Services Administration. 2008. *Results from the 2007 National Survey on Drug Use and Health: National Findings* (http://www.drugabusestatistics.samhsa.gov; retrieved February 6, 2009); Centers for Disease Control and Prevention. 2004. Prevalence of cigarette use among 14 racial/ethnic populations—United States, 1990–2001. *Morbidity and Mortality Weekly Report* 53(3): 49–52; Centers for Disease Control and Prevention. 2008. Youth Risk Behavior Surveillance—United States, 2007. *Morbidity and Mortality Weekly Report* 57(SS-4): 1–131.

at parties or when they are with friends who smoke. Health officials warn that occasional smokers are as vulnerable as other smokers to the health dangers of tobacco. Occasional smokers are also less likely to try to quit.

Most current smokers, however, seem to understand the risks of tobacco use. For example, more than 80% of adult smokers believe tobacco will shorten their life and would like to stop smoking. Each year, about 40% of smokers quit for at least a day, but nine out of ten of them resume smoking within a year.

Young People and Tobacco

Although all states ban the sale of tobacco to anyone under 18 years of age, at least 500 million packs of cigarettes and 26 million containers of chewing tobacco are consumed by minors each year.

Each day, roughly 1300 teenagers become regular smokers; at least one-third of them will die prematurely because of tobacco. In 2007, about 3.5% of 13-year-old Americans said they had used tobacco products in the last month.

QUESTIONS FOR CRITICAL THINKING AND REFLECTION
Do any of your friends or family members smoke or use smokeless tobacco? What effect has it had on their health and relationships? Have you ever discussed their tobacco use with them? Why or why not?

Among high school students, about 20% smoke cigarettes at least occasionally and 14% smoke cigars. An estimated 8%, including 10% of white male students, use spit tobacco. Male college athletes and professional baseball players report even higher rates of spit tobacco use. (The various types of tobacco products are described in detail later in this chapter.)

Tobacco and Other Drugs

Men and women with other drug-abuse problems frequently use tobacco. For example, studies show that roughly 80% of alcoholics and more than 90% of heroin addicts are heavy smokers.

Smoking also is more prevalent among people with mental disorders than among the rest of the population: 40% of people with major depression, social phobias, and generalized anxiety disorder are smokers, as are 80% of people with schizophrenia. Such findings suggest that underlying psychological or physiological traits may predispose people to drug use, including tobacco.

WHY PEOPLE USE TOBACCO

Although people start smoking for a variety of reasons, they usually become long-term smokers after becoming addicted to nicotine—the key psychoactive ingredient in tobacco smoke.

Nicotine Addiction

The primary reason people continue to use **tobacco** is that they have become addicted to a powerful psychoactive drug: **nicotine.** Although the tobacco industry long maintained that nicotine had not been proved to be addictive, scientific evidence overwhelmingly shows that nicotine is highly addictive. Many researchers consider nicotine to be the most physically addictive of all the psychoactive drugs.

Some neurological studies indicate that nicotine acts on the brain in much the same way as cocaine and heroin. Nicotine reaches the brain via the bloodstream seconds after it is inhaled or, in the case of spit tobacco, absorbed through membranes of the mouth or nose. It triggers the release of powerful chemical messengers in the brain, in-cluding epinephrine, norepinephrine, and dopamine. But unlike street drugs, most of which are used to achieve a high, nicotine's primary attraction seems to lie in its ability to modulate everyday emotions.

At low doses, nicotine acts as a stimulant. It increases heart rate and blood pressure. In adults, nicotine can enhance alertness, concentration, rapid information processing, memory, and learning. The opposite effect occurs in teens who smoke, however; they show impairment in memory and other cognitive functions.

In some circumstances, nicotine acts as a mild sedative. Most commonly, nicotine relieves symptoms such as anxiety, irritability, and mild depression in tobacco users who are experiencing withdrawal. Some studies have shown that high doses of nicotine and rapid smoking cause increases in levels of glucocorticoids and endorphins, chemicals that act in the brain to moderate moods and reduce stress. Tobacco users are able to fine-tune nicotine's effects and regulate their moods by increasing or decreasing their intake of the drug. Studies have shown that smokers experience milder mood variation than nonsmokers while performing long, boring tasks or while watching emotional movies, for example.

All tobacco products contain nicotine, and the use of any of them can lead to addiction (see the box "Nicotine Dependence: Are You Hooked?"). Nicotine addiction fulfills the criteria for substance dependence described in Chapter 9, including loss of control, tolerance, and withdrawal.

Loss of Control   Three out of four smokers want to quit but find they cannot. Although 60–80% of people who attend stop-smoking clinics are able to quit, three-quarters of them start smoking again within a year—a relapse rate similar to rates for alcoholics and heroin addicts. Quitting may be even harder for smokeless users: In one study, only 1 of 14 spit tobacco users who participated in a tobacco-cessation clinic was able to stop for more than 4 hours.

Regular tobacco users live according to a rigid cycle of need and gratification. On average, they can go no more than 40 minutes between doses of nicotine; otherwise, they begin feeling edgy and irritable and have trouble concentrating. If ignored, nicotine cravings build until getting tobacco becomes a paramount concern, crowding out other thoughts. Tobacco users may plan their daily

Nicotine Dependence: Are You Hooked?

Answer each question in the list below, giving yourself the appropriate number of points.

_____ 1. How soon after you wake up do you have your first cigarette?
   a. within 5 minutes (3)
   b. 6–30 minutes (2)
   c. 31–60 minutes (1)
   d. after 60 minutes (0)

_____ 2. Do you find it difficult to refrain from smoking in places where it is forbidden, such as the library, a theater, or a doctor's office?
   a. yes (1)
   b. no (0)

_____ 3. Which cigarette would you most hate to give up?
   a. the first one in the morning (1)
   b. any other (0)

_____ 4. How many cigarettes a day do you smoke?
   a. 10 or less (0)
   b. 11–20 (1)
   c. 21–30 (2)
   d. 31 or more (3)

_____ 5. Do you smoke more frequently during the first hours after waking than during the rest of the day?
   a. yes (1)
   b. no (0)

_____ 6. Do you smoke if you are so ill that you are in bed most of the day?
   a. yes (1)
   b. no (0)

_____ TOTAL

A total score of 7 or more indicates that you are very dependent on nicotine and are likely to experience withdrawal symptoms when you stop smoking. A score of 6 or less indicates low to moderate dependence.

SOURCE: Heatherton, T. F., et al. 1991. The Fagerstrom Test for Nicotine Dependence: A revision of the Fagerstrom Tolerance Questionnaire. *British Journal of Addictions* 86(9): 1119–1127.

schedule around opportunities to satisfy their nicotine cravings; this loss of control and personal freedom can affect all the dimensions of wellness (see the box "Tobacco Use and Religion: Global Views" on p. 304).

Tobacco users become adept, therefore, at keeping a steady amount of nicotine circulating in the blood and going to the brain. In one experiment, smokers were given cigarettes that looked and tasted alike but varied in nicotine content. The subjects automatically adjusted their rate and depth of inhalation so that they absorbed their usual amount of nicotine. In other studies, heavy smokers were given nicotine without knowing it, and they cut down on their smoking without a conscious effort. Spit tobacco users maintain blood nicotine levels as high as those of cigarette smokers.

Tolerance and Withdrawal Using tobacco builds up tolerance. Where one cigarette may make a beginning smoker nauseated and dizzy, a long-term smoker may have to chain-smoke a pack or more to experience the same effects. For most regular tobacco users, sudden abstinence from nicotine produces predictable withdrawal symptoms as well. These symptoms, which come on several hours after the last dose of nicotine, can include severe cravings, insomnia, confusion, tremors, difficulty concentrating, fatigue, muscle pains, headache, nausea, irritability, anger, and depression. Users undergo measurable changes in brain waves, heart rate, and blood pressure, and they perform poorly on tasks requiring sustained attention. Although most of these symptoms of physical dependence pass in 2 or 3 days, the craving associated with addiction

persists. Many ex-smokers report intermittent, intense urges to smoke for years after quitting.

Social and Psychological Factors

Why do tobacco users have such a hard time quitting even when they want to? Social and psychological forces combine with physiological addiction to maintain the tobacco habit. Many people, for example, have established habits of smoking while doing something else—while talking, working, drinking, and so on. The spit tobacco habit is also associated with certain situations—studying, drinking coffee, or playing sports. It is difficult for these people to break their habits because the activities they associate with tobacco use continue to trigger their urge. Such activities are called **secondary reinforcers;** they act together with the physiological addiction to keep the user dependent on tobacco.

Genetic Factors

Inherited characteristics play an important role in some aspects of tobacco use. Genetic factors may be more important than social and environmental factors in smoking initiation and in the development of nicotine dependence.

For example, a gene that influences the way in which nicotine is metabolized, or broken down in the body, helps regulate the activity of an enzyme called CYP2A6. When people with slow CYP2A6 metabolism use tobacco, the nicotine remains in their blood longer than in people

Tobacco Use and Religion: Global Views

Religious traditions can best assist adult smokers by reminding them of two principles: one, the value of liberation from any form of slavery, and two, respect for life out of deference to their god.

Tobacco Use as a Violation of Religious Principles

All religions condemn tobacco use for its damaging effects on the body. Most religions regard the human body as the dwelling place of the spirit; as such, it deserves care and respect.

The Baha'i faith, for example, strongly discourages smoking as unclean and unhealthy. Some Protestant churches consider tobacco use a violation of the body. For Hindus, smoking goes against one of the primary spiritual practices, the care of the body. The Roman Catholic Church endorses the age-old adage "a sound mind in a sound body." For Muslims, one of the five essential principles on which religious law is based is protection of the integrity of the individual. In Judaism, people are urged to "choose life" and to choose whatever strengthens the capacity to live. Buddhists believe that the body doesn't belong to the person at all—even suicide is considered murder—and one must do nothing to harm it.

Most religions also contend that dependence and addiction run counter to ideas of freedom, choice, and human dignity. Buddhism teaches a path of freedom—a way of life without dependence on anything. Hindus regard tobacco use as a dependence that is not necessary for the preservation of health. Protestant churches caution that any form of dependence is contrary to the notion of Christian freedom.

Another argument against tobacco use is the immorality of imposing secondhand smoke on nonsmokers, which is seen as inflicting harm on others. In Hinduism, harming others is sinful. In the Jewish tradition, those who force nonsmokers to breathe smoke jeopardize the lives of others, and to do so is to jeopardize the whole universe.

The Role of Individual Responsibility

Most religions focus on the role of individual responsibility in overcoming dependence on tobacco. In Buddhism, for example, people must assume responsibility for their habits; they practice introspection to understand the cause of problems within themselves and the effects of their actions on others. The principles of Islam are based on notions of responsibility and protection; you are responsible for your body and health.

Religion and Tobacco Control

Different religions share common views on how the problem of tobacco use should be approached. The Islamic view is that the campaign to control tobacco use must be based on awareness, responsibility, and justice. Developing aware-

ness means providing information on the global problem. Fostering responsibility means helping people understand what they need to do to attain well-being. Emphasizing social and human justice means helping the farmers and societies that depend on tobacco cultivation to find alternative crops.

According to the Geneva Interreligious Platform (a project involving Hindus, Buddhists, Jews, Christians, Muslims, and Baha'is), the best approach is prevention. Here, the rights of nonsmokers clearly prevail over the freedom of smokers. In support of this position, the common religious exhortation not to do unto others what you would not have them do unto you can be invoked. Further, adequate information should be provided to counter the deceptive images projected by tobacco industry advertising, especially where minors are concerned. Protection of the weak and denunciation of dishonesty are underlying values of all religious traditions.

---

who have the gene for a faster metabolizing form of the enzyme. The slow metabolizers are more likely to feel nausea or dizziness when they first use tobacco, are less likely to continue smoking if they try it, and find it easier to quit if they do become regular smokers.

Scientists have also shown that a gene called *DRD2* (associated with the brain chemical dopamine, which plays a key role in the pleasurable effects of nicotine) appears to influence the progression of smoking in adolescence. Among tenth graders who took one puff of a cigarette, those with one form of the gene were more than three times as likely as those with the other form to be regular smokers when they finished the eleventh grade.

Why Start in the First Place?

Children and teenagers constitute 90% of all new smokers in this country. Every day, 1300 teenagers and many younger children start smoking, while hundreds of others take up snuff or chewing tobacco. The average age for starting smokers is 13; for spit tobacco users, 10. Meanwhile, children—especially girls—are beginning to experiment with tobacco at ever-younger ages. The earlier people begin smoking, the more likely they are to

Most adult smokers began as teenagers.

become heavy smokers—and to die of tobacco-related disease.

Not all young people are equally vulnerable to the lure of tobacco. Research suggests that the more of the following characteristics that apply to a child or adolescent, the more likely he or she is to use tobacco:

- A parent or sibling uses tobacco.
- Peers use tobacco.
- The child comes from a blue-collar family.
- The child comes from a low-income home.
- The family is headed by a single parent.
- The child performs poorly in school.
- The child drops out of school.
- The child has positive attitudes about tobacco use.

Young people start using tobacco for a variety of reasons. Many young, white, male athletes, for example, begin using spit tobacco to emulate their favorite professional athletes. Young women commonly take up smoking because they think it will help them lose weight or stay thin. Most often, however, young people start smoking simply because their peers are already doing it; smoking gives them a way to fit in with a crowd or to look cool.

Rationalizing the Dangers Making the decision to smoke requires minimizing or denying both the health risks of tobacco use and the tremendous pain, disability, emotional trauma, family stress, and financial expense involved in tobacco-related diseases such as cancer and emphysema. A sense of invincibility, characteristic of many adolescents and young adults, also contributes to the decision to use tobacco. Young people may persuade themselves they are too intelligent, too lucky, or too healthy to be vulnerable to tobacco's dangers. "I'm not dumb enough to get hooked," they may argue. "I'll be able to quit before I do myself any real harm."

Many teenagers believe they will be able to stop smoking when they want. In fact, adolescents are more vulnerable to nicotine than are older tobacco users. Compared with older smokers, adolescents become heavy smokers and develop dependence after fewer cigarettes. Nicotine addiction can start within a few days of smoking and after just a few cigarettes. Over half of teenagers who try cigarettes progress to daily use, and about half of those who ever smoke daily progress to nicotine dependence. In polls, about 75% of smoking teens state they wish they had never started. Another survey revealed that only 5% of high school smokers predicted they would definitely be smoking in 5 years; in fact, close to 75% were smoking 7–9 years later.

Emulating Smoking in the Media Researchers have found that smoking in movies has increased significantly since 1990, to levels not seen since 1960. Between 1998 and 2000, smoking in PG-13 movies increased by 50%. Half the tobacco shots in the top movies from 2002 to 2003 were in G, PG, and PG-13 movies.

The portrayal of smoking in films does not reflect U.S. patterns of tobacco use. The prevalence of smoking among lead characters is three to four times that among comparable Americans. Films typically show the smoker as white, male, well educated, successful, and attractive. In reality, smokers tend to be poor and to have less education. In the top-grossing films in 2002–2003, smoking was portrayed in more than 73% of the films, including 82% of PG-13 films; smoking was often shown positively as a means to relieve tension or as something to do while socializing. Negative consequences resulting from tobacco use were depicted for only 3% of the major characters who used tobacco. By showing smoking in an unrealistically positive light, films may be acting as advertisement (see the box "Tobacco Advertising" on p. 307).

Does smoking on-screen affect real-life smoking habits? Studies of

13.4% of Kentucky's high school students are frequent smokers—the highest rate of any state.

—CDC, 2008

Although tobacco advertising has been severely restricted, smoking is still commonly portrayed in movies. In the 2007 movie *Atonement*, set in the 1940s, Keira Knightley is seldom without a cigarette.

adolescents have consistently found a strong association between seeing tobacco use in films and trying cigarettes. Adolescents who see more smoking in films or whose favorite movie stars frequently use tobacco on-screen have more positive attitudes about smoking and are as much as three times more likely to have tried smoking than teens with less exposure to films. Teens may be particularly sensitive to on-screen portrayals of smoking because they are in the process of developing adult identities; during this period, they may try out different personas, including those of their favorite movie stars.

Some groups suggest an automatic R rating for any film that shows tobacco use, equating smoking with violence, strong language, sexuality, and nudity in determining a film's rating.

QUESTIONS FOR CRITICAL THINKING AND REFLECTION

What has influenced your decision to smoke, not to smoke, or to quit smoking? Have you ever felt that images or messages in the media were encouraging you to use tobacco? How do you react to such messages?

HEALTH HAZARDS

Tobacco adversely affects nearly every part of the body, including the brain, stomach, mouth, and reproductive organs.

Tobacco Smoke: A Toxic Mix

Tobacco smoke contains hundreds of damaging chemical substances, including acetone (nail polish remover), ammonia, hexamine (lighter fluid), and toluene (industrial solvent). Smoke from a typical unfiltered cigarette contains about 5 billion particles per cubic millimeter—50,000 times as many as are found in an equal volume of smoggy urban air. These particles, when condensed, form a brown, sticky mass called **cigarette tar.**

Carcinogens and Poisons   At least 43 chemicals in tobacco smoke are linked to the development of cancer. Some, such as benzo(a)pyrene and urethane, are **carcinogens;** that is, they directly cause cancer. Other chemicals, such as formaldehyde, are **cocarcinogens;** they do not themselves cause cancer but combine with other chemicals to stimulate the growth of certain cancers, at least in laboratory animals. Other substances in tobacco cause health problems because they damage the lining of the respiratory tract or decrease the lungs' ability to fight off infection.

Tobacco also contains poisonous substances, including arsenic and hydrogen cyanide. In addition to being an addictive psychoactive drug, nicotine is also a poison and can be fatal in high doses. Many cases of nicotine poisoning occur each year in toddlers and infants who pick up and eat cigarette butts they find at home or on the playground.

Cigarette smoke contains carbon monoxide, the deadly gas in automobile exhaust, in concentrations 400 times greater than is considered safe in industrial workplaces. Not surprisingly, smokers often complain of breathlessness when they require a burst of energy to climb stairs or lift something. Carbon monoxide displaces oxygen in red blood cells, depleting the body's supply of oxygen needed for extra work. Carbon monoxide also impairs visual acuity, especially at night.

Additives   Tobacco manufacturers use additives to manipulate the taste and effect of cigarettes and other tobacco products. Additives account for roughly 10%, by weight, of a cigarette, and include sugars and other flavoring agents, humectants (compounds that keep tobacco from drying out), and chemicals that enhance the addicting properties of nicotine.

Added sugars—including licorice, cocoa, and honey—have a dual role. As flavor enhancers, sugars mask the harsh, bitter taste of tobacco, so smokers can inhale more smoke and absorb more nicotine. When sugars burn,

CRITICAL CONSUMER

Tobacco Advertising

Advertising is a powerful influence. In 2003, the tobacco industry spent more than $15 billion on advertising that portrayed users as confident, popular, fit, and sexually attractive. That same year, Americans smoked 400 billion cigarettes.

Youth Appeal

Young people are a prime target of tobacco ads because nicotine addiction can lead to a lifetime of purchasing tobacco. The tobacco industry also understands that young smokers are most likely to buy familiar brands. The most heavily advertised cigarettes are the choice of 90% of teen smokers. In the 1980s and 1990s, for example, R.J. Reynolds Tobacco Company's promotion of the Camel brand recruited millions of new smokers. In surveys, more than 90% of 6-year-olds recognized the Camel character ("Joe Camel"), who became as familiar to children as Mickey Mouse.

Cigarette ads don't target only children. Certain brands are designed to appeal primarily either to men or women, or to a specific ethnic group. Magazines that target African American audiences, for example, receive proportionately more revenues from cigarette ads than do other consumer magazines. Billboards advertising tobacco products are placed in black communities four or five times more often than in primarily white communities.

Limits on Ads

The federal government began regulating tobacco advertising in 1967, requiring broadcasters to air anti-smoking messages along with cigarette advertisements. Within a few years, cigarette consumption dropped by 7%. Broadcast ads for cigarettes were banned in 1971.

In 1998, controls on tobacco advertising were enacted as part of a deal to settle lawsuits brought against the tobacco industry by the attorneys general of 39 states. This settlement limits or bans the following types of marketing tools:

- Billboard and transit ads for tobacco products

- The use of cartoon characters in ads and on packaging

- Tobacco logos on T-shirts, hats, and other promotional items

- Brand-name sponsorship of sporting events

- Product placement in movies, television shows, and concerts

Regardless, the tobacco industry continues to spend billions of dollars annually to promote its product. Much of this money is spent on print ads and coupons, but a great deal is also given to retailers to help offset ever-increasing taxes levied on tobacco products by states.

The industry's promotional efforts are most apparent in neighborhood convenience stores, where tobacco products and promotions are prominently placed at checkout counters. In this carefully engineered setting, tobacco products are presented as a colorful and commonplace part of the neighborhood retail environment—as acceptable as a candy bar or a jug of milk.

---

they produce acetaldehyde, a chemical that enhances the addictive effect of nicotine and is a carcinogen.

Other flavor components, such as theobromine and glycyrrhizin, act as bronchodilators, opening the lungs' airways and making it easier for nicotine to get into the bloodstream.

Ammonia plays a complex role in tobacco products, but its chief purpose is to boost the amount of addictive nicotine delivered by cigarettes. Ammonia reduces the acidity of tobacco smoke and releases nicotine in the form of a base (alkaline) rather than a salt (acid) bound to other acid components of smoke. As a free base, nicotine is more readily absorbed into the blood.

Some additives are intended to make **sidestream smoke** (the uninhaled smoke from a burning cigarette) less obvious and objectionable. For example, potassium citrate, aluminum, and clay are added to cigarette wrappers to convert particulate ash into an invisible gas with less irritating odor than would be given off by a conventional paper wrapper. These additives serve no purpose in making cigarettes more desirable and addicting to the smoker; instead, they are intended to reduce social pressures from nonsmokers.

Nearly 600 chemicals, approved as safe when used as food additives, are used in manufacturing cigarettes. In 1994, U.S. cigarette manufacturers submitted a list of tobacco additives to the Department of Health and Human Services, which made the list public and accompanied it

QUICK STATS

Nicotine levels increased **more than 1%** per year in major cigarette brands from 1998 to 2005.

—Harvard School of Public Health, 2007

TERMS

cigarette tar   A brown, sticky mass created when the chemical particles in tobacco smoke condense.

carcinogen   Any substance that causes cancer.

cocarcinogen   A substance that works with a carcinogen to cause cancer.

sidestream smoke   The uninhaled smoke from a burning cigarette.

Cigarette making is an elaborate process involving industrial machinery and chemistry. Dozens of compounds may be added to tobacco to produce a specific brand of cigarette.

The Results of Inhaling Tobacco Smoke All smokers absorb some gases, tar, and nicotine from cigarette smoke, but smokers who inhale bring most of these substances into their bodies and keep them there. In 1 year, a typical pack-a-day smoker takes in 50,000–70,000 puffs. Smoke from a cigarette, pipe, or cigar directly assaults the mouth, throat, and respiratory tract. The nose, which normally filters about 75% of foreign matter we breathe, is completely bypassed.

In a cigarette, the unburned tobacco itself acts as a filter. As a cigarette burns down, there is less and less filter. Thus, more chemicals are absorbed into the body during the last third of a cigarette than during the first. A smoker can cut down on the absorption of harmful chemicals by with the notice that "although these ingredients are regarded as safe when ingested in foods, some may form carcinogens when heated or burned."

not smoking cigarettes down to short butts. Any gains, of course, will be offset by smoking more cigarettes, inhaling more deeply, or puffing more frequently.

"Light" and Low-Tar Cigarettes Some smokers switch to low-tar, low-nicotine, or filtered cigarettes because they believe them to be healthier alternatives. But there is no such thing as a safe cigarette, and smoking behavior is a more important factor in tar and nicotine intake than the type of cigarette smoked. Smokers who switch to a low-nicotine brand often compensate by smoking more cigarettes, inhaling more deeply, taking larger or more frequent puffs, or blocking ventilation holes with lips or fingers to offset the effects of filters.

Studies have found that people who smoke "light" cigarettes inhale up to eight times as much tar and nicotine as printed on the label. Studies also show that smokers of light cigarettes are less likely to quit than smokers of regular cigarettes, probably due to the misperception that light cigarettes are safer. Use of "light" and low-tar cigarettes does not reduce the risk of smoking-related illnesses.

Menthol Cigarettes Concerns have also been raised about menthol cigarettes. Menthol is a bronchodilator; as mentioned earlier, bronchodilators open the lungs' airways and make it easier for nicotine to enter the bloodstream. About 70% of African American smokers smoke these cigarettes, as compared to 30% of whites. Studies have found that blacks absorb more nicotine than other groups and metabolize it more slowly; they also have lower rates of successful quitting. The anesthetizing effect of menthol, which may allow smokers to inhale more deeply and hold smoke in their lungs for a longer period, may be partly responsible for these differences. Research is needed to determine if effects of menthol and differences in smoking behavior can help explain the higher rates of smoking-related diseases seen among blacks.

The Immediate Effects of Smoking

The beginning smoker often has symptoms of mild nicotine poisoning: dizziness; faintness; rapid pulse; cold, clammy skin; and sometimes nausea, vomiting, and diar-

cerebral cortex The outer layer of the brain, which controls complex behavior and mental activity.

coronary heart disease (CHD) Cardiovascular disease caused by hardening of the arteries that supply oxygen to the heart muscle; also called *coronary artery disease*.

atherosclerosis Cardiovascular disease caused by the deposit of fatty substances (called *plaque*) in the walls of the arteries.

plaque A deposit on the inner wall of blood vessels; blood can coagulate around plaque and form a clot.

TERMS

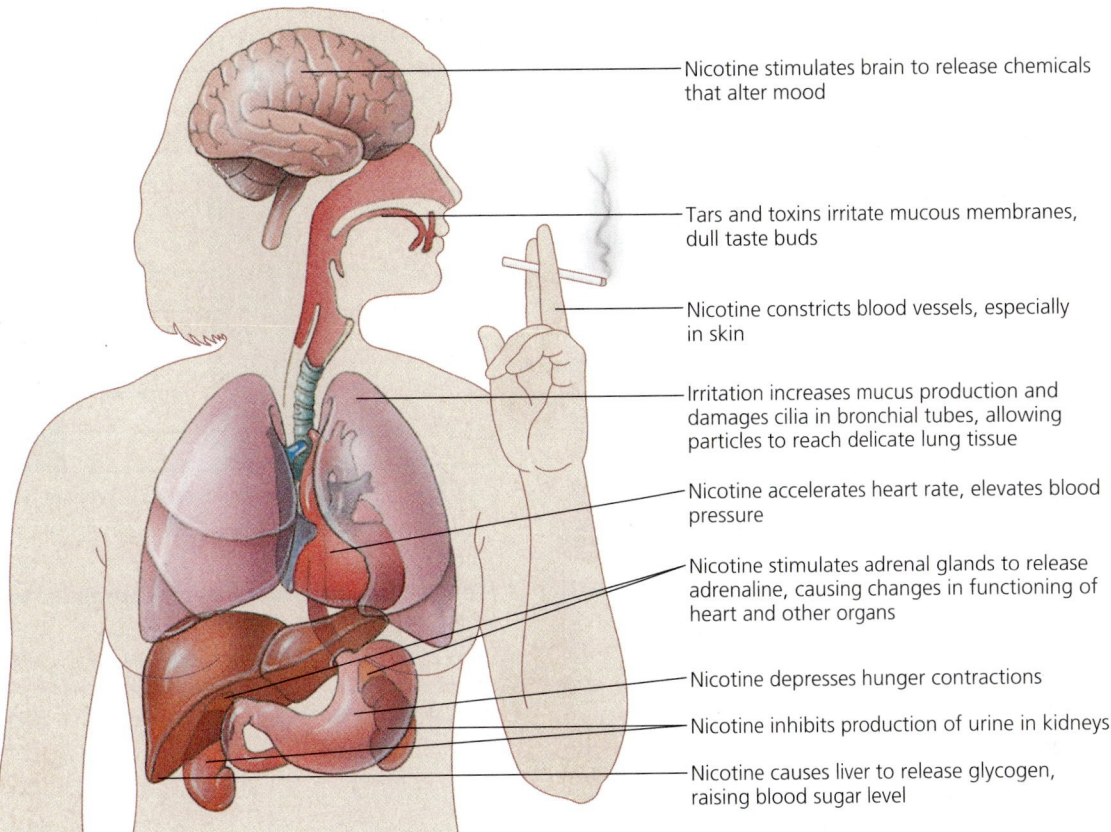

Nicotine stimulates brain to release chemicals that alter mood

Tars and toxins irritate mucous membranes, dull taste buds

Nicotine constricts blood vessels, especially in skin

Irritation increases mucus production and damages cilia in bronchial tubes, allowing particles to reach delicate lung tissue

Nicotine accelerates heart rate, elevates blood pressure

Nicotine stimulates adrenal glands to release adrenaline, causing changes in functioning of heart and other organs

Nicotine depresses hunger contractions

Nicotine inhibits production of urine in kidneys

Nicotine causes liver to release glycogen, raising blood sugar level

FIGURE 11.2   The short-term effects of smoking a cigarette.

rhea. The seasoned smoker occasionally suffers these effects of nicotine poisoning, particularly after quitting and then returning to a previous level of consumption. The effects of nicotine on smokers vary, depending greatly on the size of the nicotine dose and how much tolerance previous smoking has built up. Nicotine can either excite or tranquilize the nervous system, depending on dosage.

Nicotine has many other immediate effects (Figure 11.2). It stimulates the part of the brain called the **cerebral cortex.** It also stimulates the adrenal glands to discharge adrenaline. Nicotine inhibits the formation of urine; constricts the blood vessels, especially in the skin; accelerates the heart rate; and elevates blood pressure. Higher blood pressure, faster heart rate, and constricted blood vessels require the heart to pump more blood. In healthy people, the heart can usually meet this demand, but in people whose coronary arteries are damaged enough to interfere with the flow of blood, the heart muscle may be strained.

Smoking depresses hunger contractions and dulls the taste buds; smokers who quit often notice that food tastes much better. Smoking is not useful for weight loss, however. Smoking for decades may lessen or prevent age-associated weight gain for some smokers, but for people under 30, smoking is not associated with weight loss.

The Long-Term Effects of Smoking

Smoking is linked to many deadly and disabling diseases. Research indicates that the total amount of tobacco smoke inhaled is a key factor contributing to disease. People who smoke more cigarettes per day, inhale deeply, puff frequently, smoke cigarettes down to the butts, or begin smoking at an early age run a greater risk of disease than do those who smoke more moderately or who do not smoke at all.

As more research is done, even more diseases associated with smoking are being uncovered. The costliest ones—to society as well as to the individual—are cardiovascular diseases, respiratory diseases such as emphysema and lung cancer, and other cancers.

Cardiovascular Disease   Although lung cancer tends to receive the most publicity, one form of cardiovascular disease, **coronary heart disease (CHD),** is actually the most widespread single cause of death for cigarette smokers. CHD often results from **atherosclerosis,** a condition in which fatty deposits called **plaques** form on the inner walls of heart arteries, causing them to narrow and stiffen. Smoking and exposure to environmental tobacco smoke (ETS) permanently accelerate the rate of plaque accumulation in the coronary arteries—50% for smokers, 25% for ex-smokers, and 20% for people regularly exposed to ETS. The crushing chest pain of **angina pectoris,** a primary symptom of CHD, results when the heart muscle, or *myocardium,* does not get enough oxygen. Sometimes a plaque forms at a narrow point in a main coronary artery. If the plaque completely blocks the flow of blood to a portion of the heart, that portion may die. This type of heart attack is called a **myocardial infarction.**

CHD can also interfere with the heart's electrical activity, resulting in disturbances of the normal heartbeat rhythm. Sudden and unexpected death is a common result of CHD, particularly among smokers. (See Chapter 15 for a more extensive discussion of cardiovascular disease.)

Smokers have a death rate from CHD that is 70% higher than that of nonsmokers. Deaths from CHD associated with cigarette smoking are most common in people age 40–50. (In contrast, deaths from lung cancer caused by smoking are most likely to occur in 60–70-year-olds.) Among people *under* age 40, smokers are five times more likely than nonsmokers to have a heart attack. Cigar and pipe smokers run a lower risk than cigarette smokers.

We do not completely understand how cigarette smoking increases the risk of CHD, but researchers are beginning to shed light on the process. Smoking reduces the amount of "good" cholesterol (high-density lipoprotein, or HDL) in the blood, thereby promoting plaque formation in artery walls. Smoking may also increase tension in heart muscle walls, speeding up the rate of muscular contraction and accelerating the heart rate. The workload of the heart thus increases, as does its need for oxygen and other nutrients. Carbon monoxide produced by cigarette smoking combines with hemoglobin in the red blood cells, displacing oxygen and thus providing less oxygen to the heart. One study showed that the additional blood supply available to the heart during stress was 21% less in smokers than in nonsmokers. This reduced blood flow is an early indicator of future heart attacks or strokes.

The risks of CHD decrease rapidly when a person stops smoking; this is particularly true for younger smokers, whose coronary arteries have not yet been extensively damaged.

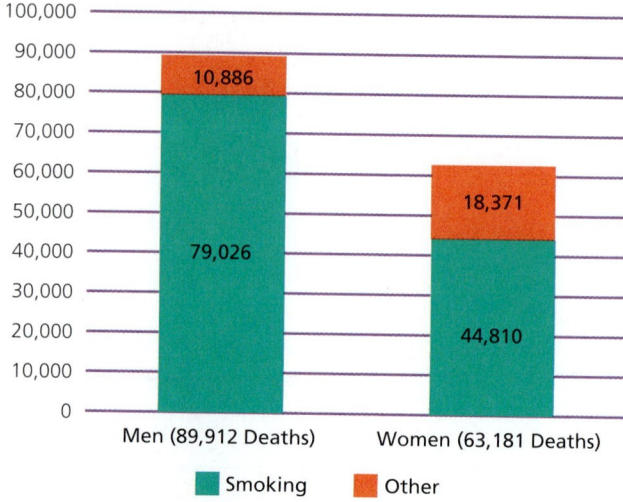

Annual Lung Cancer Deaths Attributable to Smoking or Other Causes: 1997–2001

FIGURE 11.3   Lung cancer deaths attributed to smoking versus other causes.

SOURCE: Centers for Disease Control and Prevention. 2005. Annual smoking-attributable mortality, years of potential life lost, and productivity losses—United States, 1997–2001. *Morbidity and Mortality Weekly Report* 54(24): 625–628.

Cigarette smoking has been linked to other cardiovascular diseases, including the following:

- *Stroke,* a sudden interference with the circulation of blood in a part of the brain, resulting in the destruction of brain cells

- *Aortic aneurysm,* a bulge in the aorta caused by a weakening in its walls

- *Pulmonary heart disease,* a disorder of the right side of the heart, caused by changes in the blood vessels of the lungs

Lung Cancer and Other Cancers   Cigarette smoking is the primary cause of lung cancer (Figure 11.3). A recent study identified the precise mechanism: Benzo(a)pyrene, a chemical found in tobacco smoke, causes genetic mutations in lung cells that are identical to those found in many patients with lung cancer. Those who smoke two or more packs of cigarettes a day have lung cancer death rates 12–25 times greater than those of nonsmokers. The dramatic rise in lung cancer rates among women in the past 40 years clearly parallels the increase of smoking in this group; lung cancer now exceeds breast cancer as the leading cause of cancer deaths among women. The risk of developing lung cancer increases with the number of cigarettes smoked each day, the number of years of smoking, and the age at which the person started smoking.

While cigar and pipe smokers have a higher risk of lung cancer than nonsmokers do, the risk is lower than that for cigarette smokers. Smoking filter-tipped cigarettes

TERMS

angina pectoris   Chest pain due to coronary heart disease.

myocardial infarction   A heart attack caused by the complete blockage of a main coronary artery.

emphysema   A disease characterized by a loss of lung tissue elasticity and breakup of the air sacs, impairing the lungs' ability to obtain oxygen and remove carbon dioxide.

chronic bronchitis   Recurrent, persistent inflammation of the bronchial tubes.

slightly reduces health hazards, unless the smoker compensates by smoking more, as is often the case.

Evidence suggests that after 1 year without smoking, the risk of lung cancer decreases substantially. After 10 years, the risk of lung cancer among ex-smokers is 50% lower than that of continuing smokers.

Research has also linked smoking to cancers of the trachea, mouth, pharynx, esophagus, larynx, pancreas, bladder, kidney, breast, cervix, stomach, liver, colon, and skin. For more information on cancer, see Chapter 16.

Chronic Obstructive Pulmonary Disease   The lungs of a smoker are constantly exposed to dangerous chemicals and irritants, and they must work harder to function adequately. The stresses placed on the lungs by smoking can permanently damage lung function and lead to *chronic obstructive pulmonary disease (COPD),* also known as chronic obstructive lung disease (COLD), or chronic lower respiratory disease. COPD is the fourth leading cause of death in the United States. This progressive and disabling disorder consists of several different but related diseases; emphysema and chronic bronchitis are two of the most common.

Cigarette smokers are up to 18 times more likely than nonsmokers to die from emphysema and chronic bronchitis. (Pipe and cigar smokers are more likely to die from COPD than are nonsmokers, but they have a smaller risk than cigarette smokers.) A 2006 study found that one in four heavy smokers develops COPD. The risk rises with the number of cigarettes smoked and falls when smoking ceases. For most Americans, cigarette smoking is a more important cause of COPD than air pollution, but exposure to both is more dangerous than exposure to either by itself.

EMPHYSEMA   Smoking is the primary cause of **emphysema,** a disabling condition in which the walls of the lungs' air sacs lose their elasticity and are gradually destroyed. The lungs' ability to obtain oxygen and remove carbon dioxide is impaired. A person with emphysema is breathless, is constantly gasping for air, and has the feeling of drowning. The heart must pump harder and may become enlarged. People with emphysema often die from a damaged heart. There is no known way to reverse this disease. In its advanced stage, the victim is bedridden and severely disabled.

CHRONIC BRONCHITIS   Persistent, recurrent inflammation of the bronchial tubes characterizes **chronic bronchitis.** When the cell lining of the bronchial tubes is irritated, it secretes excess mucus. Bronchial congestion is followed by a chronic cough, which makes breathing more and more difficult. If smokers have chronic bronchitis, they face a greater risk of lung cancer, no matter how old they are or how many cigarettes they smoke. Chronic bronchitis seems to be a shortcut to lung cancer.

Other Respiratory Damage   Even when the smoker shows no signs of lung impairment or disease, cigarette smoking damages the respiratory system. Normally the cells lining the bronchial tubes secrete mucus, a sticky fluid that collects particles of soot, dust, and other substances in inhaled air. Mucus is carried up to the mouth by the continuous motion of the cilia, hairlike structures that protrude from the inner surface of the bronchial tubes (Figure 11.4). If the cilia are destroyed or impaired, or if the pollution of inhaled air is more than the system can remove, the protection provided by cilia is lost.

Cigarette smoke first slows and then stops the action of the cilia. Eventually it destroys them, leaving delicate membranes exposed to injury from substances inhaled in cigarette smoke or from the polluted air in which the person lives or works. Special cells, called *macrophages,* a type of white blood cell, also work to remove foreign particles from the respiratory tract by engulfing them. Smoking appears to make macrophages work less efficiently. This interference with the functioning of the respiratory system often leads rapidly to the conditions known as smoker's throat and smoker's cough, as well as to shortness of breath. Even smokers of high school age show

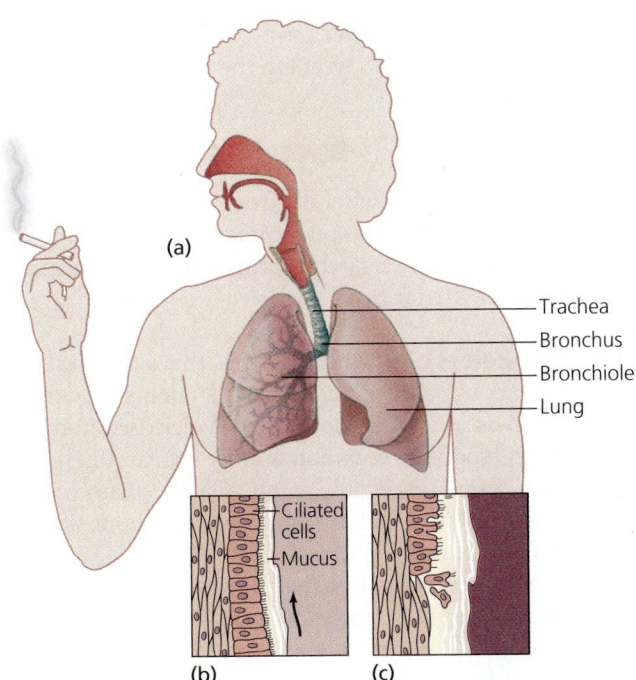

Trachea
Bronchus
Bronchiole
Lung

Ciliated cells
Mucus

(a)   (b)   (c)

FIGURE 11.4   Damage to the lungs caused by smoking.
(a) The respiratory system. (b) The inside of a bronchiole of a nonsmoker. (c) The inside of a bronchiole of a smoker.

impaired respiratory function, compared with nonsmokers of the same age. Other respiratory effects of smoking include a worsening of allergy and asthma symptoms and an increase in the smoker's susceptibility to colds.

Although cigarette smoking can cause many respiratory disorders and diseases, the damage is not always permanent. Once a person stops smoking, steady improvement in overall lung function usually takes place. Chronic coughing subsides, mucus production returns to normal, and breathing becomes easier. The likelihood of lung disease drops sharply. People of all ages, even those who have been smoking for decades, improve after they stop smoking.

Additional Health, Cosmetic, and Economic Concerns

- *Ulcers.* People who smoke are more likely to develop peptic ulcers and are more likely to die from them (especially stomach ulcers), because smoking impairs the body's healing ability. Smoking also increases the risk of gastroesophageal reflux, which causes heartburn and can, if severe, raise the risk of esophageal cancer.

- *Impotence.* Smoking affects blood flow in the veins and arteries of the penis, and it is an independent risk factor for impotence. In one recent study, smokers were twice as likely as nonsmokers to experience erectile dysfunction (impotence).

- *Reproductive health problems.* Smoking is linked to reduced fertility in both men and women. A study of 18-year-old smoking men found that they had a significantly higher proportion of abnormally shaped sperm and sperm with genetic defects than nonsmokers. In women, smoking can contribute to menstrual disorders, early menopause, and complications of pregnancy.

- *Dental diseases.* Smokers are at increased risk for tooth decay and gum and periodontal diseases, with symptoms appearing by the mid-20s.

- *Diminished physical senses.* Smoking dulls the senses of taste and smell. Over time, it increases the risk for hearing loss, and for macular degeneration and cataracts (both serious eye conditions that can result in partial or total blindness).

- *Injuries.* Smokers have higher rates of motor vehicle crashes, fire-related injuries, and back pain.

- *Cosmetic concerns.* Smoking can cause premature skin wrinkling, premature baldness, stained teeth, discolored fingers, and a persistent tobacco odor in clothes and hair.

- *Economic costs.* In 2008, the average per-pack price of cigarettes was $4.32. A pack-a-day habit costs nearly $1600 each year for cigarettes alone.

In addition, smoking contributes to osteoporosis, increases the risk of complications from diabetes, and accelerates the course of multiple sclerosis. Further research may link tobacco use to still other disorders.

Cumulative Effects The cumulative effects of tobacco use fall into two general categories. The first category is reduced life expectancy. A male who takes up smoking before age 15 and continues to smoke is only half as likely to live to age 75 as a male who never smokes. Females who have similar smoking habits also have a reduced life expectancy.

The second category involves quality of life. A national health survey begun in 1964 shows that smokers spend one-third more time away from their jobs because of illness than nonsmokers. Female smokers spend 17% more days sick in bed than female nonsmokers. Lost work days due to smoking number in the millions.

Both men and women smokers show a greater rate of acute and chronic disease than people who have never smoked (see the box "Gender and Tobacco Use"). Smokers become disabled at younger ages than nonsmokers and have more years of unhealthy life as well as a shorter life span. The U.S. Public Health Service estimates that if all people had the same rate of disease as those who never smoked, there would be 1 million fewer cases of chronic bronchitis, 1.8 million fewer cases of **sinusitis**, and 1 million fewer cases of peptic ulcers in the country every year.

Other Forms of Tobacco Use

Many smokers have switched from cigarettes to other forms of tobacco, such as spit (smokeless) tobacco, cigars and pipes, and clove cigarettes and bidis. These alternatives, however, are far from safe.

Spit (Smokeless) Tobacco More than 6.6 million adults and about 8% of all high school students are current spit tobacco users. Spit tobacco use has increased in recent years and is especially common among Native Americans, adolescent males (especially white males), male college athletes, and professional baseball players. About 80% of users start by the ninth grade.

Spit tobacco comes in two major forms: snuff and chewing tobacco (chew). In snuff, the tobacco leaf is processed

Gender and Tobacco Use

American men are currently more likely than women to smoke, but women younger than age 23 are becoming smokers at a faster rate than any other population segment. As the rate of smoking among women approaches that of men, so do rates of tobacco-related illness and death. More American women now die each year from lung cancer than from breast cancer.

Although overall risks of tobacco-related illness are similar for women and men, sex appears to make a difference in some diseases. Women, for example, are more at risk for smoking-related blood clots and strokes than are men, and the risk is even greater for women using oral contraceptives. Among men and women with the same smoking history, the odds for developing three major types of cancer, including lung cancer, is 1.2–1.7 times higher in women than in men. Women may also have a greater biological vulnerability to lung cancer.

For both men and women, tobacco use is associated with increased incidence of sex-specific health problems. Men who smoke increase their risk of erectile dysfunction and infertility due to reduced sperm density and motility. Women who smoke have higher rates of

osteoporosis (a bone-thinning disease that can lead to fractures), thyroid-related diseases, and depression.

Women who smoke also have risks associated with reproduction and the reproductive organs. Smoking is associated with greater menstrual bleeding, greater duration of painful menstrual cramps, and more variability in menstrual cycle length. Smokers have a more difficult time becoming pregnant, and they reach menopause on average a year or two earlier than nonsmokers. When women smokers become pregnant, they face increased chances of miscarriage or placental disorders that lead to bleeding and premature delivery; rates of ectopic pregnancy, preeclampsia, and stillbirth are also higher among women who smoke. Smoking is a risk factor for cervical cancer.

When women decide to try to stop smoking, they are more likely than men to join a support group. Overall, though, women are less successful than men in quitting. Women report more severe withdrawal symptoms when they stop smoking and are more likely than men to report cravings in response to social and behavioral cues associated with smoking.

For men, relapse to smoking is often associated with work or social pressure; women are more likely to relapse when sad or depressed or concerned about weight gain. Women and men also respond differently to medications: Nicotine replacement therapy appears to work better for men, whereas the nonnicotine medication bupropion appears to work better for women.

into a coarse, moist powder and mixed with flavorings. Snuff is usually sold in small tins. Users place a "pinch," "dip," or "quid" between the lower lip or cheek and gum and suck on it. In chewing tobacco, the tobacco leaf may be shredded ("leaf"), pressed into bricks or cakes ("plugs"), or dried and twisted into ropelike strands ("twists"). Chew is usually sold in pouches. Users place a wad of tobacco in their mouth and then chew or suck it to release the nicotine. All types of smokeless tobacco cause an increase in saliva production, and the resulting tobacco juice is spit out or swallowed. A recent innovation in smokeless tobacco, called *snus*, comes in a tiny pouch that is placed between the lip and gum. Snus does not require the user to spit, as do other forms of smokeless tobacco.

The nicotine in spit tobacco—along with flavorings and additives—is absorbed through the gums and lining of the mouth. Holding an average-size dip in the mouth for 30 minutes delivers about the same amount of nicotine as two or three cigarettes. Because of its nicotine content, spit tobacco is highly addictive. Some users keep it in their mouth even while sleeping.

Although not as dangerous as smoking cigarettes, the use of spit tobacco carries many health risks. Changes can occur in the mouth after only a few weeks of use. Gums and lips become dried and irritated and may bleed. White or red patches may appear inside the mouth; this condition, known as *leukoplakia,* can lead to oral cancer. About 25% of regular spit tobacco users have *gingivitis* (inflammation) and recession of the gums and bone loss around the teeth, especially where the tobacco is usually placed. The senses of taste and smell are usually dulled. In addition, other people find the presence of wads of tobacco in the mouth, stained teeth, bad breath, and behaviors such as frequent spitting to be unpleasant.

One of the most serious effects of spit tobacco is an increased risk of oral cancer—cancers of the lip, tongue, cheek, throat, gums, roof and floor of the mouth, and larynx. Spit tobacco contains at least 28 chemicals known to cause cancer, and long-term snuff use may increase the risk of oral cancer by as much as 50 times. Surgery to treat oral cancer is often disfiguring and may involve removing parts of the face, tongue, cheek, or lip.

Cigars contain more tobacco than cigarettes and so produce more tar when smoked. Cigar smokers face an increased risk of cancer even if they don't inhale the smoke.

The smoke from cigars contains many of the same toxins and carcinogens as the smoke from cigarettes, some in much higher quantities. The health risks of cigars depend on the number of cigars smoked and whether the smoker inhales. Because most cigar and pipe users do not inhale, they have a lower risk of cancer and cardiovascular and respiratory diseases than cigarette smokers. However, their risks are substantially higher than those of non-smokers. For example, compared to nonsmokers, people who smoke one or two cigars per day without inhaling have 6 times the risk of cancer of the larynx. The risks are much higher for cigar smokers who inhale: They have 27 times the risk of oral cancer and 53 times the risk of cancer of the larynx compared to nonsmokers, and their risk of heart and lung diseases approaches that of cigarette smokers. Smoking a cigar immediately impairs the ability of blood vessels to dilate, reducing the amount of oxygen delivered to tissues, including the heart muscle, especially during times of stress. Pipe and cigar smoking are also risk factors for pancreatic cancer, which is almost always fatal.

Nicotine addiction is another concern. Most adults who smoke cigars do so only occasionally, and there is little evidence that use of cigars by adults leads to addiction. The recent rise in cigar use among teens has raised concerns, however, because nicotine addiction almost always develops in the teen or young adult years. More research is needed to determine if cigar use by teens will develop into nicotine addiction and frequent use of either cigarettes or spit tobacco. In June 2000 the FTC announced an agreement to put warning labels on cigar packages, 34 years after warning labels first appeared on cigarette packages.

Dipping and chewing tobacco produce blood levels of nicotine similar to those in cigarette smokers. Other chemicals in spit tobacco are believed to pose risks to developing fetuses.

Cigars and Pipes   After decades of decline, cigar smoking increased by an estimated 148% from 1993 to 2006. The popularity of cigars is highest among white males age 18–44 with higher-than-average income and education, but women are also smoking cigars in record numbers. Cigar use is also growing among young people: In government surveys, 12% of American high school students reported having smoked at least one cigar in the previous month. Less than 1% of Americans, mostly males who also smoke cigarettes, are pipe smokers.

Cigars are made from rolled whole tobacco leaves; pipe tobacco is made from shredded leaves and often flavored. Because cigar and pipe smoke are more alkaline than cigarette smoke, users of cigars and pipes do not need to inhale in order to ingest nicotine; instead, they absorb nicotine through the gums and lining of the mouth. Cigars contain more tobacco than cigarettes and so contain more nicotine and produce more tar when smoked. Large cigars may contain as much tobacco as a whole pack of cigarettes and take 1–2 hours to smoke.

Clove Cigarettes and Bidis   Clove cigarettes, also called "kreteks" or "chicartas," are made of tobacco mixed with chopped cloves; they are imported primarily from Indonesia and Pakistan. Clove cigarettes contain almost twice as much tar, nicotine, and carbon monoxide as conventional cigarettes and so have all the same health hazards. Some chemical constituents of cloves may also be dangerous. For example, eugenol, an anesthetic compound found in cloves, may impair the respiratory system's ability to detect and defend against foreign particles. There have been a number of serious respiratory injuries and deaths from the use of clove cigarettes.

Bidis, or "beadies," are small cigarettes imported from India that contain species of tobacco different from those used by U.S. cigarette manufacturers. The tobacco in bidis is hand-rolled in Indian ebony leaves (tendu) and then often flavored; clove, mint, chocolate, and fruit varieties are available. Bidis contain up to four times more nicotine than and twice as much tar as U.S. cigarettes. Use of bidis has been growing among teens, possibly because of the flavorings they contain or because they look and smell somewhat like marijuana cigarettes (joints); they do not produce the same effects as marijuana, however.

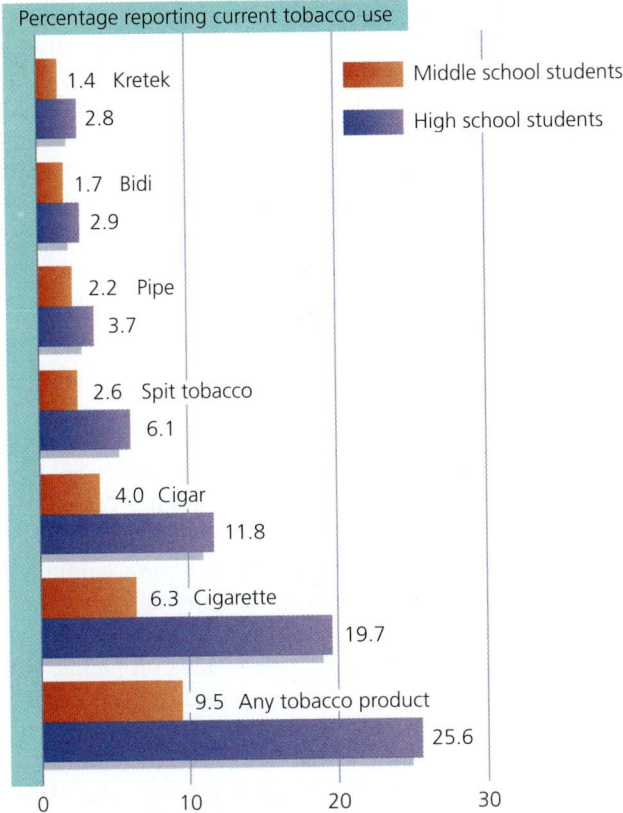

Percentage reporting current tobacco use

- Middle school students
- High school students

	Kretek	Middle	High
Kretek		1.4	2.8
Bidi		1.7	2.9
Pipe		2.2	3.7
Spit tobacco		2.6	6.1
Cigar		4.0	11.8
Cigarette		6.3	19.7
Any tobacco product		9.5	25.6

0   10   20   30

VITAL STATISTICS

FIGURE 11.5 **Tobacco use among middle school and high school students.**

SOURCE: Centers for Disease Control and Prevention. 2007. *2006 National Youth Tobacco Survey and Key Prevalence Indicators* (http://www.cdc.gov/tobacco/data _statistics/surveys/nyts/00-pdfs/indicators.pdf; retrieved October 1, 2008).

Currently, an estimated 3% of high school students use clove cigarettes or bidis (Figure 11.5). Neither is a safe or healthy alternative to conventional tobacco cigarettes.

THE EFFECTS OF SMOKING ON THE NONSMOKER

Tobacco users aren't the only ones who suffer ill effects from their habits. Tens of thousands of nonsmokers die each year because of excess exposure to secondhand smoke. Further, the medical and societal costs of tobacco use are enormous.

Environmental Tobacco Smoke

The U.S. Environmental Protection Agency (EPA) has designated **environmental tobacco smoke (ETS)**—more commonly called *secondhand smoke*—a Class A carcinogen. The Department of Health and Human Services' National Toxicology Program classifies ETS as a "known human carcinogen." These designations put ETS in the same category as notorious cancer-causing agents like asbestos. In 2006, the Surgeon General issued a report concluding that there is no safe level of exposure to ETS; even brief exposure can cause serious harm.

Environmental tobacco smoke consists of mainstream smoke and sidestream smoke. Smoke exhaled by smokers is referred to as **mainstream smoke.** Sidestream smoke enters the atmosphere from the burning end of a cigarette, cigar, or pipe. Nearly 85% of the smoke in a room where someone is smoking comes from sidestream smoke. Undiluted sidestream smoke, because it is not filtered through either a cigarette filter or a smoker's lungs, has twice as much tar and nicotine, three times as much benzo(a)pyrene, almost three times as much carbon monoxide, and three times as much ammonia.

In rooms where people are smoking, levels of carbon monoxide can exceed those permitted by Federal Air Quality Standards for outside air. In a typical home with the windows closed, it takes about 6 hours for 95% of the airborne cigarette smoke particles to clear.

The carcinogens in the secondhand smoke from a single cigar exceeds that of three cigarettes, and cigar smoke contains up to 30 times more carbon monoxide.

ETS Effects Nonsmokers subjected to ETS frequently develop coughs, headaches, nasal discomfort, and eye irritation. Other symptoms range from breathlessness to sinus problems. People with allergies tend to suffer the most (see the box "Avoiding ETS" on p. 317).

ETS causes 3000 lung cancer deaths and about 35,000 deaths from heart disease each year in people who do not smoke. As described earlier, exposure to ETS is associated with a 20% increase in the progression of atherosclerosis. ETS also aggravates asthma and increases the risk for breast and cervical cancers.

QUESTIONS FOR CRITICAL THINKING AND REFLECTION

Do you know anyone who has suffered from an illness related to tobacco use? If so, what problems did that person face? What was the outcome? Did the experience have any effect on your views about using tobacco?

TERMS

environmental tobacco smoke (ETS) Smoke that enters the atmosphere from the burning end of a cigarette, cigar, or pipe, as well as smoke that is exhaled by smokers; also called *secondhand smoke*.

mainstream smoke Smoke that is inhaled by a smoker and then exhaled into the atmosphere.

Millions of American infants and children are regularly exposed to environmental tobacco smoke.

Older children suffer, too. ETS is a risk factor for asthma in children who have not previously displayed symptoms of the disease, and it aggravates the symptoms of children who already have asthma. ETS is also linked to reduced lung function and fluid buildup in the middle ear, a contributing factor in middle-ear infections, a leading reason for childhood surgery. Children and teens exposed to ETS score lower on tests of reading and reasoning. Later in life, people exposed to ETS as children are at increased risk for lung cancer, emphysema, and chronic bronchitis.

Smoking and Pregnancy

Smoking almost doubles a pregnant woman's chance of having a miscarriage, and it significantly increases her risk of ectopic pregnancy. Maternal smoking causes an estimated 4600 infant deaths in the United States each year, primarily due to premature delivery and smoking-related problems with the placenta. Maternal smoking is a major factor in low birth weight, which puts newborns at high risk for infections and other serious problems. If a nonsmoking mother is regularly exposed to ETS, her infant is also at greater risk for low birth weight. Recent studies have also shown that babies whose mothers smoked during pregnancy had higher rates of colic, clubfoot, cleft lip and palate, and impaired lung function; they may also have genetic damage.

Babies born to mothers who smoke more than two packs a day perform poorly on developmental tests in the first hours after birth, compared to babies of nonsmoking mothers. Later in life, obesity, hyperactivity, short attention span, and lower scores on spelling and reading tests all occur more frequently in children whose mothers smoked during pregnancy than in those born to nonsmoking mothers. Prenatal tobacco exposure has also been associated with behavioral problems in children, including immaturity, emotional instability, physical aggression, and hyperactivity. Other research shows that teenagers whose mothers smoked during pregnancy have lower scores on tests of general intelligence and poorer performance on tasks requiring auditory memory than do children who were not exposed to cigarette smoke before birth. Males born to smoking mothers have higher rates of adolescent and adult criminal activity, suggesting that maternal smoking may cause brain damage that increases the risk of criminal behavior. Nevertheless, about 16% of pregnant women smoke.

Scientists have been able to measure changes that contribute to lung tissue damage and potential tumor promotion in the bloodstreams of healthy young test subjects who spend just 3 hours in a smoke-filled room. After just 30 minutes of exposure to ETS, the function in the coronary arteries of healthy nonsmokers is reduced to the same level as that of smokers. And nonsmokers can still be affected by the harmful effects of ETS hours after they have left a smoky environment. Carbon monoxide, for example, lingers in the bloodstream 5 hours later.

Infants, Children, and ETS   Recent studies have shown that infants exposed to smoke from more than 21 cigarettes a day are more than 23 times more likely to die of sudden infant death syndrome (SIDS) than babies not exposed to ETS. The National Cancer Institute recently estimated that ETS causes up to 18,600 cases of low birth weight each year. Children under 5 whose primary caregiver smokes ten or more cigarettes per day have measurable blood levels of nicotine and tobacco carcinogens.

Chemicals in tobacco smoke also show up in breast milk, and breastfeeding may pass more chemicals to the infant of a smoking mother than direct exposure to ETS.

ETS triggers 150,000–300,000 cases of bronchitis, pneumonia, and other respiratory infections in infants and toddlers up to age 18 months each year, resulting in 7,500–15,000 hospitalizations.

The Cost of Tobacco Use to Society

The annual health-related costs of smoking exceed $167 billion. These costs far exceed the tax revenues that states collect on the sale of tobacco products, even though the average cigarette tax was $1.18 per pack as of August 2008 and rising in some states.

Avoiding ETS

Given the health risks of exposure to ETS, try these strategies to keep the air around you safe:

- *Speak up tactfully.* Smokers may not know the dangers they are causing or may not know it bothers you.

- *Display reminders.* Put up signs asking smokers to refrain in your home, work area, and car.

- *Don't allow smoking in your home or room.* Get rid of ashtrays and ask smokers to light up outside.

- *Open a window.* If you cannot avoid being in a room with a smoker, at least try to provide some ventilation.

- *Sit in the nonsmoking section in restaurants and other public areas.* Complain to the manager if none exists.

- *Fight for a smoke-free work environment.* Join with your co-workers to either eliminate all smoking indoors or confine it to certain areas.

- *Discuss quitting strategies.* Social pressure is a major factor in many former smokers' decisions to quit. Help the smokers in your life by sharing quitting strategies with them.

The Master Settlement Agreement   In order to recoup public health care expenditures, 43 state attorneys general filed suit against tobacco companies. In March 1997, Liggett Group settled its part of the suit by agreeing to turn over internal documents and to pay a portion of its profits to cover tobacco-related medical expenses and anti-smoking campaigns. In November 1998, an agreement was reached that settled 39 state lawsuits and applied to seven states that never filed suit. (Four states—Florida, Minnesota, Mississippi, and Texas—settled their suits separately for a total of $40 billion.)

The 1998 Master Settlement Agreement (MSA) requires the tobacco companies to pay states $206 billion over 25 years; it also limits or bans certain types of advertising, promotions, and lobbying. Many of the provisions of the deal are designed to limit youth exposure and access to tobacco. In exchange, the tobacco industry settled the state lawsuits and is protected from future suits by states, counties, towns, and other public entities. Tobacco companies passed the costs of the settlement on to smokers.

Court Cases   The MSA, however, did not prevent individuals from suing the tobacco industry, and a number of lawsuits moved forward, some resulting in huge fines against tobacco companies. One of the most famous was a class-action suit filed in Florida in 1996, on behalf of 700,000 smokers in that state. In 2000, a jury ordered tobacco companies to pay $145 billion in punitive damages to plaintiffs in that suit. After 6 years of appeals, the Florida Supreme Court decertified the class-action suit and threw out the punitive award. The court held, however, that plaintiffs could seek damages in individual lawsuits against the tobacco companies. The court also ruled that tobacco use is a direct cause of several diseases, which frees many plaintiffs from having to prove that their illness is a result of tobacco use. In addition, the court found that tobacco companies had been selling dangerous products to the public and had attempted to conceal some of the dangers from consumers.

The court also established a $600 million trust fund, funded by the tobacco companies, to be distributed among *all* sick Florida smokers—not just the plaintiffs in the original case. To be eligible to receive a share of the fund, smokers had to register with the court by a June 2008 deadline and prove their illness was smoking-related and diagnosed

THINKING ABOUT THE ENVIRONMENT

The buildings in which you live, work, and learn are important parts of your environment, as are the skies and oceans. The health and safety of indoor air are threatened by secondhand smoke, just as the outside air is threatened by other forms of pollution.

The U.S. Surgeon General reported in 2006 that more than 40% of all nonsmokers are routinely exposed to tobacco smoke, typically indoors. Roughly 30% of indoor workers are not protected by smoke-free workplace rules. The Surgeon General also reported the following:

- Children exposed to secondhand smoke are more likely to die of sudden infant death syndrome and to develop severe infections.

- Adults exposed to secondhand smoke experience immediate harmful effects on the cardiovascular system and increased risk of coronary heart disease and lung cancer.

- There is no safe level of exposure to secondhand smoke.

- Completely eliminating indoor smoking is the only way to fully protect nonsmokers from exposure to secondhand smoke. Ventilating buildings or separating smokers from nonsmokers is not sufficient.

For more information on the environment and environmental health, see Chapter 19.

prior to November 21, 1996 (when the original class-action suit was filed).

The industry was dealt another potential blow in August 2006, when a U.S. District Court judge ordered tobacco companies to stop marketing cigarettes with labels like "light" and "low-tar." The judge found that tobacco companies had violated racketeering laws by conspiring for years to deceive the public about the health risks of smoking. At the same time, the judge said that she did not have the power to order the industry to pay billions of dollars to fund anti-smoking and education programs. Both anti-smoking advocates and tobacco companies claimed the ruling as a victory, and litigation and court cases continue.

WHAT CAN BE DONE?

There are many ways to act against this public health threat.

Action at the Local Level

Since the 1980s, local government agencies—such as city councils, school boards, and county boards of commis-

In many public spaces, such as airports, smokers can light up only in designated smoking areas. These designated zones are often outdoors, but some facilities have enclosed spaces with special ventilation to prevent smoke from escaping.

sioners—have been passing ordinances designed to discourage smoking in public places. There are now thousands of local ordinances across the nation that restrict or ban smoking in restaurants, stores, workplaces, and even public outdoor areas. An assessment made in 2006 found that 42% of Americans live in municipalities with smoke-free restaurants and 30% live in locations with smoke-free workplaces. At least 260 colleges and universities now have totally smoke-free campuses or prohibit smoking in residential buildings. As local nonsmoking laws proliferate, evidence mounts that environmental restrictions are effective in encouraging smokers to quit.

Action at the State and Federal Levels

State legislatures have passed many tough new anti-tobacco laws. As of January 2008, comprehensive smoke-free air laws were in effect in 21 states, the District of Columbia, and Puerto Rico. These laws prohibit smoking in almost all public areas, as well as in workplaces, restaurants, and bars. As of August 2008, 25 states and the District of Columbia had cigarette tax rates of at least $1.00 per pack; in 11 of those states, the tax rate was $2.00 or more per pack.

California has one of the most aggressive—and successful—tobacco control programs, combining taxes on cigarettes, graphic advertisements, and bans on smoking in bars and restaurants. California now has the second lowest rate of smoking among U.S. states, at 14.3%. Utah, with a smoking rate of 11.7%, is the first (and only) state to meet the *Healthy People 2010* target. Kentucky has the highest rate, 28.2%.

The federal government is also acting to protect nonsmokers from ETS (see the box "FDA Regulation of Tobacco"). Smoking has been banned on virtually all domestic airplane flights, and the U.S. Defense Department has banned smoking at all military work sites. The U.S. Occupational Safety and Health Administration has considered nationwide rules that would, in effect, ban smoking on the job except in specially ventilated areas.

International Action

Many countries are following the United States' lead in restricting smoking. Smoking is now banned on many international air flights, as well as in many restaurants and hotels and on public transportation in some countries. The World Health Organization has taken the lead in international anti-tobacco efforts by sponsoring the Framework Convention on Tobacco Control. Another international activity is the annual commemoration of World No Tobacco Day (May 31), on which smokers are encouraged to stop smoking for 1 day. (This is similar to the American Cancer Society's Great American Smokeout®, held each November.) The smoker who successfully takes the first step of quitting for a day may be encouraged enough to follow

FDA Regulation of Tobacco

It may seem odd that tobacco products—all of which are somehow ingested, contain psychoactive drugs, and include many of the same additives used in food products—are not regulated by the U.S. Food and Drug Administration (FDA). But, in fact, the FDA has no real authority to oversee or regulate the manufacture or sale of tobacco products.

In 1996, the FDA claimed that it had the right to regulate tobacco products under the auspices of the Food, Drug, and Cosmetic Act. At that time, the FDA's rules applied primarily to the advertising and sale of tobacco products. The tobacco industry sued to prevent enforcement of those regulations, on the grounds that Congress had not specifically empowered the FDA to regulate tobacco. The Supreme Court agreed, and all of the FDA's tobacco-related regulations were dropped.

In 2007, however, members of the U.S. Senate and the House of Representatives proposed identical pieces of legislation that would give the FDA broad regulatory powers over many aspects of the tobacco industry. Although the legislation would not give the FDA the power to ban nicotine outright, the agency would be able to dictate how much nicotine is included in tobacco products. The proposed legislation would give the FDA the power to eliminate or control levels of the thousands of chemical additives used to make tobacco more appealing and addictive. In addition, the legislation would strengthen health warnings and limit tobacco advertising.

Specifically, the proposed legislation would allow the FDA to do the following:

- Restrict advertising and promotion of tobacco products.

- Require manufacturers to provide detailed disclosure of their products' ingredients. The disclosures would include nicotine levels, specific additives used, and harmful components in the products' smoke.

- Create a content standard, which tobacco products would have to meet. If needed, the FDA could require manufacturers to modify their products to meet the standard.

- Ban all cigarette flavorings, with the exception of menthol.

- Ban the use of terms such as "light," "mild," or "low" in product advertising and packaging.

- Regulate "reduced harm" products.

- Require bigger and more informative health warnings.

- Fund FDA activity through a fee on tobacco product manufacturers.

- Overturn any existing federal rules that prevent states from creating laws regarding tobacco advertising.

- Protect states' ability to pass other tobacco control laws.

FDA regulation of tobacco has widespread support from organizations such as the American Cancer Society, American Heart Association, American Lung Association, and the Campaign for Tobacco-Free Kids. Hundreds of public health agencies, community leaders, and religious groups around the country have voiced support for the legislation.

Some opponents of the legislation contend that the FDA does not have enough resources to oversee the manufacture and sale of tobacco products. Supporters, however, say that the resources will be funded by a new federal tax on cigarettes, which is expected to generate more than $700 million a year by 2018.

The House Energy and Commerce Committee approved the proposed legislation in April 2008; in July, the House of Representatives passed the bill by a vote of 326 to 102. No timetable has been set for voting on the issue in the Senate.

---

through on the commitment and become a permanent nonsmoker. With more than 1 billion smokers worldwide, addressing the global impact of tobacco use will require a massive coordinated effort.

Action in the Private Sector

The EPA report also shook up the private sector, giving employers reason to fear worker's compensation claims based on exposure to workplace smoke. The year after the report was issued, businesses including McDonald's and Taco Bell banned smoking in thousands of their restaurants across the country. The number of smoke-free restaurants has increased dramatically in recent years, and the vast majority of the nation's shopping malls now prohibit smoking.

Such local, state, national, and international efforts represent progress, but health activists warn that tobacco industry influence remains strong. The tobacco industry contributes heavily to sympathetic legislative officeholders and candidates. Many states have relatively weak antismoking laws that are backed by the tobacco industry and include clauses that prevent the passage of stricter local ordinances. Since 1999, tobacco interests have spent more than $115 million on federal lobbying activities. During the 2005–2006 election cycle, the industry gave nearly $3 million to federal candidates.

> **QUICK STATS**
>
> At **$2.75 per pack,** New York had the highest cigarette tax rate in the United States as of August 2008.
>
> —American Lung Association, 2008

Helping a Friend or Partner Stop Using Tobacco

The U.S. Public Health Service recommends a "Five A's" approach for physicians to help patients quit tobacco use. If someone you care about uses tobacco, you can try the same strategies to help them quit.

1. **Ask** about tobacco use. How many cigarettes does your girlfriend smoke each day? How long has your roommate been dipping snuff?

2. **Advise** tobacco users to stop. Express your concern over the tobacco user's habit. "When we're close, the smell of smoke on your hair and breath bothers me. I've noticed you cough a lot and your voice is raspy. I'm worried about your health. You should stop."

3. **Assess** the tobacco user's willingness to quit. "Next week would be a good time to try to quit. Would you be willing to give it a try?"

4. **Assist** the tobacco user who is willing to stop. To coincide with your partner's quit date, take him away for a romantic weekend far from the places he associates with smoking. Offer to be an exercise partner. Call once a day to offer support and help. Bring gifts of low-calorie snacks or projects that occupy the hands. If the quitter lapses, be encouraging. A lapse doesn't have to become a relapse.

5. **Arrange** follow-up. Maintaining abstinence is an ongoing process. Celebrate milestones of 1 week, 1 month, 1 year without tobacco. Note how much better your friend's or partner's car, room, and person smell, how much healthier he or she is, and how much you appreciate not having to breathe tobacco smoke.

Keep in mind the special influence that a partner or loved one can have on someone who is trying to quit using tobacco. Recent research has shown that certain kinds of behavior by a partner are consistently related to successful quitting, whereas other behaviors are related to relapse. Behaviors linked to success include expressing pleasure at the smoker's efforts to quit, actively rewarding the smoker's efforts (for example, giving a small gift), helping to calm the smoker when he or she is feeling stressed or irritable, and actively sharing in an activity such as dancing, jogging, or hiking that serves as a distraction from smoking.

Sometimes a tobacco user's partner does things that are intended to be helpful but actually interfere with the user's efforts to quit. These behaviors include hiding ashtrays, keeping track of the amount of tobacco used, hiding or throwing out the smoker's cigarettes, frequently mentioning the health risks associated with tobacco, ignoring the smoker during efforts to quit, downplaying the difficulty of quitting, and complaining about the partner's irritability during attempts to quit.

If your partner is trying to quit and you are uncertain how to help, ask what would be most helpful. Recognize that tobacco use is your partner's problem, and although there may be things you can do to help, your partner is ultimately in control of his or her own body. If your partner asks you to back off, then do so within the limits you have established in your relationship. If your partner gets angry or irritable, recognize that this hypersensitivity is a normal but temporary side effect of nicotine withdrawal and remind yourself that it will pass. Listen to your partner, communicate your feelings as clearly as possible, and do what you can to reduce your partner's stress level, such as temporarily taking over a household chore. If you smoke, you can help your partner by not smoking in open view and by providing positive support. Even better, take inspiration from your partner's efforts and quit.

SOURCE: "Five A's" from Fiore, E. M. C., et al. 2000. *Treating Tobacco Use and Dependence.* Clinical Practice Guideline. Rockville, Md.: U.S. Department of Health and Human Services.

Individual Action

Nonsmokers have the right not only to breathe clean air but also to take action to help solve one of society's most serious public health threats. Here are just some of the many ways in which individuals can help support tobacco prevention and stop-smoking efforts.

- When a smoker violates a no-smoking designation, complain.

- If your favorite restaurant or shop doesn't have a nonsmoking policy, ask the manager to adopt one.

- If you see children buying tobacco, report this illegal activity to the facility manager or the police.

- Learn more about addiction and tobacco cessation so you can better support the tobacco users you know (see the box "Helping a Friend or Partner Stop Using Tobacco").

- Vote for candidates who support anti-tobacco measures; contact local, state, and national representatives to express your views.

- Cancel your subscriptions to magazines that carry tobacco advertising; send a letter to the publisher explaining your decision.

- Voice your opinion about other positive representations of tobacco use. (A recent study found that more than two-thirds of children's animated feature films have featured tobacco or alcohol use with no clear message that such practices were unhealthy.)

- Volunteer with the American Lung Association, the American Cancer Society, or the American Heart Association.

Table 11.2	Benefits of Quitting Smoking

Within 20 minutes of your last cigarette:
- You stop polluting the air
- Blood pressure drops to normal
- Pulse rate drops to normal
- Temperature of hands and feet increases to normal

8 hours:
- Carbon monoxide level in blood drops to normal
- Oxygen level in blood increases to normal

24 hours:
- Chance of heart attack decreases

48 hours:
- Nerve endings start regrowing
- Ability to smell and taste is enhanced

2–3 months:
- Circulation improves
- Walking becomes easier
- Lung function increases up to 30%

1–9 months:
- Coughing, sinus congestion, fatigue, and shortness of breath all decrease

1 year:
- Heart disease death rate is half that of a smoker

5 years:
- Stroke risk drops nearly to the risk for nonsmokers

10 years:
- Lung cancer death rate drops to 50% of that of continuing smokers
- Incidence of other cancers (mouth, throat, larynx, esophagus, bladder, kidney, and pancreas) decreases
- Risk of ulcer decreases

15 years:
- Risk of lung cancer is about 25% of that of continuing smokers
- Risks of heart disease and death are close to those for nonsmokers

SOURCES: American Lung Association. 2002. *Benefits of Quitting* (http://www.lungusa.org/tobacco/quit_ben.html; retrieved August 18, 2006); American Cancer Society. 2000. *Quitting Smoking* (http://www.cancer.org/tobacco/quitting.html; retrieved August 18, 2006).

HOW A TOBACCO USER CAN QUIT

Giving up tobacco is a long-term, intricate process. Heavy smokers who say they have just stopped cold turkey don't tell of the struggling and mental processes that contributed to their final conquest over this powerful addiction.

Research shows that tobacco users move through predictable stages—from being uninterested in stopping, to thinking about change, to making a concerted effort to stop, to finally maintaining abstinence. But most attempt to quit several times before they finally succeed. Relapse is a normal part of the process.

The Benefits of Quitting

Giving up tobacco provides immediate health benefits to men and women of all ages (Table 11.2). People who quit smoking find that food tastes better. Their sense of smell is sharper. Circulation improves, heart rate and blood pressure drop, and lung function and heart efficiency increase. Ex-smokers can breathe more easily, and their capacity for exercise improves. Many ex-smokers report feeling more energetic and alert. They experience fewer headaches. Even their complexion may improve.

Quitting also has a positive effect on long-term disease risk. From the first day without tobacco, ex-smokers begin to decrease their risk of cancer of the lung, larynx, mouth, pancreas, bladder, cervix, and other sites. Risk of heart attack, stroke, and other cardiovascular diseases drops quickly, too.

QUICK STATS

50.2% of all American smokers have stopped smoking.

—American Cancer Society, 2008

The younger people are when they stop smoking, the more pronounced the health improvements. And these improvements gradually but invariably increase as the period of nonsmoking lengthens. It's never too late to quit, though. According to a U.S. Surgeon General's report, people who quit smoking, regardless of age, live longer than people who continue to smoke. Even smokers who have already developed chronic bronchitis or emphysema may show some improvement when they quit.

Options for Quitting

Most tobacco users—76% in a recent survey—want to quit, and half of those who want to quit will make an attempt this year. What are their options? No single method works for everyone, but each does work for some people some of the time. In June 2000, the U.S. Public Health Service issued guidelines for medical professionals on how to help their patients quit smoking, emphasizing the benefits of both behavioral and pharmacological

Building Motivation to Quit Smoking

A common misconception among smokers is that a few cigarettes a day aren't enough to cause harm. Perhaps this is why a recent survey showed that among college students who smoke, 75% smoke ten or fewer cigarettes a day. These smokers are ignoring the very real health risks of even one cigarette. The U.S. Public Health Service suggests a "5 R's" strategy to enhance motivation to quit. If you are a smoker or are trying to help one, think about these areas of concern and see if they help develop a desire and readiness to make a real attempt at quitting.

Relevance: Think about the personal relevance of quitting tobacco use. What would the effects be on your family and friends? How would your daily life improve? What is the most important way that quitting would change your life?

Risks: There are immediate risks, such as shortness of breath, infertility, and impotence, and long-term risks, including cancer, heart disease, and respiratory problems. Remember, smoking is harmful both to you and to anyone exposed to your smoke.

Rewards: The list of the rewards of quitting is almost endless, including improving immediate and long-term health, saving money, and feeling better about yourself. You can also stop worrying about quitting and set a good example for others.

Roadblocks: What are the potential obstacles to quitting? Are you worried about withdrawal symptoms, weight gain, or lack of support? How can these barriers be overcome?

Repetition: Revisit your reasons for quitting and strengthen your resolve until you are ready to prepare a plan. Most people make several attempts to quit before they succeed. Relapsing once does not mean that you will never succeed.

SOURCES: Rigotti, N. A., J. E. Lee, and H. Wechsler. 2000. U.S. college students' use of tobacco products. *Journal of the American Medical Association* 284(6): 699–705; Fiore, M. C., et al. 2000. *Treating Tobacco Use and Dependence.* Clinical Practice Guidelines. Rockville, Md.: U.S. Department of Health and Human Services.

interventions. In 2008, the agency updated those guidelines and urged all physicians to provide anti-smoking intervention and treatment to all their patients who use tobacco. In essence, the health service set a goal of treating every American smoker—not just those who ask their doctors for help in quitting smoking.

Choosing to quit requires developing a strategy for success (see the box "Building Motivation to Quit Smoking"). Some people quit cold turkey, whereas others taper off slowly. There are over-the-counter and prescription products that help many people (see the box "Smoking Cessation Products" for more on these options). Behavioral factors that have been shown to increase the chances of a smoker's permanent smoking cessation are support from others and regular exercise. Support can come from friends and family and/or formal group programs sponsored by organizations such as the American Cancer Society, the American Lung Association, and the Seventh-Day Adventist Church or by your college health center or community hospital. Programs that combine group support with nicotine replacement therapy have rates of continued abstention as high as 35% after 1 year.

Free telephone quitlines are emerging as a popular and effective strategy to help stop smoking. Quitlines are staffed by trained counselors who help each caller plan a personal quitting strategy, usually including a combination of nicotine replacement therapy, changes in daily habits, and emotional support. Counselors provide printed materials that match the smoker's needs and schedule phone counseling sessions for key days after a smoker quits. Smokers can schedule sessions to fit their schedule, and some quitlines may provide stop-smoking medications at reduced prices. Almost all smokers make more than one attempt to stop before they succeed in quitting for good; and quitline counselors can help smokers understand what leads to relapse, review their reasons for wanting to quit, and make a better plan for the next attempt. The goal is for smokers to find a support system and techniques that work for them. In 2004, the Department of Health and Human Services established a national toll-free number, 1-800-QUITNOW (1-800-784-8669), to serve as a single access point for smokers seeking information and assistance in quitting. Callers are routed to their state's smoking cessation quitline or, in states that have not established quitlines, to one maintained by the National Cancer Institute.

Most smokers in the process of quitting experience both physical and psychological effects of nicotine withdrawal, and exercise can help with both. For many smokers, their tobacco use is associated with certain times and places—following a meal, for example. Resolving to walk after dinner instead of lighting up provides a distraction from cravings and eliminates the cues that trigger a desire to smoke. In addition, many people worry about weight

Smoking Cessation Products

Each year, millions of Americans visit their doctors in the hope of finding a drug that can help them stop smoking. Although pharmacological options are limited, the few available drugs have proved successful.

Chantix (Varinicline)

The newest smoking cessation drug, marketed under the name Chantix, works in two ways: It reduces nicotine cravings, easing the withdrawal process, and it blocks the pleasant effects of nicotine. The drug acts on neurotransmitter receptors in the brain.

Six clinical trials, which included more than 3600 long-term, chronic smokers, demonstrated that Chantix is an effective smoking cessation aid. In one of the studies, nearly 25% of Chantix users stopped smoking for a full year. Results varied with the dosage and duration of treatment.

Unlike most smoking cessation products currently on the market, Chantix is not a nicotine replacement. For this reason, smokers may be advised to continue smoking for the first few days of treatment, to avoid withdrawal and to allow the drug to build up in their system. The approved course of treatment is 12 weeks, but the duration and recommended dosage depend on several factors, including the smoker's general health and the length and severity of his or her nicotine addiction.

Side effects reported with Chantix include nausea, headache, vomiting, sleep disruptions, and change in taste perception. People with kidney problems or who take certain medications should not take Chantix, and it is not recommended for women who are pregnant or nursing. In early 2008, the FDA issued a public health advisory warning that some Chantix users suffered adverse reactions, such as behavioral changes, agitation, depression, suicidal thoughts, and attempted suicide. Anyone taking Chantix should immediately notify his or her doctor of any sudden change in mood or behavior.

Zyban (Bupropion)

Bupropion is an antidepressant (prescribed under the name Wellbutrin) as well as a smoking cessation aid (prescribed under the name Zyban). As a smoking cessation aid, bupropion eases the symptoms of nicotine withdrawal and reduces the urge to smoke. Like Chantix, it acts on neurotransmitter receptors in the brain.

Bupropion is not a nicotine replacement, so the user may need to continue smoking for the first few days of treatment. A nicotine replacement product, such as a patch or gum, may be recommended to further ease withdrawal symptoms after the user stops smoking.

Bupropion users have reported an array of side effects, but they are rare. Side effects may be reduced by changing the dosage, taking the medicine at a different time of day, or taking it with or without food. Bupropion is not recommended for people with specific physical conditions or who take certain drugs. Zyban and Wellbutrin should not be taken together.

Nicotine Replacement Products

The most widely used smoking cessation products replace the nicotine that the user would normally get from tobacco. The user continues to get nicotine, so withdrawal symptoms and cravings are reduced. Although still harmful, nicotine replacement products provide a cleaner form of nicotine, without the thousands of poisons and tars produced by burning tobacco. Less of the product is used over time, as the need for nicotine decreases.

Nicotine replacement products come in several forms, including patches, gum, lozenges, nasal sprays, and inhalers. They are available in a variety of strengths and can be worked into many different smoking cessation strategies. Most are available without a prescription.

The nicotine patch is popular because it can be applied and forgotten until it needs to be removed or changed, usually every 16 or 24 hours. Placed on the upper arm or torso, it releases a steady stream of nicotine, which is absorbed through the skin. The main side effects are skin irritation and redness. Nicotine gum and nicotine lozenges have the advantage of allowing the smoker to use them whenever he or she craves nicotine. Side effects of nicotine gum include mouth sores and headaches; nicotine lozenges can cause nausea and heartburn. Nicotine nasal sprays and inhalers are available only by prescription.

Although all these products have proved to be effective in helping users stop smoking, experts recommend them only as one part of a complete smoking cessation program. Such a program should include regular professional counseling and physician monitoring.

---

gain associated with quitting. Although most ex-smokers do gain a few pounds, at least temporarily, incorporating exercise into a new tobacco-free routine lays the foundation for healthy weight management. The health risks of adding a few pounds are far outweighed by the risks of continued smoking; it's estimated that a smoker would have to gain 75–100 pounds to equal the health risks of smoking a pack a day.

As with any significant change in health-related behavior, giving up tobacco requires planning, sustained effort, and support. It is an ongoing process, not a one-time event. The Behavior Change Strategy describes the steps that successful quitters follow.

Kicking the Tobacco Habit

You can look forward to a longer and healthier life if you join the 47 million Americans who have quit using tobacco. The steps for quitting described below are discussed in terms of the most popular tobacco product in the United States—cigarettes—but they can be adapted for all forms of tobacco.

Gather Information

Collect personal smoking information in a detailed journal about your smoking behavior. Write down the time you smoke each cigarette of the day, the situation you are in, how you feel, where you smoke, and how strong your craving for the cigarette is, plus any other information that seems relevant. Part of the job is to identify patterns of smoking that are connected with routine situations (for example, the coffee break smoke, the after-dinner cigarette, the tension-reduction cigarette). Use this information to discover the behavior patterns involved in your smoking habit.

Make the Decision to Quit

Choose a date in the near future when you expect to be relatively stress-free and can give quitting the energy and attention it will require. Don't choose a date right before or during finals week, for instance. Consider making quitting a gift: Choose your birthday as your quit date, for example, or make quitting a Father's Day or Mother's Day present. You might also want to coordinate your quit date with a buddy—a fellow tobacco user who wants to quit or a nonsmoker who wants to give up another bad habit or begin an exercise program. Tell your friends and family when you plan to quit. Ask them to offer encouragement and help hold you to your goal.

Decide what approach to quitting will work best for you. Will you go cold turkey, or will you taper off? Will you use nicotine patches or gum? Will you join a support group or enlist the help of a buddy? Prepare a contract for quitting, as discussed in Chapter 1. Set firm dates and rewards, and sign the contract. Post it in a prominent place.

Prepare to Quit

One of the most important things you can do to prepare to quit is to develop and practice nonsmoking relaxation techniques. Many smokers find that they use cigarettes to help them unwind in tense situations or to relax at other times. If this is true for you, you'll need to find and develop effective substitutes. It takes time to become proficient at relaxation techniques, so begin practicing before your quit date. Refer to the detailed discussion of relaxation techniques in Chapter 2.

Other things you can do to help prepare for quitting include the following:

- Make an appointment to see your physician. Ask about OTC and prescription aids for tobacco cessation and whether one or more might be appropriate for you.

- Make a dentist's appointment to have your teeth cleaned the day after your target quit date.

- Start an easy exercise program, if you're not exercising regularly already.

- Buy some sugarless gum. Stock your kitchen with low-calorie snacks.

- Clean out your car, and air out your house. Send your clothes out for dry cleaning.

- Throw away all your cigarette-related paraphernalia (ashtrays, lighters, etc.).

- The night before your quit day, get rid of all your cigarettes. Have fun with this—get your friends or family to help you tear them up.

- Make your last few days of smoking inconvenient: Smoke only outdoors and when alone. Don't do anything else while you smoke.

Quitting

Your first few days without cigarettes will probably be the most difficult. It's hard to give up such a strongly ingrained habit, but remember that millions of Americans have done it—and you can, too. Plan and rehearse the steps you will take when you experience a powerful craving. Avoid or control situations that you know from your journal are powerfully associated with your smoking (see the table). If your hands feel empty without a cigarette, try holding or fiddling with a small object such as a paper clip or pencil.

Social support can also be a big help. Arrange with a buddy to help you with your weak moments, and call him or her whenever you feel overwhelmed by an urge to smoke. Tell people you've just quit. You may discover many inspiring former smokers who can encourage you and reassure you that it's possible to quit and lead a happier, healthier life. Find a formal support group to join if you think it will help.

Maintaining Nonsmoking

The lingering smoking urges that remain once you've quit should be carefully tracked and controlled because they can cause relapses if left unattended. Keep track of these urges in your journal to help you deal with them. If certain situations still trigger the urge for a cigarette, change something about the situation to break past associations. If stress or boredom causes strong smoking urges, use a relaxation technique, take a brisk walk, have a stick of gum, or substitute some other activity for smoking.

Don't set yourself up for a relapse. If you allow yourself to get overwhelmed at school or work or to gain weight, it will be easier to convince yourself that now isn't the right time to quit. This *is* the right time. Continue to practice time-management and relaxation techniques. Exercise regularly, eat sensibly, and get enough sleep. These habits will not only ensure your success at remaining tobacco-free but also serve you well in stressful times throughout your life. In fact, former smokers who have quit for at least 3 months report reduced stress levels, probably because quitting smoking lowers overall arousal.

Watch out for patterns of thinking that can make nonsmoking more difficult. Focus on the positive aspects of not smoking, and give yourself lots of praise—you deserve it. Stick with the schedule of rewards you developed for your contract.

Keep track of the emerging benefits that come from having quit. Items that might appear on your list include improved stamina, an increased sense of pride at having kicked a strong addiction, a sharper sense of taste and smell, no more smoker's cough, and so on. Keep track of the money you're saving by not smoking, and spend it on things you really enjoy. And if you do lapse, be gentle with yourself. Lapses are a normal part of quitting. Forgive yourself, and pick up where you left off.

Strategies for Dealing with High-Risk Smoking Situations

Cues and High-Risk Situations	Suggested Strategies
Awakening in morning	Brush your teeth as soon as you wake up. Take a shower or bath.
Drinking coffee	Do something else with your hands. Drink tea or another beverage instead.
Eating meals	Sit in nonsmoking sections of restaurants. Get up from the table right after eating, and start another activity. Brush your teeth right after eating.
Driving a car	Have the car cleaned when you quit smoking. Chew sugarless gum or eat a low-calorie snack. Take public transportation or ride your bike. Turn on the radio and sing along.
Socializing with friends who smoke	Suggest nonsmoking events (movies, theater, shopping). Tell friends you've quit and ask them not to smoke around you, offer you cigarettes, or give you cigarettes if you ask for them.
Drinking at a bar, restaurant, or party	Try to take a nonsmoker with you, or associate with nonsmokers. Let friends know you've just quit. Moderate your intake of alcohol (it can weaken your resolve).
Encountering stressful situations	Practice relaxation techniques. Take some deep breaths. Get out of your room or house. Go somewhere that doesn't allow smoking. Take a shower, chew gum, call a friend, or exercise.

SOURCES: Strategies adapted with permission from *Postgraduate Medicine* 90(1), July 1991.

TIPS FOR TODAY AND THE FUTURE

For most smokers, quitting is one of the hardest things they'll ever do.

RIGHT NOW YOU CAN

- If you smoke, throw the pack and matches away.
- If you smoke, think about the next time you'll want a cigarette, such as while talking on the phone this afternoon or relaxing after dinner tonight. Visualize yourself enjoying this activity without smoking.
- If you use tobacco, go outside for a short walk or a stretch to limber up. Breathe deeply. Tell a friend you've just decided to quit.

IN THE FUTURE YOU CAN

- Resolve to talk to someone you know who uses tobacco, offering support and assistance if the person is interested in quitting.
- If you smoke, resolve to quit. Research your options for quitting and choose the one you think will work best for you.
- Recruit a friend or family member to help you quit smoking. Arrange to talk to this person whenever you feel the urge to smoke.

SUMMARY

- Smoking is the largest preventable cause of ill health and death in the United States. Nevertheless, millions of Americans continue to use tobacco.

- Regular tobacco use causes physical dependence on nicotine, characterized by loss of control, tolerance, and withdrawal. Habits can become associated with tobacco use and trigger the urge for a cigarette.

- People who begin smoking are usually imitating others or responding to seductive advertising. Smoking is associated with low education level and the use of other drugs.

- Tobacco smoke is made up of hundreds of different chemicals, including some that are carcinogenic or poisonous or that damage the respiratory system.

- Nicotine acts on the nervous system as a stimulant or a depressant. It can cause blood pressure and heart rate to increase, straining the heart.

- Cardiovascular disease is the most widespread cause of death for cigarette smokers. Cigarette smoking is the primary cause of lung cancer and is linked to many other cancers and respiratory diseases.

- Cigarette smoking is linked to ulcers, impotence, reproductive health problems, dental diseases, and other conditions. Tobacco use leads to lower life expectancy and to a diminished quality of life.

- The use of spit tobacco leads to nicotine addiction and is linked to oral cancers.

- Cigars, pipes, clove cigarettes, and bidis are not safe alternatives to cigarettes.

- Environmental tobacco smoke (ETS) contains high concentrations of toxic chemicals and can cause headaches, eye and nasal irritation, and sinus problems. Long-term exposure to ETS can cause lung cancer and heart disease.

- Infants and young children take in more pollutants than adults do; children whose parents smoke are especially susceptible to respiratory diseases.

- Smoking during pregnancy increases the risk of miscarriage, stillbirth, congenital abnormalities, premature birth, and low birth weight. SIDS, behavior problems, and long-term impairments in development are also risks.

- The overall cost of tobacco use to society includes the cost of both medical care and lost worker productivity.

- There are many avenues individuals and groups can take to act against tobacco use. Nonsmokers can use social pressure and legislative channels to assert their rights to breathe clean air.

- Giving up smoking is a difficult and long-term process. Although most ex-smokers quit on their own, some smokers benefit from stop-smoking programs, OTC and prescription medications, and support groups.

FOR MORE INFORMATION

BOOKS

American Lung Association. 2004. *How to Quit Smoking Without Gaining Weight.* New York: American Lung Association. *Provides methods for smokers who want to quite but are afraid they'll gain weight as a result.*

Carr, A. 2005. *The Easy Way to Stop Smoking.* New York: Sterling. *A best-selling self-help book for smokers who want to stop.*

Dean, M. 2007. *Empty Cribs: The Impact of Smoking on Child Health.* New York: Arts & Sciences Publishing. *Examines the effects of smoking on children, before and after birth.*

Jeorgensen, N. A., ed. 2006. *Passive Smoking and Health Research.* Hauppauge, N.Y.: Nova Science Publishers. *A scientific look at the health effects of environmental tobacco smoke.*

Sloan, F. A., et al. 2006. *The Price of Smoking,* New ed. Cambridge, Mass.: MIT Press. *A careful examination of the economic and social consequences of smoking.*

Vaknin, J. 2007. *Smoke Signals: 100 Years of Tobacco Advertising.* London: Middlesex University Press. *An exploration of the many ways tobacco products have been marketed to consumers.*

ORGANIZATIONS, HOTLINES, AND WEB SITES

Action on Smoking and Health (ASH). An advocacy group that provides statistics, news briefs, and other information.
http://ash.org

American Cancer Society (ACS). Sponsor of the annual Great American Smokeout; provides information on the dangers of tobacco, as well as tools for prevention and cessation for both smokers and users of spit tobacco.

http://www.cancer.org

American Lung Association. Provides information on lung diseases, tobacco control, and environmental health.

http://www.lungusa.org

CDC's Tobacco Information and Prevention Source (TIPS). Provides research results, educational materials, and tips on how to quit smoking; Web site includes special sections for kids and teens.

http://www.cdc.gov/tobacco

Environmental Protection Agency Indoor Air Quality/ETS. Provides information and links about secondhand smoke.

http://www.epa.gov/smokefree

Nicotine Anonymous. A 12-step program for tobacco users.

http://www.nicotine-anonymous.org

Smokefree.Gov. Provides step-by-step strategies for quitting as well as expert support via telephone or instant messaging.

http://www.smokefree.gov

Tobacco BBS. A resource center on tobacco and smoking issues that includes news and information, assistance for smokers who want to quit, and links to related sites.

http://www.tobacco.org

Tobacco Control Resource Center and Tobacco Products Liability Project (TPLP). Provides current information about tobacco-related court cases and legislation.

http://www.tobacco.neu.edu

World Health Organization Tobacco Free Initiative. Promotes the goal of a tobacco-free world.

http://www.who.int/tobacco/en

World No Tobacco Day (WNTD). Provides information on the annual worldwide event to encourage people to quit smoking; includes general information about tobacco use and testimonials of ex-smokers.

http://www.worldnotobaccoday.com

See also the listings for Chapters 9, 15, and 16.

SELECTED BIBLIOGRAPHY

American Cancer Society. 2008. *Cancer Facts and Figures, 2008.* Atlanta, Ga.: American Cancer Society.

American Lung Association. 2008. *State Legislated Actions on Tobacco Issues (SLATI), 19th Edition* (http://slati.lungusa.org/reports/SLATI_07.pdf; retrieved February 6, 2009).

American Lung Association. 2008. *State of Tobacco Control 2007.* New York: American Lung Association.

American Nonsmokers' Rights Foundation. 2009. *Colleges and Universities with Smokefree Air Policies: January 4, 2009.* (http://www.no-smoke.org/pdf/ smokefreecollegesuniversities.pdf; retrieved February 6, 2009).

Anthonisen, N. R., et al. 2005. The effects of a smoking cessation intervention on 14.5-year mortality: A randomized clinical trial. *Annals of Internal Medicine* 142(4): 233–239.

Campaign for Tobacco-Free Kids. 2008. *State Cigarette Tax Rates and Rank, Date of Last Increase, Annual Pack Sales and Revenues, and Related Data, August 2008* (http://tobaccofreekids.org/research/factsheets/pdf/0099.pdf; retrieved February 6, 2009).

Centers for Disease Control and Prevention. 2005. Annual smoking-attributable mortality, years of potential life lost, and productivity losses—United States, 1997–2001. *Morbidity and Mortality Weekly Report* 54(25): 625–628.

Centers for Disease Control and Prevention. 2006. Cigarette use among high school students—United States, 1991–2005. *Morbidity and Mortality Weekly Report* 55(26): 724–726.

Centers for Disease Control and Prevention. 2007. Cigarette smoking among adults—United States, 2006. *Morbidity and Mortality Weekly Report* 56(44): 1157–1161.

Centers for Disease Control and Prevention. 2008. *Behavioral Risk Factor Surveillance System Survey Data, 2007.* Atlanta, Georgia: U.S. Department of Health and Human Services, Centers for Disease Control and Prevention.

Centers for Disease Control and Prevention. 2008. *Early Release of Selected Estimates Based on Data from the January–March 2008 National Health Interview Survey* (http://www.cdc.gov/nchs/data/nhis/earlyrelease/earlyrelease200809.pdf; retrieved September 29, 2008).

Centers for Disease Control and Prevention. 2008. Surveillance for cancers associated with tobacco use—United States, 1999–2004. *Morbidity and Mortality Weekly Report* 57(SS-08): 1–33.

Centers for Disease Control and Prevention. 2008. Youth risk behavior surveillance—United States, 2007. *Morbidity and Mortality Weekly Report* 57(SS-04): 1–131.

de la Chica, R. A., et al. 2005. Chromosomal instability in amniocytes from fetuses of mothers who smoke. *Journal of the American Medical Association* 293(10): 1212–1222.

Farrelly, M. C., et al. 2005. Evidence of a dose-response relationship between "truth" antismoking ads and youth smoking prevalence. *American Journal of Public Health* 95(3): 425–431.

Fiore, M. C., et al. 2008. *Treating Tobacco Use and Dependence: 2008 Update. Clinical Practice Guideline.* Rockville, Md.: U.S. Department of Health and Human Services, Public Health Service.

Food and Drug Administration. 2008. *Consumer Update: New Safety Warnings for Chantix* (http://www.fds.gov/consumer/updates/chantix020508.html; retrieved September 27, 2008).

Gades, N. M., et al. 2005. Association between smoking and erectile dysfunction: A population-based study. *American Journal of Epidemiology* 161(4): 346–351.

Hanaoka, T., et al. 2005. Active and passive smoking and breast cancer risk in middle-aged Japanese women. *International Journal of Cancer* 114(2): 317–322.

Mannino, D. M., and A. S. Buist. 2007. Global burden of COPD: Risk factors, prevalence, and future trends. *Lancet* 370(9589): 765–773.

Office of Applied Studies, Substance Abuse and Mental Health Services Administration. 2008. *Results from the 2007 National Survey on Drug Use and Health: National Findings* (http://www.drugabusestatistics.samhsa.gov; retrieved February 6, 2009).

Shiffman, S., M. E. Di Marino, and J. L. Pillitteri. 2005. The effectiveness of nicotine patch and nicotine lozenge in very heavy smokers. *Journal of Substance Abuse Treatment* 28(1): 49–55.

Titus-Ernstoff, L., et al. 2008. Longitudinal study of viewing smoking in movies and initiation of smoking by children. *Pediatrics* 121(1): 15–21.

Trimble, C. L., et al. 2005. Active and passive cigarette smoking and the risk of cervical neoplasia. *Obstetrics and Gynecology* 105(1):174–81.

U.S. Surgeon General. 2006. *The Health Consequences of Involuntary Exposure to Tobacco Smoke* (http://www.surgeongeneral.gov/library/secondhandsmoke/ report/; retrieved May 6, 2008).

USA Today Online. 2008. *House Panel OKs FDA Tobacco Regulation* (http://www.usatoday.com/news/washington/2008-04-02-fda-tobacco_N.htm; retrieved October 1, 2008).

Vineis, P., et al. 2005. Environmental tobacco smoke and risk of respiratory cancer and chronic obstructive pulmonary disease in former smokers and never smokers in the EPIC prospective study. *British Medical Journal* 330(7486): 277.

World Health Organization. 2008. *The Global Tobacco Crisis* (http://www.who.int/tobacco/mpower/mpower_report_tobacco_crisis_2008.pdf; retrieved September 27, 2008).

Yolton, K., et al. 2005. Exposure to environmental tobacco smoke and cognitive abilities among U.S. children and adolescents. *Environmental Health Perspectives* 113(1): 98–103.

Zhang, X., et al. 2005. Association of passive smoking by husbands with prevalence of stroke among Chinese women nonsmokers. *American Journal of Epidemiology* 161(3): 213–218.

LOOKING AHEAD>>>>>

AFTER READING THIS CHAPTER, YOU SHOULD BE ABLE TO:

- List the essential nutrients, and describe the functions they perform in the body

- Describe the guidelines that have been developed to help people choose a healthy diet, avoid nutritional deficiencies, and reduce their risk of diet-related chronic diseases

- Discuss nutritional guidelines for vegetarians and for special population groups

- Explain how to use food labels and other consumer tools to make informed choices about foods

- Put together a personal nutrition plan based on affordable foods that you enjoy and that will promote wellness, today as well as in the future

TEST YOUR KNOWLEDGE

1. **It is recommended that all adults consume one to two servings each of fruits and vegetables every day.**
   True or false?

2. **How many french fries are considered to be one 1⁄2-cup serving?**
   a. 10
   b. 15
   c. 25

3. **Candy is the leading source of added sugars in the American diet.**
   True or false?

4. **Which of the following is not a whole grain?**
   a. brown rice
   b. wheat flour
   c. popcorn

5. **Nutritionists advise reduced intake of saturated and trans fats for which of the following reasons?**
   a. They increase levels of low-density lipoproteins (LDL), or "bad" cholesterol.
   b. They provide more calories than other types of fat.
   c. They increase the risk of heart disease.

ANSWERS

1. **FALSE.** For someone consuming 2000 calories, a minimum of nine servings per day—four of fruits and five of vegetables—is recommended, the equivalent of 4½ cups per day.

2. **A.** Many people underestimate the size of the portions they eat, leading to overconsumption of calories and fat.

3. **FALSE.** Regular (nondiet) sodas are the leading source of sugar and of calories, with an average of 55 gallons consumed per person per year. Each 12-ounce soda supplies about 10 teaspoons of sugar, or nearly 10% of the calories in a 2000-calorie diet.

4. **B.** Unless labeled *whole* wheat, wheat flour is processed to remove the bran and the germ and is not a whole grain.

5. **A and C.** High intake of saturated and trans fats raises LDL levels and the risk of heart disease. Saturated and trans fats provide the same number of calories as other types of fat—9 calories per gram (compared to 4 calories per gram for protein and carbohydrate).

In your lifetime, you'll spend about 6 years eating—about 70,000 meals and 60 tons of food. What you eat can have profound effects on your health and well-being. Your nutritional habits help determine your risk of major chronic diseases, including heart disease, cancer, stroke, and diabetes. Choosing foods that provide the nutrients you need while limiting the substances linked to disease should be an important part of your daily life.

Choosing a healthy diet is a two-part process. First, you have to know which nutrients you need and in what amounts. Second, you have to translate those requirements into a diet consisting of foods you like that are both available and affordable. Once you know what constitutes a healthy diet for you, you can adjust your current diet to bring it into line with your goals.

This chapter explains the basic principles of **nutrition.** It introduces the six classes of essential nutrients, explaining their roles in the functioning of the body. It also provides guidelines that you can use to design a healthy diet plan. Finally, it offers practical tools and advice to help you apply the guidelines to your own life.

NUTRITIONAL REQUIREMENTS: COMPONENTS OF A HEALTHY DIET

You probably think about your diet in terms of the foods you like to eat. What's important for your health, though, are the nutrients contained in those foods. Your body requires proteins, fats, carbohydrates, vitamins, minerals, and water—about 45 **essential nutrients.** In this context, the word *essential* means that you must get these substances from food because your body is unable to manufacture them, or at least not fast enough to meet your physiological needs. The six classes of nutrients, along with their functions and major sources, are listed in Table 12.1. The body needs some essential nutrients in relatively large amounts; these **macronutrients** include protein, fat, and carbohydrate. **Micronutrients,** such as vitamins and minerals, are required in much smaller amounts. Your body obtains these nutrients through the process of **digestion,** in which the foods you eat are broken down into compounds your gastrointestinal tract can absorb and your body can use (Figure 12.1). A diet that provides enough essential nutrients is vital because various nutrients provide energy, help build and maintain body tissues, and help regulate body functions (see the box "Eating Habits and Total Wellness" on p. 332).

Calories

The energy in foods is expressed as **kilocalories.** One kilocalorie represents the amount of heat it takes to raise the temperature of 1 liter of water 1°C. A person needs about 2000 kilocalories per day to meet his or her energy needs. In common usage, people usually refer to kilocalories as *calories,* which is technically a much smaller energy unit: (1 kilocalorie contains 1000 calories). This text uses the familiar word *calorie* to stand for the larger energy unit; you'll also find the word *calorie* used on food labels.

Of the six classes of essential nutrients, three supply energy:

- Fat = 9 calories per gram
- Protein = 4 calories per gram
- Carbohydrate = 4 calories per gram

Alcohol, though not an essential nutrient, also supplies energy, providing 7 calories per gram. (One gram equals a little less than .04 ounce.) The high caloric content of fat is one reason experts often advise against high fat consumption; most of us do not need the extra calories to meet energy needs. Regardless of their source, calories consumed in excess of energy needs are converted to fat and stored in the body.

Table 12.1	The Six Classes of Essential Nutrients	
Nutrient	**Function**	**Major Sources**
Proteins (4 calories/gram)	Form important parts of muscles, bone, blood, enzymes, some hormones, and cell membranes; repair tissue; regulate water and acid-base balance; help in growth; supply energy	Meat, fish, poultry, eggs, milk products, legumes, nuts
Carbohydrates (4 calories/gram)	Supply energy to cells in brain, nervous system, and blood; supply energy to muscles during exercise	Grains (breads and cereals), fruits, vegetables, milk
Fats (9 calories/gram)	Supply energy; insulate, support, and cushion organs; provide medium for absorption of fat-soluble vitamins	Animal foods, grains, nuts, seeds, fish, vegetables
Vitamins	Promote (initiate or speed up) specific chemical reactions within cells	Abundant in fruits, vegetables, and grains; also found in meat and dairy products
Minerals	Help regulate body functions; aid in growth and maintenance of body tissues; act as catalysts for release of energy	Found in most food groups
Water	Makes up 50–60% of body weight; provides medium for chemical reactions; transports chemicals; regulates temperature; removes waste products	Fruits, vegetables, liquids

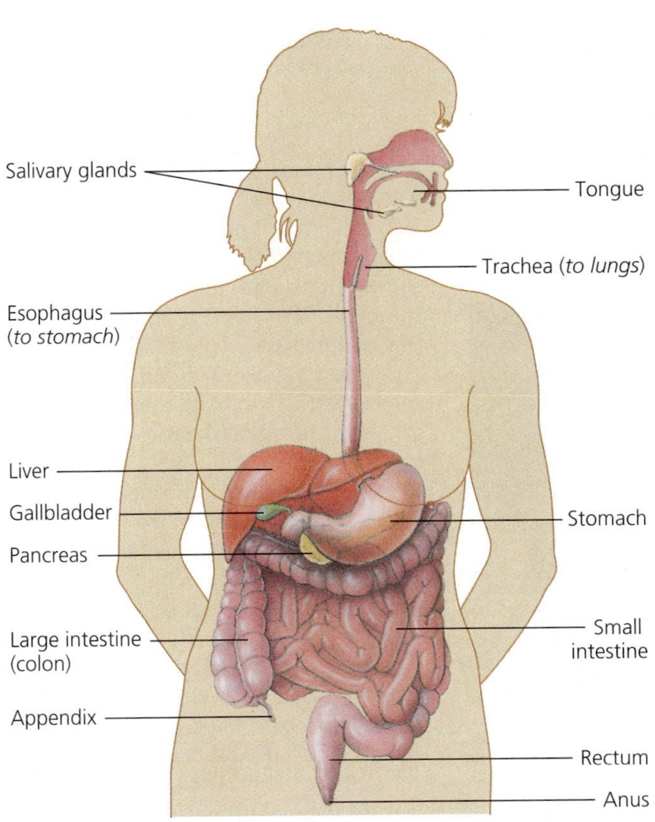

FIGURE 12.1 The digestive system. Food is partially broken down by being chewed and mixed with saliva in the mouth. After traveling to the stomach via the esophagus, food is broken down further by stomach acids and other secretions. As food moves through the digestive tract, it is mixed by muscular contractions and broken down by chemicals. Most absorption of nutrients occurs in the small intestine, aided by secretions from the pancreas, gallbladder, and intestinal lining. The large intestine reabsorbs excess water; the remaining solid wastes are collected in the rectum and excreted through the anus.

But just meeting energy needs is not enough; our bodies need enough of the essential nutrients to grow and function properly. Practically all foods contain mixtures of nutrients, although foods are commonly classified according to the predominant nutrient; for example, spaghetti is thought of as a carbohydrate. The following sections discuss the function and sources of each class of nutrients.

Proteins—The Basis of Body Structure

Proteins form important parts of the body's main structural components: muscles and bones. Proteins also form important parts of blood, enzymes, some hormones, and cell membranes. As mentioned earlier, proteins also provide energy (4 calories per gram) for the body.

Amino Acids The building blocks of proteins are called **amino acids.** Twenty common amino acids are found in food; nine of these are essential: histidine, isoleucine, leucine, lysine, methionine, phenylalanine, threonine, tryptophan, and valine. The other eleven amino acids can be produced by the body, given the presence of the needed components supplied by foods.

Complete and Incomplete Proteins Individual protein sources are considered *complete* if they supply all the essential amino acids in adequate amounts and *incomplete* if they do not. Meat, fish, poultry, eggs, milk, cheese, and soy provide complete proteins. Incomplete proteins, which come from other plant sources such as **legumes** and nuts, are good sources of most essential amino acids but are usually low in one or two.

Certain combinations of vegetable proteins, such as wheat and peanuts in a peanut butter sandwich, allow each vegetable protein to make up for the amino acids missing in the other protein. The combination yields a complete protein. Many traditional food pairings, such as beans and rice or corn and beans, emerged as dietary staples because they are complementary proteins.

It was once believed that vegetarians had to complement their proteins at each meal in order to receive the benefit of a complete protein. It is now known, however, that proteins consumed throughout the course of the day can complement each other to form a pool of amino acids the body can draw from to produce the necessary proteins. Vegetarians should include a variety of vegetable

QUICK STATS

Worldwide, 35% of childhood deaths and 11% of diseases are attributable to malnutrition.

—Lancet, 2008

TERMS

nutrition The science of food and how the body uses it in health and disease.

essential nutrients Substances the body must get from foods because it cannot manufacture them at all or fast enough to meet its needs. These nutrients include proteins, fats, carbohydrates, vitamins, minerals, and water.

macronutrient An essential nutrient required by the body in relatively large amounts.

micronutrient An essential nutrient required by the body in minute amounts.

digestion The process of breaking down foods in the gastrointestinal tract into compounds the body can absorb.

kilocalorie A measure of energy content in food; 1 kilocalorie represents the amount of heat needed to raise the temperature of 1 liter of water 1°C; commonly referred to as *calorie.*

protein An essential nutrient; a compound made of amino acids that contains carbon, hydrogen, oxygen, and nitrogen.

amino acids The building blocks of proteins.

legumes Vegetables such as peas and beans that are high in fiber and are also important sources of protein.

MIND/BODY/SPIRIT

Healthy eating does more than nourish your body—it enhances your ability to enjoy life to the fullest by improving overall wellness, both physical and mental. One study examined a group of adults who followed a healthy eating plan for four years. At the end of this period, the study subjects were more confident with their food choices and more satisfied with their lives in general than their peers who did not make any dietary changes. The reverse is also true—when people overeat, they often have feelings of guilt, anger, discouragement, and even self-loathing. Out-of-control eating can erode self-confidence and lead to depression.

Can individual foods affect the way we feel? Limited scientific evidence points to some correlation between certain foods and one's mood. Many people, especially women, seem to crave chocolate when they feel slightly depressed. Studies show that chocolate, in small quantities, may indeed give you a lift. Sugary foods tend to temporarily raise serotonin levels in the brain, which can improve mood (serotonin is a neurotransmitter associated with a calm, relaxed state). The fat found in chocolate acts to increase endorphins, brain chemicals that reduce pain and increase feelings of well-being. Chocolate also contains a variety of other less studied chemicals that may have a positive impact on mood.

A commonly held belief about the connection between food and the mind

is that eating sugary foods makes people (especially children) hyperactive. Parents often comment on the wild behavior observed at parties and festive events where lots of sweets are consumed. However, several carefully controlled studies showed no correlation between behavior and the consumption of sugary foods. Researchers speculate that high-sugar foods tend to be eaten at birthday parties and other exciting occasions when children tend to be highly stimulated regardless of what they eat.

Some recent research shows that eating certain carbohydrate-rich foods, such as a plain baked potato or a bagel with jelly, can have a temporary calming effect. This effect is most pronounced when rapidly digestible carbohydrates are consumed alone, with no fats or proteins in the meal. The practical implications of this research are uncertain.

If you are looking for a mental boost, some scientists think that eating a meal consisting primarily of protein-rich foods may be helpful. The theory is that proteins contain the amino acid tyrosine, which the body uses to make the neurotransmitters dopamine and norepinephrine. Some researchers think that eating protein-rich foods could increase the synthesis of these neurotransmitters, which can speed reaction time and increase alertness. Whether this really works, especially in well-nourished individuals who have not been lacking these nutrients to begin with, remains to be seen. In the meantime, it wouldn't hurt, and might even help, to include some protein in the meal you eat prior to your next big exam.

What we know about how food affects mood remains limited. But evidence points to the commonsense conclusion that enjoying reasonable portions of a variety of healthy and tasty foods is a great way to optimize your physical and mental health.

SOURCE: Fahey, T. D., P. M. Insel, and W. T. Roth. 2007. *Fit and Well*, 8th ed. New York: McGraw-Hill. Copyright © 2007 The McGraw-Hill Companies, Inc.

protein sources in their diets to make sure they get all the essential amino acids in adequate amounts. (Healthy vegetarian diets are discussed later in the chapter.) About two-thirds of the protein in the American diet comes from animal sources (meat and dairy products); therefore, the American diet is rich in essential amino acids.

Recommended Protein Intake Adequate daily intake of protein for adults is 0.8 gram per kilogram (0.36 gram per pound) of body weight, corresponding to 50 grams of protein per day for someone who weighs 140 pounds and 65 grams of protein for someone who weighs 180 pounds. Table 12.2 lists some popular food items and the amount of protein each provides.

Most Americans meet or exceed the protein intake needed for adequate nutrition. If you consume more protein than your body needs, the extra protein is synthesized into fat for energy storage or burned for energy requirements. A little extra protein is not harmful, but it can contribute fat to the diet because protein-rich foods are often fat-rich as well. A very high protein intake can also strain the kidneys.

A fairly broad range of protein intakes is associated with good health, and the Food and Nutrition Board recommends that the amount of protein adults eat should fall within the range of 10–35% of total daily calorie intake, depending on the individual's age. The average American diet includes about 15–16% of total daily calories as protein.

Table 12.2	Protein Content of Common Food Items	
Item		**Protein (grams)**
3 ounces lean meat, poultry, or fish		20–25
½ cup tofu		20–25
1 cup dried beans		15–20
1 cup milk, yogurt		8–12
1½ ounces cheese		8–12
1 serving of cereals, grains, nuts, vegetables		2–4

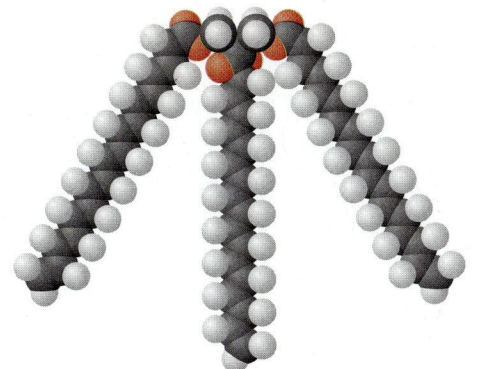

FIGURE 12.2 A triglyceride.

Fats—Essential in Small Amounts

Fats, also known as *lipids*, are the most concentrated source of energy, at 9 calories per gram. The fats stored in your body represent usable energy, they help insulate your body, and they support and cushion your organs. Fats in the diet help your body absorb fat-soluble vitamins, and add important flavor and texture to foods. Fats are the major fuel for the body during rest and light activity.

Two fats, linoleic acid and alpha-linolenic acid, are essential components of the diet. They are used to make compounds that are key regulators of such body functions as the maintenance of blood pressure and the progress of a healthy pregnancy.

Types and Sources of Fats   Most of the fats in foods are fairly similar in composition, generally including a molecule of glycerol (an alcohol) with three fatty acid chains attached to it. The resulting structure is called a *triglyceride* (see Figure 12.2). Animal fat, for example, is primarily made of triglycerides.

Within a triglyceride, differences in the fatty acid structure result in different types of fats. Depending on this structure, a fat may be unsaturated, monounsaturated, polyunsaturated, or saturated. (The essential fatty acids—linoleic and alpha-linolenic acids—are both polyunsaturated.) The different types of fatty acids have different characteristics and different effects on your health.

Food fats are usually composed of both saturated and unsaturated fatty acids; the dominant type of fatty acid determines the fat's characteristics. Food fats containing large amounts of saturated fatty acids are usually solid at room temperature; they are generally found naturally in animal products. The leading sources of saturated fat in the American diet are red meats (hamburger, steak, roasts), whole milk, cheese, hot dogs, and lunch meats. Food fats containing large amounts of monounsaturated and polyunsaturated fatty acids usually come from plant sources and are liquid at room temperature. Olive, canola, safflower, and peanut oils contain mostly monounsaturated fatty acids. Soybean, corn, and cottonseed oils contain mostly polyunsaturated fatty acids.

Hydrogenation   There are notable exceptions to these generalizations. When unsaturated vegetable oils undergo the process of **hydrogenation,** a mixture of saturated and unsaturated fatty acids is produced, creating a more solid fat from a liquid oil. Hydrogenation also changes some unsaturated fatty acids to **trans fatty acids,** unsaturated fatty acids with an atypical shape that affects their behavior in the body. Food manufacturers use hydrogenation to increase the stability of an oil so it can be reused for deep frying, to improve the texture of certain foods (to make pastries and pie crusts flakier, for example), and to extend the shelf life of foods made with oil. Hydrogenation is also used to transform a liquid oil into margarine or vegetable shortening.

Many baked and fried foods are prepared with hydrogenated vegetable oils, so they can be relatively high in saturated and trans fatty acids. Leading sources of trans fats in the American diet are deep-fried fast foods such as french fries and fried chicken (typically fried in vegetable shortening rather than oil); baked and snack foods such as pot pies, cakes, cookies, pastries, doughnuts, and chips; and stick margarine.

In general, the more solid a hydrogenated oil is, the more saturated and trans fats it contains; for example, stick margarines typically contain more saturated and trans fats than do tub or squeeze margarines. Small amounts of trans fatty acids are found naturally in meat and milk.

hydrogenation   A process by which hydrogens are added to unsaturated fats, increasing the degree of saturation and turning liquid oils into solid fats. Hydrogenation produces a mixture of saturated fatty acids and standard and trans forms of unsaturated fatty acids.

trans fatty acid   A type of unsaturated fatty acid produced during the process of hydrogenation; trans fats have an atypical shape that affects their chemical activity.

TERMS

12 American cities, including New York City and Philadelphia, have banned artificial trans fats in restaurants. In California, a statewide ban takes effect in 2011.

—*New York Times,* 2008

Hydrogenated vegetable oils are not the only plant fats that contain saturated fats. Palm and coconut oils, although derived from plants, are also highly saturated. However, fish oils, derived from an animal source, are rich in polyunsaturated fats.

Fats and Health   Different types of fats have very different effects on health. Many studies have examined the effects of dietary fat intake on blood **cholesterol** levels and the risk of heart disease. Saturated and trans fatty acids raise blood levels of **low-density lipoprotein (LDL),** or "bad" cholesterol, thereby increasing a person's risk of heart disease. Unsaturated fatty acids lower LDL. Monounsaturated fatty acids, such as those found in olive and canola oils, may also increase levels of **high-density lipoproteins (HDL),** or "good" cholesterol, providing even greater benefits for heart health. In large amounts, trans fatty acids may lower HDL. Saturated fats have been found to impair the ability of HDLs to prevent inflammation of the blood vessels, one of the key factors in vascular disease; they have also been found to reduce the ability of the blood vessels to react normally to stress. Thus, to reduce the risk of heart disease, it is important to choose unsaturated fats instead of saturated and trans fats. (See Chapter 15 for more on cholesterol.)

Most Americans consume more saturated fat than trans fat (11% versus 2–4% of total daily calories). However, health experts are particularly concerned about trans fats because of their double negative effect on heart health—they both raise LDL and lower HDL—and because there is less public awareness of trans fats. Since January 2006,

cholesterol   A waxy substance found in the blood and cells and needed for synthesis of cell membranes, vitamin D, and hormones.

low-density lipoprotein (LDL)   Blood fat that transports cholesterol to organs and tissues; excess amounts result in the accumulation of deposits on artery walls.

high-density lipoprotein (HDL)   Blood fat that helps transport cholesterol out of the arteries, thereby protecting against heart disease.

omega-3 fatty acids   Polyunsaturated fatty acids commonly found in fish oils that are beneficial to cardiovascular health.

food labels have included trans fat content. Consumers can also check for the presence of trans fats by examining the ingredient list of a food for partially hydrogenated oil or vegetable shortening.

For heart health, it's important to minimize your consumption of both saturated and trans fats. The best way to reduce saturated fat in your diet is to lower your intake of meat and full-fat dairy products (whole milk, cream, butter, cheese, yogurt, ice cream). To lower trans fats, decrease your intake of deep-fried foods and crackers, cookies, and other baked goods made with hydrogenated vegetable oils; use liquid oils for cooking; and favor tub or squeeze margarines over stick margarines. Remember, the softer or more liquid a fat is, the less saturated and trans fat it is likely to contain.

Although saturated and trans fats pose health hazards, other fats can be beneficial. When used in place of saturated fats, monounsaturated fatty acids, as found in avocados, most nuts, and olive, canola, peanut, and safflower oils, improve cholesterol levels and may help protect against some cancers.

Omega-3 fatty acids, a form of polyunsaturated fat found primarily in fish, may be even more healthful. Foods rich in omega-3s are important because they contain the essential nutrient alpha-linolenic acid. Omega-3s and the compounds the body makes from them have a number of heart-healthy effects: They reduce the tendency of blood to clot, inhibit inflammation and abnormal heart rhythms, and reduce blood pressure and risk of heart attack and stroke in some people. Because of these benefits, nutritionists recommend that Americans increase the proportion of omega-3s in their diet by eating fish two or more times a week. Salmon, tuna, trout, mackerel, herring, sardines, and anchovies are all good sources of omega-3s; lesser amounts are found in plant foods, including darkgreen leafy vegetables; walnuts; flaxseeds; and canola, walnut, and flaxseed oils.

Most of the polyunsaturated fats currently consumed by Americans are omega-6 fatty acids, primarily from corn oil and soybean oil. Foods rich in omega-6s are important because they contain the essential nutrient linoleic acid. However, some nutritionists recommend that people reduce the proportion of omega-6s they consume in favor of omega-3s. To make this adjustment, use canola oil rather than corn oil in cooking, and check for corn, soybean, or cottonseed oil in products such as mayonnaise, margarine, and salad dressing.

In addition to its effects on heart disease risk, dietary fat can affect health in other ways. Diets high in fatty red meat are associated with an increased risk of certain forms of cancer, especially colon cancer. A high-fat diet can also make weight management more difficult. Because fat is a concentrated source of calories (9 calories per gram versus 4 calories per gram for protein and carbohydrate), a high-fat diet is often a high-calorie diet that can lead to weight gain. In addition, there is some evidence that calo-

Type of Fatty Acid		Found In[a]	Possible Effects on Health
SATURATED		Animal fats (especially fatty meats and poultry fat and skin) Butter, cheese, and other high-fat dairy products Palm and coconut oils	Raises total cholesterol and LDL cholesterol levels Increases risk of heart disease May increase risk of colon and prostate cancers
TRANS		French fries and other deep-fried fast foods Stick margarines, shortening Packaged cookies and crackers Processed snacks and sweets	Raises total cholesterol and LDL cholesterol levels Lowers HDL cholesterol levels May increase risk of heart disease and breast cancer
MONOUNSATURATED		Olive, canola, and safflower oils Avocados, olives Peanut butter (without added fat) Many nuts, including almonds, cashews, pecans, and pistachios	Lowers total cholesterol and LDL cholesterol levels May reduce blood pressure and lower triglyceride levels (a risk factor for CVD) May reduce risk of heart disease, stroke, and some cancers
POLYUNSATURATED (two groups)[b]			
Omega-3 fatty acids		Fatty fish, including salmon, white albacore tuna, mackerel, anchovies, and sardines Lesser amounts in walnut, flaxseed, canola, and soybean oils; tofu; walnuts; flaxseeds; and dark green leafy vegetables	Reduces blood clotting and inflammation and inhibits abnormal heart rhythms Lowers triglyceride levels (a risk factor for CVD) May lower blood pressure in some people May reduce risk of fatal heart attack, stroke, and some cancers
Omega-6 fatty acids		Corn, soybean, and cottonseed oils (often used in margarine, mayonnaise, and salad dressing)	Lowers total cholesterol and LDL cholesterol levels May lower HDL cholesterol levels May reduce risk of heart disease May slightly increase risk of cancer if omega-6 intake is high and omega-3 intake is low

Left margin labels: *Keep Intake Low* (Saturated, Trans); *Choose Moderate Amounts* (Monounsaturated, Polyunsaturated)

[a] Food fats contain a combination of types of fatty acids in various proportions; for example, canola oil is composed mainly of monounsaturated fatty acids (62%) but also contains polyunsaturated (32%) and saturated (6%) fatty acids. Food fats are categorized here according to their predominant fatty acid.

[b] The essential fatty acids are polyunsaturated: Linoleic acid is an omega-6 fatty acid and alpha-linolenic acid is an omega-3 fatty acid.

FIGURE 12.3   Types of fatty acids and their possible effects on health.

ries from fat are more easily converted to body fat than calories from protein or carbohydrate.

Although more research is needed on the precise effects of different types and amounts of fat on overall health, a great deal of evidence points to the fact that most people benefit from keeping their overall fat intake at recommended levels and choosing unsaturated fats instead of saturated and trans fats. The types of fatty acids and their effects on health are summarized in Figure 12.3.

Recommended Fat Intake   To meet the body's demand for essential fats, adult men need about 17 grams per day of linoleic acid and 1.6 grams per day of alpha-linolenic acid; adult women need 12 grams of linoleic acid and 1.1 grams of alpha-linolenic acid. It takes only 3–4 teaspoons (15–20 grams) of vegetable oil per day incorporated into your diet to supply the essential fats. Most Americans consume sufficient amounts of the essential fats; limiting unhealthy fats is a much greater health concern.

Limits for total fat, saturated fat, and trans fat intake have been set by a number of government and research organizations. In 2002, the Food and Nutrition Board of the Institute of Medicine released recommendations for the balance of energy sources in a healthful diet. These new recommendations, called Acceptable Macronutrient Distribution Ranges (AMDRs), are based on ensuring adequate intake of essential nutrients while also reducing the risk of chronic diseases such as heart disease and cancer. As with protein, a range of levels of fat consumption is associated with good health; the AMDR for total fat is 20–35% of total calories. Although more difficult for consumers to monitor, AMDRs have also been set for omega-6 fatty acids (5–10%) and omega-3 fatty acids (0.6–1.2%) as part of total fat intake. Because any amount of saturated and trans fats increases the risk of heart disease, the Food and Nutrition Board recommends that saturated fat and trans

Three ounces of salmon provides 1.1– 1.9 grams of omega-3 fatty acids.

—American Heart Association, 2008

QUICK STATS

Setting Intake Goals for Protein, Fat, and Carbohydrate

Goals have been established by the Food and Nutrition Board to help ensure adequate intake of the essential amino acids, fatty acids, and carbohydrate. The daily goals for adequate intake for adults are as follow:

	Men	Women
Protein	56 grams	46 grams
Fat: Linoleic acid	17 grams	12 grams
Alpha-linolenic acid	1.6 grams	1.1 grams
Carbohydrate	130 grams	130 grams

Protein intake goals can be calculated more specifically by multiplying your body weight in kilograms by 0.8 or your body weight in pounds by 0.36. (Refer to the Nutrition Resources section at the end of the chapter for information for specific age groups and life stages.)

To meet your daily energy needs, you need to consume more than the minimally adequate amounts of the energy-providing nutrients listed above, which alone supply only about 800–900 calories. The Food and Nutrition Board provides additional guidance in the form of Acceptable Macronutrient Distribution Ranges (AMDRs). The ranges can help you balance your intake of the energy-providing nutrients in ways that ensure adequate intake while reducing the risk of chronic disease. The AMDRs for protein, total fat, and carbohydrate are as follow:

Protein	10–35% of total daily calories
Total fat	20–35% of total daily calories
Carbohydrate	45–65% of total daily calories

To set individual goals, begin by estimating your total daily energy (calorie) needs; if your weight is stable, your current energy intake is the number of calories you need to maintain your weight at your current activity level. Next, select percentage goals for protein, fat, and carbohydrate. You can allocate your total daily calories among the three classes of macronutrients to suit your preferences; just make sure that the three percentages you select total 100% and that you meet the minimum intake goals listed. Two samples reflecting different total energy intake and nutrient intake goals are shown in the table below.

To translate your own percentage goals into daily intake goals expressed in calories and grams, multiply the appropriate percentages by total calorie intake and then divide the results by the corresponding calories per gram. For example, a fat limit of 35% applied to a 2200-calorie diet would be calculated as follows: $0.35 \times 2200 = 770$ calories of total fat; $770 \div 9$ calories per gram = 86 grams of total fat. (Remember that, fat has 9 calories per gram and that protein and carbohydrate have 4 calories per gram.)

Two Sample Macronutrient Distributions

Nutrient	AMDR	Sample 1		Sample 2	
		Individual Goals	Amounts for a 1600-Calorie Diet	Individual Goals	Amounts for a 2800-Calorie Diet
Protein	10–35%	15%	240 calories = 60 grams	30%	840 calories = 210 grams
Fat	20–35%	30%	480 calories = 53 grams	25%	700 calories = 78 grams
Carbohydrate	45–65%	55%	880 calories = 220 grams	45%	1260 calories = 315 grams

SOURCE: Food and Nutrition Board, Institute of Medicine, National Academies. 2002. *Dietary Reference Intakes: Applications in Dietary Planning*, Washington, D.C.: National Academies Press. Reprinted with permission from the National Academies Press, Washington, D.C.

fat intake be kept as low as possible; most fat in a healthy diet should be unsaturated. American adults currently consume about 33% of total calories as fat, including 11% of calories as saturated fat and 2–4% as trans fat.

For advice on setting individual intake goals, see the box "Setting Intake Goals for Protein, Fat, and Carbohydrate" above. To determine how close you are to meeting your personal intake goals for fat, keep a running total over the course of the day. For prepared foods, food labels list the number of grams of fat, protein, and carbohydrate; the breakdown for popular fast-food items can be found in Appendix A. Nutrition information is also available in many grocery stores, in inexpensive published nutrition guides, and online (see For More Information at the end of the chapter). By checking these resources, you can keep track of the total grams of fat, protein, and carbohydrate you eat and assess your current diet.

You can still eat high-fat foods, but it makes sense to limit the size of your portions and to balance your intake with low-fat foods. For example, peanut butter is high in fat, with 8 grams (72 calories) of fat in each 90-calorie tablespoon. Two tablespoons of peanut butter eaten on whole-wheat bread and served with a banana, carrot sticks, and a glass of fat-free milk makes a nutritious lunch—high in protein and carbohydrate, and relatively low in fat (500 calories, 18 grams of total fat, 4 grams of saturated fat). Four tablespoons of peanut butter on high-fat crackers with potato chips, cookies, and whole milk is a less healthy combination (1000 calories, 62 grams of total fat, 15 grams of saturated fat). So although it's important to evaluate individual food items for their fat content, it is more important to look at them in the context of your overall diet.

Carbohydrates—An Ideal Source of Energy

Carbohydrates are needed in the diet primarily to supply energy for body cells. Some cells, such as those found in the brain and other parts of the nervous system and in blood, use only carbohydrates for fuel. During high-intensity exercise, muscles also use primarily carbohydrates for fuel.

When we don't eat enough carbohydrates to satisfy the needs of the brain and red blood cells, our bodies synthesize carbohydrates from proteins. In situations of extreme deprivation, when the diet lacks a sufficient amount of both carbohydrates and proteins, the body turns to its own organs and tissues, breaking down proteins in muscles, the heart, kidneys, and other vital organs to supply carbohydrate needs. This rarely occurs, however, because consuming the equivalent of just three or four slices of bread supplies the body's daily minimum need for carbohydrates.

Simple and Complex Carbohydrates Carbohydrates are classified into two groups: simple and complex. Simple carbohydrates include sucrose (table sugar), fructose (fruit sugar, honey), maltose (malt sugar), and lactose (milk sugar). Simple carbohydrates provide much of the sweetness in foods and are found naturally in fruits and milk and are added to soft drinks, fruit drinks, candy, and sweet desserts. There is no evidence that any type of simple carbohydrate is more nutritious than others.

Complex carbohydrates include starches and most types of dietary fiber. Starches are found in a variety of plants, especially grains (wheat, rye, rice, oats, barley, millet), legumes (dry beans, peas, and lentils), and tubers (potatoes and yams). Most other vegetables contain a mixture of complex and simple carbohydrates. Fiber, discussed in the next section, is found in grains, fruits, and vegetables.

During digestion in the mouth and small intestine, your body breaks down carbohydrates into simple sugar molecules, such as **glucose,** for absorption. Once glucose is in the bloodstream, the pancreas releases the hormone insulin, which allows cells to take up glucose and use it for energy. The liver and muscles also take up glucose to provide carbohydrate storage in the form of **glycogen.** Some people have problems controlling blood glucose levels, a disorder called *diabetes mellitus* (see Chapter 14 for more on diabetes).

Refined Carbohydrates Versus Whole Grains Complex carbohydrates can be further divided between refined, or processed, carbohydrates and unrefined carbohydrates, or whole grains. Before they are processed, all

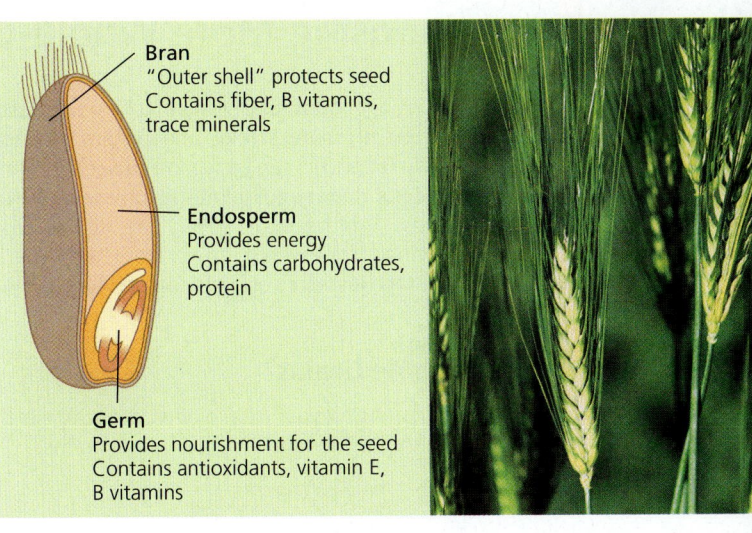

Bran
"Outer shell" protects seed
Contains fiber, B vitamins, trace minerals

Endosperm
Provides energy
Contains carbohydrates, protein

Germ
Provides nourishment for the seed
Contains antioxidants, vitamin E, B vitamins

FIGURE 12.4   The parts of a whole grain kernel.

grains are **whole grains,** consisting of an inner layer, germ; a middle layer, the endosperm; and an outer layer, bran (Figure 12.4). During processing, the germ and bran are often removed, leaving just the starchy endosperm. The refinement of whole grains transforms whole-wheat flour to white flour, brown rice to white rice, and so on.

Refined carbohydrates usually retain all the calories of their unrefined counterparts, but they tend to be much lower in fiber, vitamins, minerals, and other beneficial compounds. (Many refined grain products are enriched or fortified with vitamins and minerals, but often the nutrients lost in processing are not replaced.)

Unrefined carbohydrates tend to take longer to chew and digest than refined ones; they also enter the bloodstream more slowly. This slower digestive pace tends to make people feel full sooner and for a longer period. Also, a slower rise in blood glucose levels following consumption of complex carbohydrates may help in the management of diabetes. Whole grains are also high

carbohydrate   An essential nutrient; sugars, starches, and dietary fiber are all carbohydrates.

glucose   A simple sugar that is the body's basic fuel.

glycogen   An animal starch stored in the liver and muscles.

whole grain   The entire edible portion of a grain such as wheat, rice, or oats, consisting of the germ, endosperm, and bran. During milling or processing, parts of the grain are removed, often leaving just the endosperm.

TERMS

Choosing More Whole-Grain Foods

Whole-grain foods are good weapons against heart disease, diabetes, high blood pressure, stroke, and certain cancers. They are also low in fat and so can be a good choice for managing weight. Federal dietary guidelines recommend six or more total servings of grain products every day, with at least half of these servings from whole grains. However, Americans currently average less than one serving of whole grains per day.

What Are Whole Grains?

The first step in increasing your intake of whole grains is to correctly identify them. The following are whole grains:

whole wheat	whole-grain corn
whole rye	popcorn
whole oats	brown rice
oatmeal	whole-grain barley

More unusual choices include bulgur (cracked wheat), millet, kasha (roasted buckwheat kernels), quinoa, wheat and rye berries, amaranth, wild rice, graham flour, whole-grain kamut, whole-grain spelt, and whole-grain triticale.

Wheat flour, unbleached flour, enriched flour, and de-germinated corn meal are not whole grains. Wheat germ and wheat bran are also not whole grains, but they are the constituents of wheat typically left out when wheat is processed and so are healthier choices than regular wheat flour, which typically contains just the endosperm.

Reading Food Packages to Find Whole Grains

To find packaged foods rich in whole grains, read the list of ingredients and check for special health claims related to whole grains. The *first* item on the list of ingredients should be one of the whole grains listed above. In addition, the FDA allows manufacturers to include special health claims for foods that contain 51% or more whole-grain ingredients. Such products may contain a statement such as the following on their packaging: "Rich in whole grain," "Made with 100% whole grain," or "Diets rich in whole-grain foods may help reduce the risk of heart disease and certain cancers." However, many whole-grain products will not carry such claims. Product names and food color can be misleading. *When in doubt, always check the list of ingredients, looking for "whole" as the first word on the list.*

Incorporating Whole Grains into Your Daily Diet

• *Bread:* Look for sandwich breads, bagels, English muffins, buns, and pita breads with a whole grain listed as the first ingredient.

• *Breakfast cereals:* Check the ingredient list for whole grains. Whole-grain choices include oatmeal, muesli, shredded wheat, and some types of raisin bran, bran flakes, wheat flakes, toasted oats, and granola.

• *Rice:* Choose brown rice or rice blends that include brown rice.

• *Pasta:* Look for whole-wheat, whole-grain kamut, or whole-grain spelt pasta.

• *Tortillas:* Choose whole-wheat or whole-corn tortillas.

• *Crackers and snacks:* Some varieties of crackers are made from whole grains, including some flatbreads or crispbreads, woven wheat crackers, and rye crackers. Other whole-grain snack possibilities include popcorn, popcorn cakes, brown rice cakes, whole-corn tortilla chips, and whole-wheat fig cookies. Be sure to check food labels for fat content, as many popular snacks are high in fat.

• *Mixed-grain dishes:* Combine whole grains with other foods to create healthy mixed dishes. Possibilities include tabouli; soups made with hulled barley or wheat berries; and pilafs, casseroles, and salads made with brown rice, whole-wheat couscous, kasha, millet, wheat bulgur, or quinoa.

If your grocery store doesn't carry all of these items, try your local health food store.

---

in dietary fiber and so have all the benefits of fiber (discussed later). Consumption of whole grains has been linked to a reduced risk of heart disease, diabetes, high blood pressure, stroke, and certain forms of cancer. For all these reasons, whole grains are recommended over those that have been refined. This does not mean that you should never eat refined carbohydrates such as white bread or white rice, simply that whole-wheat bread, brown rice, and other whole grains are healthier choices. See the box "Choosing More Whole-Grain Foods" above for tips on increasing your intake of whole grains.

Glycemic Index and Glycemic Response Insulin and glucose levels rise and fall following a meal or snack containing any type of carbohydrate. Some foods cause a quick and dramatic rise in glucose and insulin levels; others have a slower, more moderate effect. A food that has a rapid effect on blood glucose levels is said to have a high **glycemic index.** Research findings have been mixed, but some studies have found that a meal containing high glycemic index foods may increase appetite, and that over the long term, diets rich in these foods may increase risk of diabetes and heart disease for some people. High glycemic index foods do not, as some popular diets claim, directly cause weight gain beyond the calories they contain.

Attempting to base food choices on glycemic index is a difficult task, however. Although unrefined complex carbohydrates and high-fiber foods generally tend to have a low glycemic index, patterns are less clear for other types of foods and do not follow an easy distinction such as that of simple versus complex carbohydrates. For example, some fruits with fairly high levels of simple carbohydrates have only a moderate effect on blood glucose levels, whereas white rice, potatoes, and white bread, which are rich in complex carbohydrates, have a high glycemic index. Watermelon has a glycemic index more than twice that of strawberries, and the glycemic index of a banana changes dramatically as it ripens. The acid and fat content of a food also affect glycemic index; the more acidic and higher in fat a food is, the lower its effect on glucose levels. The body's response to carbohydrates also depends on many other factors, such as how foods are combined and prepared and the fitness status of the individual.

This complexity is one reason major health organizations have not issued specific guidelines for glycemic index. For people with particular health concerns, glycemic index may be an important consideration; however, it should not be the sole criterion for food choices. For example, ice cream has a much lower glycemic index than brown rice or carrots—but that doesn't make it a healthier choice overall. Remember that most unrefined grains, fruits, vegetables, and legumes are rich in nutrients, have a relatively low energy density, and have a low to moderate glycemic index. Choose a variety of vegetables daily, and avoid heavy consumption of white potatoes. Limit foods that are high in added sugars but provide few other nutrients. Some studies have singled out regular soda, with its large dose of rapidly absorbable sugar, as specifically linked to increased diabetes risk.

Recommended Carbohydrate Intake   On average, Americans consume 200–300 grams of carbohydrate per day, well above the 130 grams needed to meet the body's requirement for essential carbohydrate. A range of intakes is associated with good health, and experts recommend that adults consume 45–65% of total daily calories as carbohydrate, about 225–325 grams of carbohydrate for someone consuming 2000 calories per day. The focus should be on consuming a variety of foods rich in complex carbohydrates, especially whole grains.

Although the Food and Nutrition Board set an AMDR for added sugars of 25% or less of total daily calories, many health experts recommend an even lower intake. World Health Organization guidelines suggested a limit of 10% of total daily calories from added sugars; limits set by the USDA in 2005 are even lower, with a maximum of about 8 teaspoons (32 grams) suggested for someone consuming 2000 calories per day. Foods high in added sugar are generally high in calories and low in nutrients and fiber, thus providing empty calories. To reduce your intake of added sugars, limit soft drinks, candy, sweet desserts, and sweetened fruit drinks. The simple carbohydrates in your diet should come mainly from fruits, which are excellent sources of vitamins and minerals, and from low-fat or fat-free milk and other dairy products, which are high in protein and calcium.

Athletes in training can especially benefit from high-carbohydrate diets (60–70% of total daily calories), which enhance the amount of carbohydrates stored in their muscles (as glycogen) and therefore provide more carbohydrate fuel for use during endurance events or long workouts. In addition, carbohydrates consumed during prolonged athletic events can help fuel muscles and extend the availability of the glycogen stored in muscles. Caution is in order, however, because overconsumption of carbohydrates can lead to fatigue and underconsumption of other nutrients.

Fiber—A Closer Look

Fiber is the term given to nondigestible carbohydrates provided by plants. Instead of being digested, like starch, fiber passes through the intestinal tract and provides bulk for feces in the large intestine, which in turn facilitates elimination. In the large intestine, some types of fiber are broken down by bacteria into acids and gases, which explains why consuming too much fiber can lead to intestinal gas. Because humans cannot digest fiber, it is not a source of carbohydrate in the diet; however, the consumption of fiber is necessary for good health.

Types of Fiber   The Food and Nutrition Board has defined two types of fiber: dietary fiber and functional fiber. **Dietary fiber** refers to the nondigestible carbohydrates (and the noncarbohydrate substance lignin) that are present naturally in plants such as grains, legumes, and vegetables. **Functional fiber** refers to nondigestible carbohydrates that have been either isolated from natural sources or synthesized in a lab and then added to a food product or dietary supplement. **Total fiber** is the sum of dietary and functional fiber.

Fibers have different properties that lead to different physiological effects in the body. For example, **soluble (viscous) fiber** such as that found in oat bran or legumes can delay stomach emptying, slow the movement of glucose into the blood after eating, and reduce absorption of cholesterol. **Insoluble fiber,** such as that found in wheat bran or psyllium seed, increases fecal bulk and helps prevent constipation, hemorrhoids, and other digestive

TERMS

glycemic index   A measure of how the ingestion of a particular food affects blood glucose levels.

dietary fiber   Nondigestible carbohydrates and lignin that are intact in plants.

functional fiber   Nondigestible carbohydrates either isolated from natural sources or synthesized; these may be added to foods and dietary supplements.

total fiber   The total amount of dietary fiber and functional fiber in the diet.

soluble (viscous) fiber   Fiber that dissolves in water or is broken down by bacteria in the large intestine.

insoluble fiber   Fiber that does not dissolve in water and is not broken down by bacteria in the large intestine.

disorders. A diet high in fiber can help reduce the risk of type 2 diabetes and heart disease as well as improve gastrointestinal health. Some studies have linked high-fiber diets with reduced risk of colon and rectal cancer; other studies have suggested that other characteristics of diets rich in fruits, vegetables, and whole grains may be responsible for this reduction in risk (see Chapter 16 for more on cancer and diet).

Sources of Fiber   All plant foods contain some dietary fiber. Fruits, legumes, oats (especially oat bran), and barley all contain the viscous types of fiber that help lower blood glucose and cholesterol levels. Wheat (especially wheat bran), other grains and cereals, and vegetables are good sources of cellulose and other fibers that help prevent constipation. Psyllium, which is often added to cereals or used in fiber supplements and laxatives, improves intestinal health and also helps control glucose and cholesterol levels. The processing of packaged foods can remove fiber, so it is important to rely on fresh fruits and vegetables and foods made from whole grains as your main sources of fiber.

Recommended Fiber Intake   To reduce the risk of chronic disease and maintain intestinal health, the Food and Nutrition Board recommends a daily fiber intake of 38 grams for adult men and 25 grams for adult women. Americans currently consume about half this amount. Fiber should come from foods, not supplements, which should be used only under medical supervision.

Vitamins—Organic Micronutrients

Vitamins are organic (carbon-containing) substances required in small amounts to regulate various processes within living cells (Table 12.3). Humans need 13 vitamins; 4 are fat-soluble (A, D, E, and K), and 9 are water-soluble (C, and the 8 B-complex vitamins: thiamin, riboflavin, niacin, vitamin B-6, folate, vitamin B-12, biotin, and pantothenic acid).

Solubility affects how a vitamin is absorbed, transported, and stored in the body. The water-soluble vitamins are absorbed directly into the bloodstream, where they travel freely; excess water-soluble vitamins are detected and removed by the kidneys and excreted in urine. Fat-soluble vitamins require a more complex absorptive process; they are usually carried in the blood by special proteins and are stored in the liver and in fat tissues rather than excreted.

Functions of Vitamins   Many vitamins help chemical reactions take place. They provide no energy to the body directly but help unleash the energy stored in carbohydrates, proteins, and fats. Vitamins are critical in the production of red blood cells and the maintenance of the nervous, skeletal, and immune systems. Some vitamins act as **antioxidants,** which help preserve healthy cells in the body. Key vitamin antioxidants include vitamin E, vitamin C, and the vitamin A precursor beta-carotene. (Antioxidants are described later in the chapter.)

Sources of Vitamins   The human body does not manufacture most of the vitamins it requires and must obtain them from foods. Vitamins are abundant in fruits, vegetables, and grains. In addition, many processed foods, such as flour and breakfast cereals, contain added vitamins. A few vitamins are made in certain parts of the body: The skin makes vitamin D when it is exposed to sunlight, and intestinal bacteria make vitamin K. Nonetheless, you still need to obtain vitamin D and vitamin K from foods. Table 12.3 lists good food sources of vitamins.

Vitamin Deficiencies   If your diet lacks a particular vitamin, characteristic symptoms of deficiency can develop. (Table 12.3 lists the signs of certain vitamin deficiencies.) Physicians have known about some common deficiency-related ailments for generations. For example, *scurvy* is a potentially fatal illness caused by a long-term lack of vitamin C. Children who do not get enough vitamin D can develop *rickets,* which leads to potentially disabling bone deformations. Vitamin A deficiency may cause blindness, and seizures can develop in people whose diet lacks vitamin B-6. Low intake of folate and vitamins B-6 and B-12 has been linked to an increased risk of heart disease.

New research is tying vitamin deficiencies with other health risks, as well. For example, two recent studies showed that a lack of vitamin K may contribute to bone brittleness and contribute to bone fractures. A great deal of recent research has focused on vitamin D, with surprising results. Several studies have associated vitamin D deficiency with an increased risk of cardiovascular disease in adults, and show that the vitamin plays an important role in arterial health and blood clotting. A 2008 study also raised the possibility that women with certain types of breast

TERMS

vitamins   Carbon-containing substances needed in small amounts to help promote and regulate chemical reactions and processes in the body.

antioxidant   A substance that can lessen the breakdown of food or body constituents by free radicals; actions include binding oxygen, donating electrons to free radicals, and repairing damage to molecules.

Table 12.3   Facts About Vitamins

Vitamin	Important Dietary Sources	Major Functions	Signs of Prolonged Deficiency	Toxic Effects of Megadoses
Fat-Soluble				
Vitamin A	Liver, milk, butter, cheese, and fortified margarine; carrots, spinach, and other orange and deep-green vegetables and fruits	Maintenance of vision, skin, linings of the nose, mouth, digestive and urinary tracts, immune function	Night blindness; dry, scaling skin; increased susceptibility to infection; loss of appetite; anemia; kidney stones	Liver damage, miscarriage and birth defects, headache, vomiting and diarrhea, vertigo, double vision, bone abnormalities
Vitamin D	Fortified milk and margarine, fish oils, butter, egg yolks (sunlight on skin also produces vitamin D)	Development and maintenance of bones and teeth, promotion of calcium absorption	Rickets (bone deformities) in children; bone softening, loss, and fractures in adults	Kidney damage, calcium deposits in soft tissues, depression, death
Vitamin E	Vegetable oils, whole grains, nuts and seeds, green leafy vegetables, asparagus, peaches	Protection and maintenance of cellular membranes	Red blood cell breakage and anemia, weakness, neurological problems, muscle cramps	Relatively nontoxic, but may cause excess bleeding or formation of blood clots
Vitamin K	Green leafy vegetables; smaller amounts widespread in other foods	Production of factors essential for blood clotting and bone metabolism	Hemorrhaging	None reported
Water-Soluble				
Bitoin	Cereals, yeast, egg yolks, soy flour, liver; widespread in foods	Synthesis of fat, glycogen, and amino acids	Rash, nausea, vomiting, weight loss, depression, fatigue, hair loss	None reported
Folate	Green leafy vegetables, yeast, oranges, whole grains, legumes, liver	Amino acid metabolism, synthesis of RNA and DNA, new cell synthesis	Anemia, weakness, fatigue, irritability, shortness of breath, swollen tongue	Masking of vitamin B-12 deficiency
Niacin	Eggs, poultry, fish, milk, whole grains, nuts, enriched breads and cereals, meats, legumes	Conversion of carbohydrates, fats, and protein into usable forms of energy	Pellagra (symptoms include diarrhea, dermatitis, inflammation of mucous membranes, dementia)	Flushing of the skin, nausea, vomiting, diarrhea, liver dysfunction, glucose intolerance
Pantothenic acid	Animal foods, whole grains, broccoli, potatoes; widespread in foods	Metabolism of fats, carbohydrates, and proteins	Fatigue, numbness and tingling of hands and feet, gastrointestinal disturbances	None reported
Riboflavin	Dairy products, enriched breads and cereals, lean meats, poultry, fish, green vegetables	Energy metabolism; maintenance of skin, mucous membranes, and nervous system structures	Cracks at corners of mouth, sore throat, skin rash, hypersensitivity to light, purple tongue	None reported
Thiamin	Whole-grain and enriched breads and cereals, organ meats, lean pork, nuts, legumes	Conversion of carbohydrates into usable forms of energy, maintenance of appetite and nervous system function	Beriberi (symptoms include muscle wasting, mental confusion, anorexia, enlarged heart, nerve changes)	None reported
Vitamin B-6	Eggs, poultry, fish, whole grains, nuts, soybeans, liver, kidney, pork	Metabolism of amino acids and glycogen	Anemia, convulsions, cracks at corners of mouth, dermatitis, nausea, confusion	Neurological abnormalities and damage
Vitamin B-12	Meat, fish, poultry, fortified cereals	Synthesis of blood cells; other metabolic reactions	Anemia, fatigue, nervous system damage, sore tongue	None reported
Vitamin C	Peppers, broccoli, spinach, brussels sprouts, citrus fruits, strawberries, tomatoes, potatoes, cabbage, other fruits and vegetables	Maintenance and repair of connective tissue, bones, teeth, and cartilage; promotion of healing; aid in iron absorption	Scurvy, anemia, reduced resistance to infection, loosened teeth, joint pain, poor wound healing, hair loss, poor iron absorption	Urinary stones in some people, acid stomach from ingesting supplements in pill form, nausea, diarrhea, headache, fatigue

SOURCES: Food and Nutrition Board, Institute of Medicine. 2006. *Dietary Reference Intakes: The Essential Guide to Nutrient Requirements.* Washington, D.C.: The National Academies Press. The complete Dietary Reference Intake reports are available from the National Academy Press (http://www.nap.edu); Shils, M. E., et al., eds. 2005. *Modern Nutrition in Health and Disease,* 10th ed. Baltimore: Lippincott Williams & Wilkins.

cancer may be more likely to die from their cancer if they do not get enough vitamin D.

Vitamin deficiency diseases are most often seen in developing countries, and are relatively rare in the United States because vitamins are readily available from our food supply. Still, many Americans consume less-than-recommended amounts of several vitamins, including vitamins A, C, and E. It is estimated that up to 50% of adult Americans do not get the recommended amount of vitamin D in their diets.

Even in the face of new findings, however, experts warn that there is not yet enough evidence to prove that everyone should begin taking vitamin supplements. Supplementation is discussed in detail later in this chapter.

Vitamin Excesses Extra vitamins in the diet can also be harmful, especially when taken as supplements. Megadoses of fat-soluble vitamins are particularly dangerous because the excess is stored in the body rather than excreted, increasing the risk of toxicity. Even when vitamins are not taken in excess, relying on supplements for an adequate intake of vitamins can be a problem. There are many substances in foods other than vitamins and minerals, and some of these compounds may have important health effects. Later in the chapter we discuss specific recommendations for vitamin intake and when a vitamin supplement is advisable. For now, keep in mind that it's best to get most of your vitamins from foods rather than supplements.

Keeping the Nutrient Value in Food Vitamins and minerals can be lost or destroyed during the storage and cooking of foods. To retain nutrients, consume or process vegetables as soon as possible after purchasing. Store fruits and vegetables in the refrigerator in covered containers or plastic bags to minimize moisture loss; freeze foods that won't be eaten within a few days. (Frozen and canned vegetables are usually as high in nutrients as fresh vegetables because nutrients are locked in when produce is frozen or canned.) To reduce nutrient losses during food preparation, minimize the amount of water used and the total cooking time. Develop a taste for a crunchier texture in cooked vegetables. Baking, steaming, broiling, grilling, and microwaving are all good methods of preparing vegetables.

Minerals—Inorganic Micronutrients

Minerals are inorganic (non–carbon-containing) elements you need in relatively small amounts to help regulate body functions, aid in the growth and maintenance of body tissues, and help release energy (Table 12.4). There are about 17 essential minerals. The major minerals, those that the body needs in amounts exceeding 100 milligrams per day, include calcium, phosphorus, magnesium, sodium, potassium, and chloride. The essential trace minerals, those that you need in minute amounts, include copper, fluoride, iodide, iron, selenium, and zinc.

Characteristic symptoms develop if an essential mineral is consumed in a quantity too small or too large for good health. The minerals commonly lacking in the American diet are iron, calcium, potassium, and magnesium. Iron-deficiency **anemia** is a problem in many age groups, and researchers fear poor calcium intakes in childhood are sowing the seeds for future **osteoporosis**, especially in women. See Chapter 19 for more information on osteoporosis; the box "Eating for Healthy Bones" (p. 344) has tips for building and maintaining bone density.

Water—Vital but Often Ignored

Water is the major component in both foods and the human body: You are composed of about 50–60% water. Your need for other nutrients, in terms of weight, is much less than your need for water. You can live up to 50 days without food, but only a few days without water.

Water is distributed all over the body, among lean and other tissues and in blood and other body fluids. Water is used in the digestion and absorption of food and is the medium in which most of the chemical reactions take place within the body. Some water-based fluids, like blood, transport substances around the body, whereas other fluids serve as lubricants or cushions. Water also helps regulate body temperature.

Water is contained in almost all foods, particularly in liquids, fruits, and vegetables. The foods and fluids you consume provide 80–90% of your daily water intake; the remainder is generated through metabolism. You lose water each day in urine, feces, and sweat and through evaporation from your lungs.

TERMS

minerals Inorganic compounds needed in relatively small amounts for regulation, growth, and maintenance of body tissues and functions.

anemia A deficiency in the oxygen-carrying material in the red blood cells.

osteoporosis A condition in which the bones become extremely thin and brittle and break easily.

free radical An electron-seeking compound that can react with fats, proteins, and DNA, damaging cell membranes and mutating genes in its search for electrons; produced through chemical reactions in the body and by exposure to environmental factors such as sunlight and tobacco smoke.

Table 12.4 Facts About Selected Minerals

Mineral	Important Dietary Sources	Major Functions	Signs of Prolonged Deficiency	Toxic Effects of Megadoses
Calcium	Milk and milk products, tofu, fortified orange juice and bread, green leafy vegetables, bones in fish	Formation of bones and teeth, control of nerve impulses, muscle contraction, blood clotting	Stunted growth in children, bone mineral loss in adults; urinary stones	Kidney stones, calcium deposits in soft tissues, inhibition of mineral absorption, constipation
Fluoride	Fluoridated water, tea, marine fish eaten with bones	Maintenance of tooth and bone structure	Higher frequency of tooth decay	Increased bone density, mottling of teeth, impaired kidney function
Iodine	Iodized salt, seafood, processed foods	Essential part of thyroid hormones, regulation of body metabolism	Goiter (enlarged thyroid), cretinism (birth defect)	Depression of thyroid activity, hyperthyroidism in susceptible people
Iron	Meat and poultry, fortified grain products, dark green vegetables, dried fruit	Component of hemoglobin, myoglobin, and enzymes	Iron-deficiency anemia, weakness, impaired immune function, gastrointestinal distress	Nausea, diarrhea, liver and kidney damage, joint pains, sterility, disruption of cardiac function, death
Magnesium	Widespread in foods and water (except soft water); especially found in grains, legumes, nuts, seeds, green vegetables, milk	Transmission of nerve impulses, energy transfer, activation of many enzymes	Neurological disturbances, cardiovascular problems, kidney disorders, nausea, growth failure in children	Nausea, vomiting, diarrhea, central nervous system depression, coma; death in people with impaired kidney function
Phosphorus	Present in nearly all foods, especially milk, cereal, peas, eggs, meat	Bone growth and maintenance, energy transfer in cells	Impaired growth, weakness, kidney disorders, cardiorespiratory and nervous system dysfunction	Drop in blood calcium levels, calcium deposits in soft tissues, bone loss
Potassium	Meats, milk, fruits, vegetables, grains, legumes	Nerve function and body water balance	Muscular weakness, nausea, drowsiness, paralysis, confusion, disruption of cardiac rhythm	Cardiac arrest
Selenium	Seafood, meat, eggs, whole grains	Defense against oxidative stress, regulation of thyroid hormone action	Muscle pain and weakness, heart disorders	Hair and nail loss, nausea and vomiting, weakness, irritability
Sodium	Salt, soy sauce, salted foods, tomato juice	Body water balance, acid-base balance, nerve function	Muscle weakness, loss of appetite, nausea, vomiting; deficiency is rarely seen	Edema, hypertension in sensitive people
Zinc	Whole grains, meat, eggs, liver, seafood (especially oysters)	Synthesis of proteins, RNA, and DNA; wound healing; immune response; ability to taste	Growth failure, loss of appetite, impaired taste acuity, skin rash, impaired immune function, poor wound healing	Vomiting, impaired immune function, decline in blood HDL levels, impaired copper absorption

SOURCES: Food and Nutrition Board, Institute of Medicine. 2006. *Dietary Reference Intakes: The Essential Guide to Nutrient Requirements.* Washington, D.C.: The National Academies Press. The complete Dietary Reference Intake reports are available from the National Academy Press (http://www.nap.edu); Shils, M. E., et al., eds. 2005. *Modern Nutrition in Health and Disease,* 10th ed. Baltimore: Lippincott Williams & Wilkins.

Most people can maintain a healthy water balance by consuming beverages at meals and drinking fluids in response to thirst. The Food and Nutrition Board has set levels of adequate water intake to maintain hydration; all fluids, including those containing caffeine, can count toward your total daily fluid intake. Under these guidelines, men need to consume about 3.7 total liters of water, with 3.0 liters (about 13 cups) coming from beverages; women need 2.7 total liters, with 2.2 liters (about 9 cups) coming from beverages. (See Table 1 in the Nutrition Resources section at the end of the chapter for information on specific age groups.) If you exercise vigorously or live in a hot climate, you need to consume additional fluids to maintain a balance between water consumed and water lost. Severe dehydration causes weakness and can lead to death.

Other Substances in Food

Many substances in food are not essential nutrients but may influence health.

Antioxidants When the body uses oxygen or breaks down certain fats or proteins as a normal part of metabolism, it gives rise to substances called **free radicals.**

Eating for Healthy Bones

Osteoporosis is a condition in which the bones become dangerously thin and fragile over time. An estimated 10 million Americans over age 50 have osteoporosis, and another 34 million are at risk. Women account for about 80% of osteoporosis cases. Most bone mass is built by age 18. After bone density peaks between ages 25 and 35, bone mass is lost over time. To prevent osteoporosis, the best strategy is to build as much bone as possible during your youth and do everything you can to maintain it as you age. Up to 50% of bone loss is determined by controllable lifestyle factors. Key nutrients for bone health include the following:

- **Calcium.** Consuming an adequate amount of calcium is important throughout life to build and maintain bone mass. Milk, yogurt, and calcium-fortified orange juice, bread, and cereals are all good sources.

- **Vitamin D.** Vitamin D is necessary for bones to absorb calcium; a daily intake of 5 micrograms is recommended for adults age 19–50. Vitamin D can be obtained from foods and is manufactured by the skin when exposed to sunlight. Candidates for vitamin D supplements include people who don't eat many foods rich in vitamin D; those who don't expose their face, arms, and hands to the sun (without sunscreen) for 5–15 minutes a few times each week; and people who live north of an imaginary line roughly between Boston and the Oregon–California border (the sun is weaker in northern latitudes).

- **Vitamin K.** Vitamin K promotes the synthesis of proteins that help keep bones strong. Broccoli and leafy green vegetables are rich in vitamin K.

- **Other nutrients.** Other nutrients that may play an important role in bone health include vitamin C, magnesium, potassium, manganese, zinc, copper, and boron.

On the flip side, there are several dietary substances that may have a *negative* effect on bone health, especially if consumed in excess: alcohol, sodium, caffeine, and retinol (a form of vitamin A). Drinking lots of soda, which often replaces milk in the diet and which is high in phosphorus (a mineral that may interfere with calcium absorption), has been shown to increase the risk of bone fracture in teenage girls.

The effect of protein intake on bone mass depends on other nutrients: Protein helps build bone as long as calcium and vitamin D intake are adequate; but if intake of calcium and vitamin D is low, high protein intake can lead to bone loss.

Weight-bearing aerobic exercise helps maintain bone mass throughout life, and strength training improves bone density, muscle mass, strength, and balance. Drinking alcohol only in moderation, refraining from smoking, and managing depression and stress are also important for maintaining strong bones. For people who develop osteoporosis, a variety of medications are available to treat the condition.

Environmental factors such as cigarette smoke, exhaust fumes, radiation, excessive sunlight, certain drugs, and stress can increase free radical production. A free radical is a chemically unstable molecule that reacts with fats, proteins, and DNA, damaging cell membranes and mutating genes. Free radicals have been implicated in aging, cancer, cardiovascular disease, and other degenerative diseases like arthritis.

Antioxidants found in foods can help protect the body from damage by free radicals in several ways. Some prevent or reduce the formation of free radicals; others remove free radicals from the body; still others repair some types of free radical damage after it occurs. Some antioxidants, such as vitamin C, vitamin E, and selenium, are also essential nutrients. Others—such as the carotenoids found in yellow, orange, and deep-green vegetables—are not. Researchers recently identified the top antioxidant-containing foods and beverages as blackberries, walnuts, strawberries, artichokes, cranberries, brewed coffee, raspberries, pecans, blueberries, cloves, grape juice, unsweetened baking chocolate, sour cherries, and red wine. Also high in antioxidants are brussels sprouts, kale, cauliflower, and pomegranates.

Phytochemicals   Antioxidants fall into the broader category of **phytochemicals**, substances found in plant foods that may help prevent chronic disease. Researchers have just begun to identify and study all the different compounds found in foods, and many preliminary findings are promising. For example, certain substances found in soy foods may help lower cholesterol levels. Sulforaphane, a compound isolated from broccoli and other **cruciferous vegetables**, may render some carcinogenic compounds harmless. Allyl sulfides, a group of chemicals found in garlic and onions, appear to boost the activity of cancer-fighting immune cells. Further research on phytochemicals may extend the role of nutrition to the prevention and treatment of many chronic diseases.

If you want to increase your intake of phytochemicals, it is best to eat a variety of fruits, vegetables, and grains rather than relying on supplements. Like many vitamins

QUESTIONS FOR CRITICAL THINKING AND REFLECTION

Experts say that two of the most important factors in a healthy diet are eating the "right" kinds of carbohydrates and the "right" kinds of fats. Based on what you've read so far in this chapter, which are the "right" carbohydrates and fats? How would you say your own diet stacks up when it comes to carbs and fats?

Cruciferous vegetables like broccoli are rich in phytochemicals and essential vitamins and minerals.

and minerals, isolated phytochemicals may be harmful if taken in high doses. In addition, it is likely that their health benefits are the result of chemical substances working in combination. The role of phytochemicals in disease prevention is discussed further in Chapters 15 and 16.

NUTRITIONAL GUIDELINES: PLANNING YOUR DIET

Various tools have been created by scientific and government groups to help people design healthy diets. The **Dietary Reference Intakes (DRIs)** are standards for nutrient intake designed to prevent nutritional deficiencies and reduce the risk of chronic disease. **Dietary Guidelines for Americans** have been established to promote health and reduce the risk for major chronic diseases through diet and physical activity. Further guidance symbolized by **MyPyramid** provides daily food intake patterns that meet the DRIs and are consistent with the Dietary Guidelines for Americans.

Dietary Reference Intakes (DRIs)

The Food and Nutrition Board establishes dietary standards, or recommended intake levels, for Americans of all ages. The current set of standards, called Dietary Reference Intakes (DRIs), is relatively new, having been intro-

duced in 1997. The DRIs are frequently reviewed and are updated as new nutrition-related information becomes available. The DRIs present different categories of nutrients in easy-to-read table format. An earlier set of standards, called the Recommended Dietary Allowances (RDAs), focused on preventing nutritional deficiency diseases such as anemia. The DRIs have a broader focus because of research that looked not just at the prevention of nutrient deficiencies but also at the role of nutrients in promoting health and preventing chronic diseases such as cancer, osteoporosis, and heart disease.

The DRIs include standards for both recommended intakes and maximum safe intakes. The recommended intake of each nutrient is expressed as either a *Recommended Dietary Allowance (RDA)* or *Adequate Intake (AI)*. An AI is set when there is not enough information available to set an RDA value; regardless of the type of standard used, however, the DRI represents the best available estimate of intake for optimal health. The *Tolerable Upper Intake Level (UL)* is the maximum daily intake that is unlikely to cause health problems in a healthy person. For example, the AI for calcium for an 18-year-old female is 1300 mg per day; the UL is 2500 mg per day.

Because of lack of data, ULs have not been set for all nutrients. This does not mean that people can tolerate chronic intakes of these vitamins and minerals above recommended levels (see the box "Should You Take Supplements?" on p. 346). Like all chemical agents, nutrients can produce adverse effects if intakes are excessive. There is no established benefit from consuming nutrients at levels above the RDA or AI. The DRIs can be found in the Nutrition Resources section at the end of the chapter.

Because the DRIs are too cumbersome to use as a basis for food labels, the U.S. Food and Drug Administration

TERMS

phytochemical A naturally occurring substance found in plant foods that may help prevent and treat chronic diseases like cancer and heart disease; *phyto* means plant.

cruciferous vegetables Vegetables of the cabbage family, including cabbage, broccoli, brussels sprouts, kale, and cauliflower; the flower petals of these plants form the shape of a cross, hence the name.

Dietary Reference Intakes (DRIs) An umbrella term for four types of nutrient standards. Estimated Average Requirement (EAR) is the amount estimated to meet the nutrient needs of half the individuals in a population group; Adequate Intake (AI) and Recommended Dietary Allowance (RDA) are levels of intake considered adequate to prevent nutrient deficiencies and reduce the risk of chronic disease for most individuals in a population group; Tolerable Upper Intake Level (UL) is the maximum daily intake that is unlikely to cause health problems.

Dietary Guidelines for Americans General principles of good nutrition intended to help prevent certain diet-related diseases.

MyPyramid A food-group plan that provides practical advice to ensure a balanced intake of the essential nutrients.

Should You Take Supplements?

The aim of the Dietary Reference Intakes (DRIs) is to guide you in meeting your nutritional needs primarily with food, rather than with vitamin and mineral supplements. Supplements lack potentially beneficial phytochemicals and fibers that are found only in whole foods. Most Americans can get the vitamins and minerals they need by eating a nutritionally balanced diet of various foods. The use of supplements to reduce heart disease or cancer risk remains controversial, so experts suggest that you avoid taking any nutrient at a level exceeding the Tolerable Upper Intake Level (UL).

The question of whether to take supplements is a serious one. Some vitamins and minerals are dangerous when taken in excess. Large doses of particular nutrients can also cause health problems by affecting the absorption of certain vitamins or minerals. For this reason, ask your doctor or a dietician before taking any high-dosage supplement.

In setting the DRIs, the Food and Nutrition Board recommended supplements of particular nutrients for specific groups:

• Women who are capable of getting pregnant should get 400 µg per day of folic acid (the synthetic form of the vitamin folate) from fortified foods and/or supplements in addition to folate from a varied diet. This level of folate can reduce the risk of neural tube defects in a developing fetus. Enriched breads, flours, cornmeal, rice, noodles, and other grain products are fortified with folic acid. Folate is found naturally in leafy green vegetables, legumes, oranges, and strawberries.

• People over age 50 should eat foods fortified with vitamin B-12, take a B-12 supplement, or combine the two to meet the RDA of 2.4 µg daily. Up to 30% of people over 50 may have trouble absorbing protein-bound B-12 in foods.

• Because of the oxidative stress caused by smoking, smokers should get 35 mg more vitamin C per day than the RDA set for their age and sex. Supplements aren't usually necessary, however, because this extra vitamin C can easily be found in foods. For example, one cup of orange juice has about 100 mg of vitamin C.

Supplements may be recommended in other cases. Women with heavy menstrual flows, for example, may need extra iron. Elderly people, people with dark skin, and people exposed to little sunlight may need extra vitamin D. Some vegetarians may need supplemental calcium, iron, zinc, and B-12, depending on their food choices. Other people may benefit from supplementation based on their physical conditions, the medicines they take, or their dietary habits.

Before deciding whether to take a vitamin or mineral supplement, consider

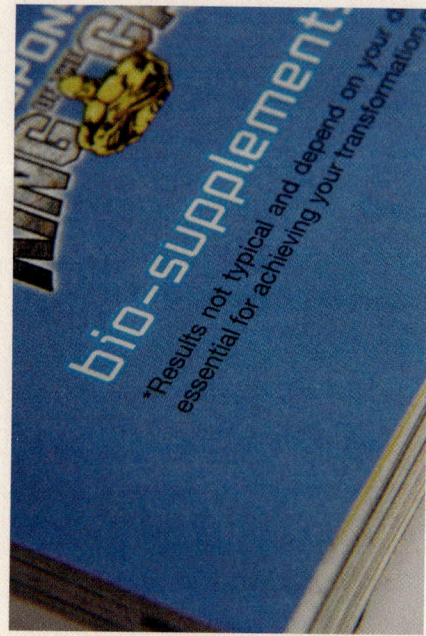

whether you already consume a fortified breakfast cereal every day. Many breakfast cereals contain almost as many nutrients as a multivitamin pill. If you elect to take a supplement, choose one that contains 50–100% of the Daily Value for vitamins and minerals. Avoid supplements containing large doses of particular nutrients.

(FDA) uses another set of dietary standards, the **Daily Values.** The Daily Values are based on several different sets of guidelines and include standards for fat, cholesterol, carbohydrate, dietary fiber, and selected vitamins and minerals. The Daily Values represent appropriate intake levels for a 2000-calorie diet. The percent Daily Value shown on a food label shows how well that food contributes to your recommended daily intake. Food labels are described in detail later in the chapter.

Dietary Guidelines for Americans

To provide general guidance for choosing a healthy diet, the U.S. Department of Agriculture (USDA) and the U.S. Department of Health and Human Services (DHHS) have jointly issued Dietary Guidelines for Americans, most recently in 2005. These guidelines are intended for healthy children age 2 and older and adults of all ages. Key recommendations include the following:

• Consume a variety of nutrient-dense foods within and among the basic food groups, while staying within energy needs.

• Control calorie intake to manage body weight.

• Be physically active every day.

• Increase daily intake of foods from certain groups: fruits and vegetables, whole grains, and fat-free or low-fat milk and milk products.

• Choose fats wisely for good health, limiting intake of saturated and trans fats.

• Choose carbohydrates wisely for good health, limiting intake of added sugars.

• Choose and prepare foods with little salt, and consume potassium-rich foods.

• If you drink alcoholic beverages, do so in moderation.

• Keep foods safe to eat.

THINKING ABOUT THE ENVIRONMENT

Environmental issues—including booming populations and changing weather patterns—have coupled with fuel shortages to create a potential global food crisis. In 2008, evidence of such a crisis began to mount, even as worldwide production of many food staples reached all-time highs.

- The growing demand for corn to create ethanol (an alternative to gasoline) has driven up corn prices and greatly reduced the amount of grain used for human and animal consumption.

- Driven by fears of future shortages, the price of rice rose by more than 75% between December 2007 and April 2008. Some rice-producing countries began restricting rice exports to meet their own needs for the staple.

- Riots erupted in Haiti, Egypt, Bangladesh, and other countries in the spring of 2008, as residents protested food shortages and high prices. Many experts warned that at current rates, the world's poorest people soon would not be able to feed themselves.

For more information on the environment and health, see Chapter 19.

Following these guidelines promotes health and reduces risk for chronic diseases, including heart disease, cancer, diabetes, stroke, osteoporosis, and obesity. Each of the recommendations in the 2005 Dietary Guidelines for Americans is supported by an extensive review of scientific and medical evidence.

Adequate Nutrients Within Calorie Needs Many people consume more calories than they need while failing to meet recommended intakes for all nutrients. The DRIs provide a foundation not only for current health but also for reducing chronic disease risk.

Two eating plans that translate nutrient recommendations into food choices are the USDA's MyPyramid and the DASH eating plan. MyPyramid is described in detail later in this chapter. The DASH plan appears in the Nutrition Resources section at the end of the chapter. You can obtain all the nutrients you need by choosing the recommended number of daily servings from basic food groups and following the advice about selecting nutrient-dense foods within the groups.

People's food choices can be affected by individual and cultural preferences, moral beliefs, the cost and availability of food, and food intolerances and allergies. But healthy eating is possible no matter how foods are prepared or combined (see the box "Ethnic Foods" on p. 348). If you avoid most or all foods from any of the major food groups, be sure to get enough nutrients from the other groups. MyPyramid can be applied to vegetarian diets.

Weight Management Overweight and obesity are a major public health problem in the United States. Calorie intake and physical activity work together to influence body weight. Most Americans need to reduce the amount of calories they consume, increase their level of physical activity, and make wiser food choices. Many adults gain weight slowly over time, but even small changes in behavior can help avoid weight gain. For more information on weight management, see Chapter 14.

Physical Activity Regular physical activity improves fitness, helps manage weight, promotes psychological well-being, and reduces risk of heart disease, high blood pressure, cancer, and diabetes. Become active if you are inactive, and maintain or increase physical activity if you are already active. The amount of daily physical activity recommended for you depends on your current health status and goals. See Chapter 13 for information on exercise and physical fitness.

Food Groups to Encourage The Dietary Guidelines for Americans and MyPyramid both emphasize eating a wide range of foods. Central to these plans are fruits, vegetables, whole grains, and low-fat and fat-free dairy products. Each of these food groups offers a nearly endless array of choices. The discussion of MyPyramid, which comes later in this chapter, provides detailed information on choices and serving sizes.

Fats The type and amount of fats consumed can make a difference for health. A diet low in saturated fat, trans fat, and cholesterol helps keep blood cholesterol low and reduces the risk for heart disease.

Goals for fat intake for most adults are as follows:

Total fat: 20–35% of total daily calories

Saturated fat: Less than 10% of total daily calories

Trans fat: As little as possible

Cholesterol: Less than 300 mg per day

TERMS

Daily Values A simplified version of the RDAs used on food labels; also included are values for nutrients with no RDA per se.

Ethnic Foods

There is no one ethnic diet that clearly surpasses all others in providing people with healthful foods. However, every diet has its advantages and disadvantages and, within each cuisine, some foods are better choices. The dietary guidelines described in this chapter can be applied to any ethnic cuisine. For additional guidance, refer to the table below.

Choose More Often	Choose Less Often
Chinese Dishes that are steamed, poached (jum), boiled (chu), roasted (kow), barbecued (shu), or lightly stir-fried Hoisin sauce, oyster sauce, wine sauce, plum sauce, velvet sauce, or hot mustard Fresh fish and seafood, skinless chicken, tofu Mixed vegetables, Chinese greens Steamed rice, steamed spring rolls, soft noodles	Fried wontons or egg rolls Crab rangoon Crispy (Peking) duck or chicken Sweet-and-sour dishes made with breaded and deep-fried meat, poultry, or fish Fried rice Fried or crispy noodles
French Dishes prepared au vapeur (steamed), en brochette (skewered and broiled), or grillé (grilled) Fresh fish, shrimp, scallops, or mussels or skinless chicken, without sauces Clear soups	Dishes prepared à la crème (in cream sauce), au gratin or gratinée (baked with cream and cheese), or en croûte (in pastry crust) Drawn butter, hollandaise sauce, and remoulade (mayonnaise-based sauce)
Greek Dishes that are stewed, broiled, or grilled, including shish kebabs (souvlaki) Dolmas (grape leaves) stuffed with rice Tzatziki (yogurt, cucumbers, and garlic) Tabouli (bulgur-based salad) Pita bread, especially whole wheat	Moussaka, saganaki (fried cheese) Vegetable pies such as spanakopita and tyropita Baba ghanoush (eggplant and olive oil) Deep-fried falafel (chickpea patties) Gyros stuffed with ground meat Baklava
Indian Dishes prepared masala (curry), tandoori (roasted in a clay oven), or tikke (pan roasted); kebabs Raita (yogurt and cucumber salad) and other yogurt-based dishes and sauces Dal (lentils), pullao or pilau (basmati rice) Chapati (baked bread)	Ghee (clarified butter) Korma (meat in cream sauce) Samosas, pakoras (fried dishes) Molee and other coconut milk–based dishes Poori, bhatura, or paratha (fried breads)
Italian Pasta primavera or pasta, polenta, risotto, or gnocchi with marinara, red or white wine, white or red clam, or light mushroom sauce Dishes that are grilled or prepared cacciatore (tomato-based sauce), marsala (broth and wine sauce), or piccata (lemon sauce) Cioppino (seafood stew) Vegetable soup, minestrone or fagioli (beans)	Antipasto (cheese, smoked meats) Dishes that are prepared alfredo, frito (fried), crema (creamed), alla panna (with cream), or carbonara Veal scaloppini Chicken, veal, or eggplant parmigiana Italian sausage, salami, and prosciutto Buttered garlic bread Cannoli
Japanese Dishes prepared nabemono (boiled), shabu-shabu (in boiling broth), mushimono (steamed), nimono (simmered), yaki (broiled), or yakimono (grilled) Sushi or domburi (mixed rice dish) Steamed rice or soba (buckwheat), udon (wheat), or rice noodles	Tempura (battered and fried) Agemono (deep fried) Katsu (fried pork cutlet) Sukiyaki Fried tofu
Mexican Soft corn or wheat tortillas Burritos, fajitas, enchiladas, soft tacos, and tamales filled with beans, vegetables, or lean meats Refried beans, nonfat or low-fat; rice and beans Ceviche (fish marinated in lime juice) Salsa, enchilada sauce, and picante sauce Gazpacho, menudo, or black bean soup Fruit or flan for dessert	Crispy, fried tortillas Dishes that are fried, such as chile relleños, chimichangas, flautas, and tostadas Nachos and cheese, chili con queso, and other dishes made with cheese or cheese sauce Guacamole, sour cream, and extra cheese Refried beans made with lard Fried ice cream
Thai Dishes that are barbecued, sautéed, broiled, boiled, steamed, braised, or marinated Sâté (skewered and grilled meats) Fish sauce, basil sauce, chili or hot sauces Bean thread noodles, Thai salad	Coconut milk soup Peanut sauce or dishes topped with nuts Mee-krob (crispy noodles) Red, green, and yellow curries, which typically contain coconut milk

SOURCES: National Heart, Lung and Blood Institute. 2006. *Guidelines on Overweight and Obesity: Electronic Textbook* (http://www.nhlbi.nih.gov/ guidelines/ obesity/e_txtbk/appndx/6a3b.htm; retrieved Feburary 9, 2009). Duyff, R. L. 2006. *The American Dietetic Association's Complete Food and Nutrition Guide*, 2nd ed. Hoboken, N.J.: Wiley.

Half of your daily grain servings should come from whole grains. To check if a food contains whole grains, read the ingredient list on the food label.

Most fats in the diet should come from sources of unsaturated fats, such as fish, nuts, and vegetable oils. When selecting and preparing meat, poultry, dry beans, and milk or milk products, make choices that are lean, low-fat, or fat-free. To reduce trans fat intake, limit intake of foods made with hydrogenated vegetable oils. (See the box "Going Trans Fat–Free").

Cholesterol is found only in animal foods. If you need to reduce your cholesterol intake, limit your intake of foods that are particularly high in cholesterol, including egg yolks, dairy fats, certain shellfish, and liver and other organ meats; watch your serving sizes of animal foods. Food labels list the fat and cholesterol content of foods.

Two servings per week of fish rich in heart-healthy omega-3 fatty acids are also recommended for people at high risk for heart disease. However, for certain groups, intake limits are set for varieties of fish that may contain mercury; see page 367 for more information. Fish rich in omega-3 fatty acids include salmon, mackerel, and trout.

Carbohydrates   Carbohydrates are an important energy source in a healthy diet. Foods rich in carbohydrates may also be rich in dietary fiber, which promotes healthy digestion and helps reduce the risk of type 2 diabetes and heart disease. Fruits, vegetables, whole grains, and fat-free or low-fat milk can provide the recommended amount of carbohydrate. Choose fiber-rich foods often—for example, whole fruits, whole grains, and legumes.

People who consume foods and beverages high in added sugars tend to consume more calories but smaller amounts of vitamins and minerals than those who limit their intake of added sugars. A food is likely high in sugar if one of the following appears first or second in the list of ingredients or if several are listed: sugar (any type, including beet, brown, invert, raw, and cane), corn syrup or sweetener, fruit juice concentrate, honey, malt syrup, molasses, syrup, cane juice, dextrose, fructose, glucose, lactose, maltose, or sucrose.

To reduce added sugar consumption, cut back on soft drinks, candies, sweet desserts, fruit drinks, and other foods high in added sugars. Watch out for specialty drinks like café mochas, chai tea, smoothies, and sports drinks, which can contain hundreds of extra calories from sugar. Drink water rather than sweetened drinks, and don't let sodas and other sweets crowd out more nutritious foods, such as low-fat milk. Regular soda is the leading source of both added sugars and calories in the American diet, but it provides little in the way of nutrients except sugar (Figure 12.5 on p. 351). The 10 teaspoons of sugar in a 12-ounce soda can exceed the recommended daily limit for added sugars for someone consuming 2000 calories per day; for more on added sugar limits, see the discussion of MyPyramid.

Sodium and Potassium   Many people can reduce their chance of developing high blood pressure or lower already elevated blood pressure by consuming less salt; reducing blood pressure lowers the risk for stroke, heart disease, and kidney disease. Salt is made up of the minerals sodium and chloride, and although both of these minerals are essential for normal body function, we need only small amounts (1500 mg per day for adults). Most Americans consume much more salt than they need. The goal is to reduce sodium intake to less than 2300 milligrams per day, the equivalent of about 1 teaspoon of salt. Certain groups, including people with hypertension, African Americans, and older adults, benefit from an even lower sodium intake (no more than 1500 mg per day).

QUICK STATS

Most Americans consume about **4000 mg** of sodium per day, which is nearly twice the recommended amount for most people.

—Johns Hopkins Medicine, 2008

Going Trans Fat–Free

What do the cities of New York, Philadelphia, and Tiburon, California, have in common? They were the first three cities in the United States to be trans fat–free. In 2004, restaurants in Tiburon, a suburb of San Francisco, voluntarily stopped using cooking oils containing trans fat. The grassroots effort in Tiburon served as a model for regulations passed in 2006 and 2007 to limit the amount of trans fat served in New York and Philadelphia restaurants. Since then, nine other American cities have enacted similar regulations. In 2008, California enacted legislation banning the use of trans fats statewide; the law, which will be in full effect in 2011, restricts the use of trans fats in restaurants and in the preparation of food for retail sale.

What Are Trans Fats?

Trans fats are unsaturated fatty acids that have at least one double bond in the *trans* configuration. This refers to the way the hydrogen atoms are arranged on either side of the double bond. Normally, these hydrogen atoms are on the same side of the double bond, but in a trans fatty acid, they are on opposite sides. This gives the fatty acid a physical structure more like a saturated fatty acid. Although trans fats are found in small amounts naturally in milk, beef, and lamb, most trans fats are formed through the process of hydrogenation. Many popular food items contain trans fat (see table).

Hydrogenation makes liquid oils into solid or semisolid fats. This is the process used to make margarine and shortening. These partially hydrogenated oils have a longer shelf life and ideal physical properties for use in baked goods such as pastries, pie crusts, pizza dough, biscuits, cookies, and crackers. Partially hydrogenated oils are used for deep-fat frying because they have a long fry life, and therefore are more cost effective than non-hydrogenated oils.

The use of partially hydrogenated oils in restaurant and commercially prepared foods grew throughout the 1960s, 1970s, and 1980s in response to public health recommendations to reduce saturated fat intake from animal fats and tropical oils (such as palm and coconut oil).

Why Worry About Trans Fats?

In the 1990s, studies began to show that trans fats had similar effects in the body as saturated fat. Further research found that trans fats were actually worse for heart health because they not only raise LDL cholesterol, but also lower HDL cholesterol. A recent study found that a 2% increase in dietary intake from trans fat was associated with a 23% increase in heart disease. Other studies suggest that trans fats may promote obesity and diabetes.

Can Trans Fats Be Eliminated?

Trans fats are not a dietary essential. Health organizations recommend that trans fat intake be as low as possible. Because there are some naturally occurring trans fats, unless you are a strict vegetarian, there is not much room in the diet for trans fats from partially hydrogenated oils. More and more products in the grocery store are available trans fat–free, and as consumer interest in trans fat–free restaurants grows, it will be easier for consumers to limit trans fats when eating out.

Denmark has made it illegal for any food to contain more than 2% trans fat, and Canada is considering a nationwide ban on trans fats in restaurants. In 2004, the Center for Science in the Public Interest petitioned the FDA to ban trans fat as a food ingredient.

Reducing Your Trans Fat Intake

Start by reading food labels; trans fat content is required to be listed. A word of caution, however: A serving of a food can contain up to 0.5 gram of trans fat and still show zero grams on the Nutrition Fact label and the words "trans fat–free" on the label. So check the ingredient list. If partially hydrogenated oil is included in the list, then the product contains trans fat.

Next, check the product's calorie and saturated fat content. Trans fat–free foods are not healthier if they contain more saturated fat or more calories from added sugars. Ask at restaurants whether trans fat–free oils are used in cooking. Proposals being considered in some states could require national chain restaurants to include information about calorie content of their foods, which could also help consumers make smart choices.

Trans Fat Content of Common Food Items

Product	Common Serving Size	Total Fat (g)	Trans Fat (g)
French fries	Medium pkg (147 g)	27	8
Stick margarine	1 tbsp	11	3
Tub margarine	1 tbsp	7	0.5
Shortening	1 tbsp	13	4
Potato chips	Small bag (42.5 g)	11	3
Doughnut	1	18	5
Candy bar	1 (40 g)	10	3
Pound cake	1 slice (80 g)	16	4.5

SOURCES: Mozaffarian, D., et al. 2006. Trans fatty acids and cardiovascular disease. *New England Journal of Medicine* 354(15): 1601–1613; Eckel, R. H., et al. 2006. Understanding the complexity of trans fatty acid reduction in the American diet. American Heart Association Trans Fat Conference 2006. Report of the *Trans Fat Conference Planning Group. Circulation* 115(16): 2231–2246; American Heart Association. 2009. *Trans Fats* (http://www.americanheart.org/presenter.jhtml?identifier=3045792; retrieved February 9, 2009); Center for Science in the Public Interest. 2009. *Trans Fat* (http://www.cspinet.org/transfat; retrieved February 9, 2009); U.S. Food and Drug Administration, Center for Food Safety and Applied Nutrition. 2006 Update. *Questions and Answers about Trans Fat Nutrition Labeling* (http://vm.cfsan.fda.gov/~dms/qatrans2.html; retrieved February 9, 2009); U.S. Food and Drug Administration. 2003. *Revealing Trans Fats* (http://www.fda.gov/FDAC/features/2003/503_fats.html; retrieved February 9, 2009).

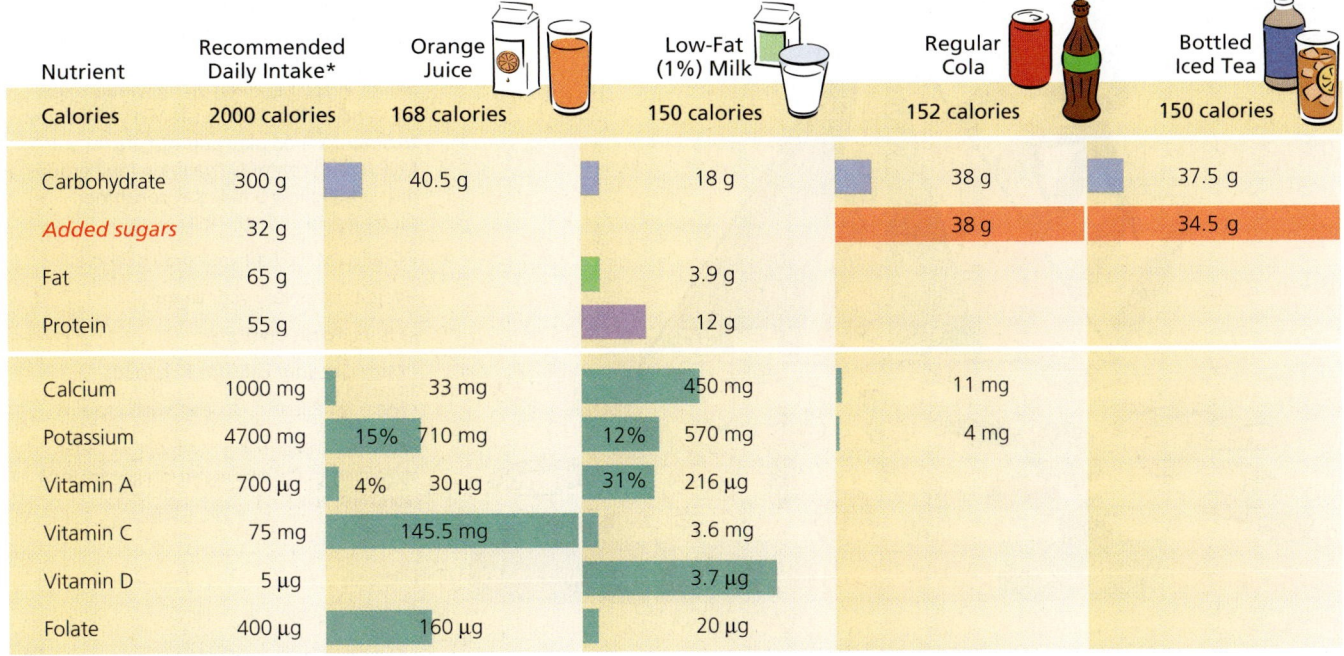

Nutrient	Recommended Daily Intake*	Orange Juice		Low-Fat (1%) Milk		Regular Cola		Bottled Iced Tea	
Calories	2000 calories	168 calories		150 calories		152 calories		150 calories	
Carbohydrate	300 g		40.5 g		18 g		38 g		37.5 g
Added sugars	32 g						38 g		34.5 g
Fat	65 g				3.9 g				
Protein	55 g				12 g				
Calcium	1000 mg		33 mg		450 mg		11 mg		
Potassium	4700 mg	15%	710 mg	12%	570 mg		4 mg		
Vitamin A	700 µg	4%	30 µg	31%	216 µg				
Vitamin C	75 mg		145.5 mg		3.6 mg				
Vitamin D	5 µg				3.7 µg				
Folate	400 µg		160 µg		20 µg				

*Recommended intakes and limits appropriate for a 20-year-old woman consuming 2000 calories per day.

FIGURE 12.5 Nutrient density of 12-ounce portions of selected beverages. Color bars represent percentage of recommended daily intake or limit for each nutrient.

Salt is found mainly in processed and prepared foods; smaller amounts may also be added during cooking or at the table. To lower your intake of salt, choose fresh or plain frozen meat, poultry, seafood, and vegetables most often; these are lower in salt than processed forms are. Check and compare the sodium content in processed foods, including frozen dinners, cheeses, soups, salad dressings, sauces, and canned mixed dishes. Add less salt during cooking and at the table, and limit your use of high-sodium condiments like soy sauce, ketchup, mustard, pickles, and olives. Use lemon juice, herbs, and spices instead of salt to enhance the flavor of foods.

Along with lowering salt intake, increasing potassium intake helps lower blood pressure. Fruits, vegetables, and most milk products are available in forms that contain no salt, and many of these are sources of potassium. Potassium-rich foods include leafy green vegetables, sweet and white potatoes, winter squash, soybeans, tomato sauce, bananas, peaches, apricots, cantaloupes, and orange juice.

Alcoholic Beverages Alcoholic beverages supply calories but few nutrients. Drinking in moderation—that is, no more than one drink per day for women and no more than two drinks per day for men—is associated with mortality reduction among some groups, primarily males age 45 and older and women age 55 and older. Among younger people, alcohol use provides little if any health benefit, and heavy drinking is associated with motor vehicle injuries and deaths, liver disease, stroke, violence, and other health problems (see Chapter 10 for more on the health risks and potential benefits of alcohol use).

USDA's MyPyramid

When the first USDA daily food guide was published, in 1916, it emphasized the importance of getting enough calories from fats and sugars to support daily activity. Today, the guidelines stress the importance of limiting fats and sugars to control calorie intake. Many Americans are familiar with the USDA Food Guide Pyramid, the food guidance system that was first released in 1992. Since the initial release of the Pyramid, scientists have updated both nutrient recommendations (the DRIs) and the Dietary Guidelines for Americans. So, as the 2005 Dietary Guidelines were prepared, the USDA reassessed its overall food guidance system and released MyPyramid in April 2005 (Figure 12.6 on p. 352).

A variety of experts have proposed other food-group plans. Some of these address perceived shortcomings in the USDA plans, and some adapt the basic 1992 Pyramid to special populations. Two alternative food plans appear in the Nutrition Resources section at the end of the chapter: The DASH eating plan and the Harvard Healthy Eating Pyramid. The USDA Center for Nutrition Policy and Promotion (www.usda.gov/cnpp) has more on alternative food plans for special populations such as young children, older adults, and people choosing particular ethnic diets. MyPyramid is available in Spanish, and there

FIGURE 12.6 USDA's MyPyramid. The USDA food guidance system, called MyPyramid, can be personalized based on an individual's sex, age, and activity level; visit MyPyramid.gov to obtain a food plan appropriate for you. MyPyramid contains five main food groups plus oils (yellow band). Key consumer messages include the following:

• Grains: Make half your grains whole

• Vegetables: Vary your veggies

• Fruits: Focus on fruits

• Milk: Get your calcium-rich foods

• Meat and Beans: Go lean with protein

SOURCE: U.S. Department of Agriculture. 2005. *MyPyramid* (http://www.mypyramid.gov; retrieved February 9, 2009).

are special adaptations of MyPyramid for children age 6–11 and for pregnant or breastfeeding women (www .MyPyramid.gov).

Another food plan that has received attention in recent years is the Mediterranean diet, which emphasizes vegetables, fruits, and whole grains; daily servings of beans, legumes, and nuts; moderate consumption of fish, poultry, and dairy products; and the use of olive oil over other types of fat, especially saturated fat. The Mediterranean diet has been associated with lower rates of heart disease and cancer, and recent studies have found a link between the diet and a greatly reduced risk of Alzheimer's disease.

Key Messages of MyPyramid   The new MyPyramid symbol has been developed to remind consumers to make healthy food choices and to be active every day. Consuming a balance of servings from each food group will not only meet nutrient needs but also help to reduce chronic disease risk. Key messages include the following:

• *Personalization* is represented by the person on the steps and the MyPyramid.gov site, which includes individualized recommendations, interactive assessments of food intake and physical activity, and tips for success.

• *Daily physical activity,* represented by the person climbing the steps, is important for maintaining a healthy weight and reducing the risk of chronic disease.

• *Moderation* of food intake is represented by the narrowing of each food group from bottom to top. The wider base stands for foods with little or no solid fats or added sugars, which should be selected more often; the narrower top represents food containing

more solid fats and added sugars, which should be limited.

• *Proportionality* is represented by the different widths of the food group bands. The widths provide a general guide for how much food a person should choose from each group.

• *Variety* is represented by the six color bands representing the five food groups of MyPyramid and oils. Foods from all groups are needed daily for good health.

• *Gradual improvement* is a good strategy; people can benefit from taking small steps to improve their diet and activity habits each day.

The MyPyramid chart in Figure 12.7 shows the food intake patterns recommended for different levels of calorie intake; Table 12.5 (p. 354) provides guidance for determining an appropriate calorie intake for weight maintenance. Use the table to identify an energy intake that is about right for you; then refer to the appropriate column in Figure 12.7. A personalized version of MyPyramid recommendations can also be found at MyPyramid.gov. Each food group is described briefly below. Past experiences have shown that many Americans have trouble identifying serving sizes, so recommended daily intakes from each group are now given in terms of cups and ounces; see the box "Judging Portion Sizes" (p. 355) for additional advice.

Grains   Foods from this group are usually low in fat and rich in complex carbohydrates, dietary fiber (if grains are unrefined), and many vitamins and minerals, including thiamin, riboflavin, iron, niacin, folic acid (if enriched or fortified), and zinc. Someone eating 2000 calories a day

Daily Amount of Food from Each Group

Food group amounts shown in cups (c) or ounce-equivalents (oz-eq), with number of daily servings (srv) shown in parentheses; vegetable subgroup amounts are per week

Calorie level		1600	1800	2000	2200	2400	2600	2800	3000
Grains		5 oz-eq	6 oz-eq	6 oz-eq	7 oz-eq	8 oz-eq	9 oz-eq	10 oz-eq	10 oz-eq
	Whole grains	3 oz-eq	3 oz-eq	3 oz-eq	3.5 oz-eq	4 oz-eq	4.5 oz-eq	5 oz-eq	5 oz-eq
	Other grains	2 oz-eq	3 oz-eq	3 oz-eq	3.5 oz-eq	4 oz-eq	4.5 oz-eq	5 oz-eq	5 oz-eq
Vegetables		2 c (4 srv)	2.5 c (5 srv)	2.5 c (5 srv)	3c (6 srv)	3 c (6 srv)	3.5 c (7 srv)	3.5 c (7 srv)	4 c (8 srv)
	Dark green	2 c/wk	3 c/wk	3 c/wk	3 c/wk	3 c/wk	3 c/wk	3 c/wk	3 c/wk
	Orange	1.5 c/wk	2 c/wk	2 c/wk	2 c/wk	2 c/wk	2.5 c/wk	2.5 c/wk	2.5 c/wk
	Legumes	2.5 c/wk	3 c/wk	3 c/wk	3 c/wk	3 c/wk	3.5 c/wk	3.5 c/wk	3.5 c/wk
	Starchy	2.5 c/wk	3 c/wk	3 c/wk	6 c/wk	6 c/wk	7 c/wk	7 c/wk	9 c/wk
	Other	5.5 c/wk	6.5 c/wk	6.5 c/wk	7 c/wk	7 c/wk	8.5 c/wk	8.5 c/wk	10 c/wk
Fruits		1.5 c (3 srv)	1.5 c (3 srv)	2 c (4 srv)	2 c (4 srv)	2 c (4 srv)	2 c (4 srv)	2.5 c (5 srv)	2.5 c (5 srv)
Milk		3 c	3 c	3 c	3 c	3 c	3 c	3 c	3 c
Lean meat and beans		5 oz-eq	5 oz-eq	5.5 oz-eq	6 oz-eq	6.5 oz-eq	6.5 oz-eq	7 oz-eq	7 oz-eq
Oils		5 tsp	5 tsp	6 tsp	6 tsp	7 tsp	8 tsp	8 tsp	10 tsp

The discretionary calorie allowances shown below are the calories remaining at each level after nutrient-dense foods in each food group are selected. Those trying to lose weight may choose not to use discretionary calories. For those wanting to maintain weight, discretionary calories may be used to increase the amount of food from each food group; to consume foods that are not in the lowest fat form or that contain added sugars; to add oil, fat, or sugars to foods; or to consume alcohol. The amounts below show how discretionary calories may be divided between solid fats and added sugars.

Discretionary calories	132	195	267	290	362	410	426	512
Solid fats	11 g	15 g	18 g	19 g	22 g	24 g	24 g	29 g
Added sugars	12 g (3 tsp)	20 g (5 tsp)	32 g (8 tsp)	38 g (9 tsp)	48 g (12 tsp)	56 g (14 tsp)	60 g (15 tsp)	72 g (18 tsp)

FIGURE 12.7 MyPyramid food intake patterns. To determine an appropriate amount of food from each group, find the column with your approximate daily energy intake. That column lists the daily recommended intake from each food group. Visit MyPyramid.gov for a personalized intake plan and for intakes for other calorie levels.

SOURCE: U.S. Department of Health and Human Services and U.S. Department of Agriculture. 2005. *Dietary Guidelines for Americans, 2005, Appendix A. Eating Patterns* (http://www.health.gov/dietaryguidelines/dga2005/document/html/appendixA.htm; retrieved February 9, 2009).

should include 6 ounce-equivalents each day, with half of those servings from whole grains such as whole-grain bread, whole-wheat pasta, high-fiber cereal, and brown rice. The following count as 1 ounce-equivalent:

- 1 slice of bread
- 1 small (2½-inch diameter) muffin
- 1 cup ready-to-eat cereal flakes
- ½ cup cooked cereal, rice, grains, or pasta
- 1 6-inch tortilla

Choose foods that are typically made with little fat or sugar (bread, rice, pasta) over those that are high in fat and sugar (croissants, chips, cookies, doughnuts).

Table 12.5	MyPyramid Daily Calorie Intake Levels		
Age (years)	Sedentary[a]	Moderately Active[b]	Active[c]
Child			
2–3	1000	1000–1400	1000–1400
Female			
4–8	1200–1400	1400–1600	1400–1800
9–13	1400–1600	1600–2000	1800–2200
14–18	1800	2000	2400
19–30	1800–2000	2000–2200	2400
31–50	1800	2000	2200
51+	1600	1800	2000–2200
Male			
4–8	1200–1400	1400–1600	1600–2000
9–13	1600–2000	1800–2200	2000–2600
14–18	2000–2400	2400–2800	2800–3200
19–30	2400–2600	2600–2800	3000
31–50	2200–2400	2400–2600	2800–3000
51+	2000–2200	2200–2400	2400–2800

[a] A lifestyle that includes only the light physical activity associated with typical day-to-day life.

[b] A lifestyle that includes physical activity equivalent to walking about 1.5 to 3 miles per day at 3 to 4 miles per hour (30–60 minutes a day of moderate physical activity), in addition to the light physical activity associated with typical day-to-day life.

[c] A lifestyle that includes physical activity equivalent to walking more than 3 miles per day at 3 to 4 miles per hour (60 or more minutes a day of moderate physical activity), in addition to the light physical activity associated with typical day-to-day life.

SOURCE: U.S. Department of Agriculture. 2005. *MyPyramid Food Intake Pattern Calorie Levels* (http://www.mypyramid.gov/downloads/ MyPyramid _Calorie_Levels.pdf; retrieved February 9, 2009).

Vegetables Vegetables contain carbohydrates, dietary fiber, vitamin A, vitamin C, folate, potassium, and other nutrients. They are also naturally low in fat. In a 2000-calorie diet, 2½ cups (5 servings) of vegetables should be included daily. Each of the following counts as 1 serving (½ cup or equivalent) of vegetables:

- ½ cup raw or cooked vegetables
- 1 cup raw leafy salad greens
- ½ cup vegetable juice

Because vegetables vary in the nutrients they provide, it is important to consume a variety of types of vegetables to obtain maximum nutrition. Many Americans consume only a few types of vegetables, with white potatoes (baked or served as french fries) being the most popular. To help boost variety, MyPyramid recommends servings from five different subgroups within the vegetables group; try to consume vegetables from several subgroups each day. (For clarity, Figure 12.7 shows servings from the subgroups in terms of weekly consumption.)

- Dark green vegetables like spinach, chard, collards, bok choy, broccoli, kale, romaine, and turnip and mustard greens
- Orange and deep yellow vegetables like carrots, winter squash, sweet potatoes, and pumpkin
- Legumes like pinto beans, kidney beans, black beans, lentils, chickpeas, soybeans, split peas, and tofu; legumes can be counted as servings of vegetables *or* as alternatives to meat
- Starchy vegetables like corn, green peas, and white potatoes
- Other vegetables; tomatoes, bell peppers (red, orange, yellow, or green), green beans, and cruciferous vegetables like cauliflower are good choices

Fruits Fruits are rich in carbohydrates, dietary fiber, and many vitamins, especially vitamin C. For someone eating a 2000-calorie diet, 2 cups (4 servings) of fruits are recommended daily. The following each count as 1 serving (½ cup or equivalent) of fruit:

- ½ cup fresh, canned, or frozen fruit
- ½ cup fruit juice (100% juice)
- 1 small whole fruit
- ¼ cup dried fruit

Good choices from this group are citrus fruits and juices, melons, pears, apples, bananas, and berries. Choose whole fruits often—they are higher in fiber and often lower in calories than fruit juices. Fruit *juices* typically contain more nutrients and less added sugar than fruit *drinks*. For canned fruits, choose those packed in 100% fruit juice or water rather than in syrup.

Milk This group includes all milk and milk products, such as yogurt, cheeses (except cream cheese), and dairy desserts, as well as lactose-free and lactose-reduced products. Foods from this group are high in protein, carbohydrate, calcium, riboflavin, and vitamin D (if fortified). Those consuming 2000 calories per day should include 3 cups of milk or the equivalent daily. Each of the following counts as the equivalent of 1 cup:

- 1 cup milk or yogurt
- ½ cup ricotta cheese
- 1½ ounces natural cheese
- 2 ounces processed cheese

Cottage cheese is lower in calcium than most other cheeses; ½ cup is equivalent to ¼ cup milk. Ice cream is

Judging Portion Sizes

Studies have shown that most people underestimate the size of their food portions, in many cases by as much as 50%. If you need to retrain your eye, try using measuring cups and spoons and an inexpensive kitchen scale when you eat at home. With a little practice, you'll learn the difference between 3 and 8 ounces of chicken or meat, and what a half-cup of rice really looks like. For quick estimates, use the following equivalents:

- 1 teaspoon of margarine = the tip of your thumb

- 1 ounce of cheese = your thumb, four dice stacked together, or an ice cube

- 3 ounces of chicken or meat = a deck of cards or an audio-cassette tape

- 1 cup of pasta = a small fist or a tennis ball

- ½ cup of rice or cooked vegetables = an ice cream scoop or one-third of a can of soda

- 2 tablespoons of peanut butter = a ping-pong ball or large marshmallow

- 1 medium potato = a computer mouse

- 1–2-ounce muffin or roll = plum or large egg

- 2-ounce bagel = hockey puck or yo-yo

- 1 medium fruit (apple or orange) = baseball

- ¼ cup nuts = golf ball

- Small cookie or cracker = poker chip

---

also lower in calcium and higher in sugar and fat than many other dairy products; one scoop counts as ⅓ cup milk. To limit calories and saturated fat in your diet, it is best to choose servings of low-fat and fat-free items from this group.

Meat and Beans This group includes meat, poultry, fish, dry beans and peas, eggs, nuts, and seeds. These foods provide protein, niacin, iron, vitamin B-6, zinc, and thiamin; the animal foods in the group also provide vitamin B-12. For someone consuming a 2000-calorie diet, 5½ ounce-equivalents is recommended. Each of the following counts as equivalent to 1 ounce:

- 1 ounce cooked lean meat, poultry, or fish
- ¼ cup cooked dry beans (legumes) or tofu
- 1 egg
- 1 tablespoon peanut butter
- ½ ounce nuts or seeds

One egg at breakfast, ½ cup of pinto beans at lunch, and a 3-ounce (cooked weight) hamburger at dinner would add up to the equivalent of 6 ounces of lean meat for the day. To limit your intake of fat and saturated fat, choose lean cuts of meat and skinless poultry, and watch your serving sizes carefully. Choose at least one serving of plant proteins, such as black beans, lentils, or tofu, every day.

Oils The Oils group represents the oils that are added to foods during processing, cooking, or at the table; oils and soft margarines include vegetable oils and soft vegetable oil table spreads that have no trans fats. These are major sources of vitamin E and unsaturated fatty acids, including the essential fatty acids. For a 2000-calorie diet, 6 teaspoons of oils per day are recommended. One teaspoon is the equivalent of the following:

- 1 teaspoon vegetable oil or soft margarine
- 1 tablespoon salad dressing or light mayonnaise

Foods that are mostly oils include nuts, olives, avocados, and some fish. The following portions include about 1 teaspoon of oil: 8 large olives, ⅙ medium avocado, ½ tablespoon peanut butter, and ⅓ ounce roasted nuts. Food labels can help consumers identify the type and amount of fat in various foods.

Discretionary Calories, Solid Fats, and Added Sugars The suggested intakes from the basic food groups in MyPyramid assume that nutrient-dense forms are selected

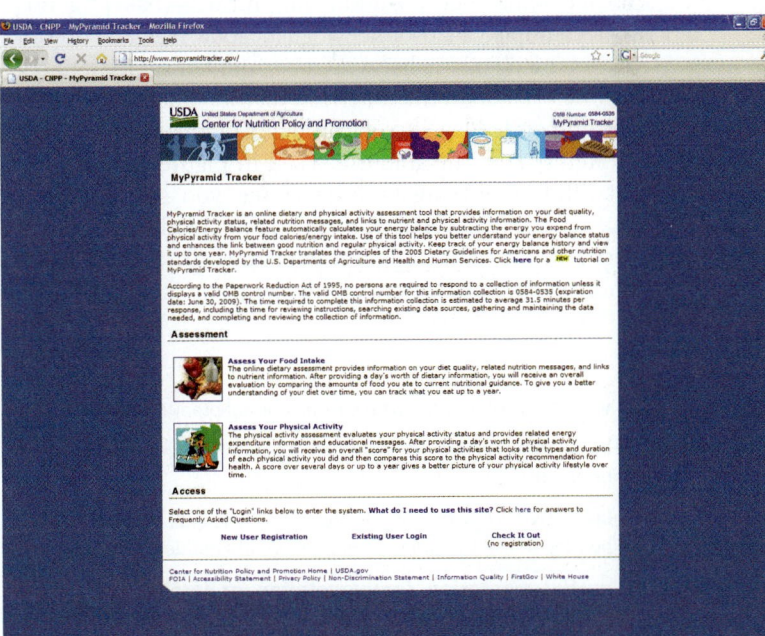

You can track your diet and physical activity and create a personal diet plan by using the online tools at MyPyramid.gov.

from each group; nutrient-dense forms are those that are fat-free or low-fat and that contain no added sugars. If this pattern is followed, then a small amount of additional calories can be consumed—the *discretionary calorie allowance*. Figure 12.7 shows the discretionary calorie allowance at each calorie level in MyPyramid.

People who are trying to lose weight may choose not to use discretionary calories. For those wanting to maintain weight, discretionary calories may be used to increase the amount of food from a food group; to consume foods that are not in the lowest fat form or that contain added sugars; to add oil, fat, or sugars to foods; or to consume alcohol. The amounts shown in Figure 12.7 show how discretionary calories may be divided between solid fats and added sugars. The values for additional fat target no more than 30% of total calories from fat and less than 10% of calories from saturated fat. Examples of discretionary solid fat calories include choosing higher-fat meats such as sausages, or chicken with skin, or whole milk instead of fat-free milk and topping foods with butter. For example, a cup of whole milk has 60 calories more than a cup of fat-free milk; these 60 calories would be counted as discretionary calories.

As described earlier in the chapter, added sugars are the sugars added to foods and beverages in processing or preparation, not the naturally occurring sugars in fruits or milk. The suggested amounts of added sugars may be helpful limits for including some sweetened foods or beverages in the daily diet without exceeding energy needs or underconsuming other nutrients. For example, in a 2000-calorie diet, MyPyramid lists 32 grams (8 teaspoons) for discretionary intake of added sugars. In the American diet, added sugars are often found in sweetened beverages (regular soda, sweetened teas, fruit drinks), dairy products (ice cream, some yogurts), and grain products (bakery goods). For example, a 20-ounce regular soda has 260 calories from added sugars that would be counted as discretionary calories. The current American diet includes higher-than-recommended levels of sugar intake (Table 12.6).

Remember, the amounts listed in Figure 12.7 for solid fats and added sugars assume that you select foods in nutrient-dense forms from the major food groups; don't just add fats and sugars to your diet. To control weight and get enough essential nutrients, it is important to

Table 12.6	Top Ten Sources of Calories in the American Diet

Food	Percent of Total Calories
Regular soft drinks	7.1
Cake, sweet rolls, doughnuts, pastries	3.6
Hamburgers, cheeseburgers, meatloaf	3.1
Pizza	3.1
Potato chips, corn chips, popcorn	2.9
Rice	2.7
Rolls, buns, English muffins, bagels	2.7
Cheese or cheese spread	2.6
Beer	2.6
French fries, fried potatoes	2.2

SOURCE: Bloc, G. 2004. Foods contributing to energy intake in the US: Data from NHANES III and NHANES 1999–2000. *Journal of Food Composition and Analysis* 17(2004): 439–447.

choose nutrient-dense forms of foods for most of your daily servings.

For an evaluation of your diet, complete the activity in the box "Your Diet Versus MyPyramid Recommendations."

The Vegetarian Alternative

Some people choose a diet with one essential difference from the diets we've already described—foods of animal origin (meat, poultry, fish, eggs, milk) are eliminated or restricted. Many do so for health reasons; vegetarian diets tend to be lower in saturated fat, cholesterol, and animal protein and higher in complex carbohydrates, dietary fiber, folate, vitamins C and E, carotenoids, and phytochemicals. Some people adopt a vegetarian diet out of concern for the environment, for financial considerations, or for reasons related to ethics or religion.

Types of Vegetarian Diets   There are various vegetarian styles; the wider the variety of the diet eaten, the easier it is to meet nutritional needs.

- **Vegans** eat only plant foods.
- **Lacto-vegetarians** eat plant foods and dairy products.
- **Lacto-ovo-vegetarians** eat plant foods, dairy products, and eggs.

Others can be categorized as **partial vegetarians, semivegetarians,** or **pescovegetarians;** these individuals eat plant foods, dairy products, eggs, and usually a small selection of poultry, fish, and other seafood. Many other people choose vegetarian meals frequently but are not strictly vegetarian. Including some animal protein (such as dairy products) in a vegetarian diet makes planning easier, but it is not necessary.

TERMS

vegan   A vegetarian who eats no animal products at all.

lacto-vegetarian   A vegetarian who includes milk and cheese products in the diet.

lacto-ovo-vegetarian   A vegetarian who eats no meat, poultry, or fish but does eat eggs and milk products.

partial vegetarian, semivegetarian, or pescovegetarian   A vegetarian who includes eggs, dairy products, and/or small amounts of poultry and seafood in the diet.

Your Diet Versus MyPyramid Recommendations

1. **Keep a food record:** To evaluate your daily diet, begin by keeping a record of everything you eat on a typical day. To help with your analysis, break down each food item into its component parts and note your portion sizes; for example, a turkey sandwich might be listed as 2 slices sourdough bread, 3 ounces turkey, 1 tomato, 1 tablespoon mayonnaise, and so on.

2. **Compare your servings to the recommendations of MyPyramid:** Complete the chart below to compare your daily diet to MyPyramid. See Figure 12.7 for the recommended daily intake for your calorie level.

Food Group	Recommended Daily, Amounts/Servings for Your Energy Intake	Your Actual Daily Intake (Amounts/Servings)	Serving Sizes and Equivalents
Grains (*total*)			1 ounce-equivalent = 1 slice of bread; 1 small muffin; 1 cup ready-to-eat cereal flakes; or ½ cup cooked cereal, rice, grains, or pasta
Whole grains			
Other grains			
Vegetables (*total*)			½ cup or equivalent (1 serving) = ½ cup raw or cooked vegetables; 1 cup raw leafy salad greens; or ½ cup vegetable juice
*Dark green**			
*Deep yellow**			
*Legumes**			
*Starchy**			
*Other**			
Fruits			½ cup or equivalent (1 serving) = ½ cup fresh, canned, or frozen fruit; ½ cup fruit juice; 1 small whole fruit; or ¼ cup dried fruit
Milk			1 cup or equivalent = 1 cup milk or yogurt; 1½ oz natural cheese; or 2 oz processed cheese
Meat and Beans			1 ounce-equivalent = 1 oz lean meat, poultry, or fish; ¼ cup cooked dry beans or tofu; 1 egg; 1 tablespoon peanut butter; or ½ oz nuts or seeds
Oils			1 teaspoon or equivalent = 1 teaspoon vegetable oil or 1 tablespoon light mayonnaise or salad dressing
Solid Fats			
Added Sugars			

*Compare your daily intake with the approximate daily intake derived from the weekly pattern given in MyPyramid (Figure 12.7).

It may be difficult to track values for added sugars and, especially, oils and fats, but be as accurate as you can. Check food labels for information on fat and sugar. (NOTE: For a more complete and accurate analysis of your diet, keep food records for 3 days and then average the results.) MyPyramid.gov has additional guidelines for counting discretionary calories.

3. **Further evaluate your food choices within the groups:** Based on the data you collected and what you learned in the chapter, what were the especially healthy choices you made (for example, whole grains and citrus fruits) and what were your less healthy choices? Identify and list foods in the latter category, as these are areas where you can make changes to improve your diet. In particular, you may want to limit your intake of the following: processed, sweetened grains; high-fat meats and poultry skin; deep-fried fast foods; full-fat dairy products; regular sodas, sweetened teas, fruit drinks; alcoholic beverages; other foods that primarily provide sugar and fat and few other nutrients.

4. **Make healthy changes:** Bring your diet in line with MyPyramid by adding servings from food groups for which you fall short of the recommendations. To maintain a healthy weight, you may need to balance these additions by reductions in other areas—by eliminating some of the fats, oils, sweets, and alcohol you consume; by cutting extra servings from food groups for which your intake is more than adequate; or by making healthier choices within the food groups. Make a list of foods to add and a list of foods to eliminate; post your lists in a prominent location.

For a more detailed analysis of your current diet, including intakes of specific nutrients, use the online MyPyramid Tracker tool available at MyPyramid.gov.

A Food Plan for Vegetarians MyPyramid can be adapted for use by vegetarians with only a few key modifications. For the meat and beans group, vegetarians can focus on the nonmeat choices of dry beans (legumes), nuts, seeds, eggs, and soy foods like tofu (soybean curd) and tempeh (a cultured soy product). Vegans and other vegetarians who do not consume any dairy products must find other rich sources of calcium (see below). Fruits, vegetables, and whole grains are healthy choices for people following all types of vegetarian diets.

A healthy vegetarian diet emphasizes a wide variety of plant foods. Although plant proteins are generally of lower quality than animal proteins, choosing a variety of plant foods will supply all of the essential amino acids. Choosing minimally processed and unrefined foods will maximize nutrient value and provide ample dietary fiber. Daily consumption of a variety of plant foods in amounts that meet total energy needs can provide all needed nutrients, except vitamin B-12 and possibly vitamin D. Strategies for obtaining nutrients of concern include the following:

- *Vitamin B-12* is found naturally only in animal foods; if dairy products and eggs are limited or avoided, B-12 can be obtained from fortified foods such as ready-to-eat cereals, soy beverages, meat substitutes, and special yeast products or from supplements.

- *Vitamin D* can be obtained by spending 5–15 minutes a day in the sun, by consuming vitamin D–fortified products like ready-to-eat cereals and soy or rice milk, or by taking a supplement.

- *Calcium* is found in legumes, tofu processed with calcium, dark green leafy vegetables, nuts, tortillas made from lime-processed corn, and fortified orange juice, soy milk, bread, and other foods.

- *Iron* can be obtained from whole grains, fortified bread and breakfast cereals, dried fruits, green leafy vegetables, nuts and seeds, legumes, and soy foods. The iron in plant foods is more difficult for the body to absorb than is the iron from animal sources; consuming a good source of vitamin C with most meals is helpful because vitamin C improves iron absorption.

- *Zinc* is found in whole grains, nuts, legumes, and soy foods.

If you are a vegetarian or considering becoming one, devote some extra time and thought to your diet. It's especially important to eat as wide a variety of foods as possible to ensure that all your nutritional needs are satisfied. Consulting with a registered dietitian will make your planning even easier. Vegetarian diets for children, teens, and pregnant and lactating women warrant professional guidance.

Dietary Challenges for Special Population Groups

The Dietary Guidelines for Americans and MyPyramid provide a basis that everyone can use to create a healthy diet. However, some population groups face special dietary challenges (see the box "How Different Are the Nutritional Needs of Women and Men?").

Children and Teenagers Young people often simply need to be encouraged to eat. Perhaps the best thing a parent can do for younger children is to provide them with a variety of foods. Add vegetables to casseroles and fruit to cereal; offer fruit and vegetable juices or homemade yogurt or fruit shakes instead of sugary drinks. Allowing children to help prepare meals is another good way to increase overall food consumption and variety. Many children and teenagers enjoy eating at fast-food restaurants; they should be encouraged to select the healthiest choices from fast-food menus (see Appendix A) and to complete the day's diet with low-fat, nutrient-rich foods.

College Students Foods that are convenient for college students are not always the healthiest choices. It is easy for students who eat in buffet-style dining halls or food courts to overeat, and the foods offered are not necessarily high in essential nutrients and low in fat. The same is true of meals at fast-food restaurants, another convenient source of quick and inexpensive meals for busy students. Although no food is entirely bad, consuming a wide variety of foods is critical for a healthy diet. See the box "Eating Strategies for College Students" on page 360 for tips on making healthy eating convenient and affordable.

Older Adults Nutrient needs do not change much as people age, but because older adults tend to become less active, they require fewer calories to maintain body weight. At the same time, the absorption of nutrients tends to be lower in older adults because of age-related changes in the digestive tract. Thus, they must consume nutrient-dense foods in order to meet their nutritional requirements. As discussed earlier, foods fortified with vitamin B-12 and/or B-12 supplements are recommended for people over age 50. Because constipation is a common problem, consuming foods high in fiber and getting adequate fluids are important goals.

Athletes Key dietary concerns for athletes are meeting their increased energy requirements and drinking enough fluids during practice and throughout the day to remain fully hydrated. Endurance athletes may also benefit from increasing the amount of carbohydrate in the diet to 60–70% of total daily calories; this increase should come in

How Different Are the Nutritional Needs of Women and Men?

connect™

When it comes to nutrition, men and women have a lot in common. Both sexes need the same essential nutrients, and the Dietary Guidelines for Americans apply equally to both. But beyond the basics, men and women need different amounts of essential nutrients and have different nutritional concerns.

Women tend to be smaller and weigh less than men, and thus have lower energy requirements and need to consume fewer calories than men to maintain a healthy weight. For most nutrients, women need the same or slightly lower amounts than men. But because women consume fewer calories, they may have more difficulty getting adequate amounts of all essential nutrients and need to focus on nutrient-dense foods.

Two nutrients of special concern to women are calcium and iron. Low calcium intake may be linked to the development of osteoporosis in later life. The *Healthy People 2010* report sets a goal of increasing from 40% to 75% the proportion of women age 20–49 who meet the dietary recommendation for calcium. Fat-free and low-fat dairy products and fortified cereal, bread, and orange juice are good choices for calcium-rich foods.

Menstruating women also have higher iron needs than other groups, and low iron intake can lead to iron-deficiency anemia. Lean red meat, green leafy vegetables, and fortified breakfast cereals are good sources of iron. As discussed earlier, all women capable of becoming pregnant should consume adequate folic acid from fortified foods and/or supplements.

Men are seldom thought of as having nutritional deficiencies because they generally have high-calorie diets. However, many men have a diet that does not follow recommended food intake patterns and includes more red meat and fewer fruits, vegetables, and whole grains than recommended. This dietary pattern is linked to heart disease and some types of cancer. A high intake of calories can lead to weight gain over time if a man's activity level decreases as he ages. To reduce chronic disease risk, men should focus on increasing their consumption of fruits, vegetables, and whole grains to obtain vitamins, minerals, fiber, and phytochemicals.

The "Fruits and Veggies—More Matters" initiative is the result of a partnership of health organizations led by the Centers for Disease Control and Prevention and the Produce for Better Health Foundation. The goal is to increase consumption of fruits and vegetables. Information found in stores, online, and on packaging will help both men and women make healthful choices.

---

the form of complex, rather than simple, carbohydrates. Athletes for whom maintaining low body weight and body fat is important—such as skaters, gymnasts, and wrestlers—should consume adequate nutrients and avoid falling into unhealthy patterns of eating. Eating for exercise is discussed in more detail in Chapter 13; refer to Chapter 14 for information on eating disorders.

People with Special Health Concerns   Many Americans have special health concerns that affect their dietary needs. For example, women who are pregnant or breast-feeding require extra calories, vitamins, and minerals (see Chapter 8). People with diabetes benefit from a well-balanced diet that is low in simple sugars, high in complex carbohydrates, and relatively rich in monounsaturated fats. People with high blood pressure need to control their weight and limit their sodium consumption. If you have a health problem or concern that may require a special diet, discuss your situation with a physician or registered dietitian.

A PERSONAL PLAN: MAKING INFORMED CHOICES ABOUT FOOD

Now that you understand the basis of good nutrition and a healthy diet, you can put together a diet that works for you. Focus on the likely causes of any health problems in your life, and make specific dietary changes to address them. You may also have some specific areas of concern, such as interpreting food labels and dietary supplement labels, avoiding foodborne illnesses and environmental contaminants, and understanding food additives. We turn to these and other topics next.

? QUESTIONS FOR CRITICAL THINKING AND REFLECTION

What factors influence your food choices—convenience, cost, availability, habit? Do you ever consider nutritional content or nutritional recommendations like those found in MyPyramid? If not, how big a change would it be for you to think of nutritional content first when choosing food? Is it something you could do easily?

Eating Strategies for College Students

General Guidelines

• Eat slowly, and enjoy your food. Set aside a separate time to eat, and don't eat while you study.

• Eat a colorful, varied diet. The more colorful your diet is, the more varied and rich in fruits and vegetables it will be. Many Americans eat few fruits and vegetables, despite the fact that these foods are typically inexpensive, delicious, rich in nutrients, and low in fat and calories.

• Eat breakfast. You'll have more energy in the morning and be less likely to grab an unhealthy snack later on.

• Choose healthy snacks—fruits, vegetables, grains, and cereals—as often as you can.

• Drink water more often than soft drinks or other sweetened beverages. Rent a mini-refrigerator for your dorm room and stock up on healthy beverages.

• Pay attention to portion sizes.

• Combine physical activity with healthy eating. You'll feel better and have a much lower risk of many chronic diseases. Even a little exercise is better than none.

Eating in the Dining Hall

• Choose a meal plan that includes breakfast, and don't skip it.

• Accept that dining hall food is not going to taste the same as home cooking. Find healthy dishes that you like.

• If menus are posted or distributed, decide what you want to eat before you get in line, and stick to your choices. Consider what you plan to do and eat for the rest of the day before making your choices.

• Ask for large servings of vegetables and small servings of meat and other high-fat main dishes. Build your meals around grains and vegetables.

• Try whole grains like brown rice, whole-wheat bread, and whole-grain cereals.

• Choose leaner poultry, fish, or bean dishes rather than high-fat meats and fried entrees.

• Ask that gravies and sauces be served on the side; limit your intake.

• Choose broth-based or vegetable soups rather than cream soups.

• At the salad bar, load up on leafy greens, beans, and fresh vegetables. Avoid mayonnaise-coated salads, bacon, croutons, and high-fat dressings. Put dressing on the side, and dip your fork into it rather than pouring it over the salad.

• Drink nonfat milk, water, mineral water, or 100% fruit juice rather than heavily sweetened fruit drinks, whole milk, or soft drinks.

• Choose fruit for dessert rather than pastries, cookies, or cakes.

• Do some research about the foods and preparation methods used in your dining hall or cafeteria. Discuss any suggestions you have with your food-service manager.

Eating in Fast-Food Restaurants

• Most fast-food chains can provide a brochure with a nutritional breakdown of the foods on the menu. Ask for it. (See also the information in Appendix A.)

• Order small single burgers with no cheese instead of double burgers with many toppings. If possible, ask for them broiled instead of fried.

• Ask for items to be prepared without mayonnaise, tartar sauce, sour cream, or other high-fat sauces. Ketchup, mustard, and fat-free mayonnaise or sour cream are better choices and are available at many fast-food restaurants.

• Choose whole-grain buns or bread for burgers and sandwiches.

• Choose chicken items made from chicken breast, not processed chicken.

• Order vegetable pizzas without extra cheese.

• If you order french fries or onion rings, get the smallest size, and/or share them with a friend. Better yet, get a salad or fruit cup instead.

Eating on the Run

Are you chronically short of time? Pack these items for a quick snack or meal: fresh or dried fruit, fruit juices, raw fresh vegetables like carrots, plain bagels, bread sticks, whole-wheat fig bars, low-fat cheese sticks or cubes, low-fat crackers or granola bars, fat-free or low-fat yogurt, snack-size cereal boxes, pretzels, rice or corn cakes, plain popcorn, soup (if you have access to a microwave), or water.

Reading Food Labels

All processed foods regulated by either the FDA or the USDA include standardized nutrition information on their labels. Every food label shows serving sizes and the amount of fat, saturated fat, trans fat, cholesterol, sodium, total carbohydrate, dietary fiber, sugars, and protein in each serving. To make intelligent choices about food, learn to read and *understand* food labels (see the box "Using Food Labels").

Fresh meat, poultry, fish, fruits, and vegetables are not required to have food labels, and many of these products

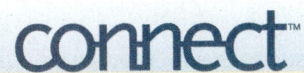

Using Food Labels

Food labels are designed to help consumers make food choices based on the nutrients that are most important to good health. In addition to listing nutrient content by weight, the label puts the information in the context of a daily diet of 2000 calories that includes no more than 65 grams of fat (approximately 30% of total calories). For example, if a serving of a particular product has 13 grams of fat, the label will show that the serving represents 20% of the daily fat allowance. If your daily diet contains fewer or more than 2000 calories, you need to adjust these calculations accordingly.

Food labels contain uniform serving sizes. This means that if you look at different brands of salad dressing, for example, you can compare calories and fat content based on the serving amount. (Food label serving sizes may be larger or smaller than MyPyramid serving size equivalents, however.) Regulations also require that foods meet strict definitions if their packaging includes the terms *light, low-fat,* or *high-fiber* (see below). Health claims such as "good source of dietary fiber" or "low in saturated fat" on packages are signals that those products can wisely be included in your diet. Overall, the food label is an important tool to help you choose a diet that conforms to MyPyramid and the Dietary Guidelines.

Selected Nutrient Claims and What They Mean

Healthy A food that is low in fat, is low in saturated fat, has no more than 360–480 mg of sodium and 60 mg of cholesterol, *and* provides 10% or more of the Daily Value for vitamin A, vitamin C, protein, calcium, iron, or dietary fiber.

Light or lite One-third fewer calories or 50% less fat than a similar product.

Reduced or fewer At least 25% less of a nutrient than a similar product; can be ap-plied to fat ("reduced fat"), saturated fat, cholesterol, sodium, and calories.

Extra or added 10% or more of the Daily Value per serving when compared to what a similar product has.

Good source 10–19% of the Daily Value for a particular nutrient per serving.

High, rich in, or excellent source of 20% or more of the Daily Value for a particular nutrient per serving.

Low calorie 40 calories or less per serving.

High fiber 5 g or more of fiber per serving.

Good source of fiber 2.5–4.9 g of fiber per serving.

Fat-free Less than 0.5 g of fat per serving.

Low-fat 3 g of fat or less per serving.

Saturated fat-free Less than 0.5 g of saturated fat and 0.5 g of trans fatty acids per serving.

Low saturated fat 1 g or less of saturated fat per serving and no more than 15% of total calories.

Cholesterol-free Less than 2 mg of cholesterol and 2 g or less of saturated fat per serving.

Low cholesterol 20 mg or less of cholesterol and 2 g or less of saturated fat per serving.

Low sodium 140 mg or less of sodium per serving.

Very low sodium 35 mg or less of sodium per serving.

Lean Cooked seafood, meat, or poultry with less than 10 g of fat, 4.5 g or less of saturated fat, and less than 95 mg of cholesterol per serving.

Extra lean Cooked seafood, meat, or poultry with less than 5 g of fat, 2 g of saturated fat, and 95 mg of cholesterol per serving.

Note: The FDA has not yet defined nutrient claims relating to carbohydrate, so foods labeled low- or reduced-carbohydrate do not conform to any approved standard.

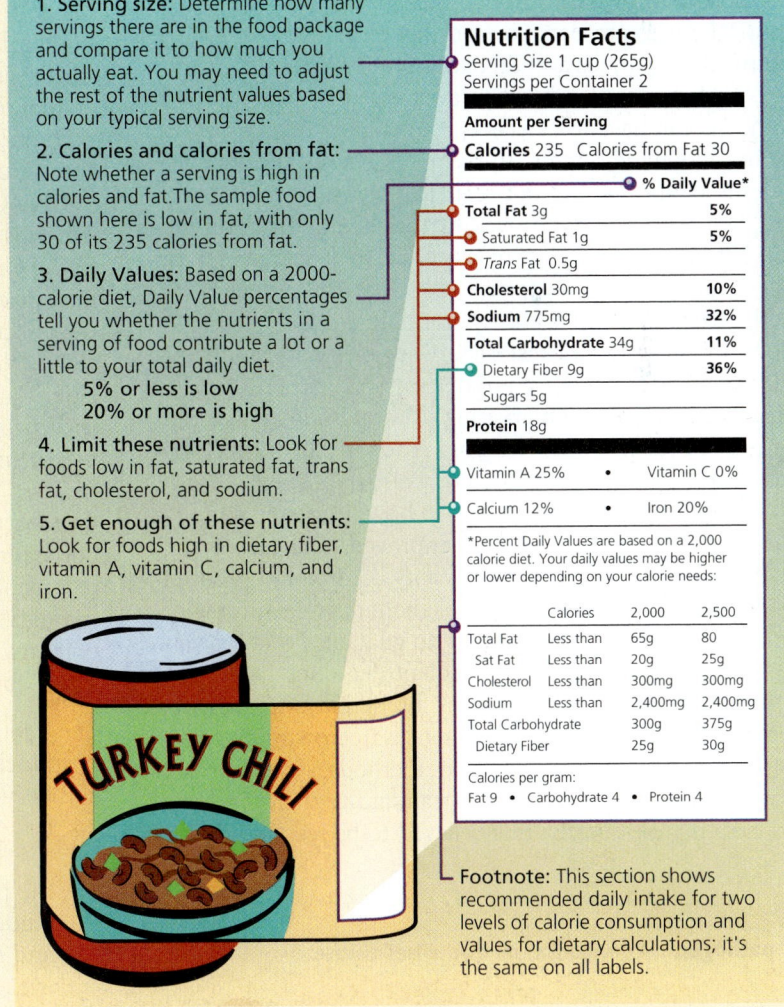

1. **Serving size:** Determine how many servings there are in the food package and compare it to how much you actually eat. You may need to adjust the rest of the nutrient values based on your typical serving size.

2. **Calories and calories from fat:** Note whether a serving is high in calories and fat. The sample food shown here is low in fat, with only 30 of its 235 calories from fat.

3. **Daily Values:** Based on a 2000-calorie diet, Daily Value percentages tell you whether the nutrients in a serving of food contribute a lot or a little to your total daily diet.
   5% or less is low
   20% or more is high

4. **Limit these nutrients:** Look for foods low in fat, saturated fat, trans fat, cholesterol, and sodium.

5. **Get enough of these nutrients:** Look for foods high in dietary fiber, vitamin A, vitamin C, calcium, and iron.

Footnote: This section shows recommended daily intake for two levels of calorie consumption and values for dietary calculations; it's the same on all labels.

Nutrition Facts
Serving Size 1 cup (265g)
Servings per Container 2

Amount per Serving

Calories 235 Calories from Fat 30

	% Daily Value*
Total Fat 3g	5%
Saturated Fat 1g	5%
Trans Fat 0.5g	
Cholesterol 30mg	10%
Sodium 775mg	32%
Total Carbohydrate 34g	11%
Dietary Fiber 9g	36%
Sugars 5g	
Protein 18g	

Vitamin A 25%	•	Vitamin C 0%	
Calcium 12%	•	Iron 20%	

*Percent Daily Values are based on a 2,000 calorie diet. Your daily values may be higher or lower depending on your calorie needs:

	Calories	2,000	2,500
Total Fat	Less than	65g	80
Sat Fat	Less than	20g	25g
Cholesterol	Less than	300mg	300mg
Sodium	Less than	2,400mg	2,400mg
Total Carbohydrate		300g	375g
Dietary Fiber		25g	30g

Calories per gram:
Fat 9 • Carbohydrate 4 • Protein 4

are not packaged. You can find information on the nutrient content of these items from basic nutrition books, registered dietitians, nutrient analysis computer software, the World Wide Web, and the companies that produce or distribute these foods. Supermarkets often have large posters or pamphlets listing the nutrient contents of these foods.

Reading Dietary Supplement Labels

Dietary supplements include vitamins, minerals, amino acids, herbs, glandular extracts, enzymes, and other compounds. They may come in the form of tablets, capsules, liquids, or powders. Surveys indicate that over half of American adults use dietary supplements at least occasionally. Although dietary supplements are often thought to be safe and "natural," they contain powerful bioactive chemicals that have the potential for harm. About one-quarter of all pharmaceutical drugs are derived from botanical sources—morphine from poppies and digoxin from foxglove, for example. And, as described earlier, even essential vitamins and minerals can have toxic effects if consumed in excess.

In the United States, supplements are not legally considered drugs and are not regulated the same way drugs are. Before they are approved by the FDA and put on the market, drugs undergo clinical studies to determine safety, effectiveness, side effects and risks, possible interactions with other substances, and appropriate dosages. The FDA does not authorize or test dietary supplements, and supplements are not required to demonstrate either safety or effectiveness prior to marketing. Although dosage guidelines exist for some of the compounds in dietary supplements, dosages for many are not well established.

There are also key differences in how drugs and supplements are manufactured. FDA-approved medications are standardized for potency, and quality control and proof of purity are required. Dietary supplement manufacture is not as closely regulated, and there is no guarantee that a product even contains a given ingredient, let alone in the appropriate amount. The potency of herbal supplements tends to vary widely due to differences in growing and harvesting conditions, preparation methods, and storage. Some manufacturers attempt to standardize their products by isolating the compounds believed to be responsible for

an herb's action. However, potency is often still highly variable, and when several compounds are thought to be responsible for an herb's effect, often only one is standardized. In addition, herbs can be contaminated or misidentified at any stage from harvest to packaging. (See Chapter 20 for more on herbal remedies.) The FDA has recalled several products due to the presence of dangerous contaminants, including heavy metals and pharmaceutical drugs.

To provide consumers with more reliable and consistent information about supplements, the FDA requires supplements to have labels similar to those found on foods (see the box "Using Dietary Supplement Labels" for more information). Label statements and claims about supplements are also regulated.

Finally, it is important to remember that dietary supplements are no substitute for a healthy diet. Supplements do not provide all the known—or yet-to-be-discovered—benefits of whole foods. Supplements should also not be used as a replacement for medical treatment for serious illnesses.

Protecting Yourself Against Foodborne Illness

Many people worry about additives or pesticide residues in their food, but a greater threat comes from microorganisms that cause foodborne illnesses. Raw or undercooked animal products, such as chicken, hamburger, and oysters, pose the greatest threat, although in recent years contaminated fruits and vegetables have been catching up.

The CDC estimates that about 76 million illnesses, 325,000 hospitalizations, and 5000 deaths occur each year in the United States due to foodborne illness. Symptoms include diarrhea, vomiting, fever, and weakness. Although the effects of foodborne illnesses are usually not serious, some groups, such as children, pregnant women, and the elderly, are more at risk for severe complications such as rheumatic diseases, seizures, blood poisoning, other ailments, and death.

Causes of Foodborne Illnesses   Most cases of foodborne illness are caused by **pathogens**, disease-causing microorganisms. Food can be contaminated with pathogens through improper handling; pathogens can grow if food is prepared or stored improperly. Causes of foodborne illness in the United States include the following pathogens:

- *Campylobacter jejuni* causes more cases of foodborne illness than any other bacteria. It is most commonly found in contaminated water, raw milk, and raw or undercooked poultry, meat, or shellfish; the majority of chickens sold in the United States test positive for the presence of *C. jejuni*. Symptoms of infection include diarrhea, fever, abdominal and muscle pain, and headache, which resolve in 7–10 days. However, in about 1 in 1000 cases, *Campylobacter* infection triggers Guillain-Barré syndrome, a neurological

Using Dietary Supplement Labels

Since 1999, specific types of information have been required on the labels of dietary supplements. In addition to basic information about the product, labels include a "Supplement Facts" panel, modeled after the "Nutrition Facts" panel used on food labels (see the label below). Under the Dietary Supplement Health and Education Act (DSHEA) and food labeling laws, supplement labels can make three types of health-related claims.

• *Nutrient-content claims,* such as "high in calcium," "excellent source of vitamin C," or "high potency." The claims "high in" and "excellent source of" mean the same as they do on food labels. A "high potency" single-ingredient supplement must contain 100% of its Daily Value; a "high potency" multi-ingredient product must contain 100% or more of the Daily Value of at least two-thirds of the nutrients present for which Daily Values have been established.

• *Health claims,* if they have been authorized by the FDA or another authoritative scientific body. The association between adequate calcium intake and lower risk of osteoporosis is an example of an approved health claim. Since 2003, the FDA has also allowed so-called *qualified* health claims for situations in which there is emerging but as yet inconclusive evidence for a particular claim. Such claims must include qualifying language such as "scientific evidence suggests but does not prove" the claim.

• *Structure-function claims,* such as "antioxidants maintain cellular integrity" or "this product enhances energy levels." Because these claims are not reviewed by the FDA, they must carry a disclaimer (see the sample label).

Tips for Choosing and Using Dietary Supplements

• Check with your physician before taking a supplement. Many are not meant for children, elderly people, women who are pregnant or breast-feeding, people with chronic illnesses, or people taking prescription or OTC medications.

• Choose brands made by nationally known food and drug manufacturers or house brands from large retail chains. Due to their size and visibility, such sources are likely to have high manufacturing standards.

• Look for the USP verification mark on the label, indicating that the product meets minimum safety and purity standards developed under the Dietary Supplement Verification Program by the United States Pharmacopeia (USP). The USP mark means that the product (1) contains the ingredients stated on the label, (2) has the declared amount and strength of ingredients, (3) will dissolve effectively, (4) has been screened for harmful contaminants, and (5) has been manufactured using safe, sanitary, and well-controlled procedures. The National Nutritional Foods Association (NNFA) has a self-regulatory testing program for its members; other, smaller associations and labs, including ConsumerLab.Com, also test and rate dietary supplements.

• Follow the cautions, instructions for use, and dosage given on the label.

• If you experience side effects, discontinue use of the product and contact your physician. Report any serious reactions to the FDA's MedWatch monitoring program (800-FDA-1088; http://www.fda.gov/medwatch).

For More Information About Dietary Supplements

ConsumerLab.Com: http://www.consumerlab.com

Food and Drug Administration: http://vm.cfsan.fda.gov/~dms/supplmnt.html

National Institutes of Health, Office of Dietary Supplements: http://dietary-supplements.info.nih.gov

Natural Products Association: http://www.naturalproductsassoc.org

U.S. Department of Agriculture: http://www.nal.usda.gov/fnic/etext/000015.html

U.S. Pharmacopeia: http://www.usp.org/uspverified/dietarysupplements

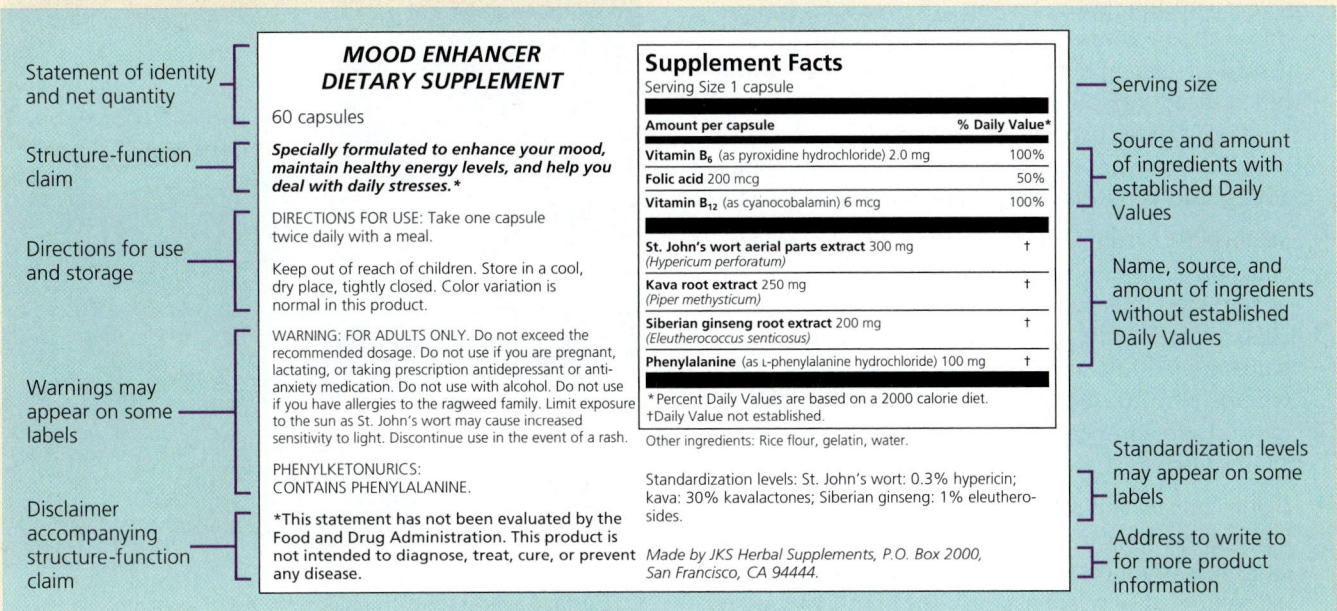

Statement of identity and net quantity

Structure-function claim

Directions for use and storage

Warnings may appear on some labels

Disclaimer accompanying structure-function claim

MOOD ENHANCER DIETARY SUPPLEMENT

60 capsules

Specially formulated to enhance your mood, maintain healthy energy levels, and help you deal with daily stresses.*

DIRECTIONS FOR USE: Take one capsule twice daily with a meal.

Keep out of reach of children. Store in a cool, dry place, tightly closed. Color variation is normal in this product.

WARNING: FOR ADULTS ONLY. Do not exceed the recommended dosage. Do not use if you are pregnant, lactating, or taking prescription antidepressant or anti-anxiety medication. Do not use with alcohol. Do not use if you have allergies to the ragweed family. Limit exposure to the sun as St. John's wort may cause increased sensitivity to light. Discontinue use in the event of a rash.

PHENYLKETONURICS: CONTAINS PHENYLALANINE.

*This statement has not been evaluated by the Food and Drug Administration. This product is not intended to diagnose, treat, cure, or prevent any disease.

Supplement Facts
Serving Size 1 capsule

Amount per capsule	% Daily Value*
Vitamin B₆ (as pyroxidine hydrochloride) 2.0 mg	100%
Folic acid 200 mcg	50%
Vitamin B₁₂ (as cyanocobalamin) 6 mcg	100%
St. John's wort aerial parts extract 300 mg *(Hypericum perforatum)*	†
Kava root extract 250 mg *(Piper methysticum)*	†
Siberian ginseng root extract 200 mg *(Eleutherococcus senticosus)*	†
Phenylalanine (as L-phenylalanine hydrochloride) 100 mg	†

* Percent Daily Values are based on a 2000 calorie diet.
†Daily Value not established.

Other ingredients: Rice flour, gelatin, water.

Standardization levels: St. John's wort: 0.3% hypericin; kava: 30% kavalactones; Siberian ginseng: 1% eleutherosides.

Made by JKS Herbal Supplements, P.O. Box 2000, San Francisco, CA 94444.

Serving size

Source and amount of ingredients with established Daily Values

Name, source, and amount of ingredients without established Daily Values

Standardization levels may appear on some labels

Address to write to for more product information

disease that can cause numbness, weakness, and (usually temporary) paralysis.

- *Salmonella* bacteria are most often found in raw or undercooked eggs, poultry, and meat; milk and dairy products; seafood; fruits and vegetables, including sprouts; and inadequately refrigerated and reheated leftovers. The recent identification of an antibiotic-resistant strain of *Salmonella* has raised concerns about a potential increase in serious illness from *Salmonella*.

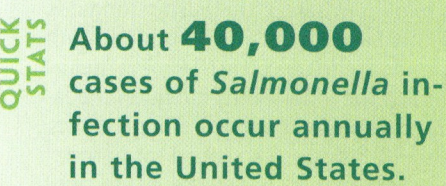
- *Shigella* bacteria are found in the human intestinal tract and usually transmitted via fecal contamination of food and water. Outbreaks are typically traced to foods, especially salads, that have been handled by people using poor personal hygiene. Contaminated water, milk, and dairy products are other possible sources of infection.

- *Escherichia coli* bacteria, found in the intestinal tracts of humans and animals, most commonly contaminate water, raw milk, raw to rare ground beef, unpasteurized juices, and fruits and vegetables. A certain strain, known as *E. coli* O157:H7, is of particular concern because it produces a toxin that causes serious illness and sometimes death. Children are particularly at risk for developing hemolytic uremic syndrome, which causes kidney failure.

- *Listeria monocytogenes* sickens about 2500 Americans a year, causing death in about 20% of cases. It is found in soft cheeses, raw milk, improperly processed ice cream, raw leafy vegetables, hot dogs and lunch meats, and other meat, poultry, and processed foods. *Listeria* is particularly dangerous for pregnant women and their fetuses, babies and children, older adults, and people with weakened immune systems.

- *Staphylococcus aureus* lives mainly in nasal passages and skin sores; it is transferred to food when people handle food or sneeze or cough over food. Foods contaminated with *S. aureus* may include cooked hams, egg and potato salads, cheese, seafood, whipped cream, and milk. *S. aureus* multiplies rapidly at room temperature to produce a toxin that causes illness.

- *Clostridium botulinum* is widely distributed in nature, but it grows only in environments with little or no oxygen; it produces a toxin that causes illness. Potential sources of *C. botulinum* include improperly canned foods, garlic in oil, sausages and other meat products, and vacuum-packed and tightly wrapped foods. Although rare, botulism is potentially fatal if untreated because the toxin affects the nervous system.

- *Norovirus,* the most common viral cause of foodborne illness, may be found in contaminated water, raw or insufficiently cooked shellfish, and salads contaminated by food handlers. Noroviruses typically cause vomiting, diarrhea, and abdominal pain, lasting 1–3 days.

Other causes of foodborne illness include the bacteria *Clostridium perfringens, Vibrio vulnificus,* and *Yersinia enterocolytica;* the hepatitis A virus; the parasites *Trichinella spiralis* (found in pork and wild game), *Anisakis* (found in raw fish), *Giardia lamblia, Cyclospora cayetanensis,* and tapeworms; and certain molds.

A potential new threat from food is bovine spongiform encephalopathy (BSE), or "mad cow disease," a fatal degenerative neurological disease caused by an abnormal protein that forms deposits in the brain. A variant form of the human version of this disease, known as Creutzfeldt-Jakob disease (CJD), is believed to be caused by eating beef contaminated with central nervous system tissue from BSE-infected cows. To date, there have been about 200 confirmed cases worldwide of this variant CJD among the

Careful food handling greatly reduces the risk of foodborne illness.

hundreds of thousands of people who may have consumed BSE-contaminated products. In December 2003, the first BSE-infected cow in the United States was identified; no meat or organs from this animal had made it into the food supply. Although the USDA states that the risk to human health from BSE is extremely low, additional steps are being taken to prevent the BSE protein from entering the food supply; visit the USDA Web site for more information (www.usda.gov).

Preventing and Treating Foodborne Illnesses Because every teaspoon of the soil that our food grows in contains about 2 billion bacteria (only some of them pathogenic), we are always exposed to the possibility of a foodborne illness. You can't tell by taste, smell, or sight whether a food is contaminated. Some studies have revealed high levels of contamination. In 2003, for example, *Consumer Reports* tested 484 chickens purchased in grocery stores and found that half were contaminated with *Campylobacter* and/or *Salmonella;* many of the strains of bacteria found were resistant to antibiotics.

Although pathogens are usually destroyed during cooking, the U.S. government is taking steps to bring down levels of contamination. In addition to new microbiological testing methods for inspection of meat and poultry processing plants, raw meat and poultry products are now sold with safe handling and cooking instructions, and all packaged, unpasteurized fresh fruit and vegetable juices carry warnings about potential contamination. Foodborne illness outbreaks associated with food-processing plants make headlines, but most cases of illness trace back to poor food handling in the home or in food-service establishments. To decrease your risk of foodborne illness, follow the guidelines in the box "Safe Food Handling" on p. 366.

If you think you may be having a bout of foodborne illness, drink plenty of clear fluids to prevent dehydration and rest to speed recovery. To prevent further contamination, wash your hands often, and always before handling food. A fever higher than 102°F, blood in the stool, or dehydration deserves a physician's evaluation, especially if the symptoms persist for more than 2–3 days. In cases of suspected botulism—characterized by symptoms such as double vision, paralysis, dizziness, and vomiting—consult a physician immediately to receive an antitoxin.

Environmental Contaminants and Organic Foods

Contaminants are also present in the food-growing environment, but few of them ever enter the food and water supply in amounts sufficient to cause health problems. Environmental contaminants include various minerals, antibiotics, hormones, pesticides, the industrial chemicals known as **PCBs (polychlorinated biphenyls),** and naturally occurring substances such as cyanogenic glycosides (found in lima beans and the pits of some fruits) and

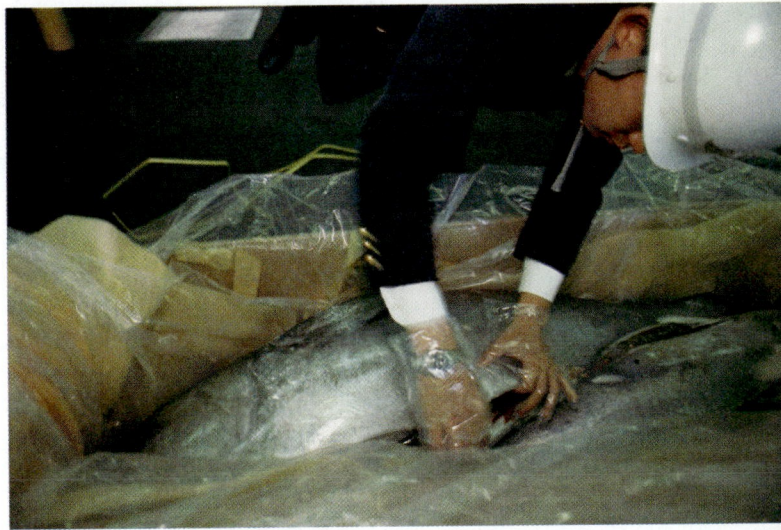

Government inspectors regularly check the U.S. food supply to ensure its safety.

certain molds. Their effects depend on many factors, including concentration, length of exposure, and the age and health status of the person involved. Safety regulations attempt to keep our exposure to contaminants at safe levels, but monitoring is difficult and many substances (such as pesticides) persist in the environment long after being banned from use.

Organic Foods Some people who are concerned about pesticides and other environmental contaminants choose to buy foods that are **organic.** To be certified as organic by the USDA, foods must meet strict production, processing, handling, and labeling criteria. Organic crops must meet limits on pesticide residues; for meat, milk, eggs, and other animal products to be certified organic, animals must be given organic feed and access to the outdoors and may not be given antibiotics or growth hormones. The use of genetic engineering, ionizing radiation, and sewage sludge is prohibited. Products can be labeled "100% organic" if they contain all organic ingredients and "organic" if they contain at least 95% organic ingredients; all such products may carry the USDA organic seal. A product with at least 70% organic ingredients can be labeled "made with organic ingredients" but cannot use the USDA seal.

polychlorinated biphenyl (PCB) An industrial chemical used as an insulator in electrical transformers and linked to certain human cancers.

organic A designation applied to foods grown and produced according to strict guidelines limiting the use of pesticides, nonorganic ingredients, hormones, antibiotics, irradiation, genetic engineering, and other practices.

TERMS

Safe Food Handling

- Don't buy food in containers that leak, bulge, or are severely dented. Refrigerated foods should be cold, and frozen foods should be solid.

- Refrigerate perishable items as soon as possible after purchase. Use or freeze fresh meats within 3–5 days and fresh poultry, fish, and ground meat within 1–2 days.

- Store raw meat, poultry, fish, and shellfish in containers in the refrigerator so that the juices don't drip onto other foods. Keep these items away from other foods, surfaces, utensils, or serving dishes to prevent cross-contamination.

- Thaw frozen food in the refrigerator or in the microwave oven, not on the kitchen counter. Cook foods immediately after thawing.

- Thoroughly wash your hands with warm soapy water for 20 seconds before and after handling food, especially raw meat, fish, shellfish, poultry, or eggs.

- Make sure counters, cutting boards, dishes, utensils, and other equipment are thoroughly cleaned before and after use using hot soapy water. Wash dishcloths and kitchen towels frequently.

- If possible, use separate cutting boards for meat, poultry, and seafood and for foods that will be eaten raw, such as fruits and vegetables. Replace cutting boards once they become worn or develop hard-to-clean grooves.

- Thoroughly rinse and scrub fruits and vegetables with a brush, if possible, or peel off the skin.

- Cook foods thoroughly, especially beef, poultry, fish, pork, and eggs; cooking kills most microorganisms. Use a food thermometer to ensure that foods are cooked to a safe temperature. Hamburgers should be cooked to 160°F. Turn or stir microwaved food to make sure it is heated evenly throughout. When eating out, order hamburger cooked well-done and make sure foods are served piping hot.

- Cook stuffing separately from poultry; or wash poultry thoroughly, stuff immediately before cooking, and transfer the stuffing to a clean bowl immediately after cooking. The temperature of cooked stuffing should reach 165°F.

- Keep hot foods hot (140°F or above) and cold foods cold (40°F or below); harmful bacteria can grow rapidly between these two temperatures. Refrigerate foods within 2 hours of purchase or preparation, and within 1 hour if the air temperature is above 90°F. Refrigerate foods at or below 40°F and freeze at or below 0°F. Use refrigerated leftovers within 3–4 days.

- Don't eat raw animal products, including raw eggs in home-made hollandaise sauce or eggnog. Use only pasteurized milk and juice, and look for pasteurized eggs, which are now available in some states.

- Cook eggs until they're firm, and fully cook foods containing eggs. Store eggs in the coldest part of the refrigerator, not in the door, and use them within 3–5 weeks.

- Because of possible contamination with *E. coli* O157:H7 and *Salmonella*, avoid raw sprouts. Even sprouts grown under clean conditions in the home can be risky because bacteria may be present in the seeds. Cook sprouts before eating them.

- Read the food label and package information, and follow safety instructions such as "Keep Refrigerated" and the "Safe Handling Instructions."

- According to the USDA, "When in doubt, throw it out." Even if a food looks and smells fine, it may not be safe. If you aren't sure that a food has been prepared, served, and stored safely, don't eat it.

Additional precautions are recommended for people at particularly high risk for foodborne illness—pregnant women, young children, older persons, and people with weakened immune systems or certain chronic illnesses. If you are a member of one of these groups, don't eat or drink any of the following products: unpasteurized juices; raw sprouts; unpasteurized (raw) milk and products made from unpasteurized milk; raw or undercooked meat, poultry, eggs, fish, and shellfish; and soft cheeses such as feta, Brie, Camembert, or blue-veined cheeses. To protect against *Listeria*, it's also important to avoid ready-to-eat foods such as hot dogs, luncheon meats, and cold cuts unless they are reheated until they are steaming hot.

Organic foods are not necessarily chemical-free, however. They may be contaminated with pesticides used on neighboring lands or on foods transported in the same train or truck. However, they do tend to have lower levels of pesticide residues than conventionally grown crops. Some experts recommend that consumers who want to buy organic fruits and vegetables spend their money on those that carry lower pesticide residues than their conventional counterparts (the "dirty dozen"): apples, bell peppers, celery, cherries, imported grapes, nectarines, peaches, pears, potatoes, red raspberries, spinach, and strawberries.

Experts also recommend buying organic beef, poultry, eggs, dairy products, and baby food. Fruits and vegetables that carry little pesticide residue whether grown conventionally or organically include asparagus, avocadoes, bananas, broccoli, cauliflower, corn, kiwi, mangoes, onions, papaya, pineapples, and peas. All foods are subject to strict pesticide limits; the debate about the health effects of small amounts of residue is ongoing.

Whether organic foods are better for your health or not, organic farming is better for the environment. It helps maintain biodiversity of crops and replenish the earth's resources; it is less likely to degrade soil, contaminate water, or expose farm workers to toxic chemicals. As multinational food companies get into the organic food business, however, consumers who want to support environmentally friendly farming methods should look for foods that are not only organic but locally grown.

Guidelines for Fish Consumption   A specific area of concern has been possible mercury contamination in fish. Overall, fish and shellfish are healthy sources of protein, omega-3 fats, and other nutrients. Prudent choices can minimize the risk of any possible negative health effects. High mercury concentrations are most likely to be found in predator fish—large fish that eat smaller fish. Mercury can cause brain damage to fetuses and young children.

In 2004, the FDA and Environmental Protection Agency (EPA) released an advisory with guidelines for certain groups. To reduce exposure to mercury, women who are or who may become pregnant and nursing mothers should follow these guidelines:

- Do not eat shark, swordfish, king mackerel, or tilefish.

- Eat up to 12 ounces a week of a variety of fish and shellfish that is lower in mercury, such as shrimp, canned light tuna, salmon, pollock, and catfish. Limit consumption of albacore tuna to 6 ounces per week.

- Check advisories about the safety of recreationally caught fish from local lakes, rivers, and coastal areas; if no information is available, limit consumption to 6 ounces per week.

The same FDA/EPA guidelines apply to children, although they should consume smaller servings.

Some experts have also expressed concern about the presence of toxins such as PCBs in farmed fish, especially farmed salmon. Although no federal guidelines have been set, some researchers suggest that consumers limit themselves to 8 ounces of farmed salmon per month. Fish should be labeled with its country of origin and whether it is wild or farmed; most canned salmon is wild.

Additives in Food

Today, some 2800 substances are intentionally added to foods to maintain or improve nutritional quality, to maintain freshness, to help in processing or preparation, or to alter taste or appearance. Additives make up less than 1% of our food. The most widely used are sugar, salt, and corn syrup; these three plus citric acid, baking soda, vegetable colors, mustard, and pepper account for 98% by weight of all food additives used in the United States.

Some additives may be of concern for certain people, either because they are consumed in large quantities or because they cause some type of reaction. Additives having potential health concerns include the following:

- *Nitrates and nitrites:* Used to protect meats from contamination with botulism. Their consumption is associated with the synthesis of cancer-causing agents in the stomach, but the cancer risk appears to be low, except for people with low stomach acid output (such as some elderly people).

- *BHA and BHT:* Used to help maintain the freshness of foods. Some studies indicate a potential link between BHT and an increased risk of certain cancers, but any risk from these agents is considered to be low. Some manufacturers have stopped using BHT and BHA.

- *Sulfites:* Used to keep vegetables from turning brown. They can cause severe reactions in some people. The FDA severely limits the use of sulfites and requires any foods containing sulfites to be clearly labeled.

- *Monosodium glutamate (MSG):* Typically used as a flavor enhancer. MSG may cause some people to experience episodes of increased blood pressure and sweating. If you are sensitive to MSG, check food labels when shopping, and ask to have it left out of dishes you order at restaurants.

Food additives pose no significant health hazard to most people because the levels used are well below any that could produce toxic effects. To avoid potential problems, eat a variety of foods in moderation. If you are sensitive to an additive, check food labels when you shop, and ask questions when you eat out.

Food Irradiation

Food irradiation is the treatment of foods with gamma rays, X rays, or high-voltage electrons to kill potentially harmful pathogens, including bacteria, parasites, insects, and fungi that cause foodborne illness. It also reduces spoilage and extends shelf life. For example, irradiated strawberries stay unspoiled in the refrigerator up to 3 weeks, versus only 3–5 days for untreated berries. The government permits the irradiation of certain foods, including wheat and flour, white potatoes, pork, herbs and spices, fruits and vegetables, raw poultry, red meat, and certain leafy green vegetables. The same irradiation process has also been used for decades on such items as plastic wrap, milk cartons, teething rings, contact lenses, and medical supplies.

food irradiation   The treatment of foods with gamma rays, X rays, or high-voltage electrons to kill potentially harmful pathogens and increase shelf life.

TERMS

Even though irradiation has been generally endorsed by agencies such as the World Health Organization, the Centers for Disease Control and Prevention, and the American Medical Association, few irradiated foods are currently on the market due to consumer resistance and skepticism. Studies haven't conclusively identified any harmful effects of food irradiation, and the newer methods of irradiation involving electricity and X rays do not require the use of any radioactive materials. Some irradiated foods may taste slightly different, just as pasteurized milk tastes slightly different than unpasteurized milk.

Studies indicate that when consumers are given information about the process of irradiation and the benefits of irradiated foods, most want to purchase them. Without such information, many remain skeptical. All primary irradiated foods (meat, vegetables, and so on) are labeled with the flower-like radura symbol and a brief information label; spices and foods that are merely ingredients do not have to be so labeled. It is important to remember that although irradiation kills most pathogens, it does not completely sterilize foods. Proper handling of irradiated foods is still critical for preventing foodborne illness.

Genetically Modified Foods

Genetic engineering involves altering the characteristics of a plant, animal, or microorganism by adding, rearranging, or replacing genes in its DNA; the result is a **genetically modified (GM) organism.** New DNA may come from related species or from entirely different types of organisms. Many GM crops are already grown in the United States: About 75% of the current U.S. soybean crop has been genetically modified to be resistant to an herbicide used to kill weeds, and about 34% of the U.S. corn crop carries genes for herbicide resistance or pest resistance. Products made with GM organisms include juice, soda, nuts, tuna, frozen pizza, spaghetti sauce, canola oil, chips, salad dressings, and soup.

The potential benefits of GM foods cited by supporters include improved yields overall and in difficult growing conditions, increased disease resistance, improved nutritional content, lower prices, and less pesticide use. Critics of biotechnology argue that unexpected effects may occur: Gene manipulation could elevate levels of naturally occurring toxins or allergens, permanently change the gene pool and reduce biodiversity, and produce pesticide-resistant insects through the transfer of genes. Experience has shown that GM products are difficult to keep separate from non-GM products; animal escapes, cross-pollination, and contamination during processing are just a few ways GM organisms could potentially appear unexpectedly in the food supply or the environment.

According to the National Academy of Sciences, there is currently no proof that the GM food already on the market is unsafe. However, experts have recommended regulatory changes and further study of key issues, particularly the environmental effects of the escape of GM animals.

Animal Cloning   In early 2008, the FDA concluded that meat and milk from cloned animals is no different from the meat and milk from naturally reproduced animals, and is thus safe for human consumption. The FDA's conclusion resulted from several years of studies of cloned and otherwise genetically modified animals.

Cloning allows producers to create animals with highly desirable characteristics, such as disease resistance and more predictable fat-to-lean meat ratios. Cloned animals are similar to identical twins. For example, scientists can produce a cloned cow by taking an egg from a female cow, removing the egg's gene-containing nucleus, and inserting genes from another cow that the scientists want to copy. The egg is then urged to create an embryo, and the embryo is implanted into the uterus of another female cow, which carries it to term and delivers it. (This surrogate cow's DNA does not affect the clone's DNA.)

The FDA's regulations regarding cloned animals state that cloned cattle, pigs, and goats (as well as their offspring) are safe for human consumption. Regulations discourage producers from introducing other cloned species into the food chain. Cloned animals will most commonly be used as breeding stock, however, rather than as food sources. In this way, the clones' desirable traits are passed down to future generations of offspring, which then may enter the food chain.

Labeling of GM Foods   Labeling has been another major concern, with surveys indicating that most Americans want to know if their food contains GM ingredients. The FDA does not require special labeling for foods from genetically modified or cloned sources. Under current rules, the FDA requires special labeling only when a food's composition is changed significantly or when a known allergen such as a peanut gene is introduced into a food. The only foods guaranteed not to contain GM ingredients are those certified as organic.

Food Allergies and Food Intolerances

For some people, consuming a particular food causes symptoms such as itchiness, swollen lips, or abdominal

---

TERMS

genetically modified (GM) organism   A plant, animal, or microorganism in which genes have been added, rearranged, or replaced through genetic engineering.

food allergy   An adverse reaction to a food or food ingredient in which the immune system perceives a particular substance (allergen) as foreign and acts to destroy it.

food intolerance   An adverse reaction to a food or food ingredient that doesn't involve the immune system; intolerances are often due to a problem with metabolism.

QUESTIONS FOR CRITICAL THINKING AND REFLECTION

What is the least healthy food you eat every day (either during meals or as a snack)? Identify at least one substitute that would be healthier but just as satisfying.

pain. Adverse reactions like these may be due to a food allergy or a food intolerance, and symptoms may range from annoying to life-threatening. If you've had an adverse reaction to a food, it's important to determine whether your symptoms are due to an allergy or an intolerance so that you can take appropriate action.

Food Allergies   A true **food allergy** is a reaction of the body's immune system to a food or food ingredient, usually a protein. The immune system perceives the reaction-provoking substance, or allergen, as foreign and acts to destroy it. This immune reaction can occur within minutes of ingesting the food, resulting in symptoms that affect the skin (hives), gastrointestinal tract (cramps or diarrhea), respiratory tract (asthma), or mouth (swelling of the lips or tongue). The most severe response is a systemic reaction called *anaphylaxis,* which involves a potentially life-threatening drop in blood pressure.

Food allergies affect only about 1.5% of the adult population and up to 6% of infants; many infants outgrow food allergies. Although numerous food allergens have been identified, just eight foods account for more than 90% of the food allergies in the United States: cow's milk, eggs, peanuts, tree nuts (walnuts, cashews, and so on), soy, wheat, fish, and shellfish. Food labels are now required to state the presence of the eight most common allergens in plain language in the ingredient list. Individuals with food allergies, especially those prone to anaphylaxis, must diligently avoid trigger foods. This involves carefully reading food labels and asking questions about ingredients when eating out. People at risk are usually advised to carry medications to treat anaphylaxis, such as injectable epinephrine. Refer to Chapter 17 for more on allergies.

Food Intolerances   Many people who believe they have food allergies may actually suffer from a much more common source of adverse food reactions, a **food intolerance.** In the case of a food intolerance, the problem usually lies with metabolism rather than with the immune system. Typically, the body cannot adequately digest a food or food component, often because of some type of chemical deficiency; in other cases, the body reacts to a particular compound in a food. Lactose intolerance is a fairly common food intolerance. A more serious condition is intolerance of gluten, a protein component of some grains; in affected individuals, consumption of gluten damages the lining of the small intestine. Sulfite, a common food additive, can produce severe asthmatic reactions in sensitive individuals. Food intolerances have also been attributed to tartrazine (a yellow food coloring), MSG, and the sweetener aspartame.

Food intolerance reactions often produce symptoms similar to food allergies, such as diarrhea or cramps, but reactions are typically localized and not life-threatening. Many people with food intolerances can consume small amounts of the food that affects them; exceptions are gluten and sulfite, which must be avoided by sensitive individuals. Through trial and error, most people with food intolerances can adjust their intake of the trigger food to an appropriate level.

If you suspect that you have a food allergy or intolerance, a good first step is to keep a food diary. Note everything you eat or drink, any symptoms you develop, and how long after eating the symptoms appear. Then make an appointment with your physician to go over your diary and determine if any additional tests are needed.

TIPS FOR TODAY AND THE FUTURE

Opportunities to improve your diet present themselves every day, and small changes add up.

RIGHT NOW YOU CAN

- Substitute a healthy snack for an unhealthy one.
- Drink a glass of water and put a bottle of water in your backpack for tomorrow.
- Plan to make healthy selections when you eat out, such as steamed vegetables instead of french fries or salmon instead of steak.

IN THE FUTURE, YOU CAN

- Visit the MyPyramid Web site at www.mypyramid.gov and use the online tools to create a personalized nutrition plan and begin tracking your eating habits.
- Learn to cook healthier meals. There are hundreds of free Web sites and low-cost cookbooks that provide recipes for healthy dishes.

Improving Your Diet by Choosing Healthy Beverages

After reading this chapter and completing the dietary assessment on p. 357, you can probably identify several changes you could make to improve your diet. Here, we focus on choosing healthy beverages to increase intake of nutrients and decrease intake of empty calories from added sugars and fat. However, this model of dietary change can be applied to any modification you'd like to make to your diet. Additional specific plans for improving diet can be found in the Behavior Change Strategies in Chapter 15 (decreasing saturated and trans fat intake) and Chapter 16 (increasing intake of fruits and vegetables).

Gather Data and Establish a Baseline

Begin by tracking your beverage consumption in your health journal. Write down the types and amounts of beverages you drink, including water. Also note where you were at the time and whether you obtained the beverage there or brought it with you. At the same time, investigate your options. Find out what other beverages you can easily obtain over the course of your daily routine. For example, what drinks are available in the dining hall where you eat lunch or at the food court where you often grab snacks? How many drinking fountains do you walk by over the course of the day? This information will help you put together a successful plan for change.

Analyze Your Data and Set Goals

Evaluate your beverage consumption by dividing your typical daily consumption between healthy and less healthy choices. Use the following guide as a basis, and add other beverages to the lists as needed.

Choose less often:

- Regular soda

- Sweetened bottled iced tea

- Fruit beverages made with little fruit juice (usually labeled fruit drinks, punches, beverages, blends, or ades)

- Whole milk

Choose more often:

- Water—plain, mineral, and sparkling

- Low-fat or fat-free milk

- Fruit juice (100% juice)

- Unsweetened herbal tea

How many beverages do you consume daily from each category? What would be a healthy and realistic goal for change? For example, if your beverage consumption is currently evenly divided between the "choose more often" and "choose less often" categories (four from each list), you might set a final goal for your behavior change program of increasing your healthy choices by two (to six from the "more often" list and two from the "less often" list).

Develop a Plan for Change

Once you've set your goal, you need to develop strategies that will help you choose healthy beverages more often. Consider the following possibilities:

- Keep healthy beverages on hand; if you live in a student dorm, rent a small refrigerator or keep bottled water, juice, fat-free milk, and other healthy choices in the dorm kitchen's refrigerator.

- Plan ahead, and put a bottle of water or 100% juice in your backpack every day.

- Check food labels on beverages for serving sizes, calories, and nutrients; comparison shop to find the healthiest choices, and watch your serving sizes. Use this information to make your "choose more often" list longer and more specific.

- If you eat out frequently, examine all the beverages available at the places you typically eat your meals. You'll probably find that healthy choices are available; if not, bring along your own drink or find somewhere else to eat.

- For a snack, try water and a piece of fruit rather than a heavily sweetened beverage.

- Create healthy beverages that appeal to you; for example, try adding slices of citrus fruit to water or mixing 100% fruit juice with sparkling water.

You may also need to make some changes in your routine to decrease the likelihood that you'll make unhealthy choices. For example, you might discover from your health journal that you always buy a soda after class when you pass a particular vending machine. If this is the case, try another route that allows you to avoid the machine. And try to guard against impulse buying by carrying water or a healthy snack with you every day.

To complete your plan, try some of the other behavior change strategies described in Chapter 1: Develop and sign a contract, set up a system of rewards, involve other people in your program, and develop strategies for challenging situations. Once your plan is complete, take action. Keep track of your progress in your health journal by continuing to monitor and evaluate your beverage consumption.

SUMMARY

- To function at its best, the human body requires about 45 essential nutrients in specific proportions. People get the nutrients needed to fuel their bodies and maintain tissues and organ systems from foods; the body cannot synthesize most of them.

- Proteins, made up of amino acids, form muscles and bones and help make up blood, enzymes, hormones, and cell membranes. Foods from animal sources provide complete proteins; plants provide incomplete proteins.

- Fats, a concentrated source of energy, also help insulate the body and cushion the organs; 1 tablespoon of vegetable oil per day supplies the essential fats. Dietary fat intake should be 20–35% of total daily calories. Unsaturated fats should be favored over saturated and trans fats.

- Carbohydrates supply energy to the brain and other parts of the nervous system as well as to red blood cells. The body needs about 130 grams of carbohydrates a day, but more is recommended.

- Fiber includes nondigestible carbohydrates provided mainly by plants. Adequate intake of fiber (38 grams per day for men and 25 grams per day for women) can help people manage diabetes and high cholesterol levels and improve intestinal health.

- The 13 vitamins needed in the diet are organic substances that promote specific chemical and cell processes within living tissue. Deficiencies or excesses can cause serious illnesses and even death.

- The approximately 17 minerals needed in the diet are inorganic substances that regulate body functions, aid in the growth and maintenance of body tissues, and help in the release of energy from foods.

- Water is used to digest and absorb food, transport substances around the body, lubricate joints and organs, and regulate body temperature.

- Foods contain other substances such as phytochemicals, which may not be essential nutrients but which reduce chronic disease risk.

- Dietary Reference Intakes (DRIs) are recommended intakes for essential nutrients that meet the needs of healthy people.

- The Dietary Guidelines for Americans address the prevention of diet-related diseases such as CVD, cancer, and diabetes. The guidelines advise us to consume a variety of foods while staying within calorie needs; manage body weight through calorie control and regular physical activity; eat more fruits, vegetables, whole grains, and reduced-fat dairy products; choose fats and carbohydrates wisely; eat less salt and more potassium; be moderate with alcohol intake; and handle foods safely.

- Choosing foods from each group in MyPyramid every day helps ensure the appropriate amounts of necessary nutrients.

- A vegetarian diet can meet human nutritional needs.

- Almost all foods have labels that show how much fat, cholesterol, protein, fiber, and sodium they contain. Serving sizes are standardized, and health claims are carefully regulated. Dietary supplements also have uniform labels.

- Foodborne illnesses are a greater threat to health than additives and environmental contaminants. Other dietary issues of concern to some people include organic foods, food irradiation, genetic modification of foods, and food allergies and intolerances.

FOR MORE INFORMATION

BOOKS

Byrd-Bredbenner, C., et al. 2009. *Wardlaw's Perspectives in Nutrition,* 8th ed. New York: McGraw-Hill. *An easy-to-understand review of major concepts in nutrition.*

Duyff, R. L. 2006. *ADA Complete Food and Nutrition Guide,* 3rd ed. Hoboken, N.J.: Wiley. *An excellent review of current nutrition information.*

Insel, P., R. E. Turner, and D. Ross. 2009. *Nutrition,* 4thd ed. Sudbury, Mass.: Jones & Bartlett. *An introductory nutrition textbook covering a variety of key topics.*

Nestle, M. 2007. *What to Eat.* New York: North Point Press. *A nutritionist examines the marketing of food and explains how to interpret food-related information while shopping.*

Selkowitz, A. 2005. *The College Student's Guide to Eating Well on Campus,* revised ed. Bethesda, Md.: Tulip Hill Press. *Provides practical advice for students, including how to make healthy choices when eating in a dorm or restaurant and how to stock a first pantry.*

Warshaw, H. 2006. *What to Eat When You're Eating Out.* Alexandria, VA.: American Diabetes Association. *A registered dietician explains how to eat well when dining in restaurants; designed especially for those trying to manage their weight or a chronic condition such as diabetes.*

NEWSLETTERS

Environmental Nutrition (800-424-7887; http://www.environmental nutrition.com)

Nutrition Action Health Letter (202-332-9110; http://www.cspinet .org/nah)

Tufts University Health & Nutrition Letter (800-274-7581; http:// www.tuftshealthletter.com)

ORGANIZATIONS, HOTLINES, AND WEB SITES

American Dietetic Association. Provides a wide variety of nutrition-related educational materials.
   http://www.eatright.org

American Heart Association: Delicious Decisions. Provides basic information about nutrition, tips for shopping and eating out, and heart-healthy recipes.
   http://www.deliciousdecisions.org

FDA Center for Food Safety and Applied Nutrition. Offers information about topics such as food labeling, food additives, dietary supplements, and foodborne illness.
   http://vm.cfsan.fda.gov

Food Safety Hotlines. Provide information on safe purchase, handling, cooking, and storage of food.
   888-SAFEFOOD (FDA)
   800-535-4555 (USDA)

Gateways to Government Nutrition Information. Provide access to government resources relating to food safety and nutrition.
   http://www.foodsafety.gov
   http://www.nutrition.gov

Harvard School of Public Health Nutrition Source. Provides recent key research findings, including advice on interpreting news on nutrition; an overview of the Healthy Eating Pyramid, an alternative to the basic USDA pyramid; and suggestions for building a healthy diet.
   http://www.hsph.harvard.edu/nutritionsource

International Food Information Council. Provides information on food safety and nutrition for consumers, journalists, and educators.

http://www.ific.org

MyPyramid.gov. Provides personalized dietary plans and interactive food and activity tracking tools.

http://www.mypyramid.gov

National Academies' Food and Nutrition Board. Provides information about the Dietary Reference Intakes and related guidelines.

http://www.iom.edu/CMS/3788.aspx

Tufts University Nutrition Navigator. Provides descriptions and ratings for many nutrition-related Web pages.

http://navigator.tufts.edu

USDA Center for Nutrition Policy and Promotion. Includes information on the Dietary Guidelines and MyPyramid.

http://www.usda.gov/cnpp

USDA Food and Nutrition Information Center. Provides a variety of materials and extensive links relating to the Dietary Guidelines, food labels, MyPyramid, and many other topics.

http://www.nal.usda.gov/fnic

Vegetarian Resource Group. Information and links for vegetarians and people interested in learning more about vegetarian diets.

http://www.vrg.org

You can obtain nutrient breakdowns of individual food items from the following sites:

Nutrition Analysis Tool, University of Illinois, Urbana/Champaign

http:/www.nat.uiuc.edu

USDA Nutrient Data Laboratory

http://www.ars.usda.gov/ba/bhnrc/ndl

See also the resources listed in the dietary supplements box on page 363 and in the For More Information sections in Chapters 13–16 and 22.

SELECTED BIBLIOGRAPHY

Aldana, S. G., et al. 2005. Effects of an intensive diet and physical activity modification program on the health risks of adults. *Journal of the American Dietetic Association* 105(3): 371–381.

American Heart Association. 2008. *Diet and Lifestyle Recommendations* (http://www.americanheart.org/presenter.jhtml?identifier=851; retrieved February 9, 2009).

American Heart Association. 2008. *Fish, Levels of Mercury and Omega-3 Fatty Acids* (http://www.americanheart.org/presenter.jhtml?identifier=3013797; retrieved February 9, 2009).

Centers for Disease Control and Prevention. 2005. *Foodborne Illness* (http://www.cdc.gov/ncidod/dbmd/diseaseinfo/files/foodborne_illness_FAQ.pdf; retrieved February 9, 2009).

Centers for Disease Control and Prevention. 2007. *vCJD (Variant Creutzfeldt-Jakob Disease)* (http://www.cdc.gov/ncidod/dvrd/vcjd/factsheet_nvcjd.htm; retrieved February 9, 2009).

Centers for Disease Control and Prevention. 2008. *Listeriosis* (http://www.cdc.gov/nczved/dfbmd/disease_listing/listeriosis_gi.html; retrieved February 9, 2009).

Clifton, P. M., J. B. Keogh, and M. Noakes. 2004. Trans fatty acids in adipose tissue and the food supply are associated with myocardial infarction. *Journal of Nutrition* 134: 874–879.

Cotton, P. A., et al. 2004. Dietary sources of nutrients among U.S. adults, 1994 to 1996. *Journal of the American Dietetic Association* 104: 921–930.

Council for Responsible Nutrition. 2005. *Dietary Supplements: Safe, Regulated and Beneficial* (http://www.crnusa.org/pdfs/CRN_FACT_DSSafeRegulatedBeneficial_07.pdf; retrieved February 9, 2009).

Food and Nutrition Board, Institute of Medicine. 2005. *Dietary Reference Intakes for Energy, Carbohydrate, Fiber, Fat, Fatty Acids, Cholesterol, Protein, and Amino Acids.* Washington, D.C.: National Academy Press.

Food and Nutrition Board, Institute of Medicine. 2005. *Dietary Reference Intakes for Water, Potassium, Sodium, Chloride, and Sulfate.* Washington, D.C.: National Academy Press.

Foote, J. A., et al. 2004. Dietary variety increases the probability of nutrient adequacy among adults. *Journal of Nutrition* 134: 1779–1784.

Foster-Powell K., et al. 2002. International table of glycemic index and glycemic load values: 2002. *American Journal of Clinical Nutrition* 76(1): 5–56.

A guide to the best and worst drinks. 2006. *Consumer Reports on Health*, July, 8–9.

Hanley, D. A., and K. S. Davison. 2005. Vitamin D insufficiency in North America. *Journal of Nutrition* 135(2): 332–337.

Harvard School of Public Health, Department of Nutrition. 2009. *The Nutrition Source: Knowledge for Healthy Eating* (http://www.hsph.harvard.edu/nutritionsource/index.html; retrieved February 9, 2009).

He, K., et al. 2004. Accumulated evidence on fish consumption and coronary heart disease mortality: A meta-analysis of cohort studies. *Circulation* 109: 2705–2711.

Hites, R. A., et al. 2004. Global assessment of organic contaminants in farmed salmon. *Science* 303(5655): 225–229.

Houston, D. K., et al. 2005. Dairy, fruit, and vegetable intakes and functional limitations and disability in a biracial cohort. *American Journal of Clinical Nutrition* 81(2): 515–522.

Kranz, S., et al. 2005. Adverse effect of high added sugar consumption on dietary intake in American preschoolers. *Journal of Pediatrics* 46(1): 105–111.

Lichtenstein, A. H., et al. 2006. Diet and Lifestyle Recommendations, Revision 2006. A Scientific Statement from the American Heart Association Nutrition Committee. *Circulation* 114(1): 82–96.

Liebman, B. 2006. Whole grains: The inside story. *Nutrition Action Health Letter* 33(4): 1–5.

Ma, Y., et al. 2005. Association between dietary carbohydrates and body weight. *American Journal of Epidemiology* 161(4): 359–367.

Mayo Clinic. 2008. *Food Pyramid: An Option for Better Eating* (http://www.mayoclinic.com/health/healthy-diet/NU00190; retrieved February 9, 2009).

Moreira N. 2005. *Soft Drinks as Top Calorie Culprit.* (http://www.sciencenews.org/articles/20050618/food.asp; retrieved May 12, 2008).

Mosaffarian, D., et al. 2006. Trans fatty acids and cardiovascular disease. *New England Journal of Medicine* 354(15): 1601–1613.

Nanney, M. S., et al. 2004. Rationale for a consistent "powerhouse" approach to vegetable and fruit messages. *Journal of the American Dietetic Association* 104(3): 352–356.

National Academy of Sciences, Institute of Medicine, Food and Nutrition Board. 2005. *Dietary Reference Intakes: Recommended Intakes for Individuals* (http://www.iom.edu/Object.File/Master/7/300/Webtablemacro.pdf; retrieved February 9, 2009).

Nicholls, S. J., et al. 2006. Consumption of saturated fat impairs the anti-inflammatory properties of high-density lipoproteins and endothelial function. *Journal of the American College of Cardiology* 48(4): 715–720.

Opotowsky, A. R., et al. 2004. Serum vitamin A concentration and the risk of hip fracture among women 50 to 74 years old in the United States. *American Journal of Medicine* 117(3): 169–174.

Pereira, M. A., et al. 2004. Dietary fiber and risk of coronary heart disease: A pooled analysis of cohort studies. *Archives of Internal Medicine* 164(4): 370–376.

Smit, E., et al. 1999. Estimates of animal and plant protein intake in US adults: Results from the Third National Health and Nutrition Examination Survey, 1988–1991. Journal of the American Dietetic Association 99(7): 813-820.

U.S. Department of Agriculture and Centers for Disease Control and Prevention. 2007. *What We Eat in America, NHANES 2003–2004 Data: Nutrient Intakes: Mean Amounts and Percentages of Calories from Protein,*

Carbohydrate, Fat and Alcohol (http://www.ars.usda.gov/Services/docs.htm?docid=14958; retrieved February 9, 2009).

U.S. Department of Health and Human Services, Office of the Surgeon General. 2004. *Bone Health and Osteoporosis: A Report of the Surgeon General* (http://www.surgeongeneral.gov/library/bonehealth; retrieved February 9, 2009).

U.S. Department of Health and Human Services and U.S. Department of Agriculture. 2005. *Dietary Guidelines for Americans 2005* (http://www.healthierus.gov/dietaryguidelines/index.html; retrieved February 9, 2009).

U.S. Department of Health and Human Services and U.S. Department of Agriculture. 2005. *Finding your way to a healthier you: Based on the Dietary Guidelines for Americans.* Home and Garden Bulletin No. 232-CP.

U.S. Food and Drug Administration. 2001. *Food Allergies: When Food Becomes the Enemy.* (http://www.fda.gov/FDAC/features/2001/401_food.html; retrieved February 9, 2009).

Vegetarian Resource Group. 2000. *How Many Vegetarians Are There?* (http://www.vrg.org/journal/vj2000may/2000maypoll.htm; retrieved February 9, 2009).

Vieth, R. 2006. What is the optimal vitamin D status for health? *Progress in Biophysics and Molecular Biology* 92(1): 26–32.

Nutrition Resources

Table 1 — Dietary Reference Intakes (DRIs): Recommended Levels for Individual Intake

Life Stage	Group	Biotin (µg/day)	Choline (mg/day)[a]	Folate (µg/day)[b]	Niacin (mg/day)[c]	Pantothenic Acid (mg/day)	Riboflavin (mg/day)
Infants	0–6 months	5	125	65	2	1.7	0.3
	7–12 months	6	150	80	**4**	1.8	0.4
Children	1–3 years	8	200	**150**	6	2	0.5
	4–8 years	12	250	**200**	8	3	0.6
Males	9–13 years	20	375	**300**	12	4	0.9
	14–18 years	25	550	**400**	16	5	1.3
	19–30 years	30	550	**400**	16	5	1.3
	31–50 years	30	550	**400**	16	5	1.3
	51–70 years	30	550	**400**	16	5	1.3
	>70 years	30	550	**400**	16	5	1.3
Females	9–13 years	20	375	**300**	12	4	0.9
	14–18 years	25	400	**400**[i]	14	5	1.0
	19–30 years	30	425	**400**[i]	14	5	1.1
	31–50 years	30	425	**400**[i]	14	5	1.1
	51–70 years	30	425	**400**[i]	14	5	1.1
	>70 years	30	425	**400**	14	5	1.1
Pregnancy	≤18 years	30	450	**600**[i]	18	6	1.4
	19–30 years	30	450	**600**[j]	18	6	1.4
	31–50 years	30	450	**600**[j]	18	6	1.4
Lactation	≤18 years	35	550	**500**	17	7	1.6
	19–30 years	35	550	**500**	17	7	1.6
	31–50 years	35	550	**500**	17	7	1.6
Tolerable Upper Intake Levels for Adults (19–70)			3500	1000[k]	35[k]		

Life Stage	Group	Thiamin (mg/day)	Vitamin A (µg/day)[d]	Vitamin B-6 (mg/day)	Vitamin B-12 (µg/day)	Vitamin C (mg/day)[e]	Vitamin D (µg/day)[f]	Vitamin E (mg/day)[g]
Infants	0–6 months	0.2	400	0.1	0.4	40	5	4
	7–12 months	0.3	500	0.3	0.5	50	5	5
Children	1–3 years	0.5	300	0.5	0.9	15	5	6
	4–8 years	0.6	400	0.6	1.2	25	5	7
Males	9–13 years	0.9	600	1.0	1.8	45	5	11
	14–18 years	1.2	900	1.3	2.4	75	5	15
	19–30 years	1.2	900	1.3	2.4	90	5	15
	31–50 years	1.2	900	1.3	2.4	90	5	15
	51–70 years	1.2	900	1.7	2.4[h]	90	10	15
	>70 years	1.2	900	1.7	2.4[h]	90	15	15
Females	9–13 years	0.9	600	1.0	1.8	45	5	11
	14–18 years	1.0	700	1.2	2.4	65	5	15
	19–30 years	1.1	700	1.3	2.4	75	5	15
	31–50 years	1.1	700	1.3	2.4	75	5	15
	51–70 years	1.1	700	1.5	2.4[h]	75	10	15
	>70 years	1.1	700	1.5	2.4[h]	75	15	15
Pregnancy	≤18 years	1.4	750	1.9	2.6	80	5	15
	19–30 years	1.4	770	1.9	2.6	85	5	15
	31–50 years	1.4	770	1.9	2.6	85	5	15
Lactation	≤18 years	1.4	1200	2.0	2.8	115	5	19
	19–30 years	1.4	1300	2.0	2.8	120	5	19
	31–50 years	1.4	1300	2.0	2.8	120	5	19
Tolerable Upper Intake Levels for Adults (19–70)			3000	100		2000	50	1000[k]

NOTE: The table includes values for the type of DRI standard—Adequate Intake (AI) or Recommended Dietary Allowance (RDA)—that has been established for that particular nutrient and life stage; RDAs are shown in **bold type**. The final row of the table shows the Tolerable Upper Intake Levels (ULs) for adults; refer to the full DRI report for information on other ages and life stages. A UL is the maximum level of daily nutrient intake that is likely to pose no risk of adverse effects. There is insufficient data to set ULs for all nutrients, but this does not mean that there is no potential for adverse effects; source of intake should be from food only to prevent high levels of intake of nutrients without established ULs. In healthy individuals, there is no established benefit from nutrient intakes above the RDA or AI.

[a]Although AIs have been set for choline, there are few data to assess whether a dietary supply of choline is needed at all stages of the life cycle, and it may be that the choline requirement can be met by endogenous synthesis at some of these stages.

[b]As dietary folate equivalents (DFE): 1 DFE 5 1 µg food folate 5 0.6 µg folate from fortified food or as a supplement consumed with food 5 0.5 µg of a supplement taken on an empty stomach.

[c]As niacin equivalents (NE): 1 mg niacin 5 60 mg tryptophan.

[d]As retinol activity equivalents (RAEs): 1 RAE 5 1 µg retinol, 12 µg β-carotene, or 24 µg α-carotene or β-cryptoxanthin. Preformed vitamin A (retinol) is abundant in animal-derived foods; provitamin A carotenoids are abundant in some dark yellow, orange, red, and deep-green fruits and vegetables. For preformed vitamin A and for provitamin A carotenoids in supplements, 1RE 5 1 RAE; for provitamin A carotenoids in foods, divide the REs by 2 to obtain RAEs. The UL applies only to preformed vitamin A.

Table 1

Life Stage	Group	Vitamin K (µg/day)	Calcium (mg/day)	Chromium (µg/day)	Copper (µg/day)	Fluoride (mg/day)	Iodine (µg/day)
Infants	0–6 months	2.0	210	0.2	200	0.01	110
	7–12 months	2.5	270	5.5	220	0.5	130
Children	1–3 years	30	500	11	340	0.7	90
	4–8 years	55	800	15	440	1	90
Males	9–13 years	60	1300	25	700	2	120
	14–18 years	75	1300	35	890	3	150
	19–30 years	120	1000	35	900	4	150
	31–50 years	120	1000	35	900	4	150
	51–70 years	120	1200	30	900	4	150
	>70 years	120	1200	30	900	4	150
Females	9–13 years	60	1300	21	700	2	120
	14–18 years	75	1300	24	890	3	150
	19–30 years	90	1000	25	900	3	150
	31–50 years	90	1000	25	900	3	150
	51–70 years	90	1200	20	900	3	150
	>70 years	90	1200	20	900	3	150
Pregnancy	≤8 years	75	1300	29	1000	3	220
	19–30 years	90	1000	30	1000	3	220
	31–50 years	90	1000	30	1000	3	220
Lactation	≤18 years	75	1300	44	1300	3	290
	19–30 years	90	1000	45	1300	3	290
	31–50 years	90	1000	45	1300	3	290
Tolerable Upper Intake Levels for Adults (19–70)			2500		10,000	10	1100

Life Stage	Group	Iron (mg/day)[l]	Magnesium (mg/day)	Manganese (mg/day)	Molybdenum (µg/day)	Phosphorus (mg/day)	Selenium (µg/day)	Zinc (mg/day)[m]
Infants	0–6 months	0.27	30	0.003	2	100	15	2
	7–12 months	11	75	0.6	3	275	20	3
Children	1–3 years	7	80	1.2	17	460	20	3
	4–8 years	10	130	1.5	22	500	30	5
Males	9–13 years	8	240	1.9	34	1250	40	8
	14–18 years	11	410	2.2	43	1250	55	11
	19–30 years	8	400	2.3	45	700	55	11
	31–50 years	8	420	2.3	45	700	55	11
	51–70 years	8	420	2.3	45	700	55	11
	>70 years	8	420	2.3	45	700	55	11
Females	9–13 years	8	240	1.6	34	1250	40	8
	14–18 years	15	360	1.6	43	1250	55	9
	19–30 years	18	310	1.8	45	700	55	8
	31–50 years	18	320	1.8	45	700	55	8
	51–70 years	8	320	1.8	45	700	55	8
	>70 years	8	320	1.8	45	700	55	8
Pregnancy	≤8 years	27	400	2.0	50	1250	60	13
	19–30 years	27	350	2.0	50	700	60	11
	31–50 years	27	360	2.0	50	700	60	11
Lactation	≤18 years	10	360	2.6	50	1250	70	14
	19–30 years	9	310	2.6	50	700	70	12
	31–50 years	9	320	2.6	50	700	70	12
Tolerable Upper Intake Levels for Adults (19–70)		45	350[k]	11	2000	4000	400	40

[e]Individuals who smoke require an additional 35 mg/day of vitamin C over that needed by nonsmokers; nonsmokers regularly exposed to tobacco smoke should ensure they meet the RDA for vitamin C.

[f]As cholecalciferol: 1 µg cholecalciferol 5 40 IU vitamin D. DRI values are based on the absence of adequate exposure to sunlight.

[g]As α-tocopherol. Includes naturally occurring RRR-α-tocopherol and the 2R-stereoisomeric forms from supplements; does not include the 2S-stereoisomeric forms from supplements.

[h]Because 10–30% of older people may malabsorb food-bound B-12, those over age 50 should meet their RDA mainly with supplements or foods fortified with B-12.

[i]In view of evidence linking folate intake with neural tube defects in the fetus. It is recommended that all women capable of becoming pregnant consume 400 µg from supplements or fortified foods in addition to consuming folate from a varied diet.

[j]It is assumed that women will continue consuming 400 µg from supplements or fortified food until their pregnancy is confirmed and they enter prenatal care, which ordinarily occurs after the end of the periconceptional period-the critical time for formation of the neural tube.

[k]The UL applies only to intake from supplements, fortified foods, and/or pharmacological agents and not to intake from foods.

[l]Because the absorption of iron from plant foods is low compared to that from animal foods, the RDA for strict vegetarians is approximately 1.8 times higher than the values established for omnivores (14 mg/day for adult male vegetarians; 33 mg/day for premenopausal female vegetarians). Oral contraceptives (OCs) reduce menstrual blood losses, so women taking them need less daily iron; the RDA for premenopausal women taking OCs is 10.9 mg/day. For more on iron requirements for other special situations, refer to *Dietary Reference Intakes for Vitamin A, Vitamin K, Arsenic, Boron, Chromium, Copper, Iodine, Iron, Manganese, Molybdenum, Nickel, Silicon, Vanadium, and Zinc* (visit http://www.nap.edu for the complete report).

[m]Zinc absorption is lower for those consuming vegetarian diets so the zinc requirement for vegetarians is approximately twofold greater than for those consuming a nonvegetarian diet.

Life Stage	Group	Potassium (g/day)	Sodium (g/day)	Chloride (g/day)	Carbohydrate RDA/AI (g/day)	Carbohydrate AMDR[o] (%)	Total Fiber RDA/AI (g/day)	Total Fat AMDR[o] (%)
Infants	0–6 months	0.4	0.12	0.18	60	ND[q]	ND	[r]
	7–12 months	0.7	0.37	0.57	95	ND[q]	ND	[r]
Children	1–3 years	3.0	1.0	1.5	130	45–65	19	30–40
	4–8 years	3.8	1.2	1.9	130	45–65	25	25–35
Males	9–13 years	4.5	1.5	2.3	130	45–65	31	25–35
	14–18 years	4.7	1.5	2.3	130	45–65	38	25–35
	19–30 years	4.7	1.5	2.3	130	45–65	38	20–35
	31–50 years	4.7	1.5	2.3	130	45–65	38	20–35
	51–70 years	4.7	1.3	2.0	130	45–65	30	20–35
	>70 years	4.7	1.2	1.8	130	45–65	30	20–35
Females	9–13 years	4.5	1.5	2.3	130	45–65	26	25–35
	14–18 years	4.7	1.5	2.3	130	45–65	26	25–35
	19–30 years	4.7	1.5	2.3	130	45–65	25	20–35
	31–50 years	4.7	1.5	2.3	130	45–65	25	20–35
	51–70 years	4.7	1.3	2.0	130	45–65	21	20–35
	>70 years	4.7	1.2	1.8	130	45–65	21	20–35
Pregnancy	≤18 years	4.7	1.5	2.3	175	45–65	28	20–35
	19–30 years	4.7	1.5	2.3	175	45–65	28	20–35
	31–50 years	4.7	1.5	2.3	175	45–65	28	20–35
Lactation	≤18 years	5.1	1.5	2.3	210	45–65	29	20–35
	19–30 years	5.1	1.5	2.3	210	45–65	29	20–35
	31–50 years	5.1	1.5	2.3	210	45–65	29	20–35
Tolerable Upper Intake Levels for Adults (19–70)			2.3	3.6				

Life Stage	Group	Linoleic Acid RDA/AI (g/day)	Linoleic Acid AMDR[o] (%)	Alpha-linolenic Acid RDA/AI (g/day)	Alpha-linolenic Acid AMDR[o] (%)	Protein[n] RDA/AI (g/day)	Protein[n] AMDR[o] (%)	Water[p] (L/day)
Infants	0–6 months	4.4	ND[q]	0.5	ND[q]	9.1	ND[q]	0.7
	7–12 months	4.6	ND[q]	0.5	ND[q]	13.5	ND[q]	0.8
Children	1–3 years	7	5–10	0.7	0.6–1.2	13	5–20	1.3
	4–8 years	10	5–10	0.9	0.6–1.2	19	10–30	1.7
Males	9–13 years	12	5–10	1.2	0.6–1.2	34	10–30	2.4
	14–18 years	16	5–10	1.6	0.6–1.2	52	10–30	3.3
	19–30 years	17	5–10	1.6	0.6–1.2	56	10–35	3.7
	31–50 years	17	5–10	1.6	0.6–1.2	56	10–35	3.7
	51–70 years	14	5–10	1.6	0.6–1.2	56	10–35	3.7
	>70 years	14	5–10	1.6	0.6–1.2	56	10–35	3.7
Females	9–13 years	10	5–10	1.0	0.6–1.2	34	10–30	2.1
	14–18 years	11	5–10	1.1	0.6–1.2	46	10–30	2.3
	19–30 years	12	5–10	1.1	0.6–1.2	46	10–35	2.7
	31–50 years	12	5–10	1.1	0.6–1.2	46	10–35	2.7
	51–70 years	11	5–10	1.1	0.6–1.2	46	10–35	2.7
	>70 years	11	5–10	1.1	0.6–1.2	46	10–35	2.7
Pregnancy	≤18 years	13	5–10	1.4	0.6–1.2	71	10–35	3.0
	19–30 years	13	5–10	1.4	0.6–1.2	71	10–35	3.0
	31–50 years	13	5–10	1.4	0.6–1.2	71	10–35	3.0
Lactation	≤18 years	13	5–10	1.3	0.6–1.2	71	10–35	3.8
	19–30 years	13	5–10	1.3	0.6–1.2	71	10–35	3.8
	31–50 years	13	5–10	1.3	0.6–1.2	71	10–35	3.8

[n]Daily protein recommendations are based on body weight for reference body weights. To calculate for a specific body weight, use the following values: 1.5 g/kg for infants, 1.1 g/kg for 1–3 years, 0.95 g/kg for 4–13 years, 0.85 g/kg for 14–18 years, 0.8 g/kg for adults, and 1.1 g/kg for pregnant (using prepregnancy weight) and lactating women.

[o]Acceptable Macronutrient Distribution Range (AMDR), expressed as a percent of total daily calories, is the range of intake for a particular energy source that is associated with reduced risk of chronic disease while providing intakes of essential nutrients. If an individual consumes in excess of the AMDR, there is a potential for increasing the risk of chronic diseases and/or insufficient intakes of essential nutrients.

[p]Total water intake from fluids and food.

[q]Not determinable due to lack of data of adverse effects in this age group and concern with regard to lack of ability to handle excess amounts. Source of intake should be from food only to prevent high levels of intake.

[r]For infants, Adequate Intake of total fat is 31 grams/day (0–6 months) and 30 grams per day (7–12 months) from breast milk and, for infants 7–12 months, complementary food and beverages.

SOURCE: Reprinted with permission from *Dietary Reference Intakes: Applications in Dietary Planning,* copyright © 2003 by the National Academy of Sciences. Reprinted with permission from the National Academies Press, Washington, D.C.

Nutrition Resources

Number of servings per day (or per week, as noted)

Food groups	1600 calories	2000 calories	2600 calories	3100 calories	Serving sizes and notes
Grains	6	6–8	10–11	12–13	1 slice bread, 1 oz dry cereal, 1/2 cup cooked rice, pasta, or cereal; choose whole grains
Vegetables	3–4	4–5	5–6	6	1 cup raw leafy vegetables, 1/2 cup cooked vegetables, 1/2 cup vegetable juice
Fruits	4	4–5	5–6	6	1/2 cup fruit juice, 1 medium fruit, 1/4 cup dried fruit, 1/2 cup fresh, frozen, or canned fruit
Low-fat or fat-free dairy foods	2–3	2–3	3	3–4	1 cup milk; 1 cup yogurt, 1-1/2 oz cheese; choose fat-free or low-fat types
Meat, poultry, fish	3–6	6 or less	6	6–9	1 oz cooked meats, poultry, or fish: select only lean; trim away visible fats; broil, roast, or boil instead of frying; remove skin from poultry
Nuts, seeds, legumes	3 servings/ week	4–5 servings/ week	1	1	1/3 cup or 1-1/2 oz nuts, 2 Tbsp or 1/2 oz seeds, 1/2 cup cooked dry beans/peas, 2 Tbsp peanut butter
Fats and oils	2	2–3	3	4	1 tsp soft margarine; 1 Tbsp low-fat mayonnaise, 2 Tbsp light salad dressing, 1 tsp vegetable oil; DASH has 27% of calories as fat (low in saturated fat)
Sweets	0	5 servings/ week or less	2	2	1 Tbsp sugar, 1 Tbsp jelly or jam, 1/2 cup sorbet, 1 cup lemonade; sweets should be low in fat

FIGURE 1   The DASH Eating Plan.   SOURCE: National Institutes of Health, National Heart, Lung, and Blood Institute. 2006. *Your Guide to Lowering Your Blood Pressure with DASH: How Do I Make the Dash?* (http://www.nhlbi.nih.gov/health/public/heart/hbp/dash/how_make_dash.html; retrieved February 9, 2009).

FIGURE 2   Healthy Eating Pyramid.   The Healthy Eating Pyramid is an alternative food-group plan developed by researchers at the Harvard School of Public Health; this pyramid reflects many major research studies that have looked at the relationship between diet and long-term health. The Healthy Eating Pyramid differentiates between the various dietary sources of fat, protein, and carbohydrate, and it emphasizes whole grains, vegetable oils, fruits and vegetables, nuts, and dry peas and beans.   **SOURCE:** Reprinted by permission of Simon & Schuster Adult Publishing Group from *Eat, Drink, and Be Healthy: The Harvard Medical School Guide to Healthy Eating* by Walter C. Willett, M.D. Copyright © 2001 by the President and Fellows of Harvard College. All rights reserved.

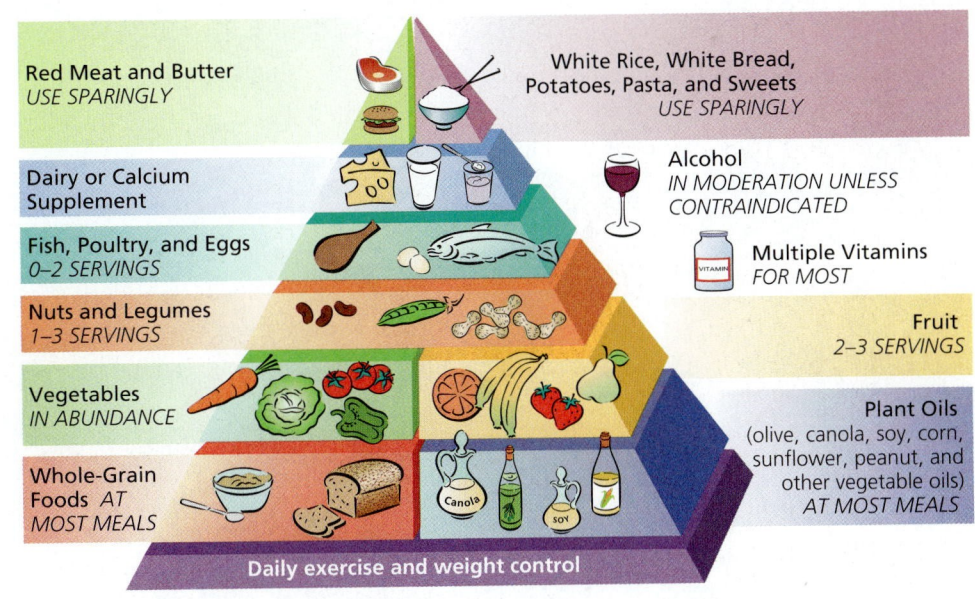

Red Meat and Butter *USE SPARINGLY*

White Rice, White Bread, Potatoes, Pasta, and Sweets *USE SPARINGLY*

Dairy or Calcium Supplement

Alcohol *IN MODERATION UNLESS CONTRAINDICATED*

Fish, Poultry, and Eggs *0–2 SERVINGS*

Multiple Vitamins *FOR MOST*

Nuts and Legumes *1–3 SERVINGS*

Fruit *2–3 SERVINGS*

Vegetables *IN ABUNDANCE*

Plant Oils (olive, canola, soy, corn, sunflower, peanut, and other vegetable oils) *AT MOST MEALS*

Whole-Grain Foods *AT MOST MEALS*

Daily exercise and weight control

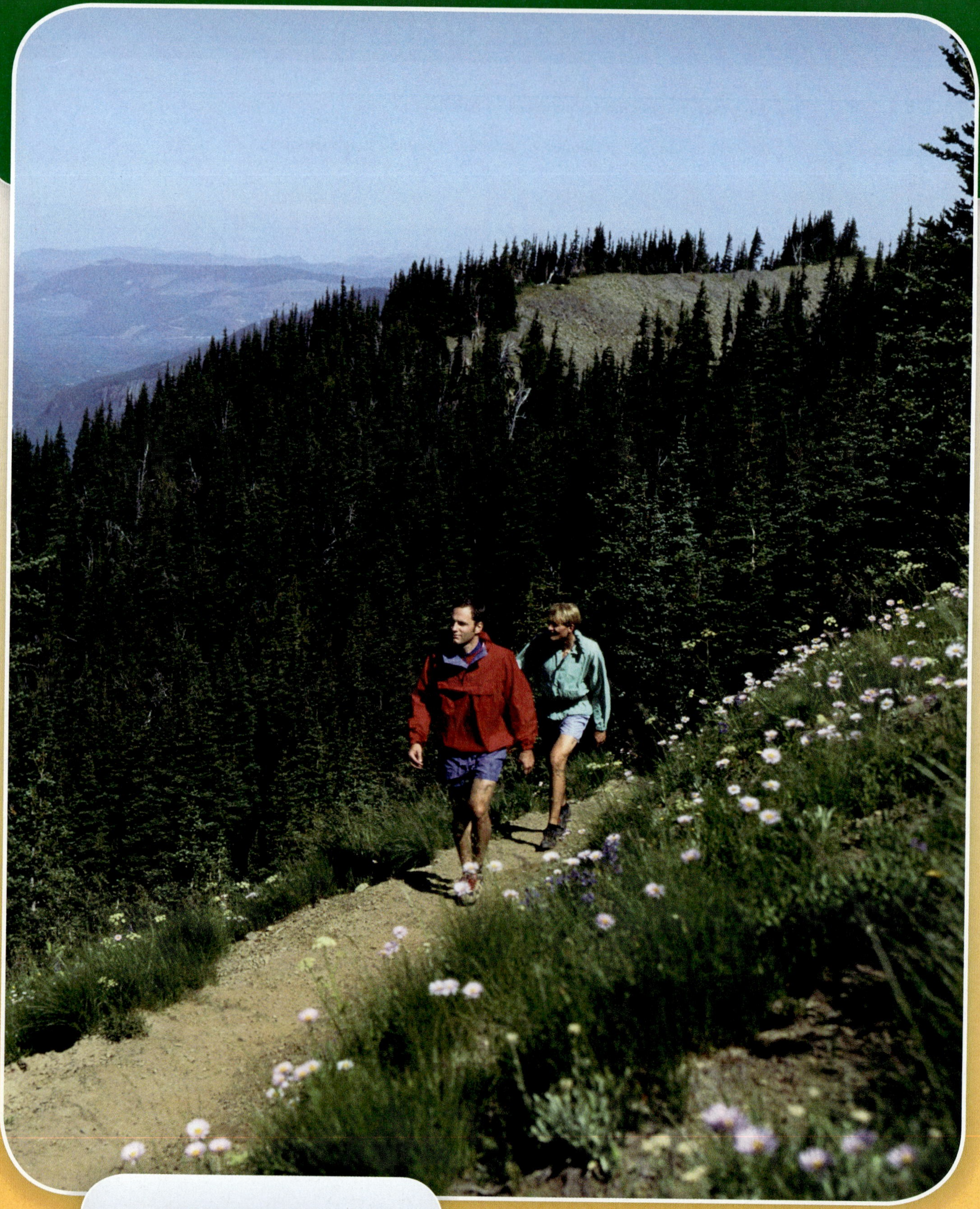

CORE CONCEPTS IN HEALTH
connect
PERSONAL HEALTH

http://www.mcgrawhillconnect.com/personalhealth

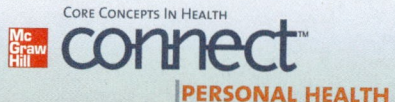

EXERCISE FOR HEALTH AND FITNESS

LOOKING AHEAD>>>>>

AFTER READING THIS CHAPTER, YOU SHOULD BE ABLE TO:

- Define physical fitness, and list the health-related components of fitness
- Explain the wellness benefits of physical activity and exercise
- Describe how to develop each of the health-related components of fitness
- Discuss how to choose appropriate exercise equipment, how to eat and drink for exercise, how to assess fitness, and how to prevent and manage injuries
- Put together a personalized exercise program that you enjoy and that will enable you to achieve your fitness goals

TEST YOUR KNOWLEDGE

1. To improve your health, you must exercise vigorously for at least 30 minutes straight, 5 or more days per week.
   True or false?

2. Which of the following is considered a form of cardiorespiratory endurance exercise?
   a. walking
   b. swimming
   c. aerobic dancing

3. Developing strength in the trunk muscles is the most important way to prevent low-back pain.
   True or false?

4. The terms *physical activity* and *exercise* mean the same thing.
   True or false?

5. Which principle of fitness states that when you stop exercising, you can lose up to 50% of fitness improvements in 2 months?
   a. FITT
   b. reversibility
   c. progressive overload

ANSWERS

1. **FALSE.** Experts recommend about 30 minutes of moderate physical activity 5 or more days per week, but activity can be done in short bouts—10-minute sessions, for example—spread out over the course of the day.

2. **ALL THREE.** You can develop cardiorespiratory endurance through activities that involve continuous, rhythmic movements of large-muscle groups, such as the legs. Many kinds of activities count as cardiorespiratory endurance exercise.

3. **FALSE.** Although muscular strength is an important factor in low-back health, muscular endurance in the trunk is actually more important to preventing low-back pain.

4. **FALSE.** Physical activity is any body movement carried out by the skeletal muscles that requires energy. Exercise is planned, structured, repetitive movement performed specifically to improve or maintain physical fitness.

5. **B.** The body adapts to any level of physical activity. The harder you exercise, the greater the improvements in fitness you will make. The reverse is also true; as you work less, your fitness drops to lower levels.

Your body is a wonderful moving machine made to work best when it is physically active. It readily adapts to practically any level of activity and exercise: The more you ask of your body—your muscles, bones, heart, lungs— the stronger and more fit it becomes. The opposite is also true. Left unchallenged, bones lose their density, joints stiffen, muscles become weak, and cellular energy systems begin to degenerate. To be truly healthy, human beings must be active.

This chapter gives you the basic information you need to put together a physical fitness program that will work for you. If approached correctly, physical activity and exercise can contribute immeasurably to overall wellness, add fun and joy to life, and provide the foundation for a lifetime of fitness.

WHAT IS PHYSICAL FITNESS?

Physical fitness is the body's ability to respond or adapt to the demands and stress of physical effort—that is, to perform moderate to vigorous levels of physical activity without becoming overly tired.

Some components of fitness are related to specific activities or sports; others relate to general health. **Health-related fitness** includes the following components:

- Cardiorespiratory endurance
- Muscular strength
- Muscular endurance
- Flexibility
- Body composition

Health-related fitness helps you withstand physical challenges and protects you from diseases.

Cardiorespiratory Endurance

Cardiorespiratory endurance is the ability to perform prolonged, large-muscle, dynamic exercise at moderate to high intensity. It depends on such factors as the lungs' ability to deliver oxygen to the bloodstream, the heart's capacity to pump blood, the ability of the nervous system and blood vessels to regulate blood flow, and the body's ability to use oxygen and process fuels for exercise.

When cardiorespiratory fitness is low, the heart has to work hard during normal daily activities and may not be able to work hard enough to sustain high-intensity physical activity in an emergency. Poor cardiorespiratory fitness is linked with heart disease, diabetes, colon cancer, stroke, depression, and anxiety.

Regular cardiorespiratory **endurance training**, however, conditions the heart. Endurance training makes the heart stronger and improves the function of the entire cardiorespiratory system. As cardiorespiratory fitness improves, related physical functions also improve:

- The heart pumps more blood per heartbeat.
- Resting heart rate slows and resting blood pressure decreases.
- Blood volume increases.
- Blood supply to tissues improves.
- The body can cool itself better.

A healthy heart can better withstand the strains of daily life, the stress of occasional emergencies, and the wear and tear of time.

Endurance training also improves the function of the body's chemical systems, particularly in the muscles and liver, enhancing the body's ability to use energy from food and to do more exercise with less effort.

You can develop cardiorespiratory endurance through activities that involve continuous, rhythmic movements of large-muscle groups, such as the legs. Such activities include walking, jogging, cycling, and aerobic dancing.

Muscular Strength

Muscular strength is the amount of force a muscle can produce with a single maximum effort. It depends on such factors as the size of muscle cells and the ability of nerves to activate muscle cells. Strong muscles are important for everyday activities, such as climbing stairs, as well as for emergencies. They help keep the skeleton in proper alignment, preventing back and leg pain and providing the support necessary for good posture. Muscular strength has obvious importance in recreational activities. Strong people can hit a tennis ball harder, kick a soccer ball farther, and ride a bicycle uphill more easily.

Muscle tissue is an important element of overall body composition. Greater muscle mass makes possible a higher rate of metabolism and faster energy use, which help to maintain a healthy body weight.

Maintaining strength and muscle mass is vital for healthy aging. Older people tend to lose muscle cells (a condition called *sarcopenia*), and many of the remaining muscle cells become nonfunctional because they lose their attachment to the nervous system. Strength training helps maintain muscle mass, function, and balance in older people, which greatly enhances their quality of life and prevents life-threatening injuries. Strength training has also been shown to benefit cardiovascular health and reduce the risk of osteoporosis (bone loss).

Cardiorespiratory endurance is a critical component of health-related fitness.

Muscular strength can be developed by training with weights or by using the weight of the body for resistance during calisthenic exercises such as push-ups and curl-ups.

Muscular Endurance

Muscular endurance is the ability to resist fatigue and sustain a given level of muscle tension—that is, to hold a muscle contraction for a long time or to contract a muscle over and over again. It depends on such factors as the size of muscle cells, the ability of muscles to store fuel, and the blood supply to muscles.

Muscular endurance is important for good posture and for injury prevention. For example, if abdominal and back muscles cannot hold the spine correctly, the chances of low-back pain and back injury are increased. In fact, good muscular endurance in the trunk muscles is more important than muscular strength for preventing back pain. Muscular endurance helps people cope with the physical demands of everyday life and enhances performance in sports and work.

Like muscular strength, muscular endurance is developed by stressing the muscles with a greater load (weight) than they are used to. The degree to which strength or endurance develops depends on the type and amount of stress that is applied.

Flexibility

Flexibility is the ability to move joints through their full range of motion. It depends on joint structure, the length and elasticity of connective tissue, and nervous system activity. Flexible, pain-free joints are important for good health and well-being. Inactivity causes the joints to become stiffer with age. Stiffness, in turn, often causes older people to assume unnatural body postures that can stress joints and muscles.

Stretching exercises can help ensure a healthy range of motion for all major joints.

Body Composition

Body composition refers to the proportion of fat and **fat-free mass** (muscle, bone, and water) in the body. Healthy body composition involves a high proportion of fat-free mass and an acceptably low level of body fat, adjusted for age and sex. A person with excessive body fat—especially in the abdomen—is more likely to experience health problems, including heart disease, high blood pressure, stroke, joint problems, diabetes, gallbladder disease, cancer, and back pain.

The best way to lose fat is through a lifestyle that includes a sensible diet and exercise. The best way to add muscle mass is through resistance training such as weight training. (Body composition is discussed in detail in Chapter 14.)

TERMS

physical fitness   The body's ability to respond or adapt to the demands and stress of physical effort.

health-related fitness   Physical capabilities that contribute to health, including cardiorespiratory endurance, muscular strength, muscular endurance, flexibility, and body composition.

cardiorespiratory endurance   The ability of the body to perform prolonged, large-muscle, dynamic exercise at moderate to high levels of intensity.

endurance training   Exercise intended specifically to improve cardiorespiratory endurance; usually involves prolonged, large-muscle, dynamic exercises.

muscular strength   The amount of force a muscle can produce with a single maximum effort.

muscular endurance   The ability of a muscle or group of muscles to remain contracted or to contract repeatedly for a long period of time.

flexibility   The ability to move joints through their full range of motion.

body composition   The proportion of fat and fat-free mass (muscle, bone, and water) in the body.

fat-free mass   The nonfat component of the human body, consisting of skeletal muscle, bone, and water.

Skill-Related Components of Fitness

In addition to the five health-related components of physical fitness, the ability to perform a particular sport or activity may depend on **skill-related fitness** components such as the following:

- *Speed*—the ability to perform a movement in a short period of time
- *Power*—the ability to exert force rapidly, based on a combination of strength and speed
- *Agility*—the ability to change the body's position quickly and accurately
- *Balance*—the ability to maintain equilibrium while either moving or stationary
- *Coordination*—the ability to perform motor tasks accurately and smoothly using body movements and the senses
- *Reaction time*—the ability to respond quickly to a stimulus

Skill-related fitness tends to be sport-specific and is best developed through practice. For example, the speed, coordination, and agility needed to play basketball are best developed by playing basketball. Some fitness experts contend that certain sports don't contribute to all the health-related components of physical fitness. Nevertheless, playing a sport can be fun, can help you build fitness, and may contribute to other areas of wellness.

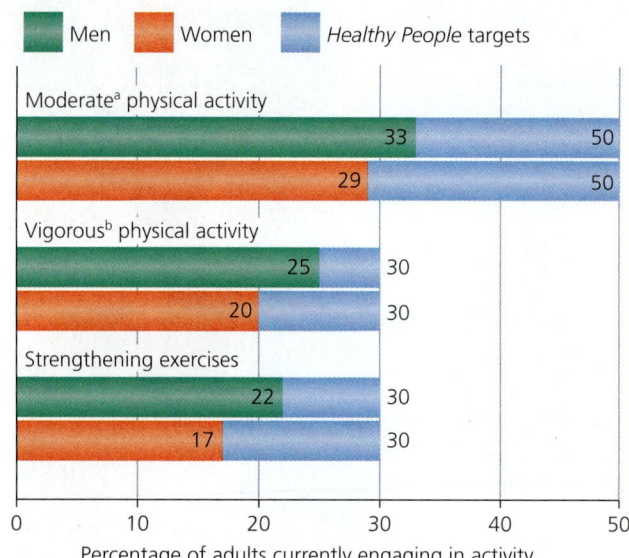

QUICK STATS

Physical inactivity contributes to **400,000** American deaths each year.

—CDC, 2004

PHYSICAL ACTIVITY AND EXERCISE FOR HEALTH AND FITNESS

Despite the many benefits of an active lifestyle, levels of physical activity remain low for all populations of Americans.

Figure 13.1 shows the percentage of Americans who regularly exercise, based on mid-2008 findings from the

? QUESTIONS FOR CRITICAL THINKING AND REFLECTION

When you think about exercise, do you think of only one or two of the five components of health-related fitness, such as muscular strength or body composition? If so, where do you think your ideas come from? What role do the media play in shaping your ideas about fitness?

VITAL STATISTICS

FIGURE 13.1 Current levels of physical activity among American adults.

SOURCES: National Center for Health Statistics. 2008. *DATA2010: The Healthy People 2010 Database*, April 2008 Edition (http://wonder.cdc.gov/data2010; retrieved February 10, 2009.

Healthy People 2010 initiative. This data shows that about 30% of adult Americans meet the *Healthy People* target of getting moderate physical activity on 5 or more days per week. When viewing statistics, however, it is important to remember that the numbers vary according to the source. For example, a December 2008 report from the CDC, based on data from the 2007 Behavioral Risk Factor Surveillance System (BRFSS) survey, showed that 49% of Americans meet the exercise objectives set in *Healthy People 2010*.

In another report released at the end of 2008, the U.S. Department of Health and Human Services (HHS) issued a new set of exercise recommendations, which differ from those established by the *Healthy People 2010* initiative. (Exercise recommendations are described in detail later in the chapter.) Using BRFSS data, the CDC and HHS estimated that 65% of adult Americans already get enough moderate or vigorous exercise to meet the new HHS recommendations.

Specific numbers aside, most surveys show large gaps in exercise habits among Americans of different ethnicities, socioeconomic status, and education level. Regardless of statistics, however, evidence is growing that for many Americans, becoming more physically active may be the single most important lifestyle change for promoting health and well-being. (See the box "Exercise and Total Wellness," on page 383.)

Exercise and Total Wellness

As you will see throughout this chapter, an active lifestyle provides a multitude of benefits. For example, physically active adults live from 2 to 4 years longer, on average, than do sedentary adults. The benefits of regular physical activity, however, go beyond longevity. They impact quality of life across multiple dimensions of wellness.

Physical Wellness

In terms of general health, exercise increases your physical capacity so that you are better able to meet the challenges of daily life with energy and vigor. Physical activity can help you do the following:

- Generate more energy.
- Increase your stamina.
- Control your weight.
- Manage stress.
- Boost your immune system.

Over the long term, even moderate physical activity can help you avoid illnesses such as heart disease, diabetes, high blood pressure, depression, osteoporosis, and some cancers. Evidence shows that exercise can even prevent premature death from several causes.

Emotional Wellness

Exercise provides psychological and emotional benefits, contributing to your sense of competence and well-being. People

who focus on staying active can also enjoy an improved self-image and a higher level of self-confidence. Such healthy self-esteem can positively affect other aspects of your life, as well. For example, a good self-image can be helpful when dealing with others or when competing.

Intellectual Wellness

Recent studies indicate that regular exercise is good for the brain—literally. One study shows that brain volume actually increases in adults who exercise regularly. Such gains in brain mass (growth or replenishment of brain matter) can improve cognitive functions and the overall health of the nervous system. Additionally, the process of mastering physical challenges—such as learning a proper golf swing—can boost intellectual fitness in the same manner as solving puzzles or engaging in other learning experiences.

Interpersonal Wellness

Joining in physical activity with a friend or a group can be a boon to your interpersonal or social wellness, too. By sharing physical challenges with others, you can make new friends, deepen your existing relationships, and build a stronger overall network of support.

Physical Activity on a Continuum

Physical activity is any body movement carried out by the skeletal muscles and requiring energy. Different types of physical activity can be arranged on a continuum based on the amount of energy they require. Quick, easy movements such as standing up or walking down a hallway require little energy or effort; more intense, sustained activities such as cycling 5 miles or running in a race require considerably more.

Exercise refers to a subset of physical activity—planned, structured, repetitive movement of the body intended specifically to improve or maintain physical fitness. Levels of fitness depend on such physiological factors as the heart's ability to pump blood and the size of muscle fibers. These factors are a function both of genetics—a person's inborn potential for physical fitness—and of behavior—the amount of exercise a person does to improve fitness. To develop fitness, a person must perform enough physical activity to stress the body and cause long-term physiological changes.

Physical activity is essential to health and confers wide-ranging health benefits, but exercise is necessary to significantly improve physical fitness. This important distinction between physical activity and exercise is a key concept in understanding the guidelines discussed in this chapter.

> **TERMS**
>
> **skill-related fitness** Physical abilities that contribute to performance in a sport or activity, including speed, power, agility, balance, coordination, and reaction time.
>
> **physical activity** Any body movement carried out by the skeletal muscles and requiring energy.
>
> **exercise** Planned, structured, repetitive movement of the body intended to improve or maintain physical fitness.

Increasing Physical Activity to Improve Health and Wellness In 1996, the U.S. Surgeon General issued *Physical Activity and Health,* a landmark report designed to encourage Americans to become more active. One of its findings was that people can enjoy significant health benefits by including a moderate amount of physical activity on most, if not all, days of the week. This finding was echoed in the 2005 Dietary Guidelines for Americans, which recommended that all adults engage in at least 30 minutes of moderate-intensity physical activity, beyond usual activity, on most days of the week, in order to improve health.

The recommendation was further refined in the publication *Physical Activity and Public Health: Updated Recommendations for Adults,* published jointly by the American College of Sports Medicine (ACSM) and the American Heart Association (AHA) in 2007. This report stated that, to promote and maintain health, adults need a minimum of 30 minutes of moderate-intensity aerobic (endurance) physical activity 5 days per week or 20 minutes of vigorous-intensity aerobic physical activity 3 days per week. Research shows that these levels of physical activity promote health and wellness in specific ways: by lowering the risk of high blood pressure, stroke, heart disease, type 2 diabetes, colon cancer, and osteoporosis and by reducing feelings of mild-to-moderate depression and anxiety.

What exactly is *moderate* physical activity? Activities such as brisk walking, dancing, swimming, cycling, and yard work can all count toward the daily total. The Surgeon General's report defines a moderate amount of activity as activity that uses about 150 calories of energy. Examples of activities that use about 150 calories are shown in Figure 13.2. You can burn the same number of calories by doing a lower-intensity activity for a longer time or higher-intensity activity for a shorter time. For more examples of light, moderate, and vigorous activities, see the box "Classifying Activity Levels" (p. 386).

The 2007 ACSM/AHA report defines moderate-intensity physical activity as activity that causes a noticeable increase in heart rate, such as a brisk walk. The report defines vigorous-intensity physical activity as activity that causes rapid breathing and a substantial increase in heart rate, as exemplified by jogging. Both the Surgeon General's report and the ACSM/AHA report also recommend that people perform strength training exercises at least twice a week to build and maintain muscular strength and endurance.

The daily total of physical activity can be accumulated in multiple bouts of 10 or more minutes—for example, two 10-minute bike rides to and from class and a brisk 10-minute walk to the store. In this lifestyle approach to physical activity, people can choose activities that they find enjoyable and that fit into their daily routine; everyday tasks at school, work, and home can be structured to contribute to the daily activity total (see the box "Making Time for Physical Activity" on p. 387). If all Americans who are currently sedentary were to increase their lifestyle physical

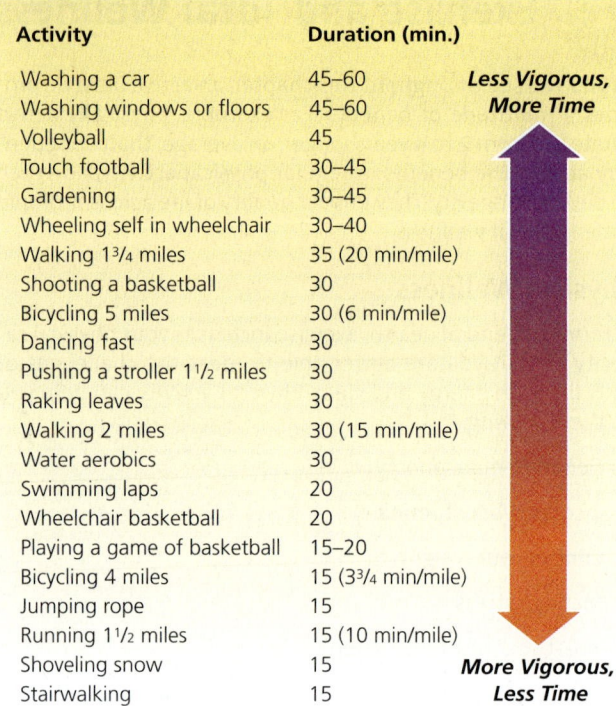

Activity	Duration (min.)	
Washing a car	45–60	*Less Vigorous, More Time*
Washing windows or floors	45–60	
Volleyball	45	
Touch football	30–45	
Gardening	30–45	
Wheeling self in wheelchair	30–40	
Walking 1¾ miles	35 (20 min/mile)	
Shooting a basketball	30	
Bicycling 5 miles	30 (6 min/mile)	
Dancing fast	30	
Pushing a stroller 1½ miles	30	
Raking leaves	30	
Walking 2 miles	30 (15 min/mile)	
Water aerobics	30	
Swimming laps	20	
Wheelchair basketball	20	
Playing a game of basketball	15–20	
Bicycling 4 miles	15 (3¾ min/mile)	
Jumping rope	15	
Running 1½ miles	15 (10 min/mile)	
Shoveling snow	15	*More Vigorous, Less Time*
Stairwalking	15	

FIGURE 13.2   Examples of moderate amounts of physical activity.   Each example uses about 150 calories.

SOURCE: Department of Health and Human Services. 1996. *Physical Activity and Health: A Report of the Surgeon General.* Atlanta: DHHS.

activity to 30 minutes per day, there would be an enormous benefit to public health and to individual well-being.

Increasing Physical Activity to Manage Weight Because two-thirds of Americans are overweight, government agencies and health organizations have also published physical activity guidelines focusing on weight management. These guidelines call for more daily physical activity than the guidelines designed for general health promotion. Table 13.1 lists recommendations for promoting health and managing weight from just a few of these organizations.

These guidelines do not conflict with those from the Surgeon General, but they do have a different emphasis. They recognize that for people who need to prevent weight gain, lose weight, or maintain weight loss, 30 minutes per day of physical activity may not be enough. Instead, they recommend 45–90 or more minutes per day of physical activity. For example, the Dietary Guidelines recommend 60 minutes of daily physical activity to manage body weight and prevent unhealthy weight gain and 60–90 minutes of daily activity to sustain weight loss. The different recommendations may seem confusing, but all major health organizations have the same message: People can improve their health by becoming more active.

Exercising to Improve Physical Fitness As mentioned earlier, moderate physical activity confers significant

Table 13.1	Summary of Physical Activity Recommendations from Selected Leading Health Organizations

Organization	Recommendation	Purpose
Centers for Disease Control and Prevention	A minimum of 30 minutes of moderate-intensity physical activity on 5 or more days of the week	Promote health and prevent chronic disease
American College of Sports Medicine	A minimum of 30 minutes of moderate activity 5 days per week or 20 minutes of vigorous activity 3 days per week. (The ACSM has separate guidelines for exercise programs to develop fitness; see pp. 390–401 and Table 13.2.)	Promote health and prevent chronic disease
U.S. Surgeon General: Report on Physical Activity and Health	A minimum of 150 calories per day expended in moderate physical activity (the equivalent of about 30 minutes of brisk walking); resistance training twice a week	Promote health and prevent chronic disease
U.S. Department of Health and Human Services and U.S. Department of Agriculture: 2005 Dietary Guidelines for Americans	30 minutes of moderate-intensity exercise on most days of the week 60 minutes of moderate-to-vigorous-intensity exercise on most days of the week 60–90 minutes of moderate-intensity exercise per day	Reduce the risk of chronic disease Manage body weight and prevent unhealthy weight gain Sustain weight loss
U.S Department of Health and Human Services: 2008 Physical Activity Guidelines for Americans	At least 2 hours and 30 minutes of moderate aerobic exercise per week or 1 hour and 15 minutes of vigorous aerobic exercise per week, plus resistance training at least 2 nonconsecutive days per week	Promote health and prevent chronic disease
Healthy People 2010	At least 30 minutes of moderate physical activity 5 or more days per week	Promote health and prevent chronic disease
Institute of Medicine, National Academies	At least 60 minutes of moderate physical activity per day	Promote health, prevent chronic disease, and control weight
International Association for the Study of Obesity	45–60 minutes of moderate physical activity per day 60–90 minutes of moderate physical activity per day	Prevent weight gain Maintain weight loss
World Health Organization	At least 30 minutes of moderate physical activity per day	Promote health, prevent chronic disease, and control weight

health and wellness benefits, especially for those who are currently sedentary and become moderately active. The Surgeon General's report, the Dietary Guidelines for Americans, and the ACSM/AHA report all conclude that people can obtain even greater health and wellness benefits by increasing the duration and intensity of physical activity. With increased activity, they will see more improvements in quality of life and greater reductions in disease and mortality risk.

More vigorous activity, as in a structured, systematic exercise program, is also needed to improve physical fitness; moderate physical activity alone is not enough. Physical fitness requires more intense movement that poses a substantially greater challenge to the body. The ACSM issued separate guidelines in 2006 for creating a formal exercise program that will develop physical fitness. These guidelines are described in detail later in the chapter.

How Much Physical Activity Is Enough?

Some experts feel that people get most of the health benefits of an exercise program simply by becoming more active over the course of the day; the amount of activity needed depends on an individual's health status and goals.

Other experts feel that the activity goal set by the lifestyle approach is too low; they argue that people should exercise long enough and intensely enough to improve their body's capacity for exercise—that is, to improve physical fitness. More research is needed to clarify the health effects of different amounts of lifestyle physical activity, of moderate-intensity versus high-intensity exercise, and of continuous versus intermittent exercise. However, there is probably some truth in both of these positions.

Where does this leave you? Most experts agree that some physical activity is better than none, but that more—as

QUESTIONS FOR CRITICAL THINKING AND REFLECTION
Does your current lifestyle include enough physical activity—30 minutes of moderate-intensity activity 5 or more days a week—to support health and wellness? Does your lifestyle go beyond this level to include enough vigorous physical activity and exercise to build physical fitness? What changes could you make in your lifestyle to start developing physical fitness?

Classifying Activity Levels

Assessing your physical activity level is easier if you know how to classify different kinds of activities. Fitness experts categorize activities into the following three levels:

• *Light activity* includes the routine tasks associated with typical day-to-day life, such as vacuuming or walking to class. You probably perform dozens of light activities every day without even thinking about it. You can gain signifi-

cant health benefits by turning light activities into moderate activities—by walking briskly instead of slowly, for example.

• *Moderate activity* causes your breathing and heart rate to accelerate but still allows for comfortable conversation, such as walking at 3–4 miles per hour. It is sometimes described as activity that can be performed comfortably for about 45 minutes. Raking leaves is an example

of moderate physical activity, as are most occupational tasks that involve extended periods of moderate effort.

• *Vigorous activity* elevates your heart rate considerably and has other physical effects that improve your fitness level. During vigorous activity you are breathing too heavily to hold a conversation very easily. An example is walking faster than 4 miles per hour.

Here are some examples:

Light	Moderate	Vigorous
Walking slowly	Walking briskly	Walking briskly uphill
Routine tasks:	Cycling moderately on level terrain	Cycling on steep uphill terrain
• Cooking	Social dancing	Heavy housework:
• Shopping	Moderate housework:	• Moving furniture
Light housework:	• Scrubbing floors	• Carrying heavy objects upstairs
• Ironing	• Washing windows	Vigorous yard work or home activities:
• Dusting	Moderate yard work or home activities:	• Shoveling snow
• Washing dishes	• Planting	• Trimming trees
Light yard work or home activities:	• Raking	• Doing construction work
• Pruning	• Painting	• Digging
• Weeding	• Washing car	Fitness activities requiring vigorous effort:
• Plumbing	Fitness activities requiring moderate effort:	• Running
Light fitness activities:	• Doing low-impact aerobics	• Doing high-impact aerobics
• Light stretching or warm-up	• Playing Frisbee	• Doing circuit weight training
• Swimming, slow treading	• Swimming	• Swimming laps
	• Playing tennis, doubles	• Playing most competitive sports

long as it does not result in injury—is better than some. To set a personal goal for physical activity and exercise, consider your current activity level, your health status, and your overall goals. At the very least, strive to become more active and meet the goal set by the Surgeon General's report of using about 150 calories a day in physical activity—the equivalent of about 30 minutes of moderate-intensity activity. Choose to be active whenever you can. If weight management is a concern for you, begin by achieving the goal of 30 minutes of activity per day and then try to raise your activity level further, to 45–90 minutes per day or more. For even better health and well-being, participate in a structured exercise program that develops physical fitness. Any increase in physical activity will contribute to your health and well-being, now and in the future.

THE BENEFITS OF EXERCISE

As mentioned earlier, the human body is very adaptable. The greater the demands made on it, the more it adjusts to meet the demands—it becomes fit. Over time, imme-

diate, short-term adjustments translate into long-term changes and improvements (Figure 13.3 on p. 388). The goal of regular physical activity is to bring about these kinds of long-term changes and improvements in the body's functioning.

Improved Cardiorespiratory Functioning

Every time you take a breath, oxygen in the air enters your lungs and is picked up by red blood cells and transported to your heart. From there, the heart pumps oxygenated blood throughout the body to organs and tissues that use it. During exercise, the cardiorespiratory system (heart, lungs, and circulatory system) must work harder to meet the body's increased demand for oxygen. Regular endurance exercise improves the functioning of the heart and the ability of the cardiorespiratory system to carry oxygen to body tissues. Exercise directly affects the health of your arteries, keeping them from stiffening or clogging with plaque and reducing the risk of cardiovascular disease. Exercise also improves sexual function and general vitality.

Making Time for Physical Activity

"Too little time" is a common excuse for not being physically active. Learning to manage your time successfully is crucial if you are to maintain a wellness lifestyle. You can begin by keeping a record of how you are currently spending your time; in your health journal, use a grid broken into blocks of 15, 20, or 30 minutes to track your daily activities. Then analyze your record: List each type of activity and the total time you engaged in it on a given day—for example, sleeping, 7 hours; eating, 1.5 hours; studying, 3 hours; and so on. Take a close look at your list of activities, and prioritize them according to how important they are to you, from essential to somewhat important to not important at all.

Based on the priorities you set, make changes in your daily schedule by subtracting time from some activities in order to make time for physical activity. Look particularly carefully at your leisure-time activities and your methods of transportation; these are areas where it is easy to build in physical activity. Make changes using a system of trade-offs. For example, you may choose to reduce the total amount of time you spend playing computer games, listening to the radio, and chatting on the phone in order to make time for an after-dinner bike ride or a walk with a friend. You may decide to watch 10 fewer minutes of television in the morning in order to change your 5-minute drive to class into a 15-minute walk. In making these kinds of changes in your schedule, don't feel that you have to miss out on anything you enjoy. You can get more from less time by focusing on what you are doing and by combining activities.

The following are just a few ways to incorporate more physical activity into your daily routine:

- Take the stairs instead of the elevator or escalator.

- Walk to the mailbox, post office, store, bank, or library whenever possible.

- Park your car a mile or even just a few blocks from your destination, and walk briskly.

- Do at least one chore every day that requires physical activity: Wash the windows or your car, clean your room or house, mow the lawn, or rake the leaves.

- Take study or work breaks to avoid sitting for more than 30 minutes at a time. Get up and walk around the library, your office, or your home or dorm; go up and down a flight of stairs.

- Stretch when you stand in line or watch TV.

- When you take public transportation, get off one stop early and walk to your destination.

- Go dancing instead of to a movie.

- Walk to visit a neighbor or friend rather than calling him or her on the phone. Go for a walk while you chat.

- Put your remote controls in storage; when you want to change TV or radio stations, get up and do it by hand.

- Take the dog for a walk (or an extra walk) every day.

- Play actively with children.

- If weather or neighborhood safety rule out walking outside, look for alternate locations—an indoor track, an enclosed shopping mall, or even a long hallway. Look for locations near or on the way to your campus, workplace, or residence.

- Remember, being busy isn't the same as being active. Seize every opportunity to get up and walk around. Move more and sit less.

Visit the U.S. Department of Health and Human Services Small Step Web site (www.smallstep.gov) for more ideas.

More Efficient Metabolism

Endurance exercise improves metabolism, the process that converts food to energy and builds tissue. This process involves oxygen, nutrients, hormones, and enzymes. A physically fit person can more efficiently generate energy, to use carbohydrates and fats for energy, and to regulate hormones. Exercise may also protect cells from damage from free radicals, which are destructive chemicals produced during normal metabolism (see Chapter 12), and from inflammation caused by high blood pressure or cholesterol, nicotine, and overeating. Training activates antioxidant enzymes that prevent free radical damage and maintain the health of the body's cells.

Improved Body Composition

Healthy body composition means that the body has a high proportion of fat-free mass and a relatively small propor-

tion of fat. Too much body fat, particularly abdominal fat, is linked to a variety of health problems, including heart disease, cancer, and diabetes. Healthy body composition can be difficult to achieve and maintain because a diet that contains all essential nutrients can be relatively high in calories, especially for someone who is sedentary. Excess calories are stored in the body as fat.

Exercise can improve body composition in several ways. Endurance exercise significantly increases daily calorie expenditure; it can also slightly raise *metabolic rate*, the rate at which the body burns calories, for several hours after an exercise session. Strength training increases muscle mass, thereby tipping the body composition ratio toward fat-free mass and away from fat. It can also help with losing fat because metabolic rate is directly proportional to fat-free mass: The more muscle mass, the higher the metabolic rate.

Physical activity reduces the risk of death regardless of its effect on body composition. That is, greater levels of

Immediate effects

Increased levels of neurotransmitters; constant or slightly increased blood flow to the brain.

Increased heart rate and stroke volume (amount of blood pumped per beat).

Increased pulmonary ventilation (amount of air breathed into the body per minute). More air is taken into the lungs with each breath and breathing rate increases.

Reduced blood flow to the stomach, intestines, liver, and kidneys, resulting in less activity in the digestive tract and less urine output.

Increased energy production in muscles.

Increased blood flow to the skin and increased sweating to help maintain a safe body temperature.

Increased systolic blood pressure; increased blood flow and oxygen transport to working skeletal muscles and the heart; increased oxygen consumption.

Long-term effects

Improved self-image, cognitive functioning, and ability to manage stress; enhanced learning, memory, energy level, and sleep; decreased depression, anxiety, and risk for stroke.

Increased heart size and resting stroke volume; lower resting heart rate. Risk of heart disease and heart attack significantly reduced.

Improved ability to extract oxygen from air during exercise. Reduced risk of colds and upper respiratory tract infections.

Increased sweat rate, earlier onset of sweating, and greater dissipation of sweat, helping to cool the body.

Decreased body fat.

Reduced risk of colon cancer and certain other forms of cancer.

Muscle cell changes that allow for greater energy production and power output during exercise. Insulin sensitivity remains constant or improves, helping to prevent type 2 diabetes. Increase or maintenance of muscle mass.

Increased density and breaking strength of bones, ligaments, and tendons; reduced risk for low-back pain, injuries, and osteoporosis; improved range of motion in joints.

Increased blood volume and capillary density; higher levels of high-density lipoproteins (HDL) and lower levels of triglycerides; lower resting blood pressure; reduced platelet stickiness (a factor in coronary heart disease); improved blood flow control; and reduced blood vessel inflammation.

FIGURE 13.3   Immediate and long-term effects of regular exercise.

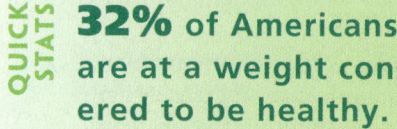

activity are associated with lower death rates among people who are overweight or obese as well as people who are at a healthy weight (Figure 13.4). Physical activity does not eliminate the health risks associated with overweight, but it reduces its effects.

Disease Prevention and Management

Regular physical activity lowers your risk of many chronic, disabling diseases.

Cardiovascular Disease   A sedentary lifestyle is one of the six major risk factors for cardiovascular disease (CVD), including heart attack and stroke. The other major risk factors are smoking, abnormal blood fats, high blood pressure, diabetes, and obesity. Most of these risk factors are linked by a group of symptoms that scientists call the *metabolic syndrome*. These symptoms include insulin resistance, high blood pressure, abnormal blood fats, abdominal fat deposits, type 2 diabetes, blood clotting abnormalities, and blood vessel inflammation (see Chapter 15 for more on metabolic syndrome). Sedentary people have CVD death rates significantly higher than those of fit individuals. Physical inactivity increases the risk of CVD by 50–240%.

The benefit of physical activity occurs at moderate levels of activity and rises with increasing levels of activity.

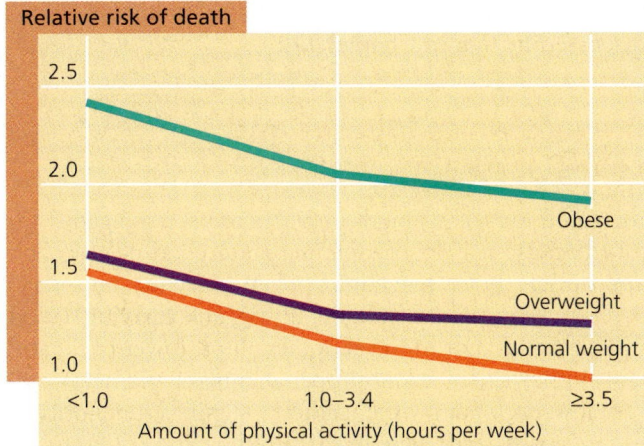

FIGURE 13.4 **Relationship among amount of physical activity, body weight, and risk of death.**

SOURCE: Hu, F. B., et al. 2004. Adiposity compared with physical activity in predicting mortality among women. *New England Journal of Medicine* 351(26): 2694–2703.

Exercise positively affects the risk factors for CVD, including cholesterol levels and high blood pressure. Exercise also directly interferes with the disease process itself, directly lowering risk of heart disease and stroke.

BLOOD FAT LEVELS Endurance exercise and strength training have a positive effect on the balance of lipids (fats) that circulate in the blood. High concentrations of lipids such as cholesterol and triglycerides are linked to heart disease because they contribute to the formation of fatty deposits on the linings of arteries. When blood clots block a narrowed artery, a heart attack or stroke can occur.

Cholesterol is carried in the blood by lipoproteins, which are classified according to size and density. Cholesterol carried by low-density lipoproteins (LDLs) sticks to the walls of coronary arteries. High-density lipoproteins (HDLs) pick up excess cholesterol in the bloodstream and carry it back to the liver for excretion from the body. High LDL levels and low HDL levels increase the risk of cardiovascular disease. High levels of HDL and low levels of LDL are associated with lower risk.

Heart disease is covered in Chapter 15. For our purposes in this chapter, it is important to know only that endurance exercise and strength training influence blood lipids in a positive way, by increasing HDL and decreasing LDL and triglycerides—reducing the risk of CVD.

HIGH BLOOD PRESSURE Regular endurance exercise tends to reduce high blood pressure (hypertension), a contributing factor in diseases such as coronary heart disease, stroke, heart failure, kidney failure, and blindness. Intense, long-duration exercise works best, but even moderate exercise can produce significant improvements. Strength training also reduces blood pressure.

CORONARY HEART DISEASE Coronary heart disease (CHD), also called coronary artery disease (CAD), involves block-

age of one of the coronary arteries. These blood vessels supply the heart with oxygenated blood, and an obstruction in one of them can cause a heart attack. Exercise directly interferes with the disease process that causes coronary artery blockage. It also enhances the function of cells lining the arteries that help regulate blood flow.

STROKE A stroke occurs when a blood vessel leading to the brain is blocked, often through the same disease process that leads to heart attacks. Regular exercise reduces the risk of stroke.

Cancer Studies have shown a relationship between increased physical activity and a reduced risk of cancer, but these findings are not conclusive. There is evidence that exercise reduces the risk of colon cancer and promising data that it reduces the risk of cancer of the breast and reproductive organs in women and prostate cancer in men. Exercise may decrease the risk of colon cancer by speeding the movement of food through the gastrointestinal tract (quickly eliminating potential carcinogens), lowering blood insulin levels, enhancing immune function, and reducing blood fats. The protective mechanism in the case of reproductive system cancers is less clear, but physical activity during the high school and college years may be particularly important for preventing breast cancer later in life. Some studies have also found that regular physical activity reduces the risk of pancreatic cancer.

Osteoporosis A special benefit of exercise, especially for women, is protection against osteoporosis, a disease that results in loss of bone density and poor bone strength. Weight-bearing exercise, which includes almost everything except swimming, helps build bone during childhood and the teens and twenties. Older people with denser bones can better endure the bone loss that occurs with aging. Strength training and impact exercises such as jumping rope can increase bone density throughout life. With stronger bones and muscles and better balance, fit people are less likely to experience debilitating falls and bone fractures. Along with exercise, a well-balanced diet containing adequate calcium and vitamin D and normal hormone function are also essential for strong bones. (One caution: Too much exercise can depress levels of estrogen, which helps maintain bone density, thereby leading to bone loss, even in young women.)

Type 2 Diabetes People with diabetes are prone to heart disease, blindness, and severe problems of the nervous and circulatory systems. Exercise prevents the development of type 2 diabetes, the most common form of the disease. Exercise burns excess sugar and makes cells more sensitive to insulin. Exercise also helps keep body fat at healthy levels. (Obesity is a key risk factor for type 2 diabetes.) For people who have diabetes, physical activity is an important part of treatment. See Chapter 14 for more on diabetes.

Improved Psychological and Emotional Wellness

People who are physically active experience many social, psychological, and emotional benefits, including the following:

• *Reduced stress.* In response to stressors, physically fit people experience milder physical responses and less emotional distress than sedentary individuals. Physical activity also provides protection against the effects of stress that have been linked to poor cardiorespiratory health. Endurance exercise decreases the secretion of hormones and neurotransmitters triggered by emotional stress. It also can diffuse hostility and alleviate feelings of stress and anxiety by providing an emotional outlet and inducing feelings of relaxation. Regular exercise can also relieve sleeping problems.

• *Reduced anxiety and depression.* Sedentary adults are much more likely to feel fatigue and depression than those who are physically active. Exercise is an effective treatment for people with depression and improves mood in non-depressed people.

• *Improved self-image.* Performing physical activities provides proof of skill and self-control, thus enhancing your self-concept. Sticking with an exercise program increases people's belief in their ability to be active, thereby boosting self-efficacy. Exercise also helps you look and feel better, boosting self-confidence and body image.

• *Learning and memory.* Exercise enhances the formation and survival of new nerve cells and the connections between nerves, which in turn improve memory and learning. Physical activity helps maintain mental functioning in older adults and may ward off dementia.

• *Enjoyment.* Exercise is fun. It offers a way to interact with other people, as well as opportunities to strive and excel. Physically fit people can perform everyday tasks with ease. They have plenty of energy and can lead lives that are full and varied.

Improved Immune Function

Exercise can have either positive or negative effects on the immune system, the physiological processes that protect us from disease. It appears that moderate endurance exercise boosts immune function, whereas excessive training depresses it. Physically fit people get fewer colds and upper respiratory tract infections than people who are not

fit. The immune system—and ways to strengthen it—is discussed further in Chapter 17.

Prevention of Injuries and Low-Back Pain

Increased muscle strength provides protection against injury because it helps people maintain good posture and appropriate body mechanics when carrying out everyday activities such as walking, lifting, and carrying. Good muscle endurance in the abdomen, hips, lower back, and legs supports the back in proper alignment and helps prevent low-back pain, which afflicts a significant majority of Americans at some time in their lives.

Improved Wellness for Life

Although people differ in the maximum levels of fitness they can achieve through exercise, the wellness benefits of exercise are available to everyone (see the box "Exercise for People with Special Health Concerns"). Exercising regularly may be the single most important thing you can do now to improve the quality of your life in the future. All the benefits of exercise continue to accrue but gain new importance as the resilience of youth begins to wane. Simply stated, exercising can help you live a longer and healthier life.

DESIGNING YOUR EXERCISE PROGRAM

The best exercise program has two primary characteristics: It promotes your health, and it's fun for you to do. Exercise does not have to be a chore. On the contrary, it can provide some of the most pleasurable moments of your day, once you make it a habit. A little thought and planning will help you achieve these goals.

Figure 13.5 (p. 392) shows a physical activity pyramid to guide you in meeting goals for physical activity. If you are sedentary, start at the bottom of the pyramid and gradually increase the moderate-intensity physical activity in your daily life. You don't have to exercise vigorously, but you should experience a moderate increase in your heart and breathing rates; appropriate activities include

QUESTIONS FOR CRITICAL THINKING AND REFLECTION

Which benefits of exercise are most important to you, and why? For example, is there a history of heart disease or diabetes in your family? Have you thought about how regular exercise could reduce your risks for specific diseases?

Exercise for People with Special Health Concerns

Regular, appropriate exercise is safe and beneficial for many people with chronic conditions or other special health concerns. For many people with special health concerns, in fact, the risks associated with *not* exercising are far greater than those associated with a moderate program of regular exercise.

If you have a special health concern and have hesitated becoming more active, one helpful strategy is to take a class or join an exercise group specifically designed for your condition. Many health centers and support groups sponsor specially tailored activity programs. Such a class or group activity can provide you with both expert advice and exercise partners who share your concerns and goals. If you prefer to exercise at home, exercise videos are available for people with a variety of conditions.

The fitness recommendations for the general population presented in this chapter can serve as general guidelines for any exercise program. However, for people with special health concerns, certain precautions and monitoring may be required. *Anyone with special health concerns should consult a physician before beginning an exercise program.* Guidelines and cautions for some common conditions are described below:

Asthma

• Carry medication during workouts and avoid exercising alone. Use your inhaler before exercise, if recommended by your physician.

• Exercise regularly, and warm up and cool down slowly to reduce the risk of acute attacks.

• When starting a fitness program, choose self-paced endurance activities, especially those involving interval training (short bouts of exercise followed by rest periods).

• When possible, avoid circumstances that may trigger an asthma attack, including cold, dry air or pollen or dust. Drink water to keep your airways moist, and in cold weather, cover your mouth with a mask or scarf to warm and humidify the air you breathe. Swimming is a good activity choice for people with asthma.

Diabetes

• Don't exercise alone; wear a bracelet identifying yourself as having diabetes.

• If you are taking insulin or another medication, you may need to adjust the timing and amount of each dose as you learn to balance your energy intake and output and your medication dosage.

• To prevent abnormally rapid absorption of injected insulin, inject it over a muscle that won't be exercised and wait at least an hour before exercising.

• Check blood sugar levels before, during, and after exercise, and adjust your diet or insulin dosage if needed. Avoid exercise if your blood sugar level is above 250 mg/dl, and ingest carbohydrates prior to exercise if your blood sugar level is below 100 mg/dl. Have high-carbohydrate foods available during a workout.

• Check your skin regularly for blisters and abrasions, especially on your feet.

Obesity

• For maximum benefit and minimum risk, begin with low- to moderate-intensity activities and increase intensity slowly as your fitness improves.

• To lose weight or maintain lost weight, exercise moderately 60 minutes or more every day; you can exercise all at once or divide your total activity time into sessions of 10 or more minutes.

• At first choose non- or low-weight-bearing activities like swimming, water exercises, cycling, or walking.

• Stay alert for symptoms of heat-related problems during exercise.

• Try to include as much lifestyle physical activity in your daily routine as possible.

• Include strength training in your program to build or maintain muscle mass.

Heart Disease and Hypertension

• Warm-up and cool-down sessions should be gradual and last at least 10 minutes.

• Exercise at a moderate rather than a high intensity; monitor your heart rate during exercise, and stop if you experience dizziness or chest pain.

• Increase exercise frequency, intensity, and time very gradually.

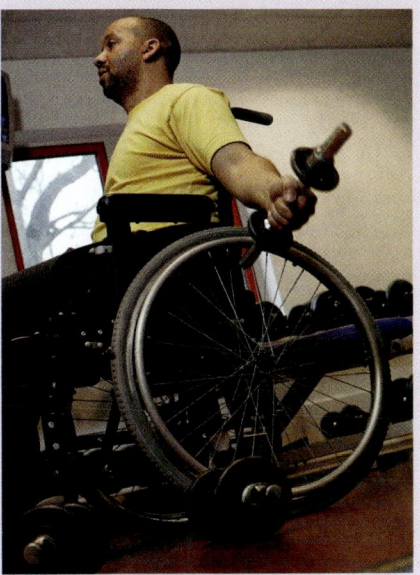

• Don't hold your breath when exercising as this can cause a sudden, steep increase in blood pressure.

• Discuss the effects of your medication with your physician; for example, certain drugs for hypertension affect heart rate. If your physician has prescribed nitroglycerine, carry it with you during exercise.

Arthritis

• Begin an exercise program as early as possible in the course of the disease.

• Warm up thoroughly before each workout to loosen stiff muscles and lower the risk of injury.

• Avoid high-impact activities that may damage arthritic joints; consider swimming or water aerobics.

• In strength training, pay special attention to muscles that support and protect affected joints; add weight very gradually.

• Perform flexibility exercises regularly.

Osteoporosis

• If possible, choose low-impact, weight-bearing activities to help safely maintain bone density.

• To prevent fractures, avoid any activity or movement that stresses the back or carries a risk of falling.

• Weight train to improve strength and balance and reduce the risk of falls and fractures, but avoid lifting heavy weights.

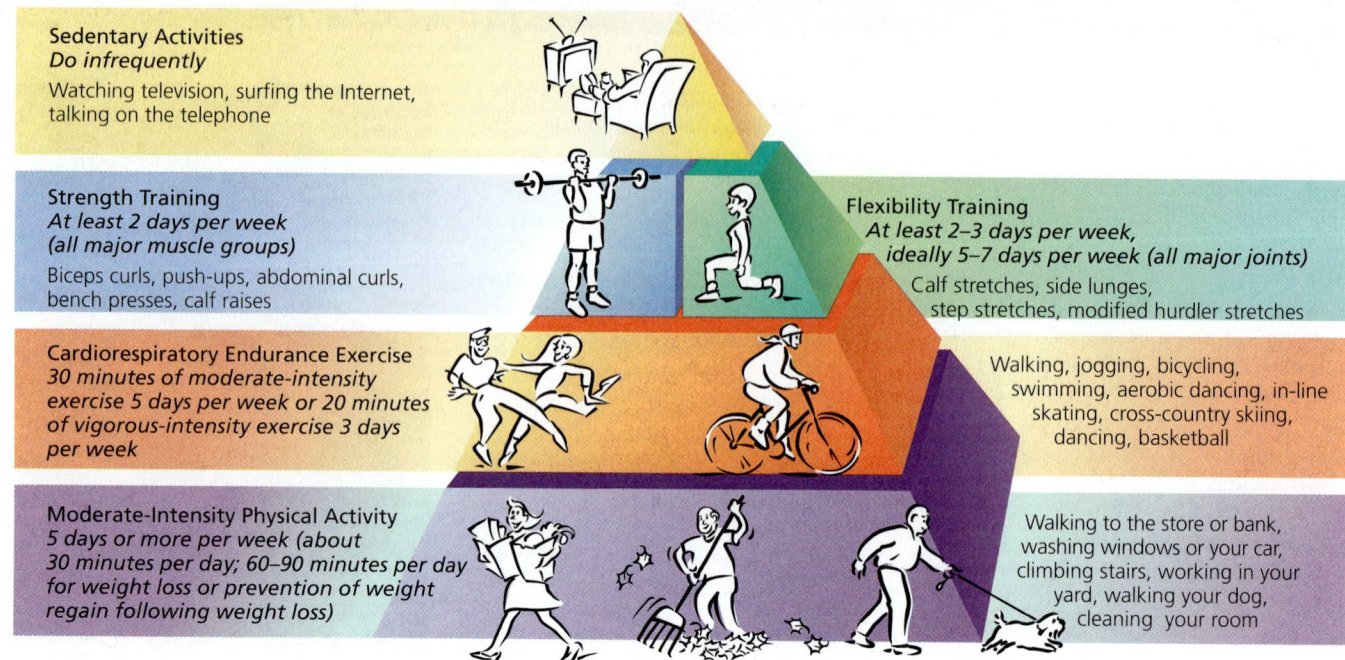

FIGURE 13.5   Physical activity pyramid.

walking, climbing stairs, doing yard work, and washing your car. As mentioned earlier, your activity time can be broken up into small blocks over the course of a day. Work up to meeting the goal of 30 minutes of moderate-intensity exercise, at least 5 days per week. Choose to be active whenever you can. If weight management is a concern for you, begin by achieving the goal of 30 minutes per day and then gradually raise your activity level to 60 minutes per day or more.

For even greater benefits, move up to the next two levels of the pyramid, which illustrate parts of a formal exercise program. The American College of Sports Medicine has established guidelines for an exercise program that includes cardiorespiratory endurance (aerobic) exercise, strength training, and flexibility training (Table 13.2). Such a program will develop all the health-related components of physical fitness. The following sections of this chapter will show you how to develop a personalized exercise program. For a summary of the health and fitness benefits of different levels of physical activity, see Figure 13.6 on page 394.

First Steps

Are you thinking about starting a formal exercise program? A little planning can help make it a success.

Medical Clearance   Previously inactive men over 40 and women over 50 should get a medical examination before beginning an exercise program. Diabetes, asthma, heart disease, and extreme obesity are conditions that may call for a modified program. If you have an increased risk of heart disease because of smoking, high blood pressure, or obesity, get a physical checkup, including an **electrocardiogram (ECG or EKG)**, before beginning an exercise program.

Basic Principles of Physical Training   To put together an effective exercise program, you should first understand the basic principles of physical training.

SPECIFICITY   To develop a fitness component, you must perform exercises that are specifically designed for that component. This is the principle of *specificity*. Weight training, for example, develops muscular strength, but is less effective for developing flexibility. Specificity also applies to the skill-related fitness components and to the different parts of the body. A well-rounded exercise program includes exercises geared to each component of fitness, to different parts of the body, and to specific activities or sports.

PROGRESSIVE OVERLOAD   Your body adapts to the demands of exercise by improving its functioning. When the amount of exercise, also called **overload**, is progressively increased, fitness continues to improve. Too little exercise will have no effect on fitness; too much may cause injury. The appropriate amount depends on your current level of fitness, your fitness goals, and the fitness components be-

Table 13.2 ACSM Exercise Recommendations for Fitness Development in Healthy Adults

Exercise to Develop and Maintain Cardiorespiratory Endurance and Body Composition

Frequency of training	3–5 days per week.
Intensity of training	55/65–90% of maximum heart rate or 40/50–85% of heart rate reserve or maximum oxygen uptake reserve. The lower intensity values (55–64% of maximum heart rate and 40–49% of heart rate reserve) are most applicable to individuals who are quite unfit. For average individuals, intensities of 70–85% of maximum heart rate or 60–80% of heart rate reserve are appropriate; see page 396 for instructions for determining target heart rate.
Time (duration) of training	20–60 total minutes of continuous or intermittent (in sessions lasting 10 or more minutes) aerobic activity. Duration is dependent on the intensity of activity; thus, low-intensity activity should be conducted over a longer period of time (30 minutes or more). Low-to-moderate-intensity activity of longer duration is recommended for nonathletic adults.
Type (mode) of activity	Any activity that uses large-muscle groups, can be maintained continuously, and is rhythmic and aerobic in nature—for example, walking-hiking, running-jogging, cycling-bicycling, cross-country skiing, aerobic dance, stair climbing, swimming, and skating.

Exercise to Develop and Maintain Muscular Strength and Endurance, Flexibility, and Body Composition

Resistance training	One set of 8–10 exercises that condition the major muscle groups should be performed at least 2 days per week. Most people should complete 8–12 repetitions of each exercise to the point of fatigue; practicing other repetition ranges (for example, 3–5 or 12–15) also builds strength and endurance; for older and frailer people (approximately 50–60 and older), 10–15 repetitions with a lighter weight may be more appropriate. Multiple-set regimens will provide greater benefits if time allows. Any mode of exercise that is comfortable throughout the full range of motion is appropriate (for example, free weights, bands, or machines).
Flexibility training	Static stretches should be performed for the major muscle groups at least 2–3 days per week, ideally 5–7 days per week. Stretch to the point of tightness, holding each stretch for 15–30 seconds; perform 2–4 repetitions of each stretch.

SOURCE: Adapted from American College of Sports Medicine. 2006. *ACSM's Guidelines for Exercise Testing and Prescription*, 7th ed. Philadelphia: Lippincott Williams & Wilkins.

ing developed. A novice, for example, might experience fitness benefits from jogging a mile in 10 minutes, but this level of exercise would cause no physical adaptations in a trained distance runner.

The amount of overload needed to maintain or improve a particular level of fitness is determined in four dimensions, represented by the acronym FITT:

Frequency

Intensity

Time

Type

• *Frequency, or how often.* Optimum exercise frequency, expressed in number of days per week, varies with the component being developed, how vigorously you exercise, and your goals. A frequency of 3–5 days per week is recommended for cardiorespiratory endurance exercise, 2 or 3 days per week for strength training, and 2 to 3 days per week (ideally 5 to 7 days per week) for stretching.

• *Intensity, or how hard.* Fitness benefits occur when you exercise harder than your normal level of activity. To develop cardiorespiratory endurance, you must raise your heart rate above normal; to develop muscular strength, you must lift a heavier weight than you normally do; to develop flexibility, you must stretch your muscles beyond their normal length. A gradual increase in intensity is recommended to avoid injury.

• *Time (duration), or how long.* If fitness benefits are to occur, exercise sessions must last for an extended period of time. Depending on the component being developed and your intensity level, a duration of 20–60 minutes is usually recommended.

• *Type, or mode of activity.* The type of exercise in which you should engage varies with each fitness component and with your personal fitness goals. To develop cardiorespiratory endurance, you need to engage in continuous activities involving large-muscle groups—walking, cycling, or swimming, for example. Resistive exercises develop muscular strength and endurance; stretching exercises build flexibility. The frequency, intensity, and time of exercise will be different for each type of activity.

These dimensions of overload are described individually as they apply to the health-related components of fitness discussed in this chapter.

TERMS

electrocardiogram (ECG or EKG) A recording of the changes in electrical activity of the heart.

overload The amount of stress placed on the body; a gradual increase in the amount of overload causes adaptations that improve fitness.

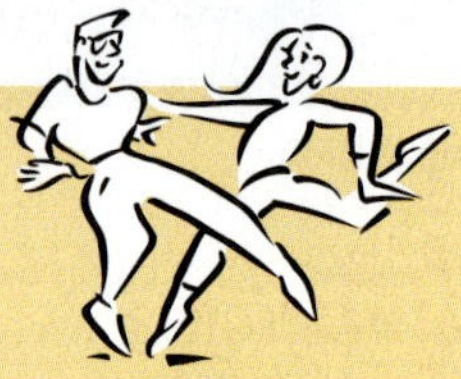 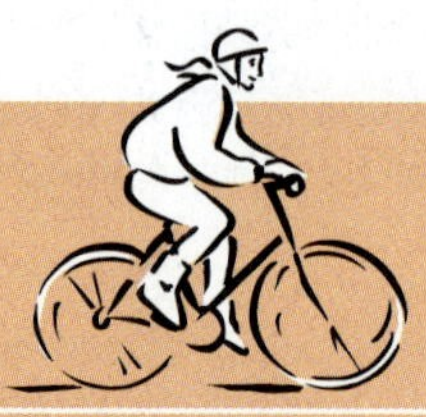 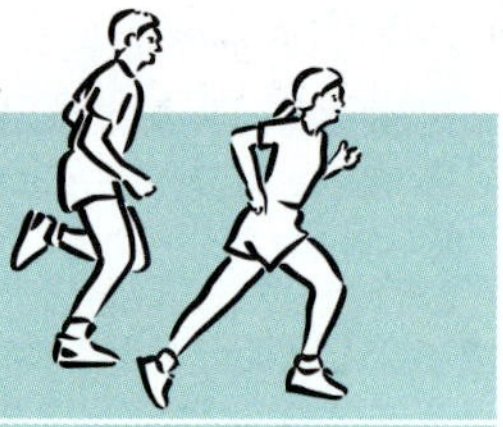

	Lifestyle physical activity	Moderate exercise program	Vigorous exercise program
Description	Moderate physical activity—an amount of activity that uses about 150 calories per day	Cardiorespiratory endurance exercise (30 minutes, 5 days per week); strength training (at least 2 nonconsecutive days per week) and stretching exercises (2 or more days per week)	Cardiorespiratory endurance exercise (20 minutes, 3 days per week); interval training; strength training (3–4 days per week); and stretching exercises (5–7 days per week)
Sample activities or program	*One of the following:* • Walking to and from work, 15 minutes each way • Cycling to and from class, 15 minutes each way • Yard work for 30 minutes • Dancing (fast) for 30 minutes • Playing basketball for 20 minutes	• Walking for 30 minutes, 5 days per week • Weight training, 1 set of 8 exercises, 2 days per week • Stretching exercises, 3 days per week	• Jogging for 45 minutes, 3 days per week • Intervals: running 400 m at high effort, 4 sets, 2 days per week • Weight training, 3 sets of 10 exercises, 3 days per week • Stretching exercises, 6 days per week
Health and fitness benefits	Better blood cholesterol levels, reduced body fat, better control of blood pressure, improved metabolic health, and enhanced glucose metabolism; improved quality of life; reduced risk of some chronic diseases Greater amounts of activity can help prevent weight gain and promote weight loss	All the benefits of lifestyle physical activity, plus improved physical fitness (increased cardiorespiratory endurance, muscular strength and endurance, and flexibility) and even greater improvements in health and quality of life and reductions in chronic disease risk	All the benefits of lifestyle physical activity and a moderate exercise program, with greater increases in fitness and somewhat greater reductions in chronic disease risk Participating in a vigorous exercise program may increase risk of injury and overtraining

FIGURE 13.6 Health and fitness benefits of different amounts of physical activity and exercise.

REVERSIBILITY The body adjusts to lower levels of physical activity in the same way it adjusts to higher levels—the principle of **reversibility.** When you stop exercising, you can lose up to 50% of fitness improvements within 2 months. Try to exercise consistently, and don't quit if you miss a few workouts. If you must temporarily curtail your training, you can maintain your fitness improvements by keeping the intensity of your workouts constant while reducing their frequency or duration.

QUICK STATS

There are 2686 YMCA branches in the United States, most of which provide a variety of individual and group exercise programs.

—YMCA, 2008

INDIVIDUAL DIFFERENCES There are limits to the potential for improvement and large individual differences in our ability to improve fitness, achieve a desirable body composition, and perform and learn sports skills. Scientists have identified specific genes that influence the capacity to alter body fat, strength, and endurance. In addition, men tend to have higher endurance capacity than women due to higher testosterone levels (which affect oxygen transport and cellular metabolism) and lower levels of body fat. However, men and women have the same capacity for improvement when gains are expressed as a percent of initial fitness.

Selecting Activities

If you have been inactive, you should begin slowly by gradually increasing the amount of moderate physical activity in your life (the bottom of

TERMS

reversibility The training principle that fitness improvements are lost when demands on the body are lowered.

maximal oxygen consumption ($\dot{V}O_{2max}$) The body's maximum ability to transport and use oxygen.

target heart rate range The range of heart rates within which exercise yields cardiorespiratory benefits.

synovial fluid Fluid found within many joints that provides lubrication and nutrition to the cells of the joint surface.

the activity pyramid). Once your body adjusts to your new level of activity, you can choose additional activities for your exercise program.

Be sure the activities you choose contribute to your overall wellness and make sense for you. Are you competitive? If so, try racquetball, basketball, or squash. Do you prefer to exercise alone? Then consider cross-country skiing or road running. Have you been sedentary? A walking program may be a good place to start. If you think you may have trouble sticking with an exercise program, find a structured activity that you can do with a buddy or a group.

Be realistic about the constraints presented by some sports, such as accessibility, expense, and time. For example, if you have to travel for hours to get to a ski area, skiing may not be a good choice for your regular exercise program. And if you've never played tennis, it will probably take some time to reach a reasonable skill level; you may be better off with a program of walking or jogging to get good workouts while you're improving your tennis game.

Cardiorespiratory Endurance Exercises

Exercises that condition your heart and lungs should have a central role in your fitness program. The best exercises for developing cardiorespiratory endurance stress a large portion of the body's muscle mass for a prolonged period of time. These include walking, jogging, running, swimming, bicycling, and aerobic dancing. Many popular sports and recreational activities, such as racquetball, tennis, basketball, and soccer, are also good if the skill level and intensity of the game are sufficient to provide a vigorous workout.

Frequency The optimal workout schedule for endurance training is 3–5 days per week. Beginners should start with 3 and work up to 5 days. Training more than 5 days a week often leads to injury for recreational athletes. Although you do get health benefits from exercising very vigorously only 1 or 2 days per week, you risk injury because your body never gets a chance to adapt fully to regular exercise training.

Intensity The most misunderstood aspect of conditioning, even among experienced athletes, is training intensity. Intensity is the crucial factor in attaining a significant training effect—that is, in increasing the body's cardiorespiratory capacity. A primary purpose of endurance training is to increase **maximal oxygen consumption** ($\dot{V}O_{2max}$). $\dot{V}O_{2max}$ represents the maximum ability of the cells to use oxygen and is considered the best measure of cardiorespiratory capacity. Intensity of training is the crucial factor in improving $\dot{V}O_{2max}$.

One of the easiest ways to determine exactly how intensely you should work involves measuring your heart rate. It is not necessary or desirable to exercise at your maximum heart rate—the fastest heart rate possible before exhaustion sets in—in order to improve your cardiorespiratory capacity. Beneficial effects occur at lower heart rates with a much lower risk of injury. **Target heart rate range** is the range of rates within which you should exercise to obtain cardiorespiratory benefits. To determine the intensity at which you should exercise, refer to the box "Determining Your Target Heart Rate Range" (p. 396) and Figure 13.7 (p. 397).

After you begin your fitness program, you may improve quickly because the body adapts readily to new exercises; the rate of improvement may slow after the first month or so. The more fit you become, the harder you will have to work to improve. By monitoring your heart rate, you will always know if you are working hard enough to improve, not hard enough, or too hard. For most people, a fitness program involves attaining an acceptable level of fitness and then maintaining that level. There is no need to keep working indefinitely to improve; doing so only increases the chance of injury. After you have reached the level you want, you can maintain fitness by exercising at the same intensity 3–5 days per week.

Time (Duration) A total time of 20–60 minutes is recommended; exercise can take place in a single session or several sessions lasting 10 or more minutes. The total duration of exercise depends on its intensity. To improve cardiorespiratory endurance during a low- to moderate-intensity activity such as walking or slow swimming, you should exercise for 45–60 minutes. For high-intensity exercise performed at the top of your target heart rate zone, a duration of 20 minutes is sufficient. Start with less vigorous activities and gradually increase intensity.

You can use these three dimensions of cardiorespiratory endurance training—frequency, intensity, and time—to develop a fitness program that strengthens your heart and lungs and provides all the benefits described earlier in this chapter. Build your program around at least 20 minutes of endurance exercise at your target heart rate 3 to 5 days a week. Then add exercises that develop the other components of fitness.

The Warm-Up and Cool-Down It is always important to warm up before you exercise and to cool down afterward. Warming up enhances your performance and decreases your chances of injury. Your muscles work better when their temperature is elevated slightly above resting level. Warming up helps your body gradually progress from rest to exercise. Blood needs to be redirected to active muscles, and your heart needs time to adapt to the increased demands of exercise. A warm-up helps spread **synovial fluid** throughout the joints, which helps protect joint surfaces from wear and tear. (It's like warming up a car to spread oil through the engine parts before shifting into gear.)

Determining Your Target Heart Rate Range

Your target heart rate is the range of rates at which you should exercise to experience cardiorespiratory benefits. Your target heart rate range is based on your maximum heart rate, which can be estimated from your age. (If you are a serious athlete or face possible cardiovascular risks from exercise, you may want to have your maximum heart rate determined more accurately through a treadmill test in a physician's office, hospital, or sports medicine laboratory.) Your target heart rate is a range: The lower value corresponds to moderate-intensity exercise, and the higher value is associated with high-intensity exercise. Target heart rate ranges are shown in the table.

You can monitor the intensity of your workouts by measuring your pulse either at your wrist or at one of your carotid arteries, located on either side of your Adam's apple. Your pulse rate drops rapidly after exercise, so begin counting immediately after you have finished exercising. You will obtain the most accurate results by counting beats for 10 seconds and then multiplying by 6 to get your heart rate in beats per minute (bpm). The 10-second counts corresponding to each target heart rate range are also shown in the table.

Age (years)	Target Heart Rate Range (bpm)*	10-Second Count (beats)*
20–24	127–180	21–30
25–29	124–176	20–29
30–34	121–171	20–28
35–39	118–167	19–27
40–44	114–162	19–27
45–49	111–158	18–26
50–54	108–153	18–25
55–59	105–149	17–24
60–64	101–144	16–24
65+	97–140	16–23

*Target heart rates lower than those shown here are appropriate for individuals with a very low initial level of fitness. Ranges are based on the following formula: Target heart rate = 0.65 to 0.90 of maximum heart rate, assuming maximum heart rate = 220 − age.

A warm-up session should include low-intensity movements similar to those in the activity that will follow. For example, hit forehands and backhands before a tennis game or jog slowly for 400 meters before progressing to an 8-minute mile. Some people like to include stretching exercises in their warm-up. Experts recommend that you stretch *after* the active part of your warm-up, when your body temperature has been elevated. Studies have found that stretching prior to exercise can temporarily decrease muscle strength and power, so if a high-performance workout is your goal, it is best to stretch after a workout. See pages 399–400 for more on stretching.

Cooling down after exercise is important to restore the body's circulation to its normal resting condition. When you are at rest, a relatively small percentage of your total blood volume is directed to muscles, but during exercise, as much as 90% of the heart's output is directed to them. During recovery from exercise, it is important to continue exercising at a low level to provide a smooth transition to the resting state. Cooling down helps regulate the return of blood to your heart.

Developing Muscular Strength and Endurance

Any program designed to promote health should include exercises that develop muscular strength and endurance (see the box "Gender Differences in Muscular Strength" on p. 398). Your ability to maintain correct posture and move efficiently depends in part on adequate muscle fitness. Strengthening exercises also increase muscle tone, which improves the appearance of your body.

Types of Strength Training Exercises Muscular strength and endurance can be developed in many ways, from weight training to calisthenics. Common exercises such as curl-ups, push-ups, pull-ups, and wall-sitting (leaning against a wall in a seated position and supporting yourself with your leg muscles) maintain the muscular strength of most people if they practice them several times a week. To condition and tone your whole body, choose exercises that work the major muscles of the shoulders, chest, back, arms, abdomen, and legs.

To increase muscular strength and endurance, you must do **resistance exercise**—exercises in which your muscles must exert force against a significant amount of resistance. Resistance can be provided by weights, exercise machines, or your own body weight.

Isometric (static) exercises involve applying force without movement, such as when you contract your abdominal muscles. This static type of exercise is valuable for toning and strengthening muscles. Isometrics can be

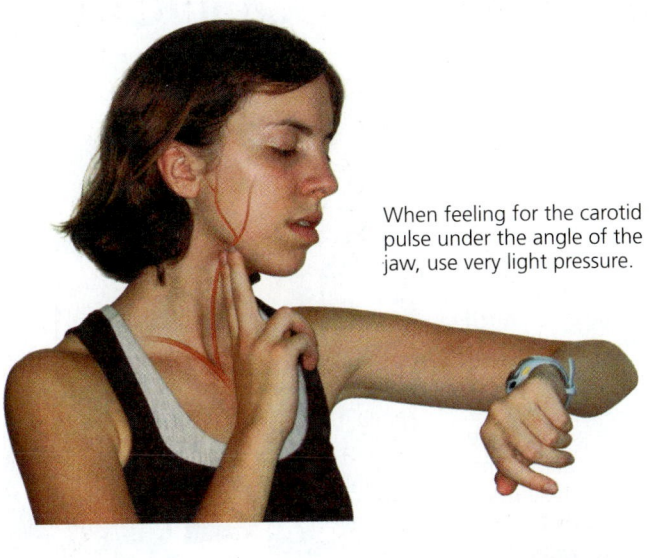

When feeling for the carotid pulse under the angle of the jaw, use very light pressure.

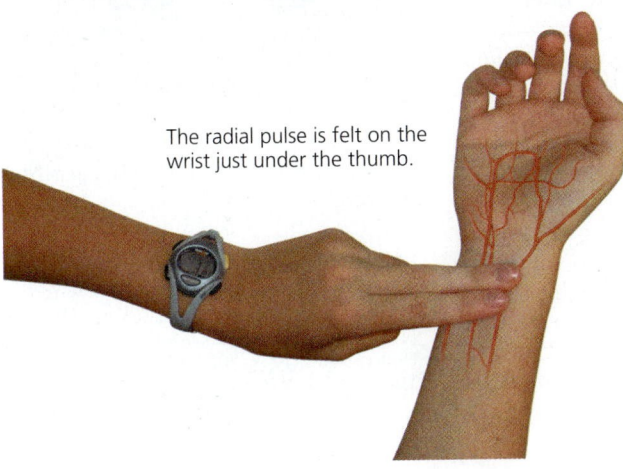

The radial pulse is felt on the wrist just under the thumb.

FIGURE 13.7 Checking your pulse. The pulse can be taken at the carotid artery in the neck (top) or at the radial artery in the wrist (bottom).

practiced anywhere and do not require any equipment. For maximum strength gains, hold an isometric contraction maximally for 6 seconds; do five to ten repetitions. Don't hold your breath—that can restrict blood flow to your heart and brain. Within a few weeks, you will notice the effect of this exercise. Isometrics are particularly useful when recovering from an injury.

Isotonic (dynamic) exercises involve applying force with movement, as in weight training exercises such as the bench press. These are the most popular type of exercises for increasing muscle strength and seem to be most valuable for developing strength that can be transferred to other forms of physical activity. They include exercises using barbells, dumbbells, weight machines, and body weight, as in push-ups or curl-ups.

Choosing Equipment Weight machines are preferred by many people because they are safe, convenient, and easy to use (see the box "Exercise Machines Versus Free Weights" on p. 399). You just set the resistance, sit down at the machine, and start working. Machines make it easy to isolate and work specific muscles. Free weights require more care, balance, and coordination to use, but they strengthen your body in ways that are more adaptable to real life. When using free weights, you need to use a spotter, someone who stands by to assist in case you lose control over a weight (see the box "Safe Weight Training" on p. 400).

Choosing Exercises A complete weight training program works all the major muscle groups: neck, upper back, shoulders, arms, chest, abdomen, lower back, thighs, buttocks, and calves. Different exercises work different muscles, so it usually takes about eight to ten exercises to get a complete workout for general fitness—for example, bench presses to develop the chest, shoulders, and upper arms; pull-ups to work the biceps and upper back; squats to develop the legs and buttocks; toe raises to work the calves; and so on. If you are also training for a particular sport, include exercises to strengthen the muscles important for optimal performance and those most likely to be injured.

Frequency For general fitness, the American College of Sports Medicine recommends a frequency of at least 2 nonconsecutive days per week. This allows your muscles one or more days of rest between workouts to avoid soreness and injury. If you enjoy weight training and would like to train more often, try working different muscle groups on alternate days.

Intensity and Time The amount of weight (resistance) you lift in weight training exercises is equivalent to intensity in cardiorespiratory endurance training; the number of repetitions of each exercise is equivalent to time. In order to improve fitness, you must do enough repetitions of each exercise to temporarily fatigue your muscles. The number of repetitions needed to cause fatigue depends on the amount of resistance: the heavier the weight, the fewer repetitions to reach fatigue. In general, a heavy weight and a low number of repetitions (1–5) build strength, whereas a light weight and a high number of repetitions (20–25) build endurance. For a general fitness program to build both strength and endurance, try to do 8–12 repetitions of each exercise; a few exercises, such as

resistance exercise Exercise that forces muscles to contract against increased resistance; also called *strength training.*

isometric (static) exercise The application of force without movement.

isotonic (dynamic) exercise The application of force with movement.

TERMS

Gender Differences in Muscular Strength

connect™

Men are generally stronger than women because they typically have larger bodies overall and a larger proportion of their total body mass is made up of muscle. But when strength is expressed per unit of muscle tissue, men are only 1–2% stronger than women in the upper body and about equal to women in the lower body. Individual muscle cells are larger in men, but the functioning of the cells is the same in both sexes.

Two factors that help explain these disparities are testosterone levels and the speed of nervous control of muscle. Testosterone promotes the growth of muscle tissue in both males and females, but testosterone levels are about 6–10 times higher in men than in women, so men develop larger muscles. Also, because the male nervous system can activate muscles faster, men tend to have more power.

Some women are concerned that they will develop large muscles from strength training. Because of hormonal differences, most women do not develop large muscles unless they train intensely over many years or take steroids. A study of average women who weight trained 2–3 days per week for 8 weeks found that the women gained about 1.75 pounds of muscle and lost about 3.5 pounds of fat. Another study followed women who trained with weights for 2 years. Not only did the women reduce their overall body fat levels but they ended up with less fat around their midsection.

Losing muscle over time is a much greater health concern for women than small gains in muscle weight in response to strength training, especially as any gains in muscle weight are typically more than balanced with loss of fat weight. Both men and women lose muscle mass and power as they age, but because men start out with more muscle when they are young and don't lose power as quickly as women, older women tend to have greater impairment of muscle function than older men. This may partially explain the higher incidence of life-threatening falls in older women.

Healthy People 2010 sets a national health objective of increasing to 30% the proportion of adults who perform strength training exercises on 2 or more days per week. In 2008, however, the CDC reported that only 22% of men and 17% of women met this goal, underscor-

ing the need for additional programs and campaigns that promote this form of exercise.

SOURCES: Fahey, T. D. 2007. *Basic Weight Training for Men and Women*, 6th ed. New York: McGraw-Hill; Centers for Disease Control and Prevention. 2006. Trends in strength training—United States, 1998–2004. *Morbidity and Mortality Weekly Report* 55(28): 769–772.

---

abdominal crunches and calf raises, may require more. (For people who are 50–60 years of age and older, 10–15 repetitions of each exercise using a lighter weight is recommended.)

The first few sessions of weight training should be devoted to learning the exercises. To start, choose a weight that you can move easily through 8–12 repetitions. Add weight when you can do more than 12 repetitions of an exercise. If adding weight means you can do only 7 or 8 repetitions before your muscles fatigue, stay with that weight until you can again complete 12 repetitions. If you can do only 4–6 repetitions after adding weight, or if you can't maintain good form, you've added too much and should take some off. As a general guideline, try increases of approximately ½ pound of additional weight for each 10 pounds you are currently lifting.

For developing strength and endurance for general fitness, a single set (group) of each exercise is sufficient, provided you use enough resistance (weight) to fatigue your muscles. Doing more than one set of each exercise may increase strength development, and most serious weight trainers do at least three sets of each exercise. If you do more than one set of an exercise, rest long enough between sets to allow your muscles to recover.

You should warm up before every weight training session and cool down afterward. You can expect to improve rapidly during the first 6–10 weeks of training; gains will then come more slowly. Factors such as age, motivation, gender, and heredity will affect your program. Your ultimate goal depends on you. After you have achieved the level of strength and muscularity that you want, you can maintain your gains by training 2–3 nonconsecutive days per week.

A Caution About Supplements No nutritional supplement or drug will change a weak person into a strong person. Those changes require regular training that

Exercise Machines Versus Free Weights

Exercise Machines		Free Weights	
Advantages	**Disadvantages**	**Advantages**	**Disadvantages**
• Are safe and convenient	• Have limited availability	• Allow dynamic movements	• Are not as safe
• Don't require spotters	• Are inappropriate for performing dynamic movements	• Allow user to develop control of weights	• Require spotters
• Don't require lifter to balance bar	• Allow limited number of exercises	• Allow greater variety of exercises	• Require more skill
• Provide variable resistance	• Train muscles rather than movements	• Are widely available, inexpensive, and convenient for home use	• Cause more blisters and calluses
• Require less skill	• Place minimal stress on core stabilizing muscles (those in torso)	• Train core stabilizing muscles	
• Make it easy to move from one exercise to the next		• Are better for building power	
• Allow easy isolation of muscles and muscle groups		• Are truer to real-life situations; strength transfers to daily activities	
• Support back (on many machines)			

stresses the body and causes physiological adaptations. Supplements or drugs that promise quick, large gains in strength usually don't work and are often either dangerous, expensive, or both (see the box "Drugs and Supplements for Improved Athletic Performance" on p. 401). Over-the-counter supplements are not carefully regulated, and their long-term effects have not been systematically studied.

Flexibility Exercises

Flexibility, or stretching, exercises are important for maintaining the normal range of motion in the major joints of the body. Some exercises, such as running, can actually decrease flexibility because they require only a partial range of motion. Like a good weight training program, a good stretching program includes exercises for all the major muscle groups and joints of the body: neck, shoulders, back, hips, thighs, hamstrings, and calves.

Proper Stretching Technique   Stretching should be performed statically. Ballistic stretching (known as "bouncing") is dangerous and counterproductive. In active stretching, a muscle is stretched under a person's own power by contracting the opposing muscles. In passive stretching, an outside force or resistance provided by yourself, a partner, gravity, or a weight helps elongate the targeted muscle. You can achieve a greater range of motion and a more intense stretch using passive stretching,

When performed regularly, stretching exercises help maintain or improve the range of motion in joints. For each exercise, stretch to the point of tightness in the muscle and hold the position for 15–30 seconds.

but there is a greater risk of injury. The safest and most convenient technique may be active static stretching with a passive assist. For example, you might do a seated stretch of your calf muscles both by contracting the

Safe Weight Training

General Strategies

• Lift weights from a stabilized body position. Protect your back from dangerous positions. Don't twist your body while lifting.

• Don't lift beyond the limits of your strength.

• Be aware of what's going on around you so that you don't bump into someone or get too close to a moving weight stack.

• Don't use defective equipment; report any equipment problems immediately.

• Don't chew gum when exercising.

• *Don't hold your breath while doing weight training exercises.* Exhale when exerting the greatest force, and inhale when moving the weight into position. (Holding your breath raises blood pressure and causes a decrease in blood returning to the heart; it can make you become dizzy and faint.)

• Rest between lifts.

• Always warm up before training and cool down afterward.

Free Weights

• Use spotters to avoid injury. A spotter can help you if you cannot complete a lift or if the weight tilts.

• Secure weight plates to barbells with a collar to prevent them from sliding off.

• Keep weights as close to your body as possible. Do most of your lifting with your legs; keep your hips and buttocks tucked in.

• Lift weights smoothly and slowly; don't bounce or jerk them. Control the weight through the entire range of motion.

• When holding barbells and dumbbells, wrap your thumbs around the bar when gripping it.

Weight Machines

• Stay away from moving parts of the machine that could pinch your skin or crush your fingers.

• Adjust each machine for your body so that you don't have to work in an awkward position.

• Beware of broken bolts, frayed cables, broken chains, or loose cushions that can give way and cause serious injury.

• Make sure the machines are clean. Carry a towel with you, and place it on the machine where you will sit or lie down.

---

muscles on the top of your shin and by grabbing your feet and pulling them toward you.

Frequency   Do stretching exercises at least 2–3 days per week, ideally 5–7 days per week. If you stretch after cardiorespiratory endurance exercise or strength training, during your cool-down, you may develop more flexibility, because your muscles are warmer then and can be stretched farther.

Intensity and Time   For each exercise, stretch to the point of tightness in the muscle, and hold the position for 15–30 seconds. Rest for 30–60 seconds, then repeat, trying to stretch a bit farther. Relax and breathe easily as you stretch. You should feel a pleasant, mild stretch as you let the muscles relax; stretching should not be painful. Do 2–4 repetitions of each exercise. A complete flexibility workout usually takes about 20–30 minutes.

Increase your intensity gradually over time. Improved flexibility takes many months to develop. There are large individual differences in joint flexibility. Don't feel you have to compete with others during stretching workouts.

Training in Specific Skills

The final component in your fitness program is learning the skills required for the sports or activities in which you choose to participate. By taking the time and effort to acquire competence, you can achieve a sense of mastery and add a new physical activity to your repertoire.

The first step in learning a new skill is getting help. Sports like tennis, golf, sailing, and skiing require mastery of basic movements and techniques, so instruction from a qualified teacher can save you hours of frustration and increase your enjoyment of the sport. Skill is also important in conditioning activities such as jogging, swimming, and cycling. Even if you learned a sport as a child, additional instruction now can help you refine your technique, get over stumbling blocks, and relearn skills that you may have learned incorrectly.

Putting It All Together

Now that you know the basic components of a fitness program, you can put them all together in a program that works for you. Remember to include the following:

TERMS   **anabolic steroids**   Synthetic male hormones used to increase muscle size and strength.

Drugs and Supplements for Improved Athletic Performance

Doping scandals have snared athletes in sports as diverse as cycling, baseball, and track and field. In 2007, cyclist Floyd Landis was stripped of his 2006 Tour de France title and banned from cycling for two years, after testing positive for synthetic testosterone. Meantime, as baseball legends Barry Bonds and Roger Clemens fought to restore reputations damaged by allegations of steroid abuse, a special congressional report accused nearly 90 professional baseball players of using steroids and other performance-enhancing drugs. That same year, Olympic sprinter Marion Jones admitted using banned substances before the 2000 Olympic games. In the wake of these and other events, the U.S. Congress, professional sports leagues, and anti-doping agencies all sought ways to rid sports of banned substances.

Professional and Olympic athletes aren't the only ones using performance-enhancing drugs. About 2–6% of high school and college students report having used anabolic steroids, and over-the-counter dietary supplements are much more popular. Many such substances are ineffective and expensive, and many are also dangerous. A few of the most widely used compounds are described below.

Anabolic Steroids These synthetic derivatives of testosterone are taken to increase strength, power, speed, endurance, muscle size, and aggressiveness. **Anabolic steroids** have dangerous side effects, including disruption of the body's hormone system, liver disease, acne, breast development and testicular shrinkage in males, masculinization in women and children, and increased risk of heart disease and cancer. Evidence links steroid use and risk of heart attack, stroke, and sudden death.

Steroid users who inject the drugs face the same health risks as other injection drug users, including increased risk of HIV infection. Steroids have been found to be a gateway to the use of other drugs.

Adrenal Androgens This group of drugs, which includes dehydroepiandrosterone (DHEA) and androstenedione, are typically taken to stimulate muscle growth and aid in weight control. The few studies of these agents done on humans show that they are of very little value in improving athletic performance, and they have side effects similar to those of anabolic steroids, especially when taken in high doses.

Ephedra and Other Stimulants These drugs may be taken to increase training intensity, to suppress hunger, to reduce fatigue, and to promote weight loss. They raise heart rate and blood pressure and, at high doses, may increase the risk of heart attack, stroke, and heat-related illness. Several stimulants, including ephedra and phenylpropanolamine, have been banned by the FDA.

Erythropoietin (EPO) A naturally occurring hormone that boosts the concentration of red blood cells, EPO is used by endurance athletes to improve performance. EPO can cause blood clots and death.

Creatine Monohydrate Creatine is thought to improve performance in short-term, high-intensity, repetitive ex-

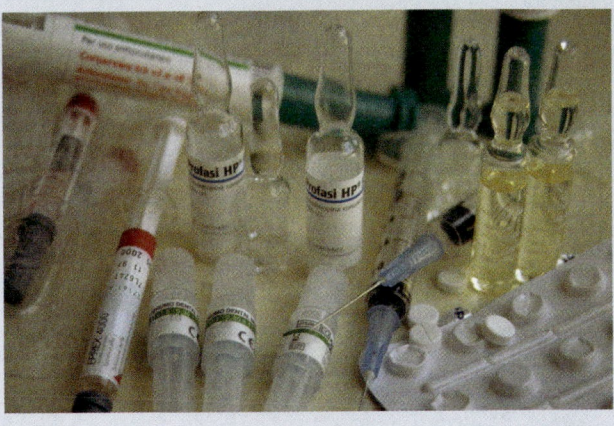

ercise and decrease the risk of injury. People vary in their responses to creatine. The long-term effects of creatine use, especially among young people, are not well established.

Protein, Amino Acid, and Polypeptide Supplements Taking protein supplements after weight training may increase muscle strength and hypertrophy. Little research supports the use of such supplements, however, even in athletes on extremely heavy training regimens. The protein requirements of athletes are not much higher than those of sedentary individuals, and most people take in more than enough protein in their diets. By substituting supplements for food sources of protein, people may risk deficiencies in other key nutrients typically found in such foods, including iron and B vitamins.

Chromium Picolinate Sold over the counter, chromium picolinate is a more easily digested form of the trace mineral chromium. Although often marketed as a means to build muscle and reduce fat, most studies have found no positive effects. Long-term use of high dosages may have serious health consequences.

- *Cardiorespiratory endurance exercise:* Do at least 20–60 minutes of aerobic exercise within your target heart rate range 3 to 5 days a week.

- *Muscular strength and endurance:* Work the major muscle groups (one or more sets of eight to ten exercises) at least 2 nonconsecutive days a week.

- *Flexibility exercise:* Do stretches at least 2 or 3 days a week, ideally 5 to 7 days a week, preferably after exercise, when your muscles are warm.

- *Skill training:* Incorporate some or all of your aerobic or strengthening exercise into an enjoyable sport or physical activity.

Table 13.3   A Summary of Sports and Fitness Activities

This table classifies sports and activities as high (H), moderate (M), or low (L) in terms of their ability to develop each of the five components of physical fitness: cardiorespiratory endurance (CRE), muscular strength (MS), muscular endurance (ME), flexibility (F), and body composition (BC). The skill level needed to obtain fitness benefits is noted: Low (L) means little or no skill is required to obtain fitness benefits; moderate (M) means average skill is needed to obtain fitness benefits; and high (H) means much skill is required to obtain fitness benefits. The fitness prerequisite, or conditioning needs of a beginner, is also noted: Low (L) means no fitness prerequisite is required, moderate (M) means some preconditioning is required, and high (H) means substantial fitness is required. The last two columns list the calorie cost of each activity when performed moderately and vigorously. To determine how many calories you burn, multiply the value in the appropriate column by your body weight and then by the number of minutes you exercise. Work up to using 300 or more calories per workout.

Sports and Activities	Components					Skill Level	Fitness Prerequisite	Approximate Calorie Cost (cal/lb/min)	
	CRE	MS*	ME*	F*	BC			Moderate	Vigorous
Aerobic dance	H	M	H	H	H	L	L	.046	.062
Backpacking	H	M	H	M	H	L	M	.032	.078
Badminton, skilled, singles	H	M	M	M	H	M	M	—	.071
Ballet (floor combinations)	M	M	H	H	M	M	L	—	.058
Ballroom dancing	M	L	M	L	M	M	L	.034	.049
Baseball (pitcher and catcher)	M	M	H	M	M	H	M	.039	—
Basketball, half court	H	M	H	M	H	M	M	.045	.071
Bicycling	H	M	H	M	H	M	L	.049	.071
Bowling	L	L	L	L	L	L	L	—	—
Calisthenic circuit training	H	M	H	M	H	L	L	—	.060
Canoeing and kayaking (flat water)	M	M	H	M	M	M	M	.045	—
Cheerleading	M	M	M	M	M	M	L	.033	.049
Elliptical exercise	H	M	H	M	H	L	L	.049	.070
Fencing	M	M	H	H	M	M	L	.032	.078
Field hockey	H	M	H	M	H	M	M	.052	.078
Folk and square dancing	M	L	M	L	M	L	L	.039	.049
Football, touch	M	M	M	M	M	M	M	.049	.078
Frisbee, ultimate	H	M	H	M	H	M	M	.049	.078
Golf (riding cart)	L	L	L	M	L	L	L	—	—
Handball, skilled, singles	H	M	H	M	H	M	M	—	.078
Hiking	H	M	H	L	H	L	M	.051	.073
Hockey, ice and roller	H	M	H	M	H	M	M	.052	.078
Horseback riding	M	M	M	L	M	M	M	.052	.065
Interval circuit training	H	H	H	M	H	L	L	—	.062
Jogging and running	H	M	H	L	H	L	L	.060	.104
Judo	M	H	H	M	M	M	L	.049	.090

*Ratings are for the muscle groups involved.

	Cardiorespiratory endurance training	Strength training	Flexibility training
Frequency	3–5 days per week	At least 2 nonconsecutive days per week	2–3 days per week (minimum); 5–7 days per week (ideal)
Intensity	55/65–90% of maximum heart rate	Sufficient resistance to fatigue muscles	Stretch to the point of tension
Time	20–60 minutes in sessions lasting 10 minutes or more	8–12 repetitions of each exercise, 1 or more sets	2–4 repetitions of each exercise, held for 15–30 seconds
Type	Continuous rhythmic activities using large muscle groups	Resistance exercises for all major muscle groups	Stretching exercises for all major joints

FIGURE 13.8   A summary of the FITT principle for the health-related components of fitness.

Table 13.3   A Summary of Sports and Fitness Activities *(continued)*

| Sports and Activities | Components | | | | | Skill Level | Fitness Prerequisite | Approximate Calorie Cost (cal/lb/min) | |
	CRE	MS*	ME*	F*	BC			Moderate	Vigorous
Karate	H	M	H	H	H	L	M	.049	.090
Lacrosse	H	M	H	M	H	H	M	.052	.078
Modern dance (moving combinations)	M	M	H	H	M	L	L	—	.058
Orienteering	H	M	H	L	H	L	M	.049	.078
Outdoor fitness trails	H	M	H	M	H	L	L	—	.060
Popular dancing	M	L	M	M	M	M	L	—	.049
Racquetball, skilled, singles	H	M	M	M	H	M	M	.049	.078
Rock climbing	M	H	H	H	M	H	M	.033	.033
Rope skipping	H	M	H	L	H	M	M	.071	.095
Rowing	H	H	H	H	H	L	L	.032	.097
Rugby	H	M	H	M	H	M	M	.052	.097
Sailing	L	L	M	L	L	M	L	—	—
Skating, ice, roller, and in-line	M	M	M	M	M	H	M	.049	.095
Skiing, alpine	M	H	H	M	M	H	M	.039	.078
Skiing, cross-country	H	M	H	M	H	M	M	.049	.104
Soccer	H	M	H	M	H	M	M	.052	.097
Squash, skilled, singles	H	M	M	M	H	M	M	.049	.078
Stretching	L	L	L	H	L	L	L	—	—
Surfing (including swimming)	M	M	M	M	M	H	M	—	.078
Swimming	H	M	H	M	H	M	L	.032	.088
Synchronized swimming	M	M	H	H	M	H	M	.032	.052
Table tennis	M	L	M	M	M	M	L	—	.045
Tennis, skilled, singles	H	M	M	M	H	M	M	—	.071
Volleyball	M	L	M	M	M	M	M	—	.065
Walking	H	L	M	L	H	L	L	.029	.048
Water polo	H	M	H	M	H	H	M	—	.078
Water skiing	M	M	H	M	M	H	M	.039	.055
Weight training	L	H	H	H	M	L	L	—	—
Wrestling	H	H	H	H	H	H	H	.065	.094
Yoga	L	L	M	H	L	H	L		

*Ratings are for the muscle groups involved.

SOURCE: Kusinitz, I., and M. Fine, *Physical Fitness for Practically Everybody,* Consumer Reports © 1983. Consumers Union of the U.S., Inc., Yonkers, NY 10703-1057, a nonprofit organization. Reprinted with permission for educational purposes only. No commercial use or reproduction permitted. www.ConsumerReports.org(r).

Refer to Figure 13.8 for a summary of the FITT principle for the health-related fitness components; the fitness benefits of a variety of activities are provided in Table 13.3 to help you plan your program.

GETTING STARTED AND STAYING ON TRACK

Once you have a program that fulfills your basic fitness needs and suits your personal tastes, adhering to a few basic principles will help you improve at the fastest rate, have more fun, and minimize the risk of injury. These principles include buying appropriate equipment, eating and drinking properly, and managing your program so it becomes an integral part of your life.

Selecting Instructors, Equipment, and Facilities

Once you've chosen the activities for your program, you may need to obtain appropriate information, instruction, and equipment or find an appropriate facility.

QUESTIONS FOR CRITICAL THINKING AND REFLECTION

Consider the list of physical activities and sports in Table 13.3. For which ones do you have the necessary fitness prerequisite (low, moderate, or high)? Given your current fitness and skill level, which ones could you reasonably incorporate into your exercise program?

Finding Help and Advice About Exercise One of the best places to get help is an exercise class, where an expert instructor can help you learn the basics of training and answer your questions. A qualified personal trainer can also get you started on an exercise program or a new form of training. Make sure that your instructor or trainer has proper qualifications, such as a college degree in exercise physiology or physical education and certification by the American College of Sports Medicine (ACSM), National Strength and Conditioning Association (NSCA), or another professional organization. Don't seek out a person for advice simply because he or she looks fit. You can further your knowledge by reading articles by experts in fitness magazines.

Many Web sites provide fitness programs, including ongoing support and feedback via e-mail. Many of these sites charge a fee, so it is important to review the sites, decide which ones seem most appropriate, and if possible go through a free trial period before subscribing. Also remember to consider the reliability of the information at fitness Web sites, especially those that also advertise or sell products. A few popular sites are listed in For More Information at the end of the chapter.

Selecting Equipment Try to purchase the best equipment you can afford. Good equipment will enhance your enjoyment and decrease your risk of injury. Appropriate safety equipment, such as pads and helmets for in-line skating, is particularly important. If you shop around, you can often find bargains through mail-order companies and discount or used equipment stores.

Before you invest in a new piece of equipment, investigate it. Try it out at a local gym to make sure that you'll use it regularly. Also check whether you have space to use and store it at home. Ask the experts (coaches, physical educators, and sports instructors) for their opinion. Better yet, educate yourself. Every sport, from running to volleyball, has its own magazine.

Footwear is an important piece of equipment for almost any activity; see the box "Choosing Exercise Footwear" for shopping strategies.

Choosing a Fitness Center Are you thinking of joining a health club or fitness center? Be sure to choose one that has the right programs and equipment available at the times you will use them. You should feel comfortable with the classes and activities available; the age, fitness level, and dress of others in the club; and the types of music used in classes. The facility and equipment should be clean and well maintained, including the showers and lockers; the staff should be well trained and helpful.

Also make sure the facility is certified; look for the displayed names American College of Sports Medicine (ACSM); National Strength and Conditioning Association (NSCA); American Council on Exercise (ACE); Aerobics and Fitness Association of America (AFAA); or International Health, Racquet, and Sportsclub Association (IHRSA). These trade associations have established standards to help protect consumer health, safety, and rights.

Ask for a free trial workout, a 1-day pass, or an inexpensive 1- to 2-week trial membership before committing to a long-term contract. Be wary of promotional gimmicks and high-pressure sales tactics.

Eating and Drinking for Exercise

Most people do not need to change their eating habits when they begin a fitness program. Many athletes and other physically active people are lured into buying aggressively advertised vitamins, minerals, and protein supplements; but, in almost every case, a well-balanced diet contains all the energy and nutrients needed to sustain an exercise program (see Chapter 12).

A balanced diet is also the key to improving your body composition when you begin to exercise more. One of the promises of a fitness program is a decrease in body fat and an increase in muscular body mass. As mentioned earlier, the control of body fat is determined by the balance of energy in the body. If more calories are consumed than are expended through metabolism and exercise, then fat increases. If the reverse is true, fat is lost. The best way to control body fat is to follow a diet containing adequate but not excessive calories and to be physically active.

One of the most important principles to follow when exercising is to drink enough water. Your body depends on water to sustain many chemical reactions and to maintain correct body temperature. Sweating during exercise depletes the body's water supply and can lead to dehydration if fluids are not replaced. Serious dehydration can cause reduced blood volume, accelerated heart rate, elevated body temperature, muscle cramps, heat stroke, and other serious problems.

Drinking fluids before and during exercise is important to prevent dehydration and enhance performance. Thirst receptors in the brain make you want to drink fluids, but during heavy or prolonged exercise or exercise in hot weather, thirst alone isn't a good indication of how much fluid you need to drink. As a rule of thumb, drink at least 2 cups (16 ounces) of fluid 2 hours before exercise and then drink enough during exercise to match fluid loss in sweat—at least 1 cup of fluid every 20–30 minutes of exercise, more in hot weather or if you sweat heavily. To determine if you're drinking the right amount of fluid, weigh yourself before and after an exercise session: Any

QUICK STATS

There are more than **29,000** health clubs in the United States, serving nearly **43 million members.**

—International Health, Racquet and Sportsclub Association, 2007

Choosing Exercise Footwear

Footwear is perhaps the most important item of equipment for most activities. Shoes protect and support your feet and improve your traction. When you jump or run, you place as much as six times more force on your feet than when you stand still. Shoes can help cushion against the stress that this additional force places on your lower legs, thereby preventing injuries. Some athletic shoes are also designed to help prevent ankle rollover, another common source of injury.

General Guidelines

When choosing athletic shoes, first consider the activity you've chosen for your exercise program. Shoes appropriate for different activities have very different characteristics. For example, running shoes typically have highly cushioned midsoles, rubber outsoles with elevated heels, and a great deal of flexibility in the forefoot. The heels of walking shoes tend to be lower, less padded, and more beveled than those designed for running. For aerobic dance, shoes must be flexible in the forefoot and have straight, nonflared heels to allow for safe and easy lateral movements. Court shoes also provide substantial support for lateral movements; they typically have outsoles made from white rubber that will not damage court surfaces.

Also consider the location and intensity of your workouts. If you plan to walk or run on trails, choose shoes with water-resistant, highly durable uppers and more outsole traction. If you work out intensely or have a relatively high body weight, you'll need thick, firm midsoles to avoid bottoming-out the cushioning system of your shoes.

Foot type is another important consideration. If your feet tend to roll inward excessively, you may need shoes with additional stability features on their inner side to counteract this movement. If your feet tend to roll outward excessively, you may need highly flexible and cushioned shoes that promote foot motion. For aerobic dancers with feet that tend to roll inward or outward, mid-cut to high-cut shoes may be more appropriate than low-cut aerobic shoes or cross-trainers (shoes designed to be worn for several different activities). Compared with men, women have narrower feet overall and narrower heels relative to the forefoot. Most women will get a better fit if they choose shoes that are specifically designed for women's feet rather than those that are downsized versions of men's shoes.

Successful Shopping

For successful shoe shopping, keep the following strategies in mind:

• Shop at an athletic shoe or specialty store that has personnel trained to fit athletic shoes and a large selection of styles and sizes.

• Shop late in the day or, ideally, following a workout. Your foot size increases over the course of the day and as a result of exercise.

• Wear socks like those you plan to wear during exercise. If you have an old pair of athletic shoes, bring them with you. The wear pattern on your old shoes can help you select a pair with extra support or cushioning in the places you need it the most.

• Ask for help. Trained salespeople know which shoes are designed for your foot type and your level of activity. They can also help fit your shoes properly.

• Don't insist on buying shoes in what you consider to be your typical shoe size. Sizes vary from shoe to shoe. In addition, foot sizes change over time, and many people have one foot that is larger or wider than the other. Try several sizes in several widths, if necessary. Don't buy shoes that are too small.

• Try on both shoes, and wear them for 10 or more minutes. Try walking on a noncarpeted surface. Approximate the movements of your activity: walk, jog, run, jump, and so on.

• Check the fit and style carefully:

Is the toe box roomy enough? Your toes will spread out when your foot hits the ground or you push off. There should be at least one thumb's width of space from the longest toe to the end of the toe box.
Do the shoes have enough cushioning? Do your feet feel supported when you bounce up and down? Try bouncing on your toes and on your heels.
Do your heels fit snugly into the shoe? Do they stay put when you walk, or do they rise up?
Are the arches of your feet right on top of the shoes' arch supports?
Do the shoes feel stable when you twist and turn on the balls of your feet? Try twisting from side to side while standing on one foot.
Do you feel any pressure points?

• If the shoes are not comfortable in the store, don't buy them. Don't expect athletic shoes to stretch over time in order to fit your feet properly.

• If you exercise at dawn or dusk, choose shoes with reflective sections for added visibility and safety.

• Replace athletic shoes about every 3 months or 300–500 miles of jogging or walking.

weight loss is due to fluid loss that needs to be replaced. Any weight gain is due to over-consumption of fluid.

Bring a bottle of water when you exercise so you can replace your fluids when they're depleted. For exercise sessions lasting less than 60–90 minutes, cool water is an excellent fluid replacement. For longer workouts, a sports drink that contains water and small amounts of electrolytes (sodium, potassium, and magnesium) and simple carbohydrates (sugar, usually in the form of sucrose or glucose) is recommended.

Managing Your Fitness Program

How can you tell when you're in shape? When do you stop improving and start maintaining? How can you stay motivated? If your program is going to become an integral

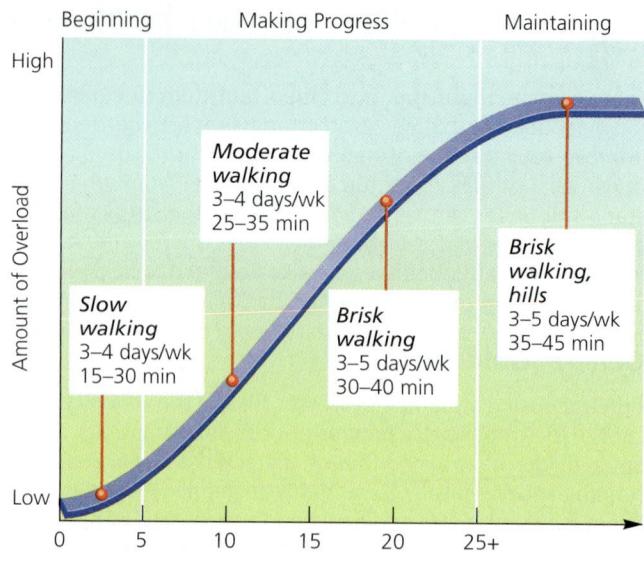

FIGURE 13.9 Progression of an exercise program. This figure shows how the amount of overload is increased gradually over time in a sample walking program. Regardless of the activity chosen, it is important that an exercise program begin slowly and progress gradually. Once you achieve the desired level of fitness, you can maintain it by exercising 3–5 days a week.

SOURCE: Progression data from American College of Sports Medicine. 2006. *ACSM's Guidelines for Exercise Testing and Prescription*, 7th ed. Philadelphia: Lippincott Williams & Wilkins.

THINKING ABOUT THE ENVIRONMENT

Wherever you see people exercising, you will see bottled water in abundance. For several years, however, a debate has been raging about the quality and safety of commercially bottled water. In recent months, new evidence has emerged showing that most bottled waters are no better for you than regular tap water, and some bottled waters may actually be bad for you.

In a 2008 analysis, the Environmental Working Group (EWG) found 38 different contaminants in ten popular brands of bottled water. Contaminants included heavy metals such as arsenic, pharmaceutical residues and other pollutants commonly found in urban wastewater, and a variety of industrial chemicals.

In recent years, government and private agencies have revealed that many commercially bottled water products are really just tap water drawn from municipal water systems. These products are priced many times higher than water from a residential tap. They also provide no benefit over standard tap water.

Further, plastic water bottles have become a huge solid waste problem, as millions of bottles end up in landfills each day. Once in a landfill, many kinds of plastic bottles will never decompose at all; at best, some types of plastic take years to biodegrade.

Experts say that when you're exercising, the cheapest and safest way to stay hydrated is to drink filtered tap water. If you need to carry water with you, buy a reusable container (preferably made of stainless steel) that can be cleaned and sterilized after each use. If you drink from plastic bottles, be sure they are recyclable and dispose of them by recycling.

For more information on the environment and environmental health, see Chapter 19.

part of your life, and if the principles behind it are going to serve you well in the future, these are key questions.

Start Slowly, Get in Shape Gradually As Figure 13.9 shows, an exercise program can be divided into three phases:

- *Beginning phase.* The body adjusts to the new type and level of activity.
- *Progress phase.* Fitness increases.
- *Maintenance phase.* The targeted level of fitness is sustained over the long term.

When beginning a program, start slowly to give your body time to adapt to the stress of exercise. Choose activities carefully, according to your fitness status; if you have been sedentary or are overweight, try an activity such as walking or swimming that won't jar the body or strain your joints.

Exercising Consistently Consistency is the key to getting into shape without injury. Steady fitness improvement comes when you overload your body consistently over a long period of time. The best way to ensure consistency is to keep a training journal in which you record the details of your workouts: how far you ran, how much weight you lifted, how many laps you swam, and so on. This record will help you evaluate your prog-

The 1.5-Mile Run-Walk Test

You can obtain a general rating of your cardiorespiratory fitness by taking the 1.5-mile run-walk test. Don't attempt this test unless you have completed at least 6 weeks of some type of conditioning activity. Also, if you are over age 35 or have questions about your health, check with your physician before taking this test.

You'll need a stopwatch, clock, or watch with a second hand and a running track or course that is flat and provides measurements of up to 1.5 miles. You may want to practice pacing yourself prior to taking the test to avoid going too fast at the start and becoming fatigued before you finish. Allow yourself a day or two to recover from a practice run before taking the test.

Warm up before taking the test with some walking, easy jogging, and stretching exercises. The idea is to cover the distance as fast as possible, at a pace that is comfortable for you. You can run or walk the entire distance or use some combination of running and walking. If possible, monitor your own pace, or have someone call out your time at various intervals to help you determine whether your pace is correct.

When you have completed the test, refer to the table for your cardiorespiratory fitness rating. Be sure to cool down by walking or jogging slowly for about 5 minutes.

Standards for the 1.5-Mile Run-Walk Test (minutes:seconds)

	Superior	Excellent	Good	Fair	Poor	Very Poor
Women						
Age: 18–29	11:00 or less	11:15–12:45	13:00–14:15	14:30–15:45	16:00–17:30	17:45 or more
30–39	11:45 or less	12:00–13:30	13:45–15:15	15:30–16:30	16:45–18:45	19:00 or more
40–49	12:45 or less	13:00–14:30	14:45–16:30	16:45–18:30	18:45–20:45	21:00 or more
50–59	14:15 or less	14:30–16:30	16:45–18:30	18:45–20:30	20:45–23:00	23:15 or more
60 and over	14:00 or less	14:15–17:15	17:30–20:15	20:30–22:45	23:00–24:45	25:00 or more
Men						
Age: 18–29	9:15 or less	9:30–10:30	10:45–11:45	12:00–12:45	13:00–14:00	14:15 or more
30–39	9:45 or less	10:00–11:00	11:15–12:15	12:30–13:30	13:45–14:45	15:00 or more
40–49	10:00 or less	10:15–11:45	12:00–13:00	13:15–14:15	14:30–16:00	16:15 or more
50–59	10:45 or less	11:00–12:45	13:00–14:15	14:30–15:45	16:00–17:45	18:00 or more
60 and over	11:15 or less	11:30–13:45	14:00–15:45	16:00–17:45	18:00–20:45	21:00 or more

SOURCES: *The Aerobics Program for Total Well Being,* by Kenneth H. Cooper, M.D. Copyright © 1982 by Kenneth H. Cooper. www.cooperaerobics.com. Used by permission of the author and Bantam Books, a division of Random House, Inc.

---

ress and plan your workout sessions intelligently. Don't increase your exercise volume by more than 5–10% per week.

Assessing Your Fitness When are you in shape? It depends. One person may be out of shape running a mile in 5 minutes; another may be in shape running a mile in 12 minutes. As mentioned earlier, your ultimate level of fitness depends on your goals, your program, and your natural ability. The important thing is to set goals that make sense for you.

If you are interested in finding out exactly how fit you are before you begin a program, the best approach is to get an assessment from a sports medicine laboratory. Such laboratories can be found in university physical education departments and medical centers. Here you will receive an accurate profile of your capacity to exercise. Typically, your endurance will be measured on a treadmill or bicycle, your body fat will be estimated, and your strength and flexibility will be tested. This evaluation will reveal whether your physical condition is consistent with good

health, and the staff members at the laboratory can suggest an exercise program that will be appropriate for your level of fitness. To assess your own approximate level of cardiorespiratory endurance, take the test in the box "The 1.5-Mile Run-Walk Test."

Preventing and Managing Athletic Injuries Although annoying, most injuries are neither serious nor permanent. However, an injury that is not cared for properly can escalate into a chronic problem. It is important to learn how to deal with injuries so they don't derail your fitness program (Table 13.4 on p. 408).

Some injuries require medical attention. Consult a physician for head and eye injuries, possible ligament injuries, broken bones, and internal disorders such as chest pain, fainting, and intolerance to heat. Also seek medical attention for apparently minor injuries that do not get better within a reasonable amount of time.

For minor cuts and scrapes, stop the bleeding and clean the wound with soap and water. Treat soft tissue injuries (muscles and joints) with the R-I-C-E principle:

Table 13.4 — Care of Common Exercise Injuries and Discomforts

Injury	Symptoms	Treatment
Blister	Accumulation of fluid in one spot under the skin	Don't pop or drain it unless it interferes too much with your daily activities. If it does pop, clean the area with antiseptic and cover with a bandage. Do not remove the skin covering the blister.
Bruise (contusion)	Pain, swelling, and discoloration	R-I-C-E: rest, ice, compression, elevation.
Fracture and/or dislocation	Pain, swelling, tenderness, loss of function, and deformity	Seek medical attention, immobilize the affected area, and apply cold.
Joint sprain	Pain, tenderness, swelling, discoloration, and loss of function	R-I-C-E. Apply heat when swelling has disappeared. Stretch and strengthen affected area.
Muscle cramp	Painful, spasmodic muscle contractions	Gently stretch for 15–30 seconds at a time and/or massage the cramped area. Drink fluids and increase dietary salt intake if exercising in hot weather.
Muscle soreness or stiffness	Pain and tenderness in the affected muscle	Stretch the affected muscle gently; exercise at a low intensity; apply heat. Nonsteroidal anti-inflammatory drugs, such as ibuprofen, help some people.
Muscle strain	Pain, tenderness, swelling, and loss of strength in the affected muscle	R-I-C-E; apply heat when swelling has disappeared. Stretch and strengthen the affected area.
Plantar fasciitis	Pain and tenderness in the connective tissue on the bottom of your feet	Apply ice, take nonsteroidal anti-inflammatory drugs, and stretch. Wear night splints when sleeping.
Shin splint	Pain and tenderness on the front of the lower leg; sometimes also pain in the calf muscle	Rest; apply ice to the affected area several times a day and before exercise; wrap with tape for support. Stretch and strengthen muscles in the lower legs. Purchase good-quality footwear and run on soft surfaces.
Side stitch	Pain on the side of the abdomen	Stretch the arm on the affected side as high as possible; if that doesn't help, try bending forward while tightening the abdominal muscles.
Tendinitis	Pain, swelling, and tenderness of the affected area	R-I-C-E; apply heat when swelling has disappeared. Stretch and strengthen the affected area.

SOURCE: Fahey, T. D., P. M. Insel, and W. T. Roth. 2009. *Fit and Well: Core Concepts and Labs in Physical Fitness and Wellness*, 8th ed. New York: McGraw-Hill. Copyright © 2009 The McGraw-Hill Companies, Inc.

Rest: Stop using the injured area as soon as you experience pain, protect it from further injury, and avoid any activity that causes pain.

Ice: Apply ice to the injured area to reduce swelling and alleviate pain. Apply ice immediately for 10–20 minutes, and repeat every few hours until the swelling disappears. Let the injured part return to normal temperature between icings, and do not apply ice to one area for more than 20 minutes (10 minutes if you are using a cold gel pack).

Compression: Wrap the injured area with an elastic or compression bandage between icings. If the area starts throbbing or begins to change color, the bandage may be wrapped too tightly. Do not sleep with the bandage on.

Elevation: Raise the injured area above heart level to decrease the blood supply and reduce swelling.

After about 36–48 hours, apply heat, if the swelling has completely disappeared, to help relieve pain, relax muscles, and reduce stiffness. Immerse the affected area in warm water or apply warm compresses, a hot water bottle, or a heating pad.

After a minor athletic injury, gradually reintroduce the stress of the activity until you are capable of returning to full intensity. Before returning to full exercise participation, you should have a full range of motion in your joints; normal strength and balance among your muscles; no injury-compensation movements, such as limping; and little or no pain.

To prevent injuries in the future, follow a few basic guidelines:

- Stay in condition; haphazard exercise programs invite injury.
- Warm up thoroughly before exercise.
- Use proper body mechanics when lifting objects or executing sports skills.
- Don't exercise when you're ill or overtrained (experiencing extreme fatigue due to overexercising).
- Use the proper equipment.
- Don't return to your normal exercise program until athletic injuries have healed.

You can minimize the risk of injury by following safety guidelines, using proper technique and equipment, re-

Maintaining Your Exercise Program

- *Set realistic goals.* Unrealistically high goals will only discourage you.

- *Sign a contract and keep a fitness journal.* A journal can help keep your program on track, identify sources of problems, and give you a continuing sense of accomplishment.

- *Start slowly, and increase your intensity and duration gradually.* Overzealous exercising can result in discouraging discomforts and injuries. Your program is meant to last a lifetime. The important first step is to break your established pattern of inactivity.

- *Make your program fun.* Participate in a variety of different activities that you enjoy. Vary the routes you take walking, running, or biking.

- *Exercise with a friend.* The social side of exercise is an important factor for many regular exercisers.

- *Focus on the positive.* Concentrate on the improvements you obtain from your program, how good you feel during and after exercise.

- *Revisit and revise.* If your program turns out to be unrealistic, revise it. Expect to make many adjustments in your program along the way.

- *Expect fluctuation.* On some days your progress will be excellent, whereas on others you'll barely be able to drag yourself through your scheduled activities.

- *Expect lapses.* Don't let lapses discourage you or make you feel guilty. Instead, feel a renewed commitment to your exercise program.

- *Plan ahead for difficult situations.* Think about what circumstances might make it tough to keep up with your fitness routine, and develop strategies for sticking with your program. For example, devise a plan for your program during vacation, travel, bad weather, and so on.

- *Reward yourself.* Give yourself frequent rewards for sticking with your program.

- *Renew your attitude.* If you notice you're slacking off, try to list the negative thoughts and behaviors that are causing noncompliance. Devise a strategy to decrease the frequency of negative thoughts and behaviors. Make changes in your program plan and reward system to help renew your enthusiasm and commitment.

- *Review your goals.* Visualize what it will be like to reach them, and keep these pictures in your mind as an incentive to stick to your program.

---

specting signals from your body that something may be wrong, and treating any injuries that occur. Warm up, cool down, and drink plenty of fluids before, during, and after exercise. Use special caution in extreme heat or humidity (over 80°F and/or 60% humidity): Exercise slowly, rest frequently in the shade, wear clothing that "breathes," and drink plenty of fluids; slow down or stop if you begin to feel uncomfortable. During hot weather, it's best to exercise in the early morning or evening, when temperatures are lowest.

Staying with Your Program Once you have attained your desired level of fitness, you can maintain it by exercising regularly at a consistent intensity, 3 to 5 days a week. You must work at the intensity that brought you to your desired fitness level. If you don't, your body will become less fit because less is expected of it. In general, if you exercise at the same intensity over a long period, your fitness will level out and can be maintained easily.

Adapt your program to changes in environment or schedule. Don't use wet weather or a new job as an excuse to give up your fitness program. If you walk in the summer, dress appropriately and walk in the winter as well. (Exercise is usually safe even in very cold temperatures as long as you dress warmly in layers and don't stay out too long.) If you can't go out because of darkness or an unsafe neighborhood, walk in a local shopping mall or on campus or join a gym and walk on a treadmill.

What if you run out of steam? Although good health is an important *reason* to exercise, it's a poor *motivator* for consistent adherence to an exercise program. A variety of specific suggestions for staying with your program are given in the box "Maintaining Your Exercise Program" and in the Behavior Change Strategy at the end of the chapter. It's a good idea to have a meaningful goal, anything from fitting into the same-size jeans you used to wear to successfully skiing down a new slope.

Varying your program is another key strategy. Some people alternate two or more activities—swimming and jogging, for example—to improve a particular component of fitness. The practice, called **cross-training**, can help prevent boredom and overuse injuries. Explore many exercise options. Consider competitive sports at the recreational level: swimming, running, racquetball, volleyball, golf, and so on. Find out how you can participate in an activity you've never done before: canoeing, hang gliding, windsurfing, backpacking. Try new activities, especially ones that you will be able to do for the rest of your life.

cross-training Participating in two or more activities to develop a particular component of fitness.

SUMMARY

- The five components of physical fitness most important to health are cardiorespiratory endurance, muscular strength, muscular endurance, flexibility, and body composition.

- Exercise improves the functioning of the heart and the ability of the cardiorespiratory system to carry oxygen to the body's tissues. It also increases the efficiency of the body's metabolism and improves body composition.

- Exercise lowers the risk of cardiovascular disease by improving blood fat levels, reducing high blood pressure, and interfering with the disease process that causes coronary artery blockage.

- Exercise reduces the risk of cancer, osteoporosis, and diabetes. It improves immune function and psychological health and helps prevent injuries and low-back pain.

- Everyone should accumulate at least 30–60 minutes per day of moderate endurance-type physical activity. Additional health and fitness benefits can be achieved through longer or more vigorous activity.

- Cardiorespiratory endurance exercises stress a large portion of the body's muscle mass. Endurance exercise should be performed 3–5 days per week for a total of 20–60 minutes per day. Intensity can be evaluated by measuring the heart rate.

- Warming up before exercising and cooling down afterward improve your performance and decrease your chances of injury.

- Exercises that develop muscular strength and endurance involve exerting force against a significant resistance. A strength training program for general fitness typically involves one set of 8–12 repetitions of 8–10 exercises, at least 2 nonconsecutive days per week.

- A good stretching program includes exercises for all the major muscle groups and joints of the body. Do a series of active, static stretches 2–3 days per week, ideally 5–7 days per week. Hold each stretch for 15–30 seconds; do two to four repetitions. Stretch when muscles are warm.

- Instructors, equipment, and facilities should be chosen carefully to enhance enjoyment and prevent injuries.

- A well-balanced diet contains all the energy and nutrients needed to sustain a fitness program. When exercising, remember to drink enough fluids.

- Rest, ice, compression, and elevation (R-I-C-E) are treatments for muscle and joint injuries.

- A desired level of fitness can be maintained by exercising 3 to 5 days a week at a consistent intensity.

- Strategies for maintaining an exercise program over the long term include having meaningful goals, varying the program, and trying new activities.

FOR MORE INFORMATION

BOOKS

Fahey, T. 2007. *Basic Weight Training for Men and Women*, 6th ed. New York: McGraw-Hill. *Weight training and plyometric exercises for fitness, weight control, and improved sports performance.*

Fahey, T., P. Insel, and W. Roth. 2009. *Fit and Well: Core Concepts and Labs in Physical Fitness and Wellness*, 8th ed. New York: McGraw-Hill. *A comprehensive guide to developing a complete fitness program.*

Fenton, M. 2008. *The Complete Guide to Walking, New and Revised: For Health, Weight Loss, and Fitness*. Guildford, Conn.: Lyons Press. *Discusses walking as a fitness method and a way to avoid diseases such as diabetes.*

Gotlin, R. 2007. *Sport Injuries Guidebook.* Champaign, Ill.: Human Kinetics. *Provides information and care instructions on many types of sports-related injuries.*

Nelson, A. G., et al. 2006. *Stretching Anatomy.* Champaign, Ill.: Human Kinetics. *A guide to stretching that features highly detailed illustrations of the muscles affected by each exercise.*

Nieman, D. C. 2007. *Exercise Testing and Prescription. A Health-Related Approach,* 6th ed. New York: McGraw-Hill. *A comprehensive discussion of the effects of exercise and exercise testing and prescription.*

ORGANIZATIONS, HOTLINES, AND WEB SITES

American Academy of Orthopaedic Surgeons. Provides fact sheets on many fitness and sports topics, including how to begin a program, how to choose equipment, and how to prevent and treat many types of injuries.

http://orthoinfo.aaos.org

American College of Sports Medicine. Provides brochures, publications, and audio- and videotapes on the positive effects of exercise.

http://www.acsm.org

American Council on Exercise. Promotes exercise and fitness for all Americans; the Web site features fact sheets on many consumer topics, including choosing shoes, cross-training, steroids, and getting started on an exercise program.

http://www.acefitness.org

American Heart Association: MyStart! Provides practical advice for people of all fitness levels plus an online fitness diary.

http://www.americanheart.org/presenter.jhtml?identifier=3040839

CDC Physical Activity Information. Provides information on the benefits of physical activity and suggestions for incorporating moderate physical activity into daily life.

http://www.cdc.gov/nccdphp/dnpa

Disabled Sports USA. Provides sport and recreation services to people with physical or mobility disorders.

http://www.dsusa.org

Federal Trade Commission: Consumer Protection—Diet, Health, and Fitness. Provides several brochures with consumer advice about purchasing exercise equipment.

http://www.ftc.gov/bcp/menus/consumer/health.shtm

Georgia State University: Exercise and Physical Fitness Page. Provides information about the benefits of exercise and how to get started on a fitness program.

http://www.gsu.edu/~wwwfit

Mayo Clinic Healthy Living Centers: Fitness. Offers information on incorporating physical activity and exercise into your daily life.

http://www.mayoclinic.com/health/fitness/SM99999

MedlinePlus: Exercise and Physical Fitness. Provides links to news and reliable information about fitness and exercise from government agencies and professional associations.

http://www.nlm.nih.gov/medlineplus/
exerciseandphysicalfitness.html

National Institute on Drug Abuse: Anabolic Steroid Abuse. Provides information and links about the dangers of anabolic steroids.

http://www.steroidabuse.org

President's Council on Physical Fitness and Sports (PCPFS). Provides information on PCPFS programs and publications.

http://www.fitness.gov
http://www.presidentschallenge.org

SmallStep.gov. Provides resources for increasing activity and improving diet through small changes in daily habits.

http://www.smallstep.gov

World Health Organization (WHO): Move for Health. Provides information about the WHO initiative to promote increased physical activity.

http://www.who.int/moveforhealth/en/

See also the listings for Chapters 12, 14, and 15.

SELECTED BIBLIOGRAPHY

American Cancer Society. 2006. *Cancer Prevention and Early Detection: Facts and Figures 2006.* Atlanta, Ga.: American Cancer Society.

American College of Sports Medicine. 2006. *ACSM's Guidelines for Exercise Testing and Prescription,* 7th ed. Philadelphia: Lippincott Williams & Wilkins.

American College of Sports Medicine. 2006. *ACSM's Resource Manual for Guidelines for Exercise Testing and Prescription,* 5th ed. Philadelphia: Lippincott Williams & Wilkins.

American Heart Association. 2008. *Heart Disease and Stroke Statistics—2008 Update.* Dallas: American Heart Association.

Armstrong, L. E., et al. 2007. American College of Sports Medicine position stand: Exertional heat illness during training and competition. *Medicine and Science in Sports and Exercise* 39(3): 556–572.

Bertoli, S., et al. 2006. Nutritional status and dietary patterns in disabled people. *Nutrition Metabolism and Cardiovascular Diseases* 16(2): 100–112.

Brooks, G. A., et al. 2005. *Exercise Physiology: Human Bioenergetics and Its Applications,* 4th ed. New York: McGraw-Hill.

Brownson, R. C., T. K. Boehmer, and D. A. Luke. 2005. Declining rates of physical activity in the United States: What are the contributors? *Annual Review of Public Health* 26: 421–443.

Burke, L. M., et al. 2006. Energy and carbohydrate for training and recovery. *Journal of Sports Science* 24(7): 675–685.

Carnathon, M. R., M. Gulati, and P. Greenland. 2006. Prevalence and cardiovascular disease correlates of low cardiorespiratory fitness in adolescents and adults. *Journal of the American Medical Association* 294(23): 2981–2988.

Centers for Disease Control and Prevention. 2008. Prevalence of self-reported physically active adults—United States, 2007. *Morbidity and Mortality Weekly Report* 57(48): 1297–1300.

Colbert, L. H., et al. 2004. Physical activity, exercise, and inflammatory markers in older adults: Findings from the health, aging and body composition study. *Journal of the American Geriatrics Society* 52: 1098–1104.

Cooper, C. B. 2006. Exercise testing does not have to be complicated. *Chronic Respiratory Disease* 3(2): 107–108.

Dal Maso, L., et al. 2006. Lifetime occupational and recreational physical activity and risk of benign prostatic hyperplasia. *International Journal of Cancer* 118(10): 2632–2635.

Dishman, R. K., et al. 2006. Neurobiology of exercise. *Obesity* (Silver Spring) 14(3): 345–356.

Dugan, S. 2005. Safe exercise for women. *ACSM Fit Society Page,* Winter.

Dunn, A. L., et al. 2005. Exercise treatment for depression: Efficacy and dose response. *American Journal of Preventive Medicine* 28(1): 1–8.

Fahey, T. D., P. M. Insel, and W. T. Roth. 2009. *Fit and Well: Core Concepts and Labs in Physical Fitness and Wellness,* 8th ed. New York: McGraw-Hill.

Fenicchia, L. M., et al. 2004. Influence of resistance exercise training on glucose control in women with type 2 diabetes. *Metabolism* 53(3): 284–289.

Food and Nutrition Board, Institute of Medicine, National Academies. 2002. *Dietary Reference Intakes for Energy, Carbohydrates, Fiber, Fat, Protein and Amino Acids (Macronutrients).* Washington, D.C.: National Academy Press.

Franco, O. H., et al. 2005. Effects of physical activity on life expectancy with cardiovascular disease. *Archives of Internal Medicine* 165(20): 2355–2360.

Gunter, M. J., and M. F. Leitzmann. 2006. Obesity and colorectal cancer: Epidemiology, mechanisms and candidate genes. *Journal of Nutritional Biochemistry* 17(3): 145–156.

Planning a Personal Exercise Program

Although most people recognize the importance of incorporating exercise into their lives, many find it difficult to do. No single strategy will work for everyone, but the general steps outlined here should help you create an exercise program that fits your goals, preferences, and lifestyle. A carefully designed contract and program plan can help you convert your vague wishes into a detailed plan of action. And the strategies for program compliance outlined here and in Chapter 1 can help you enjoy and stick with your program for the rest of your life.

Step 1: Set Goals

Setting specific goals to accomplish by exercising is an important first step in a successful fitness program because it establishes the direction you want to take. Your goals might be specifically related to health, such as lowering your blood pressure and risk of heart disease, or they might relate to other aspects of your life, such as improving your tennis game or the fit of your clothes. If you can decide why you're starting to exercise, it can help you keep going.

Think carefully about your reasons for incorporating exercise into your life, and then fill in the goals portion of the Personal Fitness Contract.

Step 2: Select Activities

As discussed in the chapter, the success of your fitness program depends on the consistency of your involvement. Select activities that encourage your commitment: The right program will be its own incentive to continue; poor activity choices provide obstacles and can turn exercise into a chore.

When choosing activities for your fitness program, consider the following:

- Is this activity fun? Will it hold my interest over time?

- Will this activity help me reach the goals I have set?

- Will my current fitness and skill level enable me to participate fully in this activity?

- Can I easily fit this activity into my daily schedule? Are there any special requirements (facilities, partners, equipment, etc.) that I must plan for?

- Can I afford any special costs required for equipment or facilities?

- If you have special exercise needs due to a particular health problem: Does this activity conform to those exercise needs? Will it enhance my ability to cope with my specific health problem?

Refer to Table 13.3, which summarizes the fitness benefits and other characteristics of many activities. Using the guidelines listed above, select a number of sports and activities. Fill in the Program Plan portion of the Fitness Contract, using Table 13.3 to include the fitness components your choices will develop and the frequency, intensity, and time standard you intend to meet for each activity. Does your program meet the criteria of a complete fitness program discussed in the chapter?

Step 3: Make a Commitment

Complete your Fitness Contract and Program Plan by signing your contract and having it witnessed and signed by someone who can help make you accountable for your progress. By completing a written contract, you will make a firm commitment and will be more likely to follow through until you meet your goals.

Step 4: Begin and Maintain Your Program

Start out slowly to allow your body time to adjust. Be realistic and patient—meeting your goals will take time. The following guidelines may help you start and stick with your program:

- Set aside regular periods for exercise. Choose times that fit in best with your schedule, and stick to them. Allow an adequate amount of time for warm-up, cool-down, and a shower.

- Take advantage of any opportunity for exercise that presents itself (for example, walk to class, take the stairs instead of the elevator).

- Do what you can to avoid boredom. Do stretching exercises or jumping jacks to music, or watch the evening news while riding your stationary bicycle.

- Exercise with a group that shares your goals and general level of competence.

- Vary the program. Change your activities periodically. Alter your route or distance if biking or jogging. Change racquetball partners, or find a new volleyball court.

- Establish minigoals or a point system, and work rewards into your program. Until you reach your main goals, a series of small rewards will help you stick with your program. Rewards should be things you enjoy that are easily obtainable.

Hambrecht, R., and S. Gielen. 2005. Essay: Hunter-gatherer to sedentary lifestyle. *Lancet* 366 (Suppl. 1): S60–S61.

Hart, L. 2006. Exercise therapy for nonspecific low-back pain: A meta-analysis. *Clinical Journal of Sports Medicine* 16(2): 189–190.

Haskell, W. L., et al. 2007. Physical activity and public health: Updated recommendations for adults from the American College of Sports Medicine and the American Heart Association. *Circulation* 116(9): 1081–1093.

John, E. M., P. L. Horn-Ross, and J. Koo. 2004. Lifetime physical activity and breast cancer risk in a multiethnic population. *Cancer Epidemiology, Biomarkers & Prevention* 12(11 Pt. 1): 1143–1152.

Kelly, C. W. 2005. Commitment to Health Scale. *Journal of Nursing Measurement* 13(3): 219–229.

Lakka, T. A., and C. Bouchard. 2005. Physical activity, obesity and cardiovascular diseases. *Handbook of Experimental Pharmacology* 2005(170): 137–163.

Larson, E. B., et al. 2006. Exercise is associated with reduced risk for incident dementia among persons 65 years of age and older. *Annals of Internal Medicine* 144(2): 73–81.

LaRoche, D. P., and D. A. Connolly. 2006. Effects of stretching on passive muscle tension and response to eccentric exercise. *American Journal of Sports Medicine* 34(6): 1000–1007.

Nattiv, A., et al. 2007. American College of Sports Medicine position stand: The female athlete triad. *Medicine and Science in Sports and Exercise* 39(10): 1867–1882.

Personal Fitness Contract

I, _____, am contracting with myself to follow an exercise program to work at the following goals. I will begin my program on _____ .

Fitness Goals

1. _____   4. _____
2. _____   5. _____
3. _____   6. _____

Program Plan

Activities	Components (Check ✔)					Frequency (Check ✔)							Intensity	Time
	CRE	MS	ME	F	BC	M	Tu	W	Th	F	Sa	Su		
1. _____														
2. _____														
3. _____														
4. _____														
5. _____														

Note: You should conduct activities for achieving CRE goals at your target heart rate.

I agree to maintain a record of my activity, assess my progress periodically, and, if necessary, revise my goals.

Signed _____   Date _____

Witness _____

Step 5: Record and Assess Your Progress

Keeping a record that notes the daily results of your program will help remind you of your ongoing commitment to your program and give you a sense of accomplishment. Create daily and weekly program logs that you can use to track your progress. Record the activity frequency, intensity, time, and type. Keep your log handy, and fill it in immediately after each exercise session. Post it in a visible place to remind you of your activity schedule and to provide incentive for improvement.

SOURCE: Adapted from Kusinitz, I., and M. Fine. 1995. *Your Guide to Getting Fit,* 3rd ed. Mountain View, Calif.: Mayfield.

Nelson, M. E., et al. 2007. Physical activity and public health in older adults: Recommendations from the American College of Sports Medicine and the American Heart Association. *Medicine and Science in Sports and Exercise* 39(8): 1435–1445.

Pescatello, L. S., et al. 2004. American College of Sports Medicine position stand: Exercise and hypertension. *Medicine and Science in Sports and Exercise* 36(3): 533–553.

Physical Activity Guidelines Advisory Committee. 2008. *Physical Activity Guidelines Advisory Committee Report, 2008.* Washington, D.C.: U.S. Department of Health and Human Services.

Sawka, M. N., et al. 2005. Human water needs. *Nutritional Reviews* 63(6 Pt. 2): S30–S39.

Sawka, M. N., et al. 2007. American College of Sports Medicine position stand: Exercise and fluid replacement. *Medicine and Science in Sports and Exercise* 39(2): 377–390.

Shehab, R., et al. 2006. Pre-exercise stretching and sports-related injuries: Knowledge, attitudes and practices. *Clinical Journal of Sports Medicine* 16(3): 228–231.

U.S. Department of Health and Human Services. 2008. *2008 Physical Activity Guidelines for Americans.* Hyattsville, Md.: U.S. Department of Health and Human Services. ODPHP Publication U0036.

Vaz, M., et al. 2005. A compilation of energy costs of physical activities. *Public Health Nutrition* 8(7A): 1153–1183.

WEIGHT MANAGEMENT

LOOKING AHEAD>>>>>

AFTER READING THIS CHAPTER, YOU SHOULD BE ABLE TO:

- Discuss different methods for assessing body weight and body composition
- Explain the health risks associated with overweight and obesity
- Explain factors that may contribute to a weight problem, including genetic, physiological, lifestyle, and psychosocial factors
- Describe lifestyle factors that contribute to weight gain and loss, including the roles of diet, exercise, and emotional factors
- Identify and describe the symptoms of eating disorders and the health risks associated with them
- Design a personal plan for successfully managing body weight

TEST YOUR KNOWLEDGE

1. **About what percentage of American adults are overweight?**
   a. 15%
   b. 35%
   c. 65%

2. **Genetic factors explain most cases of obesity.**
   True or false?

3. **The consumption of low-calorie sweeteners has helped Americans control their weight.**
   True or false?

4. **Approximately how many female high school and college students have either anorexia or bulimia?**
   a. 0%
   b. 1%
   c. 2%

5. **Which of the following is the most significant risk factor for type 2 diabetes (the most common type of diabetes)?**
   a. smoking
   b. low-fiber diet
   c. overweight or obesity
   d. inactivity

ANSWERS

1. **C.** About 66% of American adults are overweight, including approximately 33% of adult men and 35% of adult women who are obese.

2. **FALSE.** Genetic factors may increase an individual's tendency to gain weight, but lifestyle is the key contributing factor.

3. **FALSE.** Since the introduction of low-calorie sweeteners, both total calorie intake and total sugar intake have increased, as has the proportion of Americans who are overweight.

4. **C.** About 2–4% of female students suffer from bulimia or anorexia, and many more occasionally engage in behaviors associated with these eating disorders.

5. **C.** All four are risk factors for diabetes, but overweight or obesity is the most significant. It's estimated that 90% of cases of type 2 diabetes could be prevented if people adopted healthy lifestyle behaviors.

Achieving and maintaining a healthy body weight is a serious public health challenge and a source of distress for many Americans. Under standards developed by the National Institutes of Health (NIH), about 66% of American adults are overweight, including more than 34% who are obese (Figure 14.1). In 2005–2006, 33% of adult men and 35% of adult women were obese. In the United States, the number of obese adults doubled between 1980 and 2004, although obesity rates have begun leveling off since 2003. Even so, experts say that by 2015, 75% of adults will be overweight and 41% will be obese. By 2030, it is estimated that the entire American adult population will be overweight or obese. And while millions struggle to lose weight, others fall into dangerous eating patterns such as binge eating or self-starvation.

Although not completely understood, managing body weight is not a mysterious process. It's simply a matter of balancing calories consumed with calories expended in daily activities—in other words, eating a moderate diet and exercising regularly. Unfortunately, this is not as exciting as the latest fad diet or "scientific breakthrough" that promises rapid weight loss without effort. Many people fail in their efforts to manage their weight because they focus on short-term weight loss rather than permanent changes in lifestyle. Successful weight management requires the long-term coordination of many aspects of a wellness lifestyle, including proper nutrition, adequate physical activity, and stress management.

This chapter explores the factors that contribute to the development of overweight and to eating disorders. It also takes a closer look at weight management through lifestyle behaviors and suggests specific strategies for reaching and maintaining a healthy weight.

BASIC CONCEPTS OF WEIGHT MANAGEMENT

If you are like most people, you are concerned about your weight. But how do you decide if you are overweight? At what point does being overweight present a health risk? And how thin is too thin?

Body Composition

The human body can be divided into fat-free mass and body fat. Fat-free mass is composed of all the body's non-fat tissues: bone, water, muscle, connective tissue, organ tissues, and teeth. There are two types of body fat:

- **Subcutaneous fat** includes *lipids,* or fats, incorporated in the nerves, brain, heart, lungs, liver, and mammary glands. These fat deposits, which are crucial for normal body functioning, make up approximately 3–5% of total body weight in men and 8–12% in women. The

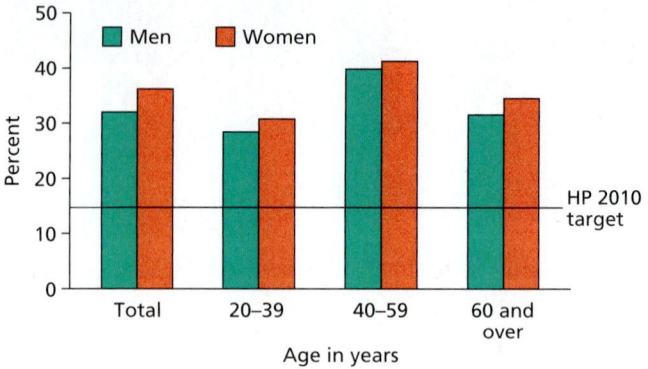

FIGURE 14.1   Obesity prevalence, by age and sex, of American adults, 2005–2006.   *Healthy People 2010 sets a target obesity prevalence of not greater than 15% for all adults.*

SOURCE: Ogden, C. L., et al. 2007. Obesity among adults in the United States. No change since 2003–2004. *NCHS Data Brief No. 1.* Hyattsville, MD: National Center for Health Statistics.

larger percentage in women is due to fat deposits in the breasts, uterus, and other sites specific to females.

- **Visceral fat** exists primarily within *adipose tissue,* or fat cells, often located just below the skin and around major organs, behind the *abdominal wall* (the wall of muscle between the skin and digestive organs). The amount of visceral fat varies from person to person based on many factors, including gender, age, heredity, metabolism, diet, and activity level. When we talk about wanting to lose weight, most of us are referring to visceral fat.

A pound of body fat is equal to 3500 calories. This means that having only an extra 10 calories per day will equal a one-pound weight gain over the course of a year. In 10 years, this would amount to a 10-pound weight

subcutaneous fat   The fats incorporated in various tissues of the body; critical for normal body functioning.

visceral fat   The fat inside the abdominal wall in and around the internal organs. An excess leads to a greater risk of heart disease, insulin resistance, and metabolic syndrome.

percent body fat   The percentage of total body weight that is composed of fat.

overweight   Body weight that falls above the recommended range for good health.

obesity   The condition of having an excess of nonessential body fat; having a body mass index of 30 or greater or having a percent body fat greater than about 25% for men and 33% for women.

body mass index (BMI)   A measure of relative body weight that takes height into account and is highly correlated with more direct measures of body fat; calculated by dividing total body weight (in kilograms) by the square of height (in meters).

TERMS

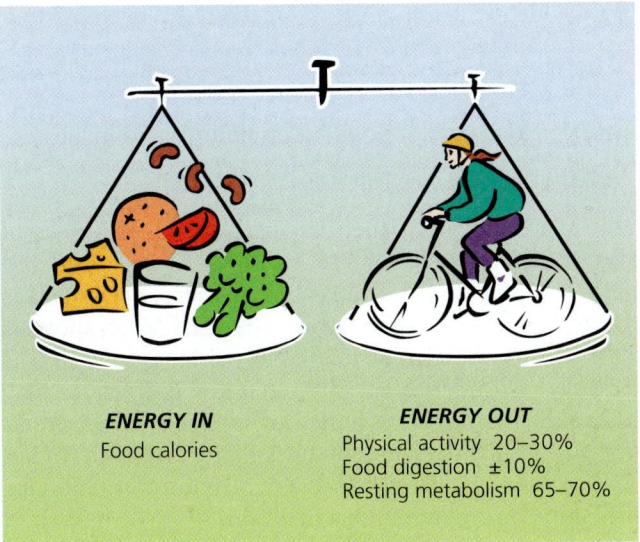

ENERGY IN
Food calories

ENERGY OUT
Physical activity 20–30%
Food digestion ±10%
Resting metabolism 65–70%

FIGURE 14.2 **The energy balance equation.**

gain. What is most important for health is not total weight but rather the proportion of the body's total weight that is fat—the **percent body fat.**

For example, two women may both be 5 feet, 5 inches tall and weigh 130 pounds. But one woman, an endurance runner, may have only 15% of her body weight as fat, whereas the other woman, who is sedentary, may have 34% body fat. Although 130 pounds is not considered overweight for women of this height by most standards, the sedentary woman may be overfat. (Methods for measuring and evaluating percent body fat are presented later in this chapter.) Because most people use the word "overweight" to describe the condition of having too much body fat, we use it in this chapter, although "overfat" is actually a more accurate term.

Energy Balance

The key to keeping a healthy ratio of fat to fat-free mass is maintaining an energy balance (Figure 14.2). You take in energy (calories) from the food you eat. Your body uses energy (calories) to maintain vital body functions (resting metabolism), to digest food, and to fuel physical activity. When energy in equals energy out, you maintain your current weight. To change your weight and body composition, you must tip the energy balance equation in a particular direction. If you take in more calories daily than your body burns (a *positive* energy balance), the excess calories will be stored as fat and you will gain weight over time. If you eat fewer calories than you burn each day (a *negative* energy balance), you will lose some of the stored fat and probably lose weight.

If we look at the energy balance equation today as expressed for the general American population, the equation is tipped heavily toward the energy-in side. Our

environment is rich in large portion sizes; high-fat, high-calorie foods; and palatable, easily available, and inexpensive foods. Unfortunately, the energy-out side of the equation has not compensated for increased energy intake; instead, we've decreased work-related physical activity, decreased activity associated with daily living, and increased time spent in sedentary pastimes like TV watching and computer use.

The good news, however, is that you control both parts of the energy balance equation. Specific strategies for altering energy balance are discussed later in the chapter.

Evaluating Body Weight and Body Composition

Overweight is usually defined as total body weight above the recommended range for good health (as determined by large-scale population surveys). **Obesity** is defined as a more serious degree of overweight. Many methods are available for measuring and evaluating body weight and percent body fat; the cutoff points for defining overweight and obesity vary with the method chosen.

Height-Weight Charts In the past, many people relied on height-weight charts to evaluate body weight. Based on insurance company statistics, these charts list a range of ideal or recommended body weights associated with the lowest mortality for people of a particular sex, age, and height. Although easy to use, height-weight charts can be highly inaccurate for some people, and they provide only an indirect measure of body fat.

Body Mass Index Body mass index (BMI) is a measure of body weight that is useful for classifying the health risks of body weight if you don't have access to more sophisticated methods. Though more accurate than height-weight tables, BMI is also based on the concept that weight should be proportional to height. Easy to calculate and rate, BMI is a fairly accurate measure of the health risks of body weight for average people. Researchers frequently use BMI in conjunction with waist circumference in studies that examine the health risks associated with body weight.

However, because BMI does not distinguish between fat weight and fat-free weight, it can be very inaccurate for some groups, including short people (under 5 feet tall), muscular athletes, and older adults with little muscle mass due to inactivity or an underlying disease. If you are in one of these groups, use one of the methods described in the next section for estimating percent body fat to assess whether your current weight and body composition are healthy. BMI is also not particularly useful for tracking changes in body composition—gains in muscle mass and losses of fat. Women are likely to have more body fat for a given BMI than men.

You can calculate your BMI by dividing your body weight (expressed in kilograms) by the square of your height (expressed in meters). You can look up your BMI by using the chart in Figure 14.3, or use the following formula to calculate it more precisely. The formula is based on a person who is 5 feet, 3 inches tall (63 inches) and weighs 130 pounds:

1. Divide your body weight in pounds by 2.2 to convert the amount to kilograms:

   $130 \div 2.2 = 59.1$

2. Multiply your height in inches by 0.0254 to convert the amount to meters:

   $63 \times 0.0254 = 1.6$

3. Multiply the result of step 2 by itself to get the square of the height measurement:

   $1.6 \times 1.6 = 2.56$

4. Divide the result of step 1 by the result of step 3 to determine your BMI:

   $59.1 \div 2.56 = 23$

An alternative equation, based on pounds and inches, is

$$BMI = [weight / (height \times height)] \times 703$$

Under standards issued by the National Institutes of Health, a BMI between 18.5 and 24.9 is considered healthy; a person with a BMI of 25 or above is classified as overweight, and a person with a BMI of 30 or above is classified as obese. A person with a BMI below 18.5 is classified as underweight, although low BMI values may be healthy in some cases if they are not the result of smoking, an eating disorder, or an underlying disease; a BMI of 17.5 or less is sometimes used as a diagnostic criterion for the eating disorder anorexia nervosa.

Body Composition Analysis   The most accurate and direct way to evaluate body composition is to determine percent body fat. A variety of methods are available, but it is worth noting that the NIH and the World Health Organization (WHO) have not established specific guidelines for body composition assessment. See Table 14.1 for body composition ratings based on percent body fat; as with BMI, the percent body fat ratings indicate cutoff points for health risks associated with underweight and obesity.

	<18.5 Underweight		18.5–24.9 Normal						25–29.9 Overweight					30–34.9 Obesity (Class I)					35–39.9 Obesity (Class II)					≥40 Extreme obesity
BMI	17	18	19	20	21	22	23	24	25	26	27	28	29	30	31	32	33	34	35	36	37	38	39	40
Height								Body Weight (pounds)																
4' 10"	81	86	91	96	101	105	110	115	120	124	129	134	139	144	148	153	158	163	168	172	177	182	187	192
4' 11"	84	89	94	99	104	109	114	119	124	129	134	139	144	149	154	159	163	168	173	178	183	188	193	198
5'	87	92	97	102	108	113	118	123	128	133	138	143	149	154	159	164	169	174	179	184	190	195	200	205
5' 1"	90	95	101	106	111	117	122	127	132	138	143	148	154	159	164	169	175	180	185	191	196	201	207	212
5' 2"	93	98	104	109	115	120	126	131	137	142	148	153	159	164	170	175	181	186	191	197	202	208	213	219
5' 3"	96	102	107	113	119	124	130	136	141	147	153	158	164	169	175	181	186	192	198	203	209	215	220	226
5' 4"	99	105	111	117	122	128	134	140	146	152	157	163	169	175	181	187	192	198	204	210	216	222	227	233
5' 5"	102	108	114	120	126	132	138	144	150	156	162	168	174	180	186	192	198	204	210	216	222	229	235	241
5' 6"	105	112	118	124	130	136	143	149	155	161	167	174	180	186	192	198	205	211	217	223	229	236	242	248
5' 7"	109	115	121	128	134	141	147	153	160	166	173	179	185	192	198	204	211	217	224	230	236	243	249	256
5' 8"	112	118	125	132	138	145	151	158	165	171	178	184	191	197	204	211	217	224	230	237	244	250	257	263
5' 9"	115	122	129	136	142	149	156	163	169	176	183	190	197	203	210	217	224	230	237	244	251	258	264	271
5' 10"	119	126	133	139	146	153	160	167	174	181	188	195	202	209	216	223	230	237	244	251	258	265	272	279
5' 11"	122	129	136	143	151	158	165	172	179	187	194	201	208	215	222	230	237	244	251	258	265	273	280	287
6'	125	133	140	148	155	162	170	177	184	192	199	207	214	221	229	236	243	251	258	266	273	280	288	295
6' 1"	129	137	144	152	159	167	174	182	190	197	205	212	220	228	235	243	250	258	265	273	281	288	296	303
6' 2"	132	140	148	156	164	171	179	187	195	203	210	218	226	234	242	249	257	265	273	281	288	296	304	312
6' 3"	136	144	152	160	168	176	184	192	200	208	216	224	232	240	248	256	264	272	280	288	296	304	312	320
6' 4"	140	148	156	164	173	181	189	197	206	214	222	230	238	247	255	263	271	280	288	296	304	312	321	329

FIGURE 14.3   Body mass index (BMI).   To determine your BMI, find your height in the left column. Move across the appropriate row until you find the weight closest to your own. The number at the top of the column is the BMI at that height and weight.

SOURCE: Ratings from National Heart, Lung, and Blood Institute. 1998. *Clinical Guidelines on the Identification, Evaluation, and Treatment of Overweight and Obesity in Adults: The Evidence Report*. Bethesda, Md.: National Institutes of Health.

Table 14.1	Percentage of Body Fat as the Criterion for Obesity	
	Percent Body Fat	
Category	Males	Females
Normal	12–20%	20–30%
Borderline	21–25%	31–33%
Obese	>25%	>33%

SOURCE: Bray, G. A. 2003. *Contemporary Diagnosis and Management of Obesity and the Metabolic Syndrome*, 3rd ed. Newton, Pa.: Handbooks in Health Care.

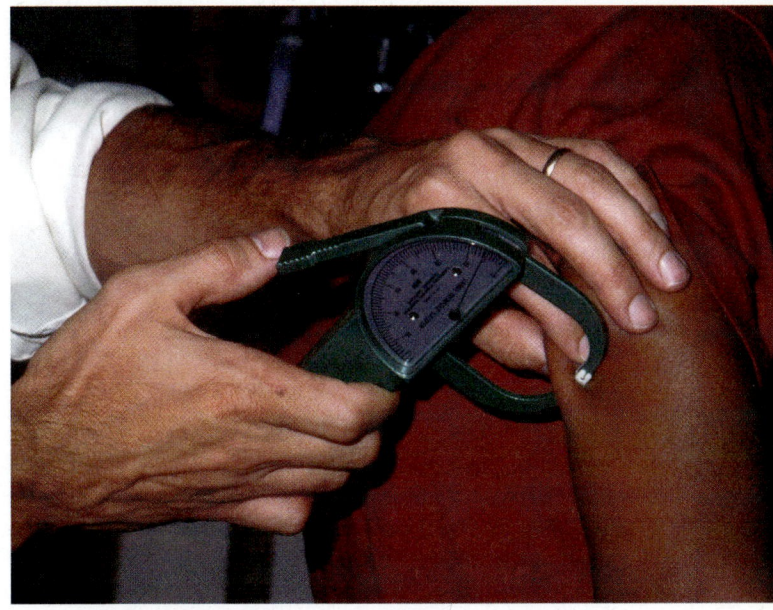

Calipers are used to perform skinfold measurements, which is a simple and inexpensive way to determine body fat levels. To assure accuracy, skinfold measurements must be done by someone with appropriate training.

HYDROSTATIC (UNDERWATER) WEIGHING AND BOD POD One of the most accurate techniques for analyzing body composition is hydrostatic weighing. In this method, a person is submerged and weighed under water. Percent body fat can be calculated from body density. Muscle has a higher density and fat a lower density than water, so people with more fat tend to float and weigh less under water, while lean people tend to sink and weigh more under water.

A specialized body composition analysis device called the Bod Pod uses air instead of water. A person sits in a chamber, and computerized pressure sensors determine the amount of air displaced by the person's body.

SKINFOLD MEASUREMENTS The skinfold thickness technique measures the thickness of fat under the skin. Measurements are taken at several sites and plugged into formulas that calculate body fat percentages.

ELECTRICAL IMPEDANCE ANALYSIS In this method, electrodes are attached to the body and a harmless electrical current is transmitted from electrode to electrode. The electrical conduction through the body favors the path of the fat-free tissues over the fat tissues. A computer can calculate fat percentages from measurements of current.

SCANNING PROCEDURES High-tech scanning procedures are highly accurate means of assessing body composition, but they require expensive equipment. These procedures include computed tomography (CT), magnetic resonance imaging (MRI), dual-energy X-ray absorptiometry (DEXA), and dual-photon absorptiometry. Other procedures include infrared reactance (Futrex 1100) and total body electrical conductivity (TOBEC).

Excess Body Fat and Wellness

The amount of fat in the body—and its location—can have profound effects on health.

The Health Risks of Excess Body Fat Obesity doubles mortality rates and can reduce life expectancy by 10–20 years. In fact, if the current trends in overweight and obe-

sity (and their related health problems) continue, scientists believe that the average American's life expectancy will soon decline by 5 years.

Obese people have a 50–100% increased risk of death from all causes, compared with normal-weight persons. Obesity is associated with unhealthy cholesterol and triglyceride levels, impaired heart function, and death from cardiovascular disease. Other health risks include hypertension, many kinds of cancer, impaired immune function, gallbladder and kidney diseases, skin problems, impotence, sleep and breathing disorders, back pain, arthritis, and other bone and joint disorders. Obesity is also associated with complications of pregnancy, menstrual irregularities, urine leakage (stress incontinence), increased surgical risk, and psychological disorders and problems (such as depression, low self-esteem, and body dissatisfaction).

There is a strong association between excess body fat and diabetes mellitus, a disease that causes a disruption of normal metabolism. The pancreas normally secretes the hormone insulin, which stimulates cells to take up blood sugar (glucose) to produce energy (Figure 14.4 on p. 420). In diabetes, this process is disrupted, causing a buildup of glucose in the bloodstream. Diabetes is associated with kidney failure; nerve damage; circulation problems and amputations; retinal damage and blindness; and increased rates of heart attack, stroke, and hypertension. Excess body fat is a major risk factor for type 2 diabetes (the most common form of diabetes). Obese people are more than three times as likely to develop diabetes, and the incidence of

Symptoms of diabetes

- Frequent urination
- Extreme thirst and hunger
- Unexplained weight loss
- Extreme fatigue
- Blurred vision
- Frequent infections
- Slow wound healing
- Tingling or numbness in hands and feet
- Dry, itchy skin

Note: In the early stages, diabetes often has no symptoms.

Esophagus

Stomach

Pancreas

Small intestine

Normal

Insulin binds to receptors on the surface of a cell and signals special transporters in the cell to transport glucose inside.

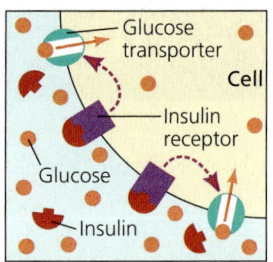

Glucose transporter

Cell

Insulin receptor

Glucose

Insulin

Type 1 diabetes

The pancreas produces little or no insulin. Thus, no signal is sent instructing the cell to transport glucose, and glucose builds up in the bloodstream.

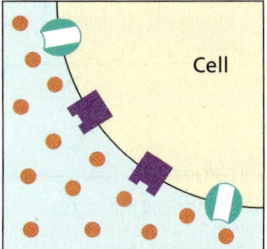

Cell

Type 2 diabetes

The pancreas produces too little insulin and/or the body's cells are resistant to it. Some insulin binds to receptors on the cell's surface, but the signal to transport glucose is blocked. Glucose builds up in the bloodstream.

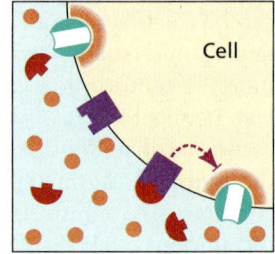

Cell

FIGURE 14.4 **Diabetes mellitus.** During digestion, carbohydrates are broken down in the small intestine into glucose, a simple sugar that enters the bloodstream. The presence of glucose signals the pancreas to release insulin, a hormone that helps cells take up glucose; once inside a cell, glucose can be converted to energy. In diabetes, this process is disrupted, resulting in a buildup of glucose in the bloodstream.

diabetes among Americans has increased dramatically as the rate of obesity has climbed. Diabetes is currently the seventh leading cause of death in the United States (see the box "Diabetes" on p. 421 for more information).

The risks from obesity increase with its severity, and they are much more likely to occur in people who are more than twice their desirable body weight. Controversy exists about the precise degree of risk at lower levels of overweight, particularly among overweight individuals who are physically active. The health risks associated with overweight depend in part on an individual's overall health and other risk factors, such as high blood pressure, unhealthy cholesterol levels, body fat distribution, and tobacco use. The NIH recommends weight loss for people whose BMI places them in the obese category and for those who are over-weight *and* have two or more major risk factors for disease. If your BMI is 25 or above, consult a physician for help in determining a healthy BMI for you.

Many people who are overweight have some of the risk factors associated with obesity. The Nurses' Health Study, in which Harvard researchers have followed more than 120,000 women since 1976, has found that even mildly to moderately overweight women have an 80% increased risk of developing CHD compared to leaner women. This study also confirmed that to reduce the risk of dying prematurely of any cause, maintaining a desirable body weight is important. This conclusion was supported by a 10-year study that ended in 2006 after following a half-million Americans in their fifties. Researchers concluded that subjects who were even slightly overweight were up to 40% more likely to die within the next decade, compared to age-matched people who had a desirable weight. But it is also important to realize that small weight losses— 5% to 10% of total body weight—can lead to significant health improvements.

Body Fat Distribution and Health The distribution of body fat (that is, the locations of fat on the body) is also

Diabetes

Types of Diabetes

About 24 million Americans (or 8% of the population) have one of two major forms of diabetes. About 5–10% of people with diabetes have the more serious form, known as *type 1 diabetes*. In this type of diabetes, the pancreas produces little or no insulin, so daily doses of insulin are required. Type 1 diabetes occurs when the body's immune system, triggered by a viral infection or some other environmental factor, mistakenly destroys the insulin-producing cells in the pancreas. It usually strikes before age 30.

The remaining 90–95% of Americans with diabetes have *type 2 diabetes,* and the prevalence is rising dramatically. This condition can develop slowly, and about 25% of affected individuals are unaware of their condition. In type 2 diabetes, the pancreas doesn't produce enough insulin, cells are resistant to insulin, or both. This condition is usually diagnosed in people over age 40, although there has been a tenfold increase in type 2 diabetes in children in the past two decades. About one-third of people with type 2 diabetes must take insulin; others may take medications that increase insulin production or stimulate cells to take up glucose.

A third type of diabetes occurs in about 7% of women during pregnancy. *Gestational diabetes* usually disappears after pregnancy, but more than half of women who experience it eventually develop type 2 diabetes.

The term *pre-diabetes* describes blood glucose levels that are higher than normal but not high enough for a diagnosis of full-blown diabetes. About 57 million Americans have pre-diabetes, and most people with the condition will develop type 2 diabetes unless they adopt preventive lifestyle measures. Pre-diabetes poses a risk to health beyond just the development of diabetes: Blood glucose levels in the pre-diabetes range increase the risk of heart attack or stroke by 50%. The insulin resistance and elevated glucose levels associated with pre-diabetes (and diabetes) are among the defining risk factors of metabolic syndrome.

The major factors involved in the development of diabetes are age, obesity, physical inactivity, a family history of diabetes, and lifestyle. Excess body fat reduces cell sensitivity to insulin, and insulin resistance is almost always a precursor of type 2 diabetes.

Ethnic background also plays a role. According to statistics released by the CDC in 2008, the rate of diagnosed diabetes cases is highest among Native Americans and Alaska Natives (16.5%), followed by blacks (11.8%), Hispanics (10.4%), Asian Americans (7.5%), and white Americans (6.6%). Across all races, about 25% of Americans age 60 and older have diabetes.

Prevention

It is estimated that 90% of cases of type 2 diabetes could be prevented if people adopted healthy lifestyle behaviors, including regular physical activity, a moderate diet, and modest weight loss. For people with pre-diabetes, lifestyle measures are more effective than medication for delaying or preventing the development of diabetes. Studies of people with pre-diabetes show that just a 5–7% weight loss can lower diabetes onset by nearly 60%. Exercise (endurance and/or strength training) makes cells more sensitive to insulin and helps stabilize blood glucose levels; it also helps keep body fat at healthy levels.

A moderate diet to control body fat is perhaps the most important dietary recommendation for the prevention of diabetes. However, the composition of the diet may also be important. Studies have linked diets low in fiber and high in sugar, refined carbohydrates, saturated fat, red meat, and high-fat dairy products to increased risk of diabetes; diets rich in whole grains, fruits, vegetables, legumes, fish, and poultry may be protective. Specific foods linked to higher risk of diabetes include soft drinks, white bread, white rice, french fries, processed meats, and sugary desserts.

Treatment

There is no cure for diabetes, but it can be successfully managed by keeping blood sugar levels within safe limits through diet, exercise, and, if necessary, medication. Blood sugar levels can be monitored using a home test; close monitoring and control of glucose levels can significantly reduce the rate of serious complications. New drug therapies include inhibitors known as DDP-4, which lower blood sugar without causing weight gain.

Nearly 90% of people with type 2 diabetes are overweight when diagnosed, including 55% who are obese. An important step in treatment is to lose weight; even a small amount of weight loss can be beneficial. People with diabetes should get their carbohydrate from whole grains, fruits, vegetables, and low-fat dairy products; carbohydrate and monounsaturated fat together should provide 60–70% of total daily calories. Regular exercise and a healthy diet are often sufficient to control type 2 diabetes.

Warning Signs and Testing

Be alert for the warning signs of diabetes:

- Frequent urination
- Extreme hunger or thirst
- Unexplained weight loss
- Extreme fatigue
- Blurred vision
- Frequent infections
- Cuts and bruises that are slow to heal
- Tingling or numbness in hands or feet
- Generalized itching with no rash

The best way to avoid complications is to recognize these symptoms and get early diagnosis and treatment. Type 2 diabetes is often asymptomatic in the early stages, however, so routine screening is recommended for people over age 45 and anyone younger who is at high risk. Screening involves a blood test to check glucose levels after either a period of fasting or the administration of a set dose of glucose. A fasting glucose level of 126 mg/dl or higher indicates diabetes; a level of 100–125 mg/dl indicates pre-diabetes.

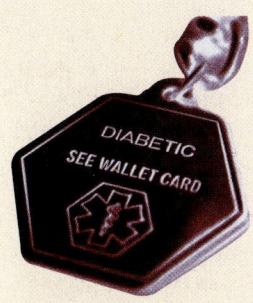

an important indicator of health. Men and postmenopausal women tend to store fat in the upper regions of their bodies, particularly in the abdominal area (the apple shape). Premenopausal women usually store fat in hips, buttocks, and thighs (the pear shape). Excess fat in the abdominal area increases risk of high blood pressure, diabetes, early-onset heart disease, stroke, certain types of cancer, and mortality. This risk is independent of a person's BMI. The reason for this increase in risk is not entirely clear, but it appears that abdominal fat is more easily mobilized and sent into the bloodstream, increasing disease-related blood fat levels.

The risks from body fat distribution are usually assessed by measuring waist circumference (the distance around the abdomen at the level of the hip bone, known as the iliac crest). Waist circumference can be used as a measure of abdominal obesity, an indicator of disease risk, and to monitor changes in body composition over time. More research is needed to determine the precise degree of risk associated with specific values for waist measurement. However, a total waist measurement of more than 40 inches (102 cm) for men and 35 inches (88 cm) for women is associated with a significantly increased risk of disease.

A person doesn't have to be technically overfat to have fat distribution be a risk factor, nor do all overfat people face this increased risk. The NIH BMI guidelines state that large waist circumference can be a marker for increased risk of diabetes, high blood pressure, and CVD even in people with a BMI in the normal range. And at any given level of overweight, people with a large waist circumference and/or additional disease risk factors are at greater risk for health problems. For example, a man with a BMI of 27, a waist circumference above 40 inches, and diabetes is at greater risk for health problems than another man who has a BMI of 27 but has a smaller waist and no other risk factors. Abdominal obesity and any two other risk factors associated with cardiovascular health put an individual at risk for metabolic syndrome. Abdominal obesity (as measured by waist circumference) is a primary component of metabolic syndrome and a forewarning of diabetes and heart disease.

Body Image The collective picture of the body as seen through the mind's eye, **body image** consists of perceptions, images, thoughts, attitudes, and emotions. A negative body image is characterized by dissatisfaction with the body in general or some part of the body in particular. Recent surveys indicate that the majority of Americans, many of whom are not actually overweight, are unhappy with their body weight or with some aspect of their appearance.

Losing weight or getting cosmetic surgery does not necessarily improve body image. However, improvements in body image may occur in the absence of changes in weight or appearance. Many experts now believe that body image issues must be dealt with as part of treating obesity and eating disorders. See pages 438–443 for more information on body image and eating disorders.

Problems Associated with Very Low Levels of Body Fat Health experts have generally viewed very low levels of body fat—less than 8–12% for women and 3–5% for men—as a threat to wellness. Extreme leanness has been linked with reproductive, circulatory, and immune system disorders. Extremely lean people may experience muscle wasting and fatigue; they are also more likely to suffer from dangerous eating disorders.

In physically active women and girls, particularly those involved in sports where weight and appearance are important (ballet, gymnastics, skating, and distance running, for example), a condition called the **female athlete triad** may develop. The triad consists of three interrelated disorders: abnormal eating patterns (and excessive exercising), followed by **amenorrhea** (absence of menstruation), followed by decreased bone density (premature osteoporosis). Prolonged amenorrhea can cause bone density to erode to a point that a woman in her twenties will have the bone density of a woman in her sixties. Left untreated, the triad can lead to decreased physical performance, increased incidence of bone fractures, disturbances of heart rhythm and metabolism, and even death.

What Is the Right Weight for You?

BMI, percent body fat, and waist circumference measurement can best serve as general guides or estimates for body weight (Table 14.2).

To answer the question of what you should weigh, let your lifestyle be your guide. Don't focus on a particular weight as your goal. Instead, focus on living a lifestyle that includes eating moderate amounts of healthful foods, getting plenty of exercise, thinking positively, and learning to cope with stress. Then let the pounds fall where they may. For most people, the result will be close to the recommended weight ranges discussed earlier. For some, their weight will be somewhat higher than societal standards—but right for them. By letting a healthy lifestyle determine your weight, you can avoid developing unhealthy patterns of eating and a negative body image.

Table 14.2   Body Mass Index (BMI) Classification and Disease Risk

Classification	BMI (kg/m²)	Obesity Class	Disease Risk Relative to Normal Weight and Waist Circumference[a]	
			Men ≤ 40 in. (102 cm) Women ≤ 35 in. (88 cm)	> 40 in. (102 cm) > 35 in. (88 cm)
Underweight[b]	<18.5		—	—
Normal[c]	18.5–24.9		—	—
Overweight	25.0–29.9		Increased	High
Obesity	30.0–34.9	I	High	Very high
	35.0–39.9	II	Very high	Very high
Extreme obesity	≥ 40.0	III	Extremely high	Extremely high

[a]Disease risk for type 2 diabetes, hypertension, and cardiovascular disease. The waist circumference cutoff points for increased risk are 40 inches (102 cm) for men and 35 inches (88 cm) for women.

[b]Research suggests that a low BMI can be healthy in some cases, as long as it is not the result of smoking, an eating disorder, or an underlying disease process. A BMI of 17.5 or less is sometimes used as a diagnostic criterion for the eating disorder anorexia nervosa.

[c]Increased waist circumference can also be a marker for increased risk, even in persons of normal weight.

SOURCE: Adapted from National Heart, Lung, and Blood Institute. 1998. *Clinical Guidelines on the Identification, Evaluation, and Treatment of Overweight and Obesity in Adults: The Evidence Report*. Bethesda, Md.: National Institutes of Health.

QUESTIONS FOR CRITICAL THINKING AND REFLECTION

Calculate your BMI using the formula given in this chapter, then compare it with the BMIs of some classmates. Do the results surprise you? How well do you think BMI reflects body composition? Why do you think it is such a commonly used measure?

FACTORS CONTRIBUTING TO EXCESS BODY FAT

Body weight and body composition may be determined by multiple factors that may vary with each individual. These factors can be grouped into genetic, physiological, lifestyle, and psychosocial factors.

Genetic Factors

Nutrigenomics is the study of how nutrients and genes interact and how genetic variations can cause people to respond differently to nutrients in food. Estimates of the genetic contribution to obesity vary widely, from about 25% to 40% of an individual's body fat. Scientists have so far identified more than 600 genes associated with obesity. Genes influence body size and shape, body fat distribution, and metabolic rate. Genetic factors also affect the ease with which weight is gained as a result of overeating and where on the body extra weight is added.

If both parents are obese, their children have an 80% risk of being obese; children with only one obese parent face a 40% risk of becoming obese. In studies that compared adoptees and their biological parents, the weights of the adoptees were found to be more like those of the biological parents than the adoptive parents, again indicating a strong genetic link.

Hereditary influences, however, must be balanced against the contribution of environmental factors. Not all children of obese parents become obese, and normal-weight parents may have overweight children. Environmental factors like diet and exercise are probably responsible for such differences. Thus, the *tendency* to develop obesity may be inherited, but the expression of this tendency is affected by environmental influences.

The message you should take from this research is that genes are not destiny. It is true that some people have a harder time losing weight and maintaining weight loss than others. However, with increased exercise and attention to diet, even those with a genetic tendency toward obesity can maintain a healthy body weight. And regardless of genetic factors, lifestyle choices remain the cornerstone of successful weight management.

body image   The mental representation a person holds about his or her body at any given moment in time, consisting of perceptions, images, thoughts, attitudes, and emotions about the body.

female athlete triad   A condition consisting of three interrelated disorders: abnormal eating patterns (and excessive exercising) followed by lack of menstrual periods (amenorrhea) and decreased bone density (premature osteoporosis).

amenorrhea   The absence of menstruation.

TERMS

Physiological Factors

Metabolism is a key physiological factor in the regulation of body fat and body weight; hormones and fat cell types also play a role.

Metabolism   Metabolism is the sum of all the vital processes by which food energy and nutrients are made available to and used by the body. The largest component of metabolism, **resting metabolic rate (RMR),** is the energy required to maintain vital body functions, including respiration, heart rate, body temperature, and blood pressure, while the body is at rest. As shown in Figure 14.2, RMR accounts for about 65–70% of daily energy expenditure. The energy required to digest food accounts for an additional ±10% of daily energy expenditure. The remaining 20–30% is expended during physical activity.

Both heredity and behavior affect metabolic rate. Men, who have a higher proportion of muscle mass than women, have a higher RMR because muscle tissue is more metabolically active than fat. Also, some individuals inherit a higher or lower RMR than others. A higher RMR means that a person burns more calories while at rest and can therefore take in more calories without gaining weight.

Weight loss or gain also affects metabolic rate. When a person loses weight, both RMR and the energy required to perform physical tasks decrease. The reverse occurs when weight is gained. One of the reasons exercise is so important during a weight-loss program is that exercise, especially resistance training, helps maintain muscle mass and metabolic rate.

Exercise has a positive effect on metabolism. When people exercise, they slightly increase their RMR—the number of calories their bodies burn at rest. They also increase their muscle mass, which is associated with a higher metabolic rate. The exercise itself also burns calories, raising total energy expenditure. The higher the energy expenditure, the more the person can eat without gaining weight. (The role of exercise in weight management is discussed in greater detail later in the chapter.)

Hormones   Hormones clearly play a role in the accumulation of body fat, especially for females. Hormonal changes at puberty, during pregnancy, and at menopause contribute to the amount and location of fat accumulation. For example, during puberty, hormones cause the development of secondary sex characteristics, including larger breasts, wider hips, and a fat layer under the skin.

One hormone thought to be linked to obesity is leptin. Secreted by the body's fat cells, leptin is carried to the brain, where it appears to let the brain know how big or small the body's fat stores are. With this information, the brain can regulate appetite and metabolic rate accordingly. Several other hormones may be involved in the regulation of appetite. Researchers hope to use these hormones to develop treatments for obesity based on appetite control; however, as most of us will admit, hunger is often *not* the primary reason we overeat. Cases of obesity based solely or primarily on hormone abnormalities do exist, but they are rare. Lifestyle choices still account for the largest proportion of the differences in body weight and body composition among individuals.

Fat Cells   The amount of fat (adipose tissue) the body can store is a function of the number and size of fat (adipose) cells. These fat cells are like little compartments that can inflate to hold body fat; when existing fat cells are filled, the body makes more, thereby increasing its ability to store fat.

Some people are born with an above-average number of fat cells and thus have the potential for storing more energy as body fat. Overeating at critical times, such as in childhood, can cause the body to create more fat cells. If a person loses weight, fat cell content is depleted, but it is unclear whether the number of fat cells can be decreased.

Further, it appears that all fat cells are not created equal. As mentioned earlier, visceral adipose tissue is located at waist level, inside the abdominal wall and surrounding the organs. This type of fat contains many biologically active substances such as inflammatory chemicals and growth factors, which can adhere to the lining of blood vessels, cause insulin resistance, and have a negative influence on cardiovascular health. The more visceral fat you have, the greater your chances of developing insulin resistance, metabolic syndrome, type 2 diabetes, and heart disease. Researchers consider visceral fat to be an active endocrine organ (like the pancreas), responsible for many of the pathological conditions of obesity. Visceral fat may also be the reason waist circumference is such a critical indicator of obesity risk.

In contrast, subcutaneous fat carries little or no health risk. Subcutaneous fat lies just under your skin, outside the abdominal wall. This fat tends to be soft and flabby (whereas visceral fat is hard) and is not metabolically active like visceral fat.

Found more often in women than men, subcutaneous fat appears on the lower body—the hips, upper thighs, and buttocks—a trait called *gynoid obesity* (Figure 14.5). As a result of their body shape, people with excess subcutaneous fat are described as "pears." People with excess visceral fat tend to carry it on their upper body (*android obesity*), and are called "apples." In terms of health risk, apples are bad and pears are good.

Lifestyle Factors

Although genetic and physiological factors may increase risk for excess body fat, they are not sufficient to explain

---

TERMS

resting metabolic rate (RMR)   The energy required to maintain vital body functions, including respiration, heart rate, body temperature, and blood pressure, while the body is at rest.

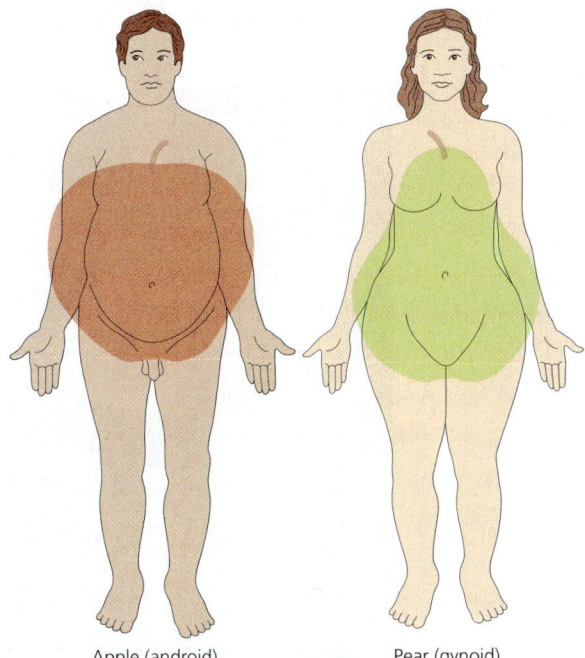

Apple (android)   Pear (gynoid)

FIGURE 14.5 Overweight men tend to have an apple (android) shape; overweight women tend to have a pear (gynoid) shape.

THINKING ABOUT THE ENVIRONMENT

Environmental factors can make weight management even more difficult for many people. In this case, it is the man-made environment, not the natural one, that creates obstacles to a healthy lifestyle:

- A noisy environment can make it difficult to sleep, and poor sleep quality has been associated with weight gain, difficulty in losing weight, and other conditions such as depression and high blood pressure.

- In some urban and high-poverty areas, it is not always easy to make ideal food choices because fresh, healthy foods may be more expensive or harder to obtain than cheaper, less healthy fast food or junk food.

- People who live in unsafe environments, such as some inner-city areas, may not get as much physical activity as they need, simply because there are not enough safe places to walk or exercise.

As you create your own weight-management program, remember to account for environmental factors that may interfere with your efforts. Creative solutions may be needed to keep your program on track.

For more information on health and the environment, see Chapter 19.

the increasingly high rate of obesity seen in the United States. The gene pool has not changed in the past 40 years, but the rate of obesity among Americans has more than doubled (see the box "Overweight and Obesity Among U.S. Ethnic Populations" on p. 426). Clearly, other factors are at work—particularly lifestyle factors such as increased eating and decreased physical activity.

QUICK STATS

Over 50% of adult, non-Hispanic black women are obese—a significantly higher rate than white or Mexican-American women.

—NCHS, 2007

Eating   Americans have access to plenty of calorie-dense foods, and many have eating habits that contribute to weight gain. Most overweight adults admit to eating more than they should of high-fat, high-sugar, high-calorie foods. Americans eat out more frequently now than in the past, and we rely more heavily on fast food and packaged convenience foods. Restaurant and convenience food portion sizes tend to be large, and the foods themselves are likely to be high in fat, sugar, and calories and low in nutrients. Studies have consistently found that people underestimate portion sizes by as much as 25%.

Americans' average calorie intake has increased by 18% since 1983. Many of those extra calories come from carbohydrates, such as refined sugars. The popularity of sugar-free soft drinks does not appear to be helping people lose weight (see the box "Are Diet Sodas Bad for You?" on p. 427). Levels of physical activity declined during this period. The result has been a substantial increase in the number of overweight and obese Americans. Eating for weight management is discussed later in this chapter.

Physical Activity   Research has shown that activity levels among Americans are declining, beginning in childhood and continuing throughout life. Many schools have cut back on physical education classes and recess. Most adults drive to work, sit all day, and then relax in front of the TV at night. One study found that 60% of the incidence of overweight can be linked to excessive television viewing. On average, Americans exercise 15 minutes per day and watch 170 minutes of TV and movies. Modern conveniences such as remote controls, elevators, and power mowers have also reduced daily physical activity.

Psychosocial Factors

Many people have learned to use food as a means of coping with stress and negative emotions. Eating can provide a powerful distraction from difficult feelings—loneliness, anger, boredom, anxiety, shame, sadness, inadequacy. It can be used to combat low moods, low energy levels, and low self-esteem (see the box "What Triggers Your Eating?" on p. 428). When food and eating become the primary

Overweight and Obesity Among U.S. Ethnic Populations

connect™

Among all population groups in the United States, the prevalence of overweight and obesity is growing. However, rates and trends vary by ethnic group and by other population characteristics.

• Certain groups, including African Americans, Latinos, and American Indians and Alaska Natives, have higher-than-average rates of obesity. Asian Americans have a low rate of obesity.

• There is considerable variation within populations grouped into general ethnic categories. For example, Asian Americans, Vietnamese Americans, and Chinese Americans have very low rates of obesity, and Asian Indians have much higher rates of obesity.

• Within all groups, women have higher rates of overweight and obesity than men.

• Low socioeconomic status is associated with higher rates of overweight and obesity. Researchers theorize that people living in poor communities are more greatly affected by a toxic food and exercise environment—meaning there are fewer opportunities to purchase healthy foods and safely engage in regular physical activity. In addition, many foods low in price are high in calorie density (fast food, for example).

• Higher or increasing socioeconomic status is associated with lower rates of obesity among some groups and constant or increased rates of obesity among other groups. Groups that are transitioning from poverty, food scarcity, and jobs that require significant energy expenditure may not have good family or community models of reducing energy intake and increasing leisure-time physical activity.

• Acculturation boosts body weight. The longer a foreign-born person lives in the United States, the more likely she or he is to become obese. BMI among immigrants begins to climb after about 10 years of U.S. residence, and after 15 years, it approaches the national average.

• Cultural factors that influence dietary and exercise behaviors appear to play a role in the development of obesity. There are also cultural differences in acceptance of larger body size and in body image perception. For example, one study found that African Americans were more likely to think they were thinner than they really were and whites were more likely to think they were fatter than they really were.

• The health consequences of obesity affect ethnic populations in different ways. At a given level of BMI, Latinos are significantly more likely to have type 2 diabetes. Obesity in African Americans is associated with increased risk of developing hypertension at a younger age and in a more severe form.

• For Asian Americans or persons of Asian descent, waist circumference is a better indicator of relative disease risk than BMI, and disease risk goes up at a lower level of BMI than for individuals of other groups. For Asian populations, WHO guidelines have a lower BMI cutoff for defining overweight (BMI 23).

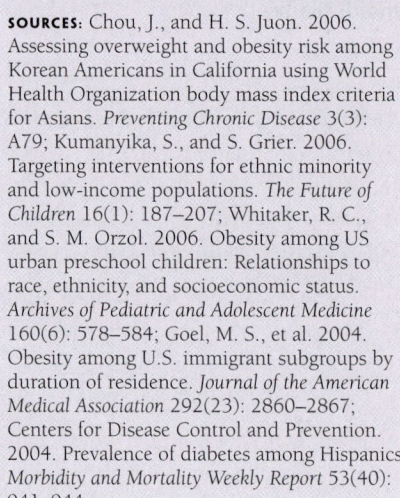

SOURCES: Chou, J., and H. S. Juon. 2006. Assessing overweight and obesity risk among Korean Americans in California using World Health Organization body mass index criteria for Asians. *Preventing Chronic Disease* 3(3): A79; Kumanyika, S., and S. Grier. 2006. Targeting interventions for ethnic minority and low-income populations. *The Future of Children* 16(1): 187–207; Whitaker, R. C., and S. M. Orzol. 2006. Obesity among US urban preschool children: Relationships to race, ethnicity, and socioeconomic status. *Archives of Pediatric and Adolescent Medicine* 160(6): 578–584; Goel, M. S., et al. 2004. Obesity among U.S. immigrant subgroups by duration of residence. *Journal of the American Medical Association* 292(23): 2860–2867; Centers for Disease Control and Prevention. 2004. Prevalence of diabetes among Hispanics. *Morbidity and Mortality Weekly Report* 53(40): 941–944.

means of regulating emotions, binge eating or other disturbed eating patterns can develop.

Obesity is strongly associated with socioeconomic status. The prevalence of obesity goes down as income level goes up. More women than men are obese at lower income levels, but men are somewhat more obese at higher levels. These differences may reflect the greater sensitivity and concern for a slim physical appearance among upper-income women, as well as greater access to information about nutrition, to low-fat and low-calorie foods, and to opportunities for physical activity. It may also reflect the greater acceptance of obesity among certain ethnic groups, as well as different cultural values related to food choices.

In some families and cultures, food is used as a symbol of love and caring. It is an integral part of social gatherings and celebrations. In such cases, it may be difficult to change established eating patterns because they are linked to cultural and family values.

ADOPTING A HEALTHY LIFESTYLE FOR SUCCESSFUL WEIGHT MANAGEMENT

When all the research has been assessed, it is clear that most weight problems are lifestyle problems. Even though more and more young people are developing weight

Are Diet Sodas Bad for You?

American soft drink consumption has grown significantly in the past 30 years, among children, adolescents, and adults. Regular soft drinks, in fact, are now the leading source of calories in the American diet.

A can of regular soda contains about 150 calories. High consumption of sugary soda has previously been linked with obesity and diabetes in children and adolescents and with high blood pressure in adults. Further, some studies have shown that the added sweeteners in soft drinks are linked to increased triglycerides in the blood, leading to a greater risk of heart disease.

Why does drinking more soda lead to obesity and insulin resistance? Researchers have attributed this effect to the following factors:

- Consuming more calories in general

- The high fructose corn syrup content in sodas

- Lower feelings of satiety (satisfaction)

- The general effect of eating a diet that is high in refined carbohydrates, including sugar

Many weight-conscious people have changed to diet soda in the hope that this is a healthier, calorie-free alternative to regular soda. But is it? Recent research indicates that drinking more than one soft drink a day, even if it is diet soda, may be associated with an increased incidence of metabolic syndrome. As described elsewhere in this text, metabolic syndrome is a cluster of risk factors linked to the development of diabetes, heart disease, and stroke. The syndrome includes high blood pressure, elevated triglyceride levels, low levels of HDL ("good") cholesterol), high fasting blood sugar levels, and excessive waist circumference.

This news came from the Framingham Heart Study, which examined more than 6000 middle-aged Americans who were initially free of metabolic syndrome. The link between diet soft drink consumption and metabolic syndrome was clear even when the researchers accounted for other factors, such as saturated fat and fiber in the diet, total calories, physical activity, and smoking.

Compared to people who did not drink soda, researchers found that people who consumed more than one soft drink per day—regular or diet—were associated with the following:

- 44% more likely to develop metabolic syndrome

- 31% more likely to be obese

- 25% more likely to have higher-than-average blood pressure

- 18% more likely to have high blood pressure

What is the possible explanation for the association? Some research has suggested that the artificial sweeteners in diet drinks make a person more prone to eat sweet, higher-calorie foods. Another theory is that the caramel content in

both regular and diet sodas may play a role in insulin resistance.

On the other hand, some contradictory studies show the benefit of diet soda consumption in overweight individuals and suggest that other factors could explain the development of risk factors for heart disease. Regardless, everyone agrees that more research should be done before a final verdict on diet soda consumption is reached.

Meanwhile, nutritionists say that this is a wake-up call for diet soda drinkers, suggesting that a zero-calorie beverage cannot undo the damage of an unhealthy diet.

---

problems, most arrive at early adulthood with the advantage of having a normal body weight—neither too fat nor too thin. In fact, many young adults get away with terrible eating and exercise habits and don't develop a weight problem. But as the rapid growth of adolescence slows and family and career obligations increase, maintaining a healthy weight becomes a greater challenge. Slow weight gain is a major cause of overweight and obesity, so weight management is important for everyone, not just for people who are currently overweight. A good time to develop a lifestyle for successful weight management is during early adulthood, when healthy behavior patterns have a better chance of taking a firm hold.

Permanent weight loss is not something you start and stop. You need to adopt healthy behaviors that you can maintain throughout life, including eating habits, level of physical activity, an ability to think positively and manage your emotions effectively, and the coping strategies you use to deal with the stresses and challenges in your life.

QUESTIONS FOR CRITICAL THINKING AND REFLECTION

How do you view your own body composition? Where do you think you've gotten your ideas about how your body should look and perform? In light of what you've read in this chapter, do the ideals and images promoted in our culture seem reasonable? Do they seem healthy?

What Triggers Your Eating?

Hunger isn't the only reason people eat. Efforts to maintain a healthy body weight can be sabotaged by eating related to other factors, including emotions, environment, and patterns of thinking. This quiz is designed to provide you with a score for five factors that describe many people's eating habits. This information will put you in a better position to manage your eating behavior and control your weight. Circle the number that indicates to what degree each situation is likely to make you start eating.

Social

	Very Unlikely									Very Likely
1. Arguing or having a conflict with someone	1	2	3	4	5	6	7	8	9	10
2. Being with others when they are eating	1	2	3	4	5	6	7	8	9	10
3. Being urged to eat by someone else	1	2	3	4	5	6	7	8	9	10
4. Feeling inadequate around others	1	2	3	4	5	6	7	8	9	10

Emotional

5. Feeling bad, such as being anxious or depressed	1	2	3	4	5	6	7	8	9	10
6. Feeling good, happy, or relaxed	1	2	3	4	5	6	7	8	9	10
7. Feeling bored or having time on my hands	1	2	3	4	5	6	7	8	9	10
8. Feeling stressed or excited	1	2	3	4	5	6	7	8	9	10

Situational

9. Seeing an advertisement for food or eating	1	2	3	4	5	6	7	8	9	10
10. Passing by a bakery, cookie shop, or other enticement to eat	1	2	3	4	5	6	7	8	9	10
11. Being involved in a party, celebration, or special occasion	1	2	3	4	5	6	7	8	9	10
12. Eating out	1	2	3	4	5	6	7	8	9	10

Thinking

13. Making excuses to myself about why it's OK to eat	1	2	3	4	5	6	7	8	9	10
14. Berating myself for being fat or unable to control my eating	1	2	3	4	5	6	7	8	9	10
15. Worrying about others or about difficulties I'm having	1	2	3	4	5	6	7	8	9	10
16. Thinking about how things should or shouldn't be	1	2	3	4	5	6	7	8	9	10

Physiological

17. Experiencing pain or physical discomfort	1	2	3	4	5	6	7	8	9	10
18. Experiencing trembling, headache, or light-headedness associated with no eating or too much caffeine	1	2	3	4	5	6	7	8	9	10
19. Experiencing fatigue or feeling overtired	1	2	3	4	5	6	7	8	9	10
20. Experiencing hunger pangs or urges to eat, even though I've eaten recently	1	2	3	4	5	6	7	8	9	10

Scoring

Total your scores for each category, and enter them below. Then rank the scores by marking the highest score 1, next highest score 2, and so on. Focus on the highest-ranked categories first, but any score above 24 is high and indicates that you need to work on that category.

Category	Total Score	Rank Order
Social (Items 1–4)	_____	_____
Emotional (Items 5–8)	_____	_____
Situational (Items 9–12)	_____	_____
Thinking (Items 13–16)	_____	_____
Physiological (Items 17–20)	_____	_____

What Your Score Means

Social A high score here means you are very susceptible to the influence of others. Work on better ways to communicate more assertively, handle conflict, and manage anger. Challenge your beliefs about the need to be polite and the obligations you feel you must fulfill.

Emotional A high score here means you need to develop effective ways to cope with emotions. Work on developing skills in stress management, time management, and communication. Practicing positive but realistic self-talk can help you handle small daily upsets.

Situational A high score here means you are especially susceptible to external influences. Try to avoid external cues and respond differently to those you cannot avoid. Control your environment by changing the way you buy, store, cook, and serve food. Anticipate potential problems, and have a plan for handling them.

Thinking A high score here means that the way you think—how you talk to yourself, the beliefs you hold, your memories, and your expectations—have a powerful influence on your eating habits. Try to be less self-critical, less perfectionistic, and more flexible in your ideas about the way things ought to be. Recognize when you're making excuses or rationalizations that allow you to eat.

Physiological A high score here means that the way you eat, what you eat, or medications you are taking may be affecting your eating behavior. You may be eating to reduce physical arousal or deal with physical discomfort. Try eating three meals a day, supplemented with regular snacks if needed. Avoid too much caffeine. If any medication you're taking produces adverse physical reactions, switch to an alternative, if possible. If your medications may be affecting your hormone levels, discuss possible alternatives with your physician.

SOURCE: Adapted from Nash, J. D. 1997. *The New Maximize Your Body Potential.* Boulder, Colorado: Bull. Reprinted with permission from Bull Publishing Company.

Diet and Eating Habits

In contrast to dieting, which involves some form of food restriction, the term *diet* refers to your daily food choices. Everyone has a diet, but not everyone is dieting. You need to develop a diet that you enjoy and that enables you to maintain a healthy body composition. Use MyPyramid or DASH as the basis for a healthy diet (see Chapter 12). For weight management, pay special attention to total calories, portion sizes, energy density, fat and carbohydrate intake, and eating habits.

Total Calories   MyPyramid suggests approximate daily energy intakes based on gender, age, and activity level. However, energy balance may be a more important consideration for weight management than total calories consumed (refer back to Figure 14.2). To maintain your current weight, the total number of calories you eat must equal the number you burn. To lose weight, you must decrease your calorie intake and/or increase the number of calories you burn; to gain weight, the reverse is true. (One pound of body fat represents 3500 calories.)

The best approach for weight loss is combining an increase in physical activity with moderate calorie restriction. Don't go on a crash diet. To maintain weight loss, you will probably have to maintain some degree of the calorie restriction you used to lose the weight. Therefore, you need to adopt a level of food intake that provides all the essential nutrients that you can live with over the long term. For most people, maintaining weight loss is more difficult than losing the weight in the first place.

Portion Sizes   Overconsumption of total calories is closely tied to portion sizes. Many Americans are unaware that the portions of packaged foods and of foods served at restaurants have increased in size, and most of us significantly underestimate the amount of food we eat. Studies have found that the larger the meal, the greater the underestimation of calories. People also commonly eat much more of the foods that they perceive as being healthy, but in the process consume far more calories than they need. Limiting portion sizes is critical for maintaining good health. For many people, concentrating on portion sizes is easier than counting calories.

To counteract portion distortion, weigh and measure your food at home for a few days every now and then. In addition, check the serving sizes listed on packaged foods. With practice, you'll learn to judge portion sizes more accurately. When eating out, try to order the smallest-sized items on the menu. It is especially important to limit serving sizes of foods that are high in calories and low in nutrients. Don't supersize your meals and snacks; although huge servings may seem like the best deal, it is more important to order just what you need. Refer to Chapter 12 for more information on choosing appropriate portion sizes.

Table 14.3	Examples of Foods Low in Energy Density	
Food	**Amount**	**Calories**
Egg substitute	¼ cup	30
Plain instant oatmeal	½ cup	80
Fresh blueberries	1 cup	80
Corn on the cob (plain)	1 ear	80
Cantaloupe	½ melon	95
Unsweetened apple sauce	1 cup	100
Pear	1 medium	100
Mixed vegetables	1 cup	110
Sweet potato	1 medium	120

Energy (Calorie) Density   Experts also recommend that you pay attention to *energy density*—the number of calories per ounce or gram of weight in a food. Studies suggest that it isn't consumption of a certain amount of fat or calories in food that reduces hunger and leads to feelings of fullness and satisfaction; rather, it is consumption of a certain weight of food. Foods that are low in energy density have more volume and bulk—that is, they are relatively heavy but have few calories (see Table 14.3). For example, for the same 100 calories, you could eat 21 baby carrots or 4 pretzel twists; you are more likely to feel full after eating the serving of carrots because it weighs 10 times as much as the serving of pretzels (10 ounces versus 1 ounce).

Fresh fruits and vegetables, with their high water and fiber content, are low in energy density, as are whole-grain foods. Fresh fruits contain less calories and more fiber than fruit juices or drinks. Meat, ice cream, potato chips, croissants, crackers, and cakes and cookies are examples of foods high in energy density. Strategies for lowering the energy density of your diet include the following:

- Eat fruit with breakfast and for dessert.
- Add extra vegetables to sandwiches, casseroles, stir-fry dishes, pizza, pasta dishes, and fajitas.
- Start meals with a bowl of broth-based soup; include a green salad or fruit salad.
- Snack on fresh fruits and vegetables rather than crackers, chips, or other energy-dense snack foods.

Limit serving sizes of energy-dense foods such as butter, mayonnaise, cheese, chocolate, fatty meats, croissants, and snack foods that are fried, high in added sugars (including reduced-fat products), or contain trans fats.

It is also important to watch out for processed foods, which can be high in fat and sodium. Even processed foods labeled "fat-free" or "reduced fat" may be high in calories; such products may contain sugar and fat substitutes (see the box "Evaluating Fat and Sugar Substitutes" on p. 430).

Evaluating Fat and Sugar Substitutes

Foods made with fat and sugar substitutes are often promoted for weight loss. But what are fat and sugar substitutes? And can they really contribute to weight management?

Fat Substitutes

A variety of substances are used to replace fats in processed foods and other products. Some contribute calories, protein, fiber, and/or other nutrients, whereas others do not. Fat replacers fall into three general categories:

• *Carbohydrate-based fat replacers* include starch, fibers, gums, cellulose, polydextrose, and fruit purees. They are the oldest and most widely used form of fat replacer and are found in dairy and meat products, baked goods, salad dressings, and many other prepared foods. Newer types such as Oatrim, Z-trim, and Nu-trim are made from types of dietary fiber that may actually lower cholesterol levels. Carbohydrate-based fat replacers contribute 0–4 calories per gram.

• *Protein-based fat replacers* are typically made from milk, egg whites, soy, or whey; trade names include Simplesse, Dairy-lo, and Supro. They are used in cheese, sour cream, mayonnaise, margarine spreads, frozen desserts, salad dressings, and baked goods. Protein-based fat replacers typically contribute 1–4 calories per gram.

• *Fat-based fat replacers* include glycerides, olestra, and other special types of fatty acids. Some of these compounds are not absorbed well by the body and so provide fewer calories per gram (5 calories compared with the standard 9 for fats); others are impossible for the body to digest and so contribute no calories at all. Olestra, marketed under the trade name Olean and used in fried snack foods, is an example of the latter type of compound. Concerns have been raised about the safety of olestra because it reduces the absorption of fat-soluble nutrients and certain antioxidants and because it causes gastrointestinal distress in some people.

Nonnutritive Sweeteners and Sugar Alcohols

Sugar substitutes are often referred to as nonnutritive sweeteners because they provide no calories or essential nutrients. By 2005, five types of nonnutritive sweeteners had been approved for use in the United States: acesulfame-K (Sunett, Sweet One), aspartame (NutraSweet, Equal, NatraTaste), saccharin (Sweet 'N Low), sucralose (Splenda), and neotame. They are used in beverages, desserts, baked goods, yogurt, chewing gum, and products such as toothpaste, mouthwash, and cough syrup. Another sweetener, stevia, is an extract of a South American shrub; it is classified as a dietary supplement and so is not regulated by the FDA.

Sugar alcohols are made by altering the chemical form of sugars extracted from fruits and other plant sources; they include erythritol, isomalt, lactitol, maltitol, mannitol, sorbitol, and zylitol. Sugar alcohols provide 0.2–2.5 calories per gram, compared to 4 calories per gram in standard sugar. They have typically been used to sweeten sugar-free candies but are now being added to many sweet foods promoted as low-carbohydrate products, often combined with other sweeteners. Sugar alcohols are digested in a way that can create gas, cramps, and diarrhea if they are consumed in large amounts—more than about 10 grams in one meal. To avoid problems, check ingredient lists to determine if a food contains sugar alcohols.

Fat and Sugar Substitutes in Weight Management

Whether fat and sugar substitutes help you achieve and maintain a healthy weight depends on your overall eating and activity habits. The increase in the availability of fat-free and sugar-free foods in the United States has *not* been associated with a drop in calorie consumption. When evaluating foods with fat and sugar substitutes, consider these issues:

• *Is the food lower in calories or just lower in fat?* Reduced-fat foods often contain extra sugar to improve the taste and texture lost when fat is removed, so such foods may be as high or even higher in total calories than their fattier counterparts. Limiting fat intake is an important goal for weight management, but so is controlling total calories.

• *Are you choosing foods with fat and/or sugar substitutes instead of foods you typically eat or in addition to foods you typically eat?* If you consume low-fat, no-sugar-added ice cream instead of regular ice cream, you may save calories. But if you add such ice cream to your daily diet simply because it is lower in fat and sugar, your overall calorie consumption—and your weight—may increase.

• *How many foods containing fat and sugar substitutes do you consume each day?* Although the FDA has given at least provisional approval to all the fat and sugar substitutes currently available, health concerns about some of these products linger. One way to limit any potential adverse effects is to read labels and monitor how much of each product you consume.

• *Is an even healthier choice available?* Many of the foods containing fat and sugar substitutes are low-nutrient snack foods. Although substituting a lower-fat or lower-sugar version of the same food may be beneficial, fruits, vegetables, and whole grains are healthier snack choices.

Otherwise, stick to the calorie and nutrient recommendations offered by the Dietary Guidelines for Americans, MyPyramid, or the DASH Diet. These guidelines are described in detail in Chapter 12.

Eating Habits Equally important to weight management is the habit of eating small, frequent meals—four to five meals per day, including breakfast and snacks—on a regular schedule. Skipping meals leads to excessive

Exercise, Body Image, and Self-Esteem

If you gaze into the mirror and wish you could change the way your body looks, consider getting some exercise—not to reshape your contours but to firm up your body image and enhance your self-esteem. In a recent study, 82 adults completed a 12-week aerobic exercise program and had 12 months of follow-up. Compared with the control group, these participants improved their fitness and also benefited psychologically in tests of mood, anxiety, and self-concept. These same physical and psychological benefits were still significant at the 1-year follow-up.

One reason for the findings may be that people who exercise regularly often gain a sense of mastery and competence that enhances their self-esteem and body image. In addition, exercise contributes to a more toned look, which many adults prefer.

Research suggests that physically active people are more comfortable with their body and their image than sedentary people are. In one workplace study, 60 employees were asked to complete a 36-session stretching program whose main purpose was to prevent muscle strains at work. At the end of the program, besides the significant increase by all participants in measurements of flexibility, their perceptions of their bodies improved and so did their overall sense of self-worth.

Similar results were obtained in a Norwegian study, in which 219 middle-aged people at risk for heart disease were randomly assigned to one of four groups: diet, diet plus exercise, exercise, and no intervention. The greater the participation of individuals in the exercise component of the program, the higher were their scores in perceived competence/self-esteem and coping.

---

hunger, feelings of deprivation, and increased vulnerability to binge eating or snacking. In addition to establishing a regular pattern of eating, set some rules to govern your food choices. Rules for breakfast might be these, for example: Choose a sugar-free, high-fiber cereal with fat-free milk on most days; have a hard-boiled egg (no more than 3 per week); save pancakes and waffles for special occasions, unless they are whole-grain. (For effective weight management, it is better to consume the majority of calories during the day rather than in the evening.)

Decreeing some foods off-limits generally sets up a rule to be broken. A more sensible principle is "everything in moderation." If a particular food becomes troublesome, place it off-limits until you gain control over it. The ultimate goal is to eat in moderation; no foods need to be entirely off-limits, though some should be eaten judiciously.

Physical Activity and Exercise

Regular physical activity is another important lifestyle factor in weight management. Physical activity and exercise burn calories and keep the metabolism geared to using food for energy instead of storing it as fat. Making significant cuts in food intake in order to lose weight is a difficult strategy to maintain; increasing your physical activity is a much better approach. Regular physical activity protects against weight gain, is essential for maintaining weight loss, and improves quality of life (see the box "Exercise, Body Image, and Self-Esteem" above). The sooner you establish good habits, the better. The key to success is making exercise an integral part of the lifestyle you can enjoy now and in the future. Chapter 13 contains many suggestions for becoming a more active, physically fit person.

Thinking and Emotions

The way you think about yourself and your world influences, and is influenced by, how you feel and how you act. In fact, research on people who have a weight problem indicates that low self-esteem and the negative emotions that accompany it are significant problems. Often, people with low self-esteem mentally compare the actual self to an internally held picture of an "ideal self," an image based on perfectionistic goals and beliefs about how they and others should be. The more these two pictures differ, the larger the impact on self-esteem and the more likely the presence of negative emotions.

Besides the internal picture we carry of ourselves, all of us carry on an internal dialogue about events happening to us and around us. This *self-talk* can be either self-deprecating or positively motivating, depending on our beliefs and attitudes. Having realistic beliefs and goals,

and practicing positive self-talk and problem solving support a healthy lifestyle.

Coping Strategies

Appropriate coping strategies help you deal with the stresses of life; they are also an important lifestyle factor in weight management. Many people use eating as a way to cope; others may cope by turning to drugs, alcohol, smoking, or gambling. Those who overeat might use food to alleviate loneliness or to serve as a pickup for fatigue, as an antidote to boredom, or as a distraction from problems. Some people even overeat to punish themselves for real or imagined transgressions.

Those who recognize that they are misusing food in such ways can analyze their eating habits with fresh eyes. They can consciously attempt to find new coping strategies and begin to use food appropriately—to fuel life's activities, to foster growth, and to bring pleasure, but *not* as a way to manage stress. For a summary of the components of weight management through healthy lifestyle choices, see the box "Lifestyle Strategies for Successful Weight Management."

APPROACHES TO OVERCOMING A WEIGHT PROBLEM

What should you do if you are overweight? You have several options.

Doing It Yourself

If you need to lose weight, focus on adopting the healthy lifestyle described throughout this book. The right weight for you will naturally evolve, and you won't have to diet. Combine modest cuts in energy intake with exercise, and avoid very-low-calorie diets. (In general, a low-calorie diet should have 1200–1500 calories per day.)

By producing a negative energy balance of 250–1000 calories per day, you will produce the recommended weight loss of 0.5–2.0 pounds per week.

Don't try to lose weight more rapidly. Most low-calorie diets cause a rapid loss of body water at first. When this phase passes, weight loss declines. As a result, dieters are often misled into believing that their efforts are not working. They then give up, not realizing that smaller, mostly fat, losses later in the diet are actually better than the initial larger, mostly fluid losses. Reasonable weight loss is 8–10% of body weight over 6 months.

For many Americans, maintaining weight loss is a bigger challenge than losing weight. Most weight lost during a period of dieting is regained. When planning a weight management program, it is extremely important to include strategies that you can maintain over the long term, both for food choices and for physical activity. Weight management is a lifelong project. A registered dietitian or nutritionist can recommend an appropriate plan for you when you want to lose weight on your own. For more tips, refer to the Behavior Change Strategy at the end of the chapter.

Diet Books

Many people who try to lose weight by themselves fall prey to one or more of the dozens of diet books on the market. Although some contain useful advice and motivational tips, most make empty promises. Here are some guidelines for evaluating and choosing a diet book:

- Reject books that advocate an unbalanced way of eating, such as a high-carbohydrate-only diet or a low-carbohydrate, high-protein diet. Also reject books promoting a single food, such as cabbage or grapefruit.
- Reject books that claim to be based on a "scientific breakthrough" or to have the "secret to success."
- Reject books that use gimmicks, such as matching eating to blood type, hyping insulin resistance as the single cause of obesity, combining foods in special ways to achieve weight loss, rotating levels of calories, or purporting that a weight problem is due to food allergies, food sensitivities, yeast infections, or hormone imbalances.
- Reject books that promise quick weight loss or that limit the selection of foods.
- Accept books that advocate a balanced approach to diet plus exercise and sound nutrition advice.

Many diets can cause weight loss if maintained; the real difficulty is finding a safe and healthy pattern of food choices and physical activity that results in long-term maintenance of a healthy body weight and reduced risk of chronic disease (see the box "Is Any Diet Best for Weight Loss?" on p. 434).

Lifestyle Strategies for Successful Weight Management

Food Choices

• Follow the recommendations in MyPyramid for eating a moderate, varied diet. Focus on making good choices from each food group.

• Favor foods with a *low energy density* and a *high nutrient density.*

• Check food labels for serving sizes, calories, and nutrient levels.

• Watch for hidden calories. Reduced-fat foods often have as many calories as their full-fat versions. Fat-based condiments like butter, margarine, mayonnaise, and salad dressings provide about 100 calories per tablespoon; added sugars such as jams, jellies, and syrup are also packed with calories.

• Drink fewer calories in the form of soda, fruit drinks, sports drinks, alcohol, and specialty coffees and teas.

• For problem foods, try eating small amounts under controlled conditions. Go out for a scoop of ice cream, for example, rather than buying half a gallon for your freezer.

Planning and Serving

• Keep a log of what you eat. Before you begin your program, your log will provide a realistic picture of your current diet and what changes you can make. Once you start your program, a log will keep you focused on your food choices and portion sizes. Track the food eaten, your hunger level, the circumstances (location, other activities), outside influences (environment, other people), and your thoughts and emotions.

• Eat 4–5 meals/snacks daily, *including breakfast,* to distribute calories throughout your day. In studies, people who eat breakfast consume fewer calories overall over the course of the day. Fix more meals yourself and eat out less often. Keep low-calorie snacks on hand to combat the "munchies": baby carrots, popcorn, and fresh fruits and vegetables are good choices.

• When shopping, make a list and stick to it. Don't shop when you're hungry. Avoid aisles that contain problem foods.

• Consume the majority of your daily calories during the day, not in the evening.

• Pay special attention to portion sizes. Use measuring cups and spoons and a food scale to become more familiar with appropriate portion sizes.

• Serve meals on small plates and in small bowls to help you eat smaller portions without feeling deprived.

• Eat only in specifically designated spots. Remove food from other areas of your home.

• When you eat, just eat—don't do anything else, such as reading or watching TV.

• Avoid late-night eating, a behavior specifically associated with weight gain among college students.

• Eat slowly. It takes time for your brain to get the message that your stomach is full. Take small bites and chew food thoroughly. Pay attention to every bite, and enjoy your

food. Between bites, try putting your fork or spoon down and taking sips of a beverage.

• When you're done eating, remove your plate. Cue yourself that the meal is over; drink a glass of water, suck on a mint, chew gum, or brush your teeth.

Special Occasions

• When you eat out, choose a restaurant where you can make healthy food choices. Ask the server not to put bread and butter on the table before the meal, and request that sauces and salad dressings be served on the side. If portion sizes are large, take half your food home for a meal later in the week. Don't choose supersized meals.

• If you cook a large meal for friends, send leftovers home with your guests.

• If you're eating at a friend's, eat a little and leave the rest. Don't eat to be polite; if someone offers you food you don't want, thank the person and decline firmly.

• Take care during the winter holidays. Research indicates that people gain less than they think during the winter holidays (about a pound) but that the weight isn't lost during the rest of the year, leading to slow, steady weight gain.

Physical Activity and Stress Management

• Increase your level of daily physical activity. If you have been sedentary for a long time or are seriously overweight, increase your level of activity slowly. Start by walking 10 minutes at a time, and work toward 30–60 minutes or more of moderate physical activity per day.

• Begin a formal exercise program that includes cardiorespiratory endurance exercise, strength training, and stretching.

• Develop techniques for handling stress. Try walking, or use a relaxation technique. Practice positive self-talk. Get adequate sleep. (See Chapter 2 for more on stress management.)

• Develop strategies for coping with nonhunger cues to eat, such as boredom, sleepiness, or anxiety. Try calling a friend, taking a shower, or reading a magazine.

• Tell family members and friends that you're changing your eating and exercise habits. Ask them to be supportive.

Visit the Small Steps site for more tips (www.smallstep.gov).

Is Any Diet Best for Weight Loss?

Experts agree that reducing calorie intake promotes weight loss. However, many popular weight-loss plans include a special hook and promote specific food choices and macronutrient (protein, fat, carbohydrate) combinations as best for weight loss. Research findings have been mixed, but two points are clear. Total calorie intake matters, and the best diet is probably the one you can stick with.

Low-Carbohydrate Diets

Some low-carb diets advocate fewer than 10% of total calories from carbohydrates, compared to the 45–65% recommended by the Food and Nutrition Board. Some suggest daily carbohydrate intake below the 130 grams needed to provide essential carbohydrates in the diet. Small studies have found that low-carbohydrate diets can help with short-term weight loss and be safe for relatively short periods of time—although unpleasant effects such as bad breath, constipation, and headache are fairly common.

Some low-carb diets tend to be very high in protein and saturated fat and low in fiber, whole grains, vegetables, and fruits (and thus lack some essential nutrients). Diets high in protein and saturated fat have been linked to an increased risk of heart disease, high blood pressure, and cancer. Other low-carb diets, though still emphasizing protein, limit saturated fats, allow most vegetables after an initial period, and advocate switching to "healthy carbs." These diets are healthier than the more extreme versions.

Low-Fat Diets

Many experts advocate diets that are relatively low in fat, high in carbohydrates, and moderate in protein. Critics of these diets blame them for rising rates of obesity and note that very-low-fat, very-high-carbohydrate diets can increase triglyceride levels and reduce levels of good (HDL) cholesterol in some people. These negative effects can be counteracted with moderate-intensity exercise, however, and low-fat diets combined with physical activity can be safe and effective for many people.

Few experts take the position that low-fat, high-carbohydrate diets, apart from overall diet and activity patterns, are responsible for the increase in obesity among Americans. However, the debate has highlighted the importance of total calorie intake and the quality of carbohydrate choices. A low-fat diet is not a license to consume excess calories, even in low-fat foods.

How Do Popular Diets Measure Up?

In one recent study, obese people on a very-low-carbohydrate, high-fat diet lost more weight over a 6-month period than people following a moderate-fat diet. After a year, however, the difference in weight loss between the two groups was no longer significant, and the dropout rate from both groups was high.

A 2005 study followed participants in four popular diets that emphasize different strategies—Weight Watchers (restricted portion sizes and calories), Atkins (low-carbohydrate, high-fat), Zone (relatively high protein, moderate fat and carbohydrate), and Ornish (very low fat). Each of these diets modestly reduced body weight and heart disease risk factors. There was no significant difference in weight loss at 1 year among the diets, and the more closely people adhered to each diet, the more

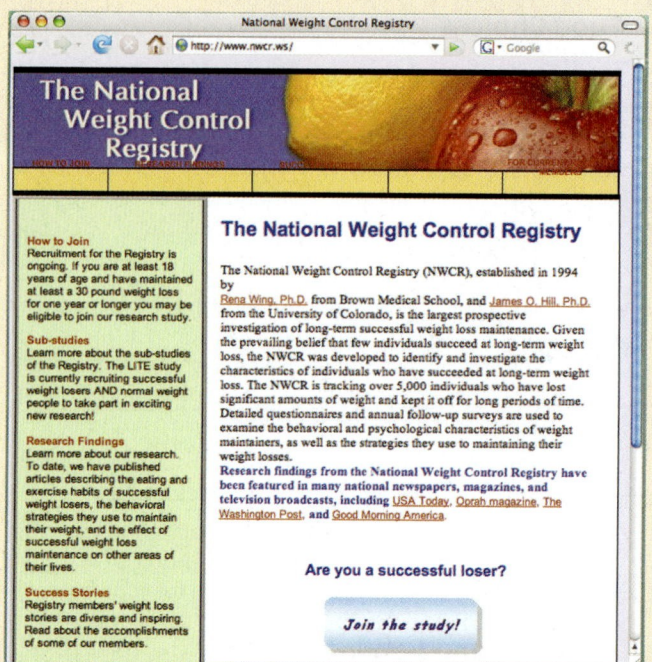

weight they lost. Dropout rates were high—about 50% for Atkins and Ornish and 35% for Weight Watchers and Zone.

Energy Balance Counts: The National Weight Control Registry

Future research may determine that certain macronutrient patterns are somewhat more helpful for disease reduction in people with particular risk profiles. In terms of weight loss, however, such differences among diets are likely overshadowed by the importance of total calorie intake and physical activity. Important lessons about energy balance can be drawn from the National Weight Control Registry, an ongoing study of people who have lost significant amounts of weight and kept it off. The average participant in the registry has lost 71 pounds and kept the weight off for more than 5 years. Nearly all participants use a combination of diet and exercise to manage their weight. Most consume diets moderate in calories and relatively low in fat and fried foods; they monitor their body weight and their food intake frequently. Participants engage in an average of 60 minutes of moderate physical activity daily. The National Weight Control Registry study illustrates that to lose weight and keep it off, you must decrease daily calorie intake and/or increase daily physical activity—and continue to do so over your lifetime.

SOURCES: Battle of the diet books II. 2006. *Nutrition Action Healthletter,* July/August; Dansinger, M. L., et al. 2005. Comparison of the Atkins, Ornish, Weight Watchers, and Zone diets for weight loss and heart disease risk reduction. *Journal of the American Medical Association* 293(1): 43–53; Hays, N. P., et al. 2004. Effects of an ad libitum low-fat, high-carbohydrate diet on body weight, body composition, and fat distribution in older men and women. *Archives of Internal Medicine* 164(2): 210–217. Hill, J., and R. Wing. 2003. The National Weight Control Registry. *Permanente Journal* 7(3): 34–37. Bravata, D. M., et al. 2003. Efficacy and safety of low-carbohydrate diets. *Journal of the American Medical Association* 289: 1837–1850; Foster, G. D., et al. 2003. A randomized trial of low-carbohydrate diet for obesity. *New England Journal of Medicine* 348: 2082–2090. Screenshot from The National Weight Control Registry reprinted with permission.

Dietary Supplements and Diet Aids

The number of dietary supplements and other weight-loss aids on the market has also increased in recent years. Promoted in advertisements, magazines, direct mail campaigns, infomercials, and Web sites, these products typically promise a quick and easy path to weight loss. Most of these products are marketed as dietary supplements and so are subject to fewer regulations than OTC medications. A 2002 report from the Federal Trade Commission stated that more than half of advertisements for weight-loss products made representations that are likely to be false. In addition, use of OTC products doesn't help in the adoption of lifestyle behaviors that can help people achieve and maintain a healthy weight over the long term.

The bottom line on nonprescription diet aids is caveat emptor—let the buyer beware. There is no quick and easy way to lose weight. The most effective approach is to develop healthy diet and exercise habits and make them a permanent part of your lifestyle. The following sections describe some commonly marketed OTC products for weight loss.

Formula Drinks and Food Bars Canned diet drinks, powders used to make shakes, and diet food bars and snacks are designed to achieve weight loss by substituting for some or all of a person's daily food intake. However, most people find it difficult to use these products for long periods, and muscle loss and other serious health problems may result if they are used as the sole source of nutrition for an extended period. Use of such products sometimes results in rapid short-term weight loss, but the weight is typically regained because users don't learn to change their eating and lifestyle behaviors.

Herbal Supplements As described in Chapter 12, herbs are marketed as dietary supplements, so there is little information about effectiveness, proper dosage, drug interactions, and side effects. In addition, labels may not accurately reflect the ingredients and dosages present, and safe manufacturing practices are not guaranteed. For example, the substitution of a toxic herb for another compound during the manufacture of a Chinese herbal weight-loss preparation caused more than 100 cases of kidney damage and cancer among users in Europe.

The FDA has banned the sale of ephedra (*ma huang*), stating that it presented a significant and unreasonable risk to human health. Ephedrine, the active ingredient in ephedra, is structurally similar to amphetamine and was widely used in weight-loss supplements. It may suppress appetite, but adverse effects have included elevated blood pressure, panic attacks, seizures, insomnia, and increased risk of heart attack or stroke, particularly when combined with another stimulant, such as caffeine. The FDA banned the synthetic stimulant phenylpropanolamine for similar reasons. Other herbal stimulants still on the market are described in Table 14.4 on p. 436.

There are many plans and supplements promoted for weight loss, but few have any research supporting their effectiveness for long-term weight management.

Other Supplements Fiber is another common ingredient in OTC diet aids, promoted for appetite control. However, dietary fiber acts as a bulking agent in the large intestine, not the stomach, so it doesn't have a pronounced effect on appetite. In addition, many diet aids contain only 3 or fewer grams of fiber, which does not contribute much toward the recommended daily intake of 25–38 grams. Other popular dietary supplements include conjugated linoleic acid, carnitine, chromium, pyruvate, calcium, B vitamins, chitosan, and a number of products labeled "fat absorbers," "fat blockers," and "starch blockers." Research has not found these products to be effective, and many have potentially adverse side effects.

Weight-Loss Programs

Weight-loss programs come in a variety of types, including noncommercial support organizations, commercial programs, Web sites, and clinical programs.

Noncommercial Weight-Loss Programs Noncommercial programs such as TOPS (Take Off Pounds Sensibly) and Overeaters Anonymous (OA) mainly provide group support. They do not advocate any particular diet but do recommend seeking professional advice for creating an individualized plan. Like Alcoholics Anonymous, OA is a 12-step program with a spiritual orientation that promotes abstinence from compulsive overeating. These types of programs are generally free. Your physician or a registered dietitian can also provide information and support for weight loss.

Table 14.4   Ingredients Commonly Found in Weight-Loss Products

Common Name	Use/Claim	Evidence/Efficacy	Safety Issues
Bitter orange extract (*Citrus aurantium*)	CNS stimulant	Limited evidence	Highly concentrated extracts may increase blood pressure; should not be used by people with cardiac problems
Caffeine	CNS stimulant; increases fat metabolism	Amplifies effects of ephedra	Generally considered safe; caution advised in caffeine-sensitive individuals
Garcinia cambogia	May interfere with fat metabolism or suppress appetite	Inconclusive evidence	Short-term use (<12 weeks) generally considered safe when used as directed
Green tea extract	Diuretic; increases metabolism	Limited evidence	Generally considered safe
Guarana	CNS stimulant; diuretic	Few clinical trials	Same as for caffeine; overdose can cause painful urination, abdominal spasms, and vomiting
Senna, cascara, aloe, buckthorn berries	Stimulant, laxative	Not effective for weight loss	Chronic use decreases muscle tone in large intestine, causes electrolyte imbalances, and leads to dependence on laxatives
Tea, kola, dandelion, bucho, uva-ursi, damiana, juniper	Diuretic	Not effective for weight loss	Chronic use can cause possible electrolyte imbalance in some people
Yerba mate	Stimulant, laxative, diuretic	Limited evidence	Long-term use as a beverage may increase risk of oral cancer

SOURCE: Adapted from Leslie, K. K. 2003. Herbal weight-loss products: Effective and appropriate? *Today's Dietician* 5(8).

Commercial Weight-Loss Programs Commercial weight-loss programs typically provide group support, nutrition education, physical activity recommendations, and behavior modification advice. Some also make available packaged foods to assist in following dietary advice.

A 2005 study evaluated major commercial weight-loss programs, including Weight Watchers, NutriSystem, Jenny Craig, and L A Weight Loss for 12 weeks or more with a 1-year follow-up assessment. Results showed Weight Watchers to be the only moderately priced commercial program with a mean loss of 5% of initial weight.

A responsible and safe weight-loss program should have the following features:

- The recommended diet should be safe and balanced, include all the food groups, and meet the DRIs for all nutrients. Physical activity and exercise should be strongly encouraged.

- The program should promote slow, steady weight loss averaging 0.5–2.0 pounds per week. (There may be some greater weight loss initially due to fluid loss.)

- If a participant plans to lose more than 20 pounds, has any health problems, or is taking medication on a regular basis, physician evaluation and monitoring should be recommended. The staff of the program should include qualified counselors and health professionals.

- The program should include plans for weight maintenance after the weight-loss phase is over.

- The program should provide information on all fees and costs, including those of supplements and prepackaged foods, as well as data on risks and expected outcomes of participating in the program.

In addition, you should consider whether a program fits your lifestyle and whether you are truly ready to make a commitment to it. A strong commitment and a plan for maintenance are especially important because only about 10–15% of program participants maintain their weight loss—the rest gain back all or more than they had lost. One study of participants found that regular exercise was the best predictor of maintaining weight loss, whereas frequent television viewing was the best predictor of weight gain.

Online Weight-Loss Programs A recent addition to the weight-loss program scene is the Internet-based program. Most such Web sites include a cross between self-help and group support through chat rooms, bulletin boards, and e-newsletters. Many sites offer online self-assessment for diet and physical activity habits as well as a meal plan; some provide access to a staff professional for individualized help. Many are free, but some charge a small weekly or monthly fee.

Preliminary research suggests that this type of program provides an alternative to in-person diet counseling and can lead to weight loss for some people. Studies found that people who logged on to Internet programs more frequently tended to lose more weight; weekly on-line contact in terms of behavior therapy proved most successful for weight loss. The criteria used to evaluate commercial programs can also be applied to Internet-based programs. In addition, make sure the program offers member-to-member support and access to staff professionals.

Clinical Weight-Loss Programs   Medically supervised clinical programs are usually located in a hospital or other medical setting. Designed to help those who are severely obese, these programs typically involve a closely monitored very-low-calorie diet. The cost of a clinical program is usually high, but insurance will often cover part of the fee.

Prescription Drugs

For a medicine to cause weight loss, it must reduce energy consumption, increase energy expenditure, and/or interfere with energy absorption. The medications most often prescribed for weight loss are appetite suppressants that reduce feelings of hunger or increase feelings of fullness. Appetite suppressants usually work by increasing levels of catecholamine or serotonin, two brain chemicals that affect mood and appetite.

All prescription weight-loss drugs have potential side effects. Those that affect catecholamine levels, including phentermine (Ionamin, Obenix, Fastin, and Adipex-P), diethylpropion (Tenuate), and mazindol (Sanorex), may cause sleeplessness, nervousness, and euphoria. Sibutramine (Meridia) acts on both the serotonin and catecholamine systems; it may trigger increases in blood pressure and heart rate. Headaches, constipation or diarrhea, dry mouth, and insomnia are other side effects.

In 1997, the FDA removed from the market two prescription weight-loss drugs, fenfluramine (Pondimin) and dexfenfluramine (Redux), after their use was linked to potentially life-threatening heart valve problems. (Fenfluramine was used most often in combination with phentermine, an off-label combination referred to as "fen/phen.") It appears that people who took these drugs over a long period or at high dosages are at greatest risk for problems, but the FDA recommends that anyone who has taken either of these drugs be examined by a physician.

Most appetite suppressants are approved by the FDA only for short-term use. Two drugs, however, are approved for longer-term use: sibutramine and orlistat (Xenical). Sibutramine's safety and efficacy record is good, but regular monitoring of blood pressure is required during therapy. Orlistat lowers calorie consumption by blocking fat ab-

sorption in the intestines; it prevents about 30% of the fat in food from being digested. Similar to the fat substitute olestra, orlistat reduces the absorption of fat-soluble vitamins and antioxidants. Therefore, taking a vitamin supplement is highly recommended if taking orlistat. Side effects include diarrhea, cramping, and other gastrointestinal problems if users do not follow a low-fat diet. In 2007, the FDA approved Alli, a lower-dose version of Orlistat that is sold over the counter. Alli is the first and only FDA-approved weight-loss medication sold over the counter.

A new drug, rimonabant (Acomplia) has been used successfully in Europe and is now awaiting FDA approval for use in the United States. Rimonabant suppresses appetite by acting on certain brain receptors. Studies show that rimonabant may lead to greater weight loss than other drugs and may help users keep weight off for a longer time. Side effects include mild diarrhea, dizziness, and nausea, although studies show that some users also suffer psychological side effects such as depression and suicidal thoughts.

These medications work best in conjunction with behavior modification. Studies have generally found that appetite suppressants produce modest weight loss—about 5–22 pounds above the loss expected with non-drug obesity treatments. Individuals respond very differently, however, and some experience more weight loss than others. Unfortunately, weight loss tends to level off or reverse after 4–6 months on a medication, and many people regain the weight they've lost when they stop taking the drug.

Prescription weight-loss drugs are not for people who just want to lose a few pounds. The latest federal guidelines advise people to try lifestyle modification for at least 6 months before trying drug therapy. Prescription drugs are recommended only in certain cases: for people who have been unable to lose weight with nondrug options and who have a BMI over 30 (or over 27 if two or more additional risk factors such as diabetes and high blood pressure are present). For severely obese people who have been unable to lose weight by other methods, prescription drugs may provide a good option.

Surgery

It is estimated that 23 million Americans have a BMI greater than 35 (obese) and 8 million have a BMI greater than 40 (severely obese). The number of severely obese people has nearly tripled in the past decade. Severe obesity is a serious medical condition that is often complicated by other health problems such as diabetes, sleep disorders, heart disease, and arthritis. Surgical intervention may be necessary as a treatment of last resort. According to the NIH, gastric bypass surgery is recommended for patients with a BMI greater than 40, or greater than 35 with obesity-related illnesses.

Due to the increasing prevalence of severe obesity, surgical treatment of obesity is growing worldwide. Obesity-related health conditions, as well as risk of premature death, generally improve after surgical weight loss. However, surgery is not without risks. A 2006 study found that patients with poor cardiorespiratory fitness prior to surgery experienced more postoperative complications, including stroke, kidney failure, and even death, than patients with higher fitness levels.

Gastric bypass surgery modifies the gastrointestinal tract by changing either the size of the stomach or how the intestine drains, thereby reducing food intake. The two most common surgeries are the Roux-en-Y gastric bypass and the vertical banded gastroplasty.

Roux-en-Y Gastric Bypass

In the *Roux-en-Y gastric bypass* procedure, the stomach is separated into two pouches, one large and one small. A "Y" segment of the small intestine is attached to the smaller pouch. The small stomach pouch restricts food intake, and the bypass of the lower stomach and part of the small intestine results in the absorption of fewer calories (and nutrients). Side effects include fat intolerance, nutritional deficiencies, and dumping syndrome, which involves gastrointestinal distress.

Vertical Banded Gastroplasty

In *vertical banded gastroplasty (VBG)*, a small gastric pouch is created in the upper part of the stomach by applying a double row of staples that essentially elongates the esophagus. This small pouch empties into the remaining stomach through an outlet that is restricted with a band. The procedure controls the gastric emptying of food and the volume of foods eaten. Common complications associated with this kind of surgery are nausea, vomiting, band slippage, gastroesophageal reflux, and stenosis (constriction of the outlet). When compared with Roux-en-Y gastric bypass, VBG has a lower initial weight loss and a greater weight regain.

In a variation of VGB, called Lap-Band, an adjustable band is placed around the stomach. The band is implanted laparoscopically, via a tube inserted through a small incision in the abdomen. The band ties off a portion of the stomach, creating a small pouch similar to that created in VGB surgery. The band is filled with saline and can be tightened or loosened by adding or removing saline through a small tube that exits through the patient's abdomen. The Lap-Band procedure has about the same success rate as VGB and is generally considered to be safe.

Weight loss from surgery generally ranges between 40% and 70% of total body weight over the course of a

QUESTIONS FOR CRITICAL THINKING AND REFLECTION

Why do you think people continue to buy into fad diets and weight-loss gimmicks, even though they are constantly reminded that the key to weight management is lifestyle change? Have you ever tried a fad diet or dietary supplement? If so, what were your reasons for trying it? What were the results?

year. In a 2006 study that included mild to moderately obese (BMI 30–35) adults, gastric banding surgery was significantly more effective in reducing weight and improving quality of life than nonsurgical methods, even after 2 years. For surgical procedures, the key to success is to have adequate follow-up and to stay motivated so that lifestyle behaviors and eating patterns are changed permanently.

Liposuction Another procedure, *liposuction,* has become popular for removing localized fat deposits. This cosmetic procedure does not improve health the way weight loss does and involves considerable pain and discomfort.

Psychological Help

When concern about body weight develops into an eating disorder, the help of a professional is recommended. In choosing a therapist, be sure to ask about credentials and experience (see Chapter 3). The therapist should have experience working with weight management, body image issues, eating disorders, addictions, and abuse issues.

BODY IMAGE

As described earlier in the chapter, body image consists of perceptions, images, thoughts, attitudes, and emotions. Developing a positive body image is an important aspect of psychological wellness and an important component of successful weight management.

Severe Body Image Problems

Poor body image can cause significant psychological distress. A person can become preoccupied with a perceived defect in appearance, thereby damaging self-esteem and interfering with relationships. Adolescents and adults who have a negative body image are more likely to diet restrictively, eat compulsively, or develop some other form of disordered eating.

When dissatisfaction becomes extreme, the condition is called *body dysmorphic disorder (BDD).* BDD affects about 2% of Americans, males and females in equal numbers; BDD usually begins before age 18 but can begin in adulthood. Sufferers are overly concerned with physical appearance, often focusing on slight flaws that are not obvious to others. Low self-esteem is common. Individuals with BDD may spend hours every day thinking about their flaws and looking at themselves in mirrors; they may desire and seek repeated cosmetic surgeries. BDD is related to obsessive-compulsive disorder and can lead to depression, social phobia, and suicide if left untreated. An individual with BDD needs to get professional evaluation and treatment; medication and therapy can help people with BDD.

In some cases, body image may bear little resemblance to fact. A person suffering from the eating disorder anorexia nervosa typically has a severely distorted body image—she believes herself to be fat even when she has become emaciated (see the next section for more on anorexia). Distorted body image is also a hallmark of *muscle dysmorphia,* a disorder experienced by some bodybuilders and other active people in which they see themselves as small and out of shape despite being very muscular. Those who suffer from muscle dysmorphia may let obsessive bodybuilding interfere with their work and relationships. They may also use steroids and other potentially dangerous muscle-building drugs.

Acceptance and Change

There are limits to the changes that can be made to body weight and body shape, both of which are influenced by heredity. The changes that can and should be made are lifestyle changes, as described throughout this chapter.

Knowing when the limits to healthy change have been reached—and learning to accept those limits—is crucial for overall wellness. Women in particular tend to measure self-worth in terms of their appearance; when they don't measure up to an unrealistic cultural ideal, they see themselves as defective and their self-esteem falls (see the box "Gender, Ethnicity, and Body Image" on p. 440). The result can be negative body image, disordered eating, or even a full-blown eating disorder. Women who view their bodies positively tend to be more intuitive eaters, relying on internal hunger and fullness cues to regulate what and how much they eat. They think more about how their bodies feel and function than how they appear to others.

Weight management needs to take place in a positive and realistic atmosphere. For an obese person, losing as few as 10 pounds can reduce blood pressure and improve mood. The hazards of excessive dieting and overconcern about body weight need to be countered by a change in attitude. A reasonable weight must take into account a person's weight history, social circumstances, metabolic profile, and psychological well-being.

EATING DISORDERS

Problems with body weight and weight control are not limited to excessive body fat. A growing number of people, especially adolescent girls and young women, experience **eating disorders,** characterized by severe disturbances in body image, eating patterns, and eating-related behaviors. The major eating disorders are anorexia nervosa, bulimia nervosa, and binge-eating disorder. Disordered eating affects an estimated 10 million American females and 1 million males.

Many more people have abnormal eating habits and attitudes about food that, although not meeting the criteria for a major eating disorder, do disrupt their lives.

Many factors are probably involved in the development of an eating disorder. Although wildly different explanations have been proposed, they share one central feature: a dissatisfaction with body image and body weight. Such dissatisfaction is created by distorted thinking, including perfectionistic beliefs, unreasonable demands for self-control, and excessive self-criticism. Dissatisfaction with body weight leads to dysfunctional attitudes about eating, such as fear of fat and preoccupation with food, and problematic eating behaviors, including excessive dieting, constant calorie counting, and frequent weighing.

Heredity appears to play a role in the development of eating disorders, accounting for more than 50% of the risk. But as with other conditions, only the tendency to develop an eating disorder is explained by heredity; the

TERMS **eating disorder** A serious disturbance in eating patterns or eating-related behavior, characterized by a negative body image and concerns about body weight or body fat.

Gender, Ethnicity, and Body Image

Body Image and Gender

Women are much more likely than men to be dissatisfied with their bodies, often wanting to be thinner than they are. In one study, only 30% of eighth-grade girls reported being content with their bodies, while 70% of their male classmates expressed satisfaction with their looks. Girls and women are much more likely than boys and men to diet, develop eating disorders, and be obese.

One reason that girls and women are dissatisfied with their bodies is that they are influenced by the media—particularly advertisements and women's fashion magazines. Most teen girls report that the media influence their idea of the perfect body and their decision to diet. In a study of adult women, viewing pictures of thin models in magazines had an immediate negative effect on their mood. In another study, 68% of female college students felt worse about their own appearance after looking through women's magazines. Some 75% of normal-weight women think they are overweight, and 90% overestimate their body size.

It is important to note that the image of the ideal woman presented in the media is often unrealistic and even unhealthy. In a review of BMI data for Miss America pageant winners since 1922, researchers noted a significant decline in BMI over time, with an increasing number of recent winners having BMIs in the "underweight" category. The average fashion model is 4–7 inches taller and almost 50 pounds lighter than the average American woman. Most fashion models are thinner than 98% of American women.

Our culture may be promoting an unattainable masculine ideal as well. Researchers have found that media consumption is positively associated with a desire for thinness and muscularity. Researchers studying male action figures such as GI Joe from the past 40 years noted that they have become increasingly muscular. A recent Batman action figure, if projected onto a man of average height, would result in someone with a 30-inch waist, 57-inch chest, and 27-inch biceps. Such media messages can be demoralizing; although not as commonly, boys and men do also suffer from body image problems.

Body Image and Ethnicity

Although some groups espouse thinness as an ideal body type, others do not. In many traditional African societies, for example, full-figured women's bodies are seen as symbols of health, prosperity, and fertility. African American teenage girls have a much more positive body image than do white girls; in one survey, two-thirds of them defined beauty as "the right attitude," whereas white girls were more preoccupied with weight and body shape.

Nevertheless, recent evidence indicates that African American women are as likely to engage in disordered eating behavior, especially binge eating and vomiting, as their Latina, American Indian, and white counterparts. These findings underscore the complex nature of eating disorders and body image.

Avoiding Body Image Problems

To minimize your risk of developing a body image problem, keep the following strategies in mind:

- Focus on healthy habits and good physical health.

- Focus on good psychological health and put concerns about physical appearance in perspective. Your worth as a human being does not depend on how you look.

- Practice body acceptance. You can influence your body size and type to some degree through lifestyle, but the basic fact is that some people are gene-

tically designed to be bigger or heavier than others.

- Find things to appreciate in yourself besides an idealized body image. Men and women whose self-esteem is based primarily on standards of physical attractiveness can find it difficult to age gracefully. Those who can learn to value other aspects of themselves are more accepting of the physical changes that occur naturally with age.

- View food choices as morally neutral—eating dessert isn't "bad" and doesn't make you a bad person. Healthy eating habits are an important part of a wellness lifestyle, but the things you really care about and do are more important in defining who you are.

- See the beauty and fitness industries for what they are. Realize that one of their goals is to prompt dissatisfaction with yourself so that you will buy their products.

expression of this tendency is affected by other factors. The home environment is one factor: Families in which there is hostility, abuse, or lack of cohesion provide fertile ground for the development of an eating disorder; a rigid or overprotective parent can also increase risk. Cultural messages, as well as family, friends, and peers, shape attitudes toward the self and others. Comparing oneself negatively with others can damage self-esteem and increase vulnerability. Young people who see themselves as lacking control over their lives are also at high risk for eating disorders. About 90% of eating disorders begin during adolescence. In recent years, however, cases of eating disorders have increased among children as young as 8.

Certain turning points in life, such as leaving home for college, often trigger an eating disorder. How a person copes with such stresses can influence risk, particularly in individuals who have few stress-management skills. An eating disorder may become a means of coping: The abnormal eating behavior reduces anxiety by producing numbness and alleviating emotional pain. Restrictive dieting is another possible trigger for the development of eating disorders.

Anorexia Nervosa

A person with **anorexia nervosa** does not eat enough food to maintain a reasonable body weight. Anorexia affects 1% of Americans, or about 3 million people, 95% of them female. Although it can occur later, anorexia typically develops between the ages of 12 and 18.

Characteristics of Anorexia Nervosa   People with anorexia have an intense fear of gaining weight or becoming fat. Their body image is so distorted that even when emaciated they think they are fat. People with anorexia may engage in compulsive behaviors or rituals that help keep them from eating, though some may also binge and **purge.** They often use vigorous and prolonged exercise to reduce body weight as well. Although they may express a great interest in food, even taking over the cooking responsibilities for the rest of the family, their own diet becomes more and more extreme. People with anorexia often hide or hoard food without eating it.

Anorexic people are typically introverted, emotionally reserved, and socially insecure. They are often model children who rarely complain and are anxious to please others and win their approval. Although school performance is typically above average, they are often critical of themselves and not satisfied with their accomplishments. For people with anorexia nervosa, their entire sense of self-esteem may be tied up in their evaluation of their body shape and weight.

Health Risks of Anorexia Nervosa   Because of extreme weight loss, females with anorexia often stop menstruating, become intolerant of cold, and develop low blood pressure and heart rate. They develop dry skin that is often covered by fine body hair like that of an infant. Their hands and feet may swell and take on a blue tinge.

Anorexia nervosa has been linked to a variety of medical complications, including disorders of the cardiovascular, gastrointestinal, endocrine, and skeletal systems. When body fat is virtually gone and muscles are severely wasted, the body turns to its own organs in a desperate search for protein. Death can occur from heart failure caused by electrolyte imbalances. About one in ten women with anorexia dies of starvation, cardiac arrest, or other medical complications—the highest death rate for any psychiatric disorder. Depression is also a serious risk, and about half the fatalities related to anorexia are suicides.

Bulimia Nervosa

A person suffering from **bulimia nervosa** engages in recurrent episodes of binge eating followed by purging. Bulimia is often difficult to recognize because sufferers conceal their eating habits and usually maintain a normal weight, although they may experience weight fluctuations of 10–15 pounds. Although bulimia usually begins in adolescence or young adulthood, it has begun to emerge at increasingly younger (11–12 years) and older (40–60 years) ages.

Characteristics of Bulimia Nervosa   During a binge, a bulimic person may rapidly consume thousands of calories. This is followed by an attempt to get rid of the food by purging, usually by vomiting or using laxatives or diuretics. During a binge, bulimics feel as though they have lost control and cannot stop or limit how much they eat. Some binge and purge only occasionally; others do so many times every day.

People with bulimia may appear to eat normally, but they are rarely comfortable around food. Binges usually occur in secret and can become nightmarish—raiding the kitchen for food, going from one grocery store to another to buy food, or even stealing food. During the binge, food acts as an anesthetic, and all feelings are blocked out. Afterward, bulimics feel physically drained and emotionally spent. They usually feel deeply ashamed and disgusted with both themselves and their behavior and terrified that they will gain weight from the binge.

Major life changes such as leaving for college, getting married, having a baby, or losing a job can trigger a binge-purge cycle. At such times, stress is high and the person may have no good outlet for emotional conflict or tension. As with anorexia, bulimia sufferers are often insecure and depend on others for approval and self-esteem. They may hide difficult emotions such as anger and disappointment from themselves and others. Binge eating and purging become a way of dealing with feelings.

Health Risks of Bulimia Nervosa The binge-purge cycle of bulimia places a tremendous strain on the body and can have serious health effects. Contact with vomited stomach acids erodes tooth enamel. Bulimic people often develop tooth decay because they binge on foods that are high in simple sugars. Repeated vomiting or the use of laxatives, in combination with deficient calorie intake, can damage the liver and kidneys and cause cardiac arrhythmia. Chronic hoarseness and esophageal tearing with bleeding may also result from vomiting. More rarely, binge eating can lead to rupture of the stomach. Although many bulimic women maintain normal weight, even a small weight loss to lower-than-normal weight can cause menstrual problems. And although less often associated with suicide or premature death than anorexia, bulimia is associated with increased depression, excessive preoccupation with food and body image, and sometimes disturbances in cognitive functioning.

Binge-Eating Disorder

Binge-eating disorder affects about 2% of American adults. It is characterized by uncontrollable eating, usually followed by feelings of guilt and shame with weight gain. Common eating patterns are eating more rapidly than normal, eating until uncomfortably full, eating when not hungry, and preferring to eat alone. Binge eaters may eat large amounts of food throughout the day, with no planned mealtimes. Many people with binge-eating disorder mistakenly see rigid dieting as the only solution to their problem. However, rigid dieting usually causes feelings of deprivation and a return to overeating.

Compulsive overeaters rarely eat because of hunger. Instead, food is used as a means of coping with stress, conflict, and other difficult emotions or to provide solace and entertainment. People who do not have the resources to deal effectively with stress may be more vulnerable to binge-eating disorder. Inappropriate overeating often begins during childhood. In some families, eating may be used as an activity to fill otherwise empty time. Parents may reward children with food for good behavior or withhold food as a means of punishment, thereby creating distorted feelings about the use of food.

Binge eaters are almost always obese, so they face all the health risks associated with obesity. In addition, binge eaters may have higher rates of depression and anxiety. To overcome binge eating, a person must learn to put food

and eating into proper perspective and develop other ways of coping with stress and painful emotions.

Borderline Disordered Eating

Eating habits and body image run a continuum from healthy to seriously disordered. Where each of us falls along that continuum can change depending on life stresses, illnesses, and many other factors. People with borderline disordered eating have some symptoms of eating disorders but do not meet the full diagnostic criteria for anorexia, bulimia, or binge-eating disorder. Behaviors such as excessive dieting, occasional bingeing or purging, or the inability to control eating turn food into the enemy and create havoc in the lives of millions of Americans.

How do you know if you have disordered eating habits? When thoughts about food and weight dominate your life, you have a problem. If you're convinced that your worth as a person hinges on how you look and how much you weigh, it's time to get help. Other danger signs include frequent feelings of guilt after a meal or snack, any use of vomiting or laxatives after meals, or overexercising or severely restricting your food intake to compensate for what you've already eaten.

If you suspect you have an eating problem, don't go it alone or delay getting help, as disordered eating habits can develop into a full-blown eating disorder. Check with your student health or counseling center—nearly all colleges have counselors and medical personnel who can help you or refer you to a specialist if needed. If you are concerned about eating habits of a family member or friend, refer to the suggestions in the box "If Someone You Know Has an Eating Disorder . . .".

Treating Eating Disorders

The treatment of eating disorders must address both problematic eating behaviors and the misuse of food to manage stress and emotions. Anorexia nervosa treatment first involves averting a medical crisis by restoring adequate body weight; then the psychological aspects of the disorder can be addressed. The treatment of bulimia nervosa or binge-eating disorder involves first stabilizing the

QUESTIONS FOR CRITICAL THINKING AND REFLECTION

Do you know someone you suspect may suffer from an eating disorder? Does the advice in this chapter seem helpful to you? Do you think you could follow it? Why or why not? Have you ever experienced disordered eating patterns yourself? If so, can you identify the reasons for it?

If Someone You Know Has an Eating Disorder . . .

Secrecy and denial are two hallmarks of eating disorders, so it can be hard to know if someone has anorexia or bulimia. Signs that someone may have anorexia include sudden weight loss, excessive dieting or exercise, guilt or preoccupation with food or eating, frequent weighing, fear of becoming fat despite being thin, and baggy or layered clothes to conceal weight loss. Signs that someone may have bulimia include excessive eating without weight gain, secretiveness about food (stealing, hiding, or hoarding food), self-induced vomiting (bathroom visits during or after a meal), swollen glands or puffy face, erosion of tooth enamel, and use of laxatives, diuretics, or diet pills to control weight.

If you decide to approach a friend with your concerns, here are some tips to follow:

• Find out about treatment resources in your community (see the For Further Exploration section for suggestions). You may want to consult a professional at your school clinic or counseling center about the best way to approach the situation.

• Arrange to speak with your friend in a private place, and allow enough time to talk.

• Express your concerns, with specific observations of your friend's behavior. Expect him or her to deny or minimize the problem and possibly to become angry with you. Stay calm and nonjudgmental, and continue to express your concern.

• Avoid giving simplistic advice about eating habits. Listen if your friend wants to talk, and offer your support and understanding. Give your friend the information you found about where he or she can get help, and offer to go along.

• If the situation is an emergency—if your friend has fainted, for example, or attempted suicide—call 911 for help immediately.

• If you are upset about the situation, consider talking to someone yourself. The professionals at the clinic or counseling center are there to help you. Remember, you are not to blame for another person's eating disorder.

---

eating patterns, then identifying and changing the patterns of thinking that led to disordered eating, and then improving coping skills. Concurrent problems, such as depression or anxiety, must also be addressed.

In 2006, a study published in the *Journal of the American Medical Association* showed that the antidepressant Prozac, which is widely used to treat anorexia, worked no better than a placebo in preventing recurrence in women recovering from the disorder. However, the anti-seizure drug topiramate has shown promise in the treatment of bulimia by reducing the urges to binge and purge.

Treatment of eating disorders usually involves a combination of psychotherapy and medical management. The therapy may be carried out individually or in a group; sessions involving the entire family may be recommended. A support or self-help group can be a useful adjunct to such treatment. Medical professionals, including physicians, dentists, gynecologists, and registered dietitians, can evaluate and manage the physical damage caused by the disorder. If a patient is severely depressed or emaciated, hospitalization may be necessary.

QUICK STATS

About 30% of people with anorexia receive treatment; only 6% of bulimics receive treatment.

—National Eating Disorders Association, 2005

TIPS FOR TODAY AND THE FUTURE
Many approaches work, but the simplest formula for weight management is moderate food intake coupled with regular exercise.

RIGHT NOW YOU CAN
- Assess your weight-management needs. Do you need to gain weight, lose weight, or stay at your current weight?
- List five things you can do to add more physical activity (not exercise) to your daily routine.
- Identify the foods you regularly eat that may be sabotaging your ability to manage your weight.

IN THE FUTURE YOU CAN
- Make an honest assessment of your current body image. Is it accurate and fair, or is it unduly negative and unhealthy? If your body image presents a problem, consider getting professional advice on how to view yourself realistically.
- Keep track of your energy needs to determine whether your energy balance equation is correct. Use this information as part of your long-term weight-management efforts.

SUMMARY

• Body composition is the relative amounts of fat-free mass and fat in the body. *Overweight* and *obesity* refer to

A Weight-Management Program

The behavior management plan described in Chapter 1 provides an excellent framework for a weight-management program. Following are some suggestions about specific ways you can adapt that general plan to controlling your weight.

Motivation and Commitment

Make sure you are motivated and committed before you begin. Failure at weight loss is a frustrating experience that can make it more difficult to lose weight in the future. Think about why you want to lose weight. Self-focused reasons, such as to feel good about yourself or to have a greater sense of well-being, are often associated with success. Trying to lose weight for others or out of concern for how others view you is a poor foundation for a weight-loss program. Make a list of your reasons for wanting to lose weight, and post it in a prominent place.

Setting Goals

Choose a reasonable weight you think you would like to reach over the long term, and be willing to renegotiate it as you get further along. Break down your long-term weight and behavioral goals into a series of short-term goals. Develop a new way of behaving by designing small, manageable steps that will get you to where you want to go.

Creating a Negative Energy Balance

When your weight is constant, you are burning approximately the same number of calories as you are taking in. To tip the energy balance toward weight loss, you must either consume fewer calories, or burn more calories through physical activity, or both. One pound of body fat represents 3500 calories. To lose weight at the recommended rate of 0.5–2.0 pounds per week, you must create a negative energy balance of 1750–7000 calories per week or 250–1000 calories per day. To generate a negative energy balance, it's usually best to begin by increasing activity level rather than decreasing your calorie consumption.

Physical Activity

Consider how you can increase your energy output simply by increasing routine physical activity, such as walking or taking the stairs. (Chapter 13 lists activities that use about 150 calories.) If you are not already involved in a regular exercise routine aimed at increasing endurance and building or maintaining muscle mass, seek help from someone who is competent to help you plan and start an appropriate exercise routine. If you are already doing regular physical exercise, evaluate your program according to the guidelines in Chapter 13.

Don't try to use exercise to spot reduce. Leg lifts, for example, contribute to fat loss only to the extent that they burn calories; they don't burn fat just from your legs. You can make parts of your body appear more fit by exercising them, but the only way you can reduce fat in any specific part of your body is to create an overall negative energy balance.

Diet and Eating Habits

If you can't generate a large enough negative energy balance solely by increasing physical activity, you may want to supplement exercise with modest cuts in your calorie intake. Don't think of this as going on a diet; your goal is to make small changes in your diet that you can maintain for a lifetime. Focus on cutting your intake of saturated and trans fats and added sugars and on eating a variety of nutritious foods in moderation. Don't skip meals, fast, or go on a very-low-calorie diet or a diet that is unbalanced.

Making changes in eating habits is another important strategy for weight management. If your program centers on a conscious restriction of certain food items, you're likely to spend all your time thinking about the forbidden foods. Focus on *how* to eat rather than *what* to eat. Refer to the box "Lifestyle Strategies for Successful Weight Management" for suggestions.

Self-Monitoring

Keep a record of your weight and behavior change progress. Try keeping a record of everything you eat. Write down what you plan to eat, in what quantity, *before* you eat. You'll find that just having to record something that is not OK to eat is likely to stop you from eating it. If you also note what seems to be triggering your urges to eat (for example, you feel bored, or someone offered you something), you'll become more aware of your weak spots and be better able to take corrective action. Also, keep track of your daily activities and your formal exercise program so you can monitor increases in physical activity.

Putting Your Plan into Action

- Examine the environmental cues that trigger poor eating and exercise habits, and devise strategies for dealing with them. For example, you may need to remove problem foods from your house temporarily or put a sign on the refrigerator reminding you to go for a walk instead of having a snack. Anticipate problem situations, and plan ways to handle them more effectively.

- Create new environmental cues that will support your new healthy behaviors. Put your walking shoes by the front door. Move fruits and vegetables to the front of the refrigerator.

- Get others to help. Talk to friends and family members about what they can do to support your efforts. Find a buddy to join you in your exercise program.

- Give yourself lots of praise and rewards. Think about your accomplishments and achievements and congratulate yourself. Plan special nonfood treats for yourself, such as a walk or a movie. Reward yourself often and for anything that counts toward success.

- If you slip, tell yourself to get back on track immediately, and don't waste time on self-criticism. Think positively instead of getting into a cycle of guilt and self-blame. Don't demand too much of yourself.

- Don't get discouraged. Be aware that although weight loss is bound to slow down after the first loss of body fluid, the weight loss at this slower rate is more permanent than earlier, more dramatic, losses.

- Remember that weight management is a lifelong project. You need to adopt reasonable goals and strategies that you can maintain over the long term.

body weight or the percentage of body fat that exceeds what is associated with good health.

- The key to weight management is maintaining a balance of calories in (food) and calories out (resting metabolism, food digestion, and physical activity).

- Standards for assessing body weight and body composition include body mass index (BMI) and percent body fat.

- Too much or too little body fat is linked to health problems; the distribution of body fat can also be a significant risk factor.

- An inaccurate or negative body image is common and can lead to psychological distress.

- Genetic factors help determine a person's weight, but the influence of heredity can be overcome with attention to lifestyle factors.

- Physiological factors involved in the regulation of body weight and body fat include metabolic rate, hormonal influences, and the size and number of fat cells.

- Nutritional guidelines for weight management include consuming a moderate number of calories; limiting portion sizes, energy density, and the intake of fat, simple sugars, refined carbohydrates, and protein to recommended levels; and developing an eating schedule and rules for food choices.

- Activity guidelines for weight management emphasize daily physical activity and regular sessions of cardiorespiratory endurance exercise and strength training.

- Weight management requires developing positive, realistic self-talk and self-esteem and a repertoire of appropriate techniques for handling stress and other emotional and physical challenges.

- People can be successful at long-term weight loss on their own, by combining diet and exercise.

- Diet books, OTC diet aids and supplements, and formal weight-loss programs should be assessed for safety and efficacy.

- Professional help is needed in cases of severe obesity; medical treatments include prescription drugs, surgery, and psychological therapy.

- Dissatisfaction with weight and shape are common to all eating disorders. Anorexia nervosa is characterized by self-starvation, distorted body image, and an intense fear of gaining weight. Bulimia nervosa is characterized by recurrent episodes of uncontrolled binge eating and frequent purging. Binge-eating disorder involves binge eating without regular use of compensatory purging.

FOR MORE INFORMATION

BOOKS

Critser, G. 2004. *Fat Land: How Americans Became the Fattest People in the World.* Boston: Mariner Books. *A look at the many factors in American life that have contributed to the rapid increase in obesity rates.*

Dillon, E. 2006. *Issues That Concern You: Obesity.* New York: Greenhaven Press. *A collection of perspectives on the causes of obesity, its management, and its impact on individuals and society.*

Ferguson, J. M., and C. Ferguson. 2003. *Habits Not Diets,* 4th ed. Boulder, Colo.: Bull. *A behavior-change approach to changing diet and activity habits that includes many helpful practical tips, assessment worksheets, and tracking forms.*

Gaesser, G. A., and K. Kratina. 2006. *It's the Calories, Not the Carbs.* Victoria, B.C.: Trafford. *Provides a detailed look at the facts behind successful weight loss by shunning fad diets and practicing sound energy balance.*

Hensrud, D. D. 2005. *Mayo Clinic Healthy Weight for Everyone.* Rochester, Minn.: Mayo Clinic. *Provides guidelines for successful weight management.*

Ihde, G. M. 2006. *Considering Weight-Loss Surgery: The Facts You Need to Know for a Healthy Recovery.* Victoria, B.C.: Trafford. *An easy-to-read guide to the benefits and risks of weight-loss surgery.*

Milchovich, S. K., and B. Dunn-Long. 2007. *Diabetes Mellitus: A Practical Handbook,* 9th. ed. Boulder, Colo.: Bull. *A user-friendly guide to diabetes.*

Schulherr, S. 2008. *Eating Disorders for Dummies.* Hoboken, NJ: Wiley. *An easy-to-understand-guide to eating disorders.*

ORGANIZATIONS, HOTLINES, AND WEB SITES

American Diabetes Association. Provides information, a free newsletter, and referrals to local support groups; the Web site includes an online diabetes risk assessment.
  http://www.diabetes.org

Calorie Control Council. Site includes a variety of interactive calculators, including an Exercise Calculator that estimates the calories burned from various forms of physical activity.
  http://www.caloriecontrol.org

FDA Center for Food Safety and Applied Nutrition: Dietary Supplements. Provides background facts and information on the current regulatory status of dietary supplements, including compounds marketed for weight loss.
  http://www.cfsan.fda.gov/~dms/supplmnt.html

Federal Trade Commission (FTC): Project Waistline. Provides advice for evaluating advertising about weight-loss products.
  http://www.ftc.gov/bcp/conline/edcams/waistline/index.html

National Heart, Lung, and Blood Institute (NHLBI): Aim for a Healthy Weight. Provides information and tips on diet and physical activity, as well as a BMI calculator.
  http://www.nhlbi.nih.gov/health/public/heart/obesity/lose_wt

National Institute of Diabetes and Digestive and Kidney Diseases (NIDDK). Provides information and referrals for problems related to obesity, weight control, and nutritional disorders.
  http://win.niddk.nih.gov/

Partnership for Healthy Weight Management. Provides information on evaluating weight-loss programs and advertising claims.

http://www.consumer.gov/weightloss

SmallStep.gov. Provides resources for increasing activity and improving diet through small changes in daily habits.

http://www.smallstep.gov

U.S. Consumer Gateway: Health—Dieting and Weight Control. Provides links to government sites with advice on evaluating claims about weight-loss products and programs.

http://www.consumer.gov/health.htm

USDA Food and Nutrition Information Center: Weight and Obesity. Provides links to recent reports and studies on the issue of obesity among Americans.

http://www.nal.usda.gov/fnic/reports/obesity.html

Resources for people concerned about eating disorders:

Eating Disorder Referral and Information Center
http://www.edreferral.com
Eating Disorders Shared Awareness
http://www.something-fishy.org
MedlinePlus: Eating Disorders
http://www.nlm.nih.gov/medlineplus/eatingdisorders.html
National Association of Anorexia Nervosa and Associated Disorders
847-831-3438 (referral line)
http://www.anad.org
National Eating Disorders Association
800-931-2237
http://www.nationaleatingdisorders.org

See also the listings in Chapters 12 and 13.

SELECTED BIBLIOGRAPHY

Adams, K. F., et al. 2006. Overweight, obesity, and mortality in a large prospective cohort of persons 50 to 71 years old. *New England Journal of Medicine* 355(8): 763–778.

Baker, B. 2006. Weight loss and diet plans. *American Journal of Nursing* 106(6): 52–59.

Behn, A., and E. Ur. 2006. The obesity epidemic and its cardiovascular consequences. *Current Opinions in Cardiology* 21(4): 353–360.

Bowman, S. A., et al. 2004. Effects of fast-food consumption on energy intake and diet quality among children in a national household survey. *Pediatrics* 113(1 Pt 1): 112–118.

Buchwald, H., et al. 2004. Bariatric surgery: A systematic review and meta-analysis. *Journal of the American Medical Association* 292(14): 1724–1737.

Centers for Disease Control and Prevention. 2006. *Diabetes Care.* Atlanta, Ga.: U.S. Department of Health and Human Services, Centers for Disease Control and Prevention.

Centers for Disease Control and Prevention. 2008. *National Diabetes Fact Sheet: General Information and National Estimates on Diabetes in the United States, 2007.* Atlanta, Ga: U.S. Department of Health and Human Services, Centers for Disease Control and Prevention.

Chandon, P., and B. Wansink. 2007. The biasing health halos of fast-food restaurant health claims: Lower calorie estimates and higher side-dish consumption intentions. *Journal of Consumer Research* 34(3): 301–314.

Dahlman, I., and P. Arner. Obesity and polymorphisms in genes regulating human adipose tissue. *International Journal of Obesity* 31(11): 1629–1641.

Dhingra, R., et al. 2007. Soft drink consumption and risk of developing cardiometabolic risk factors and the metabolic syndrome in middle-aged adults in the community. *Circulation* 116(5): 480–488.

Dong, L., G. Block, and S. Mandel. 2004. Activities contributing to total energy expenditure in the United States: Results from the NHAPS Study. *International Journal of Behavioral Nutrition and Physical Activity* 1(4).

Drewnowski, A., and F. Bellisle. 2007. Liquid calories, sugar and body weight. *American Journal of Clinical Nutrition* 85(3): 651–661.

Farshchi, H. R., M. A. Taylor, and I. A. Macdonald. 2005. Deleterious effects of omitting breakfast on insulin sensitivity and fasting lipid profiles in healthy lean women. *American Journal of Clinical Nutrition* 81(2): 388–396.

Flegal, K. M., et al. 2005. Excess deaths associated with underweight, overweight, and obesity. *Journal of the American Medical Association* 293(15): 1861–1867.

Fenicchia, L. M., et al. 2004. Influence of resistance exercise training on glucose control in women with type 2 diabetes. *Metabolism* 53(3): 284–289.

Fung, T. T., et al. 2004. Dietary patterns, meat intake, and the risk of type 2 diabetes in women. *Archives of Internal Medicine* 164(20): 2235–2240.

Graves, B. S., and R. L. Welsh. 2004. Recognizing the signs of body dysmorphic disorder and muscle dysmorphia. *ACSM's Health and Fitness Journal,* January/February.

Hamilton, M., et al. 2007. Role of low energy expenditure and sitting in obesity, metabolic syndrome, type 2 diabetes, and cardiovascular disease. *Diabetes* 56(11): 2655–2667.

Hu, F. B., et al. 2004. Adiposity as compared with physical activity in predicting mortality among women. *New England Journal of Medicine* 351(26): 2694–2703.

Kaiser Family Foundation. 2004. The role of media in childhood obesity. *Issue Brief,* February.

Kumanyika, S. K, et al. 2008. Population-based prevention of obesity: The need for comprehensive promotion of healthful eating, physical activity, and energy balance: A scientific statement from American Heart Association Council on Epidemiology and Prevention, Interdisciplinary Committee for Prevention (formerly the Expert Panel on Population and Prevention Science). *Circulation* 118(4): 428–464.

Ma, Y., et al. 2005. Association between dietary carbohydrates and body weight. *American Journal of Epidemiology* 161(4): 359–367.

McBride, B. F., et al. 2004. Electrocardiographic and hemodynamic effects of a multicomponent dietary supplement containing ephedra and caffeine. *Journal of the American Medical Association* 291(4): 216–221.

McCullough, P. A., et al. 2006. Cardiorespiratory fitness and short-term complications after bariatric surgery. *CHEST* 130: 517–525.

Muenning, P., et al. 2006. Gender and the burden of disease attributable to obesity. *American Journal of Public Health* 96(9): 1662–1668.

Nicklas, B. J., et al. 2004. Association of visceral adipose tissue with incident myocardial infarction in older men and women: The Health, Aging and Body Composition Study. *American Journal of Epidemiology* 160(8): 741–749.

O'Brien, P., et al. 2006. Treatment of mild to moderate obesity with laparoscopic adjustable gastric banding or an intensive medical program. *Annals of Internal Medicine* 144(9): 625–633.

Ogden, C. L., et al. 2007. Obesity among adults in the United States: No change since 2003–2004. *National Center for Health Statistics Data Brief* 1: 1–8.

Olshansky, S. J., et al. 2005. A potential decline in life expectancy in the United States in the 21st century. *New England Journal of Medicine* 352(11): 1138–1145.

Rubin, C. T., et al. 2007. Adipogenesis is inhibited by brief, daily exposure to high-frequency, extremely low-magnitude mechanical signals. *Proceedings of the National Academy of Sciences* 104(45): 17879–17884.

Schulze, M. B., et al. 2004. Sugar-sweetened beverages, weight gain, and incidence of type 2 diabetes in young and middle-aged women. *Journal of the American Medical Association* 292(8): 927–934.

Taylor, E. N., et al. 2005. Obesity, weight gain, and risk of kidney stones. *Journal of the American Medical Association* 293(4): 455–462.

Tsai, A. G., and T. A. Wadden. 2005. Systematic review: An evaluation of major commercial weight loss programs in the United States. *Annals of Internal Medicine* 142(1): 56–66.

van Dam, R. M., et al. 2006. The relationship between overweight in adolescence and premature death in women. *Annals of Internal Medicine* 145(2): 91–97.

Vorona, R. D., et al. 2005. Overweight and obese patients in a primary care population report less sleep than patients with a normal body mass index. *Archives of Internal Medicine* 165: 25–30.

Walsh, T. B., et al. 2006. Fluoxetine after weight restoration in anorexia nervosa. *Journal of the American Medical Association* 295(22): 2605–2612.

Wang, Y., and M. A. Beydoun. 2007. The obesity epidemic in the United States—gender, age, socioeconomic, racial/ethnic and geographical characteristics: A systematic review and meta-regression analysis. *Epidemiologic Reviews* 29: 6–28.

Wansink, B., and P. Chandon. 2006. Meal size, not body size, explains errors in estimating calorie content of meals. *Annals of Internal Medicine* 145: 326–332.

Weinstein, A. R., et al. 2004. Relationship of physical activity vs. body mass index with type 2 diabetes in women. *Journal of the American Medical Association* 292(10): 1188–1194.

Weinstein, P. K. 2006. A review of weight loss programs delivered via the Internet. *Journal of Cardiovascular Nursing* 21(4): 251–258.

Wong, S. L., et al. 2004. Cardiorespiratory fitness is associated with lower abdominal fat independent of body mass index. *Medicine and Science in Sports and Exercise* 36(2): 286–291.

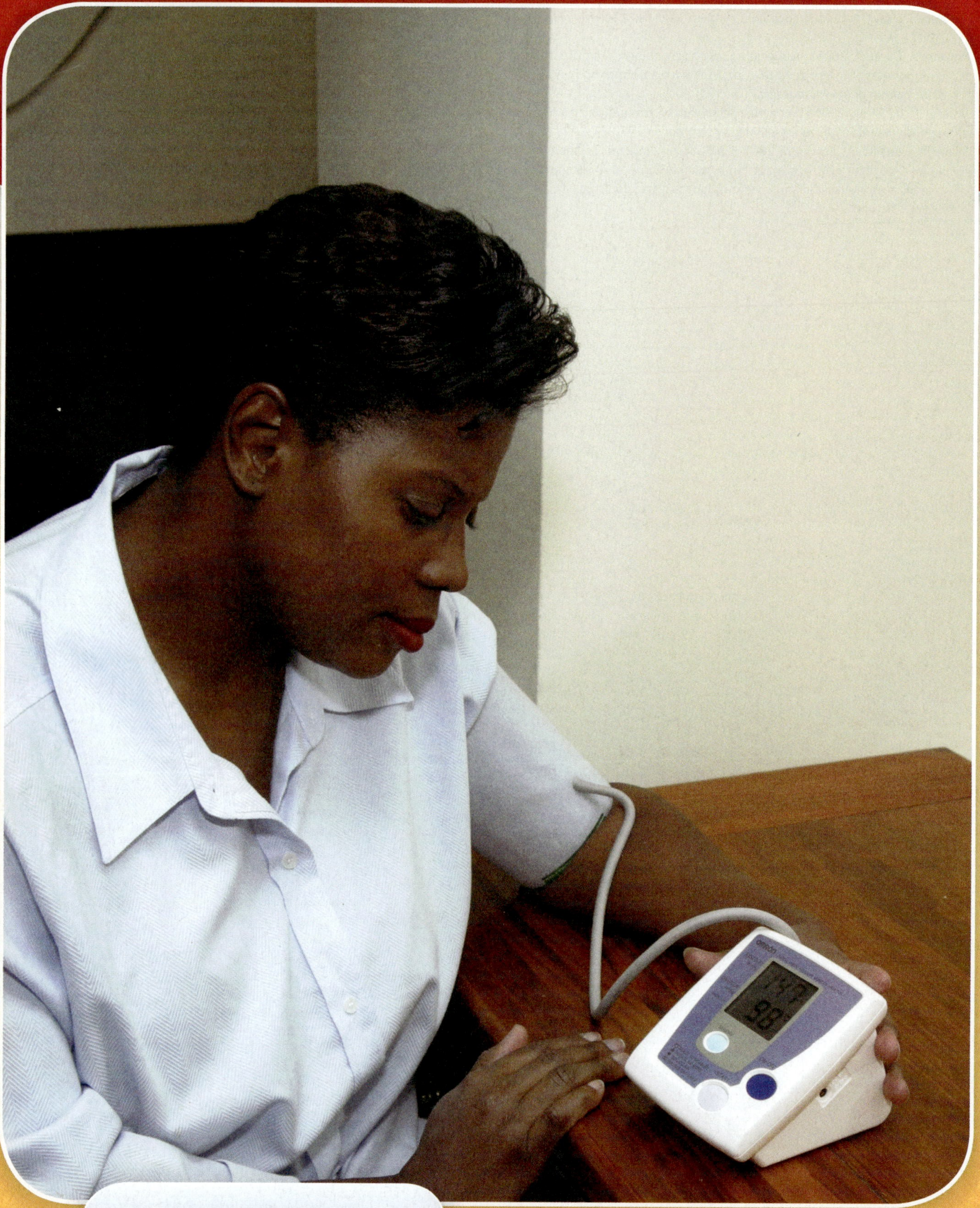

CORE CONCEPTS IN HEALTH connect PERSONAL HEALTH

http://www.mcgrawhillconnect.com/personalhealth

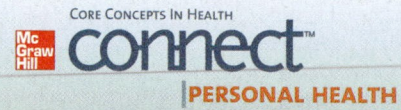

CARDIOVASCULAR HEALTH

15

LOOKING AHEAD>>>>>

AFTER READING THIS CHAPTER, YOU SHOULD BE ABLE TO:

- List the major components of the cardiovascular system and describe how blood is pumped and circulated throughout the body
- Describe the controllable and uncontrollable risk factors associated with cardiovascular disease
- Discuss the major forms of cardiovascular disease and how they develop
- List the steps you can take to lower your personal risk of developing cardiovascular disease

TEST YOUR KNOWLEDGE

1. Reducing the amount of cholesterol you eat is the most important dietary change you can make to improve your blood cholesterol levels.
   True or false?

2. Women are about as likely to die of cardiovascular disease as they are to die of breast cancer.
   True or false?

3. On average, how much earlier does heart disease develop in people who don't exercise regularly than in people who do?
   a. 6 months
   b. 2 years
   c. 6 years

4. Healthy teenagers have no signs of cardiovascular disease.
   True or false?

5. Which of the following foods would be a good choice for promoting heart health?
   a. whole grains
   b. salmon
   c. bananas

ANSWERS

1. **FALSE.** Limiting your intake of saturated and trans fats, which promote the production of cholesterol by the liver, is the key dietary change for improving blood cholesterol levels; dietary cholesterol has much less of an effect on blood cholesterol.

2. **FALSE.** Cardiovascular disease kills far more. Among American women, nearly 1 in 3 deaths is due to cardiovascular disease and about 1 in 30 is due to breast cancer.

3. **C.** Both aerobic exercise and strength training significantly improve cardiovascular health.

4. **FALSE.** Autopsy studies of young trauma victims show that narrowing of the arteries that supply the heart with blood begins in adolescence in many people.

5. **ALL THREE.** Whole grains (such as whole wheat, oatmeal, rye, barley, and brown rice), foods with omega-3 fatty acids (salmon), and foods high in potassium and low in sodium (bananas) all improve cardiovascular health.

Cardiovascular disease (CVD) affects about 80 million Americans and is the leading cause of death in the United States, claiming one life every 37 seconds—about 2400 Americans every day. Heart attacks and strokes are the number-one and number-three causes of death, respectively, making them the most common life-threatening manifestations of CVD. Though we typically think of CVD as primarily affecting men and older adults, heart attack is the number-one killer of American women, and over 17% of fatal heart attacks occur in people under age 65.

CVD is largely due to our way of life. Too many Americans eat an unhealthy diet, are overweight and sedentary, smoke, manage stress ineffectively, have uncontrolled high blood pressure or high cholesterol levels, and don't know the signs of CVD. Not all the risk factors for CVD are controllable—for example, the older you are, the greater your risk for CVD. But many key risk factors can be treated or modified, and you can reduce your risk for CVD.

This chapter introduces the workings of the cardiovascular system, explains CVD and its risks, and shows you how to keep your heart healthy for life.

THE CARDIOVASCULAR SYSTEM

The **cardiovascular system** consists of the heart and blood vessels (Figure 15.1); together, they move blood throughout the body.

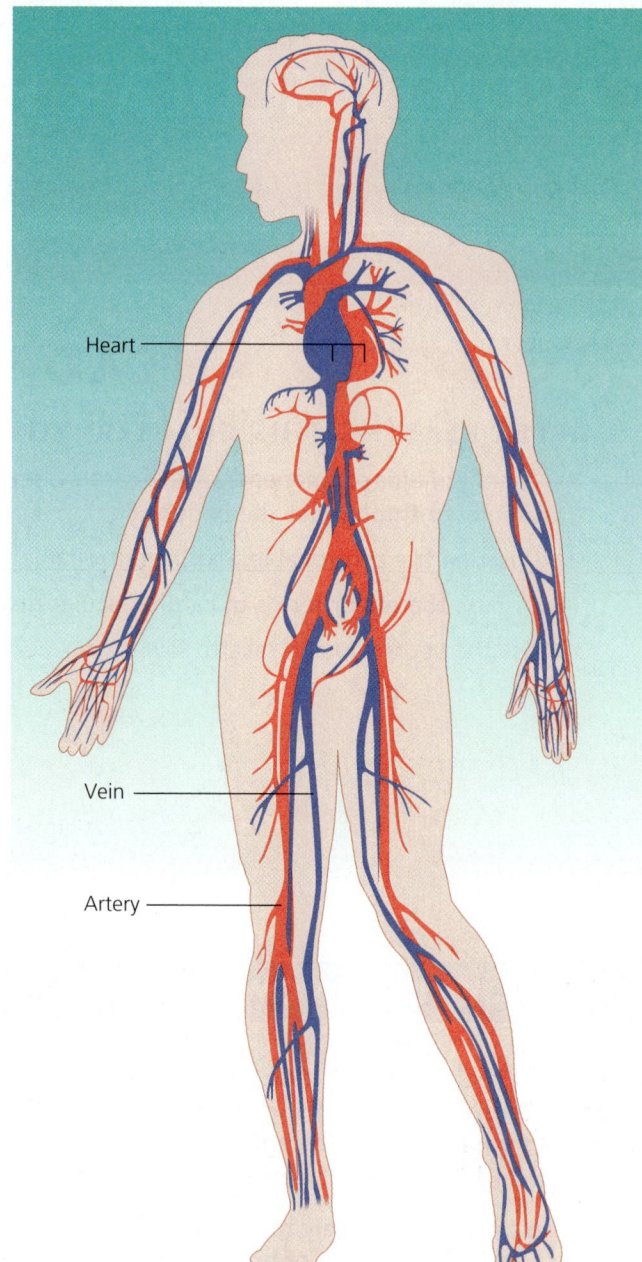

FIGURE 15.1 **The cardiovascular system.**

The Heart

The heart is a four-chambered, fist-sized muscle located just beneath the sternum (breastbone). It pumps deoxygenated (oxygen-poor) blood to the lungs and delivers oxygenated (oxygen-rich) blood to the rest of the body. Blood actually travels through two separate circulatory systems: The right side of the heart pumps blood to the lungs in what is called **pulmonary circulation,** and the left side pumps blood through the rest of the body in **systemic circulation.**

The following steps describe the path blood follows as it travels through the cardiovascular system (Figure 15.2):

TERMS

cardiovascular disease (CVD)   The collective term for various diseases of the heart and blood vessels.

cardiovascular system   The system that circulates blood through the body; consists of the heart and blood vessels.

pulmonary circulation   The part of the circulatory system governed by the right side of the heart; the circulation of blood between the heart and the lungs.

systemic circulation   The part of the circulatory system governed by the left side of the heart; the circulation of blood between the heart and the rest of the body.

vena cava   Either of two large veins through which blood is returned to the right atrium of the heart.

atria   The two upper chambers of the heart in which blood collects before passing to the ventricles.

ventricles   The two lower chambers of the heart that pump blood through arteries to the lungs and other parts of the body.

aorta   The large artery that receives blood from the left ventricle and distributes it to the body.

systole   Contraction phase of the heart.

diastole   Relaxation phase of the heart.

blood pressure   The force exerted by the blood on the walls of the blood vessels; created by the pumping action of the heart.

veins   Vessels that carry blood to the heart.

arteries   Vessels that carry blood away from the heart.

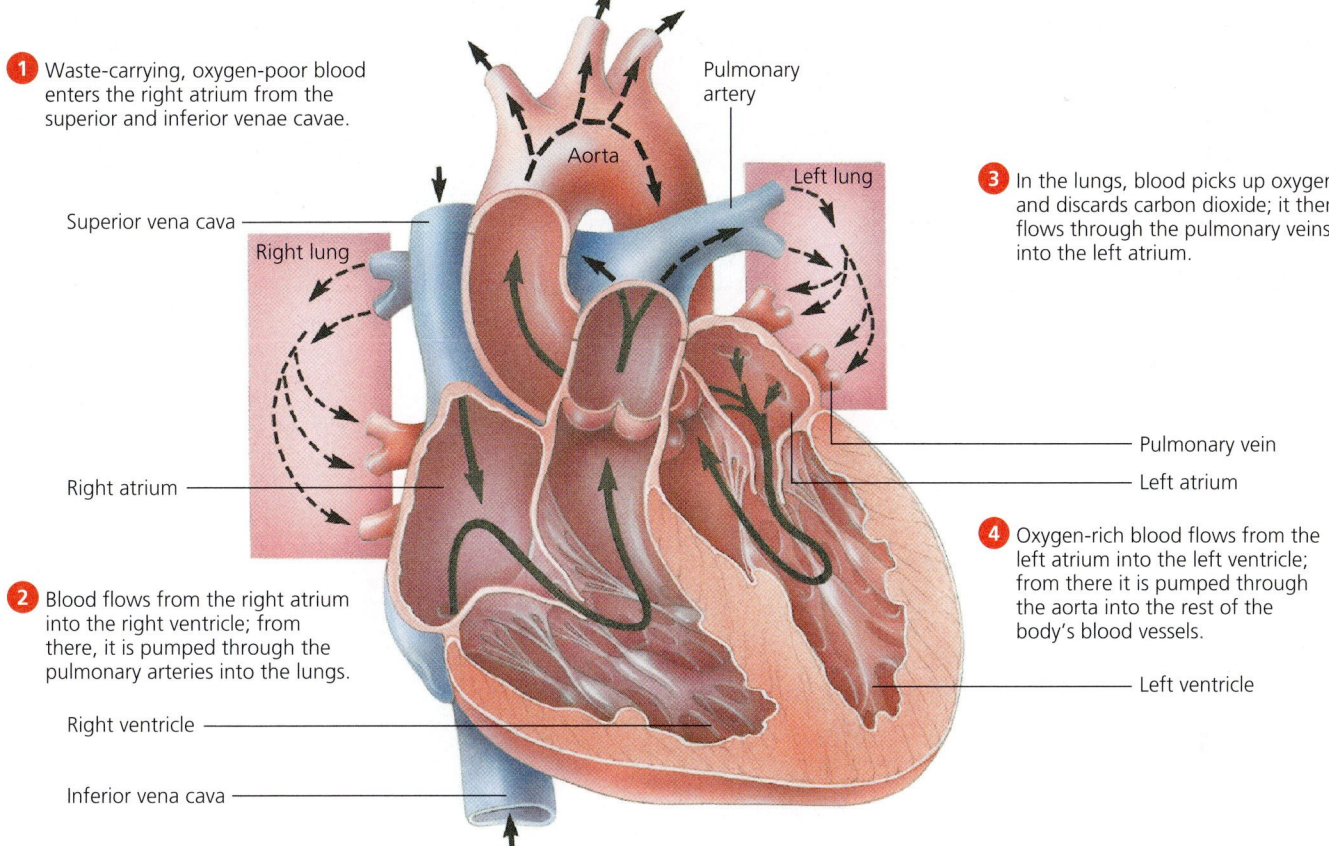

1 Waste-carrying, oxygen-poor blood enters the right atrium from the superior and inferior venae cavae.

Superior vena cava

Right lung

Right atrium

2 Blood flows from the right atrium into the right ventricle; from there, it is pumped through the pulmonary arteries into the lungs.

Right ventricle

Inferior vena cava

Pulmonary artery

Aorta

Left lung

3 In the lungs, blood picks up oxygen and discards carbon dioxide; it then flows through the pulmonary veins into the left atrium.

Pulmonary vein

Left atrium

4 Oxygen-rich blood flows from the left atrium into the left ventricle; from there it is pumped through the aorta into the rest of the body's blood vessels.

Left ventricle

FIGURE 15.2   Circulation in the heart.

1. Waste-laden, oxygen-poor blood travels through large vessels, called **venae cavae,** into the heart's right upper chamber, called the **atrium.**

2. After the right atrium fills, it contracts and pumps blood into the heart's right lower chamber, called the **ventricle.**

3. When the right ventricle is full, it contracts and pumps blood through the pulmonary artery into the lungs.

4. In the lungs, blood picks up oxygen and discards carbon dioxide.

5. The cleaned, oxygenated blood flows from the lungs through the pulmonary veins into the heart's left atrium.

6. After the left atrium fills, it contracts and pumps blood into the left ventricle.

7. When the left ventricle is full, it pumps blood through the **aorta**—the body's largest artery— for distribution to the rest of the body's blood vessels.

The period of the heart's contraction is called **systole;** the period of relaxation is called **diastole.** During systole, the atria contract first, pumping blood into the ventricles.

A fraction of a second later, the ventricles contract, pumping blood to the lungs and the body. During diastole, blood flows into the heart.

Blood pressure, the force exerted by blood on the walls of the blood vessels, is created by the pumping action of the heart; blood pressure is greater during systole than during diastole.

The heartbeat—the split-second sequence of contractions of the heart's four chambers—is controlled by nerve impulses. These signals originate in a bundle of specialized cells in the right atrium called the *sinoatrial node,* or *pacemaker.* Unless it is speeded up or slowed down by the brain in response to such stimuli as danger or the tissues' need for more oxygen, the heart produces nerve impulses at a steady rate.

The Blood Vessels

Blood vessels are classified by size and function. **Veins** carry blood to the heart. **Arteries** carry blood away from the heart. Veins have thin walls, but arteries have thick elastic walls that enable them to expand and relax with the volume of blood being pumped through them.

After leaving the heart, the aorta branches into smaller and smaller vessels. The smallest arteries branch still further

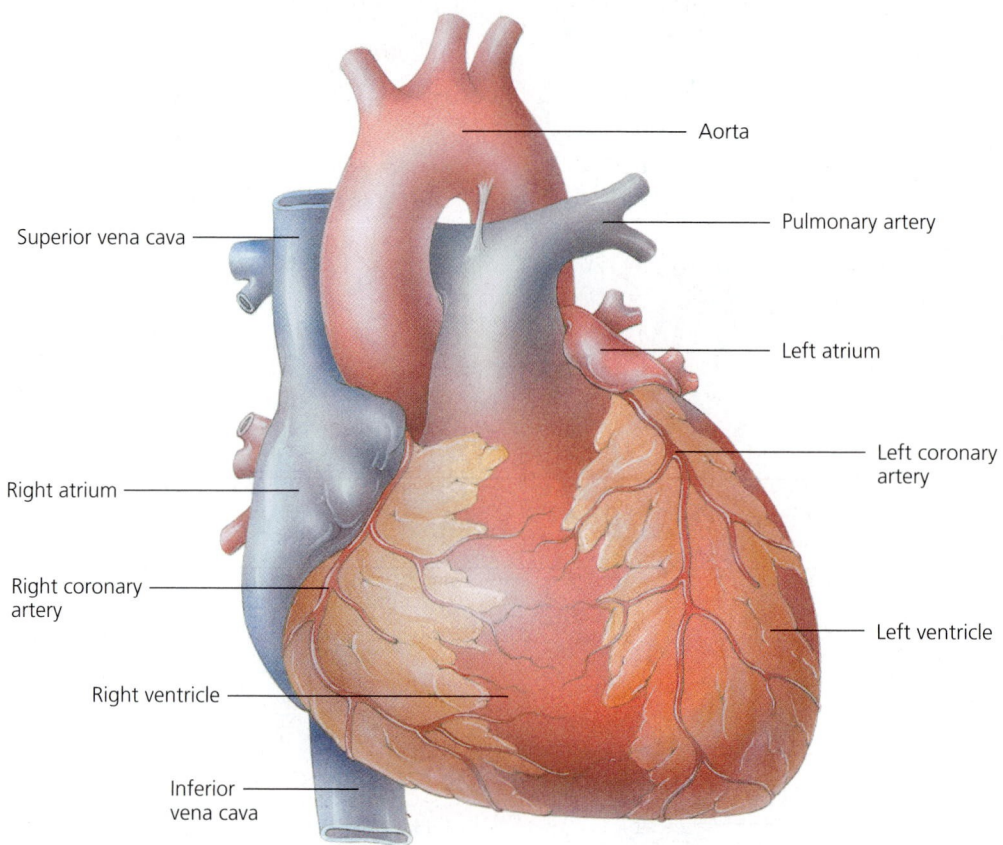

Aorta

Pulmonary artery

Left atrium

Left coronary artery

Superior vena cava

Right atrium

Left ventricle

Right coronary artery

Right ventricle

Inferior vena cava

FIGURE 15.3 Blood supply to the heart.

into **capillaries,** tiny vessels only one cell thick. The capillaries deliver oxygen and nutrient-rich blood to the tissues and pick up oxygen-poor, waste-laden blood. From the capillaries, this blood empties into small veins (*venules*) and then into larger veins that return it to the heart to repeat the cycle.

Blood pumped through the heart does not reach the cells of the heart, so the organ has its own network of arteries, veins, and capillaries (Figure 15.3). Two large vessels, the right and left **coronary arteries,** branch off the aorta and supply the heart muscle with oxygenated blood. Blockage of a coronary artery is a leading cause of heart attacks.

RISK FACTORS FOR CARDIOVASCULAR DISEASE

Researchers have identified a variety of factors associated with an increased risk of developing CVD. They are grouped into two categories: major risk factors and contributing risk factors. Some risk factors are linked to controllable aspects of lifestyle and can therefore be changed. Others are beyond your control.

Major Risk Factors That Can Be Changed

The American Heart Association (AHA) has identified six major risk factors for CVD that can be changed: tobacco use, high blood pressure, unhealthy blood cholesterol levels, physical inactivity, overweight and obesity, and diabetes.

Tobacco Use   About one in five deaths from CVD is attributable to smoking. In 2007, an estimated 71 million Americans were tobacco users, including 13.7 million college students. Smoking remains the number-one preventable cause of CVD in the United States. People who smoke a pack of cigarettes a day have twice the risk of heart attack as nonsmokers; smoking two or more packs a day triples the risk. When smokers have heart attacks, they are two to three times more likely than nonsmokers to die from them. Cigarette smoking also doubles the risk of stroke.

Smoking harms the cardiovascular system in several ways:

- It damages the lining of arteries.
- It reduces the level of high-density lipoproteins (HDL), or "good" cholesterol.
- It raises the levels of triglycerides and low-density lipoproteins (LDL), or "bad" cholesterol.
- Nicotine increases blood pressure and heart rate.
- The carbon monoxide in cigarette smoke displaces oxygen in the blood, reducing the oxygen available to the body.
- Smoking causes **platelets** to stick together in the blood stream, leading to clotting.
- Smoking speeds the development of fatty deposits in the arteries.

You don't have to smoke to be affected. The risk of death from coronary heart disease increases up to 30% among those exposed to environmental tobacco smoke (ETS) at home or at work. Researchers estimate that about 35,000 nonsmokers die from heart disease each year as a result of exposure to ETS. (See Chapter 11 for more information on smoking.)

High Blood Pressure   High blood pressure, or **hypertension,** is a risk factor for many forms of cardiovascular disease, including heart attacks and strokes, and is itself considered a form of CVD.

Blood pressure, the force exerted by the blood on the vessel walls, is created by the pumping action of the heart.

Table 15.1	Blood Pressure Classification for Healthy Adults			
Category[a]	Systolic (mm Hg)		Diastolic (mm Hg)	
Normal[b]	below 120	and	below 80	
Prehypertension	120–139	or	80–89	
Hypertension[c]				
Stage 1	140–159	or	90–99	
Stage 2	160 and above	or	100 and above	

[a]When systolic and diastolic pressure fall into different categories, the higher category should be used to classify blood pressure status.
[b]The risk of death from heart attack and stroke begins to rise when blood pressure is above 115/75.
[c]Based on the average of two or more readings taken at different physician visits. In persons over 50, systolic blood pressure greater than 140 is a much more significant CVD risk factor than diastolic blood pressure.

SOURCE: *The Seventh Report of the Joint National Committee on Prevention, Detection, Evaluation, and Treatment of High Blood Pressure.* 2003. Bethesda, Md.: National Heart, Lung, and Blood Institute. National Institutes of Health (NIH Publication No. 03-5233).

High blood pressure occurs when too much force is exerted against the walls of the arteries. Many factors affect blood pressure, such as exercise or excitement. Short periods of high blood pressure are normal, but chronic high blood pressure is a health risk.

Blood pressure is measured with a stethoscope and an instrument called a *sphygmomanometer.* It is expressed as two numbers—for example, 120 over 80—and measured in millimeters of mercury. The first number is the systolic blood pressure; the second is the diastolic blood pressure. A normal blood pressure reading for a healthy adult is below 120 systolic and below 80 diastolic; CVD risk increases when blood pressure rises above 120 over 80. High blood pressure in adults is defined as equal to or greater than 140 over 90 (Table 15.1).

CAUSES   High blood pressure results from an increased output of blood by the heart or from increased resistance to blood flow in the arteries. The latter condition can be caused by constriction of smooth muscle surrounding the arteries or by **atherosclerosis,** a disease process that causes arteries to become clogged and narrowed. (Atherosclerosis is discussed in detail later in this chapter.) High blood pressure also scars and hardens arteries, making them less elastic and further increasing blood pressure. When a person has high blood pressure, the heart must work harder than normal to force blood through the narrowed and stiffened arteries, straining both the heart and arteries. Eventually, the strained heart weakens and tends to enlarge, which weakens it even more.

HEALTH RISKS   High blood pressure is often called a silent killer, because it usually has no symptoms. A person may have high blood pressure for years without realizing it.

TERMS

capillaries   Very small blood vessels that serve to exchange oxygen and nutrients between the blood and the tissues.

coronary arteries   A system of arteries branching from the aorta that provides blood to the heart muscle.

platelets   Cell fragments in the blood that are necessary for the formation of blood clots.

hypertension   Sustained abnormally high blood pressure.

atherosclerosis   A form of CVD in which the inner layers of artery walls are made thick and irregular by plaque deposits; arteries become narrow, and blood supply is reduced.

But during that time, it damages vital organs and increases the risk of heart attack, congestive heart failure, stroke, kidney failure, and blindness. In about 90% of people with high blood pressure, the cause is unknown. This type of high blood pressure is called *primary* (or *essential*) *hypertension* and is probably due to a mixture of genetic and environmental factors, including obesity, stress, excessive alcohol intake, inactivity, and a high-fat, high-salt diet. In the remaining 10% of people, the condition is caused by an underlying illness and is referred to as *secondary hypertension*.

PREVALENCE   Hypertension is common. About 33% of adults have hypertension, and 37% have prehypertension (defined as systolic pressure of 120–139 and/or diastolic pressure of 80–89). The incidence of high blood pressure increases with age; however, it can occur among children and young adults, and women sometimes develop hypertension during pregnancy (blood pressure usually returns to normal following the pregnancy). High blood pressure is two to three times more common in women taking oral contraceptives, especially in obese and older women; this risk increases with the duration of use. The rate of hypertension is highest in African Americans (41%), in whom, compared with other groups, the disorder is often more severe, more resistant to treatment, and more likely to be fatal at an early age.

TREATMENT   Primary hypertension cannot be cured, but it can be controlled. Because hypertension has no early warning signs, it's crucial to have your blood pressure tested at least once every 2 years (more often if you have other CVD risk factors). In fact, experts now advise that anyone with hypertension or prehypertension monitor their own blood pressure several times each week. Self-monitoring is easy to do, using a low-cost digital home blood pressure monitor. Follow your physician's advice about lifestyle changes and medication.

Lifestyle changes are recommended for everyone with prehypertension and hypertension. These changes include weight reduction, regular exercise, a healthy diet, and moderation of alcohol use. The DASH diet (see Chapter 12) is recommended; it emphasizes eating more fruits, vegetables, and whole grains and increasing potassium and fiber intake. Even small increases in fruit and vegetable intake can create measurable drops in blood pressure.

Sodium restriction is also helpful for most people with hypertension. The 2005 Dietary Guidelines for Americans recommend restricting sodium consumption to less than

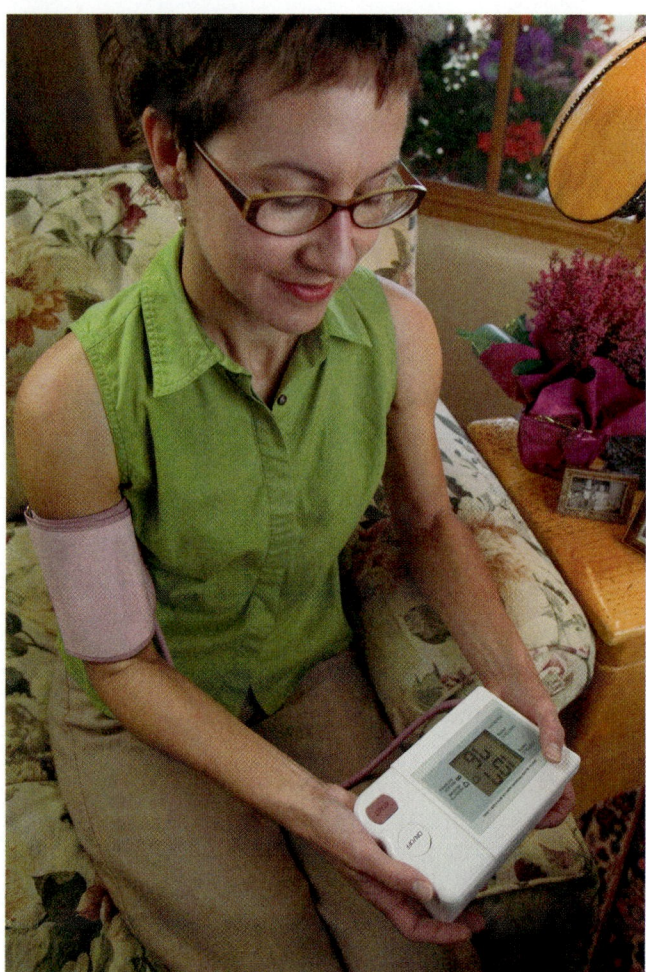

Low-cost, battery-powered home blood pressure monitors make it easy to check and track your blood pressure at home. People who plan to monitor their blood pressure at home should first see their doctor for a baseline reading and specific instructions.

2300 mg (about 1 teaspoon of salt) per day. People with hypertension, African Americans, and middle-aged and older adults should aim to consume no more than 1500 mg of sodium per day. Adequate potassium intake is also important. The recommended intake is 4.7 grams per day, which should be obtained through food. Supplements should be taken only when recommended by a physician; excessively high levels of potassium can be lethal.

For people whose blood pressure isn't adequately controlled with lifestyle changes, medication is prescribed. Many different types of antihypertensive drugs are available; the right one usually lowers blood pressure effectively with few side effects.

Recent research has shed new light on the importance of lowering blood pressure to improve cardiovascular health. Death rates from CVD begin to rise when blood pressure is above 115 over 75, well below the traditional 140 over 90 cutoff for hypertension. People with blood pressure in the prehypertension range are at increased

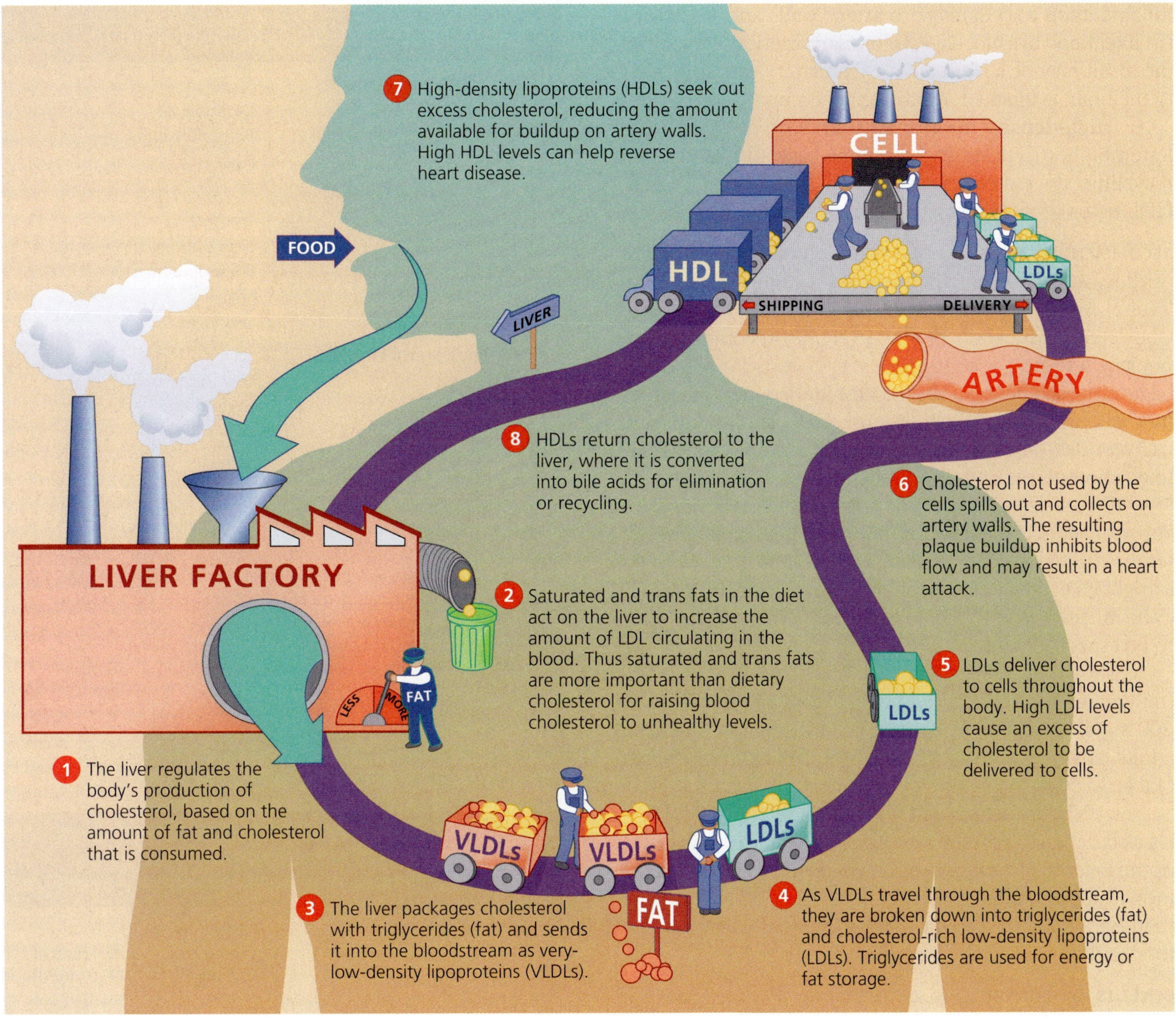

7 High-density lipoproteins (HDLs) seek out excess cholesterol, reducing the amount available for buildup on artery walls. High HDL levels can help reverse heart disease.
CELL
FOOD
HDL
LDLs
SHIPPING
DELIVERY
LIVER
ARTERY
8 HDLs return cholesterol to the liver, where it is converted into bile acids for elimination or recycling.
6 Cholesterol not used by the cells spills out and collects on artery walls. The resulting plaque buildup inhibits blood flow and may result in a heart attack.
LIVER FACTORY
2 Saturated and trans fats in the diet act on the liver to increase the amount of LDL circulating in the blood. Thus saturated and trans fats are more important than dietary cholesterol for raising blood cholesterol to unhealthy levels.
LESS
MORE
FAT
LDLs
5 LDLs deliver cholesterol to cells throughout the body. High LDL levels cause an excess of cholesterol to be delivered to cells.
1 The liver regulates the body's production of cholesterol, based on the amount of fat and cholesterol that is consumed.
VLDLs
VLDLs
LDLs
FAT
3 The liver packages cholesterol with triglycerides (fat) and sends it into the bloodstream as very-low-density lipoproteins (VLDLs).
4 As VLDLs travel through the bloodstream, they are broken down into triglycerides (fat) and cholesterol-rich low-density lipoproteins (LDLs). Triglycerides are used for energy or fat storage.

FIGURE 15.4 Cholesterol in the body.

risk of heart attack and stroke as well as at significant risk of developing full-blown hypertension.

High Cholesterol Cholesterol is a fatty, waxlike substance that circulates through the bloodstream and is an important component of cell membranes, sex hormones, vitamin D, the fluid that coats the lungs, and the protective sheaths around nerves. Adequate cholesterol is essential for the proper functioning of the body. Excess cholesterol, however, can clog arteries and increase the risk of CVD. Your liver manufactures cholesterol; you also get cholesterol from the foods you eat.

TERMS

lipoproteins Protein-and-lipid substances in the blood that carry fats and cholesterol; classified according to size, density, and chemical composition.

low-density lipoprotein (LDL) A lipoprotein containing a moderate amount of protein and a large amount of cholesterol, "bad" cholesterol.

GOOD VERSUS BAD CHOLESTEROL Cholesterol is carried in the blood in protein-lipid packages called **lipoproteins** (Figure 15.4). Two types of lipoproteins influence one's risk of heart disease:

- **Low-density lipoproteins (LDLs)** shuttle cholesterol from the liver to the organs and tissues that require it. LDL is known as "bad" cholesterol because if there is more than the body can use, the excess is deposited in the blood vessels. LDL that accumulates and becomes trapped in artery walls may be oxidized by free radicals, speeding inflammation and damage to artery walls and increasing the likelihood of a blockage. If coronary arteries are blocked, the result may be a heart attack; if an artery carrying blood to the brain is blocked, a stroke may occur.

• **High-density lipoproteins (HDLs),** or "good" cholesterol, shuttle unused cholesterol back to the liver for recycling. By removing cholesterol from blood vessels, HDL helps protect against atherosclerosis.

RECOMMENDED BLOOD CHOLESTEROL LEVELS The risk for cardiovascular disease increases with higher blood cholesterol levels, especially LDL (Table 15.2). The National Cholesterol Education Program (NCEP) recommends lipoprotein testing at least once every 5 years for all adults, beginning at age 20. The recommended test measures total cholesterol, LDL cholesterol, HDL cholesterol, and triglycerides (another blood fat). In general, high LDL, total cholesterol, and triglyceride levels combined with low HDL levels, are associated with a higher risk for CVD. You can reduce this risk by lowering LDL, total cholesterol, and triglycerides. Raising HDL is important because a high HDL level seems to offer protection from CVD even in cases where total cholesterol is high. This seems to be especially true for women.

As shown in Table 15.2, LDL levels below 100 mg/dl (milligrams per deciliter) and total cholesterol levels below 200 mg/dl are desirable. An estimated 99 million American adults have total cholesterol levels of 200 mg/dl or higher (Table 15.3).

The CVD risk associated with elevated cholesterol levels also depends on other factors. For example, an above-optimal level of LDL would be of more concern for an individual who also smokes and has high blood pressure than for someone without these additional CVD risk factors, and it is especially a concern for diabetics.

BENEFITS OF CONTROLLING CHOLESTEROL People can cut their heart attack risk by about 2% for every 1% that they reduce their total blood cholesterol levels. People who lower their total cholesterol from 250 to 200 mg/dl, for example, reduce their risk of heart attack by 40%. Studies indicate that lowering LDL and raising HDL levels not only reduces the likelihood that arteries will become clogged but may also reverse deposits on artery walls.

QUICK STATS

A **10%** decrease in total cholesterol levels could reduce the prevalence of coronary heart disease by 30%.

—American Heart Association, 2009

Your primary goal should be to reduce your LDL to healthy levels. Important dietary changes for reducing LDL levels include increasing fiber intake and substituting unsaturated for saturated and trans fats. Decreasing saturated and trans fats is particularly important because they promote the production of cholesterol by the liver. Exercising regularly and eating more fruits, vegetables, fish, and whole grains also help. Many experts believe cholesterol-lowering foods may be most effective when eaten in combination, rather than separately. You can raise your HDL levels by exercising regularly, losing weight if you are overweight, quitting smoking, and altering the amount and type of fat you consume.

Table 15.2	Cholesterol Guidelines
Total cholesterol (mg/dl)	
Less than 200	Desirable
200–239	Borderline high
240 or more	High
LDL cholesterol (mg/dl)	
Less than 100	Optimal
100–129	Near optimal/above optimal
130–159	Borderline high
160–189	High
190 or more	Very high
HDL cholesterol (mg/dl)	
Less than 40	Low (undesirable)
60 or more	High (desirable)
Triglycerides (mg/dl)	
Less than 150	Normal
150–199	Borderline high
200–499	High
500 or more	Very high

SOURCE: Expert Panel on Detection, Evaluation, and Treatment of High Blood Cholesterol in Adults. 2001. Executive Summary of the Third Report of the National Cholesterol Education Program (NCEP) Expert Panel on Detection, Evaluation, and Treatment of High Blood Cholesterol in Adults (Adult Treatment Panel III). *Journal of the American Medical Association* 285(19).

Table 15.3	Prevalence of High Cholesterol in Adult Americans	
	Total Cholesterol ≥ 200 mg/dl	Total Cholesterol ≥ 240 mg/dl
Both sexes	45.1%	15.7%
Males	42.6%	13.8%
Females	47.1%	17.3%
White males	42.1%	14.3%
White females	47.7%	18.1%
Black males	35.6%	7.9%
Black females	41.4%	13.4%
Mexican American males	52.1%	17.5%
Mexican American females	48.0%	14.5%

SOURCE: American Heart Association. 2009. *Heart Disease and Stroke Statistics, 2009 Update.* Dallas, TX.: American Heart Association.

See Chapter 12 for detailed information on nutrition and guidelines for heart-healthy eating.

Physical Inactivity   An estimated 40–60 million Americans are so sedentary that they are at high risk for developing CVD. Exercise is thought to be the closest thing we have to a magic bullet against heart disease. It lowers CVD risk by helping to decrease blood pressure and resting heart rate, increase HDL levels, maintain desirable weight, improve the condition of blood vessels, and prevent or control diabetes. One study found that women who accumulated at least 3 hours of brisk walking each week cut their risk of heart attack and stroke by more than 50%.

See Chapter 13 for detailed explanations of the benefits of physical activity and for help in creating your own exercise plan.

Obesity   As your weight increases, your risk of CVD increases. The risk of death from CVD is two to three times more likely in obese people (BMI ≥ 30) than it is in lean people (BMI 18.5–24.9), and for every 5-unit increment of BMI, a person's risk of death from coronary heart disease increases by 30%. BMI at age 18 predicts mortality due to CVD—the higher your BMI at age 18, the more likely you are to eventually die from CVD. Maintaining a healthy weight is also important. Researchers found that middle-aged women who had gained 22 pounds or more since age 18 had a significantly higher risk of subsequent death from CVD than those who were able to maintain their weight over time.

As explained in Chapter 14, excess body fat is strongly associated with hypertension, high cholesterol levels, insulin resistance, diabetes, physical inactivity, and increasing age. It is also associated with endothelial cell dysfunction and increased inflammatory markers (discussed later in this chapter). **Endothelial cells** line the inside of arteries, including the coronary arteries, and they help regulate blood flow to the heart and keep platelets and other cells from sticking to artery walls. When the endothelial cells are healthy, the coronary arteries dilate (widen) when the heart needs more blood, but when the cells are dysfunctional, the coronary arteries instead constrict, limiting blood flow to the heart. With excess weight, there is also more blood to pump and the heart has to work harder. This causes chronically elevated pressures within the heart chambers that can lead to ven-

tricular **hypertrophy** (enlargement), and eventually the heart muscle can start to fail.

Physical activity and physical fitness have a strong positive influence on cardiovascular health in those who are overweight and obese. People who are obese but have at least moderate cardiorespiratory fitness may have lower rates of cardiovascular disease than their normal-weight but unfit peers. For someone who is overweight, even modest weight reduction—5–10% of body weight—can reduce CVD risk.

Diabetes   As described in Chapter 14, diabetes is a disorder characterized by elevated blood glucose levels due to an insufficient supply or inadequate action of insulin. Diabetes doubles the risk of CVD for men and triples the risk for women. The most common cause of death in adults with diabetes is CVD, and they usually die at younger ages than people without diabetes. There is an estimated loss of 5–10 years of life in those with diabetes.

Diabetics have higher rates of other CVD risk factors, including hypertension, obesity, and unhealthy blood lipid levels (typically, high triglyceride levels and low HDL levels). The elevated blood glucose and insulin levels that occur in diabetes can damage the endothelial cells that line the arteries, making them more vulnerable to atherosclerosis; diabetics also often have platelet and blood coagulation abnormalities that increase the risk of heart attacks and strokes. People with pre-diabetes also face a significantly increased risk of CVD.

The number of people with diabetes (24 million) and pre-diabetes (57 million) continues to climb and is closely linked to obesity. It is estimated that for every kilogram increase in weight, the risk of diabetes increases by approximately 9%. The largest increase in prevalence of type 2 diabetes over the past decade has been among people age 30–39, and there has also been an alarming increase among children and adolescents. Children who are diagnosed with diabetes typically develop complications in their twenties or thirties.

Complications of diabetes mainly affect the arteries. When the larger arteries are affected, all forms of CVD result, including heart attacks, strokes, and peripheral vascular disease. Having diabetes is considered to be a heart disease risk equivalent, meaning that your CVD morbidity and mortality risk is the same as if you already had coronary artery disease (CAD). Diabetics who have CAD fare even worse; they have accelerated atherosclerosis and benefit less from common forms of treatment than nondiabetics.

In addition, evidence suggests that after a heart attack, the risk of diabetes steeply rises. A recent study demonstrated that within 3½ years after a heart attack, one-third of nondiabetic patients will develop diabetes or pre-diabetes. Thus, heart disease and elevated blood glucose are clearly linked, with each being a risk factor for the other.

Routine screening for diabetes is not currently recommended unless a person has symptoms of diabetes or

TERMS

high-density lipoprotein (HDL)   A lipoprotein containing relatively little cholesterol that helps transport cholesterol out of the arteries and thus protects against heart diseases; "good" cholesterol.

endothelial cells   Cells lining the inside of arteries; they help regulate blood flow and prevent platelets from sticking.

hypertrophy   Abnormal enlargement of an organ secondary to an increase in cell size.

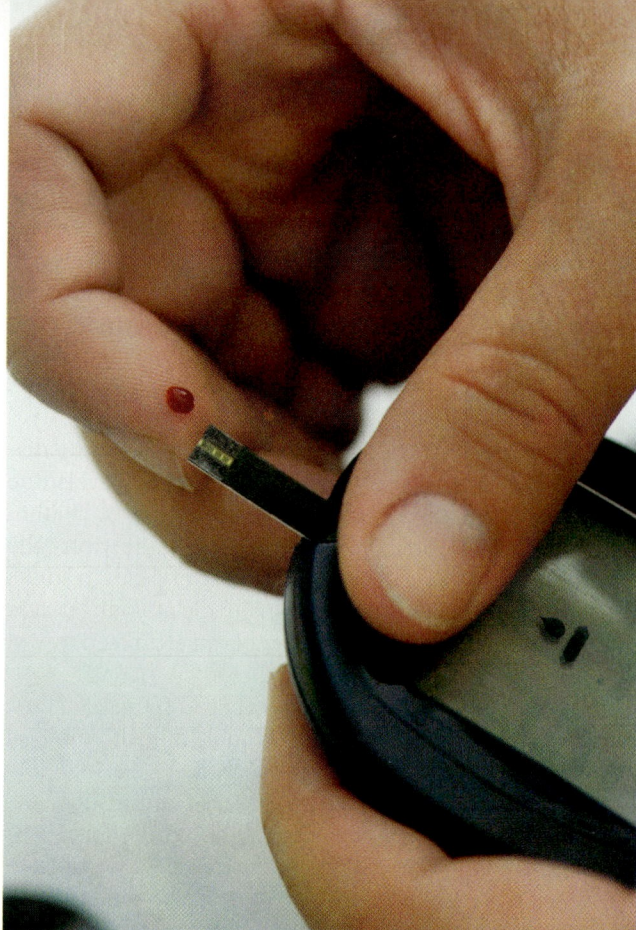

Blood glucose monitoring is important in managing diabetes and its associated risks.

predictor of heart disease, especially if associated with other risk factors, such as low HDL levels, obesity, and diabetes. Factors contributing to elevated triglyceride levels include excess body fat, physical inactivity, cigarette smoking, type 2 diabetes, excess alcohol intake, very high carbohydrate diets, and certain diseases and medications.

Much of the picture regarding triglycerides remains unclear, however. Studies have yet to show whether lowering triglyceride levels will actually decrease heart disease. Elevated triglyceride levels are most often seen in people with other lipid abnormalities; and the lifestyle modifications that help lower cholesterol also help decrease triglycerides, making it difficult to identify any potential independent benefit of lowering triglyceride levels.

A full lipid profile should include testing and evaluation of triglyceride levels (see Table 15.2). For people with borderline high triglyceride levels, increased physical activity, reduced intake of added sugars, and weight reduction can help bring levels down into the healthy range; for people with high triglyceride levels, drug therapy may be recommended. Being moderate in the use of alcohol and quitting smoking are also important.

Psychological and Social Factors Many of the psychological and social factors that influence other areas of wellness are also important risk factors for CVD. The cardiovascular system is affected by both sudden, acute episodes of mental stress and the more chronic, underlying emotions of anger, anxiety, and depression.

STRESS Excessive stress can strain the heart and blood vessels over time and contribute to CVD. When you experience stress, stress hormones activate the sympathetic nervous system. As described in Chapter 2, the sympathetic nervous system causes the fight-or-flight response; this response increases heart rate and blood pressure so that more blood is distributed to the heart and other muscles in anticipation of physical activity. Blood glucose concentrations and cholesterol also increase to provide a source of energy, and the platelets become activated so that they will be more likely to clot in case of injury. If you are healthy, you can tolerate the cardiovascular responses that take place during stress, but if you already have CVD, stress can lead to adverse outcomes such as abnormal heart rhythms (arrhythmias), heart attacks, and sudden cardiac death.

Because avoiding all stress is impossible, having healthy mechanisms to cope with it is your best defense. Instead of adopting unhealthy habits such as smoking or overeating, use healthier coping strategies such as exercising, getting enough sleep, and talking to others.

other CVD risk factors. In people with pre-diabetes, a healthy diet and exercise are more effective than medication at preventing diabetes. For people with diabetes, a healthy diet, exercise, and careful control of glucose levels are recommended to decrease chances of developing complications. Even people whose diabetes is under control face a high risk of CVD, so control of other risk factors is critical.

Contributing Risk Factors That Can Be Changed

Other factors that can be changed have been identified as contributing to CVD risk, including triglyceride levels and psychological and social factors.

High Triglyceride Levels Like cholesterol, **triglycerides** are blood fats that are obtained from food and manufactured by the body. High triglyceride levels are a reliable

triglyceride A type of blood fat that can be a predictor of heart disease.

Acute stress is associated with heart rhythm problems and deaths. The rate of arrhythmias in patients with underlying heart disease doubled in the month after the September 11, 2001, terrorist attacks.

CHRONIC HOSTILITY AND ANGER Certain traits in the hard-driving Type A personality—hostility, cynicism, and anger—are associated with increased risk of heart disease. Men prone to anger have two to three times the heart attack risk of calmer men and are much more likely to develop CVD at young ages. In a 10-year study of young adults age 18–30 years, those with high hostility levels were more than twice as likely to develop coronary artery calcification (a marker of early atherosclerosis) as those with low hostility levels. See the box "Anger, Hostility, and Heart Disease" on p. 460 for more information.

SUPPRESSING PSYCHOLOGICAL DISTRESS Consistently suppressing anger and other negative emotions may also be hazardous to a healthy heart. People who hide psychological distress appear to have higher rates of heart disease than people who experience similar distress but share it with others. People with such "Type D" personalities tend to be pessimistic, negative, and unhappy and to suppress these feelings. This Type D trait may have physical effects, or it may lead to social isolation and poor communication with physicians.

DEPRESSION Depression appears to increase the risk of CVD in healthy people, and it definitely increases the risk of adverse cardiac events in those who already have heart disease. You do not need to have a major depressive disorder to be affected: For each depressive symptom you have, the risk seems to increase in a linear fashion (see Chapter 3 for symptoms of depression).

Depression is common in people with coronary heart disease (CHD), and patients who are depressed tend to have worse outcomes than those who are not. Up to a third of patients experience major depression within 1 year of having a heart attack, and those who are depressed after having a heart attack are more likely to have another heart attack or die of a cardiac cause. Even in those with CHD who have not had a recent cardiac event, up to 20% have depression, and this number may be even higher in women. Major depressive disorder at the time of treatment for coronary artery disease is associated with both short- and long-term complications, including subsequent heart attack and death.

The relationship between depression and CHD is complex and not fully understood. Depressed people may be more likely to smoke or be sedentary. They may not consistently take prescribed medications, and they may not cope well with having an illness or undergoing a medical procedure. Depression also causes physiological changes; for example, it elevates basal levels of stress hormones, which, as described earlier, induce a variety of stress-related responses.

ANXIETY There is evidence to suggest that chronic anxiety and anxiety disorders (such as phobias and panic disorder) are associated with up to a threefold increased risk of coronary heart disease, heart attack, and sudden cardiac death. There is also some evidence that, similar to people with depression, people with anxiety are more likely to have a subsequent adverse cardiac event after having a heart attack. At the same time, people with anxiety and depression often have medically unexplained chest pain, meaning that no evidence of coronary artery disease can be found. This can create difficulties in diagnosis and disease management, but it is important to always seek medical attention if you experience unexplained chest pain.

SOCIAL ISOLATION Social isolation and low social support (living alone, or having few friends or family members) are associated with an increased incidence of CHD and poorer outcomes after the first diagnosis of CHD. Elderly men and women who report less emotional support from others before they have a heart attack are almost three times more likely to die in the first 6 months after the attack. A strong social support network is a major antidote to stress. Friends and family members can also promote and support a healthy lifestyle.

LOW SOCIOECONOMIC STATUS Low socioeconomic status and low educational attainment also increase risk for CVD. These associations are probably due to a variety of factors, including lifestyle and access to health care.

Alcohol and Drugs Although moderate drinking (defined as no more than 1–2 drinks per day for men and no

Anger, Hostility, and Heart Disease

People with a quick temper, a persistently hostile outlook, and a cynical, mistrusting attitude toward life are more likely to develop heart disease than those with a calmer, more trusting attitude. People who are angry frequently, intensely, and for long periods experience the stress response much more often than more relaxed individuals. Over the long term, the effects of stress may damage arteries and promote CVD.

Are You Too Hostile?

To help answer that question, Duke University researcher Redford Williams, M.D., has devised a short self-test. It's not a scientific evaluation, but it does offer a rough measure of hostility. Are the following statements true or false for you?

1. I often get annoyed at checkout cashiers or the people in front of me when I'm waiting in line.
2. I usually keep an eye on the people I work or live with to make sure they do what they should.
3. I often wonder how homeless people can have so little respect for themselves.
4. I believe that most people will take advantage of you if you let them.
5. The habits of friends or family members often annoy me.
6. When I'm stuck in traffic, I often start breathing faster and my heart pounds.

7. When I'm annoyed with people, I really want to let them know it.
8. If someone does me wrong, I want to get even.
9. I'd like to have the last word in any argument.
10. At least once a week, I have the urge to yell at or even hit someone.

According to Williams, five or more "true" statements suggest that you're excessively hostile and should consider taking steps to mellow out.

Managing Your Anger

Begin by monitoring your angry responses and looking for triggers—people or situations that typically make you angry. Familiarize yourself with the patterns of thinking that lead to angry or hostile feelings, and then try to head them off before they develop into full-blown anger. If you feel your anger starting to build, try reasoning with yourself by asking the following questions:

1. *Is this really important enough to get angry about?*
2. *Am I really justified in getting angry?*
3. *Is getting angry going to make a real and positive difference in this situation?*

If you answer yes to all three questions, then calm but assertive communication may be an appropriate response. If your anger isn't reasonable, try distracting

yourself or removing yourself from the situation. Exercise, humor, social support, and other stress-management techniques can also help (see Chapter 3 for additional anger-management tips). Your heart—and the people around you—will benefit from your calmer, more positive outlook.

SOURCES: Virginia Williams and Redford Williams, 1999, *Lifeskills: Lifeskills: 8 Simple Ways to Build Stronger Relationships, Communicate More Clearly, and Improve Your Health,* New York: Times Books. Reprinted by permission.

---

more than 1 drink per day for women) may have health benefits for some people, drinking too much alcohol raises blood pressure and can increase the risk of stroke and heart failure. Stimulant drugs, particularly cocaine, can also cause serious cardiac problems, including heart attack, stroke, and sudden cardiac death. Cocaine stimulates the nervous system, promotes platelet aggregation, and can cause spasm in the coronary arteries. Injection drug use can cause infection of the heart and stroke. See Chapters 9–11 for more information on the use of alcohol, tobacco, and drugs.

Major Risk Factors That Can't Be Changed

A number of major risk factors for CVD cannot be changed. They include heredity, aging, being male, and ethnicity.

Heredity Multiple genes contribute to the development of CVD and its associated risk factors, such as high cholesterol, hypertension, diabetes, and obesity. Having a favorable set of genes decreases your risk of developing CVD; having an unfavorable set of genes increases your risk. Risk, however, is modifiable by lifestyle factors such as whether you smoke, exercise, or eat a healthy diet.

Because of the genetic complexity of CVD, genetic screening is usually recommended for only a few specific conditions (for example, certain cholesterol disorders), but you can learn more about your personal risk just by assessing your family history. If you have a first-degree relative (parent, sibling, child) with CAD, for example, you have a two-fold increased risk of someday developing CAD yourself.

Don't forget the role of lifestyle factors, however. Coronary artery disease is usually the result of the interaction of several unfavorable genetic and lifestyle factors, and people with the greatest number of genetic and lifestyle risk factors will face the highest risks. People with favorable genes may not develop CAD despite having an unhealthy lifestyle, and people with many healthy habits may still develop CAD because they have an unfavorable genetic makeup. People who inherit a tendency for CVD are not destined to develop it. They may, however, have to work harder than other people to prevent CVD.

Aging   About 70% of all heart attack victims are age 65 or older, and about 75% who suffer fatal heart attacks are over 65. For people over 55, the incidence of stroke more than doubles in each successive decade. However, even people in their thirties and forties, especially men, can have heart attacks.

Being Male   Although CVD is the leading killer of both men and women in the United States, men face a greater risk of heart attack than women, especially earlier in life. Until age 55, men also have a greater risk of hypertension. The incidence of stroke is higher for males than females until age 65. Estrogen production, which is highest during the childbearing years, may protect premenopausal women against CVD (see the box "Women and CVD" on p. 462). By age 75, the gender gap nearly disappears.

Ethnicity   Rates of heart disease vary among ethnic groups in the United States, with African Americans having much higher rates of hypertension, heart disease, and stroke than other groups (see the box "Ethnicity and CVD" on p. 463). Figure 15.5 shows how rates of CVD compare among non-Hispanic whites, blacks, and Mexican Americans in the United States. Puerto Rican Americans, Cuban Americans, and Mexican Americans are also more likely to suffer from high blood pressure and angina

(a warning sign of heart disease) than non-Hispanic white Americans. Asian Americans historically have had far lower rates of CVD than white Americans.

Inflammation and C-Reactive Protein   Inflammation plays a key role in the development of CVD. When an artery is injured by smoking, cholesterol, hypertension, or other factors, the body's response is to produce inflammation. A substance called *C-reactive protein (CRP)* is released into the bloodstream during the inflammatory response, and high levels of CRP indicate a substantially elevated risk of heart attack and stroke. CRP may also be harmful to the coronary arteries themselves.

The CDC and the American Heart Association recommend testing of CRP levels for people at intermediate risk for CVD because people in this risk category who are found to have high CRP levels may benefit from additional CVD testing or treatment. (This guideline assumes that people at high risk for CVD are already receiving treatment.)

Lifestyle changes and certain drugs can reduce CRP levels. Statin drugs, widely prescribed to lower cholesterol, also decrease inflammation and reduce CRP levels; this may be one reason that statin drugs seem to lower CVD risk even in people with normal blood lipid levels. Patients who receive intensive statin treatment fare better than patients who receive less aggressive treatment that primarily targets LDL levels. The reduction in risk from decreased CRP levels is independent of changes in LDL.

The benefits of statins were confirmed in 2008, when findings were released from a study involving 18,000 patients in 26 countries. Researchers found that volunteers who took statins reduced their risk of CVD by about 50%, even if they had normal cholesterol levels. The patients had undergone a simple blood test that checked for inflammation by measuring levels of CRP; because statins lower CRP regardless of one's cholesterol levels, researchers concluded that CRP levels and inflammation are important markers of CVD risk.

Possible Risk Factors Currently Being Studied

In recent years, a number of other possible risk factors for cardiovascular disease have been identified.

Insulin Resistance and Metabolic Syndrome   When you consume carbohydrate, your blood glucose level increases. This stimulates the pancreas to secrete insulin,

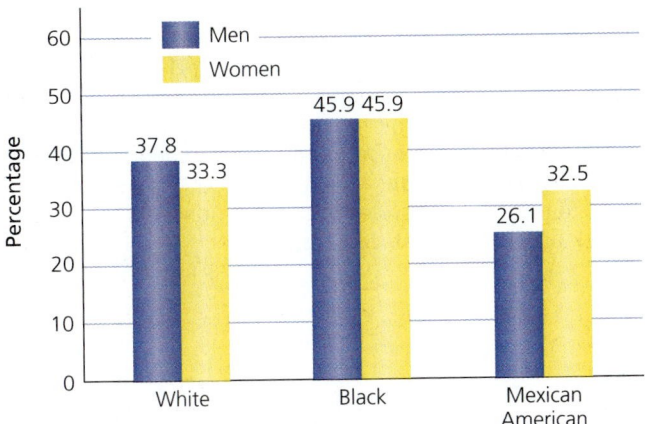

FIGURE 15.5   Percentage of adult Americans with cardiovascular disease.

SOURCE: American Heart Association. 2008. *Heart Disease and Stroke Statistics—2009 Update.* Dallas, Tex.: American Heart Association.

GENDER MATTERS

Women and CVD

CVD has traditionally been thought of as a man's disease, and until recently, this has been the justification for carrying out almost all CVD research on men. It is true that men have a higher incidence of cardiovascular problems than women, especially before age 50. On average, women live 10–15 more years free of coronary heart disease than men do. But heart disease is the leading cause of death among women, and it has killed more women than men every year since 1984.

Polls indicate that women vastly underestimate their risk of dying of a heart attack and, in turn, overestimate their risk of dying of breast cancer. In reality, nearly 1 in 3 women dies of CVD, whereas 1 in 30 dies of breast cancer. Minority women face the highest risk of developing CVD, but their awareness of heart disease as a killer of women is lower than that of white women. To help raise awareness of CVD in women, the American Heart Association launched the "Go Red for Women" campaign; visit their Web site for more information (http://www.goredforwomen.org/).

Risk factors for CVD are similar for men and women and include age, family history, smoking, hypertension, high cholesterol, and diabetes. There are some gender differences, however. HDL appears to be an even more powerful predictor of CAD risk in women than it is in men. Also, women with diabetes have a greater risk of having CVD events like heart attack and stroke than men with diabetes.

Estrogen: A Heart Protector?

The hormone estrogen, produced naturally by a woman's ovaries until menopause, improves blood lipid concentrations and other CVD risk factors. For the past several decades, many U.S. physicians encouraged menopausal women to take hormone replacement therapy (HT) to relieve menopause symptoms

and presumably reduce the risk of CVD. However, studies found that HT may actually *increase* a woman's risk for heart disease and certain other health problems, including breast cancer. Some newer studies have found a reduced risk of CVD in women who start HT in the early stages of menopause (usually the mid-40s), suggesting that outcomes may depend on several factors, including the timing of hormone use. The U.S. Preventive Services Task Force and the American Heart Association currently recommend that HT not be used to protect against CVD.

For younger women, the most common form of hormonal medication is oral contraceptives (OCs). Typical OCs contain estrogen and progestin in relatively low doses and are generally considered safe for most nonsmoking women. But women who smoke and use OCs are up to 32 times more likely to have a heart attack than nonsmoking OC users.

Postmenopausal Women: At Risk

When women have heart attacks, they are more likely than men to die within a year. One reason is that because women develop heart disease at older ages, they are more likely to have other health problems that complicate treatment. Women have smaller hearts and arteries than men, possibly making diagnosis and treatment more difficult. There may also be unknown biological or psychosocial risk factors contributing to women's mortality.

Also, medical personnel appear to evaluate and treat women less aggressively than men. Women with positive stress tests and those whose evaluation raises concern about a heart attack are less likely to be referred to further testing than are men. In addition, studies of heart attack patients have found that women usually have to wait longer than

men to receive clot-dissolving drugs in an emergency room.

Women presenting with CHD are just as likely as men to report chest pain, but are also likely to report non-chest-pain symptoms, which may obscure their diagnosis. These additional symptoms include fatigue, weakness, shortness of breath, nausea, vomiting, and pain in the abdomen, neck, jaw, and back. Women are also more likely to have pain at rest, during sleep, or with mental stress. A woman who experiences these symptoms should be persistent in seeking accurate diagnosis and appropriate treatment.

Careful diagnosis of cardiac symptoms is also key in cases of stress-induced cardiomyopathy ("broken heart syndrome"), which occurs much more commonly in women. In this condition, a severe stress response stuns the heart, producing heart-attack-like symptoms and decreased pumping function of the heart, but no damage to the heart muscle. Typically, the condition reverses quickly, and correct diagnosis is important to avoid unnecessary invasive procedures.

---

which allows body cells to pick up glucose to use for energy (see Chapter 14). The function of insulin is to maintain proper glucose levels in the body, which it does by affecting the uptake of glucose from the blood by muscle and fat tissue and by limiting the liver's production of glucose. As people gain weight and engage in less physi-

cal activity, their muscles, fat, and liver become less sensitive to the effect of insulin—a condition known as insulin resistance (or pre-diabetes). As the body becomes increasingly insulin resistant, the pancreas must secrete more and more insulin (hyperinsulinemia) to keep glucose levels within a normal range. Eventually, however, even high

Ethnicity and CVD

Although cardiovascular disease is the leading cause of death for all Americans, there is a higher prevalence of CVD and its associated risk factors in adult African Americans and Mexican Americans than in whites and Asian Americans. The reasons for these disparities likely include both genetic and environmental factors.

African Americans are at substantially higher risk for death from CVD than other groups. The rate of hypertension among African Americans is among the highest of any group in the world. Blacks tend to develop hypertension at an earlier age than whites, and their average blood pressures are much higher. African Americans have a higher risk of stroke, have strokes at younger ages, and, if they survive, have more significant stroke-related disabilities. Some experts recommend that blacks be treated with antihypertensive drugs at an earlier stage—when blood pressure reaches 130/80 rather than the typical 140/90 cutoff for hypertension.

A number of genetic and biological factors may contribute to CVD in African Americans. They may be more sensitive to dietary sodium, leading to greater blood pressure elevation in response to a given amount of sodium. African Americans may also experience less dilation of blood vessels in response to stress, an attribute that also raises blood pressure.

Heredity also plays a large role in the tendency to develop diabetes, another important CVD risk factor that is more common in blacks than whites. However, Latinos are even more likely to develop diabetes and insulin resistance, and at a younger age, than African Americans. There is variation within the Latino population, however, with a higher prevalence of diabetes occurring among Mexican Americans and Puerto Ricans and a relatively lower prevalence among Cuban Americans.

Another factor that likely contributes to the high incidence of CVD among ethnic minority groups is low income. Economic deprivation usually means reduced access to adequate health care and health insurance. Also associated with low income is low educational attainment, which often means less information about preventive health measures, such as diet and stress management. And people with low incomes tend to smoke more, use more salt, and exercise less than those with higher incomes.

Discrimination may also play a role in CVD. Physicians and hospitals may treat the medical problems of ethnic minorities differently than those of whites. Discrimination, along with low income and other forms of deprivation, may also increase stress, which is linked with hypertension and CVD. In terms of access to care, factors such as insurance coverage and availability of high-tech cardiac equipment in hospitals used most often by minorities may also play a role.

CVD risk in ethnic groups is further affected by immigration and one's place of birth. Upon immigration to the United States, an Asian's risk for CVD tends to increase and reflect that of a typical American more than a typical Asian, perhaps in part because Asian immigrants often abandon their traditional (and healthier) diets.

However, birthplace (and its associated lifestyle factors) also seems to be a strong determinant of risk. One study found that among New Yorkers born in the Northeast, blacks and whites have nearly identical risk of CVD. But black New Yorkers who were born in the South

have a sharply higher risk, and black New Yorkers born in the Caribbean have a significantly lower risk. Researchers speculate that instead of abandoning their traditional diets and lifestyles, blacks from the South instead bring these traditions with them. Some risk factors for CVD, including smoking and a high-fat diet, are more common in the South. When combined with urban stress, these factors create a lifestyle that is far from heart-healthy.

All Americans are advised to have their blood pressure checked regularly, exercise, eat a healthy diet, manage stress, and avoid smoking. These general preventive strategies may be particularly helpful for ethnic minorities. Tailoring your lifestyle to your particular ethnic risk may also be helpful in some cases. Discuss your particular risk profile with your physician to help identify lifestyle changes most appropriate for you.

---

levels of insulin may become insufficient, and blood glucose levels will also start to rise (hyperglycemia), resulting in type 2 diabetes.

Those who have insulin resistance tend to have several other related risk factors; as a group, this cluster of abnormalities is called metabolic syndrome or insulin resistance syndrome (Table 15.4). Metabolic syndrome significantly increases the risk of CVD—more so in women than in men. It is estimated that nearly 35% of the adult U.S. population has metabolic syndrome.

To reduce your risk for metabolic syndrome, choose a healthy diet and get plenty of exercise. Regular physical activity increases your body's sensitivity to insulin in addition to improving cholesterol levels and decreasing blood pressure. Reducing calorie intake to prevent weight gain or losing weight if needed will also reduce insulin resistance. The amount and type of carbohydrate intake is also important: Diets high in carbohydrates, especially high-glycemic-index foods, can raise levels of glucose and triglycerides and lower HDL, thus contributing to the development or worsening of metabolic syndrome and CVD, particularly in people who are already sedentary and overweight. For people prone to insulin resistance, eating more unsaturated fats, protein, vegetables, and fiber while limiting added sugars and starches may be beneficial.

Homocysteine   Elevated levels of homocysteine, an amino acid circulating in the blood, are associated with an increased risk of CVD. Homocysteine appears to damage the lining of blood vessels, resulting in inflammation and the development of fatty deposits in artery walls. These changes can lead to the formation of clots and blockages in arteries, which in turn can cause heart attacks and strokes. High homocysteine levels are also associated with cognitive impairment, such as memory loss.

Men generally have higher homocysteine levels than women, as do individuals with diets low in folic acid, vitamin B-12, and vitamin B-6. Many genes may cause elevated homocysteine levels, and some genes associated with small-to-moderate elevations are quite common in the general population. A recent study showed that taking folic acid will decrease homocysteine levels, but it does not lower the risk of CVD and may actually be harmful. Therefore, taking folic acid beyond the dose found in a multivitamin is not recommended. Instead, it may be more helpful to follow a diet rich in fruits, vegetables, and whole grains. Also, if your homocysteine level is high, aggressively controlling your other cardiac risk factors is that much more important.

Infectious Agents   Several infectious agents have been identified as possible culprits in the development of CVD. *Chlamydia pneumoniae,* a common cause of flulike respiratory infections, has been found in sections of clogged, damaged arteries but not in sections of healthy arteries. It does not appear that antibiotic treatment for *C. pneumo-* *niae* reduces risk, but further research is needed. Other infectious agents may also play a role in CVD.

Lipoprotein(a)   A high level of a specific type of LDL called lipoprotein(a), or Lp(a), may be a risk factor for CHD, especially when associated with high LDL or low HDL levels. Lp(a) is thought to contribute to CVD by promoting clots and by delivering cholesterol to a site of vascular injury. Lp(a) levels have a strong genetic component and are difficult to treat. Lp(a) levels tend to increase with age and vary by race, with higher levels found in African Americans than in whites. About 25% of the U.S. population has elevated lipoprotein(a) levels. Lifestyle modifications such as diet, exercise, and weight loss appear to have little effect in lowering Lp(a). High-dose niacin has been shown to decrease Lp(a), but studies are still needed to see if lower levels actually reduce the risk of CVD. In the meantime, if you have elevated Lp(a), any other cholesterol abnormalities—such as elevated LDL—should be treated even more aggressively.

LDL Particle Size   Research has shown that LDL particles differ in size and density and that the concentrations of different particles vary among individuals. LDL cholesterol profiles can be divided into three general types: People with pattern A have mostly large, buoyant LDL particles; people with pattern B have mostly small, dense LDL particles; and people with pattern C have a mixture of particle types. Small, dense LDL particles pose a greater CVD risk than large particles; thus, people with LDL pattern B are at greater risk for CVD. Exercise, a low-fat diet, and certain lipid-lowering drugs may help lower CVD risk in people with LDL pattern B. In a recent study of men who walked or jogged 12–20 miles per week, total cholesterol and LDL levels were often unchanged, but the LDL particles became larger and less dense.

Blood Viscosity and Iron   High blood viscosity (thickness) may increase the risk of CVD; excess iron stores have also been linked to higher risk, especially for men and postmenopausal women (iron stores are usually lower in younger women because of menstrual blood loss). Regular blood donation, which reduces iron stores and blood viscosity, is associated with lower CVD risk in men. Drinking five or more glasses of water a day may also reduce risk by reducing blood viscosity. On the flip side, high consumption of heme iron—found in meat, fish, and poultry—is associated with an increased risk of heart attack. Men and postmenopausal women should consult a physician before taking iron supplements.

Uric Acid   Recent research suggests a link between high blood levels of uric acid and CVD mortality, particularly among postmenopausal women and African Americans. Uric acid may raise CVD risk by increasing inflammation and platelet aggregation or by influencing the develop-

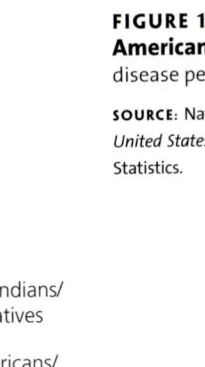

FIGURE 15.6 Heart disease death rates of Americans, 2005. Deaths due to various forms of heart disease per 100,000 people.

SOURCE: National Center for Health Statistics. 2008. Update. *Health, United States, 2007.* Hyattsville, Md.: National Center for Health Statistics.

ment of hypertension; high uric acid levels also cause gout (a type of arthritis), kidney stones, and certain forms of kidney disease. Medications to lower uric acid levels are available, but it is not yet known if they will be useful in preventing CVD.

Time of Day and Time of Year   More heart attacks and sudden cardiac deaths occur between 6:00 A.M. and noon than during other times of the day. This trend may be explained by the natural increase in adrenaline and cortisol levels that occurs in the morning and by an increase in the sympathetic nervous system activity as people hurry around at the beginning of their day. Blood pressure is often lowest during sleep and highest in the morning, and endothelial function may be impaired in the early morning.

There is also a seasonal pattern of heart attacks, with up to 50% more occurring in winter months than in summer months. Heart attacks that occur in winter also tend to be more often fatal than those that occur during summer. Possible explanations include low temperature, which can constrict blood vessels; bursts of exertion, such as snow shoveling; increased rates of smoking; increased stress and depression, including seasonal affective disorder (see Chapter 3); holiday-related episodes of high-fat eating and binge drinking; and physiological factors, including levels of cholesterol and C-reactive protein, which appear to rise

in winter. People who have symptoms of heart trouble may also be more reluctant to seek help during the holidays.

MAJOR FORMS OF CARDIOVASCULAR DISEASE

Although deaths from CVD have declined drastically over the past 60 years, it remains the leading cause of death in America. According to the CDC, heart diseases killed more than 650,000 Americans in 2005. Figure 15.6 shows the death rates among various ethnic groups due to heart disease in 2005, the most recent year for which data is available.

The main forms of CVD are atherosclerosis, heart disease and heart attack, stroke, peripheral arterial disease (PAD), congestive heart failure, congenital heart disease, rheumatic heart disease, and heart valve problems. Many forms are interrelated and have elements in common; we treat them separately here for the sake of clarity. Hypertension, which is both a major risk factor and a form of CVD, was described earlier in the chapter.

> **The estimated annual financial burden of CVD is $475.3 billion.**
> —American Heart Association, 2009
>
> QUICK STATS

Atherosclerosis

Atherosclerosis is a form of arteriosclerosis, or thickening and hardening of the arteries. In atherosclerosis, arteries become narrowed by deposits of fat, cholesterol, and other substances. The process begins when the endothelial cells (cells that line the arteries) become damaged, most likely through a combination of factors such as smoking, high blood pressure, high insulin or glucose levels, and deposits

QUESTIONS FOR CRITICAL THINKING AND REFLECTION

What risk factors do you have for cardiovascular disease? Which ones are factors you have control over, and which are factors you can't change? If you have risk factors you cannot change (such as a family history of CVD), were you aware that you can make lifestyle adjustments to reduce your risk? Do you think you will make them?

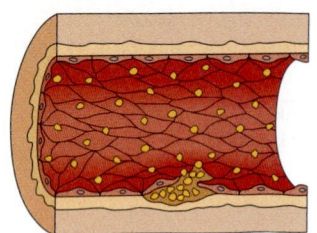 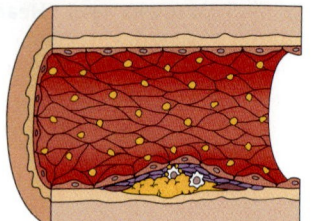 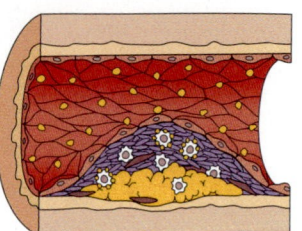 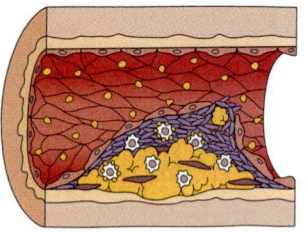

Plaque buildup begins when endothelial cells lining the arteries are damaged by smoking, high blood pressure, oxidized LDL, and other causes; excess cholesterol particles collect beneath these cells.

In response to the damage, platelets and other types of cells collect at the site; a fibrous cap forms, isolating the plaque within the artery wall. An early-stage plaque is called a fatty streak.

Chemicals released by cells in and around the plaque cause further inflammation and buildup; an advanced plaque contains LDL, white blood cells, connective tissue, smooth muscle cells, platelets, and other compounds.

The narrowed artery is vulnerable to blockage by clots. The risk of blockage and heart attack rises if the fibrous cap cracks (probably due to destructive enzymes released by white blood cells within the plaque).

FIGURE 15.7   Stages of plaque development.

of oxidized LDL particles. The body's response to this damage results in inflammation and changes in the artery lining that create a sort of magnet for LDL, platelets, and other cells; these cells build up and cause a bulge in the wall of the artery. As these deposits, called **plaques,** accumulate on artery walls, the arteries lose their elasticity and their ability to expand and contract, restricting blood flow. Once narrowed by a plaque, an artery is vulnerable to blockage by blood clots (Figure 15.7 above). The risk of life-threatening clots and heart attacks increases if the fibrous cap covering a plaque ruptures.

If the heart, brain, and/or other organs are deprived of blood and the oxygen it carries, the effects of atherosclerosis can be deadly. Coronary arteries, which supply the heart with blood, are particularly susceptible to plaque buildup, a condition called **coronary heart disease (CHD),** or *coronary artery disease (CAD)*. The blockage of a coronary artery causes a heart attack. If a cerebral artery (leading to the brain) is blocked, the result is a stroke. If an artery in a limb becomes narrowed or blocked, it causes *peripheral arterial disease,* a condition that causes pain and sometimes loss of the affected limb.

The main risk factors for atherosclerosis are cigarette smoking, physical inactivity, high levels of blood cholesterol, high blood pressure, and diabetes. Atherosclerosis often begins in childhood; in fact, autopsy studies of young trauma victims have revealed atherosclerosis of the coronary arteries in adolescents.

Heart Disease and Heart Attack

The most common form of heart disease is coronary artery disease caused by atherosclerosis. When one of the coronary arteries becomes blocked, a **heart attack,** or *myocardial infarction (MI)*, results. During a heart attack, the heart muscle (the myocardium) is damaged and part of it may die from lack of blood. Although a heart attack may come without warning, it is usually the end result of a long-term disease process.

Myocardial infarctions are a significant cause of death in the United States, especially among people age 65 and older (Table 15.5). The average age for a first heart attack is 65 for men and 70 for women.

Heart attack symptoms may include the following:

- Chest pain or pressure
- Arm, neck, or jaw pain
- Difficulty breathing
- Excessive sweating
- Nausea and vomiting
- Loss of consciousness

Most people having a heart attack suffer chest pain, but about one-third of heart attack victims do not. Women, ethnic minorities, older adults, and people with diabetes are the most likely groups to experience heart attack without chest pain (see the box "Women and CVD").

The American Heart Association estimates that 600,000 people have a first heart attack each year; 320,000 people

plaque   A deposit of fatty (and other) substances on the inner wall of the arteries.

coronary heart disease (CHD)   Heart disease caused by atherosclerosis in the arteries that supply blood to the heart muscle; also called *coronary artery disease*.

heart attack   Damage to, or death of, heart muscle, resulting from a failure of the coronary arteries to deliver enough blood to the heart; also known as *myocardial infarction (MI)*.

angina pectoris   Pain in the chest, and often in the left arm and shoulder, caused by the heart muscle not receiving enough blood.

arrhythmia   A change in the normal pattern of the heartbeat.

sudden cardiac death   A nontraumatic, unexpected death from sudden cardiac arrest, most often due to arrhythmia; in most instances, victims have underlying heart disease.

TERMS

Table 15.5	Deaths from Acute Myocardial Infarction, 2005	
Age		**Deaths**
Birth–24		88
25–44		3,126
45–64		28,623
65 and older		119,164

SOURCE: National Center for Health Statistics. 2008. *Deaths: Final Data for 2005. National Vital Statistics Reports* 56(10): 1–121. Hyattsville, Md.: National Center for Health Statistics.

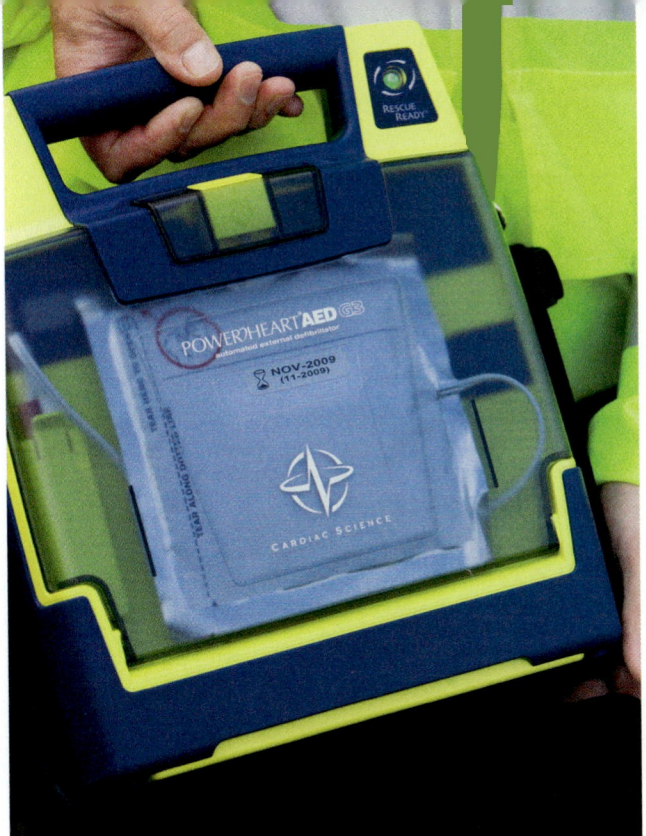

An automated external defibrillator.

have a recurrent attack. An estimated 190,000 people suffer a symptomless or "silent" heart attack each year.

Angina Arteries narrowed by disease may still be open enough to deliver blood to the heart. At times, however—during stress or exertion, for example—the heart needs more oxygen than can flow through narrowed arteries. When the need for oxygen exceeds the supply, chest pain, called **angina pectoris,** may occur.

Angina pain is usually felt as an extreme tightness in the chest and heavy pressure behind the breastbone or in the shoulder, neck, arm, hand, or back. This pain, although not actually a heart attack, is a warning that the load on the heart must be reduced. The symptoms of angina are often very difficult to distinguish from a heart attack. Any severe chest pain that lasts more than a few minutes should be considered life-threatening, and emergency medical help should be obtained immediately.

Angina may be controlled in a number of ways (with drugs and surgical or nonsurgical procedures), but its course is unpredictable. Over a period ranging from hours to years, the narrowing may go on to full blockage and a heart attack.

Arrhythmias and Sudden Cardiac Death The pumping of the heart is controlled by electrical impulses from the sinus node that maintain a regular heartbeat of 60–100 beats per minute. If this electrical conduction system is disrupted, the heart may beat too quickly, too slowly, or in an irregular fashion, a condition known as **arrhythmia.** Arrhythmia can cause symptoms ranging from imperceptible to severe and even fatal.

Sudden cardiac death, also called *cardiac arrest,* is most often caused by an arrhythmia called *ventricular fibrillation,* a kind of quivering of the ventricle that makes it ineffective in pumping blood. If ventricular fibrillation continues for more than a few minutes, it is generally fatal. Cardiac defibrillation, in which an electrical shock is delivered to the heart, can be effective in jolting the heart into a more efficient rhythm. Emergency personnel typically carry defibrillators, and automated external defibrillators (AEDs) are becoming increasingly available in public places for use by the general public. AEDs monitor the heart's rhythm and, if

appropriate, deliver an electrical shock. (Training in the use of AEDs is available from organizations such as the American Red Cross and the American Heart Association.) Sudden cardiac death most often occurs in people with coronary heart disease. Serious arrhythmias frequently develop during or after a heart attack and are often the actual cause of death in cases of a fatal MI.

Other potential causes of arrhythmia include congenital heart abnormalities, infections, drug use, chest trauma, and congestive heart failure. Some arrhythmias cause no problems and resolve without treatment; more serious arrhythmias are usually treated with medication or a surgically implanted pacemaker or defibrillator that delivers electrical stimulation to the heart to create a more normal rhythm.

Helping a Heart Attack Victim Most people who die from a heart attack do so within 2 hours from the time they experience the first symptoms. Unfortunately, half of all heart attack victims wait more than 2 hours before getting help. If you or someone you are with has any of the warning signs of heart attack listed in the box "What to Do in Case of a Heart Attack, Stroke, or Cardiac Arrest" (p. 468) take immediate action. Get help even if the person denies there is something wrong. Many experts also suggest that the heart attack victim chew and swallow one adult aspirin tablet (325 mg) as soon as possible after symptoms begin; aspirin has an immediate anticlotting effect.

What to Do in Case of a Heart Attack, Stroke, or Cardiac Arrest

Heart Attack Warning Signs

Some heart attacks are sudden and intense—the "movie heart attack," where no one doubts what's happening. But most heart attacks start slowly, with mild pain or discomfort. Often people affected aren't sure what's wrong and wait too long before getting help. Here are signs that can mean a heart attack is happening:

- **Chest discomfort.** Heart attacks often involve discomfort in the chest that lasts more than a few minutes, or that goes away and comes back. It can feel like uncomfortable pressure, squeezing, fullness, or pain.

- **Discomfort in other areas of the upper body.** Symptoms can include pain or discomfort in one or both arms, the back, neck, jaw, or stomach.

- **Shortness of breath.** May occur with or without chest discomfort.

- **Other signs:** These may include breaking out in a cold sweat, nausea, vomiting, or lightheadedness.

If you or someone you're with has chest discomfort, especially with one or more of the other signs, don't wait longer than a few minutes (no more than 5) before calling for help.

Calling 9-1-1 is almost always the fastest way to get lifesaving treatment. Emergency medical services staff can begin treatment when they arrive—up to an hour sooner than if someone gets to the hospital by car. The staff are also trained to revive someone whose heart has stopped. Patients with chest pain who arrive by ambulance usually receive faster treatment at the hospital, too.

If you can't access the emergency medical services (EMS), have someone drive you to the hospital right away. If you're the one having symptoms, don't drive yourself, unless you have absolutely no other option.

Stroke Warning Signs

The American Stroke Association says these are the warning signs of stroke:

- Sudden numbness or weakness of the face, arm, or leg, especially on one side of the body

- Sudden confusion, trouble speaking or understanding

- Sudden trouble seeing in one or both eyes

- Sudden trouble walking, dizziness, or loss of balance or coordination

- Sudden, severe headache with no known cause

If you or someone with you has one or more of these signs, don't delay! Immediately call 9-1-1 or the emergency medical services (EMS) number so an ambulance (ideally with advanced life support) can be sent for you. Also, check the time so you'll know when the first symptoms appeared. It's very important to take immediate action. If given within 3 hours of the start of symptoms, a clot-busting drug can reduce long-term disability for the most common type of stroke.

Signs of Cardiac Arrest

Cardiac arrest strikes immediately and without warning. Here are the signs:

- Sudden loss of responsiveness. No response to gentle shaking. No movement or coughing.

- No normal breathing. The victim does not take a normal breath for several seconds.

- No signs of circulation. No pulse or blood pressure.

If cardiac arrest occurs, call 9-1-1 and begin CPR immediately. If an automated external defibrillator (AED) is available and someone trained to use it is nearby, involve her or him.

For more on emergency care for cardiac arrest, see the inside back cover.

If the victim loses consciousness, a qualified person should immediately start administering emergency **cardiopulmonary resuscitation (CPR)**. Damage to the heart muscle increases with time. If the person receives emergency care quickly enough, a clot-dissolving agent can be injected to break up a clot in the coronary artery.

Detecting and Treating Heart Disease Physicians have an expanding array of tools to evaluate the condition of the heart and its arteries. Currently, the most common initial screening tool for CAD is the stress, or exercise, test, in which a patient runs or walks on a treadmill or pedals a stationary cycle while being monitored for abnormalities with an **electrocardiogram (ECG or EKG)**. Certain characteristic changes in the heart's electrical activity while under stress can reveal particular heart problems, such as restricted blood flow. Exercise testing can also be performed in conjunction with imaging techniques such as nuclear medicine or echocardiography that provide pictures of the heart, which can help pinpoint problems.

Other tests for evaluating CHD include the following:

- Electron-beam computed tomography (EBCT) uses a sweeping electron beam to produce computerized cross-sectional images; it can detect calcium in the arteries, a marker for atherosclerosis.

- Echocardiography utilizes sound waves to examine the heart's pumping function and valves.

- Multi-slice computed tomography (MSCT) is another type of CT that produces very thinly sliced images of the heart, allowing physicians to see very small structures such as the coronary arteries.
- **Magnetic resonance imaging (MRI)** uses powerful magnets to look inside the body and generate pictures of the heart and blood vessels.
- In nuclear myocardial perfusion imaging, radiotracers such as thallium-201 are injected into the bloodstream. The radiotracers' location and density in the heart can be imaged and quantified; from this data, physicians can extrapolate the blow flow (perfusion) to various areas of the heart and diagnose coronary artery disease.
- Positron Emission Tomography (PET) involves the use of positron-emitting isotopes to image and quantify regional blood flow in the heart and diagnose coronary artery disease.

If symptoms or non-invasive tests suggest coronary artery disease, the next step is usually a coronary **angiogram**, performed in a cardiac catheterization lab. In this test, a catheter (a small plastic tube) is threaded into an artery, usually in the groin, and advanced through the aorta to the coronary arteries. The catheter is then placed into the opening of the coronary artery and a special dye is injected. The dye can be seen moving through the arteries under moving X ray, and any narrowings or blockages can be identified. If a problem is found, it is commonly treated with **balloon angioplasty,** which is performed by specially trained cardiologists. In 2006, surgeons performed more than 1.3 million angioplasty

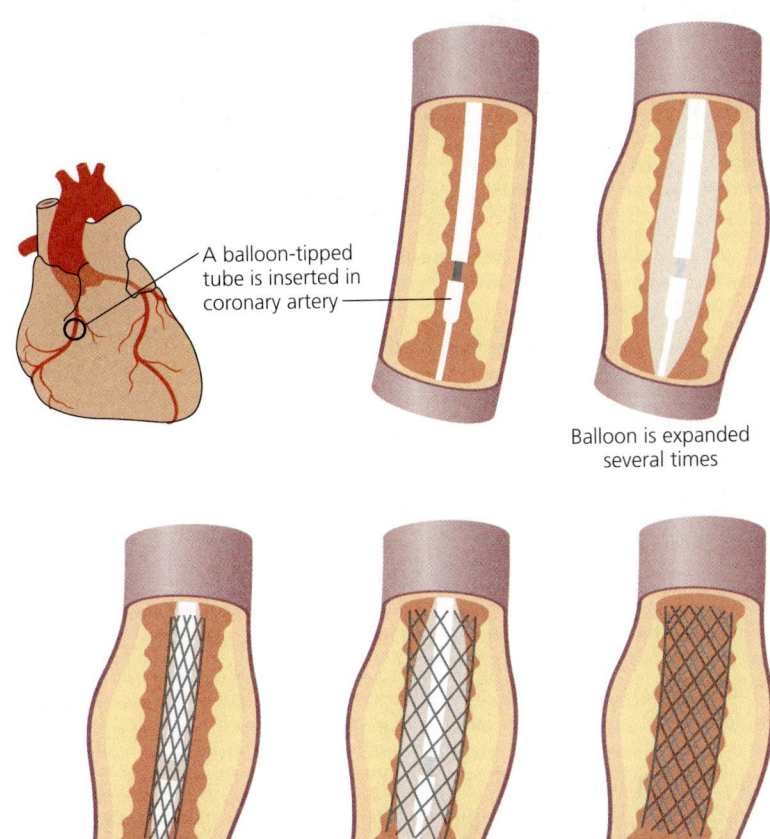

A balloon-tipped tube is inserted in coronary artery

Balloon is expanded several times

Stent insertion

Stent expansion

Stent remains in coronary artery

Balloon angioplasty and stenting.

procedures. This technique involves placing a small wire in the artery and feeding a deflated balloon over it. The balloon is advanced to the site of the narrowing and then inflated, flattening the fatty plaque and widening the arterial opening. This is generally followed by placement of a stent, a small metal tube that helps keep the artery open. Repeat clogging of the artery, known as restenosis, can occur, but the introduction of stents coated with medication, which is slowly released over a few months, significantly decreases the chance of restenosis.

Other treatments, ranging from medication to major surgery, are also available. Along with a low-fat diet, regular exercise, and smoking cessation, one frequent recommendation for people at high risk for CVD is to take a low-dose aspirin tablet every day. Aspirin has an anticlotting effect, discouraging platelets in the blood from sticking to arterial plaques and forming clots; it also reduces inflammation. (Low-dose aspirin therapy appears to help prevent first heart attacks in men, second heart attacks in men and women, and strokes in women over age 65. See the box "Aspirin and CVD" on p. 470 for more information.) Prescription drugs can help control heart rate, dilate

TERMS

cardiopulmonary resuscitation (CPR) A technique involving mouth-to-mouth breathing and/or chest compression to keep oxygen flowing to the brain.

electrocardiogram (ECG or EKG) A test to detect abnormalities by evaluating the electrical activity in the heart.

magnetic resonance imaging (MRI) A computerized imaging technique that uses a strong magnetic field and radio frequency signals to examine a thin cross section of the body.

angiogram A picture of the arterial system taken after injecting a dye that is opaque to X rays; also called *arteriogram*.

balloon angioplasty A technique in which a catheter with a deflated balloon on the tip is inserted into an artery; the balloon is then inflated at the point of obstruction in the artery, pressing the plaque against the artery wall to improve blood supply; also known as *percutaneous coronary intervention (PCI)*.

There is significant evidence that aspirin can help decrease the risk of CVD in a wide range of patients.

Aspirin functions by inactivating a clotting component of the blood called platelets. Platelets and their products play a role in virtually all events involving blocked blood vessels, including myocardial infarctions and ischemic strokes. It is believed that when atherosclerotic plaques in the blood vessels become dislodged, platelets begin accumulating at the site and ultimately form a blood clot (thrombus), which can lead to an acute cardiovascular event. Even in small amounts (75 mg/day), aspirin acts as a potent and irreversible inhibitor of platelet clotting function.

The strongest indications for aspirin are for the acute treatment of thrombotic cardiovascular events and for the prevention of further such events after an initial episode, which is called secondary prevention. There is extremely strong evidence to show that aspirin should be administered to virtually every patient with an acute MI. The benefits of aspirin for reducing the risk of subsequent MI, stroke, or vascular death are substantial, and the risks of serious bleeding and other adverse reactions are very low and treatable in an acute care hospital setting.

Guidelines from the American College of Cardiology (ACC)/American Heart Association (AHA) and the American College of Chest Physicians (ACCP), based on data from multiple randomized clinical trials, recommend that aspirin should be given in an initial dose of 162 to 325 mg to all patients with an acute MI unless there is a clear reason not to do so. The ACC/AHA and the ACCP guidelines recommend that the initial dose of aspirin should be followed by a daily dose of 75 to 162 mg, which should be continued indefinitely.

In some patients, prolonged aspirin use carries side effects such as gastrointestinal bleeding. Such people, however, are generally able to tolerate different formulations or lower doses of aspirin, although 75 mg daily is currently considered to be the lowest proven effective dose.

In January 1997, at a joint meeting of the FDA's Nonprescription Drugs and Cardiovascular and Renal Drugs Advisory Committees, the use of daily oral aspirin was recommended in patients with prior MI, unstable angina, chronic stable angina, prior occlusive stroke, and certain other conditions. In addition, the Seventh American College Chest Physicians (ACCP) Consensus Conference on Antithrombotic Therapy recommends that all patients with chronic stable angina or other clinical or laboratory evidence of coronary artery disease receive daily oral aspirin indefinitely.

Aspirin can also be used to prevent an initial thrombotic cardiovascular event, which is called primary prevention. It is vital to remember that when aspirin is used for primary prevention the benefit is much smaller than for secondary prevention while the risk of major bleeding complication such as gastrointestinal bleeding or hemorrhagic stroke is the same. In one meta-analysis looking at multiple trials on this topic, the risk of a major gastrointestinal bleeding event in those treated with aspirin was 2.30% versus 1.45% percent with placebo at an average of 28 months. Thus, in 2002 the United States Preventive Services Task Force recommended aspirin for all apparently healthy men and women whose 5-year risk of a first CVD event is 3% or greater.

Currently, the American Heart Association recommends that those with a 10% or greater risk of a primary CVD event over a 10-year period begin daily aspirin therapy. Physicians can assess the long-term risk of CVD events in their patients for the purposes of making the decision about whether to begin aspirin for primary prevention of CVD events. Risk factors include age, sex, family history, smoking, diet, alcohol and drug use, physical activity, blood pressure, body mass index, waist circumference, lipid profile, and fasting blood glucose (a measure for diabetes).

However, recent evidence has demonstrated that the use of aspirin for the primary prevention of CVD events in women is more complicated. In 2007, the American Heart Association published new CVD prevention guidelines for women that recommended low-dose aspirin (81 mg daily or 100 mg every other day) for women 65 years or older who are at increased risk of CVD. For women under 65 years of age, the guidelines recommended aspirin for the prevention of ischemic stroke in those at risk (for example, patients with TIAs), but not for the prevention of MI.

---

arteries, lower blood pressure, and reduce the strain on the heart—raising both quality and length of life in heart patients. In patients with coronary artery disease, cholesterol-lowering statins are effective in preventing heart attacks; statins also have beneficial anti-inflammatory effects.

In 2006, **coronary bypass surgery** was performed on 253,000 people. Cardiothoracic surgeons remove a healthy blood vessel, usually a vein from one of the patient's legs, and graft it from the aorta to one or more coronary arteries to bypass a blockage.

Stroke

For brain cells to function as they should, they must have a continuous supply of oxygen-rich blood. If brain cells are deprived of blood for more than a few minutes, they die. A **stroke,** also called a *cerebrovascular accident (CVA)*, occurs when the blood supply to the brain is cut off. One study found that about 2 million brain cells died per minute during a stroke and the brain aged about 3.5 years each hour.

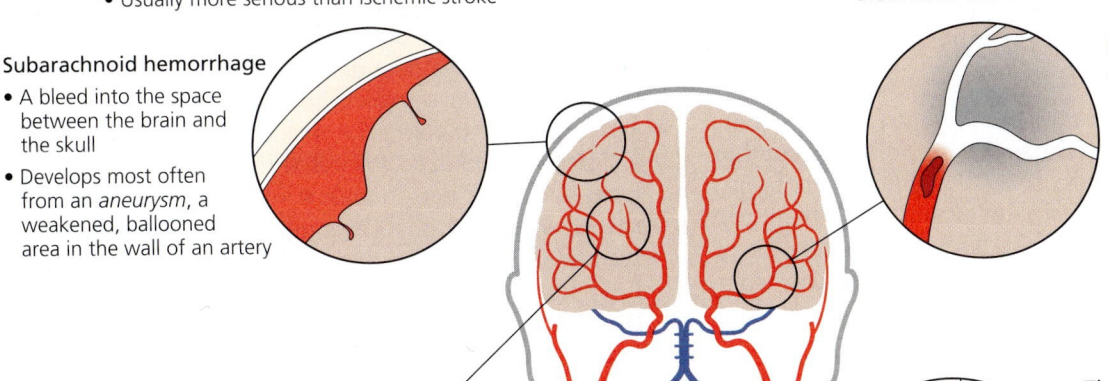

HEMORRHAGIC STROKE
- 13% of strokes
- Caused by ruptured blood vessels followed by blood leaking into tissue
- Usually more serious than ischemic stroke

ISCHEMIC STROKE
- 87% of strokes
- Caused by blockages in brain blood vessels; potentially treatable with clot-busting drugs
- Brain tissue dies when blood flow is blocked

Subarachnoid hemorrhage
- A bleed into the space between the brain and the skull
- Develops most often from an *aneurysm*, a weakened, ballooned area in the wall of an artery

Embolic stroke
- Caused by *emboli*, blood clots that travel from elsewhere in the body to the brain blood vessels
- 25% of embolic strokes are related to atrial fibrillation

Thrombotic stroke
- Caused by *thrombi*, blood clots that form where an artery has been narrowed by atherosclerosis
- Most often develops when part of a thrombus breaks away and causes a blockage in a downstream artery

Intracerebral hemorrhage
- A bleed from a blood vessel inside the brain
- Often caused by high blood pressure and the damage it does to arteries

FIGURE 15.8 **Types of stroke.**

SOURCE: Excerpted from *Harvard Health Letter,* April 2000. Reprinted with permission obtained via The Copyright Clearance Center.

In the past, not much could be done for stroke victims; today, however, prompt treatment of stroke can greatly decrease the risk of permanent disability. Everyone should know the warning signs of a stroke and seek immediate medical help, just as they would at the first sign of a heart attack.

Types of Strokes

There are two major types of strokes (Figure 15.8), which are described in the following sections.

ISCHEMIC STROKE An **ischemic stroke** is caused by a blockage in a blood vessel. There are two types of ischemic strokes:

- A *thrombotic stroke* is caused by a **thrombus,** which is a blood clot that forms in a cerebral artery that has been narrowed or damaged by atherosclerosis.
- An *embolic stroke* is cause by an **embolus,** which is a wandering blood clot that is carried in the bloodstream and may become wedged in a cerebral artery. Many embolic strokes are linked to a type of abnormal heart rhythm called *atrial fibrillation;* when this arrhythmia occurs, blood may pool in an atrium and form a clot.

Ischemic strokes, which account for 87% of all strokes, are potentially treatable with clot-busting drugs, so immediate medical help is critical to improving the victim's chances of recovery.

HEMORRHAGIC STROKE A **hemorrhagic stroke** occurs when a blood vessel in the brain bursts, spilling blood into the surrounding tissue. Cells normally nourished by the artery are deprived of blood and cannot function. In addition, accumulated blood from the burst vessel may put pressure on surrounding brain tissue, causing damage and even death. There are two types of hemorrhagic strokes:

TERMS

coronary bypass surgery Surgery in which a vein is grafted from a point above to a point below an obstruction in a coronary artery, improving the blood supply to the heart.

stroke An impeded blood supply to some part of the brain resulting in the destruction of brain cells; also called *cerebrovascular accident.*

ischemic stroke Impeded blood supply to the brain caused by the obstruction of a blood vessel by a clot.

thrombus A blood clot in a blood vessel that usually remains at the point of its formation.

embolus A blood clot that breaks off from its place of origin in a blood vessel and travels through the bloodstream.

hemorrhagic stroke Impeded blood supply to the brain caused by the rupture of a blood vessel.

- In an *intracerebral hemorrhage,* a blood vessel ruptures within the brain. About 10% of strokes are caused by intracerebral hemorrhages.

- In a *subarachnoid hemorrhage,* a blood vessel on the brain's surface ruptures and bleeds into the space between the brain and the skull. About 3% of strokes are of this type.

Hemorrhages can be caused by head injuries or the bursting of a malformed blood vessel or an **aneurysm,** which is a blood-filled pocket that bulges out from a weak spot in an artery wall. Aneurysms in the brain may remain stable and never break. But when they do, the result is a stroke. Aneurysms may be caused or worsened by hypertension.

The Effects of a Stroke

The interruption of the blood supply to any area of the brain prevents the nerve cells there from functioning—in some cases causing death. Stroke survivors usually have some lasting disability. Which parts of the body are affected depends on the area of the brain that has been damaged. Nerve cells control sensation and most of our body movements, and a stroke may cause paralysis, walking disability, speech impairment, memory loss, and changes in behavior. The severity of the stroke and its long-term effects depend on which brain cells have been injured, how widespread the damage is, how effectively the body can restore the blood supply, and how rapidly other areas of the brain can take over. Early treatment can significantly reduce the severity of disability resulting from a stroke.

Detecting and Treating Stroke

Death rates from stroke have declined significantly over the past decades—from nearly 90% in 1950 to about 19.2% today. Effective treatment requires the prompt recognition of symptoms and correct diagnosis of the type of stroke. Signs of a stroke are listed in the box on page 468; also see the box "Three Simple Ways to Recognize a Stroke."

Many people have strokes, however, without knowing it. These "silent strokes" do not cause any noticeable symptoms while they are occurring. Although they may be mild, silent strokes leave their victims at a higher risk for subsequent and more serious strokes later in life. They also contribute to loss of mental and cognitive skills. In 2008, a study of MRI scans of 2000 elderly people revealed that 11% of the subjects had brain damage from one or more strokes but did not realize they had ever had a stroke.

Some stroke victims have a **transient ischemic attack (TIA),** or ministroke, days, weeks, or months before they have a full-blown stroke. A TIA produces temporary stroke-like symptoms, such as weakness or numbness in an arm or a leg, speech difficulty, or dizziness. These symptoms are brief, often lasting just a few minutes, and do not cause permanent damage. TIAs should be taken as warning signs of a stroke, however, and anyone with a suspected TIA should get immediate medical help.

Strokes should be treated with the same urgency as heart attacks. A person with stroke symptoms should be rushed to the hospital. A **computed tomography (CT)** scan, which uses a computer to construct an image of the brain from X rays, can assess brain damage and determine the type of stroke. Newer techniques using MRI and ultrasound are becoming increasingly available and should improve the speed and accuracy of stroke diagnosis.

If tests reveal that a stroke is caused by a blood clot—and if help is sought within a few hours of the onset of symptoms—the person can be treated with the same kind of clot-dissolving drugs that are used to treat coronary artery blockages. If the clot is dissolved quickly enough, brain damage is minimized and symptoms may disappear. (The longer the brain goes without blood, the greater the risk of permanent damage.) People who have had TIAs or who are at high risk for stroke due to narrowing of the carotid arteries (large arteries on either side of the neck, which carry blood to the head) may undergo a surgical procedure called *carotid endarterectomy,* in which plaque is removed. There is also a nonsurgical procedure, similar to coronary angioplasty and stenting, that can be done in the carotid arteries.

If tests reveal that a stroke was caused by a cerebral hemorrhage, drugs may be prescribed to lower the blood pressure, which will usually be high. Careful diagnosis is crucial, because administering clot-dissolving drugs to a

TERMS

aneurysm   A sac formed by a distention or dilation of the artery wall.

transient ischemic attack (TIA)   A small stroke; usually a temporary interruption of blood supply to the brain, causing numbness or difficulty with speech.

computed tomography (CT)   The use of computerized X ray images to create a cross-sectional depiction (scan) of tissue density.

peripheral arterial disease (PAD)   Atherosclerosis in arteries in the legs (or, less commonly, arms) that can impede blood flow and lead to pain, infection, and loss of the affected limb.

pulmonary edema   The accumulation of fluid in the lungs.

congestive heart failure   A condition resulting from the heart's inability to pump out all the blood that returns to it; blood backs up in the veins leading to the heart, causing an accumulation of fluid in various parts of the body.

Three Simple Ways to Recognize a Stroke

Imagine you're at a family gathering, chatting with your grandfather. In the middle of the conversation, he becomes confused and seems to have trouble speaking. Other relatives become concerned, and someone calls 9-1-1. How can you know whether your grandfather is having a stroke? While you are waiting for help to arrive, ask him to do three simple things. His ability to respond may tell you whether the problem is a stroke.

"Give me a smile."

Ask your grandfather to smile, or just to show his teeth. If his smile droops on one side or if he is unable to move or open one side of his mouth, he may be having a stroke.

"Hold your arms out."

Ask your grandfather to close his eyes and hold his arms straight out for just a few seconds. If he cannot move one arm, or if he cannot hold one arm still, it may be a sign of a stroke.

"Say this for me."

Ask your grandfather to repeat a short, simple sentence (not a tongue-twister), like "Take me out to the ballgame." If he has difficulty speaking or cannot speak, then a stroke is possible.

If someone has trouble performing any one of these three tests, he or she may be suffering a stroke. Follow the steps for helping a stroke victim in the box "What to Do in Case of a Heart Attack, Stroke, or Cardiac Arrest" on page 468.

---

person suffering a hemorrhagic stroke would cause more bleeding and potentially more brain damage.

If detection and treatment of stroke come too late, rehabilitation is the only treatment. Although damaged or destroyed brain tissue does not normally regenerate, nerve cells in the brain can make new pathways, and some functions can be taken over by other parts of the brain. Some spontaneous recovery starts immediately after a stroke and continues for a few months.

Rehabilitation consists of physical therapy, which helps strengthen muscles and improve balance and coordination; speech and language therapy, which helps those whose speech has been damaged; and occupational therapy, which helps improve hand-eye coordination and everyday living skills. Some people recover completely in a matter of days or weeks, but most stroke victims who survive must adapt to some disability.

Peripheral Arterial Disease

Peripheral arterial disease (PAD) refers to atherosclerosis in the leg (or arm) arteries, which can eventually limit or completely obstruct blood flow. The same process that occurs in the heart arteries can occur in any artery of the body. In fact, patients with PAD frequently also have coronary artery disease and cerebrovascular disease, and they have an increased risk of death from CVD. Approximately 8 million people in the United States have PAD.

The risk factors associated with coronary atherosclerosis, such as smoking, diabetes, hypertension, and high cholesterol, also contribute to atherosclerosis in the peripheral circulation. The risk of PAD is significantly increased in people with diabetes and people who smoke. The likelihood of needing an amputation is increased in those who continue to smoke, and PAD in people with diabetes tends to be extensive and severe.

Symptoms of PAD include claudication and rest pain. *Claudication* is aching or fatigue in the affected leg with exertion, particularly walking, which resolves with rest. Claudication occurs when leg muscles do not get adequate blood and oxygen supply. *Rest pain* occurs when the limb artery is unable to supply adequate blood and oxygen even when the body is not physically active. This occurs when the artery is significantly narrowed or completely blocked. If blood flow is not restored quickly, cells and tissues die; in severe cases, amputation may be needed. PAD is the leading cause of amputation in people over age 50.

2210 heart transplants were performed in the United States in 2007.

—American Heart Association, 2009

QUICK STATS

Congestive Heart Failure

A number of conditions—high blood pressure, heart attack, atherosclerosis, alcoholism, viral infections, rheumatic fever, birth defects—can damage the heart's pumping mechanism. When the heart cannot maintain its regular pumping rate and force, fluids begin to back up. When extra fluid seeps through capillary walls, edema (swelling) results, usually in the legs and ankles, but sometimes in other parts of the body as well. Fluid can collect in the lungs and interfere with breathing, particularly when a person is lying down. This condition is called **pulmonary edema**, and the entire process is known as **congestive heart failure**. About 5.7 million Americans suffer from heart failure; the condition was associated with more than 290,000 deaths in 2005.

Congestive heart failure can be controlled. Treatment includes reducing the workload on the heart, modifying salt intake, and using drugs that help the body eliminate excess fluid. Drugs used to treat congestive heart failure improve the pumping action of the heart, lower blood pressure so the heart doesn't have to work as hard, and help the body eliminate excess salt and water. When medical therapy is ineffective, heart transplant is a solution for some patients with severe heart failure, but the need greatly exceeds the number of hearts available.

The risk of heart failure increases with age, and being overweight is a significant independent risk factor. Experts fear that the incidence of heart failure will increase dramatically over the next few decades as our population ages and becomes increasingly obese.

Other Forms of Heart Disease

Other, less common, forms of heart disease include congenital heart disease, rheumatic heart disease, and heart valve disorders.

Congenital Heart Defects   About 36,000 children born each year in the United States have a defect or malformation of the heart or major blood vessels. These conditions are collectively referred to as **congenital heart defects,** and they cause about 3600 deaths a year. Most of the common congenital defects can now be accurately diagnosed and treated with medication or surgery. Early recognition of possible heart disease in a newborn is important in saving lives. The most common congenital defects are holes in the wall that divides the chambers of the heart. Such defects cause the heart to produce a distinctive sound, making diagnosis relatively simple. Another common defect is *coarctation of the aorta,* a narrowing, or constriction, of the aorta. Heart failure may result unless the constricted area is repaired by surgery.

Hypertrophic cardiomyopathy (HCM) occurs in 1 out of every 500 people and is the most common cause of sud-

den death among athletes younger than age 35. It causes the heart muscle to become hypertrophic (enlarged), primarily in the septum, which is the area between the two ventricles. People with hypertrophic cardiomyopathy are at high risk for sudden death, mainly due to serious arrhythmias. Hypertrophic cardiomyopathy may be identified by a **murmur,** then diagnosed using echocardiography. Possible treatments include medication and a pacemaker or internal defibrillator. If the hypertrophy is mainly in the septum, some of the septum can be surgically removed or a nonsurgical procedure can be done to kill off the extra muscle.

Rheumatic Heart Disease   **Rheumatic fever,** a consequence of certain types of untreated streptococcal throat infections, is a leading cause of heart trouble worldwide. Rheumatic fever can permanently damage the heart muscle and heart valves, a condition called *rheumatic heart disease (RHD).* Many of the approximately 100,000 operations on heart valves performed annually are related to RHD, and about 3300 Americans die each year from RHD. The incidence of rheumatic fever has declined significantly in the United States since the introduction of antibiotics; rates are highest among African Americans, Latinos, and American Indians.

Symptoms of strep throat include the sudden onset of a sore throat, painful swallowing, fever, swollen glands, headache, nausea, and vomiting. Careful laboratory diagnosis is important because strep throat is treated with antibiotics, which are not useful in the treatment of far more common viral sore throats. If left untreated, up to 3% of strep infections progress into rheumatic fever. Rheumatic fever primarily affects children between the ages of 5 and 15.

Heart Valve Disorders   Congenital defects and certain types of infections can cause abnormalities in the valves between the chambers of the heart. Heart valve problems generally fall into two categories—the valve fails to open fully, or it fails to close completely. In either case, blood flow through the heart is impaired.

Treatment for heart valve disorders depends on their location and severity; serious problems may be treated with surgery to repair or replace a valve. People with certain types of heart valve defects are advised to take antibiotics prior to some types of dental and surgical procedures in order to prevent bacteria, which may be dislodged into the bloodstream during the procedure, from infecting the defective valve.

The most common heart valve disorder is **mitral valve prolapse (MVP),** which occurs in about 3% of the population. MVP is characterized by a billowing of the mitral valve, which separates the left ventricle and left atrium, during ventricular contraction; in some cases, blood leaks from the ventricle into the atrium. Most people with MVP have no symptoms; they have the same ability to exercise and live as long as people without MVP. The condition is

often diagnosed during a routine medical exam when an extra heart sound (a click) or murmur is heard; the diagnosis can be confirmed with echocardiography.

Treatment for MVP is usually unnecessary, although surgery may be needed in the rare cases where leakage through the faulty valve is severe. In the past, some people with MVP have been given antibiotics prior to certain dental or surgical procedures, to prevent an infection of the heart called *bacterial endocarditis*. However, the American Heart Association no longer recommends routine use of antibiotics prior to dental procedures or procedures involving the gastrointestinal or genitourinary tracts.

PROTECTING YOURSELF AGAINST CARDIOVASCULAR DISEASE

There are several important steps you can take now to lower your risk of developing CVD (Figure 15.9). CVD can begin very early in life. For example, fatty streaks (very early atherosclerosis) can be seen on the aorta in children younger than age 10. Also, young adults with relatively low cholesterol levels go on to live substantially longer than those with higher levels. Reducing CVD risk factors when you are young can pay off with many extra years of life and health (see the box "Are You at Risk for CVD?" on p. 476).

Eat Heart-Healthy

For most Americans, eating a heart-healthy diet involves many of the changes suggested in the 2005 Dietary Guidelines for Americans: cutting total fat intake, substituting unsaturated fats for saturated and trans fats, and increasing intake of whole grains and fiber. Such changes can lower blood levels of total cholesterol, LDL cholesterol, and triglycerides. Reducing salt intake and getting enough potassium can help lower blood pressure. A moderate amount of alcohol may also be beneficial for some people.

See Chapter 12 for a detailed discussion of nutrition and dietary guidelines. The following sections briefly discuss specific aspects of nutrition that apply directly to heart health.

Decreased Fat and Cholesterol Intake The National Cholesterol Education Program (NCEP) recommends that all Americans over age 2 adopt a diet in which total fat consumption is no more than 30% of total daily calories, with no more than one-third of total fat calories (10% of total daily calories) coming from saturated fat. The American Heart Association recommends that no more than 7% of daily calories come from saturated fat and less than 1% come from trans fats; this recommendation applies to everyone.

Do More

- Eat a diet rich in fruits, vegetable, whole grains, and low-fat or fat-free dairy products. Eat 5–9 servings of fruits and vegetables each day.

- Eat several servings of high-fiber foods each day.

- Eat 2 or more servings of fish per week; try a few servings of nuts and soy foods each week.

- Choose unsaturated fats rather than saturated and trans fats.

- Be physically active; do both aerobic exercise and strength training on a regular basis.

- Achieve and maintain a healthy weight.

- Develop effective strategies for handling stress and anger. Nurture old friendships and family ties, and make new friends; pay attention to your spiritual side.

- Obtain recommended screening tests and follow your physician's recommendations.

Do Less

- Don't use tobacco in any form: cigarettes, spit tobacco, cigars and pipes, bidis and clove cigarettes.

- Avoid exposure to environmental tobacco smoke.

- Limit consumption of fats, especially trans fats and saturated fats.

- Limit consumption of cholesterol, added sugars, and refined carbohydrates.

- Avoid excessive alcohol consumption—no more than one drink per day for women and two drinks per day for men.

- Limit consumption of salt to no more than 2300 mg of sodium per day (1500 mg if you have or are at high risk for hypertension).

- Avoid excess stress, anger, and hostility.

FIGURE 15.9 **Strategies for reducing your risk of cardiovascular disease.**

Are You at Risk for CVD?

Your chances of suffering an early heart attack or stroke depend on a variety of factors, many of which are under your control. The best time to identify your risk factors and change your behavior to lower your risk is when you are young. You can significantly affect your future health and quality of life if you adopt healthy behaviors. To help identify your risk factors, circle the response for each risk category that best describes you:

1. Gender and Age
   - 0 Female age 55 or younger; male age 45 or younger
   - 2 Female age 55 or older or male age 45 or older

2. Heredity
   - 0 Neither parent suffered a heart attack or stroke before age 60.
   - 3 One parent suffered a heart attack or stroke before age 60.
   - 7 Both parents suffered a heart attack or stroke before age 60.

3. Smoking
   - 0 Never smoked
   - 3 Quit more than 2 years ago and lifetime smoking is less than 5 pack-years*
   - 6 Quit less than 2 years ago and/or lifetime smoking is greater than 5 pack-years*
   - 8 Smoke less than ½ pack per day
   - 13 Smoke more than ½ pack per day
   - 15 Smoke more than 1 pack per day

4. Environmental Tobacco Smoke
   - 0 Do not live or work with smokers
   - 2 Exposed to ETS at work
   - 3 Live with a smoker
   - 4 Both live and work with smokers

5. Blood Pressure

   If available, average your last three readings:
   - 0 120/80 or below
   - 1 121/81–130/85
   - 3 Don't know
   - 5 131/86–150/90
   - 9 151/91–170/100
   - 13 Above 170/100

6. Total Cholesterol (mg/dl)
   - 0 Lower than 190
   - 1 190–210
   - 2 Don't know
   - 3 211–240
   - 4 241–270
   - 5 271–300
   - 6 Over 300

7. HDL Cholesterol (mg/dl)
   - 0 Over 60
   - 1 55–60
   - 2 Don't know
   - 3 45–54
   - 5 35–44
   - 7 25–34
   - 12 Lower than 25

8. Exercise
   - 0 Exercise three times a week
   - 1 Exercise once or twice a week
   - 2 Occasional exercise less than once a week
   - 7 Rarely exercise

9. Diabetes
   - 0 No personal or family history
   - 2 One parent with diabetes
   - 6 Two parents with diabetes
   - 9 Non–insulin-dependent diabetes
   - 13 Insulin-dependent diabetes

10. Body Mass Index (using the formula provided in Chapter 14)
   - 0 <23.0
   - 1 23.0–24.9
   - 2 25.0–28.9
   - 3 29.0–34.9
   - 5 35.0–39.9
   - 7 ≥40

11. Stress
   - 0 Relaxed most of the time
   - 1 Occasional stress and anger
   - 2 Frequently stressed and angry
   - 3 Usually stressed and angry

Scoring

Total your risk factor points. Refer to the list below to get an approximate rating of your risk of suffering an early heart attack or stroke.

Score	Estimated Risk
Less than 20	Low risk
20–29	Moderate risk
30–45	High risk
Over 45	Extremely high risk

*Pack-years can be calculated by multiplying the number of packs you smoked per day by the number of years you smoked. For example, if you smoked a pack and a half a day for 5 years, you would have smoked the equivalent of $1.5 \times 5 = 7.5$ pack-years.

For people with heart disease or high LDL levels, the NCEP recommends a total fat intake of 25–35% of total daily calories and a saturated fat intake of less than 7% of total calories. The higher total fat allowance is for people with insulin resistance who need to decrease their carbohydrate intake.

The NCEP recommends that most Americans limit dietary cholesterol intake to no more than 300 mg per day; for people with heart disease or high LDL levels, the suggested daily limit is 200 mg. Animal products contain cholesterol as well as saturated fat; vegetable products do not contain cholesterol.

Increased Fiber Intake

Fiber traps the bile acids the liver needs to manufacture cholesterol and carries them to the large intestine, where they are excreted. It slows the production of proteins that promote blood clotting. Fiber may also interfere with the absorption of dietary fat and may help you cut total food intake because foods rich in fiber tend to be filling. Studies have shown that a high-fiber diet is associated with a 40–50% reduction in the risk of heart attack and stroke.

To get the recommended 25–38 grams of dietary fiber per day, eat whole grains, fruits, and vegetables. Good sources of fiber include oatmeal, some breakfast cereals, barley, legumes, and most fruits and vegetables.

Decreased Sodium Intake and Increased Potassium Intake

Reducing sodium intake to recommended levels, while also increasing potassium intake, can help reduce blood pressure for many people. The recommended limit for sodium intake is 2300 mg per day; for population groups at special risk, including those with hypertension, middle-aged and older adults, and African Americans, the recommended limit is 1500 mg per day.

Potassium is also important in controlling blood pressure, and many Americans consume less than recommended amounts of the mineral. Good food sources include leafy green vegetables like spinach and beet greens, root vegetables like white and sweet potatoes, vine fruits like cantaloupe and honeydew melon, winter squash, bananas, many dried fruits, and tomato sauce.

Moderate Alcohol Consumption (For Some)

The Dietary Guidelines for Americans state that moderate alcohol consumption may lower the risk of CHD among middle-aged and older adults. (Moderate means no more than one drink per day for women and two drinks per day for men.) Moderate alcohol use may increase HDL cholesterol; it may also reduce stroke risk, possibly by dampening the inflammatory response or by affecting blood clotting.

For most people under age 45, however, the risks of alcohol use probably outweigh any health benefit. Excessive alcohol consumption increases the risk of a variety of serious health problems, including hypertension, stroke, some cancers, liver disease, alcohol dependence, and in-juries. See Chapter 10 for a detailed discussion of alcohol use, the effects of alcohol, and the importance of moderation in drinking.

Other Dietary Factors

Researchers have identified other dietary factors that may affect CVD risk:

- *Omega-3 fatty acids.* Found in fish, shellfish, and some plant foods (nuts and canola, soybean, and flaxseed oils), omega-3 fatty acids may reduce clotting, abnormal heart rhythms, and inflammation and have other heart-healthy effects, such as lowering triglycerides. The American Heart Association recommends eating fish two or more times a week; fish oil capsules may be appropriate for some people who won't eat fish or who have certain CVD risk factors. Note that omega-3 fatty acids may raise LDL levels and some fish sources may be high in mercury. Plant sources of omega-3 fatty acids are also a good choice.

- *Plant stanols and sterols.* Plant stanols and sterols, found in some types of trans fat–free margarines and other products, reduce the absorption of cholesterol in the body and help lower LDL levels. For people with high LDL levels that do not respond to changes in fat intake, the NCEP suggests an intake of 2 grams per day of plant stanols or sterols.

- *Folic acid, vitamin B-6, and vitamin B-12.* These vitamins lower homocysteine levels, and folic acid has also been found to reduce the risk of hypertension.

- *Calcium.* Diets rich in calcium may help prevent hypertension and possibly stroke by reducing insulin resistance and platelet aggregation. Good sources of calcium are low-fat and fat-free dairy products.

- *Soy protein.* Although soy itself doesn't seem to have much effect on cholesterol, replacing some animal proteins with soy protein (e.g., tofu) may help lower LDL cholesterol.

- *Healthy carbohydrates.* Most of the carbohydrates in the current American diet come from added sugars, refined grains, and starchy foods, including soft drinks, sweets, white potatoes (including french fries and chips), white bread, and refined ready-to-eat cereals; these foods are often relatively low in nutrients and have a high glycemic index (see Chapter 12). Healthier carbohydrate choices, including whole grains, fruits, and nonstarchy vegetables, typically provide more nutrients and have a lower glycemic index. Choosing healthy carbohydrates is important for people with insulin resistance, pre-diabetes, or diabetes.

- *Total calories.* Some studies have found that reducing energy intake can improve cholesterol and triglyceride levels as much as reducing fat intake does. Reduced calorie intake also helps control body weight, an extremely important risk factor for CVD.

Most experts recommend against taking nutritional supplements (especially extra folic acid and B vitamins) as a way to prevent heart disease. In fact, a 10-year-long study ending in 2008 revealed that vitamin C and E supplements provided no protection against heart disease in men. In some of the study's subjects, vitamin E supplementation was associated with an increased risk of stroke. An estimated 12% of Americans take vitamin C and E supplements, and many people do so because of a long-standing yet unproven theory that these antioxidants protect against heart disease. There is some evidence that vitamin D deficiency may increase the risk of heart disease, especially in men, but experts do not currently advise taking vitamin D supplements to prevent CVD. If you are concerned about your heart health and may not be getting the nutrition you need, ask your physician or a registered dietician for advice.

DASH A diet plan that reflects many of the recommendations described above was released as part of a study called Dietary Approaches to Stop Hypertension, or DASH. The DASH study found that a diet low in fat and high in fruits, vegetables, and low-fat dairy products reduces blood pressure. It also follows the recommendations for lowering the risk of heart disease, cancer, and osteoporosis. See Chapter 12 for details about the DASH diet plan, including specific serving information for people with different caloric needs.

Exercise Regularly

You can significantly reduce your risk of CVD with a moderate amount of physical activity. Follow the guidelines for physical activity and exercise described in Chapter 13. The American Heart Association recommends strength training in addition to aerobic exercise for building and maintaining cardiovascular health. Strength training helps lower blood pressure, reduce body fat, and improve lipid levels and glucose metabolism.

Avoid Tobacco

The number-one risk factor for CVD that you can control is smoking. If you smoke, quit. If you don't, don't start. If you live or work with people who smoke, encourage them to quit—for their sake and yours. Exposure to ETS raises your risk of CVD, and there is no safe level of exposure. If you find yourself breathing in smoke, take steps to prevent or stop the exposure. See Chapter 11 for detailed information on the effects of smoking and strategies for quitting.

Know and Manage Your Blood Pressure

If you have no CVD risk factors, have your blood pressure measured by a trained professional at least once every 2 years; yearly tests are recommended if you have other risk factors. If your blood pressure is high, follow your physician's advice on how to lower it. For those with hypertension that is not readily controlled with lifestyle changes, an array of antihypertension medications are available.

Know and Manage Your Cholesterol Levels

All people age 20 and over should have their cholesterol checked at least once every 5 years. The NCEP recommends a fasting lipoprotein profile that measures total cholesterol, HDL, LDL, and triglyceride levels. Once you know your baseline numbers, you and your physician can develop an LDL goal and lifestyle plan.

Develop Effective Ways to Handle Stress and Anger

To reduce the psychological and social risk factors for CVD, develop effective strategies for handling the stress in your life. Shore up your social support network, and try some of the techniques described in Chapter 2 for managing stress.

TIPS FOR TODAY AND THE FUTURE

Because cardiovascular disease is a long-term process that can begin when you're young, it's important to develop heart-healthy habits early in life.

RIGHT NOW YOU CAN

- Make an appointment to have your blood pressure and cholesterol levels checked.
- List the key stressors in your life, and decide what to do about the ones that bother you most.
- Plan to replace one high-fat item in your diet with one that is high in fiber. For example, replace a doughnut with a bowl of whole-grain cereal.

IN THE FUTURE YOU CAN

- Track your eating habits for one week, then compare them to the DASH eating plan. Make adjustments to bring your diet closer to the DASH recommendations.
- Sign up for a class in cardiopulmonary resuscitation (CPR). A CPR certification equips you with valuable lifesaving skills you can use to help someone who is choking, having a heart attack, or experiencing cardiac arrest.

QUESTIONS FOR CRITICAL THINKING AND REFLECTION

Do you know what your blood pressure and cholesterol levels are? If not, is there a reason you don't know? Is there something preventing you from getting this information about yourself? How can you motivate yourself to have these easy but important health checks?

SUMMARY

• The cardiovascular system pumps and circulates blood throughout the body. The heart pumps blood to the lungs via the pulmonary artery and to the body via the aorta.

• The exchange of nutrients and waste products takes place between the capillaries and the tissues.

• The six major risk factors for CVD that can be changed are smoking, high blood pressure, unhealthy cholesterol levels, inactivity, overweight and obesity, and diabetes.

• Effects of smoking include lower HDL levels, increased blood pressure and heart rate, accelerated plaque formation, and increased risk of blood clots.

• Hypertension occurs when blood pressure exceeds normal limits most of the time. It weakens the heart, scars and hardens arteries, and can damage the eyes and kidneys.

• High LDL and low HDL cholesterol levels contribute to clogged arteries and increase the risk of CVD.

• Physical inactivity, obesity, and diabetes are interrelated and are associated with high blood pressure and unhealthy cholesterol levels.

• Contributing risk factors that can be changed include high triglyceride levels and psychological and social factors.

• Risk factors for CVD that can't be changed include being over 65, being male, being African American, and having a family history of CVD.

• Atherosclerosis is a progressive hardening and narrowing of arteries that can lead to restricted blood flow and even complete blockage.

• Heart attacks are usually the result of a long-term disease process. Warning signs of a heart attack include chest discomfort, shortness of breath, nausea, and sweating.

• A stroke occurs when the blood supply to the brain is cut off by a blood clot or hemorrhage. A transient ischemic attack (TIA) is a warning sign of stroke.

• Congestive heart failure occurs when the heart's pumping action becomes less efficient and fluid collects in the lungs or in other parts of the body.

• Dietary changes that can protect against CVD include decreasing your intake of fat, especially saturated and trans fats, and cholesterol, and increasing your intake of fiber by eating more fruits, vegetables, and whole grains.

• CVD risk can also be reduced by engaging in regular exercise, avoiding tobacco and environmental tobacco smoke, knowing and managing your blood pressure and cholesterol levels, and developing effective ways of handling stress and anger.

FOR MORE INFORMATION

BOOKS

Freeman, M. W., and C. E. Junge. 2005. *Harvard Medical School Guide to Lowering Your Cholesterol.* New York: McGraw-Hill. *Information about cholesterol, including lifestyle changes and medication for improving cholesterol levels.*

Heller, M. 2005. *The DASH Diet Action Plan, Based on the National Institutes of Health Research: Dietary Approaches to Stop Hypertension.* Northbrook, Ill.: Amidon Press. *Provides background information and guidelines for adopting the DASH diet; also includes meal plans to suit differing caloric needs and recipes.*

Lipsky, M. S., et al. 2008. *American Medical Association Guide to Preventing and Treating Heart Disease.* New York: Wiley. *A team of doctors provides advice for heart health to consumers.*

Mostyn, B. 2007. *Pocket Guide to Low Sodium Foods,* 2nd ed. Olympia, Wash.: InData Publishing. *Lists thousands of low-sodium products that can be purchased in supermarkets, as well as low-sodium choices available in many restaurants.*

Phibbs, B. 2007. *The Human Heart: A Basic Guide to Heart Disease.* Philadelphia: Lippincott Williams & Wilkins. *Provides information about heart disease, treatments, and recovery for patients and their families.*

Romaine, D. S., and O. S. Randall. 2005. *The Encyclopedia of Heart and Heart Disease.* New York: Facts on File. *Includes entries on the functioning of the cardiovascular system, types and causes of heart disease, and prevention and treatment.*

ORGANIZATIONS, HOTLINES, AND WEB SITES

American Heart Association. Provides information on hundreds of topics relating to the prevention and control of cardiovascular disease; sponsors a general Web site as well as several sites focusing on specific topics.

http://www.americanheart.org (general information)
http://www.deliciousdecisions.org (dietary advice)
http://www.goredforwomen.org (information just for women)

Dietary Approaches to Stop Hypertension (DASH). Provides information about the design, diets, and results of the DASH study, including tips on how to follow the DASH diet at home.

http://www.nhlbi.nih.gov/health/public/heart/hbp/dash

The Human Heart: An On-Line Exploration. An online museum exhibit containing information on the structure and function of the heart, how to monitor your heart's health, and how to maintain a healthy heart.

http://www.fi.edu/learn/heart/index.html

Reducing the Saturated and Trans Fats in Your Diet

No more than 7% of the calories in your diet should come from saturated fats, and no more than 1% should come from trans fats. Foods high in saturated fat include meat, poultry skin, full-fat dairy products, coconut and palm oils, and hydrogenated vegetable oils. Hydrogenated fats and products such as snack foods that are made with them and deep-fried fast food are high in trans fats.

Monitor Your Current Diet

To see how your diet measures up, keep track of everything you eat for 3 days in your health journal. Information about the calorie and saturated fat content of foods is available on many food labels, in books, and on the Internet. The list below gives a few average values for foods that are rich sources of trans fats in the American diet. However, food companies are trying to reduce or eliminate trans fats from their products, so it's important to read the labels.

	Grams of trans fat/serving
Pot pie	6
French fries (large)	5
Pound cake	5
Fish sticks	5
Doughnut	4
Biscuit	4
Fried, breaded chicken	3
Danish pastry	3
Vegetable shortening	3
Margarine (stick)	2
Microwave popcorn	2
Sandwich cookies	2
Snack crackers	2
Margarine (tub)	1

At the end of the monitoring period, write in the calories and grams of saturated and trans fat for as many as possible of the foods you've eaten. Determine the percentage of daily calories as fat that you consumed for each day: multiply grams of saturated and trans fats by 9 (fat has 9 calories per gram) and then divide by total calories. For example, if you consumed 30 grams of saturated and trans fats and 2100 calories on a particular day, then your saturated and trans fat consumption as a percentage of total calories would be $30 \times 9 = 270$ calories of fat $\div$ 2100 total calories = 0.13, or 13%. If you have trouble obtaining all the data you need to do the calculations, you can still estimate whether your diet is high in saturated and trans fats by seeing how many servings of foods high in unhealthy fats you typically consume on a daily basis (see the list).

Making Heart-Healthy Changes

To reduce your intake of unhealthy fats, you may want to set a limit on the number of servings of foods high in saturated and trans fats that you consume each day. Or you may want to set a more precise goal and then continue to monitor your daily consumption. The 7% limit set by the American Heart Association and the NCEP corresponds to 12 grams of saturated and trans fats in a 1600-calorie diet, 17 grams in a 2200-calorie diet, and 22 grams in a 2800-calorie diet.

To plan healthy changes, take a close look at your food record. Do you choose many foods high in saturated and trans fats? Do you limit your portion sizes to those recommended by MyPyramid? Try making healthy substitutions. Do you have a salami and cheese sandwich for lunch? Try turkey for a change. Do you always order french fries when you eat out? Try half a plain baked potato or a different vegetable next time. Do you snack on pastries, cookies, doughnuts, chips, or fatty crackers? Try fresh fruits and vegetables instead. If you frequently eat in fast-food restaurants or other places where the majority of the menu is heavy in saturated and trans fats, trying finding an appealing alternative—and recruit some friends to join you.

When you choose foods that are rich in saturated and trans fats, *watch your portion sizes carefully.* Choose cuts of meat that have the least amount of visible fat, and trim off what you see. And try to balance your choices throughout the day: For example, if your lunch includes a hamburger and fries, choose broiled fish or poultry or a vegetarian pasta dish for dinner. There are plenty of delicious choices that are low in saturated and trans fats. Plan your diet around a variety of whole grains, vegetables, legumes, and fruits, which are nearly always low in fats and high in nutrients.

MyHeartCentral.com. Provides information for heart patients and others interested in learning how to identify and reduce their risk factors for heart disease; includes links to many related sites.

http://www.healthcentral.com/heart-disease

MedlinePlus: Blood, Heart, and Circulation Topics. Provides links to reliable sources of information on many topics relating to cardiovascular health.

http://www.nlm.nih.gov/medlineplus/heartandcirculation.html

National Heart, Lung, and Blood Institute. Provides information on and interactive applications for a variety of topics relating to cardiovascular health and disease, including cholesterol, smoking, obesity, hypertension, and the DASH diet.

http://www.nhlbi.nih.gov
http://rover.nhlbi.nih.gov/chd

National Stroke Association. Provides information and referrals for stroke victims and their families; the Web site has a stroke risk assessment.

http://www.stroke.org

See also the listings for Chapters 2, 3, and 12–14.

SELECTED BIBLIOGRAPHY

Albert, C. M., et al. 2008. Effect of folic acid and B vitamins on risk of cardiovascular events and total mortality among women at high risk for cardiovascular disease: A randomized trial. *Journal of the American Medical Association* 299(17): 2027–2036.

American Heart Association. 2009. *Heart Disease and Stroke Statistics—2009 Update.* Dallas: American Heart Association.

Instead of . . .	Try . . .
Butter, stick margarine, vegetable shortening, coconut and palm oils	Vegetable oils, trans fat–free tub or squeeze margarines
Whole or 2% milk; regular cheese, mayonnaise, and sour cream	Fat-free or 1% milk, low-fat cheese, fat-free or low-fat sour cream, yogurt, or mayonnaise
Chips, cheese puffs, crackers, buttered popcorn	Fruits, vegetables, rice cakes, plain popcorn, pretzels, fat-free chips, baked crackers
Cakes, cookies, pastries, doughnuts, cinnamon rolls, pie, regular ice cream	Fruit or a *small* serving of a low-fat sweet (angel food cake; fat-free ice cream, frozen yogurt, sherbet, or sorbet)
Biscuits, croissants, fried tortillas, regular granola, muffins, coffee cake	Whole-grain breads and rolls, baked tortillas, low-fat granola or cold cereal, English muffin, or bagel
Creamy or cheesy sauces and soups	Tomato- and other vegetable-based sauces, clam sauce, clear soups
Ground beef, hamburger patty, meatloaf, ribs, T-bone or flank steak, prime grades of beef	Ground turkey, veggie burger, extra lean ground beef, round steak, sirloin, choice or select grades of beef
Pork chops, roast, or ribs; bone-in ham; lamb chops or ribs	Pork sirloin or tenderloin, boneless ham, veal chops and cutlets, leg of lamb
Bacon, sausage, lunch meats, hot dogs	Canadian bacon; turkey ham or pastrami, other low-fat lunch meats
Poultry with skin; fried chicken or fish	Skinless poultry, especially breast or drumstick; baked, broiled, grilled, or roasted poultry or fish; ground turkey
French fries, onion rings	Baked potato or other nonfried vegetable, rice
Pizza, pot pie, macaroni and cheese, and other high-fat convenience foods	Vegetarian or turkey chili, pasta with vegetables, grilled poultry and fish dishes

SOURCES: New heart dos and don'ts. 2006. *Consumer Reports Health*, March, 49; American Heart Association. 2000. *An Eating Plan for Healthy Americans: The New 2000 Food Guidelines.* Dallas, Tex.: American Heart Association; U.S. Department of Agriculture and U.S. Department of Health and Human Services. 2000. *Nutrition and Your Health: Dietary Guidelines for Americans,* 5th ed. Home and Garden Bulletin No. 232.

Berger, J. S., et al. 2006. Aspirin for the primary prevention of cardiovascular events in women and men: A sex-specific meta-analysis of randomized controlled trials. *Journal of the American Medical Association* 295(3): 306–313.

Bonaa, K. H., et al. 2006. Homocysteine lowering and cardiovascular events after acute myocardial infarction. *New England Journal of Medicine* 354(15): 1578–1588.

Centers for Disease Control and Prevention. 2005. Differences in disability among black and white stroke survivors—United States, 2000–2001. *Morbidity and Mortality Weekly Report* 54(1): 3–9.

Centers for Disease Control and Prevention. 2005. Health disparities experienced by black or African Americans—United States. *Morbidity and Mortality Weekly Report* 54(1): 1–3.

Centers for Disease Control and Prevention. 2008. Awareness of stroke warning symptoms—13 states and the District of Columbia, 2005. *Morbidity and Mortality Weekly Report* 57(18): 481–485.

Colihan, D. 2008. *Silent Strokes Take a Toll.* (http://www.webmd.com/stroke/news/20080626/silent-strokes-take-a-toll; retrieved November 10, 2008).

Cooper, R. S., et al. 2005. An international comparative study of blood pressure in populations of European vs. African descent. *BMC Medicine* 3(1): 2.

de Torbal, A., et al. 2006. Incidence of recognized and unrecognized myocardial infarction in men and women aged 55 and older: The Rotterdam Study. *European Heart Journal* 27(6): 729–736.

Elliott, P., et al. 2006. Association between protein intake and blood pressure: The INTERMAP study. *Archives of Internal Medicine* 166(1): 79–87.

Forman, J. P., et al. 2005. Folate intake and risk of incident hypertension among U.S. women. *Journal of the American Medical Association* 293(3): 320–329.

Giovannucci, E., et al. 2008. 25-hydroxyvitamin D and risk of myocardial infarction in men; a prospective study. *Archives of Internal Medicine* 168(11): 1174–1180.

Harvard Medical School. 2008. The status of statins. *Harvard Women's Health Watch* 15(6): 1–3.

Jenkins, D. J., et al. 2006. Assessment of the longer-term effects of a dietary portfolio of cholesterol-lowering foods in hypercholesterolemia. *American Journal of Clinical Nutrition* 83(3): 582–591.

Kastrati, A., et al. 2005. Sirolimus-eluting stent or paclitaxel-eluting stent vs. balloon angioplasty for prevention of recurrences in patients with coronary in-stent restenosis. *Journal of the American Medical Association* 293(2): 165–171.

Kelemen, L. E., et al. 2005. Associations of dietary protein with disease and mortality in a prospective study of postmenopausal women. *American Journal of Epidemiology* 161(3): 239–249.

Meadows, M. 2005. Brain attack: A look at stroke prevention and treatment. *FDA Consumer,* March/April.

Mozaffarian, D., et al. 2005. Interplay between different polyunsaturated fatty acids and risk of coronary heart disease in men. *Circulation* 111(2): 157–164.

Mukamal, K. J., et al. 2005. Alcohol and risk of ischemic stroke in men: The role of drinking patterns and usual beverage. *Annals of Internal Medicine* 142(1): 11–19.

Nissen, S. E., et al. 2005. Statin therapy, LDL cholesterol, C-reactive protein, and coronary artery disease. *New England Journal of Medicine* 352(1): 29–38.

Ostrom, M. P., et al. 2008. Mortality incidence and the severity of coronary atherosclerosis assessed by computed tomography angiography. *Journal of the American College of Cardiology* 52(16): 1335–1343.

Pickering, T. G., et al. 2008. Call to action on use and reimbursement for home blood pressure monitoring: A joint scientific statement from the American Heart Association, American Society of Hypertension, and Preventive Cardiovascular Nurses Association. *Hypertension* 52(1): 10–29.

Raggi, P., et al. 2008. Coronary artery calcium to predict all-cause mortality in elderly men and women. *Journal of the American College of Cardiology* 52(1): 17–23.

Refsum, H., et al. 2006. The Hordaland Homocysteine Study: A community-based study of homocysteine, its determinants, and associations with disease. *Journal of Nutrition* 136(6 Suppl.): 1731S–1740S.

Ridker, P. M., et al. 2005. C-reactive protein levels and outcomes after statin therapy. *New England Journal of Medicine* 352(1): 20–28.

Ridker, P. M., et al. 2005. A randomized trial of low-dose aspirin in the primary prevention of cardiovascular disease in women. *New England Journal of Medicine,* 7 March [epub].

Ridker, P. M., et al. 2008. Rosuvastatin to prevent vascular events in men and women with elevated C-reactive protein. *New England Journal of Medicine* 359(21): 2195–2207.

Rothwell, P. M., and C. P. Warlow. 2005. Timing of TIAs preceding stroke: Time window for prevention is very short. *Neurology* 64(5): 817–820.

Rozanski, A. S., et al. 2005. The epidemiology, pathophysiology, and management of psychosocial risk factors in cardiac practice: The emerging field of behavioral cardiology. *Journal of the American College of Cardiology* 45(5): 637–651.

Sesso, H. D., et al. 2008. Vitamins E and C in the prevention of cardiovascular disease in men: Physician's Health Study II randomized controlled trial. *Journal of the American Medical Association* 300(18): 2123–2133.

Tufts University. 2006. Pendulum swings on estrogen and women's heart health risk. *Health & Nutrition Newsletter* 24(3): 1–2.

Turhan, H., et al. 2005. High prevalence of metabolic syndrome among young women with premature coronary artery disease. *Coronary Artery Disease* 16(1): 37–40.

University of California, Berkeley. 2008. Heart tests: low- to high-tech. *University of California, Berkeley, Wellness Letter,* August, 5.

U.S. Food and Drug Administration. 2008. *Controlling Cholesterol with Statins.* (http://www.dfa.gov/consumer/updates/statins051608.html; retrieved November 10, 2008).

Webb, D. 2005. Supplements for a healthy heart: What works, what doesn't. *Environmental Nutrition* 28(12): 1, 4.3

Willingham, S. A., and E. S. Kilpatrick. 2005. Evidence of gender bias when applying the new diagnostic criteria for myocardial infarction. *Heart* 91(2): 237–238.

Wittstein, I. S., et al. 2005. Neurohumoral features of myocardial stunning due to sudden emotional stress. *New England Journal of Medicine* 352(6): 539–548.

Yusuf, S., et al. 2005. Obesity and the risk of myocardial infarction in 27,000 participants from 52 countries: A case-control study. *Lancet* 366(9497): 1640–1649.

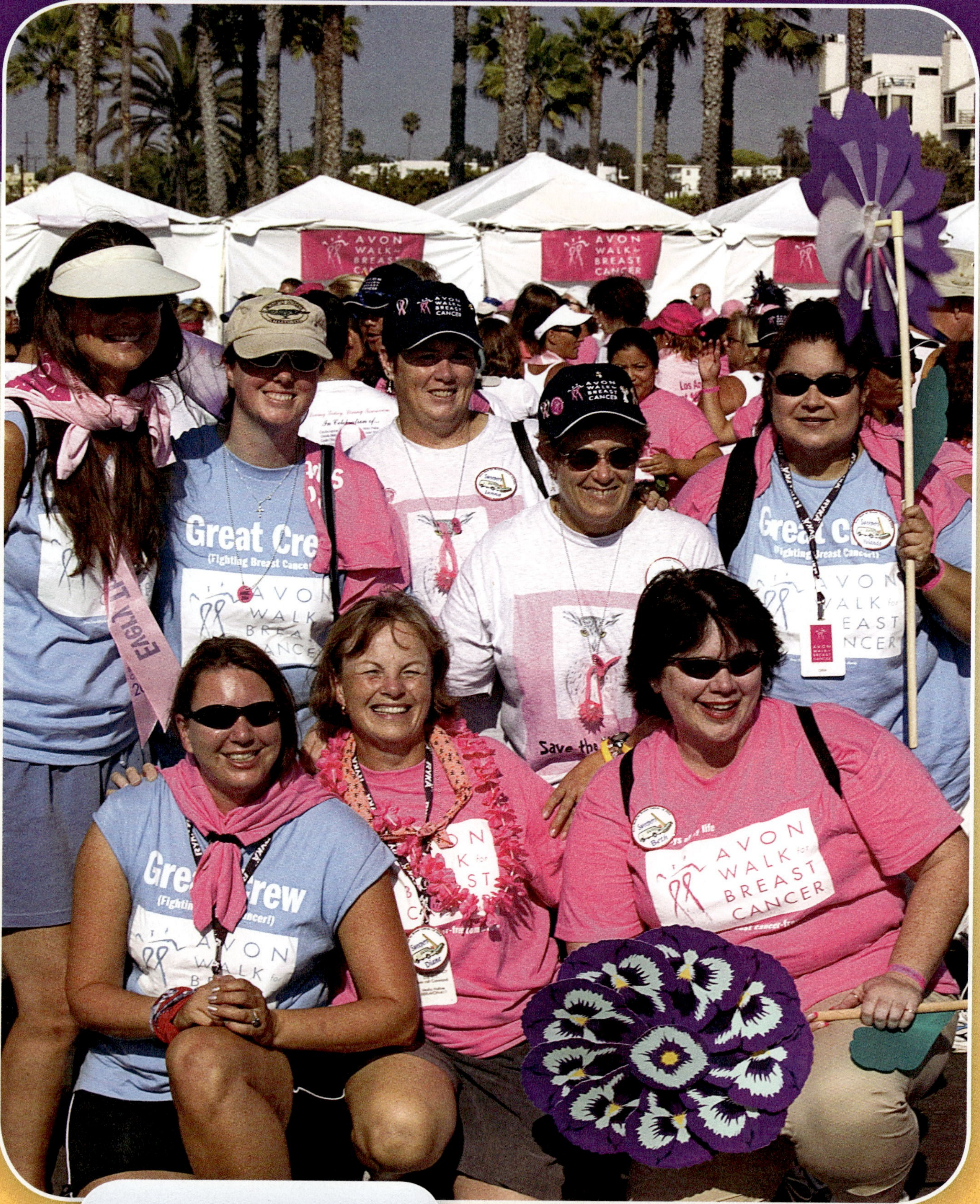

Core Concepts in Health
connect
PERSONAL HEALTH

http://www.mcgrawhillconnect.com/personalhealth

LOOKING AHEAD>>>>>

AFTER READING THIS CHAPTER, YOU SHOULD BE ABLE TO:

- Explain what cancer is and how it spreads
- List and describe common cancers—their risk factors, signs and symptoms, treatments, and approaches to prevention
- Discuss some of the causes of cancer and how they can be avoided or minimized
- Describe how cancer can be detected, diagnosed, and treated
- List specific actions you can take to lower your risk of cancer

TEST YOUR KNOWLEDGE

1. **Which type of cancer kills the most women each year?**
   a. breast cancer
   b. lung cancer
   c. ovarian cancer

2. **Which type of cancer kills the most men each year?**
   a. prostate cancer
   b. lung cancer
   c. colon cancer

3. **Testicular cancer is the most common cancer in men under age 30.**
   True or false?

4. **The use of condoms during sexual intercourse can prevent cervical cancer in women.**
   True or false?

5. **Eating which of these foods may help prevent cancer?**
   a. chili peppers
   b. broccoli
   c. oranges

ANSWERS

1. **B.** There are more cases of breast cancer each year, but lung cancer kills more women. Smoking is the primary risk factor for lung cancer.

2. **B.** There are more cases of prostate cancer, but lung cancer kills about three times as many men as prostate cancer does each year.

3. **TRUE.** Although rare, testicular cancer is the most common cancer in men under age 30. Regular self-exams may aid in its detection.

4. **TRUE.** The primary cause of cervical cancer is infection with human papillomavirus (HPV), a sexually transmitted pathogen. The use of condoms helps prevent HPV infection.

5. **ALL THREE.** These and many other fruits and vegetables are rich in phytochemicals, naturally occurring substances that may have anti-cancer effects.

Cancer is the second leading cause of death, after heart disease. In the United States, cancer is responsible for one in four deaths, claiming about 566,000 lives annually—about 1500 each day. Cancer, in its various forms, is the leading cause of disease-related death among people under age 65.

Even as medical science struggles to find a cure for cancer, mounting evidence indicates that most cancers could be prevented by simple changes in lifestyle. Tobacco use, for example, is responsible for about 30% of all cancer deaths (Figure 16.1). Poor dietary and exercise habits, and their relationship with obesity, account for another 30% of cancer deaths. Such evidence proves that individual behavior is a significant determinant of cancer risk.

This chapter introduces you to cancer, explains how the disease progresses, and identifies the factors that put people at risk for developing cancer. The following sections also discuss the lifestyle factors that can help you reduce your risk for cancer.

WHAT IS CANCER?

Cancer is the abnormal, uncontrolled multiplication of cells, which, if left untreated, can ultimately cause death.

Tumors

Most cancers take the form of tumors, although not all tumors are cancerous. A **tumor** (or *neoplasm*) is simply a mass of tissue that serves no physiological purpose. It can be benign, like a wart, or malignant, like most lung cancers

TERMS

cancer   Abnormal, uncontrolled cellular multiplication.

tumor   A mass of tissue that serves no physiological purpose; also called a *neoplasm*.

benign tumor   A tumor that is not cancerous.

malignant tumor   A tumor that is cancerous and capable of spreading.

lymphatic system   A system of vessels that returns proteins, lipids, and other substances from fluid in the tissues to the circulatory system.

biopsy   The removal and examination of a small piece of body tissue; a needle biopsy uses a needle to remove a small sample, but some biopsies require surgery.

metastasis   The spread of cancer cells from one part of the body to another.

staging   A method of classifying the progress or extent of a cancer in a patient.

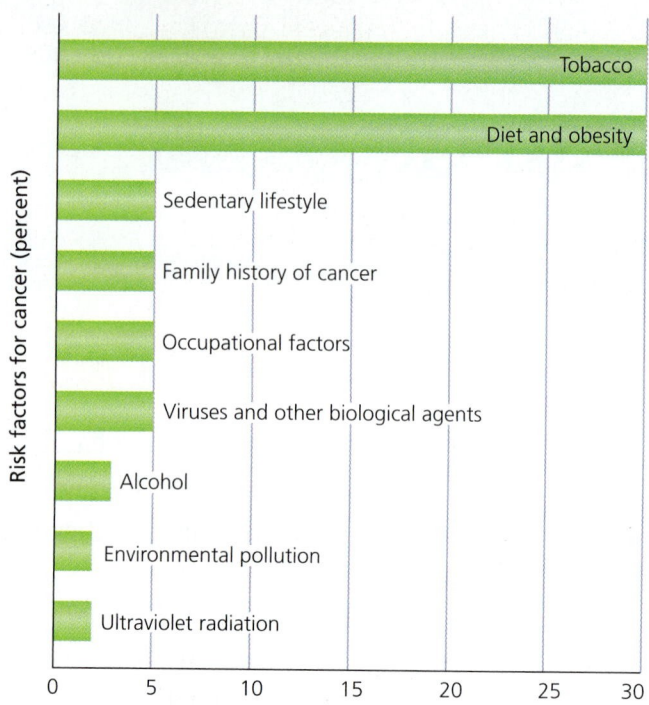

VITAL STATISTICS

FIGURE 16.1   Percentage of all cancer deaths linked to risk factors.

SOURCE: Harvard Center for Cancer Prevention. 1996. Harvard Reports on Cancer Prevention. Vol. 1: Human Causes of Cancer. *Cancer Causes and Control* 7(Suppl. 1).

Benign (noncancerous) **tumors** are made up of cells similar to the surrounding normal cells and are enclosed in a membrane that prevents them from penetrating neighboring tissues. They are dangerous only if their physical presence interferes with body functions. A benign brain tumor, for example, can cause death if it blocks the blood supply to the brain.

The term **malignant tumor** is synonymous with cancer. A malignant tumor can invade surrounding structures, including blood vessels, the **lymphatic system,** and nerves. It can also spread to distant sites via the blood and lymphatic circulation, producing invasive tumors in almost any part of the body. A few cancers, like leukemia (cancer of the blood), do not produce a mass but still have the fundamental property of rapid, uncontrolled cell multiplication; for this reason, such diseases are malignant and are considered to be a form of cancer.

Every case of cancer begins as a change in a cell that allows it to grow and divide when it should not. Normally (in adults), cells divide and grow at a rate just sufficient to replace dying cells. In contrast, a malignant cell divides without regard for normal control mechanisms and gradually produces a mass of abnormal cells, or a tumor. It takes about a billion cells to make a mass the size of a pea, so a single tumor cell must go through many divisions, often taking years, before the tumor grows to a noticeable size (Figure 16.2).

Eventually a tumor produces a sign or symptom that is determined by its location in the body. In the breast, for example, a tumor may be felt as a lump and diagnosed as cancer by an X ray or **biopsy.** In less accessible locations, like the lung, ovary, or intestine, a tumor may be noticed only after considerable growth has taken place and may then be detected only by an indirect symptom—for instance, a persistent cough or unexplained bleeding or pain. In the case of leukemia, there is no lump, but the changes in the blood will eventually be noticed as increasing fatigue, infection, or abnormal bleeding.

Metastasis

Metastasis, the spreading of cancer cells from one part of the body to another, occurs because cancer cells do not stick to each other as strongly as normal cells do and therefore may not remain at the site of the *primary tumor* (the cancer's original location). They break away and can pass through the lining of lymph or blood vessels to invade nearby tissue. Once it is established, the tumor can recruit normal cells—such as bone marrow cells—modify them, and use them as "envoys" to travel to different parts of the body and prepare other sites to receive traveling cancer cells. The envoy cells work by creating proteins that attract the free-floating cancer cells, allowing them to gather at a new site and resume replicating. This traveling and seeding process is called *metastasizing,* and the new tumors are called *secondary tumors,* or *metastases.*

The ability of cancer cells to metastasize makes early cancer detection critical. To control the cancer, every can-cerous cell must be removed. Once cancer cells enter either the lymphatic system or the bloodstream, it is extremely difficult to stop their spread to other organs of the body. In fact, counting the number of lymph nodes that contain cancer cells is one of the principal methods of predicting the outcome of the disease; the probability of a cure is much greater when the lymph nodes do not contain cancer cells.

The Stages of Cancer

Once a cancer has been diagnosed, physicians can classify the disease according to the amount of progress it has made in the victim's body. The extent or spread of the cancer is described in five **stages,** as shown in Table 16.1.

Table 16.1	Cancer Stages
Stage	**Description**
0	Early cancer, present only in the layer of cells where it originated
I, II, III	More extensive cancer, with higher numbers indicating greater tumor size and/or the degree to which the cancer has spread to nearby lymph nodes or organs adjacent to the primary tumor.
IV	Advanced cancer that has spread to another organ

SOURCE: U.S. National Institutes of Health, National Cancer Institute. 2004. *Staging: Questions and Answers* (http://www.cancer.gov/cancertopics/factsheet/detection/staging; retrieved February 15, 2009).

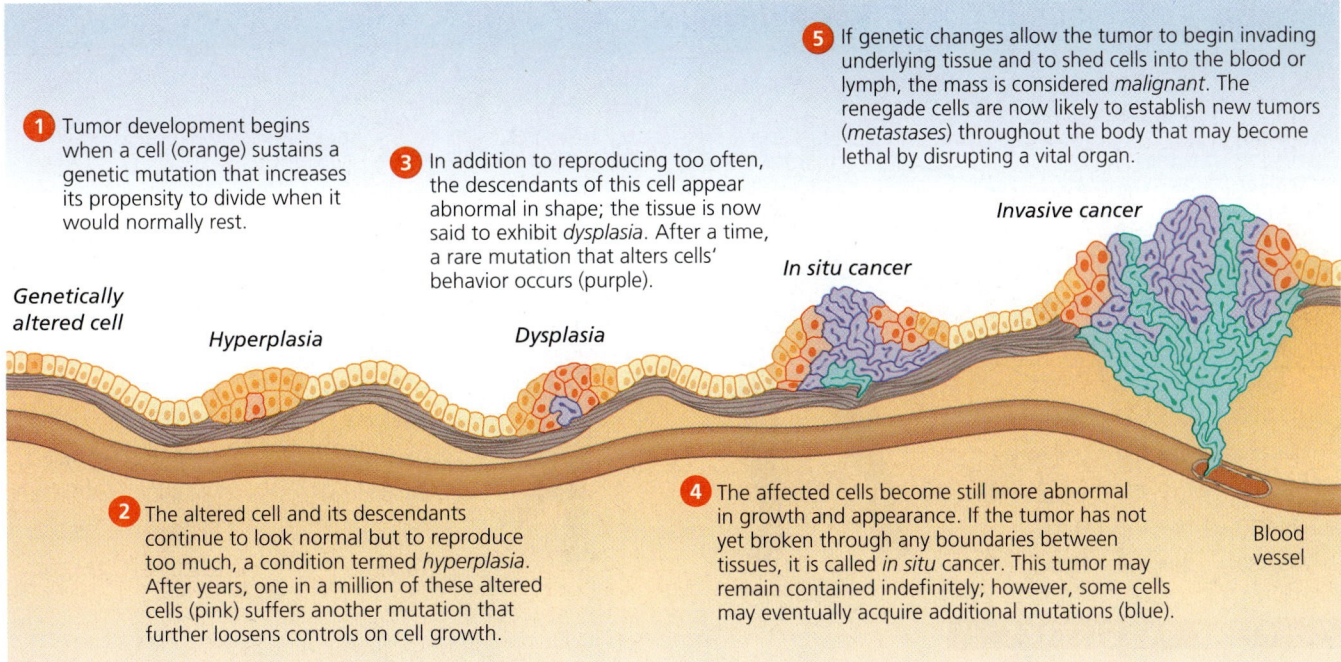

1. Tumor development begins when a cell (orange) sustains a genetic mutation that increases its propensity to divide when it would normally rest.

2. The altered cell and its descendants continue to look normal but to reproduce too much, a condition termed *hyperplasia.* After years, one in a million of these altered cells (pink) suffers another mutation that further loosens controls on cell growth.

3. In addition to reproducing too often, the descendants of this cell appear abnormal in shape; the tissue is now said to exhibit *dysplasia.* After a time, a rare mutation that alters cells' behavior occurs (purple).

4. The affected cells become still more abnormal in growth and appearance. If the tumor has not yet broken through any boundaries between tissues, it is called *in situ* cancer. This tumor may remain contained indefinitely; however, some cells may eventually acquire additional mutations (blue).

5. If genetic changes allow the tumor to begin invading underlying tissue and to shed cells into the blood or lymph, the mass is considered *malignant.* The renegade cells are now likely to establish new tumors (*metastases*) throughout the body that may become lethal by disrupting a vital organ.

Genetically altered cell

Hyperplasia

Dysplasia

In situ cancer

Invasive cancer

Blood vessel

FIGURE 16.2 Tumor development occurs in stages.

SOURCE: Weinberg, R. A. 1996. How cancer arises. *Scientific American,* September. Copyright © 1996 by Dana Burns-Pizer. Reprinted with permission.

To identify a cancer's stage, physicians assess the size or extent of the primary tumor, whether the cancer has invaded nearby lymph nodes, and whether any metastases are present. By judging the extent of each criterion, physicians can determine the cancer's current stage and choose the most appropriate treatment based on the disease's progress.

Types of Cancer

The behavior of tumors arising in different body organs is characteristic of the tissue of origin. (Figure 16.3 below shows the major cancer sites and the incidence of each type.) Because each cancer begins as a single, altered cell with a specific function in the body, the cancer retains some of the properties of the normal cell for a time. For instance, cancer of the thyroid gland may produce too much thyroid hormone and cause hyperthyroidism as well as cancer. Usually, however, cancer cells lose their resemblance to normal tissue as they continue to multiply, becoming groups of rogue cells with increasingly unpredictable behavior.

Malignant tumors are classified according to the types of cells that give rise to them:

- **Carcinomas** arise from **epithelia,** tissues that cover external body surfaces, line internal tubes and cavities, and form the secreting portion of glands. They are the most common type of cancers; major sites

include the skin, breast, uterus, prostate, lungs, and gastrointestinal tract.

- **Sarcomas** arise from connective and fibrous tissues such as muscle, bone, cartilage, and the membranes covering muscles and fat.
- **Lymphomas** are cancers of the lymph nodes, part of the body's infection-fighting system.
- **Leukemias** are cancers of the blood-forming cells, which reside chiefly in the **bone marrow.**

Cancers vary greatly in how easily they can be detected and how well they respond to treatment. For example, certain types of skin cancer are easily detected, grow slowly, and are very easy to remove; virtually all of these cancers are cured. Cancer of the pancreas, on the other hand, is very difficult to detect or treat, and very few patients survive the disease. In general, it is very difficult for an **oncologist** or **hematologist** to predict how a specific cancer will behave, because every one arises from a unique set of changes in a single cell.

The Incidence of Cancer

Each year, more than 1.4 million people in the United States are diagnosed with cancer. Most will be cured, or be able to live years longer. In fact, the American Cancer

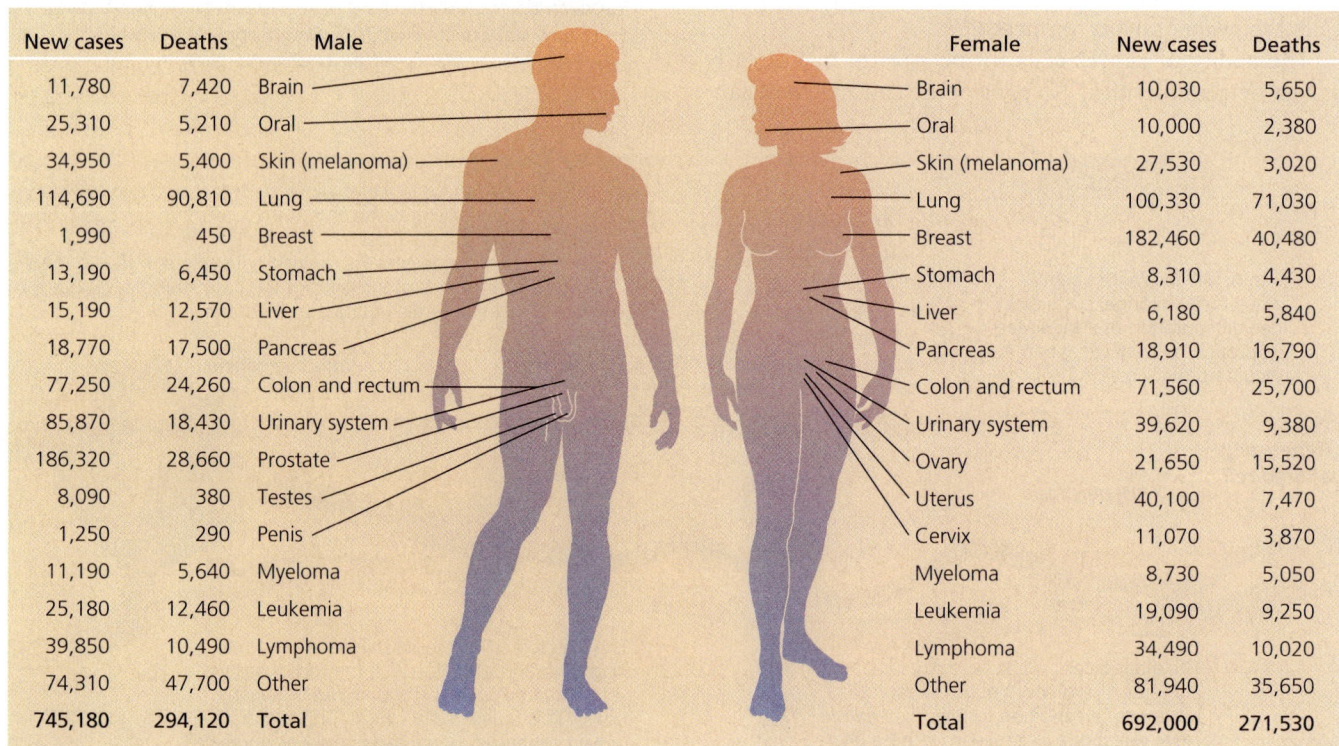

New cases	Deaths	Male		Female	New cases	Deaths
11,780	7,420	Brain		Brain	10,030	5,650
25,310	5,210	Oral		Oral	10,000	2,380
34,950	5,400	Skin (melanoma)		Skin (melanoma)	27,530	3,020
114,690	90,810	Lung		Lung	100,330	71,030
1,990	450	Breast		Breast	182,460	40,480
13,190	6,450	Stomach		Stomach	8,310	4,430
15,190	12,570	Liver		Liver	6,180	5,840
18,770	17,500	Pancreas		Pancreas	18,910	16,790
77,250	24,260	Colon and rectum		Colon and rectum	71,560	25,700
85,870	18,430	Urinary system		Urinary system	39,620	9,380
186,320	28,660	Prostate		Ovary	21,650	15,520
8,090	380	Testes		Uterus	40,100	7,470
1,250	290	Penis		Cervix	11,070	3,870
11,190	5,640	Myeloma		Myeloma	8,730	5,050
25,180	12,460	Leukemia		Leukemia	19,090	9,250
39,850	10,490	Lymphoma		Lymphoma	34,490	10,020
74,310	47,700	Other		Other	81,940	35,650
745,180	294,120	Total		Total	692,000	271,530

VITAL STATISTICS

FIGURE 16.3 Cancer cases and deaths by site and sex. The *New Cases* column indicates the number of cancers that occur annually in each site; the *Deaths* column indicates the number of cancer deaths that are annually attributed to each type.

SOURCE: American Cancer Society. 2008. *Cancer Facts and Figures, 2008.* Atlanta: American Cancer Society.

Society (ACS) estimates that the 5-year survival rate for all cancers diagnosed between 1996 and 2003 is 66%. This is significantly better than the 50% 5-year survival rate for cancers diagnosed between 1975 and 1977. These statistics exclude more than 1 million cases of the curable types of skin cancer. At current U.S. rates, nearly 1 in 2 men and more than 1 in 3 women will develop cancer at some point in their lives (see the box "Gender and Cancer" on p. 491).

Until 1991, the number of cancer deaths increased fairly steadily in the United States, largely due to a wave of lethal lung cancers among men caused by smoking. In 1991, the death rate began to fall slowly; since then it has dropped more than 18% in men and 10% in women. This trend suggests that efforts at prevention, early detection, and improved therapy are all bearing fruit. However, death rates from cancer are not declining as fast as those from heart disease, in large part because of the differing effects that quitting smoking has on disease risk. Heart-related damage of smoking reverses more quickly and more significantly than the cancer-related damage from smoking. Smoking-related gene mutations cannot be reversed, although other mechanisms can sometimes control cellular changes. Heart disease also has other risk factors like high cholesterol and blood pressure that can be tested for and controlled. If heart disease death rates continue to decline faster than cancer death rates, cancer may overtake heart disease as the leading cause of death among Americans of all ages.

Still, many more people could be saved from cancer. The American Cancer Society estimates that 90% of skin cancer could be prevented by protecting the skin from the rays of the sun and 87% of lung cancer could be prevented by avoiding exposure to tobacco smoke. Thousands of cases of colon, breast, and uterine cancer could be prevented by improving the diet and controlling body weight. Regular screenings and self-examinations have the potential to save an additional 100,000 lives per year. Although cancer may seem like a mysterious disease, there are many concrete strategies you can adopt to reduce your risk.

COMMON CANCERS

A discussion of all types of cancer is beyond the scope of this book. In this section we look at some of the most common cancers and their causes, prevention, and treatment.

QUESTIONS FOR CRITICAL THINKING AND REFLECTION

Most people think of cancer as a death sentence, but is that necessarily true? Have you or anyone you know had an experience with cancer? If so, what was the outcome? Have you ever considered whether you might be at risk for some type of cancer? Have you taken any steps to reduce your risk?

Lung Cancer

Lung cancer accounts for 15% of all new cancer diagnoses, and is the most common cause of cancer death in the United States; it is responsible for about 162,000 deaths each year. Since 1987 lung cancer has surpassed breast cancer as the leading cause of cancer death in women.

Risk Factors   The chief risk factor for lung cancer is tobacco smoke, which currently accounts for 30% of all cancer deaths and 87% of lung cancer deaths. When smoking is combined with exposure to other carcinogens, such as asbestos particles or certain pollutants, the risk of cancer can be multiplied by a factor of 10 or more.

The smoker is not the only one at risk. Environmental tobacco smoke (ETS) is a human carcinogen; even brief exposure can cause serious harm. Long-term exposure to ETS increases the risk of lung cancer. It is estimated that ETS causes about 3000 lung cancer deaths each year in nonsmokers.

Detection and Treatment   Lung cancer is difficult to detect at an early stage and hard to cure even when detected early. Symptoms of lung cancer do not usually appear until the disease has advanced to the invasive stage. Signals such as a persistent cough, chest pain, or recurring bronchitis may be the first indication of a tumor's presence.

Studies suggest that spiral CT (computed tomography) scans, a computer-assisted body imaging technique, can detect lung cancer significantly earlier than chest X rays. In cases where CT scanning is not available, a diagnosis can usually be made by chest X ray or by studying the cells in sputum. Because almost all lung cancers arise from the

carcinoma   Cancer that originates in epithelial tissue (skin, glands, and lining of internal organs).

epithelia   Tissue that covers a surface or lines a tube or cavity of the body, enclosing and protecting other parts of the body.

sarcoma   Cancer arising from bone, cartilage, or striated muscle.

lymphoma   A tumor originating from lymphatic tissue.

leukemia   Cancer of the blood or the blood-forming cells.

bone marrow   Soft vascular tissue in the interior cavities of bones that produces blood cells.

oncologist   A specialist in the study of tumors.

hematologist   A specialist in the study of blood disorders, including cancers such as leukemia and lymphoma.

TERMS

Smoking is responsible for about 30% of all cancer deaths. The benefits of quitting are substantial: Lung cancer risk decreases significantly after 1 smoke-free year and drops to half that of continuing smokers after 10 smoke-free years.

Phototherapy, gene therapy, and immunotherapy (a vaccine) are being studied in the hope of improving these statistics.

In addition, one form of lung cancer, known as small-cell lung cancer and accounting for about 13% of cases, can be treated fairly successfully with chemotherapy—alone or in combination with radiation. A large percentage of cases go into **remission,** which in some cases lasts for years.

Colon and Rectal Cancer

Another common cancer in the United States is colon and rectal cancer (also called colorectal cancer). Although there are effective screening methods for colorectal cancer, it is the third most common type of cancer.

Risk Factors   Age is a key risk factor for colon and rectal cancer, with more than 90% of cases diagnosed in people age 50 and older. Heredity also plays a role. Many cancers arise from preexisting **polyps,** small growths on the wall of the colon that may gradually develop into malignancies. The tendency to form colon polyps appears to be determined by specific genes, so many colon cancers may be due to inherited gene mutations. Chronic bowel inflammation and type 2 diabetes increase the risk of colon cancer.

Lifestyle is also a risk factor for colon and rectal cancer. Excessive alcohol use and smoking may increase the risk of colorectal cancer. Regular physical activity appears to reduce a person's risk, whereas obesity increases risk. A diet rich in red and processed meats increases risk, whereas eating fruits, vegetables, and whole grains is associated with lower risk. However, research findings on whether dietary fiber prevents colon cancer have been mixed. Studies have suggested a protective role for folic acid, magnesium, vitamin D, and calcium; in contrast, high intake of refined carbohydrates, simple sugars, and smoked meats and fish may increase risk.

Use of oral contraceptives or hormone replacement therapy may reduce risk in women. Regular use of nonsteroidal anti-inflammatory drugs such as aspirin and ibuprofen may decrease the risk of colon cancer and other cancers of the digestive tract.

Detection and Treatment   If identified early, precancerous polyps and early-stage cancers can be removed before they become malignant or spread. Because polyps may bleed as they progress, the standard warning signs of colon cancer are bleeding from the rectum and a change in bowel habits.

Regular screening tests are recommended beginning at age 50 (earlier for people with a family history of the disease). A yearly stool blood test can detect small amounts of blood in the stool long before obvious bleeding would be noticed. More involved screening tests are recommended at 5- or 10-year intervals. In sigmoidoscopy or colonoscopy (Figure 16.4), a flexible fiber-optic device is inserted through the rectum; the colon can be examined and pol-

cells that line the bronchi, tumors can sometimes be visualized by fiber-optic bronchoscopy, a test in which a flexible lighted tube is inserted into the windpipe and the surfaces of the lung passages are directly inspected.

Treatment for lung cancer depends on the type and stage of the cancer. If caught early, localized cancers can be treated with surgery. But because only about 16% of lung cancers are detected before they spread, radiation and **chemotherapy** are often used in addition to surgery. For cases detected early, 49% of patients are alive 5 years after diagnosis; but overall, the 5-year survival rate is only 15%.

TERMS

chemotherapy   The treatment of cancer with chemicals that selectively destroy cancerous cells.

remission   A period during the course of cancer in which there are no symptoms or other evidence of disease.

polyp   A small, usually harmless, mass of tissue that projects from the inner surface of the colon or rectum.

Gender and Cancer

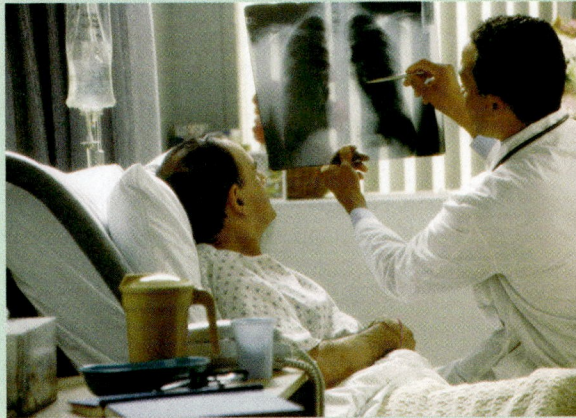

Men and women share most major risk factors for cancer, but they have a different experience because more than a third of all cancers occur in sex organs (prostate, testes, breast, ovary, uterus, cervix).

For women, this means that in addition to lifestyle factors such as smoking, diet, and exercise, hormonal factors relating to their menstrual and childbearing history are also important risk considerations. Women may also have a greater biological vulnerability to certain carcinogens, such as those in cigarettes.

Overall, however, men are more likely than women to have cancer and to die of cancer. For some cancers, the differences are especially significant. For example, men are much more likely than women to die from oral cancer, skin cancer, lung cancer, liver cancer, and urinary cancer. Here are some of the factors underlying the higher death rates among men:

• *Higher rates of tobacco use:* Particularly in the past, men had significantly higher rates of smoking than women, leading to much higher rates of the many cancers linked to smoking. Men also have much higher rates of spit tobacco and cigar use.

Lung cancer rates among men increased dramatically following significantly increased smoking rates beginning in the early 1900s (inexpensive machine-produced cigarettes were developed in the late 1800s). The lung cancer rate leveled off and (for men) started to decline after smoking rates began dropping. The smoking-related increase in lung cancer among women occurred about 20–30 years after that seen in men, as smoking among women became more socially acceptable and widespread beginning in the 1930s and 1940s.

• *Higher rates of alcohol use and abuse:* Alcohol abuse is more common in men and is a risk factor for several cancers, including oral and liver cancers.

• *Greater occupational exposure to carcinogens:* Men are more likely to work in jobs where they are exposed to chemicals—including asbestos, arsenic, coal tar, pitch, and dyes—or radiation, and such exposure is a risk factor for cancers of the bladder, lung, and skin. Men are also more likely to have outdoor jobs involving frequent sun exposure.

• *Less use of preventive measures and less contact with health care providers:* Traditional gender roles may make men more likely to minimize symptoms and less likely to seek help or to discuss cancer-related worries with a health care provider. Men may place a low status on preventive care or screenings, such as using sunscreen and wearing hats to protect the skin from the sun or performing self-exams.

Many of the factors underlying men's greater risk for cancer are controllable. It is important for both men and women to remember that there are many concrete steps they can take to significantly reduce their risk of cancer.

---

yps can be biopsied or removed without major surgery. Screening is effective; studies show it could reduce the occurrence of colorectal cancer by 80%. Still, only about one-half of adults have undergone any of these tests.

Surgery is the primary treatment for colon and rectal cancer. Radiation and chemotherapy may be used before surgery to shrink a tumor or after surgery to destroy any remaining cancerous cells. For advanced cancer, treatment with chemotherapy or monoclonal antibodies, in combination is an option. This treatment inhibits the growth of new blood vessels (angiogenesis) in tumors. The 5-year survival rate is 90% for colon and rectal cancers detected early and 64% overall.

Breast Cancer

Breast cancer is the most common cancer in women and causes almost as many deaths in women as lung cancer. In men, breast cancer occurs only rarely. In the United States, about 1 woman in 7 will develop breast cancer during her lifetime, and 1 woman in 30 will die from the disease. About 182,000 American women are diagnosed

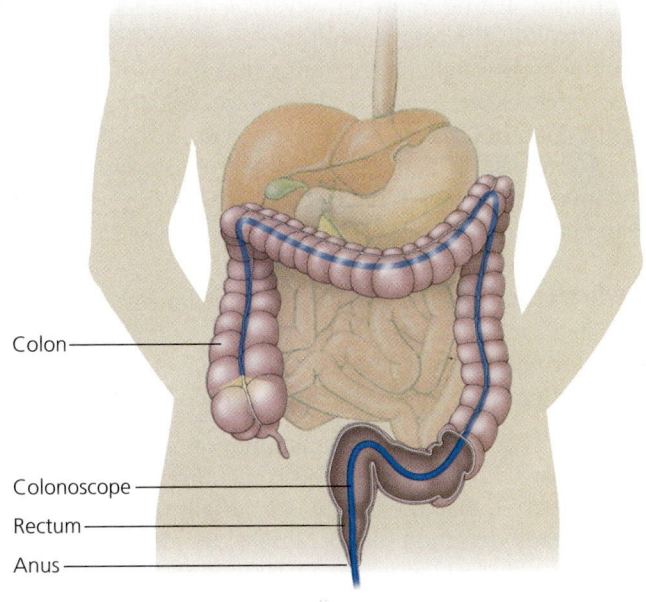

Colon

Colonoscope

Rectum

Anus

FIGURE 16.4 Colonoscopy.

with breast cancer each year. About 41,000 women die from breast cancer each year.

Less than 1% of breast cancer cases occur in women under age 30, but a woman's risk doubles every 5 years between ages 30 and 45 and then increases more slowly, by 10–15% every 5 years after age 45. More than 75% of breast cancers are diagnosed in women over 50.

Risk Factors   There is a strong genetic factor in breast cancer. A woman who has two close relatives with breast cancer is four to six times more likely to develop the disease than a woman who has no close relatives with it. However, even though genetic factors are important, only about 15% of cancers occur in women with a family history of breast cancer.

Other risk factors include early onset of menstruation, late onset of menopause, having no children or having a first child after age 30, current use of hormone replacement therapy (HT), obesity, and alcohol use. Estrogen may be a unifying element for many of these risk factors. Estrogen circulates in a woman's body in high concentrations between puberty and menopause. Fat cells also produce estrogen, and estrogen levels are higher in obese women. Alcohol can interfere with estrogen metabolism in the liver and increase estrogen levels in the blood. Estrogen promotes the growth of cells in responsive sites, including the breast and the uterus, so any factor that increases estrogen exposure may raise breast cancer risk. A dramatic drop in rates of breast cancer from 2001 to 2004 was attributed in part to reduced use of HT by women over 50 beginning in July 2002. Millions of women stopped taking the hormones after research linked HT with an increased risk of breast cancer and heart disease.

Although some of the risk factors for breast cancer cannot be changed, important lifestyle risk factors can be controlled. Eating a low-fat, vegetable-rich diet, exercising regularly, limiting alcohol intake, and maintaining a healthy body weight can minimize the chance of developing breast cancer, even for women at risk from family history or other factors. Some research has also found that long-term use of aspirin and other nonsteroidal anti-inflammatory drugs reduces risk, possibly by affecting estrogen synthesis.

Early Detection   A cure is most likely if breast cancer is detected early, so regular screening is a good investment, even for younger women. The ACS advises a three-part personal program for the early detection of breast cancer:

- The ACS recommends a **mammogram** (low-dose breast X ray) every year for women over 40 (Figure 16.5). Mammography is especially valuable as an early detection tool because it can identify about 85% of breast cancers at an early stage, before physical symptoms develop. Studies show that magnetic resonance imaging (MRI) may be better than mammography at detecting breast abnormalities in some

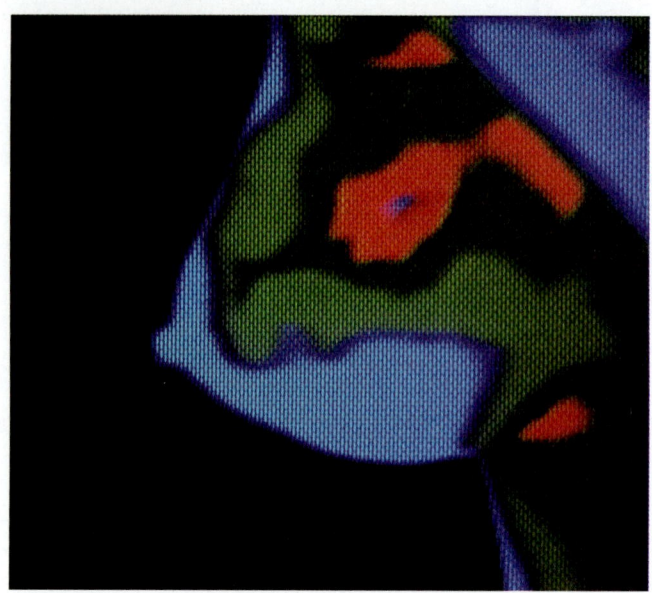

FIGURE 16.5   Mammograms can detect breast cancer in women with no symptoms.

women. The American Cancer Society recommends both an annual mammogram and MRI for women who are at high risk for breast cancer. A number of factors determine a woman's risk for developing breast cancer, and every woman should discuss her risk factors with a physician to determine what kinds of screen tests are warranted.

Unlike traditional mammography, digital mammograms are recorded on a computer disk rather than film. Digital mammograms can be enhanced and analyzed in more ways than traditional mammograms. Although digital mammography has not yet proved to be more effective at catching breast cancer in all women, there is evidence that it is more effective at spotting tumors in dense breast tissue. A National Cancer Institute study showed that digital mammography might be a better screening tool for women under age 50 who have dense breasts.

Ultrasound technology uses sound waves to create images of soft tissue. Although ultrasound is not often used as a standard screening tool for breast cancer, it is sometimes used as a follow-up investigational tool if a mammogram reveals an abnormality in breast tissue.

- *Clinical breast exam:* Women between ages 20 and 39 should have a clinical breast exam every 3 years,

mammogram   Low-dose X ray of the breasts used to check for early signs of breast cancer.

ultrasonography   An imaging method in which sound waves are bounced off body structures to create an image on a TV monitor; also called *ultrasound*.

How to Perform a Breast Self-Exam

The best time for a woman to examine her breasts is when the breasts are not tender or swollen. Women who examine their breasts should have their technique reviewed during their periodic health exams by their health care professional.

Women with breast implants can do BSE. It may be helpful to have the surgeon help identify the edges of the implant so that you know what you are feeling. There is some thought that the implants push out the breast tissue and may actually make it easier to examine. Women who are pregnant or breast-feeding can also choose to examine their breasts regularly.

It is acceptable for women to choose not to do BSE or to do BSE once in a while. Women who choose not to do BSE should still be aware of the normal look and feel of their breasts and report any changes to their doctor right away.

How to Examine Your Breasts

• Lie down and place your right arm behind your head. The exam is done while lying down, not standing up. This is because wheh lying down the breast tissue spreads evenly over the chest wall and is as thin as possible, making it much easier to feel all the breast tissue.

• Use the finger pads of the three middle fingers on your left hand to feel for lumps in the right breast. Use overlapping dime-sized circular motions of the finger pads to feel the breast tissue.

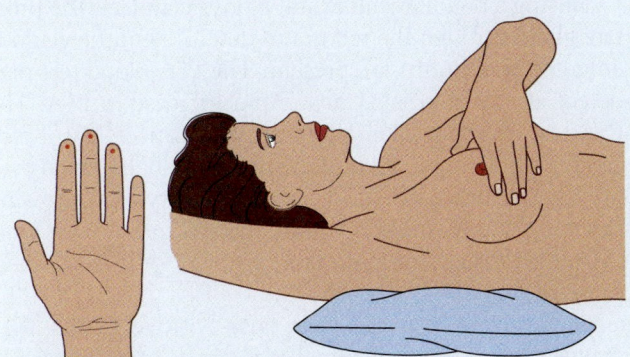

• Use three different levels of pressure to feel all the breast tissue. Light pressure is needed to feel the tissue closest to the skin; medium pressure to feel a little deeper; and firm pressure to feel the tissue closest to the chest and ribs. A firm ridge in the lower curve of each breast is normal. If you're not sure how hard to press, talk with your doctor or nurse. Use each pressure level to feel the breast tissue before moving on to the next spot.

• Move around the breast in an up-and-down pattern starting at an imaginary line drawn straight down your side from the underarm and moving across the breast to the middle of the chest bone (sternum or breastbone). Be sure to check the entire breast area going down until you feel only ribs and up to the neck or collar bone (clavicle).

• There is some evidence to suggest that the up-and-down pattern (sometimes called the vertical pattern) is the most effective pattern for covering the entire breast, without missing any breast tissue.

• Repeat the exam on your left breast, using the finger pads of the right hand.

• While standing in front of a mirror with your hands pressing firmly down on your hips, look at your breasts for any changes of size, shape, contour, or dimpling, or redness or scaliness of the nipple or breast skin. (The pressing down on the hips position contracts the chest wall muscles and enhances any breast changes.)

• Examine each underarm while sitting up or standing and with your arm only slightly raised so you can easily feel in this area. Raising your arm straight up tightens the tissue in this area and makes it harder to examine.

This procedure for doing breast self-exam is different than in previous recommendations. These changes represent an extensive review of the medical literature and input from an expert advisory group. These is evidence that this position (lying down), area felt, pattern of coverage of the breast, and use of different amounts of pressure increase a woman's ability to find abnormal areas.

and women age 40 and older should have one every year before their scheduled mammogram.

• *Breast self-exams:* Breast self-exam (BSE) allows a woman to become familiar with her breasts, so she can alert her health care provider to any changes. Women who choose to do breast self-exams should begin at age 20 (see the box "How to Perform a Breast Self-Exam").

Breast pain or tenderness is usually associated with benign conditions such as menstruation rather than breast cancer. The first physical signs of breast cancer are more likely to be a lump, swelling, or thickening; skin irritation or dimpling; or nipple pain, scaliness, or retraction. Although most breast lumps are benign, any breast lump should be brought to the attention of a health care provider.

Treatment If a lump is detected, it may be scanned by **ultrasonography** and biopsied to see if it is cancerous. In 90% of cases, the lump is found to be a cyst or other harmless growth, and no further treatment is needed. If the lump contains

77% of cancers are diagnosed in people ages 55 and older.

—American Cancer Society, 2008

QUICK STATS

cancer cells, a variety of surgeries may be called for, ranging from a lumpectomy (removal of the lump and surrounding tissue) to a mastectomy (removal of the breast). For small tumors, lumpectomy is as effective as mastectomy. To determine whether the cancer has spread, lymph nodes from the armpit may be removed and examined. If cancer cells are found, tumor cells remaining in the body can often be slowed or killed by additional therapy, such as radiation, chemotherapy, or both.

Survival of breast cancer varies, depending on the nature of the tumor and whether it has metastasized. If the tumor is discovered before it has spread to the adjacent lymph nodes, the patient has about a 98% chance of surviving more than 5 years. The survival rate for all stages is 89% at 5 years and 80% at 10 years.

New Strategies for Treatment and Prevention

A number of new drugs have been developed for the treatment or prevention of breast cancer. A family of drugs called selective estrogen-receptor modulators, or SERMs, act like estrogen in some tissues of the body but block estrogen's effects in others. One SERM, tamoxifen, has long been used in breast cancer treatment because it blocks the action of estrogen in breast tissue. In 1998, the FDA approved the use of tamoxifen to reduce the risk of breast cancer in healthy women who are at high risk for the disease. However, the drug has serious potential side effects, including increased risk of blood clots and uterine cancer, and its long-term effects are unknown. Another SERM currently being tested as a potential preventive agent is raloxifene, an osteoporosis drug that has fewer side effects than tamoxifen. Although still controversial, the use of SERMs in the prevention of breast cancer is a major breakthrough.

Women may take tamoxifen, anastrozole, or other drugs or undergo chemotherapy to help reduce the risk of recurrence. A genetic test can help predict the risk of breast cancer recurrence and help identify women who will benefit most from chemotherapy; women can then make more informed treatment decisions. For advanced cancer, treatment with trastuzumab, a monoclonal antibody, is an option for some women. Antibodies, discussed in Chapter 17, are proteins produced by the immune system that recognize and bind to foreign substances such as bacteria; monoclonal antibodies are a special type of antibody that is produced in the laboratory and designed to bind to a specific cancer-related target.

Prostate Cancer

The prostate gland is situated at the base of the bladder in men, and completely surrounds the male's urethra. It produces seminal fluid; if enlarged, it can block the flow of urine. Prostate cancer is the most common cancer in men and the second leading cause of cancer death in men. More than 186,000 new cases are diagnosed each year, and more than 28,000 American men die from the disease each year.

Risk Factors

Age is the strongest predictor of the risk, with about 64% of cases of prostate cancer diagnosed in men over age 65. Inherited genetic predisposition may be responsible for 5–10% of cases, and men with a family history of the disease should be particularly vigilant about screening. African American men have the highest rate of prostate cancer of any group in the world; both genetic and lifestyle factors may be involved.

Diets high in calories, dairy products, and animal fats and low in plant foods have also been implicated as possible culprits, as have obesity, inactivity, and a history of sexually transmitted diseases. Type 2 diabetes and insulin resistance are also associated with prostate cancer. Soy foods, tomatoes, and cruciferous vegetables are being investigated for their possible protective effects.

Detection

Early prostate cancer usually has no symptoms. Warning signs of prostate cancer can include changes in urinary frequency, weak or interrupted urine flow, painful urination, and blood in the urine.

Techniques for early detection include a digital rectal examination and the **prostate-specific antigen (PSA) blood test.** The American Cancer Society recommends that men be provided information about the benefits and limitations of the tests and that both the exam and the PSA test be offered annually, beginning at age 50 for men at average risk and age 45 for men at high risk, including African Americans and those with a family history of the disease.

During a digital rectal exam, a physician feels the prostate gland through the rectum to determine if the gland is enlarged or if lumps are present. The PSA blood test may detect an elevated level or a rapid increase in PSA. The PSA test can help catch early prostate cancer, but it also can register benign conditions (more than half of men over 50 have benign prostate disease) and very slow-growing cancers that are unlikely to kill affected individuals. Further, it is not rare for men with normal PSA levels to have prostate cancer.

Because PSA tests can yield false-positive results, they may lead men to receive further testing or treatment that is not needed. Researchers are looking for ways to make the PSA test more sensitive. A new approach involves measuring the percentage of PSA that is free-floating in the blood. PSA made by cancer cells is more likely to circulate bound to other proteins, whereas PSA from healthy prostate cells is more likely to be unbound. Thus, a low proportion of unbound, or free PSA indicates greater risk, while a high proportion of free PSA is associated with lower risk.

PSA testing has been a subject of controversy among experts for several years because of its tendency to yield misleading results, leading to further testing that can lead to harm. This is especially a concern for older men (over 75), who are more likely to die of other causes even if they have slow-growing prostate cancer. In older men, most prostate cancers are not deadly, making treatments pointless and potentially harmful.

In 2008, a review of these issues led the U.S. Preventive Services Task Force to recommend against screening men age 75 and older for prostate cancer (through PSA testing or other methods) unless they already show symptoms of the disease. The Task Force recommends that younger men talk to their doctors about the potential benefits and drawbacks of testing.

Ultrasound is used increasingly as a follow-up, to detect lumps too small to be felt and to determine their size, shape, and properties. A needle biopsy of suspicious lumps can be performed relatively painlessly, and whether the biopsied cells are malignant or benign can be determined by examining them under a microscope.

Treatment   Treatments vary based on the stage of the cancer and the age of the patient. A small, slow-growing tumor in an older man may be treated with watchful waiting because he is more likely to die from another cause before his cancer becomes life threatening; however, a recent study shows that older men who undergo treatment live longer than those who don't. More aggressive treatment would be indicated for younger men or those with more advanced cancers. Treatment usually involves radical prostatectomy, in which the prostate is removed surgically. Although radical surgery has an excellent cure rate, it is major surgery and often results in **incontinence** and/or erectile dysfunction.

A less-invasive alternative involves surgical implantation of radioactive seeds. Radiation from the seeds destroys the tumor and much of the normal prostate tissue but leaves surrounding tissue relatively untouched. Alternative or additional treatments include external radiation, hormones that shrink tumors, cryotherapy, and chemotherapy. Survival rates for all stages of this cancer have improved steadily since 1940; the 5-year survival rate is now nearly 100%.

Cancers of the Female Reproductive Tract

Because the uterus, cervix, and ovaries are subject to similar hormonal influences, the cancers of these organs can be discussed as a group.

Cervical Cancer   Cancer of the cervix occurs frequently in women in their thirties or even twenties. In the United States, more than 11,000 women are diagnosed with cervical cancer each year; the disease kills nearly 4000 annually.

Cervical cancer is at least in part a sexually transmitted disease. Most cases of cervical cancer stem from infection by the human papillomavirus (HPV), a group of about 100 related viruses that cause both common warts and genital warts. When certain types of HPV are introduced into the cervix, usually by an infected sex partner, the virus infects cervical cells, causing the cells to divide and grow. If unchecked, this growth can develop into cervical cancer. Cervical cancer is associated with multiple sex partners and is extremely rare in women who have not had heterosexual intercourse. The regular use of condoms can reduce the risk of transmitting HPV. Studies also suggest that women whose sexual partners are circumcised may be at reduced risk because circumcised men are less likely to be infected with HPV and to pass it to their partners.

Because only a very small percentage of HPV-infected women ever get cervical cancer, other factors must be involved. Two of the most important seem to be smoking and infection with genital herpes (discussed in Chapter 18 with other STDs). Both smoking and herpes infection can cause cancerous changes in cells in the laboratory and can speed and intensify the cancerous changes begun by HPV. Research suggests that women with high levels of HPV 16, a specific form of HPV, are at particularly high risk for the infection to develop into cancer. Some studies show that past exposure to the bacterium that causes the STD chlamydia may be a risk factor for cervical cancer that operates independently of HPV.

Screening for the changes in cervical cells that precede cancer is done chiefly by means of the **Pap test.** During a pelvic exam, loose cells are scraped from the cervix and examined under a microscope to see whether they are normal. If cells are abnormal but not yet cancerous, a condition commonly referred to as *cervical dysplasia*, the Pap test is repeated at intervals. Sometimes cervical cells spontaneously return to normal, but in about one-third of cases, the cellular changes progress toward malignancy. If this happens, the abnormal cells must be removed, either surgically or by destroying them with a cryoscopic (ultracold) probe or localized laser treatment. When the abnormal cells are in a precancerous state, the small patch of dangerous cells can be completely removed.

Without timely surgery, the malignant patch of cells goes on to invade the wall of the cervix and spreads to adjacent lymph nodes and to the uterus. At this stage, chemotherapy may be used with radiation to kill the fast-growing cancer cells, but chances for a complete cure are lower. Even when a cure can be achieved, it often means surgical removal of the uterus.

TERMS

prostate-specific antigen (PSA) blood test   A diagnostic test for prostate cancer that measures blood levels of prostate-specific antigen (PSA).

incontinence   The inability to control the flow of urine.

Pap test   A scraping of cells from the cervix for examination under a microscope to detect cancer.

Because the Pap test is highly effective, all sexually active women and women between ages 18 and 65 should be tested. The recommended schedule for testing depends on risk factors, the type of Pap test performed, and whether the Pap test is combined with HPV testing.

In 2006, the federal government approved a vaccine that protects against four types of HPV viruses, including two that cause about 70% of cervical cancer cases. Studies show the vaccine also protects against cancers of the vagina and vulva. The HPV/cervical cancer vaccine, named Gardasil, is given in three doses over a 6-month period. The vaccine is recommended for all girls age 11–12; the recommendation also allows for vaccination of girls as young as 9 and women through age 26. The drug is not yet known to be effective for boys or men, but it may be recommended when more information becomes available.

Uterine, or Endometrial, Cancer   Cancer of the lining of the uterus, or endometrium, most often occurs after the age of 55. Uterine cancer strikes about 40,000 American women annually, and kills about 7500 women each year.

The risk factors are similar to those for breast cancer, including prolonged exposure to estrogen, early onset of menstruation, late menopause, never having been pregnant, and obesity. Type 2 diabetes is also associated with increased risk. The use of oral contraceptives, which combine estrogen and progestin, appears to provide protection.

Endometrial cancer is usually detectable by pelvic examination. It is treated surgically, commonly by hysterectomy, or removal of the uterus. Radiation treatment, hormones, and chemotherapy may be used in addition to surgery. When the tumor is detected at an early stage, about 95% of patients are alive and disease-free 5 years later. When the disease has spread beyond the uterus, the 5-year survival rate is less than 67%.

Ovarian Cancer   Although ovarian cancer is rare compared with cervical or uterine cancer, it causes more deaths than the other two combined. There are often no warning signs of developing ovarian cancer. Early clues may include increased abdominal size and bloating, urinary urgency, and pelvic pain. It cannot be detected by Pap tests or any other simple screening method and is often diagnosed only late in its development, when surgery and other therapies are unlikely to be successful.

The risk factors are similar to those for breast and endometrial cancer: increasing age (most ovarian cancer occurs after age 60), never having been pregnant, a family history of breast or ovarian cancer, obesity, and specific genetic mutations. A high number of ovulations appears to increase the chance that a cancer-causing genetic mutation will occur, so anything that lowers the number of lifetime ovulation cycles—pregnancy, breastfeeding, or use of oral contraceptives—reduces a woman's risk of ovarian cancer. A diet rich in fruits and vegetables may be associated with reduced risk.

Women with symptoms or who are at high risk because of family history or because they harbor a mutant gene should have thorough pelvic exams at regular intervals, as recommended by their physician. Pelvic exams may include the use of ultrasound to view the ovaries.

Ovarian cancer is treated by surgical removal of both ovaries, the fallopian tubes, and the uterus. Radiation and chemotherapy are sometimes used in addition to surgery. When the tumor is localized to the ovary, the 5-year survival rate is 92%. But for all stages, the 5-year survival rate is only 45%, reflecting the difficulty of early detection.

Skin Cancer

Skin cancer is the most common cancer of all when cases of the highly curable forms are included in the count. (Usually these forms are not included, precisely because they are easily treated.) Of the more than 1 million cases of skin cancer diagnosed each year, 62,500 are of the most serious type, **melanoma**. Treatments are usually simple and successful when the cancers are caught early.

Risk Factors   Almost all cases of skin cancer can be traced to excessive exposure to **ultraviolet (UV) radiation** from the sun, including longer-wavelength ultraviolet A (UVA) and shorter-wavelength ultraviolet B (UVB) radiation. UVB radiation causes sunburns and can damage the eyes and the immune system. UVA is less likely to cause an immediate sunburn, but by damaging connective tissue it leads to premature aging of the skin, giving it a wrinkled, leathery appearance. (Tanning lamps and tanning-salon beds emit mostly UVA radiation.) Both UVA and UVB radiation have been linked to the development of skin cancer, and the National Toxicology Program has declared both solar and artificial sources of UV radiation, including sunlamps and tanning beds, to be known human carcinogens.

Both severe, acute sun reactions (sunburns) and chronic low-level sun reactions (suntans) can lead to skin cancer. People with fair skin have less natural protection against skin damage from the sun and a higher risk of developing skin cancer; people with naturally dark skin have a considerable degree of protection (see the box "What's Your UV Risk?"). Caucasians are about 10 times more likely than African Americans to develop melanoma, but African Americans and Latinos are still at risk. In general, men are more likely to develop and die from melanoma. According to a 2008 study from the National Cancer Institute, how-

What's Your UV Risk?

Your risk of skin cancer from the ultraviolet radiation in sunlight depends on several factors. Take the quiz below to see how sensitive you are. The higher your UV-risk score, the greater your risk of skin cancer—and the greater your need to take precautions against too much sun.

Score 1 point for each true statement:

_____ 1. I have blond or red hair.

_____ 2. I have light-colored eyes (blue, gray, green).

_____ 3. I freckle easily.

_____ 4. I have many moles.

_____ 5. I had two or more blistering sunburns as a child.

_____ 6. I spent lots of time in a tropical climate as a child.

_____ 7. I have a family history of skin cancer.

_____ 8. I work outdoors.

_____ 9. I spend a lot of time in outdoor activities.

_____ 10. I like to spend as much time in the sun as I can.

_____ 11. I sometimes go to a tanning parlor or use a sunlamp.

_____ Total score

Score	Risk of skin cancer from UV radiation
0	Low
1–3	Moderate
4–7	High
8–11	Very high

For self-assessments for other types of cancer, visit the Harvard Center for Cancer Prevention's Disease Risk Index Web site (http://www.diseaseriskindex.harvard.edu/update).

SOURCE: Adapted from Shear, N. 1996. What's your UV-risk score? *Consumer Reports on Health*, June. Copyright © 1996 by Consumers Union of U.S., Inc., Yonkers, N.Y. 10703–1057, a nonprofit organization. Reprinted with permission from the June 1996 issue of *Consumer Reports on Health* for educational purposes only. No commercial use or reproduction permitted. www.ConsumerReportsOnHealth.org, www.ConsumerReports.org.

ever, the rate of melanoma among women has risen 50% since 1980 while the rate among men has remained stable.

Severe sunburns in childhood have been linked to a greatly increased risk of skin cancer in later life, so children in particular should be protected. According to the American Academy of Dermatology, the risk of skin cancer doubles in people who have had five or more sunburns in their lifetime. Because of damage to the ozone layer of the atmosphere (discussed in Chapter 19), there is a chance that we may all be exposed to increasing amounts of UV radiation in the future.

Other risk factors for skin cancer include having many moles, particularly large ones; spending time at high altitudes; and a family history of the disease. Skin cancer may also be caused by exposure to coal tar, pitch, creosote, arsenic, and radioactive materials; but compared to sunlight, these agents account for only a small proportion of cases.

QUICK STATS

People with more than **50** moles are at increased risk for skin cancer.

—American Cancer Society, 2008

Types of Skin Cancer There are three main types of skin cancer, named for the types of skin cells from which they develop. **Basal cell** and **squamous cell carcinomas** together account for about 95% of the skin cancers diagnosed each year. They are usually found in chronically

Tanning, either under direct sunlight or in a tanning bed, is a known cause of skin cancer.

TERMS

melanoma   A malignant tumor of the skin that arises from pigmented cells, usually a mole.

ultraviolet (UV) radiation   Light rays of a specific wavelength emitted by the sun; most UV rays are blocked by the ozone layer in the upper atmosphere.

basal cell carcinoma   Cancer of the deepest layers of the skin.

squamous cell carcinoma   Cancer of the surface layers of the skin.

sun-exposed areas, such as the face, neck, hands, and arms. They usually appear as pale, waxlike, pearly nodules or red, scaly, sharply outlined patches. These cancers are often painless, although they may bleed, crust, and form an open sore on the skin.

Melanoma is by far the most dangerous skin cancer because it spreads so rapidly. It can occur anywhere on the body, but the most common sites are the back, chest, abdomen, and lower legs. A melanoma usually appears at the site of a preexisting mole. The mole may begin to enlarge, become mottled or varied in color (colors can include blue, pink, and white), or develop an irregular surface or irregular borders. Tissue invaded by melanoma may also itch, burn, or bleed easily.

Prevention   One of the major steps you can take to protect yourself against all forms of skin cancer is to avoid lifelong overexposure to sunlight. Blistering, peeling sunburns from unprotected sun exposure are particularly dangerous, but suntans—whether from sunlight or tanning lamps—also increase your risk of developing skin cancer later in life. People of every age, especially babies and children, need to be protected from the sun with **sunscreens** and protective clothing. For a closer look at sunlight and skin cancer, see the box "Choosing and Using Sunscreens and Sun-Protective Clothing."

Detection and Treatment   The only sure way to avoid a serious outcome from skin cancer is to make sure it is recognized and diagnosed early. More than half of all melanomas are brought to a physician's attention by patients themselves. Make it a habit to examine your skin regularly. Most of the spots, freckles, moles, and blemishes on your body are normal; you were born with some of them, and others appear and disappear throughout your life. But if you notice an unusual growth, discoloration, sore that does not heal, or mole that undergoes a sudden or progressive change, see your physician or a dermatologist immediately.

The characteristics that may signal that a skin lesion is a melanoma—asymmetry, border irregularity, color change, and a diameter greater than ¼ inch—are illustrated in Figure 16.6 above. A mole that changes in size, shape, or

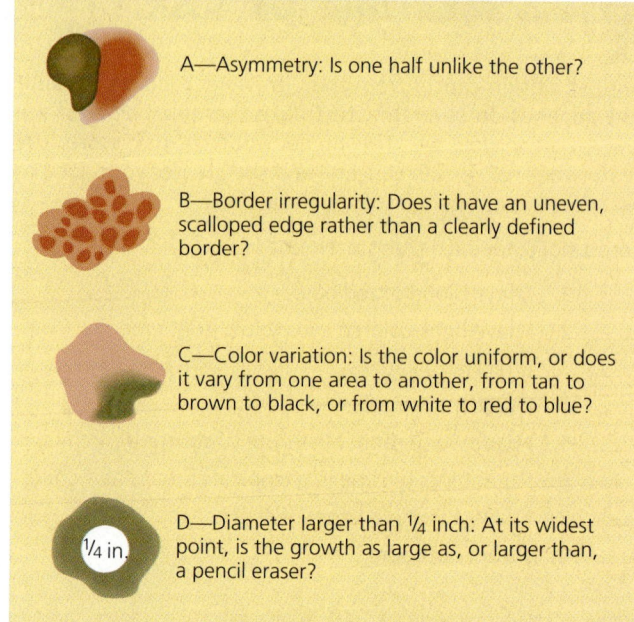

A—Asymmetry: Is one half unlike the other?

B—Border irregularity: Does it have an uneven, scalloped edge rather than a clearly defined border?

C—Color variation: Is the color uniform, or does it vary from one area to another, from tan to brown to black, or from white to red to blue?

D—Diameter larger than ¼ inch: At its widest point, is the growth as large as, or larger than, a pencil eraser?

¼ in.

FIGURE 16.6   The ABCD test for melanoma.   To see a variety of photos of melanoma and benign moles, visit the National Cancer Institute's Visuals Online site (http://visualsonline.cancer.gov).

color is also of concern. In addition, if someone in your family has had numerous skin cancers or melanomas, consult a dermatologist for a complete skin examination and discussion of your particular risk.

If you have an unusual skin lesion, your physician will examine it and possibly perform a biopsy. If the lesion is cancerous, it is usually removed surgically, a procedure that can almost always be performed in the physician's office using a local anesthetic. Occasionally, other forms of treatment may be used. Even for melanoma, the outlook after removal in the early stages is good, with a 5-year survival rate of 99% if the tumor is localized but only 65% if the cancer has spread to adjacent lymph nodes.

Oral Cancer

Oral cancer—cancers of the lip, tongue, mouth, and throat—can be traced principally to cigarette, cigar, or pipe smoking, the use of spit tobacco, and the excessive consumption of alcohol. These risk factors work together to multiply a person's risk of oral cancer. The incidence of oral cancer is twice as great in men as in women and most frequent in men over 40. Some prominent sufferers of oral cancer have included Sigmund Freud and Fidel Castro, both notorious cigar smokers. Sports figures who have cultivated a taste for spit tobacco are now also increasingly being diagnosed with oral cancer. Among long-term snuff users, the excess risk of cancers of the cheek, tongue, and gum is nearly 50-fold (see Chapter 11 for more on cigars and spit tobacco).

Oral cancers have the virtue of being fairly easy to detect, but they are often hard to cure. Furthermore, among

TERMS

sunscreen   A substance used to protect the skin from UV rays; usually applied as an ointment or a cream.

Choosing and Using Sunscreens and Sun-Protective Clothing

With consistent use of the proper clothing, sunscreens, and common sense, you can lead an active outdoor life *and* protect your skin against most sun-induced damage.

Clothing

• Wear long-sleeved shirts and long pants. Dark-colored, tightly woven fabrics provide reasonable protection from the sun. Another good choice is clothing made from special sun-protective fabrics; these garments have an ultraviolet protection factor (UPF) rating, similar to the SPF for sunscreens. For example, a fabric with a UPF rating of 20 allows only one-twentieth of the sun's UV radiation to pass through. There are three categories of UPF protection: A UPF of 15–24 provides "good" UV protection; a UPF of 25–39 provides "very good" protection; and a UPF of 40–50 provides "excellent" protection. By comparison, typical shirts provide a UPF of only 5–9, a value that drops when clothing is wet.

• Consider washing some extra sun protection into your clothes. A new laundry additive adds UV protection to ordinary fabrics; it is recommended by the Skin Cancer Foundation.

• Wear a hat. Your face, ears, neck, and scalp are especially vulnerable to the sun's harmful effects, making hats an essential weapon in the battle against sun damage. A good choice is a broad-brimmed hat or a legionnaire-style cap that covers the ears and neck. Wear sunscreen on your face even if you are wearing a hat.

• Wear sunglasses. Exposure to UV rays can damage the eyes and cause cataracts.

Sunscreen

• Use a sunscreen and lip balm with a sun protection factor (SPF) of 15 or higher. (An SPF rating refers to the amount of time you can stay out in the sun before you burn, compared with not using sunscreen. For example, a product with an SPF of 15 would allow you to remain in the sun without burning 15 times longer, on average, than if you didn't apply sunscreen.) If you're fair-skinned, have a family history of skin cancer, are at high altitude, or will be outdoors for many hours, use a sunscreen with a high SPF (301).

• Choose a broad-spectrum sunscreen that protects against both UVA and UVB radiation. The SPF rating of a sunscreen currently applies only to UVB, but a number of ingredients, especially titanium dioxide and zinc oxide, are effective at blocking most UVA radiation. In 2006, the FDA approved a product called Anthelios SX that protects against both UVA and UVB radiation. Use a water-resistant sunscreen if you swim or sweat a great deal. If you have acne, look for a sunscreen that is labeled "non-comedogenic," which means that it will not cause pimples.

• In late 2007, the FDA proposed new regulations that would require more stringent testing and labeling of commercial sunscreen products. The new system would require products to be tested for UVA protection and would implement a 4-star rating system based on those tests. The higher a product's rating in stars, the more protection it would provide against UVA radiation. The FDA also proposed placing caps on SPF ratings (which indicate how well a product protects against UVB radi-

ation), to make those ratings more consistent and meaningful to consumers.

• Shake sunscreen before applying. Apply it 30 minutes before exposure to allow it time to bond to the skin. Reapply sunscreen frequently and generously to all sun-exposed areas (many people overlook their temples, ears, and sides and backs of their necks). Most people use less than half as much as they need to attain the full SPF rating. One ounce of sunscreen is enough to cover an average-size adult in a swimsuit. Reapply sunscreen 15–30 minutes after sun exposure begins and then every 2 hours after that and/or following activities, such as swimming, that could remove sunscreen.

• If you're taking medications, ask your physician or pharmacist about possible reactions to sunlight or interactions with sunscreens. Medications for acne, allergies, and diabetes are just a few of the products that can trigger reactions. If you're using sunscreen and an insect repellent containing DEET, use extra sunscreen (DEET may decrease sunscreen effectiveness).

• Don't let sunscreens give you a false sense of security. Most of the sunscreens currently on the market allow considerable UVA radiation to penetrate the skin, with the potential for causing skin cancers (especially melanoma), as well as wrinkles and other forms of skin damage.

Time of Day and Location

• Avoid sun exposure between 10 A.M. and 4 P.M., when the sun's rays are most intense. Clouds allow as much as 80% of UV rays to reach your skin. Stay in the shade when you can.

• Consult the day's UV Index, which predicts UV levels on a 0–10+ scale, to get a sense of the amount of sun protection you'll need; take special care on days with a rating of 5 or above. UV Index ratings are available in local newspapers, from the weather bureau, or from certain Web sites.

• Be aware that UV rays can penetrate at least 3 feet in water. Thus swimmers should wear water-resistant sunscreens. Snow, sand, water, concrete, and white-painted surfaces are also highly reflective.

Tanning Salons and Sunless Tanning Products

• Stay away from tanning salons! Despite advertising claims to the contrary, the lights used in tanning parlors are damaging to your skin. Tanning beds and lamps emit mostly UVA radiation, increasing your risk of premature skin aging (such as wrinkles) and skin cancer.

• If you really want a tan, consider using a sunless tanning product. Lotions, creams, and sprays containing the color additive dihydroxyacetone (DHA) are approved by the FDA for tanning. (The FDA has not approved so-called tanning accelerators and tanning pills because these products have not been proven to be safe or effective.) DHA is for external use only and should not be inhaled, swallowed, or used around the eyes. Tanning salons that offer spraying or misting with DHA need to ensure that customers are protected from exposure to the eyes, lips, and mucous membranes as well as internal exposure. Most sunless tanning products do not contain sunscreen, so if you use them in the sun, be sure to wear sunscreen.

those who survive, a significant number will develop another primary cancer of the head and neck. The primary methods of treatment are surgery and radiation. The 5-year survival rate is about 59%.

Testicular Cancer

Testicular cancer is relatively rare, accounting for only 1% of cancer in men (about 8100 cases per year), but it is the most common cancer in men age 20–35. It is much more common among white Americans than Latinos, Asian Americans, or African Americans and among men whose fathers had testicular cancer. Men with undescended testicles are at increased risk for testicular cancer, and for this reason the condition should be corrected in early childhood. Men whose mothers took DES during pregnancy have an increased risk of undescended testicles and other genital anomalies. Thus, they may have a higher risk of testicular cancer.

Self-examination may help in the early detection of testicular cancer (see the box "Testicle Self-Examination"). Tumors are treated by surgical removal of the testicle and, if the tumor has spread, by chemotherapy. The 5-year survival rate for testicular cancer is 96%.

Other Cancers

Several other cancers affect a significant number of people each year. Some have identifiable risk factors, particularly smoking and obesity, that are controllable; causes of others are still under investigation.

Pancreatic Cancer   The pancreas, a gland found deep within the abdomen behind the stomach, produces both digestive enzymes and insulin. Because of the gland's hidden location, pancreatic cancer is usually well advanced before symptoms become noticeable. Each year there are about 38,000 new cases and about 34,000 deaths.

About three out of ten cases are linked to smoking. Other risk factors include being male, African American, obese, sedentary, or over age 60; having a family history of pancreatic cancer; having diabetes; and eating a diet high in fat and meat and low in vegetables. Pancreatic cancer can be treated in many ways, but the disease is seldom cured.

Stomach Cancer   In many parts of the world, stomach cancer is the most common form of cancer. It is relatively unusual in the United States, with about 22,000 new cases and 11,000 deaths each year. It tends to occur after the age of 50 and is almost twice as common in men as in women.

Risk factors include infection with the bacterium *Helicobacter pylori,* which has also been linked to the development of ulcers, and a diet high in smoked, salted, or pickled fish or meat. Bacteria, including *H. pylori,* can convert the nitrites in preserved foods into carcinogenic amines, and salt can break down the normal protective stomach coating, allowing these carcinogenic compounds access to the cells of the stomach wall. However, the great majority of people with *H. pylori* infection do not develop stomach cancer, particularly if they maintain a low-salt diet with plenty of fruits, vegetables, and whole grains.

There is no screening test for stomach cancer; it is usually recognized only after it has spread, and the 5-year survival rate is only 25% for all stages.

Bladder Cancer   This cancer is almost three times as common in men as in women, and smoking is the key risk factor. (Smokers are two to three times more likely to develop bladder cancer than nonsmokers.) People living in urban areas and workers exposed to chemicals used in the dye, rubber, and leather industries are also at increased risk.

There is no screening test for bladder cancer; the first symptoms are likely to be blood in the urine and/or increased frequency of urination. These symptoms can also signal a urinary infection but should trigger a visit to a physician, who can evaluate the possibility of cancer. With early detection, more than 90% of cases are curable. There are about 69,000 new cases and about 14,000 deaths each year.

Kidney Cancer   Although this cancer usually occurs in people over 50, anyone can develop it, and there are few controllable risk factors. Smoking and obesity are mild risk factors, as is a family history of the disease. Symptoms may include fatigue, pain in the side, and blood in the urine. Kidney cancer has been difficult to treat, with a 5-year survival rate of only 65% for all stages. Recently, immune cell therapies have shown some promise in the disease's advanced stage. There are about 54,000 new cases each year and about 13,000 deaths.

Brain Cancer   Tumors can arise from most of the many types of cells that are found in the brain. The vast majority of brain cancers develop for no apparent reason; one of the few established risk factors is ionizing radiation, such as X rays. Before the risks were recognized, children with ringworm of the scalp (a fungal infection) often received low-dose radiation therapy, which substantially increased their risk of brain tumors later in life. Symptoms are often nonspecific and include headaches, fatigue, behavioral changes, and sometimes seizures. There has been a slight increase in the incidence of tumors over the past 20 years, but this may be due to improved methods of diagnosis. Some brain tumors are curable by surgery or by radiation and chemotherapy, but most are not. Survival time varies, depending on the type of the tumor, from 1 to 8 years. In the United States each year there are about 22,000 new cases and 13,000 deaths.

Leukemia   Leukemia, cancer of the white blood cells, can affect both children and adults. It starts in the bone

Testicle Self-Examination

The best time to perform a testicular self-exam is after a warm shower or bath, when the scrotum is relaxed. First, stand in front of a mirror and look for any swelling of the scrotum. Then examine each testicle with both hands. Place the index and middle fingers under the testicle and the thumbs on top; roll the testicle gently between the fingers and thumbs. Don't worry if one testicle seems slightly larger than the other—that's common. Also, expect to feel the epididymis, the soft, sperm-carrying tube at the rear of the testicle.

Perform the self-exam each month. If you find a lump, swelling, or nodule, consult a physician right away. The abnormality may not be cancer, but only a physician can make a diagnosis. Other possible signs of testicular cancer include a change in the way a testicle feels, a sudden collection of fluid in the scrotum, a dull ache in the lower abdomen or groin, a feeling of heaviness in the scrotum, or pain in a testicle or the scrotum.

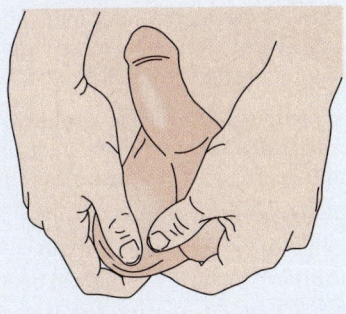

SOURCES: Testicular Cancer Resource Center. 2007. *How to Do a Testicular Self Examination* (http://www.acor.org/tcrc/tcexam.html; retrieved February 15, 2009); National Cancer Institute. 2005. *Questions and Answers About Testicular Cancer* (http://www.cancer.gov/cancertopics/factsheet/sites-types/ testicular; retrieved February 15, 2009).

---

marrow but can then spread to the lymph nodes, spleen, liver, other organs, and central nervous system. Like brain cancer, it is a complex disease with many different types and subtypes. Most people with leukemia have no known risk factors. About 20% of cases of adult leukemia are related to smoking; other possible risk factors include radiation and certain chemicals and infections. Most symptoms occur because leukemia cells crowd out the production of normal blood cells; the result can be fatigue, anemia, weight loss, and increased risk of infection. Treatment and survival rates vary, depending on the exact type and other factors. There are about 44,000 new cases and 22,000 deaths each year.

Lymphoma   Arising from the lymph cells, lymphoma begins in the lymph nodes and then may spread to almost any part of the body. There are two types—Hodgkin's disease and non-Hodgkin's lymphoma (NHL). NHL is the more common and more deadly form of the disease. It is the sixth most common cancer in the United States, with about 66,000 people diagnosed annually; about half of all patients will eventually die from the disease. Risk factors for NHL are not well understood, but people with compromised immune systems are at much greater risk, especially when exposed to radiation or certain infections and chemicals. A new therapy based on the use of antibodies has shown promise in treating patients. Rates of Hodg-

kin's disease have fallen by more than 50% since the early 1970s, and there are now about 8000 cases and 1400 deaths each year.

Multiple Myeloma   Normal plasma cells play an important role in the immune system, producing antibodies. Malignant plasma cells may produce tumors in several sites, particularly in the bone marrow; when they grow in multiple sites, they are referred to as multiple myeloma (MM). By crowding out normal bone marrow cells, MM can lead to anemia, excessive bleeding, and decreased resistance to infection. Age is the most significant risk factor: The average age at diagnosis is about 70. Other risk factors are not well understood, although MM is about twice as common among African Americans as among whites. Obesity has been associated with MM in women. There are about 20,000 new cases each year and 11,000 deaths.

THE CAUSES OF CANCER

Although scientists do not know everything about what causes cancer, they have identified genetic, environmental, and lifestyle factors. (See the box "Ethnicity, Poverty, and Cancer" on p. 502).

The Role of DNA

Heredity and genetics are important factors in a person's risk of cancer. Certain genes may predispose some people to cancer, and specific genetic mutations have been associated with cancer.

QUESTIONS FOR CRITICAL THINKING AND REFLECTION
Has anyone you know had cancer? If so, what type of cancer was it? What were its symptoms? Based on the information presented so far in this chapter, did the person have any of the known risk factors for the disease?

> **5%** of all cancers have a strong hereditary component.
> —American Cancer Society, 2008

QUICK STATS

DIMENSIONS OF DIVERSITY

Rates of cancer have declined among all U.S. ethnic groups in recent years, but significant disparities still exist.

• Among U.S. ethnic groups, African Americans have the highest incidence of and death rates from cancer.

• White women have a higher incidence of breast cancer, but African American women have the highest death rate. Black women are less likely to receive regular mammograms and more likely to experience delays in follow-up.

• African American men have a higher rate of prostate cancer than any other U.S. group and more than twice the death rate of other groups. However, black men are less likely than white men to undergo PSA testing for prostate cancer.

• Latinas have the highest incidence of cervical cancer, but African American women have the highest death rate. Language barriers and problems accessing screening services are thought to particularly affect Latinas, who have relatively low rates of Pap testing.

• Asian Americans and Pacific Islander Americans have the highest rates of liver and stomach cancers. Recent immigration helps explain these higher rates, as these cancers are usually caused by infections that are more prevalent in the recent immigrant's country of origin.

Some of the disparities in cancer risks and rates may be influenced by genetic or cultural factors. For example, certain genetic/molecular features of aggressive breast cancer are more common among African American women with the disease; they are more likely to be diagnosed at a later stage and with more aggressive tumors. Genetic factors may also help explain the high rate of prostate cancer among black men. Women from cultures where early marriage and motherhood is common are likely to have a lower risk of breast cancer.

Most of the differences in cancer rates and deaths, however, are thought to be the result of socioeconomic inequities, which influence the prevalence of many underlying cancer risk factors as well as access to early detection and quality treatment. People of low socioeconomic status are more likely to smoke, abuse alcohol, eat unhealthy foods, and be sedentary and overweight—all of which are associated with cancer. High levels of stress associated with poverty may impair the immune system, the body's first line of defense against cancer.

People with low incomes are more likely to live in unhealthy environments. For example, Latinos and Asian and Pacific Islander Americans are more likely than other groups to live in areas that do not meet federal air quality standards. Low-income people may also have jobs in which they come into daily contact with carcinogenic chemicals. They may face similar risks in their homes and schools, where they may be exposed to asbestos or other carcinogens.

People with low incomes also have less exposure to information about cancer, are less aware of the early warning signs of cancer, and are less likely to seek medical care when they have such symptoms. Lack of health insurance is a key factor explaining higher death rates among people with low incomes. A study comparing low-income Americans and Canadians found that the Canadians were more likely to survive cancer, possibly due to Canada's system of universal health care, which ensures access to treatment regardless of income. Discrimination and language and cultural barriers can also affect patients' use of the health care system.

Public education campaigns that encourage healthy lifestyle habits, routine cancer screening, and participation in clinical trials may be one helpful strategy to reduce cancer disparities. But the effects of poverty are more difficult to overcome. Some medical scientists look to policymakers for solutions and maintain that living and working conditions in the inner cities must be improved and that access to quality health care must be assured for all Americans. Then, even without new miracle drugs or medical breakthroughs, the United States could see a real decrease in cancer rates in low-income populations.

SOURCES: American Cancer Society. 2008. *Cancer Facts and Figures 2008.* Atlanta: American Cancer Society; Chlebowski, R. T., et al. 2005. Ethnicity and breast cancer: Factors influencing differences in incidence and outcome. *Journal of the National Cancer Institute* 97(6): 439–448; CDC Office of Minority Health. 2006. *Eliminate Disparities in Cancer Screening and Management* (http://www.cdc.gov/omh/AMH/factsheets/cancer.htm; retrieved February 15, 2009); National Cancer Institute. 2005. *Cancer Health Disparities: Fact Sheet* (http://www.cancer.gov/newscenter/healthdisparities; retrieved February 15, 2009).

DNA Basics The nucleus of each cell in your body contains 23 pairs of **chromosomes,** which are made up of tightly packed coils of **DNA** (deoxyribonucleic acid). DNA consists of two long strands wound around each other in a spiral structure, like a twisted ladder; scientists refer to this spiral as a double helix. The rungs of the ladder are made from four different nucleotide bases: adenine, thymine, cytosine, and guanine, or A, T, C, and G.

The arrangement of nucleotide bases along the double helix constitutes the genetic code. You can think of this code as a set of instructions for building, operating, and repairing your body.

A **gene** is a smaller unit of DNA made up of a specific sequence of nucleotide bases. Each chromosome contains hundreds, and in some cases thousands, of genes; you have about 25,000 genes in all. Each of your genes controls the production of a particular protein. The makeup of each protein—which amino acids it contains and in what sequence—is determined by its precise sequence of A, T, C, and G. Proteins build cells and make them work: They serve both as the structural material for your body and as the regulators of all chemical reactions and metabolic processes. By making different proteins at different times, genes can act as switches to alter the ways a cell works.

Cells reproduce by dividing in two, and your body makes billions of new cells every day. When a cell divides, the DNA replicates itself so that each new cell has a complete set of chromosomes. Through the proteins for which they code, some genes are responsible for controlling the rate of cell division, and some types of cells divide much more rapidly than others. Genes that control the rate of cell division often play a critical role in the development of cancer.

DNA Mutations and Cancer   A *mutation* is any change in the normal makeup of a gene. Some mutations are inherited. If the egg or sperm cell that produces a child contains a mutation, so will every one of the child's 30 trillion cells. Environmental agents can also produce mutational damage; these **mutagens** include radiation, certain viruses, and chemical substances in the air we breathe. (When a mutagen also causes cancer, it is called a carcinogen.) Some mutations are the result of copying errors that occur when DNA replicates itself as part of cell division.

A mutated gene no longer contains the proper code for producing its protein. Because a cell has two copies of each gene, it can sometimes get by with only one functioning version. In this case, the mutation may have no effect on health. However, if both copies of a gene are damaged or if the cell needs two normal copies to function properly, then the cell will cease to behave normally.

It usually takes several mutational changes over a period of years before a normal cell takes on the properties of a cancer cell. Genes in which mutations are associated with the conversion of a normal cell into a cancer cell are known as **oncogenes.** In their undamaged form, many oncogenes play a role in controlling or restricting cell growth; these are **tumor suppressor genes.** Mutational damage to these genes releases the brake on growth and leads to rapid and uncontrolled cell division—a precondition for the development of cancer.

A good example of how a series of mutational changes can produce cancer is provided by the p53 gene, located on chromosome 17. In its normal form, the protein that is coded for by this gene actually helps prevent cancer: If a cell's DNA is damaged, the p53 protein can either kill the cell outright or stop it from replicating until the damaged DNA is repaired. For example, if a skin cell's DNA is mutated by exposure to sunlight, the p53 protein activates the cell's "suicide" machinery. By thus preventing the replication of damaged DNA, the p53 protein keeps cells from progressing toward cancer. However, if the p53 gene itself undergoes a mutation, these controls are lost, and the cell can become cancerous. In fact, the damaged version of p53 can actually promote cell division and the spread of cancer. Researchers believe that damage to the p53 gene and protein may be involved, directly and indirectly, in as many as 50–60% of cancers of all types.

Hereditary Cancer Risks   One way to obtain a mutated oncogene is to inherit it. One example is *BRCA1* (breast cancer gene 1): Women who inherit a damaged copy of this suppressor gene face a significantly increased risk of breast and ovarian cancer.

In most cases, however, mutational damage occurs after birth. Although some specific genes do increase the risk for some cancers, many researchers say it is unlikely that science will identify genes that increase the risk of cancer in general. For example, only about 5–10% of breast cancer cases can be traced to inherited copies of a damaged *BRCA 1* gene. Lifestyle decisions are still important even for those who have inherited a damaged suppressor gene.

Testing and identification of hereditary cancer risks can be helpful for some people, especially if it leads to increased attention to controllable risk factors and better medical screening. For more on hereditary cancer risks and the issues involved in genetic testing, see the box "Genetic Testing for Breast Cancer" on page 504.

Cancer Promoters   Substances known as *cancer promoters* make up another important piece of the cancer puzzle. Carcinogenic agents such as UV radiation that cause mutational changes in the DNA of oncogenes are known as cancer *initiators*. Cancer *promoters*, on the other hand, don't directly produce DNA mutations. Instead, they accelerate the growth of cells without damaging or permanently altering their DNA. However, a faster growth rate means less time for a cell to repair DNA damage caused by initiators, so errors are more likely to be passed on. Estrogen, which stimulates cellular growth in the female reproductive organs, is an example of a cancer promoter. Cigarette smoke is a complete carcinogen because it acts as both an initiator and a promoter.

chromosomes   The threadlike bodies in a cell nucleus that contain molecules of DNA; most human cells contain 23 pairs of chromosomes.

DNA   Deoxyribonucleic acid, a chemical substance that carries genetic information.

gene   A section of a chromosome that contains the nucleotide base sequence for making a particular protein; the basic unit of heredity.

mutagen   Any environmental factor that can cause mutation, such as radiation and atmospheric chemicals.

oncogene   A gene involved in the transformation of a normal cell into a cancer cell.

tumor suppressor gene   A type of oncogene that normally functions to restrain cellular growth.

TERMS

IN FOCUS

Genetic Testing for Breast Cancer

Recent discoveries of disease-related genes are opening up a host of issues related to genetic testing and associated legal, financial, and ethical concerns. Tests for hereditary mutations in breast cancer genes are now commercially available, but who should be tested?

Researchers identified *BRCA1* in 1994 and *BRCA2* in 1995. About 1 or 2 in 1000 women in the general population carry a mutant copy of *BRCA1* or *BRCA2*, but in certain groups, most notably women of Ashkenazi (Eastern European) Jewish descent, as many as 3 in 100 may carry an altered gene. Defects in these genes cause breast cancer in as many as 50–80% of affected women; they also increase the risk of ovarian and other gynecological cancers. Women with an altered *BRCA* gene tend to develop breast cancer at younger ages than other women, and the cancers that develop are more malignant. The situation is complex, however, because hundreds of different mutations of *BRCA1* and *BRCA2* have been identified, and not all of them carry the same risks. Additional genes influencing risk have been identified—*TSG101* in 1997, *BRAF35* in 2001, *BASE* in 2003, *CHEK2* in 2005—and others will no doubt be found in the future.

Genetic analysis of DNA from a blood sample can identify mutant copies of *BRCA1* and *BRCA2*. The tests can be expensive, however, ranging from $350 to more than $2000. (Searching for a muta-

tion on a large gene is a bit like looking for a single typo in a novel.) Good news from a genetic test is reassuring, but it doesn't guarantee freedom from disease. Only 5–10% of all cases of breast cancer occur among women who inherit an altered version of *BRCA1* or *BRCA2*. And a woman with a family history of breast cancer must still be monitored closely, even if she carries normal versions of *BRCA1* and *BRCA2*; the cancer-causing genetic defect in her family could be located on another gene.

What about women who test positive for an altered copy of the gene? Options include close monitoring, drug treatment with a SERM such as tamoxifen, and surgical removal of currently healthy breasts or ovaries. A 2008 study showed that when women with a *BRCA1* or *BRCA2* gene mutation had their ovaries removed as a preventive measure, their risk of breast cancer fell by 47% and their risk of other gynecologic cancers fell by 88%. The benefits of such pre-emptive surgery appeared to be much greater among women with a mutation in the *BRCA2* gene than among those with a defective *BRCA1* gene. None of these strategies completely eliminates risk, and they may expose a woman to a dangerous or drastic treatment that is actually unnecessary. And those who test positive can face problems in addition to an uncertain medical future. Some health insurers may use the results of a

genetic test to justify canceling coverage. Although currently rare, such genetic discrimination could become a major problem as more and more disease-related genes are identified. Recent legislation has attempted to protect people from losing coverage due to the results of genetic tests.

The U.S. Preventive Services Task Force recommends that genetic screening be offered only to women with a definite family history of breast or ovarian cancer. The group also says no woman should undergo screening without first receiving genetic counseling.

Although much still needs to be learned about the role of genetics in cancer, it's clear that minimizing mutation damage to our DNA will lower our risk of many cancers. Unfortunately, a great many substances produce cancer-causing mutations, and we can't escape them all. By identifying the important carcinogens and understanding how

they produce their effects, we can help keep our DNA intact and avoid activating sleeping oncogenes. The careful study of oncogenes should also lead to more precise methods of assessing cancer risk and to new methods of diagnosis and treatment.

Tobacco Use

Smoking is responsible for 80–90% of lung cancers and for about 30% of all cancer deaths. The U.S. Surgeon General has reported that tobacco use is a direct cause of several types of cancer. In addition to lung and bronchial cancer (discussed earlier in this chapter and in Chapter 11), tobacco use is known to cause cancer of the larynx, mouth, pharynx, esophagus, stomach, pancreas, kidneys, bladder, and cervix. A direct causal relationship has also been established between tobacco use and acute myelogenous leukemia (AML).

TERMS

anticarcinogen An agent that destroys or otherwise blocks the action of carcinogens.

carotenoid Any of a group of yellow-to-red plant pigments that can be converted to vitamin A by the liver; many act as antioxidants or have other anti-cancer effects. The carotenoids include beta-carotene, lutein, lycopene, and zeaxanthin.

phytochemical A naturally occurring substance found in plant foods that may help prevent chronic diseases such as cancer and heart disease; *phyto* means "plant."

In a report released in 2008, the CDC stated that 2.4 million cases of tobacco-related cancer were diagnosed in the United States from 1999 to 2004. The report estimated that tobacco causes nearly 444,000 premature deaths annually in the United States—nearly one of every five deaths each year. The CDC estimates the economic burden of tobacco use at $193 billion annually, including the costs of health care and loss of productivity.

For more information on tobacco, tobacco products, and the toxic chemicals contained in these products, see Chapter 11.

Dietary Factors

Diet is one of the most important factors in cancer prevention, but it is also one of the most complex and controversial. The foods you eat contain many biologically active compounds, and your food choices affect your cancer risk by both exposing you to potentially dangerous compounds and depriving you of potentially protective ones.

The following sections examine some of the dietary factors that may affect cancer risk.

Dietary Fat and Meat   The American Cancer Society encourages everyone to limit their consumption of processed and red meats. Diets high in fat and meat appear to contribute to certain cancers, including colon, stomach, and prostate. As is true with heart disease, certain types of fats may be riskier than others. Diets favoring omega-6 polyunsaturated fats are associated with a higher risk of certain cancers than are diets favoring the omega-3 forms of fat commonly found in fish and canola oil.

For a complete discussion of nutrition, see Chapter 12.

Alcohol   Alcohol is associated with an increased incidence of several cancers. An average alcohol intake of three drinks per day is associated with a doubling in the risk of breast cancer. Alcohol and tobacco interact as risk factors for oral cancer, and heavy users of both alcohol and tobacco have a risk of oral cancer up to 15 times greater than that of people who don't drink or smoke. Alcohol also increases the risk of colon cancer. For more information on alcohol, see Chapter 10.

Fried Foods   Scientists have found high levels of the chemical acrylamide (a probable human carcinogen) in starch-based foods that had been fried or baked at high temperatures, especially french fries and certain types of snack chips and crackers.

Studies are ongoing, but the World Health Organization (WHO) has urged food companies to lower the acrylamide content of foods to reduce any risk to public health. Acrylamide levels vary widely in foods, and there are currently no warnings against eating specific foods. The wisest course may be to eat a variety of foods and avoid overindulging in any single class of foods, particularly foods like french fries and potato chips, which may contain other unhealthy substances such as saturated and trans fats. You can also limit your exposure to acrylamide by not smoking—you would likely get much more of the chemical from smoking than from food.

Fiber   Various potential cancer-fighting actions have been proposed for fiber, but none of these actions has been firmly established. Further study is needed to clarify the relationship between fiber intake and cancer risk, and experts still recommend a high-fiber diet for its overall positive effect on health.

Fruits and Vegetables   Exactly which constituents of fruits and vegetables are responsible for reducing cancer risk is not clear, but researchers have identified many mechanisms by which food components may act against cancer. Some may prevent carcinogens from forming in the first place or block them from reaching or acting on target cells. Others boost enzymes that detoxify carcinogens and render them harmless. Still other anti-cancer agents act on cells that have already been exposed to carcinogens, slowing the development of cancer or starving cancer cells of oxygen and nutrients by cutting off their blood supply.

Some essential nutrients act as **anticarcinogens.** For example, vitamin C, vitamin E, selenium, and the **carotenoids** (vitamin A precursors) may help block cancer by acting as antioxidants. As described in Chapter 12, antioxidants prevent free radicals from damaging DNA and other cell components. Vitamin C may also block the conversion of nitrites (food preservatives) into cancer-causing agents. Folic acid may inhibit the transformation of normal cells into malignant cells and strengthen immune function. Calcium inhibits cell growth in the colon and may slow the spread of potentially cancerous cells.

Many other anti-cancer agents in the diet fall under the broader heading of **phytochemicals,** substances in plants that help protect against chronic diseases. One of the first to be identified was sulforaphane, a potent anticarcinogen found in broccoli. Sulforaphane induces the cells of the liver and kidney to produce higher levels of protective enzymes, which then neutralize dietary carcinogens. Most fruits and vegetables contain beneficial phytochemicals, and researchers are just beginning to identify them. Some of the most promising are listed in Table 16.2 (p. 506).

To increase your intake of these potential cancer fighters, eat a wide variety of fruits, vegetables, legumes, and grains. Don't rely on supplements. Some practical suggestions for increasing your intake of anti-cancer agents are included in the Behavior Change Strategy at the end of the chapter.

Inactivity and Obesity

The American Cancer Society recommends maintaining a healthy weight throughout life by balancing caloric intake with physical activity, and by achieving and maintaining a healthy weight if you are currently overweight or obese.

Table 16.2   Foods with Phytochemicals

Food	Phytochemical	Potential Anticancer Effects
Chili peppers (*Note:* Hotter peppers contain more capsaicin.)	Capsaicin	Neutralizes effect of nitrosamines; may block carcinogens in cigarette smoke from acting on cells
Oranges, lemons, limes, onions, apples, berries, eggplant	Flavonoids	Act as antioxidants; block access of carcinogens to cells; suppress malignant changes in cells; prevent cancer cells from multiplying
Citrus fruits, cherries	Monoterpenes	Help detoxify carcinogens; inhibit spread of cancer cells
Cruciferous vegetables (broccoli, cabbage, bok choy, cauliflower, kale, brussels sprouts, collards)	Isothiocyanates	Boost production of cancer-fighting enzymes; suppress tumor growth; block effects of estrogen on cell growth
Garlic, onions, leeks, shallots, chives	Allyl sulfides	Increase levels of enzymes that break down potential carcinogens; boost activity of cancer-fighting immune cells
Grapes, red wine, peanuts	Resveratrol	Acts as an antioxidant; suppresses tumor growth
Green, oolong, and black teas (*Note:* Drinking burning hot tea may *increase* cancer risk.)	Polyphenols	Increase antioxidant activity; prevent cancer cells from multiplying; help speed excretion of carcinogens from body
Orange, deep yellow, red, pink, and dark green vegetables; some fruits	Carotenoids	Act as antioxidants; reduce levels of cancer-promoting enzymes; inhibit spread of cancer cells
Soy foods, whole grains, flax seeds, nuts	Phytoestrogens	Block effects of estrogen on cell growth; lower blood levels of estrogen
Whole grains, legumes	Phytic acid	Binds iron, which may prevent it from creating cell-damaging free radicals

Being overweight or obese is linked with increased risk of several kinds of cancer, including breast and colon cancer (Figure 16.7). See Chapters 13 and 14 for detailed information on physical activity and exercise.

Alarmingly, however, only 8% of Americans are aware that being overweight increases one's cancer risk (see the box "Cancer Myths and Misperceptions"). One expert estimates that if we were all to exercise for 20 minutes each day and make the dietary changes discussed in this chapter, about 40,000 cancer deaths could be prevented each year.

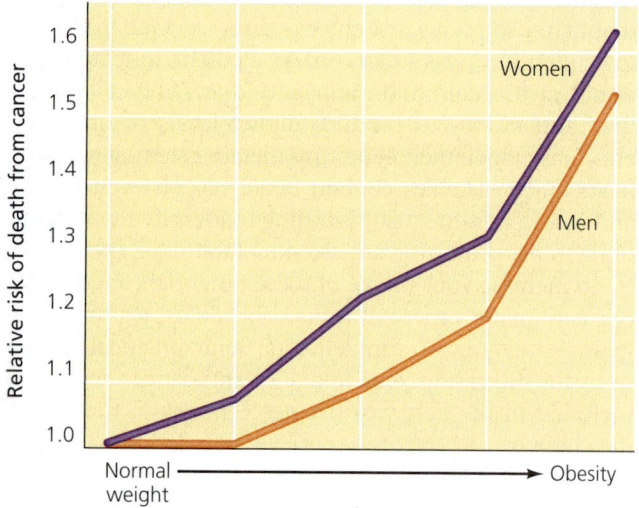

FIGURE 16.7   Body weight and cancer mortality.

SOURCE: Calle, E. E., et al. 2003. Overweight, obesity, and mortality from cancer in a prospectively studied cohort of U.S. adults. *New England Journal of Medicine* 348(17): 1625–1638.

Carcinogens in the Environment

Some carcinogens occur naturally in the environment, like viruses and the sun's UV rays. Others are manufactured or synthetic substances that show up occasionally in the general environment but more often in the work environments of specific industries.

Microbes   It is estimated that about 15% of the world's cancers are caused by microbes, including viruses, bacteria, and parasites, although the percentage is much lower in developed countries like the United States. As discussed earlier, certain types of human papillomavirus cause many cases of cervical cancer, and the *Helicobacter pylori* bacterium has been definitely linked to stomach cancer.

Viruses seem to be the main cancer causers. The Epstein-Barr virus, best known for causing mononucleosis, is also suspected of contributing to Hodgkin's disease, cancer of the pharynx, and some stomach cancers. Human herpesvirus 8 has been linked to Kaposi's sarcoma and certain types of lymphoma. Hepatitis viruses B and C together cause as many as 80% of the world's liver cancers.

Ingested Chemicals   The food industry uses preservatives and other additives to prevent food from becoming spoiled or stale (see Chapter 12). Some of these compounds are antioxidants and may actually decrease any cancer-causing properties the food might have.

Other compounds, like the nitrates and nitrites found in processed meat, are potentially more dangerous. The nitrites inhibit the growth of bacteria, which could otherwise cause food poisoning. They also preserve the pink color of the meat, which has no bearing on taste but looks

Cancer Myths and Misperceptions

Almost daily, cancer receives wide-ranging media coverage as it affects the lives of its victims and as breakthroughs create new hope for a cure. During regular checkups, doctors and dentists routinely look for signs of cancer and are quick to discuss the risks of being stricken by cancer.

Remarkably, even as we are being inundated with information about cancer, studies show that most Americans do not understand basic facts about the disease. Indeed, many still believe myths about cancer that were disproved long ago. Such misperceptions are leading Americans to ignore good advice on cancer prevention and to continue lifestyle habits that increase the risk of cancer.

Healthier Cigarettes?

Scientists have concluded that "low-tar," "low-nicotine," and "light" cigarettes are no safer than regular cigarettes. In fact, some brands of light cigarettes contain just as much nicotine and additives as regular cigarettes. Further, users of light cigarettes tend to smoke more frequently and inhale more deeply than smokers of regular cigarettes—often in the misguided belief that their chosen brand won't hurt them. In a 2006 survey, 72% of women and 63% of men said they believed light cigarettes were not as harmful as regular cigarettes. Meantime, smoking remains the leading preventable cause of cancer.

Similarly, many smokers have switched to smokeless tobacco products (such as chewing tobacco), thinking they pose no health risks. Smokeless tobacco products contribute to head, throat, and oral cancers.

Obesity and Cancer

A 2006 survey conducted for the American Cancer Society showed that only 8% of Americans are aware of the link between obesity and cancer. (Only about 15% of respondents knew their own BMI; most overweight and obese people surveyed did not view themselves as being too heavy.)

As is the case with heart disease, maintaining a healthy weight and body composition can help reduce the risk of cancer. Although scientists aren't sure how body fat works to increase cancer risk, there is bountiful evidence that overweight and obese people are in greater danger of breast, prostate, colorectal, and other cancers. In fact, obesity is the second most preventable cause of death.

Prevailing Myths

In light of such findings, it may not be surprising to learn that many Americans accept some myths about cancer, such as the following:

- *Supplements prevent cancer.* Scientists say there is no evidence that any single vitamin, mineral, or herb can boost the immune system enough to ward off cancer. The best dietary advice, they say, is to eat a wide variety of foods daily, emphasizing whole grains, fruits, and vegetables.

- *Surgery causes cancer to spread.* For generations, physicians did not have the means to detect cancer until it was advanced. As a result, doctors often performed surgery to remove a tumor from one part of the body without realizing that the cancer had already metastasized. When cancer was found again in another part of the body, many patients assumed that their surgery had "disturbed" the cancer and caused it to spread. This myth prevails even today, although it was disproved long ago. Surgery, in fact, is one of the most effective cancer treatments.

- *Stress causes cancer.* Stress has been linked to a variety of illnesses, but there is no evidence that it causes cancer.

- *Cancer cannot be prevented.* As described throughout this chapter, you can do a lot to prevent cancer, such as eating a healthy diet, exercising, controlling weight, and not smoking.

- *Cancer cannot be cured.* There are nearly 11 million cancer survivors in the United States who can dispute this myth. Treatments are more powerful than ever, and although some types of cancer are more lethal than others, there is hope for anyone whose cancer is detected early and who takes steps to get rid of it.

Surveys show that a significant percentage of Americans still believe these myths (more than 40%, in some cases). Such thinking is both wrongheaded and dangerous. The first step in preventing and treating cancer is finding good sources of reliable information and following a qualified physician's advice.

---

more appetizing to many people. While nitrates and nitrites are not themselves carcinogenic, they can combine with dietary substances in the stomach and be converted to nitrosamines, which are highly potent carcinogens. Foods cured with nitrites, as well as those cured by salt or smoke, have been linked to esophageal and stomach cancer, and they should be eaten only in modest amounts.

Environmental and Industrial Pollution Pollutants in urban air have long been suspected of contributing to the incidence of lung cancer. Fossil fuels and their combustion products, such as complex hydrocarbons, have been of special concern.

The best available data indicate that less than 2% of cancer deaths are caused by general environmental pollution, such as substances in our air and water. Exposure to carcinogenic materials in the workplace is a more serious problem. Occupational exposure to specific carcinogens may account for up to 5% of cancer deaths. With increasing industry and government regulation, we can anticipate that the industrial sources of cancer risk will continue to diminish, at least in the United States. In contrast, in the former Soviet Union and Eastern European countries, where environmental concerns were sacrificed to industrial productivity for decades, cancer rates from industrial pollution continue to climb.

Radiation   All sources of radiation are potentially carcinogenic, including medical X rays, radioactive substances (radioisotopes), and UV rays from the sun. Most physicians and dentists are quite aware of the risk of radiation, and successful efforts have been made to reduce the amount of radiation needed for mammograms, dental X rays, and other necessary medical X rays. Full-body CT scans are sometimes advertised for routine screening in otherwise well individuals in order to look for tumors. Such screening is not recommended; it is typically expensive and may have false-positive findings that lead to unnecessary and invasive additional tests. Also, the radiation in these full-body X rays may itself raise the risk of cancer; the radiation dose of one full-body CT scan is nearly 100 times that of a typical mammogram.

Sunlight is a very important source of radiation, but because its rays penetrate only a millimeter or so into the skin, it could be considered a surface carcinogen. Most cases of skin cancer are the relatively benign and highly curable basal cell carcinomas, but a substantial minority are the potentially deadly malignant melanomas. As discussed earlier, all types of skin cancer are increased by early and excessive exposure to the sun, and severe sunburn early in childhood appears to carry with it an added risk of melanoma later in life.

QUESTIONS FOR CRITICAL THINKING AND REFLECTION

What do you think your risks for cancer are? Do you have a family history of cancer, or have you been exposed to carcinogens? How about your diet and exercise habits? What can you do to reduce your risks?

DETECTING, DIAGNOSING, AND TREATING CANCER

Early cancer detection often depends on our willingness to be aware of changes in our own body and to make sure we keep up with recommended diagnostic tests. Although treatment success varies with individual cancers, cure rates have increased—sometimes dramatically—in this century.

Detecting Cancer

Unlike those of some other diseases, early signs of cancer are usually not apparent to anyone but the person who has them. Even pain is not a reliable guide to early detection, because the initial stages of cancer may be painless. Self-monitoring is the first line of defense, and the American Cancer Society recommends that you watch for the seven major warning signs shown in Figure 16.8. Remember them by the acronym CAUTION.

Although none of the warning signs is a sure indication of cancer, the appearance of any one should send you to see your physician. By being aware of the risk factors in your own life, your immediate family's cancer history, and your own history, you may bring a problem to the attention of a physician long before it would have been detected at a routine physical.

In addition to self-monitoring, the ACS recommends routine cancer checkups, as well as specific screening tests for certain cancers (Table 16.3 on p. 510).

Diagnosing Cancer

Detection of a cancer by physical examination is only the beginning. Methods for determining the exact location,

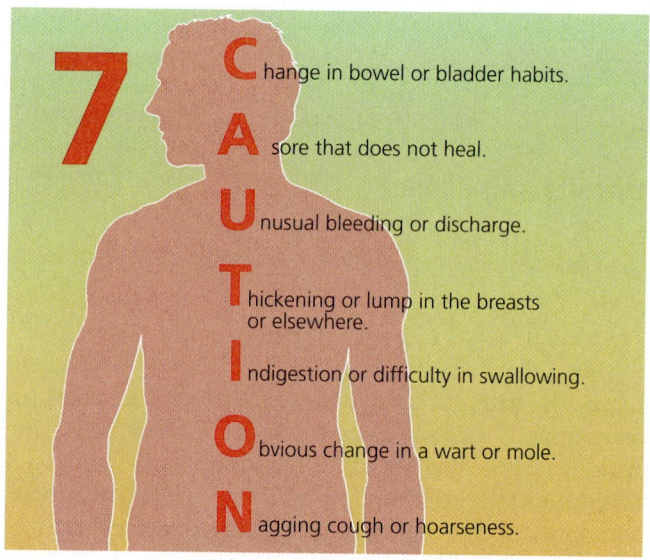

FIGURE 16.8   The seven major warning signs of cancer.

type, and degree of malignancy of a cancer continue to improve. Knowledge of the exact location and size of a tumor is necessary for precise and effective surgery or radiation therapy. This is especially true in cases where the tumor may be hard to reach, as in the brain.

Imaging studies or exploratory surgery may be performed to identify a cancer's stage. A biopsy may be performed to confirm the type of tumor. Several diagnostic imaging techniques have replaced exploratory surgery for some patients. In magnetic resonance imaging (MRI), a huge electromagnet is used to detect hidden tumors by mapping, on a computer screen, the vibrations of different atoms in the body. Computed tomography (CT) scanning uses X rays to examine the brain and other parts of the body. The process allows the construction of cross sections, which show a tumor's shape and location more accurately than is possible with conventional X rays. For patients undergoing radiation therapy, CT scanning enables the therapist to pinpoint the tumor more precisely, thereby providing more accurate radiation dosage while sparing normal tissue.

Ultrasonography has also been used increasingly in the past few years to view tumors. It has several advantages: It can be used in the physician's office, it is less expensive than other imaging methods, and it is completely safe. Prostate ultrasound (a rectal probe using ultrasonic waves to produce an image of the prostate gland) is being investigated for its ability to detect small, hidden tumors that would be missed by a digital rectal exam.

Treating Cancer

The ideal cancer therapy would kill or remove all cancerous cells while leaving normal tissue untouched. Sometimes this is almost possible, as when a surgeon removes a small superficial tumor of the skin. Usually the tumor is less accessible, and some combination of surgery, radiation therapy, and chemotherapy must be applied instead. Some patients choose to combine conventional therapies with alternative treatments (see the box "Avoiding Cancer Quackery" on p. 511).

Surgery For most cancers, surgery is the most useful treatment. In many cases, the organ containing the tumor is not essential for life and can be partially or completely removed. This is true especially for localized breast, prostate, or testicular cancer, where the surgical removal of one breast, the prostate gland, or one testicle may give a long-lasting cure. Surgery is less effective when the tumor involves cells of the immune system, which are widely distributed throughout the body, or when the cancer has already metastasized. In such cases, surgery must be combined with other techniques.

Chemotherapy Chemotherapy, or the use of cell-killing drugs to destroy rapidly growing cancer cells, has been in use since the 1940s. Many of these drugs work by interfering with DNA synthesis and replication in rapidly dividing cells. Normal cells, which usually grow slowly, are not destroyed by these drugs. However, some normal tissues such as intestinal, hair, and blood-forming cells are always growing, and damage to these tissues produces the unpleasant side effects of chemotherapy, including nausea, vomiting, diarrhea, and hair loss.

Chemotherapy drugs are often used in combinations or with surgery. Recently, in a procedure called **induction chemotherapy,** physicians have begun to use chemotherapy before surgery, both to shrink the tumor and to kill any existing small metastases as soon as possible.

Radiation In cancer radiation therapy, a beam of X rays or gamma rays is directed at the tumor, and the tumor

induction chemotherapy The use of chemotherapy prior to surgery to shrink a cancerous tumor and prevent metastasis; sometimes eliminates the need for radical surgery.

TERMS

Table 16.3   Screen Guidelines for the Early Detection of Cancer in Asymptomatic People

Site	Recommendation
Breast	• Yearly mammograms are recommended starting at age 40. The age at which screening should be stopped should be individualized by considering the potential risks and benefits of screening in the context of overall health status and longevity. • Clinical breast exam should be part of a periodic health exam about every 3 years for women in their twenties and thirties and every year for women 40 and older. • Women should know how their breasts normally feel and report any breast change promptly to their health care providers. Breast self-exam is an option for women starting in their twenties. • Screening MRI is recommended for women with an approximately 20–25% or greater lifetime risk of breast cancer, including women with a strong family history of breast or ovarian cancer and women who were treated for Hodgkin's disease.
Colon and rectum	Beginning at age 50, men and women should begin screening with one of the examination schedules below: • A fecal occult blood test (FOBT) or fecal immunochemical test (FIT) every year • A flexible sigmoidoscopy (FSIG) every 5 years • Annual FOBT or FIT and flexible sigmoidoscopy every 5 years* • A double-contrast barium enema every 5 years • A colonoscopy every 10 years *Combined testing is preferred over either annual FOBT or FIT, or FSIG every 5 years, alone. People who are at moderate or high risk for colorectal cancer should talk with a doctor about a different testing schedule.*
Prostate	The PSA test and the digital rectal examination should be offered annually, beginning at age 50, to men who have a life expectancy of at least 10 years. Men at high risk (African American men and men with a strong family history of one or more first-degree relatives diagnosed with prostate cancer at an early age) should begin testing at age 45. For men at both average risk and high risk, information should be provided about what is known and what is uncertain about the benefits and limitations of early detection and treatment of prostate cancer so that they can make an informed decision about testing.
Uterus	*Cervix:* Screening should begin approximately 3 years after a woman begins having vaginal intercourse, but no later than 21 years of age. Screening should be done every year with regular Pap tests or every 2 years using liquid-based tests. At or after age 30, women who have had three normal test results in a row may get screened every 2 to 3 years. Alternatively, cervical cancer screening with HPV DNA testing and conventional or liquid-based cytology could be performed every 3 years. However, doctors may suggest a woman get screened more often if she has certain risk factors, such as HIV infection or a weak immune system. Women age 70 and older who have had three or more consecutive normal Pap tests in the past 10 years may choose to stop cervical cancer screening. Screening after total hysterectomy (with removal of the cervix) is not necessary unless the surgery was done as a treatment for cervical cancer. *Endometrium:* The American Cancer Society recommends that at the time of menopause all women should be informed about the risks and symptoms of endometrial cancer and strongly encouraged to report any unexpected bleeding or spotting to their physicians. Annual screening for endometrial cancer with endometrial biopsy beginning at age 35 should be offered to women with or at risk for hereditary nonpolyposis colon cancer (HNPCC).
Cancer-related checkup	For individuals undergoing periodic health examinations, a cancer-related checkup should include health counseling and, depending on a person's age and gender, might include examinations for cancers of the thyroid, oral cavity, skin, lymph nodes, testes, and ovaries, as well as for some nonmalignant diseases.

SOURCE: American Cancer Society's *Cancer Facts and Figures 2008.* Copyright © 2008 American Cancer Society, Inc. www.cancer.org. Reprinted with permission.

cells are killed. Occasionally, when an organ is small enough, radioactive seeds are surgically placed inside the cancerous organ to destroy the tumor and then removed later if necessary. Radiation destroys both normal and cancerous cells, but because it can be precisely directed at the tumor it is usually less toxic for the patient than either surgery or chemotherapy, and it can often be performed on an outpatient basis. Radiation may be used as an exclusive treatment or in combination with surgery and/or chemotherapy.

New and Experimental Techniques   Many new and exciting possibilities for cancer therapy promise alternatives to the options of surgery, radiation, and chemotherapy. Although it is impossible to predict which of these new approaches will be most successful, researchers hope that cancer therapy overall will become increasingly safer and more effective.

• *Gene therapy.* Completion of the sequencing of the human genome in 2000 opened a treasure chest of new insights into cancer. Scientists have already discovered important new subtypes of tumors for breast cancer, melanoma, leukemia, and lymphomas based on patterns of gene expression. **Gene therapy** is the manipulation of gene expression in human cells. Gene therapy offers a potential treatment or cure for cancer, as well as for various genetic diseases. For gene therapy to succeed, new genes must be delivered to defective cells without dis-

Avoiding Cancer Quackery

Sometimes conventional treatments for cancer are simply not enough. A patient may be told that there is little conventional therapy can do, other than providing medication to ease pain. When therapy is available, it may be painful and even intolerable to some people. Not surprisingly, many cancer patients look for complementary and alternative therapies. As many as 80% of cancer patients report combining conventional treatments with some type of mind-body technique. A much smaller number of patients look for alternatives to the more conventional therapies. These may be therapies within the bounds of legitimate medical practice that have not yet proven themselves in clinical trials. Or, at the extreme, alternative therapies may be scientifically unsound and dangerous, as well as expensive.

Complementary therapies such as yoga, massage, meditation, music therapy, t'ai chi, and prayer can have positive physical and psychological benefits for patients and help them improve their quality of life as they deal with illness and the often difficult treatments for cancer. Mind-body practices can reduce pain and anxiety, improve sleep, and give people a sense of control and participation in their treatment; such practices may also enhance the immune system. (See Chapter 2 for more on stress and relaxation techniques.) Mind-body practices typically can be used in combination with conventional cancer therapies.

For other types of therapies, the National Cancer Institute suggests that patients and their families consider the following questions when making decisions about cancer treatment:

• *Has the treatment been evaluated in clinical trials?* Advances in cancer treatment are made through carefully monitored clinical trials. If a patient wants to try a new therapy, participation in a clinical trial may be a treatment option. (See For More Information at the end of the chapter for more on clinical trials.)

• *Do the practitioners of an approach claim that the medical community is trying to keep their cure from the public?* No one genuinely committed to finding better ways to treat a disease would knowingly keep an effective treatment secret or try to suppress such a treatment.

• *Does the treatment rely on nutritional or diet therapy as its main focus?* Although diet can be a key risk factor in the development of cancer, there is no evidence that diet alone can get rid of cancerous cells in the body.

• *Do those who endorse the treatment claim that it is harmless and painless and that it produces no unpleasant side effects?* Reputable researchers are working to develop less toxic cancer therapies, but because effective treatments for cancer must be powerful, they frequently have unpleasant side effects.

• *Does the treatment have a secret formula that only a small group of practitioners can use?* Scientists who believe they have developed an effective treatment routinely publish their results in reputable journals so they can be evaluated by other researchers.

Use special caution when evaluating cancer remedies promoted online; one recent study found that as many as one-third of cancer-related alternative medicine sites offered advice that was harmful or potentially dangerous.

One danger of alternative medicine is the very real possibility that proven therapies will be neglected while unproven, faddish alternative approaches are pursued; if alternate therapies delay proven therapies, lives may be lost. Another danger is that complementary therapies may counteract or affect conventional therapies; for example, some herbal supplements have been found to affect how cancer drugs are absorbed and used by the body. Further, some of these alternative therapies are expensive, and many patients are concerned about the cost of unproven therapies. A recent study revealed that 70% of patients using complementary therapies do not inform their physicians. However, it is essential for physicians to have this information so any side effects or harmful interactions can be prevented.

SOURCES: American Cancer Society. 2006. *Complementary and Alternative Therapies* (http://www.cancer.org/docroot/ETO/ETO_5.asp; retrieved February 15, 2009); National Cancer Institute. 2006. *Complementary and Alternative Medicine in Cancer Treatment: Questions and Answers* (http://www.cancer.gov/cancertopics/factsheet/therapy/CAM; retrieved February 15, 2009).

---

turbing the overall functioning of the cells. In the treatment of cancer, gene therapy would "turn off" the genes responsible for causing cells to divide rapidly and become malignant. Using this approach, researchers hope to develop targeted therapies for specific cancers.

• *Bone marrow and stem cell transplants.* In cancers of the blood-forming cells or lymph cells, a patient's own bone marrow may have to be eliminated by radiation or chemotherapy to rid the body of cancer cells. Bone marrow can then be restored by transplanting healthy bone marrow cells from a compatible donor. Transplant incompatibility can be a problem, but progress on this front has been made through the use of **stem cells**. These unique, unspecialized cells can divide and produce more specialized cell types, including bone marrow cells (see Chapter 22). These stem cells can be identified, purified, and grown outside the body and then transplanted back into

TERMS

gene therapy The manipulation of gene expression in human cells; offers a potential treatment or cure for cancer by "turning off" the genes responsible for causing cells to divide rapidly and become malignant.

stem cells Unspecialized cells that can divide and produce cells that differentiate into the many different types of specialized cells in the body (brain cells, muscle cells, skin cells, blood cells, and so on).

the cancer patient. This technique would allow for safe repopulation of bone marrow after radiation.

- *Biological therapies.* Biological therapies are based on enhancing the immune system's reaction to a tumor. Techniques include cancer vaccines, genetic modification of the body's immune cells, and the use of genetically engineered cytokines, which enhance immune cell function. Melanomas seem particularly susceptible to these biological approaches. Cancer vaccines are also under study for kidney cancer, lymphoma, lung cancer, and other cancers.

- *Proteasome inhibitors.* Proteasomes help control the *cell cycle*—the process through which cells divide. If proteasomes malfunction, as is often the case in cancer cells, then cells may begin multiplying out of control. Proteasome inhibitors block the action of proteasomes, halting cell division and killing the cells. One proteasome inhibitor is now being used against certain cancers, and other such drugs are in development.

- *Anti-angiogenesis drugs.* To obtain nutrients, cancer cells signal the body to produce new blood vessels, a process called angiogenesis. Drugs that block angiogenesis could keep tumors from growing and spreading.

- *Enzyme activators/blockers.* Normal cells die after dividing a given number of times. Scientists believe that the enzyme caspase triggers the death of normally functioning cells. In cancer cells, caspase activity may be blocked. Conversely, if the enzyme telomerase becomes active in cancer cells, the life/death cycle stops and the cells duplicate indefinitely. In effect, inactive caspase or active telomerase may make cancer cells "immortal." Researchers are studying compounds that can either activate caspase

or deactivate telomerase; either type of drug might lead cancer cells to self-destruct. No such drugs are now in clinical use.

Living with Cancer

There are nearly 11 million cancer survivors in the United States. The fear of cancer never disappears, however; there is always the risk of a recurrence.

Cancer survivors may suffer economic prejudice from insurers, who can refuse to issue or renew health coverage. This sort of problem can be devastating to a cancer survivor who may be struggling both psychologically and financially to restore a normal existence. Several states have passed legislation to prevent such discrimination.

Psychological support is an important factor during treatment for cancer (see the box "Coping with Cancer"). For some patients, family and friends plus a caring physician or nurse provide all the support that is necessary. For many people, an organized support group can help provide needed social and psychological support.

PREVENTING CANCER

As mentioned throughout this chapter, your lifestyle choices can radically lower your cancer risks (see Figure 16.9). Here are some guidelines:

- *Avoid tobacco.* The bloodstream carries carcinogens from tobacco smoke throughout the body, making

---

Do More

- Eat a varied, plant-based diet that is high in fiber-rich foods such as legumes and whole grains

- Eat 7–13 servings of fruits and vegetables every day, favoring foods from the following categories:
    Cruciferous vegetables
    Citrus fruits
    Berries
    Dark green leafy vegetables
    Dark yellow, orange, or red fruits and vegetables

- Be physically active

- Maintain a healthy weight

- Practice safer sex (to avoid HPV infection)

- Protect your skin from the sun with appropriate clothing and sunscreen

- Perform regular self-exams (breast self-exam, testicular self-exam, skin self-exam)

- Obtain recommended screening tests and discuss with your physician any family history of cancer.

Do Less

- Don't use tobacco in any form:
    Cigarettes
    Spit tobacco
    Cigars and pipes
    Bidis and clove cigarettes

- Avoid exposure to environmental tobacco smoke

- Limit consumption of fatty meats and other sources of saturated fat

- Avoid excessive alcohol consumption

- Limit consumption of salt

- Don't eat charred foods, and limit consumption of cured and smoked meats and meat and fish grilled in a direct flame

- Limit exposure to UV radiation from sunlight or tanning lamps or beds

- Avoid occupational exposure to carcinogens

FIGURE 16.9 Strategies for reducing your risk of cancer.

Coping with Cancer

A cancer diagnosis was once viewed as a death sentence, and patients and families were often left to face their fears alone. People were sometimes reluctant to admit to the diagnosis of cancer or share it with others because of feelings of hopelessness or irrational guilt.

Since about the 1970s, however, a cultural shift has taken place. Improved diagnostic methods and therapies have increased survival times and cures. Media attention on positive developments has created a better understanding of the scientific basis of cancer. Some of the mystery and dread of cancer has begun to abate, leading to a more positive atmosphere for cancer patients and their families.

If You Are the Patient

Each person's experience with cancer is unique, based on his or her own personality and values. Some people turn to their friends and family members for support, whereas others prefer help from other cancer patients, professional counselors, or faith-based groups. If you are a cancer patient, it is important to do what is right for you. Here are some strategies for dealing with difficult emotions that may accompany a cancer diagnosis:

• Remember that cancer doesn't always mean death. Many cancers are curable or controllable for long periods, and survivors may return to a normal, healthy life. Hope and optimism are important elements in cancer survival.

• Focus on controlling what you can. Be informed and involved with your medical care, keep your appointments, and make healthy changes in your lifestyle.

• Work toward having a positive attitude, but don't feel guilty if you can't maintain it all the time. Having cancer is difficult, and low moods will occur no matter how good you are at coping. If they become frequent or severe, seek help.

• Use strategies that have helped you solve problems and manage your emotions in the past. Some people respond to information gathering, talking with others, and prayer or meditation. Physical activity, music, art, and sharing personal stories may help lessen stress.

• Confide feelings and worries to someone close to you. Don't bottle up your feelings to spare your loved ones. If you don't feel comfortable sharing with others, consider expressing your emotions in a journal.

Finding a Support Group

Support groups may be led by cancer survivors, group members, or trained professionals. These groups typically present information, teach coping skills, and give cancer patients a place to share common concerns and obtain emotional support. Support groups may focus on education, behavioral training, or group interaction. Behavioral training can involve meditation and other techniques to reduce stress or the effects of chemotherapy or radiation therapy.

Research has shown that support groups can enhance quality of life in very practical ways. For instance, patients in breast cancer support groups were found to have improved psychological symptoms, less pain, and improved family relationships compared with patients in a control group.

Support groups vary in quality, and people with cancer may find that a support group fails to discuss topics relevant to their personal situation. Some people may find a support group upsetting because it stirs up too many uncomfortable feelings or because the leader is not skilled. Find a group that is right for you.

Online support groups can be very helpful for people living in rural areas or confined to their homes. Medical information on the Internet is highly variable in quality, however, and you should check with your physician before making any decisions based on online information.

Supporting a Person with Cancer

There is no one right way to act with a person facing cancer. Reassure the person of your love, and let him or her know that you are available for both practical and emotional support. A person with cancer may want you to be very involved in treatment or coping, or he or she may want your help in maintaining a more normal

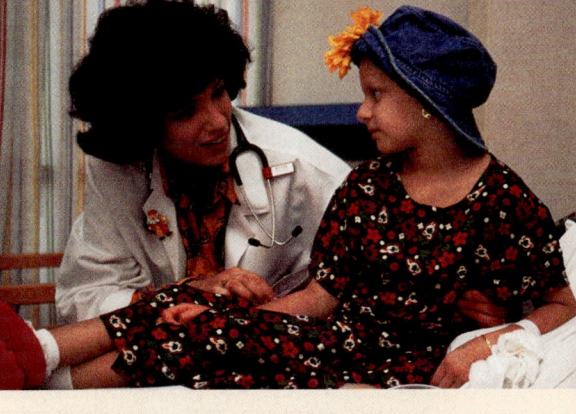

routine. Guidelines for visiting a cancer patient include the following:

• Before you visit, call to ask if it's a good time. Surprise visits are often not welcome. Don't overstay your welcome.

• Be a good listener. Allow the person to express all his or her feelings, and don't discount fears or minimize the seriousness of the situation. Let the patient decide whether the two of you talk about the illness. It's human to want to laugh and talk about other things sometimes.

• Ask "What can I get you?" or "How can I help?" instead of saying "Let me know if I can help." Make specific offers: to clean the bathroom, go grocery shopping, do laundry, or give caregivers a break.

• Refrain from offering advice. You may have heard about the latest treatment or hottest physician, but unless you are asked for suggestions, keep them to yourself.

• If you want to take food, ask about dietary restrictions ahead of time. Use a disposable container so the person won't have to return it.

• Don't be put off if your first visit gets a lukewarm reception. Many cancer victims are on an emotional roller coaster, and their feelings and needs will change over time.

Support groups also exist for friends and family members of cancer patients. These groups give people a place to express their fears about issues such as relationship changes, financial problems, and providing emotional support for the cancer patient.

SOURCES: Kissane, D. W., et al. 2004. Effect of cognitive-existential group therapy on survival in early-stage breast cancer. *Journal of Clinical Oncology* 22(21): 4255–4260; National Cancer Institute. 2002. *Your Mind and Your Feelings After Cancer Treatment* (http://www.cancer.gov/cancerinfo/life-after-treatment/page6; retrieved February 15, 2009); Goodwin, P. J., et al. 2001. The effect of group psychosocial support on survival in metastatic breast cancer. *New England Journal of Medicine* 345(24): 1719–1726; Life with cancer: How to provide support. 1996. *Women's Health Advocate*, September; Holland, J. C. 1996. Cancer's psychological challenges. *Scientific American*, September.

? QUESTIONS FOR CRITICAL THINKING AND REFLECTION

Do you know how to perform self-examinations, such as breast or testicular self-exams? Has your doctor ever suggested that you do so, or given you instructions on proper technique? Given what you know about yourself and your family's medical history, do you think self-exams could be important for you?

smoking a risk for many forms of cancer other than lung cancer. The use of spit tobacco increases the risk of cancers of the mouth, larynx, throat, and esophagus. It is also important to avoid exposure to environmental tobacco smoke.

- *Control diet and weight.* About one-third of all cancers are in some way linked to what we eat. Choose a low-fat, plant-based diet containing a wide variety of fruits, vegetables, and whole grains rich in phytochemicals. Drink alcohol only in moderation, if at all. Maintain a healthy weight.

- *Exercise.* Regular exercise is linked to lower rates of some cancers. It also helps control weight and reduce risk factors for other diseases.

- *Protect your skin.* Almost all cases of skin cancer are sun-related. Wear protective clothing when you're out in the sun, and use a sunscreen with an SPF rating of 15 or higher. Don't go to tanning salons or use tanning booths.

- *Avoid environmental and occupational carcinogens.* Try to avoid exposure to cancer-causing agents in the environment, especially in the workplace. These agents can range from secondhand smoke to pesticides and other chemicals.

Also, follow the American Cancer Society's recommendations for cancer screenings. Your doctor can help you determine the most appropriate timing and methods for screenings.

? QUESTIONS FOR CRITICAL THINKING AND REFLECTION

Review the guidelines just listed for preventing cancer. How many of these things do you do regularly? How often do you think about them? For example, do you often forget to use sunscreen before going outdoors or do you ever hang out in places where people smoke?

TIPS FOR TODAY AND THE FUTURE

A growing body of research suggests that we can take an active role in preventing many cancers by adopting a wellness lifestyle.

RIGHT NOW YOU CAN

- If you are a woman, do a breast self-exam. If you are a man, do a testicular self-exam.
- Buy multiple bottles of sunscreen and put them in places where you will most likely need them, such as your backpack, gym bag, or car.
- Check the cancer screening guidelines in this chapter and make sure you are up-to-date on your screenings.

IN THE FUTURE YOU CAN

- Learn where to find information about daily UV radiation levels in your area, and learn how to interpret the information. Many local newspapers and television stations (and their Web sites) report current UV levels every day.
- Gradually add foods with abundant phytochemicals to your diet.

SUMMARY

- A malignant tumor can invade surrounding structures and spread to distant sites via the blood and lymphatic system, producing additional tumors.

- A malignant cell divides without regard for normal growth. As tumors grow, they produce signs or symptoms that are determined by their location in the body.

- One in two men and one in three women will develop cancer.

- Lung cancer kills more people than any other type of cancer. Tobacco smoke is the primary cause.

- Colon and rectal cancer is linked to age, heredity, obesity, and a diet rich in red meat and low in fruits and vegetables. Most colon cancers arise from preexisting polyps.

- Breast cancer affects about one in seven women in the United States. Although there is a genetic component to breast cancer, diet and hormones are also risk factors.

- Prostate cancer is chiefly a disease of aging; diet and lifestyle probably are factors in its occurrence. Early detection is possible through rectal examinations, PSA blood tests, and sometimes ultrasound.

- Cancers of the female reproductive tract include cervical, uterine, and ovarian cancer. The Pap test is an effective screening test for cervical cancer.

Incorporating More Fruits and Vegetables into Your Diet

When we think about the health benefits of fruits and vegetables, we usually focus on the fact that they are rich in carbohydrates, dietary fiber, and vitamins and low in fat. A benefit that we may overlook is that they contain specific cancer-fighting compounds, phytochemicals, that help slow, stop, or even reverse the process of cancer. The National Cancer Institute (NCI) reports that people who eat five or more servings a day of fruits and vegetables have half the risk of cancer of those who eat less than two; according to the NCI, seven to nine servings or more per day is optimal. The NCI, along with industry groups, has developed a program to help more Americans increase their intake of fruits and vegetables to health-promoting levels—the "Fruits and Veggies Matter" program.

Most Americans need to double the amount of fruits and vegetables they eat every day. Begin by monitoring your diet for 1–2 weeks to assess your current intake; then look for ways to incorporate these foods into your diet in easy and tasty ways. Here are some tips to get you started.

Breakfast

- Drink 100% juice every morning.
- Add raisins, berries, or sliced fruit to cereal, pancakes, or waffles. Top bagels with tomato slices.
- Try a fruit smoothie made from fresh or frozen fruit and orange juice or low-fat yogurt.

Lunch

- Choose vegetable soup or salad with your meal.
- Replace potato chips or french fries with cut-up vegetables.
- Add extra chunks of fruits or vegetables to salads.
- Try adding vegetables such as roasted peppers, cucumber slices, shredded carrots, avocado, or salsa to sandwiches.
- Drink tomato or vegetable juice instead of soda (watch for excess sodium).

Dinner

- Choose a vegetarian main course, such as stir-fry or vegetable stew. Have at least two servings of vegetables with every dinner.
- Microwave vegetables and sprinkle them with a little bit of Parmesan cheese.
- Substitute vegetables for meat in casseroles and pasta and chili recipes.
- At the salad bar, pile your plate with healthy vegetables and use low-fat or nonfat dressing.

Snacks and On the Go

- Keep ready-to-eat-fruits and vegetables on hand (apples, plums, pears, and carrots).
- Keep small packages of dried fruit in the car (try dried apricots, peaches, and pears and raisins).
- Make ice cubes from 100% fruit juice and drop them into regular or sparkling water.
- Freeze grapes for a cool summer treat.

In the Grocery Store

- Stock up on canned, frozen, and dried fruits and vegetables when they go on sale.
- Buy fresh fruits and vegetables in season; they'll taste best and be less expensive.
- To save on preparation time, buy pre-sliced vegetables and fruits and prepackaged salads.
- Try a new fresh fruit or vegetable every week.

The All-Stars

Different fruits and vegetables contribute different vitamins, phytochemicals, and other nutrients, so be sure to get a variety. The following types of produce are particularly rich in nutrients and phytochemicals:

- Cruciferous vegetables (broccoli, cauliflower, cabbage, bok choy, brussels sprouts, kohlrabi, turnips, etc.)
- Citrus fruits (oranges, lemons, limes, grapefruit, tangerines, etc.)
- Berries (strawberries, raspberries, blueberries, etc.)
- Dark green leafy vegetables (spinach, chard, collards, beet greens, kale, mustard greens, romaine and other dark lettuces, etc.)
- Deep yellow, orange, and red fruits and vegetables (carrots, pumpkin, sweet potatoes, winter squash, red and yellow bell peppers, apricots, cantaloupe, mangoes, papayas, etc.)

SOURCES: National Cancer Institute. 2008. *Fruits and Veggies Matter* (http://www.fruitsandveggiesmatter.gov; retrieved February 15, 2009); The produce prescription. 2000. *Consumer Reports on Health,* December; Welland, D. 1999. Fruits and vegetables: Easy ways to five-a-day. *Environmental Nutrition,* June.

- Abnormal cellular changes in the epidermis, often a result of exposure to the sun, cause skin cancer, as does chronic exposure to certain chemicals. Skin cancers occur as basal cell carcinoma, squamous cell carcinoma, and melanoma.

- Oral cancer is caused primarily by smoking, excess alcohol consumption, and use of spit tobacco. Oral cancers are easy to detect but often hard to treat.

- Testicular cancer can be detected early through self-examination.

- Mutational damage to a cell's DNA can lead to rapid and uncontrolled growth of cells; mutagens include radiation, viral infection, and chemical substances in food and air.

- Cancer-promoting dietary factors include meat, certain types of fats, and alcohol.

- Diets high in fruits and vegetables are linked to a lower risk of cancer.

- Other possible causes of cancer include inactivity and obesity, certain types of infections and chemicals, and radiation.

- Self-monitoring and regular screening tests are essential to early cancer detection; early signs can be remembered by using the acronym CAUTION.

- Methods of cancer diagnosis include magnetic resonance imaging, computed tomography, and ultrasound.

- Treatment methods usually consist of some combination of surgery, chemotherapy, and radiation. Gene therapy, bone marrow and stem cell transplants, proteasome inhibitors, biological therapies, and drugs that inhibit angiogenesis or telomerase also hold promise as effective treatments.

- Strategies for preventing cancer include avoiding tobacco; eating a varied, moderate diet and controlling weight; exercising regularly; protecting skin from the sun; avoiding exposure to environmental and occupational carcinogens; and getting recommended cancer screening tests.

FOR MORE INFORMATION

BOOKS

American Cancer Society. 2003. *Cancer: What Causes It. What Doesn't.* Atlanta: American Cancer Society. *Provides basic background information about cancer and its causes.*

American Institute for Cancer Research. 2005. *The New American Plate Cookbook.* Berkeley, Calif.: U.C. Berkeley Press. *Provides guidelines and recipes for healthy eating to prevent cancer and other chronic diseases.*

Hartmann, L. C., C. L. Loprinzi, and B. S. Gostout. 2005. *Mayo Clinic: Guide to Women's Cancers.* New York: Kensington. *Provides information about a variety of women's cancers.*

McKinnell, R. G., et al. 2006. *The Biological Basis of Cancer,* 2nd ed. Boston: Cambridge University Press. *Examines the underlying causes of cancer and discusses actual cases of the disease and its impact on patients and families.*

Rosenbaum, E., et al. 2008. *Everyone's Guide to Cancer Therapy,* rev. 5th ed. Riverside, N.J.: Andrews McMeel. *Reviewed by a panel of more than 100 oncologists; provides articles on the known causes, diagnoses, and treatments for many types of cancer.*

Turkington, C., and W. LiPera. 2005. *The Encyclopedia of Cancer.* New York: Facts on File. *Includes entries on a variety of topics relating to cancer causes, prevention, diagnosis, and treatment.*

ORGANIZATIONS, HOTLINES, AND WEB SITES

American Academy of Dermatology. Provides information on skin cancer prevention.
http://www.aad.org

American Cancer Society. Provides a wide range of free materials on the prevention and treatment of cancer.
http://www.cancer.org

American Institute for Cancer Research. Provides information on lifestyle and cancer prevention, especially nutrition.
http://www.aicr.org

Cancer Guide: Steve Dunn's Cancer Information Page. Links to many good cancer resources on the Internet and advice about how to make best use of information.
http://www.cancerguide.org

Cancer News. Provides links to news and information on many types of cancer.
http://www.cancernews.com

Centers for Disease Control and Prevention: DES Update. Provides information about drugs containing DES and advice for exposed women and DES daughters and sons.
http://www.cdc.gov/DES

Clinical Trials. Information about clinical trials for new cancer treatments can be accessed at the following sites:
http://www.cancer.gov/clinicaltrials
http://www.centerwatch.com

EPA/Sunwise. Information about the UV Index and the effects of sun exposure, with links to sites with daily UV Index ratings for cities in the United States and other countries.
http://www.epa.gov/sunwise/uvindex.html

Food and Drug Administration, Center for Drug Evaluation and Research: Oncology Tools. Provides information about types of cancer, treatments, and clinical trials.
http://www.fda.gov/cder/cancer

Harvard School of Public Health: Disease Risk Index. Includes interactive risk assessments as well as tips for preventing common cancers.
http://www.diseaseriskindex.harvard.edu/update

MedlinePlus Cancer Information. Provides news and links to reliable information on a variety of cancers and cancer treatment.
http://www.nlm.nih.gov/medlineplus/cancers.html

National Cancer Institute. Provides information on treatment options, screening, and clinical trials.
http://www.cancer.gov

National Comprehensive Cancer Network (NCCN). Presents treatment guidelines for physicians and patients related to the treatment of various cancers; these guidelines were developed by a group of leading cancer centers.
http://www.nccn.org

National Toxicology Program. The federal program that creates regular reports listing those substances that are known or reasonably assumed to cause cancer in humans.
http://ntp-server.niehs.nih.gov

New York Online Access to Health (NOAH)/Cancer. Provides information about cancer—causes, symptoms, types, treatments, clinical trials—and links to related sites.
http://www.noah-health.org/en/cancer

Oncolink/The University of Pennsylvania Cancer Center Resources. Contains information on different types of cancer and answers to frequently asked questions.
http://www.oncolink.org

See also the listings in Chapters 10–14.

SELECTED BIBLIOGRAPHY

Abbasi, N. R., et al. 2004. Early diagnosis of cutaneous melanoma. *Journal of the American Medical Association* 292(22): 2771–2776.

American Cancer Society. 2008. *Cancer Facts and Figures 2008.* Atlanta: American Cancer Society.

American Cancer Society. 2008. *Cancer Prevention and Early Detection Facts and Figures 2008.* Atlanta: American Cancer Society.

American Cancer Society. 2006. *Few Americans Know Connection Between Excess Weight and Cancer Risk, Survey Finds* (http://www.cancer.org/docroot/MED/content/MED_2_1x_Few_Americans_Know_Connection_Between_Excess_Weight_and_Cancer_Risk_Survey_Finds.asp; retrieved February 15, 2009).

Baker, S., and J. Kaprio. 2006. Common susceptibility genes for cancer: Search for the end of the rainbow. *British Medical Journal* 332(7550): 1150–1152.

Bjorge, T., S. Tretli, and A. Engeland. 2004. Relation of height and body mass index to renal cell carcinoma in two million Norwegian men and women. *American Journal of Epidemiology* 160(12): 1168–1176.

Brand, T. C., et al. 2006. Prostate cancer detection strategies. *Current Urology Reports* 7(3): 181–185.

Brenner, D. J., et al. 2004. Estimated radiation risks potentially associated with full-body CT screening. *Radiology* 232(3): 735–738.

Centers for Disease Control and Prevention. 2008. Surveillance for cancers associated with tobacco use—United States, 1999–2004. *Morbidity and Mortality Weekly Report Surveillance Summaries* 57(SS-08): 1–33.

Chao, A., et al. 2005. Meat consumption and risk of colorectal cancer. *Journal of the American Medical Association* 293(2): 172–182.

Chia, K. S., et al. 2005. Profound changes in breast cancer incidence may reflect changes into a Westernized lifestyle: A comparative population-based study in Singapore and Sweden. *International Journal of Cancer* 113(2): 302–306.

de Vries, S. H., et al. 2004. Prostate cancer characteristics and prostate specific antigen changes in screening detected patients initially treated with a watchful waiting policy. *Journal of Urology* 172(6 Pt 1): 2193–2196.

Elmore, J. G., et al. 2005. Screening for breast cancer. *Journal of the American Medical Association* 293(10): 1245–1256.

Flood, A., et al. 2005. Calcium from diet and supplements is associated with reduced risk of colorectal cancer in a prospective cohort of women. *Cancer Epidemiology, Biomarkers and Prevention* 14(1): 126–132.

Garland, S. 2006. Efficacy of a quadrivalent HPV (types 6, 11, 16, 18) L1 VLP vaccine against external genital disease: Future 1 analysis. *European Journal of Obstetrics, Gynecology, and Reproductive Biology*, August 16.

Genetics and breast cancer. 2004. *Journal of the American Medical Association* 292(4): 522.

Goff, B. A., et al. 2004. Frequency of symptoms of ovarian cancer in women presenting to primary care clinics. *Journal of the American Medical Association* 291(22): 2705–2712.

Harper, D. M., et al. 2004. Efficacy of a bivalent L1 virus-like particle vaccine in prevention of infection with human papillomavirus types 16 and 18 in young women: A randomised controlled trial. *Lancet* 364(9447): 1757–1765.

Hou, L., et al. 2004. Computing physical activity and risk of colon cancer in Shanghai, China. *American Journal of Epidemiology* 160(9): 860–867.

Jee, S. H., et al. 2005. Fasting serum glucose level and cancer risk in Korean men and women. *Journal of the American Medical Association* 293(2): 194–202.

Jemal, A., et al. 2005. Cancer Statistics, 2005. *CA: A Cancer Journal for Clinicians* 55(1): 10–30.

Kaplan, R. N., et al. 2005. VEGFR1-positive haematopoietic bone marrow progenitors initiate the pre-metastatic niche. *Nature* 438(7069): 820–827.

Kauff, N. D., et al. 2008. Risk-reducing salpingo-oophorectomy for the prevention of BRCA1- and BRCA2-associated breast and gynecologic cancer: A multicenter, prospective study. *Journal of Clinical Oncology* 26(8): 1331–1337.

Kroenke, C. H., et al. 2005. Weight, weight gain, and survival after breast cancer diagnosis. *Journal of Clinical Oncology* 23(7): 1370–1378.

Laaksonen, D. E., et al. 2004. Serum linoleic and total polyunsaturated fatty acids in relation to prostate and other cancers: A population-based cohort study. *International Journal of Cancer* 111(3): 444–450.

Martinez, M. E. 2005. Primary prevention of colorectal cancer: Lifestyle, nutrition, exercise. *Recent Results in Cancer Research* 166: 177–211.

Mayo Clinic. 2006. Skin cancer epidemic. Take steps to avoid sun damage. *Mayo Clinic Health Letter* 24(4): 1–3.

Mayo Clinic. 2008. Bladder cancer: Early discovery, vigilance are key. *Mayo Clinic Health Letter* 26(10): 1–3.

Mayo Clinic. 2008. Breast imaging: Advances in earlier cancer detection. *Mayo Clinic Health Letter* 26(2): 1–3.

Meadows, M. 2004. Cancer vaccines: Training the immune system to fight cancer. *FDA Consumer,* September/October.

Melanoma. 2004. *Journal of the American Medical Association* 292(22): 2800.

Mor, G., et al. 2005. Serum protein markers for early detection of ovarian cancer. *Proceedings of the National Academy of Sciences USA,* May 12 [epub].

National Toxicology Program. 2005. *Report on Carcinogens,* Eleventh Edition. Research Triangle Park, N.C.: National Toxicology Program.

New treatments for colorectal cancer. 2004. *FDA Consumer,* May/June.

Osborn, N. K., and D. A. Ahlquist. 2005. Stool screening for colorectal cancer: Molecular approaches. *Gastroenterology* 128(1): 192–206.

Paik, S., et al. 2004. A multigene assay to predict recurrence of tamoxifen-treated, node-negative breast cancer. *New England Journal of Medicine* 351(27): 2817–2826.

Pelucchi, C., et al. 2004. Fibre intake and prostate cancer risk. *International Journal of Cancer* 109(2): 278–280.

Prostate cancer: Should you still have a PSA test? 2005. *University of California, Berkeley Wellness Letter,* January.

Putt, K. S., et al. 2006. Small-molecule activation of procaspase-3 to caspase-3 as a personalized anticancer strategy. *Nature Chemical Biology,* August.

Roden, R. B., et al. 2004. Vaccination to prevent and treat cervical cancer. *Human Pathology* 35(8): 971–982.

Seeff, L. C., et al. 2004. How many endoscopies are performed for colorectal cancer screening? Results from CDC's survey of endoscopic capacity. *Gastroenterology* 127(6): 1670–1677.

Terry, M. B., et al. 2004. Association of frequency and duration of aspirin use and hormone receptor status with breast cancer risk. *Journal of the American Medical Association* 291(20): 2433–2440.

Trimble, C. L., et al. 2005. Active and passive cigarette smoking and the risk of cervical neoplasia. *Obstetrics and Gynecology* 105(1): 174–181.

University of California, Berkeley, School of Public Health. 2006. Wellness Facts. *Wellness Letter* 22(5): 1.

U.S. Preventive Services Task Force. 2008. Screening for prostate cancer: U.S. Preventive Services Task Force recommendation statement. *Annals of Internal Medicine* 149(3): 185–191.

Van Gils, C. H., et al. 2005. Consumption of vegetables and fruits and risk of breast cancer. *Journal of the American Medical Association* 293(3): 183–193.

Velicer, C. M., et al. 2004. Antibiotic use in relation to the risk of breast cancer. *Journal of the American Medical Association* 291(7): 827–835.

Weinstein, S. J., et al. 2005. Serum alpha-tocopherol and gamma-tocopherol in relation to prostate cancer risk in a prospective study. *Journal of the National Cancer Institute* 97(5): 396–399.

World Health Organization. 2005. *Cancer: Diet and Physical Activity's Impact* (http://www.who.int/dietphysicalactivity/publications/facts/cancer/en/; retrieved Feburary 15, 2009).

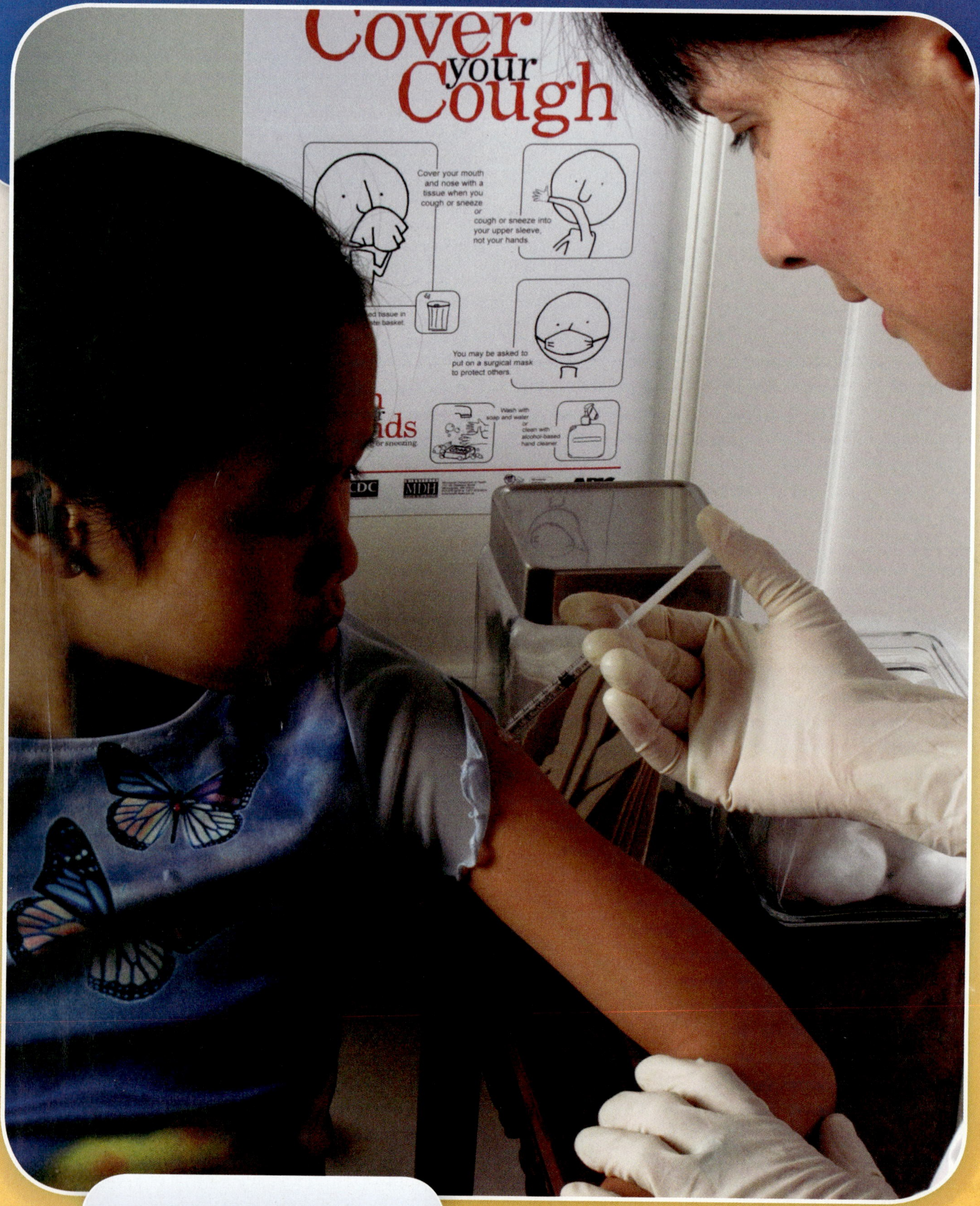

Core Concepts In Health
McGraw Hill connect™
PERSONAL HEALTH

http://www.mcgrawhillconnect.com/personalhealth

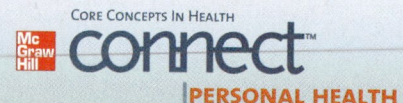

IMMUNITY AND INFECTION

17

LOOKING AHEAD>>>>>

AFTER READING THIS CHAPTER, YOU SHOULD BE ABLE TO:

- Describe the step-by-step process by which infectious diseases are transmitted
- Identify the body's physical and chemical barriers to infection
- Explain how the immune system responds to an invading microorganism
- Identify the major types of pathogens and describe the common diseases they cause
- Discuss steps you can take to prevent infections and strengthen your immune system

TEST YOUR KNOWLEDGE

1. Which of the following can transmit disease-causing pathogens (such as bacteria or viruses) from one person to another?
   a. mosquitoes
   b. doorknobs
   c. soil

2. When taking a prescription antibiotic, you should always finish the entire course of medication, even if you start feeling better before running out of medicine.
   True or false?

3. Which of the following can recognize and eliminate specific microbes (such as bacteria) that invade the body?
   a. antigens
   b. antibodies
   c. antidotes

4. Because medical facilities are sanitary, patients rarely catch bacterial infections in hospitals.
   True or false?

5. You can reduce your chances of getting sick by doing which of the following?
   a. washing your hands frequently
   b. keeping your immunizations up-to-date
   c. getting enough sleep

ANSWERS

1. **ALL THREE.** Pathogens can be transmitted directly (by contact with a sick person) or indirectly (by contact with an infected animal or insect or a contaminated object like a doorknob).

2. **TRUE.** Failing to take all your medication can lead to a relapse of the illness; taking antibiotics incorrectly also contributes to the development of antibiotic-resistant bacteria.

3. **B.** Antibodies are specialized proteins produced by the immune system, which can recognize and target specific invading organisms.

4. **FALSE.** Thousands of people die each year from infections contracted in health care settings.

5. **ALL THREE.** Frequent hand washing prevents the spread of many disease-causing agents. Immunizations prime the body to tackle an invading organism. Sleep helps support a healthy immune system.

ountless microscopic organisms live around, on, and in us. Although most microbes are beneficial, many of them can cause disease. But the constant vigilance of our immune system keeps them at bay and our bodies intact and healthy. The immune system works to keep the body from being overwhelmed, not just by external invaders that cause **infections,** but also by internal changes such as cancer.

Most people don't notice these internal skirmishes unless they become sick. But people today are more knowledgeable about the complexities of immunity because they have heard about or had experience with HIV infection, which directly attacks the immune system. The rise in other infections has caught the public's attention, too. Old scourges like tuberculosis are making comebacks—in stronger, drug-resistant forms.

This chapter introduces you to the mechanisms of immunity and infection, and shows how to keep yourself well in a world of disease-causing microorganisms.

THE CHAIN OF INFECTION

Infectious diseases are transmitted from one person to another through a series of steps—a chain of infection (Figure 17.1). New infections can be prevented by interfering with any step in this process.

Links in the Chain

The chain of infection has six major links: the pathogen, its reservoir, a portal of exit, a means of transmission, a portal of entry, and a new host.

Pathogen　The infectious disease cycle begins with a **pathogen,** a microorganism that causes disease. HIV (the virus that causes AIDS) and the tuberculosis bacterium are examples of pathogens. Many pathogens cause illness because they produce **toxins** that harm human tissue; others do so by directly invading body cells.

Reservoir　The pathogen has a natural environment—called a **reservoir**—in which it typically lives. This reservoir can be a person, an animal, or an environmental component like soil or water. A person who is the reservoir for a pathogen may be ill or may be an asymptomatic carrier who, although having no symptoms, can spread infection.

Portal of Exit　To transmit infection, the pathogen must leave the reservoir through some portal of exit. In the case of a human reservoir, portals of exit include saliva (for mumps, for example), the mucous membranes (for many sexually transmitted diseases), blood (for HIV and hepatitis), feces (for intestinal infections), and nose and throat discharges (for colds and influenza).

Means of Transmission　Transmission can occur directly or indirectly. In direct transmission, the pathogen is passed from one person to another without an intermediary. Direct transmission usually requires fairly close association with an infected host, but not necessarily physical contact. For example, sneezing and coughing can discharge infectious particles into the air, where they can be inhaled by someone nearby. Most common respiratory infections and many intestinal infections are passed directly—for example, when a person with an infectious agent on his or her hands touches someone else. Other means of direct transmission include sexual contact and contact with blood.

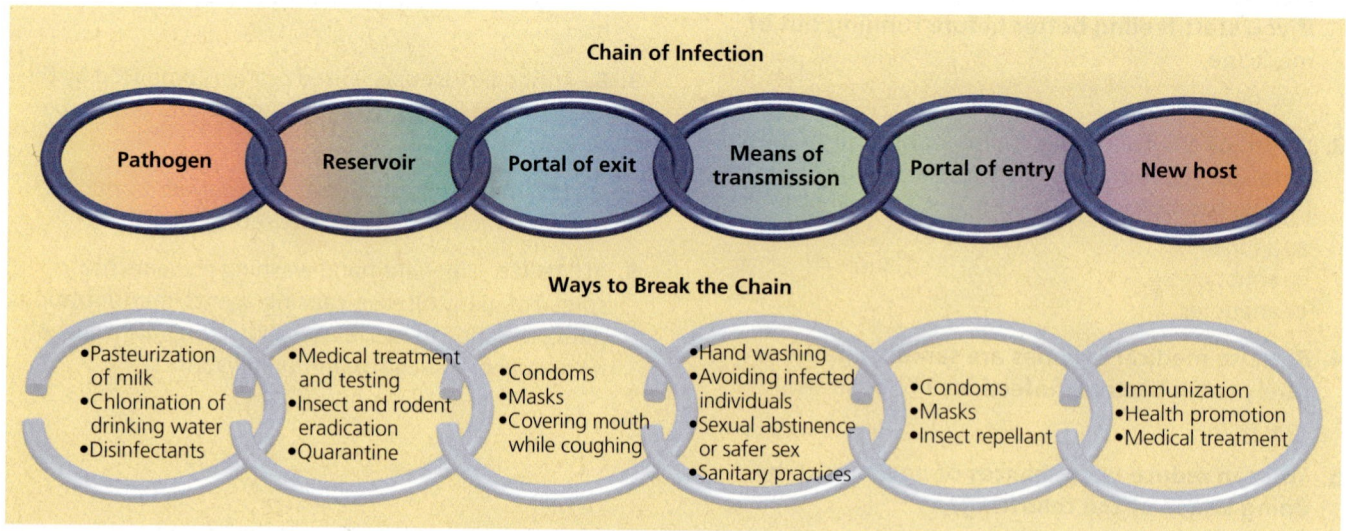

FIGURE 17.1　The chain of infection.　Any break in the chain of infection can prevent disease.

Transmission can also occur indirectly. Animals or insects such as rats, ticks, and mosquitoes can serve as **vectors**, carrying the pathogen from one host to another. Pathogens can also be transmitted via contaminated soil, food, or water or from inanimate objects, such as eating utensils, doorknobs, and handkerchiefs. Some pathogens float in the air for long periods, suspended on tiny particles of dust or droplets that can travel long distances before they are inhaled and cause infection.

Portal of Entry   To infect a new host, a pathogen must have a portal of entry into the body. Pathogens can enter in one of three general ways:

1. Direct contact with or penetration of the skin
2. Inhalation through the mouth or nose
3. Ingestion of contaminated food or water

Pathogens that enter the skin or mucous membranes can cause a local infection of the tissue, or they may penetrate into the bloodstream or lymphatic system, thereby causing a more extensive **systemic infection.** Agents that cause sexually transmitted diseases (STDs) usually enter the body through the mucous membranes lining the urethra (in males) or the cervix (in females). Organisms that are transmitted via respiratory secretions may cause upper respiratory infections or pneumonia, or they may enter the bloodstream and cause systemic infection. Foodborne and waterborne organisms enter the mouth and travel to the location that will best support their reproduction. They may attack the cells of the small intestine or the colon, causing diarrhea, or they may enter the bloodstream via the digestive system and travel to other parts of the body.

The New Host   Once in the new host, a variety of factors determine whether the pathogen will be able to establish itself and cause infection. People with a strong immune system or resistance to a particular pathogen are less likely to become ill than people with poor immunity (the concept of immunity will be discussed later in the chapter). The number of pathogens that enter the new host is also important; the body's defenses may be able to overcome a few bacteria, for example, but may be overwhelmed by thousands. If conditions are right, the pathogen will multiply and produce disease in the new host. In such a case, the new host may become a reservoir from which a new chain of infection can be started.

Breaking the Chain

Interrupting the chain of infection at any point can prevent disease. Strategies for breaking the chain include a mix of public health measures and individual action. For example, a pathogen's reservoir can be isolated or destroyed, as when a sick individual is placed under quarantine or when insects or animals carrying pathogens are killed. Public sanitation practices, such as sewage treatment and the chlorination of drinking water, can also kill pathogens. Transmission can be disrupted through strategies like hand washing and the use of face masks. Immunization and the treatment of infected hosts can stop the pathogen from multiplying, producing a serious disease, and being passed on to a new host. Some methods of breaking the chain of infection are listed in Figure 17.1.

THE BODY'S DEFENSE SYSTEM

Our bodies have very effective ways of protecting themselves against invasion by foreign organisms, especially pathogens. The body's first line of defense is a formidable array of physical and chemical barriers. When these barriers are breached, the body's **immune system** comes into play. Together, these defenses provide an effective response

TERMS

infection   Invasion of the body by a microorganism.

pathogen   A microorganism that causes disease.

toxin   A poisonous substance.

reservoir   A natural environment in which a pathogen typically lives.

vector   An insect, rodent, or other organism that carries and transmits a pathogen from one host to another.

systemic infection   An infection spread by the blood or lymphatic system to large portions of the body.

immune system   The body's collective physical and chemical defenses against foreign organisms and pathogens.

to nearly all the challenges and invasions our bodies will ever experience.

Physical and Chemical Barriers

The skin, the body's largest organ, prevents many microorganisms from entering the body. Although many bacterial and fungal organisms live on the surface of the skin, very few can penetrate it except through a cut or break.

Wherever there is an opening in the body, or an area without skin, other barriers exist. The mouth is lined with mucous membranes, which contain cells designed to prevent the passage of unwanted organisms and particles. Body openings and the fluids that cover them (for example, tears, saliva, and vaginal secretions) are rich in antibodies (discussed in detail later in the chapter) and in enzymes that break down and destroy many microorganisms.

The respiratory tract is lined not only with mucous membranes but also with cells having hairlike protrusions called *cilia*. The cilia sweep foreign matter up and out of the respiratory tract. Particles that are not caught by this mechanism may be expelled from the system by a cough. If the ciliated cells are damaged or destroyed, a cough is the body's only way of ridding the airways of foreign particles. This is one reason smokers generally have a chronic cough—to compensate for damaged airways.

The Immune System

The immune system operates through a remarkable information network involving billions of cellular defenders that rush to protect the body when a threat arises. Once the body has been invaded by a foreign organism, an elaborate system of responses is activated. Two of these responses are the inflammatory response and the immune response.

Immunological Defenders The immune response is carried out by different types of white blood cells, which are continuously being produced in the bone marrow.

- **Neutrophils,** one type of white blood cell, travel in the bloodstream to areas of invasion, attacking and ingesting pathogens.

- **Macrophages,** or "big eaters," take up stations in tissues and act as scavengers, devouring pathogens and worn-out cells.

- **Natural killer cells** directly destroy virus-infected cells and cells that have turned cancerous.

- **Dendritic cells,** which reside in tissues, eat pathogens and activate lymphocytes.

- **Lymphocytes,** of which there are several types, are white blood cells that travel in both the bloodstream and the lymphatic system.

At various places in the lymphatic system there are lymph nodes (or glands), where macrophages and den-

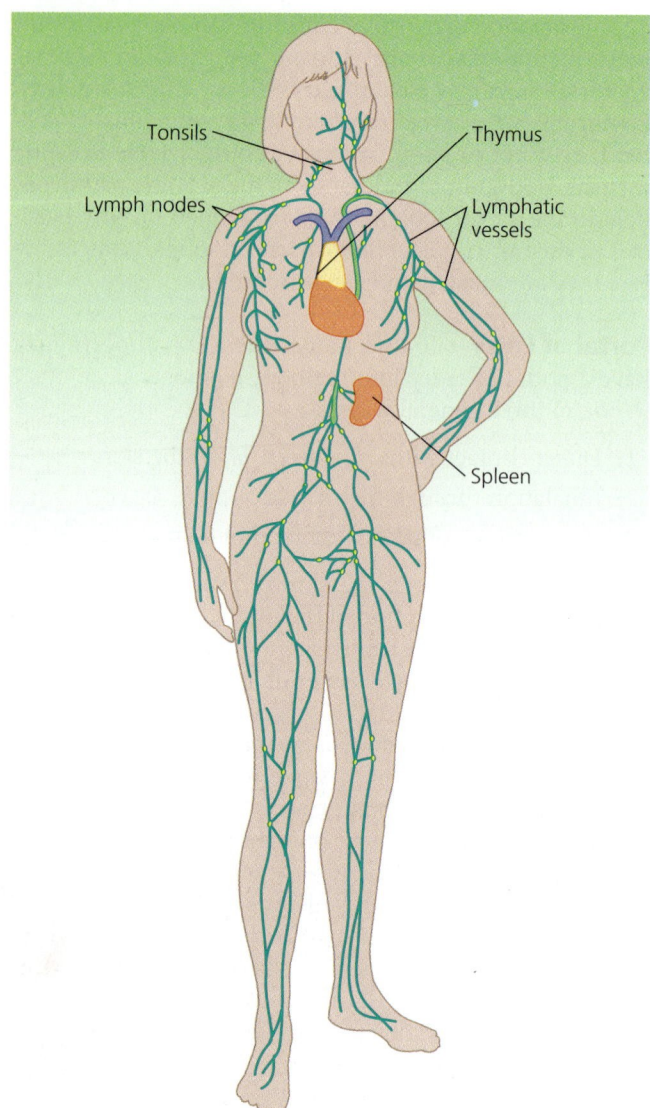

FIGURE 17.2 The lymphatic system. The lymphatic system consists of a network of vessels and organs, including the spleen, lymph nodes, thymus, and tonsils. The vessels pick up excess fluid and proteins, lipids, and other particles from body tissues. These pass through the lymph nodes, where macrophages and dendritic cells help clear the lymph (fluid) of debris and bacteria and other pathogens. The cleansed lymph is then returned to the bloodstream. The lymphatic organs are production centers for infection-fighting cells and sites for some immune responses.

dritic cells congregate and filter bacteria and other substances from the lymph (Figure 17.2). When these nodes are actively involved in fighting an invasion of microorganisms, they fill with cells; physicians use the location of swollen lymph nodes as a clue to the location and cause of an infection.

The two main types of lymphocytes are **T cells** and **B cells.** T cells are further differentiated into **helper T cells, killer T cells,** and **suppressor T cells** (also called *regulatory T cells*). B cells are lymphocytes that produce **antibodies.** The first time T cells and B cells encounter a specific invader, some of them are reserved as **memory T and B cells**, enabling the body to mount a rapid response should the same invader appear again in the future. These cells and cell products—macrophages, natural killer cells, dendritic cells, T cells, B cells and antibodies, and memory cells—are the primary players in the body's immune response.

The immune system is built on a remarkable feature of these defenders: the ability to distinguish foreign cells from the body's own cells. Because lymphocytes are capable of great destruction, it is essential that they not attack the body itself. When they do, they cause **autoimmune diseases**, such as lupus and rheumatoid arthritis.

All the cells in your body display markers on their surfaces—tiny molecular shapes—that identify them as "self" to lymphocytes that encounter them. Invading microorganisms also display markers on their surface; lymphocytes identify these as foreign, or "nonself." Nonself markers that trigger the immune response are known as **antigens**.

Antibodies have complementary surface markers that work with antigens like a lock and key. When an antigen appears in the body, it eventually encounters an antibody with a complementary pattern. The antibody locks onto the antigen, triggering a series of events designed to destroy the invading pathogen. The truly astonishing thing is that the body does not synthesize the appropriate antibody lock after it comes into contact with the antigen key. Rather, antibodies already exist for millions, if not billions, of possible antigens.

The Inflammatory Response When the body has been injured or infected, one of the body's responses is the inflammatory response. Special cells in the area of invasion or injury release **histamine** and other substances that cause blood vessels to dilate and fluid to flow out of capillaries into the injured tissue. This produces increased heat, swelling, and redness in the affected area. White blood cells, including neutrophils, dendritic cells, and macrophages, are drawn to the area and attack the invaders—in many cases, destroying them. At the site of infection there may be *pus*, a collection of dead white blood cells and debris resulting from the encounter.

The Immune Response The immune system makes two types of responses to invading pathogens: natural (innate) and acquired (adaptive).

Neutrophils, macrophages, dendritic cells, and natural killer cells are part of the natural response. They recognize pathogens as "foreign" but have no memory of past infections; they respond the same way no matter how many times a pathogen invades. These cells essentially eat the invaders, destroying them internally. Natural killer cells also destroy infected body cells, breaking the chain of reproduction of a pathogen and helping to stop an infection.

T and B cells are part of the acquired response. They change after one contact with the pathogen, developing a memory for the antigen. If the body is invaded again, they recognize the pathogen and mount a much more potent response.

Think of the immune response as having four phases (Figure 17.3, p. 524). In each phase, the system takes steps to destroy the invader and restore the body to health.

TERMS

neutrophil   A type of white blood cell that engulfs foreign organisms and infected, damaged, or aged cells; particularly prevalent during the inflammatory response.

macrophage   A large phagocytic (cell-eating) cell that devours foreign particles.

natural killer cell   A type of white blood cell that directly destroys virus-infected cells and cancer cells.

dendritic cell   A white blood cell specialized to activate T and B cells.

lymphocyte   A white blood cell that works in both the bloodstream and the lymphatic system.

T cell   A lymphocyte that arises in bone marrow and matures in the thymus (thus its name).

B cell   A lymphocyte that matures in the bone marrow and produces antibodies.

helper T cell   A lymphocyte that helps activate other T cells and may help B cells produce antibodies.

killer T cell   A lymphocyte that kills body cells that have been invaded by foreign organisms; also can kill cells that have turned cancerous.

suppressor T cell   A lymphocyte that inhibits the growth of other lymphocytes; also called *regulatory T cells*.

antibody   A specialized protein, produced by white blood cells, that can recognize and neutralize specific microbes.

memory T and B cells   Lymphocytes generated during an initial infection that circulate in the body for years, remembering the specific antigens that caused the infection and quickly destroying them if they appear again.

autoimmune disease   A disease in which the immune system attacks the person's own body.

antigen   A marker on the surface of a foreign substance that immune system cells recognize as nonself and that triggers the immune response.

histamine   A chemical responsible for the dilation and increased permeability of blood vessels in allergic reactions.

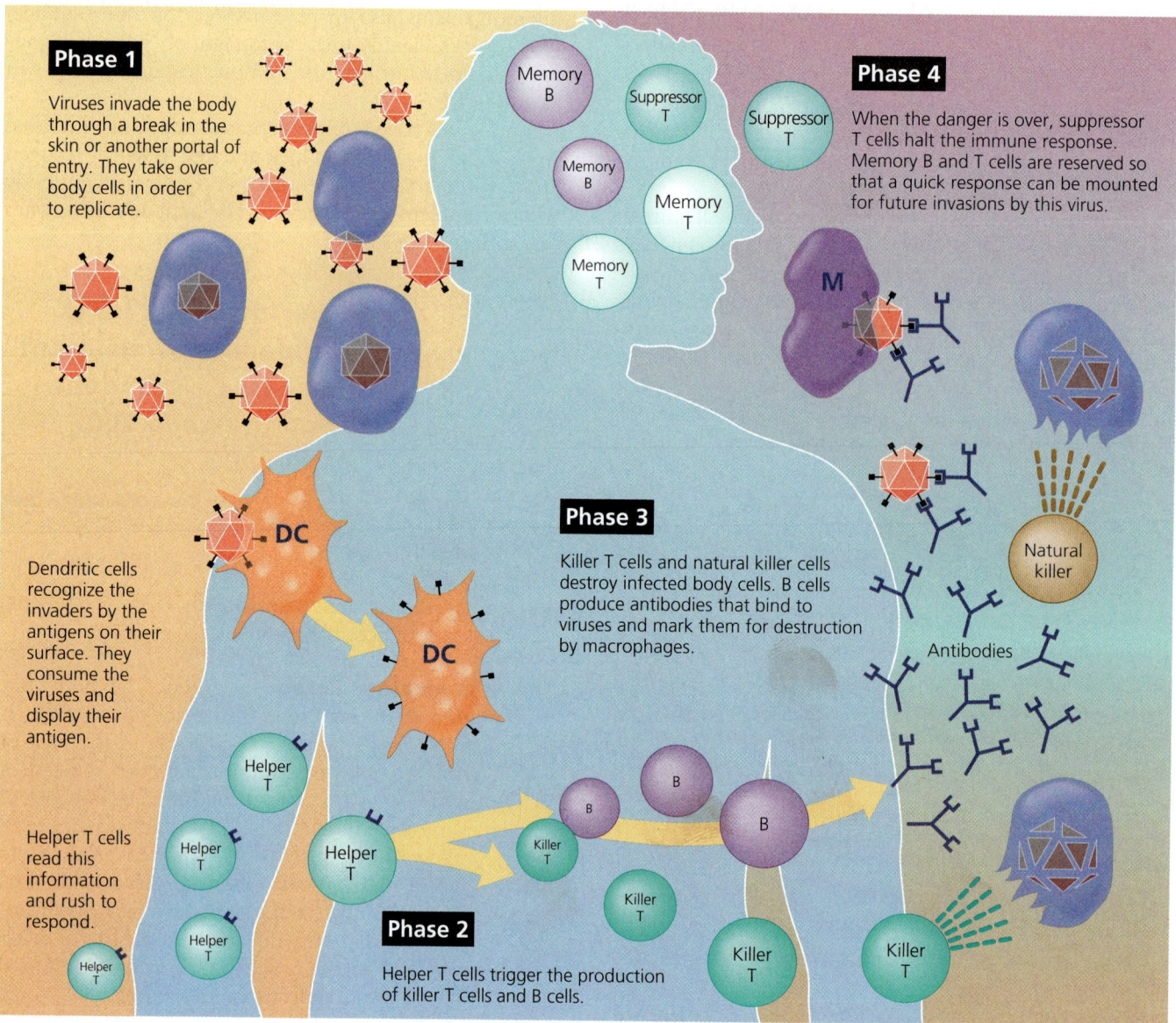

Phase 1

Viruses invade the body through a break in the skin or another portal of entry. They take over body cells in order to replicate.

Dendritic cells recognize the invaders by the antigens on their surface. They consume the viruses and display their antigen.

Helper T cells read this information and rush to respond.

Phase 2

Helper T cells trigger the production of killer T cells and B cells.

Phase 3

Killer T cells and natural killer cells destroy infected body cells. B cells produce antibodies that bind to viruses and mark them for destruction by macrophages.

Phase 4

When the danger is over, suppressor T cells halt the immune response. Memory B and T cells are reserved so that a quick response can be mounted for future invasions by this virus.

Memory B · Suppressor T · Memory B · Memory T · Memory T · Suppressor T · Memory T · M · Natural killer · Antibodies · DC · DC · Helper T · Helper T · Helper T · Helper T · Helper T · Killer T · B · B · B · Killer T · Killer T · Killer T · Killer T

FIGURE 17.3 **The immune response.** Once invaded by a pathogen, the body mounts a complex series of reactions to eliminate the invader. Pictured here are the principal elements of the immune response to a virus; not shown are the many types of cytokines that help coordinate the actions of different types of defenders.

- *Phase 1.* Dendritic cells are drawn to the site of the injury and consume the foreign cells; they then provide information about the pathogen by displaying its antigen on their surfaces. Helper T cells read this information and rush to respond.

- *Phase 2.* Helper T cells multiply rapidly and trigger the production of killer T cells and B cells in the spleen and lymph nodes. **Cytokines,** chemical messengers secreted by lymphocytes, help regulate and coordinate the immune response; *interleukins* and *interferons* are two examples of cytokines. They stimulate increased production of T cells, B cells, and antibodies; promote the activities of natural killer cells; produce fever; and have special antipathogenic properties themselves.

- *Phase 3.* Killer T cells strike at foreign cells and body cells that have been invaded and infected, identifying them by the antigens displayed on the cell surfaces. Puncturing the cell membrane, they sacrifice body cells in order to destroy the foreign organism within. This type of action is known as a *cell-mediated immune response,* because the attack is carried out by cells. Killer T cells also trigger an amplified inflammatory response and recruit more macrophages to help clean up the site.

  B cells work in a different way. Stimulated to multiply by helper T cells, they produce large quantities of antibody molecules, which are released in the bloodstream and tissues. Antibodies are Y-shaped protein molecules that bind to antigen-bearing targets and mark them for destruction by macrophages. This type of response is known as an *antibody-mediated immune response.* Antibodies work against bacteria and against viruses and other substances when they are in the body but outside cells. They do not work against infected body cells or viruses that are replicating inside cells.

- *Phase 4.* The last phase of the immune response is a slowdown of activity. During the course of the immune response, regulatory molecules and cells inhibit lymphocyte proliferation and induce lymphocyte death; this process restores "resting" levels of B and T cells. The dead cells, killed pathogens, and other debris that result from the immune response are scavenged by certain types of white blood cells; filtered out of circulation by the liver, spleen, and kidneys; and excreted from the body.

Immunity After an infection, survival often confers **immunity;** that is, an infected person will never get the same illness again. This is because some of the lymphocytes created during the second phase of the immune response are reserved as memory T and B cells. As part of the acquired immune response, they continue to circulate in the blood and lymphatic system for years or even for the rest of the person's life. If the same antigen enters the body again, the memory T and B cells recognize and destroy it before it can cause illness. This subsequent response takes only a few days to initiate and prevents illness. The ability of memory lymphocytes to remember previous infections is known as **acquired immunity.**

Symptoms and Contagion The immune system is operating at the cellular level at all times, maintaining its vigilance when you're well and fighting invaders when you're sick. How does it all feel to you, the host for these activities? How do your symptoms relate to the course of the infection and the immune response?

During **incubation,** when viruses are multiplying in the body or when bacteria are actively multiplying before

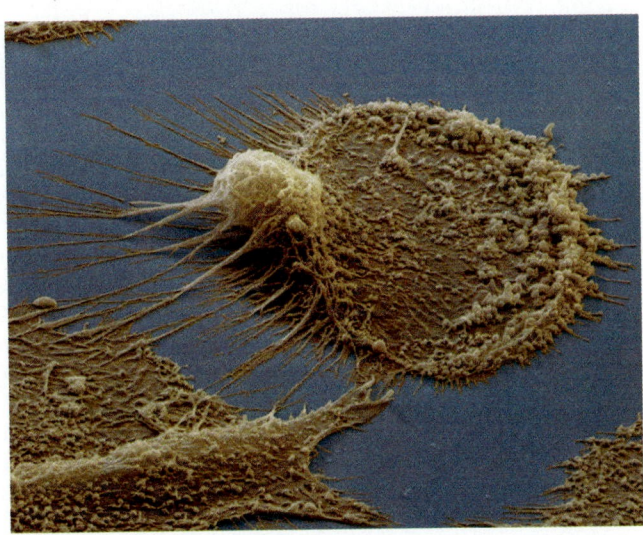

Dendritic cells are white blood cells that engulf foreign cells and display their antigens, thereby activating T and B cells. The dendritic cell shown in this scanning electron micrograph is magnified 2700 times.

the immune system has gathered momentum, you may not have any symptoms of the illness, but you may be contagious. During the second and third phases of the immune response, you may still be unaware of the infection, or you may "feel a cold coming on." Symptoms first appear during the prodromal period, which follows incubation. If the infected host has acquired immunity, the infection may be eradicated during the incubation period or the prodromal period. In this case, although you may have felt you were coming down with a cold, for example, it does not develop into a full-blown illness.

Many symptoms of an illness are actually due to the immune response of the body rather than to the actions or products of the invading organism. For example, fever is caused by the release and activation of certain cytokines in macrophages and other cells during the immune response. These cytokines travel in the bloodstream to the brain and cause the body's thermostat to be reset to a higher level. The resulting elevated temperature helps the body in its fight against pathogens by enhancing immune responses. (During an illness, it is necessary to lower a fever only if it is uncomfortably high [over 101.5°F] or if it occurs in an infant who is at risk for seizures from fever.)

Similarly, you get a runny nose when your lymphocytes destroy infected mucosal cells, leading to increased mucus production. The malaise and fatigue of the flu are caused by pro-inflammatory cytokines.

You are contagious when there are infectious microbes in your body and they can gain access to another person. This may be before a

cytokine A chemical messenger produced by a variety of cell types that helps regulate many cell functions; immune system cells release cytokines that help amplify and coordinate the immune response.

immunity Mechanisms that defend the body against infection; specific defenses against specific pathogens.

acquired immunity The body's ability to mobilize the cellular memory of an attack by a pathogen to throw off subsequent attacks; acquired through vaccination as well as the normal immune response.

incubation The period when bacteria or viruses are actively multiplying inside the body's cells; usually a period without symptoms of illness.

TERMS

27 common diseases can be prevented by vaccines.

—CDC, 2007

QUICK STATS

Table 17.1 — Immunizations for Children and Adults

Vaccine	People for Whom Immunization Is Recommended
Diphtheria	All children; booster shots recommended every 10 years
H. influenzae type b (Hib)	All children (protects against meningitis); older children and adults who have had a splenectomy or bone marrow transplant, have sickle cell disease or HIV/AIDS, or are undergoing immunosuppressant drug therapy
Hepatitis A	All children at age 1 year; injection drug users, men who have sex with men, people with clotting factor disorder or chronic liver disease, travelers to certain countries, and others at risk
Hepatitis B	All children (at birth, if possible) and unvaccinated adolescents; adults at risk, including health care workers, household contacts and sex partners of infected people, injection drug users, people with HIV or another STD, adults who have more than one sex partner, and men who have sex with men
Human papillomamvirus (HPV)	Girls age 11–12; may be given to girls as young as 9 and women through age 26 (3 doses)
Influenza	Annual vaccination for all children and teens age 6 months–18 years, caregivers of children age 6–59 months; adults age 50 and older; nursing home residents; anyone with heart, lung, or other chronic disorders (including asthma and diabetes) and others at high risk; women who will be pregnant during the influenza season; children age 6 months and over with certain risk factors; anyone over age 6 months who wishes to reduce risk of influenza; people who are immunosuppressed
Measles and mumps	All children; unvaccinated adults born after 1956 who are not immune (those who received only one dose or were vaccinated between 1963 and 1967 may need revaccination); people in high-risk groups
Meningococcal conjugate	All children at age 11–18 years or at high-school entry, unvaccinated first-year college students living in dormitories, military recruits, and others at increased risk
Pertussis (whooping cough)	All children; booster shots recommended every 10 years
Pneumococcal polysaccharide	Adults age 65 and older; anyone with chronic heart or lung disease or with no functional spleen; others at high risk, including Alaska Natives and certain American Indian groups
Pneumococcal conjugate	All children; people with chronic illness, including chronic heart, lung, kidney, or liver disease, diabetes, HIV/AIDS, sickle cell disease; anyone with a suppressed immune system
Polio	All children; adults at risk, including certain laboratory and health care workers, and travelers to polio-endemic countries
Rotavirus	All children age 6 weeks–8 months
Rubella (German measles)	All children; unvaccinated adults who are not immune, especially women
Tetanus (lockjaw)	All children; booster shots recommended every 10 years (sooner if more than 5 years has elapsed since the previous booster and the individual has a contaminated wound)
Varicella-zoster (chicken pox)	Children over age 12 months; unvaccinated adolescents and adults who have not had chicken pox
Zoster (shingles)	Unvaccinated persons age 60 and older, regardless of their history of chicken pox or shingles

For international travelers, all standard childhood immunizations should be up to date and additional vaccines considered. Further information is available from the CDC's National Immunization Program (800-232-2522; http://www.cdc.gov/nip) and the CDC's Travel Information (877-394-8747; http://www.cdc.gov/travel).

SOURCES: Centers for Disease Control and Prevention. 2009. *Recommended immunization schedules for persons aged 0 through 18 years—United States, 2009. Morbidity and Mortality Weekly Report* 57(51): Q1–Q4. Centers for Disease Control and Prevention. 2009. *Recommended adult immunization schedule—United States, 2009. Morbidity and Mortality Weekly Report* 57(53): Q1–Q4..

vigorous immune response has occurred, so at times you may be contagious before experiencing any symptoms. This means that you can transmit an illness without knowing you're infected or catch an illness from someone who doesn't appear to be sick. On the other hand, your symptoms may continue after the pathogens have been mostly destroyed, when you are no longer infectious.

Immunization

The ability of the immune system to remember previously encountered organisms and retain its strength against them is the basis for **immunization.** When a person is immunized, the immune system is primed with an antigen similar to the pathogenic organism but not as dangerous. The body responds by producing antibodies, which prevent serious infection when and if the person is exposed to the disease organism itself. The preparations used to manipulate the immune system are known as **vaccines** (Table 17.1).

immunization The process of conferring immunity to a pathogen by administering a vaccine.

vaccine A preparation of killed or weakened microorganisms, inactivated toxins, or components of microorganisms that is administered to stimulate an immune response; a vaccine protects against future infection by the pathogen.

allergy A disorder caused by the body's exaggerated response to foreign chemicals and proteins; also called *hypersensitivity.*

TERMS

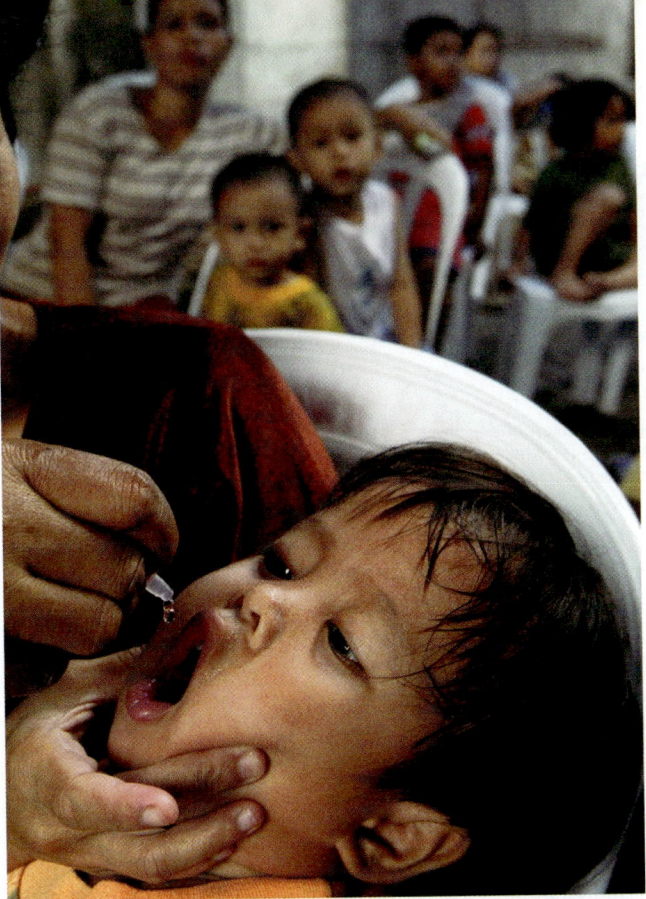

Oral vaccines have made it easier to immunize children in remote and impoverished areas of the world.

VACCINE SHORTAGES IN THE UNITED STATES Periodic shortages of influenza vaccine make the headlines, but flu vaccine is not the only one occasionally in short supply. There have been temporary shortages of most childhood vaccines in the past 5 years. Contributing factors include insufficient vaccine stockpiles, manufacturing and production problems, and the limited number of companies involved in vaccine production. Vaccines are expensive to develop and produce, carry high liability, and return relatively low profits. The influenza vaccine, which must be changed each year to match the viral strains in circulation and takes months to produce, may be particularly vulnerable to supply problems.

VACCINE SAFETY Side effects from immunization are usually mild, such as soreness at the injection site. It is estimated that an allergic reaction may occur in 1 in 1.5 million doses. Any risk from vaccines must be balanced against the risk posed by the diseases they prevent; for example, the death rate from diphtheria is about 5–10%.

The CDC monitors reports of adverse reactions to vaccines, and new formulations or types of vaccines are being developed to increase safety. For example, oral polio vaccine, which contains live but weakened polio virus, has been replaced by inactivated polio virus, which contains killed virus. The oral vaccine is somewhat more effective, but in about 1 in 2.4 million cases, it causes polio; because of the low risk for polio in the United States, the oral vaccine is no longer used.

A possible link has also been proposed between immunization and autism, a severe developmental disorder characterized by behavioral problems and impaired social and communication skills. However, a 2004 Institute of Medicine report concluded that evidence does not support such a link; a large 2006 study confirmed this conclusion. Thimerosol, a mercury-containing preservative, was withdrawn from pediatric vaccines beginning in 1999, although no clear link has been found between thimerosol-containing vaccines and autism.

> Worldwide, **2.1 million** people (mostly young children) die annually of vaccine-preventable diseases.
>
> —WHO, 2005

 QUICK STATS

Types of Vaccines

Vaccines can be made in several ways. In some cases, microbes are cultured in the laboratory in a way that attenuates (weakens) them. These live, attenuated organisms are used in vaccines against diseases such as measles, mumps, and rubella (German measles). In other cases, when it is not possible to breed attenuated organisms, vaccines are made from pathogens that have been killed in the laboratory but that still retain their ability to stimulate the production of antibodies. Vaccines composed of killed viruses are used against influenza viruses, among others.

Vaccines confer what is known as *active immunity*—that is, the vaccinated person produces his or her own antibodies to the microorganism. Another type of injection confers *passive immunity*. In this case, a person exposed to a disease is injected with the antibodies themselves, produced by other human beings or animals who have recovered from the disease. Injections of gamma globulin—a product made from the blood plasma of many individuals containing all the antibodies they have ever made—are sometimes given to people to create a rapid but temporary immunity to a particular disease. Gamma globulin is also sometimes used to treat antibody deficiency syndromes.

Immunization Concerns

Potential shortages and safety are areas of concern related to vaccines.

Allergy: The Body's Defense System Gone Haywire

An estimated 50 million Americans are affected by **allergies**. Allergies result from a hypersensitive and overactive immune system. The immune system typically defends the body against only genuinely harmful pathogens such

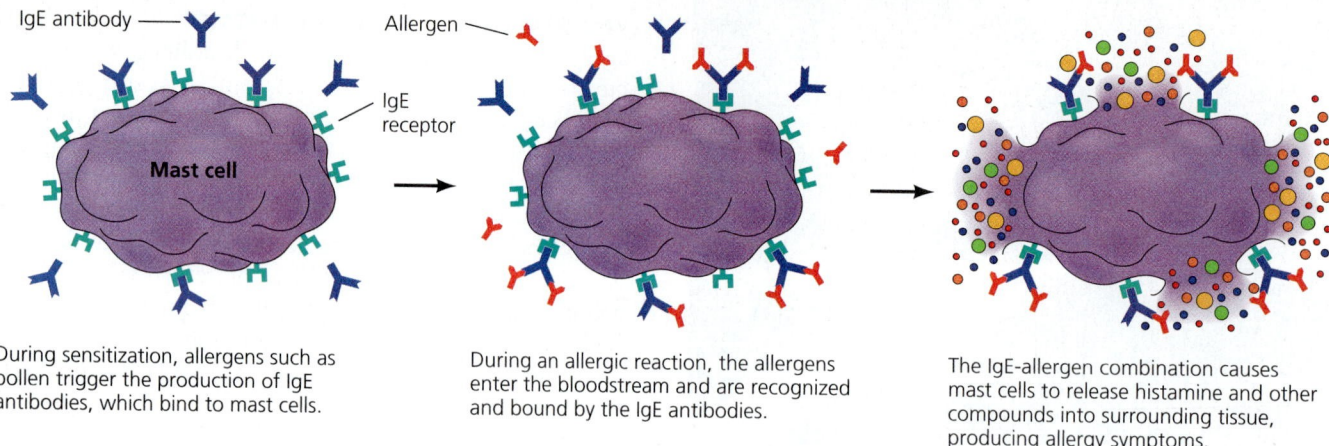

During sensitization, allergens such as pollen trigger the production of IgE antibodies, which bind to mast cells.

During an allergic reaction, the allergens enter the bloodstream and are recognized and bound by the IgE antibodies.

The IgE-allergen combination causes mast cells to release histamine and other compounds into surrounding tissue, producing allergy symptoms.

FIGURE 17.4   The allergic response.

as viruses and bacteria. However, in someone with an allergy, the immune system also mounts a response to a harmless substance such as pollen or animal dander. Allergy symptoms—stuffy nose, sneezing, wheezing, skin rashes, and so on—result primarily from the immune response rather than from the substances that provoke the response.

Allergens   Substances that provoke allergies are known as **allergens;** they may cause a response if they are inhaled or swallowed or if they come in contact with the skin. Different people have allergic reactions to different substances, but more than half of Americans age 6–59 react to at least one common allergen. Common allergens include the following:

- *Pollen:* Referred to as hay fever or allergic rhinitis, pollen allergies are widespread; weeds, grasses, and trees are common producers of allergenic pollen.

- *Animal dander:* People with animal allergies are usually allergic not to fur but to dander (dead skin flakes), urine, or a protein found in saliva; allergies to mice, dogs, and/or cats are common.

- *Dust mites and cockroaches:* The droppings of cockroaches and microscopic dust mites can trigger allergies; mites live in carpets, upholstered furniture, and bedding.

- *Molds and mildew:* The small spores produced by these fungi can trigger allergy symptoms; molds and mildew thrive in damp areas of buildings.

- *Foods:* The most common food allergens in adults include peanuts, tree nuts, fish, and shellfish.

- *Insect stings:* The venom of insects such as yellow jackets, honeybees, hornets, paper wasps, and fire ants causes allergic reactions in some people.

People may also be allergic to certain medications, plants such as poison oak, latex, metals such as nickel, and compounds found in cosmetics.

The Allergic Response   Most allergic reactions are due to the production of a special type of antibody known as immunoglobulin E (IgE). Initial exposure to a particular allergen may cause little response, but it sensitizes the immune system by causing the production of allergen-specific IgE, which binds to mast cells (Figure 17.4). Mast cells are part of the immune system and play a role in healing, the immune response, and allergic reactions. When the body is subsequently exposed to the allergen, the allergen binds to IgE, causing the mast cells to release large amounts of histamine and other compounds into surrounding tissues.

Histamine has many effects, including increasing the inflammatory response and stimulating mucus production. The precise symptoms depend on what part of the body is affected. In the nose, histamine may cause congestion and sneezing; in the eyes, itchiness and tearing; in the skin, redness, swelling, and itching; in the intestines, bloating and cramping; and in the lungs, coughing, wheezing, and shortness of breath. In some people, an allergen can trigger an asthma attack (see the box "Poverty, Ethnicity, and Asthma"). Symptoms often occur immediately, within minutes of exposure, but inflammatory reactions may take hours or days to develop and then may persist for several days.

The most serious, but rare, kind of allergic reaction is **anaphylaxis,** which results from a release of histamine throughout the body. Anaphylactic reactions can be life-threatening because symptoms may include swelling of

TERMS

allergen   A substance that triggers an allergic reaction.

anaphylaxis   A severe systemic hypersensitive reaction to an allergen characterized by difficulty breathing, low blood pressure, heart arrhythmia, seizure, and sometimes death.

Poverty, Ethnicity, and Asthma

Asthma is caused by both inflammation of the airways and spasm of the muscles surrounding the airways. The spasm causes constriction, and the inflammation causes the airway linings to swell and secrete extra mucus, which further obstructs the passages. The inflammation can become chronic, making airways even more sensitive to triggers. The symptoms of asthma—wheezing, tightness in the chest, and shortness of breath—may be mild and occur only occasionally, or they may be severe and occur daily.

An asthma attack begins when something sets off inflammation of the bronchial tubes. Usually it's an allergic reaction to an inhaled allergen, most commonly dust mites, mold, animal dander, or pollen. Anything that irritates or overtaxes the bronchial airways can also trigger spasms: exercise, cold air, pollutants, tobacco smoke, infection, or stress. In female asthmatics, hormonal changes that occur as menstruation starts may increase vulnerability to attacks.

Patterns and Prevalence

The prevalence of asthma is increasing. In the United States, more than 13.8 million adults and 6.2 million children have asthma; each year, asthma is responsible for almost 2 million emergency department visits and more than 4200 deaths. Since 1980, the number of Americans with asthma has more than doubled, and despite better treatment options, the death rate has nearly tripled.

The tendency to develop asthma may be hereditary, but some patterns appear to link it to ethnicity and socioeconomic status. Particularly affected are African Americans, American Indians, and Alaska Natives; people living in inner cities; children; and people older than age 65. Asian and Pacific Islander Americans have a relatively low incidence of asthma. African Americans' risk of being hospitalized with asthma is four times greater than that of other ethnic groups; blacks are five times more likely to die from asthma.

Much of the difference between ethnic groups disappears when poverty is factored in. People with low incomes are more often exposed to underlying risk factors and to attack triggers—higher levels of indoor air pollutants and allergens—in part because they may live in poorly ventilated housing and spend more time indoors. Higher levels of outdoor air pollution are also typically found in poor neighborhoods. Cockroach and mouse allergies are important causes of asthma-related illness among children in inner-city areas.

Treatment and Prevention of Attacks

Inhaling a muscle-relaxing medication from a bronchodilator can relieve an asthma attack immediately by opening the bronchial tubes. Inhaling an anti-inflammatory drug can treat the underlying inflammation. Both types of treatments may be needed to get asthma under control. Other medications for asthma block the actions of molecules involved in the body's inflammatory response. Asthmatics can monitor their condition by self-testing their peak air flow several times a day; a drop in peak air flow can signal an upcoming attack.

It's also a good idea to avoid allergens when possible. A recent study of urban children found that relatively small changes can reduce asthma symptoms and health care visits. In this study, allergen exposures were reduced by covering the mattresses and pillows with special covers; by using HEPA filters in vacuum cleaners and room air purifiers; and by employing professional pest control. Other researchers have found that many children with asthma live in households in which simple allergen-control methods haven't been taken, including closing windows to keep pollen out, avoiding environmental tobacco smoke, and reducing or eliminating exposure to pets.

SOURCES: Centers for Disease Control and Prevention. 2007. National surveillance for asthma: United States, 1980–2004. *Morbidity and Mortality Weekly Reports Surveillance Summaries* 56(SS-08): 1–14, 18–54; National Center for Health Statistics. 2008. *Early Release of Selected Estimates Based on Data from the January–September 2007 National Health Interview Survey.* Hyattsville, Md.: National Center for Health Statistics.

the throat, extremely low blood pressure, fainting, heart arrhythmia, and seizures. Anaphylaxis is a medical emergency, and treatment requires immediate injection of epinephrine. People at risk for anaphylaxis should wear medical alert identification and keep self-administrable epinephrine readily available.

Dealing with Allergies If you suspect you might have an allergy, visit your physician or an allergy specialist. There are three general strategies for dealing with allergies:

- *Avoidance:* You may be able to avoid or minimize exposure to allergens by making changes in your environment or behavior. For example, removing carpets from the bedroom and using special bedding can reduce dust mite contact. Pollen exposure can be limited by avoiding outdoor activities during peak pollination times, keeping windows shut, and showering and changing clothes following outdoor activities. If you can't part with a pet, keep pets out of bedrooms and frequently vacuum or damp-mop floors.

- *Medication:* A variety of medications are available for allergy sufferers. Many over-the-counter antihistamines are effective at controlling symptoms such as blocked nasal, sinus, or middle ear passages. Prescription corticosteroids delivered by aerosol markedly reduce allergy symptoms, increase effectiveness, and help limit systemic absorption and side effects.

- *Immunotherapy:* Referred to as "allergy shots," immunotherapy desensitizes a person to a particular allergen through the administration of gradually increasing doses of the allergen over a period of months or years.

PATHOGENS AND DISEASE

When pathogens enter body tissue, they can cause illness and sometimes death to the host. Worldwide, infectious diseases are responsible for more than 11 million deaths each year (Table 17.2).

Pathogens include bacteria, viruses, fungi, protozoa, parasitic worms, and prions (Figure 17.5). Infections can occur almost anywhere in or on the body. Common types of infection include bronchitis, infection of the airways (bronchi); meningitis, infection of the tissue surrounding the brain and spinal cord; conjunctivitis, infection of the layer of cells surrounding the eyes; pharyngitis, or sore throat; pneumonia, infection of the lung; gastroenteritis, infection of the gastrointestinal tract; cellulitis, infection of the soft tissues; osteomyelitis, infection of the bones; and so on, for every tissue and organ.

Bacteria

The most abundant living things on earth are **bacteria,** single-celled organisms that usually reproduce by split-

Table 17.2	Top Infectious Diseases Worldwide	
Disease		**Approximate Number of Deaths per Year**
Pneumonia		3,884,000
HIV/AIDS		2,777,000
Diarrheal diseases		1,798,000
Tuberculosis		1,566,000
Malaria		1,272,000
Measles		611,000
Pertussis (whooping cough)		294,000
Tetanus		214,000
Meningitis		173,000
Syphilis		157,000

Many of the 618,000 deaths from liver cancer each year can be traced to viral hepatitis. Overall, infectious diseases kill more than 11 million people each year, representing nearly 19% of all deaths.

SOURCE: World Health Organization. 2004. *The World Health Report 2004.* Geneva: World Health Organization.

ting in two to create a pair of identical cells. Many species of bacteria feed on dead matter and play an important role in the recycling of nutrients for other organisms; other species feed on living things and may cause disease. Bacteria are often classified according to their shape: they may be bacilli (rod-shaped), cocci (spherical), spirochete (spiral-shaped), or vibrios (comma-shaped).

We harbor both helpful and harmful bacteria on our skin and in our gastrointestinal and reproductive tracts. The human colon contains friendly bacteria that produce certain vitamins and help digest nutrients. (A large portion of feces consists of bacteria.) Friendly bacteria also keep harmful bacteria in check by competing for food and resources and secreting substances toxic to pathogenic bacteria. For example, *Lactobacillus acidophilus* resides in the vagina and produces chemicals that kill yeast and bacteria that cause vaginal infections.

Not all bacteria found in the body are beneficial, however. Pathogenic bacteria in food or drink can disrupt the normal harmony in the intestines by invading cells or producing damaging toxins. Sexual activity can introduce pathogenic bacteria into the reproductive tract. Within the bloodstream, tissues, and organs, the human body is usually aseptic—devoid of bacteria. If bacteria find their way into these areas, infection may result.

Pneumonia Inflammation of the lungs, called **pneumonia,** may be caused by infection with bacteria, viruses, or fungi or by contact with chemical toxins or irritants. Pneumonia can be serious if the alveoli (air sacs) become clogged with fluid, thus preventing oxygen from reaching the bloodstream. Pneumonia often follows another illness, such as a cold or the flu, but the symptoms are typi-

Type of Organism	Selected Pathogens	Associated Diseases
Bacteria Microscopic single-celled organisms 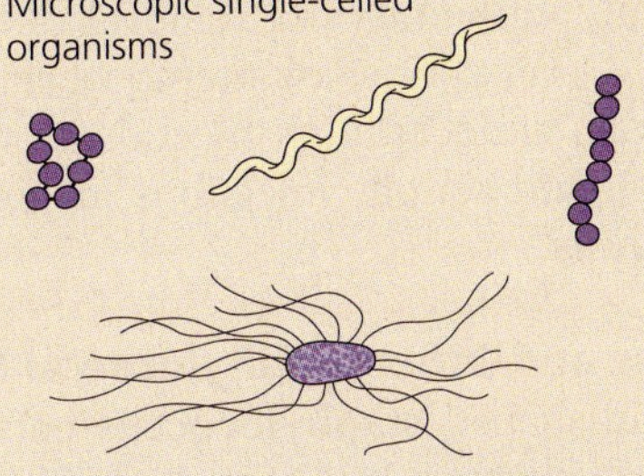	*Bordetella pertussis* *Borrelia burgdorferi* *Chlamydia* *Clostridium tetani* *Helicobacter pylori* *Legionella pneumophila* *Mycobacterium tuberculosis* Mycoplasma *Neisseria* Rickettsia Staphylococcus Streptococcus	Pertussis (whooping cough) Lyme disease Pneumonia (*C. pneumoniae*), chlamydia (*C. trachomatis*) Tetanus Peptic ulcers Legionnaire's disease Tuberculosis Pneumonia, ear infections, sore throat, urethritis Gonorrhea (*N. gonorroeae*), meningitis (*N. meningitidis*) Rocky Mountain spotted fever, typhus Boils and other skin infections, toxic shock syndrome Strep throat, skin infections, pneumonia, rheumatic fever and rheumatic heart disease, necrotizing fascitis
Viruses Infectious agents consisting of a protein shell enclosing DNA or RNA 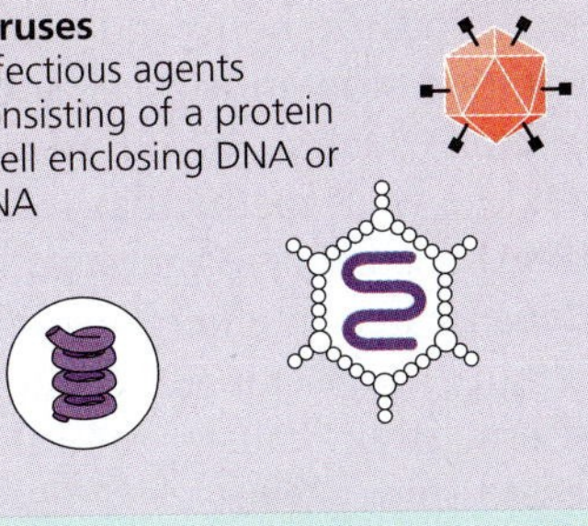	Coronavirus, rhinovirus Epstein-Barr virus Hepatitis viruses Herpes simplex 1 and 2 Human immunodeficiency virus Human papillomaviruses Influenza viruses A and B Paramyxovirus Rhabdovirus Togavirus Varicella-zoster	Severe acute respiratory syndrome (SARS), common cold Infectious mononucleosis Hepatitis (inflammation of the liver) Cold sores, genital herpes HIV/AIDS Warts, cervical cancer Flu Measles, mumps Rabies Rubella Chicken pox, shingles
Fungi Single- or multicelled organisms (e.g., yeasts, molds) 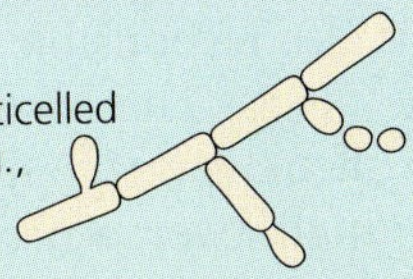	*Candida albicans* *Cryptococcus neoformans* Dermatophyte fungi *Histoplasma capsulatum* *Coccidioides immitis*	Yeast infections, thrush Pneumonia, meningitis Athlete's foot, jock itch, ringworm, nail infections Histoplasmosis Coccidioidomycosis
Protozoa Single-celled organisms 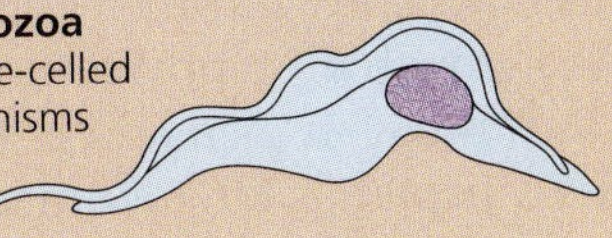	*Entamoeba histolytica* *Giardia lamblia* *Plasmodia* *Trichomonas vaginalis* *Trypanosoma brucei*	Amoebic dysentery Giardiasis Malaria Trichomoniasis African sleeping sickness
Parasitic worms Worms that feed and live on or in a host 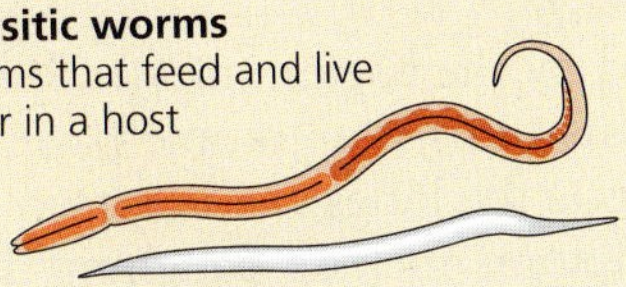	*Ancylostoma duodenale* *Ascaris lumbricoides* Beef, pork, or fish tapeworms *Enterobius vermicularis* *Necator americanus* Schistosoma	Ancylostomiasis (hookworm infection) Ascariasis (roundworm infection) Tapeworm infection Pinworm infection Hookworm infection Cercarial dermatitis (swimmer's itch), schistosomiasis
Prions Proteinaceous infectious particles	PrP^{Sc}	Creutzfeldt-Jakob disease (CJD)

FIGURE 17.5 Pathogens and associated infectious diseases.

cally more severe—fever, chills, shortness of breath, increased mucus production, and cough. Pneumonia ranks eighth among the leading causes of death for Americans; people most at risk for severe infection include those under age 2 and over age 75 and those with chronic health problems such as heart disease, asthma, or HIV. Bacterial pneumonia can be treated with antibiotics.

Pneumococcus bacteria are the most common cause of bacterial pneumonia; a vaccine is available and recommended for all adults age 65 and older and others at risk. Other bacteria that may cause pneumonia include *Streptococcus pneumoniae*, *Chlamydia pneumoniae*, and **mycoplasmas.** Outbreaks of infection with mycoplasmas are relatively common among young adults, especially in crowded settings such as dormitories.

QUICK STATS

56,000 Americans die from pneumonia each year.

—National Center for Health Statistics, 2008

Meningitis Infection of the *meninges*, the membranes covering the brain and spinal cord, is called **meningitis.**

Viral meningitis is usually mild and goes away on its own; bacterial meningitis, however, can be life-threatening and requires immediate treatment with antibiotics. Symptoms of meningitis include fever, a severe headache, stiff neck, sensitivity to light, and confusion. Before the 1990s, *Haemophilus influenzae* type b (Hib) was the leading cause of bacterial meningitis, but routine vaccination of children has reduced the occurrence of Hib meningitis. Today, *Neisseria meningitidis* and *Streptococcus pneumoniae* are the leading causes of bacterial meningitis.

In the United States, about 2700 cases of meningitis are reported each year, although the actual number is probably higher. The disease is fatal in 10% of cases, and about 10–20% of people who recover have permanent hearing loss or other serious effects. Worldwide, meningitis kills about 170,000 people each year, particularly in the so-called meningitis belt in sub-Saharan Africa.

A vaccine is available, but it is not effective against all strains of meningitis-causing bacteria. The CDC recommends routine vaccination of children 11–18 years old, previously unvaccinated adolescents at high school entry, and first-year college students who live in dormitories.

Strep Throat and Other Streptococcal Infections

The **streptococcus** bacterium is spherical-shaped and often grows in chains. Streptococcal pharyngitis, or strep throat, is characterized by a red, sore throat with white patches on the tonsils, swollen lymph nodes, fever, and headache. It is typically spread through close contact with an infected person via respiratory droplets (sneezing or coughing). If left untreated, strep throat can develop into the more serious rheumatic fever (see Chapter 15). Other streptococcal infections include scarletina (scarlet fever), characterized by a sore throat, fever, bright red tongue, and a rash over the upper body; impetigo, a superficial skin infection most common among children; and erysipelas, inflammation of skin and underlying tissues.

A particularly virulent type of streptococcus can invade the bloodstream, spread to other parts of the body, and produce dangerous systemic illness. It can also cause a serious but rare infection of the deeper layers of the skin, a condition called necrotizing fascitis, or "flesh-eating strep." This dangerous infection is characterized by tissue death and is treated with antibiotics and removal of the infected tissue or limb. Other species of streptococci are implicated in pneumonia, endocarditis (infection of the heart lining and valves), and serious infections in pregnant women and newborns.

Toxic Shock Syndrome and Other Staphylococcal Infections

The spherical-shaped **staphylococcus** bacterium often grows in small clusters. It is commonly found on the skin and in the nasal passages of healthy people. Occasionally, staphylococci enter the body and cause an infection, ranging from minor skin infections such as boils to very serious conditions such as blood infections and pneumonia. The strain known as methicillin-resistant *Staphylococcus aureus* (MRSA) has become the most common cause of skin infections treated in emergency rooms (see the box "MRSA: The Superbug?" for more information). This antibiotic-resistant strain causes painful skin lesions that resemble infected spider bites.

Staphylococcus aureus is also responsible for many cases of toxic shock syndrome (TSS). The bacteria produce a deadly toxin that causes shock (potentially life-threatening low blood pressure), high fever, a peeling skin rash, and inflammation of several organ systems. TSS was first diagnosed in women using highly absorbent tampons, which appear to allow the growth of staphylococci; however, about half of all cases occur in men and in women not using tampons. (See Chapter 6 for information on toxic shock syndrome as it relates to contraception.)

Tuberculosis

Caused by the bacterium *Mycobacterium tuberculosis,* **tuberculosis (TB)** is a chronic bacterial infection that usually affects the lungs. TB is spread via the respiratory route. Symptoms include coughing, fatigue, night sweats, weight loss, and fever.

Ten to 15 million Americans have been infected with, and therefore continue to carry, *M. tuberculosis.* Only about 10% of people with latent TB infections actually develop an active case of the disease; their immune system prevents the disease from becoming active. In the United States, active TB is most common among people infected with HIV, recent immigrants from countries where TB is **endemic,** and those who live in the inner cities. In 2007, about 13,300 cases of TB were reported in the United States—the lowest annual incidence of TB since incidence tracking began in 1953. Worldwide, about 2 billion people—one-third of the population—are infected with TB, and each year about 8.9 million develop active TB and more than 1.5 million die.

Many strains of tuberculosis respond to antibiotics, but only over a course of treatment lasting 6–12 months. Failure to complete treatment can lead to relapse and the development of strains of antibiotic-resistant bacteria. Of par-

TERMS

streptococcus Any of a genus (*Streptococcus*) of spherical bacteria; streptococcal species can cause skin infections, strep throat, rheumatic fever, pneumonia, scarlet fever, and other diseases.

staphylococcus Any of a genus (*Staphylococcus*) of spherical, clustered bacteria commonly found on the skin or in the nasal passages; staphylococcal species may enter the body and cause conditions such as boils, pneumonia, and toxic shock syndrome.

tuberculosis (TB) A chronic bacterial infection that usually affects the lungs.

endemic Persistent and relatively widespread in a given population.

MRSA: The Superbug?

Staph infections are certainly nothing new; people have been dealing with minor staph infections for generations. In fact, the CDC estimates that as many as 30% of people carry the staphylococcus (staph) bacteria in their bodies. Most of us come into contact with the germ many times during our lives, usually with little or no consequences.

In recent years, however, an antibiotic-resistant strain of staph—called methicillin-resistant *Staphylococcus aureus* (MRSA)—has changed the public's perception of staph as a relatively harmless germ. Medical experts have dubbed MRSA a "superbug" because it is highly resistant to several first-line medicines normally used to treat staph infections. These drugs include methicillin, penicillin, oxacillin, and amoxicillin, among others.

MRSA is not only virulent, it can be deadly. The CDC estimates that more Americans died from MRSA infections (18,650) than from AIDS (16,000) in 2005. That year, the CDC says that more than 94,000 Americans suffered from severe, invasive MRSA infections. Other estimates, however, say the number is much higher.

About 85% of MRSA infections affect patients in health care facilities or who have recently left a health care setting. Health care–associated MRSA victims typically have undergone an invasive surgical procedure or have an immune system weakened by illness or treatment for another disease. Experts say invasive MRSA is now the leading cause of surgical site infections, bloodstream infections, and pneumonia in hospitals and nursing homes.

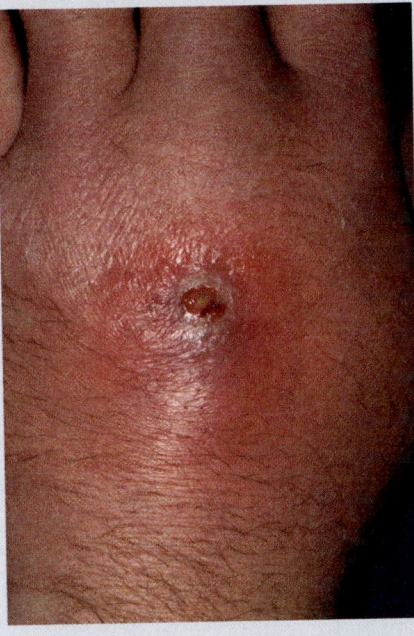

Although less common, MRSA also affects people who have not been exposed to a health care facility; such infections are called *community-associated MRSA (CA-MRSA)* infections. CA-MRSA usually is not invasive, meaning it doesn't enter the soft tissues under the skin. Instead, most community-associated infections take the form of surface abscesses and pus-filled lesions. Even though their numbers are low, community-based infections are a growing concern because they may indicate that MRSA is gaining strength "in the wild," making it more difficult to manage.

In the age of antibiotics, it's hard to imagine being infected by a germ that can't be killed. But epidemiologists say the overuse of antibiotics is one of the main reasons that bugs such as MRSA

have become so strong. When people take antibiotics inappropriately or incorrectly, as Americans have been doing for decades, bacteria have an opportunity to adapt. As a result, they can become resistant to antibiotics and the drugs lose their effectiveness.

Doctors also say that MRSA is a powerful reminder of a valuable lesson: Wash your hands. Frequent hand washing may be the most effective way to avoid infections—not just from MRSA, but from a host of other germs. Other simple but important methods for preventing infections also apply to MRSA. They include the following:

- When washing your hands, use lots of soap and scrub briskly for at least 15 seconds.

- If soap and water aren't available, carry an alcohol-based hand sanitizer with you and use it often.

- Keep your hands away from your face.

- If you have an open wound, keep it clean, dry, and covered with a bandage.

- Don't share items such as towels, razors, and tweezers; they can harbor germs and spread infection.

- If you have a skin lesion that resembles a spider bite, have it checked by a physician right away.

SOURCES: Centers for Disease Control and Prevention. 2007. Invasive MRSA (http://www.cdc.gov/ncidod/dhqp/ar_mrsa_Invasive_FS.html; retrieved February 16, 2009); Klevens, R. M., et al. 2007. Invasive methicillin-resistant *Staphylococcus aureus* infections in the United States. *Journal of the American Medical Association* 298(15): 1763–1771.

---

ticular concern is the emergence of *M. tuberculosis* with extensive resistance to second-line drugs. These drugs are more toxic than first-line drugs—the drugs primarily used against bacterial infections. From 2000 to 2004, 20% of TB bacteria isolated in labs were multidrug resistant (MDR) and 2% were extensively drug resistant (XDR). XDR TB is geographically widespread, occurring even in the United States, and is a serious threat to public health.

Tickborne Infections Some diseases are transmitted via insect vectors. Lyme disease is one such infection, and

it accounts for more than 95% of all reported vectorborne illness in the United States—more than 23,000 cases per year. It is spread by the bite of a tick of the genus *Ixodes* that is infected with the spiral-shaped bacterium *Borrelia burgdorferi*. Ticks acquire the spirochete by ingesting the blood of an infected animal; they can then transmit the microbe to their next host. The deer tick is responsible for transmitting Lyme disease bacteria to humans in the northeastern and north-central United States; on the Pacific Coast, the culprit is the western black-legged tick (Figure 17.6). Lyme disease has been reported in 48 states,

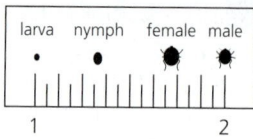

FIGURE 17.6 Deer tick (actual size).

but significant risk of infection is found in only about 100 counties in 10 states located in the northeastern and mid-Atlantic seaboard, the upper north-central region, and parts of northern California.

Symptoms of Lyme disease vary but typically occur in three stages. In the first stage, about 80% of victims develop a bull's-eye-shaped red rash expanding from the area of the bite, usually about 2 weeks after the bite occurs. The second stage occurs weeks to months later in 10–20% of untreated patients; symptoms may involve the nervous and cardiovascular systems and can include impaired coordination, partial facial paralysis, and heart rhythm abnormalities. These symptoms usually disappear on their own within a few weeks. The third stage, which occurs in about half of untreated people, can develop months or years after the tick bite and usually consists of chronic or recurring arthritis. Lyme disease can also cause fetal damage or death at any stage of pregnancy. Lyme disease is treatable at all stages, although arthritis symptoms may not completely resolve. Lyme disease is preventable by avoiding contact with ticks or by removing a tick before it has had the chance to transmit the infection.

Rocky Mountain spotted fever and typhus are caused by the *rickettsias* bacterium and are also transmitted via tick bites. Rocky Mountain spotted fever is characterized by sudden onset of fever, headache, and muscle pain, followed by development of a spotted rash. Ehrlichiosis, another tickborne disease, typically causes less severe symptoms.

Ulcers About 25 million Americans suffer from ulcers, sores in the lining of the stomach or the first part of the small intestine (duodenum). Some ulcers are caused by long-term use of nonsteroidal anti-inflammatory drugs (NSAIDs). In addition, up to 90% of ulcers are caused by infection with *Helicobacter pylori*. Ulcer symptoms include gnawing or burning pain in the abdomen, nausea, and loss of appetite. If tests show the presence of *H. pylori*, antibiotics often cure the infection and the ulcers.

Other Bacterial Infections The following are a few of the many other infections caused by bacteria:

- *Tetanus:* Also known as lockjaw, tetanus is caused by the bacterium *Clostridium tetani,* which thrives in deep puncture wounds and produces a deadly toxin. The toxin causes muscular stiffness and spasms, and infection is fatal in about 30% of cases. Due to widespread vaccination, tetanus is rare in the United States. Worldwide, however, more than 200,000 people die from tetanus each year,

primarily newborns infected through the unsterile cutting of the umbilical cord.

- *C. diff:* Another type of *Clostridium* bacteria, called *Clostridium difficile (C. diff),* has joined MRSA as a major emerging threat in American health care settings. Several varieties of *C. diff* have been known to exist for decades, and generally cause illnesses ranging from diarrhea to life-threatening colitis. Most *C. diff* bugs do their harm by damaging the mucous lining of the intestine. Since 2000, however, one specific strain of *C. diff*—named NAP1 by the Centers for Disease Control and Prevention—has emerged as a growing problem in hospitals. The NAP1 variant of *C. diff* is especially dangerous because it produces multiple toxins and generates them many times faster than other types of *C. diff*. Further, NAP1 is resistant to a wide range of antibiotics. Some experts describe the trend in *C. diff* NAP1 infections as an epidemic because infections are increasing at a rate of about 10% annually. Most *C. diff* infections occur in hospitals and commonly strike people who are already being treated with antibiotics for other infections. However, community-based infections are also on the rise, indicating that *C. diff* is spread via person-to-person contact. Infections from *C. diff* NAP1 have been reported in 37 states and result in 300,000–500,000 hospitalizations a year. More than 2% of infected people die from the disease, and the death rate has doubled over the past 5 years. The infection can be treated with a few powerful antibiotics, and treatment is most successful when the infection is caught early. The best ways to avoid *C. diff* infection are to wash your hands frequently and take antibiotics only when absolutely necessary.

- *Pertussis:* Also known as whooping cough, pertussis is a highly contagious respiratory illness caused by a toxin produced by the bacterium *Bordetella pertussis*. Pertussis is characterized by bursts of rapid coughing, followed by a long attempt at inhalation that is often accompanied by a high-pitched whoop; symptoms may persist for 2–8 weeks. The number of U.S. cases has risen steadily over the past two decades, to more than 11,000 cases per year. Those at high risk include infants and children who are too young to be fully vaccinated and those who have not completed the primary vaccination series. Adolescents and adults become susceptible when immunity from vaccination wanes, so a booster shot is recommended at 11–12 years or during adolescence and thereafter every 10 years. Adults account for about 28% of whooping cough cases.

- *Urinary tract infections (UTIs):* Infection of the bladder and urethra is most common among sexually active women but can occur in anyone. The bacterium *Escherichi coli* is the most common infectious agent, responsible for about 80% of all UTIs. Infection most often occurs when bacteria from the digestive tract that live on the skin around the anus get pushed toward the opening of the urethra during sexual intercourse; then, the bacteria travel up the urethra and into the bladder. Women who are particularly susceptible may be given a supply of antibiotics

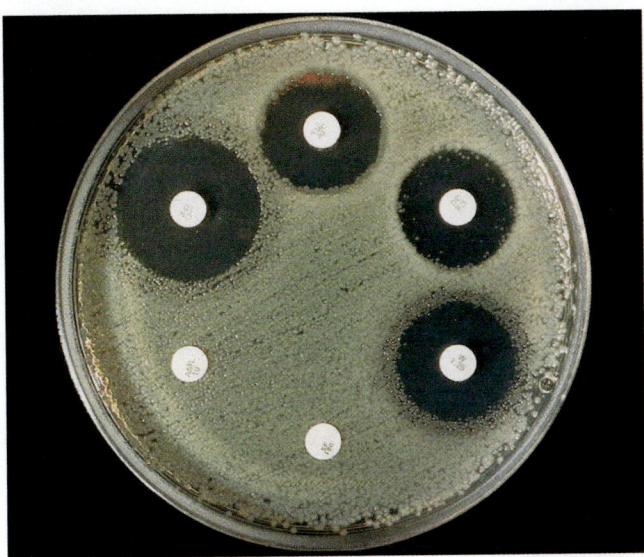

One of the dangers of antibiotic overuse is the development of bacteria resistant to drugs. Cultures of *E. coli* (a bacterium normally present in the human intestine) in this laboratory dish are sensitive to four different types of antibiotics, as indicated by the wide circles where no bacteria are growing, but they are resistant to two other types, which have no effect on their growth.

to use after intercourse or at the first sign of infection; urinating before and after intercourse may also help prevent UTIs.

Bacteria responsible for foodborne illness are described in Chapter 12; Chapter 18 discusses sexually transmitted bacterial infections such as chlamydia.

Antibiotic Treatments The body's immune system can fight off many, if not most, bacterial infections. However, while the body musters its defenses, some bacteria can cause a great deal of damage: Inflammation, caused by the gathering of white blood cells, may lead to scarring and permanently damaged tissues. To help the body deal with these infections, science and medicine have made a considerable contribution: antibiotics.

ACTIONS OF ANTIBIOTICS Antibiotics are both naturally occurring and synthetic substances that can kill bacteria. Most antibiotics work in a similar fashion: They interrupt the production of new bacteria by damaging some part of their reproductive cycle or by causing faulty parts of new bacteria to be made. Penicillins inhibit the formation of the cell wall when bacteria divide to form new cells. Other antibiotics inhibit the production of certain proteins by the bacteria, and still others interfere directly with the reading of genetic material (DNA) during the process of bacterial reproduction. Antibiotics are among the most widely prescribed and effective drugs.

ANTIBIOTIC RESISTANCE When antibiotics are misused or overused, the pathogens they are designed to treat can become resistant to their effects. A bacterium can become resistant from a chance genetic mutation or through the transfer of genetic material from one bacterium to another. When exposed to antibiotics, resistant bacteria can grow and flourish, while the antibiotic-sensitive bacteria die off. Eventually, an entire colony of bacteria can become resistant to one or more antibiotics and can become very difficult to treat. Antibiotic-resistant strains of many common bacteria have developed, including strains of gonorrhea (an STD) and salmonellosis (a foodborne illness). One strain of tuberculosis is resistant to seven different antibiotics. Antibiotic resistance is a major factor contributing to the recent rise in problematic infectious diseases.

The more often bacteria encounter antibiotics, the more likely they are to develop resistance. Resistance is promoted when people fail to take the full course of an antibiotic or when they inappropriately take antibiotics for viral infections. Another possible source of resistance is the use of antibiotics in agriculture, which is estimated to account for 50–80% of the 25,000 tons of antibiotics used annually in the United States. At least four species of antibiotic-resistant bacteria are documented to have been transmitted from food animals to humans. In 2002, the FDA issued guidelines to the pharmaceutical industry regarding the use of new antibiotics in food-producing animals. Limits may be placed on the use in animals of drugs used in human medicine as last resorts for serious or life-threatening disease.

You can help prevent the development of antibiotic-resistant strains of bacteria by using antibiotics properly:

- Don't take an antibiotic every time you get sick. They are mainly helpful for bacterial infections; they are ineffective against viruses.

- Use antibiotics as directed, and finish the full course of medication even if you begin to feel better. This helps ensure that all targeted bacteria are killed off.

- Never take an antibiotic without a prescription. If you take an antibiotic for a viral infection, take the wrong one, or take an insufficient dose, your illness will not improve, and you'll give bacteria the opportunity to develop resistance.

Viruses

Visible only with an electron (high-magnification) microscope, **viruses** lack all the enzymes essential to energy production and protein synthesis in normal animal cells,

antibiotics Synthetic or naturally occurring substances used as drugs to kill bacteria.

virus A very small infectious agent composed of nucleic acid (DNA or RNA) surrounded by a protein coat; lacks an independent metabolism and reproduces only within a host cell.

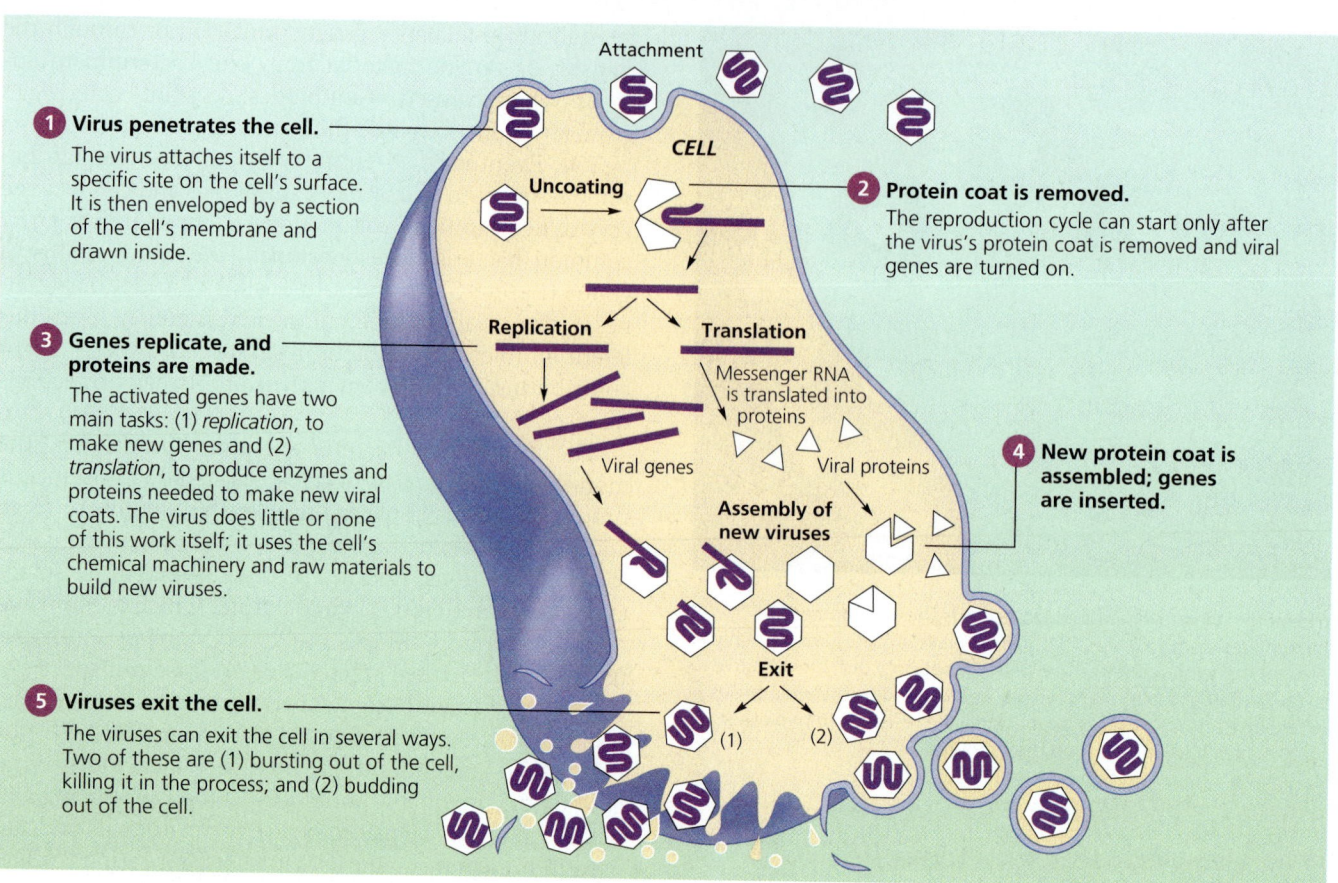

1 **Virus penetrates the cell.**

The virus attaches itself to a specific site on the cell's surface. It is then enveloped by a section of the cell's membrane and drawn inside.

2 **Protein coat is removed.**

The reproduction cycle can start only after the virus's protein coat is removed and viral genes are turned on.

3 **Genes replicate, and proteins are made.**

The activated genes have two main tasks: (1) *replication*, to make new genes and (2) *translation*, to produce enzymes and proteins needed to make new viral coats. The virus does little or none of this work itself; it uses the cell's chemical machinery and raw materials to build new viruses.

4 **New protein coat is assembled; genes are inserted.**

5 **Viruses exit the cell.**

The viruses can exit the cell in several ways. Two of these are (1) bursting out of the cell, killing it in the process; and (2) budding out of the cell.

Labels in figure: Attachment · Uncoating · CELL · Replication · Translation · Messenger RNA is translated into proteins · Viral genes · Viral proteins · Assembly of new viruses · Exit · (1) (2)

FIGURE 17.7 **Life cycle of a virus.**

and they cannot grow or reproduce by themselves. Viruses are **parasites**; they take what they need for growth and reproduction from the cells they invade. Once a virus is inside the host cell, it sheds its protein covering, and its genetic material takes control of the cell and manufactures more viruses like itself (Figure 17.7). In order to fight viruses, the cellular immunity system produces substances such as interferon; these same substances are also responsible for most of the symptoms of a viral illness.

Illnesses caused by viruses are the most common forms of **contagious disease**. Different viruses affect different kinds of cells, and the seriousness of the disease they cause depends greatly on which kind of cell is affected. The viruses that cause colds, for example, attack upper respiratory tract cells, which are constantly cast off and replaced; the disease is therefore mild. Poliovirus, in contrast, attacks nerve cells that cannot be replaced, and the consequences, such as paralysis, are severe. HIV infection, a viral illness that destroys immune system cells, can destroy the body's ability to fight infectious diseases (see Chapter 18).

The Common Cold   Although generally brief, lasting only 1–2 weeks, colds are nonetheless irritating and often interfere with one's normal activities. A cold may be caused by any of more than 200 different viruses that attack the lining of the nasal passages; rhinoviruses and coronaviruses cause a large percentage of all colds among adults.

Cold viruses are almost always transmitted by hand-to-hand contact. To lessen your risk of contracting a cold, wash your hands frequently; if you touch someone else, avoid touching your face until after you've washed your hands. Colds are not caused by exposure to cold weather or by being chilled or overheated; more colds occur in the fall and winter months, probably because of the opening of school season (children contract more colds than

TERMS

parasite   An organism that lives on or within a living host; the relationship benefits the parasite and harms the host.

contagious disease   A disease that can be transmitted from one person to another; most are viral diseases, such as the common cold and flu.

influenza   Infection of the respiratory tract by the influenza virus, which is highly infectious and adaptable; the form changes so easily that every year new strains arise, making treatment difficult; commonly known as the flu.

Preventing and Treating the Common Cold

Prevention

Colds are usually spread by hand-to-hand contact with another person or with objects such as doorknobs and telephones, which an infected person may have handled. The best way to avoid transmission is to wash your hands frequently with warm water and soap. Keeping your immune system strong is another good prevention strategy (see the guidelines provided later in the chapter).

Home Treatments

• Get some extra rest. It isn't usually necessary to stay home in bed, but you will need to slow down a little from your usual routine to give your body a chance to fight the infection.

• Drink plenty of liquids to prevent dehydration. Hot liquids such as herbal tea and clear chicken soup will soothe a sore throat and loosen secretions; gargling with a glass of slightly salty water may also help. Avoid alcoholic beverages when you have a cold.

• Hot showers or the use of a humidifier can help eliminate nasal stuffiness and soothe inflamed membranes.

Over-the-Counter Treatments

Avoid multisymptom cold remedies. Because these products include drugs to treat symptoms you may not even have, you risk suffering from side effects from medications you don't need. It's better to treat each symptom separately:

• *Analgesics*—aspirin, acetaminophen (Tylenol), ibuprofen (Advil or Motrin), and naproxen sodium (Aleve)—all help lower fever and relieve muscle aches. Use of aspirin is associated with an increased risk of a serious condition called Reye's syndrome in children and teenagers; for this reason, aspirin should be given only to adults.

• *Decongestants* shrink nasal blood vessels, relieving swelling and congestion. However, they may dry out mucous membranes in the throat and make a sore throat worse. Nasal sprays shouldn't be used for more than 2–3 days to avoid rebound congestion.

• *Cough medicines* may be helpful when your cough is non-productive (not bringing up mucus) or if it disrupts your sleep or work. Expectorants make coughs more productive by increasing the volume of mucus and decreasing its thickness, thereby helping remove irritants from the respiratory airways. Suppressants (antitussives) reduce the frequency of coughing.

• *Antihistamines* decrease nasal secretions caused by the effects of histamine, so they are much more useful in treating allergies than colds. *Caution:* Many antihistamines can make you drowsy.

Antibiotics will not help a cold unless a bacterial infection such as strep throat is also present, and overuse of antibiotics leads to the development of drug resistance. The jury is still out on whether other remedies, including zinc gluconate lozenges, echinacea, and vitamin C, will relieve symptoms or shorten the duration of a cold. Researchers are also studying antiviral drugs that target the most common types of cold viruses.

Sometimes a cold leads to a more serious complication, such as bronchitis, pneumonia, or strep throat. If a fever of 102°F or higher persists, or if cold symptoms don't get better after 2 weeks, see your physician.

---

adults) and because people spend more time indoors in the fall and winter months, making person-to-person transmission of viruses more likely.

If you catch a cold, over-the-counter cold remedies may help treat your symptoms but do not directly attack the viral cause (see the box "Preventing and Treating the Common Cold"). Sometimes it is difficult to determine whether your symptoms are due to a virus (as for colds, flu, and some sinus infections), a bacterium (as for other sinus infections), or an allergy, but this information is important for appropriate treatment (Table 17.3 on p. 538). For example, antibiotics will not help treat a cold but will help treat a bacterial sinus infection.

Influenza Commonly called the flu, **influenza** is an infection of the respiratory tract caused by the influenza virus. (Many people use the term "stomach flu" to describe gastrointestinal illnesses, but these infections are actually caused by organisms other than influenza viruses). Compared to the common cold, influenza is a more serious illness, usually including a fever and extreme fatigue. Most people who get the flu recover within 1–2 weeks, but some develop potentially life-threatening complications, such as pneumonia. The highest rates of infection occur in children. Influenza is highly contagious and is spread via respiratory droplets (see the box "The Next Influenza Pandemic—When, Not If?" on p. 539).

The most effective way of preventing the flu is through annual vaccination. The influenza vaccine consists of killed virus and provides protection against the strains of the virus currently circulating; it is updated each year in response to changes in the virus. Vaccination can be appropriate for anyone age 6 months or older who wants to reduce his or her risk of the flu. The CDC strongly recommends vaccination for all children age 6 months to 18 years, people age 50 or older, anyone age 6 months or older with long-term health conditions, anyone with a weakened immune system, women who will be pregnant during the flu season, residents of nursing homes and long-term care facilities, health care workers, and household contacts and caregivers of children up to 5 years old and persons at high risk. In addition to the injected

Table 17.3   What's Causing My Symptoms?

Symptoms	Influenza	Common Cold	Allergy	Sinusitis
Headache	Usually	Occasionally	Occasionally	Usually
Muscle aches	Usually (severe)	Usually (mild)	Rarely	Rarely
Fatigue, weakness	Usually (severe; sudden onset; may last several weeks)	Usually (mild)	Rarely	Rarely
Fever	Usually (high, typically 102–104°F; sudden onset; lasts 3–4 days)	Occasionally (mild)	Never	Occasionally
Cough	Usually (often severe)	Occasionally	Occasionally	Usually
Runny, stuffy nose	Occasionally	Usually	Usually	Usually (stuffy)
Nasal discharge	Occasionally	Usually (thick, clear to yellowish green)	Usually (watery, clear)	Usually (thick, yellowish green)
Sneezing	Occasionally	Occasionally	Usually	Rarely
Sore throat	Occasionally	Usually	Occasionally	Rarely
Itchy eyes, nose, throat	Rarely	Rarely	Usually	Never

SOURCE: Is it the flu? 2000. *Consumer Reports*, November. Copyright © 2000 by Consumers Union of U.S., Inc. Yonkers, NY 10703-1057, a nonprofit organization. Reprinted with permission from the November 2000 issue of *Consumer Reports* for educational purposes only. No commercial use or reproduction permitted. http://www.consumerreports.org/oh/index.htm.

vaccine, there is a nasal aerosol vaccine called FluMist. In 2007, the FDA approved FluMist for healthy children age 24–59 months and for nonpregnant healthy persons age 5–49 years.

A number of medications are used to treat influenza, but in most cases they can shorten the duration of illness by little more than a day and then only if treatment begins within 1–2 days after onset of symptoms. Several medications are also effective in reducing the risk of illness from influenza; however, they are less effective than the vaccine.

Measles, Mumps, and Rubella Three childhood viral illnesses that have waned in the United States due to effective vaccines are measles, mumps, and rubella (German measles). Measles and rubella are generally characterized by rash and fever. Measles can occasionally cause more severe illness, including liver or brain infection or pneumonia; worldwide, more than 600,000 people die each year from measles. Measles is a highly contagious disease, and prior to the introduction of vaccines, more than 90% of Americans contracted measles by age 15.

Rubella, if it infects a pregnant woman, can be transmitted to a fetus, causing miscarriage, stillbirth, and severe birth defects, including deafness, eye and heart defects, and mental impairment.

Mumps generally causes swelling of the parotid (salivary) glands, located just below and in front of the ears. This virus can also cause meningitis and, in males, inflammation of the testes.

Chicken Pox, Cold Sores, and Other Herpesvirus Infections The **herpesviruses** are a large group of viruses. Once infected, the host is never free of the virus. The virus lies latent within certain cells and becomes active periodically, producing symptoms. Herpesviruses are particularly dangerous for people with a depressed immune system, as in the case of HIV infection. The family of herpesviruses includes the following:

- *Varicella-zoster virus,* which causes chicken pox and shingles. Chicken pox is a highly contagious childhood disease characterized by an itchy rash made up of small blisters; the infection is usually mild, although complications are more likely to occur in young infants and adults. After the rash resolves, the virus becomes latent, living in sensory nerves. Many years later, the virus may reactivate and cause shingles; symptoms of shingles include pain in

herpesvirus A family of viruses responsible for cold sores, mononucleosis, chicken pox, and the STD known as herpes; frequently causes latent infections.

epidemic The occurrence in a particular community or region of more than the expected number of cases of a particular disease.

pandemic A disease epidemic that is unusually severe or widespread; often used to refer to worldwide epidemics affecting a large proportion of the population.

TERMS

The Next Influenza Pandemic—When, Not If?

connect™

Influenza Virus Basics

There are three main types of influenza viruses, designated A, B, and C. Influenza C usually causes only mild illness and has not been associated with widespread outbreaks. Types A and B, however, are responsible for **epidemics** of respiratory illness that occur almost every winter. Influenza A viruses are further divided into subtypes, based on differences in two surface antigens: hemagglutinin (H) and neuraminidase (N).

Influenza A viruses also differ from types B and C in that they can infect a variety of animals in addition to humans. Aquatic birds, such as ducks, are a natural reservoir for influenza A; they carry and can spread the virus but do not themselves become ill. Avian strains can infect and cause serious illness in domestic poultry and may also infect pigs, humans, and other mammals.

Antigenic Drift and Shift

Through replication errors and gene sharing, influenza viruses undergo constant change, enabling them to evade the immune system and thereby make people susceptible to influenza throughout life. A person infected with influenza does develop antibodies, but as the H and N antigens change, the antibodies no longer recognize the virus, and reinfection can occur.

Small changes in H and N antigens are referred to as *antigenic drift*; these changes are why the flu vaccine is reformulated each year. Fortunately, if the changes in H and N are small, the immune system may at least partially recognize the virus, giving many people some immune protection against the new strain.

Occasionally, an influenza A virus undergoes a sudden, dramatic change, called *antigenic shift*. Antigenic shift occurs when an avian influenza virus mixes and exchanges genes with a human virus; this mixing may occur when a human or an animal such as a pig is simultaneously infected by both human and avian strains of influenza A. If this occurs and the new virus spreads easily from person to person, a worldwide epidemic, called a **pandemic,** can occur because few people have any antibody protection against the virus.

Influenza pandemics usually occur about every 30 years or so. During the twentieth century, three major influenza pandemics occurred in humans:

- 1918–1919 ("Spanish flu"): About 20–40% of the world's population became ill, and as many as 40 million people died, including more than 500,000 Americans.

- 1957–1958 ("Asian flu")

- 1968–1969 ("Hong Kong flu")

The Next Pandemic

Many experts believe that an influenza pandemic is overdue, inevitable, and possibly imminent. Conditions that allow the mingling of flu viruses—including wild and domestic birds, humans, and other flu carriers living in crowded conditions and close proximity—exist in many parts of the world.

Scientists have been monitoring the progress of a strain of avian influenza A(H5N1) in Asia that has caused a small but deadly number of cases in humans. The initial outbreak in 1997–1998 killed 6 people in Hong Kong. Local authorities contained the outbreak quickly by tracing its source to infected chickens, ducks, and geese and then ordering the slaughter of all domestic poultry. Many experts believe that this quick action probably averted a pandemic.

The H5N1 strain doesn't pass easily to or between humans. However, when it infects humans, it is deadly. Through mid-2006, outbreaks of H5N1 avian influenza were reported among migratory birds and poultry flocks in several countries in Asia, Africa, the Middle East, and Europe, with 63% of cases occurring in Indonesia and Vietnam. Where those

outbreaks occurred, people who came into close contact with infected birds became ill or died. As of February 11, 2009, 407 people worldwide had been diagnosed with H5N1 infection and 254 of those victims died.

The more people who are infected, the greater the chance that avian and human strains will mix, producing an influenza virus that is easily transmitted between people. It is hoped that the resulting strain will be less lethal than the avian strain; human strains tend to be less deadly, and the quick death of avian hosts prevents the virus from being transmitted.

Scientists are studying the virus to determine how many mutations it would take to allow H5N1 to pass easily between humans. The avian flu virus is resistant to at least two antiviral medications—amantadine and rimantadine—which are commonly used to treat influenza. Scientists are trying to confirm whether the virus resists other currently available antiviral drugs, as well. In 2007, the Food and Drug Administration approved the first avian flu vaccine for use in humans; others are in development.

---

the affected nerves and a rash on the skin that follows the pattern of the nerve pathways (often a band over the ribs on one side of the body). A vaccine is available that prevents chicken pox in the majority of cases and results in milder illness if the disease does occur. In 2007, the CDC Advisory Committee on Immunization Practices recommended the varicella vaccine for all adults who lack immunity to varicella.

- *Herpes simplex virus (HSV) types 1 and 2*, which cause cold sores and the STD herpes (Chapter 18). Herpes

Are All Diseases Infectious?

Researchers have been identifying infectious bases for more and more diseases—even diseases that have long been thought to be caused by other factors. Some scientists feel that the role of infectious agents in the major killers of today—CVD, cancer, diabetes, and so on—has been greatly underestimated. The following are just a few examples:

- **Type 1 diabetes.** A viral infection is thought to trigger the immune system to destroy insulin-producing cells in the pancreas; when this occurs, the pancreas is no longer able to produce enough insulin to metabolize glucose.

- **Multiple sclerosis (MS).** Infection with any of several viruses has been proposed as the precipitating cause of MS, a condition characterized by damage to nerve fiber coverings and progressive muscle weakness.

- **Schizophrenia.** There is evidence that some schizophrenic cases are associated with occurrence of prior infection. A recent study found that maternal respiratory infection increases the risk for schizophrenia in offspring from three- to sevenfold.

- **Childhood obsessive-compulsive disorder (OCD).** Some cases of OCD that begin in early childhood have been found to follow infection with streptococcus bacteria. It is thought that antibodies produced to fight the infection, rather than the infection itself, may cause OCD. Some affected children improve when they are given intravenous immunoglobulin or undergo plasma exchange to remove the antibodies from their blood.

- **Heart disease.** Several infectious agents have been implicated in the inflammatory processes underlying atherosclerosis, including *Chlamydia pneumoniae* and *Cytomegalovirus*. Research is under way to determine if antibiotics can lessen the risk of heart attack in infected individuals.

- **Cancer.** A number of infections have been linked to specific types of cancer: human papillomavirus and cervical cancer; Epstein-Barr virus and Burkitt's lymphoma, nasopharyngeal cancer and some B-cell lymphomas; hepatitis B and C viruses and liver cancer; HTLV-1 and T-cell leukemia; *Helicobacter pylori* and stomach cancer; and human herpesvirus 8 and Kaposi's sarcoma.

---

infections are characterized by small, painful ulcers in the area around the mouth or genitals, at the site where a person first contracts the virus. Following the initial infection, HSV becomes latent and may reactivate again and again over time. Many infected people do not know they are infected, and the virus can be transmitted even when sores are not apparent. Antiviral medications are available to prevent recurrences of genital herpes.

- *Epstein-Barr virus (EBV),* which causes infectious mononucleosis. Mono, as it is commonly called, is characterized by fever, sore throat, swollen lymph nodes, and fatigue. It is usually spread by intimate contact with the saliva of an infected person—hence the name "kissing disease." Mono most often affects adolescents and young adults. Although EBV does reactivate throughout life, it generally does not cause any further symptoms. In a few people, especially those with HIV infection, EBV is associated with the development of cancers of the lymph system (see the box "Are All Diseases Infectious?").

Two herpesviruses that can cause severe infections in people with a suppressed immune system are cytomega-

lovirus (CMV), which infects the lungs, brain, colon, and eyes, and human herpesvirus 8 (HHV-8), which has been linked to Kaposi's sarcoma.

Viral Encephalitis HSV type 1 is a possible cause of viral **encephalitis**, inflammation of brain tissue due to a viral infection. Other possible causes include HIV and several mosquitoborne viruses, including Japanese encephalitis virus, equine encephalomyelitis virus, and West Nile virus. Mild cases of encephalitis may cause fever, headache, nausea, and lethargy; severe cases are characterized by memory loss, delirium, diminished speech function, and seizures, and they may result in permanent brain damage or death.

Viral Hepatitis Viral **hepatitis** is a term used to describe several different infections that cause inflammation of the liver. Hepatitis is usually caused by one of the three most common hepatitis viruses.

- *Hepatitis A virus (HAV)* causes the mildest form of the disease and is usually transmitted by food or water contaminated by sewage or an infected person.

- *Hepatitis B virus (HBV)* is usually transmitted sexually; it is discussed in detail in Chapter 18.

- *Hepatitis C virus (HCV)* can also be transmitted sexually, but it is much more commonly passed through direct contact with infected blood via injection drug use or, prior to the development of screening tests,

Body art procedures, such as tattooing, can lead to infection unless they are done with care.

blood transfusions. HBV and, to a lesser extent, HCV can also be passed from a pregnant woman to her child.

There are effective vaccines for hepatitis A and B, but more than 150,000 new cases of hepatitis occur in the United States each year.

Symptoms of acute hepatitis infection can include fatigue, **jaundice,** abdominal pain, loss of appetite, nausea, and diarrhea. Most people recover from hepatitis A within a month or so. However, 5–10% of people infected with HBV and 85–90% of people infected with HCV become chronic carriers of the virus, capable of infecting others for the rest of their lives. Some chronic carriers remain asymptomatic, while others slowly develop chronic liver disease, cirrhosis, or liver cancer. An estimated 4 million Americans and 500 million people worldwide may be chronic carriers of hepatitis. Each year in the United States, HBV and HCV are responsible for more than 15,000 deaths.

The extent of HCV infection has only recently been recognized, and most infected people are unaware of their condition. To ensure proper treatment and prevention, testing for HCV may be recommended for people at risk, including people who have ever injected drugs (even once), who received a blood transfusion or a donated or-

gan prior to July 1992, who have engaged in high-risk sexual behavior, or who have had body piercing, tattoos, or acupuncture involving unsterile equipment (see the box "Tattoos and Body Piercing" on p. 542). Antiviral drugs are available to treat chronic hepatitis, but they are not completely effective and may have significant side effects.

Poliomyelitis An infectious viral disease that affects the nervous system, **poliomyelitis** (polio) can cause irreversible paralysis and death in some affected individuals. As with other vaccine-preventable diseases, the incidence of polio declined dramatically in the United States following the introduction of the vaccine, and North and South America are now considered free of the disease.

>
> **Polio remains endemic in only 4 countries: Afghanistan, India, Nigeria, and Pakistan.**
> —World Health Organization, 2008

Rabies Caused by a rhabdovirus, rabies is a potentially fatal infection of the central nervous system that is most often transmitted through an animal bite. U.S. rabies-related deaths among humans declined dramatically during the twentieth century due to the widespread vaccination of domestic animals and the development of a highly effective vaccine regimen that provides immunity following exposure (post-exposure prophylaxis, or PEP).

Although rabies is rare in the United States, most recent cases have been traced to bats. The CDC recommends that PEP be considered for anyone who has had direct contact with a bat, including someone who has been in the same room with a bat and who might be unaware that contact has occurred (a sleeping child, for example). PEP consists of one dose of immunoglobulin and five doses of rabies vaccine over a 28-day period.

Human Papillomavirus (HPV) The more than 100 different types of HPV cause a variety of warts (non-cancerous skin tumors), including common warts on the

TERMS

encephalitis Inflammation of the brain; fever, headache, nausea, and lethargy are common initial symptoms, followed in some cases by memory loss, seizures, brain damage, and death.

hepatitis Inflammation of the liver, which can be caused by infection, drugs, or toxins.

jaundice Increased bile pigment levels in the blood, characterized by yellowing of the skin and the whites of the eyes.

poliomyelitis A disease of the nervous system, sometimes crippling; vaccines now prevent most cases of polio.

Tattoos and Body Piercing

Because tattooing and body piercing involve the use of needles, they carry health risks. If you are considering either procedure, you can reduce the risks by carefully choosing a body artist and following aftercare directions.

Tattoos are permanent marks applied with an electrically powered instrument that injects dye into the second layer of the skin. Pain and a little bleeding are common; a tattoo typically takes a week or two to heal and should be protected from sun exposure until then.

In piercing, the artist pushes a needle through the skin; a piece of jewelry holds the piercing open. Earlobe piercing is the most common, but people also pierce the upper ear, eyebrow, tongue, lip, nose, navel, nipples, and genitals. Healing time varies depending on the site of the piercing and other factors. Some pain and swelling are common; there may be prolonged bleeding following oral piercing because the tongue contains so many blood vessels.

Potential Health Issues

- **Infection:** There is a risk of transmission of bloodborne infectious agents, such as hepatitis and HIV, if instruments are not sterilized properly. No cases of HIV infection have been traced to tattooing or piercing. In 2006, the CDC reported an outbreak of methicillin-resistant *Staphylococcus aureus* among customers of tattoo parlors in several states. In most cases, investigators found that the tattooists had not followed proper hygiene procedures, such as changing gloves between customers. Due to the potential risks of infection, people currently cannot donate blood for 12 months following application of body art, including tattoos and some body piercings. People with heart valve problems should check with a physician prior to body piercing to determine if they should take antibiotics before the procedure.

- **Allergic reactions:** Some people may be allergic to pigments used in tattooing or to metals used in body-piercing jewelry. All jewelry should be of noncorrosive materials such as stainless steel or titanium; avoid jewelry that contains nickel.

- **Nodules and scars:** Some people may develop granulomas (nodules) or keloids (a type of scar) following tattooing or body piercing.

- **Problems relating to placement:** Tattoos may become swollen or burned if the wearer undergoes magnetic resonance imaging (MRI), and tattoos may also interfere with the quality of MRI images. Oral ornaments may obscure dental problems in dental X rays; they may also damage teeth and fillings and interfere with speech and chewing. Navel piercings may become infected more easily because tight-fitting clothes allow moisture to collect in the area.

Tattoos are meant to be permanent and so are expensive and very difficult (or impossible) to remove completely. Tattoo removal may involve scraping or cutting off the layers of tattooed skin or using laser surgery to break up the pigment in the tattoo; some scarring can occur. Body piercings may close and heal once the jewelry is removed, but they may leave a permanent scar.

Choosing a Body Artist and Studio

A body art studio should be clean and have an autoclave for sterilizing instruments. Needles should be sterilized and disposable; piercing guns should not be used, as they cannot be adequately sterilized. The body artist should wear disposable latex gloves throughout the procedure. Leftover tattoo ink should be thrown away and not reused. Ask to see references and aftercare instructions beforehand.

Some states and local health departments regulate body art facilities. Also, ask if the studio and/or artist are members of the Alliance of Professional Tattooists (http://www.safe-tattoos.com) or the Association of Professional Piercers (http://www.safepiercing.org); these organizations have developed infection-control and other guidelines for their members to follow.

---

hands, plantar warts on the soles of the feet, and genital warts around the genitalia. Depending on their location, warts may be removed using over-the-counter preparations or professional methods such as laser surgery or cryosurgery. Because HPV infection is chronic, warts can reappear despite treatment. As described in Chapter 16, HPV causes the majority of cases of cervical cancer. A vaccine was approved in 2006 and is recommended for girls age 11–12; it may be given to girls as young as 9 and women through age 26.

Treating Viral Illnesses Antiviral drugs typically work by interfering with some part of the viral life cycle; for example, they may prevent a virus from entering body cells or from successfully reproducing within cells. Antivirals are currently available to fight infections caused by HIV, influenza, herpes simplex, varicella-zoster, HBV, and HVC. Most other viral diseases must simply run their course.

Fungi

A **fungus** is an organism that absorbs food from organic matter. Fungi may be multicellular (like molds) or unicellular (like yeasts). Mushrooms and the molds that form on bread and cheese are all fungi. Only about 50 fungi out of many thousands of species cause disease in humans, and these diseases are usually restricted to the skin, mucous membranes, and lungs. Some fungal diseases are extremely difficult to treat because some fungi form spores, an especially resistant dormant stage of the organism.

Candida albicans is a common fungus found naturally in the vagina of most women. When excessive growth occurs, the result is itching and discomfort, commonly known as a yeast infection. Factors that increase the growth of *C. albicans* include the use of antibiotics, clothing that keeps the vaginal area excessively warm and moist, pregnancy, oral contraceptive use, and certain diseases, including diabetes and HIV infection. The most common symptom is usually a thick white or yellowish discharge. Prescription and OTC treatments are available. Women should not self-treat unless they are certain from a past medical diagnosis that they have a yeast infection. (Misdiagnosis could mean that a different and more severe infection goes untreated.) *C. albicans* overgrowth can occur in other areas of the body, especially in the mouth in infants (a condition known as thrush).

Other common fungal conditions, including athlete's foot, jock itch, and ringworm, affect the skin. These three conditions are usually mild and easy to cure.

Fungi can also cause systemic diseases that are severe, life-threatening, and extremely difficult to treat. Histoplasmosis, or valley fever, causes pulmonary and sometimes systemic disease and is most common in the Mississippi and Ohio River Valleys. Coccidioidomycosis is also known as valley fever because it is most frequent in the San Joaquin Valley of California. Fungal infections can be especially deadly in people with an impaired immune system.

Protozoa

Another group of pathogens is single-celled organisms known as **protozoa**. Millions of people in developing countries suffer from protozoal infections.

Malaria, caused by a protozoan of the genus *Plasmodium,* is characterized by recurrent attacks of severe flu-like symptoms (chills, fever, headache, nausea, and vomiting) and may cause anemia. The protozoan is injected into the bloodstream via a mosquito bite. Although relatively rare in the United States, malaria is a major killer worldwide; each year, there are 350–500 million new cases of malaria and more than 1 million deaths, mostly among infants and children. Drugs are available to prevent and treat malaria, but in the poorest, most remote areas, conditions make it difficult to distribute drugs. Drug-resistant strains of malaria have emerged, requiring new medicines.

Giardiasis is caused by *Giardia lamblia,* a single-celled parasite that lives in the intestines of humans and animals. Giardiasis is characterized by nausea, diarrhea, bloating, and abdominal cramps, and it is among the most common waterborne diseases in the United States. People may become infected with *Giardia* if they consume contaminated food or water or pick up the parasite from the contaminated surface of an object such as a bathroom fixture, diaper pail, or toy. People at risk include child care workers, children who attend day care, international travelers, and hikers and campers who drink untreated water. Giardiasis is rarely serious and can be treated with prescription medications.

Other protozoal infections include the following:

- *Trichomoniasis,* a common vaginal infection. Although usually mild and treatable, trich may increase the risk of HIV transmission (see Chapter 18).

- *Trypanosomiasis* (African sleeping sickness), which is transmitted through the bite of an infected tsetse fly and causes extreme fatigue, fever, rash, severe headache, central nervous system damage, and death.

- *Amoebic dysentery,* a severe form of amebiasis, infection of the intestines with the parasite *Entamoeba histolytica.* It is characterized by bloody diarrhea, stomach pain, and fever.

Parasitic Worms

The **parasitic worms** are the largest organisms that can enter the body to cause infection. The tapeworm, for example, can grow to a length of many feet. Worms, including intestinal parasites such as the tapeworm and hookworm, cause a variety of relatively mild infections. Pinworm, the most common worm infection in the United States, primarily affects young children. Pinworms are white and about the size of a staple and live in the rectum of humans; they can cause itching and difficulty sleeping. Smaller worms known as flukes infect organs such as the liver and lungs and, in large numbers, can be deadly. Worm infections generally originate from contaminated food or drink and can be controlled by careful attention to hygiene.

TERMS

fungus A single-celled or multicelled organism that absorbs food from living or dead organic matter; examples include molds, mushrooms, and yeasts. Fungal diseases include yeast infections, athlete's foot, and ringworm.

protozoan (plural, protozoa) A microscopic single-celled organism that often produces recurrent, cyclical attacks of disease.

malaria A severe, recurrent, mosquito-borne infection caused by the protozoan *Plasmodium.*

giardiasis An intestinal disease caused by the protozoan *Giardia lamblia.*

parasitic worm A pathogen that causes intestinal and other infections; includes tapeworms, hookworms, pinworms, and flukes.

Prions

In recent years, several fatal degenerative disorders of the central nervous system have been linked to **prions,** or proteinaceous infectious particles. Unlike all other infectious agents, prions appear to lack DNA or RNA and to consist only of protein; their presence in the body does not trigger an immune response. Prions have an abnormal shape and form deposits in the brain. They may spread by triggering normal proteins to change their structure to the abnormal, damaging, form.

Prions are associated with a class of diseases known as *transmissible spongiform encephalopathies (TSEs)*, which are characterized by spongelike holes in the brain; symptoms of TSEs include loss of coordination, weakness, dementia, and death. Known prion diseases include Creutzfeldt-Jakob disease (CJD) in humans; bovine spongiform encephalopathy (BSE), or mad cow disease, in cattle; and scrapie in sheep. Some prion diseases are inherited or the result of spontaneous genetic mutations, whereas others are the result of eating infected tissue or being exposed to prions during medical procedures such as organ transplants. A variant form of CJD referred to as vCJD occurs in humans who are infected by eating beef from cows with BSE.

As of 2006, there had been 200 cases of vCJD in the world, with 164 of those cases occurring in the United Kingdom. The first U.S. BSE case was identified in 2003. Several steps have been taken or proposed to reduce the number of BSE-infected cows and the likelihood of meat from an infected animal entering the human food supply. These include increased surveillance, limiting or banning the use of cattle products in feed for other cattle, prohibiting meat imports from countries with BSE-infected cattle, restricting certain people from giving blood, and banning the use of downer (nonambulatory disabled) cattle for food for human consumption. Prions present special challenges because they are resistant to heat, radiation, and chemicals that kill other pathogens and because the diseases they cause have a long incubation period. In fact, experts say BSE can take 50 years to incubate. Authorities are now concerned that many more people may harbor BSE than estimated, leading to an epidemic of vCJD in coming decades. Scientists are working to develop new tests that would detect low levels of dangerous prions in asymptomatic cattle.

Emerging Infectious Diseases

Emerging infectious diseases are those infections whose incidence in humans has increased or threatens to increase in the near future. They include both known dis-

prion Proteinaceous infectious particles thought to be responsible for a class of neurodegenerative diseases known as transmissible spongiform encephalopathies; Creutzfeldt-Jakob disease (CJD) in humans and bovine spongiform encephalopathy (BSE, or mad cow disease) are prion diseases.

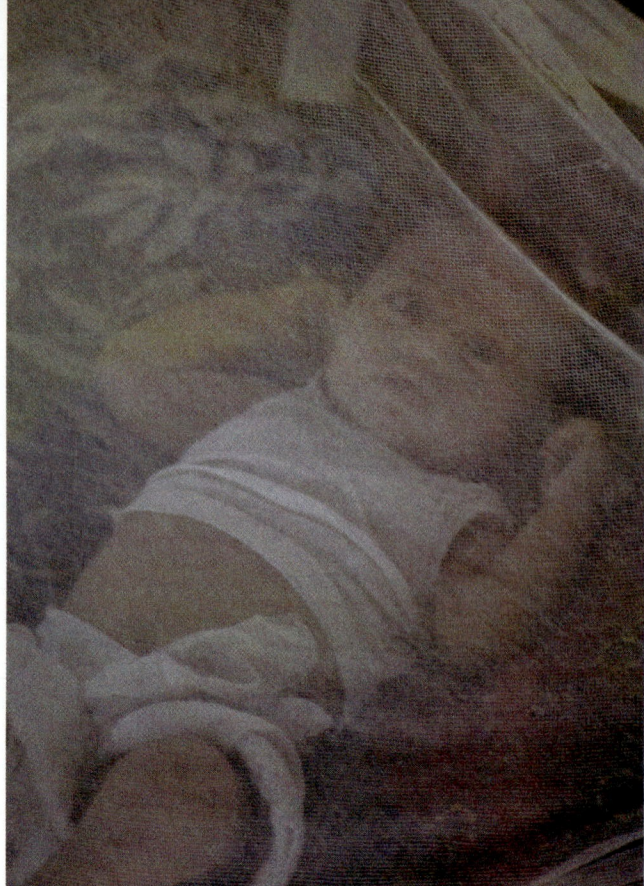

Insecticides, repellants, protective clothing, and screens are helpful in reducing mosquito bites. In developing countries, mosquito nets are a first line of defense against mosquitos.

eases that have experienced a resurgence, such as tuberculosis and cholera, and diseases that were previously unknown or confined to specific areas, such as the Ebola and West Nile viruses.

Selected Infections of Concern   Although the chances of the average American contracting an exotic infection are very low, emerging infections are a concern to public health officials and represent a challenge to all nations in the future.

WEST NILE VIRUS   A mini-outbreak of encephalitis in New York in 1999 led to identification of this virus, which had previously been restricted to Africa, the Middle East, and parts of Europe. Between 1999 and 2007, the virus spread across the United States and caused more than 27,605 illnesses and 1086 deaths. West Nile virus is carried by birds and then passed to humans when mosquitoes bite first an infected bird and then a person. Most people who are bitten have few or no symptoms, but the virus can cause permanent brain damage or death in some. Vaccines are being developed for West Nile virus, but it is important to protect yourself from mosquito bites.

SEVERE ACUTE RESPIRATORY SYNDROME (SARS)   In February 2003, SARS appeared in southern China and quickly spread to more than 15 countries; it is a form of pneumonia that is fatal in about 5–15% of cases. SARS is caused by a new type of coronavirus found in wildlife that may have crossed the species barrier when certain wildlife species were consumed as delicacies. It has reemerged several times since 2003, and by 2004 had been responsible for more than 8000 illnesses and 800 deaths. There have been no new cases reported since 2004.

ROTAVIRUS The leading viral cause of gastroenteritis, an intestinal inflammation that results in vomiting and diarrhea, rotavirus infects almost every child at one time or another. Worldwide, the virus kills about 600,000 children each year, mostly in developing countries. Left untreated, rotavirus-induced diarrhea can become severe and lead to dehydration, which can be fatal. Rotavirus spreads through poor hygiene and sanitation practices.

ESCHERICHIA COLI O157:H7 This potentially deadly strain of *E. coli,* transmitted in contaminated food, can cause bloody diarrhea and kidney damage. In 2006, more than 200 people became ill and 3 died from eating spinach from a field in California contaminated by cattle and wildlife. Other outbreaks have been linked to lettuce, alfalfa sprouts, unpasteurized juice, petting zoos, and contaminated public swimming pools. An estimated 70,000 cases and 61 deaths occur in the United States each year.

HANTAVIRUS Since first being recognized in 1993, over 300 cases of hantavirus pulmonary syndrome (HPS) have been reported in the United States. HPS is caused by the rodentborne Sin Nombre virus (SNV) and is spread primarily through airborne viral particles from rodent urine, droppings, or saliva. It is characterized by a dangerous fluid buildup in the lungs and is fatal in about 45% of cases.

EBOLA Human outbreaks of the often fatal Ebola hemorrhagic fever (EHF) have occurred only in Africa. The Ebola virus is transmitted by contact with infected blood or other body secretions, and many cases of EHF have been linked to unsanitary conditions in medical facilities. Because symptoms appear quickly and 70% of victims die, usually within a few days, the virus tends not to spread widely.

Factors Contributing to Emerging Infections What's behind this rising tide of infectious diseases? Contributing factors are complex and interrelated.

DRUG RESISTANCE New or increasing drug resistance has been found in organisms that cause malaria, tuberculosis, gonorrhea, influenza, AIDS, and pneumococcal and staphylococcal infections. Infections caused by drug-resistant organisms prolong illness, and—if not treated in time with more effective, expensive drugs—they can cause death. Some bacterial strains now appear to be resistant to all available antibiotics.

> **Nearly all** major bacterial infections are becoming resistant to common antibiotics.
>
> —CDC, 2007

QUICK STATS

POVERTY More than 1 billion people live in extreme poverty, and half the world's population have no regular access to essential drugs. Population growth, urbanization, overcrowding, and migration (including the movement of refugees) also spread infectious diseases.

BREAKDOWN OF PUBLIC HEALTH MEASURES A poor public health infrastructure is often associated with poverty and social upheaval, but problems such as contaminated water supplies can occur even in industrial countries. Inadequate vaccination has led to the reemergence of diseases such as diphtheria and pertussis. Natural disasters such as hurricanes also disrupt the public health infrastructure, leaving survivors with contaminated water and food supplies and no shelter from disease-carrying insects.

TRAVEL AND COMMERCE More than 500 million travelers cross national borders each year, and international tourism and trade open the world to infectious agents. SARS was quickly spread throughout the world by infected air travelers. The reintroduction of cholera into the Western Hemisphere is thought to have occurred through the discharge of bilge water from a Chinese freighter into the waters off Peru.

MASS FOOD PRODUCTION AND DISTRIBUTION Food now travels long distances to our table, and microbes are transmitted along with it. Mass production of food increases the likelihood that a chance contamination can lead to mass illness.

HUMAN BEHAVIORS Changes in patterns of human behavior also influence the spread of infectious diseases. The widespread use of injectable drugs rapidly transmits HIV

THINKING ABOUT THE ENVIRONMENT

Many environmental factors contribute to the spread of infectious diseases. Here are a few examples:

- In poverty-stricken regions, many people become ill as a result of unsanitary conditions and a lack of clean drinking water.

- Unsustainable development practices, such as clearing forests and draining wetlands, disturb the ecosystem and force many disease-carrying vectors (such as vermin and insects) out of their natural habitats and into contact with people.

- A shift in rainfall patterns (perhaps caused by global warming) may allow mosquito-borne diseases such as malaria to spread from the tropics into the temperate zones. Since many species of mosquito in North America can carry malaria, such changes could someday make malaria a widespread health threat to the United States.

For more information on the environment and environmental health, see Chapter 19.

infection and hepatitis. Changes in sexual behavior over the past 30 years have led to a proliferation of old and new STDs. The use of day-care facilities for children has led to increases in the incidence of several infections that cause diarrhea.

BIOTERRORISM   The deliberate release of deadly infectious agents is an ongoing concern. In 2001, infectious anthrax spores sent through the mail sickened 11 and killed 5 people in the United States. Potential bioterrorism agents that the CDC categorizes as a highest concern are those that can be easily disseminated or transmitted from person to person and that have a high mortality rate and the potential for a major public health impact; these include anthrax, smallpox, plague, botulism, and viral hemorrhagic fevers such as Ebola.

Other Immune Disorders: Cancer and Autoimmune Diseases

The immune system has evolved to protect the body from invasion by foreign microorganisms. Sometimes, as in the case of cancer, the body comes under attack by its own cells. As explained in Chapter 16, cancer cells cease to cooperate normally with the rest of the body and multiply uncontrollably. The immune system can often detect cells that have recently become cancerous and then destroy them just as it would a foreign microorganism. But if the immune system breaks down, as it may when people get older, when they have certain immune disorders (including HIV infection), or when they are receiving chemotherapy for other diseases, the cancer cells may multiply out of control before the immune system recognizes the danger. By the time the immune system gears up to destroy the cancerous cells, it may be too late.

Another immune disorder occurs when the body confuses its own cells with foreign organisms. As described earlier, the immune system must recognize many thousands of antigens as foreign and then be able to recognize the same antigens again and again. Our own tissue cells also are antigenic; that is, they would be recognized by another person's immune system as foreign. A delicate balance must be maintained to ensure that one's immune system recognizes only truly foreign antigens as enemies; erroneous recognition of one's own cells as foreign produces havoc.

This is what happens in autoimmune diseases such as rheumatoid arthritis and systemic lupus erythematosus. In this type of malady, the immune system seems to be a bit too sensitive and begins to misapprehend itself as non-

self. For reasons not well understood, these conditions are much more common in women than in men (see the box "Women and Autoimmune Diseases").

SUPPORTING YOUR IMMUNE SYSTEM

Pathogens threaten everyone's wellness, but you can take steps to prevent them from compromising your health. Here are some general guidelines for keeping pathogens at bay:

- Eat a balanced diet and maintain a healthy weight, as discussed in Chapters 12 and 14.

- Get enough sleep. Most people need 6–8 hours every night. Sleep helps your body replenish itself and encourages the production of immune system cells. Lack of sleep can actually increase your chances of getting sick.

- Exercise, but not when you're sick. Exercise helps you stay healthy, as discussed in Chapter 13. It also staves off stress, which can weaken your immune system. For more information, see the box "Immunity and Stress" on p. 548.

- Don't smoke. Smoking decreases the levels of some immune cells (see Chapter 11).

- If you drink alcohol, do so only in moderation (see Chapter 10). Excessive drinking can interfere with normal immune system functioning.

- Wash your hands frequently, as advised throughout this chapter. Antibacterial soap has not been proven

QUESTIONS FOR CRITICAL THINKING AND REFLECTION

Have you ever had any of the illnesses described in the preceding section? How were you exposed to the disease? Could you have taken any precautions to avoid it?

GENDER MATTERS

Women and Autoimmune Diseases

Although the immune systems of men and women are essentially the same, women have much higher rates of many autoimmune diseases. The reason is somewhat of a mystery. One clue may come from pregnancy: In order to conceive and carry a baby to term, a woman's body must temporarily suppress its immune response so it doesn't attack the sperm or the fetus. Another factor seems to be related to estrogen. Estrogen receptors have been found on suppressor T cells, pointing to a possible link between the glands controlling immunity and those controlling sex hormones. Women also appear to have somewhat enhanced immunity compared to men, a factor that could be linked to both longer life spans and higher rates of autoimmune disorders.

Systemic lupus erythematosus is an autoimmune disease in which the immune system attacks the body's normal tissue, causing inflammation of the joints, blood vessels, heart, lungs, brain, and kidneys. Its symptoms include painful swollen joints, a rash on the nose and cheeks, sensitivity to sunlight, chest pain, fatigue, and dizziness. There are about 1.4–2.0 million Americans with lupus, 80% of them women; the disorder is especially common among Native Ameri-can and African American women. Lupus usually begins before menopause and may flare up during pregnancy; for some women, symptoms also increase in severity during menstruation or with the use of oral contraceptives. A link between these exacerbating factors is increased levels of estrogen, but this connection is not well understood. Researchers have also identified genetic mutations that may be associated with lupus.

In rheumatoid arthritis, the body's immune system attacks the membranes lining the joints, causing pain and swelling. Among the estimated 1% of American adults with rheumatoid arthritis, women outnumber men 3 to 1. The causes of the disease are not well understood. Researchers have hypothesized that an as-yet-unidentified virus may stimulate the immune system and trigger the disease. When the disease is present in younger women, symptoms often improve during pregnancy, when estrogen levels are higher, the opposite of what is seen in the case of lupus. Therefore, although estrogen levels may play a role in these disorders, its effects appear to be influenced by many other factors.

Other autoimmune disorders more common among women than men include multiple sclerosis, a neurological

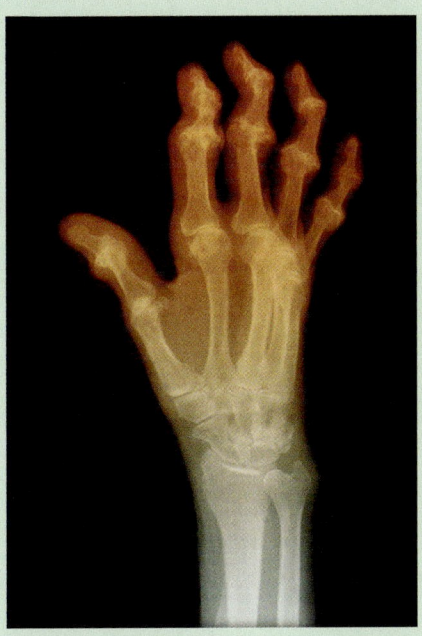

disease caused by the destruction of the protective coating around nerves; scleroderma, a connective tissue disease characterized by thickening, hardening, and tightening of the skin; and Graves' disease, characterized by an increase in the production of thyroid hormone, which affects metabolism and many body systems.

to reduce the risk of infection any better than regular soap, especially if you wash properly. Use hand sanitizer when soap and water aren't available; make sure the product is at least 60% alcohol.

- Avoid contact with people who are contagious with an infectious disease.

- Make sure you drink water only from clean sources. Unpurified water from lakes and streams can carry pathogens, even if it seems pristine.

- Avoid contact with disease carriers such as rodents, mosquitoes, and ticks. Never touch or feed wild animals or rodents.

- Practice safer sex (as described in Chapter 18).

- Do not use injectable drugs of any kind (see Chapter 9).

- Make sure you have received all your recommended vaccinations, and keep them up-to-date. Your physician can tell you exactly what immunizations you need and when you should have them.

SUMMARY

- The step-by-step process by which infections are transmitted from one person to another involves the pathogen, its reservoir, a portal of exit, a means of transmission, a portal of entry, and a new host.

- Infection can be prevented by breaking the chain at any point. Strategies include public health measures such as treatment of drinking water and individual actions such as hand washing.

- Physical and chemical barriers to microorganisms include skin, mucous membranes, and the cilia lining the respiratory tract.

- The immune response is carried out by white blood cells that are continuously produced in the bone marrow. These include neutrophils, macrophages, dendritic cells, natural killer cells, and lymphocytes.

- The immune response has four stages: recognition of the invading pathogen; rapid replication of killer T cells

Immunity and Stress

Studies have shown that rates of illness are higher for weeks or even months in people who have experienced the severe emotional trauma of divorce or the death of a loved one. But can commonplace anxieties and stresses also cause measurable changes in the immune system? And can common stress-management techniques boost the immune system? The answer to these questions appears to be yes. Consider the following research findings:

• Medical students taking final exams showed a much weaker immune response to a hepatitis vaccination than unstressed students. In other studies, stress was associated with lower T-cell responses and antibody levels following influenza vaccinations.

• People with higher levels of stress and who had a negative or pessimistic outlook developed more colds over the course of a yearlong study than individuals with lower levels of stress and a more positive outlook.

• In a study of caregivers, relaxation sessions were associated with increased secretion of cytokines in minor wounds, thus speeding healing. Relaxation and imagery have been shown to increase T-cell levels in some people.

• A study comparing parents of children with cancer (who presumably had high stress levels) with parents of healthy children found that stress appears to interfere with the body's ability to shut down the inflammatory response after it gets started. Continuing high levels of cytokines and inflammation could harm health. The same study found that social support improves the immune response.

In seeking to explain these effects, researchers are looking at the connections between stress, hormones, and immunity. Some hormones, such as cortisol, appear to impair the ability of immune cells to multiply and function. Others, such as prolactin, seem to give immune cells a boost. By matching stress levels and hormonal changes to the ups and downs of immune function, researchers hope to gain a better grasp of the shifting chemistry of mind and immunity.

---

and B cells; attack by killer T cells and macrophages; and suppression of the immune response.

• Immunization is based on the body's ability to remember previously encountered organisms and retain its strength against them.

• Allergic reactions occur when the immune system responds to harmless substances as if they were dangerous antigens.

• Bacteria are single-celled organisms; some cause disease in humans. Bacterial infections include pneumonia, meningitis, strep throat, toxic shock syndrome, tuberculosis, Lyme disease, and ulcers.

• Most antibiotics work by interrupting the production of new bacteria; they do *not* work against viruses. Bacteria can become resistant to antibiotics.

• Viruses cannot grow or reproduce themselves; different viruses cause the common cold, influenza, measles, mumps, rubella, chicken pox, cold sores, mononucleosis, encephalitis, hepatitis, polio, and warts.

• Other diseases are caused by certain types of fungi, protozoa, parasitic worms, and prions.

• Autoimmune diseases occur when the body identifies its own cells as foreign.

• The immune system needs little help other than adequate nutrition and rest, a moderate lifestyle, and protection from excessive stress. Vaccinations also help protect against disease.

FOR MORE INFORMATION

BOOKS

Barry, J. 2005. *The Great Influenza: The Epic Story of the Deadliest Plague in History.* New York: Penguin. *A compelling account of the medical, social, and political aspects of the influenza epidemic of 1918–1919.*

Bollet, A. J. 2004. *Plagues and Poxes: The Impact of Human History on Epidemic Disease.* New York: Demos Medical. *Describes how human activity affects diseases.*

Roitt, I. M., et al. 2006. *Roitt's Essential Immunology,* 11th ed. London: Blackwell. *A highly readable introduction to the science of immunology.*

Siegel, M. 2006. *Bird Flu: Everything You Need to Know About the Next Pandemic.* New York: Wiley. *A practicing physician and teacher examines the potential threat of an avian flu outbreak and explains the measures we can take to protect ourselves.*

Sompayrac, L. M. 2008. *How the Immune System Works.* 3rd ed. Malden, Mass.: Blackwell Science. *A highly readable overview of basic concepts of immunity.*

ORGANIZATIONS, HOTLINES, AND WEB SITES

Alliance for the Prudent Use of Antibiotics. Provides information on the proper use of antibiotics and tips for avoiding infections.

http://www.tufts.edu/med/apua

American Academy of Allergy, Asthma, and Immunology. Provides information and publications; pollen counts are available from the Web site.

http://www.aaaai.org

American Autoimmune-Related Diseases Association. Provides background information, coping tips, and an online knowledge quiz about autoimmune diseases.

http://www.aarda.org

American College of Allergy, Asthma, and Immunology. Provides information for patients and physicians; Web site includes an extensive glossary of terms related to allergies and asthma.

http://www.acaai.org

American Society for Microbiology. Includes a library of images and an introduction to microbes.

http://www.microbeworld.org (Microbe World online)

http://www.washup.org (Clean Hands Campaign)

CDC National Center for Infectious Diseases. Provides extensive information on a wide variety of infectious diseases.

http://www.cdc.gov/ncidod

CDC National Immunization Program. Information and answers to frequently asked questions about immunizations.

http://www.cdc.gov/nip

http://www.cdc.gov/travel

Cells Alive! Includes micrographs of immune cells and pathogens at work.

http://www.cellsalive.com

National Foundation for Infectious Diseases. Provides information about a variety of diseases and disease issues.

http://www.nfid.org

National Institute of Allergy and Infectious Diseases. Includes fact sheets about many topics relating to allergies and infectious diseases, including tuberculosis and STDs.

http://www.niaid.nih.gov

World Health Organization: Infectious Diseases. Provides fact sheets about many emerging and tropical diseases as well as information about current outbreaks.

http://www.who.int/topics/infectious_diseases/en/

See also the listings in Chapter 12 (food safety), Chapter 18, and Appendix B.

SELECTED BIBLIOGRAPHY

Andries, K., et al. 2005. A diarylquinoline drug active on the ATP synthetase of *Mycobacterium tuberculosis*. *Science* 307(5707): 223–227.

Arbes, S. J., et al. 2005. Prevalences of positive skin test responses to 10 common allergens in the US population: Results from the third National Health and Nutrition Examination Survey. *Journal of Allergy and Clinical Immunology* 116(2): 377–383.

Cashman, N. R., and B. Caughey. 2004. Prion diseases—Close to an effective therapy? *Nature Reviews: Drug Discovery* 3(12): 874–884.

Centers for Disease Control and Prevention. 2006. Pertussis—United States, 2001–2003. *Morbidity and Mortality Weekly Report* 54(50): 1283–1286.

Centers for Disease Control and Prevention. 2006. Preventing tetanus, diphtheria, and pertussis among adolescents: Use of tetanus toxoid, reduced diphtheria toxoid and acellular pertussis vaccine. *Morbidity and Mortality Weekly Report* 55(RR03): 1–34.

Centers for Disease Control and Prevention. 2006. Progress toward interruption of wild poliovirus transmission—Worldwide, January 2005–March 2006. *Morbidity and Mortality Weekly Report* 55(16): 458–462.

Centers for Disease Control and Prevention. 2007. *Healthcare-Associated Methicillin Resistant Staphylococcus Aureus (HA-MRSA)* (http://www.cdc.gov/ncidod/dhqp/ar-mrsa.html; retrieved February 16, 2009).

Centers for Disease Control and Prevention. 2007. Recommended adult immunization schedule—United States, October 2007–September 2008. *Morbidity and Mortality Weekly Report* 56(41): Q1–Q4.

Centers for Disease Control and Prevention. 2008. *Asthma: General Information* (http://www.cdc.gov/asthma/basics.htm; retrieved February 16, 2009).

Centers for Disease Control and Prevention. 2008. *BSE (Bovine Spongiform Encephalopathy, or Mad Cow Disease)* (http://www.cdc.gov/ncidod/dvrd/bse; retrieved February 16, 2009).

Centers for Disease Control and Prevention. 2008. *Flu Activity and Surveillance* (http://www.cdc.gov/flu/weekly/fluactivity.htm; retrieved February 16, 2009).

Centers for Disease Control and Prevention. 2009. Recommended immunization schedules for persons aged 0–18 years—United States, 2009. *Morbidity and Mortality Weekly Report* 57(51): Q1–Q4.

Centers for Disease Control and Prevention. 2008. Trends in tuberculosis—United States, 2007. *Morbidity and Mortality Weekly Report* 57(11): 281–285.

Centers for Disease Control and Prevention. 2008. *West Nile Virus Basics* (http://www.cdc.gov/ncidod/dvbid/westnile/index.htm; retrieved February 16, 2009).

Cieslak, P. R., K. Hedberg, and L. E. Lee. 2004. Chickenpox outbreak in a highly vaccinated school population: In reply. *Pediatrics* 114(4): 1131.

Fairweather, D., and N. R. Rose. 2004. Women and autoimmune diseases. *Emerging Infectious Diseases* 10(11): 2005–2011.

Fauci, A. S. 2004. Emerging infectious diseases: A clear and present danger to humanity. *Journal of the American Medical Association* 292(15): 1887–1888.

Gupta, R. S., et al. 2006. The widening black/white gap in asthma hospitalizations and mortality. *Journal of Allergy and Clinical Immunology* 117(2): 351–358.

Immunization Safety Review Committee. 2004. *Immunization Safety Review: Vaccines and Autism*. Washington, D.C.: National Academy Press.

Keene, W. E., A. C. Markum, and M. Samadpour. 2004. Outbreak of *Pseudomonas aeruginosa* infections caused by commercial piercing of upper ear cartilage. *Journal of the American Medical Association* 291(8): 981–985.

Larson, E. L., et al. 2004. Effect of antibacterial home cleaning and handwashing products on infectious disease symptoms: A randomized, double-blind trial. *Annals of Internal Medicine* 140(5): 321–329.

Lee, G. M., et al. 2005. Illness transmission in the home: A possible role for alcohol-based hand gels. *Pediatrics* 115(4): 852–860.

Levy, S. B., and B. Marshall. 2004. Antibacterial resistance worldwide: Causes, challenges, and responses. *Nature Medicine* 10(12 Suppl): S122–S129.

National Immunization Program. 2005. *Epidemiology and Prevention of Vaccine-Preventable Diseases*, 8th ed. Rev. Waldorf, Md.: Public Health Foundation.

Oren, W. 2005. Worrying about killer flu. *Discover*, February.

Parker, S. K., et al. 2004. Thimerosal-containing vaccines and autistic spectrum disorder: A critical review of published original data. *Pediatrics* 114(3): 793–804.

Prusiner, S. B. 2004. Detecting mad cow disease. *Scientific American*, July.

Samandari, T., B. P. Bell, and G. L. Armstrong. 2004. Quantifying the impact of hepatitis A immunization in the United States, 1995–2001. *Vaccine* 22(31–32): 4342–4350.

Smeeth, L., et al. 2004. MMR vaccination and pervasive developmental disorders: A case-control study. *Lancet* 364(9438): 963–969.

Snow, R. W., et al. 2005. The global distribution of clinical episodes of *Plasmodium falciparum* malaria. *Nature* 434: 214–217.

Vazquez, M., et al. 2004. Effectiveness over time of varicella vaccine. *Journal of the American Medical Association* 291(7): 851–855.

World Health Organization. 2004. *WHO Guidelines for the Global Surveillance of Severe Acute Respiratory Syndrome (SARS), Updated Recommendations, October 2004*. Geneva: World Health Organization.

World Health Organization. 2007. *The World Health Report 2007*. Geneva: World Health Organization.

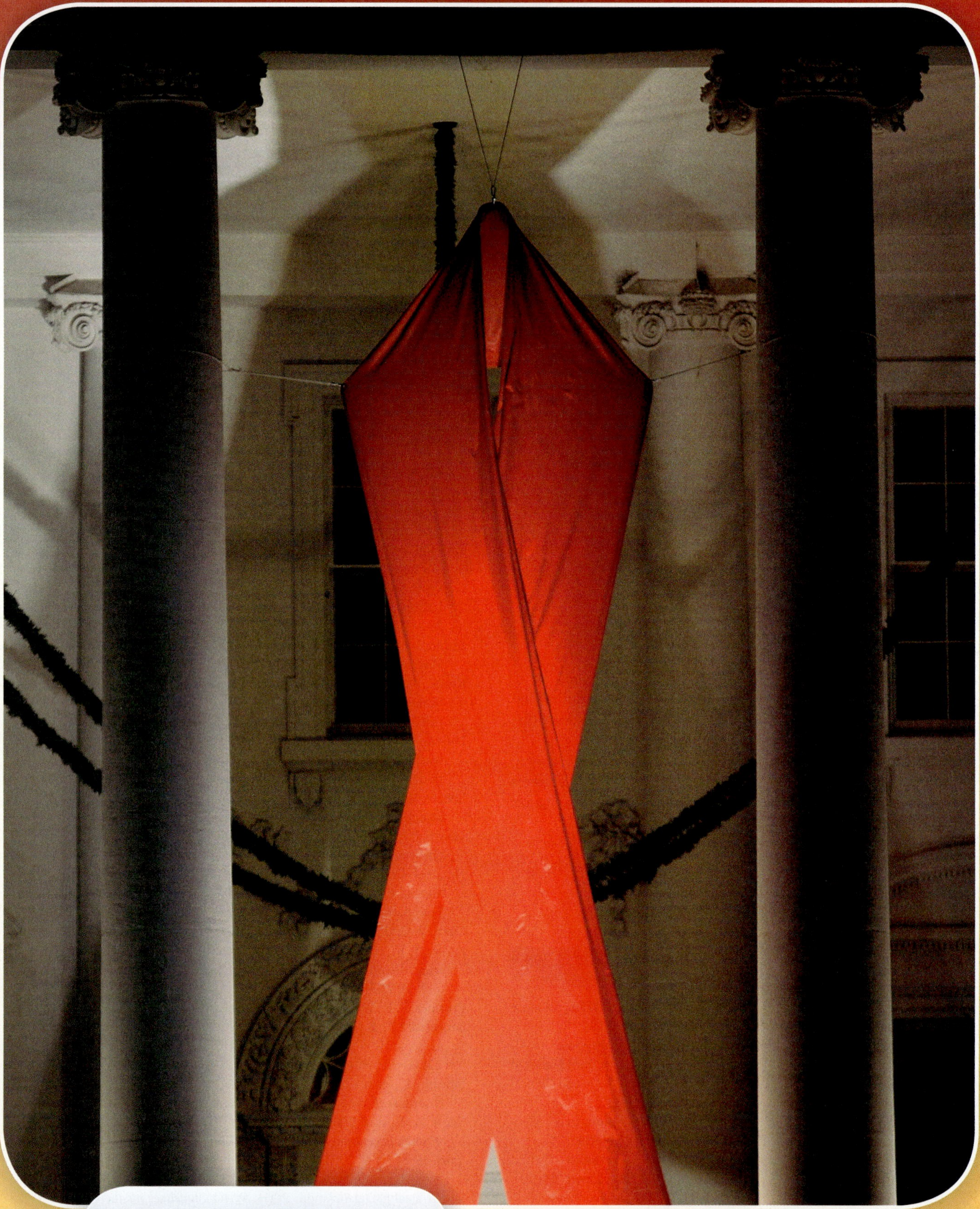

Core Concepts in Health
connect
PERSONAL HEALTH

http://www.mcgrawhillconnect.com/personalhealth

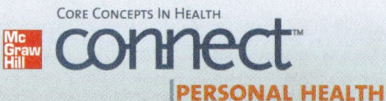

SEXUALLY TRANSMITTED DISEASES

LOOKING AHEAD>>>>>

AFTER READING THIS CHAPTER, YOU SHOULD BE ABLE TO:

- Explain how HIV infection affects the body and how it is transmitted, diagnosed, and treated
- Discuss the symptoms, risks, and treatments for the other major STDs
- List strategies for protecting yourself from STDs

TEST YOUR KNOWLEDGE

1. **If you have a sexually transmitted disease (STD), you will know it.**
   True or false?

2. **Worldwide, HIV infection is spread primarily via which of the following?**
   a. injection drug use
   b. sex between men
   c. mother-to-child transmission
   d. heterosexual sex

3. **Of the developed countries, which one has the highest rate of sexually transmitted diseases?**
   a. Germany
   b. United States
   c. Canada
   d. France

4. **A man with an STD is more likely to transmit the infection to a female partner than vice versa.**
   True or false?

5. **After you have had an STD once, you become immune to that disease and cannot get it again.**
   True or false?

ANSWERS

1. **FALSE.** Many people with STDs have no symptoms and do not know they are infected; however, they can still pass an infection to their partners.

2. **D.** The vast majority of HIV infection cases worldwide result from heterosexual contact, and nearly two-thirds of all new cases occur in teenage girls and young women.

3. **B.** The United States has the highest rate of STDs of any developed nation. If current trends continue, 50% of all Americans will contract a sexually transmitted disease by age 25.

4. **TRUE.** For many STDs, infected men are at least twice as likely as infected women to transmit an STD to their partner.

5. **FALSE.** Reinfection with STDs is very common. For example, if you are treated and cured of chlamydia and then you have sex with your untreated partner, the chances are very good that you will be infected again.

Considering the intimate nature of sexual activity, it is not surprising that many diseases can be transmitted from one person to another through sexual contact. Of course, colds, influenza, and many other infections can spread from one sexual partner to another, but sexual contact is not the primary means of transmission for these illnesses. **Sexually transmitted diseases (STDs)**—also called **sexually transmitted infections (STIs)**—spread from person to person mainly through sexual activity.

STDs are a particularly insidious group of illnesses because a person can be infected and able to transmit the disease, yet not look or feel sick; this is why the term *sexually transmitted infection (STI)* is coming into common use. (This chapter uses both terms STD and STI in discussing these illnesses.)

Everyone should have a clear understanding of what STDs are, how they are transmitted, and how they can be prevented. Many STDs can also be cured if treated early and properly. This chapter introduces the major forms of sexually transmitted diseases; it also provides information about healthy, safer sexual behavior to help you understand how to reduce the further spread of these diseases.

THE MAJOR STDS

The following seven STDs pose a major health threat:

- HIV/AIDS
- Hepatitis
- Syphilis
- Chlamydia
- Gonorrhea
- Herpes
- Human papillomavirus (HPV)

These diseases are considered major threats because they are serious in themselves, cause serious complications if left untreated, and pose risks to a fetus or newborn. STDs often result in serious long-term consequences, including chronic pain, infertility, stillbirths, genital cancers, and death.

All of these diseases have a relatively high incidence among Americans (Table 18.1). In fact, the United States

Table 18.1	Annual New Cases of STDs in the United States
STD	**New Cases**
Trichomoniasis	7,400,000
HPV	6,200,000
Chlamydia	1,100,000
Genital herpes	371,000
Gonorrhea	351,000
HIV infection	56,000
Hepatitis B	46,000
Syphilis (all stages)	41,000

SOURCES: Centers for Disease Control and Prevention, National Center for HIV/AIDS, Viral Hepatitis, STD, and TB Prevention. 2008. *2006 Disease Profile* (http://www.cdc.gov/nchhstp/Publications/docs/2006_Disease_Profile_508_FINAL.pdf; retrieved February 17, 2009). Centers for Disease Control and Prevention. 2008. *Genital HPV Infection—CDC Fact Sheet* (http://www.cdc.gov/std/hpv/stdfact-hpv.htm; retrieved February 17, 2009); Centers for Disease Control and Prevention. 2008. *Sexually Transmitted Disease Surveillance, 2007.* Atlanta: Centers for Disease Control and Prevention.

has the highest rate of STDs of any developed nation; at current rates, half of all young people will acquire an STD by age 25. A 2007 report from the Centers for Disease Control and Prevention (CDC) shows that many of the most common STDs are on the rise in the United States. In 2008, the CDC estimated that 65 million Americans were infected with an STD, and about 19 million Americans become newly infected with an STD each year.

STIs are caused by more than 30 different organisms, including viruses, bacteria, fungi, and protozoa. Table 18.2 lists the pathogens responsible for these and other STDs.

HIV Infection and AIDS

The **human immunodeficiency virus (HIV)** causes **acquired immunodeficiency syndrome (AIDS),** a disease that ultimately kills most of its victims, especially in parts of the world where adequate treatment is not available. AIDS originated in Africa sometime during the early twentieth century but was not recognized or named until 1981. The disease spread rapidly throughout the world and is now a leading cause of death globally.

An estimated total of 65 million people have been infected since the epidemic began—nearly 1% of the world's population—and tens of millions of those people have died (see the box "HIV/AIDS Around the World" on p. 554). Currently, about 33 million people are infected with HIV/AIDS worldwide (Table 18.3), and most of these people will die within the next 10 years.

For the first time in the history of the AIDS epidemic, the number of people worldwide that are living with HIV infection has begun to level off. Many experts believe that the global HIV epidemic peaked in the late 1990s, at about 3 million new infections per year, compared with an estimated 2.7 new infections in 2007. Despite a slowing of the

TERMS

sexually transmitted disease (STD) or sexually transmitted infection (STI) A disease that can be transmitted by sexual contact; some can also be transmitted by other means.

human immunodeficiency virus (HIV) The virus that causes HIV infection and AIDS.

acquired immunodeficiency syndrome (AIDS) A generally fatal, incurable, sexually transmitted viral disease.

HIV infection A chronic, progressive viral infection that damages the immune system.

CD4 T cell A type of white blood cell that helps coordinate the activity of the immune system; the primary target for HIV infection. A decrease in the number of these cells correlates with the risk and severity of HIV-related illness.

Table 18.2 — Sexually Transmitted Pathogens and Associated Diseases

Bacteria

Chlamydia trachomatis	Chlamydia, pelvic inflammatory disease, epididymitis, urethritis
Gardnerella vaginalis	Bacterial vaginosis
Haemophilus ducreyi	Chancroid
Neisseria gonorrhoeae	Gonorrhea, pelvic inflammatory disease, epididymitis, urethritis
Treponema pallidum	Syphilis

Viruses

Hepatitis B virus (HBV)	Hepatitis, cirrhosis, liver cancer
Herpes simplex viruses (HSV)	Genital herpes, oral-labial herpes (cold sores)
Human immunodeficiency virus (HIV)	HIV infection/AIDS
Human papillomavirus (HPV)	Genital warts, cervical, anal, penile, vulvar, and oral cancers

Protozoa

Trichomonas vaginalis	Trichomoniasis

Ectoparasites

Phthirus pubis	Pubic lice
Sarcoptes scabiei	Scabies

epidemic, however, AIDS remains the primary cause of death in Africa and continues to be a major cause of mortality around the world.

In the United States, about 1.1 million people have been infected with HIV and about 56,000 new HIV infections were reported in 2006. Nearly 550,000 Americans have died from AIDS since the start of the epidemic in 1981. Today, about 25% of HIV-infected Americans are unaware of their condition.

HIV is thought to be a relatively new disease in humans. In 1998, researchers discovered a group of wild chimpanzees in west equatorial Africa that carry simian immunodeficiency virus (SIV), a virus very similar to the pandemic strain of HIV seen around the world in humans. Genetic evidence shows that SIV first spread from chimpanzees to humans in the 1930s, when the trapping and butchering of chimpanzees was common. SIV is fairly benign in chimps, but as it "made the jump" to humans, it became more virulent and deadly. Poverty, the harsh environment, crowded living conditions, and unsound vaccination practices contributed to the disease's spread through local populations. Eventually, global travel allowed the disease to spread to the rest of the world.

> ### QUICK STATS
> **Worldwide, about 1 million people acquire an STD (including HIV) every day.**
> —World Health Organization (WHO), 2008

Table 18.3 — HIV/AIDS Global Summary: 2007

People Living with HIV	
Adult men	15,300,000
Adult women	15,500,000
Children (<15 years old)	2,000,000
Total	**32,800,000**
People Newly Infected with HIV	
Adults	2,330,000
Children (<15 years old)	370,000
Total	**2,700,000**
AIDS Deaths	
Adults	**1,730,000**
Children (<15 years old)	270,000
Total	**2,000,000**

SOURCES: Joint United Nations Programme on HIV/AIDS (UNAIDS). 2008. *2008 Report on the Global AIDS Epidemic.* Geneva: UNAIDS.

What Is HIV Infection? HIV infection is a chronic disease that progressively damages the body's immune system, making an otherwise healthy person less able to resist a variety of infections and disorders. Normally, when a virus or other pathogen enters the body, it is targeted and destroyed by the immune system. But HIV attacks the immune system itself, invading and taking over **CD4 T cells,** monocytes, and macrophages, which are essential elements of the immune system (Chapter 17). HIV enters a human cell and converts its own genetic material, RNA, into DNA. It then inserts this DNA into the chromosomes of the host cell. The viral DNA takes over the CD4 cell, causing it to produce new copies of HIV; it also makes the CD4 cell incapable of performing its immune functions.

Immediately following infection with HIV, billions of infectious particles are produced every day. For a time, the immune system keeps pace, also producing billions of new cells. Unlike the virus, however, the immune system cannot make new cells indefinitely; as long as the virus keeps replicating, it wins in the end. The destruction of the immune system is signaled by the loss of CD4 T cells

DIMENSIONS OF DIVERSITY

In 2006, the world marked the twenty-fifth year since AIDS, a previously unknown disease, was diagnosed in 5 young gay men in Los Angeles. We now know that HIV originated in Africa about five decades earlier. HIV is now a worldwide scourge, with 65 million people infected and 25 million deaths since the epidemic began. Although some developments in efforts to address the epidemic have been promising, the number of people living with AIDS increased in every region of the world between 2004 and 2006.

The vast majority of cases—95%—have occurred in developing countries, where heterosexual contact is the primary means of transmission, responsible for 85% of all adult infections. In the developed world, HIV is increasingly becoming a disease that disproportionately affects the poor and ethnic minorities. Worldwide, women are the fastest-growing group of newly infected people; half of adults living with HIV in 2007 were women. In addition, an estimated 2 million children are living with HIV infection and about 12 million children are AIDS orphans.

Sub-Saharan Africa remains the hardest hit of all areas of the world. Two-thirds of all adults and children with HIV live in this region, and three-quarters of all deaths due to AIDS in 2007 occurred here. However, because the epidemic started about 10 years later in Asia than in Africa, experts expect an explosion of new cases in Asia. And because Asia accounts for more than 50% of the world's population, the pool of people at risk is much larger than in Africa. India has overtaken South Africa as the country with the largest number of people living with HIV infection. HIV is also spreading rapidly in Eastern Europe, and former Soviet countries have seen a fiftyfold increase in HIV infection in the last decade.

Efforts to combat AIDS are complicated by political, economic, and cultural barriers. Education and prevention programs are often hampered by resistance from social and religious institutions and by the taboo on openly discussing sexual issues. Condoms are not commonly used in many countries, and women in many societies do not have sufficient control over their lives to demand that men use condoms during sex. Prevention approaches that have had success include STD treatment and education, public education campaigns about safer sex, and syringe exchange programs for injection drug users.

In countries where there is a substantial imbalance in the social power of men and women, empowering women is a crucial priority in reducing the spread of HIV. In particular, reducing sexual violence against women, allowing women property and inheritance rights, and increasing women's access to education and employment are essential.

International efforts are under way to make condoms more available by lowering their price and to develop effective antiviral creams that women can use without the knowledge of their partners. Other potential strategies for fighting the spread of HIV include the widespread use of drugs to suppress genital herpes simplex, an extremely common STD that can dramatically increase transmission of HIV. Also, the practice of male circumcision might be useful in reducing the spread of HIV (and chlamydia, discussed later in this chapter). Recent research has shown a 60% reduction in HIV transmission among circumcised men compared with uncircumcised men, even when controlling for other factors.

In developed nations such as the United States, new drugs are easing AIDS symptoms and lowering viral levels dramatically for some patients. In the past few years, a small but growing number of people in poor countries have gained access to antiviral drugs because of the introduction of inexpensive generic drugs and increasing international funding for HIV treatment. Still, the vast majority of people with HIV remain untreated.

(Figure 18.1 on p. 556). As CD4 cells decline, an infected person may begin to experience mild to moderately severe symptoms. A person is diagnosed with full-blown AIDS when he or she develops one of the conditions defined as a marker for AIDS or when the number of CD4 cells in the blood drops below a certain level (200/µl). People with AIDS are vulnerable to a number of serious **opportunistic (secondary) infections.** The infections that most often prove deadly for people with HIV are seldom serious in people with a healthy immune system. Opportunistic infections are usually caused by organisms that are common in the environment and generally do not cause illness in healthy people.

The first weeks after being infected with HIV are called the *primary infection* phase. Most, but not all, infected people develop flulike symptoms during this time. During primary HIV infection, people have large amounts of HIV in the bloodstream, making them much more infectious than they will be several months later when they enter the chronic infection stage. Experts believe that about half of all cases of HIV infection are acquired from people who are in the primary infection stage. The vast majority of people with primary infection have no idea they are infected, and even if they suspect infection and get tested, the most commonly used tests for HIV will be negative in this stage. Special tests can detect primary infection, and experts believe that improved detection of primary infection could help reduce the spread of the virus.

The next phase of HIV infection is the chronic **asymptomatic** (symptom-free) stage. This period can last from 2 to 20 years, with an average of 11 years in untreated adults. During this time the virus progressively infects and destroys the cells of the immune system. People infected with HIV can transmit the disease to others, even if they

TERMS

opportunistic (secondary) infection An infection caused when organisms take the opportunity presented by a primary (initial) infection to multiply and cause a new, different infection.

asymptomatic Showing no signs or symptoms of a disease.

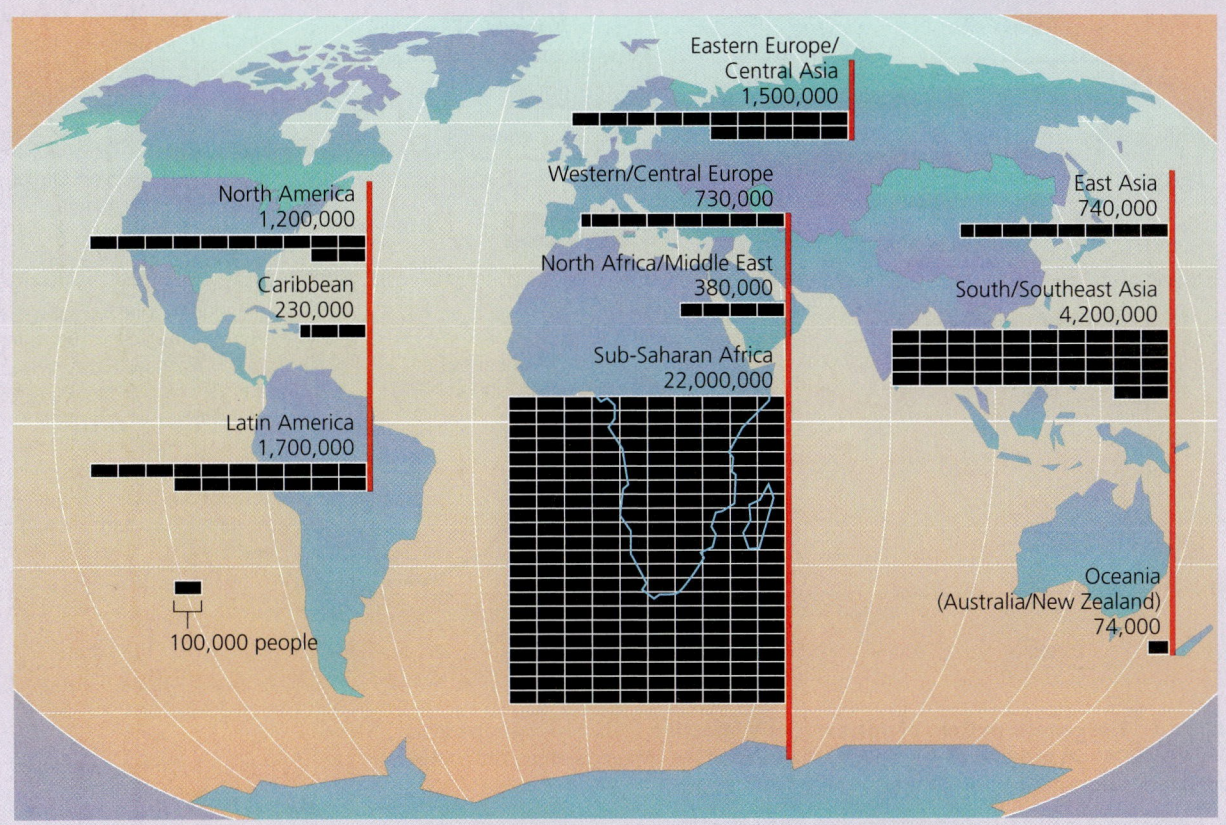

Approximate number of people living with HIV/AIDS in 2007.

SOURCE: Joint United Nations Programme on HIV/AIDS (UNAIDS). 2008. *2008 Report on the Global AIDS Epidemic.* Geneva: UNAIDS.

are symptom-free. Even if they receive treatment, they remain infectious to varying degrees throughout their lives.

Transmitting the Virus   HIV lives only within cells and body fluids, not outside the body. It is transmitted by blood and blood products, semen, vaginal and cervical secretions, and breast milk. It cannot live in air, in water, or on objects or surfaces such as toilet seats, eating utensils, or telephones. The three main routes of HIV transmission are (1) from specific kinds of sexual contact, (2) from direct exposure to infected blood, and (3) from an HIV-infected woman to her fetus during pregnancy or childbirth or to her infant during breastfeeding.

SEXUAL CONTACT   HIV is more likely to be transmitted by unprotected anal or vaginal intercourse than by other sexual activities. During vaginal intercourse, male-to-female transmission is more likely to occur than female-to-male transmission. HIV has been found in preejaculatory fluid, so transmission can occur before ejaculation. Being the receptive partner during unprotected anal intercourse is the riskiest of all sexual activities. Oral-genital contact carries some risk of transmission, although less than anal or vaginal intercourse. HIV can be transmitted through tiny tears, traumatized points, or irritated areas in the lining of the vagina, cervix, penis, anus, mouth, and throat and through direct infection of cells in these areas. Sexual assault is an important factor in the transmission of HIV both in the United States and throughout the world. Protection is almost never used during sexual assault, and tissue trauma is generally greater than in unforced sexual activity.

The presence of lesions, blisters, or inflammation from other STDs in the genital, anal, or oral areas makes it two to nine times easier for the virus to be passed. Spermicides may also cause irritation and increase the risk of HIV transmission. Recent studies of the widely used spermicide nonoxynol-9 (N-9) found that frequent use may cause vaginal and rectal irritation, increasing the risk of transmission of HIV and other STDs. The World Health Organization (WHO) recommends that spermicides containing N-9 not be used for protection against HIV and STDs. Condoms or lubricants with N-9 should never be used during

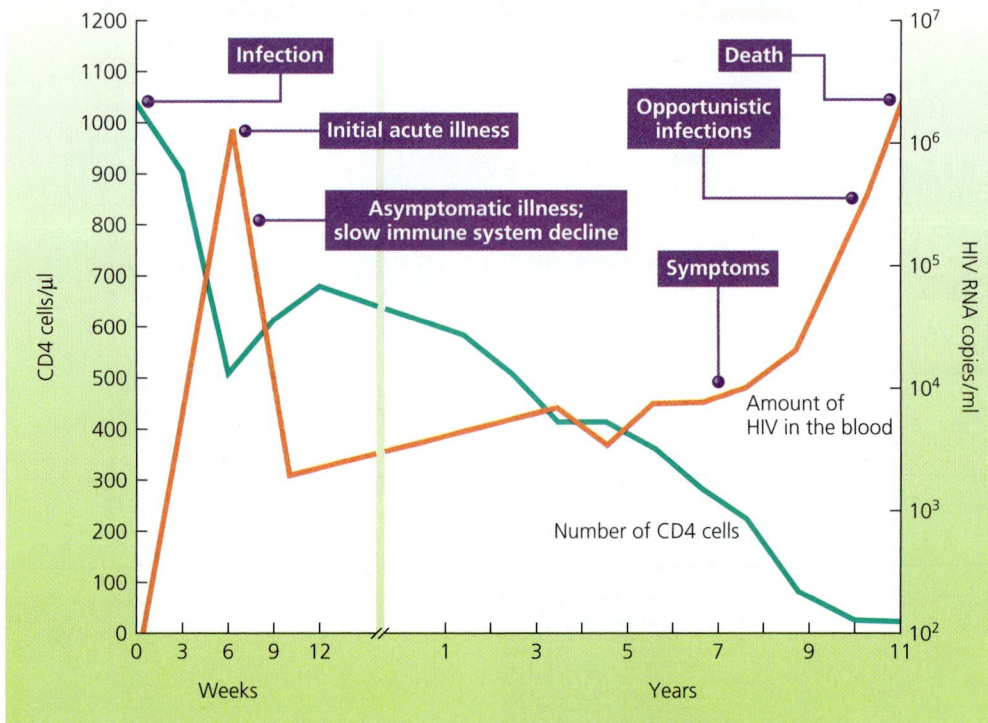

During the initial acute illness, CD4 levels fall sharply and HIV RNA levels increase; 60–90% of infected people experience flulike symptoms during this period. Antibodies to HIV usually appear 2–12 weeks after the initial infection. During the asymptomatic phase that follows, CD4 levels gradually decline, and HIV RNA levels again increase. Due to declines in immunity, infected individuals eventually begin to experience symptoms; when CD4 levels drop very low, people become vulnerable to serious opportunistic infections characteristic of full-blown AIDS. Chronic or recurrent illnesses continue until the immune system fails and death results.

FIGURE 18.1 The general pattern of untreated HIV infection. The blue line represents the number of CD4 cells in the blood, a marker for the status of the immune system. The orange line shows the amount of HIV RNA in the blood.

SOURCE: Adapted from A. S. Fauci & Giuseppe Pantaleo, 1996, "Immunopathogenic Mechanisms of HIV infection," *Annals of Internal Medicine* 124(7), 654–663, Figure 1. Reprinted with permission of the American College of Physicians.

anal intercourse because N-9 damages the lining of the rectum, providing an entry point for HIV and other STDs.

The risk of HIV transmission during oral sex increases if a person has poor oral hygiene, has oral sores, or has brushed or flossed just before or after oral sex. Some evidence suggests that recent consumption of alcohol may make the cells that line the mouth more susceptible to infection with HIV.

Studies in developing nations with high rates of HIV infection have found that circumcised males have a lower risk of HIV infection than uncircumcised males. A study in South Africa showed a 60% reduction in new infections among men who were circumcised as part of the study, and another study in Kenya and Uganda showed an approximate halving of risk among men who were circumcised. Circumcision is uncommon in most parts of the world, but these findings are heightening interest in the practice. In the United States, where circumcision is common and HIV infection rates are much lower, circumcision does not appear to offer any significant protection against HIV.

DIRECT CONTACT WITH INFECTED BLOOD Direct contact with the blood of an infected person is another major route of HIV transmission. Needles used to inject drugs (including heroin, cocaine, and anabolic steroids) are routinely contaminated by the blood of the user. If needles are shared, small amounts of one person's blood are directly injected into another person's bloodstream. HIV may be transmitted through subcutaneous and intramuscular injection as well, from needles or blades used in acupuncture, tattooing, ritual scarring, and piercing of the earlobes, nose, lip, nipple, navel, or other body part.

Nearly 20% of all new U.S. cases of HIV are caused, directly or indirectly, by sharing drug injection equipment contaminated with HIV. Drug users, their sex partners, and their children are all at extremely high risk for HIV infection. Most experts agree that syringe exchange programs combined with increased substance abuse treatment and prevention could significantly reduce the spread of HIV.

HIV has been transmitted in blood and blood products used in the medical treatment of injuries and illnesses, resulting in about 14,000 cases of AIDS in the United States. Nearly all of these cases occurred in the early days of the AIDS epidemic, before effective screening tests were available. All blood in licensed U.S. blood banks and plasma centers is now thoroughly screened for HIV. The American Blood Bank Association estimates that fewer than 1 in 2 million units of blood products is capable of transmitting HIV. Unfortunately, the blood supply is much less safe in the rest of the world. In the developing world in particular, blood is often not adequately tested and blood donors are not always appropriately screened. In these countries, the risk of contracting HIV or another serious infection from a blood transfusion is very high. The WHO estimates that about 5% of all cases of HIV infection worldwide have resulted from the transfusion of infected blood and blood products.

A small number of health care workers have acquired HIV on the job; most of these cases involve needle sticks, in which a health care worker is accidentally stuck with a needle used on an infected patient. The likelihood of a patient acquiring HIV infection from a health care worker is almost negligible; the risk to health care workers from infected patients is much greater.

What about contact with other body fluids? Trace amounts of HIV have been found in the saliva and tears of some infected people. However, researchers believe that these fluids do not carry enough of the virus to infect another person. (In the rare cases of HIV infection linked to deep kissing or biting, the virus is thought to have been transmitted in blood from oral sores rather than in saliva.) Contact with the urine or feces of an infected person may carry some risk, but contact with sweat is not believed to carry any risk. There is no evidence that HIV can be spread by insects such as mosquitoes.

MOTHER-TO-CHILD TRANSMISSION The final major route of HIV transmission is mother-to-child, also called *vertical,* or *perinatal, transmission,* which can occur during pregnancy, childbirth, or breastfeeding. About 25–30% of infants born to untreated HIV-infected mothers are also infected with the virus; testing and treatment can dramatically lower this infection rate. Worldwide, about two-thirds of vertical transmission occurs during pregnancy and childbirth and one-third through breastfeeding.

HIV-infected children rarely appear ill at birth, but they begin to develop health problems over the first months and years of life. About 20% of infected children become very ill and progress to AIDS or death by age 4; the remaining 80% develop problems more slowly. In the United States and other developed countries, new treatments to reduce vertical transmission are in use, and the number of new cases of this type of HIV infection has declined more than 90% since 1992.

NOT THROUGH CASUAL CONTACT A person is not at risk of getting HIV infection by being in the same classroom, dining room, or even household with someone who is infected. Before this was generally known, many people with HIV infection, including children, were the targets of ostracism, hysteria, and outright violence. Today, it is an acknowledged responsibility of everyone to treat people with HIV infection with respect and compassion, regardless of their age or how they became infected.

Populations of Special Concern for HIV Infection

Among Americans with AIDS, the most common means of HIV exposure is sexual activity between men; heterosexual contact and injection drug use (IDU) are the next most common (Figure 18.2, above). Although HIV transmission occurs through specific individual behaviors, dis-

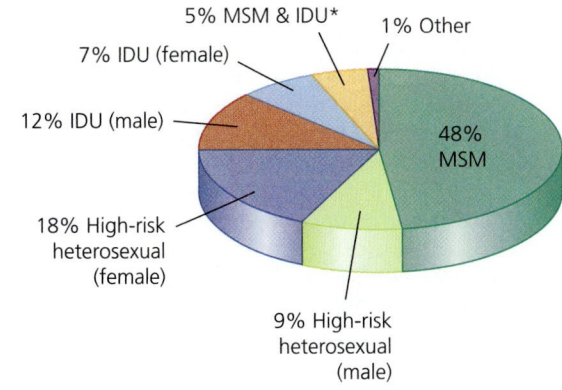

Estimated HIV Prevalence by Transmission Category, 2006

- 5% MSM & IDU*
- 1% Other
- 7% IDU (female)
- 12% IDU (male)
- 18% High-risk heterosexual (female)
- 9% High-risk heterosexual (male)
- 48% MSM

* MSM = Men who have sex with men
IDU = Injection drug users

FIGURE 18.2   Routes of HIV transmission Among Americans

SOURCE: Centers for Disease Control and Prevention. 2008. *New Estimates of U.S. HIV Prevalence, 2006.* (http://www.cdc.gov/hiv/topics/surveillance/resources/factsheets/pdf/prevalence.pdf; retrieved February 17, 2009).

proportionately high rates of infection in certain groups are tied to social, cultural, and economic factors. In 2008, the CDC estimated that 75% of HIV-positive Americans were men; the remaining 25% were women. HIV in the United States is increasingly becoming a disease that affects ethnic minorities, women, and the poor. Women, especially African American women and Latinas, make up an increasingly large proportion of all U.S. AIDS cases. Overall, African American men and women are vastly overrepresented among people newly diagnosed with AIDS. See the box "HIV/AIDS Among African Americans and Latinos" on p. 558 for more on these trends.

Another group of people at increased risk for HIV infection are young men who have sex with men. HIV infection has increased in recent years among this group, primarily because more young men are engaging in unsafe sexual practices such as unprotected anal intercourse. There are probably several factors underlying this trend. Young gay men are less likely than older men to have experienced watching friends die from AIDS and thus are more removed from the reality of the disease. They may be less afraid of acquiring HIV be-

96% of new HIV infections occur in low- and middle-income countries.

—UNAIDS, 2007

QUICK STATS

cause of advances in treatment and a false belief that a cure is just around the corner. Drug use, especially use of crystal methamphetamine or club drugs, and the practice of meeting sex partners over the Internet are also associated with increased rates of unsafe sex and HIV infection among men who have sex with men.

HIV/AIDS Among African Americans and Latinos

When HIV infection rates are examined in relation to populations, one can see that African Americans and Latinos have been disproportionately affected by the HIV/AIDS epidemic. Although whites make up the majority of the population in the United States (67%), the prevalence of HIV/AIDS is greater among African Americans and Latinos because higher percentages of those ethnic groups have become infected with HIV.

• African Americans represent 12% of the U.S. population but account for 46% of all HIV infections. According to the CDC, the overall rate of HIV infection among blacks is almost eight times as high as that of whites (see figures).

• African American men have the highest rates of HIV infection of any ethnic group, with an infection rate that is about six times higher than the rate for white men. African American women suffer an HIV infection rate that is about 18 times greater than the rate for white women.

• Latinos account for 15% of the U.S. population, but represent 18% of HIV infections. The overall rate of HIV infection among Latinos is about three times higher than the rate for whites.

• Latino men have an infection rate that is about twice the rate for white men. Latino women have an HIV infection rate that is four times the rate for white women.

In 2005, AIDS was the ninth leading cause of death among African Americans of both sexes, and the seventh leading cause of death among African American men. That year, the overall death rate from AIDS among black males was eight times higher than that of white males; among black women, the AIDS death rate was 15 times higher than that of white women. The AIDS death rate among Latinos (male and female) was twice as high as that of whites.

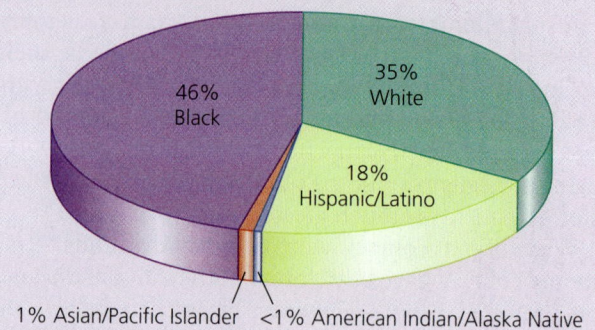

Estimated HIV Prevalence by Race/Ethnicity, 2006

46% Black
35% White
18% Hispanic/Latino
1% Asian/Pacific Islander   <1% American Indian/Alaska Native

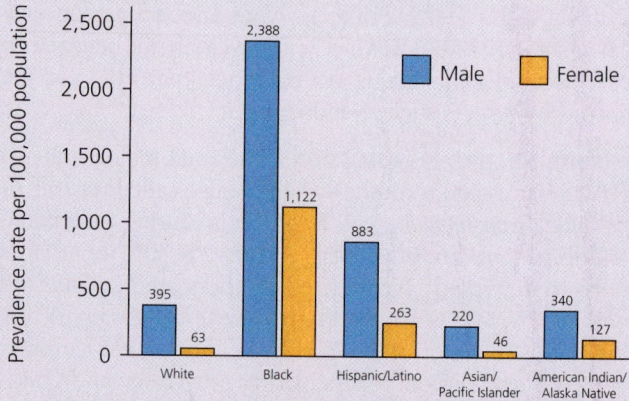

Estimated HIV Prevalence Rate (per 100,000 population) by Race/Ethnicity and Sex, United States—2006

Prevalence rate per 100,000 population

Male   Female

White: 395 / 63
Black: 2,388 / 1,122
Hispanic/Latino: 883 / 263
Asian/Pacific Islander: 220 / 46
American Indian/Alaska Native: 340 / 127

Distribution of HIV infection in the United States, by race.

There also appears to be a growing number of cases among men who acquire HIV through sex with other men but who do not identify themselves as gay. Particularly among minorities, many men who have sex with men also have sex with women, and they identify themselves as heterosexual, not gay or bisexual. Men who have sex with men and still identify themselves as heterosexual are just as likely to be infected with HIV as are gay and bisexual men who are out, but they are much less likely to know their HIV status and so may be more likely to transmit HIV to a male or female partner. Public health efforts directed toward gay men may not reach men in this group, and negative cultural attitudes toward homosexuality may make it difficult for gay and bisexual men to be honest with their partners. This trend endangers not only the men but also their male and female partners.

These patterns of HIV infection reflect complex social, economic, and behavioral factors. Reducing the rates of HIV transmission and AIDS death in minorities, women, and other groups at risk will require dealing with the difficult problems of drug abuse, poverty, and discrimination. HIV prevention programs must be tailored to meet the special needs of minority communities.

Increased testing is one of the most important aspects of HIV prevention, but knowledge of HIV status may not be enough to change behavior. Studies show that up to one-third of people who have been diagnosed with HIV continue to have unprotected sex. Testing must be coupled with strategies not only to encourage HIV-positive people to take the steps necessary to avoid infecting others but also to encourage HIV-negative people to consistently practice safer sex.

Symptoms of HIV Infection   Within a few days or weeks of infection with HIV, some people will develop symptoms of primary HIV infection. These can include fever, fatigue, rashes, headache, swollen lymph nodes, body aches, night sweats, sore throat, nausea, and diar-

Factors contributing to disparities in HIV incidence include the following:

- *Poverty, drug use, and associated problems:* Low income is linked to lack of information about safer sex and HIV testing and treatment, higher rates of injection drug use, and lack of access to health care. Women who are poor and unemployed are more likely to be financially dependent on a male partner and less likely to use condoms; they are more likely to trade sex for money or drugs. Higher rates of incarceration among minorities also contribute to the spread of HIV.

- *Distrust of physicians and public health campaigns:* Surveys suggest that a substantial proportion of blacks believe that HIV information is being withheld from the public and that a cure exists but is being withheld from the poor. These types of beliefs may deter some people from using condoms; they also highlight the need to tailor HIV prevention programs for different groups.

- *Social patterns and perception of risk*: High prevalence of infection in a group, combined with a low perception of risk, contributes to the spread of HIV as people are more likely to encounter an infected sex partner if they choose partners from a group with a high prevalence.

A recent study of young African American men who have sex with men found that despite high rates of risky behavior, most did not perceive themselves at risk for HIV infection and many thought that HIV status could be determined from someone's appearance or whether they identify themselves as straight or gay. Many men in this study did not identify as gay and/or were not open about their sexual identity, and nearly 20% had had recent female sex partners. It is unclear how large a role this pattern plays in the transmission of the virus, but it is a risky pattern for the men and their male and female sexual partners.

New approaches to prevention and treatment will likely be needed to combat the high incidence of HIV/AIDS among African Americans and Latinos. HIV prevention messages need to communicate effectively with the populations most at risk. Programs stressing ethnic and gender pride have been found effective for some groups. To overcome conspiracy beliefs, researchers recommend acknowledging the origin of such beliefs in the context of current and historical discrimination. For those who are already HIV-positive, resources such as peer networks, legal assistance, and on-site child care at clinics may help improve treatment access and success.

The Department of Health and Human Services' Minority HIV/AIDS Initiative Web site (www.omhrc.gov) has information about HIV/AIDS among minority populations and extensive links to relevant organizations.

SOURCES: Centers for Disease Control and Prevention. 2008. *New Estimates of U.S. HIV Prevalence, 2006.* (http://www.cdc.gov/hiv/topics/surveillance/resources/factsheets/pdf/prevalence.pdf; retrieved February 17, 2009); Centers for Disease Control and Prevention. 2008. HIV prevalence estimates—United States, 2006. *Morbidity and Mortality Weekly Report* 57(39): 1073–1076; National Center for Health Statistics. 2007. *Health, United States, 2007 with Chartbook on Trends in the Health of Americans.* Hyattsville, Md.: National Center for Health Statistics.

rhea. Because the symptoms of primary HIV infection are similar to those of many common viral illnesses, the condition often goes undiagnosed, even if an infected individual sees a physician.

Diagnosis of HIV at this very early stage of infection, although uncommon, is extremely beneficial. Immediate treatment is sometimes given to help preserve immune function, slow the progress of the disease, and reduce transmission of HIV to others. It is critical for people who have engaged in behavior that places them at risk for HIV infection and who then experience symptoms of primary HIV infection to immediately inform their physician of their risk status. Standard tests for HIV will usually be negative in the very early stages of infection, so specialized tests such as the **HIV RNA assay,** which directly measures the amount of virus in the body, must be used.

Other than the initial flulike symptoms associated with primary HIV infection, most people in the first months or years of HIV infection have few if any symptoms. As the immune system weakens, however, a variety of symptoms can develop—persistent swollen lymph nodes; lumps, rashes, sores, or other growths on or under the skin or on the mucous membranes of the eyes, mouth, anus, or nasal passages; persistent yeast infections; unexplained weight loss; fever and drenching night sweats; dry cough and shortness of breath; persistent diarrhea; easy bruising and unexplained bleeding; profound fatigue; memory loss; difficulty with balance; tremors or seizures; changes in vision, hearing, taste, or smell; difficulty in swallowing; changes in mood and other psychological symptoms; and persistent or recurrent pain. Obviously, many of these symptoms can also occur with a variety of other illnesses.

HIV RNA assay A test used to determine the viral load (the amount of HIV in the blood).

TERMS

Because the immune system is weakened, people with HIV infection are highly susceptible to infections, both common and uncommon. The infection most often seen in the United States among people with HIV is *Pneumocystis* pneumonia, a fungal infection. **Kaposi's sarcoma,** a previously rare form of cancer, is common in HIV-infected men. Women with HIV infection often have frequent and difficult-to-treat vaginal yeast infections. Cases of tuberculosis (TB) are increasingly being reported in people with HIV, and the CDC recommends TB testing for anyone with HIV infection.

Diagnosing HIV Infection   The most common HIV tests check for antibodies to the virus. HIV infection primarily disrupts T-cell immunity; B cells are still able to produce antibodies to HIV, which show up in tests. These antibodies, however, do not protect against the spread of the virus. For most other diseases, the presence of an antibody to a particular pathogen may indicate protective immunity. In the case of HIV, however, the presence of the antibody indicates an active case of the disease. **HIV antibody tests** are used because they are accurate and relatively inexpensive. Standard testing involves an initial test called an **ELISA;** if it is positive, a second test—either a **Western blot** or immunoflourescence assay—is done to confirm the results (see the box "Getting an HIV Test").

Not everyone with HIV infection will test positive on antibody tests. Antibodies may not appear in the blood for weeks or months after infection, so people who are newly infected are likely to have a negative antibody test. The infection can be detected with a more expensive test that directly measures the presence of the virus, such as an HIV RNA test.

The reverse situation is seen in babies born to HIV-infected mothers: They may carry HIV antibodies, passed from their mother, without being infected with HIV. Antibodies can pass through the placenta to a fetus, but in the majority of cases, even without treatment, an infant does not acquire HIV. Thus, an infant may test positive on an HIV antibody test but actually be uninfected. Further tests such as the HIV RNA assay must be done to determine if an infant is actually infected.

If a person is diagnosed as **HIV-positive,** the next step is to determine the disease's severity to plan appropriate treatment. The immune system's status can be gauged by measuring CD4 T-cells every few months. The infection itself can be monitored by tracking the viral load (the amount of virus in the body) through HIV RNA assay. Keeping track of viral load changes helps physicians evaluate the effects of treatment and can also help predict the likelihood of long-term survival in a person infected with HIV.

According to the CDC, only about one-third of adult Americans have been tested for HIV. Among those who have never been tested, nearly three-fourths say that they haven't been tested because they don't think they are at risk.

Many people are not aware that rapid HIV tests, home tests, and tests that do not require a blood sample are now available. Rapid (same-day) HIV tests are effective. As of June 2006, the CDC had given out 800,000 rapid HIV tests; nearly half of those tests had been used, identifying more than 4500 cases of HIV infection.

A new diagnostic test that may help guide treatment decisions is called HIV Replication Capacity. This test shows how fast HIV from a patient's blood sample can reproduce itself. It is a measure of viral fitness and may be helpful when used in conjunction with CD4 and viral load tests in predicting how quickly a given person may progress to more serious disease.

Being tested once is not enough. Periodic routine testing is the best way for anyone to find out if he or she has HIV. The frequency of testing depends on multiple factors. For example, the CDC recommends that men who have sex with men should be tested at least once a year. People who engage in high-risk behavior (such as unprotected anal sex) should be tested more often. Rather than testing only at-risk individuals, the CDC also recommends universal HIV testing as part of routine medical care for everyone age 13–64. The CDC hopes that routine HIV testing will increase the odds that people with HIV are diagnosed earlier. Early detection is important to minimizing the disease's effects and reducing the risks to others.

Diagnosing AIDS   AIDS is the most severe form of HIV infection. The CDC's criteria for a diagnosis of AIDS reflect the stage of HIV infection at which a person's immune system becomes dangerously compromised. Since January 1993, a diagnosis of AIDS has been made if a person is HIV-positive and either has developed an infection defined as an AIDS indicator or has a severely damaged immune system (as measured by CD4 T-cell counts).

Reporting   In the United States, all diagnosed cases of HIV or AIDS must be reported to public health authorities. Every state has laws that require doctors, clinics, and laboratories to report certain contagious diseases, so that

Getting an HIV Test

You should strongly consider being tested if any of the following apply to you or any past or current sexual partners:

- You have had unprotected sex (vaginal, anal, or oral) with more than one partner or with a partner who was not in a mutually monogamous relationship with you.
- You have used or shared needles, syringes, or other paraphernalia for injecting drugs (including steroids).
- You received a transfusion of blood or blood products between 1978 and 1985.
- You have ever been diagnosed with an STD.

You can either visit a physician or health clinic or take a home test. A big advantage to having the test performed by a physician or clinician is that you will get one-on-one counseling about the test, your results, and ways to avoid future infection or spreading the disease. If you have good reason to think you may test positive, it is probably best to be tested by a physician or clinic, where follow-up counseling and medical care will be intensive. If you suspect you have been recently exposed to HIV and might have primary infection, see your physician and ask about an HIV RNA test. The home test is a good alternative for people at low risk who just want to be sure.

Physician or Clinic Testing

Your physician, student health clinic, Planned Parenthood, public health department, or local AIDS association can arrange your HIV test. It usually costs $50–$100, but public clinics often charge little or nothing. The standard test involves drawing a sample of blood that is sent to a laboratory for analysis for the presence of antibodies; if the first stage of testing is positive, a confirmatory test is done. This standard test takes 1–2 weeks, and you'll be asked to phone or come in personally to obtain your results, which should also include appropriate counseling.

Alternative tests are available at some clinics. The Orasure test uses oral fluid, which is collected by placing a treated cotton pad in the mouth; urine tests are also available.

New rapid tests are now also available at some locations. These tests involve the use of blood or oral fluid and can provide results in as little as 20 minutes. If a rapid test is positive for HIV infection, a confirmatory test will be performed.

Before you get an HIV test, be sure you understand what will be done with the results. Results from confidential tests may still become part of your medical record and/or be reported (with your name or some other identifier) to state and federal public health agencies. If you decide you want to be tested anonymously—in which case the results will not be reported to anyone but yourself—check with your physician or counselor about how to obtain an anonymous test or use a home test.

Home Testing

Home test kits for HIV are available; they cost about $40–70. (Avoid testing kits that are not FDA-approved; unapproved kits are sold over the Internet. As of this printing, the only FDA-approved home test kit for HIV was manufactured by Home Access.) To use a home test, you prick a finger with a supplied lancet, blot a few drops of blood onto blotting paper, and mail it to the company's laboratory. In about a week (or within 3 business days for more expensive "express" tests), you call a toll-free number to find out your results. Anyone testing positive is routed to a trained counselor, who can provide emotional and medical support. The results of home test kits are completely anonymous.

Understanding the Results

A negative test result means that no antibodies were found in your sample. However, it usually takes at least a month after exposure to HIV (and possibly as long as 6 months in some people) for antibodies to appear. Therefore, an infected person may get a false-negative result. If you test negative but your risk of infection is high, ask about obtaining an HIV RNA assay, which allows very early diagnosis, and about the appropriateness of retesting in a few months.

A positive result means that you are infected. It is important to seek medical care and counseling immediately. You need to know more about your medical options; the possible psychological, social, and financial repercussions; and how to avoid spreading the disease. Rapid progress is being made in treating HIV, and treatments are potentially much more successful when begun early.

For more information about HIV testing and a national directory of testing sites, visit the CDC National HIV Testing Resources site (www.hivtest.org). You can also find a test center near you by using your mobile phone. Text-message your ZIP code to 566948. The CDC will automatically respond with a text message listing HIV test centers in your area.

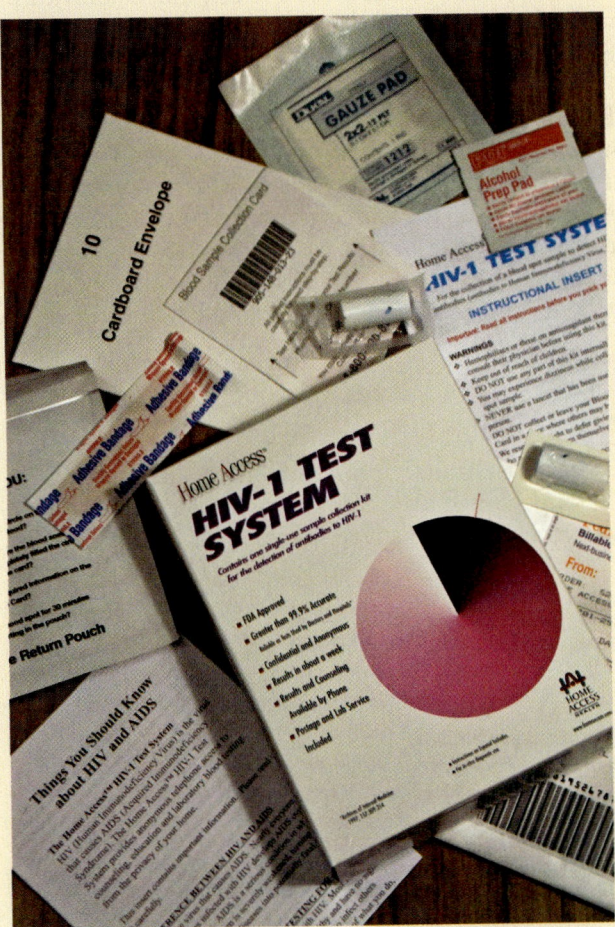

public health officials can use this information to track and attempt to prevent the spread of these diseases.

Tracking the U.S. HIV epidemic has been particularly difficult for political, social, and technical reasons. Prior to 2007, for example, estimates for newly acquired cases of HIV were based on very limited data. Until recently, national data excluded a number of large states. For example, California was not included in most national HIV data before 2006 because of its method of recording HIV data.

Another major limitation in tracking the epidemic was that, until recently, public health officials were unable to determine whether newly reported cases of HIV infection represented true recently acquired infections. Remember that a standard positive HIV test only indicates the presence of infection, so a newly diagnosed person might actually have been infected years earlier.

A new blood test makes it possible to estimate the length of time a person has been infected with HIV. The CDC now tests HIV-positive blood samples for duration of infection, allowing a much more accurate picture of the HIV epidemic in the United States.

Despite efforts to safeguard confidentiality and prohibit discrimination, mandatory reporting of HIV infection remains controversial. If people believe they are risking their jobs, friends, or social acceptability, they may be less likely to be tested. At the same time, it is essential that enough information be disclosed to monitor the epidemic. The CDC recommends that states continue to provide opportunities for people to be tested anonymously; home HIV tests also allow anonymous testing.

Treatment Although there is no known cure for HIV infection, medications can significantly alter the course of the disease and extend life. The drop in the number of U.S. AIDS deaths that has occurred since 1996 is in large part due to the increasing use of combinations of new drugs. However, this progress is irrelevant to the vast majority of AIDS sufferers worldwide, who can't afford treatment.

ANTIVIRAL DRUGS Antiviral drugs in current use to combat HIV fall into several categories based on how they block HIV replication.

- **Reverse transcriptase inhibitors,** including the widely used drug zidovudine (AZT), work by inhibiting the enzyme reverse transcriptase, which HIV

uses to integrate its genetic material into human cells (Figure 18.3).

- **Protease inhibitors** target the enzyme HIV protease, which the virus uses to create a protein coat for each new copy of itself. A similar type of drug, called a *maturation inhibitor,* also works by interfering with the processing of newly formed viral proteins. (Maturation inhibitors are not yet approved by the FDA.)

- **Entry inhibitors** block HIV from entering and infecting cells.

A new type of anti-HIV drug, called an *integrase inhibitor,* joined the arsenal of FDA-approved HIV medications in 2007. This new class of drugs blocks the incorporation of newly formed HIV DNA into the host cell's chromosomes.

Having many drugs that work against HIV in different stages of its life cycle is crucial to keeping the virus at bay. HIV is an incredibly agile virus that constantly changes, mutates, and adapts to its environment. The virus can easily become resistant to any given drug, but when an HIV-infected person takes several types of drugs that attack the virus at different stages of its life, the virus is much less likely to develop resistance.

Treatment with combinations of drugs, referred to as *highly active antiretroviral therapy,* or *HAART,* can reduce HIV in the blood to undetectable levels in many people. However, research indicates that latent virus is still present in the body and that HIV-infected people on HAART carry potentially transmissible HIV in their body fluids. Even people who respond well to HIV treatment may still be able to infect others, although successful treatment greatly reduces the risk.

HIV/AIDS treatment is becoming increasingly complex. There are now nearly 30 drugs approved specifically for use against HIV/AIDS, and many others are being developed. One way to simplify treatment is by combining medicines. For example, in June 2006, the FDA approved Atripla, the first once-a-day tablet for HIV patients; Atripla combines three medicines into one.

POSTEXPOSURE PROPHYLAXIS (PEP) Antiviral medications are being used in some cases in an attempt to prevent infection in people who have been exposed to HIV. The CDC has long recommended that health care workers who have significant exposure to HIV-infected blood or body fluids via a needle stick or other mishap consider starting antiviral medication as soon as possible (preferably within a few hours of exposure) to decrease the risk of infection. PEP is also often recommended for victims of sexual assault, and for people who are at risk for HIV infection from recent nonoccupational exposure to blood, genital secretions, or other potentially infectious body fluids of a person known to have HIV. Nonoccupational exposure refers to situations such as unprotected sex or contact with a contaminated needle. PEP consists of 28 days of HAART, which should begin as soon as possible after exposure, but always within 72 hours.

TERMS

reverse transcriptase inhibitor An antiviral drug used to treat HIV infection that works by inhibiting reverse transcriptase, the enzyme that converts viral RNA to DNA.

protease inhibitor A drug that inhibits the action of any of the protein-splitting enzymes known as proteases. Protease inhibitors have been developed to block the action of HIV protease and thus prevent the replication of HIV.

entry inhibitor An antiviral drug that blocks the entry of HIV into cells by inhibiting the fusion of viral and cell membranes.

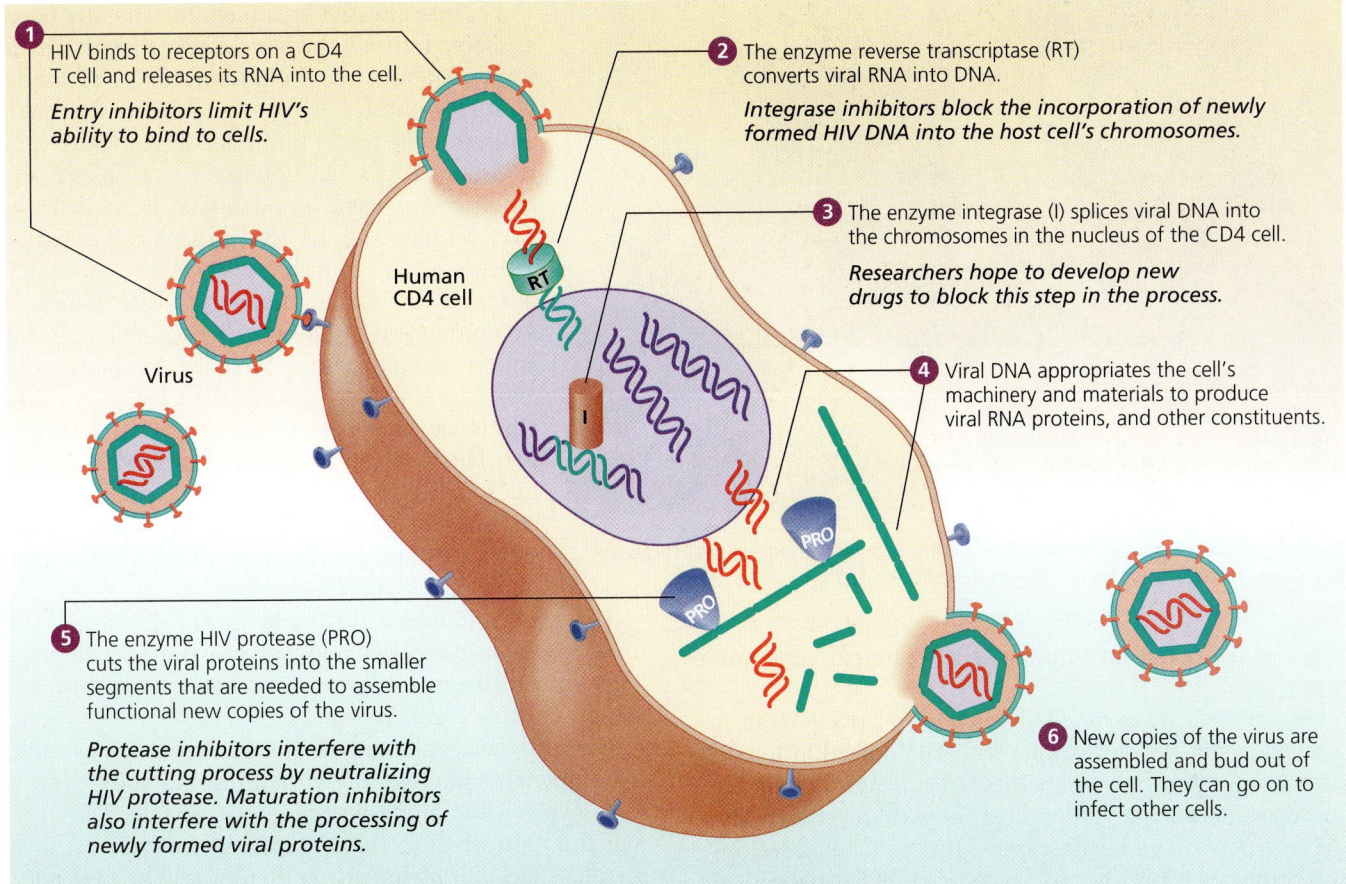

1 HIV binds to receptors on a CD4 T cell and releases its RNA into the cell.

Entry inhibitors limit HIV's ability to bind to cells.

2 The enzyme reverse transcriptase (RT) converts viral RNA into DNA.

Integrase inhibitors block the incorporation of newly formed HIV DNA into the host cell's chromosomes.

3 The enzyme integrase (I) splices viral DNA into the chromosomes in the nucleus of the CD4 cell.

Researchers hope to develop new drugs to block this step in the process.

4 Viral DNA appropriates the cell's machinery and materials to produce viral RNA proteins, and other constituents.

5 The enzyme HIV protease (PRO) cuts the viral proteins into the smaller segments that are needed to assemble functional new copies of the virus.

Protease inhibitors interfere with the cutting process by neutralizing HIV protease. Maturation inhibitors also interfere with the processing of newly formed viral proteins.

6 New copies of the virus are assembled and bud out of the cell. They can go on to infect other cells.

Virus

Human CD4 cell

FIGURE 18.3 **The life cycle of HIV: How antiviral drugs work.** Different classes of drugs block the replication of HIV at different points in the virus's life cycle.

SOURCES: A virus in action. 2001. *Scientific American*, November; Dickinson, G., et al. 1998. The latest recommendations for antiretroviral therapy. *Patient Care*, 15 August.

TREATMENTS FOR OPPORTUNISTIC INFECTIONS In addition to antiviral drugs, most patients with low CD4 T-cell counts also take a variety of antibiotics to help prevent opportunistic infections such as pneumonia and tuberculosis. A person with advanced HIV infection may need to take 20 or more pills every day. Medication side effects can become severe when so many drugs are used in combination.

HIV AND PREGNANCY Early-stage HIV infection does not appear to significantly affect a woman's chance of becoming pregnant. Without treatment, 25–30% of infants born to HIV-infected women are themselves infected with the virus. The risk of an infected mother transmitting HIV to her baby can be reduced to less than 2% by treating the mother during her pregnancy and labor, giving the baby antiretroviral drugs during the first weeks of life, avoiding breastfeeding (which can transmit HIV), and delivering the baby by cesarean section if necessary. Cesarean delivery can lower the risk of infection in women who have high blood levels of HIV; women who have undergone antiviral treatment and have very low levels of HIV can usually deliver vaginally. HIV testing is strongly recommended for all pregnant women.

Testing and the use of antiviral drugs by pregnant HIV-positive women has had a dramatic effect in the United States. Unfortunately, long-term combination antiviral therapy is very expensive and is out of reach for most of the world's HIV-positive women. As newer and less expensive drugs against HIV become available, there is hope that more pregnant women and infants will be treated, resulting in lower vertical transmission rates worldwide. Currently, some resource-poor nations are reducing the spread of HIV to infants by giving a short course of antiretroviral drugs to mother and newborn. Although not as effective as more extensive treatment, this is a major advance in HIV prevention for many developing countries.

TREATMENT CHALLENGES The cost of treatment for HIV continues to be an area of major concern. A 2006 study from Cornell University estimated the average cost of treatment for an HIV-infected person in the United States at $2100 per month. Treatment for someone with more advanced disease averaged over $4000 a month. The study estimated that in the near future, the United States will need to spend over $12 billion annually to care for HIV-infected people in this country. Meantime, the United States

Currently available treatments can significantly increase the chance that this baby, born to an HIV-infected mother, will be free of the virus.

Because effective treatment for HIV has been available for only the last decade, there is much to learn about the long-term effects of living with HIV and its treatments. Patients who take antiretroviral medications for an extended period sometimes develop serious problems including abnormal blood lipids, heart disease, liver problems, bone loss, kidney disease, and cancers. Changes in body shape and facial appearance due to alterations in fat distribution is a common and troubling side effect of long-term antiretroviral drug use. Weighing the benefits of antiretroviral drugs against their long-term side effects can make treatment decisions challenging. The National Institutes of Health has guidelines for HIV treatment that help with these decisions. Generally, people with HIV who have no symptoms and have relatively high CD4 counts may opt to delay treatment.

However, immediate treatment is still recommended for anyone who is experiencing symptoms, and for all pregnant women. Treatment for primary stage (very recent) infection remains controversial.

Currently available antiviral drugs do not appear able to completely eliminate the virus from the body, even if viral levels in the blood become undetectable. The optimal duration of drug therapy is not known, but most scientists feel that lifelong drug therapy will be necessary. It is also unclear to what degree a damaged immune system can rebound from the effects of long-term HIV infection even if the virus is brought under control with antiviral medication.

What About a Vaccine?   If an effective, safe, affordable vaccine against HIV could be developed, it might be possible to stop the worldwide HIV epidemic. Unfortunately, making a vaccine against HIV is proving to be exceedingly difficult. Methods that have been used to produce vaccines against other diseases are often ineffective or unsafe when used against HIV. Adding to the challenge is the fact that HIV comes in numerous subtypes, mutates rapidly, and destroys the very cells that normally protect the body against infectious diseases. Vaccines are being tested in humans, but experts are discouraged by recent vaccine trial failures. A licensed AIDS vaccine is now estimated to be at least a decade away, and some experts are grudgingly conceding the possibility that a fully effective AIDS vaccine may never be developed. Vaccines are also being tested as therapy for people already infected with HIV.

Researchers are making relatively rapid progress in producing a **microbicide** that could be used to prevent HIV and other STDs. A microbicide in the form of a cream, gel, sponge, ring, or suppository that could be inserted into the vagina or rectum could function as a kind of chemical condom. A microbicide could fill the urgent need for a prevention method that can be used by a woman without requiring cooperation from her partner. Several microbi-

plays a major role in funding HIV treatment programs worldwide.

These costs are tremendous even for relatively wealthy countries. But 95% of people with HIV infection live in developing countries, where these treatments are unlikely to be available to anyone except the wealthiest few. The average per-person health expenditure in many developing countries is only about $10 per year. Pharmaceutical companies and the World Bank are working to develop combination pills and to lower drug costs in developing regions, and international aid is gradually increasing; however, it is still not nearly enough to counteract the devastating impact of AIDS on these countries.

Besides financial cost, receiving HIV treatment is challenging in many other ways. The toxicity of antiretroviral drugs is a concern. Common short-term side effects include nausea, vomiting, diarrhea, and fatigue. Many of these problems improve with time, or can be circumvented with different medications. People on HIV drugs must take their medicines on time, every time, because drug resistance can develop if the medicines are taken inconsistently. Despite the challenges, these drugs make it possible for many HIV-infected people to live for decades, maybe even into old age.

TERMS   **microbicide**   An agent that destroys microorganisms; also known as an antiseptic.

cides are currently undergoing human testing for safety and effectiveness.

The female condom may someday play a larger role in HIV prevention. Female condoms are more expensive than male condoms and aren't widely available in developing countries, but they offer the advantage that women can initiate their use. Scientists are developing a cheaper, easier-to-use female condom and are evaluating whether diaphragms (in combination with microbicides) protect against HIV.

Another approach is the use of preexposure treatment as prevention. HIV-negative individuals at high risk for infection would take an anti-HIV medication prior to an activity that might expose them to HIV. This approach is controversial but might be effective in stopping the spread of HIV in highly vulnerable populations such as sex workers. Unlike a vaccine, this form of prevention could be tested and put into practice in a relatively short period of time, especially if an existing HIV drug is used.

How Can You Protect Yourself? Although AIDS is currently incurable, it is preventable. You can protect yourself by avoiding behaviors that may bring you into contact with HIV. This means making careful choices about sexual activity and not sharing needles if you inject drugs.

MAKE CAREFUL CHOICES ABOUT SEXUAL ACTIVITY In a sexual relationship, the current and past behaviors of you and your partner determine the amount of risk involved. If you are uninfected and in a mutually monogamous relationship with another uninfected person, you are not at risk for HIV. Of course, it is often hard to know for sure whether your partner is completely faithful and is truly uninfected. Having a series of monogamous relationships is not a safe prevention strategy.

For anyone not involved in a long-term, mutually monogamous relationship, abstinence from any sexual activity that involves the exchange of body fluids is the only sure way to prevent HIV infection (Figure 18.4).

Anal and vaginal intercourse are the sexual activities associated with the highest risk of HIV infection. If you have intercourse, always use a condom. Use of a lubricated condom reduces the risk of transmitting HIV during all forms of intercourse. Condoms are not perfect, and they do not provide risk-free sex; however, used properly, a condom provides a high level of protection against HIV. Experts also suggest the use of latex squares and dental dams, rubber devices that can be used as barriers during oral-genital or oral-anal sexual contact. As mentioned already, avoid using nonoxynol-9 lubricants because of the risk of tissue irritation, which can make STD transmission more likely.

Like condom use, many of the same steps you can take to avoid an unintended pregnancy can help you prevent STD and HIV infection. These methods are discussed in detail in Chapter 6 and are covered again later in this chapter.

DON'T SHARE DRUG NEEDLES People who inject drugs should avoid sharing needles, syringes, or anything that might have blood on it. Any injectable drug, legal or illegal, can be associated with HIV transmission. Needles can be decontaminated with a solution of bleach and water, but it is not a foolproof procedure, and HIV can survive in a syringe for a month or longer. (Boiling needles and syringes does not necessarily destroy HIV either.) As described in Chapter 9, obtaining sterile syringes through a syringe exchange program is much more effective than attempting to sterilize used syringes. Many prominent health organizations, including the United Nations AIDS Program and the American Medical Association, support syringe exchange programs, but these programs are unavailable and/or illegal in many parts of the world.

High Risk

Unprotected anal sex is the riskiest sexual behavior, especially for the receptive partner.

Unprotected vaginal intercourse is the next riskiest, especially for women, who are much more likely to be infected by an infected male partner than vice versa.

Oral sex is probably considerably less risky than anal and vaginal intercourse but can still result in HIV transmission.

Sharing of sex toys can be risky because they can carry blood, semen, or vaginal fluid.

Use of a condom reduces risk considerably but not completely for any type of intercourse. Anal sex with a condom is riskier than vaginal sex with a condom; oral sex with a condom is less risky, especially if the man does not ejaculate.

Hand-genital contact and deep kissing are less risky but could still theoretically transmit HIV; the presence of cuts or sores increases risk.

Sex with only one uninfected and totally faithful partner is without risk, but effective only if both partners are uninfected and completely monogamous.

Activities that don't involve the exchange of body fluids carry no risk: hugging, massage, closed-mouth kissing, masturbation, phone sex, and fantasy.

Abstinence is completely without risk. For many people, it can be an effective and reasonable method of avoiding HIV infection and other STDs during certain periods of life.

No Risk

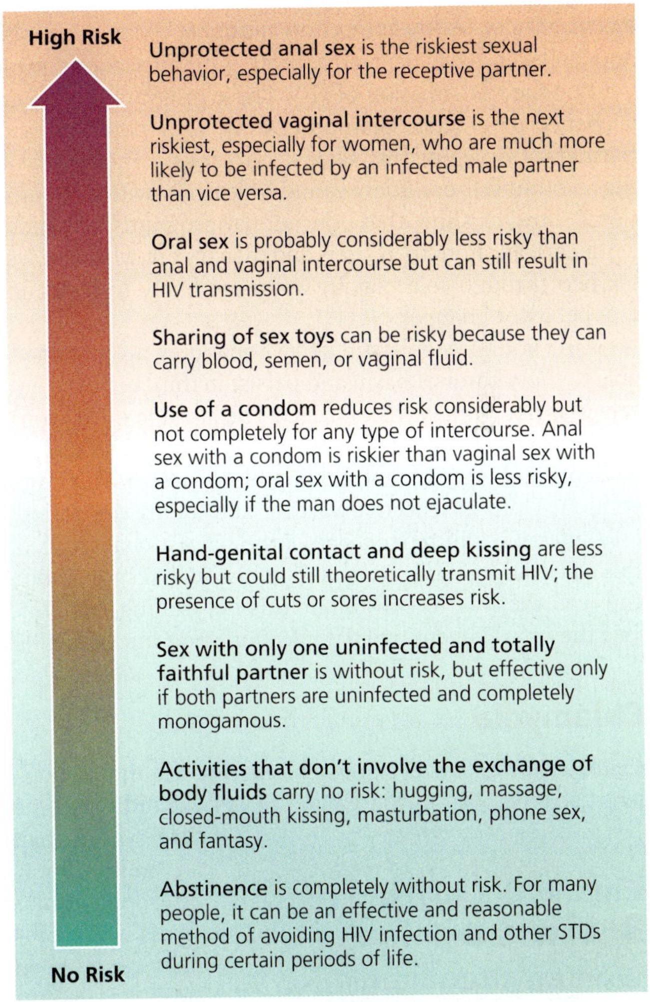

FIGURE 18.4 What's risky and what's not: The approximate relative risk of HIV transmission of various sexual activities.

Accurate information about HIV/AIDS, including where to go for testing and treatment, is available from many sources, including health professionals, community-based organizations, and national hotlines.

If you are an injection drug user, your best protection is to obtain treatment and refrain from using drugs.

PARTICIPATE IN AN HIV EDUCATION PROGRAM Many schools and colleges have peer education programs about preventing the transmission of HIV. These programs give you a chance to practice communicating with potential sex partners and negotiating safer sex, to engage in role playing to build self-confidence, and to learn how to use condoms. Studies show that educational programs in which students learn from their peers and then try out what they've learned through role playing are more likely to result in real behavior change.

Many young people still believe that they are invulnerable to most kinds of harm and persist in thinking of themselves as not being at risk for HIV. The attitude of "It won't happen to me" is pervasive among high school and college students and is a major stumbling block to HIV/AIDS prevention. Until an effective vaccine and a cure are found, HIV infection will remain one of the biggest challenges of this generation. Education and individual responsibility can lead the way to controlling this devastating epidemic (see the box "Preventing HIV Infection and Other STDs").

Chlamydia

Chlamydia trachomatis causes **chlamydia,** the most prevalent bacterial STD in the United States. According to the CDC, more than 1.1 million new cases of chlamydia were officially reported in 2007—a slight increase from the previous year.

> **QUICK STATS**
> Chlamydia affects
> **3 times** more
> women than men.
> —CDC, 2007

Many experts believe, however, that chlamydia is vastly underreported because it is often symptomless, and estimate that as many as 3 million new cases of the disease occur each year. The highest rates of infection occur in single people between ages 15 and 24. African American women experience chlamydia infections at nearly eight times the rate of white women. (Table 18.4 compares rates of common STDs among ethnic groups.) Both men and women are susceptible to chlamydia, but, as with most STDs, women bear the greater burden because of possible complications and consequences of the disease (see the box "Women Are Hit Hard by STDs" on p. 568). *C. trachomatis* can be transmitted by oral sex as well as by other forms of sexual intercourse.

In most women, chlamydia produces no early symptoms. If left untreated, it can lead to pelvic inflammatory disease (PID), which is discussed later in this chapter. Chlamydia also greatly increases a woman's risk for infertility and ectopic (tubal) pregnancy. Because rates of infection are high and most women with chlamydia have no symptoms, many physicians screen sexually active women at the time of their routine pelvic exam. The U.S. Preventive Services Task Force currently recommends routine screening for all sexually active women age 25 or younger and for older women who are at increased risk (such as those who have multiple sex partners).

Chlamydia can also lead to infertility in men, although not as often as in women. In men under age 35, chlamydia is the most common cause of **epididymitis,** inflammation of the sperm-carrying ducts. And up to half of all cases of **urethritis,** inflammation of the urethra, in men are caused by chlamydia. Despite these statistics, many infected men have no symptoms. Screening for chlamydia in heterosexual men currently is not routine, but some experts feel that

Table 18.4	Rates of Common STDs, by Race/Ethnicity: 2007*		
	Chlamydia	Gonorrhea	Syphilis[†]
Whites	162	35	2
Blacks	1399	663	14
Hispanics	473	69	4
Asians/Pacific Islanders	140	19	1
American Indians/ Alaska Natives	733	107	3

*As reported to the CDC. Rates are per 100,000 population.

[†]All stages.

SOURCE: Centers for Disease Control and Prevention. 2008. *Sexually Transmitted Disease Surveillance, 2007.* Atlanta: Centers for Disease Control and Prevention.

Preventing HIV Infection and Other STDs

For those who aren't in a long-term monogamous relationship with an uninfected partner, abstinence is the only truly safe option for avoiding STDs. Remember that it's OK to say no to sex and drugs.

Safer sexual activities that allow close person-to-person contact with almost no risk of contracting STDs or HIV include fantasy, hugging, massage, rubbing clothed bodies together, self-stimulation by both partners, and kissing with lips closed.

If you choose to be sexually active, talk with potential partners about HIV, safer sex, and the use of condoms before you begin a sexual relationship. The following behaviors will help lower your risk of exposure to STDs during sexual activities:

- Don't drink alcohol or use drugs in sexual situations. Mood-altering drugs can affect your judgment and make you more likely to take risks. Having sex when intoxicated significantly increases the risk of STDs.

- Limit the number of partners. Avoid sexual contact with people who have HIV or an STD or who have engaged in risky behaviors in the past, including unprotected sex and injection drug use.

- Use condoms during every act of intercourse and oral sex. Condoms do not provide perfect protection, but they greatly reduce your risk of contracting an infection. Multiple studies show that regular condom use can reduce the risk of several diseases, including HIV, chlamydia, and genital herpes.

- Use condoms properly to obtain maximum protection (see Chapter 6). Use a water-based lubricant; don't use oil-based lubricants such as petroleum jelly or baby oil or any vaginal product containing mineral or vegetable oil. Avoid using lubricants or condoms containing nonoxynol-9, particularly for anal intercourse. Unroll condoms gently to avoid tearing them, and smooth out any air bubbles. If you accidentally put a condom on the wrong way, remove it and throw it away; do not flip it over and try again.

- Avoid sexual contact that could cause cuts or tears in the skin or tissue. Using extra lubricant (water-based) can help prevent damage to delicate tissues.

- Get periodic screening tests for STDs and HIV. Young women need yearly pelvic exams and Pap tests.

- Get vaccinated for hepatitis B. Young women should consider getting vaccinated against HPV.

- Get prompt treatment for any STDs you contract.

If you inject drugs of any kind, don't share needles, syringes, or anything that might have blood on it. If your community has a syringe exchange program, use it. Seek treatment; stop using injectable drugs.

If you are at risk for HIV infection, don't donate blood, sperm, or body organs. Don't have unprotected sex or share needles or syringes. Get tested for HIV soon, and get treated. HIV-infected people who get early treatment generally feel better and live longer than those who delay.

---

screening young sexually active men in addition to young women would be effective in reducing chlamydia rates.

Infants of infected mothers can acquire the infection through contact with the pathogen in the birth canal during delivery. Every year, over 150,000 newborns suffer from eye infections and pneumonia as a result of untreated maternal chlamydial infections.

Symptoms   In men, chlamydia symptoms include painful urination, a slight watery discharge from the penis, and sometimes pain around the testicles. Although most women with chlamydia are asymptomatic, some notice increased vaginal discharge, burning with urination, pain or bleeding with intercourse, and lower abdominal pain. Less common symptoms in both men and women include arthritis, conjunctivitis, sore throat, and rectal inflammation and pain (in people who become infected during receptive anal intercourse). Symptoms in both men and women can begin within 5 days of infection. However, most people experience few or no symptoms, increasing the likelihood that they will inadvertently spread the infection to their partners.

Diagnosis   Chlamydia is typically diagnosed through laboratory tests on a urine sample or a small amount of fluid from the urethra or cervix. The lab test may involve growing the organism in culture, using special dyes to detect bacterial proteins, or a process that quickly copies and detects genetic material from the bacteria. Testing pregnant women and treating those with chlamydia is a highly effective way to prevent infection of newborns. A home test is currently being studied.

Treatment   Once chlamydia has been diagnosed, the infected person and his or her partner(s) are given antibiotics—usually doxycycline, erythromycin, or a newer drug, azithromycin, which can cure infection in one dose. Treatment of partners is important because people who have been treated for chlamydia are susceptible to getting the disease again if they have sexual contact with an infected person.

The CDC now recommends that women who have been treated for chlamydia be retested 3 months after

Women Are Hit Hard by STDs

Sexually transmitted diseases cause suffering for all who are infected, but in many ways, women and girls are the hardest hit, for both biological and social reasons. Among Americans, 62% of all cases of adverse health problems from STDs occur in women. Worldwide, as many women as men now die from AIDS each year, and in the hardest-hit regions of Africa, nearly 60% of HIV-positive adults are women.

Male-to-female transmission of many infections is more likely to occur than female-to-male transmission. This is particularly true of HIV: Studies show that it is three to eight times easier for an HIV-positive man to transmit the virus to a woman than it is for an HIV-positive woman to infect a man.

Teenagers have been hit especially hard by STDs. In fact, a 2008 report from the CDC states that 26% of American girls age 14–19 are infected with at least one of the most common STDs (the study looked at rates of HPV, chlamydia, herpes simplex type 2, and trichomoniasis). Young women are more vulnerable to STDs than older women because the less-mature cervix is more susceptible to injury and infection. As a woman ages, the type of cells at the opening of the cervix gradually changes so that the tissue becomes more resistant to infection. Young women are also more vulnerable for social and emotional reasons: Lack of control in relationships, fear of discussing condom use, and having an older sex partner are all linked to increased STD risk.

Once infected, women tend to suffer more consequences of STDs than men.

For example, gonorrhea and chlamydia can cause PID and permanent damage to the oviducts in women, but these infections tend to have less serious effects in men. HPV infection causes nearly all cases of cervical cancer. HPV infection is also associated with penile cancer in men, but penile cancer is much less common than cervical cancer. Women also have the added concern of the potential effects of STDs during pregnancy.

Between 1985 and 2005, the proportion of new U.S. AIDS cases in women increased from 5% to 27%. Women with HIV infection often face tremendous challenges when they are ill because they may be caring for family members who are also infected and ill. In addition, women may become sicker at lower viral loads compared with men. Women and men with HIV do about equally well if they have similar access to treatment, but in many cases women are diagnosed later in the course of HIV infection, receive less treatment, and die sooner.

Worldwide, social and economic factors play a large role in the transmission and consequences of AIDS and other STDs for women. Sexual violence against women is spreading AIDS, as are such practices as very early marriage for women, often to much older men who have had many sexual partners. Cultural gender norms that promote premarital and extramarital relationships for men, combined with women's lack of power to negotiate safer sex, make HIV a risk even for women who are married and monogamous. In addition, lack of education and economic opportunities can force women

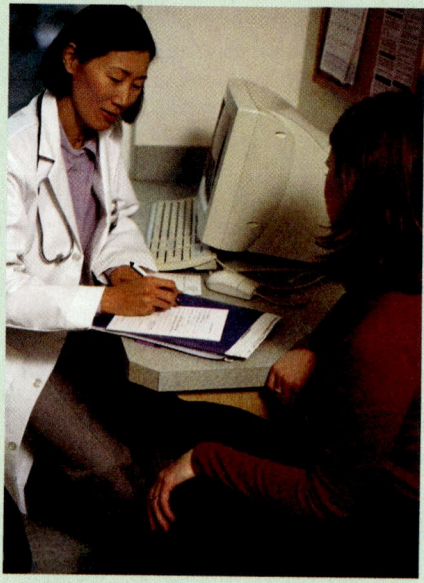

into commercial sex work, placing them at high risk for all STDs.

In some parts of the world, the stigma of AIDS hits women harder. Men with HIV are typically cared for by female family members, without being questioned about the source of their infection. Women, in contrast, may be accused of having had extramarital sex and receive less help and support. It is women who typically provide care to relatives with HIV as well as support the household financially when other earners are too ill to work. But if husbands die, women often do not inherit property and can be thrown deeper into poverty. Solutions to the STD crisis in women must include empowerment in the social sphere in addition to direct health care.

SOURCES: Ebrahim, S. H., M. T. McKenna, and J. S. Marks. 2005. Sexual behaviour: Related adverse health burden in the United States. *Sexually Transmitted Infection* 81(1): 38–40; Dunkle, K. M., et al. 2004. Gender-based violence, relationship power, and risk of HIV infection in women attending antenatal clinics in South Africa. *Lancet* 363(9419): 1415–1421; Joint United Nations Programme on HIV/AIDS. 2004. *AIDS Epidemic Update, December 2004*. Geneva: UNAIDS; World Health Organization. 2003. *Gender and HIV/AIDS*. Geneva: World Health Organization.

treatment is completed. In a 2006 study in New York City, one in eight women who had previously been diagnosed with chlamydia acquired a repeat infection within a year. A study in California yielded similar results. Both studies showed that younger women were more likely than older women to be reinfected by an untreated, infected partner.

Gonorrhea

More than 350,000 cases of **gonorrhea** were reported to the CDC in 2007, an increase of 1% over 2006. Like chla-

mydia, however, gonorrhea is underreported because it is often symptomless, and the CDC estimates the number of actual cases may be twice as high as the number of reported cases. The highest incidence is among 15–24-year-olds. Like chlamydia, untreated gonorrhea can cause PID in women and urethritis and epididymitis in men. It can also cause arthritis, rashes, and eye infections, and it occasionally involves internal organs. Being infected with gonorrhea increases the likelihood that HIV will be transmitted. A woman who is infected during pregnancy is at risk for preterm delivery and for having a baby with life-threatening gonorrheal infection of the blood or joints. An infant passing through the birth canal of an infected mother may contract **gonococcal conjunctivitis,** an infection in the eyes that can cause blindness if not treated. In most states, all newborn babies are routinely treated with antimicrobial eyedrops to prevent eye infection.

Gonorrhea is caused by the bacterium *Neisseria gonorrhoeae,* which flourishes in mucous membranes. The microbe cannot thrive outside the human body and dies within moments of exposure to light and air. Consequently, gonorrhea cannot be contracted from toilet seats, towels, or other objects.

Symptoms   In males, the incubation period for gonorrhea is brief, generally 2–7 days. The first symptoms are due to urethritis, which causes urinary discomfort and a thick, yellowish white or yellowish green discharge from the penis. The lips of the urethral opening may become inflamed and swollen. In some cases, the lymph glands in the groin become enlarged and swollen. Up to half of males have very minor symptoms or none at all.

Most females with gonorrhea are asymptomatic. Those who do have symptoms often experience pain with urination, increased vaginal discharge, and severe menstrual cramps. Up to 40% of women with untreated gonorrhea develop PID. Women may also develop painful abscesses in the Bartholin's glands, a pair of glands located on either side of the opening of the vagina.

Gonorrhea can also infect the throat or rectum of people who engage in oral or anal sex. Gonorrhea symptoms in the throat may be a sore throat or pus on the tonsils, and those in the rectum may be pus or blood in the feces or rectal pain and itching.

Diagnosis   Several tests—gram stain, detection of bacterial genes or DNA, or culture—may be performed; depending on the test, samples of urine or cervical, urethral, throat, or rectal fluids may be collected.

Treatment   Gonorrhea can be cured with antibiotics, but increasing drug resistance is a major concern. Today only one class of antibiotics, the cephalosporins, remains consistently effective against gonorrhea. People with gonorrhea often also have chlamydia, so additional antibiotics are typically given to treat chlamydia. Follow-up tests are sometimes performed to make sure the infection has been eradicated. If you have had gonorrhea and have been treated, you can still get the disease again if you have sexual contact with an infected partner.

Pelvic Inflammatory Disease

Pelvic inflammatory disease (PID) is a major complication in 10–40% of women who have been infected with either gonorrhea or chlamydia and have not received adequate treatment. PID occurs when the initial infection with gonorrhea and/or chlamydia travels upward, often along with other bacteria, beyond the cervix into the uterus, oviducts, ovaries, and pelvic cavity. PID is often serious enough to require hospitalization and sometimes surgery. Even if the disease is treated successfully, about 25% of affected women will have long-term problems such as a continuing susceptibility to infection, ectopic pregnancy, infertility, and chronic pelvic pain.

PID is the leading cause of infertility in young women, often going undetected until the inability to become pregnant leads to further evaluation. Infertility occurs in 8% of women after one episode of PID, 20% after two episodes, and 40% after three episodes. The risk of ectopic pregnancy increases significantly in women who have had PID.

Women under age 25 are much more likely to develop PID than are older women. As with all STDs, the more sex partners a woman has had, the greater her risk of PID. Smokers have twice the risk of PID as nonsmokers. Using IUDs for contraception also increases the risk of PID. Research into whether the use of other contraceptives protects against PID has yielded mixed results; OC use may reduce the severity of PID symptoms.

Symptoms   Symptoms of PID vary greatly. Some women, especially those with chlamydia, may be asymptomatic; others may feel very ill with abdominal pain, fever, chills, nausea, and vomiting. Early symptoms are essentially the same as those described earlier for chlamydia and gonorrhea. Symptoms often begin or worsen during or soon after a woman's menstrual period. Many women have abnormal vaginal bleeding—either bleeding between periods or heavy and painful menstrual bleeding.

Diagnosis   Diagnosis of PID is made on the basis of symptoms, physical examination, ultrasound, and laboratory tests. Laparoscopy may be used to confirm the diagnosis and obtain material for cultures. Cultures from the rectum or cervix may also be taken to help identify the specific organism. The symptoms of PID, ectopic pregnancy,

TERMS

gonorrhea   A sexually transmitted bacterial infection that usually affects mucous membranes.

gonococcal conjunctivitis   An inflammation of the mucous membrane lining of the eyelids, caused by the gonococcus bacterium.

pelvic inflammatory disease (PID)   An infection that progresses from the vagina and cervix to the uterus, oviducts, and pelvic cavity.

The United States has the highest STD rate of any industrialized country. Estimates released since 2004 show that half of all Americans will have at least one STD by age 25, and nearly half of all STDs that occur each year are in people age 15–24. STDs are public health challenges for many reasons.

• *STDs are stealth diseases.* Many STDs, including chlamydia, genital herpes, trichomoniasis, HPV and even early HIV infection often have few, if any, recognizable symptoms. The large number of disease carriers who are unaware of their infection makes these diseases extremely difficult to control. Experts believe that in most cases, HIV is transmitted very early in the disease, before people are aware of the infection. The fact that most people are symptom-free for the first several years of HIV infection highlights the need to frequently test people who are at risk.

• *Viral STDs are persistent and incurable.* Even if detected, most viral STDs—genital herpes, HPV infection, and HIV infection—are not curable with current therapies. This means that the number of people capable of infecting others continues to grow. The best hope for controlling viral STDs is the development and widespread use of effective vaccines. The hepatitis B vaccine provides a positive example: In the years since introduction of the vaccine, the rate of new cases of hep-atitis B has dropped by more than 75%, and further declines are expected.

• *Screening tests may be underutilized.* Nationwide, too many physicians and clinics fail to follow the CDC recommendations for screening, especially for chlamydia in young women. In addition, too many individuals are unaware of or too embarrassed to request STD screening. Testing more people for STDs could potentially bring STD rates down; it would at least provide an opportunity to counsel people about risky sexual behavior. In surveys, up to 75% of people support offering STD testing in schools. Also potentially helpful would be media messages about the benefits and availability of confidential STD screening services.

• *Young people are particularly vulnerable to STDs.* Young adults are more likely to be ignorant about STDs and safer sex, embarrassed to ask for information, and unaware of how to access appropriate STD testing and treatment services. Nearly all young adults are sexually active by age 25, but young people are more likely to be unmarried, have more than one partner over time, and/or have a partner who has an STD. Young people need medically accurate information about abstinence, condoms, and other contraceptive methods—and open communication and encouragement from family, friends, and the community to behave responsibly.

Until STDs are controllable with vaccines or effective screening and treatment, the only way to reduce your risk is to limit the number of sexual partners and to use condoms consistently (see guidelines presented earlier in the chapter). For those who choose abstinence or a mutually monogamous relationship with one uninfected partner, there is no risk of STDs.

---

and appendicitis can be quite similar, so careful evaluation is required to make the correct diagnosis.

Treatment Starting treatment of PID as quickly as possible is important in order to minimize damage to the reproductive organs. Antibiotics are usually started immediately; in severe cases, the woman may be hospitalized and antibiotics given intravenously. It is especially important that an infected woman's partners be treated. As many as 60% of the male contacts of women with PID are infected but asymptomatic.

Human Papillomavirus Infection

Human papillomavirus (HPV) infection is the most common STD in the United States (see the box "Half of Americans Will Have an STD by Age 25"). HPV infection causes a variety of human diseases, including common warts, **genital warts,** and genital cancers. HPV is the cause of virtually all cervical cancer, but also causes penile cancer and some forms of anal and oropharyngeal cancers. Genital HPV is usually spread from one person to another through sexual activity, including oral sex.

About 6.2 million Americans become infected with HPV each year; in all, more than 80% of sexually active individuals will have been infected with HPV by the age of 50. Most people with HPV infection have no symptoms at all and are unaware that they are infected and contagious. The good news is that the immune system usually clears the virus, and infection disappears without any treatment. But in some cases, the infection persists and causes genital warts or cancers.

College Students and STDs

Why Do College Students Have High Rates of STDs?

• Risky sexual behavior is common. One study of college students found that fewer than half used condoms consistently and one-third had had ten or more sex partners. Another study found that 19% of male students and 33% of female students had consented to sexual intercourse simply because they felt awkward refusing.

• College students underestimate their risk of STDs and HIV. Although students may have considerable knowledge about STDs, they often feel the risks do not apply to them—a dangerous assumption. One study of students with a history of STDs showed that more than half had unprotected sex while they were infected, and 25% of them continued to have sex without ever informing their partner(s).

• Many students are infected but don't know it. A 2006 study of asymptomatic college women revealed that nearly 10% were infected with chlamydia.

What Effect Does Alcohol or Drug Use Have on My Likelihood of Getting an STD?

• Between one-third and one-half of college students report participating in sexual activity as a direct result of being intoxicated. All too often, sexual activity while intoxicated leads to unprotected intercourse.

• Students who binge-drink are more likely to have multiple partners, use condoms inconsistently, and delay seeking treatment for STDs than students who drink little or no alcohol. Sexual assaults occur more frequently when either the perpetrator or the victim has been drinking.

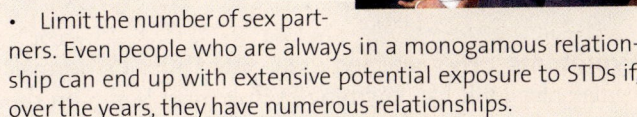

What Can Students Do to Protect Themselves Against STDs?

• Limit the number of sex partners. Even people who are always in a monogamous relationship can end up with extensive potential exposure to STDs if, over the years, they have numerous relationships.

• Use condoms consistently, and don't assume it's safe to stop after you've been with a partner for several months. HIV infection, HPV infection, herpes, and chlamydia can be asymptomatic for months or years and can be transmitted at any time. If you haven't been using condoms with your current partner, start now.

• Enjoy sexuality on your own terms. Don't let the expectations of friends and partners cause you to ignore your own feelings. Let your own wellness be your first priority. If you choose to be sexually active, learn about safer sex practices.

• Get to know your partner, and talk to him or her before becoming intimate. Be honest about yourself, and encourage your partner to do the same. But practice safer sex no matter what.

HPV is especially common in young people, with some of the highest rates of infection among college students. HPV infection is the most common STD for which diagnosis and treatment are sought in student health services (see the box "College Students and STDs" above). Many young women contract HPV infection within 3 months of becoming sexually active.

Human papillomaviruses cause many types of human warts. There are more than 100 different strains of HPV, and different strains infect specific locations. More than 30 types are likely to cause genital infections, and five of these are often implicated in cervical cancer; other strains are linked to anal, penile, and other genital cancers. The HPV strains that cause most visible genital warts are less likely to cause cancer than some of the other strains. A person can be infected with several different strains.

Genital HPV infection is quite contagious. Condoms and other barrier methods can help prevent the transmission of HPV, but HPV infection frequently occurs in areas where condoms are not fully protective. These areas are the labia in women, the base of the penis and the scrotum in men, and around the anus in both men and women. Still, a 3-year study showed that women who always use condoms cut their risk of HPV infection by 70%.

Most people who carry HPV have no visible warts or any other symptoms, and are not aware that they are infected and contagious to others. The strains of HPV that are linked with cancer are especially stealthy in that they generally do not cause warts or any obvious signs of their presence.

In 2006, the FDA approved a vaccine for HPV (Gardasil), and additional vaccines are in development. Gardasil protects against four types of HPV virus that together account for 90% of genital warts and 70% of cervical cancers; the drug has also been shown to prevent cancers of the vagina and vulva. The vaccine is not a treatment for HVP for girls or women who are infected with HPV. Vaccination is available for girls and women age 9–26. The CDC recommends the vaccine for all girls between the ages of 11 and 12. This age was chosen because the vaccine is most effec-

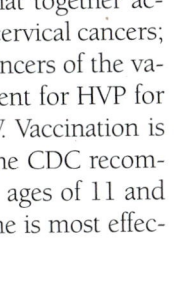

human papillomavirus (HPV) The pathogen that causes human warts, including genital warts.

genital warts A sexually transmitted viral infection characterized by growths on the genitals; also called *genital HPV infection* or *condyloma*.

TERMS

tive when given prior to exposure to genital HPV, and most girls do not become sexually active until after age 12.

The use of the vaccine for HPV has been limited by political and moral considerations, as well as its high cost. Many parents have opted not to vaccinate their daughters at least in part because they wish their daughters to choose abstinence and fear that giving the vaccine will be viewed as an endorsement for premarital sexual activity. Public health experts generally believe that giving the vaccine has little effect on girls' sexual choices, and that the vaccine offers the opportunity to prevent the majority of cases of cervical cancer. In the future, the vaccine may be recommended for boys as well as girls.

Symptoms   HPV-infected tissue often appears normal; it may also look like anything from a small bump on the skin to a large, warty growth. Depending on location and size, genital warts are sometimes painful. Untreated warts can grow together to form a cauliflower-like mass. In males, they appear on the penis and often involve the urethra, appearing first at the opening and then spreading inside. The growths may cause irritation and bleeding, leading to painful urination and a urethral discharge. Warts may also appear around the anus or within the rectum.

In women, warts may appear on the labia or vulva and may spread to the perineum, the area between the vagina and the rectum. They may also appear on the cervix.

The incubation period ranges from 1 month to 2 years from the time of contact. People can be infected with the virus and be capable of transmitting it to their sex partners without having any symptoms at all. The vast majority of people with HPV infection have no visible warts or symptoms of any kind.

Genital warts sometimes grow very large during pregnancy and can occasionally be large enough to make vaginal delivery difficult. However, most pregnant women with HPV infection can deliver vaginally. HPV infection is infrequently transmitted to an infant during delivery but can occasionally cause warts to form on the infant's vocal cords.

Diagnosis   Genital warts are usually diagnosed based on the appearance of the lesions. Sometimes examination with a special magnifying instrument or biopsy is done to evaluate suspicious lesions. HPV infection of the cervix is often detected on routine Pap tests. Special tests are now available to detect the presence of HPV infection and to distinguish among the more common strains of HPV, including those that cause most cases of cervical cancer. HPV subtypes 6 and 11 cause 90% of all cases of genital warts but do not normally cause genital cancers. HPV subtypes 16 and 18 cause most cervical cancers.

Treatment   Treatment of genital HPV infection depends on whether the infection manifests as genital warts or as a cancerous or precancerous condition. Treatment of genital warts focuses on reducing the number and size of warts, although most warts eventually disappear, even without treatment. The currently available treatments do not eradicate HPV infection. Warts may be removed by cryosurgery (freezing), electrocautery (burning), or laser surgery. Direct applications of podophyllin or other cytotoxic acids may be used, and there are treatments that patients can use at home. The success rates of methods vary, and warts often recur despite initial improvement. Warts are more likely to persist and become severe in people with an impaired immune system.

Even after treatment and the disappearance of visible warts, the individual may continue to carry HPV in healthy-looking tissue and can probably still infect others. Anyone who has ever had HPV infection should inform all partners and use condoms, even though they do not provide total protection. Because of the relationship between HPV and cervical cancer, women who have had genital warts should have Pap tests at least every 12 months. Cervical HPV infection associated with precancerous changes is treated by destroying the abnormal tissue with laser, freezing, heat, or other surgical means. Women who have regular screening exams almost never develop full-blown cervical cancer.

Genital Herpes

About one in five adults in the United States has **genital herpes,** although most of these people do not know they are infected. Worldwide, genital herpes is extremely common, and is a major factor in the transmission of HIV. Most people with HIV are also infected with HSV 2, and their herpes lesions contain large amounts of HIV, making it more likely that the virus will be transmitted. The presence of herpes lesions in an HIV-negative person increases the likelihood that she or he will be infected by an HIV-positive partner. Genital herpes may also interact with HPV infection to increase the risk of cervical cancer.

Two types of herpes simplex viruses, HSV 1 and HSV 2, cause genital herpes and oral-labial herpes (cold sores). Genital herpes is usually caused by HSV 2, and oral-labial herpes is usually caused by HSV 1, although both virus types can cause either genital or oral-labial lesions. Many people wrongly assume that they are unlikely to pick up an STD if they limit their sexual activity to oral sex, but this is not true, particularly in the case of genital herpes. HSV can also cause rectal lesions, usually transmitted through anal sex. Infection with HSV is generally lifelong; after infection, the virus lies dormant in nerve cells and can reactivate at any time.

HSV 1 infection is so common that 50–80% of U.S. adults have antibodies to HSV 1 (indicating previous exposure to the virus); most were exposed to HSV 1 during childhood. HSV 2 infection usually occurs during adoles-

genital herpes   A sexually transmitted infection caused by the herpes simplex virus.

Stress and Genital Herpes

Patients and health care workers alike have long suspected that stress and genital herpes outbreaks are related. Research into this potential link has yielded mixed results. A recent study of women with genital herpes found that persistent stressors (those lasting more than a week) and persistent high levels of anxiety were associated with increased outbreaks. Short-term stress, mood changes, and brief negative life experiences did not influence the rate of herpes outbreaks.

Experts suspect that stress has a negative impact on the immune system. Studies have shown that cell-mediated immune function and antibody levels may drop in response to psychological stress. Perhaps herpes viruses that are usually dormant in nervous system tissue become activated when immune function declines due to stress.

The next step is to investigate whether stress-reduction techniques such as meditation or exercise result in reduced rates of herpes outbreaks. Until such research becomes available, it makes sense for people who suffer recurrent genital herpes outbreaks to do what they can to reduce stress, especially long-term stress and anxiety (see Chapter 2). If you have

herpes, joining a support group may help reduce your stress and improve your ability to cope with this chronic disease. If you have several outbreaks a year, or if you have recently had your first episode of genital herpes, talk to your health care provider about suppressive antiviral medication, which can reduce outbreaks substantially. Keep in mind that regardless of stress level, genital herpes outbreaks naturally tend to become less and less frequent over time. Knowing that your outbreaks are likely to diminish can, in and of itself, help reduce your feelings of stress.

cence and early adulthood, often between ages 18 and 25. Approximately 22% of adults have antibodies to HSV 2.

HSV 2 is almost always sexually transmitted. The infection is more easily transmitted when people have active sores, but HSV 2 can be transmitted to a sex partner even when no obvious lesions are present. A recent study of women with HSV 2 showed the presence of the virus in genital secretions more than one-fourth of the time when the women were symptom-free. Because HSV is asymptomatic in 80–90% of people, the infection is often acquired from a person who does not know that he or she is infected. If you have ever had an outbreak of genital herpes, you should consider yourself always contagious and inform your partners. Avoid intimate contact when any sores are present, and use condoms during all sexual contact.

Newborns can occasionally be infected with HSV, usually during passage through the birth canal of an infected mother or due to HSV infection acquired by the mother during the third trimester of pregnancy. Without treatment, 65% of newborns with HSV will die, and most who survive will have some degree of brain damage. The risk of mother-to-child HSV transmission during pregnancy and delivery is low (less than 1%) in women with long-standing herpes infection. New herpes blood tests to screen pregnant women and their sexual partners could substantially reduce neonatal herpes infections. If an uninfected pregnant woman's partner carries HSV, abstinence or the use of condoms could prevent infection during pregnancy.

Pregnant women who have been exposed to genital herpes should inform their physician so that appropriate precautions can be taken to protect the baby from infection. These precautions sometimes include a cesarean section if active lesions are present at the time of delivery.

Symptoms   Up to 90% of people who are infected with HSV have no symptoms. Those that do develop symptoms often first notice them within 2–20 days of having

sex with an infected partner. (However, it is not unusual for the first outbreak to occur months or even years after initial exposure.) The first episode of genital herpes frequently causes flulike symptoms in addition to genital lesions. The lesions usually heal within 3 weeks, but the virus remains alive in an inactive state within nerve cells. A new outbreak of herpes can occur at any time.

On average, newly diagnosed people will experience five to eight outbreaks per year, with a decrease in the frequency of outbreaks over time. Recurrent episodes are usually less severe than the initial one, with fewer and less painful sores that heal more quickly. Outbreaks can be triggered by stress, illness, fatigue, sun exposure, sexual intercourse, and menstruation (see the box "Stress and Genital Herpes").

Diagnosis   Genital herpes is often diagnosed on the basis of symptoms; a sample of fluid from the lesions may also be sent to a laboratory for culture. This test is helpful if the specimen is obtained within about 2 days of the lesion's development. If the lesion has been around for longer than 2 days, the culture will often be negative even if the person has genital herpes.

Several blood tests can detect the presence of HSV antibodies. Older tests don't distinguish between HSV 1 and HSV 2. Because HSV 1 infection is extremely common, most people will test positive even if they have not had genital herpes. Newer tests can determine if a person is infected with HSV 1 or HSV 2 and may potentially alert many asymptomatic people to the fact that they are infected. This knowledge may help prevent transmission of HSV in couples where one partner is infected and the other is not (particularly important for uninfected women who are pregnant). The more accurate tests for HSV rely on the development of antibodies to the virus, which can take several weeks or months after exposure to the virus. For this reason, doctors often recommend that people wait for 12 to 16 weeks after possible exposure before having a blood test.

Anyone who has any STD should also be tested for HIV, but this is especially true for people who have HSV 2. Recent studies reported by the CDC revealed that adults who are infected with HSV 2 are 15 times more likely than those without HSV 2 to be infected with HIV. About 2% of all adults with HSV 2 also have HIV.

Treatment   There is no cure for herpes. Once infected, a person carries the virus for life. Antiviral drugs such as acyclovir can be taken at the beginning of an outbreak to shorten the severity and duration of symptoms. People who have frequent outbreaks can take acyclovir or similar drugs daily to suppress outbreaks and decrease viral shedding between outbreaks. Anyone diagnosed with a first episode of genital herpes should talk with a health care provider about suppressive treatment.

A person on suppressive therapy can still transmit HSV to an uninfected partner, but the risk is probably reduced by about half. Using condoms consistently and taking suppressive medication is a reasonable way to reduce the risk of passing herpes to an uninfected sexual partner. It is always important to inform a sexual partner if you have genital herpes.

A herpes vaccine is currently undergoing testing, but results to date have been frustrating because the vaccine appears to be effective only for women who have not been exposed to HSV 1 or 2, and is ineffective for men. Several microbicides are under development that may someday be available to help stop the transmission of HSV.

Hepatitis B

Hepatitis (inflammation of the liver) can cause serious and sometimes permanent damage to the liver, which can result in death in severe cases. One of the many types of hepatitis is caused by hepatitis B virus (HBV). HBV is somewhat similar to HIV; it is found in most body fluids, and it can be transmitted sexually, by injection drug use, and during pregnancy and delivery. However, HBV is much more contagious than HIV, and it can also be spread through nonsexual close contact. Health care workers who are exposed to blood are frequently infected, as are people who live in close contact with each other, such as prisoners and residents of mental health care facilities.

Hepatitis B is a potentially fatal disease with no cure, but fortunately there is an effective vaccine. The number of cases of acute hepatitis B in the United States has dropped by 75% since 1990, primarily as a result of the vaccine. In addition, mother-to-child transmission has been greatly reduced because of routine HBV screening of pregnant women. Vaccination is recommended for everyone under age 19 and for all adults at increased risk for hepatitis B, including people who have more than one sex partner in 6 months, men who have sex with other men,

those who inject illegal drugs, and health care workers who are exposed to blood and body fluids.

Other forms of viral hepatitis can also be sexually transmitted. Hepatitis A is of particular concern for people who engage in anal sex; a vaccine is available and is recommended for all people at risk. Less commonly, hepatitis C can be transmitted sexually. Experts believe that traumatic sexual activity that causes tissue damage is most likely to transmit HCV. See Chapter 17 for more on these forms of hepatitis.

Transmission   HBV is found in all body fluids, including blood and blood products, semen, saliva, urine, and vaginal secretions. It is easily transmitted through any sexual activity that involves the exchange of body fluids, the use of contaminated needles, and any blood-to-blood contact, including the use of contaminated razor blades, toothbrushes, and eating utensils. The primary risk factors for acquiring HBV are sexual exposure and injection drug use; having multiple partners greatly increases risk. As mentioned, a pregnant woman can transmit HBV to her unborn child.

Symptoms   Many people infected with HBV never develop symptoms; they have what are known as silent infections. The normal incubation period is 30–180 days. Mild cases of hepatitis cause flulike symptoms such as fever, body aches, chills, and loss of appetite. As the illness progresses, there may be nausea, vomiting, dark-colored urine, abdominal pain, and jaundice. Some people with hepatitis also develop a skin rash and joint pain or arthritis. Acute hepatitis B can sometimes be severe, resulting in prolonged illness or even death.

Most adults who have acute hepatitis B recover completely within a few weeks or months. But about 5% of adults who are infected with HBV become chronic carriers of the virus, capable of infecting others for the rest of their life. Some chronic carriers remain asymptomatic, while others develop chronic liver disease. Chronic hepatitis can cause cirrhosis of the liver, liver failure, and a deadly form of liver cancer. Hepatitis kills some 5000 Americans each year; worldwide, the annual death toll exceeds 600,000.

Diagnosis and Treatment   Blood tests can diagnose hepatitis by analyzing liver function and detecting the infecting organism. There is no cure for hepatitis B and no specific treatment for acute infections; antiviral drugs and immune system modulators may be used for cases of chronic HBV infection. For people exposed to HBV, treatment with hepatitis B immunoglobulin can provide protection against the virus.

Prevention   Preventive measures for hepatitis B are similar to those for HIV infection: Avoid sexual contact that involves sharing body fluids, including saliva; use condoms during sexual intercourse; and don't share needles. If you have tattooing or body piercing done, make sure all needles and equipment are sterile. The vaccine for hepatitis B is safe and highly effective.

Syphilis

Syphilis, a disease that once caused death and disability for millions, can now be effectively treated with antibiotics. Each year, there are about 11,000 new cases of early syphilis in the United States, and about 41,000 people are diagnosed at all stages of the disease. The number of new cases hit an all-time low in 2000 but has been on the rise since then.

The increase in syphilis has been greatest in homosexual and bisexual men, prompting health officials to call for increased education in safer sex practices among these groups. Studies have found an association between syphilis infection and the use of the Internet as a means to meet sex partners among men who have sex with men. Another recent trend is an increase in the proportion of cases of syphilis from oral sex; in nearly 15% of recent cases among gay men and 7% of cases among heterosexual men and women, the means of transmission was through oral sex. People with syphilis in the mouth may not have symptoms, or they may mistake the sores for another illness. The sores associated with syphilis, regardless of their location, dramatically increase the risk of acquiring HIV or transmitting it to someone else.

Syphilis is caused by a spirochete called *Treponema pallidum,* a thin, corkscrew-shaped bacterium. The disease is usually acquired through sexual contact, although infected pregnant women can transmit it to the fetus. The pathogen passes through any break or opening in the skin or mucous membranes and can be transmitted by kissing, vaginal or anal intercourse, or oral-genital contact. Although easy to treat, syphilis can be difficult to recognize, and if left untreated the disease can cause devastating damage to almost any system of the body.

Symptoms Syphilis progresses through several stages. *Primary syphilis* is characterized by an ulcer called a **chancre** that appears within 10–90 days after exposure. The chancre is usually found at the site where the organism entered the body, such as the genital area, but it may also appear in other sites such as the mouth, breasts, or fingers. Chancres contain large numbers of bacteria and make the disease highly contagious when present; they are often painless and typically heal on their own within a few weeks. If the disease is not treated during the primary stage, about a third of infected individuals progress to chronic stages of infections.

Secondary syphilis is usually marked by mild, flulike symptoms and a skin rash that appears 3–6 weeks after the chancre. The rash may cover the entire body or only a few areas, but the palms of the hands and soles of the feet are usually involved. Areas of skin affected by the rash are highly contagious but usually heal within several weeks or months.

If the disease remains untreated, the symptoms of secondary syphilis may recur over a period of several years; affected individuals may then lapse into an asymptomatic latent stage in which they experience no further consequences of infection. However, in about a third of cases of untreated secondary syphilis, the individual develops *late,* or *tertiary, syphilis.* Late syphilis can damage many organs of the body, possibly causing severe dementia, cardiovascular damage, blindness, and death.

In infected pregnant women, the syphilis bacterium can cross the placenta. If the mother is not treated, the probable result is stillbirth, prematurity, or congenital deformity. In many cases, the infant is also born infected (*congenital syphilis*) and requires treatment.

Diagnosis and Treatment Syphilis is diagnosed by examination of infected tissues and with blood tests. All stages can be treated with antibiotics, but damage from late syphilis can be permanent.

Other STDs

A few other diseases are transmitted sexually and require responsible sexual behavior.

Trichomoniasis (often called *trich*) is the most curable STD among young women. The CDC estimates that as many as 7.4 million new infections occur each year. The single-celled organism that causes trich, *Trichomonas vaginalis,* thrives in warm, moist conditions, making women particularly susceptible to these infections in the vagina. Women who become symptomatic with trich develop a greenish, foul-smelling vaginal discharge and severe itching and pain in the vagina. Prompt treatment with metronidazole (Flagyl) is important because studies suggest that trich may increase the risk of HIV transmission and, in pregnant women, premature delivery.

Bacterial vaginosis (BV) is the most common cause of abnormal vaginal discharge in women of reproductive age. BV occurs when healthy bacteria that normally inhabit the vagina become displaced by unhealthy species. BV is clearly associated with sexual activity and often occurs after a change in partners. Douching has been correlated with an increased risk of BV, especially in women who douche

hepatitis Inflammation of the liver, which can be caused by infection, drugs, or toxins; some forms of infectious hepatitis can be transmitted sexually.

syphilis A sexually transmitted bacterial infection caused by the spirochete *Treponema pallidum.*

chancre The sore produced by syphilis in its earliest stage.

trichomoniasis A protozoal infection caused by *Trichomonas vaginalis,* transmitted sexually and externally.

bacterial vaginosis (BV) A condition linked to sexual activity; caused by an overgrowth of certain bacteria inhabiting the vagina.

TERMS

THINKING ABOUT THE ENVIRONMENT

In some parts of the world, the human environment is far more responsible than the natural one for the spread of sexually transmitted infections.

As has been mentioned in this chapter, people in remote and poverty-stricken areas typically have little access to health care resources, information on safer sex practices, and barrier devices such as condoms. Without access to medical testing and treatment, whole populations have little means for preventing or dealing with STDs of any kind.

Making matters worse is the harsh male-dominated sexual environments found in some regions. Whether these circumstances are based on local religious or social mores, they often place women (and children, in some cases) at risk of exploitation and greatly increase the risks of STDs. For example, some cultures allow or even encourage male infidelity. In many parts of the world, women have little or no say in their sexual relationships, meaning they may not be able to use protective measures against STDs. Often, the cultures that prevent women from protecting themselves shun or punish women who become infected with a sexually transmitted disease.

See Chapter 19 for more information on the environment and environmental health.

more than once a month. Symptoms of BV include vaginal discharge with a fishy odor and sometimes vaginal irritation. BV is treated with topical and oral antibiotics.

Pubic lice (commonly known as *crabs*) and **scabies** are highly contagious parasitic infections. Treatment is generally easy, although lice infestation can require repeated applications of medications.

WHAT YOU CAN DO

You can take responsibility for your health and contribute to a general reduction in the incidence of STDs in three major areas: education, diagnosis and treatment, and prevention. To assess your current level of responsibility for STD prevention, complete the quiz in the box "Do Your Attitudes and Behaviors Put You at Risk for STDs?"

QUESTIONS FOR CRITICAL THINKING AND REFLECTION

Have you ever had sex and regretted it later? If so, what were the circumstances, and what influenced you to act the way you did? Were there any negative consequences? What preventive strategies can you use in the future to make sure it doesn't happen again?

Education

Since the AIDS epidemic began, public and private agencies have grown more serious about educating the public and increasing their awareness of all STDs. This campaign may already be paying off in changing attitudes and sexual behaviors, at least among certain segments of the population. For example, condom use among sexually active adolescents has increased over the last decade. But some groups seem to be growing weary of messages about safer sex. Many younger gay men are participating in very high risk behaviors, and a second wave of the AIDS epidemic among homosexual men can be expected if younger men fail to use preventive measures. Also discouraging is the fact that the number of cases of HIV infection among harder-to-reach groups, such as injection drug users and their partners and children, is still increasing. In particular, more educational efforts are needed among U.S. ethnic minorities.

Education efforts targeted at increasing public awareness about AIDS through the media have included public service announcements, dramatic presentations, and support from well-known public figures. Colleges offer courses in human sexuality. Free pamphlets and other literature are available from public health departments, health clinics, physicians' offices, student health centers, and Planned Parenthood, and easy-to-understand books are available in libraries and bookstores. Several national hotlines have been set up to provide free, confidential information and referral services to callers anywhere in the country.

Learning about STDs is still up to every person individually. You must assume responsibility for learning about the causes and nature of STDs and their potential effects on you, those with whom you have sexual relationships, and the children you may have. Once you know about STDs—their symptoms, how they're transmitted, and how they can be prevented—you are in a position to educate others. Providing information to your friends and partners, whether in casual conversation or in more serious decision-making discussions, is an important way that you can make a difference in both your own wellness and that of others.

Diagnosis and Treatment

Early diagnosis and treatment of STDs can help you and your sex partner(s) avoid unnecessary complications and help prevent the spread of STDs.

Get Vaccinated Every young, sexually active person should be vaccinated for hepatitis B; vaccines are available for all age groups. Men who have sex with men should be vaccinated for hepatitis A, and girls and women age 9–26 should be vaccinated for HPV.

Be Alert for Symptoms If you are sexually active, be alert for any sign or symptom of disease, such as a rash, a

Do Your Attitudes and Behaviors Put You at Risk for STDs?

To identify your STD risk factors, read the following statements and identify whether each one is true or false for you.

True or False

1. I have never been sexually active. (If false, continue. If true, you are not at risk; respond to the remaining statements based on how you realistically believe you would act.)

2. I am in a mutually monogamous relationship with an uninfected partner or am not currently sexually active. (If false, continue. If true, you are at minimal risk now; respond to the remaining statements according to your attitudes and past behaviors.)

3. I have only one sex partner.

4. I always use a condom for each act of intercourse, even if I am fairly certain my partner has no infections.

5. I do not use oil-based lubricants or other products with condoms.

6. I discuss STDs and prevention with new partners before having sex.

7. I do not use alcohol or another mood-altering drug in sexual situations.

8. I would tell my partner if I thought I had been exposed to an STD.

9. I am familiar with the signs and symptoms of STDs.

10. I regularly perform genital self-examination.

11. When I notice any sign or symptom of any STD or if I engage in risky sexual behavior, I consult my physician immediately.

12. I obtain screening for HIV and STDs regularly. In addition (if female), I obtain yearly pelvic exams and Pap tests.

13. When diagnosed with an STD, I inform all recent partners.

14. When I have a sign or symptom of an STD that goes away on its own, I still consult my physician.

15. I do not use drugs prescribed for friends or partners or left over from other illnesses to treat STDs.

16. I do not share syringes or needles to inject drugs.

False answers indicate attitudes and behaviors that may put you at risk for contracting STDs or for suffering serious medical consequences from them. (For a more detailed self-assessment, take the quiz at www.thebody.com/surveys/sexsurvey.html).

---

discharge, sores, or unusual pain, and don't hesitate to have a professional examination if you notice such a symptom. Although only a physician can make a proper diagnosis of an STD, you can perform *genital self-examination* between checkups to look for early warning signs of infection. Women should examine the entire genital area, including the area covered by pubic hair, the outer and inner lips of the vagina, the clitoris, and the area around the urinary and vaginal openings. Men should look at the entire head, shaft, and base of the penis and the scrotum. (A mirror may be helpful for checking difficult-to-see areas.)

Throughout the exam, look for bumps, sores, blisters, or warts on the skin. Bumps or blisters may be red or light colored; they may look like pimples, or they may develop into open sores. Genital warts may appear as very small bumpy spots, or they may have a fleshy, cauliflower-like appearance. Also stay alert for other signs of STDs, including pain or burning upon urination, itchiness in the genital area, abnormal discharge from the vagina or penis, pelvic pain, and, in women, bleeding between menstrual periods. Be alert for these signs or symptoms in your partner, too.

Get Tested Remember that almost all STDs—including HIV infection—can be completely asymptomatic for long periods of time. The CDC recommends that everyone between the ages of 13 and 64 be tested for HIV at least once during routine medical care. If you are sexually active, be sure to get periodic STD checks, even if you have no symptoms. If you have a risky sexual encounter,

see a physician as soon as possible (see the box "Don't Wait—Early Treatment of STDs Really Matters" on p. 578).

Sexually active young women should have pelvic exams and Pap tests at least once a year, with chlamydia and gonorrhea screening in most cases. Sexually active men, especially if they have had more than one partner, should have periodic STD screenings.

Men who have sex with men are at especially high risk for HIV and other STDs. The CDC recommends that sexually active men who have sex with men be tested annually for HIV, chlamydia (anal and urethral), syphilis, and gonorrhea (anal, urethral, and pharyngeal). Men who have multiple anonymous partners or who are injection drug users should be screened more frequently. All sexually active gay and bisexual men should be vaccinated for hepatitis A and B.

Testing for STDs is done through private physicians, public health clinics, community health agencies, and most student health services.

Inform Your Partners Telling a partner that you have exposed him or her to an STD isn't easy. You may be afraid

---

pubic lice Parasites that infest the hair of the pubic region, commonly called *crabs*.

scabies A contagious skin disease caused by a type of burrowing parasitic mite.

TERMS

Don't Wait—Early Treatment of STDs Really Matters

If you have had a recent risky sexual encounter, visit your physician, student health center, or local STD clinic and ask for testing. Don't wait for symptoms to develop—you may never have any. Permanent damage from STDs, including infertility, can occur even if you have no symptoms. Treating STDs like chlamydia and gonorrhea within a few days of infection is very likely to prevent complications such as PID and infertility. You will also be much less likely to pass the infection on to anyone else.

Unsafe sex with a person who is infected with HIV meets the criteria for PEP treatment described earlier in the chapter; if you are treated within 72 hours of possible exposure, PEP will significantly reduce your risk of HIV infection. If you develop flulike symptoms in the days or weeks following risky sexual or drug-taking behavior, see your physician and ask for an HIV RNA test in addition to standard STD tests. (HIV antibody tests may not register primary HIV infection.) If HIV treatment is begun within the first weeks of the infection, there is a good chance that damage to the immune system can be reduced or even prevented. Many physicians will not think of primary HIV infection when you describe flu-like symptoms, so be sure to speak up about your recent risky activities and your concerns about HIV.

If tests come back positive for a particular STD, you need to be tested for others, including HIV infection. Infection with any STD means that you are at higher risk for all others. Women should also have a pelvic exam and a Pap test. If you are given medication to treat an STD, take all of it as directed. Incomplete treatment can result in an incomplete cure, thereby contributing to the development of drug-resistant organisms. Do not share your medication with a partner; he or she should see a physician for testing and treatment.

Do not have sexual intercourse until your treatment—and your partner's treatment—is complete. If your partner still carries the infection, you are likely to be reinfected when you resume sexual activity. If you have an incurable STD such as herpes or HPV infection, always use a condom and make sure your partner is fully informed of the potential risks of being intimate with you, even if you are using condoms.

---

your partner will be angry or resentful, or you may worry that your partner will think less of you or reject you. At the same time, you may be feeling afraid, ashamed, embarrassed, or angry yourself. Despite the awkwardness and difficulty, it is crucial that your sex partner or partners be informed and urged to seek testing and/or treatment as quickly as possible.

You can get help telling your partner if you need it. Public health departments will notify sex partners of their possible exposure while maintaining your confidentiality and anonymity. Peer counseling and student health programs often help students with practice in role playing in these circumstances, and concerned health care personnel can provide assistance.

As emphasized throughout this chapter, undetected and untreated STDs can lead to serious medical complications and even death. In asymptomatic cases, the only way infected people can find out they have a disease is by being tested. Uninformed, untested partners can go on to spread the disease, contributing to anguish for others as well as spiraling public health problems.

Get Treated   With the exception of AIDS treatments, treatments for STDs are safe and generally inexpensive. If you are being treated, follow instructions carefully and complete all the medication as prescribed. Don't stop taking the medication just because you feel better or your symptoms have disappeared. Above all, don't give any of your medication to anyone else, including your partner. If you have an STD, your partner needs to be tested and, if necessary, treated. Taking a few of your pills is unlikely to cure your partner, and may make your treatment incomplete, leaving you both at risk for reinfection.

Being cured of an STD does not mean that you will not get it again, and exposure does not confer lasting immunity, nor does it prevent you from getting any other STD— all the more reason to be informed, to inform your partners, and to practice safer sex.

Prevention

STDs *are* preventable. As discussed earlier, the only sure way to avoid exposure to STDs is to abstain from sexual activity. But if you choose to be sexually active, the key is to think about prevention *before* you have a sexual encounter or find yourself in the heat of the moment. Find out what your partner thinks before you become sexually

The use of condoms declined as more advanced methods of contraception, such as birth control pills and IUDs, became available. But condoms are once again gaining in popularity because of the protection they provide against STDs.

Talking About Condoms and Safer Sex

The only sure way to prevent STDs, including HIV infection, is to abstain from sexual activity. If you choose to be sexually active, you should do everything possible to protect yourself from STDs. This includes good communication with your sex partner(s).

The time to talk about safer sex is before you begin a sexual relationship. However, even if you've been having unprotected sex with your partner, it is still worth it to start practicing safer sex now. If you're nervous about initiating a conversation about safer sex, rehearse what you will say first. Practice in front of a mirror or with a friend.

There are many ways to bring up the subject of safer sex and condom use with your partner. Be honest about your concerns and stress that protection against STDs means that you care about yourself and your partner. Here are a few suggestions:

- "I heard on the news that more and more people are buying and using condoms. I think it shows that people are being more responsible about sex. What do you think?"

- "I'm worried about the diseases we can get from having sex because so many don't have symptoms. I want to protect both of us by using condoms whenever we have sex."

- "I've been thinking about making love with you. But first we need to talk about how to have safer sex and be protected."

You may find that your partner shares your concerns and also wants to use condoms. He or she may be happy and relieved that you have brought up the subject of safer sex. However, if he or she resists the idea of using condoms, you may need to negotiate. Stress that you both deserve to be protected and that sex will be more enjoyable when you aren't worrying about STDs (see the suggestions to the right). If you and your partner haven't used condoms before, buy some and familiarize yourselves with how to use them. Once you feel more comfortable handling condoms, you'll be able to use them correctly and incorporate them into your sexual activity in fun ways. Consider trying the female condom.

If your partner still won't agree to use condoms, think carefully about whether you want to have a sexual relationship with him or her. Safer sex is part of a responsible, caring sexual relationship, and it's smart to say no to a partner who won't use a condom. It's up to you to protect yourself.

If your partner says . . .	Try saying . . .
"They're not romantic."	"Worrying about AIDS isn't romantic, and with condoms we won't have to worry." OR "If we put one on together, a condom could be fun."
"You don't trust me."	"I do trust you, but how can I trust your former partners or mine?" OR "It's important to me that we're both protected."
"I don't have any diseases. I've been tested."	"I'm glad you've been tested, but tests aren't foolproof for all diseases. To be safe, I always use condoms."
"I forgot to bring a condom. But it's OK to skip it just this once."	"I'd really like to make love with you, but I never have sex without a condom. Let's go get some."
"I don't like the way they feel."	"They might feel different, but let's try." OR "Sex won't feel good if we're worrying about diseases." OR "How about trying the female condom?"
"I don't use condoms."	"I use condoms every time." OR "I don't have sex without condoms."
"But I love you."	"Being in love can't protect us from diseases." OR "I love you, too. We still need to use condoms."
"But we've been having sex without condoms."	"I want to start using condoms now so we won't be at any more risk." OR "We can still prevent infection or reinfection."

SOURCE: Dialogue from San Francisco AIDS Foundation. 1998. *Condoms for Couples* (IMPACT AIDS, 3692 18th Street, San Francisco, CA 94110). Copyright © 1998 San Francisco AIDS Foundation. All rights reserved. Used with permission.

involved. Remember, you can become infected with an STD from just one unprotected encounter.

All your good intentions are likely to fly out the window if you enter into a sexual situation when you are intoxicated. If you or your partner (or both of you) is drunk, you are likely to be less cautious about sex than you would be if you were sober. Many people use alcohol and drugs as a way to deal with their anxiety in social and sexual situations. However, being intoxicated leaves you vulnerable to sexual assault and greatly increases your risk of acquiring a serious STD.

Most people don't want to think, talk, or ask questions about STDs for a variety of reasons. They may think it detracts from the appeal and excitement of the moment, that it takes away from the spontaneity of the experience, or that it will be perceived as a personal insult. For others, simply not knowing how to talk about STDs and safer sex may prevent them from bringing up the issue with a partner. (For advice on communicating with potential sex partners, see the box "Talking About Condoms and Safer Sex.")

Find out about your partner's sexual history and practices. Be honest, and ask your partner to do the same, but don't stake your health and life on assumptions about your partner's honesty. Even if your partner's past seems low-risk, still insist on using a condom every time you have sex. Any sexual activity exposes partners to everyone from their partner's sexual past as well everyone from those people's pasts. In one recent study, researchers mapped the sexual relationships of a group of high school students and found a chain of 288 one-to-one sexual relationships, meaning the teen at the end of the chain may have had direct sexual contact with only 1 person—but was indirectly exposed to 286 others.

You may find that your partner is just as concerned as you are. By thinking and talking about responsible sexual behavior, you are expressing a sense of caring for yourself, your potential partner, and your future children. Taking STDs seriously is practical, courageous, and loving; it means giving yourself the respect you deserve.

QUESTIONS FOR CRITICAL THINKING AND REFLECTION
If you are sexually active, have you talked seriously with your partner about STDs and safer sex practices? If not, why? How would you react if your partner started such a discussion?

TIPS FOR TODAY AND THE FUTURE
Because STDs can have serious, long-term effects, it's important to be vigilant about exposure, treatment, and prevention.

RIGHT NOW YOU CAN
- Make an appointment with your health care provider if you are worried about possible STD infection.
- Resolve to discuss condom use with your partner if you are sexually active and are not already using condoms.

IN THE FUTURE YOU CAN
- Learn how to communicate effectively with a partner who resists safer sex practices or is reluctant to discuss his or her sexual history. Support groups and educational classes can help.
- Make sure all your vaccinations are up-to-date; ask your doctor if you should be vaccinated against hepatitis B or any other STDs.

SUMMARY

- HIV affects the immune system, making an otherwise healthy person less able to resist a variety of infections.

- HIV is carried in blood and blood products, semen, vaginal and cervical secretions, and breast milk. HIV is transmitted through the exchange of these fluids.

- There is currently no cure or vaccine for HIV infection. Drugs have been developed to slow the course of the disease and to prevent or treat certain secondary infections.

- HIV infection can be prevented by making careful choices about sexual activity, not sharing drug needles, and learning how to protect oneself from HIV.

- Chlamydia causes epididymitis and urethritis in men; in women, it can lead to PID and infertility if untreated.

- Untreated, gonorrhea can cause PID in women and epididymitis in men, leading to infertility. In infants, untreated gonorrhea can cause blindness.

- Pelvic inflammatory disease (PID), a complication of untreated gonorrhea or chlamydia, is an infection of the uterus and oviducts that may extend to the ovaries and pelvic cavity. It can lead to infertility, ectopic pregnancy, and chronic pelvic pain.

- Human papillomavirus (HPV) causes genital warts and cervical cancer. Treatment does not eradicate the virus, which can be passed on by asymptomatic people.

- Genital herpes is a common incurable infection that can be fatal to newborns. After an initial infection, outbreaks may recur at any time.

- Hepatitis B is a viral infection of the liver transmitted through sexual and nonsexual contact. Following an initial infection, most people recover; but some become carriers and may develop serious complications.

- Syphilis is a highly contagious bacterial infection that can be treated with antibiotics. If left untreated, it can lead to deterioration of the central nervous system and death.

- Other diseases that can be transmitted sexually or are linked to sexual activity include trichomoniasis, bacterial vaginosis, pubic lice, and scabies. Any STD that causes sores or inflammation can increase the risk of HIV transmission.

- Successful diagnosis and treatment of STDs involve being alert for symptoms, getting tested, informing partners, and following treatment instructions carefully.

- All STDs are preventable; the key is practicing responsible sexual behaviors. Those who are sexually active are safest with one mutually monogamous, uninfected partner. Using a condom properly with every act of sexual intercourse helps protect against STDs.

BOOKS

Engel, J. 2007. *The Epidemic: A Global History of AIDS.* New York: Collins. *A historical, social, and cultural perspective on the AIDS epidemic, from its beginning in 1981 to the present day, from a medical historian.*

Hyde, J. S., and J. D. DeLamater. 2008. *Understanding Human Sexuality,* 10th ed. New York: McGraw-Hill. *A comprehensive, multidisciplinary introduction to human sexuality; includes material on STDs.*

Klausner, J. D., and E. W. Hook. 2007. *Current Diagnosis and Treatment of Sexually Transmitted Diseases.* New York: McGraw-Hill. *Written for the clinician; provides an easy-to-use reference of the latest diagnostic and treatment information available on STDs.*

Marr, L. 2007. *Sexually Transmitted Diseases: A Physician Tells You What You Need to Know.* Baltimore, Md.: Johns Hopkins University Press. *Practical, up-to-date information on the diagnosis, treatment, and prevention of sexually transmitted diseases of all types.*

McIlvenna, T. 2005. *The Complete Guide to Safer Sex.* Fort Lee, N.J.: Barricade Books. *Provides practical advice for STD prevention.*

Moore, E. A. 2008. *Encyclopedia of Sexually Transmitted Diseases,* Illustrated ed. Jefferson, N.C.: McFarland. *Includes a variety of information about STDs in an easy-to-use format.*

ORGANIZATIONS, HOTLINES, AND WEB SITES

American College Health Association. Offers free brochures on STDs, alcohol use, acquaintance rape, and other health issues.

http://www.acha.org

American Social Health Association (ASHA). Provides written information and referrals on STDs; sponsors support groups for people with herpes and HPV.

http://www.ashastd.org

Black AIDS Institute. Provides public health information about a variety of topics including testing, treatment, vaccines, and health care access.

http://www.blackaids.org

CDC National Prevention Information Network. Provides extensive information and links on HIV/AIDS and other STDs.

http://www.cdcnpin.org

ASHA/CDC STD and AIDS Hotlines. Callers can obtain information, counseling, and referrals for testing and treatment. The hotlines offer information on more than 20 STDs and include Spanish and TTY service.

800-227-8922

HIV InSite: Gateway to AIDS Knowledge. Provides information about prevention, education, treatment, statistics, clinical trials, and new developments.

http://hivinsite.ucsf.edu

Joint United Nations Programme on HIV/AIDS (UNAIDS). Provides statistics and information on the international HIV/AIDS situation.

http://www.unaids.org

The NAMES Project Foundation AIDS Memorial Quilt. Includes the story behind the quilt, images of quilt panels, and information and links relating to HIV infection.

http://www.aidsquilt.org

National Institute of Allergies and Infectious Disease: Sexually Transmitted Infections. Provides up-to-date fact sheets and brochures.

http://www3.niaid.nih.gov/topics/sti

Planned Parenthood Federation of America. Provides information on STDs, family planning, and contraception.

http://www.plannedparenthood.org

WHO: Sexually Transmitted Infections. Provides information on international statistics and prevention efforts.

http://www.who.int/topics/sexually_transmitted_infections/en

See also the listings for Chapters 6 and 17.

SELECTED BIBLIOGRAPHY

Agot, K. E., et al. 2004. Risk of HIV-1 in rural Kenya: A comparison of circumcised and uncircumcised men. *Epidemiology* 15(2): 157–163.

American Association of Blood Banks. 2007. *Blood Donation Frequently Asked Questions* (http://www.aabb.org/Content/Donate_Blood/Blood_Donation _FAQs/donatefaqs.htm; retrieved February 17, 2009).

American Social Health Association. 2008. *Frequently Asked Questions About Cervical Cancer/HPV Vaccine Access in the U.S.* (http://www.ashastd.org/ hpv/hpv_vaccines.cfm; retrieved February 17, 2009).

AVERT. 2009. *The Origin of AIDS and HIV and The First Cases of AIDS* (http:// www.avert.org/origins.htm; retrieved February 17, 2009).

Baeten, J. M., et al. 2005. Female-to-male infectivity of HIV-1 among circumcised and uncircumcised Kenyan men. *Journal of Infectious Diseases* 191(4): 546–553.

Brown, D. R., et al. 2005. A longitudinal study of genital human papillomavirus infection in a cohort of closely followed adolescent women. *Journal of Infectious Diseases* 191(2): 182–192.

Centers for Disease Control and Prevention. 2006. Revised recommendations for HIV testing of adults, adolescents, and pregnant women in health-care settings. *Morbidity and Mortality Weekly Report* 55(RR-14): 1–17.

Centers for Disease Control and Prevention. 2006. Trends in HIV-related risk behaviors among high school students—United States, 1991–2005. *Morbidity and Mortality Weekly Report* 55(31): 851–854.

Centers for Disease Control and Prevention. 2007. *STD Surveillance 2006* (http://www.cdc.gov/std/stats06/toc2006.htm; retrieved February 17, 2009).

Centers for Disease Control and Prevention. 2008. *Genital HPV Infection— CDC Fact Sheet* (http://www.cdc.gov/std/hpv/stdfact-hpv.htm; retrieved February 17, 2009).

Centers for Disease Control and Prevention. 2008. HIV prevalence estimates—United States, 2006. *Morbidity and Mortality Weekly Report* 57(39): 1073–1076.

Centers for Disease Control and Prevention. 2008. *New Estimates of U.S. HIV Prevalence, 2006.* (http://www.cdc.gov/hiv/topics/surveillance/ resources/factsheets/pdf/prevalence.pdf; retrieved February 17, 2009).

Centers for Disease Control and Prevention. 2008. *Sexually Transmitted Disease Surveillance, 2007.* Atlanta: Centers for Disease Control and Prevention.

Centers for Disease Control and Prevention, National Center for HIV/AIDS, Viral Hepatitis, STD, and TB Prevention. 2008. *2006 Disease Profile* (http://www.cdc.gov/nchhstp/Publications/docs/2006_Disease_Profile _508_FINAL.pdf; retrieved February 17, 2009).

Cohen, Myron. 2004. HIV and sexually transmitted diseases: A lethal synergy. *Topics in HIV Medicine* 12(4):104–107.

Crosby, R., and R.J. DiClemente. 2004. Use of recreational Viagra among men having sex with men. *Sexually Transmitted Infections* 80(6): 466–468.

Erbelding, E. J., and J. M. Zenilman. 2005. Toward better control of sexually transmitted diseases. *New England Journal of Medicine* 352(7): 720–721.

Food and Drug Administration. 2004. *FDA Approves First Oral Fluid Based Rapid HIV Test Kit* (http://www.fda.gov/bbs/topics/news/2004/NEW01042 .html; retrieved February 17, 2009).

Gupta, R., et al. 2004. Valacyclovir and acyclovir for suppression of shedding of herpes simplex virus in the genital tract. *Journal of Infectious Diseases* 190(8): 1374–1381.

Hampton, T. 2006. High prevalence of lesser-known STDs. *Journal of the American Medical Association* 295(21): 2467.

Hightow, L. B., et al. 2005. The unexpected movement of the HIV epidemic in the southeastern United States: Transmission among college students. *Journal of Acquired Immune Deficiency Syndrome* 38(5): 531–537.

Huppert, J. S. 2006. New detection methods for trichomoniasis may help curb more serious STIs. *Patient Care for the Nurse Practitioner* 40(5).

Joint United National Programme on HIV/AIDS (UNAIDS). 2008. *2008 Report on the Global AIDS Epidemic.* Geneva: UNAIDS.

Kimberlin, D., and D. Rouse. 2004. Genital herpes. *New England Journal of Medicine* 350(19): 1970–1977.

Mathers, C. D., and Loncar, D. 2006. Projections of global mortality and burden of disease from 2002 to 2030. *Public Library of Science, Medicine* 3(11):2011–2030.

Merson, M. 2006. The HIV-AIDS pandemic at 25—The global response. *New England Journal of Medicine* 354(23): 2414–2417.

Miller, W. C., et al. 2004. Prevalence of chlamydial and gonococcal infections among young adults in the United States. *Journal of the American Medical Association* 291(18): 2229–2236.

National Institutes of Allergy and Infectious Diseases. 2009. *HIV Infection in Women* (http://www3.niaid.nih.gov/topics/HIVAIDS/Understanding/Population+Specific+Information/womenHiv.htm; retrieved February 17, 2009).

Ness, R. B., et al. 2005. Douching, pelvic inflammatory disease, and incident gonococcal and chlamydial genital infection in a cohort of high-risk women. *American Journal of Epidemiology* 61(2): 186–195.

Rodriguez, B., et al. Predictive value of plasma HIV RNA level on rate of CD4 T-cell decline in untreated HIV infection. *Journal of the American Medical Association* 296(12): 1498–1506.

Sanders, G. D., et al. 2005. Cost-effectiveness of screening for HIV in the era of highly active antiretroviral therapy. *New England Journal of Medicine* 352(6): 570–585.

Sepkowitz, K. 2006. One disease, two epidemics—AIDS at 25. *New England Journal of Medicine* 354(23): 2411–2414.

Wang, C., et al. 2004. Mortality in HIV-seropositive versus -seronegative persons in the era of highly active antiretroviral therapy: Implications for when to initiate therapy. *Journal of Infectious Diseases* 190(6): 1046–1054.

Weinstock, H., S. Berman, and W. Cates. 2004. Sexually transmitted diseases among American youth: Incidence and prevalence estimates, 2000. *Perspectives on Sexual and Reproductive Health* 36(1): 6–10.

Xu, F., et al. 2006. Trends in herpes simplex virus type 1 and type 2 seroprevalence in the United States. *Journal of the American Medical Association* 296(8): 964–973.

Yeni, P. G., et al. 2004. Treatment for adult HIV infection. *Journal of the American Medical Association* 292(2): 251–265.

http://www.mcgrawhillconnect.com/personalhealth

ENVIRONMENTAL HEALTH

LOOKING AHEAD>>>>>

AFTER READING THIS CHAPTER, YOU SHOULD BE ABLE TO:

- Explain how population growth affects the earth's environment and contributes to pollution and climate change

- Discuss the causes and effects of air and water pollution, and describe strategies that people can take to protect these resources

- Discuss the issue of solid waste disposal and the impact it has on the environment and human health

- Identify key sources of chemical and radiation pollution, and discuss methods for preventing such pollution

- Explain how energy use affects the environment, and describe steps everyone can take to use energy more efficiently

TEST YOUR KNOWLEDGE

1. **The world's current population is about what?**
   a. 6 billion
   b. 6.6 billion
   c. 660 billion

2. **Air pollution can be naturally occurring, as well as human-made.**
   True or false?

3. **Worldwide, how many people do not have consistent access to safe drinking water?**
   a. 10 million
   b. 100 million
   c. 1 billion

4. **Compact fluorescent light bulbs can last ten times longer than standard incandescent light bulbs.**
   True or false?

5. **The zone around the Chernobyl accident site may not be safe for people to occupy for how many years?**
   a. 2–4 years
   b. 240 years
   c. 24,000 years

ANSWERS

1. **B.** The world's current population is about 6.6 billion, and is growing at a rate of about 76 million per year.

2. **TRUE.** There are many types of naturally occurring air pollution, such as smoke from forest fires and dust arising from dust storms.

3. **C.** According to the World Health Organization, about 1 billion people worldwide do not have reliable access to clean drinking water. About 2.6 billion do not have access to basic sanitation.

4. **TRUE.** Compact fluorescent light bulbs use 75% less energy and last up to ten times longer than regular light bulbs.

5. **C.** The explosion at the Chernobyl nuclear facility spread intense radiation over a large area, and caused hundreds of deaths and untold cases of genetic mutation. It will not be safe for humans to occupy for centuries.

We are constantly reminded of our intimate relationship with everything that surrounds us—our environment. Although the planet provides us with food, water, air, and everything else that sustains life, it also provides us with natural occurrences—earthquakes, tsunamis, hurricanes, drought, climate changes—that destroy life and disrupt society. In the past, humans frequently had to struggle against the environment to survive. Today, in addition to dealing with natural disasters, we also have to find ways to protect the environment from the by-products of our way of life.

This chapter introduces the concept of environmental health, and discusses the ways humans affect the planet and its resources. The following sections also explain how the environment affects us, and describe steps you can take to improve your personal environmental health while reducing your impact on the earth.

ENVIRONMENTAL HEALTH DEFINED

The field of **environmental health** grew out of efforts to control communicable diseases. When certain insects and rodents were found to carry microorganisms that cause disease in humans, campaigns were undertaken to eradicate or control these animal vectors. It was also recognized that pathogens could be transmitted in sewage, drinking water, and food. These discoveries led to systematic garbage collection, sewage treatment, filtration and chlorination of drinking water, food inspection, and the establishment of public health enforcement agencies.

These efforts to control and prevent communicable diseases changed the health profile of the developed world. Americans rarely contract cholera, typhoid fever, plague, diphtheria, or other diseases that once killed large numbers of people, but these diseases have not been eradicated worldwide.

In the United States, a huge, complex, public health system is constantly at work behind the scenes attending to the details of these critical health concerns. Every time the system is disrupted, danger recurs. After any disaster situation that damages a community's public health system—whether a natural disaster such as a hurricane or a human-made disaster such as a terrorist attack—prompt restoration of basic health services becomes crucial to human survival. Every time we venture beyond the boundaries of our everyday world, whether traveling to a less-developed country or camping in a wilderness area, we are reminded of the importance of these basics: clean water, sanitary waste disposal, safe food, and insect and rodent control.

Over the last few decades, the focus of environmental health has expanded and become more complex, for several reasons. We now recognize that environmental pollutants contribute not only to infectious diseases but to many chronic diseases as well. In addition, technological advances have increased our ability to affect and damage the environment. Also, rapid population growth, which has resulted partly from past environmental improvements, means that far more people are consuming and competing for resources than ever before, magnifying the effect of humans on the environment.

Environmental health is therefore seen as encompassing all the interactions of humans with their environment and the health consequences of these interactions. Funda-

Natural events—such as the 2008 cyclone that struck Myanmar—can directly kill thousands of people while wiping out essential services, polluting water, and facilitating the spread of diseases.

TERMS **environmental health** The collective interactions of humans with the environment and the short-term and long-term health consequences of those interactions.

mental to this definition is a recognition that we hold the world in trust for future generations and for other forms of life. Our responsibility is to pass on a world no worse, and preferably better, than the one we enjoy today. Although many environmental problems are complex and seem beyond the control of the individual, there are ways that people can make a difference to the future of the planet.

POPULATION GROWTH AND CONTROL

Throughout most of history, humans have been a minor pressure on the planet. About 300 million people were alive in the year A.D. 1; by the time Europeans were settling in the United States 1600 years later, the world population had increased gradually to a little over 500 million. But then it began rising exponentially—zooming to 1 billion by about 1800, more than doubling by 1930, and then doubling again in just 40 years (Figure 19.1).

The world's population, currently about 6.6 billion, is increasing at a rate of about 76 million per year—150 people every minute. The United Nations projects that world population will reach 9.1 billion by 2050 and will continue to increase until it levels off above 10 billion in 2200. Virtually all of this increase is taking place in less-developed regions. In 1950, the more-developed regions

accounted for 32% of the world's population; their share dropped to 20% in 2000 and is expected to further decline to 13% in 2050. Changes are also projected for the world's age distribution: The proportion of people age 60 and over will increase from 10% in 2000 to 22% in 2050, and by 2050 there will be more older persons than children.

This rapid expansion of population, particularly in the past 50 years, is generally believed to be responsible for most of the stress humans put on the environment. A large and rapidly growing population makes it more difficult to provide the basic components of environmental health discussed earlier, including clean and disease-free food and water. It is also a driving force behind many of the relatively more recent environmental health concerns, including chemical pollution, global warming, and the thinning of the atmosphere's ozone layer.

QUICK STATS

In 2050, the U.S. population will exceed **402 million** people.

—United Nations, 2008

How Many People Can the World Hold?

No one knows how many people the world can support, but most scientists agree that there is a limit. A 2006 report from the United Nation's Convention on Biological Diversity states that the population's demand for resources already exceed the earth's capacity by 20%. The primary factors that may eventually put a cap on human population are the following:

- *Food.* Enough food is currently produced to feed the world's entire population, but economic and sociopolitical factors have led to food shortages and famine. Food

VITAL STATISTICS

FIGURE 19.1 World population growth.
The United Nations estimates that the world's population will continue to increase dramatically until it stabilizes above 10 billion people in 2200.

SOURCES: United Nations Population Division. 2007. *World Population Prospects: The 2006 Revision.* New York: United Nations; U.S. Bureau of the Census.

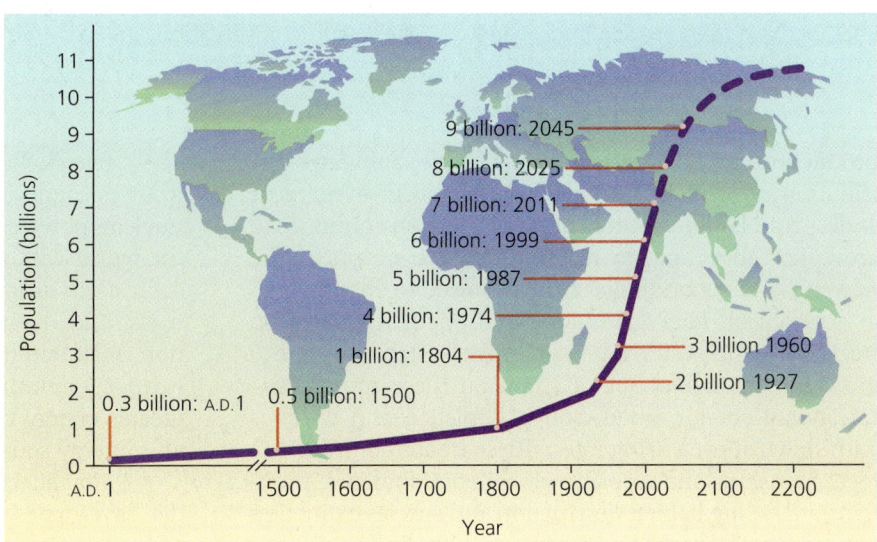

Natural Ecosystems and Biodiversity

Our world supports an abundant variety of life. Scientists have identified some 1.75 million species, but they suspect that there are probably 10–80 million more.

Different environments generate diverse life strategies, so that each **ecosystem**—from desert to tropical rainforest—contains a unique, close-knit community of organisms, linked together in a **food chain** or web. Plants use sunlight and soil for their needs. In turn, they sustain herbivores (plant eaters), which may themselves succumb to predators. When predators and surviving herbivores die, they become food for scavengers, then insect larvae, and finally bacteria, which break them down into organic substances. These substances, drawn from the soil by plants, help maintain the cycle. A similar system, based on plankton, exists in the oceans. Disruption at any point in this intricate, balanced cycle can alter or destroy an entire ecosystem.

Natural ecosystems maintain the climate and the composition of the atmosphere, cycle water and nutrients, produce food, dispose of organic wastes, generate and maintain soils, control pests, and pollinate crops. Ecosystems also support biological diversity, or **biodiversity,** represented by both the millions of different species on the earth and the genetic diversity within these species.

Biodiversity is critical as the basis for the future evolution of new species and as a genetic bank from which humans can draw useful genetic material and compounds. Although thus far we have examined few of these resources, the ones we have used provide many benefits, including medicines and pest and disease resistance for crops.

Human activity—driven by poverty and population growth in the developing world and excessive consumerism in the industrial nations—threatens biodiversity. In some cases, species and populations are being lost through direct action, such as the overharvesting of elephants, whales, and certain fish. In 2006, for example, an international team of researchers predicted the global

collapse of seafood stocks in the world's oceans within 50 years if current fishing trends continue. In other cases, species and populations are lost indirectly, through habitat destruction.

The destruction of tropical rainforests, which are disappearing at the rate of an acre every second, is of particular concern. Rainforests cover only about 7% of the planet but are thought to harbor more than half the world's species. The World Conservation Union's "red list" of animals in serious danger of extinction now includes about 16,000 species, including the polar bear and hippopotamus. The red list now includes one in four mammals, one in eight birds, one-third of all amphibians, and 70% of the world's assessed plants.

Extinction is irreversible, and species are disappearing far faster (50–100 a day) than they can be identified and assessed for useful properties. The current extinction rate is up to 10,000 times higher than expected. Cutting down on greenhouse gasses and storing carbon dioxide could save many species from vanishing. Some scientists fear that humans are precipitating a wave of mass extinction so great that the diminished stock of species will not be an adequate base on which natural selection can work to rebuild biodiversity. Even if adequate, it could take more than 10 million years for biodiversity to be restored. And because of the many ties between organisms and the physical environment, mass extinction could also threaten the functioning of the entire biological world.

What can be done to maintain biodiversity? The United States has laws that protect specific endangered species, which by indirectly preserving natural communities help maintain biodiversity. International laws and conventions also protect certain rare species, although enforcement continues to be a problem. The Convention on Biological Diversity, for example, deals specifically with the issue of biodiversity. It commits countries to preserving and managing biological resources and to integrating plant and animal preservation into economic planning.

---

production can be expanded in the future, but better distribution of food will be needed to prevent even more widespread famine as the world's population continues to grow. For all people to receive adequate nutrition, the makeup of the world's diet may also need to change.

- *Available land and water.* Rural populations rely on trees, soil, and water for their direct sustenance, and a growing population puts a strain on these resources—forests are cut for wood, soil is depleted, and water is withdrawn at ever-rising rates. These trends contribute to local hardships and to many global environmental problems, including habitat destruction and species extinction (see the box "Natural Ecosystems and Biodiversity").

- *Energy.* Currently, most of the world's energy comes from nonrenewable sources: oil, coal, natural gas, and nuclear power. As nonrenewable sources are depleted, the world will have to shift to renewable energy sources, such as hydropower and solar, geothermal, wind, biomass, and ocean power. Supporting a growing population, maintaining economic productivity, and preventing further environmental degradation will require both greater energy efficiency and an increased use of renewable energy sources.

- *Minimum acceptable standard of living.* The mass media have exposed the entire world to the American lifestyle and raised people's expectations of living at a comparable level. But such a lifestyle is supported by levels of energy consumption that the earth cannot support worldwide. The United States has about 5% of the world's population but uses 25% of the world's energy. In contrast, India has 16% of the population but uses only 3% of the energy. If *all* people are to enjoy a minimally acceptable standard of living, the population must be limited to a number that the available resources can support.

Factors That Contribute to Population Growth

Although it is apparent that population growth must be controlled, population trends are difficult to influence and manage. A variety of interconnecting factors fuel the current population explosion:

- *High fertility rates.* The combination of poverty, very high child mortality rates, and a lack of social provisions of every type is associated with high fertility rates in the developing world. Families may have to have more children to ensure that enough survive childhood to work for the household and to care for parents in old age. Most countries, both developed and developing, have experienced significant reductions in fertility as contraceptive use has increased. However, the majority of developing countries still have fertility levels that ensure substantial population growth. In a small number of countries, most of which are classified as least developed, fertility levels continue to be very high.

- *Lack of family planning resources.* Half the world's couples don't use any form of family planning.

- *Lower death rates.* Although death rates remain relatively high in the developing world, they have decreased in recent years because of public health measures and improved medical care.

Changes in any of these factors can affect population growth, but the issues are complex. Increasing death rates through disease, famine, or war might slow population growth, but few people would argue in favor of these as methods of population control. (United Nations population estimates project that there will be 344 million fewer people alive in 2050 than there would have been without deaths from HIV/AIDS.) Although the increased availabil-

ity of family planning services is a crucial part of population management, cultural, political, and religious factors also need to be considered.

To be successful, population management must change the condition of people's lives, especially poverty, to remove the pressures for having large families. Research indicates that the combination of improved health, better education, and increased literacy and employment opportunities for women works together with family planning to decrease fertility rates. Unfortunately, in the fastest-growing countries, the needs of a rapidly increasing population use up financial resources that might otherwise be used to improve lives and ultimately slow population growth.

AIR QUALITY AND POLLUTION

Air pollution is not a human invention or even a new problem. The air is polluted naturally with every forest fire, pollen bloom, and dust storm, as well as with countless other natural pollutants. To these natural sources, humans have always contributed the by-products of their activities.

Air pollution is linked to a wide range of health problems; the very young and the elderly are among those most susceptible to air pollution's effects. For people with chronic ailments such as diabetes or heart failure, even relatively brief exposures to particulate air pollution increases the risk of death by nearly 40%. Recent studies have linked exposure to air pollution to reduced birth weight in infants, reduced lung capacity in teens, and atherosclerosis (thickening of the arteries) in adults.

Air Quality and Smog

The EPA uses a measure called the **Air Quality Index (AQI)** to indicate whether air pollution levels pose a health concern. The AQI is used for five major air pollutants:

- *Carbon monoxide (CO).* An odorless, colorless gas, CO forms when the carbon in **fossil fuels** does not

TERMS

ecosystem The community of organisms (plants and animals) in an area and the nonliving physical factors with which they interact.

food chain The transfers of food energy and other substances in which one type of organism consumes another.

biodiversity The variety of living things on the earth, including all the different species of flora and fauna and the genetic diversity among individuals of the same species.

Air Quality Index (AQI) A measure of local air quality and what it means for health.

fossil fuels Buried deposits of decayed animals and plants that are converted into carbon-rich fuels by exposure to heat and pressure over millions of years; oil, coal, and natural gas are fossil fuels.

Smog tends to form over Los Angeles because of the natural geographical features of the area and because of the tremendous amount of motor vehicle exhaust in the air.

tory diseases such as asthma, NO_2 affects lung function and causes symptoms such as wheezing and shortness of breath. NO_2 exposure may also increase the risk of respiratory infections.

- *Particulate matter (PM).* Particles of different sizes are released into the atmosphere from a variety of sources, including combustion of fossil fuels, crushing or grinding operations, industrial processes, and dust from roadways. PM can accumulate in the respiratory system, aggravate cardiovascular and lung diseases, and increase the risk of respiratory infections.

- *Ground-level ozone.* At ground level, ozone is a harmful pollutant; where it occurs naturally in the upper atmosphere, it shields the earth from the sun's harmful ultraviolet rays. (The health hazards from the thinning of this protective ozone layer are discussed later in the chapter.) Ground-level ozone is formed when pollutants emitted by cars, power plants, industrial plants, and other sources react chemically in the presence of sunlight (photochemical reactions). Ozone can irritate the respiratory system, reduce lung function, aggravate asthma, increase susceptibility to respiratory infections, and damage the lining of the lungs. Short-term elevations of ozone levels have also been linked to increased death rates.

AQI values run from 0 to 500; the higher the AQI, the greater the level of pollution and associated health danger. When the AQI exceeds 100, air quality is considered unhealthy, at first for certain sensitive groups of people and then for everyone as AQI values get higher. For local areas, AQI values are calculated for each of the five pollutants listed above; the highest value becomes the AQI rating for that day. Depending on the AQI value, precautionary health advice may be provided. Local AQI information is often available in newspapers, on television and radio, on the Internet, and from state and local telephone hotlines.

The term **smog** was first used in the early 1900s in London to describe the combination of smoke and fog. What we typically call smog today is a mixture of pollutants, with ground-level ozone being the key ingredient. Major smog occurrences are linked to the combination of several factors: Heavy motor vehicle traffic, high tempera-

completely burn. The primary sources of CO are vehicle exhaust and fuel combustion in industrial processes. CO deprives body cells of oxygen, causing headaches, fatigue, and impaired vision and judgment; it also aggravates cardiovascular diseases.

- *Sulfur dioxide (SO₂).* SO_2 is produced by the burning of sulfur-containing fuels such as coal and oil, during metal smelting, and by other industrial processes; power plants are a major source. SO_2 narrows the airways, which may cause wheezing, chest tightness, and shortness of breath, particularly in people with asthma; it may also aggravate symptoms of CVD.

- *Nitrogen dioxide (NO₂).* NO_2 is a reddish-brown, highly reactive gas formed when nitric oxide combines with oxygen in the atmosphere; major sources include motor vehicles and power plants. In people with respira-

smog   Hazy atmospheric conditions resulting from increased concentrations of ground-level ozone and other pollutants.

greenhouse gas   A gas (such as carbon dioxide) or vapor that traps infrared radiation instead of allowing it to escape through the atmosphere, resulting in a warming of the earth (the greenhouse effect).

greenhouse effect   A warming of the earth due to a buildup of carbon dioxide and certain other gases.

global warming   An increase in the earth's atmospheric temperature when averaged across seasons and geographical regions; also called *climate change*.

TERMS

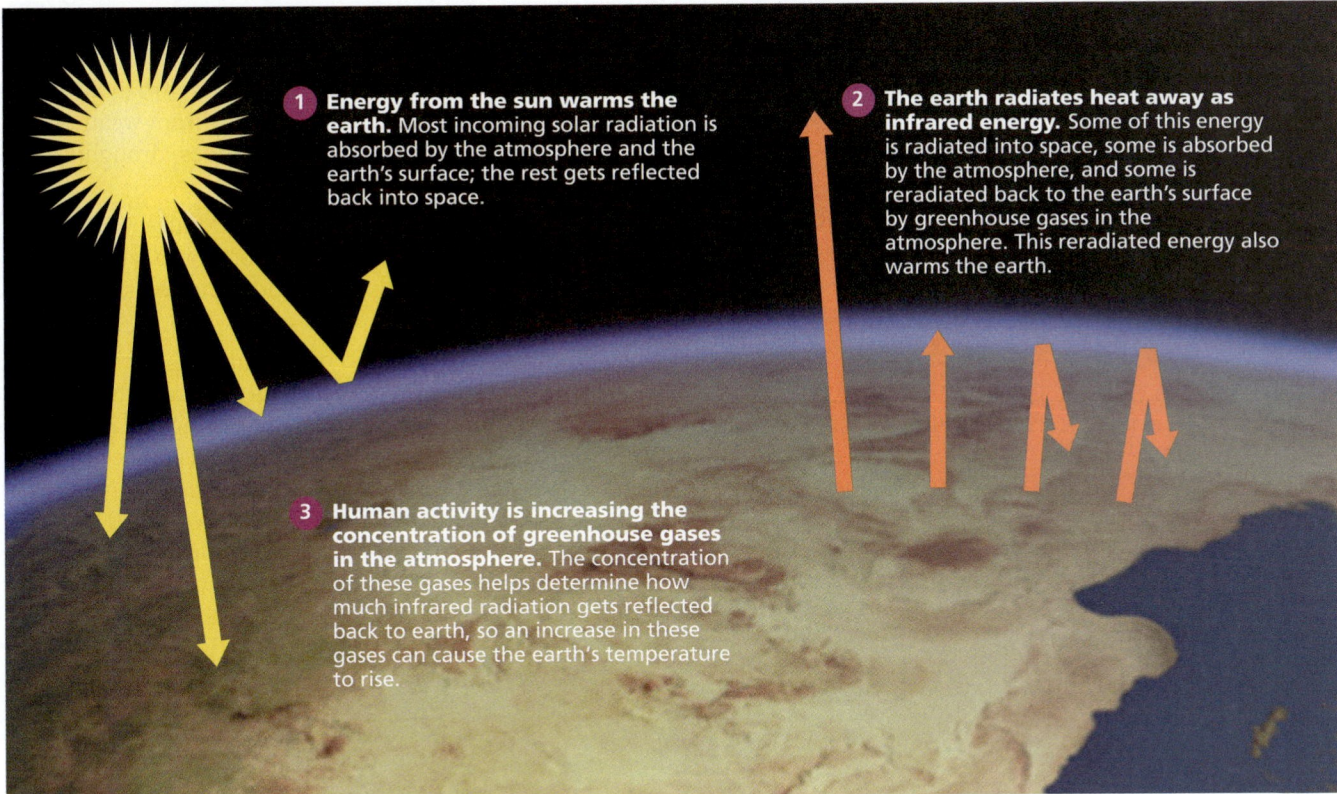

FIGURE 19.2 The greenhouse effect.

tures, and sunny weather can increase the production of ozone. Pollutants are also more likely to build up in areas with little wind and/or where a topographic feature such as a mountain range or valley prevents the wind from pushing out stagnant air.

The Greenhouse Effect and Global Warming

The temperature of the earth's atmosphere depends on the balance between the amount of energy the planet absorbs from the sun (mainly as high-energy ultraviolet radiation) and the amount of energy radiated back into space as lower-energy infrared radiation. Key components of temperature regulation are carbon dioxide, water vapor, methane, and other **greenhouse gases**—so named because, like the glass panes in a greenhouse, they let through visible light from the sun but trap some of the resulting infrared radiation and reradiate it back to the earth's surface. This reradiation causes a buildup of heat that raises the temperature of the lower atmosphere, a natural process known as the **greenhouse effect** (Figure 19.2). Without it, the atmosphere would be far cooler and much more hostile to life.

There is growing consensus that human activity is causing **global warming** or *climate change*. The concentration of greenhouse gases is increasing because of hu-

Table 19.1	Sources of Greenhouse Gases
Greenhouse Gas	**Sources**
Carbon dioxide	Fossil fuel and wood burning, factory emissions, car exhaust, deforestation
Chlorofluorocarbons (CFCs)	Refrigeration and air conditioning, aerosols, foam products, solvents
Methane	Cattle, wetlands, rice paddies, land-fills, gas leaks, coal and gas industries
Nitrous oxide	Fertilizers, soil cultivation, deforestation, animal feedlots and wastes
Ozone and other trace gases	Photochemical reactions, car exhaust, power plant emissions, solvents

man activity, especially the combustion of fossil fuels (Table 19.1). Carbon dioxide levels in the atmosphere have increased rapidly in recent decades. The use of fossil fuels pumps more than 20 billion tons of carbon dioxide into the atmosphere every year. Experts believe carbon dioxide may account for about 60% of the greenhouse effect. Analysis of ice core samples shows that carbon dioxide levels are now about 25% higher than at any other time in the last 650,000 years. The United States is responsible for one-third of the world's total emissions of carbon dioxide. Deforestation, often by burning, also sends carbon dioxide into the atmosphere and reduces

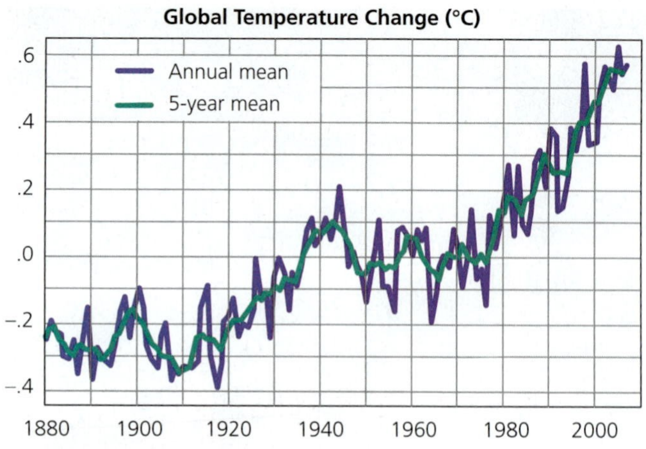

Global Temperature Change (°C)

Legend:
- Annual mean
- 5-year mean

VITAL STATISTICS

FIGURE 19.3 Trend in annual mean temperature. This graph traces the trend in the annual mean temperature relative to the 1951–1980 mean value. There has been a strong warming trend over the past 30 years.

SOURCE: Goddard Institute for Space Studies. 2009. *GISS Surface Temperature Analysis, Global Temperature Trends: 2009 Summation* (http://data.giss.nasa.gov/gistemp/2007; retrieved February 19, 2009).

the number of trees available to convert carbon dioxide into oxygen.

In 2006, the National Research Council reported that the overall global temperature had increased 0.6°C during the twentieth century (Figure 19.3). There is growing agreement among scientists that temperatures will continue to rise, although estimates vary as to how much they will change. If global warming persists, experts say the impact may be devastating (see the box "Global Warming, Local Action"). Possible consequences include the following:

- Increased rainfall and flooding in some regions, increased drought in others. Coastal zones, where

TERMS

ozone layer   A layer of ozone molecules (O_3) in the upper atmosphere that screens out UV rays from the sun.

chlorofluorocarbons (CFCs)   Chemicals used as spray-can propellants, refrigerants, and industrial solvents, implicated in the destruction of the ozone layer.

half the world's people live, would be severely affected.

- Increased mortality from heat stress, urban air pollution, and tropical diseases. Deaths from weather events such as hurricanes, tornadoes, droughts, and floods might also increase.

- A poleward shift of about 50–350 miles (150–550 km) in the location of vegetation zones, affecting crop yields, irrigation demands, and forest productivity.

- Increasingly rapid and drastic melting of the earth's polar ice caps. Arctic ice melts to some extent during the summer each year, but during the 2007 melting season, Arctic ice formations melted faster and farther than any other time since observations began. Experts predicted that as soon as 2030, the Arctic sea ice could melt away completely during the summer, but would return in the winter months. Such extensive melting could mean increased flooding in the Northern Hemisphere, further changes in weather patterns, and the elimination of habitat for species that live in the Arctic.

According to estimates from the Environmental Protection Agency (EPA), the earth's average surface temperature is likely to increase 2.0–11.5°F (1.1–6.4°C) by the end of the twenty-first century (Figure 19.4 on p. 594). Warming will not be evenly distributed around the globe. Land areas will warm more than oceans in part due to water's ability to store heat. High latitudes will warm more than low ones in part due to the effects of melting ice. Most of North America, all of Africa, Europe, Northern and Central Asia, and most of Central and South America are likely to warm more than the global average.

Thinning of the Ozone Layer

Another air pollution problem is the thinning of the **ozone layer** of the atmosphere, a fragile, invisible layer about 10–30 miles above the earth's surface that shields the planet from the sun's hazardous ultraviolet (UV) rays. Since the mid-1980s, scientists have observed the seasonal appearance and growth of a hole in the ozone layer over Antarctica. More recently, thinning over other areas—including Canada, Scandinavia, the northern United States, Russia, Australia, and New Zealand—has been noted.

The ozone layer is being destroyed primarily by **chlorofluorocarbons (CFCs)**, industrial chemicals used as coolants in refrigerators and in home and automobile air conditioners; as foaming agents in some rigid foam products, including insulation; as propellants in some kinds of aerosol sprays (most such sprays were banned in 1978); and as solvents. When CFCs rise into the atmosphere, winds carry them toward the polar regions. During winter, circular winds form a vortex that keeps the air

At current rates of consumption, we are using up the earth's resources so rapidly that they may run out sooner than anyone expects. Some experts say that humankind is already outstripping the planet's biological capacity by 20%. Indeed, a 2006 report from the Worldwatch Institute says that if fast-growing nations like China and India start using the earth's stores at the same rate as the United States, we will need the resources of *a second earth* to keep everyone satisfied.

But this problem has a second, more urgent part—that is, the way all those resources (especially minerals such as coal and oil) are being used. We use millions of tons of fossil fuel each year to power homes, cars, and factories. However unintentionally, we are also using them to destroy our planet.

Evidence of Global Warming

There is ample evidence that global warming is a reality. Here are just a few examples:

• Scientists have been measuring atmospheric carbon dioxide (CO_2) levels for years and say the amount of CO_2 is continually rising. In 2005, atmospheric CO_2 measured 380 parts per million (ppm), compared to about 290 ppm in 1850. At least one expert estimates that atmospheric CO_2 could reach 900 ppm by 2100, with a corresponding rise in global temperature of 5°–10°C.

• Glaciers and other large ice formations are melting at a quickening pace and shrinking measurably. The Greenland Ice Sheet, for example, is now melting at a rate of about 225 cubic kilometers each year. Such melting threatens to raise ocean levels around the world—possibly as much as 3 to 5 feet in the coming decades. In scenarios now envisioned, large swaths of coastline will be swamped and some small islands may disappear entirely.

• The World Health Organization says that ecological damage caused by human activities (such as burning fossil fuels and destroying forests and wetlands) is threatening our health. WHO also predicts dramatic increases in disease during the next 50 years and that climate change could have catastrophic

results in poor nations that already are unable to grow enough food or provide enough clean water for their people.

Despite the evidence, skepticism persists. Ironically, respected government agencies such as the National Oceanic and Atmospheric Administration (NOAA), NASA, and others have declared global warming to be a real phenomenon and a threat to humanity, yet many elected government officials dismiss such claims as faulty or incomplete science. In other countries, too, political and business leaders put climate change in second place after economic development. And one key component of Western-style economic development is the burning of fossil fuels to power industry and transportation.

Who Is Responsible?

To some degree, we are all responsible for climate change, just as we all stand to suffer because of it. Scientists can calculate just how much each person, house, car, appliance, and factory contributes to global warming; they call this measure an "environmental footprint." The footprint's size is determined by the amount of greenhouse gases the source generates, either directly (such as a car or factory) or indirectly (such as an electric appliance, which runs on electricity produced by a fossil-fuel-burning power plant). Here are some examples:

• For each gallon of gas your car burns, it releases about 20 pounds of CO_2 into the atmosphere. A midsize car puts out about 12,000 pounds of CO_2 per year; most SUVs put out about 22,000 pounds.

• A typical refrigerator is responsible for more than 2000 pounds of CO_2 annually. (The gas is actually released by a power plant; the amount is based on how much electricity the refrigerator uses.)

• A typical American home generates 28,000 pounds of greenhouse gases each year, both directly and indirectly.

Even though it isn't weightless, CO_2 is a gas. If you try to imagine how many CO_2 molecules it would take to make up a single pound, you can easily see why atmospheric CO_2 levels are increasing so rapidly.

What Is Being Done?

The need to slow climate change is undeniable and urgent. At the global level, many governments are taking initiatives to slow the release of greenhouse gases. One result of these efforts is the Kyoto Protocol to the United Nations Convention on Climate Change, which took effect in 2005. Under terms of this agreement, participating countries must reduce greenhouse gas emissions to an average of 5% below 1990 levels by 2012. The United States is not participating in the Kyoto Protocol, as government leaders contend the accord places too great a financial burden on industry and will stifle economic growth.

Industries are slowly getting on the bandwagon, too, although some must be forced to reduce their greenhouse emissions. Many companies are investing in cleaner fuel technology and "scrubbing" their emissions before they enter the environment. Du Pont, for example, has reduced its greenhouse gas emissions by 70% while decreasing energy use and increasing productivity.

Automakers are rapidly improving existing hybrid automobiles and making more models available, while focusing on the development of all-electric cars and hydrogen fuel cell technologies that virtually eliminate automotive pollution.

Individuals are making a difference, too. You can learn more about global warming and what it means to our future by checking out the organizations and Web sites listed in the For More Information section at the end of the chapter.

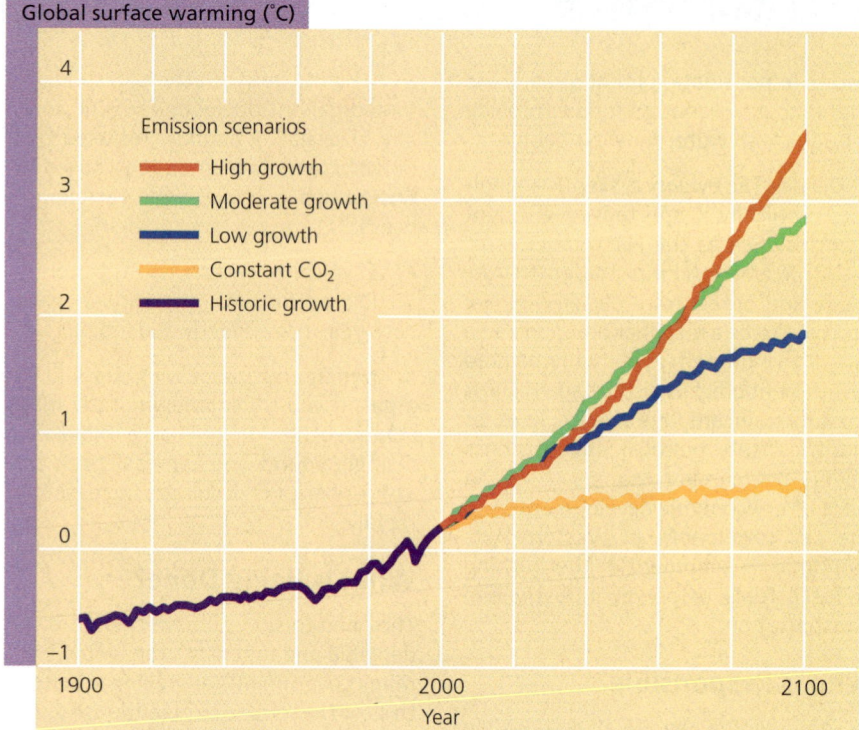

Global surface warming (°C)

Emission scenarios
High growth
Moderate growth
Low growth
Constant CO$_2$
Historic growth

Year

FIGURE 19.4 **Temperature projections to the year 2100, based on different greenhouse gas growth scenarios. The orange line shows that temperatures would change only slightly if greenhouse gas emissions stopped rising.**

SOURCE: Environmental Protection Agency, 2007. *Future Temperature Changes* (http://www.epa.gov/climatechange/science/futuretc.html; retrieved February 19, 2009).

over Antarctica from mixing with air from elsewhere. CFCs react with airborne ice crystals, releasing chlorine atoms, which destroy ozone. When the polar vortex weakens in the summer, winds richer in ozone from the north replenish the lost Antarctic ozone.

In the Northern Hemisphere, ozone levels have declined by about 10% since 1980, and certain areas may be temporarily depleted in late winter and early spring by as much as 40%. The largest and deepest ozone hole on record occurred in late September 2006, reaching 10.6 million square miles, considerably larger than the surface area of North America. The hole also had an unusual vertical extent, with nearly all the ozone between 8 and 13 miles above the earth's surface destroyed.

Without the ozone layer to absorb the sun's UV radiation, life on Earth would be impossible. (UV radiation levels under the Antarctic hole were high enough to cause sunburn within 7 minutes.) The potential effects of increased long-term exposure to UV light for humans include skin cancer, wrinkling and aging of the skin, cataracts and blindness, and reduced immune response. The United Nations Environment Programme predicts that a drop of 10% in overall ozone levels would cause a 26% rise in the incidence of nonmelanoma skin cancers. Some scientists blame ozone loss for many cases of melanoma.

UV light may interfere with photosynthesis and cause lower crop yields; it may also kill phytoplankton and krill, the basis of the ocean food chain. And because heat generated by the absorption of UV rays in the ozone layer helps create stratospheric winds, the driving force behind weather patterns, a drop in the concentration of ozone could potentially alter the earth's climate systems.

Worldwide production and use of CFCs have declined rapidly since the danger to the ozone layer was recognized. Industrialized nations agreed to eliminate CFC production and use by 2000, and limits have also been placed on other agents that destroy ozone. Metered-dose inhalers for conditions like asthma are the only significant commercial product to contain CFCs, and CFC-free inhalers are already available for some medications.

Ozone-depleting substances have very long lifetimes in the atmosphere, however, so despite these efforts, the ozone hole is not expected to recover until 2070. The gradual recovery is masked by annual variations caused by weather fluctuations over Antarctica.

Energy Use and Air Pollution

Americans are the biggest energy consumers in the world (Table 19.2). We use energy to create electricity, transport us, power our industries, and run our homes. About 85% of the energy we use comes from fossil fuels—oil, coal, and natural gas. The remainder comes from nuclear power and renewable energy sources (such as hydroelectric, wind, and solar power).

Energy consumption is at the root of many environmental problems, especially those relating to air pollution. Automobile exhaust and the burning of oil and coal by industry and by electric power plants are primary causes of smog, acid precipitation, and the greenhouse effect. The mining of coal and the extraction and transportation of oil cause pollution on land and in the water; coal miners often suffer from serious health problems related to their jobs. Nuclear power generation creates haz-

QUICK STATS

The United States consumes nearly 21 million barrels of petroleum every day.

—U.S. Energy Information Administration, 2008

<table>
<tr><td colspan="2">

Table 19.2

</td><td>

Primary Energy Consumption of Selected Countries, 2006

</td></tr>
</table>

Country	Total Consumption (quadrillion Btu*)
United States	99.856
China	73.808
Russia	30.386
Japan	22.786
India	17.677
Germany	14.629
France	11.445
United Kingdom	9.802
South Korea	9.447
Spain	6.510
Australia	5.611
South Africa	5.177
Taiwan	4.569
Thailand	3.741
World Total	**472.274**

*Includes total consumption of petroleum, dry natural gas, and coal, and net hydroelectric, nuclear, geothermal, solar, wind, and wood and waste electricity; also includes net electricity imports.

SOURCE: Energy Information Administration. 2008. International Total Primary Energy Consumption and Energy Intensity: Total Primary Energy Consumption (Quadrillion Btu): All Countries, 1980–2006 (http://www.eia.doe.gov/emeu/international/energyconsumption.html; retrieved February 19, 2009).

ardous wastes and carries the risk of dangerous releases of radiation.

Two key strategies for controlling energy use are conservation and the development of nonpolluting, renewable sources of energy. Although the use of renewable energy sources has increased in recent years, renewables still supply only a small proportion of our energy, in part because of their cost. Some countries have chosen to promote energy efficiency by removing subsidies or adding taxes on the use of fossil fuels. This strategy is reflected in the varying prices drivers pay for gasoline. According to the U.S. Energy Information Agency, the average U.S. per gallon price of unleaded gasoline was just under $2.00 in February 2009 and expected to steadily increase.

Despite increases in U.S. consumer gas prices, more than 70% of commuters drive alone to work, and low-fuel-economy sport utility vehicles (SUVs) remain popular. Every gallon of gas burned puts about 20 pounds of carbon dioxide into the atmosphere; some SUVs average fewer than 10 miles per gallon, and the largest SUVs increase greenhouse gas emissions by 6 or more tons per year more than an average car.

Alternative Fuels The U.S. Department of Energy (DOE) is encouraging researchers and automobile manufacturers to produce vehicles that can handle alternative fuels such as ethanol. Ethanol, a form of alcohol, is a re-newable and largely domestic transportation fuel produced from fermenting plant sugars such as corn, sugar cane, and other starchy agricultural products. Ethanol use reduces the amount of imported oil required to produce gasoline, reduces overall greenhouse gas emissions from automobiles, and supports the U.S. agricultural industry.

Another type of alternative fuel is E85, which is a mixture of 85% ethanol and 15% gasoline. E85 is becoming more popular in the Midwest region (the "corn belt") of the United States. E85 provides lower mileage than gasoline, though it typically costs the same as regular gasoline. Ethanol has been mixed with gasoline for years in the United States, but several other countries (such as Brazil) use ethanol much more extensively.

Ethanol, however, has its critics, who say the alternative fuel may do more harm than good. For one thing, some reports show that corn-based ethanol requires more energy to produce than it yields when burned as fuel. Other reports dispute this point, and improvements in manufacturing processes may reduce the amount of energy required to make the fuel. Regardless, ethanol made from sugar cane and other plant matter may be far more energy-efficient, say some experts.

One huge potential drawback of ethanol is the diversion of corn crops from the food supply to produce the fuel. In 2007 and 2008, this practice was blamed for skyrocketing food prices and food shortages around the world, which led to food riots in several countries. At the same time, the federal government gave billions of dollars in subsidies to corn farmers to raise the grain for ethanol production, even as grain prices soared. The food-related concerns prompted the United Nations to call for a moratorium on food-based ethanol production until nonfood sources of alternative fuels could be developed.

Hybrid and Electric Vehicles A more positive trend has been the introduction of hybrid electric vehicles (HEVs). Hybrid vehicles use two or more distinct power sources to propel the vehicle, such as an on-board energy storage system (batteries, for example) and an internal combustion engine and electric motor. The hybrid vehicle typically realizes greater fuel economy than a conventional car does, and produces fewer polluting emissions. Hybrids also tend to run with less noise than conventional vehicles. Several hybrid models are currently available in the United States, but typically cost several thousand dollars more than their conventional gas-powered counterparts. Still, hybrids are gaining popularity with consumers and are being more commonly used in both corporate and government vehicle fleets.

Researchers hope that hybrid technology can be extended to all classes of vehicles and that Americans can be convinced to use more fuel-efficient vehicles and to travel more frequently on public transportation, in carpools, or on foot.

Another type of alternative vehicle is all-electric. In these vehicles, electricity is stored in battery packs and then converted into mechanical power that runs the vehicle. After a given number of miles, the batteries must be recharged. These vehicles do not produce tailpipe emissions, but generators that produce the electricity for the batteries do emit pollutants.

Even when mass production begins, electric vehicles are expected to cost more than conventionally fueled ones. Even with lower "fuel" and maintenance costs (electric vehicles have fewer moving parts than gas-powered cars), the lead-acid battery packs must be replaced every few years, adding to the overall cost of electric vehicles.

Indoor Air Pollution

Although most people associate air pollution with the outdoors, your home may also harbor potentially dangerous pollutants. Some of these compounds trigger allergic responses, and others have been linked to cancer. Common indoor pollutants include the following:

- *Environmental tobacco smoke (ETS),* a human carcinogen that also increases the risk of asthma, bronchitis, and cardiovascular disease (see Chapter 11). Several states and cities have passed legislation known as Clean Indoor Air Acts, which state that any enclosed, indoor areas used by the public shall be smoke-free except for certain designated areas.

- *Carbon monoxide and other combustion by-products,* which can cause chronic bronchitis, headaches, dizziness, nausea, fatigue, and even death. Common sources in the home are woodstoves, fireplaces, kerosene heaters and lamps, and gas ranges. In poverty-stricken areas, especially in Asia and Africa, people commonly burn solid fuels like coal for cooking and heating their homes. The World Health Organization (WHO) says the smoke and by-products from these indoor fires kill about 1.5 million people annually—mostly children.

- *Formaldehyde gas,* which can cause eye, nose, and throat irritation; shortness of breath; headaches; nausea; lethargy; and, over the long term, cancer. This gas can seep from certain construction materials, paints, floor finishes, permanent press clothing, and nail polish.

- *Biological pollutants,* including bacteria, dust mites, mold, and animal dander, which can cause allergic reactions and other health problems. These allergens are typically found in bathrooms, damp or flooded basements, humidifiers, air conditioners, and even some carpets and furniture.

- *Indoor mold,* the fuzzy black substance growing on shower tiles and damp basement walls, is an indoor pollutant not to be taken likely. Even though more than 100 common indoor molds have been classified as potentially hazardous to people, only a few are serious threats to human health. One of the most common of these is *Stachybotrys* mold, commonly known as "toxic black bold." It is greenish black in color and appears slimy when wet. Toxic mold spores permeate the air and can cause health problems when inhaled, especially for people with asthma and other respiratory conditions.

Preventing Air Pollution

You can do a great deal to reduce air pollution. Here are a few ideas:

- Cut back on driving. Ride your bike, walk, use public transportation, or carpool in a fuel-efficient vehicle.

- Keep your car tuned up and well maintained. Use only unleaded gas, and keep your tires inflated at recommended pressures. To save energy when driving, avoid quick starts, stay within the speed limit, limit the use of air conditioning, and don't let your car idle unless absolutely necessary. Have your car's air conditioner checked and serviced by a station that uses environmentally friendly refrigerants (car air conditioners made before 1994 are a major source of CFCs).

- Buy energy-efficient appliances, and use them only when necessary. Run the washing machine, dryer, and dishwasher only when you have full loads, and do laundry in warm or cold water instead of hot; don't overdry your clothes. Clean refrigerator coils and clothes dryer lint screens frequently. Towel or air-dry your hair rather than using an electric dryer.

- Replace incandescent bulbs with compact fluorescent bulbs (not fluorescent tubes). For more information, see the box "Compact Fluorescent Light Bulbs."

- Make sure your home is well-insulated with ozone-safe agents; use insulating shades and curtains to keep heat in during winter and out during summer. Seal any openings that produce drafts. In cold weather, put on a sweater and turn down the thermostat. In hot weather, wear lightweight clothing and, whenever possible, use a fan instead of an air conditioner to cool yourself.

- Plant and care for trees in your own yard and neighborhood. Because they recycle carbon dioxide, trees

TERMS **fluoridation** The addition of fluoride to the water supply to reduce tooth decay.

Compact Fluorescent Light Bulbs

A good way to cut your home's energy use, lower your energy bills, and reduce your environmental footprint is by using energy-efficient light bulbs, commonly called *compact fluorescent light bulbs (CFLs)*.

According to the EPA, CFLs are cost-efficient because they use 75% less energy than traditional incandescent light bulbs. Although CFLs initially cost more than regular light bulbs, over the long term they save money for the user. This is because they use less energy by requiring less electricity to produce light. For example, a 15-watt CFL is equivalent to a 60-watt incandescent light bulb. CFLs also last up to ten times longer than conventional light bulbs.

The EPA also says that if every American home replaced one incandescent bulb with a CFL, enough energy would be saved in one year to light 3 million homes. It would also reduce greenhouse gas emissions by an amount equal to the output of 800,000 cars.

In spite of their positive attributes, compact fluorescent bulbs have a downside. That is, they contain a gas that in-

cludes low-pressure mercury and argon. If all the CFLs currently in use were disposed of in landfills, they could generate about 30,000 pounds of mercury that could eventually leech into the groundwater system. For this reason, it is best to take your burned-out CFLs to a community recycling center for proper disposal instead of tossing them in the trash.

Even though the amount of mercury in a single CFL is very small, you should take extra precautions when cleaning up a broken bulb. If a CFL breaks, shut off the central heating/air condition system, open a window, and clear all people and animals out of the room for at least 15 minutes. Put on rubber or latex gloves, and carefully pick up the large pieces of glass. Put the pieces in a glass jar that can be closed with a lid, or in a heavy-duty plastic bag that can be sealed. Gently sweep up the small pieces and dust using a broom and dustpan. You can use duct tape to pick up fine particles. Seal everything up (including your gloves) in the jar or bag, and take it to a recycling center for disposal.

---

work against global warming. They also provide shade and cool the air, so less air conditioning is needed.

- Before discarding a refrigerator, air conditioner, or humidifier, check with the waste hauler or your local government to ensure that ozone-depleting refrigerants will be removed prior to disposal. If you use a metered-dose inhaler, ask your physician if an ozone-safe inhaler is available for your medication.

- To prevent indoor air pollution, keep your house adequately ventilated, and buy some houseplants; they have a natural ability to rid the air of harmful pollutants.

- Keep paints, cleaning agents, and other chemical products tightly sealed in their original containers.

- Don't smoke, and don't allow others to smoke in your room, apartment, or home. If these rules are

too strict for your situation, limit smoking to a single, well-ventilated room.

- Clean and inspect chimneys, furnaces, and other appliances regularly. Install carbon monoxide detectors.

WATER QUALITY AND POLLUTION

Few parts of the world have enough safe, clean drinking water, and yet few things are as important to human health.

Water Contamination and Treatment

Many cities rely at least in part on wells that tap local groundwater, but often it is necessary to tap lakes and rivers to supplement wells. Because such surface water is more likely to be contaminated with both organic matter and pathogenic microorganisms, it is purified in water-treatment plants before being piped into the community. At treatment facilities, the water is subjected to various physical and chemical processes, including screening, filtration, and disinfection (often with chlorine), before it is introduced into the water supply system. **Fluoridation**, a water-treatment process that reduces tooth decay

? QUESTIONS FOR CRITICAL THINKING AND REFLECTION

What are your views on the issue of climate change? Do you believe it is a real problem, or that it has been overly hyped by the media and some politicians? How do you support your views?

Most communities in the United States draw on surface water for their drinking water supply. Unlike ground water, surface water is never free of contaminants and has to be treated before it is safe for humans to drink.

by 15–40%, has been used successfully in the United States for more than 60 years.

In most areas of the United States, water systems have adequate, dependable supplies, are able to control water-borne disease, and provide water without unacceptable color, odor, or taste. However, problems do occur. In 1993, more than 400,000 people became ill and 100 died when Milwaukee's drinking water was contaminated with the bacterium *Cryptosporidium*. The Centers for Disease Control and Prevention (CDC) estimate that 1 million Americans become ill and 900–1000 die each year from microbial illnesses from drinking water. Pollution by hazardous chemicals from manufacturing, agriculture, and household wastes is another concern. (Chemical pollu-

tion is discussed later in the chapter.) Worldwide, more than 2 million people, mostly children, die from water-related diseases each year.

Water Shortages

Water shortages are a growing concern in many regions of the world. Some parts of the United States are experiencing rapid population growth that outstrips the ability of local systems to provide adequate water to all. Many proposals are being discussed to relieve these shortages, including long-distance transfers; conservation; the recycling of some water, such as the water in office-building air conditioners; and the sale of water by regions with large supplies to areas with less available water.

According to the World Health Organization (WHO), 1 billion people do not have safe drinking water and 2.6 billion do not have access to basic sanitation. Less than 1% of the world's fresh water—about 0.007% of all the water on Earth—is readily accessible for direct human use.

Groundwater pumping and the diversion of water from lakes and rivers for irrigation are further reducing the amount of water available to local communities. In some areas, groundwater is being removed at twice the rate at

TERMS

septic system   A self-contained sewage disposal system, often used in rural areas, in which waste material is decomposed by bacteria.

heavy metal   A metal with a high specific gravity, such as lead, copper, or tin.

polychlorinated biphenyl (PCB)   An industrial chemical used as an insulator in electrical transformers and linked to certain human cancers.

which it is replaced. The Aral Sea, located in Kazakhstan and Uzbekistan, was once one of the world's largest inland seas. Since the 1960s, it has lost two-thirds of its volume to irrigation, and the exposed seabed is now as big as the Netherlands. People living in the area have experienced severe water and food shortages and increased rates of respiratory disease and throat cancer linked to dust storms from the dry seabed. Due to agricultural diversions, the Yellow River ran dry for the first time in China's 3000-year history in 1972, failing to reach the sea for 15 days that year; now, the dry period extends for more than half of each year. In the United States, the Colorado River is now diverted to the extent that it no longer flows into the ocean.

Sewage

Prior to the mid-nineteenth century, many people contracted diseases such as typhoid, cholera, and hepatitis A by direct contact with human feces, which were disposed of at random. Once the links between sewage and disease were discovered, practices began to change. People learned how to build sanitary outhouses and how to locate them so they would not contaminate water sources. As plumbing moved indoors, sewage disposal became more complicated. In rural areas, the **septic system,** a self-contained sewage disposal system, worked quite well. Today, many rural homes still rely on septic systems; however, many old tanks are leaking contaminants into the environment.

Different approaches became necessary as urban areas developed. Most cities have sewage-treatment systems that separate fecal matter from water in huge tanks and ponds and stabilize it so that it cannot transmit infectious diseases. Once treated and biologically safe, the water is released back into the environment. The sludge that remains behind is often contaminated with **heavy metals** and is handled as hazardous waste; if not contaminated, sludge may be used as fertilizer. If incorporated into the food chain, heavy metals, such as lead, cadmium, copper, and tin, can cause illness or death; therefore, these chemicals must be prevented from being released into the environment when sludge is burned or buried.

In addition to regulating industrial discharge, many cities have now begun expanded sewage-treatment measures to remove heavy metals and other hazardous chemicals. This action has resulted from many studies linking exposure to chemicals such as mercury, lead, and **polychlorinated biphenyls (PCBs)** with long-term health consequences, including cancer and damage to the central nervous system. The technology to effectively remove heavy metals and chemicals from sewage is still developing, and the costs involved are immense.

Protecting the Water Supply

By reducing your own water use, you help preserve your community's valuable supply and lower your monthly water bill. By taking steps to keep the water supply clean, you reduce pollution overall and help protect the land, wildlife, and other people from illness. Here are some simple steps you can take to protect your water supply:

- Take showers, not baths, to minimize your water consumption. Don't let water run when you're not actively using it while brushing your teeth, shaving, or hand-washing clothes. Don't run a dishwasher or washing machine until you have a full load.
- Install sink faucet aerators and water-efficient showerheads, which use two to five times less water with no noticeable decrease in performance.
- Purchase a water-saver toilet, or put a displacement device in your toilet tank to reduce the amount of water used with each flush.
- Fix any leaky faucets in your home. Leaks can waste thousands of gallons of water per year.
- Don't pour toxic materials such as cleaning solvents, bleach, or motor oil down the drain. Store them until you can take them to a hazardous waste collection center.
- Don't pour old medicines down the drain or flush them down the toilet. A 2008 report by the Associated Press revealed that the drinking water of some 40 million Americans may be contaminated with prescription and over-the-counter drugs. Some medications enter the water system after human excretion into sewage systems, but many people flush old or unused medicines. The EPA is working on strategies to remove medicines from drinking water, but for now says the drugs appear only in trace amounts and generally are not considered a health hazard. Still, experts say the best way to discard old medicines is to mix them with coffee grounds or cat litter, seal them in a container, and put them in the trash.

SOLID WASTE POLLUTION

Humans generate huge amounts of waste, which must be handled appropriately if the environment is to be kept safe.

? QUESTIONS FOR CRITICAL THINKING AND REFLECTION
How would you describe the quality of the water where you live? Are there lakes or streams where you can safely swim or fish? What local information sources can you find about water quality in your area?

Solid Waste

The bulk of the organic food garbage produced in American kitchens is now dumped in the sewage system by way of the mechanical garbage disposal. The garbage that remains is not very hazardous from the standpoint of infectious disease because there is very little food waste in it, but it does represent an enormous disposal and contamination problem.

What's In Our Garbage?   In 2007, Americans generated about 254 million tons of trash and recycled 85 million tons of materials. The biggest single component of household trash by weight is paper products, including junk mail, glossy mail-order catalogs, and computer printouts (Figure 19.5). Yard waste, plastic, metals, and glass are other significant components. About 1% of the solid waste is toxic; a new source of toxic waste is the disposal of computer components in both household and commercial waste. Burning, as opposed to burial, reduces the bulk of solid waste, but it may release hazardous material into the air.

Solid waste is not limited to household products. Manufacturing, mining, and other industries all produce large amounts of potentially dangerous materials that cannot simply be dumped. At Love Canal (near Buffalo, New York), toxic industrial wastes had been dumped into a waterway for years until, in the 1970s, nearby residents began to suffer from associated birth defects and cancers. The government had to step in, people had to move from their homes, and huge costs were incurred.

Disposing of Solid Waste   Since the 1960s, billions of tons of solid waste have been buried in **sanitary landfill** disposal sites (Figure 19.6). Careful site selection and daily management are an essential part of this approach to disposal. The site is thoroughly studied to ensure that it is not near groundwater, streams, or any other source of water that could be contaminated by leakage from the landfill. Sometimes protective liners are used around the site, and nearby monitoring wells are now required in most states. Layers of solid waste are regularly covered with thin layers of dirt until the site is filled. Some communities then plant grass and trees and convert the site into a park. Landfill is relatively stable; almost no decomposition occurs in the solidly packed waste.

Burying solid waste in landfills has several disadvantages. Much of this waste contains chemicals, ranging from leftover pesticides to paints and oils, which should not be released indiscriminately into the environment. Despite precautions, buried contaminants sometimes leak into the surrounding soil and groundwater. Burial is also expensive and requires huge amounts of space.

Biodegradability   *Biodegradation* is the process by which organic substances are broken down naturally by living organisms. Organic materials can be degraded either aerobically (with oxygen) or anaerobically (without oxygen). These organic materials—including plant and animal matter, substances originating from living organisms, or artificial materials similar in nature to plants and animals—are put to use by microorganisms. The term **biodegradable** means that certain products can break down naturally, safely, and quickly into the raw materials of nature, then disappear back into the environment. Table 19.3 shows the amount of time required for different types of material to biodegrade.

Recycling   Because of the expense and potential chemical hazards of any form of solid waste disposal, many communities encourage individuals and businesses to recycle their trash. In **recycling**, many kinds of waste materials are collected and used as raw materials in the production of new products. For example, waste paper can be recycled into new paper products, or an old bicycle frame can be melted down and used in the production of appliances. The number of recycling opportunities are almost limitless. Some cities offer curbside pickup of recyclables; others have recycling centers where people can bring their waste. These materials are not limited to paper, glass, and cans but also include things such as dis-

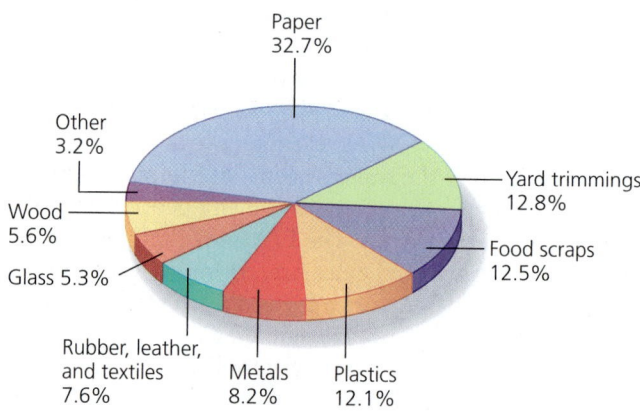

Paper
32.7%

Other
3.2%

Wood
5.6%

Glass 5.3%

Rubber, leather,
and textiles
7.6%

Metals
8.2%

Plastics
12.1%

Yard trimmings
12.8%

Food scraps
12.5%

Due to rounding, these numbers do not add up to 100%.

FIGURE 19.5   Components of municipal solid waste, by weight, before recycling.

SOURCE: Environmental Protection Agency, 2008. *Municipal Solid Waste Generation, Recycling and Disposal in the United States: Facts and Figures for 2007* (http://www.epa.gov/epawaste/nonhaz/municipal/pubs/msw07-fs.pdf; retrieved February 19, 2009).

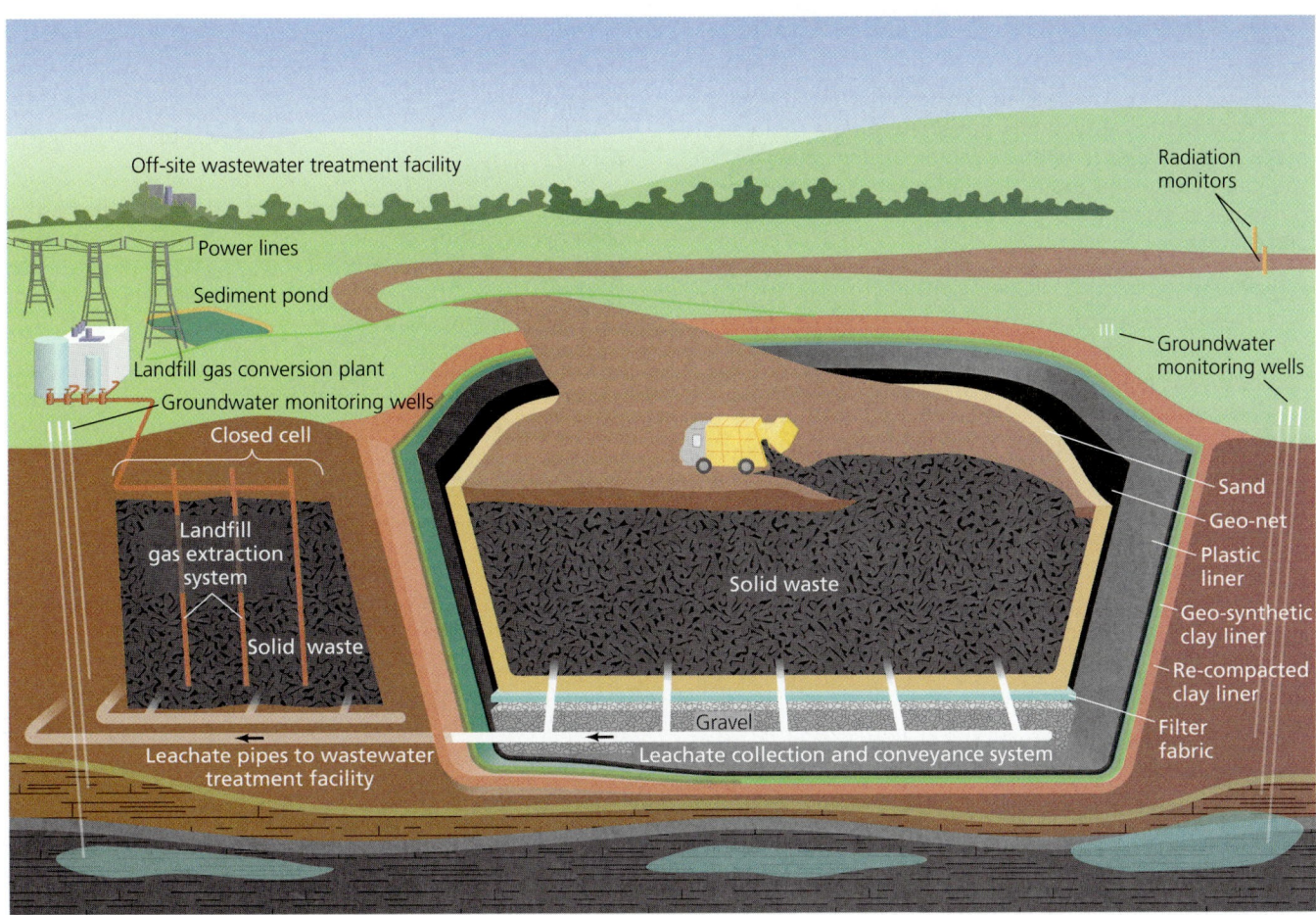

FIGURE 19.6   A sanitary landfill.

carded tires and used oils. Recycling is a good idea for two reasons. First, it puts unwanted objects back to good use. Second, it reduces the amount of solid waste sitting in landfills, some of which takes decades to decay naturally.

Even as recycling grows in popularity, however, the total amount of garbage Americans generate will probably continue to rise as the population increases. Researchers estimate that 80% of the nation's landfills will be closed within 20 years.

Discarded Technology   A newer solid waste disposal problem involves the discarding of old computers, televisions, and other electronic devices. Americans scrap about 400 million consumer electronic devices each year. This "e-waste" is the fastest-growing portion of our waste stream. Junked electronic devices are toxic, hazardous waste because they contain varying amounts of lead, mercury, and other heavy metals.

Table 19.3	Biodegrading Times of Different Objects

Item	Time Required to Biodegrade
Banana peel	2–10 days
Paper	2–5 months
Rope	3–14 months
Orange peel	6 months
Wool sock	1–5 years
Cigarette butt	1–12 years
Plastic-coated milk carton	5 years
Aluminum can	80–100 years
Plastic six-pack holder ring	450 years
Glass bottle	1 million years
Plastic bottle	Forever

TERMS

sanitary landfill   A disposal site where solid wastes are buried.

biodegradable   Refers to the ability of some materials to break down naturally and disappear back into the environment.

recycling   The use of waste materials as raw materials in the production of new products.

How to Be a Green Consumer

It may seem like a hassle to consider the environmental impact of the things you buy, but a few simple choices can make a big difference without compromising your lifestyle. You can quickly and easily develop habits that direct your consumer dollar toward environmentally friendly products and companies.

- Remember the four Rs of green consumerism:

    Reduce the amount of trash and pollution you generate by consuming and throwing away less.

    Reuse as many products as possible—either yourself or by selling them or donating them to charity.

    Recycle all appropriate materials and buy recycled products whenever possible.

    Respond by educating others about reducing waste and recycling, by finding creative ways to reduce waste and toxicity, and by making your preferences known.

- Choose products packaged in refillable, recycled, reusable containers or in readily recyclable materials, such as paper, cardboard, aluminum, or glass. Don't buy products that are excessively packaged or wrapped.

- Look for products made with the highest possible content of recycled paper, metal, glass, plastic, and other materials.

- Choose simple products containing the lowest amounts of bleaches, dyes, and fragrances. Look for organically grown foods and clothes made from organically grown cotton or Fox Fibre or another naturally colored type of cotton.

- Buy high-quality appliances that have an Energy Star seal from the EPA or some other type of certification indicating that they are energy- and water-efficient.

- Get a reusable cloth shopping bag. Don't bag items that don't need to be bagged. If you forget to bring your bag to the store, it doesn't matter much if you use a paper or plastic bag to carry your purchases home. What's important is that you reuse whatever bag you get.

- Don't buy what you don't need—borrow, rent, or share. Take good care of the things you own, repair items when they break, and replace them with used rather than new items whenever possible.

- Walk or bike when you can. If you must drive, do several errands at once to save energy and cut down on pollution.

- Look beyond the products to the companies that make them. Support those with good environmental records. If some of your favorite products are overpackaged or contain harmful ingredients, write to the manufacturer.

- Keep in mind that doing something is better than doing nothing. Even if you can't be a perfectly green consumer, doing your best on any purchase *will* make a difference.

SOURCES: U.S. Environmental Protection Agency. 2009. *Consumer Handbook for Reducing Solid Waste* (http://www.epa.gov/osw/wycd/catbook; retrieved February 19, 2009); Natural Resources Defense Council. 2009. *NRDC's Guide to Greener Living* (http:// www.nrdc.org/cities/living/gover. asp; retrieved February 19, 2009).

The e-waste problem is expected to get worse because the Federal Communications Commission (FCC) has mandated the transition to digital television broadcasting in 2009. Many consumers are expected to throw out their current televisions in order to upgrade their sets for digital reception.

Reducing Solid Waste

By recycling more and throwing away less, you can conserve landfill space and put more reusable items back into service. Here are some ideas to help you reduce solid waste:

- Buy products with the least amount of packaging you can, or buy products in bulk (see the box "How to Be a Green Consumer"). For example, buy large jars of juice, not individually packaged juice drinks. Buy products packaged in recyclable containers.

- Buy recycled or recyclable products. Avoid disposables; instead, use long-lasting or reusable products such as refillable pens and rechargeable batteries.

- Avoid using foam or paper cups and plastic stirrers by bringing your own china coffee mug and metal spoon to work or wherever you drink coffee or tea. Pack your lunch in reusable containers, and use a cloth or plastic lunch sack or a lunch box.

- To store food, use glass jars and reusable plastic containers rather than foil and plastic wrap.

- Recycle your newspapers, glass, cans, paper, and other recyclables. If you receive something packaged with foam pellets, take them to a commercial mailing center that accepts them for recycling.

- Do not throw electronic items, batteries, or fluorescent lights into the trash. Take all these to state-approved recycling centers; check with your local disposal service for more information.

- Start a compost pile for your organic garbage (non-animal food and yard waste) if you have a yard. If you live in an apartment, you can create a small composting system using earthworms, or take your organic wastes to a community composting center.

- Stop junk mail. To cancel your junk mail, send a request to Mail Preference Service, Direct Marketing Association, 1120 Avenue of the Americas, New York, NY 10036-6700 (http://www.dmaconsumers.org).

CHEMICAL POLLUTION AND HAZARDOUS WASTE

Chemical pollution is by no means a new problem. The ancient Romans were plagued by lead poisoning; industrial chemicals have claimed countless lives over the past few centuries.

Today, new chemical substances are constantly being introduced into the environment—as pesticides, herbicides, solvents, and hundreds of other products. More people and wildlife are exposed and potentially exposed to them than ever before. Many chemicals are harmless by themselves but become deadly in combination. A 2006 study of a single Nebraska cornfield revealed nine chemicals present in the soil and water; the combination was shown to cause illness, slow maturation, deformities, and higher mortality rates in nearby wildlife.

Chemical pollutants have been responsible for several environmental disasters, including thousands of deaths and injuries among people in Bhopal, India, that occurred when a powerful chemical used in manufacturing the insecticide Sevin was released from a plant. Catastrophes illustrate the short-term potential for disaster, but the long-term health consequences may be just as deadly.

The problem of chemical pollution and hazardous waste became so prominent in the 1970s that the EPA established the Superfund program to clean up the nation's uncontrolled hazardous waste sites. A national priorities list determines which locations get cleaned up. To date, the EPA has completed cleanups at 966 hazardous waste sites, accounting for 62% of the top-priority contamination sites around the country. As the Superfund program matures, so does the size, complexity, and cost of cleanup work. The EPA also pushes industrial polluters to pay the costs of cleanups. Potential polluters have agreed to conduct more than $857 million in future response work, and to reimburse the EPA for $248 million in past costs.

Asbestos

A mineral-based compound, asbestos was widely used for fire protection and insulation in buildings until the late 1960s. Microscopic asbestos fibers can be released into the air when this material is applied or when it later deteriorates or is damaged. These fibers can lodge in the lungs, causing **asbestosis,** lung cancer, and other serious lung diseases. Similar conditions expose workers to risk in the coal mining industry, from coal and silica dust (black lung disease), and in the textile industry, from cotton fibers (brown lung disease).

Asbestos can pose a danger in homes and apartment buildings, about 25% of which are thought to contain some asbestos. Areas where it is most likely to be found are insulation around water and steam pipes, ducts, and furnaces; boiler wraps; vinyl flooring; floor, wall, and ceiling insulation; roofing and siding; and fireproof board.

Lead

Thanks to better preventive efforts, lead poisoning is not as serious a problem today as it was a few years ago. Still, the CDC estimates that about 435,000 children under age 6 may have unsafe lead levels in their blood; the actual number could be much higher. Many of these children live in poor, inner-city areas (see the box "Poverty and Environmental Health" on p. 604). When lead is ingested or inhaled, it can damage the central nervous system, cause mental impairment, hinder oxygen transport in the blood, and create digestive problems. Severe lead poisoning may cause coma or even death. Neurological damage can be permanent.

Long-term exposure to low levels of lead may cause kidney disease; it can also cause lead to build up in bones, where it may be released into the bloodstream during pregnancy or when bone mass is lost from osteoporosis.

Young children can easily ingest lead from their environment by picking up dust and dirt on their hands and

asbestosis A lung condition caused by inhalation of microscopic asbestos fibers, which inflame the lung and can lead to lung cancer.

TERMS

Poverty and Environmental Health

Residents of poor and minority communities are often exposed to more environmental toxins than residents of wealthier communities, and they are more likely to suffer from health problems caused or aggravated by pollutants.

Poor neighborhoods are often located near highways and industrial areas that have high levels of air and noise pollution; they are also common sites for hazardous waste production and disposal. Residents of substandard housing are more likely to come into contact with lead, asbestos, carbon monoxide, pesticides, and other hazardous pollutants associated with peeling paint, old plumbing, poorly maintained insulation and heating equipment, and attempts to control high levels of pests such as cockroaches and rodents.

Poor people are more likely to have jobs that expose them to asbestos, silica dust, and pesticides, and they are more likely to catch and consume fish contaminated with PCBs, mercury, and other toxins.

The most thoroughly researched and documented link among poverty, the environment, and health is lead poisoning in children. Many studies have shown that children of low-income black families are much more likely to have elevated levels of lead in their blood than white children. One survey found that two-thirds of urban African American children from families earning less than $6000 a year had elevated lead levels. The CDC and the American Academy of Pediatrics recommend annual testing of blood lead levels for all children under age 6, with more frequent testing for children at special risk.

Asthma is another health threat that appears to be linked with both environmental and socioeconomic factors. The number of Americans with asthma has grown dramatically in the past 20 years; most of the increase has occurred in children, with African Americans and the poor hardest hit. Researchers are not sure what accounts for this increase, but suspects include household pollutants, pesticides, air pollution, cigarette smoke, and allergens like cockroaches. These risk factors are likely to cluster in poor urban areas where inadequate health care may worsen asthma's effects.

---

then putting their fingers in their mouth. Lead-based paints are the chief culprit in lead poisoning of children and were banned from residential use in 1978, but as many as 57 million American homes still contain lead paint. In 2006, the EPA proposed new guidelines requiring contractors to take special lead-containment measures when doing renovations, repairs, or painting in certain buildings. The use of lead in plumbing is now also banned, but some old pipes and faucets contain lead.

Pesticides

Pesticides are used primarily for two purposes: to prevent the spread of insectborne diseases and to maximize food production by killing insects that eat crops. Both uses have risks as well as benefits. Take, for example, the pesticide DDT. Recognized as a powerful pesticide in 1939, DDT was extremely important in efforts to control widespread insectborne diseases in tropical countries and increase crop yields throughout the world. In 1962, however, biologist Rachel Carson questioned the safety of DDT in her book *Silent Spring,* pointing out that the pesticide disrupts the life cycles of birds, fish, and reptiles. DDT also builds up in the food chain, increasing in concentration as larger animals eat smaller ones, a process known as **biomagnification.**

Despite its effectiveness as a pesticide, DDT was banned in the United States in 1972 because the costs associated with its use—to wildlife and potentially to humans—were too high. Most pesticide hazards to date have been a result of overuse, but there are concerns about the health effects of long-term exposure to small amounts of pesticide residues in foods, especially for children.

Mercury

A naturally occurring metal, mercury is a toxin that affects the nervous system and may damage the brain, kidneys, and gastrointestinal tract; increase blood pressure, heart rate, and heart attack risk; and cause cancer. Mercury slows fetal and child development and causes irreversible deficits in brain function. As many as 600,000 babies are born each year after being exposed to unsafe levels of mercury. Coal-fired power plants are the largest produc-

TERMS

pesticides Chemicals used to prevent the spread of diseases transmitted by insects and to maximize food production by killing insects that eat crops.

biomagnification The accumulation of a substance in a food chain.

Gender and Environmental Health

Although many environmental health risks are shared by all, some risks disproportionately affect women or men. Women and men often have different roles and responsibilities with respect to family, community, and the workforce. These differences can determine the types of environmental hazards that individuals are exposed to and what the potential risks of those exposures are.

In many societies, women are more often involved in day-to-day activities associated with the environment, including food preparation, agricultural work, and tasks around the home. These activities can expose women to greater levels of indoor air pollution, water pollution, foodborne pathogens, agricultural chemicals, and waste contamination. Indoor pollutants, especially soot from burning wood, charcoal, and other solid fuels used for home heating and cooking, are a particular risk for women. Exposure to this particulate pollution increases the risk of respiratory diseases, lung cancer, and reproductive problems.

All humans are exposed to chemicals in air, food, and drinking water, and we all carry a body load of chemicals. Some of these chemicals bioaccumulate in our bones, blood, or fatty tissues. Women are smaller than men, on average, and have a higher percentage of body fat; so chemicals that accumulate in fatty tissue may pose a relatively greater risk for women. On the other hand, men may be more likely to work in industries that involve significant occupational exposures to disease-related toxins; for example, coal miners have an increased risk of lung cancer (black lung disease).

Although any chemical exposure can be a concern for health, women face the added risk of passing pollutants to a developing fetus during pregnancy or to an infant through breastfeeding. Even relatively low exposure to pollutants can result in a significant chemical body load in an infant or young child because of their small body size. And because infants and children are still developing, the effects of chemical exposure can be significant and devastating. It is not unusual for dangerous environmental toxin exposures to be first recognized through noticeable effects on infants or children.

Reproductive risks are not limited to women and infants in developing parts of the world. Even in industrialized countries with strong environmental laws, infants and children are affected by such chemicals as lead and mercury. In 2005, scientists announced that they had found elevated levels of the rocket fuel chemical perchlorate in human breast milk in amounts above the safe dose set by the National Academy of Sciences. Many other chemicals, including PCBs and pesticides, have already been found in breast milk.

Studies are ongoing to identify and reduce environmental hazards in the United States and throughout the world. However, many of the people most directly affected by environmental health problems—women, children, and people living in poor communities—have limited economic, social, and political power. It is important that everyone affected by environmental problems be given a voice in determining environmental policies.

SOURCES: Kirk, A. B., et al. 2005. Perchlorate and iodide in dairy and breast milk. *Environmental Science and Technology,* Web release, February 22; McCally, M., ed. 2002. *Life Support: The Environment and Human Health.* Cambridge, Mass.: MIT Press; Population Reference Bureau. 2002. *Women, Men, and Environmental Change: The Gender Dimensions of Environmental Policies and Programs.* Washington, D.C.: Population Reference Bureau.

ers of mercury; other sources include mining and smelting operations and the disposal of consumer products containing mercury.

Mercury persists in the environment and, like pesticides, it is bioaccumulative. In particular, large, long-lived fish may carry high levels of mercury. Chapter 12 includes information on safe fish consumption; see the box "Gender and Environmental Health" for more on issues affecting pregnant women.

Because of health concerns, some cities and stores have banned the sale of mercury fever thermometers, a small but significant source of mercury. If a thermometer breaks or is disposed of improperly, mercury can enter the environment; if it vaporizes into the atmosphere, it can be hazardous to health. To safely clean up mercury from a broken thermometer, increase ventilation in the room and pick up the mercury with an eyedropper or scoop up the beads with a piece of heavy paper. Dispose of it and any contaminated instruments by placing them in a plastic bag and taking them to an appropriate hazardous waste disposal site. Replace mercury thermometers with one of the many mercury-free alternatives.

Other Chemical Pollutants

The list of real and potential chemical pollution problems may well be as long as the list of known chemicals. To the preceding examples we can add recent concern about arsenic in drinking water, poisonous chemicals in plastic baby bottles, hormones in streams, and other by-products of our industrial age.

As mentioned earlier, hazardous wastes are also found in the home and should be handled and disposed of properly. They include automotive supplies (motor oil, antifreeze, transmission fluid), paint supplies (turpentine, paint thinner, mineral spirits), art and hobby supplies (oil-based paint, solvents, acids and alkalis, aerosol sprays), insecticides, batteries, computer and

Hazardous chemicals accumulate in many homes, as well as in businesses and industrial sites.

electronic components, and household cleaners containing sodium hydroxide (lye) or ammonia. These chemicals are dangerous when inhaled or ingested, when they contact the skin or the eyes, or when they are burned or dumped.

Many cities provide guidelines about approved disposal methods and have hazardous waste collection days. Look in the government pages of your phone book under Hazardous Waste or Waste Disposal.

Preventing Chemical Pollution

You can take steps to reduce the chemical pollution in your community. Just as important, by reducing and eliminating the number of chemicals in your home, you may save the life of a child or animal who might encounter one of those chemicals.

- When buying products, read the labels, and try to buy the least toxic ones available. Choose nontoxic nonpetrochemical cleansers, disinfectants, polishes, and other personal and household products.

- Dispose of your household hazardous wastes properly. If you are not sure whether something is hazardous or don't know how to dispose of it, contact your local environmental health office or health department. Don't burn trash.

? QUESTIONS FOR CRITICAL THINKING AND REFLECTION

Are there any hazardous chemicals in your home, such as cleaning products, solvents, paint, or batteries? Would you know what to do if one of these chemicals spilled? How would you clean it up?

- Buy organic produce or produce that has been grown locally. Wash, scrub, and, if appropriate, peel fruits and vegetables. Consider eating less meat; animal products require more pesticides, fertilizer, water, and energy to produce.

- If you must use pesticides or toxic household products, store them in a locked place where children and pets can't get to them. Don't measure chemicals with food-preparation utensils, and wear gloves whenever handling them.

- If you have your house fumigated for pest control, be sure to hire a licensed exterminator. Keep everyone, including pets, out of the house while the crew works and, if possible, for a few days after.

RADIATION POLLUTION

Many people are afraid of **radiation,** in part because they don't understand what it is. Basically, radiation is energy. It can come in different forms, such as ultraviolet rays, microwaves, or X rays, and from different sources, such as the sun, uranium, and nuclear weapons (Figure 19.7). These forms of electromagnetic radiation differ in wavelength and energy, with shorter waves having the highest energy levels.

Of most concern to health are gamma rays produced by radioactive sources such as nuclear weapons, nuclear energy plants, and radon gas; these high-energy waves are powerful enough to penetrate objects and break molecular bonds. Although gamma radiation cannot be seen or felt, its effects at high doses can include **radiation sickness** and death; at lower doses, chromosome damage, sterility, tissue damage, cataracts, and cancer can occur. Other types of radiation can also affect health; for example, exposure to UV radiation from the sun or from tanning salons can increase the risk of skin cancer. The effects of some sources of radiation, such as cell phones, remain controversial.

Nuclear Weapons and Nuclear Energy

Nuclear weapons pose a health risk of the most serious kind to all species. Public health associations have stated that in the event of an intentional or unintentional discharge of these weapons, the casualties would run into the hundreds of thousands or millions. Reducing the stockpiles of nuclear weapons is a challenge and a goal for the twenty-first century.

Power-generating plants that use nuclear fuel also pose health problems. When **nuclear power** was first developed as an alternative to oil and coal, it was promoted as clean, efficient, inexpensive, and safe. In general, this has proven to be the case. Power systems in several parts of the world rely on nuclear power plants. However, despite all the built-in safeguards and regulating agencies, acci-

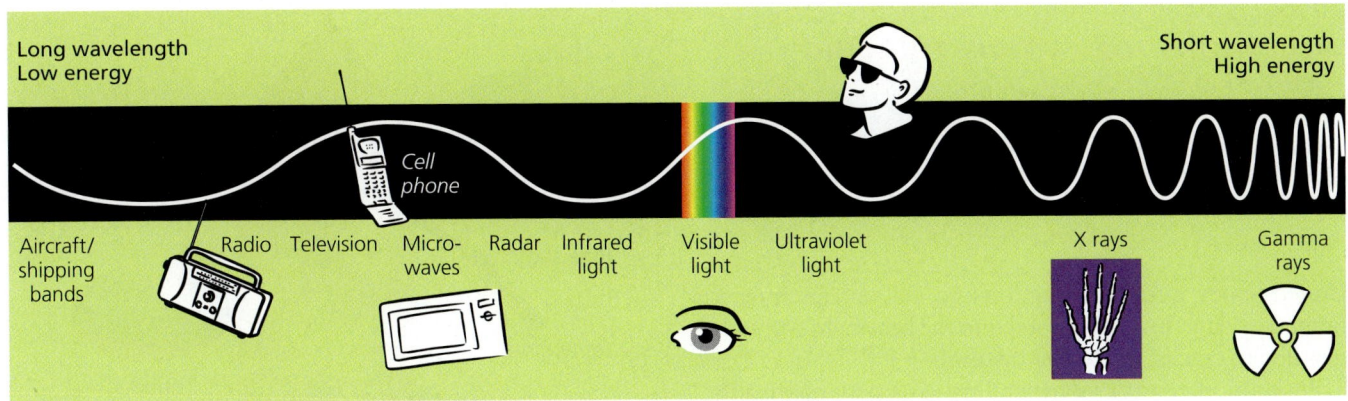

FIGURE 19.7 Electromagnetic radiation. Electromagnetic radiation takes the form of waves that travel through space. The length of the wave determines the type of radiation: The shortest waves are high-energy gamma rays; the longest are radio waves and extremely low frequency waves used for communication between aircraft, ships, and submarines. Different types of electromagnetic radiation have different effects on health.

dents in nuclear power plants do happen, many due to human error (as at Three Mile Island in the United States and Tokaimura in Japan), and the consequences of such accidents are far more serious than those of similar accidents in other types of power-generating plants. The 1986 fire and explosion at the Chernobyl nuclear power station in Ukraine caused hundreds of deaths and increased rates of genetic mutation and cancer; the long-term effects are not yet clear. The zone around Chernobyl has been sealed off to human habitation and could be unsafe for the next 24,000 years.

An additional, enormous problem is disposing of the radioactive wastes these plants generate. They cannot be dumped in a sanitary landfill because the amount and type of soil used to cap a sanitary landfill are not sufficient to prevent radiation exposure. Deposit sites have to be developed that will be secure not just for a few years but for tens of thousands of years—longer than the total recorded history of human beings on this planet. To date, no storage method has been devised that can provide infallible, infinitely durable shielding for nuclear waste.

Medical Uses of Radiation

Another area of concern is the use of radiation in medicine, primarily the X ray. The development of machines that could produce images of internal bone structures was a major advance in medicine, and applications abounded. Chest X rays were routinely given to screen for tuberculosis, and children's feet were even X rayed in shoe stores to make sure their new shoes fit properly. But, as is often the case, this new technology had disadvantages. As time passed, studies revealed that X ray exposure is cumulative and that no exposure is absolutely safe.

Early X ray machines are no longer used because of the high amounts of radiation they give off. Each new generation of X ray machines has used less radiation more effectively. From a personal health point of view, no one should

ever have a "routine" X ray examination; each such exam should have a definite purpose, and its benefits and risks should be carefully weighed.

Radiation in the Home and Workplace

Recently, there has been concern about electromagnetic radiation associated with common modern devices such as microwave ovens, computer monitors, cell phones, and even high-voltage power lines. These forms of radiation do have effects on health, but research results are inconclusive.

Another area of concern is **radon,** a naturally occurring radioactive gas found in certain soils, rocks, and building materials. When the breakdown products of radon are inhaled, they cling to lungs and bombard sensitive tissue with radioactivity. Among miners, exposure to high levels of radon has been shown to cause lung cancer; overall, it is the second leading cause of lung cancer in the

radiation Energy transmitted in the form of rays, waves, or particles.

radiation sickness An illness caused by excess radiation exposure, marked by low white blood cell counts and nausea; possibly fatal.

nuclear power The use of controlled nuclear reactions to produce steam, which in turn drives turbines to produce electricity.

radon A naturally occurring radioactive gas emitted from rocks and natural building materials that can become concentrated in insulated homes, causing lung cancer.

TERMS

QUESTIONS FOR CRITICAL THINKING AND REFLECTION

Do you live in an area where radon is a problem? If so, has your home been checked for radon?

United States, after smoking tobacco. Radon can enter a home by rising through the soil into the basement through dirt floors, cracks, and other openings.

In 2005, the Surgeon General issued a national health advisory on radon, recommending that Americans test their homes for radon every 2 years, and retest any time they move, make structural changes to a home, or occupy a previously unused level of a residence. If elevated levels of radon are found—4 or more picocuries per liter of air (pCi/L)—the problem should be dealt with as soon as possible through such measures as sealing cracks or installing basement ventilation systems. More information is available at the EPA Web site or by calling 1-800-SOS-RADON.

Avoiding Radiation

The following steps can help you avoid unneeded exposure to radiation:

- If your physician orders an X ray, ask why it is necessary. Only get X rays that you need, and keep a record of the date and location of every X ray exam. Don't have a full-body CT scan for routine screening; the radiation dose of one full-body CT scan is nearly 100 times that of a typical mammogram.
- Follow the Surgeon General's recommendations for radon testing.
- Find out if there are radioactive sites in your area. If you live or work near such a site, form or join a community action group to get the site cleaned up.

NOISE POLLUTION

We are increasingly aware of the health effects of loud or persistent noise in the environment. Concerns focus on two areas: hearing loss and stress. Prolonged exposure to sounds above 80–85 **decibels** (a measure of the intensity of a sound wave) can cause permanent hearing loss (Figure 19.8). Hearing damage can occur after 8 hours of

> **decibel** A unit for expressing the relative intensity of sounds on a scale from 0 for the average least perceptible sound to about 120 for the average pain threshold.

TERMS

Rocket launch	180
Rifle shot	160
Jet engine	
	140	Thunder overhead
Rock concert	120	**Pain threshold**
Motorcycle	100	Heavy traffic
	80	
Vacuum cleaner		
	60	Normal conversation
Birds singing	40	
		Whispering
Leaves rustling	20	
	0	Faintest audible noise

Sound intensity or loudness
(decibels)

FIGURE 19.8   The intensity of selected sounds.

exposure to sounds louder than 80 decibels. Regular exposure for longer than 1 minute to more than 100 decibels can cause permanent hearing loss. Children may suffer damage to their hearing at lower noise levels than adults.

Two common sources of excessive noise are the workplace and large gatherings of people at sporting events and rock concerts. The Occupational Safety and Health Administration (OSHA) sets legal standards for noise in

Environmental Health Checklist

The following list of statements relates to your effect on the environment. Put a checkmark next to the statements that are true for you.

_____ I ride my bike, walk, carpool, or use public transportation whenever possible.

_____ I keep my car tuned up and well maintained.

_____ My residence is well insulated.

_____ Where possible, I use compact fluorescent bulbs instead of incandescent bulbs.

_____ I turn off lights and appliances when they are not in use.

_____ I avoid turning on heat or air conditioning whenever possible.

_____ I run the washing machine, dryer, and dishwasher only when they have full loads.

_____ I run the clothes dryer only as long as it takes my clothes to dry.

_____ I dry my hair with a towel rather than a hair dryer.

_____ I keep my car's air conditioner in good working order and have it serviced by a service station that recycles CFCs.

_____ When shopping, I choose products with the least amount of packaging.

_____ I choose recycled and recyclable products.

_____ I avoid products packaged in plastic and unrecycled aluminum.

_____ I store food in glass jars and waxed paper rather than plastic wrap.

_____ I take my own bag along when I go shopping.

_____ I recycle newspapers, glass, cans, and other recyclables.

_____ When shopping, I read labels and try to buy the least toxic products available.

_____ I dispose of household hazardous wastes properly.

_____ I take showers instead of baths.

_____ I take short showers and switch off the water when I'm not actively using it.

_____ I do not run the water while brushing my teeth, shaving, or hand-washing clothes.

_____ My faucets have aerators installed in them.

_____ My shower has a low-flow showerhead.

_____ I have a water-saver toilet or a water displacement device in my toilet.

_____ I snip or rip plastic six-pack rings before I throw them out.

_____ When hiking or camping, I never leave anything behind.

Statements you have not checked can help you identify behaviors you can change to improve environmental health.

For an overall estimate of how much land and water your lifestyle requires, take the Ecological Footprint quiz at www.myfootprint.org.

---

the workplace, but no laws exist regulating noise levels at rock concerts, which can be much louder than most workplaces.

Here are some ways to avoid exposing yourself to excessive noise:

- Wear ear protectors when working around noisy machinery.
- When listening to music on a headset with a volume range of 1–10, keep the volume no louder than 6; your headset is too loud if you are unable to hear people around you speaking in a normal tone of voice. Earmuff-style headphones may be easier on the ears than earbuds, which are inserted into the ear canal. Experts warn that earbuds should not be used more than 30 minutes a day unless the volume is set below 60% of maximum; headphones can be used up to 1 hour.
- Avoid loud music. Don't sit or stand near speakers or amplifiers at a rock concert, and don't play a car radio or stereo so high that you can't hear the traffic.
- Avoid exposure to painfully loud sounds, and avoid repeated exposure to any sounds above 80 decibels.

QUESTIONS FOR CRITICAL THINKING AND REFLECTION

How often do you listen to loud music? Do you ever use headphones? At what volume level do like to listen? Do you think your listening habits pose a threat to your hearing? Would you let a child listen at the same volume level?

YOU AND THE ENVIRONMENT

Faced with a vast array of confusing and complex environmental issues, you may feel overwhelmed and conclude that there isn't anything you can do about global problems. But this is not true. If everyone made individual changes in his or her life, the impact would be tremendous. (To assess your current lifestyle, refer to the box "Environmental Health Checklist.")

Making Your Letters Count

It takes only a few minutes to write to an elected official, but it can make a difference on an environmental issue you care about. When elected officials receive enough letters or e-mails on an issue, it does influence their vote—they want to be reelected, and your vote counts! To give your letter the greatest possible influence, use these guidelines:

• Use your own words and your own stationery.

• Be clear and concise. Keep your letter to one or two paragraphs, never more than one page.

• Focus on only one subject in each letter, and identify it clearly. Refer to legislation by its name or number.

• Request a specific action—vote a particular way on a piece of legislation, request hearings, cosponsor a bill—and state your reasons for your position.

• If you live or work in the legislator's district, say so.

• Courteous letters work best. Don't be insulting or unnecessarily critical.

You can send letters via regular mail; however, increased security screenings often delay delivery. You can e-mail the president or vice president at the following addresses:

president@whitehouse.gov

vice-president@whitehouse.gov

To locate the contact information for your United States senators and representatives, visit the following Web sites:

Senate: www.senate.gov

House of Representatives: www.house.gov/writerep

At the same time, it is important to recognize that large corporations and manufacturers are the ones primarily responsible for environmental degradation. Many of them have jumped on the environmental bandwagon with public relations and advertising campaigns designed to make them look good, but they haven't changed their practices nearly enough to make a difference. To influence them, people have to become educated, demand changes in production methods, and elect people to office who consider environmental concerns along with sound business practices.

Large-scale changes and individual actions complement each other. What you do every day *does* count. Following the suggestions throughout this chapter will help you make a difference in the environment. In addition, you can become a part of larger community actions to work for a healthier world:

• Share what you learn about environmental issues with your friends and family.

• Join, support, or volunteer your time to organizations working on environmental causes that are important to you.

• Contact your elected representatives and communicate your concerns. For guidelines on how to be heard, see the box "Making Your Letters Count."

TIPS FOR TODAY AND THE FUTURE

Environmental health involves protecting ourselves from environmental dangers and protecting the environment from the dangers created by humans.

RIGHT NOW YOU CAN

■ Turn off the lights, televisions, and stereos in any unoccupied rooms.

■ Turn down the heat a few degrees and put on a sweater, or turn off the air conditioner and change into cooler clothes.

■ Check your trash for recyclable items and take them out for recycling. If your town does not provide curbside pickup for recyclable items, find out where the nearest community recycling center is.

IN THE FUTURE YOU CAN

■ As your existing light bulbs burn out, replace them with compact fluorescent light bulbs.

■ Have your car checked to make sure it runs as well as it can and puts out the lowest amount of polluting emissions possible.

■ Go online and find one of the many calculators available that can help you estimate your environmental footprint. After calculating your footprint, figure out ways to reduce it.

SUMMARY

• Environmental health encompasses all the interactions of humans with their environment and the health consequences of those interactions.

• The world's population is increasing rapidly, especially in the developing world. Factors that may eventually limit human population are food, availability of land and water, energy, and minimum acceptable standard of living.

- Increased amounts of air pollutants are especially dangerous for children, older adults, and people with chronic health problems.

- Factors contributing to the development of smog include heavy motor vehicle traffic, hot weather, and stagnant air.

- Carbon dioxide and other natural gases act as a greenhouse around the earth, increasing the temperature of the atmosphere. Levels of these gases are rising through human activity; as a result, the world's climate could change.

- The ozone layer that shields the earth's surface from the sun's UV rays has thinned and developed holes in certain regions.

- Environmental damage from energy use can be limited through energy conservation and the development of non-polluting, renewable sources of energy.

- Indoor pollutants can trigger allergies and illness in the short term and cancer in the long term.

- Concerns with water quality focus on pathogenic organisms and hazardous chemicals from industry and households, as well as on water shortages.

- Sewage treatment prevents pathogens from contaminating drinking water; it often must also deal with heavy metals and hazardous chemicals.

- The amount of garbage is growing all the time; paper is the biggest component. Recycling can help reduce solid waste disposal problems.

- Potentially hazardous chemical pollutants include asbestos, lead, pesticides, mercury, and many household products. Proper handling and disposal are critical.

- Radiation can cause radiation sickness, chromosome damage, and cancer, among other health problems.

- Loud or persistent noise can lead to hearing loss and/or stress; two common sources of excessive noise are the workplace and rock concerts.

- Most health advances today must come from lifestyle changes and improvements in the global environment. The effects of personal changes made by every concerned individual could be tremendous.

FOR MORE INFORMATION

BOOKS

Ausenda, F. 2009. *Green Volunteers: The World Guide to Voluntary Work in Nature Conservation,* 7th ed. New York: Universe. *Describes a variety of opportunities to volunteer for environmental causes, in many different parts of the world.*

Brown, M. J. 2007. *Building Powerful Community Organizations: A Personal Guide to Creating Groups That Can Solve Problems and Change the World.* Chicago: Long Haul Press. *Provides advice for facing environmental (and other) challenges through local organizing and recruiting.*

Cunningham, W. P., et al. 2007. *Environmental Science: A Global Concern,* 10th ed. New York: McGraw-Hill. *A nontechnical survey of basic environmental science and key concerns.*

Maslin, M., 2005. *Global Warming: A Very Short Introduction.* New York: Oxford University Press. *A survey of the science and politics of global warming.*

Nadakavukaren, A. 2005. *Our Global Environment: A Health Perspective,* 6th ed. Prospect Heights, Ill.: Waveland Press. *A broad survey of major environmental issues and their effects on personal and community health.*

ORGANIZATIONS, HOTLINES, AND WEB SITES

CDC National Center for Environmental Health. Provides brochures and fact sheets on a variety of environmental issues.
http://www.cdc.gov/nceh/default.htm

Earth Times. An international online newspaper devoted to global environmental issues.
http://www.earthtimes.org

Ecological Footprint. Calculates your personal ecological footprint based on your diet, transportation patterns, and living arrangements.
http://www.myfootprint.org

Energy Efficiency and Renewable Energy (EERE). U.S. Department of Energy. Provides information about alternative fuels and tips for saving energy at home and in your car.
http://www.eere.doe.gov

Fuel Economy. Provides information on the fuel economy of cars made since 1985 and tips on improving gas mileage.
http://www.fueleconomy.gov

Indoor Air Quality Information Hotline. Answers questions, provides publications, and makes referrals.
800-438-4318

National Lead Information Center. Provides information packets and specialist advice.
http://www.epa.gov/lead/index.html

National Oceanic and Atmospheric Administration (NOAA): Climate. Provides information on a variety of issues related to climate, including global warming, drought, and El Niño and La Niña.
http://www.noaa.gov/climate.html

National Safety Council Environmental Health Center. Provides information on lead, radon, indoor air quality, hazardous chemicals, and other environmental issues.
http://www.nsc.org/ehc.aspx

Student Environmental Action Coalition (SEAC). A coalition of student and youth environmental groups; the Web site has contact information for local groups.
http://www.seac.org

United Nations. Several U.N. programs are devoted to environmental problems on a global scale; the Web sites provide information on current and projected trends and on international treaties developed to deal with environmental issues.
http://www.un.org/popin (Population Division)
http://www.unep.org (Environment Programme)

U.S. Environmental Protection Agency (EPA). Provides information about EPA activities and many consumer-oriented materials. The Web site includes special sites devoted to global warming, ozone loss, pesticides, and other areas of concern.

http://www.epa.gov

Worldwatch Institute. A public policy research organization focusing on emerging global environmental problems and the links between the world economy and the environment.

http://www.worldwatch.org

There are many national and international organizations working on environmental health problems. A few of the largest and best known are listed below:

Greenpeace: 800-326-0959; http://www.greenpeace.org
National Audubon Society: 212-979-3000; http://www .audubon.org
National Wildlife Federation: 800-822-9919; http://www.nwf.org
Nature Conservancy: 800-628-6860; http://www.nature.org
Sierra Club: 415-977-5500; http://www.sierraclub.org
World Wildlife Fund—U.S.: 800-960-0993; http://www .worldwildlife.org

SELECTED BIBLIOGRAPHY

Bell, M. L., et al. 2004. Ozone and short-term mortality in 95 U.S. urban communities, 1987–2000. *Journal of the American Medical Association* 292(19): 2372–2378.

CDC National Center for Environmental Health. 2007. *Children's Blood Lead Levels in the United States* (http://www.cdc.gov/nceh/lead/research/kidsBLL.htm; retrieved February 19, 2009).

Centers for Disease Control and Prevention. 2006. Adult blood lead epidemiology and surveillance—United States, 2003–2004. *Morbidity and Mortality Weekly Report* 55(32): 876–879.

Centers for Disease Control and Prevention. 2006. Surveillance for waterborne disease and outbreaks associated with drinking water and water not intended for drinking—United States, 2003–2004. *Morbidity and Mortality Weekly Report* 55(SS12): 31–58.

Delworth-Bart, J. E., and C. F. Moore. 2006. Mercy mercy me: Social injustice and the prevention of environmental pollutant exposures among ethnic minority and poor children. *Child Development* 77(2): 247–265.

Dominici, F., et al. 2006. Fine particulate air pollution and hospital admission for cardiovascular and respiratory diseases. *Journal of the American Medical Association* 295(10): 1127–1134.

Energy Information Administration. 2005. *Impacts of Modeled Recommendations of the National Commission on Energy Policy*. Washington, D.C.: U.S. Department of Energy.

Energy Information Agency. 2009. *Gasoline and Diesel Fuel Update* (http://tonto.eia.doe.gov/oog/info/gdu/gasdiesel.asp; retrieved February 19, 2009).

Environmental Protection Agency. 2008. *Municipal Solid Waste: Basic Facts* (http://www.epa.gov.epaoswer/non-hw/muncpl/facts.htm; retrieved February 19, 2009).

Gauderman, W. J., et al. 2004. The effect of air pollution on lung development from 10 to 18 years of age. *New England Journal of Medicine* 351(11): 1057–1067.

Kunzli, N., et al. 2005. Ambient air pollution and atherosclerosis in Los Angeles. *Environmental Health Perspectives* 113(2): 201–206.

Laden, F., et al. 2006. Reduction in fine particulate air pollution and mortality: Extended follow-up of the Harvard Six Cities study. *American Journal of Respiratory and Critical Care Medicine* 173(6): 667–672.

NASA Goddard Institute for Space Studies. 2008. *Global Temperature Trends: 2007 Summation* (http://www.giss.nasa.gov/gistemp/2008; retrieved February 19, 2009).

The National Academies. 2006. *Surface Temperature Reconstructions for the Last 2,000 Years*. Washington, D.C.: National Academies Press.

National Oceanic and Atmospheric Administration. 2008. *Billion Dollar U.S. Weather Disasters, 1980–2007* (http://www.ncdc.noaa.gov/oa/reports/billionz.html; retrieved February 19, 2009).

Parker, J. D., et al. 2005. Air pollution and birth weight among term infants in California. *Pediatrics* 115(1): 121–128.

Trasande, L., P. J. Landrigan, and C. Schechter. 2005. Public health and economic consequences of methylmercury toxicity to the developing brain. *Environmental Health Perspectives* online, 28 February.

United Nations Population Division. 2007. *World Population Prospects: The 2006 Revision*. New York: United Nations.

U.S. Department of Health and Human Services. 2005. *Surgeon General Releases National Health Advisory on Radon* (http://www.surgeongeneral.gov/pressreleases/sg01132005.html; retrieved February 19, 2009).

U.S. Environmental Protection Agency. 2007. *Superfund National Accomplishments Summary Fiscal Year 2007* (http://www.epa.gov/superfund/accomp/numbers07.htm; retrieved February 19, 2009).

Virtanen, J. K., et al. 2005. Mercury, fish oils, and risk of acute coronary events and cardiovascular disease, coronary heart disease, and all-cause mortality in men in eastern Finland. *Arteriosclerosis, Thrombosis, and Vascular Biology* 25(1): 228–233.

World Health Organization. 2005. *International Decade for Action: Water for Life 2005–2015* (http://www.who.int/water_sanitation_health/2005advocguide/en/index1.html; retrieved February 19, 2009).

World Health Organization. 2006. Cholera, 2005. *Weekly Epidemiological Record* 81(31): 297–308.

World Health Organization. 2006. *Fuel for Life: Household Energy and Health*. Geneva: WHO Press.

Worldwatch Institute. 2007. *Vital Signs 2007–2008*. New York: Norton.

20

CONVENTIONAL AND COMPLEMENTARY MEDICINE

LOOKING AHEAD>>>>>

AFTER READING THIS CHAPTER, YOU SHOULD BE ABLE TO:

- Explain the self-care decision-making process and discuss options for self-treatment
- Describe the basic premises, practices, and providers of conventional medicine
- Describe the basic premises, practices, and providers of complementary and alternative medicine
- Explain how to communicate effectively with health care providers and to use their input when evaluating different types of treatment
- Discuss different types of health insurance plans

TEST YOUR KNOWLEDGE

1. **The people most likely to use complementary and alternative medicine are those without a conventional primary care physician.**

   True or false?

2. **Which practice or interest is shared by both conventional Western medicine and complementary and alternative medicine?**

   a. careful observation of symptoms
   b. treatment with remedies derived from plants
   c. concern with the patient-physician relationship

3. **Herbal remedies and dietary supplements like ginkgo biloba and St. John's wort must meet FDA standards for safety and effectiveness before they can be put on the market.**

   True or false?

4. **Generic drugs are generally less effective than brand-name drugs.**

   True or false?

5. **Approximately how many Americans have no health insurance?**

   a. 4 million
   b. 14 million
   c. 40 million

ANSWERS

1. **FALSE.** The more often a person visits a conventional primary care physician, the more likely he or she is to use complementary and alternative medicine.

2. **ALL THREE.** Although there are profound philosophical differences between the approaches, they share many characteristics.

3. **FALSE.** Manufacturers are responsible for the safety of the dietary supplements they sell; however, the FDA has the power to restrict a product if it is found to pose a health risk after it is on the market. Manufacturers are not required to prove that their products are effective.

4. **FALSE.** Price is often the only difference. The generic version of a drug has the same active ingredient as the brand-name drug, but it may have different inactive ingredients.

5. **C.** According to the National Center for Health Statistics, more than 43 million Americans had no health insurance coverage in 2007.

Today, people are becoming more empowered and confident in their ability to solve personal health problems on their own. People who manage their own health care gather information and learn skills from a variety of resources; they solicit opinions and advice, make decisions, and take action. They know how to practice safe, effective self-care, and they know how to make decisions about professional medical care, whether conventional Western medicine or complementary and alternative medicine.

This chapter will help you develop the skills both to identify and manage medical problems and to make the health care system work effectively for you.

SELF-CARE

Effectively managing medical problems involves developing several skills. First, you need to learn to be a good observer of your own body and assess your symptoms. You also must be able to decide when to seek professional advice and when you can safely deal with the problem on your own. You need to know how to safely and effectively self-treat common medical problems. Finally, you need to know how to develop a partnership with physicians and other health care providers and how to carry out treatment plans.

Self-Assessment

Symptoms are often an expression of the body's attempt to heal itself. For example, the pain and swelling that occur after an ankle injury immobilize the injured joint to allow healing to take place. A fever may be an attempt to make the body less hospitable to infectious agents. A cough can help clear the airways and protect the lungs.

Understanding what a symptom means and what is going on in your body helps reduce anxiety about symptoms and enables you to practice safe self-care that supports your body's own healing mechanisms.

Carefully observing symptoms also lets you identify those signals that suggest you need professional assistance. You should begin by noting when the symptom began, how often and when it occurs, what makes it worse, what makes it better, and whether you have any associated symptoms. You can also monitor your body's vital signs, such as temperature and heart rate. Medical self-tests for blood pressure, blood sugar, pregnancy detection, and urinary tract infections can also help you make a more informed decision about when to seek medical help and when to self-treat.

Knowing When to See a Physician

In general, you should see a physician for symptoms that you would describe as follows:

1. *Severe.* If the symptom is very severe or intense, medical assistance is advised. Examples include severe pains, major injuries, and other emergencies.

2. *Unusual.* If the symptom is peculiar and unfamiliar, it is wise to check it out with your physician. Examples include unexplained lumps, changes in a mole, problems with vision, difficulty swallowing, numbness, weakness, unexplained weight loss, and blood in sputum, urine, or stool.

3. *Persistent.* If the symptom lasts longer than expected, seek medical advice. Examples in adults include fever for more than 5 days, a cough lasting longer than 2 weeks, a sore that doesn't heal within a month, and hoarseness lasting longer than 3 weeks.

4. *Recurrent.* If a symptom tends to return again and again, medical evaluation is advised. Examples include recurrent headaches, stomach pains, and backache.

Sometimes a single symptom is not a cause for concern, but when the symptom is accompanied by other symptoms, the combination suggests a more serious problem. For example, a fever with a stiff neck suggests meningitis.

If you evaluate your symptoms and think that you need professional help, you must decide how urgent the problem is. If it is a true emergency, you should go (or call someone to take you) to the nearest emergency room (ER). Emergencies include the following:

- Major trauma or injury, such as head injury, suspected broken bone, deep wound, severe burn, eye injury, or animal bite

- Uncontrollable bleeding or internal bleeding, as indicated by blood in the sputum, vomit, or stool

- Intolerable and uncontrollable pain or severe chest pain

- Severe shortness of breath

- Persistent abdominal pain, especially if associated with nausea and vomiting

- Poisoning or drug overdose

- Loss of consciousness or seizure

- Stupor, drowsiness, or disorientation that cannot be explained

- Severe or worsening reaction to an insect bite or sting or to a medication, especially if breathing is difficult

If your problem is not an emergency but still requires medical attention, call your physician's office. Often you can be given medical advice over the phone without the inconvenience of a visit. To help you make wise medical

Expressive Writing and Chronic Conditions

The act of writing down feelings and thoughts about stressful life events has been shown to help people improve their health. In one recent study, people with asthma or rheumatoid arthritis were asked to write down their feelings about the most stressful event in their lives; they wrote for 20 minutes a day over a 3-day period. In follow-up exams 4 months later, nearly half of those who engaged in expressive writing experienced positive changes in their condition, such as improved lung function or reduced joint pain.

Investigators remain unsure why writing about one's feelings has beneficial effects. It is possible that expressing feelings about a traumatic event helps people work through the event and put it behind them. The resulting sense of release and control may reduce stress levels and have positive physical effects such as reduced heart rate and blood pressure and improved immune function. Alternatively, expressive writing may change the way people think about previous stressful events in their lives and

help them cope with new stressors. Whatever the cause, it's clear that expressive writing can be a safe, inexpensive, and effective supplement to standard treatment of certain chronic illnesses.

What about the effects of expressive writing on otherwise healthy individuals? Other studies have, in fact, found a similar benefit: People who wrote about traumatic experiences reported fewer symptoms, fewer days off work, fewer visits to the doctor, improved mood, and a more positive outlook.

If you'd like to try expressive writing to help you deal with a traumatic event, set aside a special time—15 minutes a day for 4 consecutive days, for example, or 1 day a week for 4 weeks. Write in a place where you won't be interrupted or distracted. Explore your very deepest thoughts and feelings and why you feel the way you do. Don't worry about grammar or coherence or about what someone else might think about what you're writing; you are writing just for yourself. You may find the writing exercise to be distressing in the short term—sadness

and depression are common when dealing with feelings about a stressful event— but most people report relief and contentment soon after writing for several days.

---

decisions, a Self-Care Guide for Common Medical Problems is provided in Appendix B.

Self-Treatment

When confronted with a new symptom, many people try to find some pill or potion that will relieve or cure it. However, other self-treatment options are available.

Watchful Waiting In most cases, your body itself can relieve your symptoms and heal the disorder. The prescriptions filled by your body's internal pharmacy are frequently the safest and most effective treatment, so patience and careful self-observation are often the best choices in self-treatment.

Nondrug Options Nondrug options are often easy, inexpensive, safe, and highly effective. For example, massage, ice packs, and neck exercises may at times be more helpful than drugs in relieving headaches and other pains. Getting adequate rest, increasing exercise, drinking more water, eating more or less of certain foods, using humidifiers, changes in ergonomics when working at a desk, and so on are just some of the hundreds of nondrug options for preventing or relieving many common health prob-

lems. For a variety of disorders caused or aggravated by stress, the treatment of choice may be relaxation or other stress-management strategies (see Chapter 2 and the box "Expressive Writing and Chronic Conditions").

Self-Medication Self-treatment with nonprescription medications is an important part of health care. Nonprescription or **over-the-counter (OTC) medications** are medicines that the Food and Drug Administration (FDA) has determined are safe for use without a physician's prescription. There are more than 100,000 OTC drugs on the market; about 60% of all medications are sold over the counter. In any 2-week period, nearly 70% of Americans use one or more OTC drugs.

Many OTC drugs are highly effective in relieving symptoms and sometimes in curing illnesses. In fact, many OTC drugs were formerly prescription drugs. More than 600 products sold over the counter today use ingredients or dosage strengths available only by prescription 20 years ago. With

over-the-counter (OTC) medication A medication or product that can be purchased by the consumer without a prescription.

this increased consumer choice, however, comes increased consumer responsibility for using OTC drugs safely.

Consumers also need to be aware of the barrage of OTC drug advertising aimed at them. The implication of such advertising is that every symptom can and should be relieved by a drug. Although many OTC products are effective, others are unnecessary or divert attention from better ways of coping. Many ingredients in OTC drugs—perhaps 70%—have not been proven to be effective, a fact the FDA does not dispute. And any drug may have risks and side effects.

Follow these simple guidelines to self-medicate safely:

1. Always read labels and follow directions carefully. The information on most OTC drug labels now appears in a standard format developed by the FDA (Figure 20.1). Ingredients, directions for safe use,

and warnings are clearly indicated; but, if you have any questions, ask a pharmacist or another qualified health care provider before using a product.

2. Do not exceed the recommended dosage or length of treatment unless you discuss this change with your physician.

3. Use caution if you are taking other medications or supplements, because OTC drugs and herbal supplements can interact with some prescription drugs. If you have questions about drug interactions, ask your pharmacist or another qualified health care provider *before* you mix medicines.

4. Try to select medications with one active ingredient rather than combination products. A product with multiple ingredients is likely to include drugs for symptoms you don't even have. Using single-ingredient products also allows you to adjust the dosage of each medication separately for optimal symptom relief with minimal side effects.

5. When choosing medications, try to buy **generic drugs**, which contain the same active ingredient as the brand-name product but generally at a much

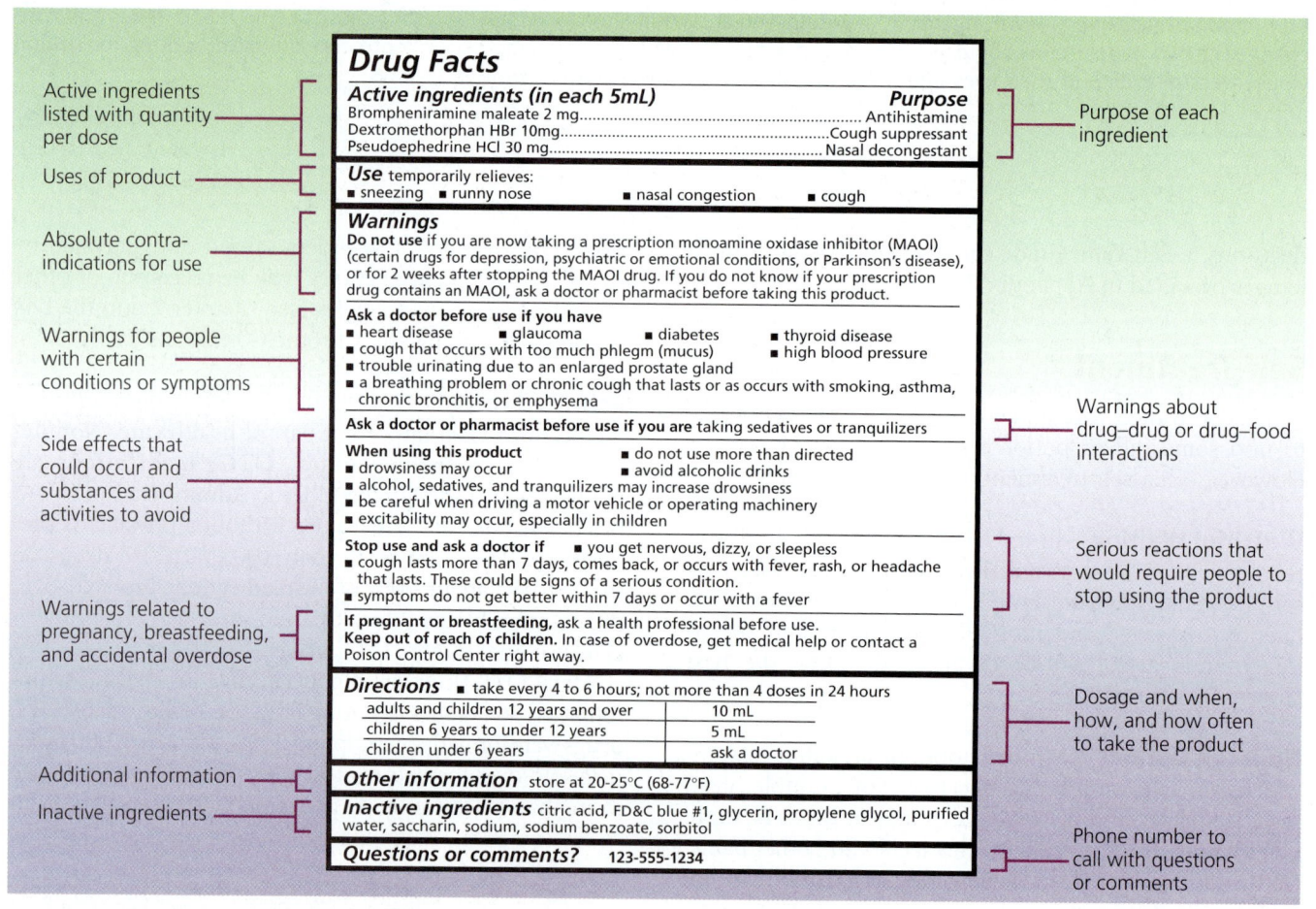

FIGURE 20.1   Reading and understanding OTC drug labels.

SOURCE: Food and Drug Administration. 1999. Over-the-counter human drugs; labeling requirements; final rule. *Federal Register* 64(51), 17 March, 13254-13303.

Closet

- Analgesic (relieves pain)
- Antacid (relieves upset stomach)
- Antibiotic ointment (reduces risk of infection)
- Antihistamine (relieves allergy symptoms)
- Antiseptic (helps stop infection)
- Fever reducer (adult and child)
- Hydrocortisone (relieves itching and inflammation)
- Decongestant (relieves stuffy nose and other cold symptoms)

Medicine Cabinet

- Adhesive bandages
- Adhesive tape
- Alcohol wipes
- Calibrated measuring spoon
- Disinfectant
- Gauze pads
- Thermometer
- Tweezers

FIGURE 20.2 Your home medical care kit. A cool, dark, and dry place such as the top of a linen closet, preferably in a locked container and out of a child's reach, is best for storing medicines. Showers and baths create heat and humidity that can cause some drugs to deteriorate rapidly. Use your bathroom medicine cabinet for supplies that aren't affected by heat and humidity.

SOURCE: Lewis, C. 2000. Your medicine cabinet needs an annual checkup, too. *FDA Consumer,* March/April.

lower cost. (Brand-name and generic drugs are discussed in more detail later in the chapter.)

6. Never take or give a drug from an unlabeled container or in the dark when you can't read what the label says.

7. If you are pregnant or nursing or have a chronic condition such as kidney or liver disease, consult your health care provider before self-medicating.

8. The expiration date marked on many medications is an estimate of how long the medication is likely to be safe and effective. However, an extensive study by the FDA found that 90% of all prescription and OTC medications are potent for several years after their stated expiration date. Exceptions include the antibiotic tetracycline, liquid antibiotics, nitroglycerine, and insulin. Expiration dates are very conservative. If a medicine is expired by more than a few years and you need to be certain that the medication is completely effective, you should purchase new medication. You can dispose of old medicine by placing it in a sealed container with coffee grounds or cat litter, but the safest way to get rid of outdated medicines is to take them to a pharmacy or hospital.

If you have any question about a medicine's expiration date, ask a pharmacist.

9. Store your medications in a cool, dry place that is out of the reach of children (Figure 20.2).

10. Use special caution with aspirin. Because of an association with a rare but serious problem known as Reye's syndrome, aspirin should not be used by children or adolescents who may have the flu, chicken pox, or any other viral illness. Outdated aspirin that has an acidic odor should be discarded.

PROFESSIONAL CARE

When self-treatment is not appropriate or sufficient, you need to seek professional medical care, whether by going to a hospital emergency room, by scheduling an appointment with your physician, or by accessing some other conventional health care. This system is a broad network of professionals and organizations, including independent practitioners, health care providers, hospitals, clinics, and public and private insurance programs.

In recent years, many Americans have also sought health care from practitioners of **complementary and alternative medicine (CAM)**, defined as those therapies and practices that do not form part of conventional, or mainstream,

generic drug A drug that is not registered or protected by a trademark; a drug that does not have a brand name.

complementary and alternative medicine (CAM) Therapies or practices that are not part of conventional or mainstream health care and medical practice as taught in most U.S. medical schools and available at most U.S. health care facilities; examples of CAM practices include acupuncture and herbal remedies.

TERMS

health care and medical practices as taught in most U.S. medical schools and offered in most U.S. hospitals. The most commonly used CAM therapies are relaxation techniques, herbal medicine, massage, and chiropractic (Table 20.1). People often use CAM therapies in addition to their conventional medical treatments, but many do not tell their physicians about it.

Consumers turn to CAM for a large variety of purposes related to health and well-being, such as boosting their immune system, lowering their cholesterol levels, losing weight, quitting smoking, or enhancing their memory. There are indications that people with chronic conditions, including cancer, asthma, autoimmune diseases, and HIV infection, are particularly likely to try CAM therapies. Despite their growing popularity, many CAM practices remain controversial, and individuals need to be critically aware of safety issues. The National Center for Complementary and Alternative Medicine (NCCAM), a branch of the National Institutes of Health (NIH), was established in the 1990s to apply rigorous scientific standards for proving or disproving the safety and effectiveness of CAM.

In the next sections of this chapter, we examine the principles and providers of both **conventional medicine**—the dominant medical system in the United States and Europe, also referred to as standard Western medicine or biomedicine—and complementary and alternative medicine, with particular attention to consumer issues.

Table 20.1	Use of Complementary and Alternative Therapies in the United States	
		Percent Who Ever Used Therapy
Prayer		55.3
Natural products (nonvitamin, nonmineral)		25.0
Chiropractic care		19.9
Deep breathing exercises		14.6
Meditation		10.2
Massage		9.3
Yoga		7.5
Diet-based therapies		6.8
Progressive relaxation		4.2
Acupuncture		4.0
Megavitamin therapy		3.9
Homeopathic treatment		3.6
Guided imagery		3.0
T'ai chi		2.5
Hypnosis		1.8
Energy healing therapy/Reiki		1.1
Biofeedback		1.0
Any therapy		**74.6**

SOURCE: Barnes, P. M., et al. 2004. Complementary and alternative medicine use among adults: United States, 2002. *Advance Data from Vital and Health Statistics* No. 343. Hyattsville, Md.: National Center for Health Statistics.

CONVENTIONAL MEDICINE

Referring to conventional medicine as standard Western medicine draws attention to the fact that it differs from the various medical systems that have developed in China, Japan, India, and other parts of the world. Calling it "biomedicine" reflects conventional medicine's foundation in the biological and physical sciences.

Premises and Assumptions of Conventional Medicine

One of the important characteristics of Western medicine is the belief that disease is caused by identifiable physical factors. Western medicine identifies the causes of disease as pathogens (such as bacteria and viruses), genetic factors, and unhealthy lifestyles that result in changes at the molecular and cellular levels. In most cases, the focus is primarily on the physical causes of illness rather than mental or spiritual imbalance.

Another feature that distinguishes Western biomedicine from other medical systems is the concept that every disease is defined by a certain set of symptoms and that these symptoms are similar in most patients suffering from this disease. Western medicine tends to treat illnesses as isolated biological disturbances that can occur in human beings, rather than as integral in some way to the individual with the illness.

Related to the idea of illness as the result of invasion by outside factors is the strong orientation toward methods of destroying pathogens or preventing them from causing serious infection. The public health measures of the nineteenth and twentieth centuries—chlorination of drinking water, sewage disposal, food safety regulations, vaccination programs, education about hygiene, and so on—are an outgrowth of this orientation.

The implementation of public health measures is one way to control pathogens; another is the use of drugs and surgery. The discovery and development of sulfa drugs, antibiotics, and steroids in the twentieth century, along with advances in chemistry that made it possible to identify the active ingredients in common plant-derived remedies, paved the way for the current close identification of Western medicine with **pharmaceuticals** (medical drugs, both

QUESTIONS FOR CRITICAL THINKING AND REFLECTION

What are your views about the use of CAM treatments and therapies? What events or information have shaped those views? At this point in your life, would you consider using complementary or alternative medicine?

prescription and over-the-counter). Western medicine also relies heavily on surgery and on advanced medical technology to discover the physical causes of disease and to correct, remove, or destroy them.

Further, Western medicine is based on the scientific method of obtaining knowledge and explaining health-related phenomena. Scientific explanations have these characteristics:

- *Empirical*—they are based on the evidence of the senses and on objective and systematic observation, often carried out under carefully controlled conditions; they must be capable of verification by others.
- *Rational*—they follow the rules of logic and are consistent with known facts.
- *Testable*—either they are verifiable through direct observation or they lead to predictions about what should occur under conditions not yet observed.
- *Parsimonious*—they explain phenomena with the fewest number of causes.
- *General*—they have broad explanatory power.
- *Rigorously evaluated*—they are constantly evaluated for consistency with the evidence and known principles, for parsimony, and for generality.
- *Tentative*—scientists are willing to entertain the possibility that their explanations are faulty, based on new, better, or connected evidence.

The scientific method is both a way of acquiring knowledge and a way of thinking that involves approaching a problem by carefully defining its parameters, seeking out relevant evidence, and subjecting proposed solutions to rigorous testing.

Western medicine translates the scientific method into practice through the research process, a highly refined and well-established approach to exploring the causes of disease and ensuring the safety and efficacy of treatments. Research ranges from case studies—descriptions of a single patient's illness and treatment—to randomized controlled trials (RTCs) conducted on large populations.

The process of drug development is equally rigorous. Drugs are developed and tested through an elaborate course that begins with preliminary research in the lab and continues through trials with human participants, review and approval by the FDA, and monitoring of the drug's effects even after it is on the market. The process may take 12 years or more, and only about 20% of drugs are eventually approved for marketing.

When results of research studies are published in medical journals, a community of scientists, physicians, researchers, and scholars has the opportunity to share the findings and enter a dialogue about the subject. Publication of research often prompts further research designed to replicate and confirm the findings, challenge the conclusions, or pursue a related line of thought or experiment. (For guidelines on how to interpret research when

Conventional Western medicine is firmly grounded in scientific explanations resulting from the application of the scientific method to a question or problem.

it is reported in the popular press, see the box "Evaluating Health News" on p. 622.)

The Providers of Conventional Medicine

Conventional medicine is practiced by a wide range of health care professionals in the United States. Several kinds of professionals are permitted to practice specific fields of medicine independently, including medical doctors, osteopaths, podiatrists, optometrists, and dentists (Table 20.2).

conventional medicine A system of medicine based on the application of the scientific method; diseases are thought to be caused by identifiable physical factors and characterized by a representative set of symptoms; also called biomedicine or standard Western medicine.

pharmaceuticals Medical drugs, both prescription and over-the-counter.

TERMS

Evaluating Health News

Health-related research is now described in popular newspapers and magazines rather than just medical journals, meaning that more and more people have access to the information. Greater access is certainly a plus, but news reports of research studies may oversimplify or exaggerate both the results and what those results mean to the average person. Researchers do not set out to mislead people, but they must often strike a balance between reporting promising preliminary findings to the public, thereby allowing people to act on them, and waiting 10–20 years until long-term studies confirm (or disprove) a particular finding.

All this can leave you in a difficult position. You cannot become an expert on all subjects, capable of effectively evaluating all the available health news. However, the following questions can help you better assess the health advice that appears in the popular media:

1. *Is the report based on research or on an anecdote?* Information or advice based on one or more carefully designed research studies has more validity than one person's experiences.

2. *What is the source of the information?* A study published in a respected peer-reviewed journal has been examined by editors and other researchers in the field, people who are in a position to evaluate the merits of a study and its results. Many journal articles also include information on the authors and funders of research, alerting readers to any possible conflicts of interest. Research presented at medical meetings should be considered very preliminary because the results have not yet undergone a thorough prepublication review; many such studies are never published. It is also wise to ask who funded a study to determine whether there is any potential for bias. Information from government agencies and national research organizations is usually considered fairly reliable.

3. *How big was the study?* A study involving many subjects is more likely to yield reliable results than a study involving only a few subjects. Another important indication that a finding is meaningful is if several studies yield the same results.

4. *Who were the participants involved in the study?* Research findings are more likely to apply to you if you share important characteristics with the participants in the study. For example, the results of a study on men over age 50 who smoke may not be particularly meaningful for a 30-year-old nonsmoking woman. Even less applicable are studies done in test tubes or on animals. Such research should be considered very preliminary in terms of its applicability to humans. Promising results from laboratory or animal research frequently cannot be replicated in human study subjects.

5. *What kind of study was it?* Epidemiological studies involve observation or interviews in order to trace the relationships among lifestyle, physical characteristics, and diseases. While epidemiological studies can suggest links, they cannot establish cause-and-effect relationships. Clinical or interventional studies or trials involve testing the effects of different treatments on groups of people who have similar lifestyles and characteristics. They are more likely to provide conclusive evidence of a cause-and-effect relationship. The best interventional studies share the following characteristics:

- *Controlled.* A group of people who receive the treatment is compared with a matched group of people (called a *control group*) who do not receive the treatment. The matched control group may receive an inert placebo or an established active treatment.

- *Randomized.* The treatment and control groups are selected randomly.

- *Double-blind.* Researchers and participants are unaware of who is receiving the treatment.

- *Multicenter.* The experiment is performed at more than one institution.

A third type of study, meta-analysis, involves combining the results of individual studies to get an overall view of the effectiveness of a treatment.

6. *What do the statistics really say?* First, are the results described as statistically significant? If a study is large and well designed, its results can be deemed statistically significant, meaning there is less than a 5% chance that the findings resulted from chance. Second, are the results stated in terms of relative or absolute risk? Many findings are reported in terms of relative risk—how a particular treatment or condition affects a person's disease risk. Consider the following examples of relative risk:

- According to some estimates, taking estrogen without progesterone can increase a postmenopausal woman's risk of dying from endometrial cancer by 233%.

- Giving AZT to HIV-infected pregnant women reduces prenatal transmission of HIV by about 90%.

The first of these findings seems far more dramatic than the second—until you also consider absolute risk, the actual risk of the illness in the population being considered. The absolute risk of endometrial cancer is 0.3%; a 233% increase based on the effects of estrogen raises it to 1%, a change of 0.7%. Without treatment, about 25% of infants born to HIV-infected women will be infected with HIV; with treatment, the absolute risk drops to about 2%, a change of 23%. Because the absolute risk of an HIV-infected mother passing the virus to her infant (25%) is so much greater than a woman's risk of developing endometrial cancer compared with (0.3%), a smaller change in relative risk translates into a much greater change in absolute risk.

7. *Is new health advice being offered?* If the media report new guidelines for health behavior or medical treatment, examine the source. Government agencies and national research foundations usually consider a great deal of evidence before offering health advice. Above all, use common sense, and check with your physician before making a major change in your health habits based on news reports.

Table 20.2	Health Care Professionals in the United States, 2007
Profession	**Number**
Pharmacists	253,110
Family/general practitioners	113,250
Dentists	85,260
Surgeons	50,260
Pediatricians	28,890
Optometrists	24,900
Psychiatrists	21,790
Obstetricians and gynecologists	21,340
Podiatrists	9,320

SOURCE: U.S. Department of Labor, Bureau of Labor Statistics. 2008. *Occupational Employment and Wages, May 2007: Healthcare Practitioner and Technical Occupations (Major Groups)* (http://www.bls.gov/oes/current/oes290000.htm; retrieved February 20, 2009).

- **Medical doctors** are practitioners who hold a doctor of medicine (M.D.) degree from an accredited medical school. In the United States, an education in medicine has several stages: 4 years of premedical education in a college or university, with an emphasis on the sciences; 4 years of medical school, which teaches basic medical skills and awards the M.D. degree; graduate medical study, called an internship and residency and lasting from 3 to 7 years, during which a specialty is chosen and studied and a medical license is obtained; and continuing medical education to keep abreast of advances in medical science. Twenty-four medical specialties are currently approved by the American Board of Medical Specialties, each with its own rule-making and certifying body.

- **Doctors of osteopathic medicine** (D.O.) receive a medical education similar to that of medical doctors, but their training places special emphasis on musculoskeletal problems and manipulative therapy. M.D.s and D.O.s are the two types of "complete" physicians in the United States, meaning they are trained and licensed to perform surgery and prescribe medication. D.O.s are graduates of osteopathic medical schools, which emphasize training students to be primary care physicians and to practice a whole-person approach to medicine.

- **Podiatrists** are practitioners who specialize in the medical and surgical care of the feet. They hold a doctor of podiatric medicine (D.P.M.) degree; the length of training is similar to that of M.D.s. They can prescribe drugs and perform surgery on the feet.

- **Optometrists** are practitioners trained to examine the eyes, detect eye diseases, and treat vision problems. They hold a doctor of optometry (O.D.) degree. All states permit optometrists to use drugs for diagnostic purposes, and most permit them to use drugs to treat minor eye problems. (Ophthalmologists are M.D. eye specialists who care for all types of eye problems and can perform eye surgery.)

- **Dentists** specialize in the care of the teeth and mouth. They are graduates of 4-year dental schools and hold the doctor of dental surgery (D.D.S.) or doctor of medical dentistry (D.M.D.) degree; specialists receive additional education. Dentists can perform surgery and prescribe drugs within the scope of their training.

In addition to these practitioners, there are millions of other trained health care professionals, known as **allied health care providers**, working in the United States. Some of them are licensed to work independently; others are permitted to work under medical supervision or medical referral. They include registered nurses (R.N.s), licensed vocational nurses (L.V.N.s), physical therapists, social workers, registered dietitians (R.D.s), physician assistants (P.A.s), nurse practitioners, and certified nurse midwives.

Choosing a Primary Care Physician

Most experts believe it is best to have a primary care physician, someone who gets to know you, who coordinates your medical care, and who refers you to specialists when you need them. Primary care physicians include those certified in family practice, internal medicine, pediatrics, and gynecology. These physicians are able to diagnose and treat the vast majority of common health problems; they also provide many preventive health services. The best time to look for a physician is before you are sick (see the box "Health Care Visits and Gender" on p. 624).

TERMS

medical doctor An independent practitioner who holds a doctor of medicine degree from an accredited medical school.

doctor of osteopathic medicine A medical practitioner who has graduated from an osteopathic medical school; osteopathy incorporates the theories and practices of scientific medicine but focuses on musculoskeletal problems and manipulative therapy.

podiatrist A practitioner who holds a doctor of podiatric medicine degree and specializes in the medical and surgical care of the feet.

optometrist A practitioner who holds a doctor of optometry degree and is trained to examine the eyes, detect eye diseases, and prescribe corrective lenses.

dentist A practitioner who holds a doctor of medical dentistry or doctor of dental surgery degree and who specializes in the prevention and treatment of diseases and injuries of the teeth, mouth, and jaws.

allied health care providers Health care professionals who typically provide services under the supervision or control of independent practitioners.

Health Care Visits and Gender

In 2006, Americans made about 902 million visits to office-based physicians. Females are more likely than males to visit a health care provider (see figure). Women age 18–44 make nearly twice as many physician visits as do men. Women are also more likely to report use of complementary and alternative therapies.

What are some of the factors underlying this difference? Reproductive health care needs may be one key factor, with women making doctor visits related to prenatal care and childbirth. Women of reproductive age may also need to make health care visits in order to obtain prescription contraceptives and have the pelvic exams and Pap tests required to obtain certain contraceptives.

Even when physician visits related to reproductive care are discounted, however, women are more likely than men to see a health care provider, especially for preventive care. Male gender roles may be a factor in this trend, with men being socialized to be strong and tough, to ignore pain or symptoms of illness, or to feel that physician visits for preventive care (when no symptoms are present) are unnecessary. And without preventive-care visits, men may be unaware of such asymptomatic conditions as high cholesterol levels or high blood pressure, which, once diagnosed, would require regular visits for monitoring and treatment.

At all ages, it is important for both men and women to obtain recommended health care screenings and immunizations. Preventive care throughout life is important to maximize wellness. Don't wait until you are ill before you see a physician.

SOURCES: Centers for Disease Control and Prevention. 2008. National Ambulatory Medical Care Survey: 2006 Summary. *National Health Statistics Reports* No. 3. Hyattsville, Md.: National Center for Health Statistics.

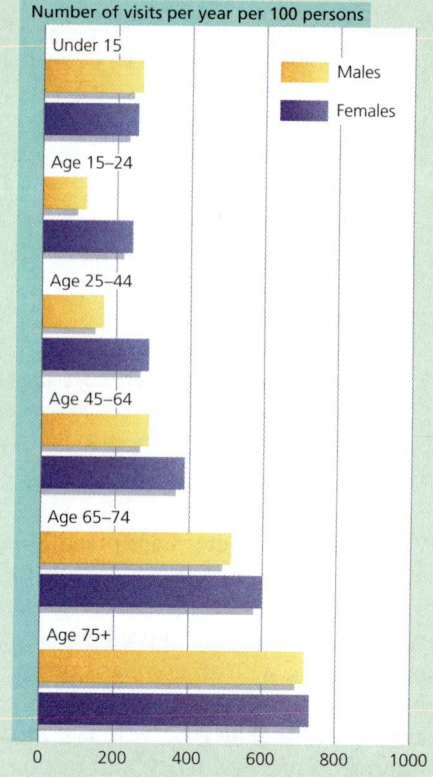

Health care visits by age and gender, 2006

To select a physician, begin by making a list of possible choices. If your insurance limits the health care providers you can see, check the plan's list first. Student health services or health maintenance organizations (discussed later) may assign you a physician. If your health plan lets you choose a physician, ask for recommendations from family, friends, coworkers, local medical societies, and the physician referral service at a local clinic or hospital. Some clinics provide brief biographies of physicians on staff who are taking new patients. If you have a particular health problem, you may want to identify physicians who are board-certified in appropriate specialties. Once you have a list of possible physicians, find out if a consumer or other independent group has rated doctors in your area; this will help you check on the quality of care they provide.

Once you have the names of a few physicians you might want to try, call their offices to find out information such as the following:

- Is the physician covered by your health plan and accepting new patients?

- What are the office hours, and when is the physician or office staff available? What do patients do if they need urgent care or have an emergency?

- Which hospitals does the physician use?

- How many other physicians are available to cover when he or she isn't available, and who are they?

- How long does it usually take to get a routine appointment?

- Does the office send reminders about preventive tests such as Pap tests?

- Does the physician (or a nurse or physician assistant) give advice over the phone for common problems?

Schedule a visit with the physician you think you would most like to use. During that first visit, you'll get a sense of how well matched you are and how well he or she might meet your medical needs.

Getting the Most Out of Your Medical Care

The key to making the health care system work for you lies in good communication with your physician and other members of the health care team. Studies show that patients who interact more with physicians and ask more questions enjoy better health outcomes.

The Physician-Patient Partnership The physician-patient relationship is undergoing an important transformation. The image of the all-knowing physician and the passive patient is fading. What is emerging is a physician-patient *partnership,* in which the physician acts more like a consultant and the patient participates more actively. You should expect your physician to be attentive, caring, and able to listen and clearly explain things to you. You also must do your part. You need to be assertive in a firm but nonaggressive manner. You need to express your feelings and concerns, ask questions and, if necessary, be persistent. If your physician is unable to communicate clearly with you despite your best efforts, you probably need to change physicians.

Your Appointment with Your Physician Physicians are often pressed for time, so prepare for your visit ahead of time. Make a written list of your key concerns and questions, along with notes about your symptoms (when they started, how long they last, what makes them better or worse, what treatments you have already tried, and so on). If there are questions you're uncomfortable about asking, practice discussing them ahead of time. Bring a list of all the medications you're taking—prescription, nonprescription, and herbal. Also bring any medical records or test results your physician may not already have.

Present your concerns at the beginning of the visit, to set the agenda. Be specific and concise about your symptoms, and be open and honest about your concerns. Share your hunches with your physician—your guesses can provide vital clues. Ask questions if you don't understand something. Let your physician know if you are taking any drugs, are allergic to any medications, are breast-feeding, or may be pregnant.

At the end of the visit, briefly repeat the physician's diagnosis, prognosis, and instructions. Make sure you understand your next steps, such as making another appointment, phoning for test results, watching for new symptoms, and so on. You may also want to ask about the possibility of using e-mail for follow-up.

The Diagnostic Process The first step in the diagnostic process is the medical history, which includes your primary reason for the visit, your current symptoms, your past medical history, and your social history (job, family life, major stressors, living conditions, and health habits). Keeping up-to-date records of your medical history can help you provide your physician with key facts about your health (see the box "Personal Health Profile" on p. 626).

The next step is the physical exam, which usually begins with a review of vital signs: blood pressure, heart rate (pulse), breathing rate, and temperature. Depending on your primary complaint, your physician may give you a complete physical, or the exam may be directed to specific areas, such as your ears, nose, and throat.

Additionally, your physician may order medical tests to complete the diagnosis. Diagnostic testing provides a wealth of information to help solve medical problems. Physicians can order X rays, biopsies, blood and urine

Good communication is a crucial factor in an effective physician-patient partnership.

tests, scans, and **endoscopies** to view, probe, or analyze almost any part of the body.

If your physician orders a test for you, be sure you know why you need it, what the risks and benefits of the test are for you, how you should prepare for it (for example, by fasting or discontinuing medications or herbal remedies), and what the test will involve. Also ask what the test results mean, because no test is 100% accurate—**false positives** and **false negatives** do occur—and interpretation of some tests is subjective. Sometimes it is important to get a second opinion on a diagnosis.

Medical and Surgical Treatments Many conditions can be treated in a variety of ways; in some cases, lifestyle changes are enough. Make sure you know the possible risks and side effects of each treatment option, as well as the likelihood that it will improve your condition.

PRESCRIPTION MEDICATIONS Each month, between 40% and 50% of Americans use at least one prescription medication;

endoscopy A medical procedure in which a viewing instrument is inserted into a body cavity or opening.

false positive A test result that incorrectly detects a disease or condition in a healthy person.

false negative A test result that fails to correctly detect a disease or condition.

TERMS

Personal Health Profile

General Information

Age: _____ Total cholesterol: _____ Blood pressure: _____ / _____ Other: _____

Height: _____ HDL: _____ Triglycerides: _____ _____

Weight: _____ LDL: _____ Glucose: _____ _____

Medical Conditions

Check any of the following that apply to you and add other conditions that might affect your health and well-being.

_____ heart disease   _____ back pain   _____ depression, anxiety, or another psychological disorder

_____ lung disease   _____ arthritis   _____ major stressors

_____ diabetes   _____ other injury or joint problem   _____ eating disorder

_____ allergies   _____ other: _____

_____ asthma   _____ substance abuse problem   _____ other: _____

Medications/Treatments

List any drugs you are taking or any medical treatments you are undergoing. Include the name of the substance or treatment and its purpose. Include both prescription and OTC drugs and any vitamin, mineral, herb, or other dietary supplement you are taking.

_____   _____   _____

_____   _____   _____

Health Care Providers

Primary care physician: name _____   phone _____

Specialist physician: name _____   phone _____

   Condition treated: _____

Other health care provider: name _____   phone _____

   Condition treated: _____

Health insurance provider and policy number: _____

To ensure that you get the most out of your medical care, you should also keep a record of your vaccinations and medical screening tests. Chapters 15–18 describe recommended vaccinations and screening tests for CVD, cancer, and STDs.

---

among those 65 and older, between 80% and 90% are current prescription drug users. Thousands of lives are saved each year by antibiotics, insulin, and other drugs, but we pay a price for having such powerful tools. A 2006 report from the Institute of Medicine (IOM) estimates that 1.5 million prescription drug-related errors—called *adverse drug events,* or ADEs—occur each year in the United States. ADEs happen for several reasons:

• *Medication errors:* Physicians may overprescribe drugs, sometimes in response to pressure by patients (see the box "Medical Errors, Adverse Events, and Their Prevention"). Adverse effects can occur if a physician prescribes the wrong drug or a dangerous combination of drugs; such problems are especially prevalent for older adults, who typically take multiple medications. The risk of ADEs increases greatly with the number of medicines you take. At the pharmacy, patients may receive the wrong drug or may not be given complete information about drug risks, side effects, and interactions. Problems can occur because of a physician's poor handwriting, misinterpretation of an abbreviated drug name, or similarities between the names and packaging of different drugs.

• *Off-label drug use:* Another potential problem is off-label use of drugs. Once a drug is approved by the FDA for

Medical Errors, Adverse Events, and Their Prevention

The Institute of Medicine (IOM) estimates that 44,000 to 98,000 deaths occur each year in hospitals due to medical errors. Even at the lower estimate, medical errors could rank as one of the ten leading causes of death in the United States. These numbers represent hospital incidents, but similar errors occur in other settings, including health clinics, urgent care centers, nursing homes, and pharmacies. The cost of medical errors to the nation is approximately $37.6 billion yearly.

The IOM defines a *medical error* as "the failure to complete a planned action as intended or the use of a wrong plan to achieve an aim." An *adverse event* is "an injury caused by medical management rather than by the underlying disease or condition of the patient."

Medical errors take a variety of forms. They may involve surgical mismanagement such as removal of the wrong kidney, misdiagnosis leading to incorrect therapy, misinterpretation of or failure to order diagnostic tests, failure to act on abnormal test results, equipment failure, blood transfusion injuries, misinterpretation of physician orders leading to use of the wrong drug or an incorrect dosage, and hospital-acquired infections.

Medication Errors

Errors involving medication are fairly common in the United States. In Massachusetts alone, the State Board of Registration in Pharmacy estimates that 2.4 million prescriptions are improperly filled each year. Nationally, about 7000 patients die each year from medication errors.

The FDA defines a *medication error* as "any preventable event that may cause or lead to inappropriate medication use or patient harm while the medication is in the control of the health care professional, patient, or consumer." Such events may be related to practice, including prescribing; order communication; and product labeling, packaging, dispensing, administration, and use.

Hospital Errors

Approximately 10 percent of all hospitalized patients acquire a significant infection. Most are caused by common bacteria that normally inhabit the skin and mucous membranes. The most common infections involve the urinary tract, surgical wounds, the respiratory tract, and skin. Proper handling of equipment and frequent hand washing by providers are the major ways to avoid such infections.

Prevention Within the System

Fortunately, most errors are in fact preventable. Major system improvements proposed in an IOM report include the following:

- *The application of standardized procedure and equipment guidelines.* For example, the error rate in anesthesia was cut by a factor of seven when standardized protocols and equipment were used.

- *Medical rounds that include a pharmacist.* By adding a pharmacist to the team, medication error rates were reduced by 66%.

- *The use of computer technology and barcodes.* In a Veteran's Hospital, wireless computer technology and barcoding reduced medication errors 70%.

Studies show that most medical errors are system-related and not attributable to negligence or misconduct by individual providers. Public awareness of these issues can be used to encourage patient participation and empowerment, and these may be the best defenses against medical errors.

Prevention Through Patient Involvement

Uninvolved and uninformed patients tend not to accept physician's recommendations or stick to treatment plans. According to the United States Agency for Healthcare Research and Quality (AHRQ), physicians often do not sufficiently help patients make informed health care decisions. Health-conscious patients inform themselves as much as possible about their condition, inquire about their health care options, and partner with their physicians, using them as information resources and health facilitators. This differs from the traditional paradigm of patients as uninformed, compliant, passive, and accepting of whatever the doctor decides. The AHRQ says the most effective way a patient can help prevent medical errors is by taking an active role in the health care team.

As a patient, you can take the following steps to prevent medical errors:

- *Take all medications exactly as prescribed, for as long as prescribed.* If you don't understand why you are being given a medication, ask your physician or pharmacist to explain.

- *If you require hospitalization, select your hospital carefully.* If possible, choose a hospital with extensive experience treating patients with your type of condition. Research has shown that patients who do this can expect better results and fewer complications.

- *When being discharged from a hospital, ask about any special care, precautions, medications, and other procedures that will be required upon returning home.* Studies show that physicians assume patients understand more about their discharge instructions than they actually do.

- *If you have doubts about the care you're getting, recruit a patient advocate.* This is someone who can give support and speak on your behalf in order to protect your rights, promote your interests, and assist you in making decisions. Formally trained patient advocates are rare, but an advocate can be a close friend or family member who is tactful, able to take accurate notes, and who has the time and concern to devote to your clinical visit or hospitalization.

- *If you require hospitalization, rely on a hospitalist.* A *hospitalist* is a physician who specializes in the care of only hospitalized patients. Hospitalists focus on advocacy and safety, and help remedy the lack of continuity that occurs among hospital providers. Hospitalists manage a patient's course through the hospital, coordinate the various providers and consultants, and stay in touch with the patient's family and primary care physician. Hospitalists help remedy many of the problems that lead to medical errors and may potentially reduce their number and seriousness.

one purpose, it can legally be prescribed (although not marketed) for purposes not listed on the label. A recent study revealed that about 20% of medications are prescribed for off-label use; three-quarters of those prescriptions are made with little or no evidence supporting such use. Many off-label uses are safe and supported by some research, but both consumers and health care providers need to take special care with off-label use of medications.

• *Online pharmacies:* Although convenient, some online pharmacies may sell products or engage in practices that are illegal in the offline world, putting consumers at risk for receiving adulterated, expired, ineffective, or counterfeit drugs. The FDA recommends that consumers avoid sites that prescribe drugs for the first time without a physical exam, sell prescription drugs without a prescription, or sell medications not approved by the FDA. You should also avoid sites that do not provide access to a registered pharmacist to answer questions or that do not provide a U.S. address and phone number to contact if there's a problem. The National Association of Boards of Pharmacy sponsors a voluntary certification program for Internet pharmacies. To be certified, a pharmacy must have a state license and allow regular inspections. Many experts recommend that consumers use online pharmacies only to obtain medicines prescribed by their usual health care provider.

• *Costs:* Spending on prescription drugs is rising faster than the rate of inflation and is now the fastest-growing portion of U.S. health care spending. Many Americans have no or limited insurance coverage for prescription drug costs. Consumers may be able to lower their drug costs by using generic versions of medications; by joining a drug discount program sponsored by a company, organization, or local pharmacy; and by investigating mail-order or Internet pharmacies.

There is ongoing controversy about the importation of lower-cost drugs from Canada. Canada imports U.S. drugs and regulates Canadian-produced drugs, so safety should theoretically not be a concern for drugs from Canada. However, companies in Canada may make drugs for export only, thus avoiding regulation, and online pharmacies may claim they are operating in Canada but may be located in another country where there is little or no regulation. U.S. regulators have found online sites advertising Canadian drugs but shipping fake or substandard versions of medications. In addition, shipping costs can be high, and U.S. generic drugs are often less expensive than Canadian drugs.

Patients also share some responsibility for problems with prescription drugs. Many people don't take their medications properly, skipping doses, taking incorrect doses, stopping too soon, or not taking the medication at all. An estimated 30–50% of the more than 3 billion prescriptions dispensed annually in the United States are not taken correctly and thus do not produce the desired results. Consumers can increase the safety and effectiveness of their treatment by carefully reading any prescription's label (Figure 20.3) and fact sheets or brochures that come with the medication. Whenever a health care provider gives you a prescription, ask the following questions:

• Are there non-drug alternatives?

• What is the name of the medication, and what is it supposed to do, within what period of time?

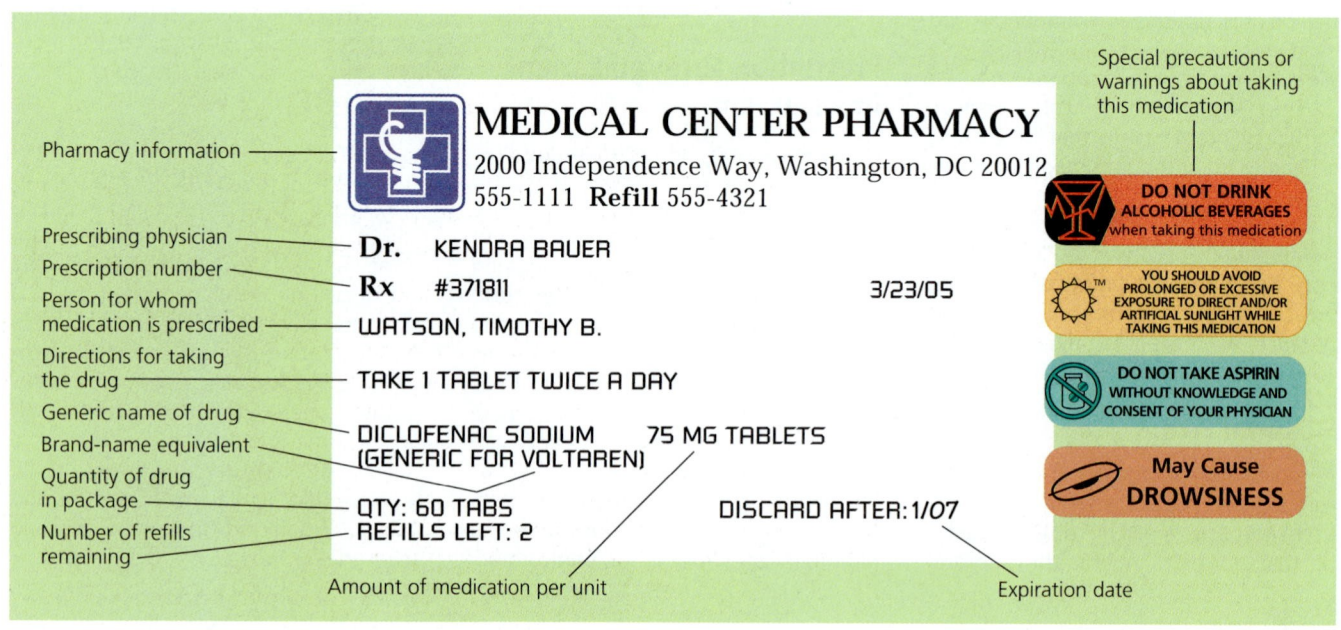

FIGURE 20.3 **Reading and understanding prescription medication labels.**

- How and when do I take the medication, how much do I take, and for how long? What should I do if I miss a dose?
- What other medications, foods, drinks, or activities should I avoid?
- What are the side effects, and what do I do if they occur?
- Can I take a generic drug rather than a brand-name one?
- Is there written information about the medication?

Remember to store your medications in a cool, dry place, out of direct light. Never share your prescription medications with anyone else, and never use an old prescription for a new ailment.

SURGERY Surgical procedures are performed more often in the United States than anywhere else in the world. Each year, more than 70 million operations and related procedures are performed. About 20% are in response to an emergency such as a severe injury, and 80% are **elective surgeries,** meaning the patient can generally choose when and where to have the operation, if at all. Many elective surgeries can be done on an **outpatient** basis, so the patient does not have to be admitted to a hospital for the procedure.

If a health care provider suggests surgery for any reason, ask the following questions:

- Why do I need surgery at this time?
- Are any nonsurgical options available, such as medicine or physical therapy?
- What are the risks and complications of the surgery?
- Can the operation be performed on an outpatient basis?
- What can I expect before, during, and after surgery?

COMPLEMENTARY AND ALTERNATIVE MEDICINE

Where conventional Western medicine tends to focus on the body, on the physical causes of disease, and on ways to eradicate pathogens in order to restore health, CAM tends to focus on an integration of mind, body, and spirit in seeking ways to restore the whole person to harmony so that he or she can regain health. Where conventional medicine is based primarily on science, CAM tends to be based on healing traditions and accumulated experience.

Many alternative medical systems with long-standing traditions have concepts and theories of medicine that once were very different from those of conventional Western medical thought. Some people consider all of CAM quackery and tell you that you can recognize a quack by his or her use of pseudoscientific language. However, the use of phrases like "bringing into harmony with nature" or "enhancing the flow of vital energy" does not necessarily mean that a practitioner is a quack; rather, it may reflect this practitioner's different concept of health and healing.

You might have heard that there are only anecdotal testimonials to support the value of many forms of CAM and that because such reports do not constitute scientific proof of effectiveness, they are therefore meaningless. Although it is correct that anecdotes and testimonials are not scientifically reliable evidence, that does not mean that they are meaningless. What is called anecdotal evidence may actually be a form of case report, a valuable and standard form of study in which a researcher describes a single patient, his or her medical history, the treatments administered, and the outcome of the case. Still, case reports alone are not sufficient to scientifically prove the effectiveness of a medical treatment. Caution is in order when choosing any mode of treatment—conventional or unconventional—that has not been scientifically evaluated for safety and effectiveness (see the box "Avoiding Health Fraud and Quackery" on p. 630).

NCCAM groups CAM practices into five domains: alternative medical systems, mind-body interventions, biological-based therapies, manipulative and body-based methods, and energy therapies (Figure 20.4, p. 630). It is impossible to discuss all of these forms fully in a single chapter. Instead, what follows is a general introduction to the types of CAM available and a brief description of some of the more widely used ones.

Alternative Medical Systems

Many cultures elaborated complete systems of medical philosophy, theory, and practice long before the current biomedical approach was developed. The complete systems that are best known in the United States are probably traditional Chinese medicine (TCM), also known as traditional Oriental medicine, and homeopathy. Traditional medical systems have also been developed in many other regions of the world, including North, Central, and South America; the Middle East; India; Tibet; and Australia. In

elective surgery A nonemergency operation that the patient can choose to schedule.

outpatient A person receiving medical attention without being admitted to the hospital.

TERMS

Avoiding Health Fraud and Quackery

According to the Federal Trade Commission, consumers waste billions of dollars on unproven, fraudulently marketed, and sometimes useless health care products and treatments. In addition, those with serious medical problems may waste valuable time before seeking proper treatment. Worse yet, some of the products they're buying may cause serious harm. Health fraud is a business that sells false hope. It preys on people with diseases that have no medical cure and on people who want shortcuts to weight loss or improvements to personal appearance.

To check out a particular product, talk to a physician or another health care professional and to family members and friends. Be wary of treatments offered by people who tell you to avoid talking to others. Check with the Better Business Bureau or local attorney general's office to see whether other consumers have lodged complaints about the product or the product's marketer. You can also check with the appropriate health professional group. For example, check with the American Diabetes Association or the National Arthritis Foundation if the products are promoted for diabetes or arthritis. Take special care with products and devices sold online; the broad reach of the Internet, combined with the ease of setting up and removing Web sites, makes online sellers particularly difficult to regulate.

If you think you have been a victim of health fraud or if you have an adverse reaction that you think is related to a particular supplement, you can report it to the appropriate agency:

- *False advertising claims:* Contact the FTC by phone (877-FTC-HELP), by mail (Consumer Response Center, Federal Trade Commission, Washington, DC 20580), or online (http://www.ftc.gov; click on File a Complaint). You can also contact your state attorney general's office, your state department of health, or the local consumer protection agency (check your local telephone directory).

- *False labeling on a product:* Contact the FDA district office consumer complaint coordinator for your geographic area. (The FDA regulates safety, manufacturing, and product labeling.)

- *Adverse reaction to a supplement:* Call a doctor or another health care provider immediately. You may also report your adverse reaction to FDA MedWatch by calling 800-FDA-1088 or by visiting the MedWatch Web site (http://www.fda.gov/medwatch).

- *Unlawful Internet sales:* If you find a Web site that you think is illegally selling drugs, medical devices, dietary supplements, or cosmetics, report it to the FDA. Problems can be reported to MedWatch or via the FDA Web site (http://www.fda.gov/oc/buyonline/buyonlineform.htm).

Domain	Characteristics	Examples
Alternative Medical Systems	Involve complete systems of theory and practice that have evolved independently of and often long before the conventional biomedical approach	Traditional Chinese medicine; Kampo; ayurveda (India); Native American, Aboriginal, African, Middle-Eastern, Tibetan, Central and South American medical systems; homeopathy; naturopathy
Mind-Body Interventions	Employ a variety of techniques designed to make it possible for the mind to affect bodily function and symptoms	Meditation, certain uses of hypnosis, prayer, mental healing
Biological-Based Therapies	Include natural and biologically based practices, interventions, and products, many of which overlap with conventional medicine's use of dietary supplements	Herbal, special dietary, orthomolecular,* and individual biological therapies
Manipulative and Body-Based Methods	Include methods that are based on manipulation and/or movement of the body	Chiropractic, osteopathy, massage therapy
Energy Therapies	Focus on energy fields within the body (biofields) or from other sources (electromagnetic fields)	Qi gong, Reiki, therapeutic touch, bioelectromagnetic-based therapies

*Orthomolecular therapies are treatments of diseases with varying, but usually high, concentrations of chemicals, including minerals (e.g., magnesium), hormones (e.g., melatonin), or vitamins.

FIGURE 20.4 The five domains of CAM practices.

many countries, these medical approaches continue to be used today—frequently alongside Western medicine and quite often by physicians trained in Western medicine.

Alternative medical systems tend to have concepts in common. For example, the concept of life force or energy exists in many cultures. In traditional Chinese medicine, the life force contained in all living things is called *qi* (sometimes spelled chi). Qi resembles the *vis vitalis* (Latin for "life force") of Greek, Roman, and European medical systems, and *prana* of ayurveda, the traditional medical system of India. Most traditional medical systems think of disease as a disturbance or imbalance not just of physical processes but also of forces and energies within the body, the mind, and the spirit. In traditional Chinese medicine, for example, the principle of balance is expressed as yin and yang, which are opposites yet complement each other. Disease is a disturbance of qi reflecting an imbalance between yin and yang. Treatment aims at reestablishing equilibrium, balance, and harmony.

Because the whole patient, rather than an isolated set of symptoms, is treated in most comprehensive alternative medical systems, it is rare that only a single treatment approach is used. Most commonly, multiple techniques and methods are employed and are continually adjusted according to the changes in the patient's health status that occur naturally or are brought about by the treatment.

Traditional Chinese Medicine Traditional Chinese medicine (TCM) is based on highly abstract concepts; a sophisticated set of techniques and methods; and individualized diagnosis, treatment, and prevention. No identical diseases exist in TCM. Two patients with the same diagnosis in Western medicine will get different diagnoses in TCM and will be given different treatments.

In TCM, the free and harmonious flow of qi produces health—a positive feeling of well-being and vitality in body, mind, and spirit. Illness occurs when the flow of qi is blocked or disturbed. TCM works to restore and balance the flow of blocked qi; the goal is not only to treat illnesses but also to increase energy, prevent disease, and support the immune system.

Two of the primary treatment methods in TCM are herbal remedies and **acupuncture.** Chinese herbal remedies number about 5800 and include plant products, animal parts, and minerals. Herbal remedies, like everything else, have yin and yang properties. When a disease is perceived to be due to a yin deficiency, remedies with more yin characteristics might be used for treatment. The use of a single medicinal botanical is rare in Chinese herbal medicine; rather, several different plants are combined in very precise proportions, often to make a tea or soup. For example, a remedy might include a primary herb that targets the main symptom, a second herb that enhances the effects of the primary herb, a third that lessens side effects, and a fourth that helps deliver ingredients to a particular body site.

Acupuncture works to correct disturbances in the flow of qi through the insertion of thin needles at appropriate points in the skin. Qi is believed to flow through the body along several *meridians*, or pathways, and there are at least 2000 acupuncture points located along these meridians. Acupuncturists use a variety of diagnostic techniques to identify the nature of the imbalance in a patient and to choose the points at which acupuncture needs to be applied. The traditional method consists of inserting the needle and leaving it in place for 20–40 minutes. Other means of stimulating acupuncture points include heat,

traditional Chinese medicine (TCM) The traditional medical system of China, which views illness as the result of a disturbance in the flow of qi, the life force; therapies include acupuncture, herbal medicine, and massage.

acupuncture Insertion of thin needles into the skin at points along meridians, pathways through which qi is believed to flow.

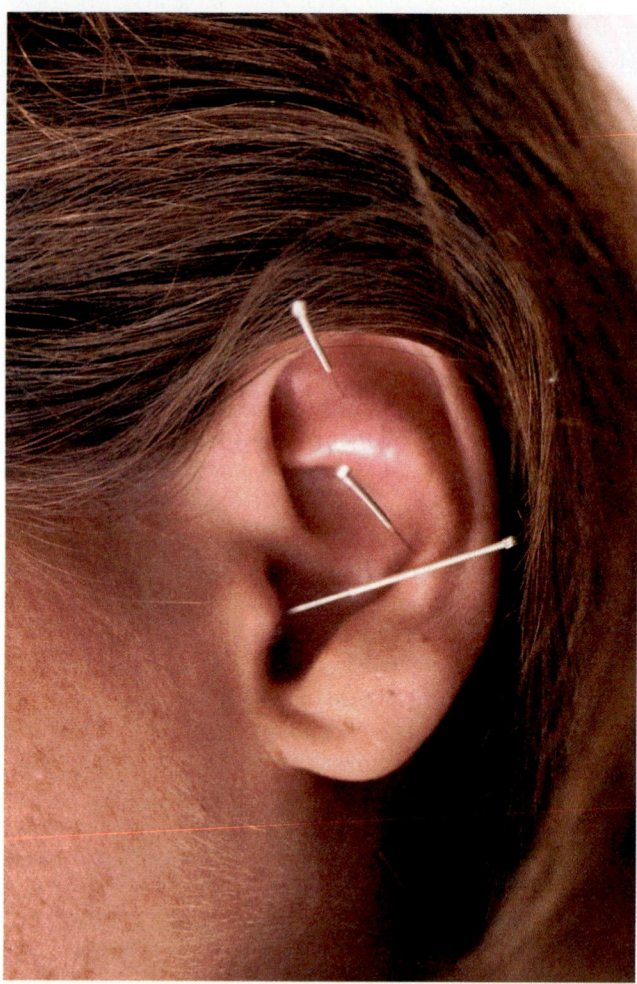

Acupuncture involves the insertion of needles at appropriate points in the skin to restore balance to the flow of qi.

surgery. Newer studies show that acupuncture may help relieve the painful symptoms of fibromyalgia and reduce the joint pain and stiffness of osteoarthritis. There is not yet enough evidence to show conclusively that acupuncture is effective for menstrual cramps, tennis elbow, carpal tunnel syndrome, asthma, or certain other conditions. Western researchers typically use a different framework for understanding the effects of acupuncture. For example, they might explain pain relief not in terms of qi but in terms of altering nervous system pathways and the release of hormones and neurotransmitters.

Very few negative side effects have been reported in conjunction with acupuncture. Nonetheless, problems can occur from the improper insertion and manipulation of needles and from the use of unsterile needles. The FDA regulates acupuncture needles like other standard medical devices and requires that they be sterile. If you consider acupuncture, you should ask your practitioner about the relative risks of the procedure and the safety practices he or she observes. Most states require licensing for acupuncture practitioners, but requirements vary widely.

Homeopathy An alternative medical system of Western origin, **homeopathy** is based on two main principles: "Like cures like," and remedies become more effective with greater dilution. "Like cures like" summarizes the concept that a substance that produces the symptoms of an illness in a healthy person can cure the illness when given in very minute quantities. Remedies containing very small quantities of a particular substance are obtained by repeatedly diluting the original solution. The extent of dilution varies, but the final extract is often so dilute that few, if any, of the original molecules are left in it. According to homeopathic thinking, such highly diluted extracts not only retain some form of biological activity but actually become more potent.

Over 1000 different substances (plant and animal parts, minerals, and chemicals) are used to prepare homeopathic remedies, and each of these substances is thought to have different effects at different dilutions. That means a homeopath must not only choose the correct remedy for a particular patient but also decide on the specific dilution of that remedy in order to achieve the desired effect.

Like other traditional systems of medicine, homeopathy constitutes a highly individualized form of therapy; that is, the treatment of each patient is determined by the overall condition of the patient rather than by specific signs and symptoms. In order to assess a patient's condition, homeopaths generally spend quite a bit of time talking with a patient and assessing his or her physical, psychological, and emotional health before deciding on the correct remedy at the proper dilution. This intensive interaction between the practitioner and the patient might play an important role in the success of the therapy. Indeed, critics of homeopathy often attribute its reported effectiveness to this nonspecific placebo effect (see the box "The Power of

pressure, friction, suction, or electric stimulation. The points chosen for acupuncture are highly individualized for each patient, and they change over the course of treatment as the patient's health status changes.

The World Health Organization has compiled a list of over 40 conditions in which acupuncture may be beneficial. At a conference called by the National Institutes of Health (NIH), a panel of experts recently analyzed the available information on the scientific evidence for the efficacy of acupuncture in many of these conditions. These experts found evidence that acupuncture was effective in relieving nausea and vomiting after chemotherapy and pain after surgery, including dental

QUICK STATS

More than **8 million** Americans have had acupuncture at least once.

—CDC, 2005

The Power of Belief: The Placebo Effect connect

A placebo is a chemically inactive substance or ineffective procedure that a patient believes is an effective therapy for his or her condition. Researchers frequently give placebos to the control group in an experiment testing the efficacy of a particular drug or other treatment. By comparing the effects of the actual treatment with the effects of the placebo, researchers can judge whether the treatment is effective.

The *placebo effect* occurs when a patient improves after receiving a placebo. In such cases, the effect of the placebo on the patient cannot be attributed to the specific actions or properties of the drug or procedure.

Researchers have consistently found that 30–40% of all patients given a placebo show improvement. This result has been observed for a wide variety of conditions or symptoms, including coughing, seasickness, depression, migraines, and angina. For some conditions, placebos have been effective in up to 70% of patients. In some cases, people given a placebo even report having the side effects associated with an actual drug. Placebos are particularly effective when they are administered by a practitioner whom the patient trusts.

A clear demonstration of the placebo effect occurred in a recent study that examined the effectiveness of a drug used to treat benign enlargement of the pros-

tate. The men who participated in the study were randomly assigned to one of two groups: One group received the medication; the other received a placebo, a look-alike dummy pill. More than half the men who got the placebo pills reported significant relief from their symptoms, including faster urine flow—despite the fact that men on the placebo actually experienced an *increase* in the size of their prostates.

How did the men in the study experience fewer symptoms despite no actual improvement in their condition? Researchers hypothesize that the patients' positive expectations of the medication's effects may have resulted in changes in nerve activity and muscle relaxation affecting the bladder, prostate, and urethra.

Studies on patients with depression and people with Parkinson's disease have found that treatment with an inactive placebo results in changes in brain function. Such changes in the electrical or chemical activity of the brain may help explain the placebo effect.

The placebo effect can be exploited by unscrupulous people who sell worthless medical treatments to the scientifically unsophisticated public. But placebo power can also be harnessed for its beneficial effects. When a skilled and compassionate medical practitioner provides a patient with a sense of confidence and hope, the positive aspects of placebo

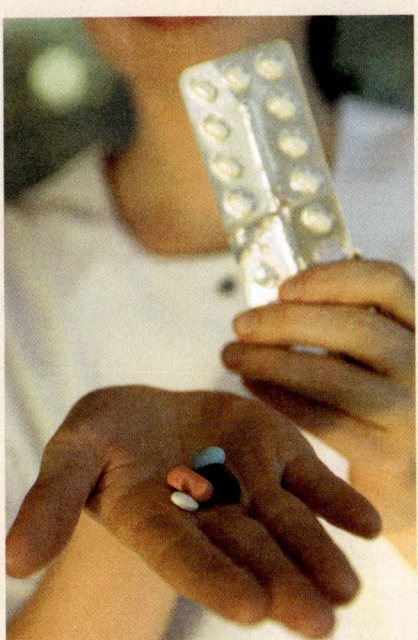

power can boost the benefits of standard medical treatment. Whenever you swallow a pill, you swallow your expectations right along with the medication or herb; imagining how the pill is helping you can stimulate a positive placebo effect. Getting well, like getting sick, is a complex process. Anatomy, physiology, mind, emotions, and the environment are all inextricably intertwined. But the placebo effect does show that belief can have both psychological and physical effects.

Belief: The Placebo Effect"). However, when the results of 185 homeopathic trials were analyzed recently, it was concluded that the clinical effects of homeopathy could not be completely explained by the placebo effect. Homeopathy remains one of the most controversial forms of CAM.

Because of the extremely dilute nature of homeopathic remedies, it is generally assumed that they are safe. To date, the FDA has not found any serious adverse events associated with the use of homeopathy, with the possible exception of situations in which a patient might have been successfully treated with standard medical approaches but chose to rely solely on homeopathy. The FDA regulates some homeopathic remedies, but they are subject to many fewer restrictions than prescription or over-the-counter drugs. Remedies designed to treat conditions such as colds and headaches can be sold over the counter; products that claim to treat serious conditions such as heart disease can be sold only by prescription. A few states require practitio-

ners to have special licenses, but most providers practice homeopathy as a specialty under another medical license, such as medical doctor or nurse practitioner.

Mind-Body Interventions

Mind-body interventions make use of the integral connection between mind and body and the effect each can have on the other. They include many of the stress-management techniques discussed in Chapter 2, including meditation, yoga, visualization, taijiquan, and biofeedback. Psychotherapy, support groups, prayer, and music, art, and dance

> **homeopathy** An alternative medical system that treats illnesses by giving very small doses of drugs that in larger doses would produce symptoms like those of the illness.
>
> **TERMS**

therapy can also be thought of as mind-body interventions. The placebo effect is one of the most widely known examples of mind-body interdependence.

Some forms of **hypnosis** are considered to be CAM therapies, although the use of hypnotherapy for certain conditions was accepted more than 40 years ago by the American Medical Association. Hypnosis involves the induction of a state of deep relaxation during which the patient is more suggestible (more easily influenced). While the patient is in such a hypnotic trance, the practitioner tries to help him or her change unwanted behavior or deal with pain and other symptoms. An NIH-sponsored report found strong evidence for the effectiveness of relaxation techniques and hypnosis in reducing chronic pain stemming from a variety of medical conditions, although subsequent studies have cast some doubt on this conclusion. Hypnosis is sometimes used in smoking cessation programs and as a nondrug approach to anxiety disorders such as phobias and chronic conditions such as irritable bowel syndrome. It has been shown to help some women deal with the pain of childbirth with less medication.

Hypnosis can be used by medical professionals (M.D.s, D.O.s, D.D.S.s) but is also offered by hypnotherapists. Physicians are certified by their own associations; many states require hypnotherapists to be licensed, but the requirements for licensing vary substantially. There is little regulation of practitioners of other relaxation techniques, but it is very rare that adverse events result from such techniques. Many studies have shown that support groups, friendships, strong family relationships, and prayer can all have a positive impact on health.

Biological-Based Therapies

Biological-based therapies include substances derived from plant or animal origin. They consist primarily of herbal therapies or remedies, botanicals, extracts from animal tissues (such as shark cartilage), and dietary supplements. Herbal therapies are sometimes referred to as *materia medica,* Latin for "medical matter," a term that can include a much larger variety of compounds than just herbs (which are plants that die down at the end of a growing season and do not produce woody tissue). Some herbal remedies are not technically herbs, such as the leaves of the *Ginkgo biloba* tree. Other substances that constitute *materia medica* are algae, bacteria, fungi, and minerals. For traditional remedies that are of plant origin, many scientists prefer to use the term *botanicals.*

Herbal remedies are a major component of all indigenous forms of medicine; prior to the development of pharmaceuticals at the end of the nineteenth century, people everywhere in the world relied on materials from nature for pain relief, wound healing, and treatment of a variety of ailments. Herbal remedies are also a common element in most systems of traditional medicine. Much of the **pharmacopoeia** of modern scientific medicine originated in the folk medicine of native peoples, and many drugs used today are derived from plants.

A majority of botanical products are sold as dietary supplements, that is, in the form of tablets, pills, capsules, liquid extracts, or teas. Like foods, dietary supplements must carry ingredient labels (see Chapter 12). As with food products, it is the responsibility of the manufacturers to ensure that their dietary supplements are safe and properly labeled prior to marketing. The FDA is responsible for monitoring the labeling and accompanying literature of dietary supplements and for overseeing their safety once they are on the market.

Well-designed clinical studies have been conducted on only a small number of biologically-based therapies. A few commonly used botanicals, their uses, and the evidence supporting their efficacy are presented in Table 20.3. Participants in clinical trials with St. John's wort, ginkgo, and echinacea experienced only minor adverse events. However, most clinical trials of this type last for only a few weeks, so the tests did not indicate whether it is safe to take these botanicals for longer periods of time. They also didn't examine the effects of different dosages or how these therapies interact with conventional drugs.

Although most drug-herb interactions are relatively minor compared to conventional drug–drug interactions, some can be potentially serious. An example is the use of herbs that have anticoagulant (anticlotting) properties, such as ginkgo biloba, when used concurrently with the commonly prescribed anticoagulant Coumadin.

Studies have shown that most people do not reveal their use of CAM therapies to their conventional health care providers, an oversight that can have severe health consequences. Any herbs or drugs used in combination should be evaluated for safety by a knowledgeable health care provider such as a pharmacist. See the box "Herbal Remedies: Are They Safe?" on p. 636.

Manipulative and Body-Based Methods

Touch and body manipulation are long-standing forms of health care. Manual healing techniques are based on the idea that misalignment or dysfunction in one part of the body can cause pain or dysfunction in that or another

Botanical	Use	Evidence	Examples of Adverse Effects and Interactions
Cranberry (Vaccinium macrocarpon)	Prevention or treatment of urinary tract disorders	May eliminate and prevent bacteria from infecting the urinary tract	None known
Dandelion (Taraxacum officinale)	As a "tonic" against liver or kidney ailments	None yet	May cause diarrhea in some users; people with gallbladder or bile duct problems should not take dandelion
Echinacea (Echinacea purpurea, E. angustifolia, E. pallida)	Stimulation of immune functions; to prevent colds and flulike diseases; to lessen symptoms of colds and flus	Some trials showed that it prevents colds and flus and helps patients recover from colds faster	Might cause liver damage if taken over long periods of time (more than 8 weeks); since it is an immune stimulant, it is not advisable to take it with immune suppressants (e.g., corticosteroids) or during chemotherapy
Evening primrose oil (Oenothera biennis L.)	Reduction of inflammation	Long-term supplementation effective in reducing symptoms of rheumatoid arthritis	None known
Feverfew (Tanacetum parthenium)	Prevention of headaches and migraines	The majority of trials indicate that it is more effective than placebo	Should not be used by people allergic to other members of the aster family; has the potential to increase the effects of warfarin and other anticoagulants
Garlic (Allium sativum)	Reduction of cholesterol	Short-term studies have found a modest effect	May interact with some medications, including anticoagulants, cyclosporine, and oral contraceptives
Ginkgo (Ginkgo biloba)	Improvement of circulation and memory	Improves cerebral insufficiency and slows progression of Alzheimer's disease and other types of senile dementia in some patients; improves blood flow in legs	Could increase bleeding time; should not be taken with nonsteroidal anti-inflammatory drugs or anticoagulants; gastrointestinal disturbance
Ginseng (Panax ginseng)	Improvement of physical performance, memory, immune function, and glycemic control in diabetes; treatment of herpes simplex 2	No conclusive evidence exists for any of these uses	Interacts with warfarin and alcohol in mice and rats, hence should probably not be used with these drugs; may cause liver damage
St. John's wort (Hypericum perforatum)	Treatment of depression	There is strong evidence that it is significantly more effective than placebo, is as effective as some standard antidepressants for mild to moderate depression, and causes fewer adverse effects	Known to interact with a variety of pharmaceuticals and should not be taken together with digoxin, theophylline, cyclosporine, indinavir, and serotonin-reuptake inhibitors
Saw palmetto (Serenoa repens)	Improvement of prostate health	Early studies showed that saw palmetto may reduce mild prostate enlargement	Has no known interactions with drugs, but should probably not be taken with hormonal therapies
Valerian (Valeriana officinalis)	Treatment of insomnia	Appears to help with sleep disorders	Interacts with thiopental and pentobarbital and should not be used with these drugs

part; correcting these misalignments can bring the body back to optimal health.

Manual healing methods are an integral part of physical therapy and osteopathic medicine, now considered a form of conventional medicine. Other physical healing methods include massage, acupressure, Feldenkrais, Rolfing, and numerous other techniques. The most commonly used CAM manual healing method is **chiropractic,** a method that focuses on the relationship between structure, primarily of joints and muscles, and function, primarily of the nervous system, to maintain or restore health. An important therapeutic procedure is the manipulation of joints, particularly those of the spinal column. However, chiropractors also use a variety of other techniques, including exercise, patient education and lifestyle modification, nutritional supplements, and orthotics (mechanical supports and braces) to treat patients. They do not use conventional drugs or surgery.

Chiropractors, or doctors of chiropractic, are trained for a minimum of four full-time academic years at accredited

Herbal Remedies: Are They Safe?

Consider the following research findings and FDA advisories:

• St. John's wort interacts with drugs used to treat HIV infection and heart disease; the herb may also reduce the effectiveness of oral contraceptives, antirejection drugs used with organ transplants, and some medications used to treat infections, depression, asthma, and seizure disorders.

• Supplements containing kava kava have been linked to severe liver damage, and anyone who has liver problems or takes medications that can affect the liver are advised to consult a physician before using kava kava–containing supplements.

• In a sample of ayurvedic herbal medicine products, 20% were found to contain potentially harmful levels of lead, mercury, and/or arsenic.

These findings highlight growing safety concerns about dietary supplements, which now represent annual sales of more than $15 billion in the United States.

Drug Interactions

Botanicals may decrease the effects of drugs, making them ineffective, or increase their effects, in some cases making them toxic. Most patients fail to tell their physicians about their use of herbal substances. Botanicals can also interact with alcohol, usually heightening alcohol's effects. Many manufacturers are offering new combinations of botanical

preparations without empirical or scientific information about the interactions of the individual products.

Lack of Standardization

The Dietary Supplement Health and Education Act of 1994 requires that dietary supplement labels list the name and quantity of each ingredient. However, confusion can result because different plant species—with distinct chemical compositions and effects—may have the same common name. The content of herbal preparations is also variable. Botanicals are naturally grown products. Herb producers do not have complete control over natural processes any more than farmers have control over the vitamin content of fruit.

As an attempt toward standardization, herb producers have identified one or two substances that indicate quality; these substances should be listed on a product's label with their corresponding concentrations, lot numbers, and purity analysis data. Avoid any herbal product whose label is missing this information. Reputable retailers sell only products with this identifying information, and some send qualified inspectors to the site of production to verify the label information.

These self-imposed quality control measures have been adopted by reputable producers and retailers to increase consumer confidence and to help divert additional government-imposed regulation. Today, this level of disclosure and standardization is rarely seen in the production of healthy foods by the agricultural industry.

The Role of Government in Safety Issues

In the United States, because herbs are considered supplements rather than food or drug products, they do not have to meet FDA food and drug standards for safety or effectiveness, nor do they currently have to meet any manufacturing standards. The manufacturer is responsible for ensuring that a supplement is safe before it is marketed; the FDA has the power to restrict a substance if it is found to pose a health risk after it is on the market.

---

chiropractic colleges and can go on to postgraduate training in many countries. Although specifically listed by NC-CAM as one of the manipulative and body-based methods of CAM, chiropractic is accepted by many health care and health insurance providers to a far greater extent than the other types of CAM therapies. Based on research showing the efficacy of chiropractic management in acute low-back pain, spinal manipulation has been included in the federal guidelines for the treatment of this condition. In fact, electrodiagnostic tests show that chiropractic is effective in controlling back pain. Promising results have also been reported with the use of chiropractic techniques in neck pain and headaches.

A caution is in order regarding chiropractic: Spinal manipulation performed by a person without proper chiropractic training can be extremely dangerous. The American Chiropractic Association can help you find a licensed chiropractor near you.

Energy Therapies

Energy therapies are forms of treatment that use energy originating either within the body (biofields) or from other sources (electromagnetic fields). Biofield therapies are based on the idea that energy fields surround and penetrate the body and can be influenced by movement, touch, pressure, or the placement of hands in or through the fields. **Qigong,** a component of traditional Chinese medicine, combines movement, meditation, and regulation of breathing to enhance the flow of qi, improve blood circulation, and enhance immune function. **Therapeutic touch** is derived from the ancient technique of laying-on of hands; it is based on the premise that healers can identify and correct energy imbalances by passing their hands over the patient's body. **Reiki** is one form of therapeutic touch; it is intended to correct disturbances in the flow of life energy (ki is the Japanese form of the Chinese qi) and enhance the body's healing powers through the use of 13 specific hand positions on the patient.

Bioelectromagnetics is the study of the interaction between living organisms and electromagnetic fields, both those produced by the organism itself and those produced by outside sources. The recognition that the body produces electromagnetic fields has led to the development of many diagnostic procedures in Western medicine, including electroencephalography (EEG), electrocardiography (ECG), and nuclear magnetic resonance (NMR) scans.

Bioelectromagnetic-based therapies involve the use of electromagnetic fields to manage pain and to treat conditions such as asthma. There are some indications that the use of electromagnetic fields might be useful in the areas of bone repair, wound healing, nerve stimulation, immune system stimulation, and modulation of the neuroendocrine (nerve and hormonal) system. Although promising, the available research is still very limited and does not allow firm conclusions about the efficacy of these therapies.

Evaluating Complementary and Alternative Therapies

Because there is less information available about complementary and alternative therapies, as well as less regulation of associated products and providers, it is important for consumers to take an active role when they are thinking about using them.

Working with Your Physician   If you are considering a CAM therapy, your first source of information should be your primary health care provider. The NCCAM advises consumers not to seek complementary therapies without first visiting a conventional health care provider for an evaluation and diagnosis of their symptoms. It's usually best to discuss and try conventional treatments that have been shown to be beneficial for your condition. If you are thinking of trying any alternative therapies, it is critically important to tell your physician in order to avoid any dangerous interactions with conventional treatments you are receiving. Areas to discuss with your physician or pharmacist include the following:

- *Safety:* Is there something unsafe about the treatment in general or for you specifically? Are there safety issues you should be aware of, such as drug-herb interactions?
- *Effectiveness:* Is there evidence-based research about the use of the therapy for your condition?

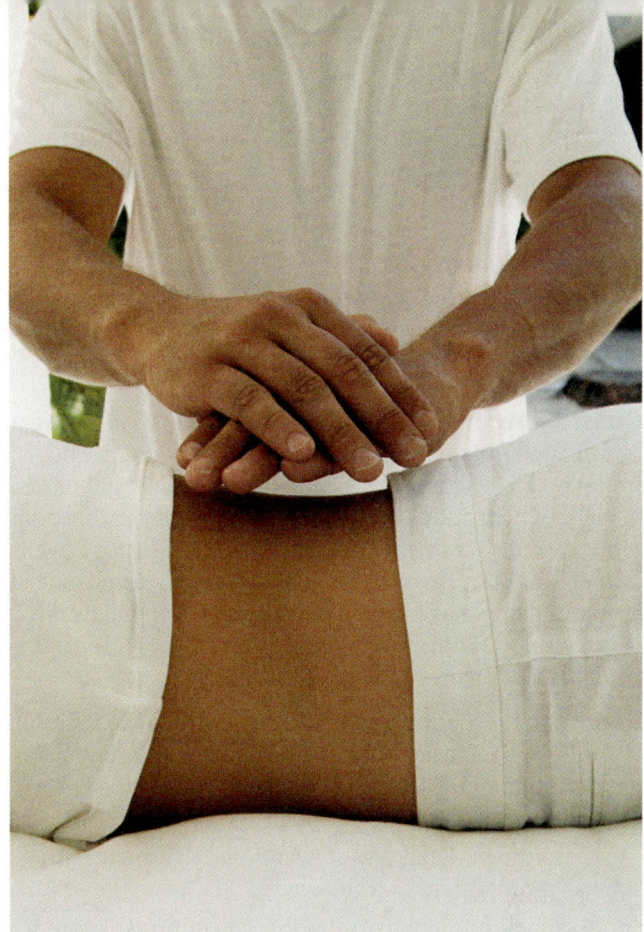

One of several touch therapies, Reiki massage has a spiritual, as well as physical, component.

- *Timing:* Is the immediate use of a conventional treatment indicated?
- *Cost:* Is the therapy likely to be very expensive, especially in light of the potential benefit?

If appropriate, schedule a follow-up visit with your physician to assess your condition and your progress after a certain amount of time using a complementary therapy.

Keep a symptom diary to more accurately track your symptoms and gauge your progress. (Symptoms such as pain and fatigue are very difficult to recall with accuracy, so an ongoing symptom diary is an important tool.) If you plan to pursue a therapy against your physician's advice, you need to tell him or her.

For supplements, particularly botanicals, pharmacists can also be an excellent source of information, if they are familiar with other medications you are taking.

Questioning the CAM Practitioner   You can also get information from individual practitioners and from schools, professional organizations, and state licensing boards. Ask about education, training, licensing, and certification. If appropriate, check with local or state regulatory agencies or the consumer affairs department to determine if any complaints have been lodged against the practitioner. Some guidelines for talking with a CAM practitioner include the following:

- Ask the practitioner why he or she thinks the therapy will be beneficial for your condition. Ask for a full description of the therapy and any potential side effects. In all cases, demand an evidence-based approach.

- Describe in detail any conventional treatments you are receiving or plan to receive.

- Ask how long the therapy should continue before it can be determined if it is beneficial.

- Ask about the expected cost of the treatment. Does it seem reasonable? Will your health insurance pay some or all of the costs?

If anything an alternative practitioner says or recommends directly conflicts with advice from your physician, discuss it with your physician before making any major changes in any current treatment regimen or in your lifestyle.

Doing Your Own Research   You can investigate CAM therapies on your own by going to the library or doing research online, although caution is in order when using Web sites for the various forms of CAM. Erroneous information about CAM is rampant among unscientific and "pop" resources. A good place to start is the Web sites of government agencies like the FDA or NCCAM and of universities and similar organizations that conduct government-sponsored research on CAM approaches (see For More Information).

? QUESTIONS FOR CRITICAL THINKING AND REFLECTION
Have you ever considered using a complementary or alternative treatment? If so, was it in addition to conventional treatment, or instead of it? What kind of research did you do before having the treatment? What advice did your primary health care provider give you about it?

If possible, also talk to people with the same condition you have who have received the same treatment. Remember, though, that patient testimonials shouldn't be used as the sole criterion for choosing a therapy or assessing its safety and efficacy. Controlled scientific trials usually provide the best information and should be consulted whenever possible. The absence of documented danger is not the same thing as proof of safety. Quite often, people working in health food stores are only too willing to give advice and make recommendations, particularly about botanical supplements. Many of these people are not qualified to give this kind of advice. Ask about qualifications (training or education) before accepting recommendations from anyone. Perhaps more so than for any other consumer products and services, the use of CAM calls for consumer skills, critical thinking, and caution.

PAYING FOR HEALTH CARE

The American health care system is one of the most advanced and comprehensive in the world, but it is also the most expensive (Figure 20.5). In 2006, the United States spent $2.1 trillion on health care, or more than $7000 per person. Many factors contribute to the high cost of health care in the United States, including the cost of advanced equipment and new technology, expensive treatments for some illnesses, the aging of the population, high earnings by some people in the health care industry, and the demand for profits by investors.

The Current System

Health care is financed by a combination of private and public insurance plans, patient out-of-pocket payments, and government assistance. Currently, private insurance and individual patients pay about 55% of the total; the government pays the rest, mainly through Medicare and Medicaid (Figure 20.6). Most nonelderly Americans receive health insurance through their employers.

Not everyone is included in this financing system. More than 43 million people, the vast majority of them employed, have no health care insurance at all in 2007 (see the box "Who Are the Uninsured?" on p. 640). Many more are underinsured, meaning they may be uninsured for periods of time, have health insurance that does not cover all needed services, and/or have high out-of-pocket costs. New government health insurance programs for children have reduced the number of Americans under age 18 who lack health insurance; still, 6.7 million American children were uninsured in 2007.

Uninsured and underinsured people use health services less often and receive poorer care when they do use the services. Children without insurance are less likely to have screening tests and immunizations. They have fewer checkups, are less likely to be treated for injuries and for

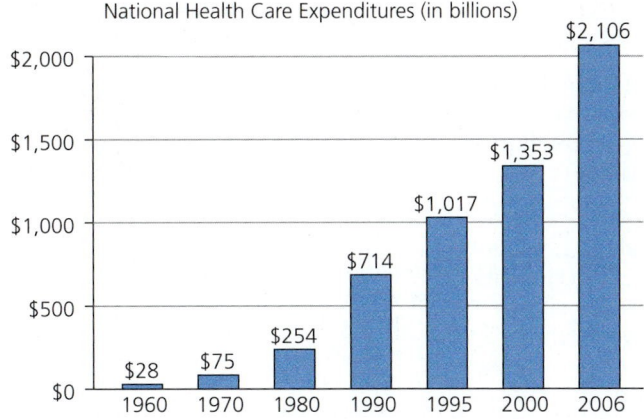

National Health Care Expenditures (in billions)

FIGURE 20.5 National health care expenditures (public and private) 1960–2006.

SOURCE: National Center for Health Statistics. 2009. *Health, United States: 2008.* Hyattsville, Md.: National Center for Health Statistics.

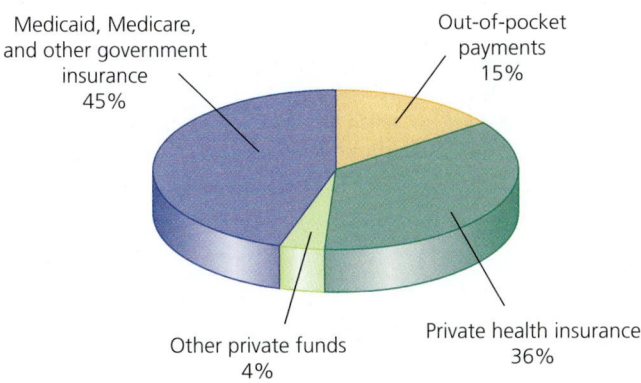

Medicaid, Medicare, and other government insurance 45%

Out-of-pocket payments 15%

Other private funds 4%

Private health insurance 36%

FIGURE 20.6 Paying for Americans' health care services, 2006.

SOURCE: National Center for Health Statistics. 2009. *Health, United States: 2008.* Hyattsville, Md.: National Center for Health Statistics.

chronic conditions such as asthma, and are more likely to go without eyeglasses and prescribed drugs.

Another problem is that national health spending is growing faster than the rest of the economy, consuming an ever-increasing share of the U.S. gross domestic product (GDP). Health care spending represented 16% of the GDP in 2006 and is projected to reach 20% by 2017. Health care costs soared in the 1980s and then were contained to some extent in the 1990s by a large-scale switch from private insurance to managed care (discussed below), which is designed to achieve cost economies. But the savings from this switch were likely a one-time phenomenon, as a large majority of insured working Americans are now covered by managed-care plans. Experts predict that health costs will increase drastically in the near future, with much of the increase borne by the government and individuals.

Health Insurance

Health insurance enables people to receive health care they might not otherwise be able to afford. Hospital care costs hundreds of dollars a day, and surgical fees can cost thousands. Health insurance is important for everyone, especially as health care costs continue to rise.

Health insurance plans are either fee-for-service (indemnity) or managed care. With both types the individual or the employer pays a basic premium, usually on a monthly basis; there are often other payments as well. Insurance policies are sold to both groups and individuals; group plans tend to cover more services and cost less. Group coverage is often available through employers to workers and their families; however, millions of workers are opting out of these company-sponsored plans because of high premiums. About 3 million fewer workers signed up for such plans in 2003 than in 1998. People who are self-employed or whose employers don't offer group policies may need to buy individual plans.

Traditional Fee-for-Service (Indemnity) Plans   In a fee-for-service, or indemnity, plan, you can use any medical provider (such as a physician or a hospital) you choose. You or the provider sends the bill to your insurance company, which pays part of it. Usually you have to pay a deductible amount each year, and then the plan will pay a percentage—often 80%—of what they consider the "usual and customary" charge for covered services. You pay the remaining 20%, which is known as coinsurance.

Freedom of choice is a major benefit of indemnity plans. You can see any physician you choose, including specialists. Your physician is paid based on the services he or she provides. Critics point to the fee-for-service payment system as a contributing factor in the rapid growth of U.S. health care costs because physicians have a financial incentive to order more tests and treatments for their patients. However, the vast majority of working Americans are now covered by managed-care plans.

Managed-Care Plans   Managed-care plans have agreements with a network of specified physicians, hospitals, and health care providers to offer a range of services to plan members at reduced cost. In general, you have lower out-of-pocket costs and less paperwork with a managed-care plan than with an indemnity plan, but you also have less freedom in choosing health care providers. Most Americans with job-based insurance are covered by managed-care plans, which may follow several different models:

managed-care plan   A health care program that integrates the financing and delivery of services by using designated providers, utilization review, and incentives for following the plan's policies; HMOs, PPOs, and POS plans are managed-care plans.

TERMS

Who Are the Uninsured?

Despite high national levels of spending on health care, many Americans under age 65—17%, or nearly 1 in 5, according to the National Center for Health Statistics—did not have health insurance in 2006. (Americans age 65 and over are often covered by government programs.) This overall statistic about the uninsured hides some important differences among groups (see table).

• *Low income:* The factor most closely associated with lack of health insurance is low income. People whose income is twice or more than the federal poverty level are significantly more likely to be insured than those below this level.

• *Age:* Young adults are less likely to be insured than older adults. Younger adults may not be regularly employed and so may not be covered by an insurance plan through work.

• *Ethnicity:* Ethnic minorities are less likely to be insured than whites. Latinos, especially persons of Mexican origin, have the lowest rates of insurance coverage. Much of the ethnic variations are explained by socioeconomic status. However, other factors may also contribute,

including language barriers, differing cultural attitudes toward medical care, living in medically underserved communities, and citizenship status.

People without health insurance receive less health care and lower quality of care. They have fewer physician visits and less preventive care. To help overcome the health gap between ethnic minorities and the general population, the U.S. Department of Health and Human Services sponsors "Take a Loved One for a Checkup Day." Held on the third Tuesday in September, this event is designed to encourage people to obtain preventive care. People are encouraged to make an appointment for themselves or for a friend or family member who hasn't seen a health care provider recently.

People who don't have a regular health care provider or who don't have health insurance can contact a local health department or local community center to find out more about free or low-cost care. For more information, visit the Closing the Health Gap Web site (http://www.omhrc.gov/healthgap/).

Uninsured Americans Under Age 65 (Percent), 2006	
Total	17.0
Income (percent of poverty level)	
Below 100%	35.7
100–149%	37.5
150–199%	34.3
200% or more	13.7
Age (years)	
Under 18	13.2
18–24	36.4
25–34	33.8
35–44	22.6
45–54	17.9
55–64	12.9
Ethnicity	
White	16.6
Asian American	18.0
African American	22.1
Latino	38.8

SOURCES: Centers for Disease Control and Prevention. 2009. *Health, United States, 2008.* Hyattsville, Md.: National Center for Health Statistics.

• **Health maintenance organizations (HMOs)** offer members a range of services for a set monthly fee. You choose a primary care physician who manages your care and refers you to specialists if you need them. If you go outside the HMO, you have to pay for the service yourself. Physicians in the HMO agree to accept a monthly per-patient fee, or **capitation,** or to charge less than standard fees for services.

• **Preferred provider organizations (PPOs)** have arrangements with physicians and other providers who have agreed to accept lower fees. If you go outside the PPO, you have to pay more.

• **Point-of-service (POS) plans** are options offered by many HMOs in which you can see a physician outside the plan and still be partially covered (for example, for a specialist outside the network).

Many managed-care plans try to reduce costs over the long term by paying for routine preventive care, such as regular checkups and screening tests and prenatal care; they may also encourage prevention by offering health education and lifestyle modification programs for members.

Other cost-cutting measures are less consumer-oriented. Consumers' choice of physicians is limited, and they may

have to wait longer for appointments and travel farther to see participating doctors or receive specialized tests. Managed-care plans may also try to discourage overtreatment through the use of gatekeepers: In many plans, patients must get preapproval from their primary care physician or a plan representative for diagnostic tests, referrals to specialists, or hospital treatments. If a patient violates the rules for obtaining services, the plan typically will not cover the cost of the services in question. Nonemergency visits to emergency rooms are also frequently not covered.

Health Savings Accounts Health savings accounts **(HSAs)** became available in 2004. An HSA includes two parts: a health plan with a high deductible (at least $1050 per individual or $2100 per family), and a tax-exempt personal savings account that is used for qualified medical expenses. The individual makes pre-tax contributions to the savings account and later uses these funds or other cash payments to cover medical expenses until the plan's deductible is met. Once the deductible is met, the plan pays remaining medical costs according to the type of policy. The savings account can also be used for certain other types of expenses not covered by the plan. An HSA

Choosing a Health Care Plan

Before you choose a health plan, it's important that you understand your options and how they affect your choice of providers and services, costs, and quality of care. The following questions can help guide you in evaluating each of the health plans you are considering:

• *How is the plan rated for quality?* Find out if consumer ratings or consumer satisfaction information is available. Possible sources include the Consumer Assessment of Health Plans (CAHPS), the Health Plan Employer Data and Information Set (HEDIS), or your state health insurance commissioner (check the phone book for contact information).

• *Is the plan accredited?* Many health plans choose to be reviewed and accredited (given a "seal of approval") by the National Committee for Quality Assurance (NCQA), the Joint Commission on Accreditation of Healthcare Organizations (JCAHO), or the American Accreditation HealthCare Commission/URAC.

• *Does the plan include the doctors and hospitals you want?* If you are happy with your current physician, find out which plans he or she is in. If going to a certain hospital is important to you, investigate where a particular physician has privileges and whether a hospital is covered by the plan.

• *Does the plan provide the benefits you need?* Determine which health care services are most important to you and your family and then check to see if the plan covers them. Possible services to consider include physician office visits, preventive services, diagnostic tests and X rays, outpatient prescription medications, inpatient medical and hospital costs, physical therapy, drug and alcohol counseling, prenatal and well baby care, eye exams and glasses or contact lenses, mental health services, complementary therapies such as acupuncture, home health care, and care for preexisting or chronic conditions.

• *Do the doctors, pharmacies, and other services in the plan have convenient times and locations?* Find out about such things as after-hours care and parking as well.

• *Does the plan fit your budget?* Consider all the applicable costs of a plan: monthly premiums, annual deductibles, and copayments for doctor and hospital visits and prescription drugs. Also find out about how much more you will need to pay if you go outside the health plan's network of physicians, hospitals, and other providers to obtain services.

SOURCE: Agency for Health Care Policy and Research. 2007. *Your Guide to Choosing Quality Health Care* (http://www.ahcpr.gov/consumer/qnt; retrieved February 20, 2009).

---

may give the consumer more control over health care spending; it can also potentially lower premiums for some people because health plans with high deductibles tend to have lower premiums.

Recent research shows that HSAs are attractive to people who need tax breaks or pay high out-of-pocket health care costs. But HSAs are less likely to be used by people who don't have extra funds to set aside for future medical expenses; they are also less likely to lower health care costs for consumers who do not have high medical expenses.

Government Programs Americans who are 65 or older and younger people with certain disabilities can be covered by **Medicare,** a federal health insurance program that helps pay for hospitalization, physician services, and prescription drugs. As a result of limits placed on payments, however, some physicians and managed-care programs have stopped accepting Medicare patients. **Medicaid** is a joint federal-state health insurance program that covers some low-income people, especially children, pregnant women, and

people with certain disabilities. The number of people and the number and cost of services covered by government programs has grown in recent years, challenging the ability of these programs to make all payments.

TERMS

health maintenance organization (HMO) A prepaid health insurance plan that offers health care from designated providers.

capitation A payment to health care providers according to the number of patients they agree to serve, rather than the amount of service rendered.

preferred provider organization (PPO) A prepaid health insurance plan in which providers agree to deliver services for discounted fees; patients can go to any provider, but using nonparticipating providers results in higher costs to the patient.

point-of-service (POS) plan A managed-care plan that covers treatment by an HMO physician but permits patients to seek treatment elsewhere with a higher copayment.

health savings account (HSA) Health insurance coverage that includes a health plan with a high deductible and a tax-exempt personal savings account that is used for qualified medical expenses.

Medicare A federal health insurance program for people 65 or older and for younger people with certain disabilities.

Medicaid A federally subsidized state-run plan of health care for people with low income.

Complying with Physicians' Instructions

Even though we sometimes have to entrust ourselves to the care of medical professionals, that doesn't mean we give up responsibility for our own behavior. Following medical instructions and advice often requires the same kind of behavioral self-management that's involved in quitting smoking, losing weight, or changing eating patterns. For example, if you have an illness or injury, you may be told to take medication at certain times of the day, do special exercises or movements, or change your diet.

The medical profession recognizes the importance of patient adherence, or compliance, and encourages different strategies to support it, such as the following:

1. Use reminders placed at home, in the car, at work, on your computer screensaver, or elsewhere that improve follow-through in taking medication and keeping scheduled appointments. To help you remember to take medications:

    ▪ Link taking the medication with some well-established routine, like brushing your teeth or eating breakfast.

    ▪ Use a medication calendar, and check off each pill.

    ▪ Use a medication organizer or pill dispenser.

    ▪ Plan ahead; don't wait until the last pill to get a prescription refilled.

2. Use a journal and other forms of self-monitoring to keep a detailed account of health-related behaviors, such as pill taking, diet, exercise, and so on.

3. Use self-reward systems so that desired behavior changes are encouraged, with a focus on short-term rewards.

4. Develop a clear image or explanation of how the medication or behavior change will improve your health and well-being.

If these strategies don't help you stick with your treatment plan, you may need to consider other possible explanations for your lack of adherence. For example, are you confused about some aspect of the treatment? Do you find the schedule for taking your medications too complicated, or do the drugs have bothersome side effects that you'd rather avoid? Do you feel that the recommended treatment is unnecessary or unlikely to help? Are you afraid of becoming dependent on a medication or that you'll be judged negatively if people know about your condition and treatment? An examination of your attitudes and beliefs about your condition and treatment plan can also help improve your compliance.

Choosing a Policy

Choosing health insurance can be complicated; it's important to evaluate the coverage provided by different plans and decide which one is best for you (see the box "Choosing a Health Care Plan"). Colleges typically provide medical services through a student health center; some require students to purchase additional insurance if they are not covered by family policies. It's usually economical to remain on a family policy as long as possible.

After college, most people secure group coverage through their place of employment or through membership in an organization. If group coverage is not available, individuals should contact several different insurance companies for information about policies. Managed-care plans tend

? QUESTIONS FOR CRITICAL THINKING AND REFLECTION
What type of health insurance coverage do you have? If you have coverage, do you know what types of medical services are fully or partially covered? What are your copayments and deductibles? If you were faced with a medical emergency, would you know how to work with your insurer to make sure your costs were covered?

TIPS FOR TODAY AND THE FUTURE
Most of the time, you can take care of yourself without consulting a health care provider. When you need professional care, you can still take responsibility for yourself by making informed decisions.

RIGHT NOW YOU CAN
▪ Make sure you have enough of your prescription medications on hand, and that your prescriptions are up-to-date.
▪ If you take any supplements (dietary or herbal), ask your pharmacist if they can interact with any prescription drugs you are taking.
▪ Stock your home and car with basic first aid supplies.

IN THE FUTURE YOU CAN
▪ Thoroughly research any form of complementary or alternative medical treatments you are using or considering; make sure it is considered safe and effective.
▪ Review your medical insurance policy and make sure you are familiar with your coverage and the policy's terms. If you have any questions about your policy, contact your insurance agent. If you don't have any medical insurance, start investigating your options.

to have lower premiums and fewer out-of-pocket costs, an advantage for young adults and families with young children. Traditional fee-for-service plans tend to cost more and involve more paperwork, but they offer a wider choice of providers. If you are choosing insurance, consider a number of different plans and use your critical thinking skills to find the one that best suits your needs.

SUMMARY

- Informed self-care requires knowing how to evaluate symptoms. It's necessary to see a physician if symptoms are severe, unusual, persistent, or recurrent.

- Self-treatment doesn't necessarily require medication, but OTC drugs can be a helpful part of self-care.

- Conventional medicine is characterized by a focus on the external, physical causes of disease; the identification of a set of symptoms for different diseases; the development of public health measures to prevent disease and of drugs and surgery to treat them; the use of rational, scientific thinking to understand phenomena; and a well-established research methodology.

- Conventional practitioners include medical doctors, doctors of osteopathic medicine, podiatrists, optometrists, and dentists, as well as allied health care providers.

- The diagnostic process involves a medical history, a physical exam, and medical tests. Patients should ask questions about medical tests and treatments recommended by their physicians.

- Safe use of prescription drugs requires knowledge of what the medication is supposed to do, how and when to take it, and what the side effects are.

- All surgical procedures carry risk; patients should ask about alternatives and get a second opinion from another physician.

- Complementary and alternative medicine (CAM) is defined as those therapies and practices that do not form part of conventional health care and medical practice as taught in most U.S. medical schools and offered in most U.S. hospitals.

- CAM is characterized by a view of health as a balance and integration of body, mind, and spirit; a focus on ways to restore the individual to harmony so that he or she can fight disease and regain health; and a body of knowledge based on accumulated experience and observations of patient reactions.

- Alternative medical systems such as traditional Chinese medicine and homeopathy are complete systems of medical philosophy, theory, and practice.

- Mind-body interventions include meditation, biofeedback, group support, hypnosis, and prayer.

- Biological-based therapies consist of herbal remedies, botanicals, animal-tissue products, and dietary supplements.

- Manipulative and body-based methods include massage and other physical healing techniques; the most frequently used is chiropractic.

- Energy therapies are designed to influence the flow of energy in and around the body; they include qigong, therapeutic touch therapies, and Reiki.

- Because there is less information available about CAM and less regulation of its practices and providers, consumers must be proactive in researching and choosing treatments, using critical thinking skills and exercising caution.

- Health insurance plans are usually described as either fee-for-service (indemnity) or managed-care plans. Indemnity plans allow consumers more choice in medical providers, but managed-care plans are less expensive.

- Government programs include Medicaid, for the poor, and Medicare, for those age 65 and over or chronically disabled.

FOR MORE INFORMATION

BOOKS

Committee on the Use of Complementary and Alternative Medicine by the American Public. 2005. *Complementary and Alternative Medicine in the United States.* Washington, D.C.: National Academy Press. *Outlines ways of integrating conventional and complementary therapies, and proposes changes to dietary supplement laws.*

Mayo Clinic. 2007. *The Mayo Clinic Book of Alternative Medicine.* New York: Time-Life. *A concise review of currently popular CAM therapies and treatments.*

Thompson, W. G. 2005. *The Placebo Effect and Health: Combining Science and Compassionate Care.* New York: Prometheus Books. *Describes the placebo effect and how it may be used to benefit health.*

PDR. 2007. *PDR for Nonprescription Drugs, Dietary Supplements, and Herbs, 2008,* 29th ed. Montvale, N.J.: Thomson Healthcare. *A reference covering the safety and efficacy of over-the-counter medications.*

Whorton, J. C. 2004. *Nature Cures: The History of Alternative Medicine in America.* New York: Oxford University Press. *Provides a history of alternative medicine in the United States, including background information on many CAM therapies.*

ORGANIZATIONS, HOTLINES, AND WEB SITES

Agency for Healthcare Research and Quality (AHRQ). Provides practical, evidence-based information on health care treatments and outcomes for consumers and practitioners.
http://www.ahrq.gov

American Board of Medical Specialties. Provides information on board certification, including information on specific physicians.
http://www.abms.org

American Chiropractic Association. Provides information on chiropractic care, consumer tips, and a searchable directory of certified chiropractors.
http://www.amerchiro.org

American Medical Association (AMA). Provides information about physicians, including their training, licensure, and board certification.

http://www.ama-assn.org

American Osteopathic Association. Provides information on osteopathic physicians, including board certification.

http://www.osteopathic.org

ConsumerLab.com. Provides information on the results of tests of dietary supplements, including information on actual ingredients and concentrations.

http://www.consumerlab.com

Food and Drug Administration: Information for Consumers. Provides materials on dietary supplements, foods, prescription and OTC drugs, and other FDA-regulated products.

http://www.fda.gov/consumer/default.htm

National Center for Complementary and Alternative Medicine (NC-CAM). Provides general information packets, answers to frequently asked questions about CAM, consumer advice for safer use of CAM, research abstracts, and bibliographies.

http://nccam.nih.gov

National Council Against Health Fraud. Provides news and information about health fraud and quackery and links to related sites.

http://www.ncahf.org

Quackwatch. Provides information on health fraud, quackery, and health decision making.

http://www.quackwatch.org

U.S. Treasury Department: Health Savings Accounts. Provides information about HSAs and links to relevant IRS forms.

http://www.treas.gov/offices/public-affairs/hsa/

See also the listings for Chapters 2 and 12; the box on dietary supplements in Chapter 12 suggests Web sites with more information on supplements.

SELECTED BIBLIOGRAPHY

American Medical Association. 2004. *Health Savings Accounts at a Glance.* Chicago: American Medical Association.

Babones, S. J. 2008. Income inequality and population health: Correlation and causality. *Social Science and Medicine* 66(7): 1614–1626.

Bach, P. B., et al. 2004. Primary care physicians who treat blacks and whites. *New England Journal of Medicine* 351(6): 575–584.

Bordens, K. S., and B. B. Abbott. 2007. *Research Design and Methods: A Process Approach,* 7th ed. New York: McGraw-Hill.

Bren, L. 2004. Study: U.S. generic drugs cost less than Canadian drugs. *FDA Consumer,* July/August.

Budetti, P. P. 2004. 10 years beyond the health security act failure: Subsequent developments and persistent problems. *Journal of the American Medical Association* 292(16): 2000–2006.

Burke, A., et al. 2006. Acupuncture use in the United States: Findings from the national health interview survey. *Journal of Alternative and Complementary Medicine* 12(7): 639–648.

Centers for Disease Control and Prevention. 2004. Complementary and alternative medicine use among adults: United States, 2002. *Advance Data from Vital and Health Statistics* No. 343. Hyattsville, Md.: National Center for Health Statistics.

Cyna, A. M., et al. 2006. Antenatal self-hypnosis for labour and childbirth: A pilot study. *Anaesthesia and Intensive Care* 34(4): 464–469.

Ernst, E. 2004. Prescribing herbal medications appropriately. *Journal of Family Practice* 53(12): 985–988.

Frazier, S. C. 2005. Health outcomes and polypharmacy in elderly individuals: An integrated literature review. *Journal of Gerontological Nursing* 31(9): 4–11.

Gan, T. J., et al. 2004. A randomized controlled comparison of electro-acupoint stimulation or ondansetron versus placebo for the prevention of postoperative nausea and vomiting. *Anesthesia and Analgesia* 99(4): 1070–1075.

Grzywaca, J. G., et al. 2008. Age-related differences in the conventional health care–complementary and alternative medicine link. *American Journal of Health Behavior* 32(6): 650–663.

Kaiser Family Foundation. 2005. *Trends and Indicators in the Changing Health Care Marketplace.* Menlo Park, Calif.: Kaiser Family Foundation.

Miller, F. G., et al. 2004. Ethical issues concerning research in complementary and alternative medicine. *Journal of the American Medical Association* 291(5): 599–604.

Morningstar, M. W. 2006. Improvement of lower extremity electro-diagnostic findings following a trail of spinal manipulation and motion-based therapy. *Chiropractic & Osteopathy* 14(1): 20.

National Academy of Sciences, Institute of Medicine. 2006. *Preventing Medication Errors.* Washington, D.C.: National Academies Press.

National Center for Health Statistics. 2008. *Early Release of Selected Estimates Based on Data from the 2007 National Health Interview Survey.* Hyattsville, Md.: National Center for Health Statistics.

National Center for Health Statistics. 2009. *Health, United States, 2008.* Hyattsville, Md.: National Center for Health Statistics.

Nissen, S. E., et al. 2006. Adverse cardiovascular effects of rofecoxib. *New England Journal of Medicine* 355(2): 203–205.

Radley, D. C., et al. 2006. Off-label prescribing among office-based physicians. *Archives of Internal Medicine* 166(9): 1021–1026.

Rados, C. 2004. FDA reiterates warning against online drug buying. *FDA Consumer,* September/October.

Remler, D. K., and S. A. Glied. 2006. How much more cost sharing will health savings accounts bring? *Health Affairs* 25(4): 1070–1078.

Saha, S., et al. 2008. Racial and ethnic disparities in the VA health care system: A systematic review. *Journal of General Internal Medicine* 23(5): 654–671.

Saper, R. B., et al. 2004. Heavy metal content of ayurvedic herbal medicine products. *Journal of the American Medical Association* 292(23): 2868–2873.

Schoen, C., et al. 2008. How many are underinsured? Trends among U.S. adults, 2003 and 2007. *Health Affairs,* 10 June [epub].

Taseng, C., et al. 2004. Cost-lowering strategies used by Medicare beneficiaries who exceed drug benefit caps and have a gap in drug coverage. *Journal of the American Medical Association* 292(8): 952–960.

The uninsured: Americans at risk. 2004. *Consumer Reports,* January.

U.S. Department of the Treasury. 2008. *Health Savings Accounts (HSAs)* (http://www.ustreas.gov/offices/public-affairs/hsa; retrieved February 20, 2009).

Wahbeh, H., S. M. Elsas, and B. S. Oken. 2008. Mind-body interventions: Applications in neurology. *Neurology* 70(24): 2321–2328.

PERSONAL SAFETY

21

LOOKING AHEAD>>>>>

AFTER READING THIS CHAPTER, YOU SHOULD BE ABLE TO:

- Identify factors that contribute to unintentional injuries
- List the most common types of unintentional injuries and strategies for preventing them
- Describe factors that contribute to violence and intentional injuries
- Discuss different forms of violence and how to protect yourself from intentional injuries
- List strategies for helping others in an emergency situation

TEST YOUR KNOWLEDGE

1. **More people are injured each year through intentional acts of violence than through unintentional injuries (accidents).**
   True or false?

2. **You should not wear a safety belt because, in a collision, your car might catch on fire or become submerged in water.**
   True or false?

3. **Your odds are greatest for being killed in**
   a. a fire
   b. a fall
   c. a plane crash

4. **Talking on a cell phone while driving increases the risk of motor vehicle crashes.**
   True or false?

5. **About what percentage of sexual assaults against women are committed by strangers?**
   a. 20%
   b. 40%
   c. 80%

ANSWERS

1. **FALSE.** Far more people are injured and killed each year through unintentional injuries than through violence. Your lifetime odds of dying from an unintentional injury are 1 in 34, while the odds of your being murdered are 1 in 217.

2. **FALSE.** These kinds of crashes are rare, and the greatest danger is the impact that precedes them.

3. **B.** The odds of being fatally injured in a fall are now estimated at 1 in 200. The odds of being killed by fire are 1 in 1167, and the odds of dying in a plane crash are 1 in 5552.

4. **TRUE.** Using a handheld or hands-free cell phone while driving decreases attentiveness and reaction time. A 20-year-old using a phone has the reaction time of a 70-year-old not using a phone.

5. **A.** The vast majority of sexual assaults against women are committed by friends, acquaintances, or intimate partners.

Each year, nearly 120,000 Americans die from injuries, and many more are temporarily or permanently disabled. The economic cost of injuries is high, with more than $650 billion spent each year for medical care and rehabilitation of injured people. Injuries also cause emotional suffering for injured people and their families, friends, and colleagues.

Luckily, many steps can be taken to reduce the risk of injuries. Engineering strategies such as safety belts can help lower injury rates, as can the passage and enforcement of safety-related laws, such as those requiring tamper-proof containers for OTC medications. Public education campaigns about risky behaviors such as driving under the influence of alcohol or smoking in bed can also help prevent injuries.

Ultimately, though, it is up to each person to take responsibility for his or her actions and make wise choices about safety behaviors. Many of the same sensible attitudes, responsible behaviors, and informed decisions that optimize your wellness can improve your chances of avoiding injuries. This chapter explains how you can protect yourself and those around you from becoming the victims of unintentional and intentional injuries.

DIFFERENTIATING INJURIES

Injuries can be intentional or unintentional. An **intentional injury** is one that is purposely inflicted, by oneself or by another person. If an injury occurs when no harm is intended, it is considered an **unintentional injury.** Motor vehicle crashes, falls, and fires often result in unintentional injuries. (Note that public health officials prefer not to use the word *accidents* to describe unintentional injuries because it suggests events beyond human control. *Injuries* are predictable outcomes of factors that can be controlled or prevented.)

Although Americans tend to express more concern about intentional injuries, unintentional injuries are actually far more common. For example, the National Safety Council (NSC) estimates that in 2006, 329 Americans died each day from unintentional injuries, whereas 89 died of suicide and 50 died from homicide. Unintentional injuries are the fifth leading cause of death among all Americans and is the leading cause of death among children and young adults.

Because unintentional injuries are so common, they account for more **years of potential life lost** than any other cause of death.

UNINTENTIONAL INJURIES

Unintentional injuries are the leading cause of death in the United States for people under age 35. Injury situations are generally categorized into four general classes, based on where they occur: motor vehicle injuries, home injuries, public injuries, and work injuries. The greatest number of deaths occur in motor vehicle crashes, but the greatest number of disabling injuries occur in the home (Table 21.1). In all of these arenas, the action you take can mean the difference between injury or death and no injury at all.

What Causes an Injury?

Most injuries are caused by a combination of human and environmental factors. Human factors are inner conditions or attitudes that lead to an unsafe state, whether physical, emotional, or psychological. Environmental factors are external conditions and circumstances, such as poor road conditions, a slippery surface, or the undertow of the ocean at the beach.

A common human factor that leads to injuries is risk-taking behavior. People vary in the amount of risk they tend to take in life; young men are especially prone to taking risks (see the box "Injuries Among Young Men"). Some people take risks to win the admiration of their peers; other people simply overestimate their physical abilities. Alcohol and drug use is another common risk factor that leads to many injuries and deaths.

Psychological and emotional factors can also play a role in injuries. People sometimes act on the basis of inadequate or inaccurate beliefs about what is safe or unsafe. For example, a person who believes that safety belts trap

Table 21.1	Unintentional Injuries in the United States	
	Deaths	**Disabling Injuries**
Motor vehicle	44,700	2,400,000
Home	42,600	10,200,000
Public	30,000	10,000,000
Work	4,988	3,700,000
All classes*	120,000	26,200,000

*Deaths and injuries for the four separate classes total more than the "All classes" figures because of rounding and because some deaths and injuries are included in more than one class.

SOURCE: National Safety Council. 2008. *Injury Facts, 2008 Edition.* Itasca, Ill.: National Safety Council.

Injuries Among Young Men

connect™

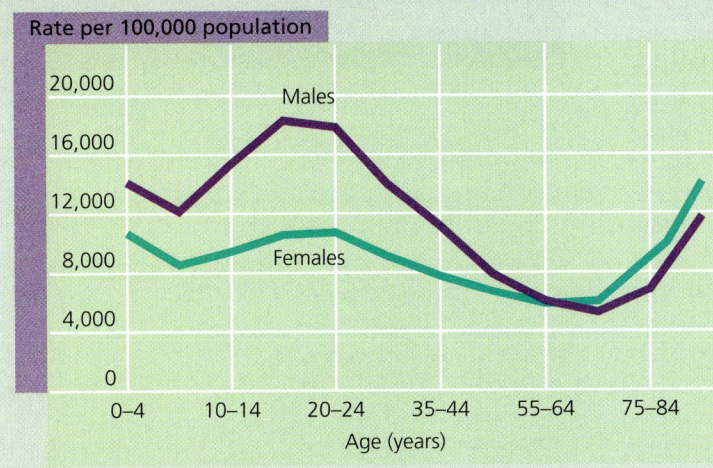

Rate per 100,000 population

Males

Females

Age (years)

Figure 1 Nonfatal injury rate by age and sex.

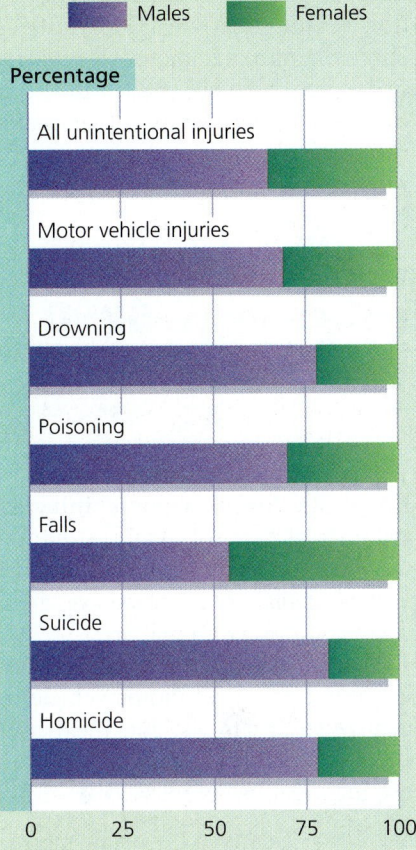

Males   Females

Percentage

- All unintentional injuries
- Motor vehicle injuries
- Drowning
- Poisoning
- Falls
- Suicide
- Homicide

Figure 2 Injury deaths: Percentage of victims by sex.

Overall, rates of injury are highest among young adults and seniors over age 85. Except among the oldest group of adults, the nonfatal injury rate is substantially higher in males than in females—and it peaks among young adult males (Figure 1). Males also significantly outnumber females in injury deaths—whether unintentional or intentional (Figure 2).

Why do men, especially young men, have such high rates of injury? Gender roles may play a key role: Traditional gender roles for males may associate masculinity with risk-taking behavior and a disregard for pain and injury, and risk-taking behavior may be particularly common among young men. Men are more likely to drive dangerously, drink and drive, binge-drink, and use aggressive behavior to control situations—all of which can lead to higher rates of fatal and nonfatal injury. Men may also have a lower perception of risk of dangerous behaviors compared with women.

Traditional gender roles may also make it more difficult for men to admit to injury or emotional vulnerability. Physical injuries may worsen or become chronic if

care is not sought promptly. Untreated depression can lead to suicide.

In addition, men may have greater exposure to some injury situations. Compared with women, men may drive more miles, have greater access to firearms, and be more likely to ride motorcycles, operate machinery, and have jobs associated with high rates of workplace injuries. They may be more likely to engage in sports and other recreational activities associated with high rates of injuries. Greater access and use of firearms plays a role in higher rates of deaths among men from assault and suicide; as described in Chapter 3, women are more likely than men to attempt suicide, but men are much more likely to succeed, primarily because they are more likely to use firearms.

Some researchers suggest that the male hormone testosterone may play a role in risky and aggressive behavior. Differences in brain structure and activity may also influence how men and women respond to stressors and how quickly and to what degree they become verbally or physically aggressive in response to anger.

Further studies are needed to identify all the factors underlying excessive risk-taking among men and how these risk behaviors can be changed to lower the rates of fatal and nonfatal injury among men.

SOURCES: Centers for Disease Control and Prevention. 2004. Surveillance for fatal and nonfatal injuries—United States, 2001. *MMWR Surveillance Summaries* 53(SS7): 1–57; World Health Organization. 2002. *Gender and Road Traffic Injuries.* Geneva: World Health Organization; Courtenay, W. 1998. College men's health: An overview and a call to action. *Journal of American College Health* 46(6): 279–290.

people in cars when a crash occurs and who therefore decides not to wear a safety belt is acting on an inaccurate belief. However, many people who have accurate information still decide to engage in risky behavior. Young people often have unsafe attitudes, such as "I won't get hurt" or "It won't happen to me." Attitudes like this can lead to risk taking and ultimately to injuries.

Environmental factors leading to injury may be natural (weather conditions), social (a drunk driver), work-related (defective equipment), or home-related (faulty wiring). Making the environment safer is an important aspect of safety. Laws are often passed to try to make our environment safer; examples include speed limits on highways and workplace safety requirements.

Motor Vehicle Injuries

According to the Centers for Disease Control and Prevention (CDC), nearly 45,000 Americans were killed and 3 million injured in motor vehicle crashes in 2006. Worldwide, motor vehicle crashes kill 1.2 million and injure up to 50 million people each year, making motor vehicle injuries the eleventh leading cause of death overall. Those most affected by motor vehicle crashes are people age 15–24. It is more likely that your death will be caused by a motor vehicle crash than by any other type of unintentional or intentional injury (Table 21.2). **Motor vehicle injuries** also result in the majority of cases of paralysis due to spinal injuries, and they are the leading cause of severe brain injury in the United States.

Factors Contributing to Motor Vehicle Injuries

Common causes of motor vehicle injuries are speeding, aggressive driving, fatigue, inexperience, cell phones and other distractions, the use of alcohol and other drugs, and the incorrect use of safety belts and other safety devices.

SPEEDING Nearly 63% of all motor vehicle crashes are caused by bad driving, especially speeding. As speed increases, momentum and the force of impact increase, and the time allowed for the driver to react (reaction time) decreases. Speed limits are posted to establish the safest maximum speed limit for a given area under ideal conditions; if visibility is limited or the road is wet, the safe maximum speed may be considerably lower. Many states have raised their highway speed limits since the 1995 repeal of the National Maximum Speed Limit, and overall motor vehicle fatalities have since increased. Raising speed limits on rural interstates has caused a 35% increase in crash death rates.

AGGRESSIVE DRIVING Speeding is also a hallmark of aggressive drivers—those who operate a motor vehicle in an unsafe and hostile manner. Aggressive driving, also known as road rage, has increased more than 50% since 1990, and one in four U.S. drivers admits to driving aggressively at least some of the time. Other characteristics of aggres-

TERMS **motor vehicle injuries** Unintentional injuries and deaths involving motor vehicles in motion, both on and off the highway or street; incidents causing motor vehicle injuries include collisions between vehicles and collisions with objects or pedestrians.

VITAL STATISTICS

Table 21.2	Lifetime Odds of Death Due to Injury

All unintentional injuries	1 in 34
Motor vehicle	1 in 84
Poisoning	1 in 180
Fall	1 in 200
Drowning	1 in 1140
Fire	1 in 1167
Choking	1 in 1173
Struck by falling object	1 in 4525
Firearm discharge	1 in 5808
Air and space transport	1 in 5552
Exposure to natural cold	1 in 5576
Electric current	1 in 9308
Exposure to natural heat	1 in 16,680
Lightning	1 in 81,949
Cataclysmic storm	1 in 59,836
Earthquake or volcano	1 in 125,655
Suicide	**1 in 116**
Homicide (assault)	**1 in 217**

SOURCE: National Safety Council. 2007. *The Odds of Dying from . . .* Itasca, Ill.: National Safety Council.

sive driving include frequent, erratic, and abrupt lane changes; tailgating; running red lights or stop signs; passing on the shoulder; and blocking other cars trying to change lanes or pass. Aggressive drivers increase the risk of crashes for themselves and others. Injuries may also occur if aggressive drivers stop their vehicles and confront each other following an incident. For more on aggressive driving, take the quiz and review the strategies in the box "Are You an Aggressive Driver?"

FATIGUE AND SLEEPINESS Driving requires mental alertness and attentiveness. Studies have shown that sleepiness causes slower reaction time, reduced coordination and vigilance, and delayed information processing. Drowsiness can be caused by not getting enough hours of sleep, by sleep disorders that prevent sleep from being refreshing, or by disruptions caused by shift work that force people to sleep at odd hours. Research shows that even mild sleep deprivation causes a deterioration in driving ability comparable to that caused by a 0.05% blood alcohol concentration—a level considered hazardous when driving. Being awake for 18 hours can impair driving ability as much as drinking two alcoholic beverages.

CELL PHONES AND OTHER DISTRACTIONS Anything that distracts a driver can increase the risk of a motor vehicle injury. Several common causes of crashes, such as disregarding stop signs, have been linked to driver distraction. Distraction is a contributing factor in 25–50% of all crashes. Cell phones are a widely documented source of

Are You an Aggressive Driver?

To find out if you are an aggressive driver, check any of the following statements that are true for you:

_____ I consistently exceed the speed limit; I'm often unaware of both my speed and the speed limit.

_____ I frequently follow closely behind the car in front of me.

_____ If I feel the car in front of me is going too slowly, I tailgate.

_____ I change lanes frequently to pass people.

_____ I seldom use my turn signal when changing lanes or turning.

_____ I often run red lights or roll through stop signs.

_____ I react to what I feel is another driver's mistake by cursing, shouting, or making rude gestures; by blocking a car from passing or changing lanes; by using high beams; or by braking suddenly in front of a tailgater.

_____ My personality changes and I become more competitive when I get behind the wheel.

_____ I often get angry or impatient with other drivers and with pedestrians.

_____ I would consider pulling over for a personal encounter with a bad driver.

Each of these statements is characteristic of aggressive drivers; the more items you checked, the greater your road rage. If you checked even one statement, consider taking some of the following steps to reduce your hostility behind the wheel:

• Allow enough time for your trip to reach your destination without speeding.

• Avoid driving during periods of heavy traffic.

• Don't drive when you are angry, tired, or intoxicated.

• Imagine that the other drivers are all people that you know and like. Be courteous and forgiving.

• Listen to soothing music or a book on tape, or practice a relaxation technique such as deep breathing (see Chapter 2).

• Take a course in anger management.

Even if you control your own aggressive impulses, you may still encounter an aggressive driver on the road. The AAA Foundation for Traffic Safety recommends the following strategies:

• Avoid behaviors that may enrage an aggressive driver; these include cutting off cars when merging, driving slowly in the left lane, tailgating, and making rude gestures.

• If you make a mistake while driving, apologize. In surveys, the most popular and widely understood gestures for apologies include raising or waving a hand and touching or knocking the head with the palm of your hand (to indicate "What was I thinking?").

• Refuse to join in a fight. Avoid eye contact with an angry driver, and put distance between your car and his or her vehicle. If you think another driver is following you, call the police on a cell phone or drive to a public place.

SOURCES: New York State Department of Motor Vehicles. 2008. *Aggressive Driving* (http://www.nysgtsc.state.ny.us/aggr-ndx.htm; retrieved February 21, 2009); AAA Foundation for Traffic Safety. 1997. *Road Rage: How to Avoid Aggressive Driving.* Washington, D.C.: AAA Foundation for Traffic Safety.

---

distraction for drivers. A 2006 study showed that drivers who use cell phones are nearly six times as likely to be involved in a crash as drivers who don't. The same study showed that sober drivers using cell phones can perform worse than drivers who are inebriated. Five states (New York, New Jersey, California, Washington, and Connecticut) and the District of Columbia have banned the use of handheld phones while driving. Other states are considering similar legislation, especially for young, inexperienced drivers (see the box "Cell Phones and Distracted Driving" on p. 652).

ALCOHOL AND OTHER DRUGS Alcohol is involved in about 40% of all fatal crashes. Alcohol-impaired driving is illegal in all states; the legal limit for blood alcohol concentration (BAC) is 0.08%, but people can be impaired at much lower BACs. A driver with a BAC between 0.05% and 0.09% is nine times more likely to have a crash than a person who has not been drinking. The combination of fatigue and alcohol use increases the risk even further. Because alcohol affects reason and judgment as well as the ability to make fast, accurate, and coordinated movements, a person who has been drinking will be less likely to recognize that he or she is impaired.

Other substances also affect judgment and driving ability. A recent study found that hay fever sufferers who had taken diphenhydramine (an antihistamine found in over-the-counter allergy medications such as Benadryl) were as impaired as if they were legally drunk. Use of many over-the-counter and all psychoactive drugs is potentially dangerous if you plan to drive (Chapters 9 and 10).

SAFETY BELTS, AIR BAGS, AND CHILD SAFETY SEATS The improper use of safety belts, air bags, and child safety seats contributes to injuries and deaths in motor vehicle crashes. Although some type of mandatory safety belt law

> **QUICK STATS**
>
> An alcohol-related traffic fatality occurs every **31 minutes** in the U.S.
>
> —NSC, 2004

Cell Phones and Distracted Driving

At any given moment, about 5% of drivers are talking on a cell phone. In 2001, New York became the first state to ban the use of handheld cellular phones while driving; drivers there must use hand-free equipment or face fines of up to $100. Since then, four other states and the District of Columbia passed similar bans, and many other states have bans under consideration. Around the world, many countries have laws against the use of handheld cell phones while driving.

Available evidence indicates that use of a cell phone while driving can increase the risk of motor vehicle crashes. In a study using a driver-training simulator, cell phone users were about 20% slower to respond to sudden hazards than were other drivers, and they were about twice as likely to rear-end a braking car in front of them. Among young adult drivers who used a cell phone, reaction time was reduced to the level of a 70-year-old driver who was not using a phone. It is unclear, however, if bans such as those in New York will help reduce the risk: Studies have not found much, if any, benefit in the use of headsets. It appears that the mental distraction of talking is a factor in crashes rather than holding the phone.

The safest strategy is not to use your phone while driving. For people who live in areas where cell phone use is legal while driving and who choose to use a phone, the following strategies may help increase safety:

- Be familiar with your phone and its functions, especially speed dial and redial.

- Store frequently called numbers on speed dial so you can place calls without looking at the phone.

- If your phone has voice-activated dialing, use it.

- Use a hands-free device so you can keep both hands on the steering wheel.

- Let the person you are speaking to know you are driving and be prepared to end the call at any time.

- Don't place or answer calls in heavy traffic or hazardous weather conditions.

- Don't take notes or look up phone numbers while driving.

- Time calls so that you can place them when you are at a stop.

- Never engage in stressful or emotional conversations while on the road. If you are discussing a complicated or emotional matter, pull off the road to complete your conversation.

Text messaging and e-mail are potentially even more distracting than talking on a cell phone. Washington, Minnesota, Alaska, California, Connecticut, Louisiana, New Jersey, and the District of Columbia prohibit text messaging while driving.

---

is in effect in 49 states (excluding New Hampshire) and the District of Columbia, only about 82% of motor vehicle occupants use safety belts even though they are the single most effective way to reduce the risk of crash-related death. Of drivers not wearing a safety belt who have been killed in automobile crashes, an estimated 60–70% would have survived if they had been wearing one. If you wear a combination lap and shoulder belt, your chance of surviving a crash is three to four times better than that of a person who doesn't wear one.

The National Highway Traffic Safety Administration (NHTSA) has mandated that, starting in 2008, all motor vehicles must have safety belts installed in the rear center seat; it is estimated that this measure will prevent about 25 deaths and 500 injuries each year.

Some people think that if they are involved in a crash they are better off being thrown free of their vehicle. In fact, the chances of being killed are 25 times greater if you are thrown from a vehicle, whether it is due to injuries caused by hitting a tree or the pavement or by being hit by another vehicle. Safety belts not only prevent you from being thrown from the car at the time of the crash but also provide protection from the second collision: If a car is traveling at 65 mph and hits another vehicle, the car stops first; then the occupants stop because they, too, are traveling at 65 mph. The second collision occurs when occupants hit something inside the car, such as the dashboard or windshield. The safety belt stops the second collision from occurring and spreads the collision's force over the body.

Since 1998, all new cars and light trucks have been equipped with dual air bags—one for the driver and one for the front passenger. Many vehicles also offer optional side air bags, which further reduce the risk of injury. Advanced air bag systems include risk-reduction technologies such as sensors to detect crash severity, seat position, passenger size, and whether a passenger is wearing a safety belt. Although air bags provide supplementary protection in the event of a collision, most are useful only in head-on collisions. They also deflate immediately after inflating and therefore do not provide protection in collisions involving multiple impacts. Air bags are not a replacement for safety belts; everyone in a vehicle should buckle up.

Air bags deploy forcefully and can injure a child or short adult who is improperly restrained or sitting too close to the dashboard, although second-generation air bags are somewhat safer for children than the older devices. To ensure that air bags work safely, always follow these basic guidelines: Place infants in rear-facing infant seats in the back seat, transport children age 12 and under in the back seat, always use safety belts or appropriate safety seats, and keep 10 inches between the air bag cover and the breastbone of the driver or passenger. If necessary, adjust the steering wheel or use seat cushions to ensure that an inflating air bag will hit a person in the chest and not in the face.

Another adjustment should be made for children who have outgrown child safety seats but are still too small for adult safety belts alone (usually age 4–8). These children should be secured using booster seats that ensure that the safety belt is positioned low across the waist. The CDC estimates that 1451 children age 12 and under were killed in car crashes in 2005; another 203,000 were injured. About 45% of the injured children were not properly restrained in the vehicle. All states have child restraint laws, and more than 30 states mandate the use of booster seats for children who are too big for child safety seats. Before driving with a child, make sure that you know your state's laws; that you have an appropriate safety seat for the child; that the seat is installed correctly; and that the child is properly secured in the seat.

In the rare event that a person needs to be exempted from air bag guidelines, permission to install an on-off switch that temporarily disables the air bag can be applied for from the National Highway Traffic Safety Administration (NHTSA). Air bags currently prevent far more injuries than they cause and are expected to save at least 3200 lives each year once they are installed in all vehicles.

Preventing Motor Vehicle Injuries   About 75% of all motor vehicle collisions occur within 25 miles of home and at speeds lower than 40 mph. Strategies for preventing motor vehicle injuries include the following:

- Obey the speed limit. If you have to speed to get somewhere on time, you're not allowing enough time.

- Always wear a safety belt. Fasten the lap belt, even if the vehicle has automatic shoulder belts. The shoulder strap should cross the collarbone, and the lap belt should fit low and snug across the hips and pelvic area. The shoulder strap should never be slipped under the arm or behind the back. Pregnant women should position the lap belt as low as possible on the pelvic area.

- Never drive under the influence of alcohol or other drugs, or ride with a driver who is.

- Keep your car in good working order.

- Always allow enough following distance. Use the 3-second rule: When the vehicle ahead passes a ref-

erence point, count out 3 seconds. If you pass the reference point before you finish counting, drop back and allow more following distance.

- Always increase your following distance and slow down if weather or road conditions are poor.

- Choose interstate highways rather than rural roads. Highways are much safer because of better visibility, wider lanes, fewer surprises, and other factors.

- Always signal when turning or changing lanes.

- Stop completely at stop signs. Follow all traffic laws.

- Take special care at intersections. Look left, right, and then left again. Make sure you have time to complete your maneuver in the intersection.

- Don't pass on two-lane roads unless you're in a designated passing area and have a clear view ahead.

Motorcycles and Mopeds   About one out of every ten traffic fatalities among people age 15–34 involves someone riding a motorcycle. In more than two-thirds of crashes involving a car and a motorcycle, the driver of the car is at fault. Injuries from motorcycle collisions are generally more severe than those involving automobiles because motorcycles provide little, if any, protection. Because head injuries are the major cause of death, the use of a helmet is critical for rider safety. Still, less than 50% of motorcyclists wear helmets that meet safety standards. Riders also need to know how to operate a motorcycle safely; operator error is a factor in 75% of fatal motorcycle crashes.

Moped riders face additional challenges. Mopeds usually have a maximum speed of 30–35 mph and have less power for maneuverability, especially in an emergency. Moped riders should use caution and learn how to handle the vehicle in traffic.

Additional strategies for preventing motorcycle and moped injuries include the following:

- Wear light-colored clothing, drive with your headlights on, and correctly position yourself in traffic.

- Develop the necessary skills. Lack of skill is a major factor in motorcycle and moped injuries. Skidding from improper braking is the most common cause of loss of control.

- Wear a helmet. Helmets should be marked with the DOT symbol, certifying that they conform to federal safety standards established by the Department of Transportation. Helmet use is required by law in nearly half of the states.

- Protect your eyes with goggles, a face shield, or a windshield.
- Drive defensively, particularly when changing lanes and at intersections, and never assume that other drivers can see you.

Bicycles   According to a 2006 estimate, bicycle crashes send more than 500,000 people to emergency rooms each year and result in about 1000 fatalities. Bicycle injuries result primarily from riders not knowing or understanding the rules of the road, failing to follow traffic laws, not having sufficient skill or experience to handle traffic conditions, or being intoxicated. Bicycles are considered vehicles; bicyclists must obey all traffic laws that apply to automobile drivers, including stopping at traffic lights and stop signs.

Head injuries are involved in about two-thirds of all bicycle-related deaths. Currently, 20 states, the District of Columbia, and nearly 150 cities have laws requiring cyclists to wear helmets. Wearing a helmet reduces the risk of head injury by 85%, but only 50% of cyclists wear helmets (see the box "Choosing a Bicycle Helmet"). Safe cycling strategies include the following:

- Wear safety equipment, including a helmet, eye protection, gloves, and proper footwear. Secure the bottom of your pant legs with clips, and secure your shoelaces so they don't get tangled in the chain.
- Wear light-colored, reflective clothing. Equip your bike with reflectors, and use lights, especially at night or when riding in wooded or other dark areas.
- Ride with the flow of traffic, not against it, and follow all traffic laws. Use bike paths when they are available.
- Ride defensively; never assume that drivers have seen you. Be especially careful when turning or crossing at corners and intersections. Watch for cars turning right.
- Stop at all traffic lights and stop signs. Know and use hand signals.
- Continue pedaling at all times when moving (no coasting) to help keep the bike stable and to maintain your balance.

Pedestrians   Pedestrians are no match for motor vehicles. About one in eight motor vehicle deaths involves pedestrians, and more than 70,000 pedestrians are injured each year. The highest rates of death and injury occur among the very young and the elderly. About 65% of pedestrian deaths occur when people cross or enter the roadway between intersections. Alcohol intoxication plays a significant role in up to half of all adult pedestrian fatalities.

The following strategies can help prevent injuries when you're walking or jogging:

- Walk or jog in daylight.
- Wear light-colored, reflective clothing.
- Face traffic when walking or jogging along a road, and follow traffic laws.
- Avoid busy roads or roads with poor visibility.
- Cross only at marked crosswalks and intersections.
- Don't use headphones while walking.
- Don't hitchhike; it places you in a potentially dangerous situation.

Home Injuries

A person's place of residence, whether a house, an apartment, a trailer, or a dormitory, is considered home. People spend a great deal of time at home and feel that they are safe and secure there. However, home can be a dangerous place. The most common fatal **home injuries** are the result of falls, fires, poisoning, suffocation, and unintentional shootings.

Falls   About 90% of fatal falls involve people age 45 and over, but falls are a significant cause of unintentional death for people under 25. Most deaths occurring from falls involve falling on stairs or steps or from one level to another. Falls also occur on the same level, from tripping, slipping, or stumbling. Alcohol is a contributing factor in many falls. Strategies for preventing falls include the following:

- Install handrails and nonslip surfaces in the shower and bathtub.
- Keep floors, stairs, and outside areas clear of objects or conditions that could cause slipping or tripping, such as ice, snow, electrical cords, and toys.
- Put a light switch by the door of every room so no one has to walk across a room to turn on a light. Use night lights in bedrooms, halls, stairs, and bathrooms.
- When climbing a ladder, use both hands. Never stand higher than the third step from the top. When using a stepladder, make sure the spreader brace is in the locked position. With straight ladders, set the base out 1 foot for every 4 feet of height.
- Don't use chairs to reach things.
- If there are small children in the home, place gates at the top and bottom of stairs. Never leave

home injuries   Unintentional injuries and deaths that occur in the home and on home premises to occupants, guests, domestic servants, and trespassers; falls, burns, poisonings, suffocations, unintentional shootings, drownings, and electrical shocks are examples.

TERMS

CRITICAL CONSUMER

Choosing a Bicycle Helmet

Wearing a bicycle helmet can help you avoid serious head injury, brain damage, or even death in the event of a collision or fall. Helmets have a layer of stiff foam, which absorbs shock and cushions a blow to your head, covered by a thin plastic shell that will skid along the ground. For maximum protection, it's important to select a correctly fitting helmet. When you go shopping, remember the four S's: size, strap, straight, and sticker.

• *Size:* Try on several different sizes before making your selection; it may take several tries before you find the most comfortable fit. The helmet should be very snug but not overly tight on your head. Pads are usually provided to help adjust the fit. A good salesperson can also help you get the right fit. When

the helmet is strapped onto your head, it should not move more than an inch in any direction, and you should not be able to pull or twist it off no matter how hard you try.

• *Strap:* Be sure that the chin strap fits snugly under your chin and that the V in the strap meets under your ear. Avoid thin straps, which can be uncomfortable. Check to be sure that the buckle is strong and won't pop open and that the straps are sturdy.

• *Straight:* The helmet should sit straight on your head, not tilted back or forward. A rule of thumb is that the rim should be about two finger widths above your eyebrows (depending on the height of your forehead).

• *Sticker:* Since March 1999, helmets sold in the United States must meet uniform safety standards established by the U.S. Consumer Product Safety Commission (CPSC). Look for a sticker or label that says the helmet meets the CPSC standard. If a helmet does not have one, it does not meet federal safety standards and should not be used.

You are more likely to wear your helmet if it is comfortable, so be sure that vents on the helmet provide airflow to promote cooling and sweat control. You will be safer with a brightly colored helmet that makes you more visible to drivers, especially in rainy, foggy, or dark conditions. Reflective tape will also increase your visibility. Finally, a helmet is a good place to put emergency information (your name, address, and phone number, plus any emergency medical conditions and an emergency contact).

If you are involved in a crash, replace your helmet. Even if the helmet doesn't have any visible signs of damage, its ability to protect your head may be compromised.

SOURCES: Bicycle Helmet Safety Institute. 2009. *A Consumer's Guide to Bicycle Helmets* (http://www.helmets.org/guide.htm; retrieved February 21, 2009); Bicycle Helmet Safety Institute. 2007. *How to Fit a Bicycle Helmet* (http://www.helmets.org/fit.htm; retrieved February 21, 2009).

a baby unattended on a bed or table. Install window guards to prevent children from falling out of windows.

Fires Approximately 80% of fire deaths and 65% of fire injuries occur in the home; a death caused by a residential fire occurs every 143 minutes. Most fires begin in the kitchen, living room, or bedroom. Cooking is now the leading cause of home fire injuries; careless smoking is the leading cause of fire deaths, followed by problems with heating equipment and arson.

To prevent fires, it's important to dispose of all cigarettes in ashtrays and to never smoke in bed. Other strategies include proper maintenance of fireplaces, furnaces, heaters, chimneys, and electrical outlets, cords, and ap-

pliances. If you use a portable heater, keep it at least 3 feet away from curtains, bedding, or anything else that might catch fire. Never leave heaters on unattended.

It's important to be adequately prepared to handle fire-related situations. Plan at least two escape routes out of each room, and designate a location outside the home as a meeting place. For practice, stage a home fire drill; do it at night, as that's when most deadly fires occur.

Install smoke detectors on every level of your home. Your risk of dying in a fire is almost twice as high if you do not use them. Clean the detectors and check the batteries once a month, and replace the batteries at least once a year. Be sure that all residents are familiar with the sound of the smoke detector's alarm; when it goes off, take it seriously.

These strategies can help prevent injuries in a fire:

- Get out as quickly as possible, and go to the designated meeting place. Don't stop for a keepsake or a pet. Never hide in a closet or under a bed. Once outside, count heads to see if everyone is out. If you think someone is still inside the burning building, tell the firefighters. Never go back inside a burning building.

- If you're trapped in a room, feel the door. If it is hot or if smoke is coming in through the cracks, don't open it; use the alternative escape route. If you can't get out, go to the window and shout for help.

- Smoke inhalation is the largest cause of death and injury in fires. To avoid inhaling smoke, crawl along the floor away from the heat and smoke. Cover your mouth and nose, ideally with a wet cloth, and take short, shallow breaths.

- If your clothes catch fire, don't run. Drop to the ground, cover your face, and roll back and forth to smother the flames. Remember: stop-drop-roll.

Although house fires cause the most deaths, hot water causes the most nonfatal burns. Set your water heater no higher than 120°F. Young children are particularly at risk of being burned. Place barriers around stoves and radiators, and keep young children out of the kitchen, where they might be burned by spills. Put pans on rear burners, and turn pot handles toward the back of the stove. Keep hot foods away from the edge of counters and tables, and don't put them on a tablecloth that a small child can pull. Always test the contents of a baby bottle; when bottles are heated in microwave ovens, the liquid can become scalding before the outside of the bottle gets very hot.

Poisoning   More than 2.4 million poisonings and over 19,000 poison-related deaths occur every year in the United States; nearly 85% of poison exposures are unintentional. Poisons come in many forms, some of which are not typically considered poisons. For example, even honey can be poisonous to children less than a year old. Medications are safe when used as prescribed, but overdosing or incorrectly combining medications with another substance may result in poisoning. Other poisonous substances include cleaning agents, petroleum-based products, insecticides and herbicides, cosmetics, nail polish and remover, and many houseplants. All potentially poisonous substances should be used only as directed and stored out of the reach of children.

Install smoke detectors on every floor of your home, check them monthly, and replace the batteries at least once a year.

The most common type of poisoning by gases is carbon monoxide poisoning. Carbon monoxide gas is emitted by motor vehicle exhaust and some types of heating equipment. The effects of exposure to this colorless, odorless gas include headache, blurred vision, and shortness of breath, followed by dizziness, vomiting, and unconsciousness. Carbon monoxide detectors (similar to smoke detectors) are available for home use; they should be used according to the manufacturer's instructions. To prevent poisoning by gases, never operate a vehicle in an enclosed space, have your furnace inspected yearly, and use caution with any substance or device that produces potentially toxic fumes.

Keep the national poison control hotline number (800-222-1222) in a convenient location. A call to the national hotline will be routed to a local Poison Control Center, which provides expert emergency advice 24 hours a day. If a poisoning does occur, it's important that you act quickly. Remove the poison from contact with the victim's eyes, skin, or mouth, or move the victim away from contact with poisonous gases. Call the Poison Control Center immediately for instructions; do not follow the emergency instructions on product labels because they may be incorrect. Depending on the situation, you may be instructed to give the victim water to drink, or to flush affected parts of the skin or eyes with water. Do not induce vomiting. If you are advised to go to an emergency room, take the poisonous substance or container with you.

Suffocation and Choking Suffocation and choking account for about 3000 deaths annually. Children can suffocate if they put small items in their mouth, get tangled in their crib bedding, or get trapped in airtight appliances like old refrigerators. Keep small objects out of reach of children under age 3, and don't give them raw carrots, hot dogs, popcorn, gum, or hard candy. Examine toys carefully for small parts that could come loose; don't give plastic bags or balloons to small children.

Adults can also become choking victims, especially if they fail to chew food properly, eat hurriedly, or try to talk and eat at the same time. Many choking victims can be saved with the **Heimlich maneuver.** The American Red Cross recommends abdominal thrusts as the easiest and safest thing to do when an adult is choking (see the inside back cover). Back blows in conjunction with abdominal thrusts are an acceptable procedure for dislodging an object from the throat of an infant.

Firearms About 40% of all unintended firearm deaths occur among people age 5–29. People who use firearms should remember the following:

- Always treat a gun as though it were loaded, even if you know it isn't.
- Never point a gun—loaded or unloaded—at anything you do not intend to shoot.
- Always unload a gun before storing it. Store unloaded firearms under lock and key, in a place separate from the ammunition.
- Always inspect firearms carefully before handling.
- If you ever plan to handle a gun, take a firearms safety course first.
- If you own a gun, buy and use a gun lock designed specifically for that weapon.

Proper storage is critical. Do not assume that young children cannot fire a gun. Even children as young as 3 can have enough finger strength to pull a trigger. Every year, about 120 Americans are unintentionally shot to death by children under 6. About 8.3 million children live in households with unlocked guns, including 2.6 million who live in households where guns are stored loaded or with ammunition nearby.

Probably the best advice for anyone who picks up a gun is to assume it is loaded. Too many deaths and injuries occur when someone unintentionally shoots a friend while under the impression that the gun he or she is handling is not loaded. If you plan to handle a gun, avoid alcohol and drugs, which affect judgment and coordination.

Leisure Injuries

Leisure activities encompass a large part of our free time, so it is not surprising that **leisure injuries** are a significant health-related problem in the United States. Key factors in leisure injuries include misuse of equipment, lack of experience and skill, use of alcohol or other drugs, and failure to use appropriate safety equipment. Specific safety strategies for activities associated with leisure injuries include the following:

- Don't swim alone, in unsupervised places, under the influence of alcohol, or for an unusual length of time. Use caution when swimming in unfamiliar surroundings or in water colder than 70°F. Check the depth of water before diving. Make sure that residential pools are fenced and that children are never allowed to swim unsupervised.
- Always use a **personal flotation device** (also known as a life jacket) when on a boat.
- For all sports and recreational activities, make sure facilities are safe, follow the rules, and practice good sportsmanship. Develop adequate skill in the activity, and use proper safety equipment, including, where appropriate, a helmet, eye protection, correct footwear, and knee, elbow, and wrist pads.
- If using equipment such as skateboards, snowboards, mountain bikes, or all-terrain vehicles, wear a helmet and other safety equipment, and avoid excessive speeds and unsafe stunts. Playground equipment should be used only for those activities for which it is designed.
- If you are active in excessively hot and humid weather, drink plenty of fluids, rest frequently in the shade, and slow down or stop if you feel uncomfortable. Danger signals of heat stress include excessive perspiration, dizziness, headache, muscle cramps, nausea, weakness, rapid pulse, and disorientation.
- Do not use alcohol or other drugs during recreational activities—such activities require coordination and sound judgment.

For more on exercise safety, see Chapter 13.

In-Line Skating Injuries More than 26 million Americans use in-line skates, and more than 250,000 are injured badly enough each year to wind up in an emergency room. Injuries to the wrist and head are most common; many occur because users do not wear appropriate safety

Heimlich maneuver A maneuver developed by Henry J. Heimlich, M.D., to help force an obstruction from the airway.

leisure injuries Unintentional injuries and deaths that occur in public places or places used in a public way, not involving motor vehicles; includes most sports and recreation deaths and injuries; falls, drownings, burns, and heat and cold stress are examples.

personal flotation device A device designed to save a person from drowning by buoying up the body while in the water.

TERMS

Safe inline skating requires several pieces of gear, including a helmet and pads for the wrists, knees, and elbows.

gear. Researchers estimate that more than one-third of all serious injuries could be prevented if all skaters wore helmets and wrist and elbow protection.

To reduce your risk of being injured while rollerblading, wear a helmet, elbow and knee pads, wrist guards, a long-sleeved shirt, and long pants. Alcohol use appears to be a significant factor in in-line skating injuries that occur on college campuses. Because in-line skating involves skill, judgment, and coordination, it makes sense not to mix skating and drinking.

Scooter Injuries   Scooters are lightweight and have low-friction wheels for quickness and portability. Along with their skyrocketing popularity have come scooter-related injuries. Over 30,000 people are treated for scooter-related injuries in hospital emergency rooms each year, and several deaths related to scooter use have been reported. The most common injuries are arm or hand fractures and dislocations, cuts and bruises, and sprains; 85% of injuries involve children under the age of 15. Viewing

scooters as toys more than transportation may lead riders to ignore important safety precautions:

- Wear a helmet that meets bicycle helmet standards, along with knee and elbow pads.
- Be sure that handlebars, the steering column, and all nuts and bolts are securely fastened.
- Ride on smooth, paved surfaces away from motor vehicle traffic. Avoid streets and surfaces with water, sand, gravel, or dirt.
- Don't ride after dark.
- Closely supervise young children.

Work Injuries

Since 1912, when industrial records were first kept in the United States, the work site has become a much safer place, as evidenced by a nearly 90% reduction in the unintentional death rate. That figure becomes even more impressive when you realize that the size of the labor force has more than doubled and production has increased more than tenfold. One very significant factor to account for such a marked decline in **work injuries** has been the Occupational Safety and Health Act of 1970. As a result of that act, the Occupational Safety and Health Administration (OSHA) was created within the U.S. Department of Labor to ensure a safer and healthier environment for workers.

According to the Bureau of Labor Statistics, 4.1 million Americans suffered injuries on the job in 2006. Certain types of injuries, including skin disorders and repetitive strain injuries, are increasing. Although laborers make up less than half of the workforce, they account for more than 75% of all work-related injuries and illnesses. Their jobs usually involve extensive manual labor and lifting, neither of which is addressed in OSHA safety standards. Skin disorders account for nearly 40% of reported occupational illnesses; the introduction of more hazardous chemicals at the work site means that these disorders are of increasing concern. Most fatal occupational injuries

work injuries   Unintentional injuries and deaths that arise out of and in the course of gainful work, such as falls, electrical shocks, exposure to radiation and toxic chemicals, burns, cuts, back sprains, and loss of fingers or other body parts in machines.

repetitive strain injury (RSI)   A musculoskeletal injury or disorder caused by repeated strain on the hand, arm, wrist, or other part of the body; also called *cumulative trauma disorder (CTD)*.

carpal tunnel syndrome   Compression of the median nerve in the wrist, often caused by repetitive use of the hands, such as in computer use; characterized by numbness, tingling, and pain in the hands and fingers; can cause nerve damage.

TERMS

QUICK STATS

26 million Americans age 20–64 suffer frequent back pain.

—American Pain Foundation, 2007

involve crushing injuries, severe lacerations, burns, and electrocutions; among women, the leading cause of workplace injury deaths is homicide.

Back Injuries   Back problems accounted for about 280,000 work injuries in 2004; many of these could be prevented through proper lifting technique (Figure 21.1).

- Avoid bending at the waist. Remain in an upright position and crouch down if you need to lower yourself to grasp the object. Bend at the knees and hips.

- Place feet securely about shoulder-width apart; grip the object firmly.

- Lift gradually, with straight arms. Avoid quick, jerky motions. Lift by standing up or pushing with your leg muscles. Keep the object close to your body.

- If you have to turn, change the position of your feet. Twisting is a common and dangerous cause of injury. Plan ahead so that your pathway is clear and turning can be minimized.

- Put the object down gently, reversing the steps for lifting.

Repetitive Strain Injuries   Musculoskeletal injuries and disorders in the workplace include **repetitive strain**

FIGURE 21.1   Correct lifting technique.   Stay upright, bending at the knees and hips.

injuries (RSIs). RSIs are caused by repeated strain on a particular part of the body. Twisting, vibrations, awkward postures, and other stressors may contribute to RSIs. **Carpal tunnel syndrome** is one type of RSI that has increased in recent years due to increased use of computers, both at work and in the home (see the box "Carpal Tunnel Syndrome" on p. 660 for more information).

VIOLENCE AND INTENTIONAL INJURIES

Violence—the use of physical force with the intent to inflict harm, injury, or death upon oneself or another—is a major public health concern in the United States. According to

THINKING ABOUT THE ENVIRONMENT

Every year, thousands of people are killed and injured by weather-related events such as floods and hurricanes. Earthquakes and tsunamis can cause massive destruction and loss of life, while leaving thousands or even millions of people homeless and injured.

In May 2008, a cyclone struck Myanmar (formerly Burma), leaving nearly 135,000 people dead or missing. That same month, an earthquake measuring 7.9 on the Richter scale struck Sichuan Province in China, killing 12,000 and injuring countless others.

But weather emergencies usually are not on such a vast scale. For example, about 60 Americans die each year after being struck by lightning, almost always in isolated incidents. According to the National Weather Service, 1159 tornadoes strike in the United States each year, causing an average of 62 deaths annually.

For more information on the environment and environmental health, see Chapter 19.

QUESTIONS FOR CRITICAL THINKING AND REFLECTION

Think of one injury you have suffered. What were you doing when you were injured? Thinking back on the injury, was there anything you could have done to avoid or minimize it? How did the experience change your attitudes or behaviors?

Carpal Tunnel Syndrome

Carpal tunnel syndrome (CTS) is a repetitive strain injury characterized by pressure on the median nerve in the wrist. It is the most commonly reported work-related medical problem, accounting for about half of all work-related injuries. Women are about twice as likely as men to be affected by CTS.

The median nerve travels from the forearm to the hand through a tunnel in the wrist formed by the carpal (wrist) bones and associated tendons and cov-

ered by a ligament (see the figure). The median nerve can become compressed for a variety of reasons, including swelling of the surrounding tendons caused by pregnancy, diabetes, arthritis, or repetitive wrist motions during activities such as typing, cutting, or carpentry work. Symptoms of CTS include numbness, tingling, burning, and/or aching in the hand, particularly in the thumb and the first three fingers. The pain may worsen at night and may shoot up from the hand as far as the shoulder.

Many cases of carpal tunnel syndrome clear up on their own or with minimal treatment. Modification of the movement that is causing the problem is critically important. For example, adjusting the height of a computer keyboard so that the wrists can be held straight during typing can help relieve pressure on the wrists. CTS is often first treated by immobilizing the wrist with a splint during the night. People may also be given anti-inflammatory drugs or injections of cortisone in the wrist to reduce swelling. In a small percentage of severe cases, surgery to cut the ligament and reduce the pressure on the nerve may be recommended.

If you engage in activities like typing or cutting that involve repetitive motions, there are some strategies you can try to reduce your risk of developing carpal tunnel syndrome. Begin by modifying your work environment to reduce

the stress on your wrists. Alternate activities to avoid spending long stretches of time engaged in the same motion. Warm up your wrists before you begin any repetitive motion activity, and take frequent breaks to stretch and flex your wrists and hands:

- Extend your arms out in front of you and stretch your wrists by pointing your fingers to the ceiling; hold for a count of five. Then straighten your wrists and relax your fingers for a count of five.

- With arms extended, make a tight fist with both hands and then bend your wrists so your knuckles are pointed toward the floor; hold for a count of five. Then straighten your wrists and relax your fingers for a count of five.

Repeat these stretches several times, and finish by letting your arms hang loosely at your sides and shaking them gently for several seconds.

SOURCES: Ly-Pen, D., et al. 2005. Surgical decompression versus local steroid injection in carpal tunnel syndrome: A one-year, prospective, randomized, open, controlled clinical trial. *Arthritis and Rheumatism* 52(2): 612–619; Carpal tunnel syndrome. 2002. *Journal of the American Medical Association* 288(10): 1310; American Academy of Orthopaedic Surgeons. 2007. *Ask an Orthopaedic Surgeon about Carpal Tunnel Syndrome* (http://orthoinfo.aaos.org/topic.cfm?topic=A00009; retrieved February 21, 2009).

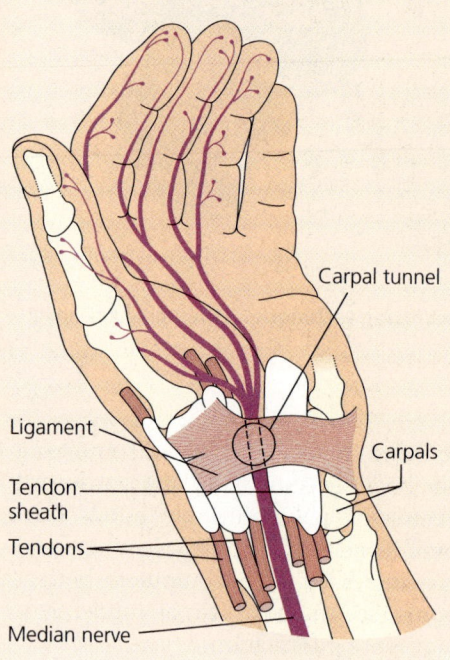

Carpal tunnel

Ligament

Carpals

Tendon sheath

Tendons

Median nerve

---

the Federal Bureau of Investigation (FBI), over 1.4 million violent crimes occurred in the United States in 2007. Worldwide, interpersonal violence is the third leading cause of death among people age 15–44. Examples of types of violence are assault, homicide, sexual assault, domestic violence, suicide, and child abuse.

It is difficult to determine the overall level of violence in our society because the major sources of data, police reports and victim surveys, are often at odds. In comparison to other industrialized countries, U.S. rates of violence are unusually high in only two areas—homicide and firearm-related deaths. The U.S. homicide death rate is four to ten times that of similar countries, and the firearm death rate is eight times that of other developed countries.

Factors Contributing to Violence

Most intentional injuries and deaths are associated with an argument or the committing of another crime. However, there are a great many forms of violence, and no single factor can explain all of them.

Social Factors   Rates of violence are not the same throughout society; they vary by geographic region, neighborhood, socioeconomic level, and many other factors. According to the FBI, violence was highest in the South in 2007, followed closely by the West. Neighborhoods that are disadvantaged in status, power, and economic resources are typically the ones with the most violence. Rates of violence are highest among young people and minorities, groups that have relatively little power. In 2007, people under age 25 accounted for 45% of the arrests for violent crime in the United States and 50% of the arrests for homicide.

People who feel a part of society (have strong family and social ties), who are economically integrated (have a reasonable chance at getting a decent job), and who grow up in areas where there is a feeling of community (good schools, parks, and neighborhoods) are significantly less likely to engage in violence. American society, where more than one-third of all children live in poverty and where the gap between rich and poor keeps growing, should be expected to breed violence. Many criminologists feel we have a growing underclass of people who cannot expect to have even the worst permanent jobs. That absence of hopes and dreams, combined with family devastation and poverty, certainly contributes to violent behavior.

Studies have shown that the environment on college campuses can contribute to violence. The nature of college campuses—transitory communities rather than permanent places where people work and live together over the long term—means that there is less incentive for people to cooperate and coexist amicably. Some campus groups even promote the ideas of bigotry and bias toward others, particularly toward individuals about whom they know little or with whom they have had little contact. Ignorance and insensitivity to differences can be precursors to acts of violence.

Violence in the Media The mass media play a major role in exposing audiences of all ages to violence as an acceptable and effective means of solving problems. Children may view as many as 10,000 violent acts on television and in movies each year. Computer and video games also include many violent acts, leading to concern that children's exposure to violence will make them more accepting or tolerant of it. The consequences of violence are depicted much less frequently.

A 2005 study linked TV viewing to bullying among children. Researchers found that the more hours per day that a 4-year-old spent watching TV, the more likely the child was to engage in bullying behavior in later years. Factors that reduced the rate of bullying included cognitive stimulation, such as parents reading to a child, and emotional support and attention. It is thought that emotional support from parents helps children develop empathy, social competence, and self-regulation—skills that enable them to deal with peers without resorting to aggressive or bullying behavior.

Researchers have found that exposure to media violence at least temporarily increases aggressive feelings in children, making them more likely to engage in violent or fearful behavior; the direct, short-term effects on teens and adults are less clear. It makes sense for parents to be aware of the potential influence of the media on their children. A child may not clearly understand the distinctions between the fantasy world portrayed in the media and the complexities of the real world. Parents should monitor the TV shows, movies, video games, music, and other forms of media to which children are exposed. Watching programs with children gives parents the opportunity to talk to children about violence and its consequences, to explain that violence is not the best way to resolve conflicts or solve problems, and to point out examples of positive behaviors such as kindness and cooperation.

Gender In most cases, violence is committed by men (Figure 21.2). Males are nine times more likely than females to commit murder, and three times more likely than females to be murdered. Male college students are

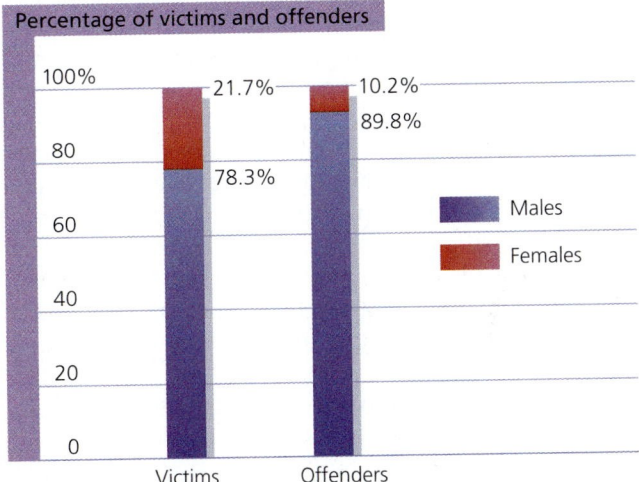

(a) Homicide victims and offenders by sex, 2007

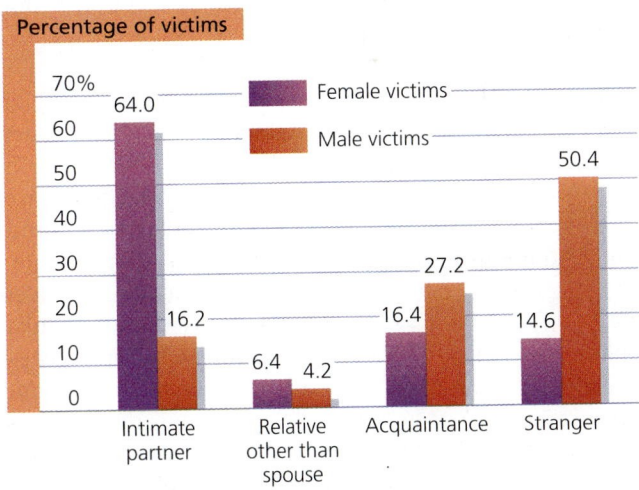

(b) Adult victims of violence by victim-offender relationship and sex of victim

FIGURE 21.2 Facts about violence in the United States.

SOURCES: Federal Bureau of Investigation. 2008. *Crime in the United States 2007.* Washington, D.C.: U.S. Department of Justice; Tjaden, P., and N. Thoennes. 2000. *Full Report of the Prevalence, Incidence, and Consequences of Violence Against Women.* Washington, D.C.: U.S. Department of Justice.

twice as likely to be the victim of violence as female students. Some researchers have suggested that the male hormone testosterone is in some way linked to aggressive behavior. Others point to prevailing cultural attitudes about male roles (men as dominant and controlling) as an explanation for the high rate of violence among men. However, these theories do not explain why it is that violent men are more likely to live in the West, belong to minorities, be poor, and be young.

Women do commit acts of violence, including a small but substantial proportion of murders of spouses. This fact has been used to argue that women have the same capacity to commit violence as men, but most researchers note substantial differences. Men often kill their wives as the culmination of years of violence or after stalking them; they may kill their entire family and themselves at the same time. Women virtually never kill in such circumstances; rather, they kill their husbands after repeated victimization or while being beaten.

Interpersonal Factors   Although most people fear attack from strangers, the majority of victims are acquainted with their attacker. Approximately 60% of murders of women and 80% of sexual assaults are committed by someone the woman knows. Crime victims and violent criminals tend to share many characteristics—that is, they are likely to be young, male, in a minority, and poor.

Alcohol and Other Drugs   Substance abuse and dependence are consistently associated with interpersonal violence and suicide. Intoxication affects judgment and may increase aggression in some people, causing a small argument to escalate into a serious physical confrontation. On college campuses, alcohol is involved in about 95% of all violent crimes.

Firearms   Many criminologists feel that the high rate of homicide in the United States is directly related to the fact that we are the only industrialized country in which handguns are widespread and easily available. Simply put, most victims of assaults with other weapons don't die, but the death rate from assault by handgun is extremely high. The use of a handgun can change a suicide attempt to a completed suicide and a violent assault to a murder.

Over 100,000 deaths and injuries occur in the United States each year as a result of the use of firearms. Firearms are used in more than two-thirds of homicides, and studies reveal a strong correlation between the incidence of gun ownership and homicide rates for a given area of the

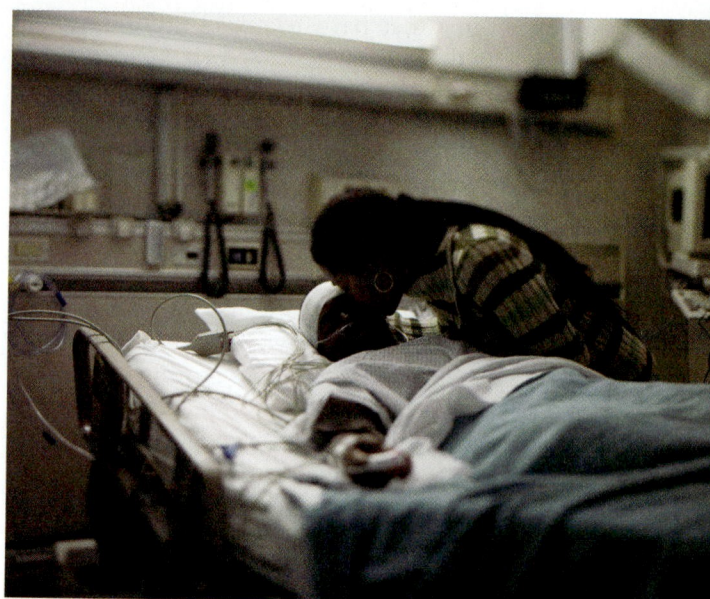

The victims of most types of violence are statistically likely to be young (under age 25), poor, in a minority, urban, and—except for rape and domestic violence—male.

country. Over half of all suicides involve a firearm, and people living in households in which guns are kept have a risk of suicide that is five or more times greater than that of people living in households without guns. Men between ages 15 and 34 have the highest risk of death from homicide and suicide when guns are the weapon used.

Research indicates that of all firearms, handguns are the murder weapon of choice, used in about 75% of homicides involving firearms. Teenagers and young adults are at particularly high risk for being murdered by handguns.

Assault

Assault is the use of physical force by a person or persons to inflict injury or death on another; homicide, aggravated assault, and robbery are examples of assault. Research indicates that the victims of assaultive injuries and their perpetrators tend to resemble one another in terms of ethnicity, educational background, psychological profile, and reliance on weapons. In many cases, the victim actually magnifies the confrontation through the use of a weapon.

Homicide

The FBI estimates that nearly 17,000 Americans were murdered in 2007. Men, teenagers, young adults, and members of minority groups, particularly African Americans and Latinos, are most likely to be murder victims. Although homicide rates for African Americans have declined dramatically in the past 25 years, the murder rate for black males is about six times higher than the rate for

> **QUICK STATS**
>
> In 2007, **21%** of aggravated assaults involved the use of a firearm.
>
> —FBI, 2008

the U.S. population as a whole. Poverty and unemployment have been identified as key factors in homicide, and this may account for the high rates of homicide among blacks and other minority groups.

Most homicides are committed with a firearm, occur during an argument, and occur among people who know one another. Intrafamilial homicide, where the perpetrator and victim are related, accounts for about one out of every eight homicides. About 40% of family homicides are committed by spouses, usually following a history of physical and emotional abuse directed at the woman. Wives are more likely to be murdered than husbands, and when a wife kills her husband, it is usually in self-defense.

Gang-Related Violence

Violence results from more than just the acts of individuals, as evidenced by the number of injuries and deaths resulting from gang activities. Gangs are most frequently associated with large cities, but gang activity also extends to the suburbs and even to rural areas. It is estimated that more than 1 million Americans belong to gangs; the average age for joining a gang is 14. Most gangs control a particular territory and will oppose other gangs, as well as police and community efforts to eliminate them. Gangs may be involved in illegal drug trade, extortion, and protection schemes. Gang members are more likely than non–gang members to possess weapons, and violence may result from conflicts over territory or illegal activities.

Gangs are more common in areas that are poor and suffer from high unemployment, population density, and crime. In these areas, an individual may feel that his or her hope of legitimate success in life is out of reach and know that involvement in the drug market makes some gang members rich. Often, gangs serve as a mechanism for companionship, self-esteem, support, and security; indeed, in some areas gang membership may be viewed as the only possible means of survival.

Hate Crimes

When bias against another person's race or ethnicity, national origin, religion, sexual orientation, or disability motivates a criminal act, the offense is classified as a hate crime. Hate crimes may be committed against people or property. Those against people may include intimidation, assault, and even rape or murder. Crimes against property most frequently involve graffiti, the desecration of churches or synagogues, cross burnings, and other acts of vandalism or property damage.

About 7700 hate crimes were reported in 2006; many more go unreported. The FBI estimates that hate crimes rose by 8% from 2005 to 2006. Crimes against people made up about 60% of all incidents; intimidation and assault are the most common offenses. Racial or ethnic bias was cited as a motivation in 52% of the hate crimes reported in 2006.

National origin or ethnicity was cited in 13% of cases, religion in 19%, and sexual orientation in 16%.

Hate crimes may be extremely brutal acts perpetrated at random on total strangers by multiple offenders. Suspects frequently are not identified, but research indicates that a substantial number of hate crimes are committed by males under age 20. Hate crimes are frequently, but not always, associated with fringe groups that have extremist ideologies, such as the Ku Klux Klan and neo-Nazi groups. The Southern Poverty Law Center tracks more than 880 hate groups and group chapters currently active in the United States; the rapid growth of hate sites on the Internet is another area of concern.

A variety of factors lead to the prejudice and intolerance that are a major force behind hate crimes. The FBI has reported a substantial increase in hate-motivated crimes in the past few years, especially since the terrorist attacks of September 11, 2001. Hate crimes against lesbian, gay, bisexual, and transgender (LGBT) people have more than tripled in recent years. A social context of unemployment and hard economic times, an influx of immigrants, and the growth of visible minority rights movements have been associated with the recent increases in hate crimes in the United States.

School Violence

Tragedies like the shootings at Columbine High School in Colorado and Red Lake Senior High School in Minnesota have brought national attention to the problem of violence in elementary, middle, and high schools. According to the National School Safety Center, about 450 school-associated violent deaths of students, faculty, and administrators have occurred since 1992. Most of these deaths occurred in urban areas, at high schools, and involved use of a firearm. As with other types of violence, both victims and offenders were predominantly young men. Homicide and suicide are the most serious but least common types of violence in schools; an estimated 400,000 less serious incidents of violence and crime occur each year, including theft, vandalism, and fights not involving weapons.

How risky is the school environment for students? Children are actually much safer at school than away from it. Less than 1% of all homicides among youths age 5–19 occur at school, and 90% of schools report no incidents of serious violence. Children and adolescents are far more likely to be killed by an adult in their own home or away from school than they are to die as a result of school-associated violence. According to the CDC, the overall number of violent incidents has decreased steadily since 1992; however, the number of multiple-victim events may have increased.

Recent school shootings received so much attention in part because they were unusual—they took place in predominantly suburban or rural schools and involved multiple victims. Despite declines in violence-related behaviors, about 6% of high school students in the 2007 Youth

Risk Behavior Survey reported carrying a weapon (gun, knife, club) to school at least once in the month before the survey, and 8% reported being threatened or injured with a weapon on school grounds in the past year.

Although schools are basically safe places overall, there are steps that can be taken to identify at-risk youths and improve safety for all students. Characteristics associated with youths who have caused school-associated violent deaths include the following:

- Uncontrollable angry outbursts
- Violent and abusive language and behavior
- Isolation from peers
- Depression and irritability
- Access to and preoccupation with weapons
- Lack of support and supervision from adults

Being a victim of teasing, bullying, or social exclusion (rejection) may lead to aggressive behavior and violence.

Recommendations for reducing school violence include offering classroom training in anger management, social skills, and improved self-control; providing mental health and social services for students in need; developing after-school programs that help students build self-esteem and make friends; and keeping guns out of the hands of children and out of schools.

Workplace Violence

Each year U.S. workers experience an average of 1.5 million minor assaults, 400,000 serious assaults, 85,000 robberies, 50,000 sexual assaults, and 700 homicides. In about 60% of cases, workplace violence is committed by strangers; acquaintances account for nearly 40% of cases, and intimates for 1%. Most of the perpetrators of workplace violence are white males over age 21. Firearms are used in more than 80% of workplace homicides, and the majority of these homicides occur during the commission of a robbery or other crime.

Police and corrections officers have the most dangerous jobs, followed by taxi drivers, security guards, bartenders, mental health professionals, and workers at gas stations and convenience and liquor stores. According to the U.S. Department of Labor, workers in state government offices experience more workplace violence of all types than do workers in local government or private industry.

General crime prevention strategies, including use of surveillance cameras and silent alarms and limiting the amount of cash on hand, can help reduce workplace violence related to robberies. A highly stressed workplace is a risk factor in cases of violence between acquaintances or coworkers; clear guidelines about acceptable behavior and prompt action after any threats or incidents of violence can help control this type of workplace violence.

Terrorism

In 2001, more Americans died as a result of terrorism than in any prior year; the attacks on September 11 killed more than 3000 people, including citizens of 78 countries. The FBI defines terrorism as the unlawful use of force or violence against persons or property to intimidate or coerce a government, the civilian population, or any segment thereof in furtherance of political or social objectives (see the box "Violence and Health: A Global View"). Terrorism can be either domestic, carried out by groups based in the United States, or international. It comes in many forms, including biological (see Chapter 17), chemical, nuclear, and cyber. Its intent is to promote helplessness by instilling fear of harm or destruction.

Terrorism-prevention activities occur at all levels of government. U.S. government efforts include close work with the diplomatic, law-enforcement, intelligence, economic, and military communities. The mission of the Department of Homeland Security is to help prevent, protect against, and respond to acts of terrorism on U.S. soil. It is coordinating efforts to protect electric and water supply systems, transportation, gas and oil, emergency services, the computer infrastructure, and other systems.

One step you can take is to put together an emergency plan and kit for your family or household that can serve for any type of emergency or disaster (see the box "Emergency Preparedness" on p. 666). See Chapters 2, 3, and 23 for advice on coping with the stress of terrorism, violence on campus, and recognizing post-traumatic stress disorder.

Family and Intimate Violence

Violence in families challenges some of our most basic assumptions about the family. Family violence generally refers to any rough and illegitimate use of physical force, aggression, or verbal abuse by one family member toward another. Such abuse may be physical and/or psychological in nature. Based on reported cases, an estimated 5–7 million women and children are abused each year in the United States.

Battering   Studies reveal that 95% of domestic violence victims are women; 20–35% of women who visit medical emergency rooms are there for injuries related to ongoing abuse. Violence against wives or intimate partners, or battering, occurs at every level of society but is more common at lower socioeconomic levels. It occurs more frequently in relationships with a high degree of conflict—an

Violence and Health: A Global View

connect™

In 2002, the World Health Organization (WHO) issued its *World Report on Violence and Health*, which examines the magnitude and impact of violence throughout the world. Each year, more than 1.6 million people die from violent acts: Suicide claims a life every 40 seconds, homicide every minute, and armed conflict every 2 minutes. Violence is among the leading causes of death for people age 15–44, accounting for 14% of deaths among males and 7% of deaths among females. Millions more victims of violence survive but are left with physical, psychological, and reproductive problems, including lost limbs, paralysis, depression, alcohol and drug abuse, sexual dysfunction, and STDs and other reproductive health problems. Beyond individual misery, violence has devastating social and economic consequences.

Interpersonal Violence

WHO defines *interpersonal violence* as the intentional use of physical force or power, threatened or actual, against another person that is likely to result in injury, death, psychological harm, or deprivation. Each year, more than 500,000 people die from interpersonal violence, and more than 60 million children and elderly adults are maltreated. It's estimated that 10–70% of women experience physical violence at the hands of an intimate partner during their lifetime; in addition, forced prostitution, child marriage, sexual trafficking, and female genital mutilation are prevalent in some areas of the world.

Worldwide, adolescents and young adults are the primary victims and perpetrators of interpersonal violence. Individual risk factors for violence highlighted in the WHO report include being young, male, and poor; being intoxicated; and having easy access to firearms. At the community and social levels, risk factors include low social capital (norms and networks that promote coordination and cooperation), high crime rates, rapid social change, poverty, poor rule of law and corruption, gender inequality, firearm availability, and armed conflict.

Collective Violence

WHO applies the term *collective violence* to violence inflicted by one group against another group to achieve political, economic, or social objectives. Collective violence includes armed conflict within or between states; genocide, repression, and other human rights abuses; terrorism; and organized violent crime. Characteristics of countries with increased risk of violent conflict include long-standing tensions between groups, a lack of democratic processes, unequal access to power, unequal distribution and control of resources, and rapid demographic changes.

In the twentieth century, an estimated 191 million people—well over half of them civilians—lost their lives directly or indirectly as a result of armed conflict, and many more were injured. In addition to directly causing deaths and injuries, collective violence destroys infrastructure and disrupts trade, food production, and vital services, thus setting the stage for famine, increased rates of infectious diseases, and mass movements of refugees. The resulting social turmoil also increases rates of interpersonal violence.

What Can Be Done?

The WHO report emphasizes that violence is neither an inevitable part of the human condition nor an intractable social problem. Rather, the wide variation in violence within and among nations over time suggests that violence is the product of a complex but modifiable set of social and environmental factors. Potential strategies to reduce violence include the following:

• Individual and relationship approaches to encourage healthy attitudes and behaviors, such as training in social,

parenting, and relationship skills and conflict resolution; mentoring programs; and treatment for people who suffer from depression or who have inflicted abuse on partners or children

• Community-based efforts to raise public awareness and address local social and material causes of violence, such as creating safe places for children to play and adopting community policing

• Societal approaches to change underlying cultural, social, and economic factors, such as new laws and international treaties, policy changes to reduce poverty and inequality, efforts to change harmful social and cultural norms (for example, ethnic discrimination or gender inequality), and disarmament and demobilization programs in countries emerging from conflict

SOURCES: World Health Organization. 2002. *The World Health Report 2002: Reducing Risks, Promoting Healthy Life.* Geneva: World Health Organization; World Health Organization. 2002. *World Report on Violence and Health.* Geneva: World Health Organization.

apparent inability to resolve arguments through negotiation and compromise. About 25% of women report having been physically assaulted or raped by an intimate partner, and more than 50% report having experienced some type of abuse—physical or psychological—in a relationship. In more than 10% of cases, the domestic violence continues for 20 years or longer. The problem of intimate violence is even apparent among young people; each year, 1.5 million high school students are victims of physical violence while on a date, according to the CDC.

In any given year, some part of the United States may be hit by a hurricane, flooding, tornadoes, or a mass power outage. These all-too-real situations—and the fear of potential threats such as terrorist strikes or an outbreak of widespread violence—underscore the need for everyone to be prepared for an emergency. Two key elements of emergency preparedness are a well-stocked emergency supply kit and a well-reasoned emergency plan.

Emergency Supplies

An emergency supply kit should include everything you'll need to make it on your own for at least 3 days. You'll need nonperishable food, water, first aid supplies, essential medications, a battery-powered radio, toiletries, clothing, a flashlight or candles and matches, cash, keys, copies of important documents, and supplies for sleeping outdoors in any season/weather (blankets, sleeping bags, tent, and so on). Don't forget about special-needs items for infants, seniors, and pets.

In the case of certain types of terrorist attacks or industrial disasters, you may need supplies to "shelter in place"—to create a barrier between yourself and any dangerous airborne materials. These supplies might include filter masks or folded cotton towels that can be placed over the mouth and nose. Plastic sheeting and duct tape can be used to seal windows and doors.

You may want to create several kits of emergency supplies. The primary one would contain supplies for home use. Put together a smaller, lightweight version that you can take with you if you are forced to evacuate your residence and kits for your car and office.

A Family or Household Plan

You and the members of your household may not be together when a disaster strikes. You should have a plan about where to meet and how to communicate. Choose at least two potential meeting places—one in your neighborhood and one or more in other areas. Your community may also have set locations for community shelters.

Where you go may depend on the circumstances of the emergency situation. Use your common sense, and listen to the radio or television for instructions from emergency officials about whether to evacuate or stay in place. In addition, know all the transportation options in the vicinity of your home, school, and workplace; roadways and public transit may be affected, so keep walking shoes in your emergency kit.

Everyone in the household should also have the same emergency contact person to call, preferably someone who lives outside the immediate area. Local phone service may be significantly disrupted, so long-distance calls may be more likely to go through. Everyone should carry the relevant phone numbers and addresses at all times.

Check the emergency plans at any location where you or family members spend time, including schools and workplaces. For each location, know the safest place to be for different types of emergencies—for example, near load-bearing interior walls during an earthquake, the basement during a tornado, or a safe location miles away from a hur-

ricane (assuming there will be enough time to get there). Also know how to turn off water, gas, and electricity in case of damaged utility lines; keep the needed tools next to the shutoff valves.

Other steps you can take to help prepare for emergencies include taking a first aid class and setting up an emergency response group in your neighborhood or building. More complete information about emergency preparedness is available from the following sources:

American Red Cross (www.redcross.org)

Federal Emergency Management Agency (www.fema.gov)

U.S. Department of Homeland Security (www.ready.gov)

At the root of much of this abusive behavior is the need to control another person. Abusive partners are controlling partners. They not only want to have power over another person, but also believe they are entitled to it, no matter what the cost to the other person. Abuse includes behavior that physically harms, arouses fear, prevents a person from doing what she wants, or compels her to behave in ways she does not freely choose. Controlling people use a variety of psychological, emotional, and physical tactics to keep their partners bound to them.

Early in a relationship, a person's tendency to be controlling may not be obvious (see the box "Recognizing the Potential for Abusiveness in a Partner" on p. 667).

In abusive relationships, the abuser (in most cases a man) usually has a history of violent behavior, traditional beliefs about gender roles, and problems with alcohol abuse. He has low self-esteem and seeks to raise it by dominating and imposing his will on another person. Research has revealed a three-phase cycle of battering, consisting of a period of increasing tension, a violent explo-

Recognizing the Potential for Abusiveness in a Partner

There are no sure ways to tell whether someone will become abusive or violent toward an intimate partner, but there are warning signs that you can look for. (Remember that, although most abusive relationships involve male violence directed at a woman, women can also be abusive, as can partners in a same-sex relationship. Because most abusers are male, the following material refers to the abuser as "he.") If you are concerned that a person you are involved with has the potential for violence, observe his or her behavior, and ask yourself these questions:

• What is this person's attitude toward women? How does he treat his mother and his sister? How does he work with female students, female colleagues, or a female boss? How does he treat your women friends?

• What is his attitude toward your autonomy? Does he respect the work you do and the way you do it? Or does he put it down, tell you how to do it better, or encourage you to give it up? Does he tell you he'll take care of you?

• How self-centered is he? Does he want to spend leisure time on your interests or his? Does he listen to you? Does he remember what you say?

• Is he possessive or jealous? Does he want to spend every minute with you? Does he cross-examine you about things you do when you're not with him?

• What happens when things don't go the way he wants them to? Does he blow up? Does he always have to get his way?

• Is he moody, mocking, critical, or bossy? Do you feel as if you're walking on eggshells when you're with him?

• Do you feel you have to avoid arguing with him?

• Does he drink too much or use drugs?

• Does he refuse to use condoms or take other precautions for safer sex?

Listen to your own uneasiness, and stay away from any man who disrespects women, who wants or needs you intensely and exclusively, and who has a knack for getting his own way almost all the time.

If you are in a serious relationship with a controlling person, you may already have experienced abuse. Consider the following questions:

• Does your partner constantly criticize you, blame you for things that are not your fault, or verbally degrade you?

• Does he humiliate you in front of others?

• Is he suspicious or jealous? Does he accuse you of being unfaithful or monitor your mail or phone calls?

• Does he track all your time? Does he discourage you from seeing friends and family?

• Does he prevent you from getting or keeping a job or attending school? Does he control your shared resources or restrict your access to money?

• Has he ever pushed, slapped, hit, kicked, bitten, or restrained you? Thrown an object at you? Used a weapon on you?

• Has he ever destroyed or damaged your personal property or sentimental items?

• Has he ever forced you to have sex or to do something sexually you didn't want to do?

• Does he anger easily when drinking or taking drugs?

• Has he ever threatened to harm you or your children, friends, pets, or property?

• Has he ever threatened to blackmail you if you leave?

If you answered yes to one or more of these questions, you may be experiencing domestic abuse. If you believe you or your children are in imminent danger, look in your local telephone directory for a women's shelter, or call 9-1-1. If you want information, referrals to a program in your area, or assistance, contact one of the organizations listed in For More Information at the end of the chapter.

SOURCES: Family Violence Prevention Fund. 2006. *It's Your Business.* San Francisco:Family Violence Prevention Fund; South Dakota Network Against Family Violence and Sexual Assault. 2005. *Are You in an Abusive Situation?* (http://www.sdnafvsa.com/abusive_relationship.php; retrieved June 16, 2008); National Coalition Against Domestic Violence. 2006. *2005 Domestic Violence Facts* (http://www.ncadv.org/files/DV_Facts.pdf; retrieved June 16, 2008).

---

sion and loss of control, and a period of contriteness in which the man begs forgiveness and promises it will never happen again. The batterer is drawn back to this cycle over and over again, but he never succeeds in changing his feelings about himself.

Battered women often stay in violent relationships for years. They may be economically dependent on their partners, feel trapped or fear retaliation if they leave, believe their children need a father, or have low self-esteem themselves. They may love or pity their husband, or they may believe they'll eventually be able to stop the violence. They usually leave the relationship only when they become determined that the violence must end. Battered women's shelters offer physical protection, counseling, support, and other assistance.

Many batterers are arrested, prosecuted, and imprisoned. Treatment programs are helpful in some cases but not all. Programs focus on stress management, communication and conflict-resolution skills, behavior change, and individual and group therapy. A crucial factor in changing

Education, counseling, and support can help the victims of family violence.

violent behavior seems to be a partner's adamant insistence that the abuse stop.

Stalking and Cyberstalking Battering is closely associated with **stalking,** characterized by harassing behaviors such as following or spying on a person and making verbal, written, or implied threats. In the United States, it is estimated that 1 million women and 400,000 men are stalked each year; about 87% of stalkers are men. About half of female victims are stalked by current or former intimate partners; of these, 80% had been physically or sexually assaulted by that partner during the relationship. Research suggests that stalking among female college students may be greater than that experienced by the general population. A stalker's goal may be to control or scare the victim or to keep her or him in a relationship. Most stalking episodes last a year or less.

The use of the Internet, e-mail, chat rooms, and other electronic communications devices to stalk another person is known as **cyberstalking.** As with offline stalking, the majority of cyberstalkers are men, and the majority of victims are women, although there have been same-sex cyberstalking incidents. Online incidents of harassment or abuse are becoming more common and more serious, and the U.S. Department of Justice estimates that over one-half million people each year experience cyberstalking. As the seriousness of the crime is being recognized, several states have passed cyberstalking or related laws, and a federal law is under consideration. The impersonal nature of electronic communication may lower the barriers to harassment and threats, because a cyberstalker does not have to physically confront the victim, and thus may make stalking more common. The popularity of online dating sites may also increase cyberstalking.

Cyberstalkers may send harassing or threatening e-mails or chat room messages to the victim, or they may encour-age others to harass the victim—for example, by impersonating the victim and posting inflammatory messages and personal information on bulletin boards or in chat rooms. Guidelines for staying safe online include the following:

- Never use your real name as an e-mail username or chat room nickname. Select an age- and gender-neutral identity.
- Avoid filling out profiles for accounts related to e-mail use or chat room activities with information that could be used to identify you.
- Do not share personal information in public spaces anywhere online or give it to strangers.
- Learn how to filter unwanted e-mail messages.
- If you experience harassment online, do not respond to the harasser. Log off or surf elsewhere.

If you receive unwanted online contact, make it clear to that person that you want all contact to stop. If harassment continues, contact the harasser's Internet service provider (ISP) by identifying the domain of the stalker's account (after the "@" sign); most ISPs have an e-mail address for complaints. Often, an ISP can try to stop the conduct by direct contact with the harasser or by closing his or her account. Save all communications for evidence, and contact your ISP and your local police department. Many states have laws against cyberstalking.

Violence Against Children Violence is also directed against children. Every year, at least 1 million American children are physically abused by their parents, and another 1 to 2 million are victims of neglect.

Parents who abuse children tend to have low self-esteem, to believe in physical punishment, to have a poor marital relationship, and to have been abused themselves (although many people who were abused as children do not grow up to abuse their own children). Poverty, unemployment, and social isolation are characteristics of families in which children are abused. External stressors related to socioeconomic and environmental factors are most closely associated with neglect, whereas stressors related to interpersonal issues are more closely associated with physical abuse. Single parents, both men and women, are at especially high risk for abusing their children. Very often one child, whom the parents consider different in some way, is singled out for violent treatment.

When government agencies intervene in child-abuse situations, their goals are to protect the victims and to assist and strengthen the families. Successful programs emphasize education and early intervention, such as home visits to high-risk first-time mothers. Educational efforts focus on stress management, money management, job-finding skills, and information about child behavior and development. Parents may receive counseling and be referred to substance-abuse treatment programs. Support groups like Parents Anonymous are effective for parents committed to changing their behavior.

Elder Abuse   According to the National Center on Elder Abuse, each year, 1–2 million older adults are abused, exploited, or mistreated by someone who is supposed to be giving them care and protection; only one in six incidents is reported. Most abusers are family members who are serving as caregivers.

Elder abuse can take different forms: physical, sexual, or emotional abuse; financial exploitation; neglect; or abandonment. Neglect accounts for about 55% of reported cases. Elders who have lost some mental or physical functions and must rely on others for care are most at risk and may suffer malnutrition, dehydration, mismanaged medication, or infection due to poor hygiene. Physical abuse accounts for about 15% of reported cases, and financial exploitation for about 13%. Experts also cite a growing concern about self-neglect among the elderly population. This includes behavior that threatens one's own health or safety, and can include refusing to comply with doctors' orders or neglecting to eat a balanced diet.

Abuse often occurs when caring for a dependent adult becomes too stressful for the caregiver, especially if the elder is incontinent, has suffered mental deterioration, or is violent. Abuse may become an outlet for frustration. Many believe that the solution to elder abuse is support in the form of greater social and financial assistance, such as adult day-care centers and education and public care programs.

Sexual Violence

The use of force and coercion in sexual relationships is one of the most serious problems in human interactions. The most extreme manifestation of sexual coercion— forcing a person to submit to another's sexual desires—is rape, but sexual coercion occurs in many subtler forms, including sexual harassment.

Sexual Assault: Rape   Sexual coercion that relies on the threat and use of physical force or takes advantage of

circumstances that render a person incapable of giving consent (such as when drunk) constitutes **sexual assault** or **rape.** When the victim is younger than the legally defined age of consent, the act constitutes **statutory rape,** whether or not coercion is involved. Coerced sexual activity in which the victim knows or is dating the rapist is often referred to as **date rape,** or *acquaintance rape.* Most victims know their assailant, but less than one-third of all sexual crimes are reported.

Any woman—or man—can be a rape victim. Between 100,000 and 130,000 cases of rape are reported each year. It is estimated that nearly 700,000 women are raped each year and that 1 in 6 women and 1 in 33 men has experienced an attempted or completed rape at some point in their lives. A study of college students found that between 1 in 4 and 1 in 5 college women experience a completed or attempted rape during their college years. Most male-on-male rapes do not occur in prison.

> Only **6%** of rapists ever spend a day in jail for their offense.
>
> QUICK STATS
>
> —Rape, Abuse, & Incest National Network, 2008

WHO COMMITS RAPE?   Men who commit rape may be any age and come from any socioeconomic group. Some rapists are exploiters in the sense that they rape on the spur of the moment and mainly want immediate gratification. Some attempt to compensate for feelings of sexual inadequacy and an inability to obtain satisfaction otherwise. Others are more hostile and sadistic and are primarily interested in hurting and humiliating a particular woman or women in general. Often, the rapist is more interested in dominance, control, and power than in sexual satisfaction.

Most women are in much less danger of being raped by a stranger than of being sexually assaulted by a man they know or date. Surveys suggest that as many as 25% of women have had experiences in which the men they were dating persisted in trying to force sex despite pleading, crying, screaming, or resisting. Surveys have also found that more than 60% of all rape victims were raped by a current or former spouse, boyfriend, or date.

Most cases of date rape are never reported to the police, partly because of the subtlety of the crime. Usually no weapons are involved, and direct verbal threats may not have been made. Rather than being terrorized, the victim usually is attracted to the man at first. Victims of date rape tend to shoulder much of the responsibility for the incident, questioning their own judgment and behavior rather than blaming the aggressor.

Sometimes husbands rape their wives. Strong evidence suggests that 15% of American women who have ever married have been raped by their husbands or ex-husbands; as many as 60% of battered women may have been raped by

TERMS

stalking   Repeatedly harassing or threatening a person through behaviors such as following a person, appearing at a person's residence or workplace, leaving written messages or objects, making harassing phone calls, or vandalizing property; frequently directed at a former intimate partner.

cyberstalking   The use of e-mail, chat rooms, bulletin boards, or other electronic communications devices to stalk another person.

sexual assault or **rape**   The use of force to have sex with someone against that person's will.

statutory rape   Sexual interaction with someone under the legal age of consent.

date rape   Sexual assault by someone the victim knows or is dating; also called *acquaintance rape.*

their husbands. A charge of spousal rape can now be taken to court in all states.

FACTORS CONTRIBUTING TO DATE RAPE Although the general status of women in society has improved, it is still a commonly held cultural belief that nice women don't say yes to sex (even when they want to) and that real men don't take no for an answer.

Men and women also differ in their perception of romantic encounters and signals. In one study, researchers found that men interpreted women's actions on dates, such as smiling or talking in a low voice, as indicating an interest in having sex, whereas the women interpreted the same actions as just being friendly. Men's thinking about forceful sex also tends to be unclear. One psychologist reports that men find "forcing a woman to have sex against her will" more acceptable than "raping a woman," even though the former description is the definition of rape.

Men who rape their dates tend to have certain attributes, including hostility toward women, a belief that dominance alone is a valid motive for sex, and an acceptance of sexual violence. They may feel that force is justified in certain circumstances, such as if they are sexually involved with a woman and she refuses to have sex, if the woman is known to have had sex with other men, or if the woman shows up at a party where people are drinking and taking drugs. The man often primes himself to force himself sexually on his date by drinking, which lowers his ordinary social inhibitions. Many college men who have committed date rape tried to seduce their dates by plying them with alcohol first.

DATE-RAPE DRUGS A 2006 study showed that drugs are a factor in more than 60% of sexual assaults and about 5% of victims are given date-rape drugs. Also called predator drugs, the drugs used in date rapes include flunitrazepam (Rohypnol), gamma hydroxybutyrate (GHB), and ketamine hydrochloride ("Special K"). Rohypnol is not legal in the United States, but Ketamine and GHB can be legally obtained because they are used for legitimate medical purposes.

These drugs have a variety of effects, including sedation; if slipped surreptitiously into a drink, they can incapacitate a person within about 20 minutes and make her or him more vulnerable to assault. Rohypnol, GHB, and other drugs also often cause anterograde amnesia, meaning victims have little memory of what happened while they were under the influence of the drug. (See Chapter 9 for more on the effects of these and other psychoactive drugs.)

The Drug-Induced Rape Prevention and Punishment Act of 1996 adds up to 20 years to the prison sentence of any rapist who uses a drug to incapacitate a victim. Supporters of the law likened dropping a drug in a victim's drink to putting a knife to her throat. The makers of Rohypnol are modifying the pills so they will be a more noticeable color and will dissolve more slowly, thereby reducing the likelihood that Rohypnol can be used as a date-rape drug; however, other drugs in powdered or liquid form can be slipped into drinks unnoticed. Strategies such as the following can help ensure that your drink is not tampered with at a bar or party:

- Check with campus or local police to find out if drug-facilitated sexual assault has occurred in your area and, if so, where.

- Drink moderately and responsibly. Avoid group drinking and drinking games.

- Be wary of opened beverages—alcoholic or nonalcoholic—offered by strangers. When at an unfamiliar bar, watch the bartender pour your drink.

- Let your date be the first to drink from the punchbowl at a bar, club, or rave.

- If an opened beverage tastes, looks, or smells strange, do not drink it. If you leave your drink unattended, such as when you dance or use the restroom, obtain a fresh drink when you return to your table.

- If you go to a party, club, or bar, go with friends. Have a prearranged plan for checking on each other visually and verbally. If you feel giddy or lightheaded, get assistance.

Both males and females can take actions that will reduce the incidence of acquaintance rape; see the box "Preventing Date Rape" for specific suggestions.

DEALING WITH A SEXUAL ASSAULT Experts disagree about whether a woman who is faced with a rapist should fight back or give in quietly to avoid being injured or to gain time in the hope of escaping. Some rapists say that if a woman had screamed or resisted loudly, they would have run; others report they would have injured or killed her. (If a rapist is carrying a weapon, most experts advise against fighting unless absolutely necessary.) A woman who is raped by a stranger is more likely to be physically injured than a woman raped by someone she knows. Each situation is unique, and a woman should respond in whatever way she thinks best. If a woman chooses not to resist, it does not mean that she has not been raped.

If you are threatened by a rapist and decide to fight back, here is what Women Organized Against Rape (WOAR) recommends:

- Trust your gut feeling. If you feel you are in danger, don't hesitate to run and scream. It is better to feel foolish than to be raped.

- Yell—and keep yelling. It will clear your head and start your adrenaline going; it may scare your attacker and also bring help. Don't forget that a rapist is also afraid of pain and afraid of getting caught.

- If an attacker grabs you from behind, use your elbows for striking his neck, his sides, or his stomach.

- Try kicking. Your legs are the strongest part of your body, and your kick is longer than his reach. Kick

Preventing Date Rape

Guidelines for Women

• Believe in your right to control what you do. Set limits, and communicate these limits clearly, firmly, and early. Say no when you mean no.

• Be assertive with someone who is sexually pressuring you. Men often interpret passivity as permission.

• If you are unsure of a new acquaintance, go on a group date or double date. If possible, provide your own transportation.

• Remember that some men assume sexy dress and a flirtatious manner mean a desire for sex.

• Remember that alcohol and drugs interfere with clear communication about sex.

• Use the statement that has proven most effective in stopping date rape: "This is rape, and I'm calling the police."

Guidelines for Men

• Be aware of social pressure. It's OK to not score.

• Understand that no means no. Don't continue making advances when your date resists or tells you she wants to stop. Remember that she has the right to refuse sex.

• Don't assume sexy dress and a flirtatious manner are invitations to sex, that previous permission for sex applies to the current situation, or that your date's relationships with other men constitute sexual permission for you.

• Remember that alcohol and drugs interfere with clear communication about sex.

---

with your rear foot and with the toe of your shoe. Aim low to avoid losing your balance.

• His most vulnerable spot is his knee; it's low, difficult to protect, and easily knocked out of place. Don't try to kick a rapist in the crotch; he has been protecting this area all his life and will have better protective reflexes there than at his knees.

• Once you start fighting, keep it up. Your objective is to get away as soon as you can.

• Remember that ordinary rules of behavior don't apply. It's OK to vomit, act crazy, or claim to have a sexually transmitted disease.

If you are raped, tell what happened to the first friendly person you meet. Call the police, tell them you were raped, and give your location. Try to remember as many facts as you can about your attacker; write down a description as soon as possible. Don't wash or change your clothes, or you may destroy important evidence. The police will take you to a hospital for a complete exam; show the physician any injuries. Tell the police simply, but exactly, what happened. Be honest, and stick to your story.

If you decide that you don't want to report the rape to the police, be sure to see a physician as soon as possible. You need to be checked for pregnancy and STDs.

THE EFFECTS OF RAPE Rape victims suffer both physical and psychological injury. For most, physical wounds heal within a few weeks. Psychological pain may endure and be substantial. Even the most physically and mentally strong are likely to experience shock, anxiety, depression, shame, and a host of psychosomatic symptoms after being victimized. These psychological reactions following rape comprise rape trauma syndrome, which is characterized by fear, nightmares, fatigue, crying spells, and digestive upset. (Rape trauma syndrome is a form of post-traumatic stress disorder; see Chapter 3.) Self-blame is very likely; society has contributed to this tendency by perpetuating the myths that women can actually defend themselves and that no one can be raped if she doesn't want to be. Fortunately, these false beliefs are dissolving in the face of evidence to the contrary.

Many organizations offer counseling and support to rape victims. Look in the telephone directory under Rape or Rape Crisis Center for a hotline number to call. Your campus may have counseling services or a support group.

Child Sexual Abuse Child sexual abuse is any sexual contact between an adult and a child who is below the legal age of consent. Adults and older adolescents are able to coerce children into sexual activity because of their authority and power over them. Threats, force, or the promise of friendship or material rewards may be used to manipulate a child. Sexual contacts are typically brief and consist of genital manipulation; genital intercourse is much less common.

Sexual abusers are usually male, heterosexual, and known to the victim. The abuser may be a relative, a

> **15%** of rape and sexual assault victims are less than 12 years old.
>
> —Rape, Abuse, & Incest National Network, 2008

QUICK STATS

friend, a neighbor, or another trusted adult acquaintance. Child abusers are often pedophiles, people who are sexually attracted to children. They may have poor interpersonal and sexual relationships with other adults and feel socially inadequate and inferior.

One highly traumatic form of sexual abuse is **incest**, sexual activity between people too closely related to legally marry. The most common forms of incest are father-daughter (which includes stepfather-stepdaughter) abuse, brother-sister abuse (usually an adolescent boy abusing a preadolescent girl), and uncle-niece abuse; mother-son sexual activity is rare. Adults who commit incest may be pedophiles, but very often they are simply sexual opportunists or people with poor impulse control and emotional problems.

Most sexually abused children are between ages 8 and 12 when the abuse first occurs. More girls are sexually abused than boys. The degree of trauma for the child can be very serious, but it varies with the type of encounters, their frequency, the child's age and relationship to the abuser, and the parents' response. Father-daughter abuse may be the most traumatic form, in part because it is a violation of the basic parent-child relationship and because the abuse tends to be more frequent. Abused children may be depressed or moody, exhibit hyperactivity, play violently with others or with inanimate objects, talk nonsense, or unintentionally injure themselves.

Child sexual abuse is often unreported. Surveys suggest that as many as 27% of women and 16% of men were sexually abused as children. An estimated 150,000–200,000 new cases of child sexual abuse occur each year. It can leave lasting scars; victims are more likely to suffer as adults from low self-esteem, depression, anxiety, eating disorders, self-destructive tendencies, sexual problems, and difficulties in intimate relationships.

If you were a victim of sexual abuse as a child and feel it may be interfering with your functioning today, you may want to address the problem. A variety of approaches can help, such as joining a support group of people who have had similar experiences, confiding in a partner or friend, or seeking professional help.

Sexual Harassment   Unwelcome sexual advances, requests for sexual favors, and other verbal, visual, or physical conduct of a sexual nature constitute **sexual harassment** if such conduct explicitly or implicitly does any of the following:

- Affects academic or employment decisions or evaluations
- Interferes with an individual's academic or work performance
- Creates an intimidating, hostile, or offensive academic, work, or student living environment

Extreme cases of sexual harassment occur when a manager, professor, or other person in authority uses his or her ability to control or influence jobs or grades to coerce people into having sex or to punish them if they refuse. A hostile environment can be created by conduct such as sexual gestures, displaying of sexually suggestive objects or pictures, derogatory comments and jokes, sexual remarks about clothing or appearance, obscene letters, and unnecessary touching or pinching. Sexual harassment can occur between people of the same or opposite sex.

Although sexual harassment is forbidden by law, many cases go unreported. In a survey of 17,000 federal employees, 42% of women and 15% of men reported having been sexually harassed.

If you have been the victim of sexual harassment, you can take action to stop it. Be assertive with anyone who uses language or actions you find inappropriate. If possible, confront your harasser either in writing, over the telephone, or in person, informing him or her that the situation is unacceptable to you and you want the harassment to stop. Be clear. "Do not *ever* make sexual remarks to me" is an unequivocal statement. If assertive communication doesn't work, assemble a file or log documenting the harassment, noting the details of each incident and information about any witnesses who may be able to support your claims. You may discover others who have been harassed by the same person, which will strengthen your case. Then file a grievance with the harasser's supervisor or employer, such as someone in the dean's office if you are a student or someone in the human resources office if you are an employee.

If your attempts to deal with the harassment internally are not successful, you can file an official complaint with your city or state Human Rights Commission or Fair Employment Practices Agency, or with the federal Equal Employment Opportunity Commission. You may also wish to pursue legal action under the Civil Rights Act or under

TERMS

incest   Sexual activity between close relatives, such as siblings or parents and their children.

sexual harassment   Unwelcome sexual advances, requests for sexual favors, and other conduct of a sexual nature that affects academic or employment decisions or evaluations; interferes with an individual's academic or work performance; or creates an intimidating, hostile, or offensive academic, work, or student living environment.

Staying Safe on Campus

College campuses can be the site of criminal activity and violence just as any other environment or living situation can be—and so they require the same level of caution and awareness that you would use in other situations. Two key points to remember: 80% of campus crimes are committed by a student against a fellow student, and alcohol or drug use is involved in 90% of campus felonies. Drinking or drug use can affect judgment and lower inhibitions, so be aware if you or another person is under the influence. Here are some suggestions for keeping yourself safe on campus:

• Don't travel alone after dark. Many campuses have shuttle buses that run from spots on campus such as the library and the dining hall to residence halls and other locations. Escorts are often available to walk with you at night.

• Be familiar with well-lit and frequently traveled routes around campus if you do need to walk alone.

• If you have a car, follow the usual precautions about parking in well-lit areas, keeping the doors locked while you are driving, and never picking up hitchhikers.

• Always have your keys ready as you approach your residence hall, room, and car. Don't lend your keys to others.

• Let friends and family members know your schedule of classes and activities to create a sort of buddy system.

• Be sure the doors and windows of your dorm room have sturdy locks, and use them.

• Don't prop open doors or hold doors open for nonstudents or nonresidents trying to enter your dorm. Be aware of non-residents around your dorm. If someone says that he or she is meeting a friend inside, that person should be able to call the friend from outside the building.

• Keep valuables and anything containing personal information—credit cards, wallets, jewelry, and so on—hidden. Secure expensive computer and stereo equipment with cables so that it can't be easily stolen. Use a quality U-shaped lock whenever you leave a bicycle unattended.

• Be alert when using an ATM, and don't display large amounts of cash.

• Stay alert and trust your instincts. Don't hesitate to call the police or campus security if something doesn't seem or feel right.

The Jeanne Clery Disclosure of Campus Security Policy and Campus Crime Statistics Act, named for a Lehigh University student who was murdered in her residence hall in 1986, requires colleges and universities to collect and report campus crime statistics. You can now review this information online at the Crime Statistics Web site of the U.S. Department of Education's Office of Postsecondary Education (http://ope.ed.gov/security/Search.asp).

local laws prohibiting employment discrimination. Very often, the threat of a lawsuit or other legal action is enough to stop the harasser.

What You Can Do About Violence

It is obvious that violence in our society is not disappearing and that it is a serious threat to our collective health and well-being. This is especially true on college campuses, which in a sense are communities in themselves but sometimes lack the authority or guidance to tackle the issue of violence directly (see the box "Staying Safe on Campus"). Schools are now providing training for conflict resolution and are educating people about the diverse nature of our society, thereby encouraging tolerance and understanding. New programs are being developed at the grass-roots level to deal with problems of violence directly.

As with any public health problem, one potential approach is to identify and target high-risk groups for intervention. Violence prevention programs currently focus on conflict-resolution training and the development of social skills. These measures have proven effective, but for behavior change to be lasting, the focus of such programs must expand beyond individual intervention to include social and environmental factors.

Reducing gun-related injuries may require changes in the availability, possession, and lethality of the 8–12 million firearms sold in the United States each year. As part of the Brady gun control law, computerized instant background checks are performed for most gun sales to prevent purchases by convicted felons, people with a history of mental instability, and certain other groups. In some states, waiting periods are required in addition to the background checks. Some groups advocate a complete and universal federal ban on the sale of all handguns.

Safety experts also advocate the adoption of consumer safety standards for guns, including features such as childproofing and indicators to show if a gun is loaded. Technologies are now available to personalize handguns to help prevent unauthorized use. Magnetic encoding, touch memory, radio frequency, and fingerprint reading are ways to identify the owner and prevent use by others. Education about proper storage is also important. Surveys indicate that more than 40% of homes with children contain guns; in about 23% of gun-owning households, the weapon is stored loaded, and in 28% the gun is kept hidden but not locked. To be effective, any approach to

firearm injury prevention must have the support of law enforcement and the community as a whole.

PROVIDING EMERGENCY CARE

No matter how hard you try to avoid them, some injuries will inevitably occur. Therefore, it is important to prepare for situations when you may need to provide emergency care for yourself or others. If you are prepared to help, you can improve someone else's chances of surviving or avoiding permanent disability.

A course in **first aid** can help you respond appropriately when someone is injured. One important benefit of first aid training is learning what *not* to do in certain situations. For example, a person with a suspected neck or back injury should not be moved unless other life-threatening conditions exist. A trained person can assess emergency situations accurately before acting.

Emergency rescue techniques can save the lives of people who are choking, who have stopped breathing, or whose hearts have stopped beating. As described earlier, the Heimlich maneuver is used when a victim is choking (see the inside back cover). Pulmonary resuscitation (also known as rescue breathing, artificial respiration, or mouth-to-mouth resuscitation) is used when a person is not breathing. Cardiopulmonary resuscitation (CPR) is used when a pulse cannot be found. Training is required before a person can perform CPR, and in 2005, significant changes were made to the guidelines for lay rescuer CPR. Courses are offered by the American Red Cross and the American Heart Association.

A new feature of some of these courses is training in the use of automatic external defibrillators (AEDs), which monitor the heart's rhythm and, if appropriate, deliver an electrical shock to restart the heart. Because of the impor-

tance of early use of defibrillators in saving heart attack victims, these devices are being installed in public places, including casinos, airports, and many office buildings.

As a person providing assistance, you are the first link in the **emergency medical services (EMS) system**. Your responsibility may be to render first aid, provide emotional support for the victim, or just call for help. It is important to remain calm and act sensibly. The basic pattern for providing emergency care is check-call-care:

- *Check the situation:* Make sure the scene is safe for both you and the injured person. Don't put yourself in danger; if you get hurt too, you will be of little help to the injured person.

- *Check the victim:* Conduct a quick head-to-toe examination. Assess the victim's signs and symptoms, such as level of responsiveness, pulse, and breathing rate. Look for bleeding and any indications of broken bones or paralysis.

- *Call for help:* Call 9-1-1 or a local emergency number. Identify yourself and give as much information as you can about the condition of the victim and what happened.

- *Care for the victim:* If the situation requires immediate action (no pulse, shock, etc.), provide first aid if you are trained to do so.

QUESTIONS FOR CRITICAL THINKING AND REFLECTION

What kinds of emergency training have you had? What kinds of skills do you have that would enable you to help someone who was hurt, trapped, or needed some other kind of assistance?

SUMMARY

- Injuries are caused by a dynamic interaction of human and environmental factors. Risk-taking behavior is associated with a high rate of injury.

- Key factors in motor vehicle injuries include aggressive driving, speeding, a failure to wear safety belts, alcohol and drug intoxication, fatigue, and distraction.

- Motorcycle, moped, and bicycle injuries can be prevented by developing appropriate skills, driving or riding defensively, and wearing proper safety equipment, especially a helmet.

- Most fall-related injuries are a result of falls at floor level, but stairs, chairs, and ladders are also involved in a significant number of falls.

- Careless smoking and problems with cooking or heating equipment are common causes of home fires. Being prepared for fire emergencies means planning escape routes and installing smoke detectors.

- The home can contain many poisonous substances, including medications, cleaning agents, plants, and fumes from cars and appliances.

- Performing the Heimlich maneuver can prevent someone from dying from choking.

- The proper storage and handling of firearms can help prevent injuries; assume that any gun is loaded.

- Many injuries during leisure activities result from the misuse of equipment, lack of experience, use of alcohol, and a failure to wear proper safety equipment.

- Most work-related injuries involve extensive manual labor; back problems and repetitive strain injuries are most common.

- Factors contributing to violence include poverty, the absence of strong social ties, the influence of the mass media, cultural attitudes about gender roles, problems in interpersonal relationships, alcohol and drug abuse, and the availability of firearms.

- Types of violence include assault, homicide, gang-related violence, hate crimes, school violence, workplace violence, and terrorism.

- Battering and child abuse occur at every socioeconomic level. The core issue is the abuser's need to control other people.

- Most rape victims are women, and most know their attackers. Factors in date rape include different standards of appropriate sexual behavior for men and women and different perceptions of actions.

- Child sexual abuse often results in serious trauma; usually the abuser is a trusted adult.

- Sexual harassment is unwelcome sexual advances or other conduct of a sexual nature that affects academic or employment performance or evaluations or that creates an intimidating, hostile, or offensive academic, work, or student living environment.

- Strategies for reducing violence include conflict-resolution training, social skills development, and education programs that foster tolerance and understanding among diverse groups.

- Steps in giving emergency care include making sure the scene is safe for you and the injured person, conducting a quick examination of the victim, calling for help, and providing emergency first aid.

FOR MORE INFORMATION

BOOKS

Becker, N. 2005. *Popular Mechanics Home Safety Handbook: Practical Tips for Safe Living*. Red Oak, IA: Popular Mechanics. *Provides tips on living safely and how to prevent accidents and injuries in your home.*

Dacey, J. S., and L. B. Fiore. 2006. *The Safe Child Handbook*. San Francisco: Jossey-Bass. *A practical handbook for keeping your family safe and coping with the stress and fear associated with many real-world dangers.*

Henry, J., H. Larson, and J. Rubin. 2007. *Home Emergency Pocket Guide*. Tigard, OR.: Informed Publishing. *A small, spiral-bound guide that provides critical information to help in dealing with a variety of emergencies.*

MacPherson, J. 2003. *AAA Auto Guide: Driving Survival. How to Stay Safe on the Road*. Heathrow, Fl: AAA Publishing. *Provides helpful strategies for choosing and maintaining a safe vehicle and for handling a variety of driving situations.*

McGrew, J. 2005. *Think Safe: Practical Measures to Increase Security at Home, at Work, and Throughout Life*. Hilton Head Island, S.C.: Cameo Publications. *A general guide to safety and crime and violence prevention.*

National Safety Council. 2007. *Standard First Aid, CPR, and AED*. Itasca, Ill.: National Safety Council. *An everyday guide to the most current first aid and emergency resuscitation techniques, with instructions for using automatic defibrillators.*

ORGANIZATIONS, HOTLINES, AND WEB SITES

American Automobile Association Foundation for Traffic Safety. Provides consumer information about all aspects of traffic safety; Web site has online quizzes and extensive links.
   http://www.aaafts.org

Adopting Safer Habits

Why do you get injured? What human and environmental factors contribute to injuries? Identifying those factors is one step toward making your lifestyle safer. Changing unsafe behaviors before they lead to injuries is an even better way of improving your chances.

For the next 7–10 days, keep track of any mishaps you are involved in or injuries you receive, recording them on a daily behavior record like the one shown in Chapter 1. Count each time you cut, burn, or injure yourself, fall down, run into someone, or have any other potentially injury-causing mishap, no matter how trivial. Also record any risk-taking behaviors, such as failing to wear your safety belt or bicycle helmet, drinking and driving, exceeding the speed limit, putting off home or bicycle repairs, and so on. For each entry (injury or incidence of unsafe behavior), record the date, the time, what you were doing, who else was there and how you were influenced by him or her, what your motivations were, and what you were thinking and feeling at the time.

At the end of the monitoring period, examine your data. For each incident, determine both the human factors and the environmental factors that contributed to the injury or unsafe behavior. Were you tired? Distracted? Did you not realize this situation was dangerous? Did you take a chance? Did you think this incident couldn't happen to you? Was visibility poor? Were you using defective equipment? Then consider each contributing factor carefully, determining why it existed and how it could have been avoided or changed. Finally, consider what preventive actions you could take to avoid such incidents or to change your behaviors in the future.

As an example, let's say that you usually don't use a safety belt when you run local errands in your car and that several factors contribute to this behavior: You don't really think you could be involved in a crash so close to home, you only go on short trips, you just never think to use it, and so on. One of the contributing factors to your unsafe behavior is inadequate knowledge. You can change this factor by obtaining accurate information about auto crashes (and their usual proximity to a victim's home) from this chapter and from library or Internet research. Just acquiring information about auto crashes and safety belt use may lead you to examine your beliefs and attitudes about safety belts and motivate you to change your behavior.

Once you're committed, you can use behavior change techniques described in Chapter 1, such as completing a contract, asking family and friends for support, and so on, to build a new habit. Put a note or picture reminding you to buckle up in your car where you can see it clearly. Recruit a friend to run errands with you and to remind you about using your safety belt. Once your habit is established, you may influence other people—especially people who ride in your car—to use safety belts all the time. By changing this behavior, you have reduced the chances that you or your passengers will suffer a serious injury or even die in a vehicle crash.

American Bar Association: Domestic Violence. Provides information on statistics, research, and laws relating to domestic violence.
http://www.abanet.org/domviol/home.html

Consumer Product Safety Commission. Provides information and advice about safety issues relating to consumer products.
http://www.cpsc.gov

CyberAngels. Provides information on online safety and help and advice for victims of cyberstalking.
http://www.cyberangels.org

Insurance Institute for Highway Safety. Provides information about crashes on the nation's highways, as well as reports on topics such as speeding and crashworthiness of vehicles.
http://www.iihs.org

National Center for Injury Prevention and Control. Provides consumer-oriented information about unintentional injuries and violence.
http://www.cdc.gov/injury

National Center for Victims of Crime. An advocacy group for crime victims; provides statistics, news, safety strategies, tips on finding local assistance, and links to related sites.
http://www.ncvc.org

National Highway Traffic Safety Administration. Supplies materials about reducing deaths, injuries, and economic losses from motor vehicle crashes.
http://www.nhtsa.dot.gov

National Safety Council. Provides information and statistics about preventing unintentional injuries.
http://www.nsc.org

National Violence Hotlines. Provide information, referral services, and crisis intervention.
800-799-SAFE (domestic violence)
800-422-4453 (child abuse)
800-656-HOPE (sexual assault)

National Youth Violence Prevention Resource Center. Provides information about violence related to college students.
http://www.safeyouth.org/scripts/topics/college.asp

Occupational Safety and Health Administration. Provides information about topics related to health and safety issues in the workplace.
http://www.osha.gov

Prevent Child Abuse America. Provides statistics, information, and publications relating to child abuse, including parenting tips.
http://www.preventchildabuse.org

Rape, Abuse, and Incest National Network (RAINN). Provides guidelines for preventing and dealing with sexual assault and abuse.
http://www.rainn.org

SafeUSA. Provides information about safety at home, in schools, at work, on the road, and in communities.
http://www.safeusa.org

Tolerance.Org: 10 Ways to Fight Hate on Campus. Offers suggestions for fighting hate and promoting tolerance; sponsored by the Southern Poverty Law Center.

http://www.tolerance.org/campus/index.jsp

World Health Organization: Violence and Injury Prevention. Provides statistics and information about the consequences of intentional and unintentional injuries worldwide.

http://www.who.int/violence_injury_prevention

The following sites provide statistics and background information on violence and crime in the United States:

Bureau of Justice Statistics: http://www.ojp.usdoj.gov/bjs
Federal Bureau of Investigation: http://www.fbi.gov
Justice Information Center: http://www.ncjrs.org

SELECTED BIBLIOGRAPHY

Browne, K. D., and C. Hamilton-Giachritsis. 2005. The influence of violent media on children and adolescents: A public-health approach. *Lancet* 365(9460): 702–710.

Carr, J. L. 2005. *American College Health Association Campus Violence White Paper.* Baltimore, Md.: American College Health Association.

Centers for Disease Control and Prevention. 2004. Impact of primary laws on adult use of safety belts—United States, 2002. *Morbidity and Mortality Weekly Report* 53(12): 257–260.

Centers for Disease Control and Prevention. 2004. Surveillance for fatal and nonfatal injuries—United States, 2001. *MMWR Surveillance Summaries* 55(SS-7): 1–57.

Centers for Disease Control and Prevention. 2004. Violence-related behaviors among high school students—United States, 1991–2003. *Morbidity and Mortality Weekly Report* 53(29): 651–655.

Centers for Disease Control and Prevention. 2005. Increase in poisoning deaths caused by nonillicit drugs. *Morbidity and Mortality Weekly Report* 54(2): 33–36.

Centers for Disease Control and Prevention. 2005. Unintentional non-fire-related carbon monoxide exposures—United States, 2001–2003. *Morbidity and Mortality Weekly Report* 54(2): 36–39.

Centers for Disease Control and Prevention. 2006. Nonfatal injuries and restraint use among child passengers—United States, 2004. *Morbidity and Mortality Weekly Report* 55(22): 624–627.

Centers for Disease Control and Prevention. 2006. Notice to Readers: Buckle Up America Week—May 22–29, 2006. *Morbidity and Mortality Weekly Report* 55(19): 535–536.

Centers for Disease Control and Prevention. 2006. Physical dating violence among high school students—United States, 2003. *Morbidity and Mortality Weekly Report* 55(19): 532–535.

Commission for Global Road Safety. 2008. *Global Road Safety Fact File* (http://www.fiafoundation.com/commissionforglobalroadsafety/factfile/index.html; retrieved February 21, 2009).

Cummings, P., and F. P. Rivara. 2004. Car occupant death according to the restraint use of other occupants. *Journal of the American Medical Association* 291(3): 343–349.

Cummings, P., et al. 2006. Changes in traffic crash mortality rates attributed to use of alcohol, or lack of a seat belt, air bag, motorcycle helmet, or bicycle helmet, United States, 1982–2001. *Injury Prevention* 12(3): 148–154.

Federal Bureau of Investigation. 2007. *Hate Crime Statistics, 2006.* Washington, D.C.: U.S. Department of Justice.

Federal Bureau of Investigation. 2008. *Crime in the United States. Uniform Crime Reports, 2007.* Washington, D.C.: U.S. Department of Justice.

Graffunder, C. M., et al. 2004. Through a public health lens. Preventing violence against women: An update from the U.S. Centers for Disease Control and Prevention. *Journal of Women's Health* 13(1): 5–15.

Gray-Vickrey, P. 2004. Combating elder abuse. *Nursing* 34(10): 47–51.

Grossman, D. C., et al. 2005. Gun storage practices and risk of youth suicide and unintentional firearm injuries. *Journal of the American Medical Association* 293(6): 707–714.

Iudice, A., et al. 2005. Effects of prolonged wakefulness combined with alcohol and hands-free cell phone divided attention tasks on simulated driving. *Human Psychopharmacology* 20(2): 125–132.

Kilpatrick, D. 2004. Interpersonal violence and public policy: What about the victims? *Journal of Law, Medicine, and Ethics* 32(1): 73–81.

Krug, E. G. 2004. Injury surveillance is key to preventing injuries. *Lancet* 364(9445): 1563–1566.

National Center for Health Statistics. 2008. Deaths: Preliminary data for 2006. *National Vital Statistics Reports* 56(16).

National Safety Council. 2008. *Injury Facts 2008.* Itasca, Ill.: National Safety Council.

National School Safety Center. 2008. *Report on School Associated Violent Deaths* (http://www.schoolsafety.us/pubfiles/savd.pdf; retrieved February 21, 2009).

National Traffic Safety Administration. 2007. *Traffic Safety Facts Research Note: Driver Cell Phone Use in 2006—Overall Results.* Washington, D.C.: National Traffic Safety Administration.

Olson, C. M., et al. 2006. Association of first- and second-generation air bags with front occupant death in car crashes: A matched cohort study. *American Journal of Epidemiology* 164(2): 161–169.

Quinlan, K. P., et al. 2005. Alcohol-impaired driving among U.S. adults, 1993–2002. *American Journal of Preventive Medicine* 28(4): 346–350.

Silverman, J. G., A. Raj, and K. Clements. 2004. Dating violence and associated sexual risk and pregnancy among adolescent girls in the United States. *Pediatrics* 114(2): e220–225.

Strayer, D. L., et al. 2006. A comparison of the cell phone driver and the drunk driver. *Human Factors* 48(2): 381–391.

Thompson, R. S., et al. 2006. Intimate partner violence: Prevalence, types and chronicity in adult women. *American Journal of Preventive Medicine* 30(6): 447–457.

UC Berkeley School of Public Health. 2006. Cycling: Use your head. *University of California, Berkeley, Wellness Letter* 22(9): 6.

World Health Organization. 2004. *World Report on Road Traffic Injury Prevention.* Geneva: World Health Organization.

Zimmerman, F. J., et al. 2005. Early cognitive stimulation, emotional support, and television watching as predictors of subsequent bullying among grade-school children. *Archives of Pediatrics and Adolescent Medicine* 59(4): 384–388.

AGING: A VITAL PROCESS

LOOKING AHEAD>>>>>

AFTER READING THIS CHAPTER, YOU SHOULD BE ABLE TO:

- List strategies for healthful aging
- Explain the physical, social, and mental changes that may accompany aging and discuss how people can best confront these changes
- Describe practical considerations of older adults and caregivers, including housing, finances, health care, communication, and transportation

TEST YOUR KNOWLEDGE

1. **Women do not need to take preventive measures against osteoporosis until after menopause.**
   True or false?

2. **What is the leading cause of disability in the United States?**
   a. heart disease
   b. arthritis
   c. dementia

3. **On average, a woman will spend more time caring for an aging relative than raising children.**
   True or false?

4. **Exercise is beneficial for older people because it**
   a. protects against osteoporosis.
   b. maintains alertness and intelligence.
   c. prevents falls.

5. **Alcohol abuse is rare among older adults.**
   True or false?

ANSWERS

1. **FALSE.** Everyone—but especially women—needs to pay attention to diet and exercise in younger years in order to build bone mass.

2. **B.** According to the Centers for Disease Control and Prevention, arthritis is the leading cause of disability in the United States.

3. **TRUE.** The average woman will spend 17 years raising children and 18 years caring for an aging relative.

4. **ALL THREE.** Even for people over 80, exercise can improve physical functioning and balance and reduce falls and injuries.

5. **FALSE.** Alcohol abuse affects about 10% of elderly people. It often goes undetected because its symptoms may mimic those of other conditions, such as Alzheimer's disease.

Aging is the process of becoming older, a process that is genetically determined but profoundly affected by one's environment. Your grandparents or great-grandparents may be examples of how these two determinants play a role in the aging process.

Aging does not begin at some specific point in life, and there is no precise age at which a person becomes "old." Rather, aging is a normal process of development that occurs throughout life. It happens to everyone, but at different rates for different people. Some people are "old" at 25, and others are still "young" at 75.

Although youth is not entirely a state of mind, your attitude toward life and your attention to your health significantly influence the satisfaction you will get from life. This is especially true when new physical, mental, and social challenges occur in later years. If you optimize wellness during young adulthood, you can exert great control over the physical and mental aspects of aging, and you can better handle your response to events that might be out of your control.

This chapter discusses the aging process and describes some of the major effects increasing age can have on one's life.

GENERATING VITALITY AS YOU AGE

As we age, physical and mental changes occur gradually, over a lifetime. Biological aging includes all the normal, progressive, irreversible changes to one's body that begin at birth and continue until death. Psychological aging and social aging usually involve more abrupt changes in circumstance and emotion: relocating, changing homes, losing a spouse and friends, retiring, having a lower income, and changing roles and social status. These changes represent opportunities for growth throughout life.

Not all of them happen to everybody, and their timing varies, partly depending on how we have prepared for our later days. Some people never have to leave their homes and appear to be in good health until the day they die. Others have tremendous adjustments to make—to entirely new surroundings with fewer financial resources, to new acquaintances, to the changing physical condition of their bodies and new health problems, and possibly to loneliness and loss of self-esteem.

Successful aging requires preparation. People need to establish good health habits in their teens and twenties. During their twenties and thirties, they usually develop important relationships and settle into a particular lifestyle. By their mid-forties, they generally know how much money they need to support the lifestyle they've chosen. At this point, they must assess their financial status and perhaps adjust their savings in order to continue enjoying that lifestyle after retirement. In their mid-fifties, they need to reevaluate their health insurance plans and may want to think about retirement housing. In their seventies

Table 22.1	Americans Who Rate Their Health as Fair or Poor, 2007	
Age Group	**Percentage**
18–24	9.7%
25–34	10.4%
35–44	11.9%
45–54	16.5%
55–64	22.5%
65–74	25.0%
75 and older	31.4%

SOURCE: Centers for Disease Control and Prevention, National Center for Chronic Disease Prevention and Health Promotion. 2008. *Health Related Quality of Life* (http://www.cdc.gov/hrqol; retrieved February 22, 2009).

and beyond, they need to consider ways of sharing their legacy with the next generation. Throughout life, people should cultivate interests and hobbies they enjoy, both alone and with others.

What Happens as You Age?

A significant number of older Americans describe themselves as being in poor health (Table 22.1). Many of the characteristics associated with aging are not due to aging at all. Rather, they are the result of neglect and abuse of our bodies and minds. These assaults lay the foundation for later psychological problems and chronic conditions like arthritis, heart disease, diabetes, hearing loss, and hypertension. We sacrifice our health by smoking, having poor nutrition, overeating, abusing alcohol and drugs, bombarding our ears with excessive noise, and exposing our bodies to too much ultraviolet radiation from the sun. We also jeopardize our bodies through inactivity, encouraging our muscles and even our bones to wither and deteriorate. And we endure abuse from the toxic chemicals in our environment.

But even with the healthiest behavior and environment, aging inevitably occurs. It results from biochemical processes we don't yet fully understand. The physiological changes in organ systems are caused by a combination of gradual aging and impairment from disease. Because of redundancy in most organ systems, the body's ability to function is not affected until damage is fairly extensive. Studies of healthy people indicate that functioning remains essentially constant until after age 70. Further research may help pinpoint the causes of aging and aid in the development of therapies to repair damage to aging organs (see the box "Stem Cells").

Life-Enhancing Measures: Age-Proofing

You can prevent, delay, lessen, or even reverse some of the changes associated with aging through good habits. Simple things you can do daily will make a vast difference to

Nearly all the cells in the body are differentiated, meaning they are committed to specific functions. We have heart cells, skin cells, nerve cells—more than 260 kinds in all. Stem cells, on the other hand, are undifferentiated; they can renew themselves by continuing to divide in their undifferentiated state for long periods, or they can develop into specialized cells as needed. The ability to develop into almost any type of tissue gives stem cells great therapeutic potential.

Theoretically, stem cells can be used to create replacement cells for many diseased or injured tissues. For example, if scientists can coax stem cells into differentiating, they may be able to create insulin-producing cells to treat diabetes, cardiac muscle cells to repair a damaged heart, or healthy brain cells for people with Parkinson's disease. Experts hope that stem cells can be widely produced and matched to a patient's cellular makeup. Before this can happen, however, technical and ethical problems must be solved.

Embryonic Stem Cells

As their name suggests, embryonic stem cells are derived from embryos. About 4–5 days after fertilization, an embryo is a microscopic ball of cells, called a *blastocyst*. At this stage, the embryo contains about 30 stem cells; scientists can remove these cells and grow them, producing millions of embryonic stem cells.

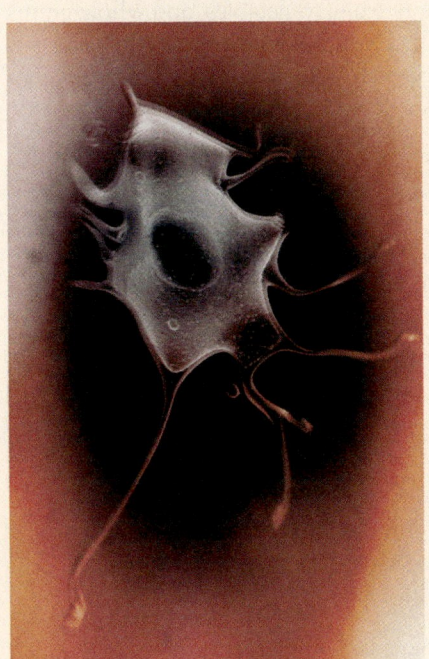

This method kills the embryo, however, and gives rise to the ethical debate that swirls around stem cell research. Most embryonic stem cells used in research are derived from eggs that have been fertilized in vitro, then donated to research; they are not taken from embryos fertilized in the womb.

In mid-2006, a team of researchers announced that a single stem cell (called a *blastomere*) could be taken from a 2- or 3-day-old embryo without destroying the embryo. This soon after fertilization, the embryo contains only 8 cells. The technique, in fact, is sometimes performed on embryos created through in vitro fertilization. Scientists allow the blastomere to multiply, then test the cells for defects before implanting the embryo—which has continued developing from the 7 remaining cells—in the mother's womb. Fertilization experts report that such embryos develop into healthy babies.

Currently there are no approved treatments or human trials using these cells. Theoretically, they offer the greatest potential for regeneration and tissue replacement after disease or serious injury.

Adult Stem Cells

Some organs and tissues in the adult body can replace cells, while others do not seem to have this ability. Researchers now believe that cellular repair is carried out by adult stem cells that lie dormant in tissues until they are needed.

Adult stem cells seem to have some *plasticity* (the ability to differentiate). For example, hematopoietic stem cells in bone marrow can turn into all the different types of blood cells. There is only limited evidence to suggest that adult stem cells from one tissue can turn into functional cells of another type of tissue.

The hematopoietic stem cell is the most studied type of adult stem cell and the only one widely used in clinical applications. These cells are used in transplants to restore blood and immune components to the bone marrow of people being treated for cancer and other diseases. Hematopoietic stem cells for transplant can be collected from a donor, but they are also sometimes derived from umbilical cord blood.

Although transplant success rates have improved, rejection remains a major problem, and success depends on finding a close cellular match between donor and recipient. Another avenue of stem cell re-

search—and a possible solution to rejection—is *somatic cell nuclear transfer*. In this technique, the nucleus from a somatic (body) cell is placed in an egg whose nucleus has been removed. The egg is allowed to grow into a blastocyst, and then the resulting stem cells are removed. This process, also called *therapeutic cloning*, produces a line of stem cells that are genetically matched to the original cell's donor; using these stem cells for transplant should eliminate problems with rejection. (This technique is distinct from reproductive cloning, in which an embryo is created through somatic cell transfer, then implanted into a woman's uterus and allowed to develop. This process results in an offspring who is genetically identical to the donor of the original somatic cell.)

The Stem Cell Controversy

Many experts believe that research into both embryonic and adult stem cells is needed to advance the therapeutic potential of stem cell research. However, the use of human embryos for such research is controversial. Some people advocate a complete ban; others would permit the use of existing stem cell lines, the use of extra embryos produced through in vitro fertilization, or the use of embryos created from eggs and sperm donated specifically for research.

Federal officials have been wrangling with the stem cell issue since 2000; federal guidelines now place severe restrictions on funding for stem cell research and limit researchers' access to stem cells. The result is a confusing patchwork of state laws regarding stem cells. Meanwhile, Taiwan and several European countries have jumped into the stem cell arena, providing funding for research and approving laws supporting stem cell use. As a result, many prominent American researchers have gone abroad in hopes of continuing their work under more favorable circumstances.

In 2007, scientists at Wake Forest University found a new type of stem cell in amniotic fluid. This discovery could provide an alternative to embryonic stem cells. Additional research is being conducted, and preliminary tests show opportunities for future cell development and transplantation. Clinical trials have shown promise in treating heart failure, lupus, and other blood and bone diseases.

your level of energy and vitality—your overall wellness. The following suggestions have been mentioned throughout this text. But because they are profoundly related to health in later life, we highlight them here.

Challenge Your Mind   Numerous studies show that older adults who stay mentally active have a lower risk of developing dementia. Reading, doing puzzles, learning language, and studying music are good ways to stimulate the brain. The more complex the activity, the more protective it may be.

Develop Physical Fitness   Exercise significantly enhances both psychological and physical health. A 2006 study showed that elderly people who burned extra calories through daily activity had a much lower mortality rate than their peers who did not exercise. The positive effects of exercise include the following:

- Lower blood pressure and healthier cholesterol levels
- Better protection against heart attacks and an increased chance of survival should one occur

Regular exercise is a key to successful, healthy aging.

- Sustained or increased lung capacity
- Weight control through less accumulation of fat
- Maintenance of strength, flexibility, and balance
- Protection against osteoporosis and type 2 diabetes
- Increased effectiveness of the immune system
- Maintenance of mental agility and flexibility, response time, memory, and hand-eye coordination

The stimulus that exercise provides also seems to protect against the loss of **fluid intelligence,** the ability to find solutions to new problems. Fluid intelligence depends on rapidity of responsiveness, memory, and alertness. Individuals who exercise regularly are also less susceptible to depression and dementia.

Regular physical activity also fends off *sarcopenia,* which is age-related loss of muscle mass, strength, and function (see Chapter 13). The weaker a person becomes, the less he or she can do; this condition can rob one of self-sufficiency and lead to greater dependence on others. The muscle wasting that occurs in sarcopenia also leads to weight gain because muscle burns more calories than fat, even at rest.

Regular physical activity is essential for healthy aging. Table 22.2 shows specific exercise recommendations for healthy adults age 65 or older, and for adults age 50–64 with chronic conditions such as arthritis. Older individuals who have been sedentary should be encouraged to become more active. It's never too late to start exercising. Even in people over 80, endurance and strength training can improve balance, flexibility, and physical functioning and reduce the potential for dangerous falls.

Eat Wisely   Good health at any age is enhanced by eating a varied diet full of nutrient-rich foods. Follow the recommendations in the 2005 Dietary Guidelines for Americans to get enough essential nutrients while maintaining a healthy weight (Chapter 12). For many adults, that means eating more fruits, vegetables, and whole grains while eating fewer foods high in saturated and trans fats and added sugars. Special guidelines for older adults include the following:

- Get enough vitamin B-12 and extra vitamin D from fortified foods or supplements.
- To help control blood pressure, limit sodium intake to 1500 mg per day and get enough potassium (4700 mg per day). Older adults tend to have higher blood pressure and to be salt-sensitive.
- Consume foods rich in dietary fiber and drink plenty of water to help prevent constipation, which may occur in up to 20% of older adults. A diet rich in whole grains, vegetables, and fruits can meet the recommended goals for fiber.
- Pay special attention to food safety; older adults tend to be more susceptible to foodborne illness (see Chapter 12).

Table 22.2	Exercise Recommendations for Older Adults	
Type of Exercise	Days per Week	Duration
Moderate-intensity aerobic exercise *or*	At least 5	At least 30 minutes
Vigorous-intensity aerobic exercise	At least 3	At least 20 minutes
Strength training	At least 2	8–10 exercises, 10–15 repetitions each
Flexibility training	At least 2	At least 10 minutes

SOURCE: Nelson M. E., et al. 2007. Physical activity and public health in older adults: Recommendation from the American College of Sports Medicine and the American Heart Association. *Medical Science in Sports and Exercise* 39(8): 1435–1445.

Maintain a Healthy Weight   Weight management is especially difficult if you have been overweight most of your life. A sensible program of expending more calories through exercise, cutting calorie intake, or a combination of both will work for most people who want to lose weight, but there is no magic formula. Obesity is not physically healthy, and it leads to premature aging (see Chapter 14).

Control Drinking and Overdependence on Medications   Alcohol abuse ranks with depression as a common hidden mental health problem, affecting about 10% of older adults. (The ability to metabolize alcohol decreases with age.) The problem is often not identified because the effects of alcohol or drug dependence can mimic disease, such as Alzheimer's disease. Signs of potential alcohol or drug dependence include unexplained falls or frequent injuries, forgetfulness, depression, and malnutrition. Older people who retire or lose a spouse are especially at risk. Problems can be avoided by not using alcohol to relieve anxiety or emotional pain and not taking medication when safer forms of treatment are available.

Don't Smoke   The average pack-a-day smoker can expect to live about 13–14 years less than a nonsmoker. Furthermore, smokers suffer more illnesses that last longer, and they are subject to respiratory disabilities that limit their total vigor for many years before their death. Premature balding, skin wrinkling, and osteoporosis have been linked to cigarette smoking. Smokers at age 50 often have wrinkles resembling those of a person of 60.

Schedule Physical Examinations to Detect Treatable Diseases   When detected early, many diseases, including hypertension, diabetes, and many types of cancer, can be successfully controlled by medication and lifestyle changes. Regular testing for **glaucoma** after age 40 can prevent blindness from this eye disease. Recommended immunizations, including those for influenza and pneumococcus, can protect you from preventable infectious diseases. (See Chapters 14–17 for screening and immunization guidelines.)

Recognize and Reduce Stress   Stress-induced physiological changes increase wear and tear on your body. Cut down on the stresses in your life. Don't wear yourself out through lack of sleep, substance abuse or misuse, or overwork. Practice relaxation, using the techniques described in Chapter 2. If you contract a disease, consider it your body's attempt to interrupt your life pattern; reevaluate your lifestyle, and perhaps slow down.

> **42%** of older Americans say their health is a serious problem.
> —National Council on Aging, 2003
>
> QUICK STATS

The health behaviors you practice *now* are more influential in determining how long and how well you will live than your behaviors at a later age. Retiring from your life's occupation with a physically healthy body will allow far more options for enjoying yourself than will retiring with frail health or disabilities. Preventable poor health drains finances, emotions, and energy and contributes to poor psychological health. By enhancing your wellness today, you're ensuring some wellness for the future.

DEALING WITH THE CHANGES OF AGING

The changes that occur with aging have repercussions that must be grappled with and resolved. Just as you can act now to prevent or limit the physical changes of aging, you can also begin preparing yourself psychologically, socially, and financially for changes that may occur later in life. If you have aging parents, grandparents, and friends,

> **? QUESTIONS FOR CRITICAL THINKING AND REFLECTION**
> How do you feel about the prospect of growing old? Would you say that you look forward to it, or are you anxious about it? What influences have shaped your feelings about aging?

> **fluid intelligence**   The ability to develop a solution when confronted with a new problem.
>
> **glaucoma**   A disease in which fluid inside the eye is under abnormally high pressure; can lead to the loss of peripheral vision and blindness.
>
> TERMS

the following information may give you insight into their lives and encourage you to begin cultivating appropriate and useful behaviors now.

Planning for Social Changes

Retirement marks a major change in the second half of life. As Americans' longevity has increased, people spend a larger proportion of their lives—17 years or more—in retirement. This has implications for reestablishing important relationships, developing satisfying interests outside work, and saving for an adequate retirement income. People who have well-developed leisure pursuits adjust better to retirement than those with few interests outside work.

Changing Roles and Relationships   Changes in social roles are a major feature of middle age. Children become young adults and leave home, putting an end to daily parenting. Parents experiencing this empty-nest syndrome must adapt to changes in their customary responsibilities and personal identities. And although retirement may be a desirable milestone for most people, it may also be viewed as a threat to prestige, purpose, and self-respect—the loss of a valued or customary role—and will probably require some adjustment.

Retirement and the end of child rearing also bring about changes in the relationship between marriage partners. The amount of time a couple spends together will increase and activities will change. Couples may need a period of adjustment, in which they get to know each other as individuals again. Discussing what types of activities each partner enjoys can help couples set up a mutually satisfying routine of shared and independent activities.

Increased Leisure Time   Although retirement confers the advantages of leisure time and freedom from deadlines, competition, and stress, many people do not know how to enjoy their free time. If you have developed diverse interests, retirement can be a joyful and fulfilling period of your life. It can provide opportunities for expanding your horizons by giving you the chance to try new activities, take classes, and meet new people. Volunteering in your community can enhance self-esteem and allow you to be a contributing member of society (see the box "Help Yourself by Helping Others").

The retirement years can be the best part of one's life, socially, with increased opportunities to meet and interact with new and different people.

The Economics of Retirement   Retirement is usually accompanied by a new economic situation. It may mean a severely restricted budget or possibly even financial disaster if you don't take stock of your finances and plan ahead. Financial planning for retirement should begin early in life. People in their twenties and thirties should estimate how much money they need to support their standard of living, calculate their projected income, and begin a savings program. The earlier people begin such a program, the more money they will have at retirement.

Financial planning for retirement is especially critical for women. American women are much less likely than men to be covered by pension plans, reflecting the fact that many women have lower-paying jobs or work part-time during their childbearing years. They tend to have less money vested in other types of retirement plans as well. Although the gap is narrowing, women currently outlive men by about 5–6 years, and they are more likely to develop chronic conditions that impair their daily activities later in life. The net result of these factors is that older women are almost twice as likely as older men to live in poverty. Women should investigate their retirement plans and take charge of their finances to be sure they will be provided for as they get older.

Help Yourself by Helping Others

Choosing to help others—whether as a volunteer for a community organization or through spontaneous acts of kindness—can enhance emotional, social, spiritual, and physical wellness. Surveys and studies indicate that the sense of purpose and service and the feelings of generosity and kindness that go with helping others may be as important a consideration for wellness as good nutrition and regular exercise. Volunteer activities result in many of the same benefits as regular exercise, such as increased energy and vitality. Older adults who volunteer have higher levels of emotional and social wellness and lower rates of death.

In a national survey of volunteers from all fields, helpers reported the following benefits:

• Helper's high—physical and emotional sensations such as sudden warmth, a surge of energy, and a feeling of euphoria that occur immediately after helping

• Feelings of increased self-worth, calm, and relaxation

• A perception of greater physical health

• Fewer colds and headaches, improved eating and sleeping habits, and some relief from the pain of chronic diseases such as asthma and arthritis

Just how might helping benefit the health of the helper? By helping others, we may relieve our own distress and guilt over their problems. We focus on things other than our own problems, and we get a special kind of attention from the people we help. Helping others can be effective at banishing a bad mood or a case of the blues. Helping others can also expand our perspective and enhance our appreciation for our own lives. Helping may benefit physical health by providing a temporary boost to the immune system and by combating stress and hostile feelings linked to the development of chronic diseases.

Helping others doesn't require a huge time commitment or a change of career. To get the most out of helping, keep the following guidelines in mind:

• *Make contact.* Choose an activity that involves personal contact.

• *Help as often as possible.* If your schedule allows, volunteer at least once a week. Any amount of time helping is better than none.

• *Make helping voluntary.* Voluntary helping has positive results, whereas obligatory helping situations can actually increase stress.

• *Volunteer with others.* Working with a group enables you to form bonds with other helpers who can support your interests and efforts. The health benefits of volunteering are strongest for people who otherwise have low levels of social interaction.

• *Focus on the process, not the outcome.* We can't always measure or know the results of our actions.

• *Practice random acts of kindness.* Smile, let people go ahead of you in line, pick up litter, and so on.

• *Adopt a pet.* Several studies suggest that pet owners enjoy better health, perhaps by feeling needed or by having a source of unconditional love and affection.

• *Avoid burnout.* Recognize your own limits, pace yourself, and try not to feel guilty or discouraged. Take pride in being a volunteer or caregiver.

Adapting to Physical Changes

As described earlier in the chapter, there are many things a person can do to avoid or minimize the effects of the physical changes associated with aging. However, some changes in physical functioning are inevitable, and successful aging involves anticipating and accommodating these changes.

Decreased energy and changes in health mean that older people have to develop priorities for how to use their energy. Rather than curtailing activities to conserve energy, they need to learn how to generate energy. This usually involves saying yes to enjoyable activities and paying close attention to the need for rest and sleep.

Adapting, rather than giving up, favorite activities may be the best strategy for dealing with physical limitations. For example, if **arthritis** interferes with playing an instrument, a person can continue to enjoy music by taking up a different instrument or attending concerts.

Hearing Loss   The loss of hearing is a common physical change that can have a particularly strong effect on the

> **arthritis**   Inflammation of a joint or joints, causing pain and swelling.

TERMS

lives of older adults. Some people lose their hearing slowly as they age—a condition known as *presbycusis*. Hearing loss affects a person's ability to interact with others and can lead to a sense of isolation and depression. Hearing loss should be assessed and treated by a health care professional; in some cases, hearing can be completely restored by dealing with the underlying cause of hearing loss. In other cases, hearing aids may be prescribed.

Protect your hearing by avoiding exposure to noises above 90 decibels, such as lawn mowers, motorcycles, gun shots, and loud music (Chapter 19). Wear ear plugs when you must be around loud noises, limit your time of exposure, and stay as far as possible from the sound's source.

Vision Changes   Vision usually declines with age. For some individuals this can be traced to conditions such as glaucoma or **age-related macular degeneration (AMD)** that can be treated medically. For others, the effects of a decline in vision can be managed using strategies to make the most of remaining vision.

Glaucoma is caused by increased pressure within the eye due to built-up fluid. The optic nerve can be damaged by this increased pressure, resulting in a loss of side vision and, if untreated, blindness. Medication can relieve the pressure by decreasing the amount of fluid produced or by helping it drain more efficiently. Laser and conventional surgery are other options. Of the 4 million Americans with glaucoma, only half know that they have it; others lose the opportunity to control it and preserve their sight. People over 60, African Americans over 40, and anyone with a family history of glaucoma are at risk.

AMD is a slow disintegration of the *macula,* the tissue at the center of the retina where fine, straight-ahead detail is distinguished. AMD affects more than 1.5 million Americans over 40 and is the leading cause of blindness in people over age 75. Losing this vision makes it difficult to read, drive, or perform other close-up activities. Risk factors for AMD are age, gender (women may be at higher risk than men), smoking, elevated cholesterol levels, and family history. Some cases of AMD can be treated with laser surgery. Both glaucoma and AMD can be detected with regular screening.

Vision can also be affected by conditions that are products of aging. By the time they reach their forties, many people have developed **presbyopia,** a gradual decline in the ability to focus on objects close to them. This occurs because the lens of the eye no longer expands and contracts as readily. **Cataracts,** a clouding of the lens caused by lifelong oxidation damage (a by-product of normal body chemistry), may dim vision by the sixties.

Arthritis   More than 46 million American adults are estimated to have some form of arthritis. This degenerative disease causes joint inflammation leading to chronic pain, swelling, and loss of mobility. Its warning signs include swelling, pain, redness, warmth, tenderness, changes in joint mobility, early-morning stiffness, and unexplained weight loss, fever, or weakness in combination with joint pain.

There are more than 100 different types of arthritis; osteoarthritis (OA) is by far the most common. (Rheumatoid arthritis, an autoimmune disorder, is described in Chapter 17.) In a person with OA, the cartilage that caps the bones in joints wears away, forming sharp spurs (Figure 22.1). It most often affects the hands and weight-bearing joints of the body—knees, ankles, and hips.

Strategies for reducing the risk of arthritis and, for those who already have OA, for managing it include exercise, weight management, and avoidance of heavy or repetitive muscle use. Exercise lubricates joints and strengthens the muscles around them, protecting them from further damage. Swimming, walking, and t'ai chi are good low-impact exercises; knitting and crocheting are excellent for the hands. Maintaining an appropriate weight is important to avoid placing stress on the hips, knees, and ankles. Assistive devices such as kitchen utensils and repair tools with large handles can also help.

It is also important to visit a physician as soon as arthritis symptoms occur so appropriate treatment can be started to reduce pain and swelling, keep joints moving safely, and prevent further joint damage. If joints are severely dam-

Macular degeneration makes many daily tasks difficult or impossible. This photo shows how things look to someone with AMD.

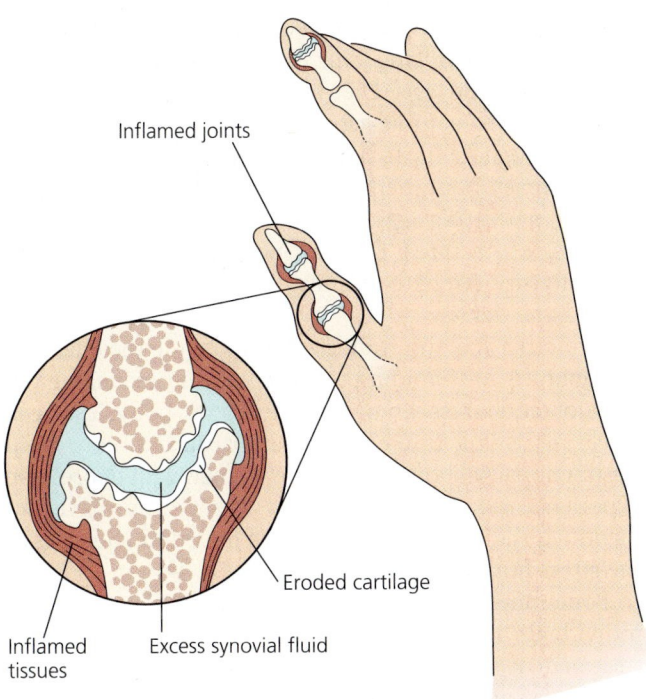

Inflamed joints

Eroded cartilage

Excess synovial fluid

Inflamed tissues

FIGURE 22.1 Osteoarthritis. When cartilage wears away within a joint, sharp spurs form and the amount of fluid increases, causing pain and swelling.

SOURCE: Clayman, C., ed. 1995. *The Human Body: An Illustrated Guide to Its Structure, Function, and Disorders.* New York: DK.

aged and activity is limited, surgery to repair or replace joints may be considered, but medication is usually the first treatment. Many people with OA take medication to relieve inflammation and reduce pain. Because arthritis is a chronic condition, researchers are trying to find medications that are effective and safe when used over the long term. Nonsteroidal anti-inflammatory drugs like ibuprofen can help but can irritate the digestive tract; prescription drugs that relieve pain without damaging the stomach have been found to have other dangerous side effects. Acetaminophen can also reduce pain without upsetting the stomach, but exceeding the recommended dosage can cause liver damage.

Menopause The natural process of menopause usually occurs during a woman's forties or fifties. The ovaries gradually stop functioning, estrogen levels drop, and eventually menstruation ceases. Several years before a woman stops menstruating, her periods usually become irregular, and she may experience hot flashes, vaginal dryness, sleep disturbances, and mood swings. This period, called *perimenopause,* can be troublesome for many women, some more than others. A 5-year study that concluded in 2006 showed that African American women are 60% more likely than white women to suffer aggravating or painful symptoms.

During the 1990s, about one-third of menopausal women used hormone replacement therapy (HT) to alleviate the symptoms of menopause and possibly prevent chronic diseases such as CVD and osteoporosis. Many experts believed that HT would substantially reduce a woman's risk for CVD because estrogen has a favorable influence on blood lipids and overall cardiovascular health. The benefits of HT came into serious question, however, when a large-scale government-funded HT study (part of the Women's Health Initiative) was halted in 2002, after a significant number of participants suffered cardiovascular problems. This decision led many physicians to stop recommending HT for menopausal women. Newer data, however, are reopening the debate about HT. For example, a 2006 study published in the *Journal of Women's Health* reported that women who started HT near the beginning of menopause had a significantly lower risk of heart disease than women who did not take hormones. No benefit was found for women who started HT at older ages. Thus, age and the number of years a woman has been in menopause before starting therapy may be key considerations. Researchers are studying variations in the timing, duration, and composition of HT to see if these changes will improve its effects on health. HT is effective for controlling severe menopausal symptoms, and it has been shown to reduce the risk of bone fractures and colon cancer. Decisions about HT should be made by individual women in consultation with their physicians, taking into account their overall health. Currently, the U.S. Preventive Services Task Force and the American Heart Association recommend that HT not be used to protect against CVD.

Drugs called selective estrogen-receptor modulators (SERMs) mimic estrogen's effects on some body tissues while blocking its effects on others. Researchers hope to develop SERMs that provide all estrogen's beneficial effects without the risks associated with HT. Some antidepressants and blood pressure medications may reduce hot flashes, but a 2006 study showed the effects of such drugs to be minimal—probably not enough to outweigh their potential side effects. In another study, however, the progesterone-like drug MPA reduced hot flashes by about 70%. Phytoestrogens, plant-based substances similar to estrogen, may

QUICK STATS

67 million Americans are expected to have arthritis by 2030.

—CDC, 2007

TERMS

age-related macular degeneration (AMD) A deterioration of the macula (the central area of the retina) leading to blurred vision and sensitivity to glare; some cases can lead to blindness.

presbyopia The inability of the eyes to focus sharply on nearby objects, caused by a loss of elasticity of the lens that occurs with advancing age.

cataracts Opacity of the lens of the eye that impairs vision and can cause blindness.

provide the protective effects of estrogen without its drawbacks. Black cohosh and vitamin E are also being studied.

Lifestyle strategies to reduce menopause-related problems include many of the healthy habits discussed throughout the text: stop smoking, exercise, eat a healthy diet, lose excess weight, and perform relaxation techniques regularly.

Osteoporosis   As described in Chapter 12, **osteoporosis** is a condition in which bones become dangerously thin and fragile over time. Fractures are the most serious consequence of osteoporosis; up to 20% of all people who suffer a hip fracture die within a year. Other problems associated with osteoporosis are loss of height and a stooped posture due to vertebral fractures, severe back and hip pain, and breathing problems caused by changes in the shape of the skeleton.

Osteoporosis affects about 10 million Americans, 80% of whom are women. Women are at greater risk than men for osteoporosis because they have 10–25% less bone in their skeleton. As they lose bone mass with age, women's bones become dangerously thin sooner than men's bones (although more men will probably develop osteoporosis in the future as they live into their eighties and nineties). Bone loss accelerates in women during the first 5–10 years after the onset of menopause because of the drop in estrogen production. (Estrogen improves calcium absorption and reduces the amount of calcium the body excretes.) Black women have higher bone density and fewer fractures than white or Asian women but may be at increased risk of osteoporosis due to lack of vitamin D (a condition caused by high levels of melatonin). Other risk factors include a family history of osteoporosis, early menopause (before age 45), abnormal or irregular menstruation, a history of anorexia, and a thin, small frame. Thyroid medication, corticosteroid drugs for arthritis or asthma, and long-term use of certain contraceptives can also have a negative effect on bone mass.

TERMS

osteoporosis   The loss of bone density, causing bones to become weak, porous, and more prone to fractures.

dementia   Deterioration of mental functioning (including memory, concentration, and judgment) resulting from a brain disorder; often accompanied by emotional disturbances and personality changes.

Alzheimer's disease   A disease characterized by a progressive loss of mental functioning (dementia), caused by a degeneration of brain cells.

Preventing osteoporosis requires building as much bone as possible during your young years and then maintaining it as you age. Diet and exercise play key roles. Weight-bearing aerobic activities must be performed regularly throughout life to have lasting effects. Strength training improves bone density, muscle mass, strength, and balance, protecting against both bone loss and falls, a major cause of fractures. Even for people in their seventies, low-intensity strength training has been shown to improve bone density.

Two other lifelong strategies for reducing the effects of osteoporosis are avoiding tobacco use and managing depression and stress. Smoking reduces the body's estrogen levels and is linked to earlier menopause and more rapid postmenopausal bone loss. Some women with depression experience significant bone loss. Researchers have not identified the reason, but it may be linked to increases in the stress hormone cortisol.

Bone mineral density testing can be used to gauge an individual's risk of fracture and help determine if any treatment is needed. It is recommended for all women over age 65 and for younger postmenopausal women who have a fracture or one or more risk factors. Below-normal bone density may be classified as *osteopenia*, which is usually treated with exercise and nutrition. A greater loss of bone mass is classified as full-blown osteoporosis and is often treated with medications.

Handling Psychological and Mental Changes

Many people associate old age with forgetfulness, and slowly losing one's memory was once considered an inevitable part of growing old. However, we now know that most older adults in good health remain mentally alert and retain their full capacity to learn and remember new information. Occasional confusion or forgetfulness may indicate only a temporary information overload, fatigue, or response to medications. Many people become smarter as they become older and more experienced.

Dementia   Severe and significant brain deterioration in elderly individuals, termed **dementia,** affects about 7% of people under age 80 (the incidence rises sharply for people in their eighties and nineties). Early symptoms include slight disturbances in a person's ability to grasp the situation he or she is in. As dementia progresses, memory failure becomes apparent, and the person may forget conversations, the events of the day, or how to perform simple tasks. It is important to have any symptoms evaluated by a health care professional because some of the over 50 known causes of dementia are treatable (for example, depression, dehydration, malnutrition, vitamin B-12 deficiency, alcoholism, and misuse of medications).

The two most common forms of dementia among older people—**Alzheimer's disease** and multi-infarct demen-

Alzheimer's Disease

Alzheimer's disease (AD) is a fatal brain disorder that causes physical and chemical changes in the brain. As the brain's nerve cells are destroyed, the system that produces the neurotransmitter acetylcholine breaks down, and communication among parts of the brain deteriorates. Autopsies reveal that the interiors of the affected neurons are filled with clusters of proteins known as *tangles:* the spaces between the neurons are filled with protein deposits called *amyloid plaques.*

Almost 5 million Americans have Alzheimer's disease, and that number is expected to quadruple in the next 50 years, as more people live into their eighties and nineties. AD usually occurs in people over 60 but can occur in people as young as 40.

Symptoms

The first symptoms of AD are forgetfulness and inability to concentrate. A person may have difficulty performing fa-

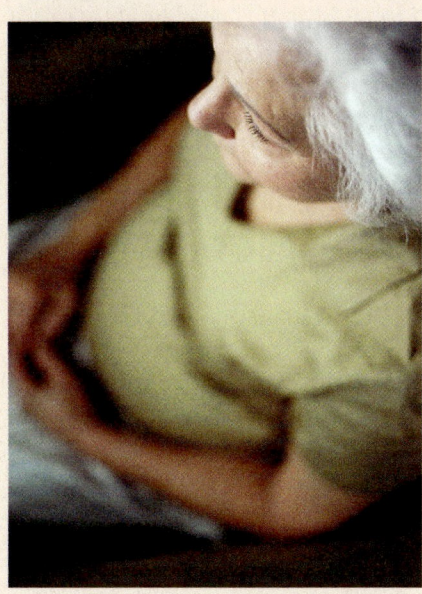

miliar tasks at home and work and have problems with abstract thinking. As the disease progresses, people experience severe memory loss, especially for recent events. They may vividly remember events from their childhood but be unable to remember the time of day or their location. Depression and anxiety are also common.

In the later stages, people with AD are disoriented and may even hallucinate; some experience personality changes—becoming very aggressive or very docile. Eventually, they lose control of physical functioning and are completely dependent on caregivers. On average, a person will survive 8 years after the development of the first symptoms.

Causes

Scientists do not yet know what causes Alzheimer's disease. Age is the main risk factor, although about 10% of cases seem tied to inherited gene mutations. Inherited familial AD generally strikes people before age 65, while the more common late-onset AD occurs in people 65 and older. Some evidence suggests that many of the same factors that affect heart disease risk also apply to AD. In women, low levels of estrogen in the brain may contribute to AD. A mutation of the protein apolipoprotein E, which can destroy neural cells, may be a cause of the disease in some people.

A great deal of research is focusing on the role of a peptide molecule known as amyloid-beta, which may play a role in the development of plaques in the brain. Scientists are looking for genetic factors that cause certain people to develop high levels of amyloid-beta. Some evidence links excess amyloid-beta production to obesity.

People who regularly take nonsteroidal anti-inflammatory drugs (NSAIDs) like ibuprofen (often to control arthritis) and people who regularly consume fish rich in omega-3 fatty acids appear to have lower rates of AD, indicating a possible protective effect of substances that reduce inflammation. Some studies indicate that vitamin E and other antioxidants may reduce risk for AD or slow the progress of the disease, suggesting that oxidative stress caused by free radicals may also play a role.

Diagnosis and Treatment

Currently, the only certain way to diagnose AD is to examine brain tissue during an autopsy. In most cases, physicians use a combination of medical history, neurological and psychological tests, physical exams, blood and urine tests, and a brain-imaging scan. Good early results have also been seen using a test that measures levels of a specific protein in spinal fluid, and less invasive blood tests to measure the same proteins are under development.

For people with mild to moderate AD, there are several drugs that provide modest improvements in memory. Several medications help maintain cognitive function by inhibiting the breakdown of the neurotransmitter acetylcholine but do not alter the course of the disease. These so-called cholinesterase inhibitors include Aricept (donepezil), Cognex (tacrine), Exelon (rivastigmine), and Reminyl (galantamine). Scientists are also developing new treatments to slow the production of amyloid-beta or to block its effects on brain cells. Other medicines now under investigation may stop Alzheimer's progress before it can cause too much damage. People with AD may also be prescribed antidepressant or antianxiety medications.

---

tia—are irreversible. Alzheimer's disease is characterized by changes in brain nerve cells. Multi-infarct dementia results from a series of small strokes or changes in the brain's blood supply that destroy brain tissue. Even for the incurable forms of dementia, however, treatment can improve an affected person's quality of life (see the box "Alzheimer's Disease").

There is evidence that some cases of dementia are hereditary, but experts say genetics are not always a sure sign that a person will develop the disease. You can also take lifestyle steps to help ward off dementia, such as controlling weight and blood pressure, eating a balanced diet (including adequate B vitamins and omega-3 fatty acids), exercising, practicing stress reduction techniques, maintaining social contacts, and cultivating a variety of mental pursuits, such as doing crossword puzzles. Strong evidence links the Mediterranean diet with reduced risk of Alzheimer's disease (see Chapter 12).

Suicide Among Older Men

One group of Americans is more than twice as likely to commit suicide than any other. From mass media accounts, you might imagine this group to be adolescents; however, suicide is much more common among the elderly—especially white males over age 65. Among men over age 65, the rate of suicide among whites is more than double that of any other group. Women and minorities of all ages have much lower rates of suicide than older white men.

Why is this so? One explanation is that because white men generally have greater power and status in our society, aging and retirement represent a relatively greater loss for them. Women, more accustomed to lesser status, are not as threatened by the loss of economic and social power. Another

theory is that white men tend to have weaker social ties than women or than men from other cultural groups and as they retire their increasing social isolation leads to depression and suicide. Indeed, depression is probably the single most significant factor associated with suicidal behavior in older adults. Men who commit suicide are more likely to have a physical illness and be widowed or divorced.

Why are rates for other groups lower? In general, women are more likely than men to attempt suicide, but men are more likely to succeed, due in large part to their choice of more lethal methods. Some cultural groups, particularly Latinos and African Americans, afford greater respect and status to older people, who are valued for their wisdom and experience. Cultural

groups that emphasize family and social ties also seem to have lower rates of suicide. See Chapter 3 for more on risk and protective factors for suicide.

Grief   Another psychological and emotional challenge of aging is dealing with grief and mourning. Aging is associated with loss—the loss of friends, peers, physical appearance, possessions, and health. Grief is the process of getting through the pain of loss, and it can be one of the loneliest and most intense times in a person's life. It can take a year or two or more to completely come to terms with the loss of a loved one. (See Chapter 23 for more information about responses to loss and how to support a grieving person.)

Unresolved grief can have serious physical and psychological or emotional health consequences and may require professional help. Signs of unresolved grief include hostility toward people connected with the death (physicians or nurses, for example), talking about the death as if it occurred yesterday, and unrealistic or harmful behavior (such as giving away all of one's own belongings). Many people become depressed after the loss of a loved one or when confronted with retirement or a chronic illness. But after a period of grieving, people are generally able to resume their lives.

Depression   Unresolved grief can lead to depression, a common problem in older adults (see Chapter 3). If you

notice the signs of depression in yourself or someone you know, consult a mental health professional. A marked loss of interest in usually pleasurable activities, decreased appetite, insomnia, fatigue, and feelings of worthlessness are signs of depression. Listen carefully when an older friend or relative complains about being depressed; it may be a request for help. Suicide rates are relatively high among the elderly, and depression should be taken seriously (see the box "Suicide Among Older Men" above).

AGING AND LIFE EXPECTANCY

Life expectancy is the average length of time we can expect to live. It is calculated by averaging mortality statistics, the ages at death of a group of people over a certain period. In 2006, life expectancy for the total population was 78.1 years, but those who reach age 65 can expect to live even longer—18 more years or longer—because they have already survived hazards to life in the younger years. Women have a longer life expectancy than men (see the box "Why Do Women Live Longer?"). Life expectancy also varies among ethnic groups; reasons for these differences include socioeconomic, genetic, and lifestyle factors.

Life expectancy in the United States increased dramatically in the twentieth century, as described in Chapter 1. This does not mean that every American lives longer now than in 1900; rather, far fewer people die young now, because childhood and infectious diseases are better controlled and diet and sanitation are much improved. Only 30% of people born in 1900 would live to age 70; of those born in 2004, closer to 77% can expect to live that long.

How long can humans expect to live in the best of circumstances? It now seems possible that our maximum

? QUESTIONS FOR CRITICAL THINKING AND REFLECTION
Have you watched someone you know grow old? How did the aging process affect that person? In what ways did the person's physical and mental health change? In what ways were you affected, as you watched him or her age?

Why Do Women Live Longer?

Women live longer than men in most countries around the world, even in places where maternal mortality rates are high. In the United States, women on average can expect to live about 5 years longer than men (see table). Worldwide, among people over age 100, women outnumber men about 9 to 1.

The reason for the gender gap in life expectancy is not entirely understood but may be influenced by biological, social, and lifestyle factors. Estrogen production and other factors during a woman's younger years may protect her from early heart disease and from age-related declines in the pumping power of the heart. Women may have lower rates of stress-related illnesses because they cope more positively with stress by seeking social support.

The news for women is not all good, however, because not all their extra years are likely to be healthy years. They are more likely than men to suffer from chronic conditions like arthritis and osteoporosis. Women's longer life spans, combined with the facts that men tend to marry younger women and that wid-owed men remarry more often than widowed women, means there are many more single older women than men. Older men are more likely to live in family settings, whereas older women are more likely to live alone. Older women are also less likely to be covered by a pension or to have retirement savings, so they are more likely to be poor.

Increased male mortality can be traced in part to higher rates of behaviors such as smoking and alcohol and drug abuse. Testosterone production may be partly responsible in that it is linked to aggressive and risky behavior and to unhealthy cholesterol levels. Men have much higher rates of death than women from car crashes and other unintentional injuries, firearm-related deaths, homicide, suicide, AIDS, and early heart attack. Gender roles that promote risky behavior among young men are a factor in many of these causes of death. Indeed, among people who have made it to age 65, the gender longevity gap is smaller.

Social and behavioral factors may be more important than physiological causes in explaining the gender gap; for example, among the Amish, a religious sect that has strict rules against smoking and drinking, men usually live as long as women. This suggests that the longevity gap could be substantially narrowed through lifestyle changes.

Life Expectancy

Year	Men	Women
At birth		
1900	46.3	48.3
1950	65.6	71.1
2000	74.3	79.7
2006	75.4	80.7
At age 65		
1900	11.5	12.2
1950	12.8	15.0
2000	16.2	19.3
2006	17.4	20.3

SOURCES: U.S. Census Bureau. 2005. *We the People: Women and Men in the United States.* Washington, D.C.: U.S. Census Bureau; National Center for Health Statistics. 2007. *Health, United States, 2007.* Hyattsville, Md.: National Center for Health Statistics; World Health Organization. 2003. *Gender, Health, and Aging.* Geneva: World Health Organization.

potential **life span** is 100–120 years. One's **health span,** by contrast, is the period of life when one is generally healthy and free from chronic or serious disease. The major difference between life span (how long you live) and health span (how long you stay healthy) is freedom from chronic or disabling disease. Failure to achieve that span in good health results to some degree from destructive environmental and behavioral factors—factors over which we can exert considerable control. Longevity appears to be influenced very little by genetics. Studies of identical twins and other research suggest that life span is only about 3% heritable, meaning that the age at which one's parents die has only a 3% effect on one's own age at death.

Long life does not necessarily mean a longer period of disability, either. People often live longer because they have been well longer. A healthy old age is very often an extension of a healthy middle age. However, behavior changes cannot extend the maximum human life span, which seems to be built into our genes.

No one really knows how and why people change as they get older. Different theories claim that aging is caused by accumulated injuries from ultraviolet light, wear and tear on the body, by-products of metabolism, and so on. Other theories view aging as a predetermined, genetically programmed process.

No theory, however, sufficiently explains all the changes of the aging process. Aging is complex and varies in how it affects different people and even different organs. Most gerontologists (scientists

life expectancy The average length of time a person is expected to live.

life span A theoretically projected length of life based on the maximum potential of the human body in the best environment.

health span The period of life when one is generally healthy and free from chronic or serious disease.

TERMS

who study aging and its effects) feel that aging is the cumulative result of the interaction of many lifelong influences, including heredity, environment, culture, diet, exercise and leisure, past illnesses, and many other factors.

LIFE IN AN AGING AMERICA

As life expectancy increases, a larger proportion of the population will be in their later years. This change will necessitate new government policies and changes in our general attitudes toward older adults.

America's Aging Minority

People over 65 are a large minority in the American population—over 37.3 million people, about 12% of the total population in 2006. That number is expected to nearly double by the year 2030 (Figure 22.2). Many older people are happy, healthy, and self-sufficient. Changes that come with age, including negative ones, normally occur so gradually that most people adapt, some even gracefully (see the box "Baby Boomers: Redefining Age and Retirement").

The enormous increase in the over-55 population is markedly affecting our stereotypes of what it means to grow old. The misfortunes associated with aging— frailty, forgetfulness, poor health, isolation—occur in fewer people in their sixties and seventies and are shifting instead to burden the very old, those over 85.

> **QUICK STATS**
>
> **43%** of American women over age 65 are widows.
>
> —Administration on Aging, 2008

About 81% of older Americans own their homes. Their living expenses are lower after retirement because they no longer support children and have fewer work-related expenses; they consume and buy less food. They are more likely to continue practicing their expertise for years after retirement: Thousands of retired consultants, teachers, technicians, and craftspeople work until their middle and late seventies. They receive greater amounts of assistance, such as Medicare, pay proportionately lower taxes, and have greater net worth from lifetime savings.

Even so, according to the Administration on Aging (AOA), nearly 10% (3.4 million) of elderly people live below the poverty level; another 6.2% (2.2 million) are "near poor," with incomes reaching 125% of the poverty level. Older women are nearly twice as likely to live in poverty as older men. People over 65 who live alone are much more likely to be poor than those who live with families.

As the aging population increases proportionately, however, the number of older people who are ill and dependent rises. Health care remains the largest expense for older adults. On average, they visit a physician 10–12 times a year and are hospitalized more frequently and require twice as many prescription drugs as the general population. Most older Americans have at least one chronic condition; many have more than one. Table 22.3 lists the most commonly reported conditions among the elderly.

Retirement finds many older people with their incomes reduced to subsistence levels. This is especially true of the very old and women. The majority of older Americans live with fixed sources of income, such as pensions, that are eroded by inflation. Expenses tend to increase more rapidly, especially those due to circumstances over which people have little or no control, such as deteriorating health. **Social Security** benefits constitute 90% of the total income for one-third of Americans over age 65. Social Security was intended to serve as a supplement to personal savings and private pensions, not as a sole source of income. It is vital to plan for an adequate retirement income.

Number of persons (millions)

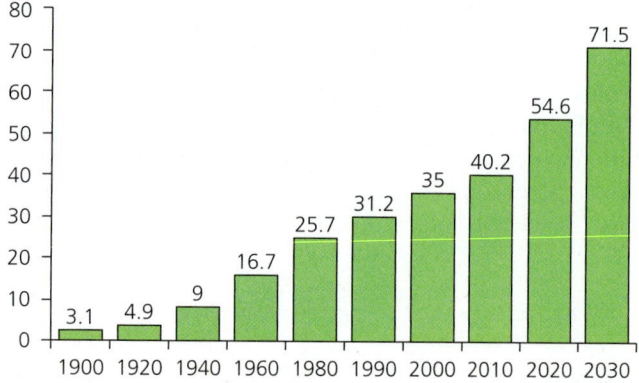

FIGURE 22.2   Increase in Americans over age 65, 1900–2030.

SOURCE: U.S. Department of Health and Human Services, Administration on Aging. 2008. *A Statistical Profile of Older Americans Aged 65+* (http://www.aoa.gov/press/prodsmats/fact/pdf/ss_stat_profile.pdf; retrieved February 22, 2009).

Table 22.3	Percentage of Older Americans with Chronic Conditions, 2005
Condition	**Percentage**
Hypertension	48%
Arthritis	47%
Heart disease	29%
Cancer	20%
Diabetes	16%
Sinusitis	14%

SOURCE: U.S. Department of Health and Human Services, Administration on Aging. 2008. *A Statistical Profile of Older Americans Aged 65+* (http://www.aoa.gov/press/prodsmats/fact/pdf/ss_stat_profile.pdf; retrieved February 22, 2009).

Baby Boomers: Redefining Age and Retirement

connect™

If you are a college student age 18–24, chances are good that one or both of your parents are members of the *baby boom* generation—Americans born between 1946 and 1964. Chances are also good that the boomers in your life will reach retirement age in the next decade or two. That doesn't mean, however, that they'll actually retire.

Living Longer, Living Younger

In general, baby boomers are living longer than their parents did. As a result, the average boomer's retirement period is longer. In 1950, for example, a 65-year-old man could expect to live another 13 years; today, that number has been extended to about 20 years. And it's becoming increasingly common for people to live into their eighties and nineties. Boomers "live younger" than their parents, too, meaning they tend to be healthier than their parents and enjoy better long-term prospects for good health.

Redefining Notions of Age

What are baby boomers doing with all that extra time and health? As it turns out, they aren't contemplating retirement, and they don't consider age 60 or 65 to be the start of their "golden years." As they reach age 60 and beyond, boomers are re-inventing themselves and their lives, leaving long-held notions of aging in the dust.

Experts describe previous generations of Americans as having lived a *linear life*—an undemarcated, continuous march of years between life and death. Baby boomers, conversely, are living a *staged life,* and each stage is clearly defined, such as adolescence, college, early career, mid-career, and so on. The end of each stage marks the beginning of a new one, filled with new opportunities. Surveys show that boomers don't equate years of life with old age; rather, they view it as an extension of their youth, and they want to put their longer life to good use.

Age Doesn't Equate to Retirement

According to the 1995 *Merrill Lynch New Retirement Survey,* only about 20% of baby boomers actually plan to retire. In fact, boomers increasingly see retirement as an artifact of the Great Depression—which, in fact, it is. In the first half of the twentieth century, government and industry urged older workers to retire in order to make room for a growing crop of younger, more able-bodied workers. Prior to the industrialization of America, in fact, retirement was not the norm. As the practice grew, however, it became a widely held assumption that *all* workers would retire at some point. Indeed, after the creation of the Social Security system, Americans came to view retirement as a fact of life, an inevitable end to a lifetime of work, regardless of whether that work had been enriching or thankless, fulfilling or frustrating.

Children of the Depression, to a large extent, began to think of retirement as a duty to be planned for. As Americans became more educated, employers devised pensions and retirement plans as enticements for the best workers. After decades of matching funds, 401(k) plans, and Individual Retirement Accounts, millions of Americans came to view retirement not as the slamming of a door on their productive life but as an entitlement to be carefully protected. Even today, workers volunteer by the thousands for early retirement rather than face the prospect of being cut from the workforce.

A Shift in Thinking

Traditional views of retirement are starting to change, primarily due to the cost of retiring. Most Americans do not save enough money to fund 20 or more years of leisure time. Further, younger workers, especially baby boomers, don't necessarily see retirement as being all that attractive. Many would prefer to continue working, volunteer their time to good causes, further their education, or even start a new career.

This has led many older Americans to practice what experts call revolving or cycling retirement—periods of work interspersed with extended periods of leisure. Following this strategy, older people can work only as required to support their lifestyle or to maintain benefits that would otherwise be too costly, such as health insurance. When not working, they can pursue other interests. Economists applaud this approach to retirement because it could save the government billions of dollars. (Federal spending on programs for older adults is expected to double by 2030.)

Of course, this scenario can play out only if one stays relatively healthy. While older Americans are fitter than ever, continued good health is not a given. If current positive trends continue, however, baby boomers may be just the first of many generations not only to live longer but to put off retirement altogether.

Family and Community Resources for Older Adults

With help from friends, family members, and community services, people in their later years can remain active and independent. About 66% of noninstitutionalized older Americans live with a spouse or other family member

Social Security   A government program that provides financial assistance to people who are unemployed, disabled, or retired (and over a certain age); financed through taxes on business and workers.

TERMS

Environmental conditions that are difficult for young people can be especially tough on the elderly. Both the natural and human-made environments pose many threats to the well-being of older adults.

Particulate air pollution and ozone, for example, aggravate breathing-related conditions such as asthma and chronic obstructive pulmonary disease (COPD). In older people with such disorders, even brief exposure to dirty air can result in hospitalization. Indoor air can be just as hazardous, especially if it contains lingering mold or dust particles.

Environmental factors can be a special concern for elderly people with diabetes. When a diabetic is exposed to hot weather, for example, the body can lose its ability to regulate its temperature—a condition that can be fatal. Air pollution can affect the ability of a diabetic's blood vessels to control blood flow. Several types of air pollution have been associated with an increased risk of cardiovascular problems in people with diabetes.

For more information on the environment and environmental health, see Chapter 19.

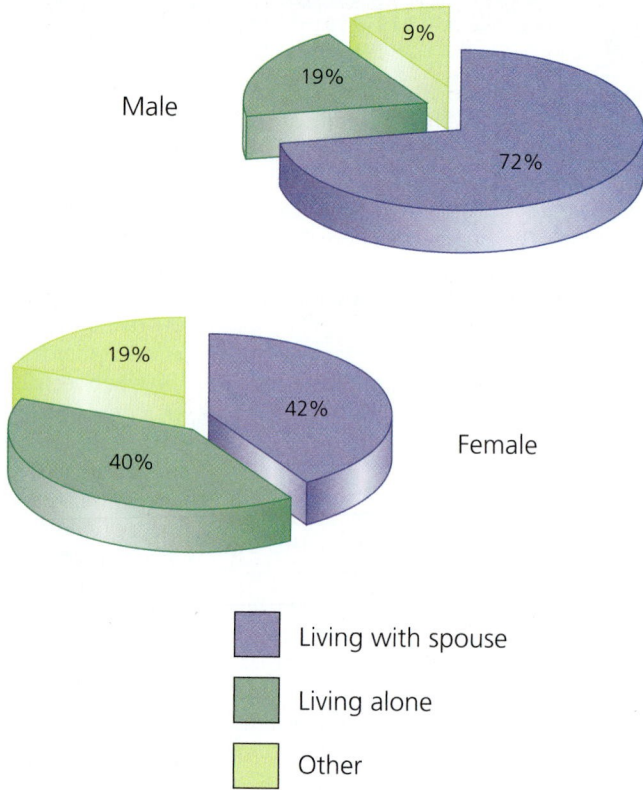

FIGURE 22.3   Living arrangements of Americans over age 65, 2006.

SOURCE: U.S. Department of Health and Human Services, Administration on Aging. 2008. *A Statistical Profile of Older Americans Aged 65+* (http://www.aoa.gov/press/prodsmats/fact/pdf/ss_stat_profile.pdf; retrieved February 22, 2009).

(Figure 22.3); the other 30% live alone. Only 4% live in institutional settings, but among those over age 85, about 15% live in a nursing home.

Family Involvement in Caregiving   Studies show that in about three out of four cases, a spouse, a grown daughter, or a daughter-in-law assumes a caregiving role for elderly relatives. With more parents living into their eighties and with fewer children per family, many people, especially women, will face the dilemma of how best to care for an aging relative. Recent surveys indicate that the average woman will spend about 17 years raising children and 18 years caring for an aging relative.

Caregiving can be rewarding, but it is also hard work. If the experience is stressful and long-term, family members may become emotionally exhausted. Corporations are increasingly responsive to the needs of their employees who are family caregivers by providing services such as referrals, flexible schedules and leaves, and on-site adult care. Professional health care advice is another critical part of successful home care. Caregivers need to give special consideration to issues such as hearing and vision loss, which can make an elderly person feel disconnected or isolated, and dementia, which can make caregiving an extremely challenging prospect.

The caregiver must work with the older person's doctors and pharmacists to ensure that medication is available and taken as prescribed. (Studies show that older adults commonly skip their cholesterol and blood pres-

sure medications, for example.) The caregiver may need to acquire a legal status called *medical power of attorney,* which enables him or her to make decisions about the patient's medical care.

The best thing a family can do is talk honestly about the obligations, time, and commitment required by caregiving. Families should also explore the community resources and professional assistance that may be available to reduce the stress in this difficult job.

Other Living and Care Options   If living together is not possible for aging parents and adult children, other living and care options are available. There are agencies that recruit and match like-minded individuals for shared living situations. Homesharing offers older adults who are in fairly good health the opportunity for new relationships, either with peers or with a younger family. Intergenerational homesharing may relieve elders of transportation problems and demanding physical tasks, which can be taken care of by younger household members. Conversely, elders in good health can help busy, working families with child care and household chores.

Retirement communities are an option for individuals in good health and with a good income who want to main-

Choosing a Place to Live

Later in life many older people need help with everyday activities like shopping, cooking, walking, or bathing. Help from family and friends may be all some people need to stay active and healthy in their own homes, while others may choose to move to a place that offers more services. A variety of options are available:

• *Retirement communities* allow maximum independence with very little supervision. They may offer transportation, activities, and other services but do not routinely offer assistance with basic needs.

• *Residential care homes* are licensed to provide services to three or more residents in a smaller environment, typically in a private home. They may provide assistance with medications, bathing, dressing, transportation, daily laundry, daily housekeeping, and meals.

• *Assisted living facilities* allow independence with supervision and are licensed by the state. They provide some meals, housekeeping and laundry, transportation, and activities.

• *Nursing homes* provide 24-hour medical care and rehabilitation for residents, who are mostly very frail or suffer from the later stages of dementia.

Some providers offer all levels of care at one site. These continuing-care communities allow people to move from one level to another as their needs change.

Finding the right place to live takes some investigation. Because the best homes often have a waiting list, plan ahead. Don't wait until your family member is too sick to function. Once you have an initial list of facilities in your area, start visiting the homes, keeping the following evaluation points in mind:

• Ask questions about specific facilities. Doctors, friends, relatives, local hospital discharge planners, social workers, and religious organizations can help. The ombudsperson at your state's office of long-term care can let you know if there have been problems in a particular nursing home. Residential care homes and assisted living facilities do not follow the same licensing requirements as nursing homes. Talk to people in the community to find out about these options.

• Contact the places that interest you. Ask basic questions about vacancies, number of residents, cost, and any services of interest to you, such as transportation and meals.

• Visit several places. Talk to the staff, residents, and, if possible, family members of residents. Set up an appointment, but also go unannounced and at different times of the day. Make sure residents are clean, well groomed, involved in activities, and treated with respect.

• Evaluate the facility's financial agreements. Have a lawyer look them over before you sign. Nursing homes may accept Medicare or Medicaid, but most other facilities are private-pay only. Costs can range from $1500 per month to $5500 per month or more.

• Moving is a big change that affects the whole family. Talk about how you feel. Once a family member has moved to a new home, visit often and pay attention to the quality of care. Say something nice when care is good, and speak up when care is poor. If you have trouble resolving a complaint, your local ombudsperson or citizen advocacy groups may be able to help.

---

tain home ownership. Other types of facilities are available for people who need more assistance with daily living (see the box "Choosing a Place to Live" above).

Community Resources Community resources are available to help older adults remain active and in their own homes. Typical services include the following:

• *Senior citizens' centers or adult day-care centers* provide meals, social activities, and health care services for those unable to be alone during the day.

• *Homemaker services* offer housekeeping, cooking, errand running, and escort service.

• *Visiting nurses* provide basic health care.

• *Household services* perform household repairs.

• *Friendly visitor or daily telephone reassurance services* provide contacts for older people who live alone.

• *Home food delivery services* provide meals to homebound people.

• *Adult day hospital care* provides day care plus physical therapy and treatment for chronic illnesses.

• *Low-cost legal aid* helps manage finances and health care.

• *Transportation services* offer rides at low rates.

• *Case management* helps seniors navigate confusing health care services.

Services are in the phone book under local government agencies or senior citizens' services.

Transportation Older drivers usually have safe driving records compared with young adults because they tend to be more cautious; however, crashes in the older age group are more likely to be fatal. Many states require special driver's testing for people over age 70 and may restrict some drivers as to the time, area, and distances they may drive. Because of changes in vision or other health problems, some older drivers may be required to give up their license before they feel ready. Elderly people report that the loss of a driver's license, and the loss of independence it brings, is one of the most severe hardships they face.

Government Aid and Policies

The federal government helps older Americans through several programs, such as food stamps, housing subsidies, Social Security, Medicare, and Medicaid. Social Security, the life insurance and old-age pension plan, has saved many from destitution, although it is intended not as a sole source of income but as a supplement to other income. Social Security funds have been used to cover other government financial deficits, so the future solvency of the program is uncertain.

Medicare is a major health insurance program for the elderly and the disabled. It has two parts: Part A is financed by part of the payroll (FICA) tax that also pays for Social Security; Part B is financed by monthly premiums paid by people who choose to enroll. Part A helps pay for inpatient hospital care, some inpatient care in a skilled nursing facility, and some types of home and hospice care. Medicare Part B helps pay for physicians' services and other services not covered by Part A.

Medicare pays about 30% of the medical costs of older Americans. It provides basic health care coverage for acute episodes of illness that require skilled professional care; it pays for some preventive services, including an initial physical exam, vaccinations, and screenings for CVD, certain cancers, osteoporosis, diabetes, and glaucoma. It does not pay for many office visits, dental care, and dentures. Over 1.6 million older people currently live in nursing homes, but Medicare pays less than 2% of nursing home costs, and private insurers pay less than 1%, creating a tremendous financial burden for nursing home residents and their families. As of 2006, Medicare subscribers could enroll in privately managed prescription drug coverage plans, known as Medicare Part D, but the program is controversial for several reasons. The plans are complex and confusing, they leave gaps that enrollees must fill, and, according to some studies, they may actually drive up the cost of drugs for many people.

When their financial resources are exhausted, people may apply for Medicaid. A 1965 amendment to the Social Security Act, Medicaid provides medical insurance to low-income people of any age. Funded by state and federal contributions, the services vary from state to state but typically include hospital, nursing home and home health care, physician services, and some medical supplies and services.

A crucial question regarding aid for the elderly is who will pay for it. The government picks up many of the health care expenses, primarily through Medicare and Medicaid. Total health care expenditures are 16% of the U.S. gross domestic product; about one-third of these expenditures go to care for older Americans.

Health care policy planners hope that rising medical costs for older adults will shrink dramatically through education and prevention. Health care professionals, including **gerontologists** and **geriatricians,** are beginning to practice preventive medicine, just as pediatricians do. They advise older people about how to avoid and, if necessary, how to manage disabilities.

Some individuals defy all preconceived ideas about age and continue to live vigorous and productive lives into their seventies, eighties, and beyond.

Changing the Public's Idea of Aging

Aging people may be one of our least used and least appreciated resources. (For another view, see the box "Multicultural Wisdom About Aging.") How can we use the knowledge and productivity of our growing numbers of older citizens, particularly those now leaving the work force through mandatory early retirement?

To start, we must change our thinking about what aging means. We must learn to judge productivity rather than age. Capacity to function should replace age as a criterion for usefulness. Instead of singling out 65 as a magic number, we could consider ages 50–75 as the third quarter of life. Changes occur around 50 that signal a new era: Children are usually grown and gone, and a person has often achieved a level in

Multicultural Wisdom About Aging

The following is excerpted from an article written by Dr. Robert Coles, a professor of psychiatry and medical humanities at Harvard Medical School.

Why are so many Americans afraid of growing old? This question occurred to me often during the three years my wife and I lived in New Mexico and Arizona. Not a day went by when we weren't reminded of how much Native American and Hispanic families value old age. These are cultures that grant dignity and authority to their elders.

One young Hispanic woman described to us her relationship with her parents, both in their seventies, in this way: "When I am wondering what to do about a problem, I turn to my mother or my father. Even if they are not here, I still turn to them. I picture them in my mind and I hear them saying words that make good sense." One day, this woman's father made a show of his humorous and practical good sense before his young grandson. "You know what my son said to me that night when he was going to bed?" the woman asked. "He told me he wished he could be old like his grandpapa!"

To be old is to "last" oneself—to go through ups and downs, to survive bad luck and avoid all sorts of hazards. To be old is to be blessed by fate, by chance and circumstance. Pueblo Indians know that. One Hopi child drew me a picture of an old woman shaking hands with the moon. Then she explained, "When you're old, you're a full moon; you make the night a little less dark." For Hopi children, an older person is a source of encouragement, instruction, inspiration, a part of nature's awesome presence.

For many young people living in other parts of America, old age is regarded not as a major achievement but rather as a last, sad, brief way station. One boy in Boston commented, "It's no fun to be old; it's the worst thing in the world, except to die." To many of us, old age means abandonment, rejection, loneliness, a loss of respect from others, and subsequently a loss of self-respect. This is not the case, though, in Hispanic and Native American cultures. The elders we met in New Mexico and Arizona showed a great deal of self-confidence, and in general they seemed contented with their lives. In their contentment and harmony with nature lies a lesson for all of us.

SOURCE: Adapted from Coles, R. 1989. Full-moon wisdom. *New Choices for the Best Years,* September. Reprinted with permission of Robert Coles, James Agee Professor of Social Ethics, Harvard University.

career, earnings, and accomplishments that meets his or her ambitions. The upper end of the quarter is determined by the fact that most people today are vigorous, in good health, mentally alert, and capable of making a productive contribution until they are at least in their seventies.

However we define old age, the costs of losing what older adults can contribute to our national productivity and quality of life are too high. Through their early retirement, we forfeit substantial income tax and Social Security tax revenues on their earnings. Those who retire at 62 start using their Social Security benefits earlier than otherwise.

A far better arrangement would be to make available full-time and part-time volunteer and paid employment. We would benefit by providing retraining programs for both occupational and leisure time activities. Volunteer opportunities, such as preparing recordings for the blind, helping with activities for the disabled, and performing necessary tasks in hospitals, could be expanded. At the same time, we could possibly change both public and private pension programs to make partial retirement possible. In such cases we could allow people to borrow against their Social Security benefits to finance retraining or enrollment in new educational programs.

There can be benefits to aging, but they don't come automatically. They require planning and wise choices earlier in life. One octogenarian, Russell Lee, founder of a medical clinic in California, perceived the advantages of aging as growth: "The limitations imposed by time are compensated by the improved taste, sharper discretion, sounder mental and esthetic judgment, increased sensitivity and compassion, clearer focus—which all contribute to a more certain direction in living. . . . The later years can be the best of life for which the earlier ones were preparation."

? QUESTIONS FOR CRITICAL THINKING AND REFLECTION

What do you want your life to be like when you are old? Do you hope to retire, or keep working indefinitely? Where would you like to live? How much time do you spend thinking about these questions? Have you done any planning yet for old age?

gerontologist One who studies the biological, psychological, and social phenomena associated with aging and old age.

geriatrician A physician specializing in the diseases, disabilities, and care of older adults.

TERMS

TIPS FOR TODAY AND THE FUTURE

The best way to ensure a high-quality life in later years is by cultivating healthy habits in your younger years.

RIGHT NOW YOU CAN

- Review your financial situation, and start thinking about a plan for the future.
- Think about any unhealthy habits you have and resolve to change them. Review the information in this text to devise strategies for change.
- If you know any older people, speak to them about what aging has meant to them, and see what lessons you can learn from them.

IN THE FUTURE YOU CAN

- Learn a new skill, such as a language or a game of strategy.
- Volunteer with a nonprofit group in your community; consider a literacy campaign, a soup kitchen, a youth mentoring program, or a group that helps the elderly in some manner.

SUMMARY

- People who take charge of their health during their youth have greater control over the physical and mental aspects of aging.

- Biological aging takes place over a lifetime, but some of the other changes associated with aging are more abrupt.

- A lifetime of interests and hobbies helps maintain creativity and intelligence.

- Exercise and a healthy diet throughout life enhances physical and psychological health.

- Alcohol abuse is a common but often hidden problem, as is overdependence on medications. Tobacco use not only shortens life but also may cause severe health impairment for many years.

- Regular physical examinations help detect conditions that can shorten life and make old age less healthy.

- Stress increases wear and tear on the body; getting enough sleep, avoiding drugs, and practicing relaxation help reduce stress.

- Retirement can be a fulfilling and enjoyable time of life for those who adjust to their new roles, enjoy participating in a variety of activities, and have planned ahead for financial stability.

- Successful aging involves anticipating and accommodating physical changes and limitations.

- Slight confusion and forgetfulness are not signs of a serious illness; however, severe symptoms may indicate Alzheimer's disease or another form of dementia.

- Resolving grief and mourning and dealing with depression are important tasks for older adults.

- Older adults can be role models for the successful integration of life's experiences and the ability to adapt to challenges.

- People over 65 form a large minority in the United States, and their status is improving. But older adults who are ill and dependent—often those who were already poor—experience major social and economic problems.

- Family and community resources can help older adults stay active and independent.

- Government aid to the elderly includes food stamps, housing subsidies, Social Security, Medicare, and Medicaid.

FOR MORE INFORMATION

BOOKS

Beers, M. H. 2005. *Merck Manual of Health and Aging: The Complete Home Guide to Healthcare and Healthy Aging for Older People and Those Who Care About Them.* New York: Ballantine. *Provides information on fundamentals of aging and preventive care.*

Johns Hopkins Medical Center. 2007. *The Johns Hopkins Medical Guide to Health After 50.* New York: Black Dog & Leventhal. *A practical guide to healthy aging for all wellness dimensions.*

Lazarus, R. S., and B. N. Lazarus. 2006. *Coping with Aging.* New York: Oxford. *Explores the experience of aging from the standpoint of the individual.*

National Institute on Aging. 2006. *Fitness Over Fifty: An Exercise Guide from the National Institute on Aging,* book and DVD ed. New York: Hatherleigh Press. *A practical guide to physical activity and exercise, with specific guidelines for safe exercise for older adults.*

Weil, A. 2007. *Healthy Aging: A Lifelong Guide to Your Physical and Spiritual Well-Being.* New York: Anchor. *One of America's best-known complementary care physicians discusses the aging process and explains methods for maintaining health during the latter years of life.*

ORGANIZATIONS AND WEB SITES

AARP. Provides information on all aspects of aging, including health promotion, health care, and retirement planning.
   http://www.aarp.org

Aging Well. A practical resource for seniors that includes information on diet, exercise, safety, and medical care.
   http://www.aging.ny.gov

Alliance for Aging Research. A nonprofit organization supporting medical and psychological research on aging.
   http://www.agingresearch.org

Alzheimer's Association. Offers tips for caregivers and patients and information on the causes and treatment of Alzheimer's disease.
   http://www.alz.org

American Association of Homes and Services for the Aging (AAHSA). Provides information about living and care arrangements available for older adults.

http://www.aahsa.org

Arthritis Foundation. Provides information about arthritis, including free brochures, referrals to local services, and research updates.

http://www.arthritis.org

FirstGov.gov: Senior Citizens' Resources. A gateway to government resources on the Internet for older Americans.

http://www.usa.gov/Topics/Seniors.shtml

Medicare. Provides information about Medicare.

http://www.medicare.gov

National Council on Aging. Provides helpful information on retirement planning, health promotion, and lifelong learning.

http://www.ncoa.org

National Institute on Aging. Provides fact sheets and brochures on aging-related topics.

http://www.nih.gov/nia

http://nihseniorhealth.gov

National Osteoporosis Foundation. Provides information on the causes, prevention, detection, and treatment of osteoporosis.

http://www.nof.org

U.S. Administration on Aging. Provides fact sheets, statistical information, and Internet links to other resources on aging.

http://www.aoa.gov

SELECTED BIBLIOGRAPHY

Americans over 50 at risk for bone fractures. 2005. *FDA Consumer,* January/February.

Anderson, K., et al. 2005. Depression and the risk of Alzheimer's disease. *Epidemiology* 16(2): 233–238.

Arnold, W. 2006. Singapore acts as haven for stem cell research. *New York Times,* 17 August.

Beyond menopause: Life after estrogen. 2005. *Mayo Clinic Health Letter Supplement,* February.

Centers for Disease Control and Prevention. 2005. Racial/ethnic differences in the prevalence and impact of doctor-diagnosed arthritis—United States, 2002. *Morbidity and Mortality Weekly Report* 54(5): 119–123.

Centers for Disease Control and Prevention. 2006. Prevalence of doctor-diagnosed arthritis and arthritis-attributable activity limitation—United States, 2003–2005. *Morbidity and Mortality Weekly Report* 55(40): 1089–1092.

Cirillo, D., et al. 2005. Effect of estrogen therapy on gallbladder disease. *Journal of the American Medical Association* 293(3): 330–339.

Congdon, N., et al. 2004. Causes and prevalence of visual impairment among adults in the United States. *Archives of Ophthalmology* 144(4): 477–485.

Curtis, L. H., et al. 2004. Inappropriate prescribing for elderly Americans in a large outpatient population. *Archives of Internal Medicine* 164(15): 1621–1625.

Cushman, M., et al. 2004. Estrogen plus progestin and risk of venous thrombosis. *Journal of the American Medical Association* 292: 1573–1580.

Ettinger, B., et al. 2004. Effects of ultralow-dose transdermal estradiol on bone mineral density: A randomized clinical trial. *Obstetrics and Gynecology* 104(3): 443–451.

Evans, M. L., et al. 2004. Management of postmenopausal hot flushes with venlafaxine hydrochloride: A randomized, controlled trial. *Obstetrics and Gynecology* 105(1): 161–166.

Harvard Medical School. 2006. Minding your mind: 12 ways to keep your brain young with proper care and feeding. *Harvard Men's Health Watch* 10(10): 1–4.

Heyn, P. C., et al. 2008. Endurance and strength training outcomes on cognitively impaired and cognitively intact older adults: A meta-analysis. *Journal of Nutrition, Health & Aging* 12(6): 401–409.

Jager, R. D., et al. 2008. Age-related macular degeneration. *New England Journal of Medicine* 258(24): 2606–2617.

Kado, D. M., et al. 2005. Homocysteine versus the vitamins folate, B(6), and B(12) as predictors of cognitive function and decline in older high-functioning adults: MacArthur Studies of Successful Aging. *American Journal of Medicine* 118(2): 161–167.

Kolata, G. 2006. Live long? Die young? Answer isn't just in genes. *New York Times,* 31 August.

Lanza, R., and N. Rosenthal. 2004. The stem cell challenge. *Scientific American,* June.

Mayo Clinic. 2006. Osteoporosis: Treatments for men and women. *Mayo Clinic Health Letter* 24(6): 4–5.

Mudge, A. M., et al. 2008. Exercising body and mind: An integrated approach to functional independence in hospitalized older people. *Journal of the American Geriatrics Society* 56(4): 630–635.

Nelson, H. D., et al. 2006. Nonhormonal therapies for menopausal hot flashes: Systematic review and meta-analysis. *Journal of the American Medical Association* 295(17): 2057–2071.

Rosengren, A., et al. 2005. Body mass index, other cardiovascular risk factors, and hospitalization for dementia. *Archives of Internal Medicine* 165(3): 321–326.

Scarmeas, N., et al. 2006. Mediterranean diet, Alzheimer disease, and vascular mediation. *Archives of Neurology* 63: December [early online release].

Sorrell, J. M. 2008. As good as it gets? Rethinking old age. *Journal of Psychosocial Nursing and Mental Health Services* 46(5): 21–24.

Tufts University. 2006. Pendulum swings on estrogen and women's heart health risk. *Tufts University Health & Nutrition Letter* 24(3): 1–2.

U.S. Department of Health and Human Services. 2004. *Bone Health and Osteoporosis: A Report of the Surgeon General.* Washington, D.C.: U.S. Department of Health and Human Services.

Ward, E. M. 2006. A weekly to-do list to help delay or prevent dementia. *Environmental Nutrition* 29(5): 2.

Welland, D. 2006. Keeping an eye on your diet may help save your sight. *Environmental Nutrition* 29(5): 1, 6.

Whitmer, R. A., et al. 2005. Midlife cardiovascular risk factors and risk of dementia in late life. *Neurology* 64(2): 277–281.

Wilson, R. S., et al. 2005. Proneness to psychological distress and risk of Alzheimer disease in a biracial community. *Neurology* 64(2): 380–382.

Wolfe, M. S. 2006. Shutting down Alzheimer's. *Scientific American* 294(5): 72–79.

Yaffe, K., et al. 2004. The metabolic syndrome, inflammation, and risk of cognitive decline. *Journal of the American Medical Association* 292(18): 2237–2242.

CORE CONCEPTS IN HEALTH

connect™

| PERSONAL HEALTH

http://www.mcgrawhillconnect.com/personalhealth

DYING AND DEATH

LOOKING AHEAD>>>>>

AFTER READING THIS CHAPTER, YOU SHOULD BE ABLE TO:

- Identify the physical, mental, social, behavioral, and spiritual dimensions of dying and death
- Describe various ways of defining death and the components of a mature concept of death
- Understand personal considerations in preparing for death, including making a will, assessing choices for end-of-life care, and making arrangements for a funeral or memorial service
- Describe the experience of living with a life-threatening illness and list ways to support a person who is dying
- Explain the grieving process and how support can be offered to adults and children who have experienced a loss

TEST YOUR KNOWLEDGE

1. **How many Americans die without leaving a will?**
   - a. 1 in 10
   - b. 4 in 10
   - c. 7 in 10

2. **If you die in a car crash, your organs will automatically be donated to people waiting for transplants.**
   True or false?

3. **How many Americans die each day while waiting for an organ transplant?**
   - a. 3
   - b. 9
   - c. 19

4. **Physician-assisted suicide is considered murder and is illegal in all 50 states.**
   True or false?

5. **The best way to help a friend who is grieving is to distract her or him from the loss by talking about sports, gossip, or other lighthearted topics.**
   True or false?

ANSWERS

1. **C.** In such cases, the deceased person's estate is distributed according to state law, which may not reflect what the individual would have wanted.

2. **FALSE.** For your organs to be donated, you must have authorized it prior to your death (for example, by completing an organ donor card), or the donation must be authorized by relatives at the time of your death.

3. **C.** Every day in the United States, about 77 people receive an organ transplant, but another 19 people die while waiting for a needed organ. The number of patients waiting for organs is several times greater than the number of organs donated each year.

4. **FALSE.** Physician-assisted suicide (PAS) is legal in Oregon, where the Death with Dignity Act was approved in 1997. By 2007, more than 292 terminally ill people participating in PAS had died from lethal doses of prescription medication.

5. **FALSE.** Most people who are grieving need to talk about their loss, and a friend who will let them talk freely is very valuable. The best strategy is simply to be a good listener.

hether it is a powerful hurricane devastating New Orleans, a man in a crowded restaurant having a heart attack, or an elderly woman dying peacefully with her family close by, images of death are easy to envision. Nevertheless, very rarely do we think about the inevitability of death in our own lives. Accepting and dealing with death are important tasks that present unique challenges to our sense of self, our relationships with others, and our understanding of the meaning of life itself.

Although times of pain and distress may accompany the dying process, facing death also presents an opportunity for growth as well as affirmation of the preciousness of simple aspects of our daily lives. The way we choose to confront death can greatly influence how we live our lives.

This chapter discusses some of the many questions surrounding one's end of life. The following sections explain steps everyone can take to make their own death a bit easier for their loved ones and describes tasks you may need to consider in preparing for your own passing. This chapter also examines the process of grieving and provides advice that can help in dealing with the death of a loved one.

WHY IS THERE DEATH?

Ultimately, there is no completely satisfying answer to the question of why death exists. When we look at the big picture, we see that death promotes variety through the evolution of species. The average human life is long enough to allow us to reproduce and ensure that our species continues. Yet it is brief enough to allow for new genetic combinations, thereby providing a means of adaptation to changing conditions in the environment. From the perspective of species survival, the cycle of life and death makes sense.

From a personal point of view, however, death challenges our emotional and intellectual security. We may acknowledge the fact that all living things eventually die and that this is nature's way of renewal, but this recognition offers little comfort when death touches our own lives. Questions about the meaning of death and what happens when we die are central concerns of the great religions and philosophies. Some promise a better life after death. Others teach that everyone is evolving toward perfection or divinity, a goal reached after successive rounds of death and rebirth. There are also those who suggest that it is not possible to know what happens—if anything—after death and that any judgment about life's worth must be made on the basis of satisfactions or rewards that we create for ourselves in our lifetime.

It is worth noting that, even in modern secular societies, religion plays a major role in shaping our attitudes and behaviors toward death. Religion offers solace to the extent that it suggests some meaning in dying. The mourning ceremonies associated with various religious practices ease the pangs of grief for many people. Dying and death are more than biological events; they have social and spiri-

Death awaits all of us at the end of our lives, and accepting and dealing with death are difficult but important tasks.

tual dimensions. Our beliefs—religious or philosophical—can be a key to how we relate to the prospect of our own death as well as the deaths of others.

UNDERSTANDING DEATH AND DYING

Death forces us to puzzle out an understanding of its meaning in our lives. We may choose not to think about some issues, such as the possibility of an afterlife, but we cannot keep from facing the reality of dying and death. Regardless of our explanations or efforts to minimize its effects, death can be challenging and painful—both to the person who is dying and to those left behind. However, it also offers an opportunity for remarkable growth and a deepening appreciation of relationships and the myriad aspects of life itself.

Defining Death

Traditionally, death has been defined as cessation of the flow of vital body fluids. This occurs when the heart stops beating and breathing ceases. These traditional signs are adequate for determining death in most cases. However, the use of respirators and other **life-support systems** in modern medicine allows some body functions to be artificially sustained. In such cases, making a determination of death requires the presence or absence of a physical response other than heartbeat or breathing. The concept of **brain death** was developed to determine whether a person is alive or dead when the traditional signs are inadequate because of supportive medical technology.

According to the standards published by a Harvard Medical School committee, brain death involves four characteristics: (1) lack of receptivity and response to external stimuli, (2) absence of spontaneous muscular movement and spontaneous breathing, (3) absence of observable reflexes, and (4) absence of brain activity, as signified by a flat **electroencephalogram (EEG)**. The Harvard criteria require a second set of tests to be performed after 24 hours have elapsed, and they exclude cases of hypothermia (body temperature below 90°F) and situations involving central nervous system depressants, such as barbiturates.

In contrast to **clinical death**, which is determined by either the cessation of heartbeat and breathing or the criteria for establishing brain death, **cellular death** refers to a gradual process that occurs when heartbeat, respiration, and brain activity have stopped. It encompasses the breakdown of metabolic processes and results in complete nonfunctionality at the cellular level. In a biological sense, therefore, death can be defined as the cessation of life due to irreversible changes in cell metabolism.

The way in which death is defined has potential legal and social consequences in a variety of areas, including criminal prosecution, inheritance, taxation, treatment of the corpse, and even mourning. It also affects the practice of organ transplantation, because some organs—hearts, most obviously—must be harvested from a human being who is legally determined to be dead. Timing is critical in removing a heart from someone who has been declared dead and transplanting it into a person whose life can thereby be saved. Safeguards are necessary to ensure that the determination of death occurs without regard to any plans for subsequent transplantation of the deceased's organs.

Learning About Death

Our understanding of death changes as we grow and mature, as do our attitudes toward it. Very young children view death as an interruption and an absence, but their lack of a mature time perspective means that they do not understand death as final and irreversible. A child's understanding of death evolves greatly from about age 5 to age 9. During this period, most children come to understand that death is final, universal, and inevitable. A child who consciously recognizes these facts is said to possess a **mature understanding of death**. This understanding of death is further refined during the years of adolescence and young adulthood by considering the impact of death

on close relationships and contemplating the value of religious or philosophical answers to the enigma of death.

Based on work done by Mark Speece and Sandor Brent, a formal statement of the empirical, or observable, facts about death includes four components:

1. **Universality.** All living things eventually die. Death is all-inclusive, inevitable, and unavoidable (although unpredictable with respect to its exact timing).
2. **Irreversibility.** Organisms that die cannot be made alive again.
3. **Nonfunctionality.** Death involves the cessation of all physiological functioning, or signs of life.
4. **Causality.** There are biological reasons for the occurrence of death.

It is important to add, however, that individuals who possess a mature understanding of death commonly hold nonempirical ideas about it as well. Such nonempirical ideas—that is, ideas not subject to scientific proof—deal mainly with the notion that human beings survive in some form beyond the death of the physical body. What happens to an individual's personality after he or she dies? Does the self or soul continue to exist after the death of the physical body? If so, what is the nature of this afterlife? Developing personally satisfying answers to such questions, which involve what Speece and Brent term **noncorporeal continuity**, is also part of the process of acquiring a mature understanding of death.

Denying Versus Welcoming Death

Understanding death in a mature fashion does not imply that we never experience anxiety about the deaths of those we love or about the prospect of our own death. The news of a friend's or loved one's serious illness can shock us into an encounter with mortality that creates a need to cope not only with the painful reality of our friend's or loved one's illness, but also with our own eventual death. Our ability to find meaning and comfort in the face of mortality depends not only on our having an understanding of the facts of death, but also on our attitudes toward it.

Many people seek to avoid any thought or mention of death. The sick and old are often isolated in hospitals and nursing homes. Relatively few Americans have been present at the death of a loved one. Where the reality of death is concerned, "out of sight, out of mind" often appears to be the rule of the day. Instead of facing death directly, we tend to amuse ourselves with unrealistic portrayals on television and movie screens.

The fictitious deaths of characters we barely know do not cause us to confront the reality of death as it is experienced in real life. Moreover, such faked death is often presented as reversible. Children watch a daily fare of superhuman heroes, invincible to bullets and other weapons. In their games, they reenact these false ideas about death—falling down dead and jumping up again unharmed. Cartoons and video games present death in a two-dimensional world where one can die and then be reborn to play another day.

Although some commentators characterize the predominant attitude toward death in the United States as "death denying," others are reluctant to generalize so broadly. People often maintain conflicting or ambivalent attitudes toward death. Those who come to view death as a relief or release from insufferable pain may have at least a partial sense of welcoming death. Few people wholly avoid or wholly welcome death. Problems can arise, however, when avoidance or denial fosters the notion that death happens to others, but not to you or me. (For another perspective, see the box "El Día de los Muertos: The Day of the Dead.")

PLANNING FOR DEATH

Acknowledging the inevitability of death allows us to plan for it. Adequate planning can help ensure that a sudden, unexpected death is not made even more difficult for survivors. Even when death is not sudden, individuals with a debilitating illness may become unable to make decisions. Many decisions can be anticipated, considered, and discussed with close relatives and friends.

Basic tasks in planning for death include making a will, anticipating medical care needs and expressing preferences for end-of-life care, considering whether to become an organ donor, and helping survivors plan tasks that will be carried out after we die. It is reasonable to begin such planning during the college years and to periodically review and revise one's decisions throughout life.

Making a Will

Surveys indicate that about seven out of ten Americans die without leaving a will. Whatever the reason, dying without a will can lead to unnecessary hardships for survivors, even when an estate is modest in size.

A **will** is a legal instrument expressing a person's intentions and wishes for the disposition of his or her property after death. It is a declaration of how one's **estate**—that is, money, property, and other possessions—will be distributed after death. During the life of the **testator** (the person making the will), a will can be changed, replaced, or revoked. Upon the testator's death, it becomes a legal instrument governing the distribution of the testator's estate.

When a person dies **intestate**—that is, without having left a valid will—property is distributed according to rules set up by the state. The failure to execute a will may result in a distribution of property that is not compatible with a person's wishes nor best suited to the interests and needs of heirs. If you haven't yet made a will, start thinking about how you'd like your property distributed in the case of your death. If you have a will, consider whether it needs to be updated in response to a key life event such as marriage, the birth of a child, or the purchase of a home. In making a will, it is generally advisable to involve close family members to prevent problems that can arise when actions are taken without the knowledge of those who will be affected.

You can also help your family members by completing a *testamentary letter;* this document includes information

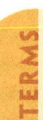
TERMS

will A legal instrument expressing a person's intentions and wishes for the disposition of his or her property after death.

estate The money, property, and other possessions belonging to a person.

testator The person who makes a will.

intestate Referring to the situation in which a person dies without having made a legal will.

El Día de los Muertos: The Day of the Dead

In contrast to the solemn attitude toward death so prevalent in the United States, a familiar and even ironic attitude is more common among Mexicans and Mexican Americans. In the Mexican worldview, death is another phase of life, and those who have passed into it remain accessible. Ancestors are not forever lost, nor is the past dead. This sense of continuity has its roots in the culture of the Aztecs, for whom regeneration was a central theme. When the Spanish came to Mexico in the sixteenth century, their beliefs about death, along with symbols such as skulls and skeletons, were absorbed into the native culture.

Mexican artists and writers confront death with humor and even sarcasm, depicting it as the inevitable fate that all— even the wealthiest—must face. At no time is this attitude toward death livelier than at the beginning of each November on the holiday known as Día de los Muertos, "the Day of the Dead." This holiday coincides with All Souls' Day, the Catholic commemoration of the dead, and represents a unique blending of indigenous ritual and religious dogma.

The celebration in honor of the dead typically spans two days—one day devoted to dead children, one to adults. It reflects the belief that the dead return to Earth in spirit once a year to rejoin their families and partake of holiday foods prepared especially for them. The fiesta usually begins at midday on October 31, with flowers and food—candies, cookies, honey, milk—set out on altars in each house for the family's dead. The next day, family groups stream to the graveyards, where they have cleaned and decorated the graves of their loved ones, to celebrate and commune with the dead. They bring games, music, and special food. People sit on the graves, eat, sing, and talk with the departed ones. Tears may be shed as the dead are remembered, but mourning is tempered by the festive mood of the occasion.

During the season of the dead, graveyards and family altars are decorated with yellow candles and yellow marigolds—the "flower of death." In some Mexican villages, yellow flower petals are strewn along the ground, connecting the graveyard with all the houses visited by death during the year. Wherever Mexican Americans have settled in the United States, Día de los Muertos celebrations keep the traditions alive.

Keeping death in the forefront of consciousness may provide solace to the living, reminding them of their loved ones and assuring them that they themselves will not be forgotten

when they die. Yearly celebrations and remembrances may help people keep in touch with their past, their ancestry, and their roots. The festive atmosphere may help dispel the fear of death, allowing people to look at it more directly. Although it is possible to deny the reality of death even when surrounded by images of it, such practices as Día de los Muertos may help people face death with more equanimity.

SOURCES: Adapted from DeSpelder, L., and A. Strickland. 2007. *The Last Dance*, 8th ed. New York: McGraw-Hill; Azcentral. 2000. *Día de los Muertos* (http://www.azcentral.com/rep/dead; retrieved September 14, 2006); Puente, T. 1991. Día de los Muertos. *Hispanic*, October; Milne, J. 1965. *Fiesta Time in Latin America*. Los Angeles: Ward Ritchie Press.

---

about your personal affairs, such as bank accounts, credit cards, the location of documents and keys, the names of your professional advisers, the names of people who should be notified of your death, and so on.

Considering Options for End-of-Life Care

An appropriate balance in end-of-life care may involve a combination of home care, hospital stays, and hospice or palliative care. By becoming aware of our options, we and our families are empowered to make informed, meaningful choices.

Home Care Many people express a preference to be cared for at home during the end stage of a terminal illness. An obvious advantage of home care is the fact that the dying person is in a familiar setting, ideally in the company of family and friends. For home care to be an option, however, support generally must be provided not only by family and friends, but also by skilled, professional caregivers.

Home care is a full-time job, and it is not always possible to provide a sufficient level of care in the home. Success depends on adequate preparation and commitment. When a patient requires sophisticated medical procedures, does not have access to qualified caregivers, or intends to be an organ donor, institutional care may be more appropriate. When suitable, however, home care is arguably the most satisfying option for care as a person's life comes to a close. Currently, about 25% of Americans die at home (about 25% die in nursing facilities, and about 50% die in hospitals, including more than 20% in intensive care units).

Hospital-Based Palliative Care Although hospitals are primarily organized to provide short-term intensive treatment for acute injury and illness, they are also adopting the principles of **palliative care** for patients who require comprehensive care at the end of life. Unlike acute care, which involves taking active measures to sustain life, palliative care focuses on controlling pain and relieving suffering by caring for the physical, psychological, spiritual, and existential needs of the patient. Although the emphasis is generally placed on comfort care, palliative therapies can be combined with cure-oriented treatment approaches in some cases. In all cases, the goal of palliative care is to achieve the best possible quality of life for patients and their families.

Hospice Programs As a comprehensive program of care offering a set of services designed to support terminally ill patients and their families, **hospice** is a well-known form of palliative care. Although the term *hospice* sometimes refers to a freestanding medical facility to which terminally ill patients are admitted, most hospice care takes place in patients' homes with family members as primary caregivers. Entering hospice care usually means affiliating with a hospice program—that is, arranging to receive the services of a local hospice. Such hospices are generally community-based organizations that coordinate a range of palliative care services that may be provided in nursing homes and hospitals, as well as in patients' homes (see the box "Hospice: Comfort and Care for the Dying"). Qualifying for hospice care usually requires a doctor's certification that a patient's life expectancy is 6 months or less,

and both patient and physician agree to forgo treatment aimed at prolonging life.

Hospice (and palliative care generally) involves a team-oriented approach to care that typically includes physicians, nurses, social workers, home health aides, pharmacists, chaplains, physical and occupational therapists, and trained volunteers. This team-oriented approach seeks to provide state-of-the-art care to prevent or relieve pain and other distressing symptoms, as well as to offer emotional and spiritual support to both patient and family.

Hospice care allows many people to choose where they die, a comforting fact for patients and families. A 2006 study revealed that nursing home residents who chose hospice care were 50% less likely to spend their final 30 days of life in a hospital. Hospitalization can negatively impact a dying person's quality of life. In addition to helping patients achieve a good or peaceful death, an important gift of hospice care is the potential to help patients and families discover how much can be shared at the end of life through personal and spiritual connections.

Deciding to Prolong Life or Hasten Death

The decision to limit treatment, to stop doing everything that can be done, is often a difficult one for patients and their families. Many people owe their lives to the advanced medical technologies now available. Yet a medical stance that strives to keep people alive by all means and at any cost is increasingly being questioned.

Modern medicine can keep the human organism alive despite the cessation of normal heart, brain, respiratory, or kidney function. But should a patient without any hope of recovery be kept alive by means of artificial life support? At what point does such treatment become futile? What if a patient has fallen into a **persistent vegetative state**, a state of profound unconsciousness, lacking any sign of normal reflexes and unresponsive to external stimuli, with no reasonable hope of improvement?

Ethical questions about a person's right to die have become prominent since the landmark case of Karen Ann Quinlan in 1975. At age 22, she was admitted in a comatose state to an intensive care unit, where her breathing was sustained by a respirator. When she remained unresponsive, in a persistent vegetative state, her parents asked that the respirator be disconnected, but the medical staff responsible for Karen's care denied their request. The request to withdraw treatment eventually reached the New

TERMS

palliative care A form of medical care aimed at reducing the intensity or severity of a disease by controlling pain and other discomforting symptoms.

hospice A program of care for dying patients and their families.

persistent vegetative state A condition of profound unconsciousness in which a person lacks normal reflexes and is unresponsive to external stimuli, lasting for an extended period with no reasonable hope of improvement.

Hospice: Comfort and Care for the Dying

Hospice is a special kind of care for people in the final phase of a terminal illness. Instead of being in a hospital, where the emphasis is on curing disease, most hospice patients stay in their home or another homelike setting surrounded by family and friends. The goals of hospice care include the following:

• To make every terminally ill patient as pain-free as possible

• To support the patient and family as a unit

• To respect the feelings and beliefs about death held by patients and their families

• To involve patients in decision making regarding their care

• To help patients and family members deal with feelings of loneliness and fears of abandonment

• To counsel family members after a patient's death

The first hospice program in the United States began in 1974. Today there are more than 4100 such programs, serving an estimated 1.2 million terminally ill patients and their families each year. Once a patient can no longer benefit from medical treatment based on curing disease, the primary physician may refer the patient to hospice. Referrals can also be made by family members, friends, clergy, or health professionals.

Most patients receive care at home, with the primary caregiver often a part-ner or family member. Providing medical care and other types of support is a team of trained professionals—physicians, nurses, counselors, therapists, social workers, home health aides, and volunteers. The emphasis of care is on enhancing the quality of life rather than extending its length. Most hospice patients have a life expectancy of 6 months or less at the time they enter hospice, and about 65% of them are over 75 years old. Cancer continues to be the most common diagnosis for hospice patients (46%); the next two biggest groups suffer from heart disease (12%) and dementia (9.8%). The median length of hospice service is about 26 days.

Hospice care can be less expensive than conventional care—high-cost technology is much less likely to be used, and family, friends, and volunteers provide much of the day-to-day patient care at home. Because a principle of hospice is to offer services based on need rather than the ability to pay, many hospices rely on grants, donations, and a large volunteer staff. At the same time, hospice has grown into a more formal, regulated industry. Hospice care is a covered benefit under most private insurance plans, Medicare, and, in many states, Medicaid.

Some experts believe hospice could serve many more patients than it does. There are several stumbling blocks, however. Physicians may be reluctant to stop treatment and tell patients and their families that nothing further can be done to effect a cure. Establishing a specific time-

line for a patient's expected death is difficult. Patients and family members may be reluctant to face an imminent death.

In addition, under Medicare rules, a physician must certify that the patient will likely die in 6 months or less. Although the rules do provide for extensions, many hospices feel pressured to accept only patients near death, turning away those who may linger beyond the half-year cutoff. The 6-month rule is supposed to be based on life expectancy at the time of the physician's certification, not an absolute deadline by which the patient must die. Nevertheless, some hospices have been subjected to audits that have left them feeling bitter and suspicious about how Medicare benefits are administered. Nearly everyone agrees that there is a need for eligibility criteria that are not time-dependent, so that hospice services can be extended to more patients and their families.

SOURCES: National Hospice and Palliative Care Organization (NHPCO). 2005. *NHPCO's Facts and Figures—2005 Findings* (http://www.nhpco.org; retrieved June 17, 2008); Hospice: A healthy way to let go. 2004. *Consumer Reports on Health*, May; Hospice care. 1997. *Mayo Clinic Health Letter*, July.

Jersey Supreme Court, which ruled that artificial respiration could be discontinued.

Since then, courts have ruled on removing other types of life-sustaining treatment, including artificial feeding mechanisms that provide nutrition and hydration to permanently comatose patients who are able to breathe on their own. Most notable was the case of Nancy Beth Cruzan, heard before the U.S. Supreme Court in 1990. As a result of injuries she received in 1983, Cruzan was in a persistent vegetative state. To provide nourishment, Nancy's physicians implanted a feeding tube, the only form of life support she was receiving. Nancy's parents asked that the tube be removed, but the hospital refused. In this case,

the U.S. Supreme Court upheld the right to refuse treatment, even if it sustains life. However, the court said states can require that such refusal come from the patient; because Nancy had not expressed her wishes, the state did not have to honor the family's request. Later testimony from Nancy's friends convinced a state court that she would have refused life support, so permission was granted to remove her feeding tube.

In 2003, the Terri Schiavo case presented a similar dilemma. Terri had been diagnosed as being in a persistent vegetative state. Contending that she would not want to continue living on life support, Terri's husband requested that her feeding tube be removed. Terri's parents contested the request, and a series of legal actions ensued. Finally, in 2005, after intervention by the U.S. Supreme Court, doctors were allowed to remove the tube. Cases like those of Nancy Cruzan and Terri Schiavo highlight the importance of expressing one's wishes about life-sustaining treatment, in writing, before the need arises.

Withholding or Withdrawing Treatment   The right of a competent patient to refuse unwanted treatment is now generally established in both law and medical practice. The consensus is that there is no medical or ethical distinction between withholding (not starting) a treatment and withdrawing (stopping) a treatment once it has been started. The choice to forgo life-sustaining treatment involves refusing treatments that would be expected to extend life. The right to refuse treatment remains constitutionally protected even when a patient is unable to communicate. Although specific requirements vary, all states authorize some type of written advance directive to honor the decisions of individuals unable to speak for themselves but who have previously recorded their wishes in an appropriate legal document. (Advance directives are discussed later in this chapter.)

The practice of withholding or withdrawing a treatment that could potentially sustain life is sometimes termed **passive euthanasia,** although many people consider this term a misnomer because it tends to confuse the widely accepted practice of withholding or withdrawing treatment with the generally unacceptable and unlawful practice of taking active steps to cause death. It can be argued that passive euthanasia is not euthanasia at all, but rather letting nature take its course. This distinction is sometimes phrased as the difference between "killing" and "allowing to die."

QUICK STATS

85 prescriptions were written for lethal drugs under Oregon's Death with Dignity Act in 2006; 46 patients took the drugs.

—Oregon Department of Human Services, 2008

Assisted Suicide and Active Euthanasia   In contrast to withdrawing or withholding treatment, assisted suicide and active euthanasia refer to practices that intentionally hasten the death of a person. Although some ethicists argue that the constitutional basis for the right to refuse treatment provides the same basis for a right to active euthanasia, this argument has not been accepted by the Supreme Court or by health care practitioners.

In **physician-assisted suicide (PAS),** a physician provides lethal drugs or other interventions—at the patient's request—with the understanding that the patient plans to use them to end his or her life. The patient administers the fatal dose.

In 1997, the Supreme Court reviewed two cases relating to physician-assisted suicide. The decisions in these cases (*Washington v. Glucksberg* and *Vacco v. Quill*) are important for several reasons. First, the Court upheld the distinction between, on the one hand, withholding or withdrawing treatment and, on the other hand, physician-assisted suicide. In doing so, the Court clarified its ruling in the Cruzan case, noting that the right to refuse treatment is based on the right to *maintain one's bodily integrity,* not on a right to *hasten one's death.* When treatment is withheld or withdrawn, the Court said, the intent is to honor the patient's wishes, not cause death, unlike with PAS, where the patient dies from the lethal medication. Second, the Court affirmed the rights of states to craft policy concerning physician-assisted suicide, either prohibiting it, as most states now do, or permitting it under a regulatory system.

Oregon is currently the only state where PAS is permitted. The Death with Dignity Act, a ballot initiative, was passed by Oregon voters in 1994 and, after surviving judicial challenges, was reaffirmed in 1997. During its first 9 years of implementation, 292 people were reported to have legally committed suicide with the assistance of their physicians. These patients exhibited strong beliefs in personal autonomy and a determination to control the end of their lives. The decision to request a prescription for lethal medication was associated mainly with concerns about loss of autonomy and control. Specific quality-of-life concerns included decreasing ability to participate in activities that make life enjoyable, losing control of bodily functions, and physical suffering. The Death with Dignity Act withstood Supreme Court scrutiny in 2006, when the court ruled that the federal government could not block Oregon physicians from prescribing lethal drugs to patients who qualified for PAS under the act's provisions.

A third finding of importance in the Supreme Court's 1997 rulings about PAS relates to the concept of **double effect** in the medical management of pain. The doctrine of double effect states that a harmful effect of treatment, even if it results in death, is permissible if the harm is not intended and occurs as a side effect of a beneficial action. Sometimes the dosages of medication needed to relieve a patient's pain (especially those in the end stage of some diseases) must be increased to levels that can cause respiratory depression, resulting in the patient's death. Thus, the relief of suffering, the intended good effect, may have a potential bad effect, which is foreseen but is not the primary intention. The Court said that such medication for pain, even if it hastens death, is not physician-assisted suicide if the intent is to relieve pain.

Unlike physician-assisted suicide, **active euthanasia** is the intentional act of killing someone who would otherwise suffer from an incurable and painful disease. Active euthanasia can be involuntary, nonvoluntary, or voluntary. *Involuntary euthanasia* (or involuntary active euthanasia) refers to the ending of a patient's life by a medical practitioner without the patient's consent. The most notorious example of this is the medical killing programs of the Nazi regime. *Nonvoluntary euthanasia* occurs when a surrogate decision maker (not the patient) asks a physician for assistance to end another person's life.

Voluntary euthanasia (also known as voluntary active euthanasia, or VAE) is the intentional termination of life at the patient's request by someone other than the patient. In practice, this generally means that a competent patient requests direct assistance to die, and he or she receives assistance from a qualified medical practitioner. Voluntary active euthanasia is legal in Belgium and the Netherlands, but is currently unlawful in the United States. Taking active steps to end someone's life is a crime—even if the motive is mercy.

Many people believe that the emphasis on a right to die results from inattention to the needs of the dying by the health care system. Inadequate pain management has been called "the shame of American medicine." The advocates of hospice and palliative care have highlighted the need for adequate pain management, not only for patients with terminal illness, but for all patients with untreated or undertreated pain and suffering. Increasingly, pain is being viewed as a "fifth vital sign," one that should be added to the four vital signs—temperature, pulse, respiration, and blood pressure—now recorded and assessed as a standard part of patient care.

Unfortunately, there is tremendous variation among health care providers with respect to assessing and managing pain adequately. In fact, a 2005 survey by the University of California–Davis Medical Center showed that most general surgeons had no training in palliative care techniques. A 2006 survey of Oregon hospices, however, showed that doctors who consistently work in hospice settings are gaining experience in palliative care practice. National studies show that many physicians are willing to prescribe strong painkillers (such as opioids) to terminally ill patients but count on patients or their families to communicate the degree of pain being suffered.

Completing an Advance Directive

To make your preferences known about medical treatment, you need to document them through a written **advance directive.** In a general sense, an advance directive is any statement made by a competent person about choices for medical treatment should he or she become unable to make such decisions or communicate them at some time in the future.

Two forms of advance directives are legally important. First is the **living will,** which enables individuals to provide instructions about the kind of medical care they wish to receive if they become incapacitated or otherwise unable to participate in treatment decisions (Figure 23.1 on p. 710). Many people believe that living wills are appropriate only for stating a desire to forgo life-sustaining procedures or to avoid medical heroics when death is imminent; indeed, most standard forms for completing a living will reflect this purpose. In fact, however, a living will can be drafted to express very different ideas about the kinds of treatment a person would or would not want, and they can be written to cover various contingencies.

The second important form of advance directive is the **health care proxy,** which is also known as a *durable power of attorney for health care.* This document makes it possible to appoint another person to make decisions about medical treatment if you become unable to do so. This decision maker, also known as a **surrogate,** may be a family member, close friend, or attorney with whom you have discussed your treatment preferences. The proxy is expected to act in accordance with your wishes as stated in an advance directive or as otherwise made known. A 2006 survey showed that nearly 50% of people would name someone other than their spouse (or even their standard emergency contact) as their proxy. Only about 5% of the population will ever need a surrogate, but everyone

FIGURE 23.1 Sample living will. Because of differences in state law, each state has its own format for advance directives.

SOURCE: Valid copies of this and other state-specific advance directives can be found at www.caringinfo.org. Reprinted with permission of The National Hospice and Palliative Care Organization. Copyright © 2005 National Hospice and Palliative Care Organization 2007 Revised. All rights reserved. Reproduction and distribution by an organization or organized group without the written permission of the National Hospice and Palliative Care Organization is expressly forbidden.

should name one, just in case. If no proxy is chosen, most states assign the task to the patient's spouse or parents.

For advance directives to be of value, you must do more than merely complete the paperwork. Discuss your wishes ahead of time with caregivers and family members as well as with your physician.

Becoming an Organ Donor

A human body is a valuable resource. Of all the advances in medical techniques for helping patients who were formerly beyond recovery, perhaps the best known is the transplantation of human organs. Yet the demand for organs continues to drastically outpace the number of organ donations. Each day about 77 people receive an organ transplant while another 19 people on the waiting list die because not enough organs are available (Figure 23.2). There are currently more than 98,000 Americans waiting for organ transplants, including more than 13,000 people under age 35. For more information about organ donation, see the box "What Can Be Done About the Shortage of Organ Donors?" on p. 712.

If you decide to become a donor, the first step is to indicate your wish by completing a **Uniform Donor Card** (Figure 23.3); alternatively, you can indicate your wish on your driver's license. Because relatives are called on to make decisions about organ and tissue donation at the time of a loved one's death, your second step is to discuss your decision with your family. If your family does not know your wishes, they are likely to refuse organ donation. In a 2005 survey, 92% of respondents said they would donate a family member's organs if they knew that was what their loved one wanted.

Planning a Funeral or Memorial Service

Funerals and memorial services are rites of passage that commemorate a person's life and acknowledge his or her passing from the community. Funerals and memorials allow survivors to support one another as they cope with their loss and express their grief. The presence of death rites in every human culture suggests that they serve innate human needs.

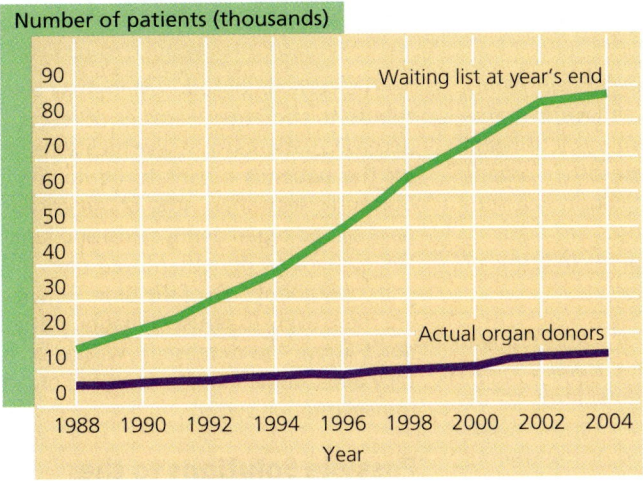

Number of patients (thousands)

Waiting list at year's end

Actual organ donors

1988 1990 1992 1994 1996 1998 2000 2002 2004
Year

VITAL STATISTICS

FIGURE 23.2 The need for organ donors. As organ transplants have become an option for more and more patients, the number of people waiting for transplants has increased. The number of actual donations has not grown nearly as significantly.

SOURCE: United Network for Organ Sharing (http://www.unos.org).

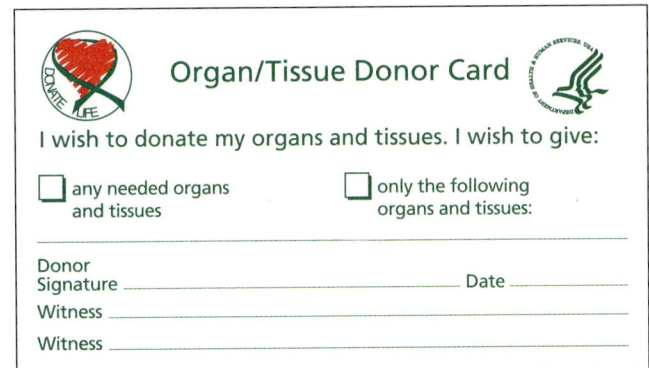

Organ/Tissue Donor Card

I wish to donate my organs and tissues. I wish to give:

☐ any needed organs and tissues

☐ only the following organs and tissues:

_____

Donor
Signature _____ Date _____
Witness _____
Witness _____

FIGURE 23.3 A sample organ/tissue donor card.

SOURCE: U.S. Department of Health and Human Services (http://www.organdonor.gov/donor/index.htm; retrieved June 17, 2008).

Disposition of the Body

When a death occurs, one of the immediate concerns of survivors is the disposition of the corpse. Although corpses must be disposed of for sanitary reasons, the disposition of a body is surrounded by a web of social, cultural, religious, psychological, and interpersonal considerations.

People generally have a preference about the final disposition of their body. For most Americans, the choice is either burial or cremation. *Burial* usually involves a grave dug into the soil or entombment in a mausoleum. *Cremation* involves subjecting a body to intense heat, thereby reducing its organic components to a mineralized skeleton. The remaining bone fragments are then usually put through a cremulator, which reduces them to a granular state, often referred to as ashes (which actually resemble coarse coral sand). Cremated remains can be buried, placed in a columbarium niche, put into an urn kept by the family or interred in an urn garden, or scattered at sea or on land. If the body is to be viewed during a wake or will be present at the funeral, **embalming** is generally done.

Arranging a Service

In commemorating a person's life and death, the choice of last rites may involve a traditional funeral ceremony or a simple memorial service. Whereas the casketed body is typically present at a funeral, it is not at a memorial service. In some cases, both a funeral and a memorial service are held, the former occurring within a few days after death and the latter being held sometime later (perhaps in a different town where the deceased had a large social network). Although it is becoming more common for individuals and families to express a preference for

THINKING ABOUT THE ENVIRONMENT

By some estimates, there are more than 22,000 cemeteries in the United States, covering hundreds of thousands of acres of land. These burial grounds hold millions of graves, some of which are hundreds of years old.

In the face of a long-standing tradition, however, many Americans are rethinking the notion of burying the dead in sealed caskets, placed in permanent concrete vaults. The practice, say environmentalists, needlessly consumes vast tracts of land, and chemicals from embalmed bodies and caskets slowly leach into the soil and water. Despite the notion that cremation solves these problems, the practice uses a great deal of energy and pollutes the air.

One solution is the natural, or "green," burial now being offered in many cemeteries. In a green burial, the body is wrapped in cloth and buried directly in the ground. There is no embalming or use of chemicals, and no casket or vault to prevent decomposition. Experts say the method is environmentally friendly; generally, however, most states require unembalmed bodies to be disposed of quickly.

What Can Be Done About the Shortage of Organ Donors?

Since the first organ, a kidney, was successfully transplanted in 1954, the transplanting of organs into people whose organs have failed has become almost commonplace. As transplant techniques and other medical care have improved, however, an acute shortage of available organs has developed.

Sources of Organs and Tissues

Organs and tissues for transplant have several sources.

• *Self-donation (autograft).* This type of transplant involves taking part of the patient's own tissue and using it to replace damaged tissue in another area. An example is moving skin from the thigh to replace skin elsewhere that has been burned. Autografts are free from rejection problems (described below) but are not a source of replacement organs.

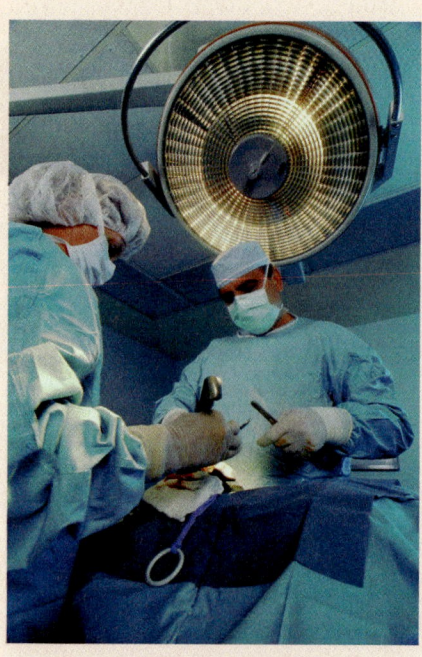

• *Deceased donor (cadaveric transplant).* A typical scenario for cadaveric transplant involves a young injury victim who is brain-dead but whose other organs are still functioning. Rejection is a serious problem, and attempts are made to match donors and recipients in terms of blood and immune factors.

• *Living donor.* Organs from siblings, parents, and other close relatives are less likely than cadaveric transplants to be rejected by the body of the recipient. Because of their own need, living donors can donate only bone marrow, liver lobes, lung lobes, and kidneys.

• *Animal donor (xenotransplantation).* There is a potentially much greater supply of animal organs than human organs, but xenotransplantation has both ethical and scientific problems. Organ rejection is very likely, and scientists fear the introduction of animal viruses into humans.

Rejection occurs when a patient's body recognizes a transplanted organ as foreign and the immune system attacks and destroys it. Autografts are almost always successful, and tissues or organs transplanted from close relatives are the next best alternative. To help prevent rejection, transplant recipients often must take powerful drugs to suppress their immune systems.

Causes of the Organ Shortage

There are many reasons for the current shortage of donor organs. First, more people are now waiting for transplants because new technologies and drugs are keeping people with serious health problems alive longer. Another reason is that fewer brain-dead donors are available because safety belts and motorcycle helmets have reduced injury deaths.

The current consent system may contribute to shortages. Families of recently deceased patients must give their consent for the patient's organs to be donated. Currently, less than 40% of Americans have signed organ donor cards, and families consent to donating loved ones' organs only about 50% of the time. Families are more likely to refuse donation if they don't know the deceased's wishes or if they don't understand or trust the organ transplantation system.

Possible Solutions to the Organ Shortage

Several possible solutions to the donor organ shortage have been adopted or are being considered:

• Education initiatives to encourage people to talk with their families and complete organ donor cards.

• Financial or other incentives for families of donors.

• Adoption of a system of presumed consent, in which organs are donated unless the family denies permission.

• Development of transgenic animals (those that have been genetically engineered to carry human proteins instead of animal proteins) to allow broader use of xenotransplantation.

• Greater use of devices such as heart pacemakers and insulin pumps that replace organ functions.

• Development of bioartifical organs, which are made up of both genetically engineered living cells and mechanical components.

• Stem cells, which could eventually be used to replace cells in damaged or diseased organs.

---

no services, bereaved relatives and friends can derive important benefits from having an opportunity to honor the deceased and express their grief through ceremony.

Decisions about your last rites are ideally made with a view to the needs and wishes of your survivors. It can be worthwhile to consider such decisions early in life, so you can gather information about options and discuss plans with family members (see the box "A Consumer Guide to Funerals" on p. 713). Religious and cultural or ethnic traditions play a major role in shaping the way people honor their dead. The diversity of life and death in the United States calls for a diversity of rites. A meaningful funeral or memorial service can be designed in many ways.

Making at least some plans ahead of time and discussing the options with family members can help reduce the burden on survivors who find themselves facing a number of tasks and decisions once death occurs (see the box "Tasks for Survivors" on p. 714).

A Consumer Guide to Funerals

Funerals are a consumer product. They are also among the most expensive purchases many consumers will ever make. A traditional funeral with a casket costs about $6000, and many funerals cost $10,000 or more. When no preplanning has been done, as often occurs, family members have to make decisions under time pressure and in the grip of strong feelings. As a result, they may make poor decisions and spend more than they need to.

To avoid these problems, millions of consumers are now making funeral arrangements in advance, comparing prices and services so they can make well-informed purchasing decisions. Many people see funeral planning as an extension of will and estate planning. It is also possible to prepay some or all of the expenses involved.

A federal law called the Funeral Rule, enforced by the Federal Trade Commission, regulates the funeral provider business. It includes many requirements designed to protect consumers from unprofessional business practices. To ensure that you make the best possible decisions, follow these guidelines:

• Plan ahead. Think about what type of funeral you want—simple or elaborate, public or private, religious or secular. Do you want your funeral to be held in a house of worship, a funeral home, or a private setting? Also think about the disposition of the body—do you want your remains to be buried or cremated?

• Shop around. Look for a funeral home that belongs to the National Funeral Directors Association (NFDA), and compare prices from at least two funeral homes. You are not legally required to use a funeral home, but many people find it makes arrangements easier.

• Ask for a price list. The Funeral Rule requires funeral directors to give you an itemized price list when you ask either in person or over the telephone. Many funeral homes offer package funerals that cost less than individual items, but you may not need or want everything included in the package.

• Decide on the goods and services you want. Basic services include planning the funeral and coordinating arrangements with the cemetery or crematory. Embalming is not necessary or legally required if the body is buried or cremated shortly after death. The casket is usually the single most expensive item; an average casket costs slightly more than $2000, but some caskets sell for as much as $10,000. You do not have to buy the casket from the funeral home you use. The Funeral Rule prohibits funeral directors from claiming that some caskets can preserve a body indefinitely; they can't.

• Resist pressure to buy goods and services you don't really want or need. Funeral directors are required to inform you that you need buy only those goods and services you want.

• In choosing a cemetery, take into consideration its location; its religious affiliation, if any; the types of monuments allowed; and cost. Visit the cemetery ahead of time to make sure it's suitable.

• Once you have made decisions, put them in writing, give copies to family members, and keep a copy accessible. It's a good idea to review your decisions every few years and revise them if necessary.

• If you need help dealing with a funeral home, contact consumer protection agencies listed in the telephone book, the Funeral Consumer's Alliance (800-765-0107 or http://www.funerals.org), or the Funeral Service Consumer Assistance Program (800-662-7666). To file a complaint about a funeral home, contact the Federal Trade Commission at 877-FTC-HELP or http://www.ftc.gov.

QUESTIONS FOR CRITICAL THINKING AND REFLECTION

Have you ever been involved in a funeral? What role did you play? Did you feel that the service reflected the values and beliefs of the deceased person? Did the experience cause you to think about your own funeral and what it should be like?

COPING WITH DYING

There is no one right way to live with or die of a life-threatening illness. Every disease has its own set of problems and challenges, and each person copes with these problems and challenges in his or her own way. Much of the suffering experienced by people with a life-threatening illness comes from overwhelming feelings of loss on all levels. Besides the emotional havoc, there are usually concerns about costly medical care, loss of income, hospitalization, and physical pain. How a person copes with such an experience is likely to reflect his or her personality and life history, as well as the nature of family relationships and patterns of interaction in the person's wider social environment.

Awareness of Dying

Living with an illness that is life-threatening and incurable can be described as a living-dying experience. From the time discomforting symptoms are first noticed and a person's worst fears confirmed by a diagnosis, through the ups and downs of treatment, and on to the final days or hours of life, hope and honesty are often delicately balanced—honesty to face reality as it is, hope for a positive outcome. The object of hope changes. The early hope that the symptoms are not really serious gives way to hope that a cure is possible. When the illness is deemed incurable, there is hope for more time. As time begins to run out, one hopes for a pain-free death, a "good death" (see the box "In Search of a Good Death" on p. 715).

Tasks for Survivors

Some of the following tasks must be attended to soon after a death occurs, whereas others take weeks or months to complete. Many of these tasks, especially those that need to be dealt with in the first hours and days following the death, can be taken care of by friends and relatives of the immediate survivors.

- Prepare a list of relatives, friends, and colleagues, and telephone them about the death as soon as possible. Friends can help with notifications.

- Find out if the deceased left instructions for disposition of the body or for a funeral or memorial service.

- If no prior plan exists, contact a mortuary or memorial society for help in making arrangements. Clergy, friends, and other family members can be asked to help decide what is most appropriate.

- If flowers are to be omitted from the funeral or memorial service, choose an appropriate charity or other memorial to which gifts can be made.

- Write the obituary. Include the deceased's age, birthplace, cause of death, occupation, academic degrees, memberships, military service, accomplishments, names and relationships of nearest survivors, and the time and place of the funeral or memorial service.

- Arrange for family members or close friends to take turns welcoming mourners who come in person and responding to those who telephone their condolences.

- Ask friends to help coordinate the supplying of meals for the first few days following the death, as well as the management of other household tasks and child care, if necessary.

- Arrange hospitality for relatives and friends who are visiting from out of town.

- If a funeral ceremony is planned, choose the individuals who are to be pallbearers, and notify them that you would like their participation.

- Send handwritten or printed notes of acknowledgment to the people who have provided assistance or who have sent flowers, contributions, or their condolences.

- Notify the lawyer, accountant, and other personal representatives who will be helping to settle the deceased's estate.

- With the help of a lawyer or an accountant, review all insurance policies as well as other sources of potential death benefits, such as Social Security, military service, fraternal organizations, and unions.

- Review all debts, mortgages, and installment payments. Some may carry clauses that cancel debt in the event of death. If payments must be delayed, contact creditors to arrange for a grace period.

Psychiatrist Avery Weisman described this process of coping as involving **middle knowledge,** with patients and their families seeking a balance between sustaining hope and acknowledging the reality. Maintaining a sense of self-worth, setting goals and striving to reach them, engaging in fruitful interactions with one's environment—all of these reflect a coping strength that sustains the will to live fully despite a bleak prognosis.

The Tasks of Coping

In her 1969 book *On Death and Dying,* Elisabeth Kübler-Ross suggested that the response to an awareness of imminent death involves five psychological stages: denial, anger, bargaining, depression, and acceptance. The notion that these five stages occur in a linear progression has since become a kind of modern myth of how people *ought* to cope with dying. Unfortunately, this can lead to the idea that it is a person's task to move sequentially through these stages, one after another, and that if this is not accomplished, the person has somehow failed. In fact, however, Kübler-Ross said that individuals go back and forth among the stages during the course of an illness and different stages can occur simultaneously.

The stage-based model devised by Kübler-Ross more than three decades ago has been a stimulus toward a better understanding of how people cope with dying. The notion of stages, however, has been deemphasized in favor of highlighting the tasks that deserve attention in coping with a life-threatening illness. Charles Corr, for example, distinguishes four primary dimensions in coping with dying:

1. *Physical:* Satisfying bodily needs and minimizing physical distress

2. *Psychological:* Maximizing a sense of security, self-worth, autonomy, and richness in living

3. *Social:* Sustaining significant relationships and addressing the social implications of dying

4. *Spiritual:* Identifying, developing, or reaffirming sources of meaning and fostering hope

Contemplating these dimensions gives us a framework for considering the specific tasks that need to be addressed in coping with dying. In addition to an *acute* phase initiated by the diagnosis, a *chronic* phase of living with the disease, and a *terminal* phase that involves coping with impending death, there are sometimes two other phases: first, a *pre-diagnostic* phase, during which a person suspects the illness

In Search of a Good Death

Participants in a recent study were asked to discuss the deaths of family members, friends, or patients and reflect on what made their deaths good or bad. From these discussions, six major themes emerged as components of a good death.

The first component was pain and symptom management. Many people fear dying in pain, and portrayals of bad deaths usually included inadequate pain management. Every health care provider in the study told regret-filled stories of patients who died in pain. Patients were concerned with pain control; when reassured that pain could be managed, they were less anxious.

The second component of a good death was clear decision making. Both providers and families feared entering a medical crisis without knowing the patient's preferences. Patients and families who had good communication with health care providers and had discussed treatment decisions ahead of time felt empowered, and providers felt they were giving good care. Although all uncertainty about end-of-life decisions cannot be eliminated, tolerance for uncertainty may increase if values and preferences are clarified.

The third component was preparation for death. Patients expressed satisfaction when they had time to prepare their wills and help plan their funeral arrangements. Many times, providers avoided end-of-life discussions to prevent their patients from losing hope, thus depriving them of the opportunity to plan ahead. Patients and families also wanted to know what to expect during the course of the illness

and what physical and psychosocial changes would take place as death approached. It was important for providers and families to have reached some personal comfort with death so they felt prepared when death occurred.

The fourth component was completion, the opportunity to review one's life, to resolve conflicts, to spend time with loved ones, and to say good-bye. Participants confirmed the deep importance of spirituality or meaningfulness at the end of life. Many times, patients were able to view their experience of dying as part of a broader life trajectory and thus continue to grow emotionally and spiritually in their last days. Issues of faith were often mentioned as important to healing, but participants emphasized that the cues about the particular expression of faith must be taken from the patient.

The fifth component was contributing to others. Patients wanted to know that they still had something to offer to others, whether it was making someone laugh or lightening the load of someone closer to death. Many patients found that as they reflected on their lives, what they valued most was their personal relationships with family and friends, and they were anxious to impart this wisdom to others.

The sixth component of a good death was affirmation of the whole person. Patients appreciated empathic health care providers, and family members were comforted by those who treated their loved ones as unique and whole people, rather than as a disease. The quality of dying is related to the acknowledgment that

people die in character, that is, as an extension of who they have been in their lives. Health care providers also focused on their personal relationships with patients and family members as important to a satisfying death.

The study affirmed that most people think of death as a natural part of life, not as a failure of technology. Although the biomedical aspects of end-of-life care are crucial, they merely provide a point of departure toward a good death. When pain is properly managed and the practical aspects of dying are taken care of, patients and their families have the opportunity to address the important emotional, psychological, and spiritual issues that all human beings face at the end of life.

---

and may seek medical attention; and, second, a *recovery* phase following a cure or remission of a previously life-threatening disease. Even as the threat of dying recedes into the background, however, there can be a need to cope with the fact that one has had a potentially terminal illness.

In addition, though, we must remember that a person's death is as unique as his or her life. Thus, although models can help us gain understanding, they need to be balanced by paying attention to the dying person's own unfolding *life* story. Each person's pathway through life-threatening illness is determined by factors such as the specific disease and its course, his or her personality, and the available supportive resources.

People who apparently cope best with life-threatening illness often exhibit a fighting spirit that views the illness not only as a threat but also as a challenge. These people strive to inform themselves about their illness and take an active part in treatment decisions. They are optimistic and have a capacity to discover positive meaning in ordinary events. Holding to a positive outlook despite distressing circumstances involves creating a sense of meaning that is bigger than the threat. In the context of life-threatening illness, this encompasses a person's ability to comprehend the implications an illness has for the future, as well as for his or her ability to accomplish goals, maintain relationships, and sustain a sense of personal vitality, competence, and power. Although life-threatening illness disrupts virtually all aspects of a person's life, there is a vital link between finding meaning and achieving a sense of mastery.

The Trajectory of Dying

Our expectations about dying may be quite different from what most people actually experience. The concept of a **trajectory of dying** is useful for understanding patients' experiences as they near death. Although sudden death from an unexpected cause—a massive heart attack or an accident, for example—is one type of dying trajectory, our focus here is on deaths that occur when there is forewarning. Among these, some trajectories involve a steady and fairly predictable decline. This is the case with many cancers, which tend to follow the course of a progressive disease with a terminal phase. Other kinds of advanced, chronic illness involve a long period of slow decline marked by episodes of crisis, the last of which proves to be "suddenly" fatal.

We can also distinguish between different stages in a dying trajectory, namely, a period when a person is known to be terminally ill but is living with a life expectancy of perhaps weeks or months, possibly years, and a later period when dying is imminent and the person is described as actively dying. The way in which such trajectories are estimated—their duration and expected course—can affect both patients and caregivers and influence their actions. Deaths that occur out of time (too quickly or too slowly) may pose special difficulties.

When a person is actively dying, his or her death is expected to occur within hours or, at most, a few days. During the last phase of a fatal illness, a dying person may exhibit irregular breathing or shortness of breath, decreased appetite and thirst, nausea and vomiting, incontinence, restlessness and agitation, disorientation and confusion, and diminished consciousness. These symptoms usually can be managed by skilled palliative care. Pain, if it is present, should be treated aggressively as part of a comprehensive approach to comfort care. Since most patients are more comfortable without eating or drinking at the end of life, forcing food or liquids is usually not beneficial. The stopping of eating and drinking has always been part of the last phase of a terminal condition. Near the time of death, relaxation of the throat muscles or secretions in the throat may cause the person's breathing to become noisy, resulting in a sound called the death rattle. Other signals may be noticeable as death draws closer. For example, the patient's extremities may feel cold to the touch; lips, fingers, and ears may appear bluish; urination becomes less frequent; or the ability to communicate may be lost. In the final hours, purple blotches (mottling) may appear on the legs

or arms. Simple steps—such as repositioning the patient, covering him or her with blankets, dimming the room's lighting, or just holding hands—can provide great relief and reassurance in the last moments. Just before death, the person may take a breath and sigh or shudder.

Supporting a Dying Person

People often feel uncomfortable in the presence of a person who is close to dying. What can we say? How should we act? It may seem that any attempt to be comforting could result only in words that are little more than stale platitudes. Yet we want to express concern and establish meaningful contact with the person who is facing death. In such circumstances, the most important gift we can bring is that of listening. Offering the dying person opportunities to speak openly and honestly about his or her experience can be crucial, even when such conversation is initially painful.

We tend to place dying people in a special category, but the reality is that their needs are not fundamentally different from anyone else's, although their situation is perhaps more urgent. Dying people need to know that they are val-

The simple act of listening can be extremely supportive to someone who is facing death.

QUESTIONS FOR CRITICAL THINKING AND REFLECTION

What is your notion of a "good death"? In what setting does it take place, and who is there? In the last days of your life, what do you think you'll need to say, and to whom will you want to say it? If you were terminally ill, what would be the most supportive things others could do for you?

ued, that they are not alone, that they are not being unfairly judged, and that those closest to them are also striving to come to terms with a difficult situation. As with any relationship, there are opportunities for growth on both sides.

Besides friends and family, the dying person may need other supportive resources. These may include counselors and clergy. Many hospitals, hospices, and other health care providers sponsor programs for dying patients and their families, offering opportunities for them to share their concerns in a supportive and validating atmosphere. Programs of this kind can be located by asking hospital staff or other medical personnel. Local chapters of support groups affiliated with organizations such as the American Cancer Society and Make Today Count also can be found in many cities.

COPING WITH LOSS

Even if we have not experienced the death of someone close, we are all survivors of losses that occur in our lives because of changes and endings. The loss of a job, the ending of a relationship, transitions from one school or neighborhood to another—these are examples of the kinds of losses that occur in all our lives. Such losses are sometimes called little deaths and, in varying degrees, they all involve grief.

Experiencing Grief

Grief is the reaction to loss. It encompasses thoughts and feelings, as well as physical and behavioral responses. Mental distress may involve disbelief, confusion, anxiety, disorganization, and depression. The emotions that can be present in normal grief include not only sorrow and sadness, but also relief, anger, and self-pity, among others. Bereaved people experience a range of feelings, even conflicting ones. Recognizing that grief can involve many different feelings—not just sadness—makes us more able to cope with it. Common behaviors associated with grief include crying, searching for the deceased, and talking incessantly about the deceased and the circumstances of the death. Bereaved people may be restless, as if not knowing what to do with themselves. Physically, grief may involve frequent sighing, insomnia, and loss of appetite. Grief may also evoke a reexamination of religious or spiritual beliefs as a person struggles to make meaning of the loss. All such

manifestations of grief can be present as part of one's total response to **bereavement**—that is, the event of loss.

Mourning is closely related to grief and is often used as a synonym for it. However, mourning refers not so much to the *reaction* to loss but to the *process* by which a bereaved person adjusts to loss and incorporates it into his or her life. How this process is managed is determined, at least partly, by cultural and gender norms for the expression of grief (see the box "Grief and Gender" on p. 718). Considered jointly, grief and mourning are the means to healing the pain of loss.

Tasks of Mourning Experiencing grief is part of the process by which a bereaved person integrates a significant loss into his or her life. Psychologist William Worden has identified four tasks that must be attended to:

1. *Accepting the reality* of the loss
2. *Working through the pain* of grief
3. *Adjusting to a changed environment* in which the deceased is absent
4. *Emotionally relocating the deceased and moving on with life*

Accomplishing the fourth task does not mean dishonoring the deceased's memory or denying normal feelings of connection that persist beyond death. Finding healthy ways to maintain bonds with the deceased is a testimony to the enduring strength of love. When this task is managed successfully, however, the bereaved is not stuck in the past. Making the journey of grief and attending to the various tasks along the way, we come to a place where we learn how to keep a special place for the deceased in our hearts and memories while moving forward with our lives.

The Course of Grief Grieving, like dying, is highly individual. In the first hours or days following a death, a bereaved person is likely to experience overwhelming shock and numbness, as well as a sense of disbelief. There is often a period of denial—"No! This can't be true!"—especially if the death was unexpected. Consider the ways in which people die: the aged grandmother, dying quietly in her sleep; the young child pronounced DOA after a bicycle crash; the despondent executive who commits suicide; a young soldier killed in battle; the chronically ill

trajectory of dying The duration and nature of a person's experience in approaching death as influenced by the underlying cause of dying.

grief A person's reaction to loss as manifested physically, emotionally, mentally, and behaviorally.

bereavement The objective event of loss.

mourning The process whereby a person actively copes with grief in adjusting to a loss and integrating it into his or her life.

Grief and Gender

The loss of a loved one generates a broad range of reactions—physical, emotional, and behavioral. But do women and men react differently to the loss of someone close to them? Some clinicians say yes, and studies now support the idea that there can be different gender patterns in grief.

Data suggest that a greater proportion of women may be vulnerable to the more distressing and disruptive symptoms characteristic of severe grief reactions. In general, women have a higher lifetime incidence and prevalence of depressive and anxiety disorders, so it is thus not surprising that at times of great stress, such as the loss of a loved one, these gender differences would be present.

In a study of gender differences in grief among parents who have lost a child, researchers found that compared with fathers, mothers showed greater feelings of being hurt, cheated, and depressed, while also revealing greater irritability and anger. The women also cried more, experienced greater numbness and confusion, were more preoccupied with thoughts of the deceased, and felt more guilt both for having failed to prevent the death and for having survived. They also experienced more physical symptoms such as insomnia and loss of appetite.

In a study of people who had lost a spouse, researchers similarly found that women had a higher level of emotional distress in reaction to loss. Women who lost a husband had higher levels of traumatic grief, depression, and anxiety than men who had lost a wife. These findings persisted at least 2 years following the death of the spouse.

Physiological factors contributing to these gender differences might include hormonal differences, subtle differences in brain chemistry or function, or genetic influences. Gender roles and cultural expectations also likely play a role. Women are often readier to express emotion and seek out social support and opportunities to talk about loss, whereas men may

be more reticent to admit to any psychological distress or allow the appearance of excessive emotionality.

person who dies a lingering death. The cause or mode of death—natural, accidental, homicide, or suicide—has an influence on how grief is experienced (see the box "Profound Trauma and Loss" on p. 719). Even when a death is anticipated, grief is not necessarily diminished when the loss becomes real.

The sense of disorganization experienced by survivors during the early period of grief is set against the need to attend to decisions and actions surrounding the disposition of the deceased's body. As family and friends gather to offer mutual support, funeral ceremonies are held. Engaging in such activities promotes accepting the reality of the death and moving beyond the initial shock and numbness.

In its middle phase, the course of grief is characterized by anxiety, apathy, and pining for the deceased. The pangs of grief are felt as the bereaved person deeply experiences the pain of separation. There is often a sense of despair as a person repeatedly goes over the events surrounding the loss, perhaps fantasizing that somehow everything could be undone and be as it was before. During this period, the bereaved also begins looking toward the future and taking the first steps toward building a life without the deceased.

This can be a difficult time in grieving. Yet the bereaved often find themselves without the social support of the relatives and friends who were present during the initial period. Grief occurs within a particular social or cultural context, and individual grievers differ in their particular styles of grieving. This leads to the recognition that there is no standard way of coping with loss. Colin

Murray Parkes points to three main influences on a person's course of grieving:

1. The urge to look back, cry, and search for what is lost

2. The urge to look forward, explore the world that emerges out of the loss, and discover what can be carried forward from the past into the future

3. The social and cultural pressures that influence how the first two urges are inhibited or expressed

As these influences interact in various ways, at times the bereaved tries to avoid the pain of grief and at other times confronts it. The goal is to achieve a balance between avoidance and confrontation that facilitates coming to terms with the loss. Attaining this goal can be seen as an oscillation between what Margaret Stroebe and Henk Schut call loss-oriented and restoration-oriented mourning. From this perspective, looking at old photographs and yearning for the deceased are examples of loss-oriented coping, whereas doing what is needed to reorganize life in the wake of the loss—for example, learning to do tasks that the deceased had always managed, such as finances—is part of restoration-oriented coping.

In moving toward the restoration of one's well-being, the last phase of active grief involves resolution. The acute pain and emotional turmoil of grief subside. Physical and mental balance is reestablished. The bereaved becomes increasingly reintegrated into his or her social world. Sadness

Profound Trauma and Loss

Profoundly traumatic events—Hurricane Katrina, the 2004 tsunami in Southeast Asia, the terrorist attacks of September 11, 2001, the deaths and destruction resulting from the wars in Iraq and Afghanistan—all represent a category of loss far beyond normal comprehension. Experiencing traumatic loss in such extraordinary circumstances can cause severe and disruptive reactions in emotion and behavior.

World War I veterans often developed psychological symptoms that collectively were described as shell shock. However, it was not until after the Vietnam War that the medical community became fully aware of how disruptive and enduring the psychological effects could be for those experiencing profound traumatic loss.

It is now widely recognized that significant psychological symptoms can follow the experiencing of loss in traumatic circumstances. Elements commonly seen in a customary reaction to grief, such as sadness, disbelief, crying, insomnia, and loss of appetite, are frequently exaggerated in the aftermath of profoundly traumatic events and will often include more pronounced symptoms, such as overwhelming distress, numbness, doubt, despair, guilt, and disabling depression and anxiety.

Depending on the severity of exposure and a person's underlying vulnerability, the symptoms can persist long after the original trauma. Memories and images of the event may suddenly pop into the victim's mind, causing anxiety, depression, and anger. Insomnia and nightmares can disrupt the sleep-wake cycle. The person may start avoiding everything that serves as a reminder of the event and, as a kind of self-protection, may begin to become numb, to lose all feelings. Such people may startle easily and have difficulty concentrating. Their work life, social life, and intimate relationships may become markedly impaired. People experiencing these severe symptoms are said to have posttraumatic stress disorder (PTSD), which can persist for months or years.

The events of September 11, 2001, are an example of a profound trauma that caused PTSD in affected people. As described in Chapter 3, PTSD symptoms occurred among survivors, rescue workers,

passersby, residents of Manhattan, and some people exposed to the events through repeated television images. Researchers who interviewed residents of Manhattan found that about 7.5% reported symptoms consistent with a diagnosis of PTSD and 9.7% reported symptoms consistent with new onset of depression; these numbers are about twice as high as the expected rates in surveys of this type. Among people who lived closest to the World Trade Center, the prevalence of PTSD was as high as 20%.

Another dramatic example is a flood that devastated the 17 communities of Buffalo Creek, West Virginia, on February 26, 1972. Following several days of rain, a dam owned by a coal company burst and released millions of gallons of black water—a wall of water described by some to be 30 feet high. Survivors of the flood described houses pushed from their foundations and thrown against one another, railroad tracks torn from the ground, and children swept from the arms of parents. Nearly 60% of survivors of the tragedy developed PTSD, and in 25% of survivors, PTSD persisted at least 14 years after the flood. Comparable effects can be expected for many of the survivors of natural disasters and traumatic events.

Many people experience disabling depression or anxiety but do not meet the full criteria for PTSD. More persistent and severe grief reactions, unexplained physical symptoms, and the increased use of

alcohol and drugs are frequent occurrences for people who have undergone such trauma. In addition, family and interpersonal conflict and financial strain are commonly seen. All too frequently, in war or natural disasters, the primary wage earner of the family dies or the family's house and belongings are destroyed.

How long will an individual's symptoms last after experiencing an event like September 11 or witnessing a friend killed by a roadside bomb in Iraq? Factors such as the severity of the trauma, the individual's proximity to the event, and his or her emotional closeness to those who have died can all play important roles in the magnitude and duration of the reaction to traumatic loss. In general, though, symptoms will diminish with time, especially in the absence of new threats and traumatic losses. Studies of those who have developed full-blown PTSD suggest that approximately half of the cases resolve within 2 years but that nearly a third never fully recover.

Psychological support and treatment can greatly help many of those who suffer from disabling emotional symptoms in reaction to traumatic loss. Building on research and work done with Vietnam veterans in the 1970s and 1980s, clinicians have developed multiple therapeutic strategies involving group therapy, individual psychological support, and pharmacologic intervention to treat persistent symptoms.

SOURCES: Coker, A. L., et al. 2006. Social and mental health needs assessment of Katrina evacuees. *Disaster Management and Response* 4(3): 88-94; Watanabe, T., et al. 2006. Acute stress syndrome in a victim of the Indian Ocean Tsunami. *Psychiatry and Clinical Neurosciences* 60(5): 644; Galea, S., and H. Resnick. 2005. Posttraumatic stress disorder in the general population after mass terrorist incidents: Considerations about the nature of exposure. *CNS Spectrums* 10(2): 107–115; Galea, S., et al. 2002. Psychological sequelae of the September 11 terrorist attacks in New York City. *New England Journal of Medicine* 346(13): 982–987; Shuster, M., et al. 2001. A national survey of stress reactions after the September 11, 2001, terrorist attacks. *New England Journal of Medicine* 345(20): 1507–1512; Ornstein, R. D., and R. K. Pitman, section eds. 2000. Trauma and post-traumatic stress disorder. In *Massachusetts General Hospital Psychiatry Update and Board Preparation*, 2nd ed., eds. T. A. Stern and J. B. Herman. New York: McGraw-Hill.

Coping with Grief

- Recognize and acknowledge the loss.

- React to grief by accepting and expressing it.

- Take time for nature's process of healing.

- Know that powerful, overwhelming feelings will change with time.

- Review and remember the relationship with the deceased.

- Share your pain by accepting support from others.

- Surround yourself with life: plants, animals, friends.

- Make use of mementos to promote your mourning, not to live in the past.

- Avoid major decisions, if possible, and give yourself time to readjust.

- Adapt to a new world without forgetting the old.

- Prepare for change, new interests, new friends, creativity, and growth.

- Reinvest in life.

SOURCES: The Centre for Living with Dying (554 Mansion Park Dr., Santa, Clara, CA 95054; 408-980-9801); Rando, T. A. 1993. *The Treatment of Complicated Mourning.* Champaign, Ill.: Research Press.

doesn't go away completely, but it recedes into the background. Although reminders of the loss stimulate active grieving from time to time, the main focus is the present, not the past. Adjusting to loss may sometimes feel like a betrayal of the deceased loved one, but it is healthy to engage again in ongoing life and the future (see the box "Coping with Grief").

Some people, however, have more trouble resolving their grief than others. Such people may get stuck in the grieving process for months or even years, sometimes becoming so burdened with loss that they lose the ability to cope with daily living. Experts call this long-term, unresolved grief *complicated grief* and describe it as truly debilitating. Complicated grief is most likely to occur when a person has lost a loved one in a sudden, violent manner (such as homicide) or experienced an untimely death (such as the loss of a child). Grief counseling or therapy can help people work through complicated grief.

Supporting a Grieving Person

In experiencing a significant loss, a person initially may feel and behave much like a frightened, helpless child. He or she may respond best to the kind of loving support that is given by a parent. A hug may be more comforting than any words. Also, because talking about a loss is an important way that survivors cope with the changed reality, simply listening can be very helpful. The key to being a good listener is to refrain from making judgments about whether the feelings expressed by a survivor are right or wrong, good or bad. The emotions, thoughts, and behaviors evoked by loss may not be the ones we expect, but they can nonetheless be valid and appropriate within a survivor's experience of loss.

Talking and crying, even yelling in rage, are among the ways of coping with intense feelings of grief. Bereaved per-

sons should not be urged to hold back their feelings or to be strong and brave. Expressions of grief are healing. On the other hand, the bereaved need not pretend to grieve or exaggerate his or her feelings to satisfy others' expectations. Funerals and other ceremonies generally help survivors gain a sense of closure and begin to integrate a loss into their lives. For some, funerals are occasions of weeping and wailing; for others, stoic and subdued emotions are the rule. Different styles of mourning can be equally valid and appropriate.

Social support for the bereaved is as critical during the later course of grief as it is during the first days after a loss. In offering support, we can reassure them that grief is normal, permissible, and appropriate. They may also need permission to occasionally give themselves a break from grieving. As they move forward in life, the bereaved may need encouragement from others to face the world confidently. An extended need for support often continues through the first year or two of mourning. The first anniversary following a significant loss can be a time of renewed grieving when the support of others is important and appreciated. Knowing that others remember the loss and that they take time to touch base is usually perceived as very helpful.

Bereaved people also may want to share their stories and concerns through organized support groups, such as those for widows and widowers. Many support groups are organized around some specific type of bereavement. Compassionate Friends, for example, is a nationwide organization composed of parents who have experienced a child's death.

Helping Children Cope with Loss

Children tend to cope with loss in a healthier fashion when they are included as part of their family's experience of grief and mourning. Although adults may be uncomfortable about sharing potentially disturbing or painful news with children, a child's natural curiosity usually negates the option of withholding information. Sudden changes in family communication patterns without any explanation can alarm a child and create anxiety. When children are asked about their experiences of family crises involving death, many say that the most difficult times occurred when they did not know what was happening. Mounting evidence shows that it is best to include children from the beginning—as soon as a terminal prognosis is made, for example—to help them understand what is happening. Children should spend time with the dying person, if possible, to learn, share, and offer and receive comfort. Such visits can be made under the guidance of a mental health professional, working with the child's best interests in mind, if deemed appropriate.

In talking about death with children, the most important guideline is to be honest. Set the explanation you are offering at the child's level of understanding. In general, it's advisable to keep the explanation simple, stick to basics, and verify what the child has understood from your explanation. A child's readiness for more details can usually be assessed by paying attention to his or her questions.

COMING TO TERMS WITH DEATH

We may wish we could keep death out of view and not make a place for it in our lives. But this wish cannot be fulfilled. With the death of a beloved friend or relative, we are confronted with emotions and thoughts that relate not only to the immediate loss but also to our own mortality.

Our encounters with dying and death teach us that relationships are more important than things and that life offers no guarantees. In discovering the meaning of death in our own lives, we find that life is both precious and precarious.

Allowing ourselves to make room for death, we discover that it touches not only the dying or bereaved person and his or her family and friends but also the wider community of which we are all part. We recognize that dying and death offer opportunities for extraordinary growth in the midst of loss. Denying death, it turns out, results in denying life.

TIPS FOR TODAY AND THE FUTURE

Facing death clear-sightedly, despite our fears and discomfort, can deepen our appreciation of life.

RIGHT NOW YOU CAN

- Think about how you want your body to be disposed of when you die.
- Think about how you would want your worldly goods to be distributed if you were to die soon.
- Think about organ donation. If you want to be an organ donor, start making the appropriate arrangements now, as described in this chapter.

IN THE FUTURE YOU CAN

- Talk to your parents or grandparents about their wishes for end-of-life care and funeral arrangements, and discuss ways you can be involved.
- Investigate your own options for end-of-life care, funeral arrangements, and so on. It may seem too early in life to start such planning, but now is a good time to begin.

SUMMARY

- Although death makes rational sense in terms of species survival and evolution, there may be no completely satisfying answer to the question of why death exists from a personal point of view.

- Dying and death are more than biological events; they have social and spiritual dimensions.

- The traditional criteria for determining death focus on vital signs such as breathing and heartbeat. Brain death is characterized by a lack of physical responses other than breathing and heartbeat.

- Between ages 5 and 9, most children develop a mature understanding of death; that is, they come to understand death as final, universal, and inevitable.

- A mature understanding of death can include ideas about the survival of the human personality after death.

- Problems arise when avoidance or denial of death fosters the notion that it happens only to others.

- Many basic tasks in preparing for death can and should be accomplished while one is young.

- A will is a legal instrument that governs the distribution of a person's estate after death.

- End-of-life care may involve a combination of home care, hospital stays, and hospice or palliative care.

? QUESTIONS FOR CRITICAL THINKING AND REFLECTION

Have you ever been in the position of being supportive to a bereaved person? What kind of support did he or she seem to appreciate most? Why do you think that was the case? How did the experience affect you?

- Palliative care is devoted to making dying patients comfortable by controlling pain and relieving suffering.

- Hospice programs apply a team-oriented approach to caring for dying patients and their families with the goal of helping people live as fully as possible until the end of their lives.

- Exercising choices about end-of-life care can involve making decisions about prolonging life or hastening death.

- The practice of withholding or withdrawing potentially life-sustaining treatment is sometimes termed passive euthanasia.

- Physician-assisted suicide occurs when a physician provides lethal drugs or other interventions, at a patient's request, with the understanding that the patient plans to use them to end his or her life. Voluntary active euthanasia refers to the intentional ending of a patient's life, at his or her request, by someone other than the patient.

- Advance directives, such as living wills and health care proxies, are used to express one's wishes about the use of life-sustaining treatment.

- People can donate their bodies or specific organs for transplantation and other medical uses after death.

- For Americans, the decision about what to do with the body after death usually involves either burial or cremation.

- Bereaved people usually benefit from participating in a funeral or memorial service to commemorate a loved one's death.

- Coping with dying involves physical, psychological, social, and spiritual dimensions.

- It is useful for patients and caregivers to understand the trajectory, or course, of dying.

- In offering support to a dying person, the gift of listening can be especially important.

- Grief encompasses thoughts and feelings, as well as physical and behavioral responses.

- Mourning, the process by which a person integrates a loss into his or her life, is determined partly by social and cultural norms for expressing grief.

- Children tend to cope with death in a healthier fashion when they are included in their family's experience of grief and mourning.

- Dying and death offer opportunities for growth in the midst of loss.

FOR MORE INFORMATION

BOOKS

Albom, M. 2005. *Tuesdays with Morrie: An Old Man, A Young Man, and Life's Greatest Lesson.* New York: Anchor. *A young man reconnects with an old professor in his last months of life and learns some of the greatest lessons that life has to offer.*

Batuello, J. T. 2003. *End of Life Decisions: A Practical Guide.* College Station, Tx.: Virtualbookworm. *A guide to end-of-life decisions, including those related to pain relief and palliative and hospice care.*

DeSpelder, L. A., and A. L. Strickland. 2009. *The Last Dance: Encountering Death and Dying,* 8th ed. New York: McGraw-Hill. *A comprehensive and readable text highlighting a broad range of topics related to dying and death.*

Shannon, J. B. 2006. *Death and Dying Sourcebook,* 2nd ed. Detroit: Omnigraphics. *A wide-ranging discussion of topics relating to terminal illness, care for the dying, and the practical realities of death.*

Turner, M. 2006. *Talking with Children and Young People about Death and Dying,* 2nd ed. London: Jessica Kingsley Publishers. *A workbook designed to help parents explain death, loss, and grief to their children.*

ORGANIZATIONS AND WEB SITES

Association for Death Education and Counseling (ADEC). Provides resources for education, bereavement counseling, and care of the dying.
http://www.adec.org

The Dougy Center. Offers education about childhood bereavement and support groups for bereaved children.
http://www.dougy.org

Dying Well. A Web site focused on wellness through the end of life.
http://www.dyingwell.org

GriefNet. A site where you can communicate with others via e-mail support groups in the areas of death, grief, and major loss.
http://www.griefnet.org

Growth House. Offers an extensive directory of Internet resources relating to life-threatening illness and end-of-life care.
http://www.growthhouse.org

Hospice Foundation of America. Promotes the hospice concept of care through education and leadership.
http://www.hospicefoundation.org

Longwood College Library: Doctor Assisted Suicide—A Guide to Web Sites and the Literature. Information on physician-assisted suicide and links to related sites.
http://www.longwood.edu/library/suic.htm

National Funeral Directors Association (NFDA). Provides resources related to funerals and funeral costs, body disposition, and bereavement support.
http://www.nfda.org

National Hospice and Palliative Care Organization (NHPCO). Provides information about hospice care and advance directives, including an online national directory of hospices listed by state and city.
http://www.nhpco.org

Nolo Press: Wills and Estate Planning. Provides answers to questions about planning for death, from writing a basic will to organ donation.
http://www.nolo.com

On Our Own Terms: Public Broadcasting System. A companion Web site to the Bill Moyers PBS series on improving end-of-life care.
http://www.pbs.org/wnet/onourownterms

Oregon Department of Health and Human Services. Provides information about Oregon's Death with Dignity Act.
http://egov.oregon.gov/DHS/ph/pas

Soros Foundation: Project on Death in America. A Web site focusing on different approaches to achieving a good death.
http://www.soros.org/initiatives/pdia

The following organizations provide information about organ donation and donor cards.

Coalition on Donation
   http://www.donatelife.net
National Kidney Foundation
   800-622-9010
   http://www.kidney.org
Organ Procurement and Transplantation Network
   http://www.optn.org
U.S. Department of Health and Human Services: Donate Life
   http://www.organdonor.gov

SELECTED BIBLIOGRAPHY

Angus, D. C., et al. 2004. Use of intensive care at the end of life in the United States: An epidemiologic study. *Critical Care Medicine* 32(3): 638–643.

Annas, G. J. 2005. "Culture of life" politics at the bedside—the case of Terri Schiavo. *New England Journal of Medicine,* 23 March [epub].

Bender, E. 2005. Palliative care. *Journal of the American Medical Association* 294(14): 1850.

Casarett, D., et al. 2005. Making difficult decisions about hospice enrollment: What do patients and families want to know? *Journal of the American Geriatrics Society* 53(2): 249–254.

Chochinov, H. M. 2006. Dying, dignity, and new horizons in palliative end-of-life care. *CA: A Cancer Journal for Clinicians* 56(2): 84–103.

Christ, G. H., and A. E. Christ. 2006. Current approaches to helping children cope with a parent's terminal illness. *CA: A Cancer Journal for Clinicians* 56(4): 197–212.

Donatelli, L. A., et al. 2006. Ethical issues in critical care and cardiac arrest: Clinical research, brain death, and organ donation. *Seminars in neurology* 26(4): 452–459.

DuBois, J. M., and E. E. Anderson. 2006. Attitudes toward death criteria and organ donation among healthcare personnel and the general public. *Progress in Transplantation* 16(1): 65–73.

Field, N. P. 2006. Unresolved grief and continuing bonds: An attachment perspective. *Death Studies* 30(8): 739–756.

Galante, J. M., et al. 2005. Experience and attitudes of surgeons toward palliation in cancer. *Archives of Surgery* 140(9): 873–878.

Gozalo, P. L., and S. C. Miller. 2006. Hospice enrollment and evaluation of its causal effect on hospitalization of dying nursing home patients. *Health Services Research,* 17 August [online early ed.].

Harvard Medical School. 2005. Living wills and health care proxies. *Harvard Health Letter* 30(8): 1–3.

Jansen-van der Weide, M. C., et al. 2005. Granted, undecided, withdrawn, and refused requests for euthanasia and physician-assisted suicide. *Archives of Internal Medicine* 165(15): 1698–1704.

Kohara, H., et al. 2005. Sedation for terminally ill patients with cancer with uncontrollable physical distress. *Journal of Palliative Medicine* 8(1): 20–25.

Lipkin, K. M. 2006. Identifying a proxy for health care as part of routine medical inquiry. *Journal of General Internal Medicine,* 17 July [online early ed.].

Mayo Clinic. 2005. Advance directives: A plan for end of life. *Mayo Clinic Health Letter* 23(2): 6.

Melhem, N. M., et al. 2004. Traumatic grief among adolescents exposed to a peer's suicide. *American Journal of Psychiatry* 161(8): 1411–1416.

National Hospice and Palliative Care Organization (NHPCO). 2005. *NHPCO's Facts and Figures—2005 Findings* (http://www.nhpco.org; retrieved February 23, 2009).

Onrust, S., et al. 2006. Predictors of psychological adjustment after bereavement. *International Psychogeriatrics,* 14 September, 1–15.

Oregon Department of Health and Human Services, Public Health Division. 2008. *"Death With Dignity Act" Annual Report: Year 9—2006 Summary* (http://www.oregon.gov/dhs/ph/pas/index.shtml; retrieved June 16, 2008).

Organ transplants. 2004. *Mayo Clinic Health Letter Supplement,* October.

Owen, A. M., et al. 2006. Detecting awareness in the vegetative state. *Science* 313(5792): 1402.

Patel, K. 2004. Euthanasia and physician-assisted suicide policy in the Netherlands and Oregon: A comparative analysis. *Journal of Health and Social Policy* 19(1): 37–55.

Pivar, I. L., and N. P. Field. 2004. Unresolved grief in combat veterans with PTSD. *Journal of Anxiety Disorders* 18(6): 745–755.

Rabow, M. W., J. M. Hauser, and J. Adams. 2004. Supporting family caregivers at the end of life. *Journal of the American Medical Association* 291(4): 483–491.

Rietjens, J. A., et al. 2004. Physician reports of terminal sedation without hydration or nutrition for patients nearing death in the Netherlands. *Annals of Internal Medicine* 141(3): 178–185.

Rietjens, J. A., et al. 2006. Terminal sedation and euthanasia: A comparison of clinical practices. *Archives of Internal Medicine* 166(7): 749–753.

Satel, S. 2006. Death's waiting list. *New York Times,* 15 May.

Schulz, R., et al. 2006. Predictors of complicated grief among dementia caregivers: A prospective study of bereavement. *American Journal of Geriatric Psychiatry* 14(8): 650–658.

Searight, H. R., and J. Gafford. 2005. Cultural diversity at the end of life: Issues and guidelines for family physicians. *American Family Physician* 71(3): 515–522.

Siminoff, L. A., et al. 2006. Racial disparities in preferences and perceptions regarding organ donation. *Journal of General Internal Medicine* 21(9): 995–1000.

U.S. Department of Health and Human Services. 2008. *Organ Donor Card* (http://www.organdonor.gov/donor/index.htm; retrieved February 23, 2009).

Wijdicks, E. F., et al. 2006. Practice parameter: Prediction of outcome in comatose survivors after cardiopulmonary resuscitation (an evidence-based review): Report of the Quality Standards Subcommittee of the American Academy of Neurology. *Neurology* 67(2): 203–210.

Arby's

	Serving size	Calories	Protein	Total fat	Saturated fat	Trans fat	Total carbohydrate	Sugars	Fiber	Cholesterol	Sodium	Vitamin A	Vitamin C	Calcium	Iron	% calories from fat
	g		g	g	g	g	g	g	g	mg	mg		% Daily Value			
Regular roast beef	154	320	21	14	5	.5	34	5	2	44	953	0	0	6	20	39
Super roast beef	198	398	21	19	6	.5	40	10	2	44	1060	7	10	7	21	43
Junior roast beef	125	272	16	10	4	0	34	5	2	29	740	0	0	6	17	33
Market Fresh® Ultimate BLT	294	779	23	45	11	0.5	75	18	6	51	1571	16	28	17	26	52
Market Fresh® Roast Turkey & Swiss	345	708	41	30	8	0.5	74	17	5	83	1677	13	17	36	29	37
Market Fresh® Southwest chicken wrap	246	581	32	31	10	1	45	4	7	77	1719	12	10	37	28	48
Chicken fillet sandwich (grilled)	244	395	32	17	3	0	38	8	2	60	1002	10	17	8	17	39
Chopped turkey club salad (w/o dressing)	293	233	22	11	6	0.5	10	0	3	54	6	81	50	25	14	34
Balsamic vinaigrette dressing	43	130	0	12	2	0	5	4	0	0	460	-	-	-	-	83
Curly fries (medium)	156	496	7	29	5	0.5	55	0	6	0	1160	11	12	6	14	53
Jalapeno Bites®, regular (5)	110	305	5	21	9	1	29	3	2	28	526	14	1	3	5	63
Apple turnover	128	380	4	14	7	0.5	58	37	3	0	287	1	3	1	7	33
Chocolate shake, regular	397	507	13	13	8	0	83	81	0	34	357	8	9	51	3	23

SOURCE: Arby's © 2008, Arby's, Inc. (http://www.arbysrestaurant.com). Used with permission of Arby's, Inc.

Burger King

	Serving size	Calories	Protein	Total fat	Saturated fat	Trans fat	Total carbohydrate	Sugars	Fiber	Cholesterol	Sodium	Vitamin A	Vitamin C	Calcium	Iron	% calories from fat
	g		g	g	g	g	g	g	g	mg	mg		% Daily Value			
Original Whopper®	290	680	29	40	11	1.5	51	11	3	75	1020	10	15	15	30	53
Original Double Whopper® w/cheese	398	1010	53	66	24	2.5	52	11	3	160	1530	15	15	30	45	59
Original Whopper Jr.®	158	370	16	21	6	1	31	6	2	40	570	4	6	8	20	51
Whopper® Junior w/o mayonnaise	147	290	16	12	4.5	0.5	31	6	2	35	500	4	6	8	20	38
Original Chicken Sandwich	219	660	24	40	8	2.5	52	5	4	65	1430	2	2	10	20	55
Chicken Tenders® (8 pieces)	123	370	24	23	6	3.5	18	<1	<1	55	870	2	0	2	6	57
French fries (medium, salted)	116	360	4	20	4.5	4.5	41	1	4	0	590	0	15	2	4	45
Onion rings (medium)	91	310	4	15	3.5	2.5	37	4	3	0	440	0	0	6	6	45
Tendergrill™ Chicken Garden Salad	292	240	33	9	3.5	0	8	3	4	80	720	200	60	15	15	33
Croissan'wich® w/bacon, egg & cheese	122	340	15	20	7	2	27	15	5	155	890	10	0	15	15	53
Hershey®'s sundae pie	79	300	3	18	12	1.5	31	23	1	10	190	2	0	4	6	53
Vanilla shake (value)	228	310	6	11	7	0	44	43	0	45	180	8	4	30	0	32

SOURCE: BURGER KING® trademarks and nutritional information used with permission from Burger King Brands, Inc.

Jack in the Box

	Serving size (g)	Calories	Protein (g)	Total fat (g)	Saturated fat (g)	Trans fat (g)	Total carbohydrate (g)	Sugars (g)	Fiber (g)	Cholesterol (mg)	Sodium (mg)	Vitamin A (% DV)	Vitamin C (% DV)	Calcium (% DV)	Iron (% DV)	% calories from fat
Breakfast Jack®	125	290	17	12	4.5	0	29	4	1	220	760	N/A	N/A	N/A	N/A	38
Supreme croissant	151	450	18	25	9	3.5	36	5	1	235	860	N/A	N/A	N/A	N/A	51
Hamburger	109	280	14	12	4.5	0.5	30	6	1	30	580	N/A	N/A	N/A	N/A	39
Jumbo Jack® w/cheese	286	690	25	42	16	1.5	54	12	3	70	1310	N/A	N/A	N/A	N/A	54
Sourdough Jack®	245	710	17	51	18	3	36	7	3	75	1230	N/A	N/A	N/A	N/A	65
Chicken fajita pita w/ whole grain, no salsa	193	300	23	9	3.5	0	33	4	4	60	1090	N/A	N/A	N/A	N/A	27
Sourdough grilled chicken club	266	530	36	28	7	2	34	5	3	85	1430	N/A	N/A	N/A	N/A	47
Deli Trio Pannido™	271	645	30	34	8.5	0	53	4	2	95	2530	N/A	N/A	N/A	N/A	47
Jack's Spicy Chicken®	270	620	25	31	6	3	61	8	4	50	1100	N/A	N/A	N/A	N/A	46
Monster taco	112	240	8	14	5	2	20	4	3	20	390	N/A	N/A	N/A	N/A	54
Egg rolls (3)	170	400	14	19	6	3	44	4	6	15	920	N/A	N/A	N/A	N/A	43
Chicken strips, crispy (4)	201	500	35	25	6	6	36	1	3	80	1260	N/A	N/A	N/A	N/A	44
Stuffed jalapeños (7)	168	530	15	30	13	4.5	51	5	4	45	1600	N/A	N/A	N/A	N/A	51
Barbeque dipping sauce	28	45	0	0	0	0	11	4	0	0	330	N/A	N/A	N/A	N/A	0
Seasoned curly fries (medium)	125	400	6	23	5	7	45	1	5	0	890	N/A	N/A	N/A	N/A	52
Onion rings	119	500	6	30	6	10	51	3	3	0	420	N/A	N/A	N/A	N/A	54
Side salad	123	50	3	3	1.5	0	5	2	2	10	60	N/A	N/A	N/A	N/A	50
Ranch dressing	57	310	1	33	5	1	3	2	0	20	470	N/A	N/A	N/A	N/A	96
Oreo® cookie ice-cream shake (small)	339	770	12	40	26	1.5	88	69	1	115	240	N/A	N/A	N/A	N/A	47

SOURCE: Jack in the Box, Inc. 2008 (http://www.jackinthebox.com). The following trademarks are owned by Jack in the Box, Inc.: Breakfast Jack,® Jumbo Jack,® Sourdough Jack,® Jack in the Box.® Reproduced with permission from Jack in the Box, Inc.

KFC

	Serving size (g)	Calories	Protein (g)	Total fat (g)	Saturated fat (g)	Trans fat (g)	Total carbohydrate (g)	Sugars (g)	Fiber (g)	Cholesterol (mg)	Sodium (mg)	Vitamin A (% DV)	Vitamin C (% DV)	Calcium (% DV)	Iron (% DV)	% calories from fat
Original Recipe® Chicken breast	161	360	37	21	5	0	7	0	0	115	1020	2	2	8	6	53
Original Recipe® Chicken thigh	126	330	20	24	6	0	8	0	0	110	870	4	2	4	8	67
Extra Crispy™ Chicken breast	162	440	34	27	6	0	15	0	0	105	970	2	2	6	6	57
Extra Crispy™ thigh	114	370	18	28	6	0	12	0	0	85	850	2	0	2	6	68
Tender Roast® sandwich w/ sauce	236	380	37	13	3	0	29	4	2	80	1180	6	15	8	15	32
Tender Roast® sandwich w/o sauce	217	300	37	4.5	1.5	0	28	3	2	70	1060	6	15	8	15	13
Hot Wings™ (5 pieces)	112	350	20	24	5	0	14	0	2	105	740	4	0	4	8	63
Popcorn chicken (large)	160	550	29	35	6	0	30	0	3	80	1600	4	2	4	10	58
Chicken pot pie	423	770	33	40	15	14	70	2	5	115	1680	200	0	0	20	47
Roasted Caesar Salad w/o dressing and croutons	301	220	30	8	4.5	0	6	3	3	70	830	45	35	25	10	36
KFC® creamy parmesan caesar dressing	57	260	2	26	5	0	4	2	0	15	540	2	0	6	2	88
Corn on the cob (5.5")	162	150	6	3	1	0	26	10	7	0	10	0	10	6	6	17
Mashed potatoes w/gravy	151	140	1	5	1	0.5	20	1	1	0	560	2	2	4	8	32
Baked beans	136	220	20	1	0	0	45	20	7	0	730	6	2	10	15	5
Cole slaw	130	180	4	10	1.5	0	22	18	3	5	270	10	20	4	4	50
Biscuit (1)	57	220	2	11	2.5	3.5	24	2	1	0	640	2	0	4	10	45
Potato salad	128	180	6	9	1.5	0	22	6	2	5	470	2	10	0	2	45

SOURCE: KFC Corporation, 2008. Nutritional information provided by KFC Corporation from its web site (www.kfc.com) as of July 30, 2008 and subject to the conditions listed therein. KFC and related marks are registered trademarks of KFC Corporation. Reproduced with permission from KFC Corporation.

McDonald's

	Serving size	Calories	Protein	Total fat	Saturated fat	Trans fat	Total carbohydrate	Sugars	Fiber	Cholesterol	Sodium	Vitamin A	Vitamin C	Calcium	Iron	% calories from fat
	g		g	g	g	g	g	g	g	mg	mg	\% Daily Value				
Hamburger	100	250	12	9	3.5	0.5	31	6	2	25	528	0	2	10	15	40
Quarter Pounder®	169	410	24	19	7	1	37	8	3	65	730	2	4	15	20	41
Quarter Pounder® w/cheese	198	510	29	26	12	1.5	40	9	3	90	1190	10	4	30	25	45
Big Mac®	214	540	25	29	10	1.5	45	9	3	75	1040	6	2	25	25	48
Big N' Tasty®	206	460	24	24	8	1.5	37	8	3	70	720	6	8	15	25	47
Filet-O-Fish®	142	380	15	18	3.5	0	38	5	2	40	640	2	0	15	10	45
McChicken®	143	360	14	16	3	0	40	5	2	35	830	0	2	10	15	42
Medium French Fries	117	380	4	19	2.5	0	48	0	5	0	270	0	10	2	6	45
Chicken McNuggets® (6 pieces)	95	280	14	17	3	0	16	0	0	40	600	2	2	2	4	57
Chicken Select® Premium Breast Strips (5 pieces)	219	660	38	40	6	0	39	0	0	85	1680	0	6	4	8	55
Tangy Honey Mustard Sauce	43	70	1	2.5	0	0	13	9	0	5	170	0	0	0	1	29
Bacon Ranch Salad w/Grilled Chicken (w/o dressing)	321	260	33	9	4	0	12	5	3	90	1010	130	50	15	10	35
Caesar Salad w/Crispy Chicken (w/o dressing)	314	330	130	17	4.5	0	20	6	3	60	840	130	50	20	10	46
Newman's Own® Ranch Dressing (2 oz)	59	170	1	15	2.5	0	9	4	0	20	530	0	0	4	0	76
Egg McMuffin®	139	300	18	12	5	0	30	3	2	260	820	10	2	30	20	37
Sausage Biscuit w/ Egg	163	510	18	33	14	0	36	2	2	250	1170	6	0	8	20	57
Hotcakes (w/o syrup & margarine)	151	350	8	9	2	0	60	14	3	20	590	2	0	15	15	23
Fruit 'n Yogurt Parfait	149	160	4	2	1	0	31	21	1	5	85	0	15	15	4	13
Chocolate Triple Thick® Shake (16 oz)	444	580	13	14	8	1	102	84	1	50	250	20	0	45	10	21

SOURCE: McDonald's Corporation, 2008. (http://www.mcdonalds.com). Used with permission from McDonald's Corporation. For the most current information, visit the McDonald's Web site.

Subway

Based on standard formulas with 6-inch subs on Italian or wheat bread

	Serving size	Calories	Protein	Total fat	Saturated fat	Trans fat	Total carbohydrate	Sugars	Fiber	Cholesterol	Sodium	Vitamin A	Vitamin C	Calcium	Iron	% calories from fat
	g		g	g	g	g	g	g	g	mg	mg	\% Daily Value				
6" Italian BMT®	242	450	23	21	8	0	47	8	5	55	1770	10	35	15	25	42
6" Meatball marinara	377	560	24	24	11	1	63	13	8	45	1590	15	60	20	40	39
6" Prime rib	278	400	29	12	6	0.5	48	9	6	60	1110	10	40	15	40	27
Subway Melt®	254	380	26	12	5	0	48	8	5	45	1600	10	35	15	25	29
Tuna	250	530	22	31	7	0.5	44	7	4	45	1010	10	35	15	30	53
Sweet onion chicken teriyaki wrap	304	480	26	90	10	3.5	70	14	2	50	1450	8	40	8	25	19
Roast beef wrap	248	400	19	10	4	0	15	3	2	15	1150	8	30	5	35	23
Turkey breast wrap	248	380	18	80	9	3	37	2	2	20	1250	8	35	6	25	21
Veggie Delite® wrap	192	330	9	8	2.5	0	55	2	2	0	750	8	35	6	25	20
Turkey Breast salad (w/o dressing)	378	110	12	2.5	0.5	0	13	6	4	20	580	60	50	6	10	20
New England style clam chowder	310	150	6	5	1	0	20	2	4	10	990	0	-	4	6	30
Chili con carne	310	290	19	8	3.5	0	35	13	12	25	990	15	20	8	20	25
Chocolate chip cookie	45	210	2	10	6	0	30	18	1	15	150	6	0	0	6	43

SOURCE: Subway U.S. Nutrition Info as found on http://www.subway.com, 7/30/2008. Reprinted by permission of Doctor's Associates, Inc.

Taco Bell

	Serving size	Calories	Protein	Total fat	Saturated fat	Trans fat	Total carbohydrate	Sugars	Fiber	Cholesterol	Sodium	Vitamin A	Vitamin C	Calcium	Iron	% calories from fat
	g		g	g	g	g	g	g	g	mg	mg		% Daily Value			
Crunchy Taco	92	150	7	8	2.5	0	13	1	3	20	370	4	2	8	6	47
Crunchy Taco Supreme®	113	210	9	13	6	.5	15	2	3	40	370	10	6	10	6	57
Soft taco, beef	113	180	8	70	7	3	21	2	3	20	650	4	2	10	10	39
Gordita Supreme®, steak	153	290	15	13	5	0	28	6	2	40	530	6	6	10	15	41
Grilled steak soft taco	128	160	10	4.5	1.5	0	20	3	2	20	550	4	10	8	10	25
Gordita Baja®, chicken	153	320	17	16	3.5	0	28	6	3	40	800	8	6	10	10	44
Chalupa Supreme, beef	153	380	14	23	7	0.5	30	4	3	40	620	8	6	15	15	55
Chalupa Supreme, chicken	153	360	17	20	5	0	29	4	2	45	650	6	8	10	15	49
1/2 lb. Beef combo burrito	241	440	21	18	7	1	51	4	8	45	1630	15	6	20	30	36
Bean burrito	198	350	13	9	3.5	0.5	54	4	8	5	1190	10	8	20	25	23
Burrito Supreme®, chicken	248	400	20	13	6	0.5	49	5	6	45	1360	15	15	20	25	30
Grilled stuffed burrito, beef	325	680	27	30	10	1	76	6	9	55	2120	15	4	30	40	40
Tostada	170	240	11	10	3.5	0.5	27	2	7	15	730	10	8	20	10	39
Zesty Chicken Border Bowl™ w/dressing	418	640	22	35	6	1	60	4	10	30	1800	15	15	15	25	37
Express taco salad	475	610	25	32	10	1.5	56	8	14	65	1420	20	20	30	25	48
Steak quesadilla	184	520	26	28	13	1	39	4	3	70	1300	10	0	45	20	50
Nachos Supreme	191	440	12	26	6	1	40	3	7	30	790	8	8	10	10	52
Nachos BellGrande®	305	770	19	44	8	1	77	5	12	30	1270	8	8	20	20	51
Pintos 'n cheese	128	160	9	6	3	0.5	19	1	7	15	670	10	6	15	8	31
Mexican rice	85	110	2	3	0	0	19	0	1	0	460	15	6	10	8	23

SOURCE: Taco Bell Corporation, 2008. (http://www.tacobell.com). Reproduced courtesy of Taco Bell Corporation.

Wendy's

	Serving size	Calories	Protein	Total fat	Saturated fat	Trans fat	Total carbohydrate	Sugars	Fiber	Cholesterol	Sodium	Vitamin A	Vitamin C	Calcium	Iron	% calories from fat
	g		g	g	g	g	g	g	g	mg	mg	% Daily Value				
Classic Single® w/everything	226	430	25	20	7	1	39	9	2	75	870	8	8	4	25	42
Jr. Hamburger	98	230	13	8	3	0	27	5	1	30	490	0	0	2	20	30
Jr. Bacon Cheeseburger	136	320	17	16	6	0.5	26	5	1	50	670	10	6	10	20	44
Ultimate Chicken Grill Sandwich	211	320	28	7	1.5	0	36	8	2	70	950	6	10	4	20	19
Spicy Chicken Sandwich	223	440	28	16	2.5	0	46	6	3	60	1300	6	8	4	15	34
Homestyle Chicken Fillet Sandwich	226	430	25	16	2.5	0	48	6	2	45	1120	6	8	4	15	33
10 Piece Chicken Nuggets	150	460	24	30	6	0	24	0	0	70	1040	0	0	2	6	59
Caesar Side Salad (no toppings or dressing)	142	260	8	19	4	0	14	2	2	490	270	100	35	10	6	57
Mandarin Chicken® Salad w/grilled chicken fillet	402	540	31	25	3	0.5	50	31	5	65	1260	70	50	6	10	43
Southwest Taco Salad (no toppings or dressing)	520	640	30	39	16	1	44	12	9	110	1570	80	35	45	20	55
Creamy ranch dressing	64	200	1	20	3.5	0	4	2	0	15	400	0	0	4	2	87
Reduced fat creamy ranch dressing	64	90	1	7	1.5	0	6	3	1	10	400	0	0	6	2	70
Large French Fries	184	550	7	26	4	0	73	0	7	0	480	4	15	2	10	42
Sour Cream & Chive Baked Potato	308	320	8	4	2	0	63	4	7	10	50	4	60	8	15	11
Strawberry Frosty™ shake, small	325	390	7	11	7	0.5	67	58	0	35	170	2	2	22	6	26
Chili, small, plain	227	190	14	6	2.5	0	19	6	5	40	830	4	4	8	15	32
Crispy Chicken Nuggets™ (5)	75	230	12	15	3	0	12	0	0	35	520	0	0	0	2	59
Barbecue sauce (1 packet)	28	45	1	0	0	0	10	8	0	0	170	0	0	0	4	0
Vanilla Frosty™, medium	298	410	11	10	6	0.5	68	57	0	45	240	20	0	40	20	22

SOURCE: Wendy's International, Inc., 2008. (http://www.wendys.com). Reproduced with permission from Wendy's International, Inc. The information contained in Wendy's International Information is effective as of July 30, 2008. Wendy's International, Inc., its subsidiaries, affiliates, franchises, and employees do not assume responsibility for a particular sensitivity or allergy (including peanuts, nuts or other allergies) to any food product provided in our restaurants. We encourage anyone with food sensitivities, allergies, or special dietary needs to check on a regular basis with Wendy's Consumer Relations Department to obtain the most up-to-date information.

Information on additional foods and restaurants is available online; see the Web sites listed in this appendix and the following additional sites: **Hardees:** http://www.hardees.com; **White Castle:** http://www.whitecastle.com

This self-care guide will help you manage some of the most common symptoms and medical problems:

- Fever
- Sore throat
- Cough
- Nasal congestion
- Ear problems
- Nausea, vomiting, or diarrhea
- Heartburn and indigestion
- Headache
- Low-back pain
- Strains and sprains
- Cuts and scrapes

Each symptom is described here in terms of what is going on in your body. Most symptoms are part of the body's natural healing response. Self-care advice is also given, along with guidelines for getting professional advice. Symptoms are usually self-limiting; that is, they resolve on their own with time and simple self-care.

No medical advice is perfect. You must decide whether to self-treat or get professional help. This guide is intended to give you information so you can make better, more informed decisions. If the advice here differs from that of your physician, discuss the differences with him or her.

The guidelines given here apply to *generally healthy adults*. If you are pregnant or nursing or if you have a chronic disease, particularly one that requires medication, check with your physician for appropriate self-care advice. Additionally, if you have an allergy or suspected allergy to any recommended med ica-tion, check with your physician before using it.

If you have several symptoms, read about your primary symptom first and then proceed to secondary symptoms. If you are particularly concerned about a symptom or confused about how to manage it, call your physician to get more information.

FEVER

A fever is an abnormally high body temperature, usually over 100°F (37.7°C). It is most commonly a sign that your body is fighting an infection. Fever may also be due to an inflammation, an injury, or a drug reaction. Chemicals released into your bloodstream during an infection reset the thermostat in the hypothalamus of your brain. The message goes out to your body to turn up the heat. The blood vessels in your skin constrict, and you curl up and throw on extra blankets to reduce heat loss. Meanwhile, your muscles may begin to shiver to generate additional body heat. The resulting rise in body temperature is a fever. Later, when your brain senses that the temperature is too high, you start sweating. As the sweat evaporates, it carries heat away from the body.

A fever may help you fight infections by making the body less hospitable to bacteria and viruses. A high body temperature appears to bolster the immune system and may inhibit the growth of infectious microorganisms.

Most generally healthy people can tolerate a fever as high as 103–104°F (39.5–40°C) without problems. If you are essen-tially healthy, there is little need to reduce a fever unless you are very uncomfortable. Older adults and those with chronic health problems such as heart disease may not tolerate a high fever, so fever reduction may be advised.

In small children (especially infants), even a low-grade fever can be a sign of a serious problem. Seek immediate medical help for any infant less than 3 months old whose temperature is 100.4°F (38°C) or higher, or for any child older than 3 months whose temperature is greater than 102°F (38.8°C). In small children, temperature should be checked with a digital rectal thermometer. Do not attempt to take a baby's temperature orally; if you have trouble taking a child's temperature for any reason, contact a medical professional right away.

Most problems with fevers are due to loss of fluids from evaporation and sweating, which may cause dehydration.

Self-Assessment

1. If you are sick, take your temperature several times through-out the day. Oral temperatures should not be measured for at least 10 minutes after smoking, eating, or drinking a hot or cold liquid. Don't use a glass thermometer that contains mercury. Digital thermometers are accurate, easy to read, and inexpensive. Follow your thermometer's directions.

    "Normal" temperature varies from person to person, so it is important to know what is normal for you. Your normal tem-perature will also vary throughout the day, being lowest in the early evening. If you exercise or if it is a hot day, your tem-perature may normally rise. Women's body temperature typi-cally varies by a degree or more through the menstrual cycle, peaking around the time of ovulation. Rectal temperatures normally run about 0.5–1.0°F higher than oral temperatures.

    If your recorded temperature is more than 1.0–1.5°F above your normal baseline temperature, you have a fever.

2. Watch for signs of dehydration: excessive thirst; very dry mouth; infrequent urination with dark, concentrated urine; and light-headedness.

Self-Care

1. Drink plenty of fluids to prevent dehydration—at least 8 ounces of water, juice, or broth every 2 hours.
2. Take a sponge bath using lukewarm water; this will in-crease evaporation and help reduce body temperature nat-urally. Don't use alcohol rubs to reduce temperature.
3. Dress lightly. Bundling up decreases the body's ability to lose excess heat.
4. Take aspirin substitute (acetaminophen, ibuprofen, or naproxen sodium) to reduce the fever and the associated headache and achiness. Follow the product's dosage in-structions carefully. Do not give aspirin to anyone younger than age 20 because some younger people with chicken pox, influenza, or other viral infections have developed a

life-threatening complication, Reye's syndrome, after taking aspirin.

When to Call the Physician

1. Fever over 103°F (39.5°C), or 102°F (38.8°C) in a person over 60 years old
2. If you have a fever that lasts more than 3 days
3. Recurrent unexplained fevers
4. Fever accompanied by a rash, stiff neck, severe headache, difficulty breathing, discolored sputum, severe pain in the side or abdomen, painful urination, convulsions, or confusion
5. Fever with signs of dehydration
6. Fever after starting a new medication

SORE THROAT

A sore throat—called *pharyngitis*—is caused by inflammation of the throat lining resulting from an infection, allergy, or irritation (especially from cigarette smoke). If you have an infection, you may also notice some hoarseness from swelling of the vocal cords and "swollen glands," which are enlarged lymph nodes that produce white blood cells to help fight the infection. Lymph nodes may become tender and remain swollen for weeks after the infection subsides.

Most throat infections are caused by viruses, so antibiotics are not effective against them. Most viral sore throats clear up in about a week with no treatment. But if a sore throat is accompanied by other symptoms (like a high fever, fatigue, aches, rash, or localized swelling), a more serious viral illness is possible, such as the flu, mononucleosis, or measles. These conditions should be diagnosed and treated by a physician.

About 20–30% of throat infections (called "strep throat") are due to streptococcal bacteria. This type of microbe can cause complications such as rheumatic fever and rheumatic heart disease and therefore should be diagnosed by a physician and treated with antibiotics. Strep throat is usually characterized by very sore throat, high fever, swollen lymph nodes, and a whitish discharge at the back of the throat.

Allergy-related sore throats may come with a runny nose, sneezing, and watery, itchy eyes.

Self-Assessment

1. Take your temperature.
2. Look at the back of your throat in a mirror. Is there a whitish discharge on the tonsils or in the back of the throat?
3. Feel the front and back of your neck. Do you feel enlarged, tender lymph nodes?

Self-Care

1. If you smoke, stop.
2. Drink plenty of liquids to soothe your inflamed throat.
3. Gargle with warm salt water (1/4 tsp salt in 4 oz water) every 1–2 hours to help reduce swelling and discomfort.
4. Suck on throat lozenges, cough drops, or hard candies to keep your throat moist.
5. Use throat lozenges, sprays, or gargles that contain an anesthetic to make swallowing less painful.

6. Try aspirin substitute to ease throat pain.
7. For an allergy-related sore throat, try an antihistamine such as chlorpheniramine or loratadine.

When to Call the Physician

1. Great difficulty swallowing saliva or breathing
2. Sore throat with fever over 101°F (38.3°C), especially if you do not have other cold symptoms such as nasal congestion or a cough
3. Sore throat with a skin rash
4. Sore throat with whitish pus on the tonsils
5. Sore throat and recent contact with a person who has had a positive throat culture for strep
6. Enlarged lymph nodes lasting longer than 3 weeks
7. Hoarseness lasting longer than 3 weeks

COUGH

A cough is a protective mechanism of the body to help keep the airways clear. There are two types of cough: a dry cough (without mucus) and a productive cough (with mucus). Common causes of cough include infection (viral or bacterial), allergies, and irritation from smoking and pollutants. If you have a cold, the cough may be the last symptom to improve, because the airways may remain irritated for several weeks after the infection has resolved.

Your airways are lined with hairlike projections called *cilia*, which move back and forth to help clear the airways of mucus, germs, and dust. Infections and cigarette smoking paralyze and damage this vital defensive mechanism.

Self-Assessment

1. Take your temperature.
2. Observe your mucus. Thick brown or bloody mucus suggests a bacterial infection.

Self-Care

1. If you smoke, stop.
2. Drink plenty of liquids (at least six 8-ounce glasses a day) to help thin mucus and loosen chest congestion.
3. Use moist heat from a hot shower or vaporizer to help loosen chest congestion.
4. Suck on cough drops, throat lozenges, or hard candy to moisten your throat and relieve a dry, tickling cough.
5. If you have a dry, nonproductive cough or the cough keeps you from sleeping, you can use a cough syrup or lozenge that contains the nonprescription cough suppressant dextromethor phan. If your cough is productive, ask your physician before using a cough suppressant. Productive coughs are often protective.

When to Call the Physician

1. Cough with thick brown or bloody sputum
2. Cough with high fever—above 102°F (38.8°C)—and shaking chills
3. Severe chest pains, wheezing, or shortness of breath
4. Cough that lasts longer than 3 weeks (a chronic cough)

NASAL CONGESTION

Nasal congestion is most commonly caused by infection or allergies. With infection, the nasal passages become congested because of increased blood flow and mucus production. This congestion is actually part of the body's defense to fight infection. The increased blood flow raises the temperature of the nasal passages, making them less hospitable to germs. The nasal secretions are rich in white blood cells and antibodies to help fight and neutralize the invading organisms and flush them away. Nasal congestion associated with sore throat, cough, and fever usually indicates a viral infection. Green nasal discharge is common with viral infections; it does not mean you need an antibiotic.

Nasal congestion caused by allergies is often accompanied by a thin watery discharge, sneezing, and itchy eyes; it is sometimes associated with a seasonal pattern. In an allergic reaction, the offending allergen (such as pollen, dust, mold, or dander) triggers the release of histamine and other chemicals from the cells lining the nose, throat, and eyes. These chemicals cause swelling, discharge, and itching. Antihistamine drugs block the release of these irritating chemicals.

Self-Assessment

1. Take your temperature.
2. Observe your nasal secretions. Thick brown or bloody discharge suggests a bacterial infection.
3. Tap with your fingers over the sinus cavities above and below the eyes. If the tapping causes increased pain, you may have a bacterial sinus infection.

Self-Care

1. If you smoke, stop.
2. Use moist heat from a hot shower or vaporizer to help liquefy congested mucus.
3. Use a decongestant nasal spray or drops to temporarily relieve congestion. However, if these decongestants are used for more than 3 days, they can cause "rebound congestion" that actually creates more nasal congestion. As an alternative, use saltwater nose drops (¼ tsp salt in ½ cup boiled water, cooled before using) or a commercial saline spray several times a day.
4. Try an oral decongestant such as pseudoephedrine (60 mg every 6 hours) to help shrink swollen mucous membranes and open nasal passages. In some people, these medications can cause nervousness, sleeplessness, or heart palpitations. If you have uncontrolled high blood pressure, heart disease, or diabetes, check with your physician before using decongestants.

When to Call the Physician

1. Nasal congestion with severe pain and tenderness in the forehead, cheeks, or upper teeth and a high fever (above 102°F or 38.8°C)
2. Thick brown or bloody nasal discharge
3. Nasal congestion and discharge unresponsive to self-care treatment and lasting longer than 3 weeks

EAR PROBLEMS

Ear symptoms include earache, discharge, itching, stuffiness, and hearing loss. They may be caused by problems in the external ear canal, eardrum, middle ear, or eustachian tube (the passageway that connects the middle ear space to the back of the throat). The ear canal can become blocked by excess wax, producing hearing loss and a sense that the ear is plugged. An infection of the external ear canal due to excessive moisture and trauma is often referred to as "swimmer's ear." It can cause pain, a sense of fullness, discharge, and itching. Congestion and blockage of the eustachian tube by a cold or allergy can result in pain, a sense of fullness, and hearing loss. A middle ear infection often produces severe pain, hearing loss, and fever.

Self-Assessment

1. Check for fever, which may be a sign of infection.
2. Have someone look into the ear canal with a flashlight or otoscope. Look for wax blockage or a red, swollen canal indicating an external ear infection.
3. Wiggle the outer part of the ear. If this increases the pain, an infection or inflammation of the external canal is the likely cause.

Self-Care

1. If blockage of the ear canal with wax is the problem, first try a hot shower to liquefy the wax, and use a wash cloth to wipe out the ear canal. You can also use a few drops of an over-the-counter wax softener and then flush the canal gently with warm water in a bulb syringe. Do not use sharp objects or cotton swabs; they can scratch the canal or push the wax in deeper.
2. To treat mild infections of the external ear canal, you must thoroughly dry the ear canal. A few drops of a drying solution (1 part rubbing alcohol, 1 part white vinegar) on a piece of cotton gently inserted into the canal can act as a wick to dry the canal.
3. To relieve congestion and blockage of the eustachian tube, try a decongestant like pseudoephedrine or a nasal spray (but for no longer than 3 days). Hot showers or a vaporizer may help loosen secretions, and yawning or swallowing may help open the eustachian tube. For a mild plugging sensation without fever or pain, pinch your nostrils and blow gently into your nose (not through your mouth) to force air up the eustachian tube and "pop" your ears.

When to Call the Physician

1. Severe earache with fever
2. Puslike or bloody discharge from the ear
3. Sudden hearing loss, especially if accompanied by ear pain or recent trauma to the ear
4. Ringing in the ears or dizziness
5. Any ear symptom lasting longer than 2 weeks

NAUSEA, VOMITING, OR DIARRHEA

Nausea, vomiting, and diarrhea usually are defensive reactions of your body to rapidly clear your digestive tract of irritants.

These symptoms may be caused by a viral infection, foodborne illness, medications, or other types of infection. Vomiting dramatically ejects irritants from your stomach, and nausea (feeling discomfort in the stomach or the sensation that you may vomit) discourages eating to allow the stomach to rest. With diarrhea, overstimulated intestines flush out the offending irritants.

The major complications of vomiting and diarrhea are dehydration from fluid losses and decreased fluid intake and a risk of bleeding from irritation of the digestive tract.

Self-Assessment

1. Take your temperature. A fever is often a clue that an infection is causing the symptoms.
2. Note the color and frequency of vomiting and diarrhea. This will help you estimate the severity of fluid losses and check for bleeding (red, black, or "coffee grounds" material in the stool or vomit; iron tablets and Pepto-Bismol can also cause black stools).
3. Watch for signs of dehydration: very dry mouth; excessive thirst; infrequent urination with dark, concentrated urine; and light-headedness.
4. Look for signs of hepatitis, an infection of the liver: a yellow color in the skin and the white parts of the eyes.

Self-Care

1. To replace fluids, take frequent, small sips of clear liquids such as water, noncitrus juice, broths, flat ginger ale, or ice chips.
2. When the vomiting and diarrhea have subsided for at least 6 hours, try nonirritating, constipating foods like the BRAT diet: bananas, rice, applesauce, and toast.
3. For several days, avoid alcohol, milk products, fatty foods, aspirin, and other medications that might irritate the stomach. Do not stop taking regularly prescribed medications without discussing this change with your physician.
4. Medications are not usually advised for vomiting. Loperamide, available without a prescription, can ease diarrhea.

When to Call the Physician

1. Inability to retain any fluids for 12 hours or signs of dehydration
2. Severe abdominal pains not relieved by the vomiting or diarrhea
3. Blood in the vomit (red or "coffee grounds" material) or in the stool (red or black tarlike material)
4. Vomiting or diarrhea with a high fever (above 102°F or 38.8°C)
5. Yellow color in skin or white parts of the eyes
6. Vomiting with severe headache and a recent head injury
7. Vomiting or diarrhea that lasts 3 days without improvement
8. If you are pregnant or have diabetes
9. Recurrent vomiting and/or diarrhea

HEARTBURN AND INDIGESTION

Indigestion and heartburn are usually a result of irritation of the stomach or the esophagus, the tube that connects the mouth to the stomach. The stomach lining is usually protected from stomach acids, but the esophagus is not. Therefore, if stomach acids "reflux," or back up into the esophagus, the result is usually a burning discomfort in the chest and throat. The esophagus is normally protected by a muscular valve that allows food to enter the stomach but prevents stomach contents from flowing upward into the esophagus. Certain foods (including chocolate, garlic, and onions), medications, and smoking can loosen and open this protective sphincter valve. Overeating, lying down, or bending over can also cause the stomach acids to gain access to the sensitive lining of the esophagus.

Self-Assessment

1. Look for a pattern in the symptoms. Do they occur after eating certain foods, taking certain medications, or when you bend over or lie down? Do certain foods or an antacid relieve the symptoms?
2. Observe your bowel movements. Black tarlike stools may indicate bleeding in the stomach (iron tablets and Pepto-Bismol can also cause black stools).

Self-Care

1. Avoid irritants such as smoking, aspirin, ibuprofen, naproxen sodium, alcohol, caffeine (coffee, tea, cola), chocolate, onions, carbonated beverages, spicy or fatty foods, acidic foods (vinegar, citrus fruits, tomatoes), or any other foods that seem to make your symptoms worse.
2. Take nonabsorbable antacids such as Maalox, Mylanta, or Gelusil every 1–2 hours and especially before bedtime, or try an acid reducer, now available without a prescription (Pepcid, Tagamet, Zantac, or Prilosec). These drugs work in different ways, so ask your physician to help you choose the right medication for you.
3. Avoid tight clothing.
4. Avoid overeating; eat smaller, more frequent meals.
5. Don't lie down for 1–2 hours after a meal. Elevate the head of your bed with 4- to 6-inch blocks of wood or bricks. Adding extra pillows usually makes things worse by creating a posture that increases pressure on the stomach. Try sleeping on your left side, which may reduce reflux compared to sleeping on your back or right side.
6. If you are overweight in the abdominal area, weight loss may help. Abdominal obesity can increase pressure on the stomach when you are lying down.

When to Call the Physician

1. Stools that are black and tarlike or vomit that is bloody or contains material that looks like coffee grounds
2. Severe abdominal or chest pain
3. Pain that goes through to the back
4. No relief from antacids
5. Difficulty swallowing solid foods
6. Symptoms lasting longer than 3 days

Recurrent or persistent abdominal pain may be a symptom of an ulcer, a raw area in the lining of the stomach or duodenum (the first part of the small intestine). About one in five men and one in ten women develop an ulcer at some time in their lives. Most ulcers are linked to infection with the bacterium *Helicobacter pylori;* people who regularly take nonsteroidal anti-inflammatory drugs like aspirin or ibuprofen are also at risk for ulcers because these drugs irritate the lining of the stomach. *H. pylori* infection is relatively easy to diagnose and treat, and other medications are available to treat ulcers linked to other causes. Many of the self-care measures described above are also frequently recommended for people with ulcers.

HEADACHE

Headache is one of the most common symptoms. There are four major types of headache: tension, migraine, cluster, and sinus. Tension headaches, migraines, and cluster headaches are described in Chapter 2. Sinus headaches are caused by blockage of the sinus cavities with resulting pressure and pain in the cheeks, forehead, and upper teeth. Headache caused by elevated blood pressure is very uncommon and occurs only with very high pressures.

Self-Assessment

1. Take your temperature. The presence of fever may indicate a sinus infection. Fever, severe headache, and a very stiff neck suggest meningitis, a rare but serious infection around the brain and spinal cord.
2. Tap with your fingers over the sinus cavities in your cheeks and forehead. If this causes increased pain, it may indicate a sinus infection.
3. For recurrent headaches, keep a headache journal. Record how often and when your headaches occur, associated symptoms, activities that precede the headache, and your food and beverage intake. Look for patterns that may provide clues to the cause(s) of your headaches.

Self-Care

1. Try applying ice packs or heat on your neck and head.
2. Gently massage the muscles of your neck and scalp.
3. Try deep relaxation or breathing exercises.
4. Take aspirin or aspirin substitute for pain relief. Over-the-counter products containing a combination of aspirin, acetaminophen, and caffeine are approved by the FDA for treating migraines.
5. If pain is associated with nasal congestion, try a decongestant medication like pseudoephedrine.
6. Try to avoid emotional and physical stressors (such as poor posture and eyestrain).
7. Try avoiding foods that may trigger headaches, such as aged cheeses, chocolate, nuts, red wine, alcohol, avocados, figs, raisins, and any fermented or pickled foods.

When to Call the Physician

1. Unusually severe headache or one that occurs suddenly
2. Headache accompanied by fever and a very stiff neck
3. Headache with sinus pain, tenderness, and fever
4. Severe headache following a recent head injury
5. Headache associated with slurred speech, visual disturbance, or numbness or weakness in the face, arms, or legs
6. Headache persisting longer than 3 days

7. Recurrent unexplained headaches
8. Increasing severity or frequency of headaches
9. Severe migraine headaches (In recent years, many new prescription medications have been approved for the prevention and treatment of migraines.)

LOW-BACK PAIN

Pain in the lower back is a very common condition; it is most often due to a strain of the muscles and ligaments along the spine, often triggered by bending, lifting, or other activity. Low-back pain can also result from bone growths (spurs) irritating the nerves along the spine or pressure from ruptured or protruding discs, the "shock absorbers" between the vertebrae. Sometimes back pain is caused by an infection or stone in the kidney. Fortunately, however, simple muscular strain is the most common cause of low-back pain and can usually be effectively self-treated.

Self-Assessment

1. Take your temperature. Back pain with high fever may indicate a kidney or other infection.
2. Check for blood in your urine or frequent, painful urination, which may also indicate a kidney problem.
3. Observe for tingling or pain traveling down one or both legs *below* the knee when you bend, cough, or sneeze. These symptoms suggest a disc problem.

Self-Care

1. Lie on your back or in any comfortable position on the floor or a firm mattress, with knees slightly bent and supported by a pillow. Rest for a day if the pain persists.
2. Use ice packs on the painful area for the first 3 days, and then continue with cold or change to heat, whichever gives more relief.
3. Take aspirin or aspirin substitute for pain relief.
4. After the acute pain has subsided, begin gentle back and stomach exercises. Practice good posture and lifting techniques to protect your back. Try to resume gentle, everyday activities like walking as soon as possible. Bed rest beyond 1 day is no longer advised and may even make things worse; try gentle stretching and resume activities that don't aggravate the problem. To learn more about proper back exercises and use of your back, consult a physical therapist or your physician.

When to Call the Physician

1. Back pain following a severe injury such as a car crash or fall
2. Back pain radiating down the leg *below* the knee on one or both sides
3. Persistent numbness, tingling, or weakness in the legs or feet
4. Loss of bladder or bowel control
5. Back pain associated with high fever (above 101°F or 38.3°C), frequent or painful urination, blood in the urine, or severe abdominal pain
6. Back pain that does not improve after 72 hours of self-care

STRAINS AND SPRAINS

Missteps, slips, falls, and athletic misadventures can result in a variety of strains, sprains, and fractures. A *strain* occurs when you overstretch a muscle or tendon (the connective tissue that attaches muscle to bone). *Sprains* are caused by overstretching or tearing ligaments (the tough fibrous bands that connect bone to bone). Depending on the severity and location, a sprain may actually be more serious than a fracture, because bones generally heal very strongly whereas ligaments may remain stretched and lax after healing. After a sprain, it may take 6 weeks for the ligament to heal.

After most injuries, you can expect pain and swelling. This is the body's way of immobilizing and protecting the injured part so that healing can take place. The goal of self-assessment is to determine whether you have a minor injury that you can safely self-treat or a more serious injury to an artery, nerve, or bone that should be treated by your physician.

Self-Assessment

1. Watch for coldness, blue color, or numbness in the limb beyond the injury. These may be signs of damage to an artery or a nerve.
2. Look for signs of a possible fracture, which include a misshapen limb, reduced length of the limb on the injured side compared to the uninjured side, an inability to move or bear weight, a grating sound with movement of the injured area, extreme tenderness at one point along the injured bone as you press with your fingers, or a sensation of snapping at the time of the injury.
3. Gently move the injured area through its full range of motion. Immobility or instability suggests a more serious injury.

Self-Care

1. Immediately immobilize, protect, and rest the injured area until you can bear weight on it or move it without pain. Remember: If it hurts, don't do it.
2. To decrease pain and swelling, immediately apply ice (a cold pack or ice wrapped in a cloth) for 15 minutes every hour for the first 24–48 hours. Then apply ice or heat as needed for comfort.
3. Immediately elevate the injured limb above the level of your heart for the first 24 hours to decrease swelling.
4. Immobilize and support the injured area with an elastic wrap or splint. Be careful not to wrap so tightly as to cause blueness, coldness, or numbness.
5. Take aspirin or aspirin substitute for pain as needed.

When to Call the Physician

1. An injury that occurred with great force, such as a high fall or motor vehicle crash
2. Hearing or feeling a snap at the time of the injury
3. A limb that is blue, cold, or numb
4. A limb that is bent, twisted, or crooked
5. Tenderness at specific points along a bone
6. Inability to move the injured area
7. A wobbly, unstable joint
8. Marked swelling of the injured area
9. Inability to bear weight after 24 hours
10. Pain that increases or lasts longer than 4 days

CUTS AND SCRAPES

Cuts and scrapes are common disruptions of the body's skin. Fortunately, the vast majority of these wounds are minor and don't require stitches, antibiotics, or a physician's care. An *abrasion* involves a scraping away of the superficial layers of skin. Abrasions, though less serious than cuts, are often more painful because they disrupt more skin nerves. There are two types of cuts: lacerations (narrow slices of the skin) and puncture wounds (stabs into deeper tissues).

Normal healing of a cut or abrasion is a remarkable process. After the bleeding stops, small amounts of serum, a clear yellowish fluid, may leak from the wound. This fluid is rich in antibodies to help prevent an infection. Redness and swelling may normally occur as more blood is shunted to the area, bringing white blood cells and nutrients to speed healing. There may also be some swelling of nearby lymph nodes, which are another part of your body's defense against infection. Finally, a scab forms. This is "nature's bandage," which protects the area while it heals.

The main concerns about cuts are the possibility of damage to deeper tissues and the risk of infection. Damage to underlying blood vessels may lead to severe bleeding as well as blueness and coldness in areas beyond the wound. Injured nerves may produce numbness and a loss of the ability to move parts of the body beyond the injured area. Damaged muscles, tendons, and ligaments can also result in inability to move areas beyond the cut.

Wound infection usually does not take place until 24–48 hours after an injury. Signs of infection include increasing redness, swelling, pain, pus, and fever. One of the most serious, though fortunately uncommon, complications of puncture wounds is tetanus ("lockjaw"). This bacterial infection thrives in areas not exposed to oxygen, so it is more likely to develop in deep puncture wounds or dirty wounds. Tetanus is not likely to develop in minor cuts or wounds caused by clean objects like knives. You need a tetanus immunization shot following a cut under the following conditions:

- If you have never had the recommended tetanus immunization injections
- If you have a dirty or contaminated wound and it has been longer than 5 years since your last injection
- If you have a clean, minor wound and it has been longer than 10 years since your last injection

Self-Assessment

1. Look for warning signs of complications: persistent bleeding, numbness, an inability to move the injured area, or the later development of pus, increasing redness, and fever.
2. Measure the size of the cut. If your cut is shallow, less than ¼ inch deep, less than an inch long, and not in a high-stress area (such as a joint, which bends) and you can easily hold the edges of the wound closed, it probably won't need stitches.

Self-Care

1. Apply direct pressure over the wound until the bleeding stops. The only exception is puncture wounds, which should be encouraged to bleed freely (unless spurting a large amount of blood) for a few minutes to flush out bacteria and debris.

2. When bleeding stops, wash your hands thoroughly with soap and water, then carefully cleanse the wound with clean water. Avoid getting soap in the wound, as it can irritate exposed tissues. Experts now advise against pouring hydrogen peroxide into a wound, as it may damage sensitive tissue. Do not try to remove visible dirt, debris, or objects (such as splinters or shards) from the wound; such cleaning should be done by a medical professional. If you don't see anything in the wound but suspect something may be there, see a doctor immediately.

3. Pat the area dry with a clean towel, then apply an antiseptic ointment and a clean bandage.

4. If it is an abrasion, cover the area with a sterile adhesive bandage until a scab forms. For minor lacerations, close the cut with a butterfly bandage or a sterile adhesive tape, drawing the edges close together but not overlapping. If there is an extra flap of clean skin, leave it in place for extra protection. Do not attempt to close a puncture wound. Instead, soak the wound in warm water for 15 minutes several times a day for several days. Soaking helps keep the wound open and thus prevents infection.

When to Call the Physician

1. Bleeding that can't be controlled with direct pressure
2. Numbness, weakness, or an inability to move the injured area
3. Any large, deep wound
4. A cut in an area that bends and with edges that cannot easily be held together
5. Cuts on the hands or face unless clean and shallow
6. A contaminated wound from which you cannot remove the foreign material
7. Any human or animal bite
8. If you need a tetanus immunization (see indications noted earlier)
9. Development of increasing redness, swelling, pain, pus, or fever 24 hours or more after the injury
10. If the wound is not healing well after 3 weeks

PHOTO CREDITS

INDEX

Boldface numbers indicate pages on which glossary definitions appear.

AA (Alcoholics Anonymous), 1, 262–263, 286
AAP (American Academy of Pediatrics), 126, 262
AASECT (American Association of Sex Educators, Counselors, and Therapists), 149
ABCD test, melanoma, 498
abortifacients, **161**, 191–192
abortion, 185–199, **186**. *See also* miscarriage
  adoption and, 190, 191
  complications of, 195–198
  concerns of, 186–190
  history of, U. S., 186, 187
  legislation on, 186–188, 193
  methods of, 191–192, 194–195
  myths about, 197
  personal considerations for, 189–191
  pill, 187
  pregnancies after, 197
  public opinion on, 188–189
abstinence, 143, **170, 171**, 171–172, 176, 179, 565
  celibacy, **143**
abuse. *See* alcohol abuse; drug abuse, defined; violence
academic stress, 41
Acamprosate (Campral), 287
Acceptable Macronutrient Distribution Ranges (AMDRs), 335, 336
acceptance, **64**, 64–66
acculturation stress, 44
Accutane, 221
ACME (Association for Couples in Marriage Enrichment), 121
acne, **131**, 221
ACOG (American College of Obstetricians and Gynecologists), 162, 212
acquired immune deficiency syndrome (AIDS), **552**. *See also* HIV infection; HIV/AIDS
  deaths from, 562
  diagnosis of, 560
  origin of, 552–553, 554
  sexual orientation and, 12
acquired immunity, **525**
ACSM (American College of Sports Medicine), 404
action stage, behavior change and, 20–21
active euthanasia, 708–709, **709**
active listening, 90
acupuncture, **631**, 631–632
acute myelogenous leukemia (AML), 504
addiction, **236, 237**. *See also* addictive behaviors; psychoactive drugs; substance dependence
  nicotine, 302–303, 305, 314
addictive behaviors, **236**, 236–246
additives in food, 367
Adequate Intake (AI), 345
ADHD (attention-deficit/hyperactivity disorder), **84**, 255
Adiana, 175
adolescence
  Erikson's stages of development, 66
  sexuality in, 139–140
adoption, 190, 191
adrenal androgens, 401
adrenal glands, **127**
adult sexuality, 140

adulthood
  development of adult identity, **66**, 66–67
  Erikson's stages of development, 66
advance directive, **709**
advertising
  alcohol, 290, 292
  films as, 305
  tobacco, 301, 305, 307
AEDs (automated external defibrillators), 467
AFP (alpha-fetoprotein), 216
Africa, HIV/AIDS origin in, 552, 554
African Americans
  alcohol use by, 288
  cancer among, 494
  cancer in, 500
  cancer incidence in, 502
  drug use/dependence among, 261
  genetic diseases in, 205
  health concerns of, 8, 11
  HIV/AIDS among, 557, 558–559
  life expectancy in, 691
  sexual behavior and, 143
  sodium consumption and, 454
  tobacco use among, 301, 308
age
  alcohol abuse and, 679
  cancer and, 492
  contraception use according to, 176
  first-time mothers, 202
  gonorrhea and, **568**
  heart attack average, 466
  injuries by sex and, nonfatal, 649
  marriage and, 111
  pregnancy, 203
  redefining, baby boomers', 693
  sexual intercourse appropriate, 175, 177
  STDs and, 570
  suicide rate by, 79
  tobacco use and, 300, 304
age-related macular degeneration (AMD), **686**
aggressive driving, injuries from, 650
aging, 679–699
  cardiovascular disease and, 461
  care options for, 694–695, 706, 707
  community resources and, 695
  culture and, 697
  diet and, 682
  life expectancy and, 690–692, **691**
  life-enhancing measures, 680–683
  medication dependence and, 683
  physical changes with, 685–688
  physical fitness and, 682
  psychological changes with, 688–690
  public perception of, 696–697
  retirement issues with, 684, 693
  sexuality and, 131–132
  social changes with, 684
  weight management and, 683
aging male syndrome, 132
agoraphobia, **74**
AI. *See* Adequate Intake
AIDS. *See* acquired immune deficiency syndrome
air bags, 651–653
air pollution, 589–597. *See also* chemical pollution; pollution
  energy use and, 594–596
  global warming, 14, 591–592

  greenhouse effect, 14, **590**, 591–592
  ground-level ozone, 590
  hotline on, 611
  indoor, 596
  ozone layer thinning and, 592, 594
  particulate matter, 590
  prevention of, 596–597
  smog, 589–591, **590**
Air Quality Index (AQI), **589**, 590
Al-Anon, 286–287
alarm, stress stage, 38
Alaska Natives
  alcohol use/abuse, 261
  drug use/dependence among, 261
  health concerns of, 11
  tobacco use among, 301
alcohol, **272**, 272–278
  absorption of, 273
  advertising for, 290, 292
  BAC, **274**, 274–276, **275**, 279
  caloric content of, 272–273
  diet planning and, 351
  dose-response function from, 279
  intake, 274–275
  poisoning, 276
  psychoactive ingredient in, 272
alcohol abuse, 261, 279–281, **283**, 283–289, 295, 679
alcohol use, 114, 123, 271–296, 651
  aggression and, 277–278
  benefits of, possible, 282–283
  body fat and, 275
  brain effects from, 273–274, 281
  cancer and, 281, 491, 505
  cardiovascular disease and, 459–460, 477
  cardiovascular system effects of, 281
  chronic abuse in, 279–281
  deaths from, 1, 5, 276, 280, 281
  digestive system and, 279–280
  driving and, 278–279
  drugs with, 277
  employment and, 260
  ethnicity and, 288–289
  gender differences in, 9, 275
  injuries and, 277, 651
  in lifestyle assessment, 16
  moderation in, 290–291
  pregnancy and, 204, 219, 281–282
  responsible drinking, 291–292
  stress and, 55–56
  violence and, 277, 662, 670
  wellness and, 275–283
Alcohol Use Disorders Test (AUDIT), 291
Alcoholics Anonymous (AA), 262–263, 286
alcoholism, **283**, 283–294
alcohol-related neurodevelopmental disorder (ARND), **282, 283**
allergens, **528**
allergic response, 528–529
allergies, **526**, 527–530
  contraceptive sponge, 170
  food, **368**, 368–369
  latex, 164–165
  stress and, 40
  vaccines and, 528–529
allied health care providers, **623**
allostatic load, **39**

alpha-fetoprotein (AFP), 216
altered states of consciousness, **258**
alternative fuels, 595
alternative medical systems, 629–633
    acupuncture, **631**, 631–632
    depression and, 83
    homeopathy, 632–633, **633**
Alzheimer's disease, 352, **688**, 689
AMD (age-related macular degeneration), **686**
AMDRs. *See* Acceptable Macronutrient Distribution Ranges
amebic dysentery, 543
amenorrhoea, **423**
American Academy of Pediatrics (AAP), 126, 262
American Association for Marriage and Family Therapy, 121
American Association for Sex Educators, counselors, and Therapists (AASECT), 149
American Cancer Society, 494, 505, 509
American College of Obstetricians and Gynecologists (ACOG), 162, 212
American College of Sports Medicine (ACSM), 404
American Heart Association, 478
American Indians
    aging and, 697
    alcohol use by, 289
    drug use/dependence among, 261
    health concerns of, 11
    tobacco use among, 301
American Medical Association, 565
American Psychiatric Association (APA), 58, 240
American Psychological Association, 43, 58
Americans. *See also* Dietary Guidelines for Americans
    alternative medical system use by, 632
    contraception use among women, 178
    drug use among, 236
    energy use by, 594–595
    ethnic groups of, 8, 10
    health disparities among, **6**, 6–12
    HIV routes of transmission among, 557
    leisure time in adult, statistics on, 47
    physical activity of, 382
    statistics on causes of deaths among, 5–6
    uninsured, 640
    whole grain consumption among, 337
amino acids, **331**, 401, 464
AML (acute myelogenous leukemia), 504
ammonia, tobacco additive, 308
amniocentesis, **216**, 217
amniotic fluid, **215**
amniotic sac, **215**
amphetamines, 253–255
anabolic steroids, **401**
anal intercourse, 144, 565
anaphylaxis, **528–529**
anaphylaxis, 369
anatomy, sexual, 124–127
androgen insensitivity syndrome, 128
androgens, **127**
androgyny, **138–139**
andropause, 132
anemia, **342**
anesthetics, **251**, 259
anger, 72–73, 459
angina pectoris, **310**, 467
angiogram, **469**
animal cloning, 368
anorexia nervosa, **441**
Antabuse. *See* Disulfram
anti-acne medications, 221
anti-angiogenesis medications, 512
antibiotics, **535**
    resistance to, 535, 545
antibodies, **522–523**, 524–525

antibody-mediated immune response, 525
anticarcinogens, **504, 505**
anti-dementia medications, 84
antidepressants, 84, 85, 86, 136–137, 221
antigen, **523**
antigenic drift, 539
antihistamines, 530
antioxidants, **340**, 343–344, 478
antipsychotics, 84
anti-tobacco legislation, 318–321
antiviral medications, HIV/AIDS treatment with, 562, 563
anxiety, **73, 74,** 80, 459. *See also* stress
    test, 35, 59
anxiety disorders, 73–78
    gender differences in, 80
    generalized anxiety disorder, **75**
    obsessive-compulsive disorder, **76**
    panic disorder, **74**
    post-traumatic stress disorder, 40, 45, **76,** 76–77
    treating, 78
anxious/ambivalent attachment, 96
anxious/avoidant attachment, 96
aortic aneurysm, 310
APA (American Psychiatric Association), 58, 240
Apgar score, **226**
appreciation, 118
AQI (Air Quality Index), **589,** 590
ARND (alcohol-related neurodevelopmental disorder), **282, 283**
arousal. *See* sexual arousal
arrhythmias, **467**
ART (assisted reproductive technology), 208
arteries, **451**
arteriosclerosis, 465
arthritis, 391, **685,** 686–687
    rheumatoid, 547
artificial insemination, **208,** 208–209
artificial trans fats, 334
asbestosis, **603**
Asian Americans
    cancer incidence in, 502
    drug use by, 261
    family life/education values of, 261
    testicular cancer in, 500
aspirin, 470, 619
assertiveness, **71**
assessments, self. *See also* evaluation
    contraceptive method selection, 180
    diet/MyPyramid recommendations, 357
    drug use, 266
    eating habits, 428
    emergencies, 616–617
    emotional intelligence, 101
    family health tree, 207
    health information evaluation, 18
    lifestyle, 16–17
    sexual attitude, 142
    sexually-transmitted disease risk, 577
    stress level, 33
    symptoms, 616
    values, 68
assisted reproductive technology (ART), 208, 210
Association for Couples in Marriage Enrichment (ACME), 121
asthma, 391, 604
asymptomatic diseases, **554**
atherosclerosis, **308, 309,** 453, 465–466. *See also* peripheral arterial disease
athletes, dietary challenges with, 359
atrium, **451**
attachment, **96,** 96–97
    postpartum period and, 229
attention-deficit/hyperactivity disorder (ADHD), 84, 255

AUDIT (Alcohol Use Disorders Test), 291
auditory hallucinations, 82
authenticity, **65**
authoritarian parent, 116
autoeroticism, **143**
autoimmune diseases, **523,** 546
    women and, 547
automated external defibrillators (AEDs), 467
autonomic nervous system, **32,** 33
autonomy, **65**
AZT (zidovudine), 562

B cells, **522–523**
baby boomer, age redefined by, 693
BAC (blood alcohol concentration), **274,** 274–276, **275,** 279
back injuries, 659
bacteria, **530,** 530–542
    foodborne illness types of, 362, 364
    STDs and, 553
    water contamination, 598
bacterial vaginosis (BV), **575,** 575–576
balloon angioplasty, **469**
barrier method, **154,** 154–155
basal cell carcinoma, **497**
battering, 664–668
BDD (body dysmorphic disorder), 438–439
beans, 355
beer, 272
behavior. *See* addictive behaviors; sexual behavior
behavior change, 15, **15**
    cycle of, 21
    goal-setting for, 22–23
    maintenance of, 21, 25–26
    motivation for, 19–20, 25
    personal contract for, 24–25
    personalized plans for, 22–25
    readiness for, 20–21
    relapse in, 21–22
    rewards for, 24
    self-efficacy in, **19**
    social influences in, 25
    spiral model of stages in, 22
    stress barrier to, 25
    target behavior, 17–18
    techniques/effort in, 25
behavior change strategies
    alcohol use, 294
    beverages and, 370
    dietary, 480
    drug use, 266
    social anxiety, 90
    test anxiety, 59
    tobacco use/smoking, 324–325
    weight management, 444
behavioral model, 85
    exposure, **85**
benign tumors, **486**
Benson-Henry Institute for Mind Body Medicine, 58
bereavement, 718, **719**
beverages, 256, 272–273, 351, 370, 435
bicycles, 653–654, 655
bidis, clove cigarettes and, 314–315
binge drinking, 282, **283,** 283–285
binge-eating disorder, **442**
biodegradability, **600,** 601
biodiversity, **588, 589**
bioelectromagnetic-based therapies, 637, **637**
biofeedback, **54**
biological model, 83–85
biological pollutants, 596
biological therapies, 512
biological-based therapies, **634**
biomagnification, **604**

biopsy, **486**, 509
bioterrorism, 546
bipolar disorder, **81**
birth control, **154**. *See also* childbirth; contraception
  pills, 130, 156–158
birth rate, 179
bisexuality, **141**
bladder cancer, 500
blaming, behavior change and, 26
blastocyst, 206, **214**
blindness, 686
blood
  cardiovascular system, 451–452
  glucose levels in, 337
  HIV transmission through, 556–557
  viscosity, 464
blood alcohol concentration (BAC), **274**, 274–276,
  275, 279
blood fat levels, 389
blood pressure, **451**, 453. *See also* high blood
  pressure
blood tests
  HIV infection, 562
  HSV, 573
  prenatal care and, 218–219
BMI. *See* body mass index
Bod Pod, 419
body composition, **381**, 387–388, 416–419
  analysis, 418
body dysmorphic disorder (BDD), 438–439
body fat
  alcohol use and, 275
  body composition and, 416–417
  distribution, 420, 422
  excess, 419–420, 423–426
  low levels of, 422
  percent, **416**, **417**
  wellness and, 419–420, 422
body image, **423**, 438–439, 440
body mass index (BMI), **416**, **417**, 417–418, 422,
  423
body weight, 417–419, 474. *See also* body fat;
  weight management
  blood alcohol concentration and, 274, 275
  BMI and, 417–418
  finding right, 422
  gender differences in, 9
  genetic factors in, 423
  lifestyle factors in, 424–425
  low birth, 316
  physiological factors in, 424
  psychosocial factors in, 425–426
bone marrow, **489**
  transplants, 511
bones, 603
  bone mineral density testing, 688
  nutrition and, 344
  osteoporosis, 342, **342**, 380, 389, 391, **688**
botanicals. *See* herbal remedies
brain
  alcohol effects on, 273–274, 281
  cancer, 500
  damage, 281
  hormones and, 128
  psychoactive drug influence on, 246–247
  sexual orientation and, 142
  stress and, 41
brain death, **703**
Brent, Sandor, 703
breast cancer, 197, 491–494, 504
  detection/diagnosis of, 492–493, 504
breast self exams (BSE), 493–494
breastfeeding, 228–229
breathing, **53**, 54
Brent, Sandor, 703
BSE (breast self-exams), 493–494

built environment, 249
bulimia nervosa, **441**, 441–442
Bupropion (Zyban), 323
burials, 713
burnout, **43**
buying, compulsive, 239

C. diff (clostridium difficile), 534
C. pneumoniae, 464
CAD. *See* coronary artery disease
caffeine, 47, 255–256
  beverage content of, 256
  decreasing use of, 266
  pregnancy and, 204, 220
calcium, 130, 477
calories, 330–331, 355–357, 429–430
  in alcohol, 272–273
  cardiovascular disease and, 477
  density of, 429–430
  diet soda, 427
  discretionary calorie allowance, 356
  food labels and, 361
  nutrients and, 347
  reducing total, 477
  weight management and, 347
CAM. *See* complementary medicine
Campral (Acamprosate), 287
Campylobacter jejuni, 362
Canada, medications from, 628
cancer, 389, 485–516, **486**, 604
  age and, 492
  alcohol use and, 281, 491, 505
  bladder, 500
  brain, 500
  breast, 197, 491–494, 504
  carcinomas, **488**, **489**, **497**
  causes of, 501–508
  cervical, 495–496
  colon/rectal, 490–491
  coping with, 513
  diabetes and, 494, 496
  diagnosis of, 490–491, 508–509
  diet and, 334, 490, 492, 494, 505
  DNA role in, 501–504
  endometrial, 496
  ethnicity and, 500, 501, 502
  female reproductive tract, 495–496
  gender differences in, 491
  heredity and, 501, 503
  hormone replacement therapy and, 492
  immune system and, 546
  incidence of, 488–489
  kidney, 500
  leukemia, **488**, **489**, 500–501, 504
  lifestyle and, 512–513
  living with, 512
  lung, 309, 310–311, 315, 489–490, 504–505, 603
  lymphomas and, **488**, **489**, 501
  melanoma and, **496**, **497**, 498
  metastasis and, **486**
  obesity and, 490, 505–506
  oral, 313, 498, 500
  ovarian, 496
  pancreatic, 500
  pollution factor in, 506–508
  poverty and, 502
  prevention of, 494, 498, 512, 514
  promoters, 503
  prostate, 494–495
  quackery, 511
  radiation treatment of, 509–510
  sarcomas and, **488**, **489**, **560**
  sexually transmitted diseases and, 495
  skin, 496–499, 508
  stages of, 487–488

  stomach, 500
  testicular, 136, 500
  tobacco use and, 306, 313, 491, 504–505
  treatment of, 509–512
  tumors and, **486–487**, 503
  types of, 488
  uterine, 496
  vaccines for, 489, 496, 512
  viruses and, 165, 486, 495
cannabis products, marijuana/other, 256–257
capacity for intimacy, **65**
capillaries, **451–452**, **453**
carbohydrates, 336–339, **337**
  AMDRs for protein/fat and, 336
  cardiovascular disease and, 477
  diet planning with, 349
  energy from, 337–339
  glycemic index for, **338**
  recommended intake of, 339
  simple/complex, 337
  whole grains v. refined, 337–338
carbon dioxide (CO2), 591, 593
carbon monoxide (CO), 307, 316, 589–590, 656
carcinogens, **306**, **307**, 313
  air pollution, 506–508
  environmental tobacco smoke, 315
  tobacco smoke, **306**, **307**, 315
  UV radiation, 496, 594
carcinoma, 488, **489**, 497
cardiac arrest, 468. *See also* sudden cardiac death
cardiac myopathy, **281**
cardiopulmonary resuscitation (CPR), **468**, **469**
cardiorespiratory endurance exercises, **380**, 386,
  395–396, 401, 402
cardiovascular disease (CVD), **40**, 386, 388–389,
  450, 452–465. *See also* atherosclerosis; heart
  attack; stroke
  aging and, 461
  alcohol consumption and, 459–460, 477
  aspirin and, 470
  blood viscosity/iron and, 464
  calories and, 477
  cholesterol and, 455–456, 475, 477
  congenital heart defects, **474**
  diabetes and, 457–458
  dietary factors for, 477–478
  drug use and, 459–460
  ethnicity and, 461, 463
  exercise and, 388–389, 478
  fiber intake and, 477
  gender differences in, 461, 462
  heredity and, 460–461
  high blood pressure and, 453–455
  homocysteine and, 464
  hormone replacement therapy and, 462
  infectious agents and, 464
  inflammation/C-Reactive protein and, 461
  insulin resistance and, 461–464
  LDL particle size and, 464
  lipoproteins and, 464
  major forms of, 465–475
  metabolic syndrome, 461–464
  obesity and, 457
  peripheral arterial disease, **473**
  physical inactivity and, 457
  postmenopausal women and, 462
  prevention of, 470, 475–478
  psychological/social factors in, 458–459
  rheumatic fever, **474**
  risk assessment for, 476
  sodium intake and, 477
  stress and, 458–459
  tobacco use and, 309–310, 453, 478
  triglyceride levels and, 458
  uric acid and, 464–465

cardiovascular system, **450**, 450–452
   alcohol effects on, 281
   blood vessels, 451–452
   heart, 450–451
caregiving, 694–695, **706**, 707
carotenoids, **504, 505**
carpal tunnel syndrome, **658**, 660
cataracts, 686, **687**
Caucasians
   cancer incidence in, 496, 502
   drug use/dependence among, 261
   genetic diseases in, 205
   life expectancy of, 691
   sexual behavior and, 143
   skin cancer likelihood in, 496
   tobacco use among, 301
causality, death and, 703
CD4 T cell, **552, 553**
CDC. *See* Center for Disease Control
celibacy, **143**
cell phones, 650–651, 652
cells
   B, **522–523**
   dendritic, **522**
   endothelial, **457**, 465
   fat, 424
   germ, **124, 125**
   helper T, **522–523**
   killer T, **522–523**
   memory T/B, **523**
   natural killer, **522**
   nerve cell communication, 81
   stem, **511**, 681
   T, **522–523**, 522–524, **552, 553**
cell-mediated immune response, 524
cellular death, **703**
Center for Disease Control (CDC), 362, 382, 537,
    539, 546, 653, 665
   AIDS diagnosis criteria of, 560
   gonorrhea cases reported to, **568**
   HIV recommendations by, 562
   lead poisoning estimated by, 603
   water contamination reports by, 598
Center for Young Women's Health, 149
Central Americans, tobacco use among, 301
central nervous system (CNS), **248**. *See also* depres-
    sants, CNS; stimulants, CNS
cerebral cortex, **308, 309**
cervical cancer, 495–496
cervical chlamydia, 157
cervical dysplasia, 495
cervix, **125**
cesarian section, **226, 227**, 227–228
CFCs (chlorofluorocarbons), 591, **592**, 596
chain of infection, 520–521
chancre, **575**
Chantix (varinicline), 323
CHD. *See* coronary heart disease
chemical pollution
   asbestosis, **603**
   ETS, 316
   hazardous waste and, 603–606
   ingested, 506–507
   lead, 603–604
   mercury, 604–605
   pesticides and, 366, 604
   preventing, 606
   tobacco smoke, 306, 308, 316
chemotherapy, **490**, 509
Chernobyl, 585
chewing tobacco, 312, 313
chicken pox, 538–539
chickens, contamination/foodborne illness with, 364
child abuse, 668, 671–672
child care, 203

child safety seats, 651–653
childbirth, 179, 224–228, 231. *See also* birth
    control
   birth defects and, 219
   cesarean section, **226, 227**, 227–228
   electronic fetal monitoring of, **226**
   methods of, 224–225
   multiple births, 204
   planning, 226
   postpartum period after, **228**, 228–229
   premature, **224**
   preparing for, 222, 226
children
   congenital heart defects in, **474**
   cost of raising, 201, 202, 203
   death of, motor vehicle injury, 653
   death understood by, 703–704
   depression and, 86
   dietary challenges with, 358
   expectations of, 116
   grief in, 720–721
   HIV transmission to, 557
   media violence and, 661
   without parents, 118
   of permissive parents, 116
   school violence and, 663–664
   sexual assault of, 671–672
   suffocation/choking and, 657
   temperaments of, 117
   violence against, 668, 671–672
children of alcoholics (COAs), 278
chiropractic, **634**, 635–636
chlamydia, 495, 566–568
Chlamydia pneumoniae, 464
chloasma ("mask" of pregnancy), 157
chlorofluorocarbons (CFCs), 591, **592**, 596
choking, 657
cholera, 586
cholesterol, **334**, 349, 389, 455–456, 475, 477,
    478
   good v. bad, 455–456
   guidelines, 456
   LDL particle size and, 464
   smoking and, 310
chorionic villi, 215
chorionic villus sampling (CVS), **217**
chromium picolinate, 401
chromosomes, **127, 502, 503**
chronic bronchitis, **310, 311**
chronic disease, **4**
chronic liver disease, 280
chronic obstructive pulmonary disease (COPD),
    311
chronic prostatitis, 136
cigar smoking, 310, 314
cigarette tar, **306, 307**, 308
cigarette tax, 316
cigarettes. *See also* smoking, cigarette; tobacco/to-
    bacco use
   clove/bidis, 314–315
   light/low-tar, 308
   menthol, 308
cilia, 522
circumcision, **126**, 556
cirrhosis, **280, 281**
civil unions, same-sex marriage and, 112
Clean Indoor Air Acts, 596
clinical death, **703**
clitoris, **124, 125**
cloning, 210, **211**
Clostridium botulinum, 364
Clostridium difficile (C. diff), 534
Clostridium sepsis, 195
clove cigarettes, 314–315
club drugs, 251, 252, 557

cluster headaches, 42
CMV (cytomegalovirus), 540
CNS. *See* central nervous system
CO (carbon monoxide), 307, 316
CO2 (carbon dioxide), 591, 593
COAs (children of alcoholics), 278
cocaine, 247, 248, 249, 251–253
cocarcinogens, **306, 307**, 313, 491
codependency, **263**, 263–264
coercion, sexual, **144, 145**
coffee, caffeine content in, 256
cognitive distortion, **69**, 70
cognitive model, 85–86
cognitive techniques, stress management through,
    50–52
cohabitation, **109**, 109–110
cold sores, 539–540
collective violence, 665
college students
   alcohol abuse among, 285, 289
   binge drinking by, 285
   dietary challenges with, 358
   drug use by, 242
   eating disorders among, 439
   eating strategies for, 360
   sexual behavior and, 145
   stressors on, 41–42
   test anxiety of, 35
   violence on campus and, 45
   wellness concerns of, 13
colon/rectal cancer, 490–491
colostrum, **228**
combination pill, 156
commercial sexuality, 145–146
commitment
   family life success and, 118
   love and, 98, 100, 113–114, 116, 120
   marriage and, 113–114
   unequal/premature, 100
common cold, 536–537, 538
communication
   contraception and, 177
   ethnicity and, 10
   family life and, 118–119
   gender differences in, 104, 106
   guidelines for effective, 105
   honest, 71–72
   "I" statements, 105
   intimate relationships, 103–107
   nerve cell, 81
   nonverbal, 103
   organizations/web sites on intimacy and, 121
   safer sex/condoms, 579
   sexual behavior and, 146–147
   stress management through, 46
community resources, aging and, 695
companionship, 97
competitiveness, 100
complementary medicine (CAM), **619**, 619–620,
    629–638
   acupuncture, **631**, 631–632
   alternative medical systems and, 629–633
   biological-based therapies, **634**
   chiropractic, **634**, 635–636
   energy therapies, 636–637
   evaluation of, 637–638
   homeopathy, 632–633, **633**
   hypnosis and, **634**
   manipulative/body-based methods, 634–636
   mind-body interventions, 633–634
   Qigong, 636–637, **637**
   traditional Chinese medicine, 629, **631**,
    631–632
compulsion, **76**, 237, 238–239
compulsive exercise, 46–47, 238–239

computed tomography (CT) scanning, 509, 608
conception, **154**, 204, 206. *See also* preconception care
condoms
    female, 165–166
    male, **164**, 164–165
    STDs and, 565, 567
    trends in use of, 178, 578
confidants, statistics on, 97–98
conflict/conflict resolution, 104–107
congenital heart defect, **474**
congenital malformations, **219**
congestive heart failure, **473**, 473–474
consciousness. *See* altered states of consciousness
constructive thinking, 50
consumerism, responsible/green, 602
contagion, 525–526
contagious disease, **536**
contamination
    environmental, organic foods and, **365**, 365–367
    food, 364–365
    water, 597–598
contemplation, **20**, 21
continuation rate, **154**, **155–156**
contraception, 147, 153–183, **154**
    abstinence, 143, **170**, **171**, 171–172, 176, 179
    age of use by type of, 176
    barrier method, **154**, 154–155
    combining methods of, 172
    continuation rate, **154**, 155–156
    contraceptive failure rate, **154**, 155
    emergency, **161**, 161–163, 182, 191–192
    ethnicity and, 176
    fertility awareness method (FAM), **170**, **171**, 171–172
    gender and, 177–178
    health risks and, 180
    issues in, 175, 177–180
    myths about, 155
    natural method, **154**, **155**
    organizations/web sites on, 182
    partner communication about, 177
    permanent/sterilization, **172**, 172–175, 176
    principles of, 154–156
    reversible, 156–172
    sexually transmitted diseases and, 157, 159, 160, 167, 168, 172, 173, 178
    spermicide, **164**, 166, 170–171
    teenager education on, 178–180
    use among American women, 178
    withdrawal, **172**
contraceptives, **154**, 187
    choosing, 180–181
    condom, 164–166, 178, 565, 567, 578
    diaphragm, **167**, 167–169
    failure rate, **154**, **155**, 173
    fallopian tube blockage, 175
    FemCap, **169**
    health clinics and, 158
    hormonal method, **154**, 155
    hysterectomy, **174**, **175**
    implants, 160
    injectable, 160–161
    intrauterine device, **163**, 163–164, 176, 180
    IUD, 163–164, 180
    laparoscopy, **174**, 174–175
    Lea's Shield, 169
    male condom, **164**, 164–165
    oral, **156**, 156–158, **157**
    Plan B, 161, 162, 166
    risk statistics on, 159
    skin patch, 158–159
    socioeconomic status and, 176
    sponge, 166, 169, **169**
    surgical method, **154**, **155**

    teenager access to, 179
    trends in, 176
    vaginal contraceptive ring, 159–160
    vaginal spermicides, 164, 166, 170–171, 555
    vasectomy, **173**, 173–174
contractions, labor, **225**
controversy
    ART, 210
    prostate-specific antigen blood test, 494
    stem cell, 681
conventional medicine, 620–629
COPD (chronic obstructive pulmonary disease), 311
Copper T-380A (ParaGard), 163
coronary arteries, **453**
coronary artery disease (CAD), 460–461, 468
coronary bypass surgery, **470**
coronary heart disease (CHD), 282, **308**, **309**, 309–310, 389, 456, 468
    lipoproteins) and, 464
    plaques and, **466**
    tobacco use and, 309–310
corpus luteum, **129**
cortisol, **33**
costs
    childraising, 201, 202, 203
    drug abuse, 259
    health care, 638–642
    HIV/AIDS, 564
    injuries, 648
    prescription drug spending, 628
    smoking, 312
    tobacco use, 316–318
counseling, 119
court cases, tobacco company, 317–318
Cowper's glands, **126**
CPR. *See* cardiopulmonary resuscitation
craving, 237
C-reactive protein (CRP), 461
cream, prostaglandin, 137
Creatine Monohydrate, 401
creativity, self-actualization and, **65**
crime, psychoactive drugs and, 259–260
cross-training, **409**
CRP (C-reactive protein), 461
cruciferous vegetables, **344**, 344–345, **345**
cryopreservation, ovarian tissue, 210
cryptosporidium, 598
CT (computed tomography) scans, 509, 608
culture
    aging and, 697
    drug use and, 261
    ethnicity and, 10
    gender identity/gender roles and, 138
    lifestyle and, 10–11
    STDs and, 576
    stress and, 36
cunnilingus, **144**
CVD. *See* cardiovascular disease
CVS (chorionic villus sampling), **217**
cybersex, **146**
cyberstalking, **668**
cycle of behavior change, 21
CYP2A6 enzyme, 303–304
cystic fibrosis, 8, 14–15, 205
cytokine, **524**, **525**
cytomegalovirus (CMV), 540
cytoplasm, injection of, 210

D & C. *See* dilation and curettage
D & E. *See* dilation and evacuation
Daily Values, **346**
DASH diet, 351–352, 377, 454, 478
date rape, **669**, 669–670, 671
date rape drugs, 252, 670
dating, 107–108, 109, 242

Day of the Dead, 705
DDT, 604
death, causes of. *See also* suicide
    AIDS, 562
    alcohol use, 1, 5, 276, 280, 281
    among Americans, statistics on, 5–6
    cancer, 488, 500, 502, 508, 509
    cardiovascular disease, 454–455, 458
    chronic liver disease, 280
    congestive heart failure, 473
    diabetes, 420
    ethnicity and, 11
    ETS and, 315
    ground-level ozone, 590
    indoor fires, 596
    infant mortality among ethnic groups and, 11
    infectious disease, 530, 534, 544
    injuries, 648
    lifestyle choices and, 4, 5
    lung cancer, 310, 315, 489
    natural disasters/tornadoes, 659
    obesity, 1, 419
    physical inactivity, 382
    poisoning, 656
    teens, 4
    tobacco use, 1, 5, 300, 309–310
    in U.S., statistics on, 5
    violence, interpersonal, 660
    water contamination, 598
Death with Dignity Act, 708
death/dying, 701–724
    awareness of dying, 713–714
    coping with dying, 713–717
    defining death, 702–703
    denying v. welcoming, 704
    disposition of body, 711
    end-of-life care options, 694–695, 706, 707
    four components of, 703
    funeral/memorial service planning, 711–713, 714
    grief and, **717**, 717–720
    home v. hospital care and, 706
    hospice care and, **706**, 707
    life-sustaining treatment, 707–708
    organ donors, 710–711, 712
    pain-relief medications and, 709
    physician-assisted suicide and, 708–709, **709**
    prolonging/hastening death, 706–708
    tasks of mourning, 718–719
    trajectory of dying, **715**, 715–717
    treatment withholding/withdrawing, 708
    will preparation and, 704–706, 709
decibels, **608**
deep breathing, **53**
deer tick, 533, 534
defense mechanisms, **70**, **71**
defensiveness, 70–71
deforestation, 591–592
dehydroepiandrosterone (DHEA), 133
delirium tremens (the DTs), **284**, **285**
delusions, 82
dementia, **688**, 688–689
dendritic cells, **522**
dental disease, from smoking, 312
dentist, **623**
deoxyribonucleic acid (DNA), 501–504, **502**
Department of Health and Human Services (DHHS), 308, 323, 346
Department of Homeland Security, 664
depersonalization, marijuana and, 256
Depo-Provera, 160–161
depressants, CNS, **248**, **249**, 249–251
depression, 77, **78**, 78–81, 690
    cardiovascular disease and, 459
    childhood, 86

gender differences in, 9, 80
herbal remedies/alternative medical systems for, 83
postpartum, **228**
during pregnancy, 213
suicide and, 80
treating, 79, 83
designated driver, 279
development
addiction, 237–238
embryonic, early, 206
fetal, 213–217
sexual behavior, 138–140
tumor, 487
development stages, 66, 67
developmental tests, tobacco use and, 316
DHEA (dehydroepiandrosterone), 133
DHSS (Department of Health and Human Services), 308, 323, 346
diabetes, 391
cancer and, 494, 496
cardiovascular disease and, 457–458
gestational, **223**, 421
mellitus, 419, **420**
prevention/treatment of, 421, 422
statistics on, 12, 16, 389
symptoms of, 420
Type 1, 420, 421
Type 2, 389–390, 419, 422, 494, 496
diagnostic process, 625
diaphragm, contraceptive, **167**, 167–169
diastole, **451**
diet(s). *See also* dietary supplements; food(s)
aging and, 682
aids, 435
alcoholic beverages and, 351
behavior change strategy, 480
cancer and, 334, 490, 492, 494, 505
carbohydrates in, 349
cardiovascular disease and, 477–478
challenges for specific populations, 358–359
college student strategies for, 360
DASH, 351–352, 377, 454, 478
death statistics and, 5
eating habits and, 56, 332, 428, 444
ethnic foods in, 348
exercise and, 404
grains in, 337–338, 352–353
incorporating fruits/vegetables into, 515
lifestyle assessment and, 16
Mediterranean, 352
MyPyramid, **345**, 351–356, 351–357
nutritional guidelines for planning, 345–359
nutritional requirements of healthy, 330–345
popular, 434
portion sizes and, 355, 357
pregnancy, 220
special population groups, 358–359
unhealthy eating habits, **56**
USDA guidelines for, 351–356
vegetarian, 331, 356–358
weight loss, 434
weight management/eating habits and, 429–431, 444
diet books, 432
diet sodas, 427
dietary fat, 333–337, 347, 349, 350, 355–356. *See also* body fat; fat(s)
AMDRs for carbohydrate/protein and, 336
blood fat levels, 389
cholesterol and, **334**
health and, 334–335
high-density lipoprotein, 310, **334**, 389, 427, **456**, 463–464, 478
hydrogenation of, **333**

low-density lipoprotein, **334**, 389, **455**, 464, 477
recommended intake of, 335–337
dietary fiber, **339**
Dietary Guidelines for Americans, **345**, 346–351, 454
Dietary Reference Intakes (DRIs), **345**, 345–346, 351, 374–376
Dietary Supplement Health and Education Act (DSHEA), 363
Dietary Supplement Verification Program, 363
dietary supplements, 477–478
club drugs sold as, 252
diet aids and, 435
exercise and, 398–399
food v., 346
labels on, 362, 363
performance-enhancing, 401
prenatal care, 220
differentiation
embryo, 127–128, 215
sexual, 127–128
digestion, 330, **331**
digestive system, 279–280, **331**
digital mammography, 492
digital rectal exam, 494
dilation and curettage (D & C), 192
dilation and evacuation (D & E), **194**
disabilities, 12, 140, 391, 679
discretionary calorie allowance, 356
discrimination
racial, 11, 44
stress and, 44
diseases. *See also* chronic disease; genetic diseases; illness; infectious diseases; psychological disorders; *specific diseases*
asymptomatic, **554**
endemic, **532**, 541
exercise for prevention/management of, 388–390
pathogens and, 530–546
sexuality and, 140
viruses causing, 531
disparities, health, **6**, 6–12
disposition of body, death/dying and, 711
distress, **38**
Disulfram (Antabuse), 287
diversity
bio-, **588**, 589
genetics and, 7
stress and, 44
divorce, 114–115
DMT, hallucinogen, 258
DNA (deoxyribonucleic acid), 501–504, **502**, **503**, 553
doctors of osteopathic medicine (D. O.), **623**
dominant gene, 205
donor eggs/embryos, 210
dopamine, 247
dose-response function, **247–248**, 279
double effect, **709**
douche, 155, **170**
Dr. Drew, 149
drinking. *See* binge drinking; water
DRIs (Dietary Reference Intakes), **345**, 345–346, 351, 374–376
driving
alcohol use and, 278–279
blood alcohol concentration and, 279
cell phone use during, 652
injuries from aggressive, 650
drug abuse, defined, **240–241**. *See also* psychoactive drugs
drug(s), defined, **236**. *See also* medications; psychoactive drugs
drug use. *See also* medications; psychoactive drugs
assessment of, 266
cardiovascular disease and, 459–460

emergencies, 245, 253, 260
ethnicity and, 261
families/family life, 242, 259–260, 261
gender differences in, 242, 243
health care and, 260
injection, 246, 557
legal consequences of, 246
legislation on, 242, 260
pregnancy and, 203, 219, 220–221, 253
prevention of, 264–265
socioeconomic status and, 248–249, 254, 261
spirituality and, 244
stress and, 55–56
time-action function effect, **248**
Drug-Induced Rape Prevention and Punishment Act, 670
drug-treatment programs, choosing, 263
drunk driving, 278–279
DSHEA. *See* Dietary Supplement Health and Education Act
DTs (delirium tremens), **284, 285**
dual (co-occurring) disorder, **244**
duration, exercise principle, 393
dysentery, amebic, 543
dysmenorrhea, **130, 131**
dysthymic disorder, 78

E. coli, 545
E. I. Q. *See* emotional intelligence
E. Q. *See* emotional intelligence
Eastern European Americans, 8, 205
eating. *See* diet(s); nutrition
eating disorders, 438, **439**, 439–443
EBCT. *See* electron-beam computed tomography
ebola, 545
EC (emergency contraception), **161**, 161–163, 191–192
ECG/EKG (electrocardiogram), **392, 393, 468, 469**
eclampsia, **223**
ecosystem, **588, 589**
ECT (electroconvulsive therapy), 79
ectoparasites, 553
ectopic pregnancy, **222, 223**
education
drug use and, 261
HIV, 566
inequality, 11–12
physical activity and, 382
STDs, 576
teenage sexuality/contraception, 178–180
tobacco use profile by age/ethnicity/level of, 300
EEG (electroencephalogram), **703**
ejaculation, **164**
premature, **136**
ejaculatory ducts, **126**
elder abuse, 669
elective surgery, **629**
electrical impedance analysis, 419
electrocardiogram (ECG/EKG), **392, 393, 468, 469**
electroconvulsive therapy (ECT), 79
electroencephalogram (EEG), **703**
electron-beam computed tomography (EBCT), 468
electronic fetal monitoring (EFM), **226**
ELISA (enzyme-linked immunosorbent assay), **560**
embalming, **711, 713**
embryo, **214, 215**. *See also* stem cells
ART/freezing of, 210
differentiation of, 127–128, 215
donor, 210
early development of, 206
emergencies
alcohol, 277
alcohol/alcohol-drug combination, 277
assessment of, 616–617
average number of, per minute, 616

emergencies (continued)
  bicycle crash, 653–654
  drug use, 245, 253, 260
  poisonings, 656
  scooter injuries, 658
emergency care, 674
emergency contraception (EC), **161**, 161–163, 191–192
emergency medical services (EMS) system, **674**
emotion(s)
  gender differences in, 80
  parenthood readiness and, 202
  pregnancy and, 212–213
  sexual stimulation and, 134
  stress and, 34–36
  strong, 101
  weight management and, 431–432
emotional intelligence (E. Q./E. I. Q.), 101
emotional wellness, **3**, 16, 383, 390
emphysema, **310, 311**
employment, alcohol/drug use and, 260
EMS. *See* emergency medical services
enabling behavior, 263–264
encephalitis, **540**
endemic diseases, **532**, 541
endocrine system, **32**, 32–33
endometrial cancer, 496
endometriosis, 197
endometriosis, 135–136
endometrium, **129**
endorphins, **33**
endoscopy, **625**
endothelial cells, **457**, 465
endurance training, **380**, 386–387, 389
energy
  drinks, 256
  nuclear, 606–607
  radiation as, **606**
energy therapies, 636–637, **637**
  Qigong, 636–637, **637**
  Reiki, **637**
  therapeutic touch, **637**
energy use
  air pollution and, 594–596
  carbohydrates for, 337–339
  nutrients supplying, 330
  population and, 588, 589
  U. S. use of, 589
entry inhibitor, **562**
environment, 14, **15**. *See also* air pollution; chemical pollution; pollution
  built, 249
  burials/embalming influence on, 713
  carcinogens in, 506–508
  contaminants in, 365–367
  food crisis and, 347
  infectious diseases and, 545
  miscarriage related to, 189
  parents instilling values of, 110
  pregnancy and, 219–221
  sexual problems and, 127
  STDs and, 576
  stress and, 37, 44
  substance abuse and, 249
  target behaviors and, 20
environmental contaminants, organic foods and, **365**, 365–367
environmental health, 585–612, **586**
Environmental Protection Agency (EPA), 367, 603, 612
environmental tobacco smoke (ETS), 309–310, **315**, 315–316, 317
  legislation on, 318, 596
environmental wellness, **3**
enzyme activators/blockers, 512
enzyme-linked immunosorbent assay (ELISA), **560**

EPA (Environmental Protection Agency), 367, 603, 612
ephedra (ma huang), 401
ephedrine, 255
epididymitis, **126, 127, 566**
epinephrine, **33**
episiotomy, **226**
epithelia, **488, 489**
EPO (Erythropoietin), 401
equipment, exercise, 397, 404
erectile dysfunction, 123, **136**, 137, 313
Erikson, Erik, 66, 67
erogenous zones, **134**
erotic fantasy, **143**
Erythropoietin (EPO), 401
escalation, addictive behavior characteristic, 237
Escherichia coli, 364, 545
essential nutrients, **330**, 330–343
  antioxidant, 344
  carbohydrates, **337**, 337–339
  fats, 333–337
  minerals, **342**
  proteins, 331–332
  six classes of, 330
  water, 342–343
estate, **704**
estrogen, **127**, 462, 492
estrogenic phase, menstrual cycle, **129**
ethanol (ETOH), 262
ethnic foods, 348
ethnicity, 7–8
  alcohol abuse and, 288–289
  body image and, 440
  cancer and, 500, 501, 502
  cardiovascular disease and, 461, 463
  causes of death and, 11
  contraception and, 176
  defined, **8**
  diabetes and, 12
  distribution in U.S., 8
  drug use and, 261
  gender and, 79
  genetic diseases and, 205
  hate crimes and, 663
  health disparities among minorities, **6**, 6–12
  heart attack and, 12
  HIV/AIDS and, 557, 558
  income/education and, 11–12
  obesity and, 425
  psychological disorders and, 75
  sexual behavior/decision making and, 143
  STDs and, 566
  stress and, 45
  suicide and, 8, 79
  tobacco use and, 300, 301, 308
ETOH (ethyl alcohol), 272
ETS. *See* environmental tobacco smoke
euphoria, 247, **248, 249**
eustress, **38**
euthanasia, 708–709, **709**
evaluation
  complementary medicine, 637–638
  health information, 18, 622
  statistics, 622
examinations
  contraception and, 158
  STDs self, 577
excitement phase, sexual response cycle, 134
exercise(s), 16, 379–413, **383**
  benefits of, 386–390
  breathing, 53, 54
  cardiovascular disease and, 388–389, 478
  compulsive, 46–47
  diet and, 404
  dietary supplements and, 398–399
  endurance, 386–387

equipment for, 397
  flexibility, **381**, 392, 399–400, 401
  footwear for, 405
  immune system and, 390
  injuries and, 407–409
  isometric, **396–397**
  isotonic, **397**
  prenatal care and, 221–222
  resistance, **396, 397**
  special health concerns and, 391
  statistics on, 23
  stress management through, 46–47, 390
  water drinking and, 404, 406
  weight management and, 431
exercise program, 390–413
  activity selection for, 394–395
  choosing exercises for, 397
  consistency in, 406–407
  designing, 390–403, 412–413
  disabilities and, 391
  equipment for, 397, 404
  fitness centers and, 404
  flexibility exercises in, 399–400, 401
  frequency and, 397
  intensity and, 393, 397–398
  management/maintenance of, 406–409
  medical clearance for, 392
  muscular strength/endurance and, **381**, 396–399, 401, 402
  personalizing, 400–403
  physical fitness assessment and, 380–386
  principles of physical training and, 392–394
  progression of, 406
  RICE and, 407–409
  specific skills and, 400
exhaustion, GAS stage, 39
expectations
  of children, 116
  of partner, 100–101
exposure, **85**

fallopian tube, **125**
  Adiana for blocking, 175
  ectopic pregnancy in, 222
  gamete intrafallopian transfer (GIFT), **208**
  zygote intrafallopian transfer, **208**, 208–209
falls, injury from, 654–655
false negative, test result, **625**
false positive, test result, **625**
FAM. *See* fertility awareness method
families/family life, 115–119. *See also* marriage; parents/parenting
  cycle, 117
  drug use and, 242, 259–260, 261
  dysfunctional, drug use in, 242
  marriage and, 115–119
  single-parent, 117–118
  step-, 118
  successful, 118–119
  violence in, 664–669
family health tree, 207
family history, 13
FAS (fetal alcohol syndrome), **219**
fast-food restaurants, 360
fat(s). *See also* body fat; dietary fat
  blood fat levels, 389
  saturated, 480
  trans, 350, 354, 480
  trans fatty acids, **333**, 334, 350
  types/sources of, 333
  unsaturated, 349
fat cells, 424
fat substitutes, 430
fat-free mass, **381**
fathers, pregnancy tasks for, 213
fatigue, motor vehicle injuries and, 650

fat-soluble vitamins, 341
fatty acids, omega-3, **334**, 477
FBI. *See* Federal Bureau of Investigation
FDA. *See* Food and Drug Administration
Federal Bureau of Investigation (FBI), 246, 259–260, 659–660, 664
federal legislation. *See* legislation
feedback, communication skill, 104
fee-for-service plans, 639
fellatio, **144**
female athlete triad, **423**
female reproductive tract cancer, 495–496
female sexual arousal disorder, 137
females. *See also* women
    caloric intake for, 347
    condoms for, 165–166
    infertility in, 208
    menstrual cycle, 128–131
    motivation for drug use, 243
    physical changes in, 128
    sex organs in, 124–125
    sexual maturation in, 128–131
    sterilization in, 174–175, 176
FemCap, 169
fertility, 155, **157**, 176, 204–206, 589
fertility awareness method (FAM), **170**, **171**, 171–172
fertilization, **204**
    in vitro, **208**
fertilized egg, **204**
fetal alcohol syndrome (FAS), **219**, **281**
fetal development, 213–217
fetal programming, 217
fetus, **203**
    multi-fetal pregnancy reduction, **194**
    viable stage of, **186**
fiber, 339–342, 477, 505
    recommended intake of, 340
    sources of, 340
    types of, 339–340
fight-or-flight reaction, **33–34**
films, portrayal of tobacco use in, 305–306
financial planning, 684
    pregnancy, 213
financial wellness, **4**
firearms, 662, 663, 673–674, 675
firefighters, 656
fires, 596, 655–656
first aid, **674**
first stage of labor, 225
fish, 349, 367, 477
flashbacks, LSD-induced, **258**
flexibility exercises, **381**, 392, 399–400, 401, 402
fluid intelligence, **683**
flunitrazepam (Rohypnol), 252, 670
fluoridation, **596**, **597**
FOCA (Freedom of Choice Act), 187
folic acid, cardiovascular disease and, 477
follicle, **129**
follicle-stimulating hormone (FSH), 129
food(s)
    additives in, 367
    allergies/intolerances to, **368**, 368–369
    antioxidants in, 343–344
    chemicals in, 506–507
    contamination of, 364–365
    environment and, 347
    ethnic, 348
    fried, 505
    genetically modified, 368
    groups, 347
    irradiation, **367**, 367–368
    labels on, 360–362
    organic, **365**, 365–367
    other substances in, 343–345
    personal choices about, 359–370

pesticides in, 366
phytochemicals in, **344**, 344–345
population and, 587–588
processed, 351, 360
protein content of common, 333
safe handling of, 366
safety hotlines, 371
supplements v., 346
trans fat content of common, 350, 480
vegetarian food plan, 358
vitamins in, 341
whole grain, **337**, 337–338
food allergy, **368**, 368–369
Food and Drug Administration (FDA), 130, 133, 137, 175, 252
    animal cloning viewed by, 368
    dietary guidelines set by, 345–346
    dietary supplement labels and, 363
    drug warnings/pregnancy and, 221
    food labeling and, 360
    GM food labeling regulations, 368
    medical abortion and, 195
    OTC medications recognized by, 618
    Plan B emergency contraceptive approved by, 162
    on prescription drugs, 628
    tobacco regulation by, 319
Food and Nutrition Board, 332, 335, 336, 345
food bars, 435
food chain, **588**, **589**
food intolerance, **368**, 369
food packages, reading, 338
food plan, personal, 359–370
    dietary supplement labels and, 362, 363
    food additives and, 367
    food irradiation and, **367**, 367–368
    food labels and, 360–362
    foodborne illnesses and, 362, 364–365
food safety, pregnancy and, 220
foodborne illnesses, 362, 364–365
    bacteria causing, 362, 364
    Guillain-Barré syndrome, 362, 364
    treating/preventing, 364–365
footwear, exercise, 405
foreplay, 143–144, **144**
formaldehyde gas, 596, 605
fossil fuels, **589**, 589–590
Framework Convention on Tobacco Control, 318
fraternal twins, **206**
free radicals, **343**, 343–344
Freedom of Access to Clinics Act, 187
Freedom of Choice Act (FOCA), 187
French Canadian Americans, health concerns of, 8
frequency, exercise program, 397
friendship, 97–98, 120
fruits, 354, 505, 515
FSH (follicle-stimulating hormone), 129
fuels
    alternative, 595
    fossil, **589**, 589–590
functional fiber, **339**
funerals, 711–713, 714
fungus, **542**, 542–543

GAD (generalized anxiety disorder), **75**
gambling, compulsive, 238
gamete intrafallopian transfer (GIFT), **208**
gamma hydroxybutyrate (GHB), 670
gammahydroxybutyrate (GHB), 252
gangs, 663
garbage, 600
GAS (general adaptation syndrome), **37**, 38, 39
gas, formaldehyde, 596, 605
gasoline, 595
gastroenteritis, 545
GDM (gestational diabetes), **223**

gender
    alcohol abuse and, 287–288
    alcohol and, 9, 275
    body image and, 440
    cancer and, 491
    cardiovascular disease and, 461, 462
    communication and, 104, 106
    contraception and, 177–178
    defined, **8**
    depression/anxiety disorders and, 80
    health care visits and, 624
    injuries and, 649
    nutritional needs according to, 359
    physiology and, 38
    psychoactive drugs and, 242, 243
    sexual response cycle and, 134
    stress and, 9, 36, 37, 38
    suicide and, 79
    tobacco use and, 9, 301, 312, 313
    violence and, 661–662
    wellness factors related to, 9
gender identity, **138**, 138–139
gender roles, 9, **36**, **96**, 138–139
gene(s), **14**, 13–14, **206**, **502**, **503**
    dominant/recessive, 205
    errors in, 14–15
    tobacco use and, **304**
gene therapy, **510**, 510–511
general adaptation syndrome (GAS), **37**, 38, 39
generalized anxiety disorder (GAD), **75**
generic drugs, 618–619, **619**, 628
genetic diseases, 204
    ethnicity and, 205
    preimplantation genetic diagnosis and, 210
    susceptibility to, 207
genetically modified (GM) foods, 368
genetically modified organism (GMO), **368**
genetics
    body weight and, 423
    diversity and, 7
    tobacco use and, 303–304
genital herpes, 539–540, **572**, 573
genital self examination, 577
genital warts, **570**
genome, **14**, 14
geography, statistics on residential, 12
geriatricians, 696, **697**
germ cells, **124**, **125**
gerontologists, 696, **697**
gestation period, 206
gestational diabetes (GDM), **223**, 421
GHB (gammahydroxybutyrate), 252, 670
giardiasis, **543**
GIFT. *See* gamete intrafallopian transfer
gingivitis, 313
glaciers, global warming effect on, 592, 593
glans, **126**
glaucoma, **683**
global warming, 14, **590**, **591**, 591–592, 593
glucose, **337**
glycemic index, **338**
glycogen, **337**
GMO. *See* genetically modified organism
goal-setting, behavior change, 22–23
gonads, **124**, **125**
gonococcal conjunctivitis, **569**
gonorrhea, **568**, 568–569
government aid, aging and, 696
government, health insurance programs, 641
grains, 352–353. *See also* whole grains
greenhouse effect, 14, **590**, **591**, 591–592
greenhouse gases, **590**, **591**
    sources of, 591
grief, 690, **717**, 717–720
    in children, 720–721
ground-level ozone, 590

Guillain-Barré syndrome, 362, 364
Guttmacher Institute, 162, 179
Gynecology Devices Panel, 175

HAART (highly active antiretroviral therapy), 562
habits, health, 13, 16–17, 49. *See also* diet(s)
habituation, **236, 237**
hallucinations, 82, **284,** 285
hallucinogens, **256,** 257–258, 261
hangover, alcohol, 276
hantavirus, 545
hardiness, personality, **36**
harm-reduction strategies, 263
Harvard Healthy Eating Pyramid, 352, 377
hate crimes, 663
Hatha yoga, 53, 54
hazardous waste, 603–606
HCG (human chorionic gonadotropin), **211,** 216
HCM (hypertrophic cardiomyopathy), **474**
HCV (hepatitis C virus), 280
HDL (high-density lipoprotein), 310, **334,** 389,
    427, **456,** 463–464, 478
headaches, 9, 42
health. *See also* environmental health; psychological
    health; wellness
    contraception and, 180
    defined, **2, 3**
    disparities, **6,** 6–12
    environmental, 585–612, **586**
    fats and, 334–335
    habits, 13, 16–17, 49
    profile, 626
health care, 158. *See also* health insurance
    access to, 15
    caregiving, 694–695, **706,** 707
    cost of, 638–642
    drug use and, 260
    ethnicity and, 12
    gender and, 624
    home medical care kit, 619
    proxy, 710, **711**
health care professionals, in U. S., 623
health information, evaluating, 18, 622
health insurance, 638, 639–642
    fee-for-service plans, 639
    government programs for, 641
    policy selection, 641–642
    uninsured Americans, 640
Health maintenance organizations (HMOs), 640,
    641
health news, evaluating, 622
health savings accounts (HSAs), 640–641, **641**
health span, **691**
health-related fitness, **380**
Healthy Eating Pyramid, Harvard, 352, 377
Healthy People, 6–7
hearing loss, aging and, 685–686
heart
    cardiovascular system and, 450–451
    circulation in, 451, 452
    congenital heart defects, **474**
heart attack, **466,** 466–470
    ethnicity and, 12
    gender differences in, 9
    myocardial infarction, **310,** 466
heart disease, 391, 466–470. *See also* cardiovascular
    disease
    anger/hostility and, 459
    angina pectoris, **467**
    arrhythmias, **467**
    diagnosis/treatment of, 468–470
    hormone therapy and, 132
    pulmonary, 310
    tobacco use and, 309–310
    vitamin deficiencies linked to, 340
heavy metal, **598, 599**

height, gender and, 9
Heimlich maneuver, **657**
helmets, bicycle, 655
helper T cells, **522–523**
hematologist, **488, 489**
hemochromatosis, 205
hemorrhagic stroke, **471,** 471–472
hepatitis, 540–541, **541, 574**
hepatitis B, 574–575
hepatitis C virus (HCV), 280
herbal remedies, 435, 615, 635
heredity, 13
    cancer and, 501, 503
    cardiovascular disease and, 460–461
heroin, 247, 249
herpes simplex virus (HSV) types 1/2, 539–540,
    572–573
    genital herpes, **572,** 573
herpesviruses, **538**
heterosexual, **110**
heterosexuality, **141**
hierarchy of needs, **64**
high blood pressure, 389, 453–455
high, from drug use, **248**
high-density lipoprotein (HDL), 310, **334,** 389,
    427, **456,** 463–464, 478
highly active antiretroviral therapy (HAART), 562
hippocampus, 41
histamine, **523**
history
    abortion, 186, 187
    family, 13
HIV. *See* human immunodeficiency virus
HIV antibody test, **560**
HIV infection, **552,** 553–566. *See also* acquired
    immune deficiency syndrome; HIV/AIDS
    definition of, 553–555
    diagnosis of, 560
    DNA and, 553
    education programs, 566
    gonorrhea and, **568,** 568–569
    mother-child transmission of, 557
    phases of, 553–555, 563
    populations of special concern for, 557–558
    pregnancy and, 563–564
    revealing to partner of, 565
    sexual contact and, 555–556, 557–558
    symptoms of, 558–559
    transmission of, 555–558, 572
    untreated, general pattern of, 556
    vaccine for, 564–565
HIV RNA assay, **559**
HIV/AIDS, **552,** 552–570
    cost of, economic, 564
    global summary, 553, 554, 555
    number people living with, 555
    prevention of, 565–566, 567
    reporting cases of, 560, 562
    treatment of, 562–566
HIV-positive, **560,** 565
HMOs (health maintenance organizations), 640,
    641
Hodgkin's disease, 501
home
    hazardous wastes in, 605–606
    injuries, **654,** 654–657
    radiation in, 607–608
home care
    end-of-life care options, 706
    home medical care kit, 619
home pregnancy test kit, 210
homeopathy, 632–633, **633**
homeostasis, **33**
homeostatic resiliency, 36
homicide, 662–663
homocysteine, 464

homophobia, 110
homosexual, **110**
homosexuality, **141,** 142, 576
honesty, 100
hormonal method, contraception, **154, 155**
hormone(s), **32**
    body weight and, 424
    follicle-stimulating, 129
    luteinizing, 129
    sexual differentiation and, 128
    sexual orientation and, 142
    stress, **48**
hormone replacement therapy (HRT), 462
    cancer and, 492
hormone therapy (HT), 131–132
hospice, **706,** 707
hospitalist, 627
hotlines
    air quality information, 611
    alcohol abuse, 295
    drug use, 268
    emergency contraception, 182
    food safety, 371
    STDs, 581
    tobacco use, 323, 326
    violence, 676
HPV. *See* human papillomavirus
HRT. *See* hormone replacement therapy
HSAs (health savings accounts), 640–641, **641**
HT (hormone therapy), 131–132
human chorionic gonadotropin (HCG), **211,** 216
human immunodeficiency virus (HIV), 536, 546,
    552. *See also* HIV infection
    birth control pills and, 157
    circumcision and, 126, 556
    contraception methods and, 170
    ethnicity and, 11
    sexual orientation and, 12
human papillomavirus (HPV), 495–496, 541–542,
    570, 570–572
    diagnosis of, 572
hunger condition, 349
hydrogenation, **333**
hydrostatic weighing, 419
hymen, **124, 125**
hypertension, 391, **453.** *See also* high blood
    pressure
hypertrophic cardiomyopathy (HCM), **474**
hypertrophy, **457**
hypnosis, **634**
hypothalamus, **127**
hysterectomy, **174, 175**

"I" statements, 105
ICSI. *See* intracytoplasmic sperm injection
identical twins, **206**
identity
    crisis, **67**
    development of adult, **66,** 66–67
    gender, **138,** 138–139
IDU. *See* injection drug use
IED (intermittent explosive disorder), 72–73
illness
    foodborne, 362, 364–365
    sexuality during, 140
immune system, **521,** 521–530
    allergies and, **526,** 527–530
    cancer and, 546
    chain of infection, 520–521
    exercise and, 390
    gender differences in, 9
    immune response in, 523–525
    immunization, **526,** 526–527
    immunological defenders in, 522–523
    inflammatory response of, **523**
    mother's, sexual orientation and, 142

pathogens/disease and, 530–546
PNI and, 40
relationships influence on, 114
stress and, 573
supporting, 546–547
symptoms/contagion, 525–526
T cells, 522–524, **523**
immunity, 525, 548
stress and, 548, 573
immunization, **526**, 526–527
immunotherapy, 530
implants, contraceptive, 160
impotence, from smoking, 312
in vitro fertilization (IVF), **208**
incest, **672**
income inequality, 11–12
incontinence, **495**
incubation, virus, **525**
indemnity plans. *See* fee-for-service plans
induction chemotherapy, **509**
inequality, income/education, 11–12
infants
    ETS and, 316
    HSV in, 573
    infant mortality, **224**
infatuation, 98
infection, **521**. *See also* HIV infection; sexually
        transmitted diseases
    chain of, 520–521
    hospital errors and, 627
    opportunistic, **554**, 563
    sexually transmitted, **552**
    streptococcal, 532
    systemic, **521**
    vaginal, 543
infectious agents, cardiovascular disease and, 464
infectious diseases, **3**, 204, 586. *See also* HIV
        infection
    amebic dysentery, 543
    antibiotics for treating, 535
    bacteria causing, **530**, 530–542
    chicken pox, 538–539
    Clostridium difficile, 534
    cold sores, 539–540
    common cold, 536–537
    contagion in, 525–526, 536
    emerging, 534, 544–546
    encephalitis, **540**
    fungus, **542**, 542–543
    giardiasis, **543**
    hepatitis, 540–541, **541**
    herpes simplex virus (HSV) types 1/2,
        539–540
    human papillomavirus, 495–496, 541–542
    influenza, **537**, 537–538
    malaria, **543**
    measles/mumps/rubella, 538
    meningitis, **531–532**
    parasites, **536**, 553, **576**
    parasitic worms, **543**
    pertussis, 534
    pneumonia, **530**, 530–531
    poliomyelitis, **541**
    poliovirus, 536
    prions, **544**
    protozoa, **543**
    rabies, 541
    staphylococcus, **532**
    strep throat/streptococcal infections, **532**, **532**
    symptoms for, overview of, 538
    tetanus, 534
    tickborne infections, 533–534
    toxic shock syndrome, **168**, **169**, 532
    transmission of, 520–521
    trichomoniasis, 543
    trypanosomiasis, 543

tuberculosis, **532**, 532–533
    ulcers, 312, 534
    viral encephalitis, 540
    viruses, **535**, 535–542
infertility, **206**, 208–209
    treatment for, 208–209
inflammation, 465
    cardiovascular disease and, 461
inflammatory response, **523**
influenza, **537**, 537–538, 539
inhalants, 258–259
inhaling, tobacco smoke, 308
injectable contraceptives, 160–161
injectable naltrexone (Vivtrol), 287
injection drug use (IDU), 246, 557
injection of cytoplasm, 210
injuries, 648–659
    alcohol-related, 277, 651
    back, 659
    causes of, 648–649
    emergency care for, 674
    exercise-related, 407–409
    falls, 654–655
    fires, 596, 655–656
    gender and, 649
    home, **654**, 654–657
    intentional v. unintentional, 648
    leisure, **657**
    motor vehicle, **650**, 650–654
    motorcycles/mopeds, 653
    pedestrian, 654
    poisoning, 656
    prevention of, 390
    repetitive strain, **659**
    scooter, 658
    skating, in-line, 657–658
    smoking causing, 312
    suffocation/choking, 657
    unintentional, **648**, 648–659
    work, **658**, 658–659
in-line skating injuries, 657–658
insemination
    artificial, **208**, 208–209
    intrauterine, 208
insoluble fiber, **339**
insomnia, 48, 50
Institute of Medicine, 335
insulin resistance, 461–464
insurance. *See* health insurance
intact dilation and extraction, 194
intellectual wellness, 383
intensity, exercise, 393, 397–398
intentional injuries, **648**. *See also* violence
intercourse. *See* sexual intercourse
interferons, 524
interleukins, 524
intermittent explosive disorder (IED), 72–73
internal stressors, 44
Internet addiction, 239
interpersonal stress, 41
interpersonal violence. *See* violence
interpersonal wellness, **3**, 383
intestate, **704**
intimate relationships, 95–121
    capacity for, **65**
    challenges in, 99–101
    choosing partner, 107
    commitment and, 98, 100, 113–114, 116, 120
    communication in, 103–107
    conflict/conflict resolution in, 104–107
    dating, 107–108, 109, 242
    developing, 67, 96–103
    ending, 102–103
    friendship and, 97–98
    interfaith/intrafaith, 108
    jealousy in, 101

love/sex/intimacy in, 98–99, 120
    same-sex, 110–111
    self-concept/self-esteem in, 96–97
    unhealthy, 101–102
intolerances, food allergies and, **368**, 368–369
intoxication, **236**, 245–246
intracerebral hemorrhage, 472
intracytoplasmic sperm injection (ICSI), 210
intrauterine device (IUD), **163**, 163–164, 176, 180
intrauterine insemination, 208
involuntary euthanasia, 709
iron
    cardiovascular disease and, 464
irreversibility, death and, 703
isometric exercises, **396–397**
isotonic exercises, **397**
IUD (intrauterine device), **163**, 163–164, 176, 180
IVF. *See* in vitro fertilization

jaundice, 541
jealousy, 101
job-related stressors, 42–43
journaling, 23, 56
    on stressor identification, 57

Kaposi's sarcoma, 540, **560**
ketamine, 252
kidney cancer, 500
killer T cells, **522–523**
kilocalories, **330**, 331
Koop, C. Everett, 197
Kübler-Ross, Elizabeth, 714

labels
    dietary supplement, 362, 363
    food/dietary supplement, 360–362, 363, 368
    GM food, 368
    nutrient claims on, 361
    "organic," 365
    OTC medications, 618–619
    USP verification on, 363
labor, **225**
    contractions, **225**
    delivery and, 225–228
    first stage of, 225
    pain relief during, 227
    preterm, 223
    second stage of, 225–226
    third stage of, 226–227
    transition stage of, **225**
labor induction, **194**, 223
lactation, **228**
lacto-ovo-vegetarians, **356**
lactose intolerance, 205
lacto-vegetarian, **356**
land, population and, 588
laparoscopy, **174**, 174–175
Latinos/Latinas, 8, 45
    alcohol use by, 288–289
    cancer incidence in, 502
    drug use/dependence among, 261
    health care for, 12
    health concerns of, 8–9
    HIV/AIDS among, 557, 558
    sexual behavior and, 143
    stress and, 45
    testicular cancer among, 500
    tobacco use among, 301
LBW. *See* low birth weight
LDL (low-density lipoprotein), **334**, 389, **455**, 464,
        477
lead, 603–604
Lea's Shield, 169
legal consequences
    drug use/abuse, 246, 260
    drunk driving, 279

legislation. *See also* government aid, aging and
abortion, 186–188, 193
anti-tobacco, 318–321
artificial trans fats, 334
dietary supplement, 363
double effect, **709**
drug use, 242, 260
emergency contraception, 162
environmental tobacco smoke, 318, 596
firearms, 673–674
indoor air pollution, 596
life-sustaining treatment, 707–708
Master Settlement Agreement on, 317
legumes, **331**
leisure
injuries, **657**
statistics on, 47
leisure time, aging and, 684
leukemia, **488, 489**, 500–501, 504
leukoplakia, 313
Levitra. *See* vardenafil
Levonorgestral IUD (Mirena), 163
life cycle, virus, 524
life expectancy, 6, 690–692, **691**
gender differences in, 9
life purpose, 67
life span, 690–691, **691**
lifestyle, **4**
aging and, 680–683
assessment of, 16–17
body weight and, 424–425
cancer and, 512–513
college students and, 13
culture and, 10–11
death causes and, 4, 5
leisure time statistics and, 47
for successful weight management, 426–432
weight management strategies, 433
wellness, 15–26
life-support systems, **703**, 707–708
light bulbs, compact fluorescent, 596, 597
lightening, **213**
lipoproteins, 310, **334**, 389, 427, **455**, 464, 477
liposuction, 438
listening, communication skill, 90, 103, 105
Listeria monocytogenes, 364
liver, 455. *See also* hepatitis
disease, 280
inflammation of, 574
living will, **709**, 710
lobbying, tobacco, 319
locus of control, **19**
loneliness, 72
loss of control
addictive behavior, 237
nicotine and, 302–303
love
addiction to sex and, 239
commitment and, 98, 100, 113–114, 116, 120
intimacy/sex and, 98–99, 120
pleasure/pain of, 98–99
transformation of, 99
low birth weight (LBW), **224**, 316
low-back pain, 390
low-carbohydrate diets, 434
low-density lipoprotein (LDL), **334**, 389, **455**, 464, 477
low-fat diets, 434
loyalty, friendship and, 97
LSD (lysergic acid diethylamide), 252, 258
lung cancer, 309, 310–311, 489–490
asbestos causing, 603
diagnosis/treatment of, 489–490
ETS cause of, 315
risk factors for, 489
smoking and, 310–311, 489, 504–505

luteinizing hormone (LH), 129
Lyme disease, 533–534
lymphatic system, **486**, 522
lymphocytes, **522**
lymphoma, **488, 489**, 501
lysergic acid diethylamide (LSD), 252

ma huang (ephedra), 401
macronutrient, **331**
macrophages, 311, **522**
magnetic resonance imaging (MRI), **469**, 509
mainstream smoke, **315**
maintenance, behavior change, 21, 25–26
malaria, **543**
males
aging male syndrome in, 132
alcohol abuse by, 288
caloric intake for, 347
condoms for, **164**, 164–165, 178, 565, 567, 578
infertility in, 208
menopause in, 132
motivation for drug use, 243
sex organs of, 125–127
sexual maturation in, 131
sterilization and, 173–174
malignant tumors, **486**
mammogram, **492, 493**
managed-care plans, **639**, 639–640
management, exercise program, 406–409
mania, **81**
manic depression, 77
manipulative/body-based methods, CAM and, 634–636
manual vacuum aspiration (MVA), **192**
MAOI (monoamine oxidase inhibitor), 84
marijuana, 56, 240
cannabis products, 256–257
dependence on, 257
medical, 56
physical effects from, 257
pregnancy and, 257
marital satisfaction, 117
marriage, 113–115. *See also* intimate relationships
abusive partners in, 664–668
benefits of, 113
cohabitation and, 110
family life and, 115–119
issues in, 113
median age of, 111
role of commitment in, 113–114
same-sex, 112
sterilization contraception and, 176
wellness and, 114
"mask" of pregnancy (chloasma), 157
Maslow, Abraham, 64–65
Master Settlement Agreement (MSA), 317
masturbation, **137**
mature understanding of death, **703**
maximal oxygen consumption (VO2max), **394, 395**
McDonald's, 319
MDMA. *See* methylenedioxymethamphetamine
measles/mumps/rubella, 538
meat, 355, 505
media
global warming in, 593
stress from, 45
tobacco use as emulating, 305–306
violence in, 661
Medicaid, **641**
medical abortion, 194–195
medical doctor, **623**
medical marijuana, 56
medical radiation, 607
medical treatment, 625–629

Medicare, **641**
medications. *See also* drug(s), defined; drug use
abortifacients, **161**, 191–192
aging and, 683
alcoholism treatment, 287
allergy, 530
anti-acne, 221
anti-angiogenesis, 512
anti-dementia, 84
anti-dementia drugs, 84
antidepressant, 84, 136–137
antipsychotics, 84
antiviral, HIV/AIDS treatment with, 562, 563
Canadian, 628
Death with Dignity Act and, 708
drug dependence and, 262, 683
errors in, 626, 627
fetus harmed by certain, 203
generic, 618–619, **619**, 628
HIV, 562
MAOI, 84
marijuana as, 257
medical abortion, 195
mood stabilizers, 84
nitrate, 137
over-the-counter, 161, 166, 363, 530, **617**, 619
pain-relief, 249, 709
PMS/PMDD, 130
pregnancy and, 203
resistance to, 545
sleep, 48, 145
taking, 627
Viagra-like, 133
medicine, 615–644
complementary, **619**, 619–620, 629–638
conventional, 620–629
diagnostic process and, 625
professional care, 619–620
self-care and, 616–619
self-medication and, 617–619
meditation, **52**, 53
Mediterranean diet, 352
melanoma, **496, 497**, 498
memorial service, 711–713, 714
memory T/B cells, **523**
men
communication advice for, 106
injuries among, 649
nutritional needs of, 359
sexual assault and, 669–670
suicide in older, 690
transsexual, 138
menarche, **128, 129**
meningitis, **531–532**
menopause, **131**
male, 132
menses, **129**
menstrual cycle, **128**, 128–131, **129**
amenorrhea/absence of, **423**
estrogenic phase of, **129**
four phases of, 128–130, 148
menses in, **129**
ovulation in, **129**, 155
pregnancy symptoms and, 211
progestational phase of, **130**
menstrual problems
dysmenorrhea, **130**
mental health. *See* psychological health
menthol
cigarettes, 308
mercury, 604–605
metabolic rate, 387
metabolic syndrome, 388, 427, 461–464
metabolism
alcohol, **272, 273**, 273–274
body weight and, 424

endurance exercise for efficient, 387
nicotine, 303–304, 308
metastasis, **486**
methamphetamine, 240
methicillin-resistant staphylococcus aureus
    (MRSA), 532, 533
Methotrexate, 195
methylenedioxymethamphetamine (MDMA), 252
methylphenidate (Ritalin), 255
MFPR (multi-fetal pregnancy reduction), **194**
MI (myocardial infarction), **310**
microbes, 506
microbicide, **564**
micronutrients, **330, 331**
    vitamins/organic, 340
middle knowledge, **713**, 713–714
mifepristone (RU-486), 187, 195
migraines, 42
milk, 354–355
mind-body interventions, 633–634
mindfulness, 101
mindfulness meditation, 52
minerals, **342**, 343
minority, America's aging, 692
Mirena (Levonorgestral IUD), 163
miscarriage, **186**, 222–223
    Clostridium sepsis from, 195
    environmental factors in, 189
misoprostol, 195
mitral valve prolapse (MVP), **474**
MM (multiple myeloma), 501
mode of activity, exercise principle, 393
models, therapeutic change, 83–87
    behavioral, 85
    biological, 83–85
    cognitive, 85–86
    combining, 87
    psychodynamic, 87
Moderation Management, 286
mold, 596
moments of relaxation, 49
monoamine oxidase inhibitor (MAOI), 84
mood disorders, 74, **78**, 78–81
    depression, **78**, 78–81
    mania/bipolar, **81**
    SAD, **80**, 80–81
mood stabilizers, 84
morbid obesity, 437
mother-child transmission, HIV, 557
mothers, age of first-time, 202
motivation
    for change, 19–20, 25
    drug use, 243–244
    quitting smoking, 322
    tobacco use, 302–306
motor vehicle injuries, **650**, 650–654
motorcycles/mopeds, 653
mourning, 718–719, **719**
MRSA (methicillin-resistant staphylococcus au-
    reus), 532, 533
MSA (Master Settlement Agreement), 317
mucus method, fertility awareness methods, 172
multi-fetal pregnancy reduction (MFPR), **194**
multiple births, 204
multiple myeloma (MM), 501
multiple sclerosis, 547
mumps, 538
murmur, **474**
muscular endurance, **381**, 396–399
muscular strength, **380**, 396–399, 401, 402
music, relaxation technique, 54
mutagens, **503**
mutuality, friendship and, 97
MVA (manual vacuum aspiration), **192**
MVP (mitral valve prolapse), **474**
mycoplasmas, **530**

myocardial infarction (MI), **310**, 466
MyPyramid, **345**, 351–357
    calories/fats/sugar and, 355–356
    fruits and, 354
    grains in, 352–353
    key messages of, 352
    meat/beans and, 355
    milk, 354–355
    oils and, 355
    self assessment according to, 357
    vegetables and, 354
myths
    abortion, 197
    contraception, 155
    suicide, 82

NA (Narcotics Anonymous), 262–263
Naltrexone, 287
Narcotics Anonymous (NA), 262–263
National Cholesterol Education Program (NCEP),
    475, 478
National Highway Traffic Safety Administration
    (NHTSA), 652, 676
National Institute for Occupational Safety and
    Health (NIOSH), 58
National Institute of Mental Health (NIMH), 58
National Institutes of Health (NIH), 632, 634
National Weight Control Registry, 434
Native Americans. *See* American Indians
Native Hawaiians, 11, 261. *See also* ethnicity
natural killer cells, **522**
natural method, contraception, **154, 155**
NCEP (National Cholesterol Education Program),
    475, 478
nervous system, 32, 81
neurotransmitters, **247**
neutrophils, **522**
NHL (non-Hodgkin's lymphoma), 501
NHTSA (National Highway Traffic Safety Adminis-
    tration), 652, 676
nicotine, **302**, 307, 313
    addiction to, 302–303, 305, 314
    clove cigarettes/bidis, 314
    loss of control and, 302–303
    metabolism of, 303–304, 308
    replacement, 313, 323
NIH (National Institutes of Health), 632, 634
nitrate medications, 137
nitrogen dioxide (NO2), 590
nitrous oxide, 591
nocturnal emissions (wet dream), 138, **139**
noise pollution, 608–609
noncorporeal continuity, **703**
nonfunctionality, death and, 703
non-Hodgkin's lymphoma (NHL), 501
non-rapid eye movement (non-REM) sleep, **47**
nonreactive resiliency, 36
nonverbal communication, 103
norepinephrine, **32**
normality, compared with psychological health, **65**
Norovirus, 364
Northern Europeans, 8, 205
nuclear power, **606**, 606–607, **607**
nuclear transfer, ART, 210
nutrition, 56, **330**, 330–372
    antioxidants, **340**, 343–344
    calories and, 330–331, 347
    carbohydrates, 336–339, **337**, 349
    DASH diet, 351–352, 377, 454, 478
    diet planning for, 345–359
    Dietary Guidelines for Americans, **345**, 346–351,
        454
    Dietary Reference Intakes, **345**, 345–346, 351,
        374–376
    DRIs for, **345**, 345–346
    energy and, 330

essential nutrients and, **330**, 330–343
ethnic foods and, 348
fast-food restaurant eating strategy for, 360
fats and, 333–337, 347, 349, 350, 355–356
fiber, 339–342
fish-consumption guidelines, 367
food allergy/intolerance, **368**, 368–369
gender differences in, 359
genetically modified foods and, 368
healthy diet components and, 330–345
Healthy Eating Pyramid, 352, 377
kilocalories, **330, 331**
labeling of foods/dietary supplements, 360–362,
    363, 368
minerals, **342**, 343
for older adults, 358
personal food plan for, 359–370
prenatal, 219
six classes of essential nutrients, **330**
stress management through, 47

OA. *See* osteoarthritis
obesity, 385, 391, **416, 417**, 426, 437. *See also*
    body fat; weight management
    aging and, 683
    BMI for determining, **416, 417**, 417–418, 422
    cancer and, 490, 505–506
    cardiovascular disease and, 457
    deaths from, 1, 419
    Dietary Guidelines for Americans for, 346–347
    ethnicity and, 425
    type 2 diabetes and, 419
    waist circumference and, 417, 422, 423
obsession, **76**
obsessive-compulsive disorder (OCD), **76**
Occupational Safety and Health Administration
    (OSHA), 608–609, 658
occupational wellness, **4**
OCD (obsessive-compulsive disorder), **76**
OCs. *See* oral contraceptives
oils, 355
omega-3 fatty acids, **334**, 477
oncogenes, **503**
oncologist, **488, 489**
one drink, **272**
online pornography, 146
online relationships, 109
openness, 100
opioids, **248, 249**
opportunistic infection, **554, 563**
opposite-sex twins, 128
optimism, 71
optometrist, **623**
oral cancer, 313, 498, 500
oral contraceptives (OCs), 130, **156**, 156–158,
    157, 176
oral-genital stimulation, 144
organ donors, 710–711, 712
organic foods, **365**, 365–367. *See also* micronutrients
organizations, websites and
    aging-related, 698–699
    alcohol use, 295
    cancer, 516
    cardiovascular disease information, 479–480
    childbirth-related, 231
    communication/intimacy, 121
    contraception-related, 182
    death/dying-related, 723
    drug use, 267–268
    environmental health, 611–612
    infectious diseases, 549
    injuries/violence, 676–677
    leading health, physical activity
        recommendations by, 385
    nutrition-related, 371–372
    physical fitness-related, 411

organizations, websites and (continued)
   preconception care/pregnancy-related, 231
   sexuality resources, 149–150
   STDs-related, 581
   tobacco use, 326–327
   weight management-related, 445–446
orgasm, 132–133, **134**
orgasmic dysfunction, **136**
orgasmic phase, sexual response cycle, 134
OSHA. *See* Occupational Safety and Health Administration
osteoarthritis (OA), 686
osteoporosis, 342, **342**, 380, 389, 391, **688**
OTC. *See* over-the-counter medications
outpatient, **629**
ovarian cancer, 496
ovary, **125**, 210
overgeneralizing, 7
overload, 392–393
over-the-counter (OTC) medications, 161, 166, 363, 530, **617**, 619
ovulation, **129**, 155
ovum, **125**
ozone, ground-level, 590
ozone layer, **592**, 594

pacemaker, 451
Pacific Islander Americans
   cancer incidence in, 502
   drug use/dependence among, 261
   health concerns of, 11
   tobacco use among, 301
PAD (peripheral arterial disease), **473**
pain relief
   during labor, 227
   medications, 249, 709
pairing, singlehood and, 107–113
palliative care, **706**
pancreatic cancer, 500
pandemic, influenza, 539
panic disorder, **74**
Pap test, **157**, **495**, 495–496, 577
papillomavirus, 157
ParaGard (Copper T-380A), 163
paraphilia, 145
parasites, **536**, **576**
   ecto-, 553
parasitic worms, **543**
parasomnia, 145
parasympathetic division, **32**
parents/parenting, 115–118
   becoming, 115–116
   environmental values instilled by, 119
   family life cycle in, 117
   preparation for, 202–204
   single, 117–118
   styles of, 116–117
   wellness and, 202
The Partial Birth Abortion Ban Act, 187
partial vegetarians, **356**
particulate matter (PM), 590
partners
   abusive, 664–668
   choosing, 107
   civil unions/ same-sex marriage and, 112
   communication about safer sex/condoms with, 579
   contraception communication with, 177
   deciding to be sexual with, 140
   expectations of, 100–101
   HIV-positive, revealing by, 565
   informing, STDs and, 565, 577–578
   physician-patient, 624–625
   same-sex, 110–111
   separation/divorce and, 114–115
   support during pregnancy from, 212, 213

PAS (physician-assisted suicide), 708–709, **709**
passion, 98–99
passive euthanasia, 708, **709**
pathogens, **362**, **520**, 530–546
   sexually transmitted diseases associated, 553
PCBs (polychlorinated biphenyls), **365**
PCP, hallucinogen, 258
peer counseling, 88, 262–263
pelvic inflammatory disease (PID), 136, 157, **569**, 569–570
penis, **125**
PEP (postexposure prophylaxis), 562
percent body fat, **416**, 417
performance-enhancing drugs, 401
peripheral arterial disease (PAD), **473**
permanent contraception, **172**, 172–175
permissiveness, parental, 116–117
persistent vegetative state, **706**, 706–707
personal contract, behavior change, 24–25
personal flotation device, **657**
personal health profile, 626
personal safety, 17, 646–677
   CAM and, 637
   food, 371
   food handling, 366
   sex, 147, 565
personality
   stress and, **35**, 35–36
   type A, B, and C, 35–36
   type D, 459
personalized plans
   behavior change, 22–25
   stress management, 56–57
pertussis, 534
pescovegetarians, **356**
pesticides, 127, 366, 604, **604**
pharmaceuticals, 620–621, **621**
pharmacological properties
   drugs, **247**
pharmacological therapy, issues in use of, 84–85
pharmacology, **240**, **241**
pharmacopoeia, **634**
pharmacy, **240**, **241**
phobia
   simple, **74**
   social, **74**
   specific, **74**
phthalates, 127
physical abuse, 664–668
physical activity, 347, 382–386, **383**. *See also* exercise
   cardiovascular disease and, 388–389, 457
   classifying levels of, 386
   continuum concept of, 383–385
   making time for, 387
   recommended amounts of, 385–386
   stress management and, 433
   weight management and, 384, 431
physical changes, aging, 685–688
physical dependence, **241**
physical fitness, 380–386. *See also* exercise; exercise program
   aging and, 682
   amount of physical activity for, 385–386
   assessment of, 380–386
   body composition in, **381**
   cardiorespiratory endurance and, **380**, 386, 395–396, 401, 402
   definition of, 380–382
   fitness centers, 404
   flexibility in, **381**
   muscular strength/endurance in, **381**, 396–399, 401, 402
   skill-related, **382**
   sports/fitness activity summary, 402–403
physical wellness, 2, 3, 383

physician-assisted suicide (PAS), 708–709, **709**
physician-patient partnership, 624–625
physicians, 616–617, 623–624, 625, 634, 637–638, 642
physiological factors, body weight, 424
physiology, gender differences in, 38
phytochemicals, **344**, 344–345, **345**, **504**, **505**
PID. *See* pelvic inflammatory disease
pinworms, 543
pipe smoking, 310, 314
pituitary gland, **127**
PKC enzyme, 40
placebo, 83
   effect, **248**, 633
placenta, 215
placenta previa, **223**
placental abruption, **223**
Plan B, contraceptives, 161, 162, 166
Planned Parenthood, 162
plant stanols/sterols, 477
plant sterols. *See* plant stanols/sterols
plaques, **308**, **309**, 466
plateau phase, sexual response cycle, 134
platelets, **453**
PM. *See* particulate matter
PMDD (premenstrual dysphoric disorder), **130**, **131**
PMS (premenstrual syndrome), **130**
Pneumocystis pneumonia, **560**
pneumonia, **530**, 530–531
   Pneumocystis, **560**
PNI (psychoneuroimmunology), **39**, 40
podiatrist, **623**
Point-of-service (POS) plans, 640, **641**
Poison Control Center, 656
poisoning, 656
   alcohol, 276
   lead, 603
poliomyelitis, **541**
poliovirus, 536
pollution. *See also* air pollution; chemical pollution
   cancers from, 506–508
   chemical, 306, 308, 316, 366, 506–507, 603–606
   noise, 608–609
   radiation, **606**, 606–608
   solid waste, 599–603
   water quality and, 597–599
polychlorinated biphenyls (PCBs), **365**, 598
polypeptide supplements, 401
polyps, **490**
population(s)
   aging, increase in, 692
   current/rate of, 585
   energy resources and, 588, 589
   food and, 587–588
   growth, 585, 587–589
   HIV infection special concern, 557–558
   land/water resources and, 588
   special, dietary challenges for, 358–359
   special health concerns, 358–359, 391, 557–558
   U. S., 587, 589
pornography, **146**
portion sizes, 355, 357, 429
POS (Point-of-service) plans, 640, **641**
positive attitude, 49, **49**, 51. *See also* self-concept
positive growth resiliency, 36
postexposure prophylaxis (PEP), 562
postpartum depression, **228**, 229
postpartum period, **228**, 228–229
post-traumatic stress disorder (PTSD), 40, 45, **76**, 76–77
potassium, 349, 351
poverty, 188, 243, 502, 545
   violence and, 663

PPOs (preferred provider organizations), 640, **641**
preconception care, 203, 203–204, 231
precontemplation, **20**, 21
pre-diabetes, 421
preeclampsia, **223**
preexisting conditions, pregnancy and, 203
preferred provider organizations (PPOs), 640, **641**
pregnancy, 209–224, 230, 231
  abortion/future, 197
  age and, 203
  alcohol use during, 204, 219, 281–282
  caffeine during, 204, 220
  changes in woman's body during, 210–212
  childbirth planning during, 226
  cocaine use during, 253
  complications of, 222–224
  depression during, 213
  diet during, 220
  dietary supplements during, 220
  drug use during, 203, 219, 220–221, 253
  early stages of, 210–212
  ectopic, **222, 223**
  emotional responses to, 212–213
  environmental hazards during, 219–221
  fathers' tasks during, 213
  finance and, 213
  food safety during, 220
  genital herpes and, 573
  HIV infection and, 563–564
  infections and, 204, 563–564
  later stages of, 212
  loss of, 222–224
  marijuana use during, 257
  "mask" of, 157
  nutrition during, 219
  preexisting conditions and, 203
  premature birth, **224**
  prenatal care, 217–222
  prior, 203
  rate, 179
  signs/symptoms of, early, 211
  STDs and, 221
  tests, 210
  tobacco use during, 201, 204, 219–220, 316
  unplanned, 180–181, 190, 202
  weight gain during, 212
preimplantation genetic diagnosis, 210
premature birth, **224**
premature ejaculation, **136**
premenstrual dysphoric disorder (PMDD), **130, 131**
premenstrual syndrome (PMS), **130, 131**
premenstrual tension, **130, 131**
prenatal care, 217–222
preparation, parenthood, 202–204
prepuce, **124, 125**
presbyopia, 686, **687**
prescription drugs. *See also* medications
  spending on, annual, 628
  weight-loss, 437
president, email address, 610
preterm labor, 223
prevention
  air pollution, 596–597
  cancer, 494, 498, 512, 514
  cardiovascular disease, 470, 475–478
  chemical pollution, 606
  date rape, 670, 671
  diabetes, 421, 422
  disease management and, 388–390
  drug use, 264–265
  foodborne illness, 364–365
  hepatitis B, 574–575
  HIV infection/STDs, 565–566, 567
  HIV/AIDS, 565–566, 567
  influenza, 537

motor vehicle injury, 653
  through patient involvement, 627
  skin cancer, 498
  STDs, 567, 578–579
primary care physician, choosing, 623–624
prions, **544**
private sector, anti-tobacco action in, 319
problem solving, 50–51
processed foods, 351
  labels on, 360
  salt content of, 351
procrastinating, behavior change, 25
professional care, 619–620
professional help, for psychological disorders, 89
progestational phase, menstrual cycle, **130**
progesterone, **128, 129**
progestins, **127**
progressive overload, exercise principle, 392
progressive relaxation, **52**
proof value, **272**
prostaglandin cream, 137
prostate cancer, 494–495
prostate gland, **126**
prostate-specific antigen (PSA), **494, 495**
prostatitis, 136
prostitution, **146**
protease inhibitor, **562**
proteasome inhibitors, cancer treatment with, 512
proteins, **331,** 331–332
  AMDRs for carbohydrate/fat and, 336
  complete/incomplete, 331–332
  dietary supplement, 401
  recommended intake of, 332, 336
  soy, 477
protozoa, **543,** 553
PSA. *See* prostate-specific antigen
psychiatrists, number practicing, 88
psychoactive drugs, 235–269, **236,** 302. *See also*
      nicotine
  addictive behavior and, **236,** 236–246, 240–246
  alcohol ingredients and, 272
  alcohol use with, 277
  behavior change strategy and, 266
  club drugs, 251, 252, 557
  commonly used, 250
  cost of, economic, 259
  crime and, 259–260
  date rape drugs, 252, 670
  decision to use, 263
  dependence on, 240–241, 262–264
  depressants, **248, 249,** 249–251
  dose-response function in, **247–248**
  drug testing and, 260, 262
  drug/substance abuse definition and, **240–241**
  effects on body of, 246–249
  families/family life, 259–260, 261
  future issues for, 259–265
  gender and, 242, 243
  hallucinogens, **256,** 257–258, 261
  health care and, 260
  inhalants, 258–259
  legalization of, 242, 260
  methods of use of, 253
  motivation for using, 243–244
  opioids, **248, 249**
  pain-relief medications and, 249
  performance-enhancing, 401
  pharmacological properties of, **247**
  religion/spirituality motivation for using, 244
  representative, 249–259
  risks of, 245–246
  side effects from, unexpected, 246
  stimulants, 84, **251,** 251–256
  tolerance and, **241**
  unknown contents in, 246
  user/nonuser profiles, 241–243

psychodynamic model, 87
psychological abuse, 664–668
psychological disorders, 73–92
  ADHD, **84**
  agoraphobia, **74**
  anxiety disorder, 73–78
  choosing mental health professional, 89
  dysthymic disorder, 78
  ethnicity and, 75
  medications for, 84
  models for therapeutic change, 83–87
  mood disorder, **74**
  mood disorders, **74,** 78–81
  nerve cell communication and, 81
  panic disorder, **74**
  professional help for, 89
  schizophrenia, **82,** 82–83
  self-help for, 87–88
  summary of, 89–90
psychological distress, suppression of, 459
psychological health, 63–91, **64**
  achieving self-esteem in, 68–70
  anger and, 72–73
  communication and, 71–72
  defining, **64**–66
  growing up and, 66–67
  intimacy and, 65, 67
  loneliness and, 72
  normality v., 65
  optimism and, 71
  self-actualization and, 64–65
  values and, 67
psychological normality, **65**
psychology
  aging and, 688–690
  stress and, 40
psychoneuroimmunology (PNI), **39,** 40
psychosis, 255
psychosocial factors, body weight, 425–426
psychotherapy, 57, 79
PTSD (post-traumatic stress disorder), 40, 45, **76,**
      76–77
puberty, **128, 129**
pubic lice, **576, 577**
public health systems, 5
Puerto Rican Americans, 10
  tobacco use among, 301
pulmonary circulation, **450**
pulmonary disease, chronic obstructive, 311
pulmonary edema, **473**
pulmonary heart disease, 310
purging, **441**

Qigong, 636–637, **637**
QMS. *See* quadruple marker screen
quadruple marker screen (QMS), **216, 217**
Quinlan, Karen Ann, 707
quitting, tobacco use, 321–325
  benefits of, 321
  options for, 321–325

R. J. Reynolds Tobacco Company, 307
rabies, 541
race, STD rates by, 566
racial discrimination, 11, 44
radiation, **607.** *See also* ultraviolet (UV) radiation
  avoiding, 608
  cancer treatment form of, 509–510
  in home/workplace, 607–608
  medical uses of, 607
  pollution, **606,** 606–608
radiation sickness, **606, 607**
radon, **607**
rainforests, 588
rape. *See* sexual assault
rapid eye movement (REM), **47**

Rational Recovery, 286
rationalization, 26, 305
RDA. *See* Recommended Dietary Allowance
realism
    self-actualization and, **64**
    self-talk, 70
recessive gene, 205
reciprocity, friendship and, 97
Recommended Dietary Allowance (RDA), 345
recommended intake
    fat, 335–337
    protein, 332
    sodium/potassium, 349, 351
    water, 343
rectal cancer. *See* colon/rectal cancer
rectal exam, digital, 494
recycling, **600**, 600–601
refined carbohydrates, whole grains v., 337–338
refractory period, sexual response cycle, 134
regulations, trans fat, 350
Reiki, **637**
reinforcement
    addictive behavior characteristic, 237
    behavioral model, **85**
relapse, behavior change, 21–22
relationships. *See also* intimate relationships
    abusive, 664–668
    aging and, 684
    competitiveness in, 100
    depression and, 80
    immune system influenced by, 114
    online, 109
    parenthood and, 202
relaxation
    moments of, **49**
    music for, 54
    progressive, **52**
    response, **52**, 53
    techniques for, 52–55
religion, 51
    circumcision and, **126**, 556
    death and, 702
    drug use and, 244
    intimate relationships and, 108
REM (rapid eye movement), 47
repetitive strain injuries (RSIs), **659**
reporting
    HIV/AIDS, 560, 562
    sexual assault, 672
    STD, 560, 562, 568
    water contamination, 598
representative psychoactive drugs, 249–259
reproductive health problems
    female reproductive tract cancer, 495–496
    from smoking, 312
reproductive technology, 210
    artificial insemination, **208**, 208–209
    assisted, 208
research evaluation, 622
reservoir, **520**, **521**
residential geography, statistics on, 12
resiliency, 36
resistance, **38**
    exercises, **396**, **397**
resolution phase, sexual response cycle, 134
resources. *See* organizations, websites and
respect, 97
respiratory system, 250, 252, 255, 257, 300, 307, 308, 311–312, 590, 605, 627, 707
response, behavioral model, **85**
restaurants, fast-food, 360
resting metabolic rate (RMR), **424**
retarded ejaculation, **136**
retirement, 684, 693
reverse transcriptase inhibitors, **562**
reversibility, exercise principle, **394**

reversible contraception, 156–172
Rh factor, **218**, **219**
RHD (rheumatic heart disease), 474
rheumatic heart disease (RHD), 474
rheumatoid arthritis, 547
RICE (rest/ice/compression/elevation) principle, 407–409
risk factors, **2**, **3**
risk-taking behavior, 648
Ritalin (methylphenidate), 255
RMR. *See* resting metabolic rate
Roe v. Wade, 186
Rohypnol (flunitrazepam), 252, 670
role models, 20
rooming-in, **226**
rotavirus, 545
roux-en-Y gastric bypass, 438
RSIs (repetitive strain injuries), **659**
RU-486 (mifepristone), 187, 195
rubella, 538

SAD (seasonal affective disorder), 80, 80–81
SADD. *See* Students Against Destructive Decisions
safer sex, 147, 565, 579
safety. *See* personal safety
safety belts, 17, 651–653
St. John's wort, 83
salmon, omega-3 fatty acids in, 335
Salmonella, 364
salt
    processed foods and, 351
    sodium/potassium and, 349, 351
same-sex marriage
    civil unions and, 112
    states allowing, 112
same-sex partnerships, 110–111
SAMHSA (Substance Abuse and Mental Health Services Administration), 242
sanitary landfill, **600**, **601**
sarcoma, **488**, **489**, **560**
sarcopenia, 380, 682
SARS. *See* severe acute respiratory syndrome
saturated fats, 480
scabies, **576**, **577**
scanning procedures, body composition analysis, 419
schizophrenia, 21, **82**, 82–83
school violence, 663–664
scooter injuries, 658
scrotum, **125**
SDM (Standard Days Method), 171
seasonal affective disorder (SAD), 80, 80–81
second stage of labor, 225–226
secondary reinforcers, **302**, **303**
sedation, **250–251**
sedative-hypnotics, **248**, **249**, 249–251
selective estrogen-receptor modulators (SERMs), 494
selective serotonin reuptake inhibitors (SSRIs), 130
self assessment. *See* assessments, self
self-actualization, 64–65
self-assessment. *See* assessments, self
self-care, 616–619
self-concept, **64**, 68, 96–97
self-disclosure, 103, 147
self-efficacy, **19**
self-esteem, **64**, 64–65, 68–70, 96–97
self-help groups
    peer counseling and, 262–263
self-help, psychological disorders, 87–88
self-medication, 617–619
self-talk, 20, 51, 69, **69**, 70
self-treatment, 617–619
semen, **134**
seminal vesicles, 126
semivegetarians, 356

sense of humor, 51
senses, smoking causing diminished, 312
separation, divorce and, 114–115
SEPs (syringe exchange programs), 246, 263
September 11 attacks, PTSD following, 77
septic system, **598**, **599**
serial bisexuality, 141
SERMs (selective estrogen-receptor modulators), 494
serotonin re-uptake inhibitors (SSRIs), 84, 86
serving size, food labels and, 361
severe acute respiratory syndrome (SARS), 544–545
sewage, 599
sex, **8**. *See also* sexual intercourse
    addiction to love and, 239
    chromosomes, **127**
    cybersex, **146**
    defined, **8**
    enhancement products, 133
    HIV infection transmission through, 555–556, 557–558
    injuries by age and, nonfatal, 649
    love/intimacy and, 98–99, 120
    safer, 147, 565, 579
    sober, 147–148
    twins of opposite, 128
sexsomnia (sleep sex disorder), 145
sexual anatomy, 124–127
sexual arousal, 145
    female sexual arousal disorder, 137
sexual assault, 162, 163, **669**, 669–672
    alcohol use and, 277, 670
    child sexual abuse, 671–672
    date rape, **669**, 669–670, 671
    dealing with, 670–671
    effects of, 671
sexual behavior, 137–148
    agreed-on, 147
    atypical/problematic, 145
    celibacy and, **143**
    communication about, 146–147
    cunnilingus, **144**
    decision making about, 140, 143, 278
    development of, 138–140
    erotic fantasy/autoeroticism, **143**
    ethnicity and, 143
    fellatio, **144**
    foreplay, 143–144, **144**
    privacy and, 147
    prostitution and, **146**
    responsible, 146–148
    sexual coercion, **144**, **145**
    touching in, 143–144
    varieties of, 143–145
sexual coercion, **144**, **145**
sexual differentiation, hormones/brain and, 128
sexual dysfunctions, **134**, **136**, 136–137
    treating, 136–137
sexual functioning, 132–137
    masturbation and, 137
    products for enhancing, 133
    sexual stimulation and, 133–134
sexual harassment, **672**, 672–673
sexual intercourse, **144**, 144–145
    abstinence from, 143, **170**, **171**, 171–172, 176, 179, 565
    anal sex and, 144, 565
    first experience of, 175, 177
sexual maturation
    aging and, 131–132
    female, 128–131
    male, 131–132
sexual orientation, 12, **110**, 140–143
    AIDS and, 12
    androgyny and, **138–139**

origins of, 141–142
  same-sex partnerships and, 110–111
sexual problems, 135–137
  common, 135–136
  environmental factor in, 127
sexual response cycle, 134
sexual stimulation, 133–134
  physical, 133–134
  psychological, 134
sexual violence, 669–673
sexuality, **124, 125,** 137–150
  adolescent, 139–140
  adult, 140
  aging and, 131–132
  commercial, 145–146
  communication about, 147
  education for teenagers on, 178–180
  in illness/disability, 140
Sexuality Information and Education Council of the United States (SIECUS), 149
sexually transmitted diseases (STDs), **154,** 535, 551–581, **552.** *See also* acquired immune deficiency syndrome; human immunodeficiency virus
  age and, 570
  annual cases of, 552
  bacterial vaginosis, **575,** 575–576
  cancer and, 495
  chlamydia, 495, 566–568
  circumcision and, 126, 556
  condoms and, 565
  contraception and, 157, 159, 160, 167, 168, 170, 172, 173, 178
  diagnosis of, 576
  education concerns, 576
  ethnicity and, 566
  gender differences and, 9
  gonorrhea, **568,** 568–569
  hepatitis B, 574–575
  HIV infection/AIDS, **552,** 552–570
  homosexuality and, 576
  human papillomavirus, 495–496, 541–542, **570,** 570–572
  pathogens/diseases associated with, 553
  pregnancy and, 221
  prevention of, 567, 578–579
  rates by race/ethnicity for common, 566
  reporting of, 560, 562, 568
  safe sex and, 147
  self assessment for risk of, 577
  seven major, list of, 552
  symptoms of, 570, 576–577
  syphilis, **575**
  treatment of, 578
  trichomoniasis, **575**
  vaccines for, 564–565
  women and, 557, 566, 568, 576
sexually transmitted infection (STI), **552**
Shigella, 364
shock therapy. *See* electroconvulsive therapy
shopping, compulsive, 239
shyness, 90
sickle-cell disease, 8, 205
sidestream smoke, **308**
SIDS. *See* sudden infant death syndrome
SIECUS (Sexuality Information and Education Council of the United States), 149
sildenafil citrate (Viagra), 133, 137
Silicon Valley Psychotherapy Center, 149
simple phobia, **74**
single parents, 117–118
singlehood
  pairing and, 107–113
  statistics on, 111
sinoatrial node, 451
sinusitis, **312**

skating, injuries from, 657–658
skill-related fitness, **382, 383**
skin cancer, 496–499, 508
skin, immune system and, 522
skin patch, contraceptive, 158–159
skinfold measurements, 419
sleep
  deprivation, 47
  phases/mechanics of, 47
  problems, **48,** 50, 145
  REM/non-REM, **47**
  sex during, 145
sleep apnea, **48**
sleep sex disorder *(sexsomnia),* 145
sleeping pills, 48
smog, 589–591, **590**
smoke. *See* tobacco smoke
smokeless tobacco. *See* spit tobacco
smoking
  cessation products, 323
  cigar/pipe, 310, 314
  health care costs of, annual, 316
  during pregnancy, 201, 204, 219–220, 316
smoking, cigarette
  benefits of, 321
  cholesterol and, 310
  chronic bronchitis from, **310, 311**
  chronic obstructive pulmonary disease from, 311
  cigar/pipe v., 310
  cumulative effects from, 312
  effects on nonsmokers, 315–318
  emphysema from, **310, 311**
  immediate effects of, 308–312
  long-term effects of, 309–312
  lung cancer from, 310–311, 489, 504–505
  options for, 321–325
  during pregnancy, 201, 204, 219–220
  respiratory system damage from, 311–312
snacks, 515
snuff, 312–313
SO₂. *See* sulfur dioxide
sober sex, 147–148
social anxiety, behavior change for, 90
social changes, aging and, 684
social phobia, **74**
social security, 692–693, **693,** 697
social stressors, 43
social support
  spiritual wellness through, 49
  stress reduced by, 45–46
socioeconomic status
  asthma and, 604
  cancer and, 502
  cardiovascular disease and, 459
  contraceptive use and, 176
  drug use and, 248–249, 254, 261
  health insurance and, 640
  obesity and, 426
  tobacco use and, 303
  violence and, 660–661
sodas
  caffeine content in, 256
  diet, 427
sodium, 349, 351, 454, 477
solid waste. *See also* hazardous waste
  components of, 600
  disposal of, 600
  pollution, 599–603
  reducing, 602–603
  technology devices as, 601–602
soluble fibers (viscous), **339**
somatic nervous system, **35**
sonogram, **216, 217**
soul, belief in, 703
sounds, intensity of selected, 608
South Africa, 197

South Americans
  tobacco use among, 301
soy protein, 477
special health concerns
  exercise and, 391
  populations with, 358–359, 391, 557–558
species, extinct, 588
specific phobia, **74**
specificity, exercise principle, 392
Speece, Mark, 703
speeding, injuries from, 650
sperm, **124, 125,** 155
  count, normal, 126
spermicide, **164, 166, 167,** 167–169, 555
sphygmomanometer, 453
spiritual wellness, **3,** 49–50, 51
spirituality
  drug use motivation of, 244
spit tobacco (smokeless), 302, 312–314
sponge, contraceptive, 166, **169,** 169–170
spontaneous abortion (miscarriage), 186, 195, 222–223
sports activities, summary of, 402–403
squamous cell carcinoma, **497**
SSRIs (serotonin re-uptake inhibitors), 84, 86, 130
stability, self-concept and, 68
Stachybotrys mold, 596
staging, **486**
stalking, **668**
Standard Days Method (SDM), 171
standard of living, 588–589
staphylococcus, **532**
Staphylococcus aureus, 364
statistics. *See also* costs
  abortion, 185, 188, 189, 191, 193, 196–197
  adoption, 190
  alcohol use, 271, 277, 282, 283, 285
  alternative medical system use by Americans, 632
  antidepressant use, 85
  artificial insemination, 208, 209
  asbestos, 603
  back pain, 659
  bicycle crash, 653–654
  breast cancer, 492
  cancer, 488–489, 492, 494, 495, 496, 508
  cardiovascular disease, 461
  on causes of deaths among Americans, 5–6
  cell phone use while driving, 652
  cervical cancer, 495
  child sexual assault, 671–672
  children without parents, 118
  chiropractic care use, 636
  cholera, 586
  chronic disease, 692
  chronic liver disease, 280
  cohabitation, 109, 110
  college student binge drinking, 285
  college student health concerns, 13
  complementary medicine U. S. use of, 620
  confidants/friendship, 97–98
  congenital heart defects in children, **474**
  contraception, 169, 176, 178
  contraceptive failure, 173
  contraceptive risk, 159
  death causes, 1, 4, 5, 79, 280, 382
  depression, 213
  diabetes, 12, 16, 389
  dietary supplement spending, 362
  diet-related, 337
  drug use, 236, 243, 245, 247, 255, 258, 260, 262
  drunk driving, 278
  eating disorder, 439, 442, 443
  education, 261
  energy use, 589
  erectile dysfunction, 123

statistics (continued)
  ETS, 316
  evaluation of, 622
  exercise, 53, 392
  on exercise, 23
  friendship, 97–98
  gonorrhea, **568**, 569
  hate crimes, 663
  health insurance, 638, 639
  heart attack, 466–467
  heart transplant, 473
  hepatitis B, 574
  high blood pressure, 454
  HIV/AIDS, 552, 553, 554, 555, 557, 564
  hospice use, 706
  hunger condition, 349
  infectious diseases, 533–534
  inhalants use, 259
  injuries from motor vehicle crashes, 654
  injuries in U. S., unintentional, 648, 649, 654, 657, 658
  Internet addiction, 239
  lead poisoning, 603
  leisure time of adult Americans, 47
  leukemia, 501
  life expectancy, 690–691
  mammogram diagnosis success, 492
  marijuana use, 56, 257
  marriage, 110, 111
  miscarriage, 222
  motor vehicle injuries, 650–651
  nutrition, 362
  obesity, 416, 417, 437
  organ donation, 710
  osteoporosis, 688
  osteoporosis in, 342
  Pap tests, 496
  physical activity of Americans, 382
  population, 585, 587
  practicing psychiatrists, 88
  preconception care availability, 203
  pregnancy, 202, 213
  prescription drug spending in U. S., 628
  prostate cancer, 494
  psychological disorders, 78
  on psychological disorders, 73, 74
  PTSD, 77
  recycling, 600
  Ritalin, 255
  schizophrenia, 21
  separation/divorce, 115
  sexual assault, 669, 671–672
  sexual behavior, 145
  single parent, 117
  singlehood, 111
  sleeping pill prescription, 48
  sodium consumption, 349
  STDs, 568, 569, 574
  suicide rate, 79
  teen death, 4
  teenage sexual behavior, 139
  tobacco use, 1, 5, 21, 300, 302, 305, 315
  twins, 208
  uterine cancer, 496
  vegetarian diet, 358
  violence against women, 664–665
  violence in U. S., 661, 663, 664–665
  violence, interpersonal, 660
  whole grain consumption among Americans, 337
  work injuries, 658
  workplace drug abuse, 260
  workplace violence, 664
statutory rape, **669**
STDs. *See* sexually transmitted diseases
stem cells, **511**, 681

Stenberg v. Carhart, 187
stepfamilies, 118
stereotyping, 7
sterilization, **172**, 172–175, 176
  female, 174–175, 176
  male, 173–174
steroids. *See* anabolic steroids
STI. *See* sexually transmitted infection (STI)
stillbirth, 223
stimulants, CNS, 84, **251**, 251–256
  amphetamines, 253–255
  caffeine, 47, 255–256
  cocaine, 247, 248, 249, 251–253
  ephedrine, 255
  methods of use of, 253
  nicotine as, 302
stimulus, behavioral model, **85**
stomach cancer, 500
STP, hallucinogen, 258
strength training exercises, 396–399, 401, 402
  isometric exercises, **396–397**
  resistance exercises, **396**, **397**
strep throat, **532**
streptococcus, **532**
stress, 31–60
  academic, 41
  alarm stage of, 38
  alcohol use and, 55–56
  behavior change and, 25
  brain and, 41
  campus violence and, 45
  cardiovascular disease and, 458–459
  common sources of, 41–44
  conditions linked to, specific, 39–41
  counterproductive coping strategies, 55–56, 57
  defined, 32–37
  discrimination and, 44
  drug use and, 55–56
  environment and, 37, 44
  ethnicity and, 45
  exercise for reduced, 46–47, 390
  experience as a whole of, 36–37
  gender differences in, 9, 36, 37, 38
  genital herpes and, 573
  hormones, **48**
  immunity and, 548, 573
  interpersonal, 41
  journal, 57
  media response, 45
  meditation and, **52**, 53
  past experiences and, 36
  perceptions of, 38
  personality and, **35**, 35–36
  PKC enzyme and, 40
  post-traumatic stress disorder, 40, 45, **76**, 76–77
  psychological problems related to, 40
  sense of humor and, 51
  symptoms of, 42
  test anxiety, 35
  weight management and, 432
  wellness and, 37–41
  women and, 37, 38
stress management, 44–56
  cognitive techniques in, 50–52
  communication and, 46
  exercise for, 46–47
  nutrition for, 47
  overview of strategies for, 37
  personalized plan for, 56–57
  problem solving for, 50–51
  relaxation techniques for, 52–55
  social support for, 45–46
  support groups for, 57
  time management and, 48–49
  writing and, 50

stress response, **32**
stressors, **32**, 50
  college, 41–42
  emotional/behavioral responses to, 34–36
  environmental, 44
  identifying, 56, 57
  internal, 44
  job-related, 42–43
  physical responses to, 32–34
  social, 43
stretch marks, 212
stretching, proper technique for, 399–400
stroke, 389, 470–473
  diagnosis/treatment of, 472–473
  gender and, 9
  from smoking, 310
  stypes of, 471–472
  warning signs for, 468, 473
Students Against Destructive Decisions (SADD), 292
subarachnoid hemorrhage, 472
subcutaneous fat, **416**
substance abuse, 240–241, 249
Substance Abuse and Mental Health Services Administration (SAMHSA), 242
substance dependence, **240**, **240–241**, 244–245, 261. *See also* codependency
  alcohol abuse and, 283–289
  amphetamine, 255
  cocaine, 253
  marijuana, 257
  medication, 683
  psychoactive drugs, 240–241, 262–264
  psychosis from, **255**
success rehearsal, for test anxiety, 59
suction curettage, **192**, 195
sudden cardiac death (cardiac arrest), **467**
sudden infant death syndrome (SIDS), 316
suffocation, 657
sugar, 349, 355–356
  substitutes, 430
suicide, 65
  depression and, 80
  ethnicity and, 8, 79
  gender and, 79
  myths about, 82
  among older men, 690
  physician-assisted, 708–709, **709**
  rate, 79
  SSRIs and, 86
  warning signs of, 78–79
sulfur dioxide (SO2), 590
sunscreen, **498**, 499
supplements. *See* dietary supplements; herbal remedies
support groups, 43
  cancer-related, 513
  peer counseling and, 88
  quitting smoking, 322–323
  stress management and, 57
supportiveness, 101, 102, 212, 213
suppressor T cells, **522–523**
surgery, 509, 625–629
  coronary bypass, **470**
  elective, **629**
  weight loss, 437–438
surgical method, contraception, **154**, **155**
surrogate, 710, **711**
sympathetic division, **32**
synesthesia, **258**
synovial fluid, **394**, **395**
syphilis, **575**
syringe exchange programs (SEPs), 246, 263
systematic desensitization, for test anxiety, 59
systemic circulation, **450**
systemic infection, 521

systemic lupus erythematosus, 547
systole, **451**

T cells, 522–524, **523, 552, 553,** 553–554
Taco Bell, 319
Tai chi, **53**
tanning salons, 499
target behaviors, 17–18, 20
target heart rate range, **394,** 396
tasks of mourning, 718–719
tax, cigarette, 316
Tay-Sachs disease, 8, 205
TB. *See* tuberculosis
TCM. *See* traditional Chinese medicine
tea, caffeine content in, 256
technology
   reproductive, 210
   solid waste from discarded, 601–602
teenagers
   contraceptive access for, 179
   dietary challenges with, 358
   divorce and, 114
   sexual behavior in/statistics on, 139
   sexuality/contraception education for, 178–180
   statistics on, 4
   tobacco use by, 301–302, 305–306, 315
television, 661
temperature method, contraception, 171
temperature, trends in average, 592
tension headaches, 42
tension-release breathing, 54
teratogens, **219**
terrorism, 77, 664
test(s)
   Alcohol Use Disorders, 291
   blood, 218–219
   breast self exam, 493–494
   developmental, 316
   drug, 260, 262
   false negative result, **625**
   false positive result, **625**
   genetic breast cancer, 504
   HIV antibody, **560**
   Pap, **495,** 495–496, 577
   pregnancy, 210
   prostate-specific antigen, 494
test anxiety, 35, 59
testator, **704**
testes, **125**
testicular cancer, 136, 500
testis, **125,** 131
testosterone, **129**
tetanus, 534
thalassemia, 205
THC, 257
therapeutic touch, **637**
therapies. *See also* complementary medicine; *specific*
   therapies
   bioelectromagnetic-based, 637, **637**
   biological-based, **634**
   energy, 636–637, **637**
Thornburgh v. American College of Obstetricians and
   Gynecologists, 187
tickborne infections, 533–534
time management, 48–49, 100–101
time pressures, 42
time-action function, drug use effect, **248**
time/duration, exercise principle, 393
tips for today
   abortion, 198
   aging, 698
   alcohol use, 293
   cancer, 514
   cardiovascular disease, 479
   contraception, 181

   death/dying, 722
   diet, 369
   environment, 610
   exercise, 410
   health care, 642
   immune system, 546
   intimate relationships, 120
   pregnancy, 230
   psychoactive drugs, 265
   psychological health, 89
   sexuality, 148
   STDs, 580
   stress management, 57
   tobacco use, 322
   violence, 675
   weight management, 443
   wellness, 27
tobacco companies, 317–318
tobacco smoke
   carbon monoxide in, 307, 316
   chemicals in, 306, 308
   environmental, 309–310, **315,** 315–316, 596
   nonsmokers and, 308
   results of inhaling, 308
   sidestream smoke, **308**
tobacco/tobacco use, 299–327, **302**
   additives in, 307–308
   advertising of, 301, 305, 307
   age and, 300, 304
   behavior change strategy and, 324–325
   cancer and, 306, 313, 491, 504–505
   cardiovascular disease and, 453, 478
   cigarette tar, **306**
   cost to society of, 316–318
   deaths from, 1, 5, 300, 309–310
   ethnicity and, 300, 301, 308
   gender differences in, 9, 301, 312, 313
   genetic factors in, 303–304
   hotlines for quitting, 323, 326
   individual action against, 320
   legislation on, 318–321
   lifestyle assessment and, 16
   lung cancer and, 489
   mainstream smoke, **315**
   motivation for, 302–306
   MSA on, 317
   nicotine addiction and, 302–303, 305, 314
   organizations related to, 326–327
   other forms of, 312–315
   portrayal in films of, 305–306
   during pregnancy, 201, 204, 219–220, 316
   quitting, 321–325
   rationalizing dangers of, 305
   smokeless, 301
   smoking as, physical effects of, 308–312
   smoking cessation products, 323
   social/psychological factors in, 303
   start of, 304–306
   teenagers and, 301–302, 305–306, 315
   user profile by ethnicity/age/education, 300
Tolerable Upper Intake Level (UL), 345
tolerance
   drug abuse and, **241**
   nicotine, 303
   withdrawal and, 303
tornadoes, 659
total fiber, **339**
touching, 143–144
   foreplay and, **143**
   therapeutic touch, **637**
toxic shock syndrome (TSS), **168, 169,** 532
toxin, **521**
traditional Chinese medicine (TCM), 629, **631,**
   631–632
   Qigong, 636–637, **637**

trajectory of dying, **715,** 715–717
tranquilizers, **251**
trans fats, 334, 350, 480
trans fatty acids, **333**
transition, labor stage, **225**
transplants, bone marrow/stem cell, 511
transsexuality, 138
trauma, loss and, 720
treatment centers, 262
trichomoniasis, 543, **575**
tricyclics, 84
triglycerides, **458,** 463
trimesters, **209.** *See also* fetal development
trypanosomiasis, 543
TSS (toxic shock syndrome), **168, 169,** 532
tubal sterilization, **174,** 174–175
tuberculosis (TB), **532,** 532–533
tumors, **486,** 486–487
   tumor suppressor genes, **503**
12-step programs, 263
twins, 128, 142, 206, 208
Type 1 diabetes, 420, 421
Type 2 diabetes, 389–390, 419, 494, 496

U. S. Department of Agriculture (USDA), 346,
   351–356, 360, 365
U. S. Preventive Services Task force, 494–495
U. S. Public Health Service, 321
UL. *See* Tolerable Upper Intake Level
ulcers, 312, 534
ultrasonography, **216, 217, 493,** 509
ultrasound, 492
ultraviolet (UV) radiation, **496,** 496–497, **497,**
   508, 594
umbilical cord, **215**
Uniform Donor Card, 710–711, **711**
uninsured, 640
unintentional injuries, **648,** 648–659
United Nations, 587
United Nations AIDS Program, 565
United States (U. S.)
   abortion history in, 186, 187
   birth/pregnancy rate in, 179
   complementary medicine use in, 620
   drug use trends in, 240
   ethnic distribution of, 8
   health care cost in, 638
   health care professionals in, 623
   nuclear power plants in, 607
   osteoporosis in, 342
   population of, 587, 589
   prescription drug spending in, 628
   unintentional injuries in, **648,** 648–659
   unplanned pregnancies in, 202
   violence in, 661, 663
   workplace violence in, 664
United States Pharmacopeia (USP), 363
universality, death and, 703
unsaturated fats, 349
urethra, **124, 125**
urethritis, **566,** 567
uric acid, 464–465
urinary tract infections (UTIs), 126, 534–535
USDA (U. S. Department of Agriculture), 346
USDA Center for Nutrition Policy, 352
user factors, physical effects of drug use, 248
uterine cancer, 496
uterus, **125**
UTIs (urinary tract infections), 126
UV (ultraviolet) radiation, **496,** 496–497, **497,**
   508, 594

vaccines, **526,** 537, 542
   allergies and, 528–529
   cancer, 489, 496, 512

vaccines (*continued*)
   hepatitis B, 574
   HIV infection, 564–565
VAE (voluntary euthanasia), 709
vagina, **125**
vaginal contraceptive ring, 159–160
vaginal infections, 543
vaginal spermicides, 164, 166, 167–169, 170–171, 555
vaginitis, 135
values, **67**, 68
vardenafil (Levitra), 137
varicella-zoster virus, 538
varinicline (Chantix), 323
vas deferens, **126**
vasa deferentia, **173–174**
vasectomy, **173**, 173–174
vasocongestion, **134**
VBG (vertical banded gastroplasty), 438
vectors, **521**
vegans, **356**
vegetables, 354, 505, 515
   cruciferous, **344**, 344–345, **345**
vegetarians, 331, 356–358
vehicles, hybrid/electric, 595–596
veins, **451**
venae cave, **451**
ventricle, **451**
vertical banded gastroplasty (VBG), 438
viable fetus, **186**
Viagra (sildenafil citrate), 133, 137
violence, 146, 659–675, 676–677
   alcohol use and, 277, 662, 670
   assault, 662
   campus, 45
   child abuse, 668, 671–672
   against children, 668, 671–672
   collective, 665
   date rape, **669**, 669–670
   elder abuse, 669
   family, 664–669
   firearms and, 662, 663, 673–674, 675
   gang-related, 663
   gender differences in, 661–662
   hate crimes, 663
   homicide, 662–663
   media on, 661
   poverty and, 663
   school, 663–664
   sexual, 162, 163, **669**, 669–672
   social factors in, 660–661
   terrorism, 77, 664
   in U. S., 661
   workplace, 664
viral encephalitis, 540
viral hepatitis, 540–541
viruses, 525, **535**, 535–542. *See also* human papillomavirus
   cancer and, 165, 486, 495
   diseases from, 531
   emerging diseases from, 544–545
   life cycle of, 524
   STDs and, 553
visceral fat, **416**
viscous fibers (soluble), **339**
vision, aging and, 686
visualization, 20, **52**

vitamin B-6, 477
vitamin B-12, 477
vitamins, **340**, 340–342
   deficiencies in, 340, 342
   dietary sources of, 341
   excesses, **340**, 340–342
   functions/sources of, 340
   toxic effect of megadoses of, 341
Vivtrol (injectable naltrexone), 287
VO$_{2max}$ (maximal oxygen consumption), **394**, **395**
voluntary euthanasia (VAE), 709
volunteering, 50
vulva, **124**, **125**

warts, 541–542
   genital, **570**
water
   contamination/treatment of, 597–598
   exercise and, 404, 406
   population and, 588
   protecting supply of, 599
   quality, 597–599
   recommended intake for, 343
   shortages of, 598–599
water-soluble vitamins, 341
websites. *See* organizations, websites and
Webster v. Reproductive Health Services, 187
weight management, 347, 415–447
   acceptance/change and, 439
   aging and, 683
   approaches to, 432, 435–438
   basic concepts, 416–423
   behavior change strategy for, 444
   body composition and, **381**, 387–388, 416–419
   body fat and, 419–420, 422, 423–426
   body image and, 438–439, 440
   body mass index and, 422
   diet and, 335, 432
   diet sodas and, 427
   diet/eating habits and, 429–431, 444
   discretionary calorie allowance and, 356
   emotions and, 431–432
   energy balance in, 417
   lifestyle for successful, 426–432
   obesity definition and, **416**, **417**
   physical activity for, 384
   physical activity/exercise and, 431
   pregnancy, 212
   stress and, 432
   surgery and, 437–438
   weight problem approaches, 432, 435–438
   weight-loss programs for, 435–437
weight-loss programs
   clinical, 437
   commercial, 436
   noncommercial, 435
   online, 436–437
   prescription drugs, 437
   surgery, 437–438
Weisman, Avery, 713–714
wellness, 2–27. *See also* psychological health
   alcohol use and, 275–283
   body fat distribution and, 420, 422
   college students concerns for, 13
   continuum, 2
   eating habits and, 56, 332, 429–431, 444
   emotional, **3**, 390

   environmental, **3**
   excess body fat and, 419–420, 422
   exercise for total, 383
   financial, **4**
   gender and, 9
   interpersonal, **3**, 383
   for life, 26–27
   lifestyle and, 15–26
   marriage and, 114
   occupational, **4**
   parenthood and, 202
   physical, **2**, 3
   risk factors of, **2**
   self-care and, 616–619
   sexual orientation influencing, 12
   spiritual, **3**, 49–50, 51
   stress and, 37–41
   target behaviors for, 17–18
   violence and, 665
West Nile virus, 544
Western blot, **560**
Western medicine. *See* conventional medicine
wet dreams, 138, **139**
WHO (World Health Organization), 126, 193, 318, 555–556, 593
whole grains, **337**, 337–338
widows, 692
will, preparation for death, **704**, 704–706
   living will, **709**, 710
withdrawal, **241**, 249, 285, 303
withdrawal method, contraception, **172**
WOAR (Women Organized Against Rape), 670
women, 149. *See also* females; pregnancy; sexual assault
   alcohol abuse by, 288
   autoimmune diseases and, 547
   cardiovascular disease and, 462
   communication advice for, 106
   contraception use among American, 178
   financial planning and, 684
   HIV/AIDS in, 557
   nutritional needs of, 359
   STDs and, 557, 566, 568, 576
   stress and, 37, 38
   transsexual, 138
   widowed, 692
Women Organized Against Rape (WOAR), 670
Worden, William, 718
work addiction, 239
work injuries, **658**, 658–659
workplace
   drug use/testing in, 260
   radiation in, 607–608
   violence in, 664
World Health Organization (WHO), 126, 193, 318, 555–556, 593, 598
worry, 42

years of potential life lost, **648**
yoga, **53**, 54

zidovudine (AZT), 562
ZIFT (zygote intrafallopian transfer), **208**, 208–209
Zyban (Bupropion), 323
zygote intrafallopian transfer (ZIFT), **208**, 208–209